LONDON
STREET ATLAS

CONTENTS

Key to Map Pages 2-3
Key to Map Symbols 4-5
Central London Maps 6-21
Main London Maps 22-104
Theatres and Cinemas Map 105
Shopping Map 105
Bus Map.. 106
Index to Places of Interest 107-108
Index to Place Names 109-110
Index to Street Names 111

Nicholson
An *Imprint* of HarperCollins*Publishers*

Nicholson
HarperCollins*Publishers*
77-85 Fulham Palace Road
London W6 8JB

First published 1994
© Nicholson 1994

Generated from the Bartholomew London Digital
Database.

The Ordnance Survey is not responsible for the
accuracy of the National Grid in this publication.

London Underground Map by permission of London
Regional Transport LRT Registered User Number
94/1496

Printed in Hong Kong.

ISBN 0 7028 1328 1

Great care has been taken throughout this atlas
to be accurate but the publishers cannot accept
responsibility for any errors which appear or
their consequences. Queries or information
regarding the London Street Atlas should be
addressed to the Publishing Director at the above
address.

All rights reserved. No part of this publication
may be reproduced, stored in a retrieval system,
or transmitted, in any form or by any means,
electronic, mechanical, photocopying, recording
or otherwise, without the prior permission of the
publisher.

F/J 6375

RNB

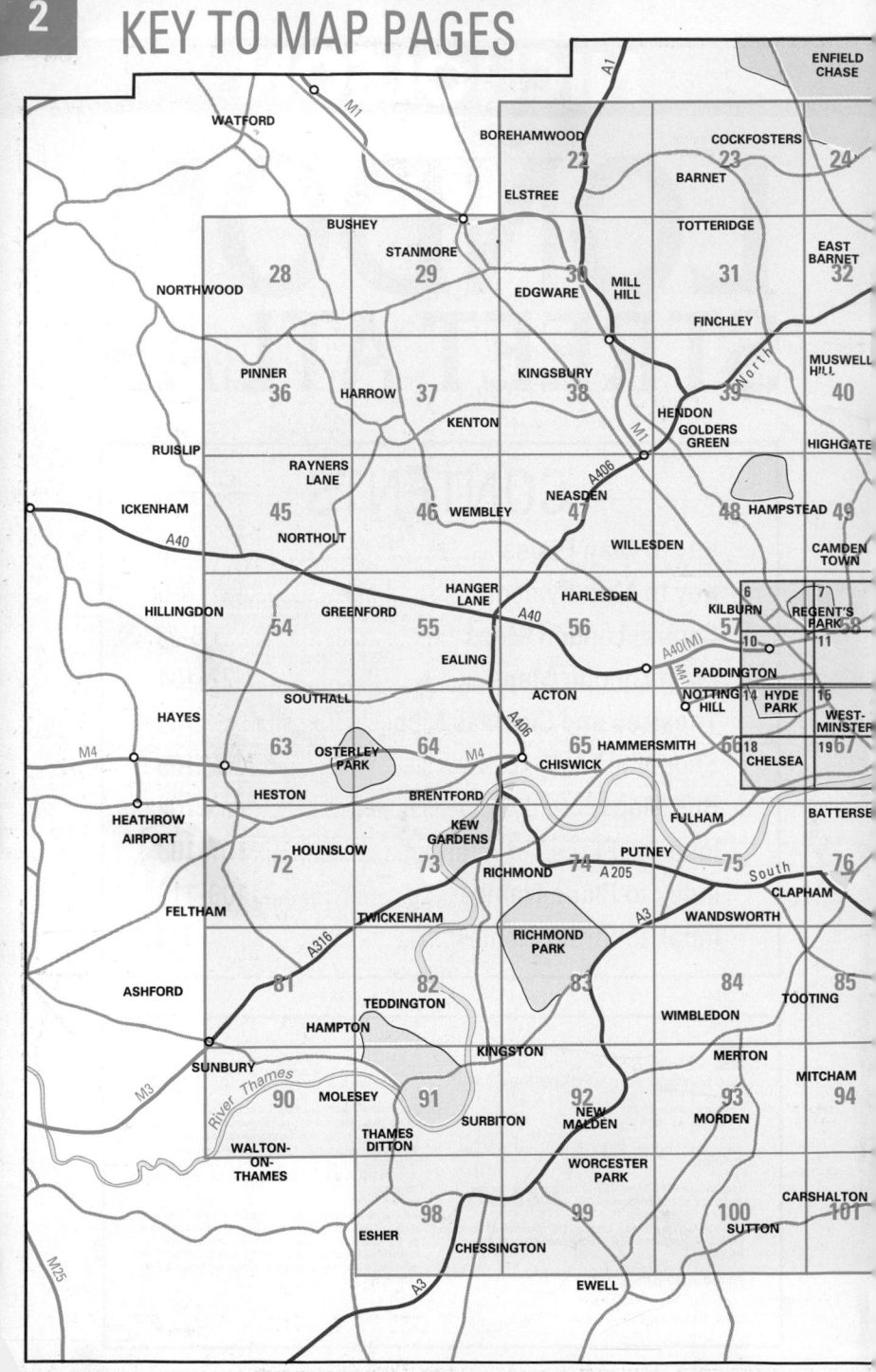

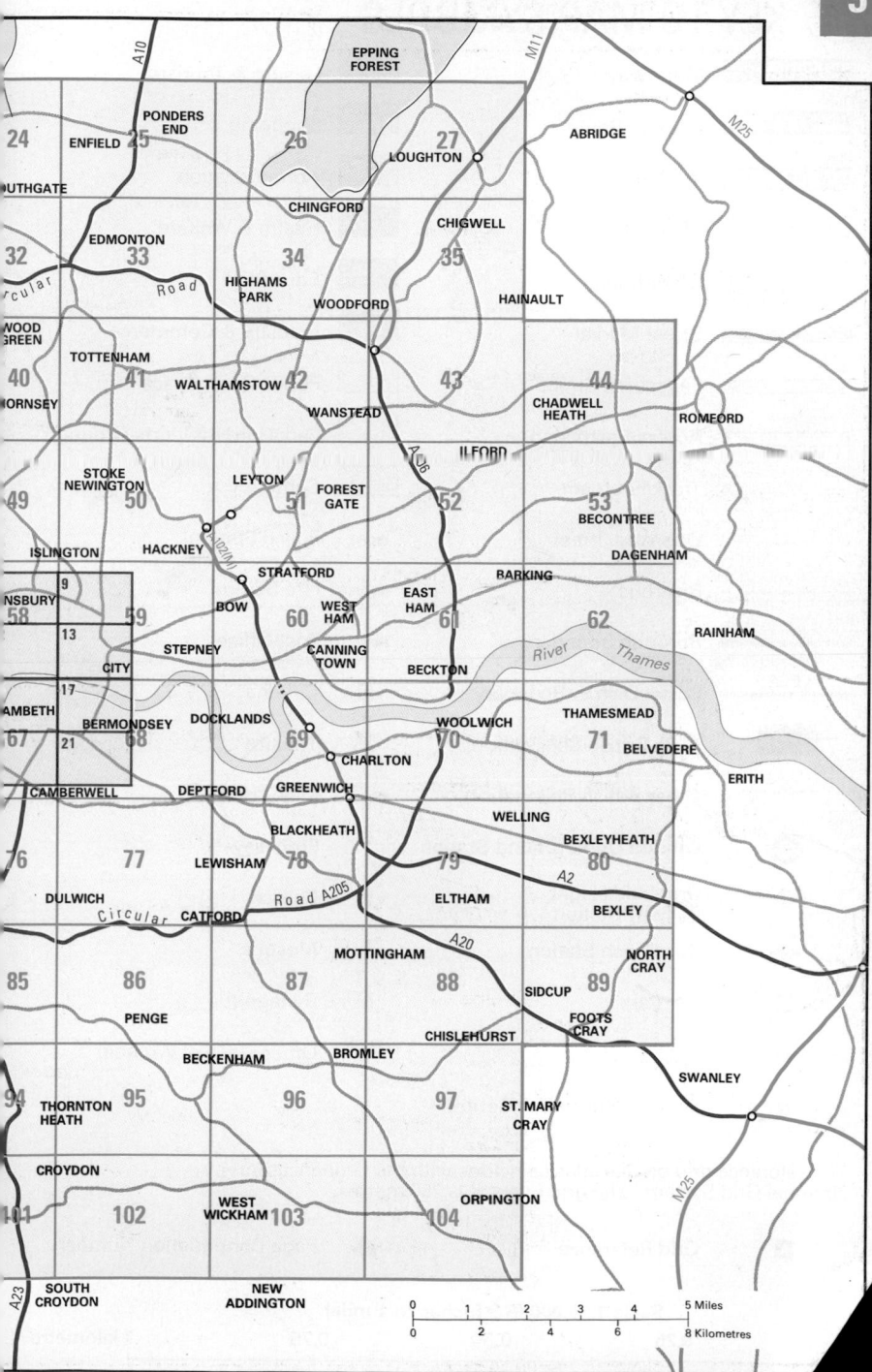

24 ENFIELD **25** PONDERS END

26 CHINGFORD

27 LOUGHTON

ABRIDGE

EPPING FOREST

OUTHGATE

32 EDMONTON **33** HIGHAMS PARK **34** WOODFORD **35**

CHIGWELL

HAINAULT

rcular Road

WOOD GREEN

40 TOTTENHAM **41** WALTHAMSTOW **42** WANSTEAD **43** CHADWELL HEATH **44** ROMFORD

HORNSEY

49 STOKE NEWINGTON **50** LEYTON **51** FOREST GATE **52** BECONTREE **53**

ISLINGTON HACKNEY

ILFORD

DAGENHAM

58 NSBURY **9** **59** BOW **60** WEST HAM STRATFORD **61** EAST HAM BARKING **62** RAINHAM

13 STEPNEY CANNING TOWN BECKTON

CITY **17**

River Thames

AMBETH **67** BERMONDSEY **21** **68** DOCKLANDS **69** WOOLWICH **70** THAMESMEAD **71** BELVEDERE

CHARLTON

CAMBERWELL DEPTFORD GREENWICH

ERITH

WELLING

BLACKHEATH

76 **77** LEWISHAM **78** **79** BEXLEYHEATH **80**

DULWICH CATFORD Circular Road A205 ELTHAM A2 BEXLEY

85 **86** PENGE **87** MOTTINGHAM **88** A20 **89** NORTH CRAY

SIDCUP FOOTS CRAY

BECKENHAM BROMLEY CHISLEHURST

94 THORNTON HEATH **95** **96** **97** ST. MARY CRAY SWANLEY

CROYDON

101 **102** WEST WICKHAM **103** ORPINGTON **104**

A23 SOUTH CROYDON NEW ADDINGTON

| 0 | 1 | 2 | 3 | 4 | 5 Miles |
| 0 | 2 | 4 | 6 | 8 Kilometres |

4

KEY TO MAP SYMBOLS

A40(M)	Motorway
Dual **A4**	Primary Route
Dual **A40**	'A' Road
B504	'B' Road
	Other Road
	Street Market
	Pedestrian Street
•————————•	Access Restriction
:::::::::: -------	Track/Footpath
→	One Way Street
– – – – – –	Riverbus
CITY	Borough Boundary
EC2	Postal District Boundary
⊟✦⊟	Main British Rail Station
–✦–	Other British Rail Station
⊖	London Underground Station
–○–	Docklands Light Railway Station
●	Bus/Coach Station
P	Car Park
WC	Public Toilet
i	Tourist Information Centre

▢	Leisure & Tourism
▢	Shopping
▢	Administration
▢	Health & Welfare
▢	Education
▢	Industry & Commerce
▢	Public Open Space
▢	Park/Garden/Sports Ground
† † †	Cemetery
■ POL	Police Station
■ Fire Sta	Fire Station
■ PO	Post Office
⚏	Cinema
♝	Theatre
⊠	Major Hotel
⅂	Embassy
+	Church
☾	Mosque
✡	Synagogue
Mormon ■	Other Place of Worship

The reference grid on this atlas coincides with the Ordnance Survey National Grid System. The grid interval is 250 metres.

A	Grid Reference	**8**	Page Continuation Number

Scale 1:10,000 (6.3 inches to 1 mile)

0.25	0.50	0.75	1 kilometre
¼		½ mile	

KEY TO MAP SYMBOLS

5

M41	Motorway		Leisure & Tourism
Dual **A4**	Primary Route	USA	Administration & Law Embassy
Dual **A40**	'A' Road		Health & Welfare
B504	'B' Road		Education
	Other Road		Industry & Commerce
	Toll		Cemetery
	Street Market		Golf Course
	Pedestrian Street		Public Open Space/Allotments
	Cycle Path		Park/Garden/Sports Ground
	Track/Footpath		Wood/Forest
	One Way Street	Pol	Police Station
P	Pedestrian Ferry	Fire Sta	Fire Station
V	Vehicle Ferry	PO	Post Office
	County/Borough Boundary	Lib	Library
	Postal District Boundary	▲	Youth Hostel
	Main British Rail Station	□	Tower Block
	Other British Rail Station	i	Tourist Information Centre
	London Underground Station	⊕	Heliport
	Docklands Light Railway Station	✗	Windmill
	Bus/Coach Station	+	Church
P	Car Park	☾	Mosque
WC	Public Toilet	✡	Synagogue

The reference grid on this atlas coincides with the Ordnance Survey National Grid System. The grid interval is 500 metres.

A	Grid Reference	24	Page Continuation Number

Scale 1:20,000 (3.2 inches to 1 mile)

25	OS National Grid Kilometre Square	0 0.25 0.50 0.75 1 kilometre
		0 ¼ ½ mile

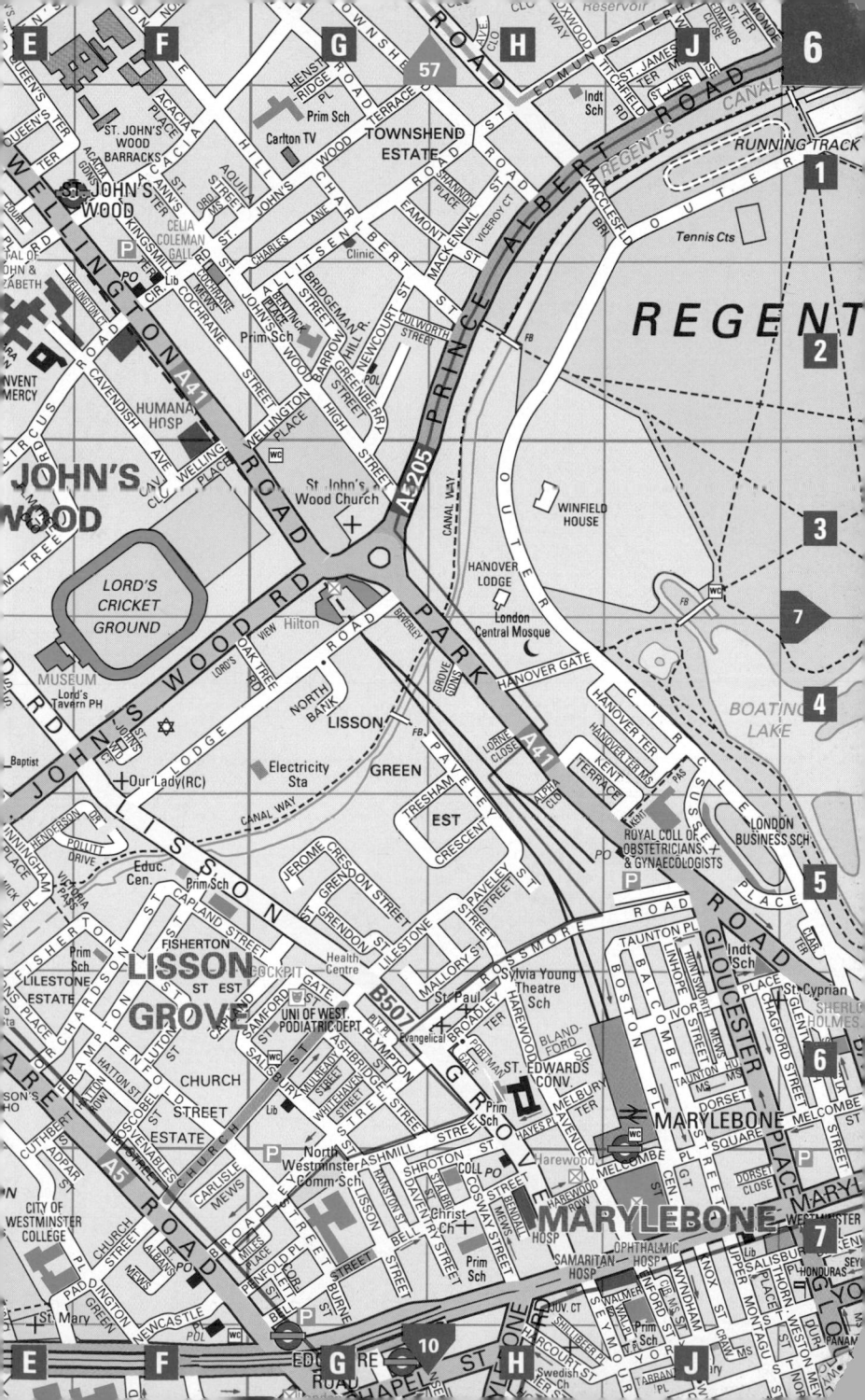

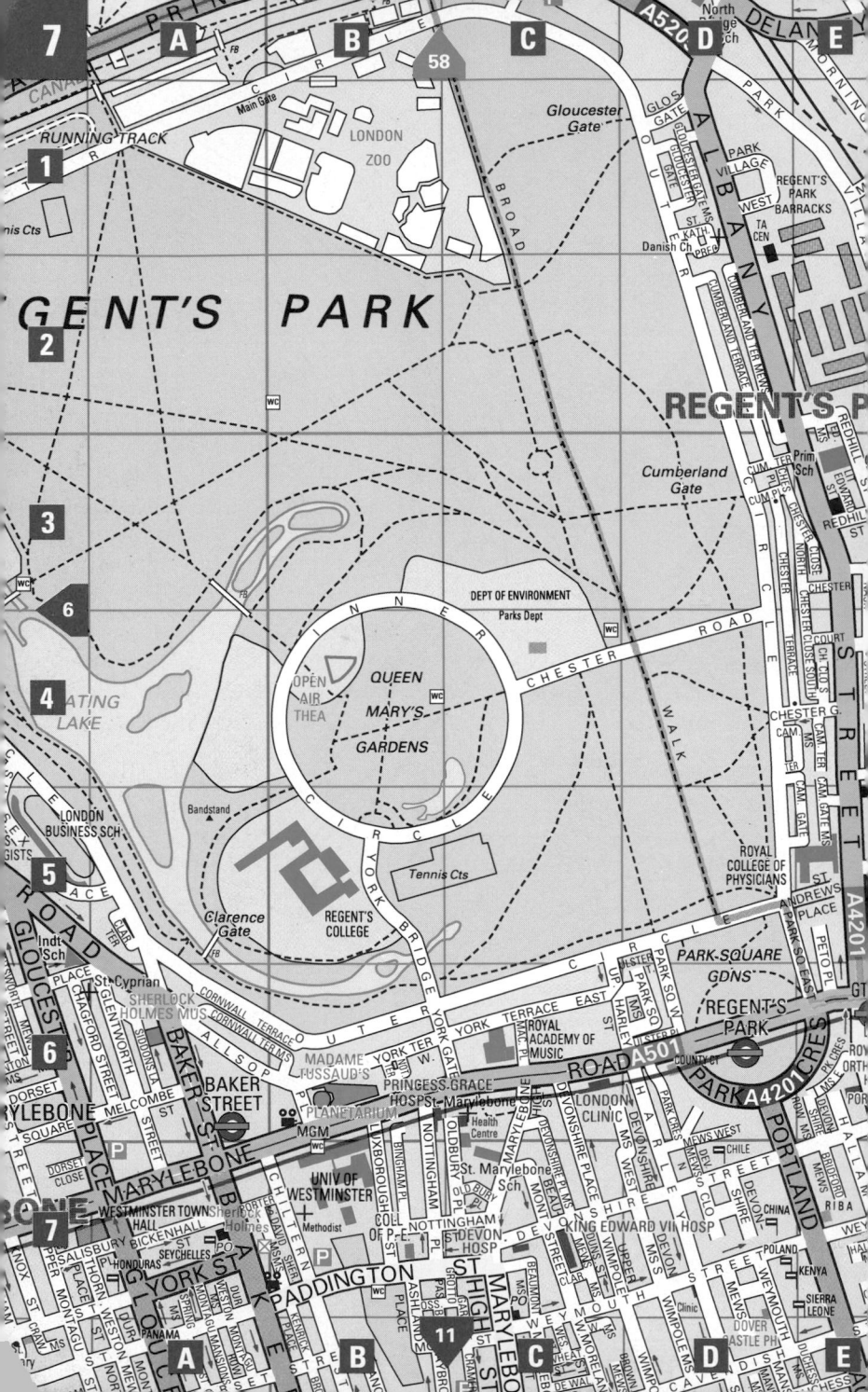

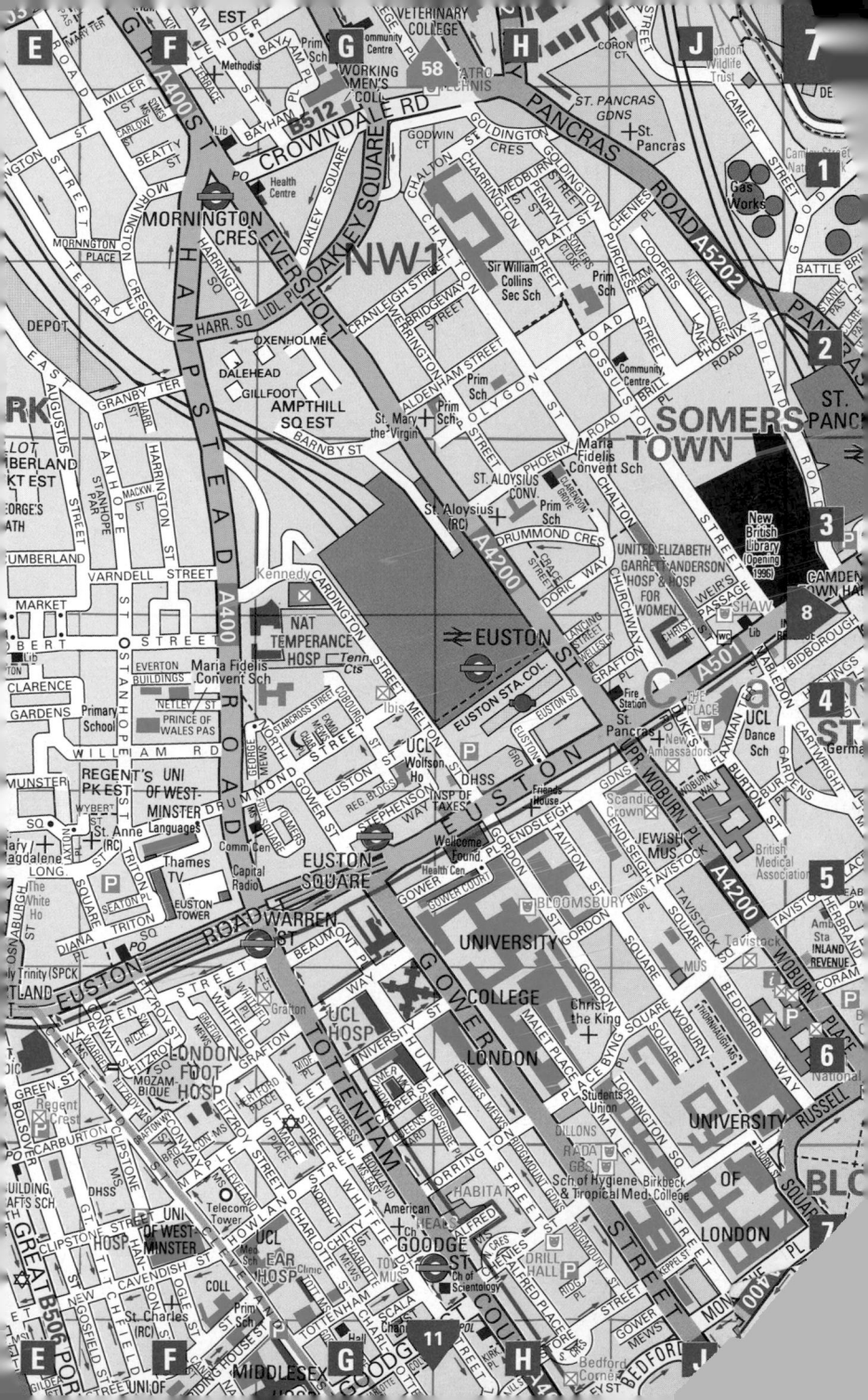

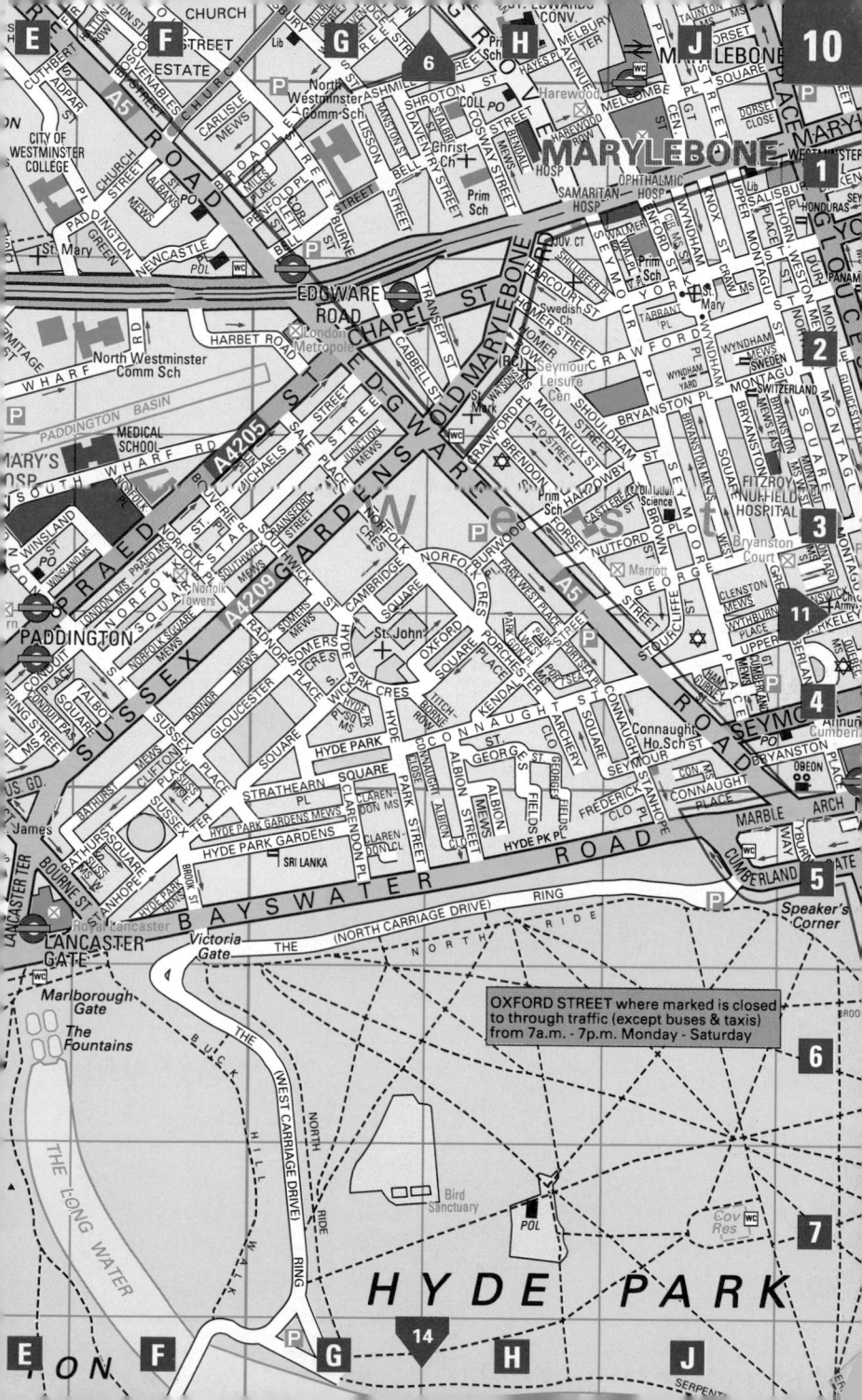

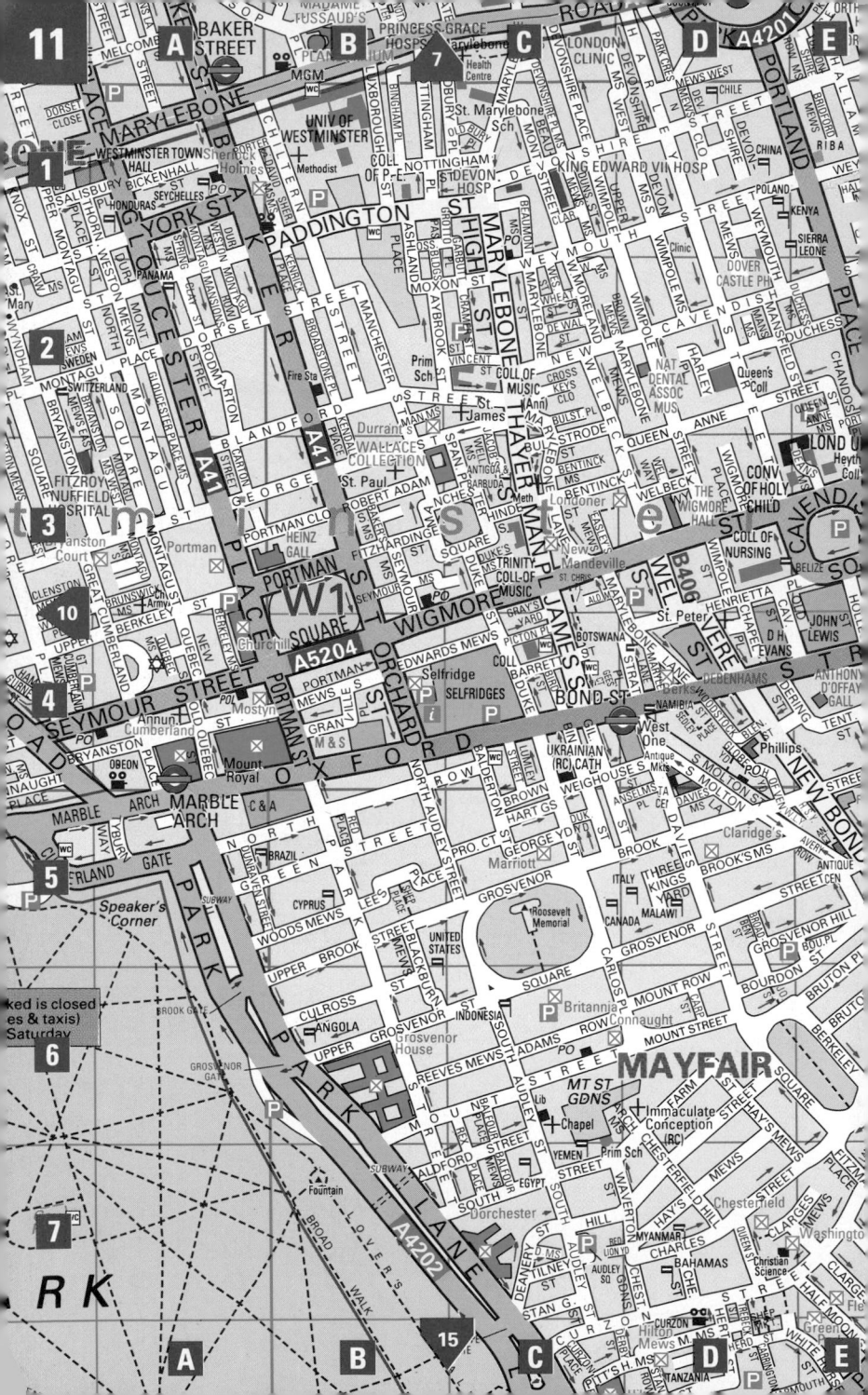

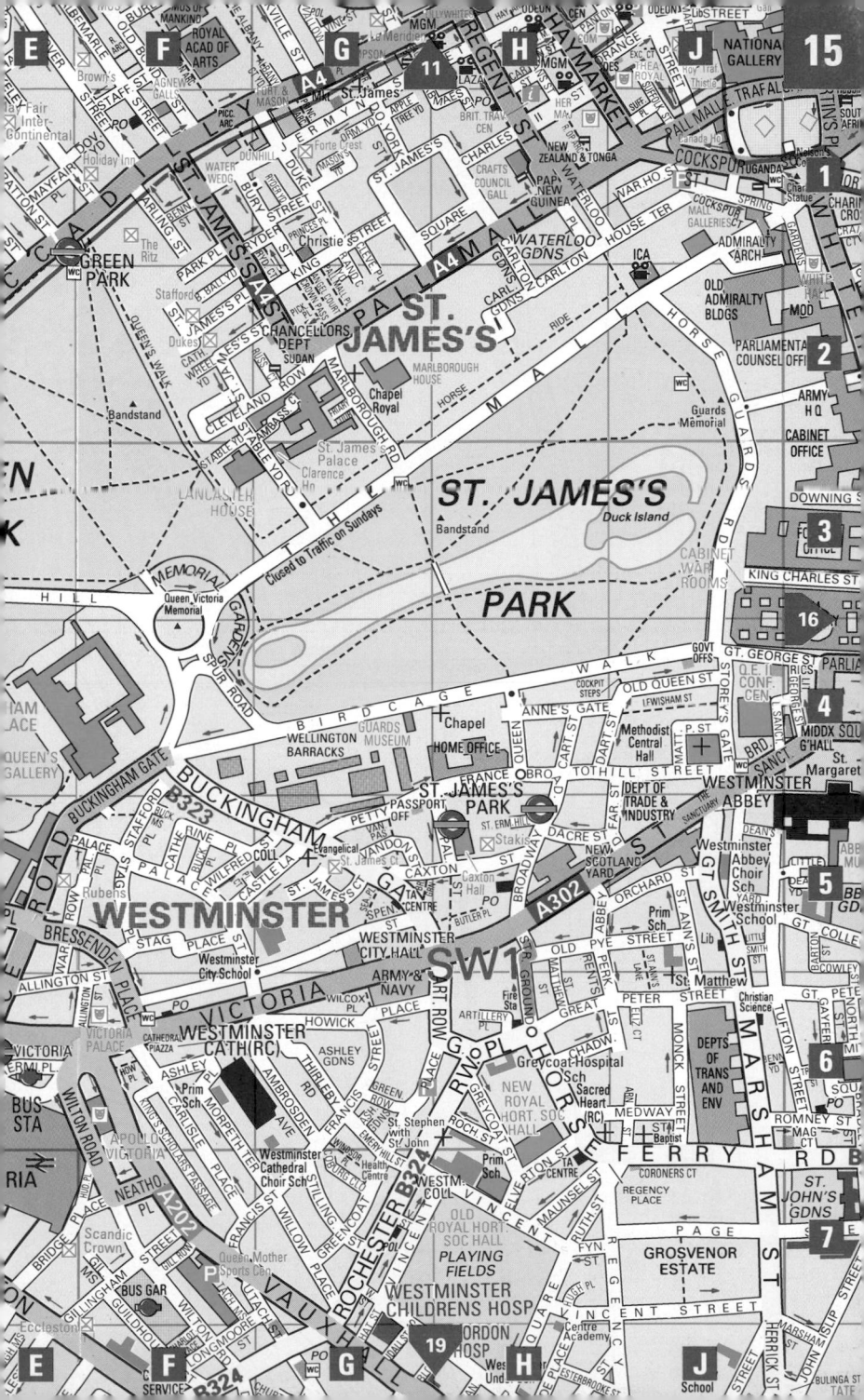

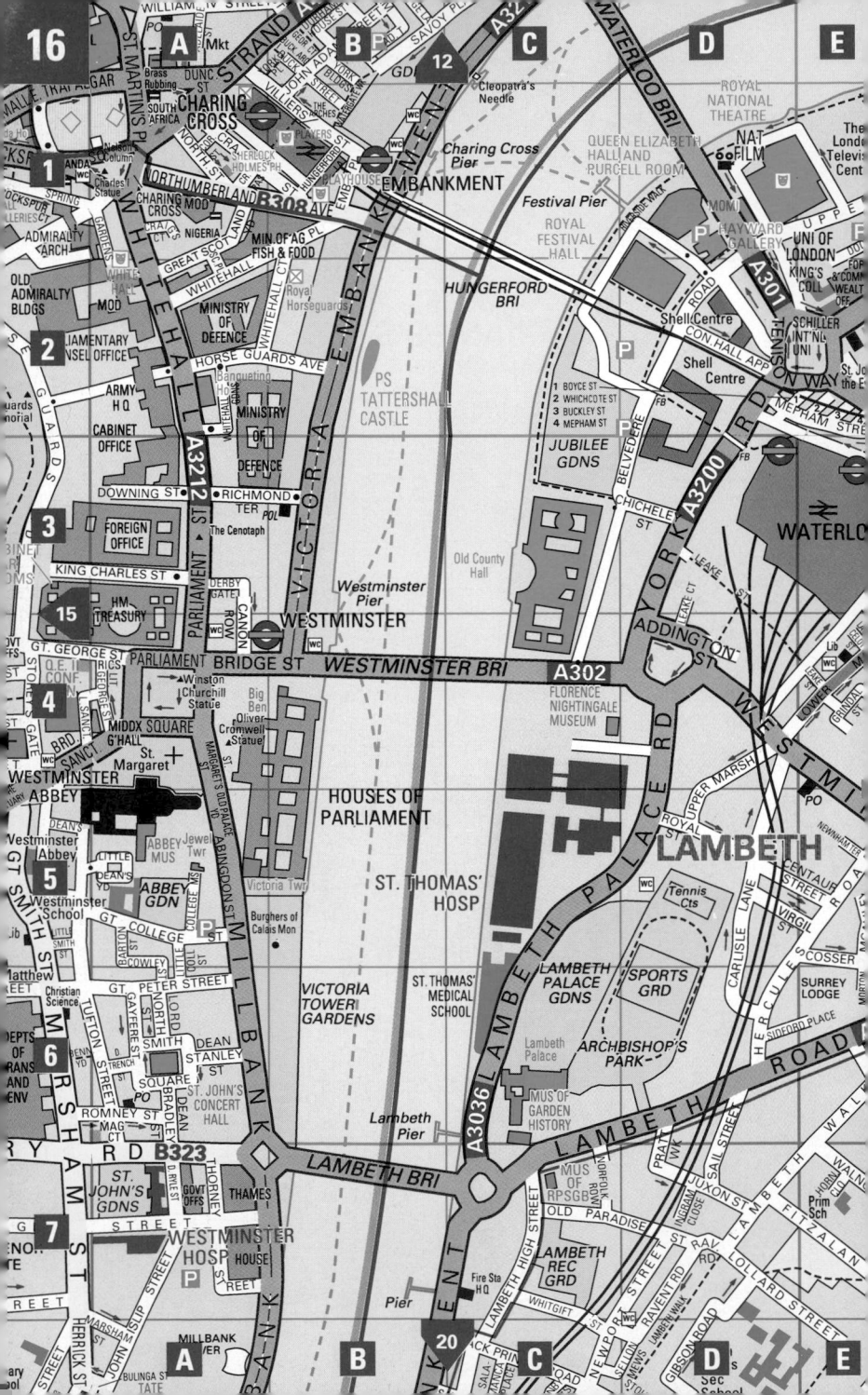

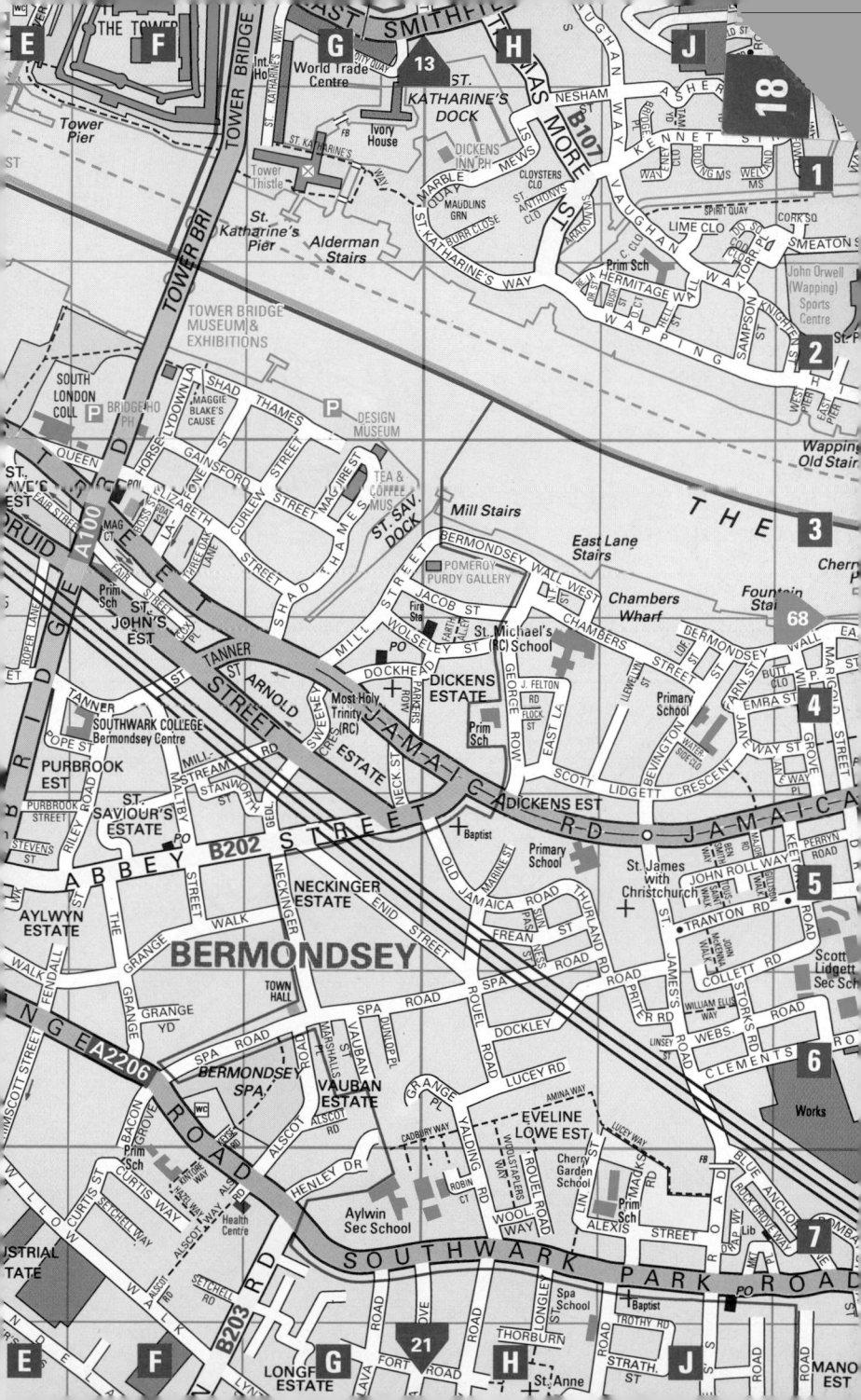

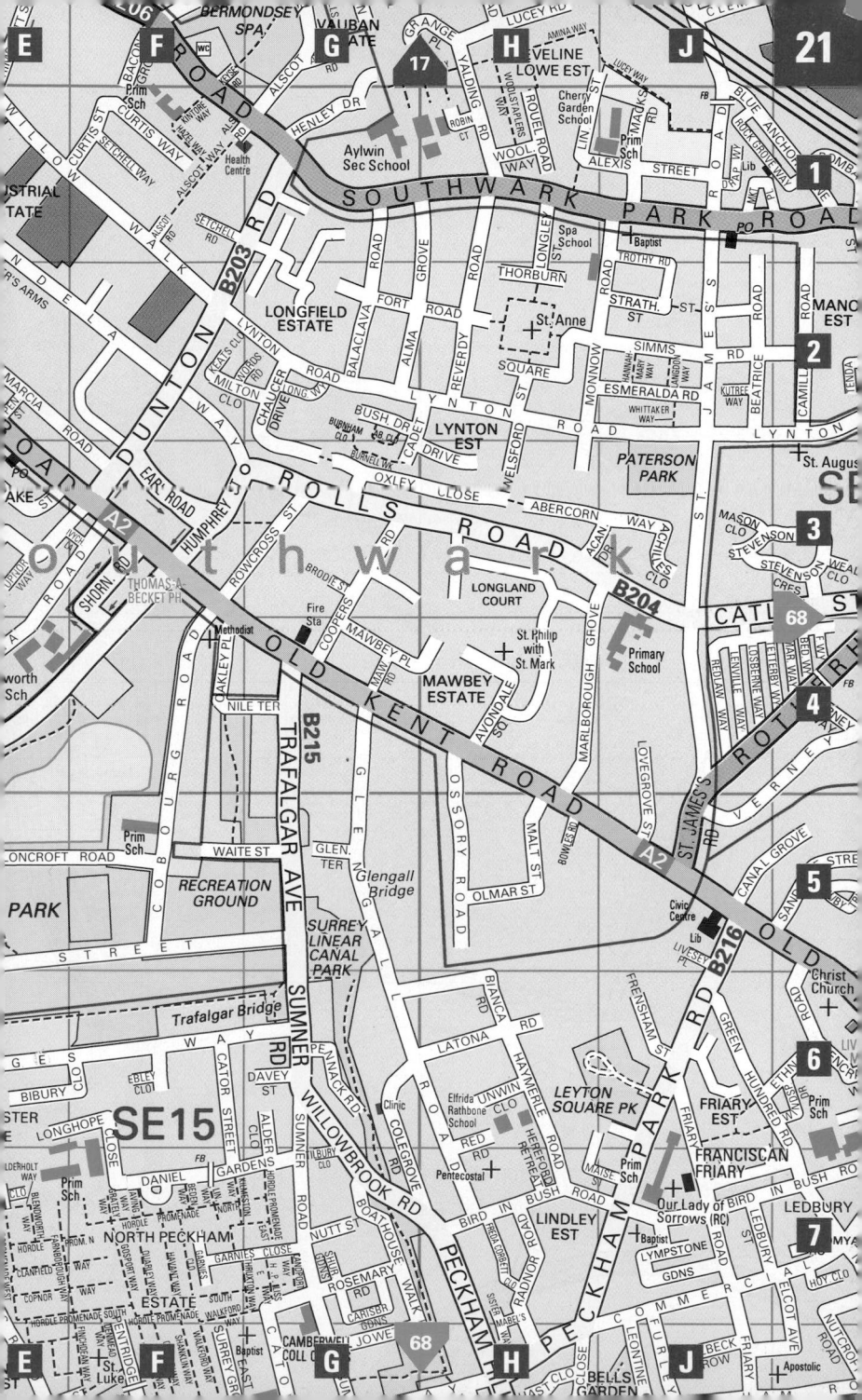

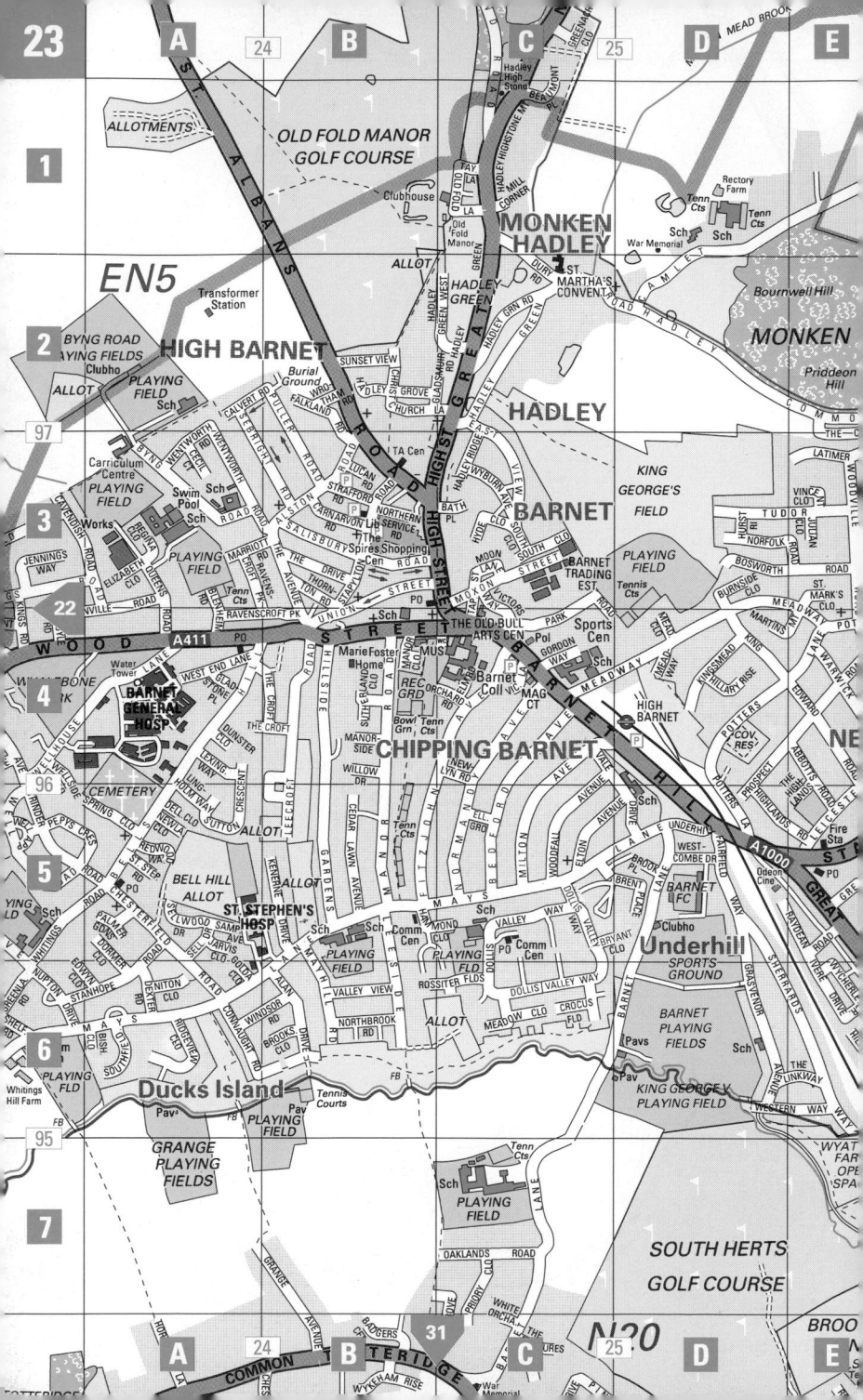

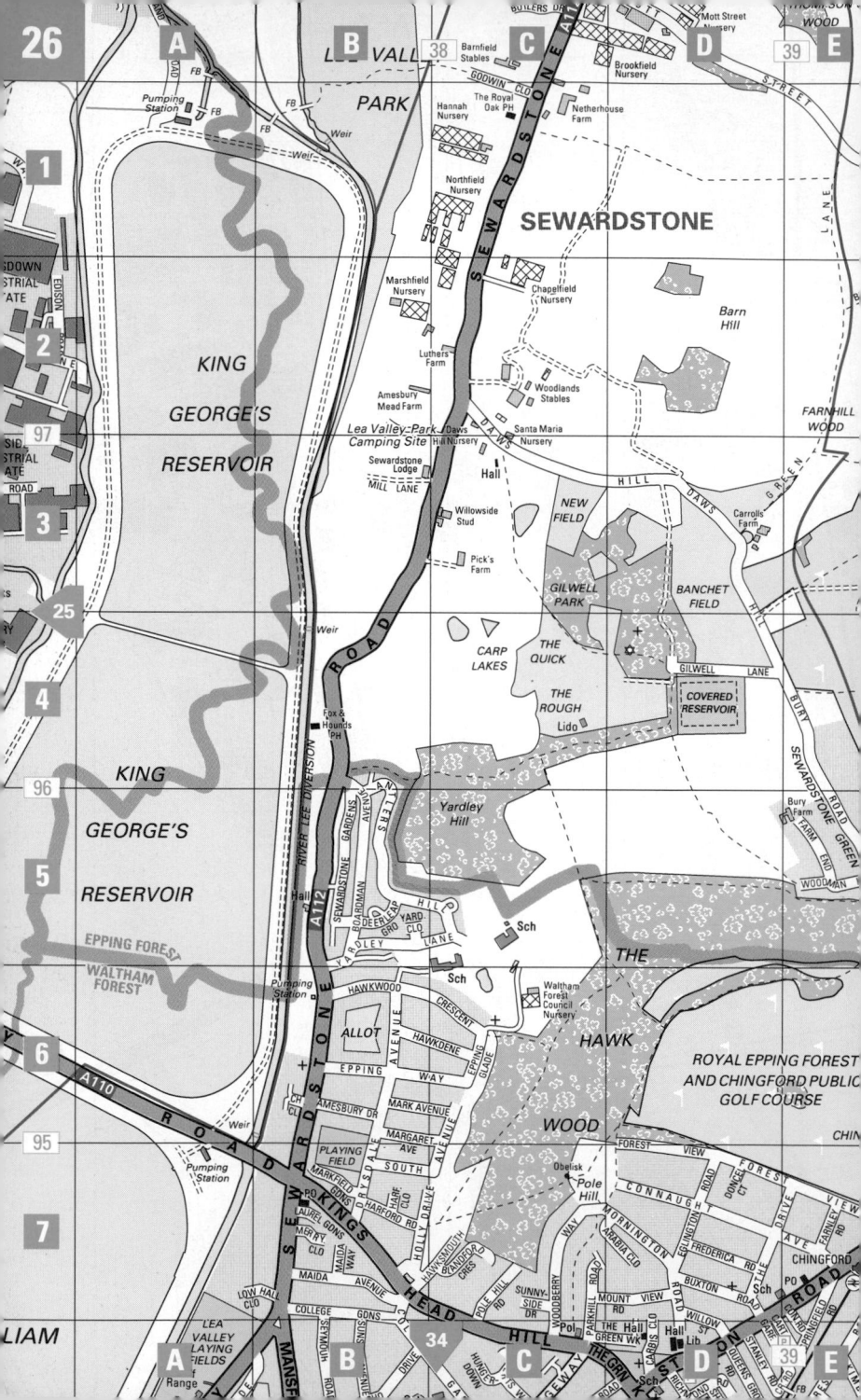

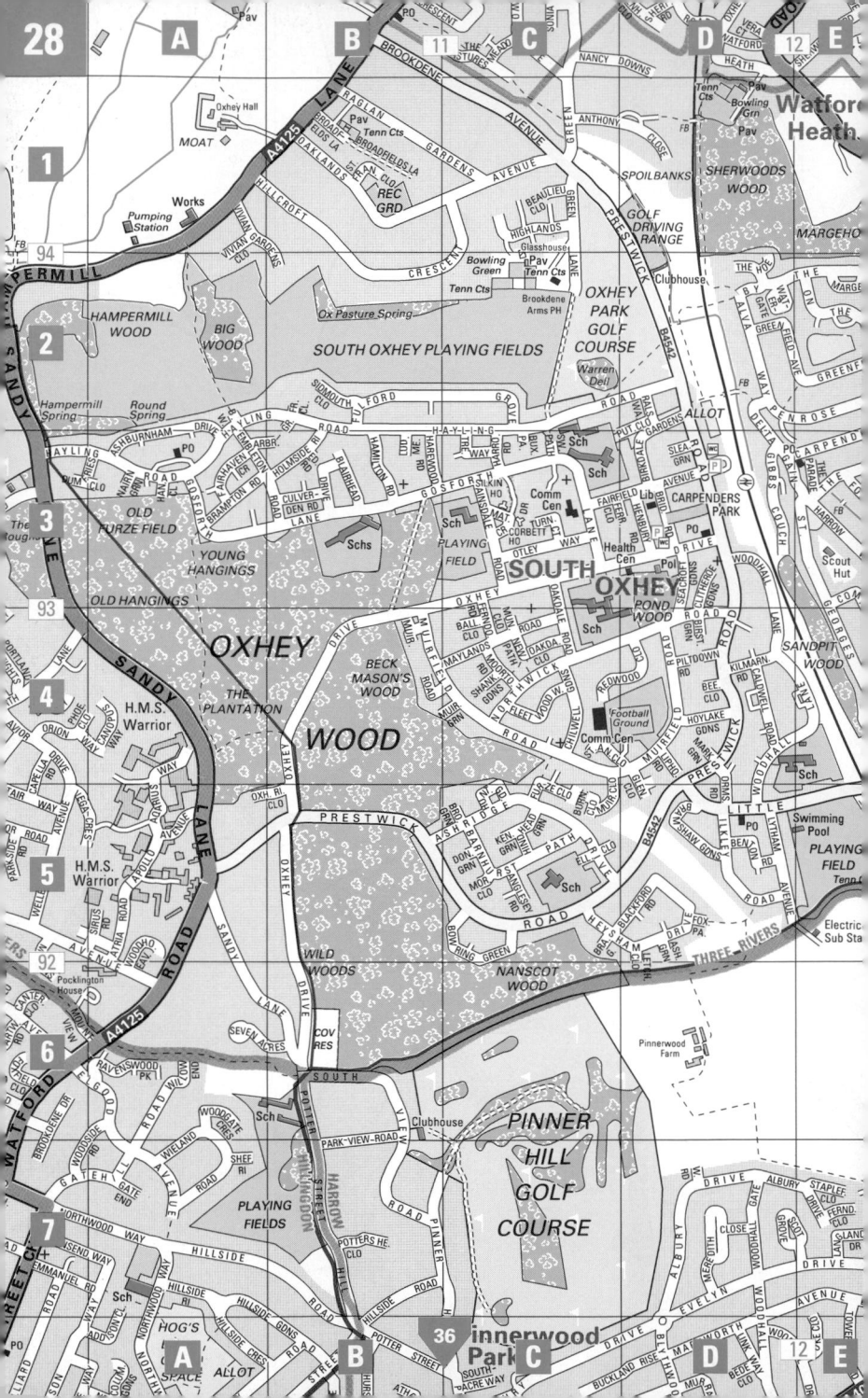

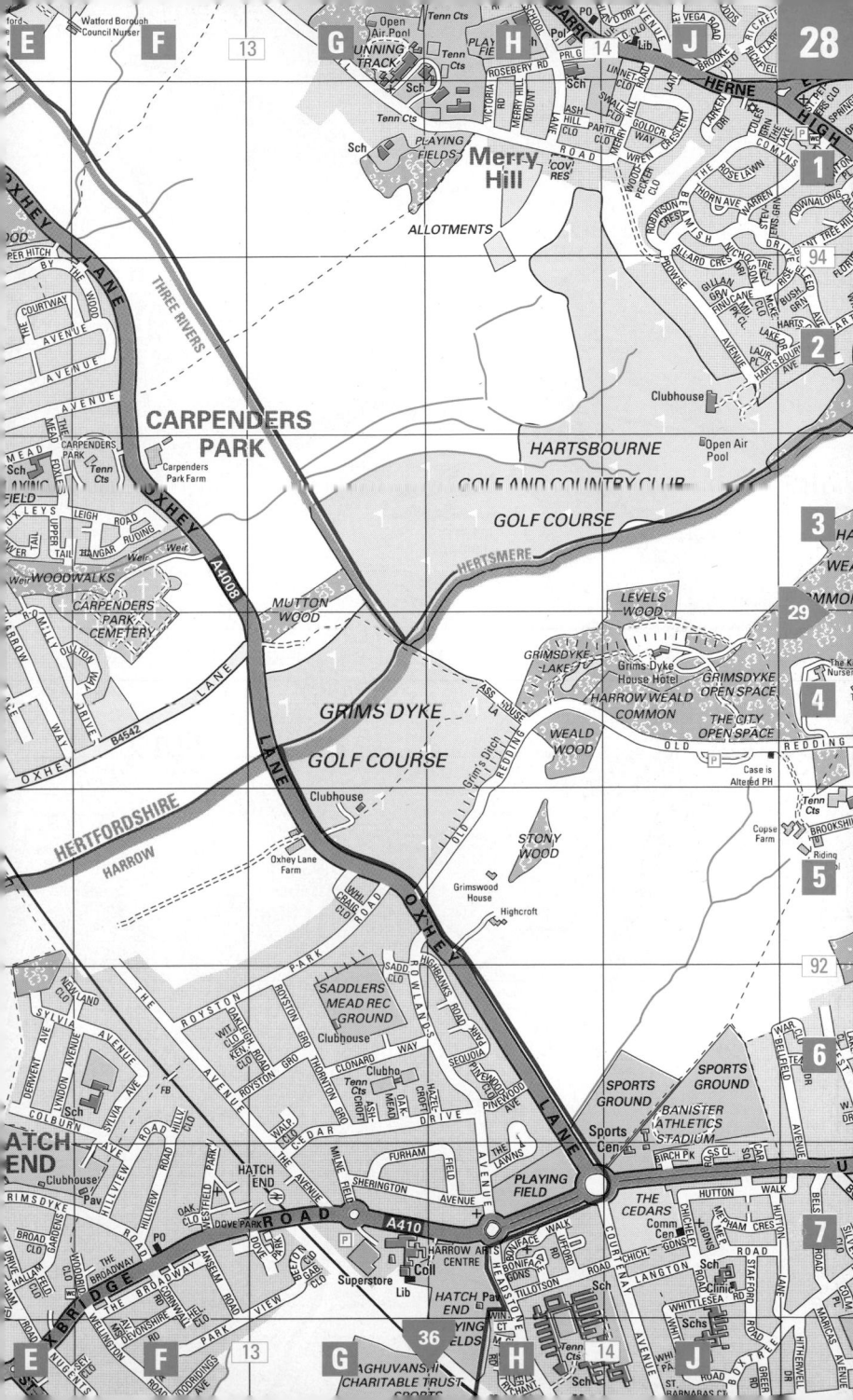

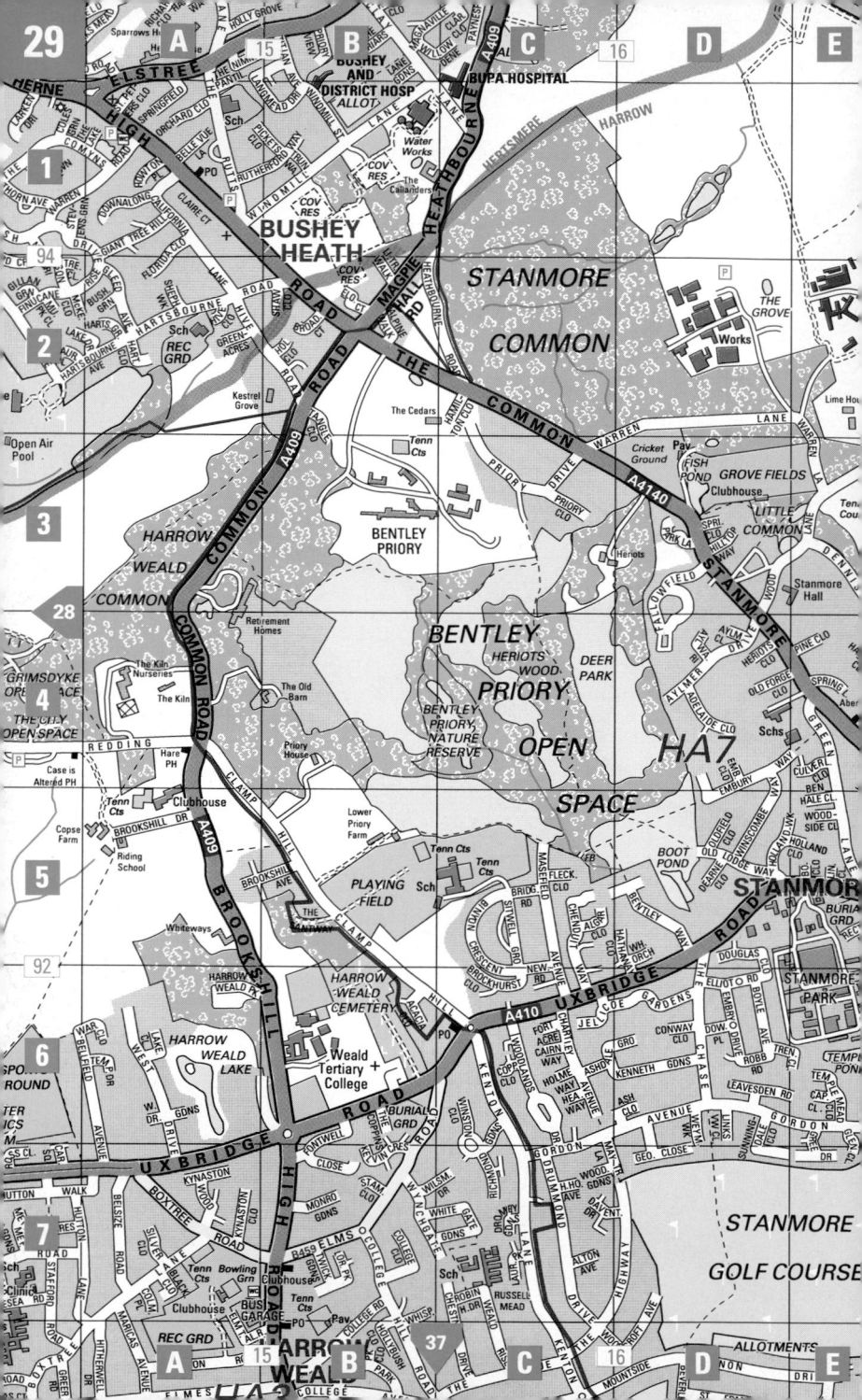

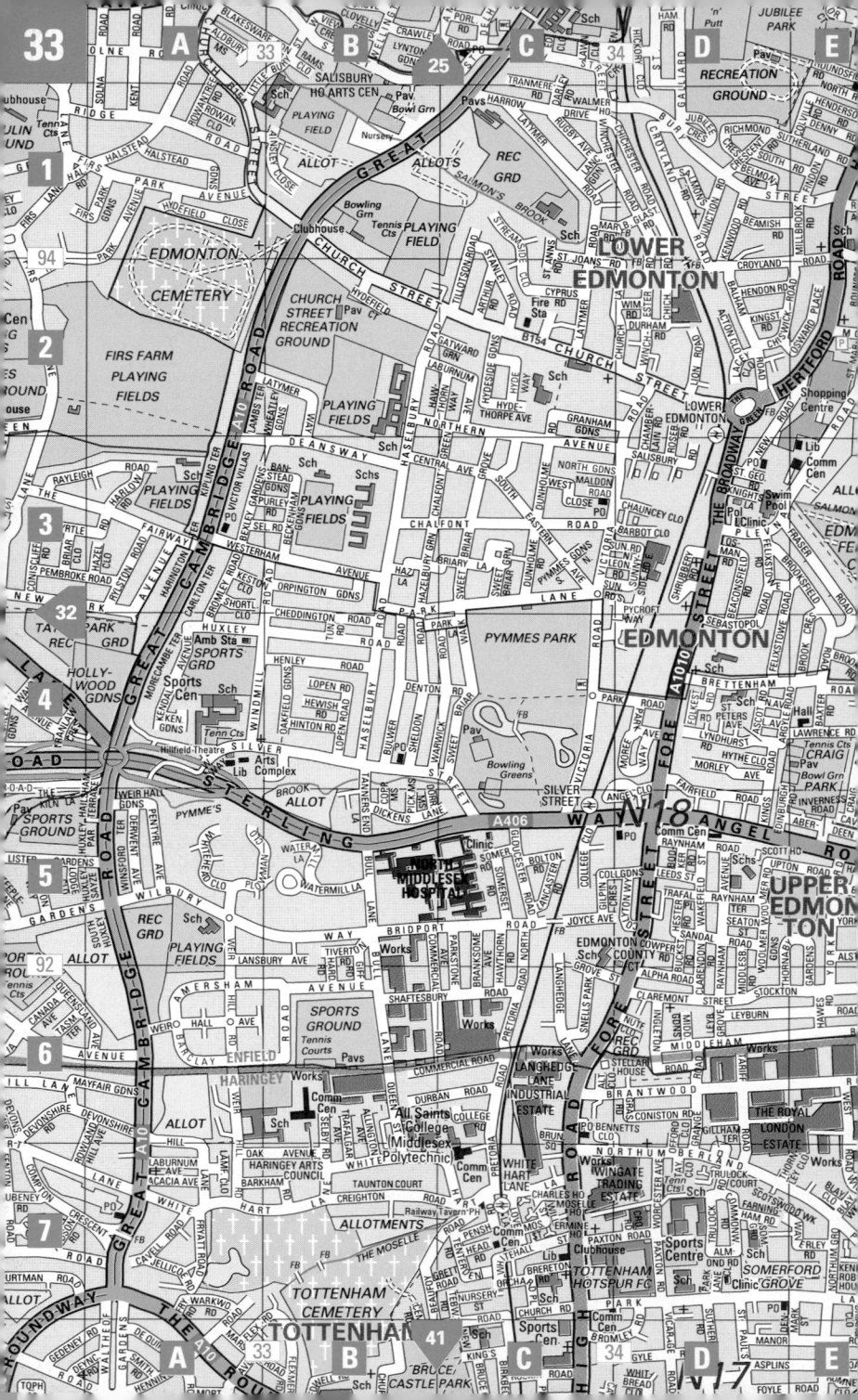

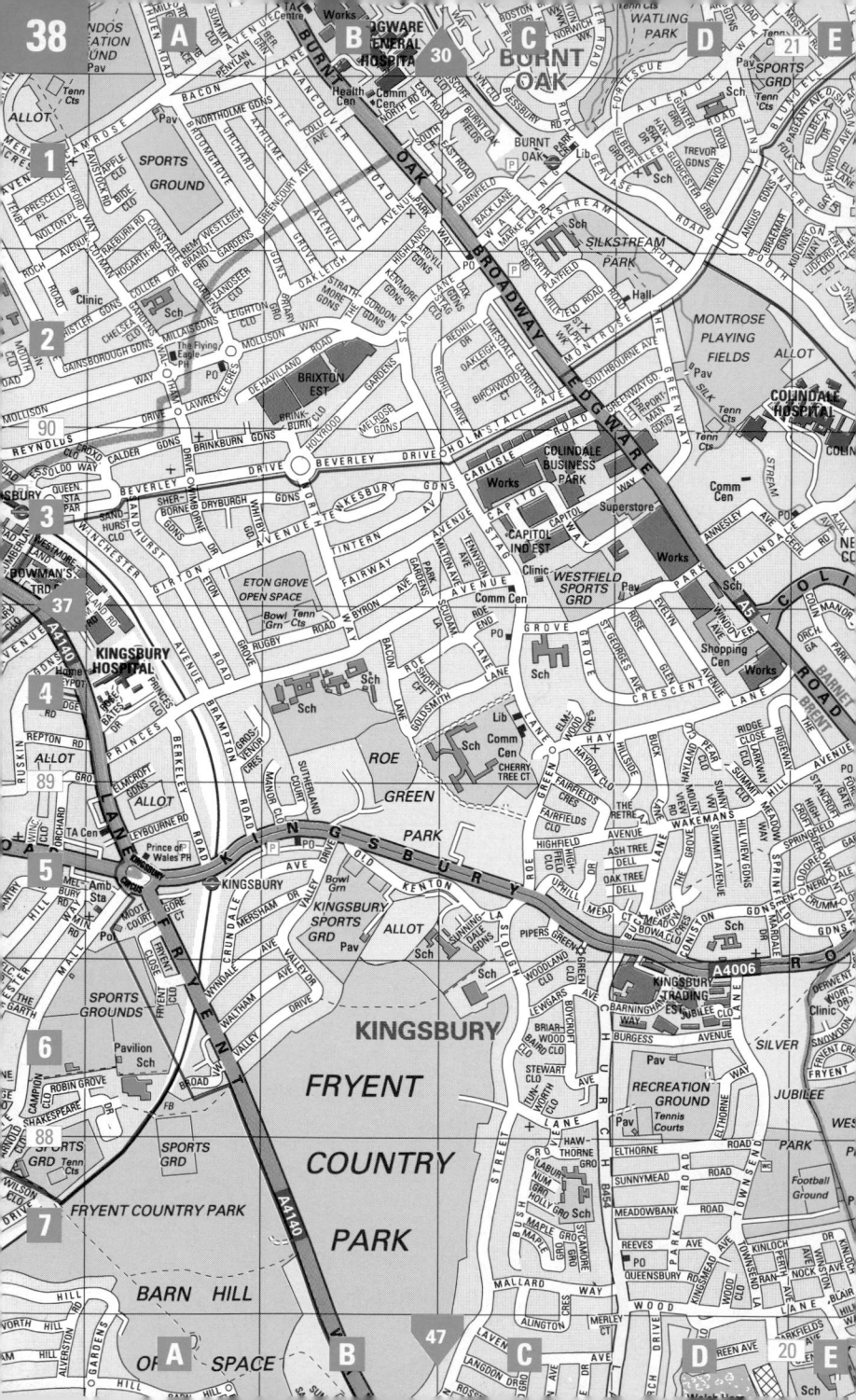

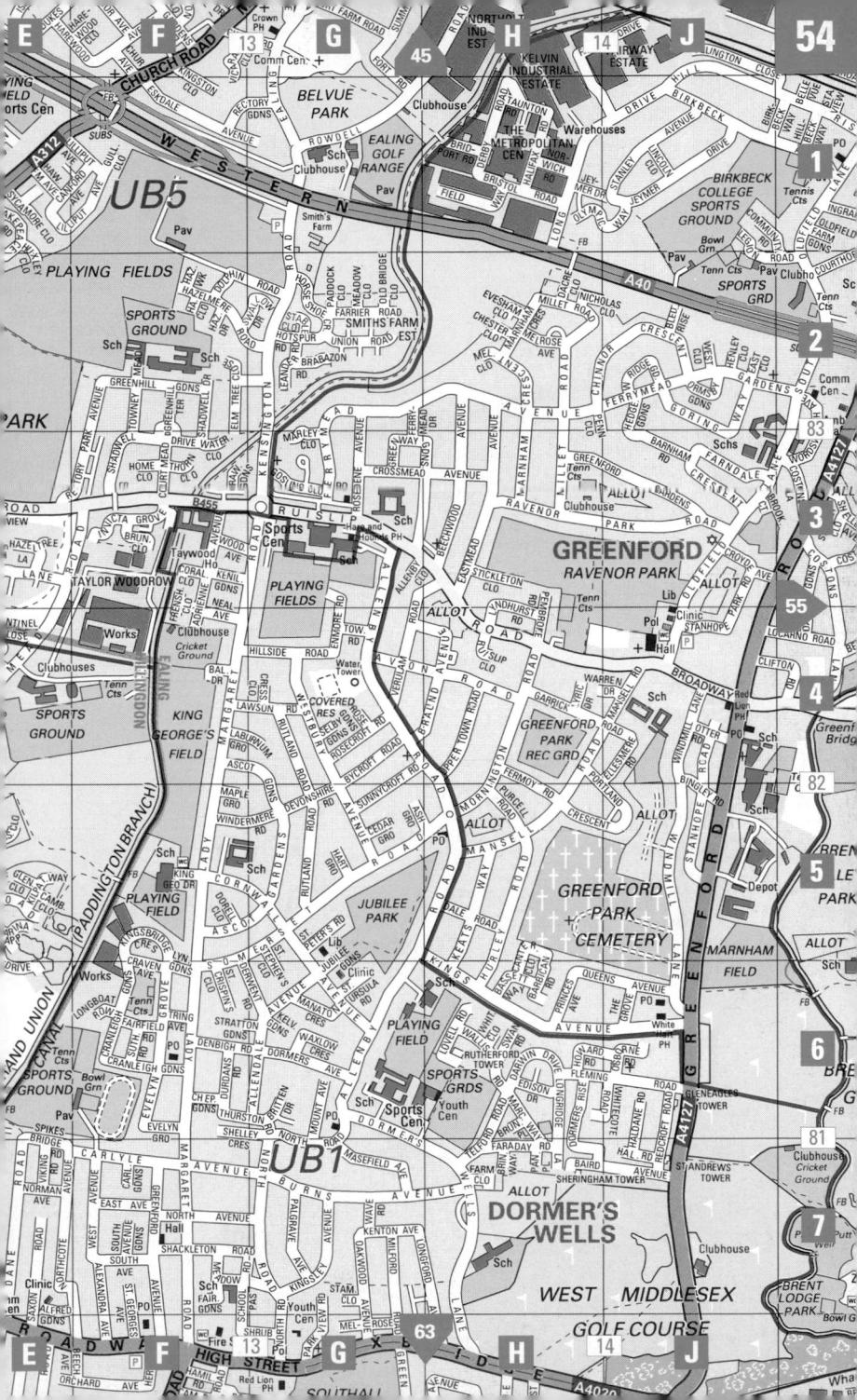

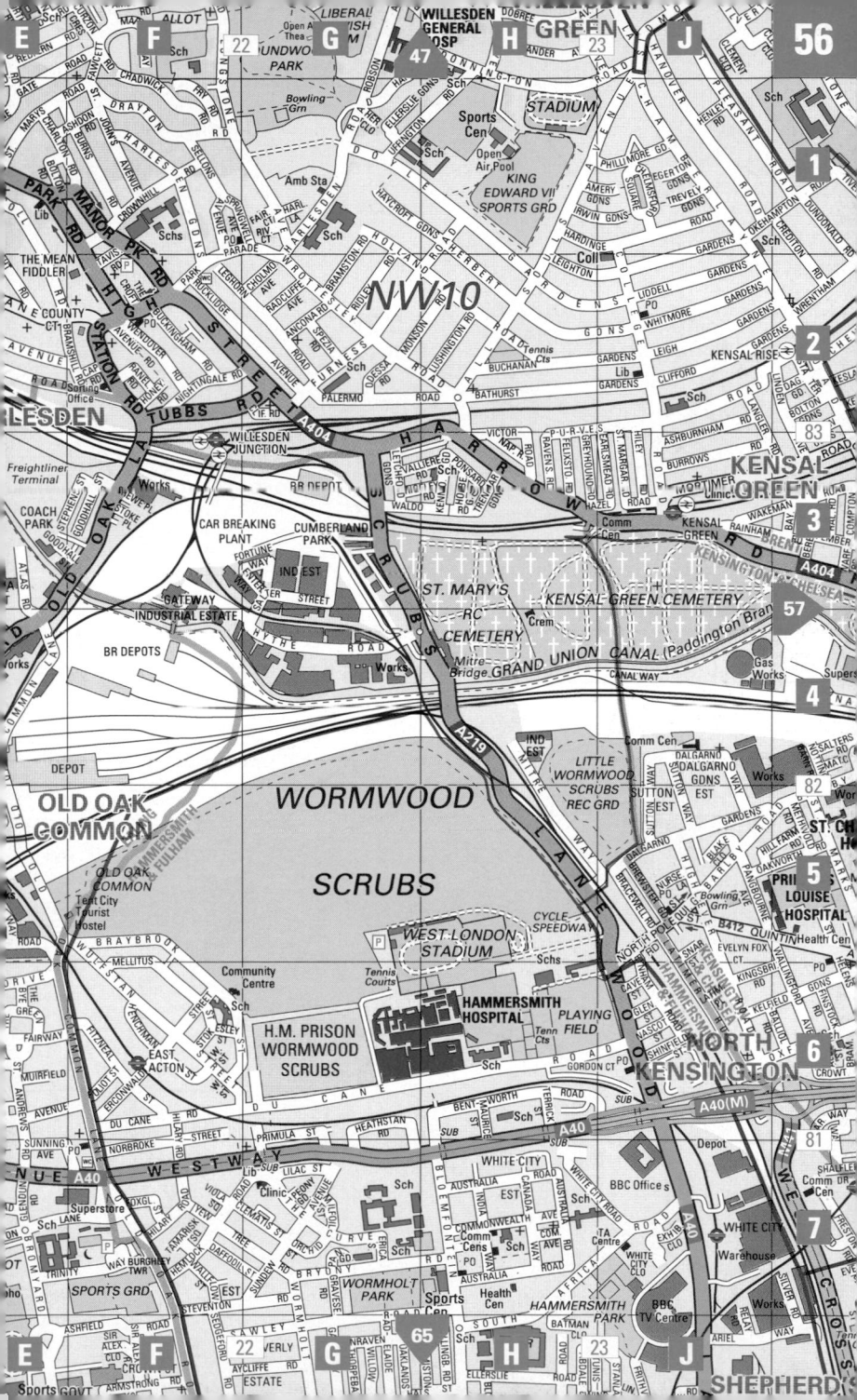

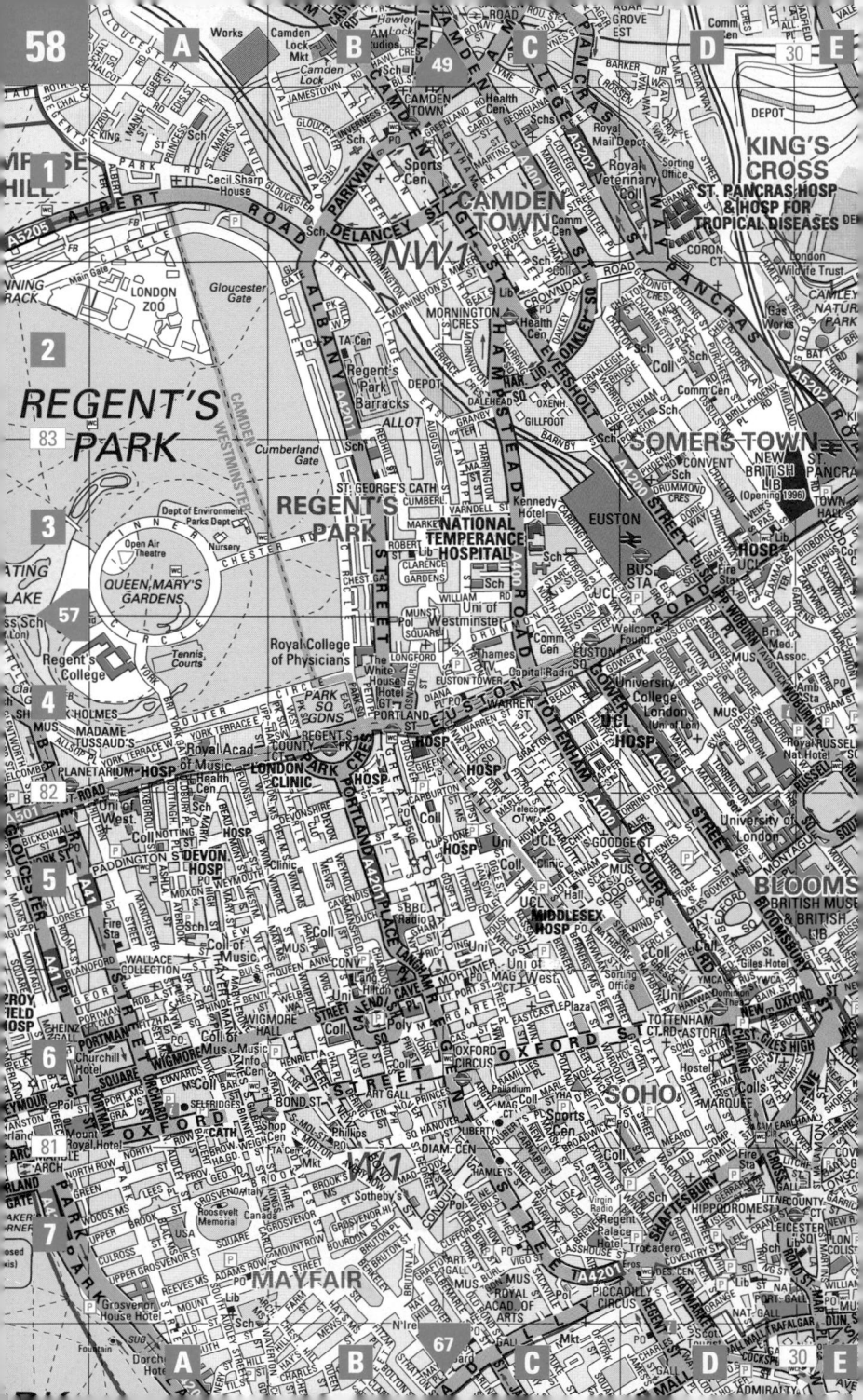

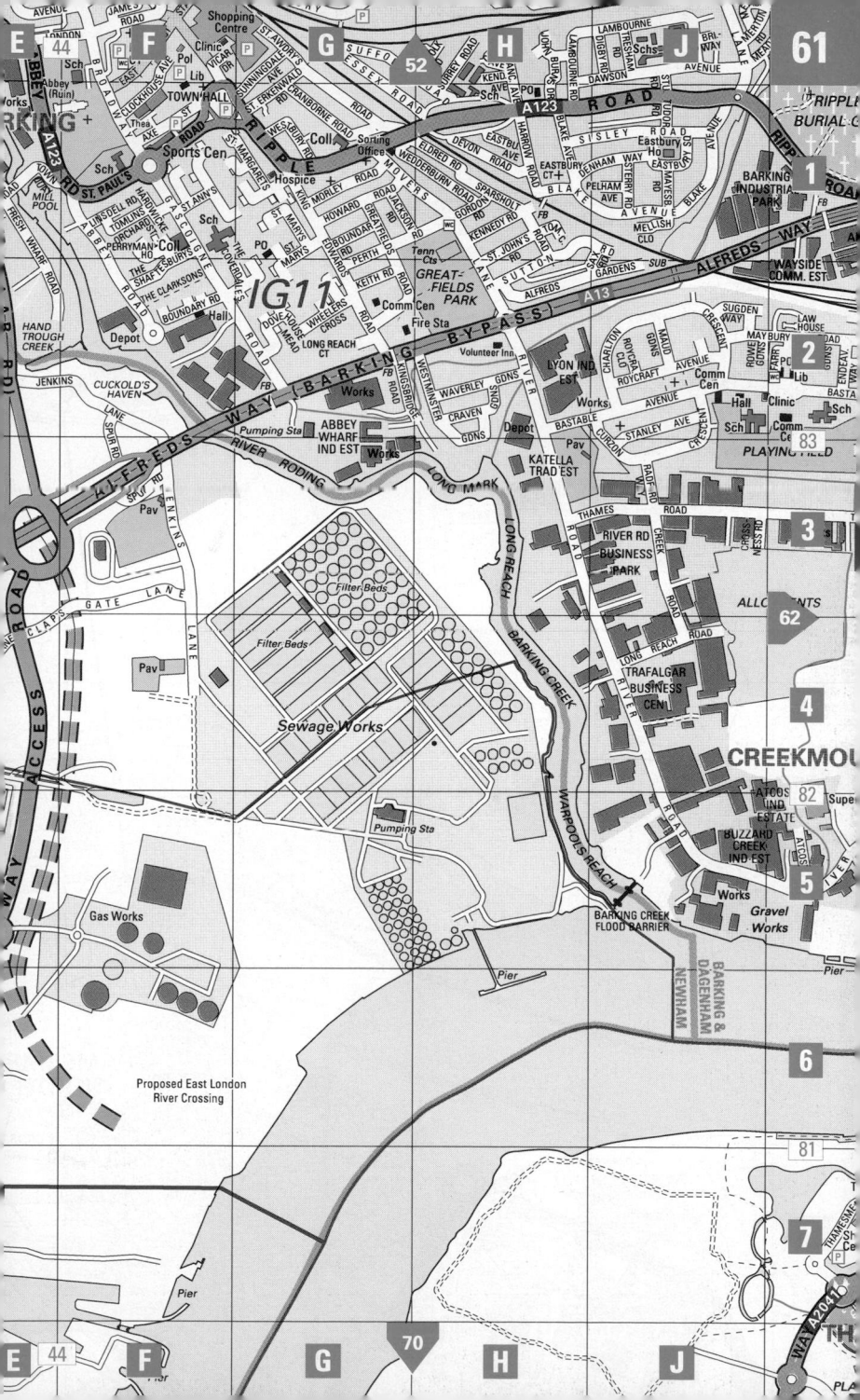

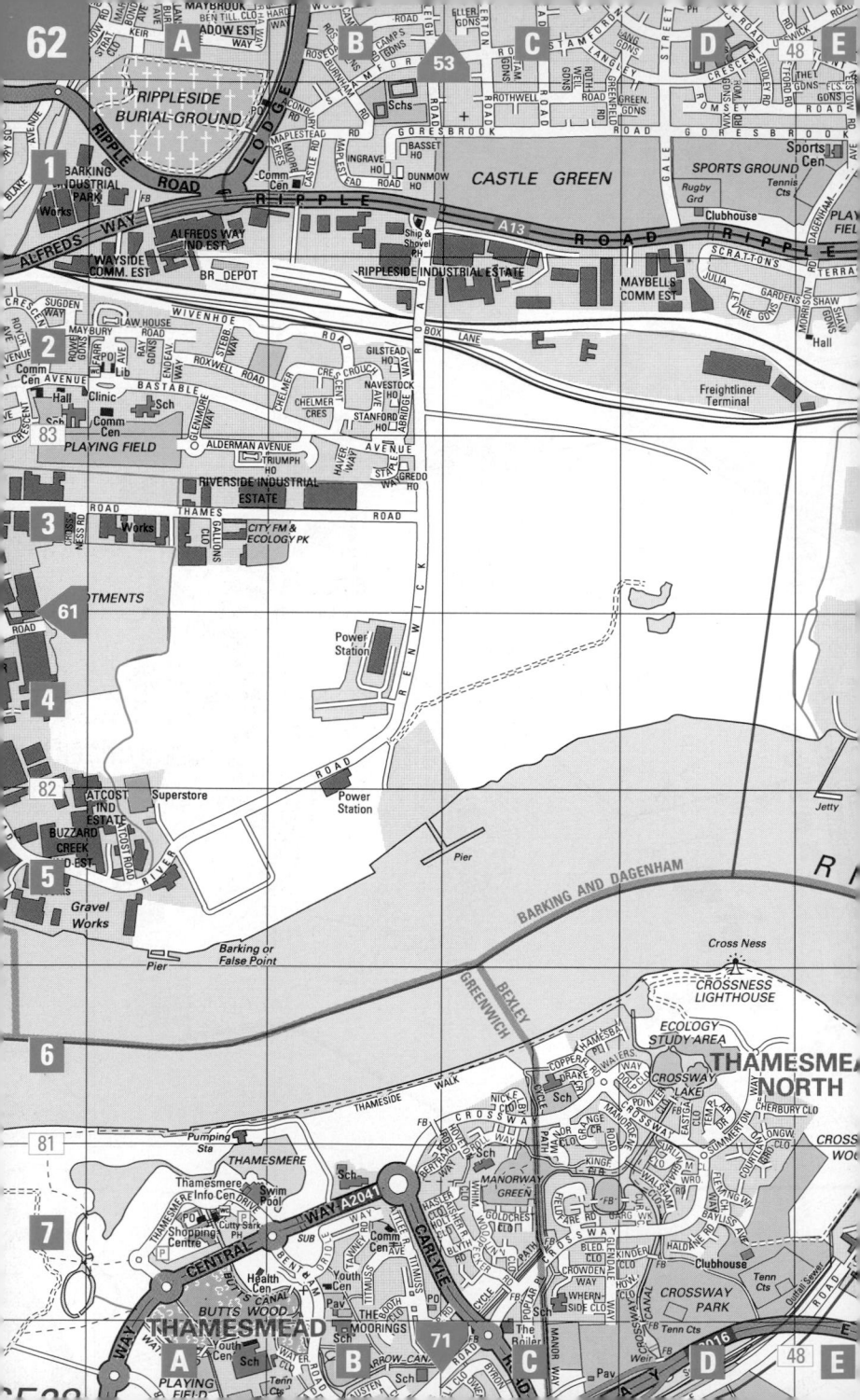

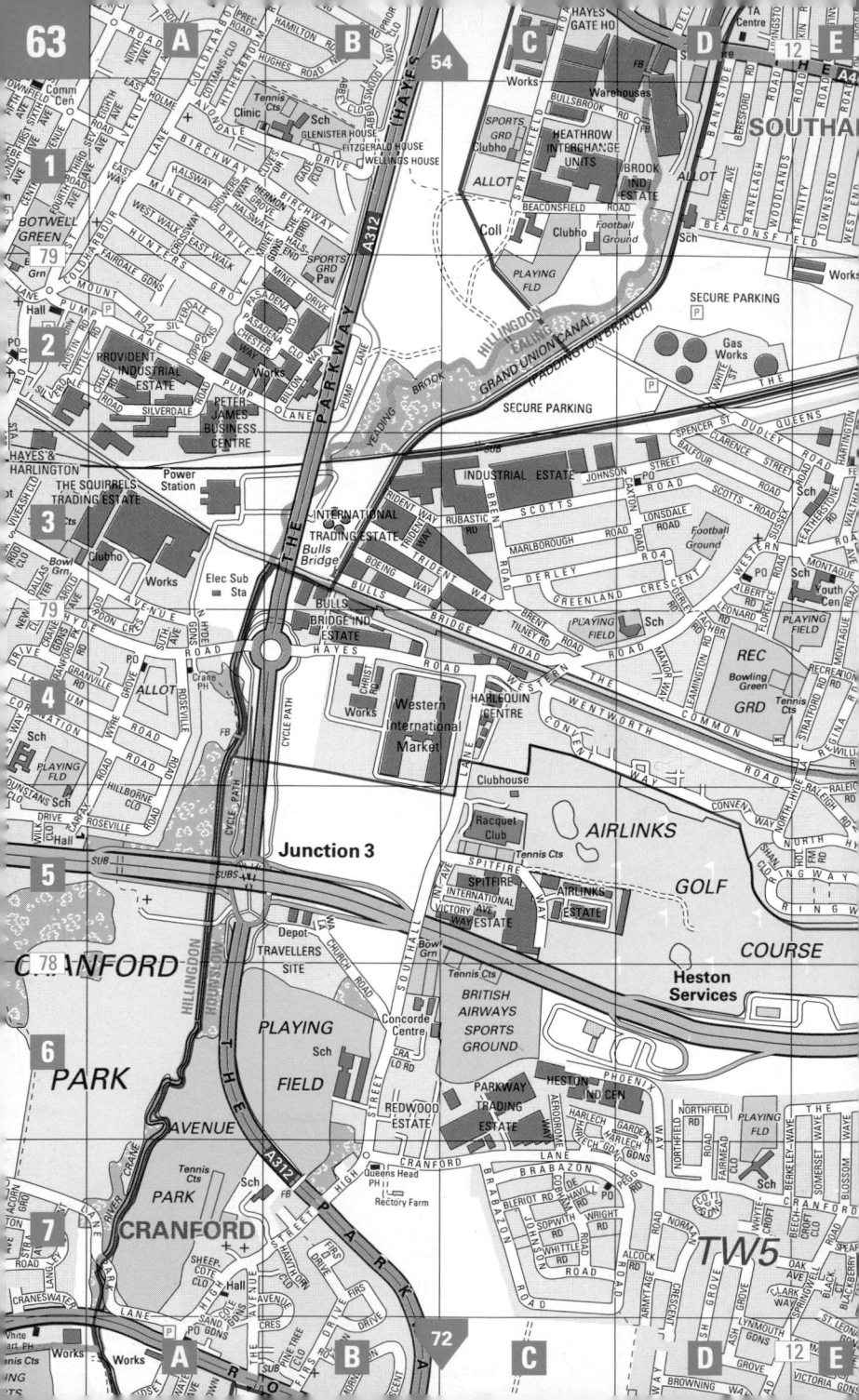

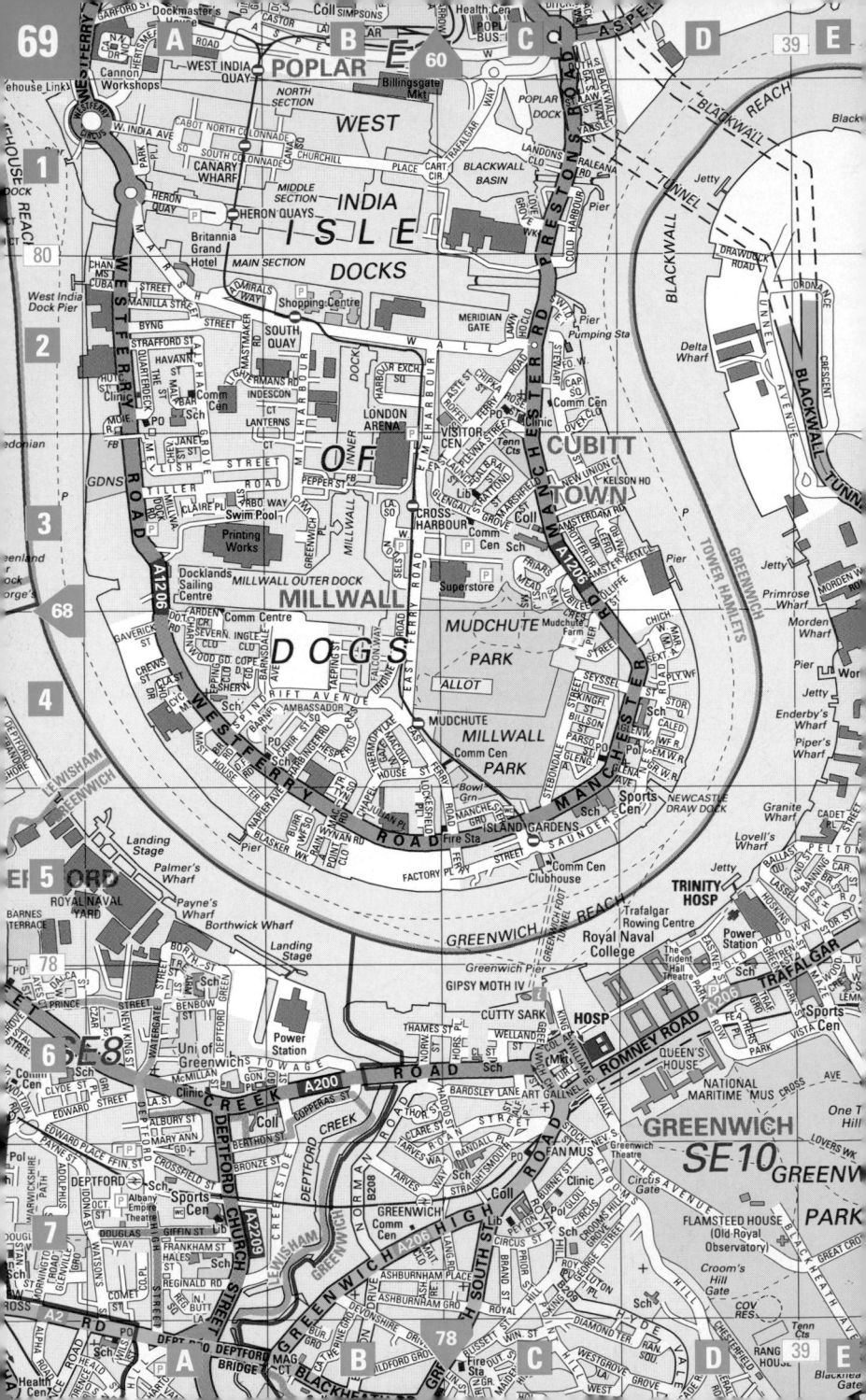

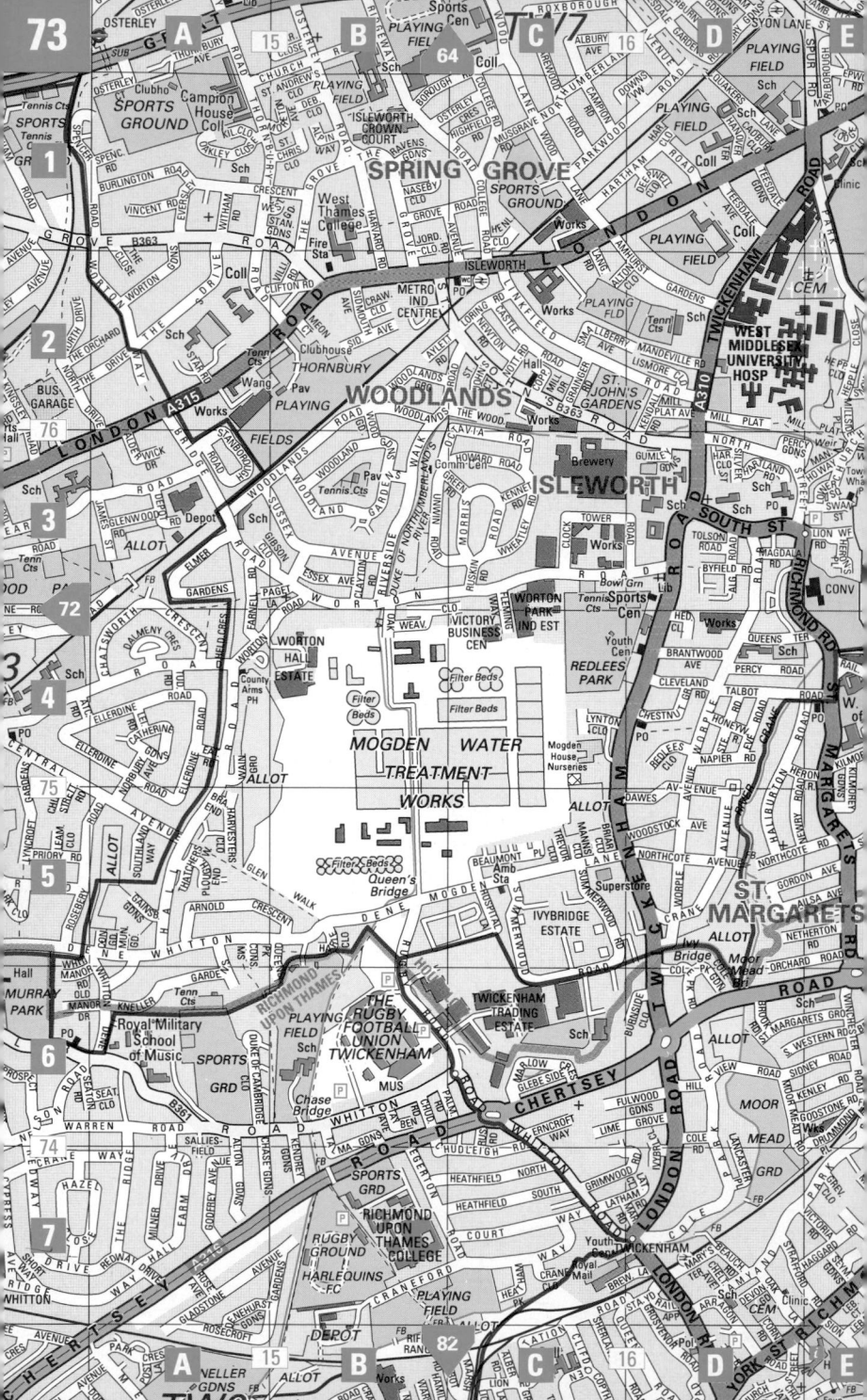

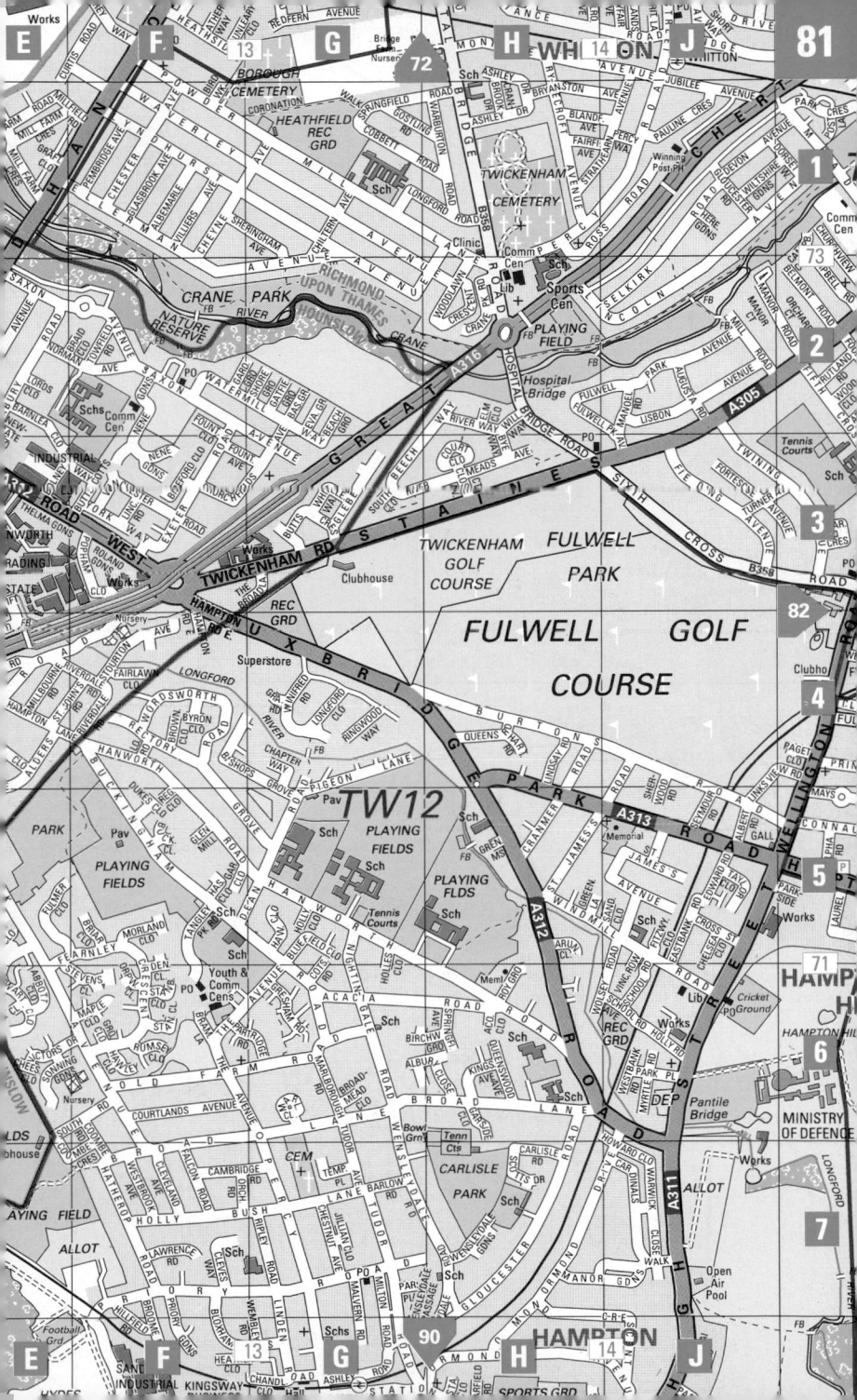

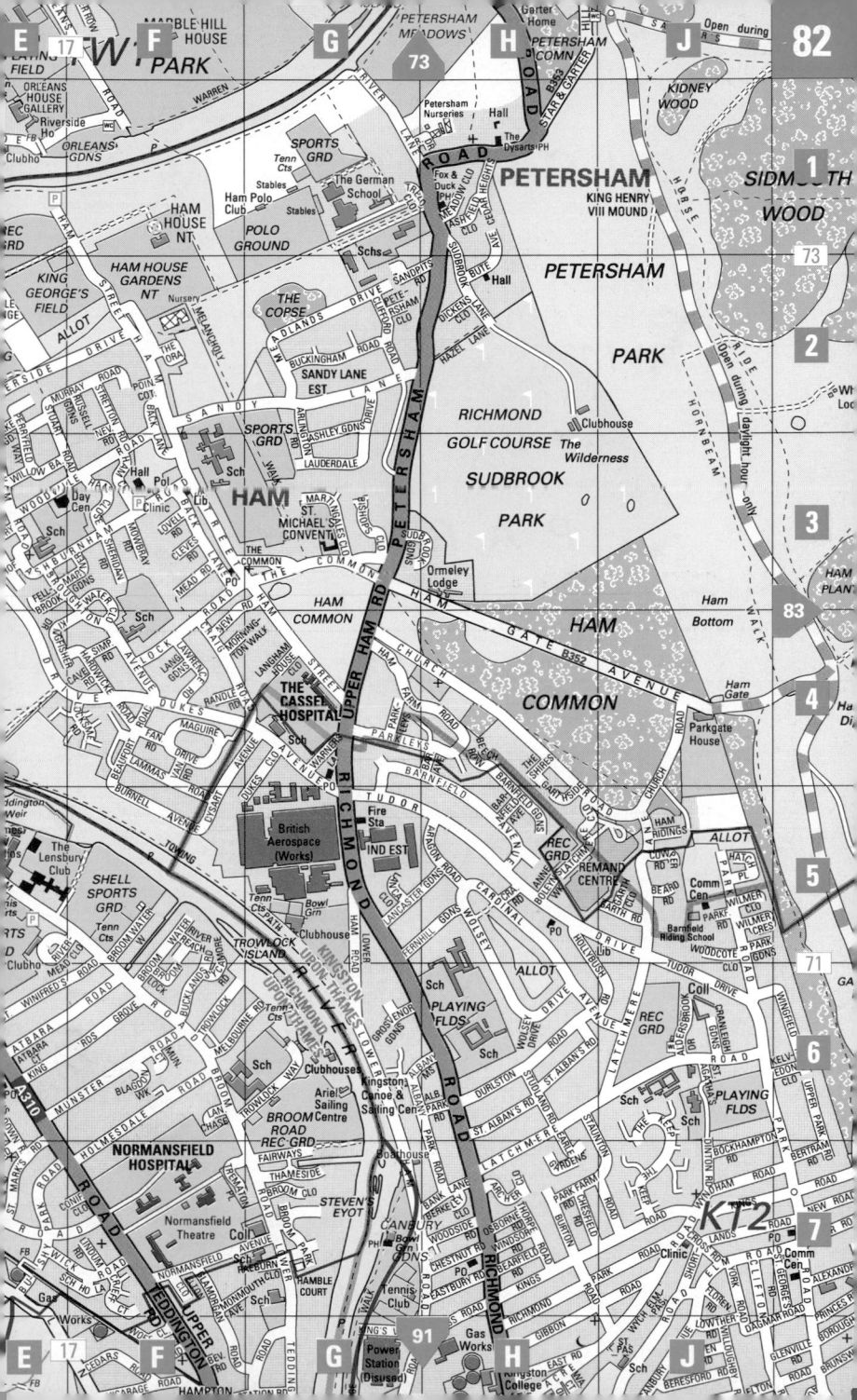

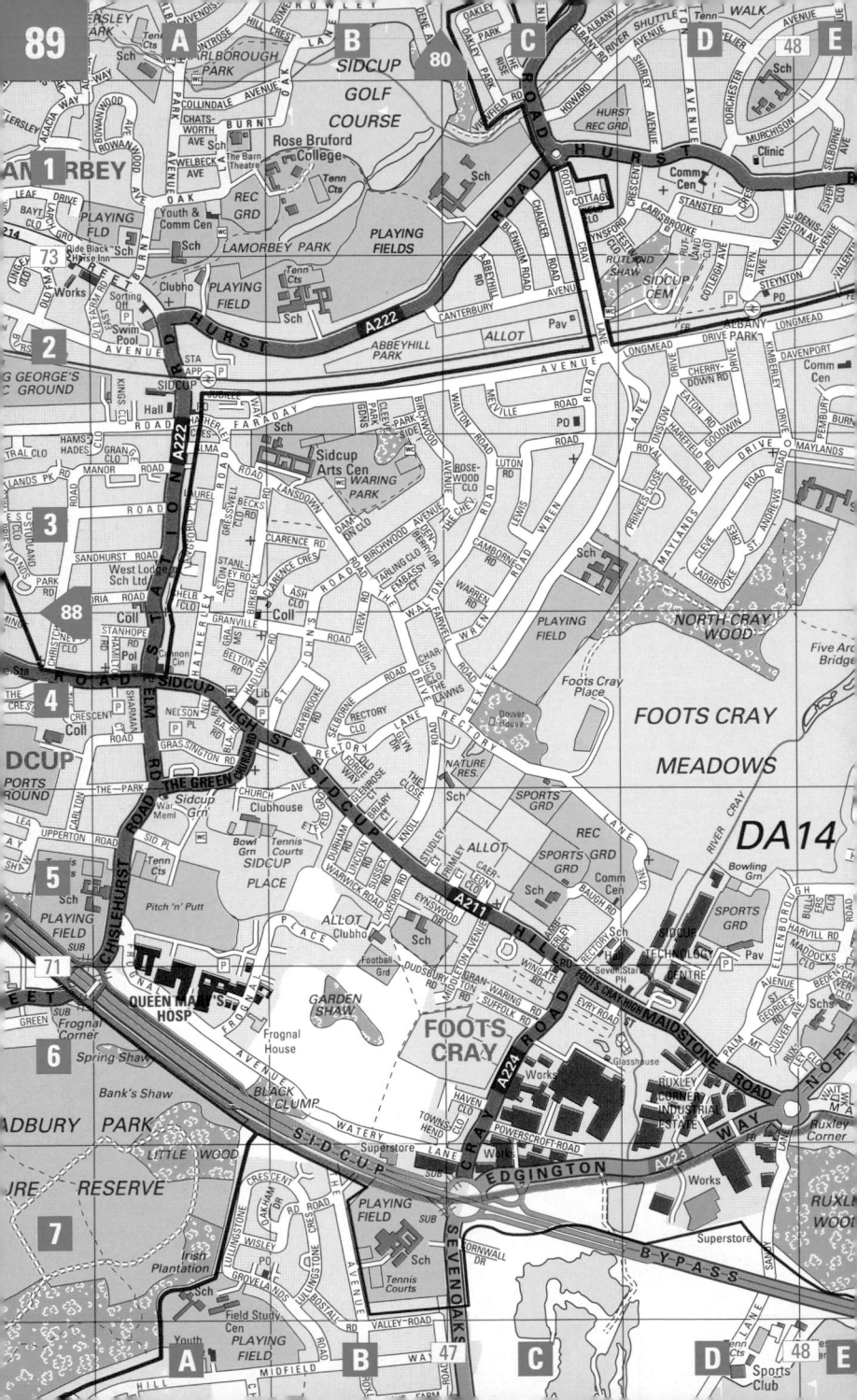

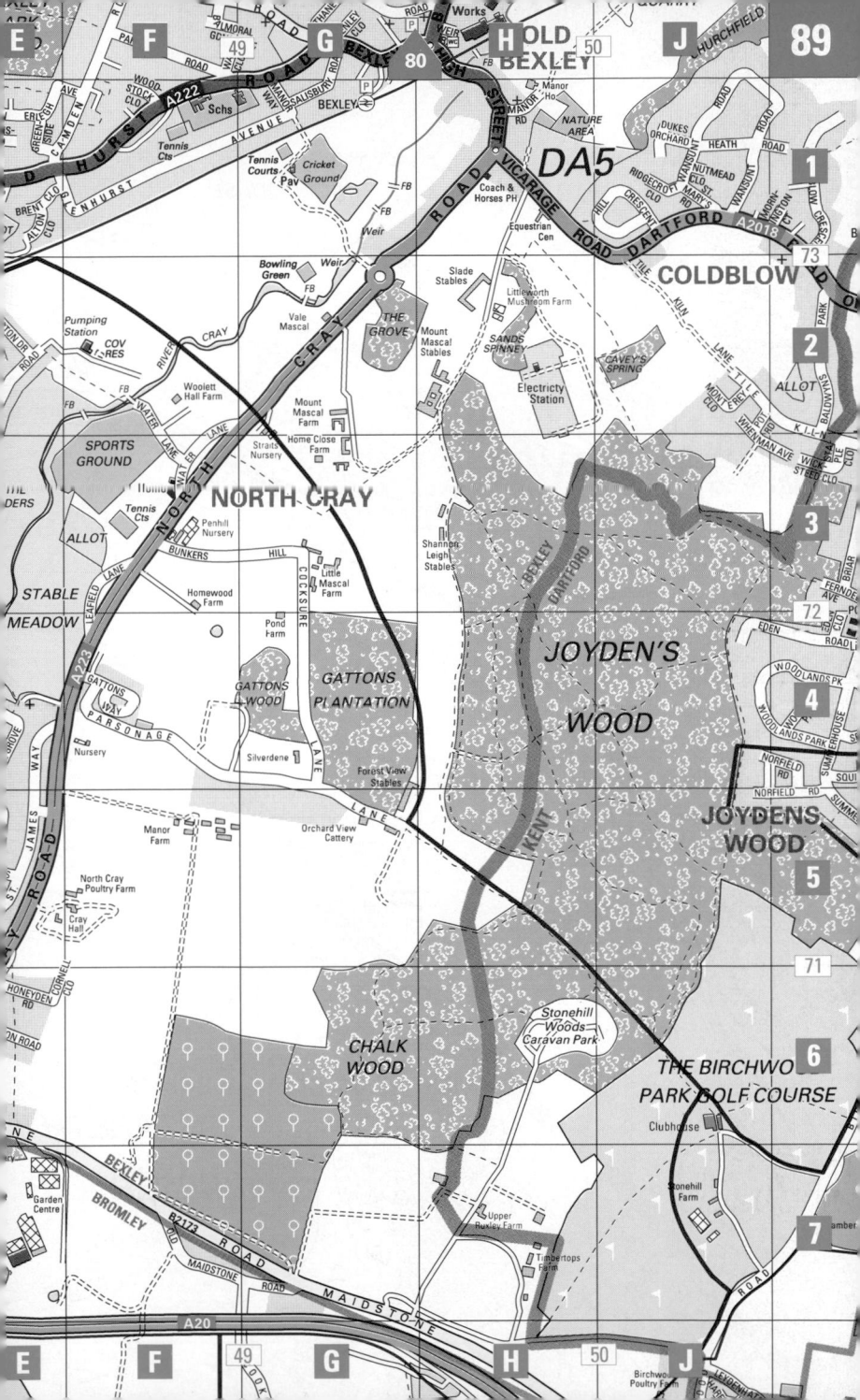

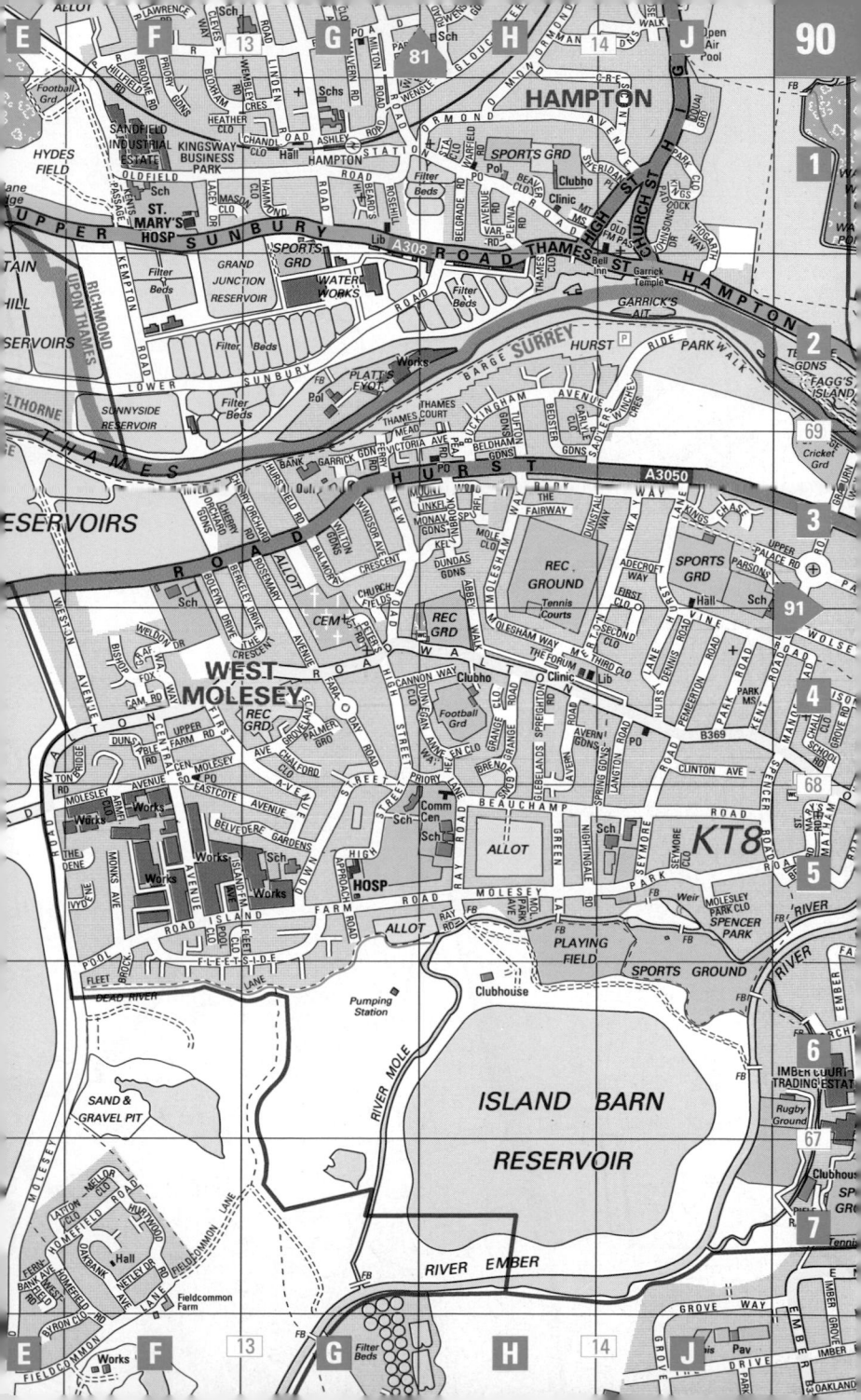

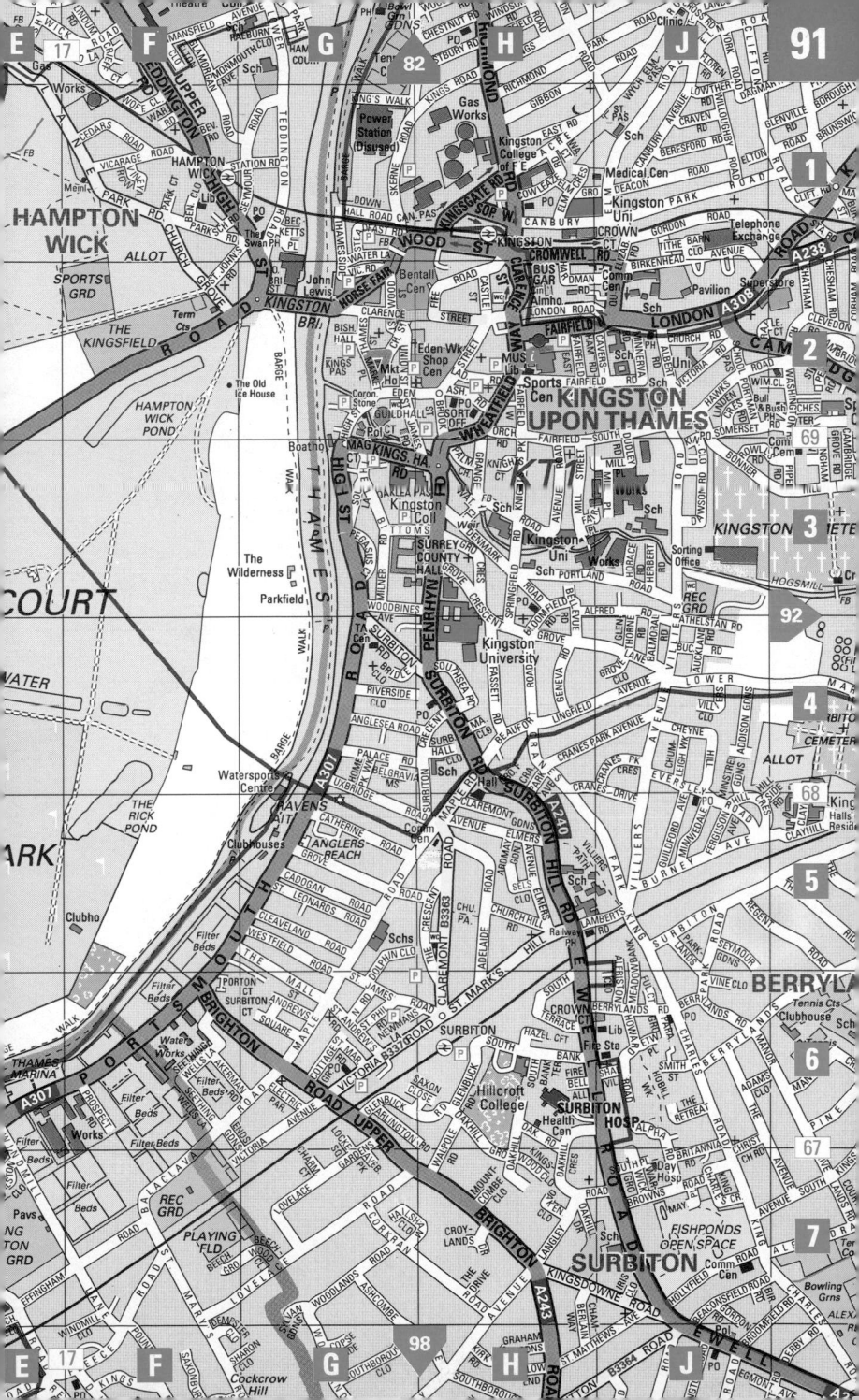

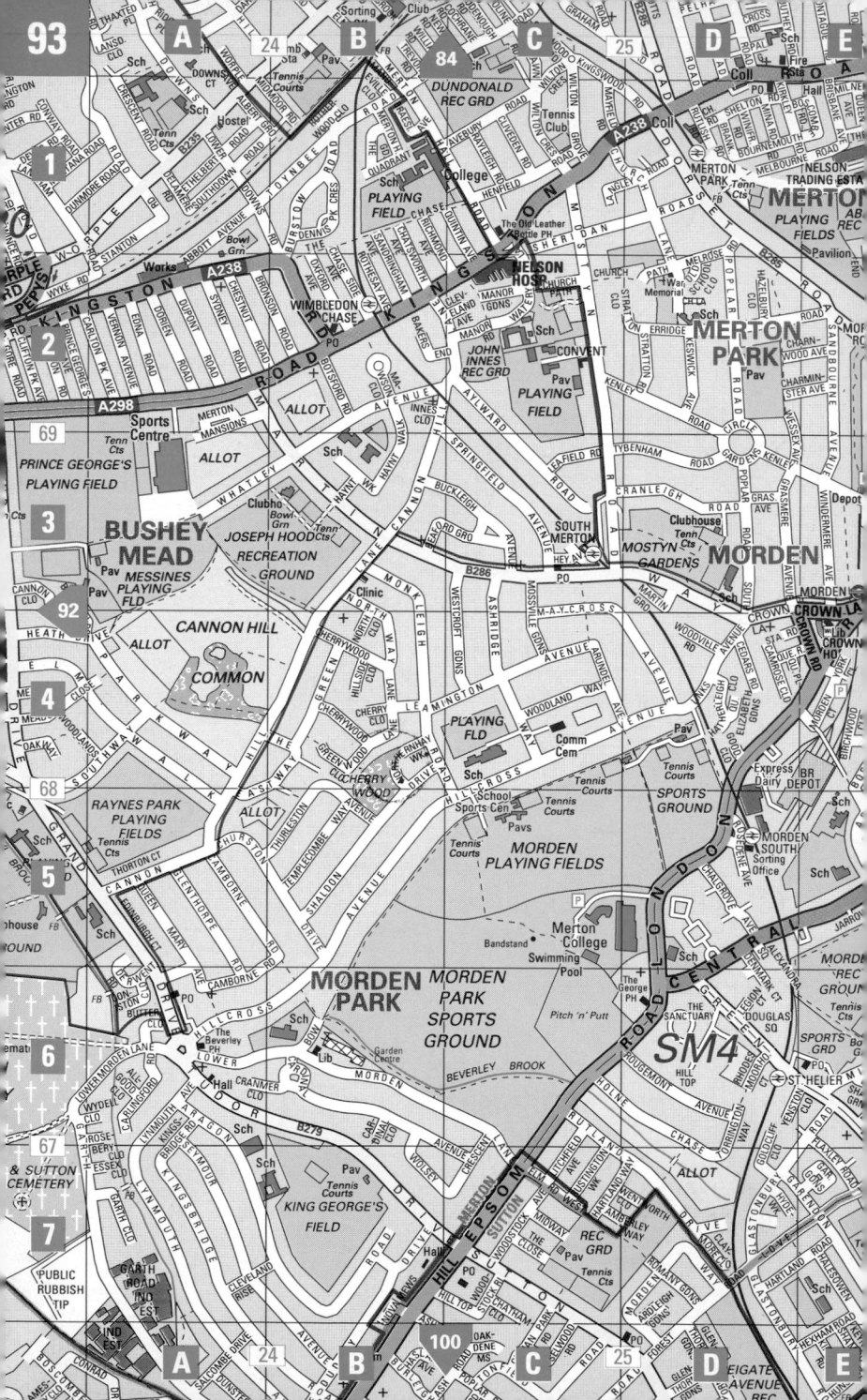

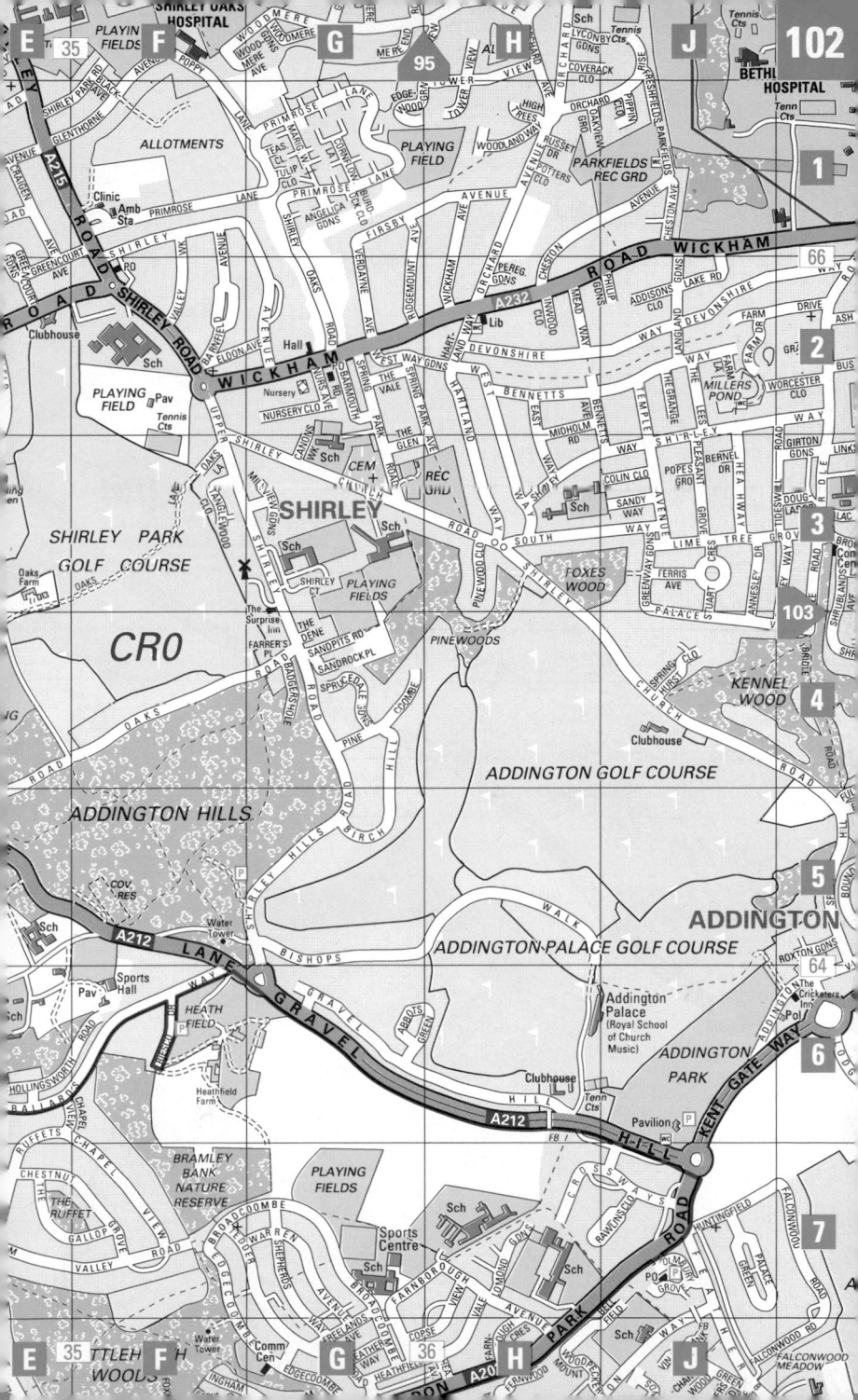

WEST END THEATRES & CINEMAS

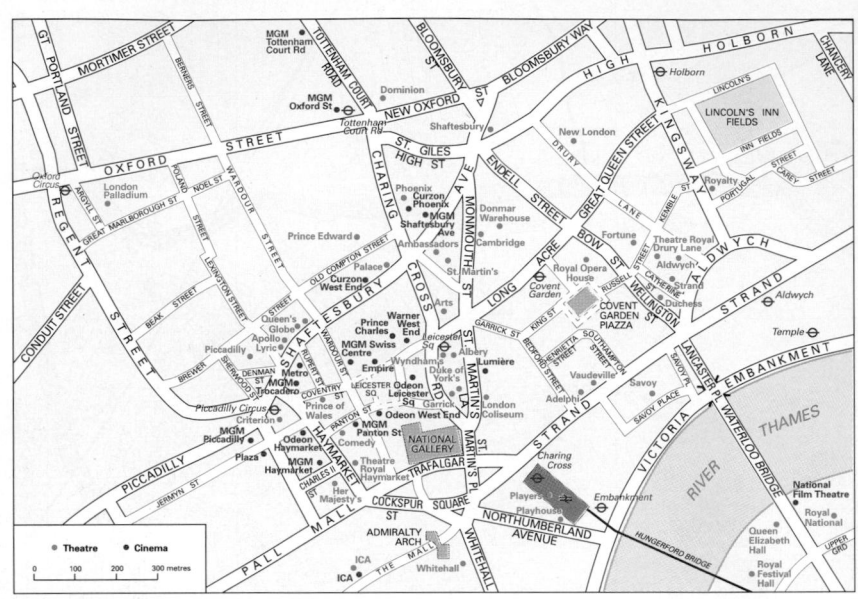

THEATRES

Adelphi *071 334 0055*
Albery *071 867 1115*
Aldwych *071 836 6404*
Ambassadors *071 836 1171*
Apollo *071 494 5070*
Arts *071 836 2132*
Cambridge *071 379 5299*
Comedy *071 867 1045*
Criterion *071 839 4488*
Dominion *071 580 9562*
Donmar Warehouse
   071 867 1150
Duchess *071 494 5075*
Duke of York's *071 836 5122*
Fortune *071 836 2238*
Garrick *071 494 5085*
Globe *071 494 5065*
Her Majesty's *071 494 5400*
ICA *071 930 3647*
London Coliseum
   071 836 3161
London Palladium
   071 494 5020
Lyric *071 494 5045*
New London *071 405 0072*
Palace *071 434 0909*
Phoenix *071 867 1044*
Piccadilly *071 867 1118*
Players *071 839 1134*
Playhouse *071 839 4401*

Prince Edward *071 734 8951*
Prince of Wales
   071 839 5987
Queen Elizabeth Hall
   071 928 3002
Queen's *071 494 5040*
Royal Festival Hall
   071 928 8800
Royal National *071 928 2252*
Royal Opera House
   071 240 1066
Royalty *071 494 5090*
St. Martin's *071 836 1443*
Savoy *071 836 8888*
Shaftesbury *071 379 5399*
Strand *071 930 8800*
Theatre Royal, Drury Lane
   071 494 5000
Theatre Royal, Haymarket
   071 930 8800
Vaudeville *071 836 9987*
Whitehall *071 867 1119*
Wyndham's *071 867 1116*

CINEMAS

Curzon Phoenix *071 240 9661*
Curzon West End *071 439 4805*
Empire *071 437 1234*

ICA *071 930 3647*
Lumière *071 836 0691*
Metro *071 437 0757*
MGM Haymarket
   071 839 1527
MGM Oxford St
   071 636 0310
MGM Panton St *071 930 0631*
MGM Piccadilly *071 437 3561*
MGM Shaftesbury Avenue
   071 836 6279
MGM Swiss Centre
   071 439 4470
MGM Tottenham Court Rd
   071 636 6148
MGM Trocadero *071 434 0031*
National Film Theatre
   071 633 0274
Odeon Haymarket
   0426 915343
Odeon Leicester Sq
   0426 915683
Odeon Mezzanine
   (Odeon Leicester Sq)
   0426 915683
Odeon West End *0426 915574*
Plaza *071 437 1234*
Prince Charles *071 437 8181*
Warner West End
   071 437 4343

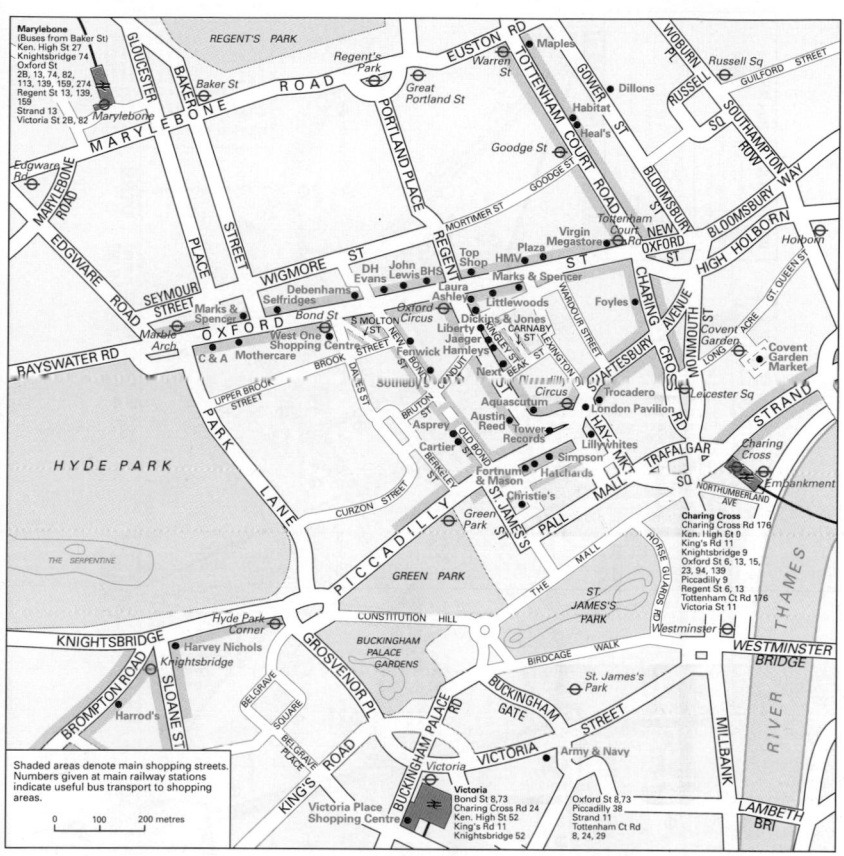

Shaded areas denote main shopping streets. Numbers given at main railway stations indicate useful bus transport to shopping areas.

0   100   200 metres

SHOPS

Aquascutum *071 734 6090*
Army & Navy *071 834 1234*
Asprey *071 493 6767*
Austin Reed *071 734 6789*
BHS(Oxford St) *071 629 2011*
C & A *071 629 7272*
Cartier *071 793 3962*
Christie's *071 839 9060*
Covent Garden Market
    071 836 9137
DH Evans *071 629 8800*
Debenhams *071 580 3000*
Dickins & Jones *071 734 7070*
Dillons *071 636 1577*
Fenwick *071 629 9161*
Fortnum & Mason
    071 734 8040
Foyles *071 437 5660*

Habitat (Tottenham Court Rd)
    071 631 3880
Hamleys *071 734 3161*
Harrod's *071 730 1234*
Harvey Nichols
    071 235 5000
Hatchards *071 439 9921*
Heal's *071 636 1666*
HMV *071 631 3423*
Jaeger *071 734 8211*
John Lewis *071 629 7711*
Laura Ashley (Regent St)
    071 437 9760
Liberty *071 734 1234*
Lillywhites *071 930 3181*
Littlewoods *071 434 4301*
London Pavilion
    071 437 1838

Maples *071 387 7000*
Marks & Spencer
    (Marble Arch) *071 935 7954*
Marks & Spencer (Oxford St)
    071 437 7722
Mothercare *071 629 6621*
Next (Regent St) *071 434 2515*
Plaza on Oxford St
    071 637 8811
Selfridges *071 629 1234*
Simpson *071 734 2002*
Sotheby's *071 493 8080*
Top Shop *071 636 7700*
Tower Records *071 439 2500*
Trocadero *071 439 1791*
Victoria Place Shopping
    Centre *071 931 8811*
Virgin Megastore *071 631 1234*

WEST END & CITY BUS ROUTES

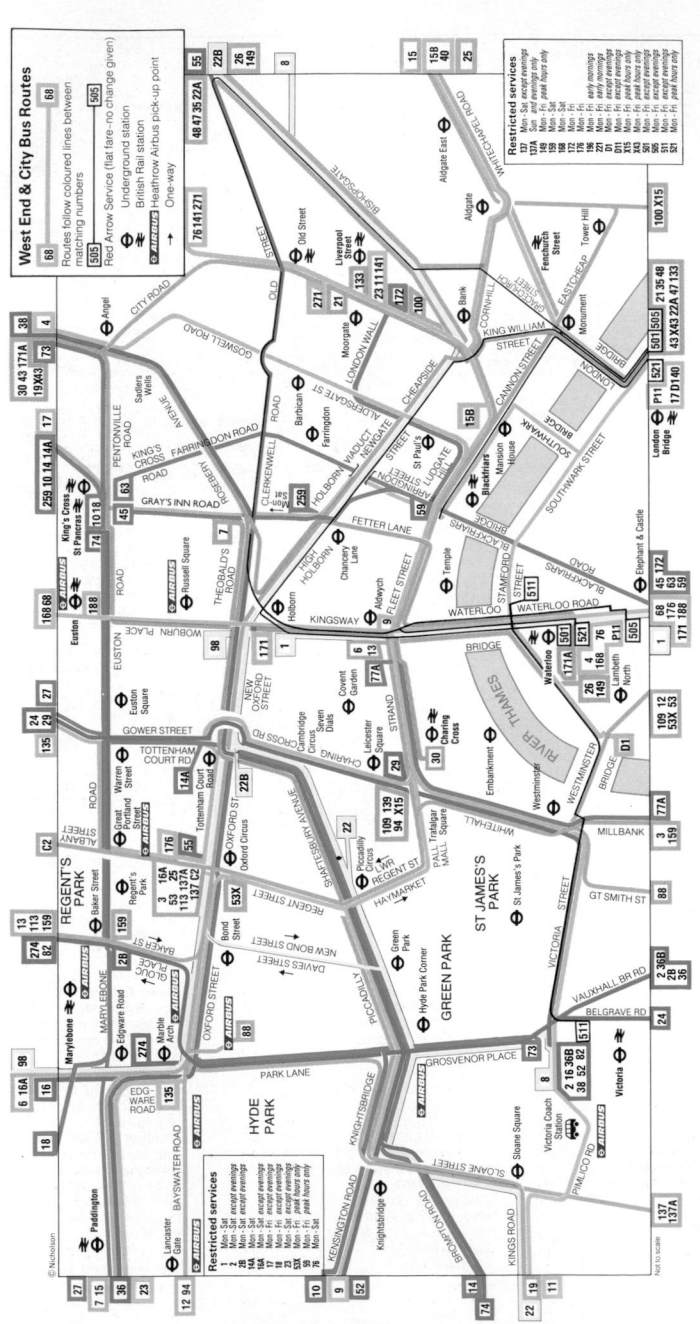

Admiralty Arch	15	J1
Agnew Galleries	15	F1
Albert Memorial	14	E3
Alexandra Palace	40	D3
Angel Centre, The	8	F2
Angel Information Centre	58	H1
Anthony d'Offay Gallery	11	E4
Apollo Victoria	15	F6
Apothecaries' Hall	12	G4
Apsley House,	15	C3
Wellington Museum		
Armourers' and Brasiers' Hall	13	B2
Arsenal Football Club	49	H4
Ashby Windmill	76	E6
Avery Hill Park, Eltham	79	F6
Baden Powell House	18	D1
Baker Street	7	A6
Bank of England	13	B4
Bank of England Museum	13	C4
Bankside Gallery	12	H6
Banqueting House	16	A2
Barbican Arts and	13	A1
Conference Centre		
Barnes Common	74	G3
Battersea Park	66	J7
Bentley Priory, Harrow	25	B3
Bermondsey Market	17	D4
Bethnal Green Museum of	59	F3
Childhood		
Big Ben	16	B4
Billingsgate Fish Market	69	B1
Blackheath	78	D1
Bloomsbury Square	12	B2
Borough Market	17	B2
Brentford Football Club	64	G6
British Dental Association	11	D2
Museum, Wimpole St.		
British Library	12	A2
British Medical Association	7	J5
British Museum	12	A2
British Travel Centre	15	H1
Broadgate Ice and Arena	13	D2
Brockwell Park	76	H6
Brompton Oratory,	14	G6
Brompton Rd.		
Bruce Castle Museum,	41	B1
Tottenham		
Brunel Engine House,	68	F2
Railway Ave.		
Buckingham Palace	15	E4
Burlington Arcade,	11	F6
Burlington Gdns.		
Bushy Park	91	C1
Business Design Centre	58	G1
Cabaret Mechanical Theatre,	12	B5
Covent Garden Market		
Cabinet Office	16	A3
Cabinet War Rooms	16	J3
Camden Lock (Waterbuses)	49	B7
Camden Lock Market	49	B7
Camley Street Natural Park	8	A1
Carlyle's House	18	G6
Carnaby Street	11	F4
Caxton Hall	15	H5
Cenotaph, The	16	A3
Central Criminal Court	12	H3
(Old Bailey)		
Centrepoint	11	J3
Charing Cross Road	11	J4
Charlton Athletic	69	J5
Football Club		
Charterhouse	12	H1
Chelsea Antique Market	18	G5
Chelsea Flower Show,	19	B5
Royal Hospital Grounds		
Chelsea Football Club	18	A7
Chelsea Old Town Hall	18	G4
Chelsea Physic Garden	18	J5
Chinatown, Gerrard Street	11	J5
Chiswick House	65	E6
Church Farm House	38	H3
Museum, Hendon		
City University	8	G4
Clapham Common	76	A4
Clarence House	15	G3
Cleopatra's Needle	12	C6
Clissold Park	50	A2
Clothworkers' Hall	13	E5
Coliseum, The	12	A6
College of Arms	12	J5
Conference Forum, The	13	G3
Court Dress Collection,	14	B2
Kensington Palace		
Courtauld Institute Galleries	12	C5
Covent Garden	12	B5
Crafts Council Gallery,	15	H1
Waterloo Pl.		
Crystal Palace Football Club	95	B4
Crystal Palace National	86	D6
Sport Centre		
Crystal Palace Park	86	C5
Cuming Museum	20	J2
Custom House	13	D6
Cutty Sark	69	C6
Danson Park, Welling	80	C4
Department of Trade	15	J5
and Industry		
Department of Transport	15	J6
and Environment		
Design Centre	11	H6
Design Museum	17	G3
Dickens House, Doughty St.	8	D6
Doctor Johnson's House,	12	F3
Gough Sq.		
Dominion	11	J3
Downing Street	16	A3
Drapers' Hall	13	C3
Dulwich College Picture	77	B7
Gallery		
Dulwich Park	77	C7
Ealing Common	64	H1
Earls Court Exhibition	66	D5
Centre		
Eel Pie Island	82	D1
Eltham Palace	79	B7
Epping Forest	26	J1
Eros	11	H6
Faraday Museum	11	F6
(The Royal Institution),		
Albemarle St.		
Fenton House, Hampstead	48	F3
Festival Pleasure Gardens,	19	B7
Battersea Park		
Finsbury Park	40	H7
Fishmongers' Hall	13	C6
Fitzroy Square	7	F6
Flamstead House Museum,	69	D7
Greenwich		
Fleet Street	12	F4
Florence Nightingale	16	C4
Museum		
Flower Market	20	A5
Foreign Office	16	A3
Fortnum and Mason	15	G1
Freightliners City Farm	49	G6
Freud Museum,	48	G6
Maresfield Gdns.		
Fulham Football Club	75	A1
Fulham Palace	75	B2
Geological Museum	14	F6
George Inn,	17	B2
Borough High St.		
Gipsy Moth IV	69	C6
Golders Hill Park	48	D2
Goldsmiths' Hall	12	J3
Gray's Inn	12	D1
Green Park	15	E3
Greenwich Park	69	D7
Greenwich Pier	69	C6
Grocers' Hall	13	B4
Guildhall	13	B3
Gunnersbury Park, Ealing	64	J4
H.M. Treasury	16	A3
H.M.S. 'Belfast'	17	E1
H.M.S. 'President'	12	F5
Haberdashers' Hall	13	A3
Hackney Marshes	50	J4
Haggerston City Farm	9	H2
Ham House	82	F1
Hamleys	11	F5
Hammersmith Palais	65	J4
Hampstead Heath	48	G2
Hampton Court Palace	91	B3
Harrods	14	J5
Harrow School	46	B1
Hay's Galleria	17	D1
Hayward Gallery	16	D1
Heinz Gallery, R.I.B.A.	11	B3
Hogarths House,	65	E6
Hogarth La.		
Holland Park	66	C2
Home Office	15	H4
Horniman Museum	86	E1
Horse Guards Parade	16	A2
Hospital Museum,	19	B4
Chelsea Royal Hospital		
Hounslow Heath	72	E6
Houses of Parliament	16	B4
Hyde Park	14	G1
Hyde Park Corner	15	C3
Imperial College,	14	E5
University of London		
Imperial War Museum	16	F6
Institute of Contemporary	15	J2
Arts		
Ironmongers' Hall	12	J2
Ismaili Centre	18	F1
Jack Straw's Castle P.H.	48	F3
Jewel Tower,	16	A5
Houses of Parliament		
Jewish Museum	7	J5
Jubilee Gardens	16	C3
Keats House, Hampstead	48	H4
Kempton Park Racecourse	81	C7
Kensington Gardens	14	D2
Kensington Palace	14	B2
Kenwood House,	48	H1
Hampstead		
Kew Bridge Steam Museum	64	H3
Kew Gardens	64	G5
Kew Observatory	73	E3
Kings Road, Chelsea	18	F5
Lambeth Palace	16	C6
Lancaster House	15	F3
Leadenhall Market	13	D4
Leicester Square	11	J6
Leighton House,	66	C3
Holland Park Rd.		
Lesnes Abbey (ruins)	71	D4
Leyton Orient Football Club	51	B3
Liberty	11	F4
Lincoln's Inn	12	D3
Linley Sambourne House,	66	D2
Stafford Ter.		
Little Venice (Waterbuses)	10	C1
Livesey Museum	68	E6
Lloyds of London	13	D4
London Brass Rubbing	12	A6
Centre, St. Martin-in-the-		
Fields Church		
London Bridge	17	C1
London Central Mosque	6	H4
London College of Printing	16	H6
London Diamond Centre	11	E4
London Dungeon	17	C2
London Palladium	11	F4
London Peace Pagoda,	19	A6
Battersea Park		
London Silver Vaults	12	E2
London Stone	13	B5
London Toy and Model	10	D5
Museum, Craven Hill		
London Transport Museum,	12	B5
Covent Gdn.		
London Zoo	7	B1
Lord's Cricket Ground	6	F3
and Museum		
Madame Tussaud's	7	B6
Mall Galleries	15	J1
Mansion House	13	B4
Marble Arch	11	A5
Marble Hill House,	73	F7
Twickenham		
Marlborough House	15	G2
Master Mariners' Hall,	12	E6
H.Q.S. 'Wellington'		
Mercers' Hall	13	B4
Merchant Taylors' Hall	13	C4
Methodist Central Hall	15	J4
Middlesex Guildhall	16	A4
Millbank Tower	20	A2
Millwall Football Club	68	G6
Ministry of Agriculture,	16	B1
Fisheries and Food		

Ministry of Defence	16	A2
Monument, The	13	C5
Morden College	78	G2
Museum of Garden History	16	C6
Museum of Instruments, Royal College of Music	14	E5
Museum of London	12	J2
Museum of Mankind, Burlington Gdns.	11	F6
Museum of the Moving Image (M.O.M.I.)	16	D1
Museum of the Royal Pharmaceutical Society of Great Britain (R.P.S.G.B.)	16	C6
Music Information Centre	11	C4
Musical Museum, High St., Brentford	64	H6
National Army Museum	19	A6
National Gallery	11	J6
National Maritime Museum	69	D6
National Portrait Gallery	11	J6
National Postal Museum	12	H3
National Westminster Tower	13	D3
Natural History Museum	14	E6
Nelson's Column	16	A1
New Covent Garden Market	67	D7
New Scotland Yard	15	H5
North Woolwich Station Museum	70	D2
Northern Ireland Tourist Board	15	E1
Notting Hill Carnival, Ladbroke Gro.	57	B6
Old Admiralty Buildings (M.o.D.)	15	J2
Old County Hall	16	C3
Old Curiosity Shop	12	C4
Old Deer Park, Richmond	73	G3
Olympia	66	B3
Operating Theatre Museum	17	C2
Orleans House Gallery, Twickenham	82	E1
Oscar Wilde's House	19	A5
Osterley Park House	63	J5
Oval, The (Cricket Ground)	20	D5
Oxford Circus	11	F4
Oxford Street	11	A4
P.S. 'Tattershall Castle'	16	B2
Pall Mall	15	G2
Passmore Edwards Museum	51	F6
Passport Office	15	G5
Patent Office	12	E3
Percival David Foundation of Chinese Art, Gordon Sq.	7	J6
Peter Pan Statue	14	E1
Petticoat Lane (Market)	13	E2
Petts Wood	97	G3
Photographers' Gallery, Great Newport Street	11	J5
Piccadilly Circus	11	H6
Planetarium	7	B6
Pollock's Toy Museum	11	G1
Pomeroy Purdy Gallery	17	H3
Primrose Hill	57	J1
Prince Henry's Room	12	E4
Public Record Office	12	E3
Public Record Office Museum	12	E4
Q.P.R. Football Club	65	H1
Queen Elizabeth Hall and Purcell Room	16	D1
Queen Elizabeth II Conference Centre	15	J4
Queen Elizabeth's Hunting Lodge, Epping Forest	26	F7
Queen Victoria Memorial	15	F4
Queen's Gallery	15	E4
Queen's Ice Rink	10	B6
Queen's Tower	14	E5
Queens Club (Tennis Centre)	66	B5
R.A.A.B. Gallery	19	J3
R.A.F. Museum, Hendon	38	F2
Regent Street	11	E3
Regent's Park	6	J2
Richmond Palace (remains)	73	F5
Richmond Park	83	A1
Roman Bath, Strand	12	D5
Rotunda Museum of Artillery, Woolwich	70	C5
Royal Academy of Arts	11	F6
Royal Academy of Dramatic Art (R.A.D.A.)	11	H1
Royal Academy of Music	7	C6
Royal Albert Hall	14	E4
Royal Botanic Gardens	64	G5
Royal College of Art	14	E4
Royal College of Music	14	E5
Royal College of Surgeons	12	D3
Royal Courts of Justice	12	D4
Royal Exchange (L.I.F.F.E.)	13	C4
Royal Festival Hall	16	D2
Royal Geographical Society	14	F4
Royal Horticultural Society (New Hall)	15	H6
Royal Horticultural Society (Old Hall)	19	H1
Royal Mews	15	E5
Royal National Theatre	16	D1
Royal Naval College	69	D6
Royal Opera House	12	B4
Saatchi Collection	57	E1
St. Bartholomew-the-Great Church, Cloth Fair	12	H2
St. Bride's Church and Crypt Museum	12	G4
St. Bride's Printing Library, Bride La.	12	G4
St. Clement Danes Church, Strand	12	D4
St. James's Palace	15	G2
St. James's Park	15	H3
St. John's Gate and Museum of the Order of St. John	8	G6
St. Katharine's Dock	17	H1
St. Lawrence Jewry Church, Gresham St.	13	A3
St. Martin-in-the-Fields Church, Trafalgar Square	12	A6
St. Mary at Hill Church, Lovat La.	13	D5
St. Mary-le-Bow Church	13	A4
St. Paul's Cathedral	12	J4
Salters' Hall	13	A2
Salvation Army International Headquarters, Queen Victoria St.	12	J5
Schooner Kathleen and May	17	B1
Science Museum	14	F6
Science Reference Library	12	E2
Scottish Tourist Board	15	J1
Selfridges	11	C4
Serpentine Gallery	14	F2
Serpentine, The	14	G2
Shakespeare Globe Museum	16	J1
Shell Centre	16	D2
Sherlock Holmes Museum	7	A6
Sir John Soane's Museum, Lincoln's Inn Fields	12	C3
Skinners' Hall, Dowgate Hill	13	B5
Smithfield Central Market	12	G2
Soho	11	H5
Somerset House	12	C5
Sotheby's	11	E5
South Bank	16	D1
South London Art Gallery, Peckham Rd.	77	B1
Southwark Cathedral	17	B1
Southwark Park	68	F4
Speaker's Corner	11	A5
Spitalfields Community Farm	9	H6
Stepping Stones Farm	59	G5
Stock Exchange	13	C4
Story of Telecommunications	12	H5
Strand, The	16	A1
Surrey Docks Farm	68	J2
Syon House, Brentford	73	F1
Tate Gallery	20	A2
Telecom Tower	11	F1
Temple Bar	12	E4
Temple of Mithras, Victoria St.	13	A4
Temple, The	12	E5
Thames Flood Barrier	70	A2
Thames House	20	A1
Theatre Museum, Tavistock Street	12	B5
Theatre Royal, Drury La.	12	B4
Tottenham Hotspur Football Club	33	C7
Tower Bridge Museum and Exhibitions	17	F2
Tower Hill	13	F6
Tower Pier	17	E1
Tower of London	13	F6
Toynbee Hall	13	G3
Trafalgar Square	16	A1
Trent Park, Enfield	24	B2
Trinity House	13	F5
Trocadero	11	H6
Twickenham Rugby Ground	73	B6
University College London	7	H5
University of London	7	J6
Victoria Coach Station	19	D2
Victoria Embankment Gardens	16	B1
Victoria Park	59	H1
Victoria Tower, Houses of Parliament	16	A5
Victoria and Albert Museum	14	F6
Vintners' Hall	13	A5
Wallace Collection	11	C3
Walworth City Farm	20	H4
Waterlow Park, Highgate	49	B1
Wellington Arch	15	C3
Wellington Museum	15	C3
Wembley Conference Centre	46	J4
Wembley Stadium	47	A5
Wesley's House	9	C5
West Ham United Football Club	61	A2
Westminster Abbey	16	A5
Westminster Abbey Museum	16	A5
Westminster Cathedral	15	F6
Westminster City Hall	15	G5
Westminster Pier	16	B3
Whitbread Brewery	13	A1
Whitbread Shire Horse Stables, Garrett St.	9	A5
Whitechapel Art Gallery	13	G3
Whitehall	16	A2
William Morris Gallery, Lloyd Park	42	A3
Wimbledon (All England Tennis Club)	84	B4
Wimbledon Common	83	F4
Wimbledon Football Club	84	E4
Woolwich Common	70	C7
World Trade Centre	13	G6
Y.H.A., Carter Lane	12	H4
Y.H.A., Earl's Court	18	A3
Y.H.A., Holland House	66	C2
Y.H.A., Oxford Street	11	G4
Y.M.C.A.	11	J3
Y.W.C.A.	11	J3
Zamana Gallery, Ismaili Centre	18	F1

Abbey Wood SE2	71	B3	Chingford E4	34	B1	Haggerston E2	59	C2
Acton W3	65	A1	Chingford Green E4	34	F1	Hainault, Chig.	35	J4
Addington, Croy.	102	J5	Chingford Hatch E4	34	D4	Hale End E4	34	D6
Addiscombe, Croy.	102	C1	Chipping Barnet, Barn.	23	B4	Ham, Rich.	82	F3
Aldborough Hatch, Ilf.	43	H3	Chislehurst, Chis.	88	D7	Hammersmith W6	65	J5
Aldersbrook E12	51	H2	Chislehurst West, Chis.	88	D5	Hampstead NW3	48	G4
Alperton, Wem.	55	H1	Chiswick W4	65	D6	Hampstead Garden Suburb	39	F5
Anerley SE20	95	E2	Church End N3	39	C1	N2		
Arkley, Barn.	22	G5	Church End NW10	47	E6	Hampton, Hmptn.	90	H1
Avery Hill SE9	79	F6	Clapham SW4	76	B3	Hampton Hill, Hmptn.	82	A6
Balham SW12	84	J1	Clapham Park SW4	76	C6	Hampton Wick, Kings.T.	91	E1
Banstead, Bans.	93	E2	Claygate, Esher	98	B7	Hanwell W7	64	C1
Barbican EC2	**13**	**A2**	Clayhall, Ilf.	43	C2	Hanworth, Felt.	81	D4
Barking, Bark.	61	E1	**Clerkenwell EC1**	**8**	**G6**	Harlesden NW10	56	C2
Barkingside, Ilf.	43	E3	Clerkenwell EC1	58	H4	Harringay N8	40	G5
Barnes SW13	74	G2	Cockfosters, Barn.	23	H4	Harrow, Har.	37	A7
Barnet, Barn.	23	C3	Coldblow, Bex.	89	J2	Harrow on the Hill, Har.	46	B1
Barnet Gate, Barn.	22	F6	Collier Row, Rom.	44	G1	Harrow Weald, Har.	37	B1
Barnsbury N1	49	G6	Collier's Wood SW19	84	G7	Hatch End, Pnr.	28	E7
Battersea SW11	76	A2	Coombe, Kings.T.	83	C7	Hayes, Brom.	96	H7
Bayswater W2	**10**	**C4**	Copse Hill SW20	83	G7	Headstone, Har.	36	J4
Bayswater W2	57	E6	Cottenham Park SW20	92	G1	Hendon NW4	38	H4
Beacontree, Dag.	53	D3	Cranbrook, Ilf.	52	C1	Herne Hill SE24	76	J5
Beacontree Heath, Dag.	53	G1	Cranford, Houns.	63	A7	Heston, Houns.	63	F7
Beckenham, Beck.	96	B1	Cricklewood NW2	48	A3	High Barnet, Barn.	23	A2
Beckton E6	61	D5	Crouch End N8	40	C6	High Beach, Loug.	26	G1
Beddington, Wall.	101	D2	Croydon, Croy.	102	A2	Highams Hill E17	41	H2
Beddington Corner, Mitch.	94	A7	Cubitt Town E14	69	C3	Highams Park E4	34	D5
Bedford Park W4	65	D3	Custom House E16	61	A6	Highbury N5	49	H5
Belgravia SW1	**19**	**C1**	Dagenham, Dag.	53	G6	Highgate N6	40	B7
Belgravia SW1	67	A3	Dalston E8	50	B7	Highwood Hill NW7	30	G2
Bell Green SE6	86	J3	Dartmouth Park NW5	49	B3	Hinchley Wood, Esher	98	C3
Bellingham SE6	87	A3	Debden, Loug.	27	G3	Hither Green SE13	78	E6
Belmont, Har.	37	D2	Deptford SE8	68	J5	**Holborn WC2**	**12**	**C3**
Belsize Park NW3	48	H6	Dollis Hill NW2	47	H3	Holborn WC2	58	F6
Belvedere, Belv.	71	H4	Dormer's Wells, Sthl.	54	H7	Holders Hill NW4	39	A2
Bonhilton, Sutt.	100	F2	Downham, Brom.	87	F4	Holloway N7	49	E4
Bermondsey SE1	**17**	**F5**	Ducks Island, Barn.	23	A6	Homerton E9	50	H5
Bermondsey SE1	68	C3	Dulwich SE21	77	B7	Honor Oak SE23	77	F6
Berrylands, Surb.	91	J6	Ealing W5	55	F7	Honor Oak Park SE4	77	G6
Bethnal Green E2	59	J2	Earls Court SW5	66	C5	Hornsey N8	40	F3
Bexley, Bex.	80	G6	Earlsfield SW18	84	F1	Hounslow, Houns.	72	F4
Bexleyheath, Bexh.	80	F5	East Acton W3	56	E7	Hounslow, West Houns.	72	D3
Bickley, Brom.	97	C3	East Barnet, Barn.	23	H6	**Hoxton N1**	**9**	**D2**
Blackfen, Sid.	79	J7	East Dulwich SE22	77	D6	Hoxton N1	59	A2
Blackheath SE3	78	E1	East Finchley N2	39	G4	Hyde, The NW9	38	F3
Blackheath Park SE3	78	G4	East Ham E6	61	B2	Ilford, Ilf.	52	F3
Bloomsbury WC1	**12**	**A1**	East Molesey, E.Mol.	91	A3	Isleworth, Islw.	73	C3
Bloomsbury WC1	58	D5	East Sheen SW14	74	D4	Islington N1	58	G1
Borehamwood, Borwd.	22	B3	East Wickham, Well.	89	A3	Joydens Wood, Bex.	89	J3
Borough, The SE1	**16**	**J4**	Eastcote, Pnr.	36	C6	**Kennington SE11**	**20**	**E6**
Borough, The SE1	67	J2	Eastcote Village, Pnr.	36	B5	Kennington SE11	67	G6
Bow E3	59	J2	Eden Park, Beck.	96	A5	Kensal Green NW10	56	J3
Bowes Park N22	32	E6	Edgware, Edg.	30	B5	Kensal Rise NW6	57	A2
Brentford, Brent.	64	F6	Edmonton N9	33	D4	Kensal Town W10	57	A4
Brimsdown, Enf.	25	H3	Elmers End, Beck.	95	G3	Kensington W8	66	C1
Brixton SW2	76	E4	Elmstead, Chis.	88	A5	Kentish Town NW5	49	C6
Broad Green, Croy.	94	G6	Eltham SE9	79	A6	Kenton, Har.	37	E5
Broadgate EC2	**13**	**C1**	Enfield, Enf.	25	C3	Kew, Rich.	65	A6
Brockley SE4	77	H5	Enfield Highway, Enf.	25	F2	Kidbrooke SE3	78	J2
Bromley E3	60	B4	Enfield Town, Enf.	25	A2	Kilburn NW6	57	C2
Bromley, Brom.	96	F2	Epsom, Epsom	83	C7	King's Cross N1	58	D1
Bromley Common, Brom.	97	C7	Falconwood, Well.	79	G3	Kingsbury NW9	38	B6
Bromley Park, Brom.	96	E1	Farnborough, Orp.	104	E5	Kingston upon Thames,	91	H2
Brompton SW3	**14**	**G6**	Feltham, Felt.	81	A2	Kings.T.		
Brompton SW3	66	H3	Finchley N3	39	E1	Kingston Vale SW15	74	E6
Brondesbury NW2	48	A6	**Finsbury EC1**	**8**	**F3**	Ladywell SE13	78	A5
Brondesbury Park NW6	48	A7	Finsbury EC1	58	H3	**Lambeth SE1**	**16**	**D5**
Brunswick Park N11	31	J2	Finsbury Park N4	49	G1	Lambeth SE1	67	F3
Buckhurst Hill, Buck.H.	26	J7	Forest Gate E7	51	G5	Lamorbey, Sid.	88	J1
Burnt Oak, Edg.	30	C7	Forest Hill SE23	86	G1	Lampton, Houns.	72	H1
Bush Hill Park, Enf.	25	B5	Friday Hill E4	34	D2	Lea Bridge E5	50	G3
Bushey Heath, Wat.	29	B1	Friern Barnet N11	31	H4	Lee SE12	78	F6
Bushey Mead SW20	93	A3	Fullwell Cross, Ilf.	43	G1	Lessness Heath, Belv.	71	H5
Camberwell SE5	67	J7	Furzedown SW17	85	A5	Lewisham SE13	78	B3
Camden Town NW1	58	C1	Gants Hill, Ilf.	43	D5	Leyton E11	51	B1
Canning Town E16	60	G6	Golders Green NW11	39	D7	Leytonstone E11	42	D7
Canons Park, Edg.	29	H7	Goodmayes, Ilf.	53	B2	Limehouse E14	59	H7
Carpenters Park, Wat.	28	F2	Gospel Oak NW5	49	A4	**Lisson Grove NW8**	**6**	**F5**
Carshalton, Cars.	100	H5	Grange Hill, Chig.	35	G6	Little Ealing W5	64	C4
Carshalton on the Hill, Cars.	101	J1	Grange Park N21	24	H5	Long Ditton, Surb.	98	F1
Castelnau SW13	65	G6	Greenford, Grnf.	54	H3	Longlands, Chis.	88	F3
Catford SE6	87	B1	Greenwich SE10	69	D6	Loughton, Loug.	27	C5
Chadwell Heath, Rom.	44	D6	Grove Park SE12	87	G2	Lower Clapton E5	50	F4
Charlton SE7	69	J6	Grove Park W4	65	C7	Lower Edmonton N9	33	C1
Cheam, Sutt.	100	A6	Gunnersbury W4	65	B4	Lower Holloway N7	49	F5
Chelsea SW3	**18**	**E5**	Hackbridge, Wall.	101	B2	Lower Sydenham SE26	86	G4
Chelsea SW3	66	G6	Hackney E8	50	E6	Loxford, Ilf.	52	F5
Chessington, Chess.	98	H6	Hackney Wick E9	50	J5	Maida Hill W9	57	C4
Chigwell, Chig.	35	E3	Hadley, Barn.	23	C2	**Maida Vale W9**	**6**	**B5**
Childs Hill NW2	48	D2	**Haggerston E2**	**9**	**H1**	Maida Vale W9	57	E4

Manor Park E12	52	B5
Mark's Gate, Rom.	44	E2
Marylebone NW1	**10**	**H1**
Marylebone NW1	57	H4
Mayfair W1	**11**	**D6**
Mayfair W1	58	A7
Merry Hill, Wat.	28	H1
Merton SW19	93	D1
Merton Park SW19	93	D2
Mile End E1	59	H3
Mill Hill NW7	30	G5
Millwall E14	69	B3
Mitcham, Mitch.	94	A3
Monken Hadley, Barn.	23	C1
Monks Orchard, Croy.	95	J7
Morden, Mord.	93	D3
Morden Park, Mord.	93	B6
Mortlake SW14	74	C3
Motspur Park, N.Mal.	92	G6
Mottingham SE9	87	J2
Muswell Hill N10	40	B3
Neasden NW2	47	E3
New Barnet, Barn.	23	E4
New Beckenham, Beck.	86	J6
New Charlton SE7	69	J4
New Cross SE14	77	H1
New Cross Gate SE14	77	G1
New Eltham SE9	88	D2
New Malden, N.Mal.	92	D3
New Southgate N11	32	D4
Newbury Park, Ilf.	43	G5
Newington SE17	**20**	**J1**
Newington SE17	67	J3
Nine Elms SW8	**19**	**G7**
Noel Park N22	40	G2
Norbiton, Kings.T.	92	B2
Norbury SW16	94	F1
Nork, Bans.	93	A1
North Acton W3	56	D4
North Cheam, Sutt.	100	A3
North Cray, Sid.	89	F3
North Finchley N12	31	G5
North Harrow, Har.	36	G6
North Hyde, Sthl.	63	E4
North Kensington W10	56	J6
North Sheen, Rich.	74	A2
North Wembley, Wem.	46	E2
North Woolwich E16	70	B2
Northolt, Nthlt.	45	E7
Northumberland Heath, Erith	71	J7
Norwood Green, Sthl.	63	G4
Norwood New Town SE19	85	J6
Notting Hill W11	57	B6
Nunhead SE15	77	F3
Oakleigh Park N20	31	G1
Oakwood N14	24	D6
Old Bexley, Bex.	80	H7
Old Ford E3	59	J1
Old Malden, Wor.Pk.	99	D1
Old Oak Common NW10	56	E5
Orpington, Orp.	104	J1
Osidge N14	32	B1
Osterley, Islw.	64	A7
Paddington W2	**10**	**C2**
Paddington W2	57	E5
Palmers Green N13	32	G3
Park Langley, Beck.	96	C5
Park Royal NW10	56	A2
Parsons Green SW6	75	C1
Peckham SE15	68	C7
Penge SE20	86	F7
Pentonville N1	**8**	**E2**
Pentonville N1	58	G2
Perivale, Grnf.	55	F1
Petersham, Rich.	82	H1
Petts Wood, Orp.	97	G5
Pimlico SW1	**19**	**F3**
Pimlico SW1	67	B5
Pinner, Pnr.	36	E4
Pinner Green, Pnr.	36	C2
Pinnerwood Park, Pnr.	36	C1
Plaistow E13	60	H3
Plaistow, Brom.	87	F6
Plumstead SE18	70	H5
Ponders End, Enf.	25	G5
Poplar E14	60	B7
Poverest, Orp.	97	J5
Preston, Wem.	46	G1
Primrose Hill NW8	57	J1
Putney SW15	74	J5
Putney Heath SW15	74	J6
Putney Vale SW15	83	F3
Queensbury, Har.	37	G3
Rayners Lane, Har.	45	F1
Raynes Park SW20	92	H3
Redbridge, Ilf.	43	C6
Regent's Park NW1	**7**	**D2**
Regent's Park NW1	58	B3
Richmond, Rich.	73	H6
Roehampton SW15	74	G5
Rosehill, Sutt.	100	E1
Rotherhithe SE16	68	G3
Rowley Green, Barn.	22	F4
Roxeth, Har.	46	A2
Ruislip Manor, Ruis.	45	A2
Rush Green, Rom.	44	J7
St. Helier, Cars.	93	G7
St. James's SW1	**15**	**G2**
St. James's SW1	67	C1
St. John's SE8	78	A2
St. John's Wood NW8	**6**	**E3**
St. John's Wood NW8	57	F2
St. Luke's EC1	**9**	**A5**
St. Luke's EC1	58	J4
St. Margarets, Twick.	73	D5
St. Pancras WC1	**8**	**A4**
St. Pancras WC1	58	E3
Sands End SW6	75	F1
Selhurst SE25	95	B6
Seven Kings, Ilf.	43	H7
Sewardstone E4	26	C1
Sewardstonebury E4	26	E4
Shacklewell N16	50	C4
Shadwell E1	59	F7
Shepherd's Bush W12	65	J1
Shirley, Croy.	102	G3
Shooter's Hill SE18	79	F1
Shoreditch E1	**9**	**F6**
Shoreditch E1	59	C4
Shortlands, Brom.	96	E3
Sidcup, Sid.	88	J4
Silvertown E16	69	J2
Snaresbrook E11	42	E5
Soho W1	**11**	**H5**
Soho W1	58	C6
Somers Town NW1	**7**	**J2**
Somers Town NW1	58	D3
South Acton W3	65	B3
South Beddington, Wall.	101	D6
South Chingford E4	33	J5
South Croydon, S.Croy.	101	J6
South Hackney E9	59	F1
South Hampstead NW6	48	E7
South Harrow, Har.	45	H3
South Kensington SW7	**18**	**C2**
South Kensington SW7	66	E3
South Lambeth SW8	76	E1
South Norwood SE25	95	C3
South Oxhey, Wat.	28	C3
South Ruislip, Ruis.	45	C4
South Tottenham N15	41	B5
South Wimbledon SW19	84	D7
South Woodford E18	42	F2
Southall, Sthl.	63	D1
Southborough, Brom.	97	C6
Southend SE6	87	C4
Southfields SW18	84	D1
Southgate N14	32	C2
Southwark SE1	**16**	**H2**
Southwark SE1	67	H1
Spring Grove, Islw.	73	B2
Stamford Hill N16	50	C1
Stanmore, Stan.	29	D5
Stepney E1	59	F5
Stockwell SW9	76	D3
Stoke Newington N16	50	B2
Stonebridge NW10	56	B1
Stoneleigh, Epsom	99	G5
Strand WC2	**12**	**A5**
Strand WC2	58	E7
Stratford E15	51	C6
Strawberry Hill, Twick.	82	B3
Streatham SW16	85	E4
Streatham Hill SW2	85	F1
Streatham Park SW16	85	C4
Streatham Vale SW16	85	D7
Stroud Green N8	40	F6
Sudbury, Wem.	46	D5
Summerstown SW17	84	E4
Sunbury, Sun.	90	B3
Sundridge, Brom.	87	J6
Surbiton , Surb.	91	H7
Sutton, Sutt.	100	D6
Sydenham SE26	86	E5
Teddington, Tedd.	82	D6
Thames Ditton, T.Ditt.	91	D7
Thamesmead SE28	71	A1
Thamesmead North SE28	62	D6
Thamesmead West SE18	70	F3
Thornton Heath, Th.Hth.	94	H4
Tokyngton, Wem.	47	J5
Tolworth, Surb.	99	A2
Tooting Graveney SW17	84	H6
Tottenham N17	41	B1
Tottenham Hale N17	41	D1
Totteridge N20	31	B1
Tufnell Park N7	49	D4
Tulse Hill SE21	85	J1
Twickenham, Twick.	82	D2
Underhill , Barn.	23	D5
Upper Clapton E5	50	E1
Upper Edmonton N18	33	D5
Upper Elmers End Beck.	95	J5
Upper Holloway N19	49	C3
Upper Norwood SE19	86	A7
Upper Sydenham SE26	86	D4
Upper Tooting SW17	84	H3
Upper Walthamstow E17	42	C4
Upton E7	51	H7
Upton Park E6	60	J1
Vauxhall SW8	**20**	**C6**
Vauxhall SW8	67	D6
Waddon, Croy.	101	G2
Walham Green SW6	66	E7
Wallington, Wall.	101	C5
Walthamstow E17	42	B2
Walworth SE17	**20**	**J3**
Walworth SE17	68	A5
Wandsworth SW18	75	C5
Wanstead E11	42	H4
Wapping E1	68	D1
Watford Heath, Wat.	28	D1
Wealdstone, Har.	37	C3
Welling, Well.	80	A3
Wembley, Wem.	46	H5
Wembley Park , Wem.	46	J2
West Barnes, N.Mal.	92	H4
West Brompton SW10	**18**	**A5**
West Brompton SW10	66	D6
West Dulwich SE21	86	A3
West Ewell, Epsom	99	E7
West Green N15	40	J4
West Ham E15	51	F7
West Hampstead NW6	48	E5
West Harrow, Har.	36	J7
West Heath SE2	71	D6
West Kilburn W9	57	C3
West Molesey, W.Mol.	90	F4
West Norwood SE27	85	J3
West Wickham, W.Wick.	103	C3
Westbourne Green W2	57	D5
Westminster SW1	**15**	**F5**
Westminster SW1	67	C3
Weston Green, T.Ditt.	98	C1
Whetstone N20	31	E2
Whitechapel E1	**13**	**H4**
Whitechapel E1	59	D6
Whitton , Twick.	72	H7
Widmore, Brom.	96	J3
Willesden NW10	47	F6
Willesden Green NW10	47	H7
Wimbledon SW19	84	B6
Wimbledon Park SW19	84	C3
Winchmore Hill N21	24	F7
Wood Green N22	40	E1
Woodford, Wdf.Grn.	34	H6
Woodford Bridge, Wdf.Grn.	35	C7
Woodford Green, Wdf.Grn.	34	G5
Woodford Wells , Wdf.Grn.	34	H3
Woodlands, Islw.	73	B2
Woodmansterne , Bans.	93	H1
Woodside, Croy.	95	C6
Woolwich SE18	70	C5
Worcester Park, Wor.Pk.	99	F2
World's End, Enf.	24	G3
Wrythe, The, Cars.	100	H2
Yeading, Hayes	54	B3

INDEX TO STREET NAMES

General Abbreviations

All	Alley	Embk	Embankment	Pas	Passage
Allot	Allotments	Est	Estate	Pav	Pavilion
Amb	Ambulance	Ex	Exchange	Pk	Park
App	Approach	FB	Footbridge	Pl	Place
Arc	Arcade	FC	Football Club	Prec	Precinct
Ave	Avenue	Fld	Field	Prom	Promenade
Bdy	Broadway	Flds	Fields	Quad	Quadrant
Bldgs	Buildings	Fm	Farm	Pt	Point
Bowl	Bowling	Gall	Gallery	RC	Roman Catholic
Bri	Bridge	Gar	Garage	Rd	Road
C of E	Church of England	Gdn	Garden	Rds	Roads
Cath	Cathedral	Gdns	Gardens	Rec	Recreation
Cem	Cemetery	Govt	Government	Res	Reservoir
Cen	Central, Centre	Gra	Grange	Ri	Rise
Cft	Croft	Grd	Ground	S	South
Ch	Church	Grds	Grounds	Sch	School
Chyd	Churchyard	Grn	Green	Shop	Shopping
Cin	Cinema	Gro	Grove	Sq	Square
Circ	Circus	Gros	Groves	St	Street
Clo	Close	Ho	House	St,	Saint
Co	County	Hos	Houses	Sta	Station
Coll	College	Hosp	Hospital	SUB	Subway
Comm	Community	Ind	Industrial	Swim	Swimming
Conv	Convent	Junct	Junction	TA	Territorial Army
Cor	Corner	La	Lane	Tenn	Tennis
Cors	Corners	Las	Lanes	Ter	Terrace
Coron	Coroners	Lo	Lodge	Thea	Theatre
Cotts	Cottages	Lwr	Lower	Trd	Trading
Cov	Covered	Mag	Magistrates	Twr	Tower
Crem	Crematorium	Mans	Mansions	Twrs	Towers
Cres	Crescent	Meml	Memorial	Vill	Villas
Ct	Court	Mkt	Market	Vw	View
Ctyd	Courtyard	Mkts	Markets	W	West
Dep	Depot	Ms	Mews	Wd	Wood
Dr	Drive	Mt	Mount	Wds	Woods
Dws	Dwellings	Mus	Museum	Wf	Wharf
E	East	N	North	Wk	Walk
Ed	Education	PH	Public House	Wks	Works
Elec	Electricity	Par	Parade	Yd	Yard

Abbreviations of District Names

Ash.	Ashtead	Grnf.	Greenford	Sid.	Sidcup
Bark.	Barking	Har.	Harrow	Sthl.	Southall
Barn.	Barnet	Hmptn.	Hampton	Stan.	Stanmore
Beck.	Beckenham	Houns.	Hounslow	Sun.	Sunbury-on-Thames
Belv.	Belvedere	Ilf.	Ilford	Surb.	Surbiton
Bex.	Bexley	Islw.	Isleworth	Sutt.	Sutton
Bexh.	Bexleyheath	Kes.	Keston	T.Ditt.	Thames Ditton
Borwd.	Borehamwood	Kings.T.	Kingston upon Thames	Tedd.	Teddington
Brent.	Brentford	Loug.	Loughton	Th.Hth.	Thornton Heath
Brom.	Bromley	Mitch.	Mitcham	Twick.	Twickenham
Buck.H.	Buckhurst Hill	Mord.	Morden	Uxb.	Uxbridge
Cars.	Carshalton	N.Mal.	New Malden	W.Mol.	West Molesey
Chess.	Chessington	Nthlt.	Northolt	W.Wick	West Wickham
Chig.	Chigwell	Nthwd.	Northwood	Wall.	Wallington
Chis.	Chislehurst	Orp.	Orpington	Walt.	Walton-on-Thames
Croy.	Croydon	Pnr.	Pinner	Wat.	Watford
Dag.	Dagenham	Pot.B.	Potters Bar	Wdf.Grn.	Woodford Green
Dart.	Dartford	Rain.	Rainham	Well.	Welling
E.Mol.	East Molesey	Rich.	Richmond	Wem.	Wembley
Edg.	Edgware	Rom.	Romford	Wey.	Weybridge
Enf.	Enfield	Ruis.	Ruislip	Wor.Pk.	Worcester Park
Epp.	Epping	S.Croy.	South Croydon		
Felt.	Feltham	Sev.	Sevenoaks		

NOTES

This index contains some street names in standard text which are followed by another street named in italics. In these cases the street in standard text does not actually appear on the map due to insufficient space but can be located close to the street named in italics.

Abbess Clo. E6 | 61 B5
Oliver Gdns.
Abbess Clo. SW2 | 85 G1
Abbeville Rd. N8 | 40 D4
Barrington Rd.
Abbeville Rd. SW4 | 76 C6
Abbey Ave., Wem. | 55 H2
Abbey Clo., Hayes | 63 B1
Abbey Clo., Nthlt. | 54 F3
Invicta Gro.
Abbey Clo., Pnr. | 36 B3
Abbey Cres., Belv. | 71 G4
Abbey Dr. SW17 | 85 A5
Church La.
Abbey Gdns. NW8 | **6 C2**
Abbey Gdns. NW8 | 57 F2
Abbey Gdns. W6 | 66 B6
Abbey Gro. SE2 | 71 B4
Abbey La. E15 | 60 C2
Abbey La., Beck. | 87 A7
Abbey Manufacturing | 55 J1
Est., Wem.
Abbey Orchard St. | **15 J5**
SW1
Abbey Orchard St. | 67 D3
SW1
Abbey Par. W5 | 55 J3
Hanger La.
Abbey Pk., Beck. | 87 A7
Abbey Rd. E15 | 60 D2
Abbey Rd. NW6 | 48 E7
Abbey Rd. NW8 | 57 E1
Abbey Rd. NW10 | 56 B2
Abbey Rd. SE2 | 71 D4
Abbey Rd. SW19 | 84 F7
Abbey Rd., Bark. | 52 E7
Abbey Rd., Belv. | 71 D4
Abbey Rd., Bexh. | 80 E4
Abbey Rd., Croy. | 101 H3
Abbey Rd., Enf. | 25 B5
Abbey Rd., Ilf. | 43 G5
Abbey Rd., Stan. | 29 F7
Abbey Rd. Est. NW8 | **57 E1**
Abbey St. E13 | 60 G4
Abbey St. SE1 | **17 E5**
Abbey St. SE1 | 68 C3
Abbey Ter. NW8 | 55 J2
Abbey Ter. SE2 | 71 D4
Abbey Vw. NW7 | 30 F3
Abbey Wk., W.Mol. | 90 H3
Abbey Way SE2 | 71 D2
Wolvercote Rd.
Abbey Wd. Rd. SE2 | 71 B4
Abbeydale Rd., Wem. | 56 A1
Abbeyfield Rd. SE16 | 68 F4
Abbeyfields Clo. | 56 A2
NW10
Abbeyhill Rd., Sid. | 89 C2
Abbot St. E8 | 50 C6
Abbots Clo. N1 | 49 J6
Alwyne Rd.
Abbots Clo., Orp. | 104 F1
Abbots Clo., Ruis. | 24 E7
Abbots Cres., Enf. | 24 H2
Abbots Dr., Har. | 45 H1
Abbots Gdns. N2 | 39 G4
Abbots Grn., Croy. | 102 G6
Abbots La. SE1 | **17 E2**
Abbots Manor Est. | **19 D3**
SW1
Abbots Pk. SW2 | 85 G1
Abbot's Pl. NW6 | 57 E1
Abbot's Rd. E6 | 61 A1
Abbots Rd., Edg. | 30 C7
Abbots Ter. N8 | 40 E6
Abbots Way, Beck. | 95 H5
Abbotsbury Clo. E15 | 60 C2
Abbotsbury Clo. W14 | 66 C2
Abbotsbury Gdns., | 36 C6
Pnr.
Abbotsbury Rd. | 66 B2
W14
Abbotsbury Rd., | 103 F2
Brom.
Abbotsbury Rd., | 93 E5
Mord.
Abbotsford Ave. N15 | 40 J4
Abbotsford Gdns., | 34 G7
Wdf.Grn.
Abbotsford Rd., Ilf. | 53 A2
Abbotshall Ave. N14 | 32 C3
Abbotshall Rd. SE6 | 87 D1
Abbotsleigh Clo., | 100 E7
Sutt.
Abbotsleigh Rd. | 85 C4
SW16
Abbotsmede Clo., | 82 C2
Twick.
Abbotstone Rd. | 74 J3
SW15
Abbotswell Rd. SE4 | 77 J5

Abbotswood Clo., | 71 E3
Belv.
Coptefield Dr.
Abbotswood Gdns., | 43 C3
Ilf.
Abbotswood Rd. | 85 D3
SW16
Abbotswood Way, | 63 B1
Hayes
Abbott Ave. SW20 | 93 A1
Abbott Clo., Hmptn. | 81 E6
Abbott Clo., Nthlt. | 45 F6
Abbott Rd. E14 | 60 C6
Abbotts Clo., Rom. | 44 H3
Abbotts Cres. E4 | 34 D4
Abbotts Dr., Wem. | 46 E2
Abbotts Pk. Rd. E10 | 42 C7
Abbotts Rd., Barn. | 23 E4
Abbotts Rd., Mitch. | 94 C4
Abbotts Rd., Sthl. | 63 E1
Abbotts Rd., Sutt. | 100 B4
Abbotts Wk., Bexh. | 71 D7
Abchurch La. EC4 | 13 C5
Abchurch La. EC4 | 59 A7
Abchurch Yd. EC4 | **13 B5**
Abdale Rd. W12 | 65 H1
Aberavon Rd. E3 | 59 H3
Abercairn Rd. SW16 | 85 C7
Aberconway Rd., | 93 E3
Mord.
Abercorn Clo. NW7 | **6 C3**
Abercorn Clo. NW8 | 57 F3
Abercorn Cres., Har. | 45 H2
Abercorn Gdns., Har. | 37 G7
Abercorn Gdns., | 44 B6
Rom.
Abercorn Pl. NW8 | **6 C3**
Abercorn Pl. NW8 | 57 F3
Abercorn Rd. NW7 | 31 B7
Abercorn Rd., Stan. | 29 F7
Abercorn Way SE1 | **21 H3**
Abercorn Way SE1 | 68 D5
Abercrombie St. | 75 H2
SW11
Aberdare Clo., | 103 C2
W.Wick.
Aberdare Gdns. NW6 | 48 E7
Aberdare Gdns. NW7 | 31 A7
Aberdare La., Enf. | 25 F4
Aberdeen La. N5 | 49 J5
Aberdeen Par. N18 | 33 E5
Angel Rd.
Aberdeen Pk. N5 | 49 J5
Aberdeen Pk. Ms. N5 | 49 J4
Aberdeen Pl. NW8 | **6 E5**
Aberdeen Pl. NW8 | 57 G4
Aberdeen Rd. N5 | 49 J4
Aberdeen Rd. N18 | 33 E5
Aberdeen Rd. NW10 | 47 F5
Aberdeen Rd., Croy. | 101 J4
Aberdeen Rd., Har. | 37 C2
Aberdeen Ter. SE3 | 78 D2
Aberdour Rd., Ilf. | 53 B3
Aberdour St. SE1 | **21 D1**
Aberdour St. SE1 | 68 B4
Aberfeldy St. E14 | 60 C6
Aberford Gdns. SE18 | 79 B1
Aberford Rd., Borwd. | 22 A2
Aberfoyle Rd. SW16 | 85 D6
Abernethy Rd. SE13 | 78 E4
Abersham Rd. E8 | 50 C5
Abery St. SE18 | 70 H4
Abingdon Clo. NW1 | 49 D6
Camden Sq.
Abingdon Rd. SE1 | **21 G2**
Abingdon Rd. SW16 | 84 F6
Abingdon Rd. N3 | 39 F2
Abingdon Rd. W8 | 66 D3
Abingdon St. SW1 | **16 A5**
Abingdon St. SW1 | 67 E3
Abingdon Vill. W8 | 66 D3
Abinger Clo., Bark. | 97 B3
Abinger Clo., Ilf. | 53 A4
Abinger Clo., Wall. | 101 E5
Abinger Gdns., Islw. | 73 B3
Sussex Ave.
Abinger Gro. SE8 | 68 J6
Abinger Ms. W9 | 57 D4
Warlock Rd.
Abinger Rd. W4 | 65 E3
Ablett St. SE16 | 68 F5
Abney Gdns. N16 | 50 C2
Stoke Newington
High St.
Aboyne Dr. SW20 | 92 G2
Aboyne Est. SW17 | 84 G3
Aboyne Rd. NW10 | 47 E3
Aboyne Rd. SW17 | 84 G3
Abridge Rd., Chig. | 27 G6
Abridge Way, Bark. | 62 B2

Abyssinia Clo. SW11 | 75 H4
Cairns Rd.
Acacia Ave. N17 | 33 A7
Acacia Ave., Brent. | 64 E7
Acacia Ave., Mitch. | 94 B2
Acacia Ave., Wem. | 45 A1
Acacia Ave., Wem. | 46 H5
Acacia Clo. SE20 | 95 D2
Selby Rd.
Acacia Clo., Orp. | 97 G5
Acacia Clo., Stan. | 29 B6
Acacia Dr., Sutt. | 100 C1
Acacia Gdns. NW8 | **6 F1**
Acacia Gdns., | 103 C2
W.Wick.
Acacia Gro. SE21 | 86 A2
Acacia Gro., N.Mal. | 92 E3
Acacia Pl. NW8 | **6 F1**
Acacia Pl. NW8 | 57 G2
Acacia Rd. E11 | 51 E2
Acacia Rd. E17 | 41 H6
Acacia Rd. N22 | 40 G1
Acacia Rd. NW8 | **6 F1**
Acacia Rd. NW8 | 57 G2
Acacia Rd. SW16 | 94 E1
Acacia Rd. W3 | 56 C7
Acacia Rd., Beck. | 95 J3
Acacia Rd., Enf. | 25 A1
Acacia Rd., Hmptn. | 81 G6
Acacia Rd., Mitch. | 94 A2
Acacia Way, Sid. | 88 J1
Academy Gdns., | 102 C1
Croy.
Academy Gdns., | 54 D2
Nthlt.
Academy Pl. SE18 | 79 C1
Academy Rd. SE18 | 79 C1
Acanthus Dr. SE1 | **21 H3**
Acanthus Dr. SE1 | 68 D5
Acanthus Rd. SW11 | 76 A3
Accommodation Rd. | 39 C7
NW11
Acfold Rd. SW6 | 75 E1
Achilles Clo. SE1 | **21 J3**
Achilles Clo. SE1 | 68 D5
Achilles Rd. NW6 | 48 D5
Achilles St. SE14 | 68 H7
Achilles Way W1 | **15 C2**
Acklam Rd. W10 | 57 C6
Portobello Rd.
Acklington Dr. NW9 | 38 E1
Ackmar Rd. SW6 | 75 D1
Ackroyd Dr. E3 | 59 J5
Ackroyd Rd. SE23 | 77 G7
Ackworth Clo. N9 | 25 F7
Acland Cres. SE5 | 77 A4
Acland Rd. NW2 | 47 H6
Acol Cres., Ruis. | 45 B5
Acol Rd. NW6 | 48 D7
Aconbury Rd., Dag. | 62 B1
Acorn Clo. E4 | 34 B5
The Lawns
Acorn Clo., Chis. | 88 F5
Acorn Clo., Enf. | 24 H1
Acorn Clo., Stan. | 29 E7
Acorn Ct., Ilf. | 43 H6
Acorn Gdns. SE19 | 95 C1
Acorn Gdns. W3 | 56 D5
Acorn Par. SE15 | 68 E7
Carlton Gro.
Acorn Wk. SE16 | 68 H1
Acorn Way SE23 | 86 G3
Acorn Way, Orp. | 104 E4
Acorns, The, Chig. | 35 H4
Acorns Clo., Hmptn. | 81 H6
Acre La. SW2 | 76 E4
Acre La., Cars. | 101 A4
Acre La., Wall. | 101 A4
Acre Rd. SW19 | 84 G6
Acre Rd., Dag. | 63 H7
Acre Rd., Kings.T. | 91 H1
Acris St. SW18 | 75 F5
Acton Clo. N9 | 33 D2
Acton La. NW10 | 56 C3
Acton La. W3 | 65 C2
Acton La. W4 | 65 C4
Acton Ms. E8 | 59 D1
Acton Pk. Ind. Est. W3 | 65 D2
Acton St. WC1 | **8 C4**
Acton St. WC1 | 58 F3
Acuba Rd. SW18 | 84 F1
Acworth Clo. N9 | 25 F7
Turin Rd.
Ada Gdns. E14 | 60 D6
Ada Gdns. E15 | 60 F1
Ada Pl. E2 | 59 D1
Ada Rd. SE5 | 68 B7
Ada Rd., Wem. | 46 F3
Ada St. E8 | 59 E1
Adair Clo. SE25 | 95 E3
Adair Rd. W10 | 57 B4
Adair Twr. W10 | 57 B4
Appleford Rd.

Adam & Eve Ct. W1 | **11 G3**
Adam & Eve Ms. W8 | 66 D3
Adam Ct. SW7 | **18 D1**
Adam Pl. N16 | 50 C2
High St.
Adam St. WC2 | **12 B6**
Adam St. WC2 | 58 E7
Adam Wk. SW6 | 65 J7
Adams Clo. N3 | 31 D7
Falkland Ave.
Adams Clo. NW9 | 47 B2
Adams Clo., Surb. | 91 J6
Adams Ct. EC2 | **13 C3**
Adams Gdns. Est. | 68 F2
SE16
St. Marychurch St.
Adams Pl. E14 | 69 B1
North Colonnade
Adams Pl. N7 | 49 F5
Georges Rd.
Adams Rd. N17 | 41 A3
Adams Rd., Beck. | 95 H5
Adams Row W1 | **11 C6**
Adams Row W1 | 58 A7
Adams Sq., Bexh. | 80 E3
Regency Way
Adams Way, Croy. | 95 C6
Adamson Rd. E16 | 60 G6
Adamson Rd. NW3 | 48 G7
Adamsrill Clo., Enf. | 25 A5
Adamsrill Rd. SE26 | 86 H4
Adare Wk. SW16 | 85 F3
Adastral Est. NW9 | 38 E1
Adcock Wk., Orp. | 104 J4
Borkwood Pk.
Adderley Gdns. SE9 | 88 D4
Adderley Gro. SW11 | 76 A5
Culmstock Rd.
Adderley Rd., Har. | 37 C1
Adderley St. E14 | 60 C6
Addington Ct. SW14 | 74 D3
Addington Dr. N12 | 31 F6
Addington Gro. SE26 | 86 H4
Addington Rd. E3 | 60 A3
Addington Rd. E16 | 60 E4
Addington Rd. N4 | 40 G6
Addington Rd., | 101 G1
Croy.
Addington Rd., | 103 C4
W.Wick.
Addington Sq. SE5 | **21 A7**
Addington Sq. SE5 | 68 A6
Addington St. SE1 | **16 D4**
Addington Village | 102 J6
Rd., Croy.
Addis Clo., Enf. | 25 G1
Addiscombe Ave., | 95 D7
Croy.
Addiscombe Clo., | 37 F5
Har.
Addiscombe Ct. Rd., | 102 B1
Croy.
Addiscombe Gro., | 102 B2
Croy.
Addiscombe Rd., | 102 B2
Croy.
Addison Ave. N14 | 24 B6
Addison Ave. W11 | 66 B1
Addison Ave., Houns. | 72 J1
Addison Bri. Pl. W14 | 66 C4
Addison Clo., Nthwd. | 36 A1
Addison Clo., Orp. | 97 F6
Addison Cres. W14 | 66 B3
Addison Dr. SE12 | 78 H5
Eltham Rd.
Addison Gdns. W14 | 66 A3
Addison Gdns., | 91 J4
Surb.
Addison Gro. W4 | 65 E3
Addison Pl. W11 | 66 B1
Addison Pl., Sthl. | 54 G7
Longford Ave.
Addison Rd. E11 | 42 G6
Addison Rd. E17 | 42 B5
Addison Rd. SE25 | 95 D4
Addison Rd. W14 | 66 B3
Addison Rd., Brom. | 96 J5
Addison Rd., Enf. | 25 F1
Addison Rd., Ilf. | 43 F1
Addison Rd., Tedd. | 82 E6
Addison Way NW11 | 39 C4
Addison Way, Hayes | 54 A6
Addisons Clo., Croy. | 102 J2
Addle Hill EC4 | **12 H4**
Addle St. EC2 | **13 A2**
Adecroft Way, | 90 J3
W.Mol.
Adela Ave., N.Mal. | 92 H5
Adela St. W10 | 57 B4
Kensal Rd.
Adelaide Ave. SE4 | 77 J4
Adelaide Clo., Stan. | 29 D4
Adelaide Cotts. W7 | 64 C2

Adelaide Gdns., 44 E5
Rom.
Adelaide Gro. W12 65 G1
Adelaide Rd. E10 51 C3
Adelaide Rd. NW3 48 G7
Adelaide Rd. W13 64 D1
Adelaide Rd., Chis. 88 E5
Adelaide Rd., Houns. 72 E1
Adelaide Rd., Ilf. 52 E2
Adelaide Rd., Rich. 73 J4
Adelaide Rd., Sthl. 63 E4
Adelaide Rd., Surb. 91 H5
Adelaide Rd., Tedd. 82 C6
Adelaide St. WC2 12 A6
Adelaide Ter., Brent. 64 G5
Adelaide Wk. SW9 76 G4
Sussex Wk.
Adelina Gro. E1 59 F5
Adelina Ms. SW12 85 D1
Kings Ave.
Adeline Pl. WC1 11 J2
Adeline Pl. WC1 58 D5
Adelphi Ter. WC2 12 B6
Adelphi Ter. WC2 58 E7
Aden Gro. N16 50 A4
Aden Rd., Enf. 25 H4
Aden Rd., Ilf. 43 E7
Aden Ter. N16 50 A4
Adeney Clo. W6 66 A6
Adenmore Rd. SE6 78 A7
Adie Rd. W6 65 J3
Adine Rd. E13 60 H4
Adler St. E1 10 I10
Adler St. E1 59 D6
Adley St. E5 50 H4
Admaston Rd. SE18 70 F6
Admiral Pl. SE16 68 H1
Admiral Seymour Rd. 79 C4
SE9
Admiral Sq. SW10 75 F1
Admiral St. SE8 78 A1
Admirals Clo. E18 42 H4
Admirals Wk. NW3 48 F3
Admirals Way E14 69 A2
Admiralty Rd., Tedd. 82 C6
Adolf St. SE6 87 B4
Adolphus Rd. N4 49 H1
Adolphus St. SE8 68 J7
Adomar Rd., Dag. 53 D3
Adpar St. W2 10 E1
Adpar St. W2 57 G5
Adrian Ave. NW2 47 H1
North Circular Rd.
Adrian Ms. SW10 18 B5
Adrian Ms. SW10 66 E6
Adrienne Ave., Sthl. 54 F3
Adys Rd. SE15 77 C3
Aerodrome Rd. NW4 38 G3
Aerodrome Rd. NW9 38 F3
Aerodrome Way, 63 C6
Houns.
Aeroville NW9 38 E2
Affleck St. N1 8 D2
Afghan Rd. SW11 75 H2
Agamemnon Rd. 48 C5
NW6
Agar Clo., Surb. 98 J2
Agar Gro. NW1 49 C7
Agar Gro. Est. NW1 49 C7
Agar Pl. NW1 49 C7
Agar St. WC2 12 A6
Agar St. WC2 58 E7
Agate Clo. E16 61 A6
Agate Rd. W6 65 J3
Agatha Clo. E1 68 E1
Penang St.
Agaton Rd. SE9 88 F2
Agave Rd. NW2 47 J4
Agdon St. EC1 8 G5
Agdon St. EC1 58 H4
Agincourt Rd. NW3 48 J4
Agnes Ave., Ilf. 52 E4
Agnes Clo. E6 61 D7
Agnes Gdns., Dag. 53 D4
Agnes Rd. W3 65 F1
Agnes St. E14 59 J6
Agnew Rd. SE23 77 G7
Agricola Pl., Enf. 25 C5
Aidan Clo., Dag. 53 E4
Aileen Wk. E15 51 F7
Devenay Rd.
Ailsa Ave., Twick. 73 D5
Ailsa Rd., Twick. 73 E5
Ailsa St. E14 60 C5
Ainger Ms. NW3 48 J7
Ainger Rd.
Ainger Rd. NW3 48 J7
Ainsdale Clo., Orp. 104 G1
Ainsdale Cres., Pnr. 36 G3
Ainsdale Rd. W5 55 G4
Ainsdale Rd., Wat. 28 C3
Ainsley Ave., Rom. 44 H6
Ainsley Clo. N9 33 B1

Ainslie St. E2 59 E3
Ainslie Wk. SW12 76 B7
Balham Gro.
Ainslie Wd. Cres. E4 34 B5
Ainslie Wd. Gdns. E4 34 B5
Ainslie Wd. Rd. E4 34 A5
Ainsworth Clo. NW2 47 G3
Ainsworth Rd. E9 50 F7
Ainsworth Rd., 101 H2
Croy.
Ainsworth Way NW8 57 F1
Aintree Ave. E6 61 B1
Aintree Cres., Ilf. 42 G7
Aintree Est. SW6 66 B7
Dawes Rd.
Aintree Rd., Grnf. 55 B7
Aintree St. SW6 66 B7
Air St. W1 11 G6
Air St. W1 58 C7
Airdrie Clo. N1 49 F7
Airdrie Clo., Hayes 54 E5
Glencoe Rd.
Airedale Ave. W4 65 F4
Airedale Ave. S. W4 65 F5
Netheravon Rd. S.
Airedale Rd. SW12 75 J7
Airedale Rd. W5 64 F3
Airlie Gdns. W8 66 D1
Campden Hill Rd.
Airlie Gdns., Ilf. 52 E1
Airlinks Est., Houns. 63 C5
Airthrie Rd., Ilf. 53 B2
Aisgill Ave. W11 66 C6
Aisher Rd. SE28 62 C7
Aislibie Rd. SE12 78 E4
Aitken Clo. E8 59 D1
Pownall Rd.
Aitken Rd. SE6 87 B2
Aitken Rd., Barn. 22 J5
Ajax Ave. NW9 38 E3
Ajax Rd. NW6 48 C5
Akenside Rd. NW3 48 G5
Akerman Rd. SW9 76 H2
Akerman Rd., Surb. 91 F6
Alabama St. SE18 70 G7
Alacross Rd. W5 64 F2
Alan Dr., Barn. 23 B6
Alan Gdns., Rom. 44 G7
Alan Rd. SW19 84 B5
Alandale Dr., Pnr. 36 B2
Alanthus Clo. SE12 78 F5
Alaska St. SE1 16 E2
Alba Clo., Hayes 54 D4
Ramulis Dr.
Alba Gdns. NW11 39 B6
Alba Pl. W11 57 C6
Portobello Rd.
Albacore Cres. SE13 78 B6
Alban Cres., Borwd. 22 A1
Albany, The W1 11 F6
Wdf.Grn.
Albany, The, 34 F4
Wdf.Grn.
Albany Clo. N15 40 H4
Albany Clo. SW14 74 B4
Albany Clo., Bex. 80 C7
Albany Ct. E4 26 B6
Chelwood Clo.
Albany Ctyd. W1 11 G6
Albany Cres., Edg. 30 A7
Albany Cres., Esher 98 B6
Albany Mans. SW11 66 H7
Albert Bri. Rd.
Albany Ms. SE5 21 A6
Albany Ms., Kings.T. 82 G6
Albany Ms., Enf. 25 F1
Albany Pk. Rd., 82 G6
Kings.T.
Albany Pas., Rich. 73 J5
Albany Pl. N7 49 G4
Benwell Rd.
Albany Pl., Brent. 64 H6
Albany Rd. E10 42 A7
Albany Rd. E12 52 A4
Albany Rd. E17 41 H6
Albany Rd. N4 40 F6
Albany Rd. N18 33 F5
Albany Rd. SE5 21 B6
Albany Rd. SE5 68 A6
Albany Rd. SW19 84 E5
Albany Rd. W13 55 E7
Albany Rd., Belv. 71 F6
Albany Rd., Bex. 80 C7
Albany Rd., Brent. 64 G6
Albany Rd., Chis. 88 E5
Albany Rd., N.Mal. 92 D4
Albany Rd., Rich. 73 J5
Albert Rd.
Albany Rd., Rom. 44 H6
Albany St. NW1 7 D1
Albany St. NW1 58 B3
Albany Vw., Buck.H. 34 G1
Albatross St. SE18 70 H7

Albatross Way SE16 68 G2
Needleman St.
Albemarle SW19 84 A2
Albemarle App., Ilf. 43 E6
Albemarle Gdns., 43 E6
Ilf.
Albemarle Gdns., 92 D4
N.Mal.
Albemarle Pk., Stan. 29 F5
Albemarle Rd., Barn. 23 H7
Albemarle Rd., Beck. 90 B1
Albemarle St. W1 11 F6
Albemarle St. W1 58 C7
Albemarle Way EC1 8 G6
Albermarle Ave., 81 F1
Twick.
Alberon Gdns. NW11 39 C4
Albert Ave. E4 34 A4
Albert Ave. SW8 67 F7
Albert Bri. SW3 18 H6
Albert Bri. SW3 66 H6
Albert Bri. SW11 18 H7
Albert Bri. SW11 66 H7
Albert Bri. Rd. SW11 18 H7
Albert Bri. Rd. SW11 66 H7
Albert Carr Gdns. 85 E5
SW16
Albert Clo. E9 59 E1
Northiam St.
Albert Clo. N22 40 D1
Albert Ct. SW7 14 E4
Albert Ct. SW7 66 G2
Albert Dr. SW19 84 B2
Albert Embk. SE1 20 B4
Albert Embk. SE1 67 G5
Albert Gdns. E1 59 G6
Albert Gro. SW20 93 A1
Albert Hall Mans. 14 E4
SW7
Albert Mans. SW11 75 J1
Albert Bri. Rd.
Albert Ms. W8 14 C5
Albert Pl. N3 39 D1
Albert Pl. N17 41 C3
High Rd.
Albert Pl. W8 14 B4
Albert Pl. W8 66 E2
Albert Rd. E10 51 C2
Albert Rd. E16 70 B1
Albert Rd. E17 42 A5
Albert Rd. E18 42 H3
Albert Rd. N4 49 F1
Albert Rd. N15 41 B6
Albert Rd. N22 40 C1
Albert Rd. NW4 39 A4
Albert Rd. NW6 57 C2
Albert Rd. NW7 30 F5
Albert Rd. SE9 88 B3
Albert Rd. SE20 86 G6
Albert Rd. SE25 95 D4
Albert Rd. W5 55 E4
Albert Rd., Barn. 23 G4
Albert Rd., Belv. 71 F5
Albert Rd., Bex. 80 G6
Albert Rd., Brom. 97 A5
Albert Rd., Buck.H. 35 A2
Albert Rd., Dag. 53 G1
Albert Rd., Hmptn. 81 J5
Albert Rd., Har. 36 J3
Albert Rd., Houns. 72 G4
Albert Rd., Ilf. 52 D7
Albert Rd., Kings.T. 91 J2
Albert Rd., Mitch. 93 J3
Albert Rd., N.Mal. 92 F4
Albert Rd., Rich. 73 H5
Albert Rd., Sthl. 63 D3
Albert Rd., Sutt. 100 G5
Albert Rd., Tedd. 82 C6
Albert Rd., Twick. 82 C1
Albert Rd. Est., Belv. 71 F5
Albert Sq. E15 51 E5
Albert Sq. SW8 67 F7
Albert St. N12 31 F5
Albert St. NW1 58 B1
Albert Ter. NW1 58 A1
Albert Ter. NW10 56 D1
Albert Ter., Buck.H. 35 A2
Albert Ter. Ms. NW1 58 A1
Regents Pk. Rd.
Albert Wk. E16 70 D2
Pier Rd.
Alberta Ave., Sutt. 100 B4
Alberta Est. SE17 20 H3
Alberta Est. SE17 67 H5
Alberta Rd., Enf. 25 C6
Alberta Rd., Erith 80 J1
Alberta St. SE17 20 G3
Alberta St. SE17 67 H5
Albion Ave. N10 40 A1
Albion Ave. SW8 76 D2
Albion Clo. W2 10 H5
Albion Dr. E8 50 C7

Albion Est. SE16 68 F2
Albion Gdns. W6 65 H4
Albion Gro. N16 50 B4
Albion Hill, Loug. 26 J5
Albion Ms. N1 49 G7
Albion Ms. NW6 48 C7
Kilburn High Rd.
Albion Ms. W2 10 H5
Albion Ms. W2 57 H6
Albion Pk., Loug. 27 A5
Albion Pl. EC1 12 G1
Albion Pl. EC1 58 H5
Albion Pl. EC3 13 C2
Albion Rd. E17 42 C3
Albion Rd. N16 50 A4
Albion Rd. N17 41 D2
Albion Rd., Bexh. 80 F4
Albion Rd., Houns. 72 G4
Albion Rd., Kings.T. 92 C1
Albion Rd., Sutt. 100 G6
Albion Rd., Twick. 82 B1
Albion Sq. E8 50 C7
Albion St. SE16 68 F2
Albion St. W2 10 H4
Albion St. W2 57 H6
Albion St., Croy. 101 H1
Albion Ter. E8 50 C7
Albion Vill. Rd. SE26 86 F3
Albion Way EC1 12 J2
Albion Way SE13 78 C4
Albion Way, Wem. 47 B3
North End Rd.
Albrighton Rd. SE22 77 B2
Albuhera Clo., Enf. 24 G1
Albury Ave., Bexh. 80 E2
Albury Ave., Islw. 64 C7
Albury Ave., Hmptn. 81 G6
Albury Dr., Pnr. 36 C1
Albury Ms. E12 51 J1
Albury Rd., Chess. 98 H5
Albury St. SE8 69 A6
Albyfield, Brom. 97 C3
Albyn Rd. SE8 78 A1
Alcester Cres. E5 50 E2
Alcester Rd., Wall. 101 B4
Alcock Clo., Wall. 101 D7
Alcock Rd., Houns. 63 D7
Alconbury Rd. E5 50 D2
Alcorn Clo., Sutt. 100 D2
Alcott Clo. W7 55 C5
Westcott Cres.
Alcuin Ct., Stan. 29 F6
Aldborough Rd., Dag. 53 J6
Aldborough Rd. N., 43 J5
Ilf.
Aldborough Rd. S., 52 H1
Ilf.
Aldbourne Rd. W12 65 F1
Aldbridge St. SE17 21 E3
Aldbridge St. SE17 68 B5
Aldburgh Ms. W1 11 C3
Aldbury Ave., Wem. 47 B7
Aldbury Ms. N9 25 A7
Aldebert Ter. SW8 67 E7
Aldeburgh Clo. E5 50 E2
Southwold Rd.
Aldeburgh Pl., 34 G4
Wdf.Grn.
Aldeburgh St. SE10 69 G5
Alden Ave. E15 60 F4
Aldenham Dr., Uxb. —
Aldenham St. NW1 7 G2
Aldenham St. NW1 58 C2
Aldensley Rd. W6 65 H3
Alder Clo. SE15 21 G6
Alder Clo. SE15 68 C6
Alder Gro. NW2 47 G2
Alder Ms. N19 49 C2
Bredgar Rd.
Alder Rd. SW14 74 D3
Alder Rd., Sid. 88 J3
Alderbrook Rd. SW12 76 B6
Alderbury Rd. SW13 65 G6
Aldergrove Gdns., 72 E2
Houns.
Bath Rd.
Alderholt Way SE15 21 E7
Alderman Ave., Bark. 62 A3
Alderman Judge 91 H2
Mall, Kings.T.
Eden St.
Aldermanbury EC2 13 A3
Aldermanbury EC2 58 J6
Aldermanbury Sq. 13 A2
EC2
Aldermans Hill N13 32 E4
Alderman's Wk. EC2 13 D2
Aldermary Rd., Brom. 96 G1
Aldermaston St. W10 57 A6
Aldermoor Rd. SE6 86 J3
Alderney Ave., 63 H7
Houns.
Alderney Gdns., 45 F7
Nthlt.

Alderney Rd. E1 59 G4
Alderney St. SW1 19 E3
Alderney St. SW1 67 B4
Alders, The N21 24 G6
Alders, The, Felt. 81 E4
Alders, The, Hous. 63 F6
Alders, The, W.Wick. 103 B1
Alders Ave., Wdf.Grn. 34 E6
Alders Clo. E11 51 H2
Aldersbrook Rd.
Alders Clo. W5 64 G3
Alders Clo., Edg. 30 C5
Alders Gro., E.Mol. 90 H4
Esher Rd.
Alders Rd., Edg. 30 C5
Aldersbrook Ave., 25 B2
Enf.
Aldersbrook Dr., 82 J6
Kings.T.
Aldersbrook La. E12 52 C3
Aldersbrook Rd. E11 51 H2
Aldersbrook Rd. E12 51 H2
Aldersey Gdns., 52 G6
Bark.
Aldersford Clo. SE4 77 G5
Aldersgate St. EC1 12 J1
Aldersgate St. EC1 58 J5
Aldersgrove Ave. 87 J3
SE9
Aldershot Rd. NW6 57 C1
Aldersmead Ave., 95 G6
Croy.
Aldersmead Rd., 86 H7
Beck.
Alderson St. W10 57 B4
Kensal Rd.
Alderton Clo. NW10 47 D3
Alderton Clo., Loug. 27 D4
Alderton Cres. NW4 38 H5
Alderton Hall La., 27 D4
Loug.
Alderton Hill, Loug. 27 B5
Alderton Ri., Loug. 27 D4
Alderton Rd. SE24 76 J3
Alderton Rd., Croy. 95 C7
Alderton Way NW4 38 H5
Alderton Way, Loug. 27 C5
Alderville Rd. SW6 75 C2
Alderwick Dr., 73 A3
Hous.
Alderwood Rd. SE9 79 G6
Aldford St. W1 15 B1
Aldford St. W1 67 A1
Aldgate EC3 13 F4
Aldgate EC3 59 B6
Aldgate Ave. E1 13 F3
Aldgate High St. EC3 13 F4
Aldgate High St. EC3 59 C6
Aldine Ct. W12 65 J1
Aldine St.
Aldine Pl. W12 65 J1
Uxbridge Rd.
Aldine St. W12 65 J1
Aldington Clo., Dag. 44 C7
Aldington Rd. SE18 70 A3
Aldis Ms. SW17 84 H5
Aldis St.
Aldis St. SW17 84 H5
Aldred Rd. NW6 48 D5
Aldren Rd. SW17 84 F3
Aldrich Ter. SW18 84 F2
Lidiard Rd.
Aldriche Way E4 34 C6
Aldridge Ave., Edg. 30 B3
Aldridge Ave., Ruis. 45 D2
Aldridge Ave., Stan. 37 H1
Aldridge Ri., N.Mal. 92 E7
Aldridge Rd. Vill. 57 C5
W11
Aldridge Wk. N14 24 E7
Aldrington Rd. SW16 85 C4
Aldsworth Clo. W9 6 A6
Aldsworth Clo. W9 57 E4
Aldwick Clo. SE9 88 G3
Aldwick Rd., Croy. 101 F3
Aldworth Gro. SE13 78 C6
Aldworth Rd. E15 51 E7
Aldwych WC2 12 C5
Aldwych WC2 58 F7
Aldwych Ave., Ilf. 43 F4
Alers Rd., Bexh. 80 D5
Aleston Beck Rd. E16 61 A6
Fulmer Rd.
Alexa Ct. W8 66 D4
Lexham Gdns.
Alexander Ave. 47 H7
NW10
Alexander Clo., Barn. 23 G4
Alexander Clo., 103 G1
Brom.
Alexander Clo., Sid. 79 H6
Alexander Clo., 82 C7
Twick.

Alexander Ms. W2 10 A3
Alexander Pl. SW7 18 G1
Alexander Pl. SW7 66 H4
Alexander Rd. N19 49 E3
Alexander Rd., Bexh. 80 D2
Alexander Rd., Chis. 88 E5
Alexander Sq. SW3 18 G1
Alexander Sq. SW3 66 H4
Alexander St. W2 57 D6
Victoria Rd.
Alexandra Ave. N22 40 D1
Alexandra Ave. SW11 76 A1
Alexandra Ave. W4 65 D7
Alexandra Ave., Har. 45 F1
Alexandra Ave., Sthl. 54 F7
Alexandra Ave., 100 D3
Sutt.
Alexandra Clo., Har. 45 G3
Alexandra Ave.
Alexandra Cotts. 77 J1
SE14
Alexandra Ct. N14 24 C5
Alexandra Ct., Wem. 46 J4
Alexandra Cres., 87 F6
Brom.
Alexandra Dr. SE19 86 B5
Alexandra Dr., Surb. 92 A7
Alexandra Est. NW8 57 E1
Alexandra Gdns. N10 40 B4
Alexandra Gdns. W4 65 E7
Alexandra Gdns., 72 H2
Houns.
Alexandra Gro. N4 49 H1
Alexandra Gro. N12 31 E5
Alexandra Ms. N2 39 J3
Fortis Grn.
Alexandra Pk. Rd. 40 B2
N10
Alexandra Pk. Rd. 40 C1
N22
Alexandra Pl. NW8 57 F1
Alexandra Pl. SE25 95 A5
Alexandra Pl., Croy. 102 B1
Alexandra Rd.
Alexandra Rd. E6 61 D3
Alexandra Rd. E10 51 C3
Alexandra Rd. E17 41 J6
Alexandra Rd. E18 42 H3
Alexandra Rd. N8 40 G3
Alexandra Rd. N9 25 E7
Alexandra Rd. N10 40 B1
Alexandra Rd. N15 41 A5
Alexandra Rd. NW4 39 A4
Alexandra Rd. NW8 48 F7
Alexandra Rd. SE26 86 G6
Alexandra Rd. SW14 74 D3
Alexandra Rd. SW19 84 C6
Alexandra Rd. W4 65 D2
Alexandra Rd., 64 G6
Brent.
Alexandra Rd., Croy. 102 B1
Alexandra Rd., Enf. 25 G4
Alexandra Rd., 72 H2
Houns.
Alexandra Rd., 83 A7
Kings.T.
Alexandra Rd., Mitch. 84 H7
Alexandra Rd., Rich. 73 J2
Alexandra Rd. 44 D6
(Chadwell Heath),
Rom.
Alexandra Rd., T.Ditt. 91 C5
Alexandra Rd., Twick. 73 F6
Alexandra Sq., Mord. 93 D5
Alexandra St. E16 60 G5
Alexandra St. SE14 68 H7
Alexandra Wk. SE19 86 B5
Alexandria Rd. W13 55 D7
Alexis St. SE16 21 J1
Alexis St. SE16 68 D4
Alfearn Rd. E5 50 F4
Alford Grn., Croy. 103 D6
Alford Pl. N1 9 A2
Alford Rd. SW8 76 D1
Alford Rd., Erith 71 J5
Alfoxton Ave. N15 40 H4
Alfreda Gdns., Sthl. 54 E7
Love Vk.
Alfred Ms. W1 11 H1
Alfred Ms. W1 58 D5
Alfred Pl. WC1 11 H1
Alfred Pl. WC1 58 D5
Alfred Prior Ho. E12 52 D4
Alfred Rd. E15 51 F5
Alfred Rd. SE25 95 D5
Alfred Rd. W2 57 D5
Alfred Rd. W3 65 C1
Alfred Rd., Belv. 71 F5
Alfred Rd., Buck.H. 35 A2
Alfred Rd., Felt. 81 C2
Alfred Rd., Kings.T. 91 H3
Alfred Rd., Sutt. 100 F5
Alfred St. E3 59 J3
Alfred St. E16 60 F7

Alfreda St. SW11 76 B1
Alfreds Gdns., Bark. 61 H2
Alfreds Way, Bark. 61 F3
Alfreds Way Ind. Est., 62 A1
Bark.
Alfreton Clo. SW19 84 A3
Alfriston Ave., Croy. 94 E7
Alfriston Ave., Har. 36 G6
Alfriston Clo., Surb. 91 J5
Alfriston Rd. SW11 75 J5
Algar Clo., Islw. 73 D3
Algar Rd.
Algar Clo., Stan. 29 C5
Algar Rd., Islw. 73 D3
Algarve Rd. SW18 84 E1
Algernon Rd. NW4 38 G6
Algernon Rd. NW6 57 D1
Algernon Rd. SE13 78 B3
Algers Clo., Loug. 27 A5
Algers Mead, Loug. 27 A5
Algers Rd., Loug. 27 A5
Algiers Rd. SE13 78 A4
Alibon Gdns., Dag. 53 G5
Alibon Rd., Dag. 53 F5
Alice Gilliatt Ct. W14 66 C5
Alice Ms., Tedd. 82 C5
Luther Rd.
Alice St. SE1 17 D6
Alice St. SE1 68 B3
Alice Way, Houns. 72 H4
Alicia Ave., Har. 37 E4
Alicia Clo., Har. 37 F4
Alicia Gdns., Har. 37 E4
Alie St. E1 13 G4
Alie St. E1 59 C6
Alington Cres. NW9 57 C1
Alison Clo. E6 61 D6
Alison Clo., Croy. 102 G1
Shirley Oaks Rd.
Aliwal Rd. SW11 75 H4
Alkerden Rd. W4 65 E5
Alkham Rd. N16 50 C1
All Hallows Rd. N17 41 B1
Victoria Rd.
All Saints Clo. N9 33 D2
All Saints Dr. SE3 78 E2
All Saints Ms., Stan. 29 B6
Uxbridge Rd.
All Saints Pas. SW18 75 E5
Wandsworth High St.
All Saints Rd. SW19 84 F7
All Saints Rd. W3 65 C3
All Saints Rd. W11 57 C6
All Saints Rd., Sutt. 100 E3
All Saints St. N1 8 C1
All Saints St. N1 58 F2
All Saints Twr. E10 42 B7
All Souls Ave. NW10 56 H2
All Souls Pl. W1 11 E2
All Souls Pl. W1 41 C6
Allan Barclay Clo. 41 C6
N15
Allan Clo., N.Mal. 92 D5
Allan Way W3 56 C5
Allandale Ave. N3 39 B3
Allard Cres. 28 J1
(Bushey), Wat.
Allardyce St. SW4 76 F4
Allbrook Clo., Tedd. 82 B5
Allcroft Rd. NW5 49 A5
Allen Ct., Grnf. 46 C5
Allen Edwards Dr. 76 E1
SW8
Allen Pl., Twick. 82 D1
Church St.
Allen Rd. E3 59 J2
Allen Rd. N16 50 B4
Allen Rd., Beck. 95 G2
Allen Rd., Croy. 101 F1
Allen Rd., Sun. 90 B1
Allen St. W8 66 D3
Allenby Rd., Grnf. 54 G3
Allenby Rd. SE23 86 H3
Allenby Rd., Sthl. 54 G3
Allendale Ave., Sthl. 54 G6
Allendale Clo. SE5 77 A1
Albacore Cres.
Allendale Clo. SE26 86 G4
Allendale Rd., Grnf. 46 E6
Allens Rd., Enf. 25 H5
Allensbury Pl. NW1 49 D7
Allenswood Rd. SE9 79 B3
Allerford Ct., Har. 36 H5
Allerford Rd. SE6 87 B3
Allerton Rd. N16 49 J2
Allerton Wk. N7 49 F2
Durham Rd.
Allestree Rd. SW6 75 B7
Alleyn Cres. SE21 86 A2
Alleyn Pk. SE21 86 A2
Alleyn Pk., Sthl. 63 G5
Alleyn Rd. SE21 86 A3

Alleyndale Rd., Dag. 53 C2
Allfarthing La. SW18 75 E6
Allgood Clo., Mord. 93 A6
Allgood St. E2 9 G2
Allgood St. E2 59 C2
Allhallows La. EC4 13 B6
Allhallows Rd. E6 61 B5
Alliance Clo., Wem. 46 G4
Milford Gdns.
Alliance Rd. E13 60 D4
Alliance Rd. SE18 71 A6
Alliance Rd. W3 56 B4
Allied Ind. Est. W3 65 E2
Allied Way W3 65 E2
Larden Rd.
Allingham Clo. W7 55 C7
Allingham St. N1 8 J1
Allingham St. N1 58 J2
Allington Ave. N17 33 B6
Allington Clo., Grnf. 45 J7
Allington Ct. SW19 84 A5
High St.
Allington Ct., Enf. 25 G5
Allington Rd. NW4 38 H5
Allington Rd. W10 57 B2
Allington Rd., Har. 36 J5
Allington Rd., Orp. 104 G2
Allington St. SW1 15 E6
Allington St. SW1 67 B3
Allison Clo. SE10 78 C1
Dartmouth Hill
Allison Gro. SE21 86 B1
Allison Rd. N8 40 G5
Allison Rd. W3 56 C6
Allitsen Rd. NW8 6 G2
Allitsen Rd. NW8 57 H2
Allnutt Way SW4 76 D5
Alloa Rd. SE8 68 H5
Alloa Rd., Ilf. 53 A2
Allonby Gdns., Wem. 46 F1
Windermere Ave.
Alloway Rd. E3 59 H3
Allsop Pl. NW1 7 A6
Allsop Pl. NW1 57 J4
Allum Way N20 31 F1
Allwood Clo. SE26 86 G4
Alma Ave. E4 34 C7
Alma Cres., Sutt. 100 B5
Alma Gro. SE1 21 G2
Alma Gro. SE1 68 C4
Alma Pl. NW10 56 H3
Harrow Rd.
Alma Pl. SE19 86 C7
Church Rd.
Alma Pl., Th.Hth. 94 G5
Alma Rd. N10 32 B7
Alma Rd. SW18 75 F4
Alma Rd., Cars. 100 H5
Alma Rd., Enf. 25 H3
Alma Rd., Esher 89 B1
Alma Rd., Sid. 89 A3
Alma Rd., Sthl. 54 E7
Alma Sq. NW8 6 D3
Alma Sq. NW8 57 F3
Alma St. E15 51 D6
Alma St. NW5 49 B6
Alma Ter. SW18 75 G7
Almack Rd. E5 50 F4
Almeida St. N1 49 H7
Almer Rd. SW20 83 G7
Almeric Rd. SW11 75 J4
Almington St. N4 49 E1
Almond Ave. W5 64 H3
Almond Ave., Cars. 100 J2
Almond Clo. SE15 77 D2
Almond Clo., Brom. 97 D7
Almond Gro., Brent. 64 E7
Almond Rd. N17 33 D7
Almond Rd. SE16 68 E4
Almond Way, Borwd. 22 B4
Almond Way, Brom. 97 D7
Almond Way, Har. 36 H2
Almond Way, Mitch. 94 D5
Almonds Ave., 34 G2
Buck.H.
Almorah Rd. N1 50 A7
Almorah Rd., Houns. 72 D1
Alnwick Gro., Mord. 93 E4
Bordesley Rd.
Alnwick Rd. E16 60 J6
Alnwick Rd. SE12 78 H7
Alperton La., Grnf. 55 G2
Alperton La., Wem. 55 G2
Alperton St. W10 57 B4
Alpha Clo. NW1 6 H4
Alpha Gro. E14 69 A2
Alpha Pl. NW6 57 D2
Alpha Pl. SW3 18 H5
Alpha Pl. SW3 66 H6
Alpha Rd. E4 34 A3
Alpha Rd. N18 33 D6
Alpha Rd. SE14 77 J1

Alpha Rd., Croy. 102 B1
Alpha Rd., Enf. 25 H4
Alpha Rd., Surb. 91 J6
Alpha Rd., Tedd. 82 A5
Alpha St. SE15 77 D2
Alphea Clo. SW19 84 H7
Courtney Rd.
Alpine Ave., Surb. 99 C2
Alpine Clo., Croy. 102 B3
Alpine Copse, Brom. 97 D2
Alpine Rd. SE16 68 F4
Alpine Rd., Walt. 90 A7
Alpine Vw., Sutt. 100 H5
Alpine Way E6 61 D5
Alric Ave. NW10 47 D7
Alric Ave., N.Mal. 92 E3
Alroy Rd. N4 40 G7
Alsace Rd. SE17 21 D3
Alscot Rd. SE1 21 G1
Alscot Rd. SE1 68 C4
Alscot Way SE1 21 F1
Alscot Way SE1 68 C4
Alsike Rd. SE2 71 D3
Alsike Rd., Erith 71 E3
Alsom Ave., Wor.Pk. 99 F4
Alston Clo., Surb. 91 E7
Alston Rd. N18 33 E5
Alston Rd. SW17 84 G4
Alston Rd., Barn. 23 B3
Alt Gro. SW19 84 C7
St. George's Rd.
Altair Clo. N17 33 C6
Altash Way SE9 88 C2
Altenburg Ave. W13 64 E3
Altenburg Gdns. 75 J4
SW11
Altham Rd., Pnr. 28 E7
Althea St. SW6 75 E2
Althorne Gdns. E18 42 F4
Althorne Way, Dag. 53 G2
Althorp Rd. SW17 84 J1
Althorpe Ms. SW11 75 G1
Westbridge Rd.
Althorpe Rd., Har. 36 J5
Altmore Ave. E6 52 C7
Alton Ave., Stan. 29 C7
Alton Clo., Bex. 89 E1
Alton Clo., Islw. 73 C2
Alton Gdns., Beck. 87 A7
Alton Gdns., Twick. 73 A4
Alton Rd. N17 41 A3
Alton Rd. SW15 83 G1
Alton Rd., Croy. 101 G3
Alton Rd., Rich. 73 H4
Alton St. E14 60 B5
Altyre Clo., Beck. 95 J4
Altyre Rd., Croy. 102 A2
Altyre Way, Beck. 95 J6
Alva Way, Wat. 28 D2
Alvanley Gdns. NW6 48 E5
Alverston Gdns. 95 B5
SE25
Alverstone Ave. 84 D2
SW19
Alverstone Ave., 23 H7
Barn.
Alverstone Gdns. 88 F1
SE9
Alverstone Rd. E12 52 D4
Alverstone Rd. NW2 47 J7
Alverstone Rd., 92 F4
N.Mal.
Alverstone Rd., Wem. 46 J1
Alverton St. SE8 68 J5
Alveston Ave., Har. 37 E3
Alvey Est. SE17 21 D2
Alvey St. SE17 21 D3
Alvey St. SE17 68 B5
Alvia Gdns., Sutt. 100 F4
Alvington Cres. E8 50 C5
Alway Ave., Epsom 99 C5
Alwold Cres. SE12 78 H6
Alwyn Ave. W4 65 D5
Alwyn Clo., Croy. 103 B7
Alwyn Gdns. NW4 38 G4
Alwyn Gdns. W3 56 B6
Alwyne La. N1 49 H7
Canonbury Rd.
Alwyne Pl. N1 49 J6
Alwyne Rd. N1 49 J7
Alwyne Rd. SW19 84 C6
Alwyne Rd. W7 55 B7
Alwyne Sq. N1 49 J6
Alwyne Vill. N1 49 H7
Alyth Gdns. NW11 39 D6
Alzette Ho. E2 59 G2
Mace St.
Amalgamated Dr., 64 D6
Brent.
Amanda Clo., Ilf. 35 G6
Amazon St. E1 59 E6
Hessel St.

Ambassador Clo., 72 E2
Houns.
Ambassador Gdns. 61 C5
E6
Ambassador Sq. E14 69 B4
Cahir St.
Ambassador's Ct. 15 G2
SW1
Amber Ave. E17 41 H1
Amer St. E15 51 D6
Salway Rd.
Amberden Ave. N3 39 D3
Ambergate Ct. E5 50 H4
Ambergate St. SE17 20 H3
Ambergate St. SE17 67 H5
Warnford Rd.
Amberley Clo., Pnr. 36 F3
Amberley Ct., Sid. 89 C5
Amberley Gdns., Enf. 25 B7
Amberley Gdns., 99 F4
Epsom
Amberley Gro. SE26 86 E5
Amberley Gro., Croy. 95 C7
Amberley Rd. E10 42 A7
Amberley Rd. N13 32 F2
Amberley Rd. SE2 71 D6
Amberley Rd. W9 57 D5
Amberley Rd., 34 J1
Buck.H.
Amberley Rd., Enf. 25 C7
Amberley Way, 72 C5
Houns.
Amberley Way, Mord. 93 C7
Amberley Way, Rom. 44 H4
Amberwood Ri., 92 E6
N.Mal.
Amblecote Clo. SE12 87 H3
Amblecote Rd. SE12 87 H3
Ambler Rd. N4 49 H3
Ambleside, Brom. 87 D6
Ambleside Ave. 85 D4
SW16
Ambleside Ave., 95 H6
Beck.
Ambleside Clo. E9 50 F5
Churchill Wk.
Ambleside Cres., Enf. 25 G3
Ambleside Gdns., 43 B4
Ilf.
Ambleside Gdns., 100 F6
Sutt.
Ambleside Gdns., 46 G1
Wem.
Ambleside Rd. NW10 47 F7
Ambleside Rd., Bexh. 80 G2
Ambrooke Rd., Belv. 71 G3
Ambrosden Ave. 15 G6
SW1
Ambrosden Ave. 67 C3
SW1
Ambrose Ave. NW11 39 B7
Ambrose Clo. E6 61 B5
Lovage App.
Ambrose Clo., Orp. 104 J3
Stapleton Rd.
Ambrose Ms. SW11 75 J2
Abercrombie St.
Ambrose St. SE16 68 E4
Ambrose Wk. E3 60 A2
Malmesbury Rd.
Amelia St. SE17 20 J3
Amelia St. SE17 67 H5
Amen Cor. EC4 12 H4
Amen Cor. SW17 84 J6
Amen Ct. EC4 12 H3
America Sq. EC3 13 F5
America St. SE1 16 J2
Amerland Rd. SW18 75 C5
Amersham Ave. N18 33 A6
Amersham Gro. SE14 68 J7
Amersham Rd. SE14 77 J1
Amersham Rd., Croy. 94 J6
Amersham Vale SE14 68 J7
Amery Gdns. NW10 56 H1
Amery Rd., Har. 46 D2
Amesbury Ave. SW2 85 E2
Amesbury Clo., 99 J1
Wor.Pk.
Amesbury Dr. E4 26 B6
Amesbury Rd., Brom. 97 A3
Amesbury Rd., Dag. 53 D7
Amesbury Rd., Felt. 81 D2
Amethyst Rd. E15 51 D4
Amherst Ave. W13 55 F6
Amherst Dr., Orp. 97 J4
Amherst Rd. W13 55 F6
Amhurst Gdns., Islw. 73 C1
Amhurst Pk. N16 41 A7
Amhurst Pas. E8 50 D5
Amhurst Rd. E8 50 E5
Amhurst Rd. N16 50 C4
Amhurst Ter. E8 50 D4

Amhurst Wk. SE28 71 A1
Pitfield Cres.
Amidas Gdns., Dag. 53 B4
Amiel St. E1 59 F4
Amies St. SW11 75 J3
Amina Way SE16 17 H6
Amis Ave., Epsom 99 A6
Amity Gro. SW20 92 J1
Amity Rd. E15 60 F1
Ammanford Gdn. 38 E6
NW9
Ruthin Clo.
Amner Rd. SW11 76 A6
Amoco Ho. W5 55 H3
Amor Rd. W6 65 J3
Amott Rd. SE15 77 D3
Amoy Pl. E14 60 A6
Ampere Way, Croy. 94 F7
Ampleforth Rd. SE2 71 B2
Ampthill Sq. Est. NW1 7 G2
Ampton Pl. WC1 8 C4
Ampton Pl. WC1 58 F3
Ampton St. WC1 8 C4
Ampton St. WC1 58 F3
Amroth Clo. SE23 86 E1
Amsterdam Rd. E14 69 C3
Amwell Clo., Enf. 25 A5
Amwell Ct. Est. N4 49 J1
Amwell St. EC1 8 E3
Amwell St. EC1 58 G3
Amyand Cotts. 73 E6
Twick.
Amyand La., Twick.
Marble Hill Gdns.
Amyand Pk. Gdns., 73 E7
Twick.
Amyand Pk. Rd.
Amyand Pk. Rd., 73 D7
Twick.
Amyruth Rd. SE4 78 A5
Anatola Rd. N19 49 B2
Dartmouth Pk. Hill
Ancaster Cres., 92 G6
N.Mal.
Ancaster Rd., Beck. 95 G3
Ancaster St. SE18 70 H7
Anchor & Hope La. 69 J4
SE7
Anchor Ms. SW12 76 B6
Hazelbourne Rd.
Anchor St. SE16 68 E4
Anchor Yd. EC1 9 A5
Anchorage Clo. 84 D5
SW19
Ancill Clo. W6 66 B6
Ancona Rd. NW10 56 G2
Ancona Rd. SE18 70 G5
Andace Pk. Gdns., 96 J1
Brom.
Andalus Rd. SW9 76 E3
Ander Clo., Wem. 46 G4
Anderson Clo. W3 56 D6
Anderson Pl., Houns. 72 H4
Anderson Rd. E9 50 G6
Anderson Rd., 43 A3
Wdf.Grn.
Anderson Pl. SW3 18 J3
Anderson St. SW3 66 J5
Anderson Way, Belv. 71 H2
Anderton Clo. SE5 77 A3
Andover Clo., Grnf. 54 H4
Ruislip Rd.
Andover Pl. NW6 6 A1
Andover Rd. N7 49 F2
Andover Rd., Orp. 104 H2
Andover Rd., Twick. 82 A1
Andre St. E8 50 D5
Andrew Borde St. 11 J3
WC2
Andrew Pl., Ilf. 35 G6
Andrew Pl. SW8 76 D1
Cowthorpe Rd.
Andrew St. E14 60 C6
Andrews Clo. E6 61 B6
Linton Gdns.
Andrews Clo., 34 J2
Buck.H.
Andrews Clo., Har. 37 A7
Bessborough Rd.
Andrews Clo., 99 J2
Wor.Pk.
Andrews Crosse WC2 12 E4
Andrews Pl. SE9 79 E6
Andrew's Rd. E8 59 E1
Andrew's Wk. SE17 20 H6
Andwell Clo. SE2 71 B2
Anerley Gro. SE19 86 C7
Anerley Hill SE19 86 C6
Anerley Pk. SE20 86 D7

Anerley Pk. Rd. SE20 86 E7
Anerley Rd. SE19 86 D7
Anerley Rd. SE20 86 D7
Anerley Sta. Rd. 95 E1
SE20
Anerley St. SW11 75 J2
Anerley Vale SE19 86 C7
Anfield Clo. SW12 76 C7
Belthorn Cres.
Angel All. E1 13 G3
Angel Clo. N18 33 C5
Angel Ct. EC2 13 C3
Angel Ct. SW1 15 G2
Angel Ct. SW17 84 J4
Angel Hill, Sutt. 100 E3
Sutton Common Rd.
Angel Hill Dr., Sutt. 100 E3
Angel La. E15 51 D6
Angel Ms. N1 8 F2
Angel Ms. N1 58 G2
Angel Pas. EC4 13 B6
Angel Pl. N18 33 D5
Angel Clo.
Angel Pl. SE1 17 B3
Angel Rd. N18 33 D5
Angel Rd., Har. 37 B6
Angel Rd., T.Ditt. 91 D7
Angel Rd. Wks. N18 33 F5
Angel St. EC1 12 J3
Angel St. EC1 58 J6
Angel Wk. W6 65 J5
Angelfield, Houns. 72 H4
Angelica Gdns. 102 G1
Croy.
Angelica Clo. 76 G3
SW9
Angell Pk. Gdns. 76 G3
SW9
Angell Rd. SW9 76 G3
Angerstein La. SE3 78 F1
Burnside Rd.
Anglers Clo., Rich. 82 F4
Locksmeade Rd.
Angler's La. NW5 49 B6
Angles Rd. SW16 85 E4
Anglesea Ave. SE18 70 E4
Anglesea Rd. SE18 70 E4
Anglesea Rd., 91 G4
Kings.T.
Anglesey Ct. Rd. 101 A6
Cars.
Anglesey Gdns. 101 A6
Cars.
Anglesey Rd., Enf. 25 E4
Anglesey Rd., Wat. 28 C5
Anglesmede Cres., 36 E3
Pnr.
Anglesmede Way, 36 E3
Pnr.
Anglia Ho. E14 59 H6
Anglo Rd. E3 59 J2
Angrave Ct. E8 59 C1
Angrave Pas. E8 59 C1
Haggerston Rd.
Angus Clo., Chess. 99 A5
Angus Dr., Ruis. 45 C4
Angus Gdns. NW9 38 D1
Angus Rd. E13 60 J3
Angus St. SE14 68 H7
Anhalt Rd. SW11 18 H7
Anhalt Rd. SW11 66 H7
Ankerdine Cres. 79 E1
Anlaby Rd., Tedd. 82 B5
Anley Rd. W14 66 A2
Anmersh Gro., Stan. 37 G1
Ann La. SW10 18 E7
Ann La. SW10 66 G7
Ann St. SE18 70 F5
Anna Clo. E8 59 C1
Anna Neagle Clo. E7 51 G4
Dames Rd.
Annabel Clo. E14 60 B6
Annandale Rd. SE10 69 F5
Annandale Rd. W4 65 E5
Annandale Rd., 102 D2
Croy.
Annandale Rd., Sid. 79 H7
Anne Boleyn's Wk., 82 H5
Kings.T.
Anne Boleyn's Wk., 100 A7
Sutt.
Anne Case Ms., 92 D3
N.Mal.
Sycamore Gro.
Anne St. E13 60 G4
Anne Way, Ilf. 35 F6
Anne Way, W.Mol. 90 H4
Annesley Ave. NW9 38 D3
Annesley Clo. NW10 47 E3
Annesley Dr., Croy. 102 J4
Annesley Rd. SE3 78 H1
Annesley Rd. N19 49 C2
Macdonald Rd.
Annett Rd., Walt. 90 A7

Annette Clo., Har. 37 B2
  Spencer Rd.
Annette Cres. N1 49 J7
  Essex Rd.
Annette Rd. N7 49 F3
Annie Besant Clo. E3 59 J1
Anning St. EC2 9 E5
Annington Rd. N2 39 J3
Annis Rd. E9 50 H6
Ann's Clo. SW1 15 A4
Ann's Pl. E1 13 F2
Annsworthy Ave., 95 A3
  Th.Hth.
  Grange Pk. Rd.
Ansdell Rd. SE15 77 F2
Ansdell St. W8 14 B5
Ansdell St. W8 66 E3
Ansdell Ter. W8 14 B5
Ansell Gro., Cars. 101 A1
Ansell Rd. SW17 84 H3
Anselm Clo., Croy. 102 C3
  Park Hill Ri.
Anselm Rd. SW6 66 D6
Anselm Rd., Pnr. 28 F7
Ansford Rd., Brom. 87 C5
Ansleigh Pl. W11 57 A7
Anson Clo., Rom. 44 H2
Anson Rd. N7 49 C4
Anson Rd. NW2 47 H5
Anstey Rd. SE15 77 D3
Anstey Wk. N8 40 H4
Anstice Clo. W4 65 E7
Anstridge Path SE9 79 G6
  Anstridge Rd.
Anstridge Rd. SE9 79 G6
Antelope Rd. SE18 70 C3
Anthony Clo. NW7 30 E4
Anthony Clo., Wat. 28 C1
Anthony Rd. SE25 95 D6
Anthony Rd., Grnf. 55 B2
Anthony Rd., Well. 80 A1
Anthony St. E1 59 E6
Antigua Clo. SE19 86 A5
  Salters Hill
Antill Rd. E3 59 H3
Antill Rd. N15 41 D4
Antill Ter. E1 59 G6
Antlers Hill E4 26 B4
Anton Cres., Sutt. 100 D3
Anton St. E8 50 D5
Antoneys Clo., Pnr. 36 D2
Antrim Gro. NW3 48 J6
Antrim Mans. NW3 48 J6
  Antrim Rd.
Antrim Rd. NW3 48 J6
Antrobus Clo., Sutt. 100 C5
Antrobus Rd. W4 65 C4
Anvil Rd., Sun. 90 A4
Anworth Clo., 34 H6
  Wdf.Grn.
Apex Clo., Beck. 96 B1
Apex Twr., N.Mal. 92 E3
Aplin Way, Islw. 73 B1
Apollo Ave., Brom. 96 H1
  Rodway Rd.
Apollo Clo., Nthwd. 28 A5
Apollo Pl. SW10 18 E7
Apollo Way SE28 70 G3
  Broadwater Rd.
Apothecary St. EC4 12 G4
Appach Rd. SW2 76 G5
Appel Garth, Brent. 64 G4
Apple Gro., Chess. 98 H4
Apple Gro., Enf. 25 B3
Apple Mkt., Kings.T. 91 G2
  Eden St.
Apple Tree Yd. SW1 15 G1
Appleby Clo. E4 34 B6
Appleby Clo. N15 41 A5
Appleby Clo., Twick. 82 A2
Appleby Rd. E8 50 D7
Appleby Rd. E16 60 F6
Appleby St. E2 9 F2
Appleby St. E2 59 C2
Appledore Ave., 80 J1
  Bexh.
Appledore Ave., Ruis. 45 C3
Appledore Clo. SW17 84 J2
Appledore Clo., 96 F5
  Brom.
Appledore Clo., Edg. 38 A1
Appledore Cres., 88 H3
  Sid.
Appleford Rd. W10 57 B4
Applegarth, Croy. 103 B7
Applegarth, Esher 98 C5
Applegarth Dr., Ilf. 43 J4
Applegarth Rd. SE28 71 B1
Applegarth Rd. W14 66 A3
Appleton Gdns., 92 G6
  N.Mal.
Appleton Rd. SE9 79 B3
Appleton Rd., Loug. 27 E3

Appleton Sq., Mitch. 93 H1
Appletree Gdns., 23 H4
  Barn.
Applewood Clo. N20 31 H1
Applewood Clo. NW2 47 H3
Appold St. EC2 13 D1
Appold St. EC2 59 B5
Apprentice Way E5 50 E4
  Clarence Rd.
Approach, The NW4 39 A5
Approach, The W3 56 D6
Approach, The, Enf. 25 E2
Approach, The, Orp. 104 J2
Approach Rd. E2 59 F2
Approach Rd. SW20 92 J2
Approach Rd., Barn. 23 F4
Approach Rd., W.Mol. 90 G5
Aprey Gdns. NW4 38 J4
April Clo. W7 55 B7
April Clo., Felt. 81 A3
April Clo., Orp. 104 J5
  Briarswood Way
April Glen SE23 86 G3
April St. E8 50 C4
Apsley Clo., Har. 36 J5
Apsley Rd. SE25 95 E4
Apsley Rd., N.Mal. 92 C3
Apsley Way W1 15 C3
Aquarius Way, 28 A5
  Nthwd.
Aquila St. NW8 6 F1
Aquila St. NW8 57 G2
Aquinas St. SE1 16 F2
Arabella Dr. SW15 74 E4
Arabia Clo. E4 26 C7
Arabin Rd. SE4 77 H4
Aragon Ave., T.Ditt. 91 C5
Aragon Clo., Brom. 104 C1
  Seymour Dr.
Aragon Dr., Har. 35 F7
Aragon Dr., Ruis. 45 D1
Aragon Ms. E1 17 H1
Aragon Rd., Kings.T. 82 H5
Aragon Rd., Mord. 93 A6
Aran Dr., Stan. 29 F4
Arandora Cres., Rom. 44 B7
Arbery Rd. E3 59 H3
Arbor Clo., Beck. 96 B2
Arbor Rd. E4 34 D3
Arbour Rd., Enf. 25 G4
Arbour Sq. E1 59 G6
Arbroath Grn., Wat. 28 A3
Arbroath Rd. SE9 79 B3
Arbury Ter. SE26 86 E3
  Oaksford Ave.
Arbuthnot La., Bex. 80 E6
Arbuthnot Rd. SE14 77 G2
Arbuthnot St. E8 59 C1
Arcade, The EC2 13 D2
Arcadia Ave. N3 39 D1
Arcadia St. E14 60 A6
Arcadian Ave., Bex. 80 E6
Arcadian Ave., Bex. 80 E6
Arcadian Gdns. N22 32 F7
Arcadian Rd., Bex. 80 E6
Arch St. SE1 16 J6
Arch St. SE1 67 J3
Archangel St. SE16 68 G2
Archbishops Pl. SW2 76 F6
Archdale Rd. SE22 77 C5
Archel Rd. W14 66 C6
Archer Clo., Kings.T. 82 H7
Archer Ho. SW11 75 G1
  Vicarage Cres.
Archer Rd. SE25 95 E4
Archer St. W1 11 H5
Archers Dr., Enf. 25 F2
Archers Wk. SE15 77 C1
  Exeter Rd.
Archery Clo. W2 10 H4
Archery Clo. W2 57 H6
Archery Clo., Har. 37 C3
Archery Rd. SE9 79 C5
Arches, The SW6 75 C2
  Munster Rd.
Arches, The WC2 16 B1
Arches, The, Har. 45 H2
Archibald Ms. W1 11 D6
Archibald Ms. W1 58 A7
Archibald Rd. N7 49 D4
Archibald St. E3 60 A3
Archway Clo. N19 49 C2
  St. Johns Way
Archway Clo. SW19 84 E4
Archway Clo., Wall. 101 D3
Archway Mall N19 49 C2
  Magdala Ave.
Archway Rd. N6 39 J5
Archway Rd. N19 49 C1
Archway Rd. SW13 74 H3
Arcola St. E8 50 C5
Arctic St. NW5 48 B5
  Gillies St.

Arcus Rd., Brom. 87 E6
Ardbeg Rd. SE24 77 A5
Arden Clo., Har. 46 A3
Arden Ct. Gdns. N2 39 G6
Arden Cres. E14 69 A4
Arden Cres., Dag. 53 C7
Arden Est. N1 9 D2
Arden Est. N1 59 B2
Arden Gro., Orp. 104 E4
Arden Mhor, Pnr. 36 B4
Arden Rd. N3 39 B3
Arden Rd. W13 55 F7
Ardent Clo. SE25 95 B3
Ardfern Ave. SW16 94 G3
Ardfillan Rd. SE6 87 D1
Ardgowan Rd. SE6 78 E7
Ardilaun Rd. N5 49 J4
Ardleigh Gdns., Sutt. 93 D7
Ardleigh Ho., Bark. 61 F1
  St. Ann's
Ardleigh Ms., Ilf. 52 E3
  Bengal Rd.
Ardleigh Rd. E17 41 J1
Ardleigh Rd. N1 50 B6
Ardleigh Ter. E17 41 J1
Ardley Clo. NW10 47 E3
Ardley Clo. SE6 86 H3
Ardlui Rd. SE27 85 J2
Ardmay Gdns., Surb. 91 H5
Ardmere Rd. SE13 78 D6
Ardmore La., Buck.H. 26 H7
Ardoch Rd. SE6 87 D2
Ardra Rd. N9 33 G3
Ardrossan Gdns., 93 G3
  Wor.Pk.
Ardwell Ave., Ilf. 43 F5
Ardwell Rd. SW2 85 E2
Ardwick Rd. NW2 48 D4
Argall Ave. E10 41 G7
Argent St. SE1 16 H3
Argon Ms. SW6 66 D7
Argus Clo., Rom. 44 H1
Argus Way W3 65 B3
Argus Way, Nthlt. 54 E3
Argyle Ave., Houns. 72 G6
Argyle Clo. W13 55 D4
Argyle Pas. N17 41 C1
  Argyle Rd.
Argyle Pl. W6 65 H4
Argyle Rd. E1 59 G4
Argyle Rd. E15 51 E5
Argyle Rd. E16 60 H6
Argyle Rd. N12 31 D5
Argyle Rd. N17 41 D1
Argyle Rd. N18 33 D4
Argyle Rd. W13 55 D5
Argyle Rd., Barn. 22 J4
Argyle Rd., Grnf. 55 C3
Argyle Rd., Har. 36 H6
Argyle Rd., Houns. 72 H5
Argyle Rd., Ilf. 52 D2
Argyle Rd., Tedd. 82 B5
Argyle Sq. WC1 8 B3
Argyle Sq. WC1 58 E3
Argyle St. WC1 8 A3
Argyle St. WC1 58 E3
Argyle Wk. WC1 8 A4
Argyll Ave., Sthl. 63 H1
Argyll Clo. SW9 76 F3
  Dalyell Rd.
Argyll Gdns., Edg. 38 B2
Argyll Rd. W8 66 D2
Argyll St. W1 11 F4
Argyll St. W1 58 C6
Arica Rd. SE4 77 H4
Ariel Rd. NW6 48 D6
Ariel Way W12 65 J1
Aristotle Rd. SW4 76 D3
Arkell Gro. SE19 85 H7
Arkindale Rd. SE6 87 C3
Arkley Cres. E17 41 J5
Arkley Dr., Barn. 22 G4
Arkley La., Barn. 22 G3
Arkley Rd. E17 41 J5
Arkley Vw., Barn. 22 H4
Arklow Rd. SE14 68 J6
Arkwright Rd. NW3 48 F5
Arlesford Rd. SW9 76 E3
Arlesey Clo. SW15 75 B6
  Lytton Gro.
Arlingford Rd. SW2 76 F4
Arlington N12 31 D3
Arlington Ave. N1 9 A1
Arlington Ave. N1 58 J1
Arlington Clo., Sid. 79 H7
Arlington Clo., Sutt. 100 D3
Arlington Clo., Twick. 73 F6
Arlington Dr., Cars. 100 J2
Arlington Gdns. W4 65 D5
Arlington Gdns., Ilf. 52 D1
Arlington Lo. SW2 76 F4

Arlington Ms., Twick. 73 E6
  Arlington Rd.
Arlington Rd. N14 32 B2
Arlington Rd. NW1 58 B1
Arlington Rd. W13 55 E6
Arlington Rd., Rich. 82 G2
Arlington Rd., Surb. 91 G6
Arlington Rd., Tedd. 82 C4
Arlington Rd., Twick. 73 F6
Arlington Rd., 34 G7
  Wdf.Grn.
Arlington Sq. N1 58 J1
Arlington St. SW1 15 F1
Arlington St. SW1 67 C1
Arlington Way EC1 8 F3
Arlington Way EC1 58 G3
Arliss Way, Nthlt. 54 C1
Arlow Rd. N21 32 G1
Armada Ct. SE8 69 A6
  Watergate St.
Armada St. SE8 69 A6
Armadale Clo. N17 41 E4
Armadale Rd. SW6 66 D7
Armadale Rd., Felt. 72 A5
Armagh Rd. E3 59 J1
Armfield Clo., W.Mol. 90 F5
Armfield Cres., Mitch. 93 J2
Armfield Rd., Enf. 25 A1
Arminger Rd. W12 65 H1
Armitage Rd. NW11 48 B3
Armitage Rd. SE10 69 F5
Armour Clo. N7 49 F6
  Roman Way
Armoury Way SW18 75 D5
Armstead Wk., Dag. 53 G7
Armstrong Ave., 34 G3
  Wdf.Grn.
Armstrong Clo. E6 61 C6
  Porter Rd.
Armstrong Clo., Dag. 53 D1
  Palmer Rd.
Armstrong Clo., Pnr. 36 A6
Armstrong Cres., 23 G3
  Barn.
Armstrong Rd. SW7 14 E6
Armstrong Rd. SW7 66 G3
Armstrong Rd. W3 65 F1
Armstrong Rd., Felt. 81 E5
Armstrong Rd., 63 H2
  Sthl.
Armytage Rd., 63 D7
  Houns.
Arnal Cres. SW18 75 E6
Arndale Cen., The 75 E6
  SW18
Arndale Wk. SW18 75 E5
  Garratt La.
Arne Gro., Orp. 104 J3
Arne St. WC2 12 B4
Arne St. WC2 58 E6
Arne Wk. SE3 78 F4
Arneway St. SW1 15 J6
Arneways Ave., Rom. 44 D4
Arnewood Clo. SW15 83 G1
Arney's La., Mitch. 94 A6
Arngask Rd. SE6 78 D7
Arnham Way SE22 77 B5
  East Dulwich Gro.
Arnison Rd., E.Mol. 91 A4
Arnold Circ. E2 9 F4
Arnold Circ. E2 59 C3
Arnold Clo., Har. 37 J7
Arnold Cres., Islw. 73 A5
Arnold Est. SE1 17 G4
Arnold Est. SE1 68 C2
Arnold Gdns. N13 32 H5
Arnold Rd. E3 60 A3
Arnold Rd. N15 41 C3
Arnold Rd. SW17 84 J7
Arnold Rd., Dag. 53 F7
Arnold Rd., Nthlt. 45 D6
Arnos Gro. N14 32 D4
Arnos Rd. N11 32 C5
Arnott Clo. SE28 62 C7
  Applegarth Rd.
Arnott Clo. W4 65 D4
  Fishers La.
Arnould Ave. SE5 77 A4
Arnsberg Way, Bexh. 80 G4
Arnside Gdns., Wem. 46 G1
Arnside Rd., Bexh. 80 G1
Arnside St. SE17 21 A5
Arnside St. SE17 67 J6
Arnulf St. SE6 87 B4
Arnulls Rd. SW16 85 G6
Arodene Rd. SW2 76 F6
Arragon Gdns. SW16 85 E7
Arragon Gdns., 103 B3
  W.Wick.
Arragon Rd. E6 61 A1
Arragon Rd., Twick. 73 D7
Arran Clo., Wall. 101 C4
Arran Dr. E12 52 A1

Arran Ms. W5 64 J1
Arran Rd. SE6 87 B2
Arran Wk. N1 49 J7
Arras Ave., Mord. 93 F5
Arrol Rd., Beck. 95 F3
Arrow Rd. E3 60 B3
Arrowscout Wk., Nthlt. 54 E3
Argus Way
Arrowsmith Clo., Chig. 35 J5
Arrowsmith Path, Chig. 35 H5
Arrowsmith Rd., Chig. 35 H5
Arrowsmith Rd., Loug. 27 B3
Arsenal Rd. SE9 79 C2
Arterberry Rd. SW20 83 J7
Artesian Clo. NW10 47 D7
Artesian Rd. W2 57 D6
Arthingworth St. E15 60 E1
Arthur Ct. W2 10 A3
Arthur Gro. SE18 70 F4
Arthur Henderson Ho. SW6 75 C2
Arthur Rd. E6 61 C2
Arthur Rd. N7 49 F4
Arthur Rd. N9 33 C2
Arthur Rd. SW19 84 B5
Arthur Rd., Kings.T. 83 A7
Arthur Rd., N.Mal. 82 H5
Arthur Rd., Rom. 44 D6
Arthur St. EC4 13 C5
Arthurdon Rd. SE4 78 A5
Artichoke Hill E1 59 E7
Pennington St.
Artichoke Pl. SE5 77 A1
Artillery Clo., Ilf. 43 F6
Horns Rd.
Artillery La. E1 13 E2
Artillery La. E1 59 B5
Artillery Pas. E1 13 E2
Artillery Pl. SE18 70 C4
Artillery Pl. SW1 15 H6
Artillery Row SW1 15 H6
Artillery Row SW1 67 D3
Artington Clo., Orp. 104 F4
Artizan St. E1 13 E3
Arundel Ave., Mord. 93 C4
Arundel Clo. E15 51 E4
Arundel Clo. SW11 75 H5
Chivalry Rd.
Arundel Clo., Bex. 80 F6
Arundel Clo., Croy. 101 H3
Arundel Clo., Hmptn. 81 H5
Arundel Ct. N12 31 H6
Arundel Ct., Har. 45 G4
Arundel Dr., Borwd. 22 B5
Arundel Dr., Har. 45 F4
Arundel Dr., Wdf.Grn. 34 G2
Arundel Gdns. N21 32 G1
Arundel Gdns. W11 57 C7
Arundel Gdns., Edg. 30 D7
Arundel Gdns., Ilf. 53 A2
Arundel Great Ct. WC2 12 D5
Arundel Gro. N16 50 B5
Arundel Pl. N1 49 G6
Arundel Rd., Barn. 23 H3
Arundel Rd., Croy. 95 A6
Arundel Rd., Houns. 72 C3
Arundel Rd., Kings.T. 92 B2
Arundel Rd., Sutt. 100 B7
Arundel Sq. N7 49 G6
Arundel St. WC2 12 D5
Arundel St. WC2 58 F7
Arundel Ter. SW13 65 H6
Arvon Rd. N5 49 G5
Ascalon St. SW8 67 C7
Ascham Dr. E4 34 B7
Rushcroft Rd.
Ascham End E17 41 H1
Ascham St. NW5 48 C5
Aschurch Rd., Croy. 95 C7
Ascot Clo., Borwd. 22 A5
Ascot Clo., Ilf. 35 H6
Ascot Clo., Nthlt. 45 G6
Ascot Gdns., Sthl. 54 F4
Ascot Rd. E6 61 C3
Ascot Rd. N15 41 A5
Ascot Rd. N18 33 D4
Ascot Rd. SW17 85 A6
Ascot Rd., Orp. 97 J4
Ascott Ave. W5 64 H2
Ash Clo. SE20 95 F2
Ash Clo., Cars. 100 J2
Ash Clo., Edg. 30 C4
Ash Clo., N.Mal. 92 D2
Ash Clo., Orp. 97 G5
Ash Clo., Sid. 89 B3
Ash Clo., Stan. 29 D6

Ash Ct., Epsom 99 C4
Ash Gro. E8 59 E1
Ash Gro. N13 32 J3
Ash Gro. NW2 48 A4
Ash Gro. SE20 95 F2
Ash Gro. W5 64 H2
Ash Gro., Enf. 25 B7
Ash Gro., Houns. 72 D1
Ash Gro., Sthl. 54 G5
Ash Gro., Wem. 46 D4
Ash Gro., W.Wick. 103 C2
Ash Hill Clo. (Bushey), Wat. 28 H1
Ash Hill Dr., Pnr. 36 C3
Ash Island, E.Mol. 91 A3
Ash La., Croy. 101 H4
Ash Rd. E15 51 E5
Ash Rd., Croy. 103 A2
Ash Rd., Orp. 104 J7
Ash Rd., Sutt. 93 B7
Ash Row, Brom. 97 D7
Ash Tree Clo., Croy. 95 H6
Ash Tree Clo., Surb. 98 H1
Ash Tree Dell NW9 38 D5
Ash Tree Way, Croy. 95 H5
Ash Wk. SW2 85 F1
Ash Wk., Wem. 46 F3
Ashbourne Ave. E18 42 H4
Ashbourne Ave. N20 31 J2
Ashbourne Ave. NW11 39 C5
Ashbourne Ave., Bexh. 71 E7
Ashbourne Ave., Har. 46 A2
Ashbourne Clo. N12 31 E4
Ashbourne Clo. W5 56 A5
Ashbourne Ct. E5 50 H4
Daubeney Rd.
Ashbourne Gro. NW7 30 D5
Ashbourne Gro. SE22 77 C5
Ashbourne Gro. W4 65 E5
Ashbourne Ri., Orp. 104 G4
Ashbourne Rd. W5 55 J4
Ashbourne Rd., Mitch. 85 A6
Ashbourne Ter. SW19 84 D7
Ashbourne Way NW11 39 C5
Ashbourne Ave.
Ashbridge Rd. E11 42 E7
Ashbridge St. NW8 6 G6
Ashbridge St. NW8 57 H4
Ashbrook Rd. N19 49 D1
Ashbrook Rd., Dag. 53 H3
Ashburn Gdns. SW7 18 C1
Ashburn Gdns. SW7 66 F4
Ashburn Pl. SW7 18 C1
Ashburn Pl. SW7 66 F4
Ashburnham Ave., Har. 37 C6
Ashburnham Clo. N2 39 G3
Ashburnham Clo., Wat. 28 A3
Ashburnham Dr.
Ashburnham Dr., Wat. 28 A3
Ashburnham Gdns., Har. 37 C6
Ashburnham Gro. SE10 69 B7
Ashburnham Pl. SE10 69 B7
Ashburnham Retreat SE10 69 B7
Ashburnham Rd. NW10 56 J3
Ashburnham Rd. SW10 18 D7
Ashburnham Rd. SW10 66 F7
Ashburnham Rd., Belv. 71 J4
Ashburnham Rd., Rich. 82 E2
Ashburton Ave., Croy. 102 E1
Ashburton Ave., Ilf. 52 H4
Ashburton Clo., Croy. 102 D1
Ashburton Ct., Pnr. 36 D3
Ashburton Gdns., Croy. 102 D2
Ashburton Gro. N7 49 G4
Ashburton Rd. E16 60 G6
Ashburton Rd., Croy. 102 D2
Ashburton Rd., Ruis. 45 A2
Ashburton Ter. E13 60 G2
Grasmere Rd.
Ashbury Gdns., Rom. 44 D5
Ashbury Rd. SW11 75 J3
Ashby Ave., Chess. 99 A6
Ashby Gro. N1 49 J7

Ashby Ms. SE4 77 J2
Ashby Rd. N15 41 D5
Ashby Rd. SE4 77 J2
Ashby St. EC1 8 H4
Ashby Wk., Croy. 94 J6
Ashchurch Gro. W12 65 G3
Ashchurch Pk. Vill. W12 65 G3
Ashchurch Ter. W12 65 G3
Ashcombe Ave., Surb. 91 G7
Ashcombe Gdns., Edg. 30 A4
Ashcombe Pk. NW2 47 E3
Ashcombe Rd. SW19 84 D5
Ashcombe Rd., Cars. 101 A6
Ashcombe Sq., N.Mal. 92 C3
Ashcombe St. SW6 75 E2
Ashcroft, Pnr. 28 B2
Ashcroft Ave., Sid. 80 A6
Ashcroft Cres., Sid. 80 A6
Ashcroft Rd. E3 59 H3
Ashcroft Rd., Chess. 98 J3
Ashcroft Sq. W6 65 J4
King St.
Ashdale Clo., Twick. 72 J7
Ashdale Gro., Stan. 29 C6
Ashdale Rd. SE12 87 H1
Ashdale Way, Twick. 72 J7
Ashdale Clo.
Ashdene SE15 77 E1
Carlton Gro.
Ashdene, Pnr. 36 C3
Ashdon Clo., Wdf.Grn. 34 H6
Ashdon Rd. NW10 56 F1
Ashdown Clo., Beck. 96 B2
Ashdown Cres. NW5 49 A5
Queens Cres.
Ashdown Rd., Enf. 25 F3
Ashdown Rd., Kings.T. 91 H2
Ashdown Wk. E14 69 A4
Charnwood Gdns.
Ashdown Way, Rom. 44 H2
Ashdown Way SW17 85 A2
Ashen E6 50 F5
Ashen Gro. SW19 84 D3
Ashenden Rd. E5 50 H5
Asher Way E1 17 J1
Asher Way E1 68 D1
Ashfield Ave., Felt. 81 B1
Ashfield Clo., Rich. 82 H1
Ashfield La., Chis. 88 F6
Ashfield Par. N14 32 D1
Ashfield Rd. N4 32 C3
Ashfield Rd. N14 32 C3
Ashfield Rd. W3 65 F1
Ashfield St. E1 59 E5
Ashfields, Loug. 18 C2
Ashford Ave. N8 40 E4
Ashford Ave., Hayes 54 D6
Ashford Clo. E17 41 J6
Ashford Cres., Enf. 25 F2
Ashford Grn., Wat. 28 D5
Ashford Rd. E6 52 D6
Ashford Rd. E18 42 H2
Ashford Rd. NW2 38 J3
Ashford St. N1 9 D3
Ashgrove Rd., Brom. 87 D6
Ashgrove Rd., Ilf. 52 J1
Ashington Clo. E4 34 C3
Ashington Rd. SW6 75 C2
Ashlake Rd. SW16 85 E4
Ashland Pl. W1 11 B1
Ashland Pl. W1 58 A5
Ashlar Pl. SE18 70 E4
Masons Hill
Ashleigh Gdns., Sutt. 100 E2
Ashleigh Rd. SE20 95 E3
Ashleigh Rd. SW14 74 E3
Ashley Ave., Ilf. 42 E3
Ashley Ave., Mord. 93 D5
Ashley Clo. NW4 38 J2
Ashley Clo., Pnr. 36 B2
Ashley Cres. N22 40 G2
Ashley Cres. SW11 76 A3
Ashley Dr., Borwd. 22 C5
Ashley Dr., Islw. 64 B6
Ashley Dr., Twick. 81 H1
Ashley Gdns. N13 32 J4
Ashley Gdns. SW1 15 G6
Ashley Gdns., Orp. 104 H5
Ashley Gdns., Rich. 82 G2
Ashley Gdns., Wem. 46 H2
Ashley Gro., Loug. 27 B3
Staples Rd.
Ashley La. NW4 38 J2
Ashley La., Croy. 101 H4
Ashley Pl. SW1 15 F6
Ashley Pl. SW1 67 C3

Ashley Rd. E4 34 A5
Ashley Rd. E7 51 J7
Ashley Rd. N17 41 D3
Ashley Rd. N19 49 E1
Ashley Rd. SW19 84 E6
Ashley Rd., Enf. 25 F2
Ashley Rd., Hmptn. 90 G1
Ashley Rd., Rich. 73 H3
Jocelyn Rd.
Ashley Rd., T.Ditt. 91 C6
Ashley Rd., Th.Hth. 94 F4
Ashley Wk. NW7 30 J7
Ashlin Rd. E15 51 D4
Ashling Rd., Croy. 102 D1
Ashlone Rd. SW15 74 J3
Ashlyns Way, Chess. 98 G6
Ashmead N14 24 C5
Ashmead Gate, Brom. 96 J1
Ashmead Rd. SE8 78 A2
Ashmead Rd., Felt. 81 A1
Ashmere Ave., Beck. 96 D2
Ashmere Clo., Sutt. 99 J5
Ashmere Gro. SW2 76 E4
Ashmill St. NW1 10 G1
Ashmill St. NW1 57 H5
Ashmole Pl. SW8 20 D6
Ashmole Pl. SW8 67 F6
Ashmole St. SW8 20 D6
Ashmole St. SW8 67 F6
Ashmore Ct., Hounis. 63 G6
Wheatlands
Ashmore Gro., Well. 79 G3
Ashmore Rd. W9 57 C2
Ashmount Rd. N15 41 C5
Ashmount Rd. N19 40 C7
Ashmount Ter. W5 64 G4
Murray Rd.
Ashneal Gdns., Har. 46 A3
Ashness Gdns., Grnf. 46 E6
Ashness Rd. SW11 75 J5
Ashridge Clo., Har. 37 F6
Ashridge Cres. SE18 70 F7
Ashridge Dr., Wat. 28 B5
Ashridge Gdns. N13 32 D5
Ashridge Gdns., Pnr. 36 E4
Ashridge Way, Mord. 93 C3
Ashridge Way, Sun. 81 A6
Ashtead Rd. E5 41 D7
Ashton Clo., Sutt. 100 D4
Ashton Gdns., Hounis. 72 F4
Ashton Gdns., Rom. 44 E6
Ashton Rd. E15 51 D5
Ashton St. E14 60 C7
Ashtree Ave., Mitch. 93 G2
Ashurst Clo. SE20 95 E1
Ashurst Dr., Ilf. 43 E6
Ashurst Rd. N12 31 H5
Ashurst Rd., Barn. 23 J5
Ashurst Wk., Croy. 102 E2
Ashvale Rd. SW17 84 J5
Ashville Rd. E11 51 D2
Ashwater Rd. SE12 87 G1
Ashwell Clo. E6 61 B6
Northumberland Rd.
Ashwin St. E8 50 C6
Ashwood Gdns., Croy. 103 B6
Ashwood Rd. E4 34 D3
Ashworth Clo. SE5 77 A2
Denmark Hill
Ashworth Rd. W9 6 B4
Ashworth Rd. W9 57 E3
Aske St. N1 9 D3
Askern Clo., Bexh. 80 D4
Askew Cres. W12 65 F2
Askew Rd. W12 65 F1
Askham Ct. W12 65 G1
Askham Rd. W12 65 G1
Askill Dr. SW15 75 B5
Keswick Rd.
Asland Rd. E15 60 D1
Aslett St. SW18 75 E7
Asmara Rd. NW2 48 B5
Asmuns Hill NW11 39 D5
Asmuns Pl. NW11 39 C5
Aspen Clo. N19 49 C2
Hargrave Pk.
Aspen Clo. W5 64 J2
Aspen Copse, Brom. 97 C2
Aspen Dr., Wem. 46 D4
Aspen Gdns. W6 65 H5
Aspen Gdns., Mitch. 94 A5
Aspen Grn., Erith 71 F3
Aspen La., Nthlt. 54 E3
Aspen Way E14 60 C7
Aspen Way, Felt. 81 B3
Aspenlea Rd. W6 66 A6
Aspern Rd. NW3 48 H5
Aspinall Rd. SE4 77 G3
Aspinden Rd. SE16 68 E4
Aspley Rd. SW18 75 E5
Asplins Rd. N17 41 D1

Asquith Clo., Dag.	53	C1
Crystal Way		
Ass Ho. La., Har.	28	H4
Assam St. E1	**13**	**H3**
Assembly Pas. E1	59	F5
Assembly Wk., Cars.	93	H7
Assurance Cotts.,	71	F5
Belv.		
Heron Hill		
Astall Clo., Har.	37	B1
Sefton Ave.		
Astbury Rd. SE15	77	F1
Aste St. E14	69	C2
Astell St. SW3	**18**	**H3**
Astell St. SW3	66	H5
Asteys Row N1	49	H7
River Pl.		
Asthall Gdns., Ilf.	43	F4
Astle St. SW11	76	A2
Astley Ave. NW2	47	J5
Aston Ave., Har.	37	F7
Aston Clo., Sid.	89	A3
Aston Grn., Houns.	72	C2
Aston Ms., Rom.	44	C7
Reynolds Ave.		
Aston Rd. SW20	92	J2
Aston Rd. W5	55	G6
Aston Rd., Esher	98	B5
Aston St. E14	59	H6
Astonville St. SW18	84	D1
Astor Ave., Rom.	44	J6
Astor Clo., Kings.T.	83	B6
Astoria Wk. SW9	76	G3
Astrop Ms. W6	65	J3
Astrop Ter. W6	65	J2
Astwood Ms. SW7	**18**	**B1**
Astwood Ms. SW7	66	E4
Asylum Rd. SE15	68	E7
Atalanta St. SW6	75	A1
Atbara Ct., Tedd.	82	E6
Atbara Rd., Tedd.	82	E6
Atcham Rd., Houns.	72	J4
Atcost Rd., Bark.	62	A5
Atheldene Rd. SW18	75	F7
Athelney St. SE6	87	A3
Athelstan Rd.,	91	J4
Kings.T.		
Athelstane Gro. E3	59	J2
Athelstone Rd., Har.	37	A2
Athena Clo., Har.	46	B2
Byron Hill Rd.		
Athenaeum Pl. N10	40	B3
Fortis Grn. Rd.		
Athenaeum Rd. N20	31	F1
Athenlay Rd. SE15	77	G5
Athens Gdns. W9	57	D4
Elgin Ave.		
Atherden Rd. E5	50	F4
Atherfold Rd. SW9	76	E3
Atherley Way,	72	F7
Houns.		
Atherstone Ms. SW7	**18**	**D1**
Atherstone Ms. SW7	66	F4
Atherton Dr. SW19	84	A4
Atherton Heights,	46	F6
Wem.		
Atherton Ms. E7	51	F6
Atherton Pl., Har.	37	A3
Atherton Pl., Sthl.	54	H7
Longford Ave.		
Atherton Rd. E7	51	F6
Atherton Rd. SW13	65	G7
Atherton Rd., Ilf.	43	B2
Atherton St. SW11	75	H2
Athlon Rd., Wem.	55	G2
Athlone, Esher	98	B6
Athlone Clo. E5	50	E4
Goulton Rd.		
Athlone Rd. SW2	76	F7
Athlone St. NW5	49	A6
Athol Clo., Pnr.	36	B1
Athol Gdns., Pnr.	36	B1
Athol Rd., Erith	71	J5
Athol Sq. E14	60	C6
Atholl Gdns., Enf.	25	B5
Atholl Rd., Ilf.	44	A7
Atkins Dr., W.Wick.	103	D2
Atkins Rd. E10	42	B6
Atkins Rd. SW12	76	D7
Atkinson Rd. E16	60	J5
Atlantic Rd. SW9	76	G4
Atlas Gdns. SE7	69	J4
Atlas Ms. E8	50	C6
Tyssen St.		
Atlas Ms. N7	49	F6
Atlas Rd. E13	60	G2
Atlas Rd. NW10	56	E3
Atlas Rd., Wem.	47	C4
Atley Rd. E3	60	A1
Atney Rd. SW15	75	B4
Atria Rd., Nthwd.	28	A5
Atterbury Rd. N4	40	G6
Atterbury St. SW1	**20**	**A2**
Atterbury St. SW1	67	E4
Attewood Ave. NW10	47	E3
Attewood Rd., Nthlt.	45	E6
Attfield Clo. N20	31	G2
Attlee Clo., Hayes	54	B3
Attlee Rd. SE28	62	B7
Attlee Rd., Hayes	54	A3
Attlee Ter. E17	42	B4
Attneave St. WC1	**8**	**E4**
Atwater Clo. SW2	85	G1
Atwell Clo. E10	42	B6
Belmont Pk. Rd.		
Atwell Rd. SE15	77	D2
Rye La.		
Atwood Ave., Rich.	74	A2
Atwood Rd. W6	65	H4
Aubert Pk. N5	49	G4
Aubert Rd. N5	49	G4
Aubrey Pl. NW8	**6**	**C2**
Aubrey Rd. E17	42	A2
Aubrey Rd. N8	40	E5
Aubrey Rd. W8	66	C1
Aubrey Wk. W8	66	C1
Aubyn Hill SE27	85	J4
Aubyn Sq. SW15	74	G4
Auckland Clo. SE19	95	C1
Auckland Gdns. SE19	95	B1
Auckland Hill SE27	85	J4
Auckland Ri. SE19	95	B1
Auckland Rd. E10	51	B3
Auckland Rd. SE19	95	C1
Auckland Rd. SW11	75	H4
Auckland Rd., Ilf.	52	E1
Auckland Rd.,	91	J4
Kings.T.		
Auckland St. SE11	**20**	**C4**
Auden Pl. NW1	58	A1
Audleigh Pl., Chig.	35	D6
Audley Clo. SW11	76	A3
Audley Clo., Borwd.	22	A3
Audley Ct. E18	42	F4
Audley Ct., Pnr.	36	C2
Audley Gdns., Ilf.	52	J2
Audley Gdns., Loug.	27	F2
Audley Pl., Sutt.	100	E7
Audley Rd. NW4	38	G6
Audley Rd. W5	55	J5
Audley Rd., Enf.	24	H2
Audley Rd., Rich.	73	J5
Audley Sq. W1	**15**	**C1**
Audrey Clo., Beck.	96	B6
Audrey Gdns., Wem.	46	E2
Audrey Rd., Ilf.	52	E3
Audrey St. E2	**9**	**J1**
Audrey St. E2	59	D2
Audric Clo., Kings.T.	92	A1
Augurs La. E13	60	H3
Augusta Rd., Twick.	81	J2
Augusta St. E14	60	B6
Augustine Rd. W14	66	A3
Augustine Rd., Har.	36	H1
Augustus Clo., Brent.	64	G7
Augustus Rd. SW19	84	A1
Augustus St. NW1	**7**	**E2**
Augustus St. NW1	58	B2
Aulton Pl. SE11	**20**	**F4**
Aultone Way, Cars.	100	J3
Aultone Way, Sutt.	100	E2
Aurelia Gdns., Croy.	94	F5
Aurelia Rd., Croy.	94	E6
Auriga Ms. N16	50	A5
Auriol Clo., Wor.Pk.	99	E3
Auriol Pk. Rd.		
Auriol Dr., Grnf.	46	A7
Auriol Pk. Rd.,	99	E3
Wor.Pk.		
Auriol Rd. W14	66	B4
Austell Gdns. NW7	30	E3
Austen Clo. SE28	71	B1
Austen Clo., Loug.	27	G3
Austen Ho. NW6	57	D3
Austen Rd., Har.	45	H2
Austin Ave., Brom.	97	B5
Austin Clo. SE23	71	J7
Austin Clo., Twick.	73	F5
Austin Ct. E6	60	J1
Kings Rd.		
Austin Friars EC2	**13**	**C3**
Austin Friars EC2	59	A6
Austin Friars Pas.		
EC2		
Austin Friars Sq. EC2	**13**	**C3**
Austin Rd. SW11	76	A1
Austin St. E2	**9**	**F4**
Austin St. E2	59	C3
Austral St. SE11	**20**	**G1**
Austral St. SE11	67	H4
Australia Rd. W12	56	H7
Austyn Gdns., Surb.	99	B1
Autumn Clo., Enf.	25	D1
Autumn St. E3	60	A1
Avalon Clo. W13	55	D5
Avalon Clo., Enf.	24	G2
Avalon Rd. SW6	75	E1
Avalon Rd. W13	55	D4
Avard Gdns., Orp.	104	F4
Avarn Rd. SW17	84	J6
Ave Maria La. EC4	**12**	**H4**
Ave Maria La. EC4	58	H6
Avebury Ct. N1	59	A1
Poole St.		
Avebury Pk., Surb.	91	G7
Avebury Rd. E11	51	D1
Southwest Rd.		
Avebury Rd. SW19	93	C1
Avebury Rd., Orp.	104	G3
Avebury St. N1	59	A1
Poole St.		
Aveline St. SE11	**20**	**E4**
Aveline St. SE11	67	G5
Aveling Pk. Rd. E17	42	A2
Avenell Rd. N5	49	H3
Avening Rd. SW18	75	D7
Brathway Rd.		
Avening Ter. SW18	75	D6
Avenons Rd. E13	60	G4
Avenue, The E4	34	D6
Avenue, The E11	42	H6
Avenue, The N3	39	D2
Sylvan Ave.		
Avenue, The N8	40	G3
Avenue, The N10	40	C2
Avenue, The N11	32	B5
Avenue, The N17	41	B2
Avenue, The NW6	57	A1
Avenue, The SE7	69	A7
Avenue, The SE10	69	D7
Avenue, The SW4	76	A5
Avenue, The SW11	75	J7
Bellevue Rd.		
Avenue, The SW18	75	H7
Avenue, The W4	65	E3
Avenue, The W13	55	E7
Avenue, The, Barn.	23	B3
Avenue, The, Beck.	96	B1
Avenue, The, Bex.	80	D6
Avenue, The, Brom.	97	A3
Avenue, The, Cars.	101	A7
Avenue, The, Croy.	102	B3
Avenue, The, Epsom	99	H7
Avenue, The, Esher	96	A5
Avenue, The, Hmptn.	81	F6
Avenue, The, Har.	37	C1
Avenue, The, Houns.	72	H5
Avenue, The	72	A1
(Cranford), Houns.		
Avenue, The, Kes.	104	A3
Avenue, The, Loug.	27	A6
Avenue, The, Orp.	104	J2
Avenue, The, Orp.	89	B7
(St. Paul's Cray)		
Avenue, The, Pnr.	36	F6
Avenue, The, Pnr.	28	F6
(Royston Parke Rd.)		
Avenue, The, Rich.	73	J2
Avenue, The, Sun.	90	B1
Avenue, The, Surb.	91	J6
Avenue, The	99	J7
(Cheam), Sutt.		
Avenue, The, Twick.	73	E5
Avenue, The, Wem.	46	H1
Avenue, The,	96	C7
W.Wick.		
Avenue, The, Wor.Pk.	99	F2
Avenue Clo. N14	24	C6
Avenue Clo. NW8	57	H1
Avenue Clo., Houns.	72	A1
The Ave.		
Avenue Cres. W3	65	B2
Avenue Cres.,	63	B7
Houns.		
Avenue Elmers,	91	H5
Surb.		
Avenue Gdns. SE25	95	D3
Avenue Gdns. SW14	74	E3
Avenue Gdns. W3	65	B2
Avenue Gdns.,	63	A7
Houns.		
The Ave.		
Avenue Gdns., Tedd.	82	C7
Avenue Ind. Est. E4	33	J6
Avenue Ms. N10	40	B3
Avenue Pk. Rd. SE27	85	H2
Avenue Rd. E7	51	H4
Avenue Rd. N6	40	C7
Avenue Rd. N12	31	F4
Avenue Rd. N14	24	B7
Avenue Rd. N15	41	A5
Avenue Rd. NW3	48	G7
Avenue Rd. NW8	48	G7
Avenue Rd. NW10	56	F2
Avenue Rd. SE20	95	F1
Avenue Rd. SE25	95	C2
Avenue Rd. SW16	94	D2
Avenue Rd. SW20	92	H2
Avenue Rd. W3	65	B2
Avenue Rd., Beck.	95	G1
Avenue Rd., Belv.	71	J4
Avenue Rd., Bexh.	80	E4
Avenue Rd., Brent.	64	F5
Avenue Rd., Erith	71	J7
Avenue Rd., Hmptn.	90	H1
Avenue Rd., Islw.	73	C1
Avenue Rd., Kings.T.	91	H3
Avenue Rd., N.Mal.	92	E4
Avenue Rd., Pnr.	36	E3
Avenue Rd., Rom.	53	B1
(Chadwell Heath)		
Avenue Rd., Sthl.	63	F2
Avenue Rd., Tedd.	82	D7
Avenue Rd., Wall.	101	C7
Avenue Rd.,	34	J6
Wdf.Grn.		
Avenue S., The,	91	J7
Surb.		
Avenue Ter., N.Mal.	92	C3
Kingston Rd.		
Averil Gro. SW16	85	H6
Averill St. W6	66	A6
Avern Gdns., W.Mol.	90	H4
Avern Rd., W.Mol.	90	H4
Avery Fm. Row SW1	**19**	**D2**
Avery Gdns., Ilf.	43	C5
Avery Hill Rd. SE9	79	G6
Avery Row W1	**11**	**E5**
Avery Row W1	58	B7
Aviary Clo. E16	60	F5
Aviemore Clo., Beck.	95	J5
Aviemore Way, Beck.	95	H5
Avignon Rd. SE4	77	G3
Avington Gro. SE20	86	F7
Avington Way SE15	**21**	**F7**
Avis Sq. E1	59	G6
Avoca Rd. SW17	85	A4
Avocet Ms. SE28	70	G3
Avon Clo., Hayes	54	C4
Avon Clo., Sutt.	100	F4
Avon Clo., Wor.Pk.	99	G2
Avon Ct., Grnf.	54	H4
Braund Ave.		
Avon Ms., Pnr.	36	F1
Avon Pl. SE1	**17**	**A4**
Avon Rd. E17	42	D3
Avon Rd. SE4	78	A3
Avon Rd., Grnf.	54	G4
Avon Way E18	42	G3
Avondale Ave. N12	31	E5
Avondale Ave. NW2	47	E3
Avondale Ave.,	31	J1
Barn.		
Avondale Ave.,	98	D3
Esher		
Avondale Ave.,	99	F1
Wor.Pk.		
Avondale Clo., Loug.	27	C7
Avondale Ct. E11	51	E1
Avondale Ct. E16	60	E5
Avondale Rd.		
Avondale Ct. E18	42	H1
Avondale Cres., Enf.	25	H3
Avondale Cres., Ilf.	43	A5
Avondale Dr., Hayes	63	A1
Avondale Dr., Loug.	27	C7
Avondale Gdns.,	72	F5
Houns.		
Avondale Ms., Brom.	87	G6
Avondale Rd.		
Avondale Pk. Gdns.	57	B7
W11		
Avondale Pk. Rd.	57	B7
W11		
Avondale Ri. SE15	77	C3
Avondale Rd. E16	60	E5
Avondale Rd. E17	42	A7
Avondale Rd. N3	39	F1
Avondale Rd. N13	32	G2
Avondale Rd. N15	40	H5
Avondale Rd. SE9	88	B2
Avondale Rd. SW14	74	D3
Avondale Rd. SW19	84	E5
Avondale Rd., Brom.	87	E6
Avondale Rd., Har.	37	C3
Avondale Rd.,	101	J7
S.Croy.		
Avondale Rd., Well.	80	C2
Avondale Sq. SE1	**21**	**H4**
Avondale Sq. SE1	68	D5
Avonley Rd. SE14	68	F7
Avonmore Pl. W14	66	B4
Avonmore Rd.		
Avonmore Rd. W14	66	B4
Avonmouth St. SE1	**16**	**J5**
Avonmouth St. SE1	67	J3
Avonwick Rd.,	72	H2
Houns.		
Avril Way E4	34	C5

Avro Way, Wall. 101 E7
Awlfield Ave. N17 41 A1
Awliscombe Rd., 79 J2
Well.
Axe St., Bark. 61 F1
Axholme Ave., Edg. 38 A1
Axminster Cres., 79 J2
Well.
Axminster Rd. N7 49 E3
Aybrook St. W1 11 B2
Aybrook St. W1 58 A5
Aycliffe Clo., Brom. 97 C4
Aycliffe Rd. W12 65 F1
Ayles Rd., Hayes 54 B3
Aylesbury Clo. E7 51 H6
Atherton Rd.
Aylesbury Est. SE17 21 C4
Aylesbury Rd. SE17 21 C4
Aylesbury Rd. SE17 68 A5
Aylesbury Rd., Brom. 96 G3
Aylesbury St. EC1 8 G6
Aylesbury St. EC1 58 H4
Aylesbury St. NW10 47 D3
Aylesford Ave., Beck. 95 H2
Aylesford St. SW1 19 H4
Aylesford St. SW1 67 D5
Aylesham Rd., Orp. 97 J7
Aylestone Ave. NW6 48 A7
Aylett Rd. SE25 95 E4
Belfast Rd.
Aylett Rd., Islw. 73 B2
Ayley Cft., Enf. 25 D5
Aylmer Clo., Stan. 23 D4
Aylmer Dr., Stan. 29 D4
Aylmer Rd. E11 51 F1
Aylmer Rd. N2 39 H5
Aylmer Rd. W12 65 F2
Aylmer Rd., Dag. 53 E3
Ayloffe Rd., Dag. 53 F6
Aylton Est. SE16 68 F2
Renforth St.
Aylward Rd. SE23 86 G2
Aylward Rd. SW20 93 C2
Aylward St. E1 59 F6
Aylwards Ri., Stan. 29 D4
Aylwyn Est. SE1 17 E5
Aylwyn Est. SE1 68 B3
Aynhoe Rd. W14 66 A4
Aynscombe La. 74 C3
SW14
Aynscombe Path 74 C2
SW14
Thames Bank
Ayr Ct. W3 56 A5
Monks Dr.
Ayres Clo. E13 60 G3
Ayres Cres. NW10 47 D7
Ayres St. SE1 17 A3
Ayres St. SE1 67 J2
Ayrsome Rd. N16 50 B3
Ayrton Rd. SW7 14 E5
Aysgarth Rd. SE21 77 B6
Aytoun Pl. SW9 76 F2
Aytoun Rd. SW9 76 F2
Azalea Clo. W7 64 C1
Azalea Wk., Pnr. 36 B5
Azenby Rd. SE15 77 C2
Azile Everitt Ho. 70 F5
SE18
Vicarage Pk.
Azof St. SE10 69 E4

B

Baalbec Rd. N5 49 H5
Babbacombe Clo., 98 G5
Chess.
Babbacombe Gdns., 43 J4
Ilf.
Babbacombe Rd., 96 G1
Brom.
Baber Dr., Felt. 72 C6
Babington Ri., Wem. 47 A6
Babington Rd. NW4 38 H4
Babington Rd. SW16 85 D5
Babington Rd., Dag. 53 C5
Babmaes St. SW1 15 H1
Bacchus Wk. N1 9 D2
Baches St. N1 9 C4
Baches St. N1 59 A3
Back Ch. La. E1 13 J4
Back Ch. La. E1 59 D7
Back Hill EC1 8 E6
Back Hill EC1 58 G4
Back La. N8 40 E5
Back La. NW3 48 F4
Heath La.
Back La., Bex. 80 G7
Back La., Brent. 64 G6
Back La., Edg. 38 C1
Back La., Rich. 82 F3
Back La., Rom. 44 E7
St. Chads Rd.

Back Rd., Sid. 89 A4
Back St. W3 65 B1
Steyne Rd.
Backhouse Pl. SE17 21 E2
Bacon Gro. SE1 17 F6
Bacon Gro. SE1 68 C3
Bacon La. NW9 38 B4
Bacon La., Edg. 38 A1
Bacon St. E1 9 G5
Bacon St. E1 59 C4
Bacon St. E2 9 G5
Bacon St. E2 59 C4
Bacons La. N6 49 A1
Bacton NW5 49 A5
Bacton St. E2 59 F3
Digby St.
Baddow Clo., Dag. 62 G1
Baddow Clo., 35 A6
Wdf.Grn.
Baden Pl. SE1 17 B3
Baden Powell Clo., 98 J2
Surb.
Baden Rd. N8 40 D4
Baden Rd., Ilf. 52 E5
Badger Clo., Felt. 81 A3
Sycamore Clo.
Badger Clo., Houns. 72 C3
Badgers Clo., Enf. 24 H3
Badgers Clo., Har. 37 A6
Badgers Copse, Orp. 104 J2
Badgers Copse, 99 F2
Wor.Pk.
Badgers Cft. N20 31 D1
Badgers Cft. SE9 88 D3
Badgers Hole, Croy. 102 G4
Badgers Wk., N.Mal. 92 E2
Badlis Rd. E17 42 A2
Badminton Clo., 22 A2
Borwd.
Badminton Clo., Har. 37 B4
Badminton Clo., 45 G7
Nthlt.
Badminton Rd. SW12 76 A6
Badsworth Rd. SE5 76 J1
Bagley's La. SW6 75 E1
Bagleys Spring, Rom. 44 E4
Bagshot Ct. SE18 79 D1
Prince Imperial Rd.
Bagshot Rd., Enf. 25 C7
Bagshot St. SE17 21 E4
Bagshot St. SE17 68 B5
Baildon St. SE8 69 A7
Watson's St.
Bailey Clo. E4 34 C4
Bailey Pl. SE26 86 G6
Baillies Wk. W5 64 G2
Liverpool Rd.
Bainbridge Rd., Dag. 53 F4
Bainbridge St. WC1 11 J3
Bainbridge St. WC1 58 D6
Baird Ave., Sthl. 54 H7
Baird Clo. NW9 38 G6
Baird Gdns. SE19 86 B4
Baird Rd., Enf. 25 E4
Baird St. EC1 9 A5
Baizdon Rd. SE3 78 E2
Baker La., Mitch. 94 A2
Baker Pas. NW10 56 E1
Acton La.
Baker Rd. NW10 56 E1
Baker Rd. SE18 79 B1
Baker St. NW1 7 A6
Baker St. NW1 57 J4
Baker St. W1 11 A1
Baker St. W1 57 J5
Baker St., Enf. 25 A3
Bakers Ave. E17 42 B6
Bakers Ct. SE25 95 B3
Bakers End SW20 93 B2
Bakers Fld. N7 49 D4
Crayford Rd.
Bakers Hill E5 50 E1
Bakers Hill, Barn. 23 E2
Bakers La. N6 39 J6
Baker's Ms. W1 11 B3
Bakers Ms., Orp. 104 J6
Bakers Pas. NW3 48 F4
Heath St.
Baker's Rents E2 9 F4
Baker's Row E15 60 E2
Baker's Row EC1 8 E6
Bakery Pl. SW11 75 J4
Altenburg Gdns.
Bakewell Ct. E5 50 H3
Mandeville St.
Bakewell Way, N.Mal. 92 E2
Bala Gdn. NW9 38 E6
Snowdon Dr.
Balaam St. E13 60 G4
Balaams La. N14 32 D2
Balaclava Rd. SE1 21 G2
Balaclava Rd. SE1 68 C4

Balaclava Rd., Surb. 91 F7
Balben Path E9 50 G7
Speldhurst Rd.
Balcaskie Rd. SE9 79 C5
Balchen Rd. SE3 79 A2
Balchier Rd. SE22 77 E6
Balcombe St. NW1 6 J5
Balcombe St. NW1 57 J4
Balcon Way, Borwd. 22 C1
Balcorne St. E9 50 F7
Balder Ri. SE12 87 H2
Balderton St. W1 11 C4
Balderton St. W1 58 A6
Baldock St. E3 60 B2
Baldry Gdns. SW16 85 E6
Baldwin Cres. SE5 76 J1
Baldwin St. EC1 9 B4
Baldwin St. EC1 59 A3
Baldwin Ter. N1 8 J1
Baldwin Ter. N1 58 J2
Baldwin's Gdns. EC1 12 E1
Baldwin's Gdns. EC1 58 G5
Baldwins Hill, Loug. 27 C2
Baldwyn Gdns. W3 56 D7
Balfe St. N1 8 B2
Balfe St. N1 58 E2
Balfern Gro. W4 65 E5
Balfern St. SW11 75 H2
Balfour Ave. W7 64 C1
Balfour Gro. N20 31 J3
Balfour Ho. W10 58 A6
St. Charles Sq.
Balfour Ms. N9 33 D3
Balfour Ms. W1 15 C1
Balfour Pl. SW15 74 H4
Balfour Pl. W1 11 C6
Balfour Rd. N5 49 J4
Balfour Rd. SE25 95 D5
Balfour Rd. SW19 84 E7
Balfour Rd. W3 56 C5
Balfour Rd. W13 64 D2
Balfour Rd., Brom. 97 A5
Balfour Rd., Cars. 100 J7
Balfour Rd., Har. 37 A5
Balfour Rd., Houns. 72 H3
Balfour Rd., Ilf. 52 E2
Balfour Rd., Sthl. 63 D3
Balfour St. SE17 21 B1
Balfour St. SE17 68 A4
Balgonie Rd. E4 34 D1
Balgowan Clo., 92 E4
N.Mal.
Balgowan Rd., Beck. 95 H3
Balgowan St. SE18 70 J4
Balham Gro. SW12 76 A7
Balham High Rd. 85 A1
SW12
Balham High Rd. 85 A3
SW17
Balham Hill SW12 76 B7
Balham New Rd. 76 B7
SW12
Balham Pk. Rd. 84 J1
SW12
Balham Rd. N9 33 D2
Balham Sta. Rd. 85 B1
SW12
Balkan Wk. E1 59 E7
Pennington St.
Ballamore Rd., Brom. 87 G3
Ballance Rd. E9 50 G6
Ballantine St. SW18 76 A7
Ballard Clo., Kings.T. 83 D7
Ballards Clo., Dag. 62 H1
Ballards Fm. Rd., 102 D6
Croy.
Ballards Fm. Rd., 102 D6
S.Croy.
Ballards La. N3 39 D1
Ballards La. N12 31 F6
Ballards Ms., Edg. 30 A6
Ballards Ri., S.Croy. 102 D6
Ballards Rd. NW2 47 G2
Ballards Rd., Dag. 62 H1
Ballards Way, Croy. 102 E6
Ballards Way, 102 D6
S.Croy.
Ballast Quay SE10 69 D5
Ballater Clo., Wat. 28 C4
Ballater Rd. SW2 76 E4
Ballater Rd., S.Croy. 102 C5
Ballina St. SE23 77 C2
Ballingdon Rd. SW11 76 A6
Ballinger Pt. E3 60 B3
Bromley High St.
Balliol Ave. E4 34 E4
Balliol Rd. N17 41 B1
Balliol Rd. W10 57 A6
Balliol Rd., Well. 80 B2
Balloch Rd. SE6 87 D1
Ballogie Ave. NW10 47 E4
Ballow Clo. SE5 68 B7
Harris St.

Balls Pond Pl. N1 50 A6
Balls Pond Rd.
Balls Pond Rd. N1 50 A6
Balmain Clo. W5 64 G1
Balmer Rd. E3 59 J2
Balmes Rd. N1 59 A1
Balmoral Ave., Beck. 95 H4
Balmoral Clo. SW15 75 A6
Westleigh Ave.
Balmoral Cres., 90 G3
W.Mol.
Balmoral Dr., Borwd. 22 D5
Balmoral Dr., Sthl. 54 F4
Balmoral Gdns. W13 64 D3
Balmoral Gdns., Bex. 80 F7
Balmoral Gdns., Ilf. 52 J1
Balmoral Gro. N7 49 F6
Balmoral Ms. W12 65 F3
Balmoral Rd. E7 51 J4
Balmoral Rd. E10 51 B2
Balmoral Rd. NW2 47 G5
Balmoral Rd., Har. 45 G4
Balmoral Rd., 91 J4
Kings.T.
Balmoral Rd., 99 H3
Wor.Pk.
Balmore Cres., Barn. 24 A5
Balmore St. N19 49 B2
Balmuir Gdns. SW15 74 J4
Balnacraig Ave. 47 E4
NW10
Baltic Clo. SW19 84 G7
Baltic Ct. SE16 68 G2
Timber Pond Rd.
Baltic St. EC1 8 J6
Baltic St. EC1 58 J4
Baltimore Pl., Well. 79 J2
Balvernie Gro. SW18 75 C7
Bamber Ho., Bark. 61 F1
St. Margarets
Bamborough Gdns. 65 J2
W12
Bamford Ave., Wem. 55 J1
Bamford Ct. E15 51 B5
Clays La.
Bamford Rd., Bark. 52 F6
Bamford Rd., Brom. 87 C5
Bampfylde Clo., 101 C3
Wall.
Bampton Rd. SE23 86 G3
Banavie Gdns., Beck. 96 C1
Banbury Ct. WC2 12 A5
Banbury Ct., Sutt. 100 D7
Banbury Enterprise 101 H2
Cen., Croy.
Factory La.
Banbury Rd. E9 50 G7
Banbury Rd. E17 33 H7
Banbury St. SW11 75 H2
Banchory Rd. SE3 69 H7
Bancroft Ave. N2 39 H5
Bancroft Ave., 34 G2
Buck.H.
Bancroft Gdns., Nthlt. 54 C1
Bancroft Gdns., Har. 36 J1
Bancroft Gdns., Orp. 104 J1
Bancroft Rd. E1 59 G3
Bancroft Rd., Har. 36 J1
Bandon Ri., Wall. 101 D5
Bangalore St. SW15 74 J3
Bangor Rd., Nthlt. 45 H5
Banim St. W6 65 H4
Banister Rd. W10 57 A3
Bank, The N6 49 B1
Highgate High St.
Bank, The N19 49 B1
Cholmeley Pk.
Bank Ave., Mitch. 93 G2
Bank End SE1 17 A1
Bank End SE1 67 J1
Bank La. SW15 74 E5
Bank La., Kings.T. 82 H7
Bankfoot Rd., Brom. 87 E4
Bankhurst Rd. SE6 77 J7
Banks La., Bexh. 80 H
Banks Rd., Borwd. 22 C2
Banksia Rd. N18 33 F5
Banksian Wk., Islw. 73 B1
The Gro.
Bankside SE1 12 J6
Bankside SE1 58 J7
Bankside, Enf. 24 H1
Bankside, S.Croy. 102 C6
Bankside, Sthl. 63 D1
Bankside Ave., Nthlt. 54 A2
Townson Ave.
Bankside Clo., Cars. 100 H6
Bankside Dr., T.Ditt. 98 E3
Bankside Way SE19 86 B6
Lunham Rd.
Bankton Rd. SW2 76 G4

Bankwell Rd. SE13 78 E4
Banner St. EC1 **9 A6**
Banner St. EC1 58 J4
Bannerman Ho. SW8 20 C6
Bannerman Ho. SW8 67 H6
Banning St. SE10 69 E5
Bannister Clo. SW2 85 G1
Ewen Cres.
Bannister Clo., Grnf. 46 A5
Bannister Ho. E9 50 G5
Homerton High St.
Bannockburn Rd. 70 H4
SE18
Banstead Gdns. N9 33 B3
Banstead St. SE15 77 F3
Banstead Way, Wall. 101 E5
Banstock Rd., Edg. 30 B6
Banton Clo., Enf. 25 E2
Central Ave.
Bantry St. SE5 68 A7
Banwell Rd., Bex. 80 D6
Woodside La.
Banyard Rd. SE16 68 E3
Southwark Pk. Rd.
Baptist Gdns. NW5 49 A6
Queens Cres.
Barandon Wk. W11 57 A7
Whitchurch Rd.
Barb Ms. W6 65 J3
**Barbara Brosnan Ct. 6 E2
NW8**
Barbauld Rd. N16 50 B3
Barber Clo. N21 24 G7
Barber's All. E13 60 H3
Barbers Rd. E15 60 B2
Barbican, The EC2 12 J1
Barbican, The EC2 58 J5
Barbican Rd., Grnf. 54 H6
Barbon Clo. WC1 12 B1
Barbot Clo. N9 33 D3
Barchard St. SW18 75 E5
Barchester Clo. W7 64 C1
Barchester Rd., Har. 37 A2
Barchester St. E14 60 B5
Barclay Clo. SW6 66 D7
Barclay Oval, 34 G4
Wdf.Grn.
Barclay Rd. E11 51 E1
Barclay Rd. E13 60 J4
Barclay Rd. E17 42 C5
Barclay Rd. N18 33 A6
Barclay Rd. SW6 66 D7
Barclay Rd., Croy. 102 A3
Barclay Way SE22 77 D7
Lordship La.
Barcombe Ave. SW2 85 E2
Bard Rd. W10 57 A7
Barden St. SE18 70 H7
Bardfield Ave., Rom. 44 D3
Bardney Rd., Mord. 93 E4
Bardolph Rd. N7 49 E4
Bardolph Rd., Rich. 73 J3
St. Georges Rd.
Bardsey Pl. E1 59 F5
Bardsey Wk. N1 49 J6
Marquess St.
Bardsley Clo., Croy. 102 C3
Bardsley La. SE10 69 C6
Barfett St. W10 57 C4
Barfield Ave. N20 31 J2
Barfield Rd. E11 51 F1
Barfield Rd., Brom. 97 D3
Barfields, Loug. 27 D4
Barfields Gdns. 27 D4
Loug.
Barfields
Barfields Path, Loug. 27 D4
Barford Clo. NW4 38 G1
Barford St. N1 58 G1
Barforth Rd. SE15 77 E3
Barfreston Way SE20 95 E1
Bargate Clo. SE18 70 J5
Bargate Clo., N.Mal. 92 G7
Barge Ho. Rd. E16 70 E2
Barge Ho. St. SE1 16 F1
Barge Wk., E.Mol. 91 G2
Barge Wk., Kings.T. 91 G2
Barge Wk., Walt. 90 C3
Bargery Rd. SE6 87 B1
Bargrove Clo. SE20 86 D7
Bargrove Cres. SE6 86 J2
Elm La.
Barham Clo., Brom. 104 B3
Barham Clo., Chis. 88 E5
Barham Clo., Rom. 44 H2
Barham Clo., Wem. 46 E6
Barham Rd. SW20 83 G7
Barham Rd., Chis. 88 E5
Barham Rd., S.Croy. 101 J4
Baring Clo. SE12 87 G2
Baring Rd. SE12 78 G7
Baring Rd., Barn. 23 G4
Baring Rd., Croy. 102 D1

Baring St. N1 59 A1
Bark Pl. W2 10 A5
Bark Pl. W2 57 E7
Barker Dr. NW1 49 C7
Barker St. SW10 18 C5
Barker St. SW10 66 F6
Barker Way SE22 86 D1
Dulwich Common
Barkham Rd. N17 33 A7
Barking Ind. Pk., Bark. 61 J1
Barking Rd. E6 61 A2
Barking Rd. E13 60 G4
Barking Rd. E16 60 E5
Barkis Way SE16 68 E5
Egan Way
Barkston Gdns. SW5 **18 A2**
Barkston Gdns. SW5 66 E4
Barkway Ct. N4 49 J3
Queens Dr.
Barkwood Clo., Rom. 44 J5
Barlborough St. 68 G7
SE14
Barlby Gdns. W10 57 A4
Barlby Rd. W10 56 J5
Barley La., Ilf. 44 A7
Barley La., Rom. 44 B4
Barley Mow Pas. EC1 12 H2
Barley Mow Pas. W4 65 D5
Heathfield Ter.
Barleycorn Way E14 59 J7
Barleyfields Clo., 44 B6
Rom.
Barlow Clo., Wall. 101 E6
Cobham Clo.
Barlow Pl. W1 11 E6
Barlow Rd. NW6 48 C6
Barlow Rd. W3 65 B1
Barlow Rd., Hmptn. 81 G7
Barlow St. SE17 21 C2
Barmeston Rd. SE6 87 B2
Barmor Clo., Har. 36 H2
Barmouth Ave., Grnf. 55 C2
Barmouth Rd. SW18 75 F6
Barmouth Rd., Croy. 102 F2
Barn Clo., Nthlt. 54 C2
Barn Cres., Stan. 29 F6
Barn Elms Pk. SW15 74 J2
Barn Hill, Wem. 47 A1
Barn Ms., Har. 45 G3
Barn Ri., Wem. 47 A1
Barn St. N16 50 B3
Stoke Newington Ch. St.
Barn Way, Wem. 47 A1
Barnabas Ct. N21 24 G5
Cheyne Wk.
Barnabas Rd. E9 50 G5
Barnaby Clo., Har. 45 J2
Barnaby Way, Chig. 35 D3
Barnard Clo. SE18 70 D3
Barnard Clo., Chis. 97 G1
Barnard Clo., Sun. 81 B7
Oak Gro.
Barnard Clo., Wall. 101 D7
Alcock Clo.
Barnard Gdns. 54 B4
Hayes
Barnard Gdns. 92 G4
N.Mal.
Barnard Gro. E15 51 F7
Vicarage La.
Barnard Hill N10 40 B1
Barnard Ms. SW11 75 H4
Barnard Rd. SW11 75 H4
Barnard Rd., Enf. 25 E2
Barnard Rd., Mitch. 94 A3
Barnardo St. E1 59 G6
Devonport St.
Barnby Sq. E15 60 E1
Barnby St. NW1 7 G3
Barnby St. NW1 58 C3
Barncroft Clo., Loug. 27 C5
Barncroft Grn., Loug. 27 D5
Barncroft Rd., Loug. 27 D5
Barnehurst Ave., 80 J1
Bexh.
Barnehurst Ave., 80 J1
Erith
Barnehurst Clo., 80 J1
Erith
Barnehurst Rd., 80 J2
Bexh.
Barnes All., Hmptn. 90 J2
Hampton Ct. Rd.
Barnes Ave. SW13 65 G7
Barnes Ave., Sthl. 63 F4
Barnes Bri. SW13 74 E2
Barnes Bri. W4 74 E2
Barnes Clo. E12 52 A4
Barnes Ct. E16 60 J5
Ridgewell Rd.
Barnes Ct., Wdf.Grn. 35 A5
Barnes End, N.Mal. 92 G5

Barnes High St. 74 F2
SW13
Barnes Ho., Bark. 61 G1
St. Marys
Barnes Rd. N18 33 F4
Barnes Rd., Ilf. 52 F5
Barnes St. E14 59 H6
Barnes Ter. SE8 68 J5
Barnesbury Ho. SW4 76 D6
Barnet Bypass, Barn. 22 E1
Barnet Dr., Brom. 104 B2
Barnet Gate La., Barn. 22 F6
Barnet Gro. E2 9 H3
Barnet Gro. E2 59 D3
Barnet Hill, Barn. 23 C4
Barnet Ho. N20 31 F2
Barnet La. N20 31 C1
Barnet La., Barn. 23 D6
Barnet Rd. 22 D6
(Arkley), Barn.
Barnet Trd. Est., 23 C3
Barn.
Barnet Way NW7 30 D3
Barnet Wd. Rd., 103 H2
Brom.
Barnett St. E1 59 E6
Kinder St.
Barney Clo. SE7 69 J5
Barnfield, N.Mal. 92 E6
Barnfield Ave., Croy. 102 F2
Barnfield Ave., 82 H5
Kings.T.
Barnfield Ave., Mitch. 94 B4
Barnfield Clo. N4 40 E7
Crouch Hill
Barnfield Gdns. SE18 70 E6
Plumstead Common Rd.
Barnfield Gdns., 82 H5
Kings.T.
Barnfield Pl. E14 69 A4
Barnfield Rd. SE18 70 E6
Barnfield Rd. W5 55 F4
Barnfield Rd., Edg. 38 C1
Barnfield Wd. Clo., 96 D6
Beck.
Barnfield Wd. Rd., 96 D6
Beck.
Barnham Rd., Grnf. 54 J3
Barnham St. SE1 17 E3
Barnham St. SE1 68 B2
Barnhill, Pnr. 36 C5
Barnhill Ave., Brom. 96 F5
Barnhill La., Hayes 54 B4
Barnhill Rd., Hayes 54 B4
Barnhill Rd., Wem. 47 C3
Barnhurst Path, Wat. 28 C5
Barningham Way 38 D6
NW9
Barnlea Clo., Felt. 81 E2
Barnmead Gdns., 53 F5
Dag.
Barnmead Rd., Beck. 95 H1
Barnmead Rd., Dag. 53 F5
Barnsbury Clo., 92 C4
N.Mal.
Barnsbury Cres., 99 B1
Surb.
Barnsbury Gro. N7 49 F6
Barnsbury La., Surb. 99 B2
Barnsbury Rd. N1 8 E1
Barnsbury Rd. N1 58 G2
Barnsbury Sq. N1 49 G7
Barnsbury St. N1 49 G7
Barnsbury Ter. N1 49 F7
Barnscroft SW20 92 H3
Barnsdale Ave. E14 69 B4
Barnsdale Rd. W9 57 C4
Barnsley St. E1 59 E4
Barnstaple Rd., Ruis. 45 C3
Barnwell Rd. SW2 76 G5
Barnwood Clo. W9 6 A6
Barnwood Clo. W9 57 E4
Barnwood Clo. E16 69 G1
North Woolwich Rd.
Baron Gdns., Ilf. 43 F3
Baron Gro., Mitch. 93 H4
Baron Rd., Dag. 53 D1
Baron St. N1 8 E2
Baron St. N1 58 G2
Baron Wk. E16 60 F5
Star La.
Baron Wk., Mitch. 93 H4
Baroness Rd. E2 9 G3
Baronet Gro. N17 41 D1
St. Paul's Rd.
Baronet Rd. N17 41 D1
Barons, The, Twick. 73 E6
Barons Ct. Rd. W14 66 B5
Barons Gate, Barn. 23 H6
Barons Keep W14 66 B5

Barons Mead, Har. 37 B4
Barons Pl. SE1 16 F4
Barons Pl. SE1 67 G2
Barons Wk., Croy. 95 H6
Baronsfield Rd., 73 E6
Twick.
Baronsmead Rd. 74 G1
SW13
Baronsmede W5 64 J2
Baronsmere Rd. N2 39 H4
Barque Ms. SE8 69 A6
Watergate St.
Barrack Rd., Houns. 72 D4
Barracks La., Barn. 23 B3
High St.
Barratt Ave. N22 40 F2
Barratt Ind. Pk., Sthl. 63 G2
Barratt Way, Har. 37 A3
Tudor Rd.
Barrenger Rd. N10 39 J1
Barrett Rd. E17 42 C4
Barrett St. W1 11 C4
Barrett St. W1 58 A6
Barretts Grn. Rd. 56 C3
NW10
Barretts Gro. N16 50 B5
Barrhill Rd. SW2 85 E2
Barrie Est. W2 10 E5
Barrie Twr. W3 65 C2
Barriedale SE14 77 H2
Barrier App. SE7 70 A3
Barringer Sq. SW17 85 A4
Barrington Clo. NW5 49 A5
Grafton Rd.
Barrington Clo., Ilf. 43 C1
Barrington Clo., 27 F4
Loug.
Barrington Clo.
Barrington Grn., 27 F4
Loug.
Barrington Rd. E12 52 D6
Barrington Rd. N8 40 D5
Barrington Rd. SW9 76 H3
Barrington Rd., Bexh. 80 D2
Barrington Rd., Loug. 27 F4
Barrington Rd., Sutt. 100 D5
Barrington Vill. SE18 79 D1
Barrow Ave., Cars. 100 J4
Barrow Clo. N21 32 H3
Barrow Hedges Clo., 100 H7
Cars.
Barrow Hedges Way, 100 H7
Cars.
Barrow Hill, Wor.Pk. 99 E2
Barrow Hill Clo., 99 E2
Wor.Pk.
Barrow Hill
Barrow Hill Rd. NW8 6 G2
Barrow Hill Rd. NW8 57 H2
Barrow Pt. Ave., Pnr. 36 E2
Barrow Pt. La., Pnr. 36 E2
Barrow Rd. SW16 85 D6
Barrow Rd., Croy. 101 G5
Barrow Wk., Brent. 64 F5
Glenhurst Rd.
Barrow Way N7 49 F3
Barrowdene Clo., Pnr. 36 E2
Paines La.
Barrowell Grn. N21 32 H2
Barrowfield Clo. N9 33 E3
Barrowgate Rd. W4 65 C5
Barrs Rd. NW10 47 D7
Barry Ave. N15 41 C6
Craven Pk. Rd.
Barry Ave., Bexh. 71 E7
Barry Clo., Orp. 104 H3
Barry Rd. E6 61 B6
Barry Rd. NW10 47 C7
Barry Rd. SE22 77 D6
Barset Rd. SE15 77 F3
Barson Clo. SE20 86 F7
Barston Rd. SE27 85 J2
Barstow Cres. SW2 85 F1
Barter St. WC1 12 B2
Barter St. WC1 58 E5
Barters Wk., Pnr. 36 E3
High St.
Barth Rd. SE18 70 H4
Bartholomew Clo. 12 J2
EC1
Bartholomew Clo. 58 J5
EC1
Bartholomew Clo. 75 F4
SW18
Bartholomew La. EC2 13 C4
Bartholomew Pl. EC1 12 J2
Bartholomew Rd. 49 C6
NW5
Bartholomew Sq. E1 59 E4
Coventry Rd.
Bartholomew Sq. EC1 9 A5
Bartholomew Sq. EC1 58 J4

Bartholomew St. SE1 17 C6
Bartholomew St. SE1 68 A3
Bartholomew Vill. 49 C6
NW5
Bartle Ave. E6 61 B2
Bartle Rd. W11 57 B6
Bartlett Clo. E14 60 A6
Bartlett Ct. EC4 12 F3
Bartlett St., S.Croy. 102 A5
Barton Ave., Rom. 53 H1
Barton Clo. E6 61 C6
Brandreth Rd.
Barton Clo. E9 50 F5
Churchill Wk.
Barton Clo. SE15 77 E3
Kirkwood Rd.
Barton Clo., Bexh. 80 E5
Barton Clo., Chig. 35 F2
Barton Grn., N.Mal. 92 D2
Barton Meadows, Ilf. 43 E4
Barton Rd. W14 66 B5
Barton Rd., Sid. 89 E6
Barton St. SW1 16 A5
Barton Way, Borwd. 22 A2
Bartram Rd. SE4 77 H5
Barwick Rd. E7 51 H4
Barwood Ave., 103 B1
W.Wick.
Basden Gro., Felt. 81 G2
Basedale Rd., Dag. 53 B7
Baseing Clo. E6 61 D7
Bashley Rd. NW10 56 D4
Basil Ave. E6 81 D5
Basil Gdns., Croy. 102 G1
Primrose La.
Basil St. SW3 14 J5
Basil St. SW3 66 J3
Basildene Rd., Houns. 72 D3
Basildon Ave., Ilf. 43 D1
Basildon Rd. SE2 71 A5
Basildon Rd., Bexh. 80 E2
Basing Clo., T.Ditt. 91 C7
Basing Ct. SE15 77 C1
Basing Dr., Bex. 80 F6
Basing Hill NW11 48 C1
Basing Hill, Wem. 46 J2
Basing Ho., Bark. 61 G1
St. Margarets
Basing Ho. Yd. E2 9 E3
Basing Pl. E2 9 E3
Basing St. W11 57 C6
Basing Way N3 39 D3
Basing Way, T.Ditt. 91 C7
Basingdon Way SE5 77 A4
Basingfield Rd., T.Ditt.91 C7
Basinghall Ave. EC2 13 B2
Basinghall Ave. EC2 59 A5
Basinghall St. EC2 13 B3
Basinghall St. EC2 58 J5
Basire St. N1 58 J1
Baskerville Rd. SW18 75 H7
Basket Gdns. SE9 79 B5
Baslow Clo., Har. 37 A1
Baslow Wk. E5 50 G4
Overbury St.
Basnett Rd. SW11 76 A3
Bassano St. SE22 77 C5
Bassant Rd. SE18 70 J6
Bassein Pk. Rd. W12 65 F2
Basset Ho., Dag. 60 H1
Bassett Gdns., Islw. 63 J7
Bassett Rd. W10 57 A6
Bassett St. NW5 49 A6
Bassett Way, Grnf. 54 H6
Bassetts Clo., Orp. 104 E3
Bassetts Way, Orp. 104 E4
Bassingham Rd. 75 F7
SW18
Bassingham Rd., 46 G6
Wem.
Basswood Clo. SE15 77 E3
Linden Gro.
Bastable Ave., Bark. 61 H2
Bastion Rd. SE2 71 A5
Baston Manor Rd., 103 H3
Brom.
Baston Rd., Brom. 103 H1
Bastwick St. EC1 8 J5
Bastwick St. EC1 58 J4
Basuto Rd. SW6 75 D1
Batavia Clo., Sun. 90 C1
Batavia Ms. SE14 68 H7
Clifton Ri.
Batavia Rd. SE14 68 H7
Batavia Rd., Sun. 90 B1
Batchelor St. N1 8 F1
Batchelor St. N1 58 G2
Bate St. E14 59 J7
Three Colt St.
Bateman Clo., Bark. 52 F6
Glenny Rd.
Bateman Ho. SE17 20 G6
Bateman Rd. E4 34 A6

Bateman St. W1 11 H4
Bateman's Bldgs. W1 11 H4
Bateman's Row EC2 9 E5
Bateman's Row EC2 59 B4
Bates Cres. SW16 85 C7
Bates Cres., Croy. 101 G5
Bath Clo. SE15 68 E7
Asylum Rd.
Bath Ct. EC1 8 E6
Bath Ho. Rd., Croy. 101 E1
Bath Pas., Kings.T. 91 G2
St. James's Rd.
Bath Pl., Barn. 23 C3
Bath Rd. E7 52 A6
Bath Rd. N9 33 E2
Bath Rd. W4 65 E4
Bath Rd., Houns. 72 D2
Bath Rd., Mitch. 93 G3
Bath Rd., Rom. 44 E6
Bath St. EC1 9 A4
Bath St. EC1 58 J3
Bath Ter. SE1 16 J6
Bath Ter. SE1 67 J3
Bathgate Rd. SW19 84 A3
Baths Rd., Brom. 97 A4
Bathurst Ave. SW19 93 E1
Brisbane Ave.
Bathurst Gdns. NW10 56 H2
Bathurst Ms. W2 10 F5
Bathurst Rd., Ilf. 52 E1
Bathurst St. W2 10 F5
Bathurst St. W2 57 G7
Batley Pl. N16 50 C3
Batley Rd. N16 50 C3
Stoke Newington
High St.
Batley Rd., Enf. 25 A1
Batman Clo. W12 65 H1
Batoum Gdns. W6 65 J3
Batson St. W12 65 G2
Batsworth Rd., Mitch. 93 G3
Batten Clo. E6 61 C6
Savage Gdns.
Batten St. SW11 75 H3
Battenburg Wk. SE19 86 B5
Brabourne Clo.
Battersby Rd. SE6 87 D2
Battersea Bri. SW3 18 F7
Battersea Bri. SW3 66 G7
Battersea Bri. SW11 18 G7
Battersea Bri. SW11 66 H7
Battersea Bri. Rd. 66 H7
SW11
Battersea Ch. Rd. 75 G1
SW11
Battersea High St. 75 G1
SW11
Battersea Pk. SW11 66 J7
Battersea Pk. Rd. 76 B1
SW8
Battersea Pk. SW11 75 H2
SW11
Battersea Pk. Rd. 75 G5
Battery Rd. SE28 70 H2
Battishill St. N1 49 H7
Waterloo Ter.
Battle Bri. La. SE1 17 D2
Battle Bri. La. SE1 68 B1
Battle Bri. Rd. NW1 8 A2
Battle Bri. Rd. NW1 58 E2
Battle Clo. SW19 84 F6
North Rd.
Battle Rd., Belv. 71 J4
Battle Rd., Erith 71 J4
Battledean Rd. N5 49 H5
Batty St. E1 13 J3
Batty St. E1 59 D6
Baudwin Rd. SE6 87 E2
Baugh Rd., Sid. 89 C5
Baulk, The SW18 75 D7
Bavant Rd. SW16 94 F2
Bavaria Rd. N19 49 E2
Bavent Rd. SE5 76 J2
Bawdale Rd. SE22 77 C5
Bawdsey Ave., Ilf. 43 J4
Bawtree Rd. SE14 68 H7
Bawtry Rd. N20 31 J3
Baxendale N20 31 F2
Baxendale St. E2 9 H3
Baxendale St. E2 59 D3
Baxter Rd. E16 60 J6
Baxter Rd. N1 50 A6
Baxter Rd. N18 33 E4
Baxter Rd. NW10 56 E4
Baxter Rd., Ilf. 52 E5
Bay Ct. W5 64 H3
Popes La.
Bay Tree Clo., Brom. 96 J1
Bayes Clo. SE26 86 F5
Bayfield Rd. SE9 79 A4
Bayford Ms. E8 50 E7
Bayford St.

Bayford Rd. NW10 57 A3
Bayford St. E8 50 E7
Bayham Pl. NW1 58 C1
Bayham Rd. W4 65 D3
Bayham Rd. W13 55 E7
Bayham Rd., Mord. 93 E4
Bayham Rd., Sid. 88 D5
Bayham St. NW1 58 C1
Bayley St. WC1 11 H2
Bayley St. WC1 58 D5
Bayley Wk. SE2 71 E5
Woolwich Rd.
Baylis Rd. SE1 16 E4
Baylis Rd. SE1 67 G2
Bayliss Ave. SE28 62 D7
Bayne Clo. E6 61 C6
Savage Gdns.
Baynes Clo., Enf. 25 D1
Baynes Ms. NW3 48 G6
Belsize La.
Baynes St. NW1 49 D7
Baynham Clo., Bex. 80 F6
Bayonne Rd. W6 66 B6
Bayston Rd. N16 50 C3
Bayswater Rd. W2 10 A6
Bayswater Rd. W2 57 E7
Baythorne St. E3 59 J5
Baytree Clo., Sid. 88 J1
Baytree Rd. SW2 76 F4
Bazalgette Clo., 92 D5
N.Mal.
Bazalgette Gdns., 92 D5
N.Mal.
Bazile Rd. N21 24 G6
Beach Gro., Felt. 81 G2
Beacham Clo. SE7 70 A5
Beachborough Rd., 87 C4
Brom.
Beachcroft Rd. E11 51 E3
Beachcroft Way N19 49 D1
Beachy Rd. E3 51 A7
Beacon Gro., Cars. 101 A4
Beacon Hill N7 49 E5
Beacon Rd. SE13 78 D6
Beacons Clo. E6 61 B5
Oliver Gdns.
Beaconsfield Clo. N11 32 A5
Beaconsfield Clo. 69 G6
SE3
Beaconsfield Clo. W4 65 C5
Beaconsfield Rd. E10 51 C2
Beaconsfield Rd. E16 60 F4
Beaconsfield Rd. E17 41 A6
Beaconsfield Rd. N9 33 D3
Beaconsfield Rd. N11 32 A3
Beaconsfield Rd. N15 41 B4
Beaconsfield Rd. 47 F6
NW10
Beaconsfield Rd. SE3 69 F7
Beaconsfield Rd. SE9 88 B2
Beaconsfield Rd. 21 C4
SE17
Beaconsfield Rd. 68 A6
SE17
Beaconsfield Rd. W4 65 D3
Beaconsfield Rd. W5 64 A2
Beaconsfield Rd., 97 A3
Brom.
Beaconsfield Rd., 95 A6
Croy.
Beaconsfield Rd., 98 B7
Esher
Beaconsfield Rd., 63 C1
Hayes
Beaconsfield Rd., 92 D2
N.Mal.
Beaconsfield Rd., 63 D1
Sthl.
Beaconsfield Rd., 91 J7
Surb.
Beaconsfield Rd., 73 E6
Twick.
Beaconsfield Ter., 44 D6
Rom.
Beaconsfield Ter. Rd. 66 B3
W14
Beaconsfield Wk. E6 61 D6
East Ham Manor Way
Beaconsfield Wk. 75 C1
SW6
Parsons Grn. La.
Beacontree Ave. E17 42 D1
Beacontree Rd. E11 42 F7
Beadlow Clo., Cars. 93 G6
Olveston Wk.
Beadman St. SE27 85 H4
Beadnell Rd. SE23 86 G1
Beadon Rd. W6 65 J4
Beadon Rd., Brom. 96 G4
Beaford Gro. SW20 93 B3
Beagle Clo., Felt. 81 B4
Beak St. W1 11 G5
Beak St. W1 58 C7

Beal Clo., Well. 80 A1
Beal Rd., Ilf. 52 D2
Beale Clo. N13 32 H5
Beale Pl. E3 59 J2
Beale Rd. E3 59 J1
Beam Ave., Dag. 62 H1
Beaminster Gdns., Ilf. 43 G2
Beamish Dr. 28 J1
(Bushey), Wat.
Beamish Rd. N9 33 D1
Bean Rd., Bexh. 80 D4
Beanacre Clo. E9 50 J6
Beanshaw SE9 88 D4
Beansland Gro., Rom. 44 E2
Bear All. EC4 12 G3
Bear Gdns. SE1 16 J1
Bear La. SE1 16 H2
Bear La. SE1 67 H1
Beard Rd., Kings.T. 82 J5
Beardell St. SE19 86 C6
Beardow Gro. N14 24 C6
Beard's Hill, Hmptn. 90 G1
Beard's Hill Clo., 90 G1
Hmptn.
Beard's Hill
Beardsfield E13 60 G1
Valetta Gro.
Beardsley Way W3 65 D2
Bearfield Rd., 82 H7
Kings.T.
Bearstead Ri. SE4 77 J5
Beatrice Ave. SW16 94 F2
Beatrice Ave., Wem. 46 H5
Beatrice Clo. E13 60 G4
Chargeable La.
Beatrice Clo., Pnr. 36 A4
Reid Clo.
Beatrice Ct., Buck.H. 35 A2
Beatrice Ct., Wem. 46 J4
Beatrice Pl. W8 14 A6
Beatrice Rd. E17 42 A5
Beatrice Rd. N4 40 G7
Beatrice Rd. N9 25 F7
Beatrice Rd. SE1 21 J2
Beatrice Rd. SE1 68 D4
Beatrice Rd., Rich. 73 J5
Albert Rd.
Beatrice Rd., Sthl. 63 F1
Beatson Wk. SE16 68 H1
Beattock Ri. N10 40 B4
Beatty Rd. N16 50 B4
Beatty Rd., Stan. 29 F6
Beatty St. NW1 7 F1
Beatty St. NW1 58 C2
Beattyville Gdns., Ilf. 43 D2
Beauchamp Clo. W4 65 C3
Church Path
Beauchamp Pl. SW3 14 H5
Beauchamp Rd. E7 52 A1
Beauchamp Rd. SE19 95 A1
Beauchamp Rd. 75 H4
SW11
Beauchamp Rd., 90 H5
E.Mol.
Beauchamp Rd., 100 D4
Sutt.
Beauchamp Rd., 73 D7
Twick.
Beauchamp Rd., 90 H5
W.Mol.
Beauchamp Ter. 74 H3
SW15
Dryburgh Rd.
Beauclerc Rd. W6 65 H3
Beauclerk Clo., Felt. 81 B1
Florence Rd.
Beaufort Ave., Har. 37 D4
Beaufort Clo. E4 34 B6
Higham Sta. Ave.
Beaufort Clo. SW15 74 H7
Beaufort Clo. W5 55 J5
Beaufort Clo., Rom. 44 J4
Beaufort Clo., Rich. 82 F4
Beaufort Rd.
Beaufort Dr. NW11 39 D4
Beaufort Gdns. NW4 38 J6
Beaufort Gdns. SW3 14 H5
Beaufort Gdns. SW16 85 F7
Beaufort Gdns., 72 E1
Houns.
Beaufort Gdns., Ilf. 52 D1
Beaufort Ms. SW6 66 C6
Lillie Rd.
Beaufort Pk. NW11 39 D4
Beaufort Rd. W5 55 J5
Beaufort Rd., Kings.T. 91 H4
Beaufort Rd., Rich. 82 F4

Beaufort Rd., Twick. 73 F7
Beaufort St. SW3 18 F6
Beaufort St. SW3 66 G6
Beaufort Way, Epsom 99 G7
Beaufoy Rd. N17 33 B7
Beaufoy Wk. SE11 20 D2
Beaufoy Wk. SE11 67 F4
Beaulieu Ave. SE26 86 E4
Beaulieu Clo. NW9 38 E3
Beaulieu Clo. SE5 77 A3
Beaulieu Clo., 72 F5
  Houns.
Beaulieu Clo., Mitch. 94 A1
Beaulieu Clo., Twick. 73 G6
Beaulieu Clo., Wat. 28 C1
Beaulieu Dr., Pnr. 36 D6
Beaulieu Gdns. N21 24 J7
Beaumanor Gdns. 88 D4
  SE9
  Beanshaw
Beaumaris Dr., 35 A7
  Wdf.Grn.
Beaumont Ave. W14 66 C5
Beaumont Ave., Har. 36 H6
Beaumont Ave., Rich. 73 J3
Beaumont Ave., 46 F5
  Wem.
Beaumont Clo., 83 A7
  Kings.T.
Beaumont Cres. W14 66 C5
Beaumont Gdns. 48 D3
  NW3
Beaumont Gro. E1 59 G4
Beaumont Ms. W1 11 C1
Beaumont Pl. W1 7 G5
Beaumont Pl. W1 58 C4
Beaumont Pl., Barn. 23 C1
Beaumont Pl., Islw. 73 C5
Beaumont Ri. N19 40 D7
Beaumont Rd. E10 42 B7
Beaumont Rd. E13 60 H3
Beaumont Rd. SE19 85 J6
Beaumont Rd. SW19 75 B7
Beaumont Rd. W4 65 C3
Beaumont Rd., Orp. 93 J6
Beaumont Sq. E1 59 G4
Beaumont St. W1 11 C1
Beaumont St. W1 58 A5
Beaumont Wk. NW3 48 J7
Beauvais Ter., Nthlt. 54 D3
Beauval Rd. SE22 77 C6
Beaver Clo. SE20 86 D7
  Lullington Rd.
Beaver Clo., Hmptn. 90 H1
Beaver Gro., Nthlt. 54 E3
  Jetstar Way
Beaverbank Rd. SE9 88 G1
Beavers Cres. 72 D4
  Houns.
Beavers La., Houns. 72 C2
  Houns.
Beaverwood Rd., 88 H6
  Chis.
Beavor La. W6 65 G4
Bebbington Rd. SE18 70 H4
Bebletts Clo., Orp. 104 J5
Bec Clo., Ruis. 45 D3
Beccles Dr., Bark. 52 H6
Beccles St. E14 59 J7
Beck Clo. SE13 78 B1
Beck Ct., Beck. 95 G3
Beck La., Beck. 95 G3
Beck Rd. E8 59 E1
Beck Way, Beck. 95 J3
Beckenham Gdns. N9 33 B3
Beckenham Gro. 96 D2
  Brom.
Beckenham Hill Rd. 87 C5
  SE6
Beckenham Hill Rd., 87 B5
  Beck.
Beckenham La., 96 E2
  Brom.
Beckenham Pl. Pk., 87 B7
  Beck.
Beckenham Rd., 95 G1
  Beck.
Beckenham Rd., 96 B7
  W.Wick.
Beckers, The N16 50 D3
  Rectory Rd.
Becket Ave. E6 61 D3
Becket Clo. SE25 95 D6
Becket Fold, Har. 37 C5
  Courtfield Cres.
Becket Rd. N18 33 F4
Becket St. SE1 17 B5
Beckett Clo. NW10 47 D6
Beckett Clo. SW16 85 D2
Beckett Clo., Belv. 71 E3
  Tunstock Way
Beckett Wk., Beck. 86 H6
Becketts Clo., Felt. 72 B6
Becketts Clo., Orp. 104 J3

Becketts Pl., Kings.T. 91 G1
Beckford Rd., Croy. 95 C6
Becklow Gdns. W12 65 G2
  Becklow Rd.
Becklow Rd. W12 65 F2
Becks Rd., Sid. 89 A3
Beckton Retail Pk. E6 61 D5
Beckton Rd. E16 60 F5
Beckway Rd. SW16 94 D2
Beckway St. SE17 21 D2
Beckway St. SE17 68 A4
Beckwith Rd. SE24 77 A6
Beclands Rd. SW17 85 A6
Becmead Ave. SW16 85 D4
Becmead Ave., Har. 37 E5
Becondale Rd. SE19 86 B5
Becontree Ave., Dag. 53 B4
Bective Pl. SW15 75 C4
  Bective Rd.
Bective Rd. E7 51 G4
Bective Rd. SW15 75 B4
Becton Pl., Erith 71 H7
Bedale St. SE1 17 B2
Bedale St. SE1 68 A1
Beddington Fm. Rd., 94 E7
  Croy.
Beddington Gdns., 101 A6
  Cars.
Beddington Gdns., 101 B6
  Wall.
Beddington Grn., 97 J1
  Orp.
Beddington Gro., 101 D5
  Wall.
Beddington La., 94 C5
  Croy.
Beddington Path, 97 J1
  Orp.
Beddington Rd., Ilf. 43 J7
Beddington Rd., Orp. 97 H1
Bede Clo., Pnr. 36 D1
Bede Rd., Rom. 44 C6
Bedenham Way SE15 21 F7
Bedens Rd., Sid. 89 E6
Bedfont Clo., Mitch. 94 A2
Bedford Ave. WC1 11 J2
Bedford Ave. WC1 58 D5
Bedford Ave., Barn. 23 C5
Bedford Ave., Hayes 54 B6
Bedford Clo. N10 32 A7
Bedford Cor. W4 65 E4
  The Ave.
Bedford Ct. WC2 12 A6
Bedford Gdns. W8 66 D1
Bedford Hill SW12 85 B1
Bedford Ho. SW4 76 E4
Bedford Pk., Croy. 101 J1
Bedford Pl. WC1 12 A1
Bedford Pl. WC1 58 E5
Bedford Pl., Croy. 102 A1
Bedford Rd. E6 61 D1
Bedford Rd. E17 42 A2
Bedford Rd. E18 42 G2
Bedford Rd. N2 39 H3
Bedford Rd. N8 40 D6
Bedford Rd. N9 25 E7
Bedford Rd. N15 41 B4
Bedford Rd. N22 40 E1
Bedford Rd. NW7 30 E2
Bedford Rd. SW4 76 E3
Bedford Rd. W4 65 D3
Bedford Rd. W13 55 E7
Bedford Rd., Har. 36 J6
Bedford Rd., Ilf. 52 E3
Bedford Rd., Sid. 88 H3
Bedford Rd., Twick. 82 A3
Bedford Rd., Wor.Pk. 99 J2
Bedford Row WC1 12 D1
Bedford Row WC1 58 F5
Bedford Sq. WC1 11 J2
Bedford Sq. WC1 58 D5
Bedford St. WC2 12 A5
Bedford St. WC2 58 E7
Bedford Way WC1 7 J6
Bedford Way WC1 58 D4
Bedfordbury WC2 12 A6
Bedgebury Gdns. 84 B2
  SW19
Bedgebury Rd. SE9 79 A4
Bedivere Rd., Brom. 87 G3
Bedlow Way, Croy. 101 F4
Bedonwell Rd. SE2 71 E6
Bedonwell Rd., Belv. 71 E6
Bedonwell Rd., 80 F1
  Bexh.
Bedser Dr., Grnf. 46 A5
Bedster Gdns., 90 H2
  W.Mol.
Bedwardine Rd. SE19 86 B7
Bedwell Rd. N17 41 B1
Bedwell Rd., Belv. 71 G5
Bedwin Way SE16 68 E5
  Catlin St.

Beeby Rd. E16 60 H5
Beech Ave. N20 31 H1
Beech Ave. W3 65 E1
Beech Ave., Brent. 64 E7
Beech Ave., Buck.H. 34 H2
Beech Ave., Ruis. 45 B1
Beech Ave., Sid. 80 A1
Beech Clo. N9 25 D6
Beech Clo. SE8 68 J6
  Clyde St.
Beech Clo. SW15 74 G7
Beech Clo. SW19 83 J6
Beech Clo., Cars. 100 J2
Beech Clo., Sun. 90 D2
  Harfield Rd.
Beech Copse, Brom. 97 C2
Beech Copse, 102 B5
  S.Croy.
Beech Ct. E17 42 D3
Beech Ct. SE9 79 B6
Beech Ct., Ilf. 52 D3
  Riverdene Rd.
Beech Dell, Kes. 104 C4
Beech Dr. N2 39 J2
Beech Gdns. W5 64 F2
Beech Gdns., Dag. 53 H7
Beech Gro., Ilf. 35 H6
Beech Gro., Mitch. 94 D5
Beech Gro., N.Mal. 92 D3
Beech Hall Cres. E4 34 D7
Beech Hall Rd. E4 34 C7
Beech Hill, Barn. 23 F1
Beech Hill Ave. 23 F1
  Barn.
Beech Ho., Croy. 96 A2
Beech Ho. Rd., Croy. 102 A3
Beech La., Buck.H. 34 H2
Beech Lawns N12 31 G5
Beech Rd. N11 32 E6
Beech Rd. SW16 94 E2
Beech Row, Rich. 82 H4
Beech St. EC2 12 J1
Beech St. EC2 58 G2
Beech St., Rom. 44 J4
Beech Tree Glade E4 34 F1
  Forest Side
Beech Wk. NW7 30 E6
Beech Way NW10 47 D7
Beech Way, Twick. 81 G3
Beechcroft, Chis. 88 D7
Beechcroft Ave. 70 A6
  NW11
Beechcroft Ave., Har. 36 G7
Beechcroft Ave., 92 C1
  N.Mal.
Beechcroft Ave., Sthl. 63 F1
Beechcroft Clo., 63 E7
  Hounes.
Beechcroft Clo., Orp. 104 G4
Beechcroft Gdns., 46 J3
  Wem.
Beechcroft Rd. E18 42 H2
Beechcroft Rd. SW14 74 C3
  Elm Rd.
Beechcroft Rd. SW17 84 H2
Beechcroft Rd., 98 J4
  Chess.
Beechcroft Rd., Orp. 104 G4
Beechdale N21 32 F2
Beechdale Rd. SW2 76 F6
  Hope Pk.
Beechen Cliff Way, 73 C1
  Islw.
  Henley Clo.
Beechen Gro., Pnr. 36 F3
Beeches Ave., The, 100 H7
  Cars.
Beeches Clo. SE20 95 F1
  Genoa Rd.
Beeches Rd. SW17 84 H3
Beeches, Sutt. 100 B1
Beechfield Cotts., 96 J2
  Brom.
  Widmore Rd.
Beechfield Gdns., 44 J7
  Rom.
Beechfield Rd. N4 40 J6
Beechfield Rd. SE6 86 J1
Beechfield Rd., 96 J2
  Brom.
Beechhill Rd. SE9 79 D5
Beechmont Clo., 87 E5
  Brom.
Beechmore Gdns., 100 A2
  Sutt.
Beechmore Rd. SW11 75 J1
Beechmount Ave. W7 55 A5
Beecholme Ave., 94 B1
  Mitch.
Beecholme Est. E5 50 E3
  Prout Rd.
Beechtree Clo., Stan. 29 F5
Beechtree Pl., Sutt. 100 E5
  St. Nicholas Way

Beechvale Clo. N12 31 H5
Beechway, Bex. 80 D6
Beechwood Ave. N3 39 C3
Beechwood Ave., 54 H3
  Grnf.
Beechwood Ave., 45 H3
  Har.
Beechwood Ave., 104 H5
  Orp.
Beechwood Ave., 74 A1
  Rich.
Beechwood Ave., 81 A6
  Sun.
Beechwood Ave., 94 H4
  Th.Hth.
Beechwood Clo. NW7 30 D5
Beechwood Clo., 91 G7
  Surb.
Beechwood Ct., Sun. 81 A6
Beechwood Cres., 80 C1
  Bexh.
Beechwood Dr., Kes. 104 A4
Beechwood Dr., 34 F5
  Wdf.Grn.
Beechwood Gdns. 55 J3
  NW10
  North Circular Rd.
Beechwood Gdns., 45 H3
  Har.
Beechwood Gdns., 43 C5
  Ilf.
Beechwood Gro., 91 F7
  Surb.
Beechwood Ms. N9 33 D2
  Winchester Rd.
Beechwood Pk. E18 42 G3
Beechwood Ri., Chis. 88 E4
Beechwood Rd. E8 50 C6
Beechwood Rd. N8 40 D4
Beechwoods Ct. 86 C5
  SE19
  Crystal Palace Par.
Beechworth Clo. 48 D2
  NW3
Beecroft Rd. SE4 77 H5
Beehive La., Ilf. 43 C5
Beehive Pas. EC3 13 D4
Beehive Pl. SW9 76 G3
Beeleigh Rd., Mord. 93 E4
Beeston Clo. E8 50 D5
  Ferncliff Rd.
Beeston Clo., Wat. 28 D4
Beeston Pl. SW1 15 E6
Beeston Pl. SW1 67 B3
Beeston Rd., Barn. 23 G6
Beeston Way, Felt. 72 C6
Beethoven St. W10 57 B3
Beeton Clo., Pnr. 28 G7
Begbie Rd. SE3 78 J1
Beggars Roost La., 100 D6
  Sutt.
Begonia Clo., Hmptn. 81 G6
  Gresham Rd.
Begonia Wk. W12 56 F6
  Du Cane Rd.
Beira St. SW12 76 B7
Bekesbourne St. E14 59 H6
  Ratcliffe La.
Belcroft Clo., Brom. 87 F7
Beldham Gdns., 90 H3
  W.Mol.
Belfairs Dr., Rom. 44 C7
Belfairs Grn., Wat. 28 D5
  Haysham Dr.
Belfast Rd. N16 50 C2
Belfast Rd. SE25 95 E4
Belfont Wk. N7 49 E4
Belford Gro. SE18 70 D4
Belfort Rd. SE15 77 F2
Belgrade Rd. N16 50 B4
Belgrade Rd., Hmptn. 90 H1
Belgrave Clo. N14 24 C5
  Prince George Ave.
Belgrave Clo. W3 65 C2
  Avenue Rd.
Belgrave Cres., Sun. 90 B1
Belgrave Gdns. N14 24 D5
Belgrave Gdns. NW8 57 E1
Belgrave Gdns., Stan. 29 F5
  Copley Rd.
Belgrave Ms. N. SW1 15 B4
Belgrave Ms. S. SW1 15 C5
Belgrave Ms. W. SW11 15 B5
Belgrave Ms. W. SW1 67 A3
Belgrave Pl. SW1 15 C5
Belgrave Pl. SW1 67 A3
Belgrave Rd. E11 51 G2
Belgrave Rd. E13 60 J3
Belgrave Rd. E17 42 A5

Belgrave Rd. SE25 95 D4
Belgrave Rd. SW1 19 F2
Belgrave Rd. SW1 67 B4
Belgrave Rd. SW13 65 F7
Belgrave Rd., Houns. 72 F3
Belgrave Rd., Ilf. 52 C1
Belgrave Rd., Mitch. 93 G3
Belgrave Rd., Sun. 90 B1
Belgrave Sq. SW1 15 B5
Belgrave Sq. SW1 67 A3
Belgrave St. E1 59 G5
Belgrave Ter., 34 G3
 Wdf.Grn.
Belgrave Wk., Mitch. 93 G3
Belgrave Yd. SW1 15 D6
Belgravia Gdns., 87 E6
 Brom.
Belgravia Ho. SW4 76 D6
Belgravia Ms., 91 G4
 Kings.T.
Belgrove St. WC1 8 B3
Belgrove St. WC1 58 E3
Belham Wk. SE5 77 A1
 D'Eynsford Rd.
Belinda Rd. SW9 76 H3
Belitha Vill. N1 49 F7
Bell Clo., Pnr. 36 C2
Bell Ct., Surb. 99 B2
 Barnsbury La.
Bell Dr. SW18 75 B7
Bell Fm. Ave., Dag. 53 J3
Bell Grn. SE26 86 J3
Bell Grn. La. SE26 86 J5
Bell Ho. Rd., Rom. 53 J1
Bell Inn Yd. EC3 13 C4
Bell La. E1 13 F2
Bell La. E1 59 C5
Bell La. E16 69 G1
Bell La. NW4 38 J4
Bell La., Twick. 82 D1
Bell Meadow SE19 86 B4
 Dulwich Wd. Ave.
Bell Rd., E.Mol. 91 A5
Bell Rd., Enf. 25 A1
Bell Rd., Houns. 72 H3
Bell St. NW1 10 G1
Bell St. NW1 57 H5
Bell Water Gate SE18 70 D3
Bell Yd. WC2 12 E4
Bell Yd. WC2 58 G6
Bellamy Clo. W14 66 C5
 Aisgill Ave.
Bellamy Dr., Stan. 37 E1
Bellamy Rd. E4 34 B6
Bellamy Rd., Enf. 25 A2
Bellamy St. SW12 76 B7
Bellasis Ave. SW2 85 E2
Belle Staines 34 A2
 Pleasaunce E4
Belle Vue, Grnf. 55 A1
Belle Vue Est. NW4 38 J4
Belle Vue La. 29 A1
 (Bushey), Wat.
Belle Vue Rd. E17 42 D2
Bellefields Rd. SW9 76 F3
Bellegrove Clo., Well. 79 J2
Bellegrove Rd., Well. 79 H2
Bellenden Rd. SE15 77 C3
Belleville Rd. SW11 75 H5
Bellevue Ms. N11 32 A5
 Bellevue Rd.
Bellevue Pk., Th.Hth. 94 J3
Bellevue Pl. E1 59 F4
 Cleveland Way
Bellevue Rd. N11 32 A4
Bellevue Rd. SW13 74 G2
Bellevue Rd. SW17 84 H1
Bellevue Rd. W13 55 E4
Bellevue Rd., Bexh. 80 F5
Bellevue Rd., Kings.T. 91 H3
Bellew St. SW17 84 F3
Bellfield, Croy. 102 J7
Bellfield Ave., Har. 39 G5
Bellflower Clo. E6 61 B5
 Sorrell Gdns.
Bellgate Ms. NW5 49 B3
 York Ri.
Bellingham Grn. SE6 87 A3
Bellingham Rd. SE6 87 C3
Bellot St. SE10 69 E5
Bellring Clo., Belv. 71 G6
Bells All. SW6 75 D2
Bells Gdn. Est. SE15 68 D7
 Buller Clo.
Bells Hill, Barn. 23 A5
Belltrees Gro. SW16 85 F5
Bellwood Rd. SE15 77 G4
Belmarsh Rd. SE28 70 H2
 Western Way
Belmont Ave. N9 33 D1
Belmont Ave. N13 32 E5
Belmont Ave. N17 40 J3
Belmont Ave., Barn. 23 J5

Belmont Ave., N.Mal. 92 G5
Belmont Ave., Sthl. 63 E3
Belmont Ave., Well. 79 H2
Belmont Ave., Wem. 55 J1
Belmont Circle, Har. 37 E2
 Kenton La.
Belmont Clo. E4 34 D5
Belmont Clo. N20 31 E1
Belmont Clo. SW4 76 C3
Belmont Clo., Barn. 23 J4
Belmont Clo., 34 H4
 Wdf.Grn.
Belmont Ct. NW11 39 C5
Belmont Gro. SE13 78 D3
Belmont Hall Ct. 78 D3
 SE13
 Belmont Gro.
Belmont Hill SE13 78 C3
Belmont La., Chis. 88 F5
Belmont La., Stan. 29 F7
Belmont Pk. SE13 78 D4
Belmont Pk. Clo. 78 D4
 SE13
 Belmont Pk.
Belmont Pk. Rd. E10 42 B6
Belmont Ri., Sutt. 100 C7
Belmont Rd. N15 40 J3
Belmont Rd. N17 40 J3
Belmont Rd. SE25 95 E5
Belmont Rd. SW4 76 C3
Belmont Rd. W4 65 D4
Belmont Rd., Beck. 95 J2
Belmont Rd., Chis. 89 E5
Belmont Rd., Erith 71 G7
Belmont Rd., Har. 37 C3
Belmont Rd., Ilf. 52 F3
Belmont Rd., Twick. 82 A2
Belmont Rd., Wall. 101 B5
Belmont St. NW1 49 A7
Belmont Ter. W4 65 D4
 Belmont Rd.
Belmor, Borwd. 22 A5
Belmore Ave., Hayes 54 A6
Belmore La. N7 49 D5
Belmore St. SW8 78 D1
Beloe Clo. SW15 74 G3
Belper Ct. E5 50 G4
 Pedro St.
Belsham St. E9 50 F6
Belsize Ave. N13 32 F6
Belsize Ave. NW3 48 G6
Belsize Ave. W13 64 E3
Belsize Cres. NW3 48 G6
Belsize Gdns., Sutt. 100 E4
Belsize Gro. NW3 48 H6
Belsize La. NW3 48 G6
Belsize Pk. NW3 48 G6
Belsize Pk. Gdns. 48 H6
 NW3
Belsize Pk. Ms. NW3 48 G6
 Belsize La.
Belsize Pl. NW3 48 G6
 Belsize La.
Belsize Rd. NW6 57 E1
Belsize Rd., Har. 29 A7
Belsize Sq. NW3 48 G6
Belsize Ter. NW3 48 G6
Belson Rd. SE18 70 C4
Beltane Dr. SW19 84 A3
Belthorn Cres. SW12 76 C7
Belton Rd. E7 51 H7
Belton Rd. E11 51 E4
Belton Rd. N17 41 B3
Belton Rd. NW2 47 G6
Belton Rd., Sid. 89 A4
Belton Way E3 60 A5
Beltran Rd. SW6 75 E2
Beltwood Rd., Belv. 71 J4
Belvedere Ave. SW19 84 B5
Belvedere Ave., Ilf. 43 E2
Belvedere Bldgs. SE1 16 H4
Belvedere Clo., 82 B5
 Tedd.
Belvedere Ct. N2 39 G5
Belvedere Dr. SW19 84 B5
Belvedere Gdns., 90 F5
 W.Mol.
Belvedere Gro. SW19 84 B5
Belvedere Ho., Felt. 81 A1
Belvedere Ind. Est., 71 J3
 Belv.
Belvedere Pl. SE1 16 H4
Belvedere Rd. E10 50 H1
Belvedere Rd. SE1 16 D3
Belvedere Rd. SE1 67 F2
Belvedere Rd. SE2 71 D1
Belvedere Rd. SE19 86 C7
Belvedere Rd. W7 64 B3
Belvedere Rd., Bexh. 80 F3
Belvedere Sq. SW19 84 B5
Belvedere Strand 38 F2
 NW9
Belvedere Way, Har. 37 H6

Belvoir Clo. SE9 88 B3
Belvoir Rd. SE22 77 D7
Belvue Clo., Nthlt. 45 G7
Belvue Rd., Nthlt. 45 G7
Bembridge Clo. NW6 48 B7
Bemerton St. N1 49 E7
Bemerton St. N1 58 F1
Bemish Rd. SW15 75 A3
Bempton Dr., Ruis. 45 B2
Bemsted Rd. E17 41 J3
Ben Hale Clo., Stan. 29 E4
Ben Jonson Rd. E1 59 G5
Ben Smith Way SE16 17 J5
Ben Tillet Clo., Bark. 53 A7
Benares Rd. SE18 70 J4
Benbow Rd. W6 65 H3
Benbow St. SE8 69 A6
Benbury Clo., Brom. 87 C5
Bench Fld., S.Croy. 102 C6
Bencroft Rd. SW16 85 C7
Bencurtis Pk., 103 D3
 W.Wick.
Bendall Ms. NW1 10 H1
Bendemeer Rd. 75 A3
 SW15
Bendish Rd. E6 52 B7
Bendmore Ave. SE2 71 A5
Bendon Valley SW18 75 E7
Benedict Clo., 104 H3
 Orp.
Benedict Clo., Belv. 71 E3
 Tunstock Way
Benedict Dr., Felt. 72 F4
Benedict Rd. SW9 76 F3
Benedict Rd., Mitch. 93 G3
Benedict Way N2 39 F3
Benenden Grn., 96 F5
 Brom.
Benett Gdns. SW16 94 E2
Benfleet Clo., Sutt. 100 F3
Bengal Rd., Ilf. 52 E4
Bengarth Dr., Har. 37 A2
Bengarth Rd., Nthlt. 54 D1
Bengeworth Rd. SE5 76 J3
Bengeworth Rd., Har. 46 D4
Benham Clo. SW11 75 G3
Benham Gdns., 72 F4
 Houns.
Benham Rd. W7 55 B5
Benhams Pl. NW3 48 F4
 Holly Wk.
Benhill Ave., Sutt. 100 E4
Benhill Rd. SE5 68 A7
Benhill Rd., Sutt. 100 F3
Benhill Wd. Rd., 100 F4
 Sutt.
Benhilton Gdns., 100 E3
 Sutt.
Benhurst Ct. SW16 85 G5
Benhurst La. SW16 85 G5
Benin St. SE13 78 D7
Benjafield Clo. N18 33 E4
 Brettenham Rd.
Benjamin Clo. E8 59 D1
Benjamin St. EC1 12 G1
Benjamin St. EC1 58 H5
Benledi St. E14 60 D6
Benn St. E9 50 H6
Bennerley Rd. SW11 75 H5
Bennets Copse, Chis. 88 B6
Bennet's Hill EC4 12 H5
Bennett Clo., Kings.T. 91 F1
Bennett Clo., Well. 80 A2
Bennett Gro. SE13 78 B1
Bennett Pk. SE3 78 F3
Bennett Rd. E13 60 J4
Bennett Rd. N16 50 B4
Bennett Rd., Rom. 44 E6
Bennett St. SW1 15 F1
Bennett St. W4 65 E6
Bennetts Ave., Croy. 102 H2
Bennetts Ave., Grnf. 55 B1
Bennetts Castle La., 53 C4
 Dag.
Bennetts Clo. N17 33 C6
Bennetts Way, Croy. 102 H2
Bennetts Yd. SW1 15 J6
Benningholme Rd., 30 E1
 Edg.
Bennington Rd. N17 41 B1
Bennington Rd., 34 E7
 Wdf.Grn.
Benn's Wk., Rich. 73 H4
 Rosedale Rd.
Benrek Clo., Ilf. 43 F1
Bensbury Clo. SW15 74 J7
Bensham Clo., 94 J4
 Th.Hth.
Bensham Gro., 94 J2
 Th.Hth.
Bensham La., Croy. 94 H7
Bensham La., Th.Hth. 94 H4
Bensham Manor Rd., 94 J4
 Th.Hth.
Bensley Clo. N11 31 J5

Benson Ave. E6 60 J2
Benson Clo., Houns. 72 G4
Benson Quay E1 59 F7
 Garnet St.
Benson Rd. SE23 86 F1
Benson Rd., Croy. 101 G3
Bentfield Gdns. SE9 87 J3
 Aldersgrove Ave.
Benthal Rd. N16 50 D2
Bentham Rd. E9 50 G6
Bentham Rd. SE28 62 B7
Bentham Wk. NW10 47 C5
Bentinck Ms. W1 11 C3
Bentinck Pl. NW8 6 G2
Bentinck St. W1 11 C3
Bentinck St. W1 58 A6
Bentley Dr., Ilf. 43 F6
Bentley Rd. N1 50 B6
 Tottenham Rd.
Bentley Way, Stan. 29 D5
Bentley Way, 34 G3
 Wdf.Grn.
Benton Rd., Ilf. 52 G1
Benton Rd., Wat. 28 D5
Bentons La. SE27 85 J4
Bentons Ri. SE27 86 A5
Bentry Clo., Dag. 53 E2
Bentry Rd., Dag. 53 E2
Bentworth Rd. W12 56 H6
Benwell Ct., Sun. 90 A1
Benwell Rd. N7 49 G4
Benwick Clo. SE16 68 E4
Benworth St. E3 59 J3
Benyon Rd. N1 59 A1
 Southgate Rd.
Berber Rd. SW11 75 J5
Bercta Rd. SE9 88 F2
Bere St. E1 59 G7
 Cranford St.
Berenger Wk. SW10 18 E7
Berens Rd. NW10 57 A3
Berens Way, Chis. 97 J4
Beresford Ave. N20 31 J2
Beresford Ave. W7 55 A5
Beresford Ave., Surb. 99 D1
Beresford Ave., 73 F6
 Twick.
Beresford Ave., 55 J1
 Wem.
Beresford Dr., 97 B3
 Brom.
Beresford Dr., 34 J4
 Wdf.Grn.
Beresford Gdns., Enf. 25 B4
Beresford Gdns., 72 F5
 Houns.
Beresford Gdns., 44 E5
 Rom.
Beresford Rd. E4 34 E1
Beresford Rd. E17 42 B1
Beresford Rd. N2 39 H3
Beresford Rd. N5 50 A5
Beresford Rd. N8 40 G5
Beresford Rd., Har. 37 A5
Beresford Rd., 91 J1
 Kings.T.
Beresford Rd., N.Mal. 92 C4
Beresford Rd., Sthl. 63 D1
Beresford Rd., Sutt. 100 C7
Beresford Sq. SE18 70 E4
Beresford St. SE18 70 E3
Beresford Ter. N5 49 J5
Berestede Rd. W6 65 F5
Bergen Sq. SE16 68 H3
 Norway Gate
Berger Clo., Orp. 97 G6
Berger Rd. E9 50 G6
Berghem Ms. W14 66 A3
 Blythe Rd.
Bergholt Ave., Ilf. 43 B5
Bergholt Cres. N16 41 B7
Bergholt Ms. NW1 49 C7
 Rossendale Way
Bering Wk. E16 61 A6
Berkeley Ave., Bexh. 80 D1
Berkeley Ave., Grnf. 46 A6
Berkeley Ave., Houns. 72 A1
Berkeley Ave., Ilf. 43 D2
Berkeley Clo., Borwd. 22 A5
Berkeley Clo., 82 H7
 Kings.T.
Berkeley Clo., Orp. 97 H7
Berkeley Clo., Ruis. 45 A3
Berkeley Ct. N14 24 C6
Berkeley Cres., Barn. 23 G5
Berkeley Gdns. N21 25 A7
Berkeley Gdns. W8 66 D1
 Brunswick Gdns.
Berkeley Gdns., 98 D6
 Esher
Berkeley Ho. E3 60 A3
 Wellington Way
Berkeley Ms. W1 11 A4

Berkeley Pl. SW19 84 A6
Berkeley Rd. E12 52 B5
Berkeley Rd. N8 40 D5
Berkeley Rd. N15 41 A6
Berkeley Rd. NW9 38 A4
Berkeley Rd. SW13 74 G1
Berkeley Sq. W1 11 E6
Berkeley Sq. W1 58 E7
Berkeley St. W1 15 E1
Berkeley St. W1 67 B1
Berkeley Wk. N7 49 F2
Durham Rd.
Berkeley Waye, 63 D7
Houns.
Berkhampstead Rd., 71 G5
Belv.
Berkhamsted Ave., 46 J6
Wem.
Berkley Dr., W.Mol. 90 F3
Berkley Gro. NW1 48 J7
Berkley Rd.
Berkley Rd. NW1 48 J7
Berkshire Gdns. N13 32 G6
Berkshire Gdns. N18 33 E5
Berkshire Rd. E9 50 J6
Berkshire Way, 94 E4
Mitch.
Bermans Way NW10 47 E4
Bermondsey Sq. SE1 17 E5
Bermondsey St. SE1 17 E5
Bermondsey St. SE1 68 D2
Bermondsey Wall E. 17 J4
SE16
Bermondsey Wall E. 68 D2
SE16
Bermondsey Wall W. 17 H3
SE16
Bermondsey Wall W. 68 D2
SE16
Bernal Clo. SE28 62 D7
Haldane Rd.
Bernard Ave. W13 64 E3
Bernard Cassidy St. 60 F5
E16
Bernard Gdns. SW19 84 C5
Bernard Rd. N15 41 C5
Bernard Rd., Rom. 44 J7
Bernard Rd., Wall. 101 B5
Bernard St. WC1 8 A6
Bernard St. WC1 58 E4
Bernards Clo., Ilf. 25 F7
Bernays Gro. SW9 76 F4
Berne Rd., Th.Hth. 94 H5
Bernel Dr., Croy. 102 J3
Berners Dr. W13 55 D6
Berners Ms. W1 11 G2
Berners Ms. W1 58 C5
Berners Pl. W1 11 G3
Berners Pl. W1 58 C6
Berners Rd. N1 58 G1
Berners Rd. N22 40 G1
Berners St. W1 11 G2
Berners St. W1 58 C5
Berney Rd., Croy. 95 A7
Bernville Way, Har. 37 J5
Kenton Rd.
Bernwell Rd. E4 34 E3
Berridge Grn., Edg. 30 B7
Berridge Rd. SE19 86 B5
Berriman Rd. N7 49 F3
Berriton Rd., Har. 45 F1
Berry Clo. N21 32 H1
Berry Clo. NW10 47 E2
Berry Ct., Houns. 72 F5
Berry Hill, Stan. 29 G4
Berry La. SE21 86 A4
Berry Pl. EC1 8 H4
Berry St. EC1 8 H5
Berry St. EC1 58 H4
Berry Way W5 64 H3
Berrybank Clo. E4 34 C2
Greenbank Clo.
Berrydale Rd., Hayes 54 E4
Berryfield Clo. E17 42 B4
Berryfield Clo., Brom. 97 B1
Berryfield Rd. SE17 20 H3
Berryfield Rd. SE17 67 H5
Berryhill SE9 79 E4
Berryhill Gdns. SE9 79 E4
Berrylands SW20 92 J3
Berrylands, Surb. 91 J6
Berrylands Rd., Surb. 91 J6
Berryman Clo., Dag. 53 C3
Bennetts Castle La.
Berrymans La. SE26 86 G4
Berrymead Gdns. W3 65 C2
Berrymede Rd. W4 65 D3
Bert Rd., Th.Hth. 94 J5
Bert Way, Enf. 25 C4
Bertal Rd. SW17 84 G4
Berthon St. SE8 69 A7
Bertie Rd. NW10 47 G6

Bertie Rd. SE26 86 G6
Bertram Cotts. SW19 84 D7
Hartfield Rd.
Bertram Rd. NW4 38 G6
Bertram Rd., Enf. 25 D4
Bertram Rd., Kings.T. 83 A7
Bertram St. N19 49 B2
Bertram Way, Enf. 25 C4
Bertrand St. SE13 78 B3
Bertrand Way SE28 62 B7
Berwick Clo., Hayes 54 D6
Berwick Clo., Stan. 29 C7
Gordon Ave.
Berwick Cres., Sid. 79 H6
Berwick Rd. E16 60 H6
Berwick Rd. N22 40 H1
Berwick Rd., Well. 80 B1
Berwick St. W1 11 G3
Berwick St. W1 58 C6
Berwyn Ave., Houns. 72 H1
Berwyn Rd. SE24 85 H1
Berwyn Rd., Rich. 74 B4
Beryl Ave. E6 61 B5
Beryl Rd. W6 66 A5
Berystede, Kings.T. 83 B7
Besant Ct. N1 50 A5
Mildmay Gro.
Besant Rd. NW2 48 B4
Besant Wk. N7 49 F2
Newington Barrow Way
Besant Way NW10 47 C5
Besley St. SW16 85 C7
Bessborough Gdns. 19 J3
SW1
Bessborough Gdns. 67 D5
SW1
Bessborough Pl. SW1 19 H3
Bessborough Pl. SW1 67 D5
Bessborough Rd. 83 G1
SW15
Bessborough Rd., 46 A1
Har.
Bessborough St. SW1 19 H3
Bessborough St. SW1 67 D5
Bessemer Rd. SE5 76 J2
Bessie Lansbury Clo. 61 D6
E6
Bessingby Rd., Ruis. 45 B2
Bessingham Wk. SE4 77 G4
Frendsbury Rd.
Besson St. SE14 77 F1
Bessy St. E2 59 F3
Roman Rd.
Bestwood St. SE8 68 G4
Beswick Ms. NW6 48 E6
Lymington Rd.
Betchworth Clo., 100 G5
Sutt.
Turnpike La.
Betchworth Rd., Ilf. 52 H2
Betham Rd., Grnf. 55 A3
Bethecar Rd., Har. 37 B5
Bethel Rd., Well. 80 C3
Bethell Ave. E16 60 F4
Bethell Ave., Ilf. 43 D7
Bethersden Clo., 86 J7
Beck.
Bethnal Grn. Rd. E1 9 F5
Bethnal Grn. Rd. E1 59 C4
Bethnal Grn. Rd. E2 9 J4
Bethnal Grn. Rd. E2 59 C4
Bethune Ave. N11 31 J4
Bethune Rd. N16 41 A7
Bethune Rd. NW10 56 D4
Bethwin Rd. SE5 20 H7
Bethwin Rd. SE5 67 H7
Betjeman Clo., Pnr. 36 G4
Betony Clo., Croy. 102 G1
Primrose La.
Betoyne Ave. E4 34 E4
Betstyle Rd. N11 32 B4
Betterton Dr., Sid. 89 E2
Betterton Rd. WC2 12 A4
Betterton St. WC2 58 E6
Bettons Pk. E15 60 E1
Bettridge Rd. SW6 75 C2
Betts Clo., Beck. 95 H2
Kendall Rd.
Betts Rd. E16 60 H7
Victoria Dock Rd.
Betts St. E1 59 E7
The Highway
Betts Way SE20 95 E1
Betts Way, Surb. 98 E1
Beulah Ave., Th.Hth. 94 F4
Beulah Rd.
Beulah Clo., Edg. 30 B3
Beulah Cres., Th.Hth. 94 J2
Beulah Gro., Croy. 94 J6
Beulah Hill SE19 85 H6
Beulah Path E17 42 B5
Addison Rd.

Beulah Rd. E17 42 B5
Beulah Rd. SW19 84 C7
Beulah Rd., Sutt. 100 D4
Beulah Rd., Th.Hth. 94 J3
Bev Callender Clo. 76 B3
SW8
Daley Thompson Way
Bevan Ave., Bark. 53 A7
Bevan Ct., Croy. 101 G5
Bevan Rd. SE2 71 B5
Bevan Rd., Barn. 23 J4
Bevan St. N1 58 J1
Bevenden St. N1 9 C3
Bevercote Wk., Belv. 71 F6
Osborne Rd.
Beveridge Rd. NW10 47 E7
Curzon Cres.
Beverley NW8 6 G4
Beverley Ave. SW20 92 F1
Beverley Ave., 72 F4
Houns.
Beverley Ave., Sid. 79 J7
Beverley Clo. N21 32 J1
Beverley Clo. SW11 75 G4
Maysoule Rd.
Beverley Clo. SW13 74 F2
Beverley Clo., Chess. 98 F4
Beverley Clo., Enf. 25 B4
Beverley Ct. N14 24 C7
Beverley Ct. SE4 77 J3
Beverley Cres., 42 H1
Wdf.Grn.
Beverley Dr., Edg. 38 A3
Beverley Gdns. NW11 39 B7
Beverley Gdns. SW13 74 F3
Beverley Gdns., Stan. 37 D1
Beverley Gdns., 46 J1
Wem.
Beverley Gdns., 99 G1
Wor.Pk.
Green La.
Beverley La. SW15 83 F3
Beverley La., 83 E7
Kings.T.
Beverley Path SW13 74 F2
Beverley Rd. E4 34 D6
Beverley Rd. E6 61 A3
Beverley Rd. SE20 95 E2
Beverley Rd. SW13 74 F3
Beverley Rd. W4 65 F5
Beverley Rd., Bexh. 80 J2
Beverley Rd., Brom. 104 B3
Beverley Rd., Dag. 53 E4
Beverley Rd., 91 F1
Kings.T.
Beverley Rd., Mitch. 94 D4
Beverley Rd., N.Mal. 92 G4
Beverley Rd., Ruis. 45 A2
Beverley Rd., Sthl. 63 E4
Beverley Rd., Wor.Pk. 99 J2
Beverley Way SW20 92 F1
Beverley Way, N.Mal. 92 F1
Beversbrook Rd. N19 49 D3
Beverstone Rd. SW2 76 F5
Beverstone Rd., 94 G4
Th.Hth.
Bevill Allen Clo. 84 J5
SW17
Bevin Clo. SE16 68 H1
Bevin Rd., Hayes 54 A3
Bevin Way WC1 8 E3
Bevington Rd. W10 57 B5
Bevington Rd., Beck. 96 B2
Bevington St. SE16 17 J4
Bevington St. SE16 68 D2
Bevis Marks EC3 13 E3
Bevis Marks EC3 59 B6
Bewcastle Gdns., Enf. 24 E4
Bewdley St. N1 49 G7
Bewick St. SW8 76 B2
Bewley St. E1 59 E7
Bewlys Rd. SE27 85 H5
Bexhill Clo., Felt. 81 E2
Bexhill Rd. N11 32 D5
Bexhill Rd. SE4 77 J6
Bexhill Rd. SW14 74 C3
Bexhill Wk. E15 60 E2
Mitre Rd.
Bexley Gdns. N9 33 A3
Bexley High St., Bex. 80 G7
Bexley La., Sid. 89 C4
Bexley Rd. SE9 79 E5
Bexley Rd., Erith 71 J7
Beynon Rd., Cars. 100 J5
Bianca Rd. SE15 21 H6
Bianca Rd. SE15 68 C6
Bibsworth Rd. N3 39 C2
Bibury Clo. SE15 21 E6
Bibury Clo. SE15 68 B6
Bicester Rd., Rich. 74 A3
Bickenhall St. W1 11 A1
Bickenhall St. W1 57 J5

Bickersteth Rd. SW17 84 J6
Bickerton Rd. N19 49 C2
Bickley Cres., Brom. 97 B4
Bickley Pk. Rd., Brom. 97 B3
Bickley Rd. E10 42 B7
Bickley Rd., Brom. 97 A2
Bickley St. SW17 84 H5
Bicknell Rd. SE5 76 J3
Bicknoller Rd., Enf. 25 B1
Bicknor Rd., Orp. 97 H7
Bidborough Clo., 96 F5
Brom.
Bidborough St. WC1 8 A4
Bidborough St. WC1 58 E3
Biddenden Way SE9 88 D4
Bidder St. E16 60 E5
Biddestone Rd. N7 49 F4
Biddulph Rd. W9 6 A4
Biddulph Rd. W9 57 E3
Bideford Ave., Grnf. 55 E2
Bideford Clo., Edg. 38 A4
Bideford Clo., Felt. 81 F3
Bideford Gdns., Enf. 25 B7
Bideford Rd., Brom. 87 F3
Bideford Rd., Ruis. 45 B3
Bideford Rd., Well. 71 B7
Bidwell Gdns. N11 32 C7
Bidwell St. SE15 77 E1
Big Hill E5 50 E1
Bigbury Rd. N17 33 B7
Barkham Rd.
Biggerstaff Rd. E15 60 C1
Biggerstaff St. N4 49 G2
Biggin Ave., Mitch. 93 J1
Biggin Hill SE19 94 H1
Biggin Way SE19 85 H7
Bigginwood Rd. 85 H7
SW16
Biggs Row SW15 75 A3
Felsham Rd.
Bigland St. E1 59 E6
Bignell Rd. SE18 70 E5
Bignold Rd. E7 51 G4
Bigwood Rd. NW11 39 E5
Bill Hamling Clo. SE9 88 C2
Billet Clo., Rom. 44 D3
Billet Rd. E17 41 G1
Billet Rd., Rom. 44 B4
Billing Pl. SW10 18 B7
Billing Pl. SW10 66 E7
Billing Rd. SW10 18 B7
Billing Rd. SW10 66 E7
Billing St. SW10 18 B7
Billing St. SW10 66 E7
Billingford Clo. SE4 77 G4
Billington Rd. SE14 68 G7
Billiter Sq. EC3 13 E4
Billiter St. EC3 13 E4
Billiter St. EC3 59 B6
Billockby Clo., Chess. 98 J6
Billson St. E14 69 C4
Bilsby Gro. SE9 88 A4
Bilton Rd., Grnf. 55 D1
Bilton Way, Enf. 25 H1
Bilton Way, Hayes 63 B2
Bina Gdns. SW5 18 C2
Bina Gdns. SW5 66 F4
Bincote Rd., Enf. 24 F3
Binden Rd. W12 65 F3
Bindon Grn., Mord. 93 E4
Bayham Rd.
Binfield Rd. SW4 76 E1
Binfield Rd., S.Croy. 102 C5
Bingfield St. N1 58 E1
Bingham Pl. W1 11 B1
Bingham Rd., Croy. 102 G1
Bingham St. N1 50 A6
Bingley Rd. E16 60 J6
Bingley Rd., Grnf. 54 J4
Bingley Rd., Sun. 81 A7
Binney St. W1 11 C4
Binney St. W1 58 A6
Binns Rd. W4 65 E5
Binsey Wk. SE2 71 C2
Binyon Cres., Stan. 29 C5
Birbeck Gdns. 34 F2
Wdf.Grn.
Birbetts Rd. SE9 88 C2
Birch Ave. N13 32 J3
Birch Clo. E16 60 E5
Birch Clo. N19 49 C2
Hargrave Pk.
Birch Clo. SE15 77 D2
Birch Clo., Brent. 64 E7
Birch Clo., Buck.H. 35 A3
Birch Clo., Rom. 44 H3
Birch Clo., Tedd. 82 D5
Birch Gdns., Dag. 53 J3
Birch Gro. SW9 30 E7
Clayton Fld.
Birch Gro. SE12 78 F7
Birch Gro. W3 65 A1
Birch Gro., Well. 80 A4

Birch Hill, Croy. 102 G5
Birch Mead, Orp. 104 D2
Birch Pk., Har. 28 J7
Birch Rd., Felt. 81 D5
Birch Rd., Rom. 44 H3
Birch Row, Brom. 97 D7
Birch Tree Ave., 103 F5
W.Wick.
Birch Tree Way, 102 E2
Croy.
Birch Wk., Borwd. 22 A1
Grove Rd.
Birch Wk., Erith 71 J6
Birch Wk., Mitch. 94 B1
Bircham Path SE4 77 G4
St. Norbert Rd.
Birchanger Rd. SE25 95 D5
Birchdale Gdns., 44 D7
Rom.
Birchdale Rd. E7 51 J5
Birchdene Dr. SE28 71 A1
Birchen Clo. NW9 47 D2
Birchen Gro. NW9 47 D2
Birchend Clo., 102 A6
S.Croy.
Sussex Rd.
Birches, The N21 24 F6
Birches, The SE7 69 H6
Birches, The, Orp. 104 D4
Birches Clo., Mitch. 93 J3
Birches Clo., Pnr. 36 E5
Birchfield St. E14 60 A7
Birchin La. EC3 13 C4
Birchin La. EC3 59 A6
Birchington Clo., 80 H1
Bexh.
Birchington Rd. N8 40 D6
Birchington Rd. NW6 57 D1
Birchington Rd., 91 J7
Surb.
Birchlands Ave. 75 J7
SW12
Birchmead Ave., Pnr. 36 C4
Birchmere Row SE3 78 F2
Birchmore Wk. N5 49 J3
Highbury Quad.
Birchville Ct. 29 B1
(Bushey), Wat.
Heathbourne Rd.
Birchway, Hayes 63 A1
Birchwood Ave. N10 40 A3
Birchwood Ave., 95 J4
Beck.
Birchwood Ave., Sid. 89 B2
Birchwood Ave., 101 A3
Wall.
Birchwood Clo., 93 E4
Mord.
Birchwood Ct. N13 32 H5
Birchwood Clo., Edg. 38 C2
Birchwood Dr. NW3 48 E3
Birchwood Gro., 81 G6
Hmptn.
Birchwood Rd. SW17 85 B5
Birchwood Rd., Orp. 97 G4
Bird in Bush Rd. 21 H7
SE15
Bird in Bush Rd. SE15 68 D7
Bird St. W1 11 C4
Bird Wk., Twick. 81 F1
Bird-in-hand La., 97 A2
Brom.
Bird-in-hand Pas. 86 F2
SE23
Dartmouth Rd.
Birdbrook Clo., Dag. 53 J7
Birdbrook Rd. SE3 78 J3
Birdcage Wk. SW1 15 G4
Birdcage Wk. SW1 67 C2
Birdham Clo., Brom. 97 B5
Birdhurst Ave., 102 A4
S.Croy.
Birdhurst Gdns., 102 A4
S.Croy.
Birdhurst Ri., 102 B5
S.Croy.
Birdhurst Rd. SW18 75 F4
Birdhurst Rd. SW19 84 B4
Birdhurst Rd., 102 B5
S.Croy.
Birdlip Clo. SE15 21 D6
Birdlip Clo. SE15 68 B6
Birds Fm. Ave., Rom. 44 H1
Birdsfield La. E3 59 J1
Birdwood Clo., Tedd. 82 B4
Birkbeck Ave. W3 56 C7
Birkbeck Ave., Grnf. 54 J1
Birkbeck Gdns., 34 F2
Wdf.Grn.
Birkbeck Gro. W3 65 D2
Birkbeck Hill SE21 85 H2
Birkbeck Ms. E8 50 C5
Sandringham Rd.

Birkbeck Pl. SE21 85 J1
Birkbeck Rd. E8 50 C5
Birkbeck Rd. N8 40 E4
Birkbeck Rd. N12 31 F5
Birkbeck Rd. N17 41 C1
Birkbeck Rd. NW7 30 F5
Birkbeck Rd. SW19 84 E5
Birkbeck Rd. W3 65 D1
Birkbeck Rd. W5 72 A4
Birkbeck Rd., Beck. 95 E2
Birkbeck Rd., Enf. 25 A1
Birkbeck Rd., Ilf. 43 G5
Birkbeck Rd., Sid. 89 A3
Birkbeck St. E2 59 E3
Cambridge Heath Rd.
Birkbeck Way, Grnf. 54 J1
Birkdale Ave., Pnr. 36 G3
Birkdale Clo., Orp. 97 G7
Birkdale Gdns., Wat. 28 D3
Birkdale Rd. SE2 71 A4
Birkdale Rd. W5 55 H4
Birkenhead Ave., 91 J2
Kings.T.
Birkenhead St. WC1 8 B3
Birkenhead St. WC1 58 E3
Birkhall Rd. SE6 87 D1
Birkwood Clo. SW12 76 D7
Birley Rd. N20 31 F2
Birley St. SW11 76 A2
Birnam Rd. N4 49 F2
Birse Cres. NW10 47 E4
Birstall Grn., Wat. 28 D4
Birstall Rd. N15 41 B6
Biscay Rd. W6 66 A5
Biscoe Clo., Houns. 63 G6
Biscoe Way SE13 78 D3
Bisenden Rd., Croy. 102 B2
Bisham Clo., Cars. 93 J7
Bisham Gdns. N6 49 A1
Bishop Fox Way, 90 F4
E.Mol.
Bishop Ken Rd., Har. 37 C2
Bishop Kings Rd. 66 B4
W14
Bishop Rd. N14 24 B7
Bishop St. N1 58 J1
Bishop Way NW10 47 J7
Bishop's Ave. E13 60 H1
Bishops Ave. SW6 75 A2
Bishops Ave., Brom. 96 J2
Bishops Ave., Rom. 44 C6
Bishops Ave., The 39 G7
N2
Bishops Bri. W2 10 D3
Bishops Bri. W2 57 F5
Bishops Bri. Rd. W2 10 B3
Bishops Bri. Rd. W2 57 E6
Bishops Clo. E17 42 B4
Bishops Clo. SE9 88 F2
Bishops Clo., Barn. 23 A6
Bishops Clo., Enf. 25 E2
Central Ave.
Bishops Clo., Rich. 82 G3
Bishops Clo., Sutt. 100 D3
Bishops Gro. N2 39 G6
Bishops Gro., Hmptn. 81 F4
Bishop's Hall, 91 G2
Kings.T.
Bishops Hill, Walt. 90 A7
Bishop's Pk. Rd. SW6 75 A2
Bishops Pk. Rd. 94 E1
SW16
Bishops Rd. N6 40 A6
Bishops Rd. SW6 75 B1
Bishops Rd. W7 64 A4
Bishops Rd., Croy. 94 H7
Bishops Ter. SE11 20 F1
Bishops Ter. SE11 67 G4
Bishops Wk., Chis. 97 F1
Bishop's Wk., Croy. 102 G5
Bishop's Wk., Pnr. 36 E3
High St.
Bishops Way E2 59 E2
Bishopsford Rd., 93 F7
Mord.
Bishopsgate EC2 13 E2
Bishopsgate EC2 59 B6
Bishopsgate Chyd. 13 D3
EC2
Bishopsthorpe Rd. 86 G4
SE26
Bishopswood Rd. N6 39 J7
Bisley Clo., Wor.Pk. 99 J1
Bispham Rd. NW10 55 J3
Bisson Rd. E15 60 C2
Bisterne Ave. E17 42 D3
Bittacy Clo. NW7 31 A6
Bittacy Hill NW7 31 A6
Bittacy Pk. Ave. NW7 31 A6
Bittacy Ri. NW7 30 J6
Bittacy Rd. NW7 31 A6

Bittern St. SE1 16 J4
Bittoms, The, 91 G3
Kings.T.
Bixley Clo., Sthl. 63 F4
Black Boy La. N15 40 J5
Black Fan Clo., Enf. 24 J1
Black Friars Ct. EC4 12 G5
Black Friars La. EC4 12 G5
Black Friars La. EC4 58 H6
Black Gates, Pnr. 36 F3
Church La.
Black Horse Ct. SE1 17 C5
Black Lion La. W6 65 G4
Black Path E10 41 G7
Black Prince Rd. SE1 20 B2
Black Prince Rd. SE1 67 F4
Black Prince Rd. SE11 20 D2
Black Prince Rd. SE11 67 F4
Black Swan Yd. SE1 17 D3
Blackall St. EC2 9 D5
Blackberry Fm. Clo., 63 E7
Houns.
Blackbird Hill NW9 47 C2
Blackbird Yd. E2 9 G3
Blackborne Rd., Dag. 53 G6
Blackbrook La., 97 D3
Brom.
Blackburn Rd. NW6 48 E6
Blackburne's Ms. W1 11 B5
Blackburne's Ms. W1 58 A7
Blackbush Ave., 44 D5
Rom.
Blackbush Clo., Sutt. 100 E7
Blackdown Ter. SE18 70 C7
Blackett St. SW15 75 A3
Blackfen Rd., Sid. 79 H6
Blackford Rd., Wat. 28 D5
Blackford's Path 74 G7
SW15
Roehampton High St.
Blackfriars Bri. EC4 12 G6
Blackfriars Bri. EC4 58 H7
Blackfriars Bri. SE1 12 G6
Blackfriars Bri. SE1 58 H7
Blackfriars Pas. EC4 12 G5
Blackfriars Rd. SE1 67 H1
Blackheath Ave. 69 D7
SE10
Blackheath Gro. SE3 78 F2
Blackheath Hill SE10 78 C1
Blackheath Pk. SE3 78 F3
Blackheath Ri. SE13 78 C2
Blackheath Rd. SE10 78 B1
Blackheath Vale SE3 78 E2
Blackheath Village 78 F2
SE3
Blackhorse La. E17 41 G4
Blackhorse La., Croy. 95 D7
Blackhorse Rd. E17 41 G4
Blackhorse Rd. SE8 68 H5
Blackhorse Rd., Sid. 89 A4
Blackland Ter. SW3 18 J2
Blackland Ter. SW3 66 J4
Blacklands Rd. SE6 87 C4
Blackmore Ave., Sthl. 64 A1
Blackmore Rd., 27 B7
Buck.H.
Blackmores Gro., 82 D6
Tedd.
Blackness La., Kes. 104 A7
Blackpool Rd. SE15 77 E2
Blacks Rd. W6 65 J4
Queen Caroline St.
Blackshaw Pl. N1 50 B7
Hertford Rd.
Blackshaw Rd. SW17 84 F4
Blacksmiths Clo., 44 C6
Rom.
Blackstock Ms. N4 49 H2
Blackstock Rd.
Blackstock Rd. N4 49 H2
Blackstock Rd. N5 49 H2
Blackstone Est. E8 50 D7
Blackstone Rd. NW2 47 J5
Blackthorn Ct., 63 E7
Houns.
Blackthorn Gro., 80 E3
Bexh.
Blackthorne St. E3 60 A4
Blackthorne Ave., 102 F1
Croy.
Blackthorne Dr. E4 34 D4
Blacktree Ms. SW9 76 G3
Blackwall La. SE10 69 E5
Blackwall Tunnel 69 D1
E14
Blackwall Tunnel 69 E2
App. SE10
Blackwall Tunnel 60 A2
Northern App. E3
Blackwall Tunnel 60 C4
Northern App. E14

Blackwall Way E14 60 C7
Blackwater Rd., Sutt. 100 E4
High St.
Blackwater St. SE22 77 C5
Blackwell Clo. E5 50 H4
Blackwell Clo., Har. 29 A7
Blackwell Gdns., Edg. 30 A3
Blackwood St. SE17 21 B3
Blackwood St. SE17 68 A5
Blade Ms. SW15 75 C4
Deodar Rd.
Bladindon Dr., Bex. 80 C7
Bladon Gdns., Har. 36 H6
Blagdens Clo. N14 32 C2
Blagdens La. N14 32 D2
Blagdon Rd. SE13 78 B6
Blagdon Rd., N.Mal. 92 F4
Blagdon Wk., Tedd. 82 F6
Blagrove Rd. W10 57 B5
Blair Ave. NW9 38 E7
Blair Clo. N1 49 J6
Blair Clo., Sid. 79 H5
Blair St. E14 60 C6
Blairderry Rd. SW2 85 G2
Blairhead Dr., Wat. 28 B3
Blake Ave., Bark. 61 H1
Blake Clo. W10 56 J5
Blake Clo., Well. 79 H1
Blake Gdns. SW6 75 E1
Blake Hall Cres. E11 51 G1
Blake Hall Rd. E11 42 G7
Blake Ho., Beck. 87 A6
Blake Rd. E16 60 F1
Blake Rd. N11 32 C7
Blake Rd., Croy. 102 B2
Blake Rd., Mitch. 93 H3
Blake St. SE8 69 A6
Watergate St.
Blakeden Dr., Esher 98 C6
Blakehall Rd., Cars. 100 J6
Blakemore Rd. SW16 85 E3
Blakemore Rd., 94 F5
Th.Hth.
Blakemore Way, Belv. 71 E3
Blakeney Ave., 95 J1
Beck.
Blakeney Clo. E8 50 D5
Ferncliff Rd.
Blakeney Clo. N20 31 F1
Blakeney Clo. NW1 49 D7
Rossendale Way
Blakeney Rd., Beck. 95 J1
Blakenham Rd. SW17 84 J4
Blaker Ct. SE7 69 J7
Fairlawn
Blaker Rd. E15 60 C1
Blakes Ave., N.Mal. 92 F5
Blake's Grn., 103 C1
W.Wick.
Blakes La., N.Mal. 92 F5
Blakes Rd. SE15 21 E7
Blakes Rd. SE15 68 A6
Blakes Ter., N.Mal. 92 G5
Blakesley Ave. W5 55 F6
Blakesley Wk. SW20 93 C2
Blakesware Gdns. N9 25 D1
Blakewood Clo., Felt. 81 C4
Blanch Clo. SE15 68 F7
Clifton Way
Blanchard Clo. SE9 88 B3
Blanchard Way E8 50 D6
Blanche St. E16 60 F4
Blanchedowne SE5 77 A4
Blanchland Rd., 93 E5
Mord.
Bland St. SE9 79 A4
Blandfield Rd. SW12 76 A6
Blandford Ave., Beck. 95 H2
Blandford Ave., 81 H1
Twick.
Blandford Clo. N2 39 F5
Blandford Clo., 101 A3
Croy.
Wandle Rd.
Blandford Clo., Rom. 44 H4
Blandford Cres. E4 26 C7
Blandford Rd. W4 65 E3
Blandford Rd. W5 64 G2
Blandford Rd., Beck. 95 H2
Blandford Rd., Sthl. 63 G4
Blandford Rd., Tedd. 82 A5
Blandford Sq. NW1 6 H6
Blandford Sq. NW1 57 H4
Blandford St. W1 11 A3
Blandford St. W1 57 J6
Blandford Waye, 54 C6
Hayes
Blaney Cres. E6 63 E1
Blanmerle Rd. SE9 88 E1
Blann Clo. SE9 79 A6
Blantyre St. SW10 18 E7
Blantyre St. SW10 66 G7
Blantyre Wk. SW10 18 E7

Blashford NW3 48 J7
Blashford St. SE13 78 D7
Blasker Wk. E14 69 A5
Blawith Rd., Har. 33 E7
Blaydon Clo. N17 33 E7
Blaydon Wk. N17 33 E7
Bleak Hill La. SE18 70 J6
Blean gro. SE20 86 F7
Bleasdale Ave., Grnf. 55 D2
Blechynden St. W10 57 A7
Bramley Rd.
Blechynden St. W11 57 A7
Bramley Rd.
Bleddyn Clo., Sid. 80 C6
Bledlow Clo. SE28 62 C7
Bledlow Ri., Grnf. 54 J2
Bleeding Heart Yd. 12 F2
EC1
Blegborough Rd. 85 C6
SW16
Blendon Dr., Bex. 80 D6
Blendon Path, Brom. 87 F7
Hope Pk.
Blendon Rd., Bex. 80 C6
Blendon Ter. SE18 70 F5
Blendworth Way 21 E7
SE15
Blenheim Ave., Ilf. 43 D6
Blenheim Clo. N21 32 J1
Elm Pk. Rd.
Blenheim Clo. SW20 92 J3
Blenheim Clo., Grnf. 55 A2
Leaver Gdns.
Blenheim Clo., Rom. 44 J4
Blenheim Clo., Wall. 101 C7
Blenheim Ct. N19 49 E2
Marlborough Rd.
Blenheim Ct., Sid. 88 G3
Blenheim Cres. W11 57 B7
Blenheim Cres., 101 J7
S.Croy.
Blenheim Dr., Well. 79 J1
Blenheim Gdns. NW2 47 J6
Blenheim Gdns. SW2 76 F6
Blenheim Gdns., 83 B7
Kings.T.
Blenheim Gdns., 101 C6
Wall.
Blenheim Gdns., 46 H3
Wem.
Blenheim Gro. SE15 77 D2
Blenheim Pas. NW8 6 C1
Blenheim Ri. N15 41 C4
Talbot Rd.
Blenheim Rd. E6 61 A3
Blenheim Rd. E15 51 E4
Blenheim Rd. E17 41 G3
Blenheim Rd. NW8 6 D1
Blenheim Rd. NW8 57 F2
Blenheim Rd. SE20 86 F7
Maple Rd.
Blenheim Rd. SW20 92 J3
Blenheim Rd., Barn. 23 A3
Blenheim Rd., Brom. 97 B4
Blenheim Rd., Har. 36 H6
Blenheim Rd., Nthlt. 45 H6
Blenheim Rd., Sid. 89 C1
Blenheim Rd., Sutt. 100 D3
Blenheim St. W1 11 D4
Blenheim Ter. NW8 6 C1
Blenheim Ter. NW8 57 F2
Blenkarne Rd. SW11 75 J6
Bleriot Rd., Houns. 63 C7
Blessbury Rd., Edg. 38 C1
Blessington Clo. 78 D3
SE13
Blessington Rd. SE13 78 D4
Bletchingley Clo., 94 H4
Th.Hth.
Bletchley Ct. N1 9 A2
Bletchley St. N1 9 A2
Bletchley St. N1 58 J2
Bletsoe Wk. N1 9 A1
Blincoe Clo. SW19 84 A2
Blind La., Loug. 26 E2
Bliss Cres. SE13 78 E4
Coldbath St.
Blissett St. SE10 78 C1
Blisworth Clo., Hayes 54 E4
Braunston Dr.
Blithbury Rd., Dag. 53 B6
Blithdale Rd. SE2 71 A4
Blithfield St. W8 14 A6
Blithfield St. W8 66 E3
Blockley Rd., Wem. 46 E2
Bloemfontein Ave. 65 H1
W12
Bloemfontein Rd. 56 H7
W12
Blomfield Rd. W9 10 B1
Blomfield Rd. W9 57 E5
Blomfield St. EC2 13 C2

Blomfield St. EC2 59 A5
Blomfield Vill. W2 10 B2
Blomfield Vill. W2 57 E5
Blomville Rd., Dag. 53 E3
Blondel St. SW11 76 A2
Blondin Ave. W5 64 F4
Blondin St. E3 60 A2
Bloom Gro. SE27 85 H3
Bloomburg St. SW1 19 G2
Bloomfield Cres., Ilf. 43 E6
Bloomfield Pl. W1 11 E5
Bloomfield Rd. N6 40 A6
Bloomfield Rd. SE18 70 E5
Bloomfield Rd., 97 A5
Brom.
Bloomfield Rd., 91 H4
Kings.T.
Bloomfield Ter. SW1 19 C3
Bloomfield Ter. SW1 67 A5
Bloomhall Rd. SE19 86 A5
Bloomsbury Clo. W5 55 J7
Bloomsbury Ct. WC1 12 B2
Bloomsbury Ct., Pnr. 36 F3
Bloomsbury Ho. SW4 76 D6
Bloomsbury Pl. SW18 75 F5
Fullerton Rd.
Bloomsbury Pl. WC1 12 B1
Bloomsbury Sq. WC1 12 B2
Bloomsbury St. WC1 11 J2
Bloomsbury St. WC1 58 D5
Bloomsbury Way 12 A3
WC1
Bloomsbury Way 58 E5
WC1
Blore Clo. SW8 76 D1
Thessaly Rd.
Blore Ct. W1 11 H5
Blossom Clo. W5 64 H2
Almond Ave.
Blossom Clo., Dag. 62 F1
Blossom Clo., 102 C5
S.Croy.
Melville Ave.
Blossom La., Enf. 24 J1
Blossom St. E1 9 E6
Blossom St. E1 59 B4
Blossom Waye, 63 E7
Houns.
Blount St. E14 59 H5
Bloxam Gdns. SE9 79 B5
Bloxhall Rd. E10 50 J1
Bloxham Cres., 81 F7
Hmptn.
Bloxworth Clo., Wall.101 C3
Blucher Rd. SE5 67 J7
Blue Anchor All., 73 H4
Rich.
Kew Rd.
Blue Anchor La. SE16 21 J1
Blue Anchor La. SE16 68 D4
Blue Anchor Yd. E1 13 H5
Blue Anchor Yd. E1 59 D7
Blue Ball Yd. SW1 15 F2
Bluebell Clo. SE26 86 C4
Bluebell Clo., Orp. 104 F7
Bluebell Clo., Wall. 101 B1
Bluefield Clo., Hmptn. 81 G5
Bluegates, Epsom 99 G7
Bluehouse Rd. E4 34 E3
Blundell Rd., Edg. 38 D1
Blundell St. N7 49 E7
Blunden Clo., Dag. 53 C1
Blunts Rd. SE9 79 D5
Blurton Rd. E5 50 F4
Blyth Clo. E14 69 D4
Saunders Ness Rd.
Blyth Rd. E17 41 J7
Blyth Rd. SE28 62 C7
Blyth Rd., Brom. 96 F1
Blythe Clo. SE6 77 J7
Blythe Clo., Twick. 73 C7
Grimwood Rd.
Blythe Hill SE6 77 J7
Blythe Hill, Orp. 97 J1
Blythe Hill La. SE6 77 J7
Blythe Rd. W14 66 A3
Blythe St. E2 58 J3
Blythe Vale SE6 86 J1
Blythswood Rd., Ilf. 53 A1
Blythwood Rd. N4 40 E7
Blythwood Rd., Pnr. 36 D1
Boadicea St. N1 58 F1
Copenhagen St.
Boardman Ave. E4 26 B5
Boar's Head Yd., 64 G7
Brent.
Brent Way
Boathouse Wk. SE15 21 G7
Boathouse Wk. SE15 68 C7
Boathouse Wk., Rich. 73 G1
Kew Rd.

Bob Anker Clo. E13 60 G3
Chesterton Rd.
Bob Marley Way 76 G4
SE24
Marcus Garvey Way
Bobbin Clo. SW4 76 C3
Bockhampton Rd., 82 J7
Kings.T.
Bocking St. E8 59 E1
Boddicott Clo. SW19 84 B2
Bodia Rd. SW16 84 J6
Bodiam Clo., Enf. 25 A2
Bodiam Rd. SW16 85 D7
Bodley Clo., N.Mal. 92 E5
Bodley Manor Way 76 G7
SW2
Papworth Way
Bodley Rd., N.Mal. 92 D6
Bodmin Clo., Har. 45 F3
Bodmin Gro., Mord. 93 E4
Bodmin St. SW18 84 D1
Bodnant Gdns. SW20 92 H3
Bodney Rd. E8 50 E5
Boeing Way, Sthl. 63 B3
Boevey Path, Belv. 71 F5
Orchard Ave.
Bogey La., Orp. 104 C7
Bognor Gdns., Wat. 28 C5
Bowring Grn.
Bognor Rd., Well. 80 D1
Bohemia Pl. E8 50 F6
Bohun Gro., Barn. 23 H6
Boileau Rd. SW13 65 G7
Boileau Rd. W5 55 J6
Bolden St. SE8 78 B2
Bolderwood Way, 103 B2
W.Wick.
Boldmere Rd., Pnr. 36 C7
Boleyn Ave., Enf. 25 F1
Boleyn Clo. E17 42 A4
Boleyn Ct., Buck.H. 34 G1
Boleyn Dr., Ruis. 45 D2
Boleyn Dr., W.Mol. 90 F3
Boleyn Gdns., Dag. 53 J7
Boleyn Gdns., 103 B2
W.Wick.
Boleyn Gro., 103 C2
W.Wick.
Boleyn Rd. E6 61 A2
Boleyn Rd. E7 51 G7
Boleyn Rd. N16 50 B5
Boleyn Way, Barn. 23 F3
Boleyn Way, Ilf. 35 F6
Bolina Rd. SE16 68 F5
Bolingbroke Gro. 75 J6
SW11
Bolingbroke Rd. W14 66 A3
Bolingbroke Wk. 75 G1
SW11
Bolliger Ct. NW10 56 C4
Park Royal Rd.
Bollo Bri. Rd. W3 65 B3
Bollo La. W3 65 B2
Bollo La. W4 65 C4
Bolney St. SW8 67 F7
Bolney Way, Felt. 81 E3
Bolsover St. W1 7 E6
Bolsover St. W1 58 B4
Bolstead Rd., Mitch. 94 B1
Bolt Ct. EC4 12 F4
Boltmore Clo. NW4 39 A3
Bolton Clo. SE20 95 D2
Selby Rd.
Bolton Clo., Chess. 98 G6
Bolton Cres. SE5 20 F7
Bolton Cres. SE5 67 H6
Bolton Gdns. NW10 57 A2
Bolton Gdns. SW5 18 A3
Bolton Gdns. SW5 66 E5
Bolton Gdns., Brom. 87 F6
Bolton Gdns., Tedd. 82 B6
Bolton Gdns. Ms. 18 B3
SW10
Bolton Gdns. Ms. 66 E5
SW10
Bolton Rd. E15 51 F6
Bolton Rd. N18 33 C5
Bolton Rd. NW8 57 E1
Bolton Rd. NW10 56 E1
Bolton Rd. W4 65 C7
Bolton Rd., Chess. 98 G6
Bolton Rd., Har. 36 J3
Bolton St. W1 15 E1
Bolton St. W1 66 B1
Bolton Wk. N7 49 F2
Durham Rd.
Boltons, The SW10 18 C3
Boltons, The SW10 66 E5
Boltons, The, Wem. 46 C4
Boltons, The, 34 G4
Wdf.Grn.
Bombay St. SE16 68 E4
Bomore Rd. W11 85 B7

Bon Marche Ter. 86 B4
SE27
Gipsy Rd.
Bonar Pl., Chis. 88 B7
Bonar Rd. SE15 68 D7
Bonchester Clo., 88 D7
Chis.
Bonchurch Clo., 100 E7
Sutt.
Bonchurch Rd. W10 57 B5
Bonchurch Rd. W13 64 E1
Bond Ct. EC4 13 B4
Bond Gdns., Wall. 101 C4
Bond Rd., Mitch. 93 H2
Bond Rd., Surb. 98 J1
Bond St. E15 51 E5
Bond St. W4 65 E4
Bond St. W5 55 G7
Chiswick Common Rd.
Bondfield Rd. E6 61 B5
Lovage App.
Bondfield Rd., Hayes 54 A5
Bonding Yd. Wk. 68 H2
SE16
Finland St.
Bondway SW8 20 B5
Bondway SW8 67 E6
Boneta Rd. SE18 70 C3
Bonfield Rd. SE13 78 C4
Bonham Gdns., Dag. 53 D2
Bonham Rd. SW2 76 F5
Bonham Rd., Dag. 53 D2
Bonheur Rd. W4 65 D2
Bonhill St. EC2 9 C6
Bonhill St. EC2 59 A4
Boniface Gdns., Har. 28 H7
Boniface Wk., Har. 28 H7
Bonner Hill Rd., 91 J3
Kings.T.
Bonner Rd. E2 59 F2
Bonner St. E2 59 F2
Bonnersfield Clo., 37 C6
Har.
Bonnersfield La., 37 C6
Har.
Bonneville Gdns. 76 G3
SW4
Bonnington Sq. SW8 20 C5
Bonnington Sq. SW8 67 E6
Bonnington Twr., 97 B6
Brom.
Bonny St. NW1 49 C7
Bonser Rd., Twick. 82 C2
Bonsor St. SE5 68 B7
Bonville Gdns. NW4 38 G4
Handowe Clo.
Bonville Rd., Brom. 87 F5
Book Ms. WC2 11 J4
Booker Clo. E14 59 J5
Wallwood St.
Booker Rd. N18 33 D5
Boone Ct. N9 33 F3
Boone St. SE13 78 E4
Boones Rd. SE13 78 E4
Boord St. SE10 69 E3
Boot St. N1 9 D4
Boot St. N1 59 B3
Booth Clo. SE28 62 B7
Booth Rd. NW9 38 D2
Booth Rd., Croy. 101 H2
Waddon New Rd.
Boothby Rd. N19 49 D2
Booth's Pl. W1 11 G2
Bordars Rd. W7 55 B5
Bordars Wk. W7 55 B5
Borden Ave., Enf. 25 A6
Border Cres. SE26 86 E5
Border Gdns., Croy. 103 B4
Border Rd. SE26 86 E5
Bordergate, Mitch. 93 J1
Borders La., Loug. 27 D4
Bordesley Rd., Mord. 93 E4
Bordon Wk. SW15 74 C4
Boreas Wk. N1 8 H2
Boreham Ave. E16 60 G6
Boreham Clo. E11 51 C1
Hainault Rd.
Boreham Rd. N22 40 J2
Borehamwood Ind. 22 D2
Pk., Borwd.
Borer's Pas. E1 13 E3
Borgard Rd. SE18 70 C3
Borkwood Pk., Orp. 104 J4
Borkwood Way, Orp. 104 H4
Borland Rd. SE15 77 F4
Borland Rd., Tedd. 82 E6
Borneo St. SW15 74 J3
Borough High St. 17 A4
SE1
Borough High St. 67 J2
SE1
Borough Hill, Croy. 101 H3
Borough Rd. SE1 17 H5

Borough Rd. SE1 67 H3
Borough Rd., Islw. 73 B1
Borough Rd., 92 A1
Kings.T.
Borough Rd., Mitch. 93 H2
Borough Sq. SE1 16 J4
Borrett Clo. SE17 20 J4
Borrodaile Rd. SW18 75 E6
Borrowdale Ave., 37 D2
Har.
Borrowdale Clo., Ilf. 43 B4
Borrowdale Ct., 24 J1
Borthwick Ms. E15 51 E4
Borthwick Rd.
Borthwick Rd. E15 51 E4
Borthwick Rd. NW9 38 F6
West Hendon Bdy.
Borthwick St. SE8 69 A5
Borwick Ave. E17 41 J3
Bosbury Rd. SE6 87 C3
Boscastle Rd. NW5 49 B3
Boscobel Pl. SW1 19 C1
Boscobel Pl. SW1 67 A4
Boscobel St. NW8 6 F6
Boscobel St. NW8 57 G4
Boscombe Ave. E10 42 D7
Boscombe Clo. E5 50 H5
Boscombe Gdns. 85 E6
SW16
Boscombe Rd. SW17 85 A6
Boscombe Rd. SW19 93 D1
Boscombe Rd. W12 65 G1
Boscombe Rd., 99 J1
Wor.Pk.
Bosgrove E4 34 C1
Boss St. SE1 17 F3
Bostal Row, Bexh. 80 F3
Harlington Rd.
Bostall Hill SE2 71 A5
Bostall Hill Rd. SE2 71 C6
Bostall La. SE2 71 B5
Bostall Manorway 71 B4
SE2
Bostall La.
Bostall Pk. Ave., 71 E7
Bexh.
Bostall Rd., Orp. 89 B7
Boston Gdns. W4 65 E6
Boston Gdns., Brent. 64 D4
Boston Manor Rd., 64 E4
Brent.
Boston Pk. Rd., Brent. 64 F5
Boston Pl. NW1 6 J6
Boston Pl. NW1 57 J4
Boston Rd. E6 61 B3
Boston Rd. E17 42 A6
Boston Rd. W7 64 B1
Boston Rd., Croy. 94 F6
Boston Rd., Edg. 30 C7
Boston Vale W7 64 D4
Bostonthorpe Rd. W7 64 B2
Boswell Ct. WC1 12 B1
Boswell Rd., 94 J4
Th.Hth.
Boswell St. WC1 12 B1
Boswell St. WC1 58 E5
Bosworth Clo. E17 41 J1
Bosworth Rd. N11 32 D6
Bosworth Rd. W10 57 B4
Bosworth Rd., Barn. 23 D3
Bosworth Rd., Dag. 53 G3
Botany Bay La., Chis. 97 F2
Boteley Clo. E4 34 D2
Botha Rd. E13 60 H5
Botham Clo., Edg. 30 C7
Pavilion Way
Bothwell Clo. E16 60 F5
Bothwell St. W6 66 A6
Delorme St.
Botolph All. EC3 13 D5
Botolph La. EC3 13 D5
Botsford Rd. SW20 93 B2
Botts Ms. W2 57 D6
Chepstow Rd.
Botts Pas. W2 57 D6
Chepstow Rd.
Boucher Clo., Tedd. 82 C5
Boughton Ave., 96 F7
Brom.
Boughton Rd. SE28 70 H3
Boulcott St. E1 59 G6
Boulevard, The, Pnr. 36 G4
Pinner Rd.
Boulogne Rd., Croy. 94 J6
Boulton Ho., Brent. 64 H5
Boulton Rd., Dag. 53 E3
Boultwood Rd. E6 61 C6
Bounces La. N9 33 E2
Bounces Rd. N9 33 E2
Boundaries Rd. SW12 84 J2
Boundaries Rd., Felt. 81 C1
Boundary Clo. SE20 95 D2
Haysleigh Gdns.

Boundary Clo., Ilf. 52 H4
Loxford La.
Boundary Clo., 92 B3
Kings.T.
Boundary Clo., Sthl. 63 G5
Boundary La. E13 61 A3
Boundary La. SE17 21 A5
Boundary La. SE17 67 J6
Boundary Par. N8 40 E6
Boundary Pas. E2 9 F5
Boundary Rd. E13 60 J2
Boundary Rd. E17 41 J7
Boundary Rd. N9 25 F6
Boundary Rd. N22 40 H3
Boundary Rd. NW8 57 E1
Boundary Rd. SW19 84 G6
Boundary Rd., Bark. 61 G1
Boundary Rd., Cars. 101 A7
Boundary Rd., Pnr. 36 D7
Boundary Rd., Sid. 79 H5
Boundary Rd., Wall. 101 B6
Boundary Row SE1 16 G3
Boundary St. E2 9 F4
Boundary St. E2 59 C4
Boundary Way, 103 A5
Croy.
Boundfield Rd. SE6 87 E3
Bounds Grn. Rd. N11 32 C6
Bounds Grn. Rd. N22 32 E7
Bourchier St. W1 11 H5
Bourdon Pl. W1 11 F5
Bourdon Rd. SE20 95 F2
Bourdon St. W1 11 D6
Bourdon St. W1 58 B7
Bourke Clo. NW10 47 E6
Mayo Rd.
Bourke Clo. SW4 76 E6
Bourlet Clo. W1 11 F2
Bourn Ave. N15 41 A4
Bourn Ave., Barn. 23 G5
Bournbrook Rd. SE3 79 A3
Bourne, The N14 32 D1
Bourne Ave. N14 32 J2
Bourne Ave., Ruis. 45 C5
Bourne Clo., Ruis. 45 B5
Bourne Dr., Mitch. 93 G2
Bourne Est. EC1 11 E1
Bourne Est. EC1 58 G5
Bourne Gdns. E4 34 B4
Bourne Hill N13 32 F2
Bourne Hill Clo. N13 32 F2
Bourne Hill
Bourne Mead, Bex. 80 J5
Bourne Pl. W4 65 D5
Dukes Ave.
Bourne Rd. E7 51 F3
Bourne Rd. N8 40 E6
Bourne Rd., Bex. 80 F7
Bourne Rd., Brom. 97 A4
Bourne St. SW1 19 B2
Bourne St. SW1 67 A4
Bourne St., Croy. 101 H2
Waddon New Rd.
Bourne Ter. W2 10 A1
Bourne Ter. W2 57 E5
Bourne Vale, Brom. 103 F1
Bourne Vw., Grnf. 46 C6
Bourne Way, Brom. 103 G2
Bourne Way, Epsom 99 C4
Bourne Way, Sutt. 100 C5
Bournemead Ave., 54 A2
Nthlt.
Bournemead Clo., 54 A3
Nthlt.
Bournemead Way, 54 B2
Nthlt.
Bournemouth Rd. 77 D2
SE15
Bournemouth Rd. 93 D1
SW19
Bourneside Cres. N14 32 D1
Bourneside Gdns. 87 C5
SE6
Bournevale Rd. SW16 85 E4
Bournewood Rd. 71 A7
SE18
Bournville Rd. SE6 78 A7
Bournwell Clo., Barn. 23 J3
Bourton Clo., Hayes 63 A1
Avondale Dr.
Bousfield Rd. SE14 77 G2
Boutflower Rd. SW11 75 H4
Bouverie Gdns., Har. 37 G6
Bouverie Ms. N16 50 B2
Bouverie Rd.
Bouverie Pl. W2 10 F3
Bouverie Rd. N16 50 B1
Bouverie Rd., Har. 36 J6
Bouverie St. EC4 12 F4
Bouverie St. EC4 58 G6
Boveney Rd. SE23 77 G7
Bovill Rd. SE23 77 G7

Bovingdon Ave., 47 A6
Wem.
Bovingdon La. NW9 38 E1
Bovingdon Rd. SW6 75 E1
Bow Chyd. EC4 13 A4
Bow Common La. E3 59 H4
Bow Ind. Est. E15 51 B7
Bow La. EC4 13 A4
Bow La. EC4 58 J6
Bow La. N12 31 F7
Bow La., Mord. 93 B6
Bow Rd. E3 59 J3
Bow St. E15 51 E5
Bow St. WC2 12 B4
Bow St. WC2 58 E6
Bowater Clo. NW9 38 D5
Bowater Clo. SW2 76 E6
Bowater Pl. SE3 69 H7
Bowater Rd. SE18 58 E6
Bowden St. SE11 20 F3
Bowden St. SE11 67 G5
Bowditch SE8 68 J5
Bowdon Rd. E17 42 A7
Bowen Dr. SE21 86 B3
Bowen Rd., Har. 36 J7
Bowen St. E14 60 B6
Bower Ave. SE10 78 E1
Bower Clo., Nthlt. 54 C2
Bower St. E1 59 G6
Bowerdean St. SW6 75 E1
Bowerman Ave. SE14 68 H6
Bowers Wk. E6 61 C6
Northumberland Rd.
Bowes Clo., Sid. 80 B6
Bowes Rd. N11 32 B5
Bowes Rd. N13 32 E5
Bowes Rd. W3 56 E7
Bowes Rd., Dag. 53 C4
Bowfell Rd. W6 65 J6
Bowford Ave., Bexh. 80 E1
Bowhill Clo. SW9 20 F7
Bowhill Clo. SW9 67 G7
Bowie Clo. SW4 76 D7
Bowland Rd. SW4 76 D4
Bowland Rd., 34 J6
Wdf.Grn.
Bowland Yd. SW1 15 A4
Bowles Rd. SE1 21 H5
Bowley Clo. SE19 86 C5
Bowley Rd. SE19 86 C8
Farquhar Rd.
Bowling Grn. Clo. 74 H7
SW15
Bowling Grn. Ct. EC2 9 E6
Bowling Grn. Ct. EC2 59 B4
Bowling Grn. La. EC1 8 F5
Bowling Grn. La. EC1 58 G4
Bowling Grn. Pl. SE1 17 B3
Bowling Grn. Pl. SE1 68 A2
Bowling Grn. Row 70 C3
SE18
Samuel St.
**Bowling Grn. St. 20 E5
SE11**
Bowling Grn. St. 67 G6
SE11
Bowling Grn. Wk. N1 9 D3
Bowls, The, Chig. 35 H4
Bowls Clo., Stan. 29 E5
Bowman Ave. E16 60 F7
Bowman Ms. SW18 84 C1
Bowmans Clo. W13 64 E1
Bowmans Lea SE23 77 F7
Bowmans Meadow, 101 B3
Wall.
Bowmans Ms. E1 11 H5
Bowmans Ms. N7 49 E3
Seven Sisters Rd.
Bowmans Pl. N7 49 E3
Hercules St.
Bowman's Trd. Est. 37 J3
NW9
Bowmead SE9 88 C2
Bowmore Wk. NW1 49 D7
Agar Gro.
Bowness Clo. E8 50 C6
Beechwood Rd.
Bowness Cres. SW15 83 E5
Bowness Dr., Houns. 72 E4
Bowness Rd. SE6 78 B7
Bowness Rd., Bexh. 80 H2
Bowood Rd. SW11 76 A5
Bowood Rd., Enf. 25 G2
Bowring Grn., Wat. 28 C5
Bowrons Ave., Wem. 46 G7
Bowsprit Pt. E14 60 C3
Bowyer Pl. SE5 21 A7
Bowyer St. SE5 21 A7
Bowyer St. SE5 67 J7
Box La., Bark. 62 E2
Boxall Rd. SE21 86 B6

Boxgrove Rd. SE2 71 B2
Boxley Rd., Mord. 93 F4
Boxley St. E16 69 H1
Boxmoor Rd., Har. 37 E4
Boxoll Rd., Dag. 53 F4
Boxted Clo., Buck.H. 35 B1
Boxtree La., Har. 36 J1
Boxtree Rd., Har. 29 A7
Boxworth Gro. N1 58 F1
Richmond Ave.
Boyard Rd. SE18 70 E5
Boyce St. SE1 16 E2
Boyce Way E13 60 G4
Boycroft Ave. NW9 38 C6
Boyd Ave., Sthl. 63 F1
Boyd Clo., Kings.T. 83 A7
Crescent Rd.
Boyd Rd. SW19 84 G6
Boyd St. E1 13 J4
Boyd St. E1 59 F6
Boydell Ct. NW8 48 G7
St. John's Wd. Pk.
Boyfield St. SE1 16 H4
Boyfield St. SE1 67 H2
Boyland Rd., Brom. 87 F5
Boyle Ave., Stan. 29 D6
Boyle Fm. Rd., T.Ditt. 91 D6
Boyle St. W1 11 F5
Boyne Ave. NW4 39 A4
Boyne Rd. SE13 78 C3
Boyne Rd., Dag. 53 G3
Boyne Ter. Ms. W11 66 C1
Bracewell Rd.
Boyson Rd. SE17 21 B5
Boyson Rd. SE17 68 A6
Boythorn Way SE16 68 E5
Credon Rd.
Boyton Clo. E1 59 G4
Stayners Rd.
Boyton Clo. N8 40 E3
Boyton Rd. N8 40 E3
Brabant Ct. EC3 13 D5
Brabant Rd. N22 40 F2
Brabazon Ave., Wall. 101 E7
Brabazon Rd., 63 C7
Houns.
Brabazon Rd., Nthlt. 54 G2
Brabazon St. E14 60 B6
Brabourn Gro. SE15 79 F2
Brabourne Clo. SE19 86 B5
Brabourne Cres., 71 F6
Bexh.
Brabourne Heights 30 E3
NW7
Brabourne Ri., Beck. 96 C5
Bracewell Ave., Grnf. 46 D6
Bracewell Rd. W10 56 J5
Bracewood Gdns., 102 C3
Croy.
Bracey St. N4 49 E2
Bracken Ave. SW12 76 A6
Bracken Ave., Croy. 103 A3
Bracken Clo. E6 61 C5
Bracken Clo., Twick. 72 G7
Hedley Rd.
Bracken Dr., Chig. 35 E6
Bracken End, Islw. 73 A5
Bracken Gdns. SW13 74 G2
Bracken Hill Clo., 96 F1
Brom.
Bracken Hill La.
Bracken Hill La., 96 F1
Brom.
Bracken Ind. Est., Ilf. 35 J7
Bracken Ms., Rom. 44 H6
Brackenbridge Dr., 45 D3
Ruis.
Brackenbury Gdns. 65 D3
W6
Brackenbury Rd. N2 39 F3
Brackenbury Rd. W6 65 H3
Brackendale N21 32 F2
Brackendale Clo., 72 H1
Houns.
Brackenfield Clo. E5 50 E4
Tiger Way
Brackens, The, Enf. 25 B7
Brackenwood, Sun. 90 A1
Brackley Clo., Wall. 101 E7
Brackley Rd. W4 65 E5
Brackley Rd., Beck. 66 E5
Brackley Sq., 35 A7
Wdf.Grn.
Brackley St. EC1 13 A1
Brackley Ter. W4 65 E5
Bracklyn Ct. N1 9 B1
Bracklyn St. N1 9 B1
Bracklyn St. N1 59 A2
Brackwell Clo. N22 40 G1
Bracknell Gdns. NW3 48 F4
Bracknell Gate NW3 48 E5
Bracknell Way NW3 48 E4
Bracondale Rd. SE2 71 A4

Brad St. SE1 16 F2
Bradbourne Rd., Bex. 80 G7
Bradbourne St. SW6 75 D2
Bradbury Clo., 22 B1
 Borwd.
Bradbury Clo., Sthl. 63 F4
Bradbury St. N16 50 B5
Braddon Rd., Rich. 73 J3
Braddyll St. SE10 69 E5
Braden St. W9 6 A6
Bradenham Ave., 80 A4
 Well.
Bradenham Clo. SE17 21 B5
Bradenham Clo. SE17 68 A6
Bradenham Rd., Har. 37 E4
Bradfield Dr., Bark. 53 A5
Bradfield Rd. E16 69 G2
Bradfield Rd., Ruis. 45 E5
Bradford Clo. SE26 86 E4
 Coombe Rd.
Bradford Clo., Brom. 104 C1
Bradford Dr., Epsom 93 F6
Bradford Rd. W3 65 E2
 Warple Way
Bradford Rd., Ilf. 52 G1
Bradgate Rd. SE6 78 A6
Brading Cres. E11 51 H2
Brading Rd. SW2 76 F7
Brading Rd., Croy. 94 F6
Bradiston Rd. W9 57 C3
Bradley Clo. N1 8 F1
Bradley Clo. N7 49 F6
 Sutterton St.
Bradley Gdns. W13 55 E6
Bradley Ms. SW17 84 J1
 Bellevue Rd.
Bradley Rd. N22 40 F2
Bradley Rd. SE19 85 J6
Bradman Row, Edg. 30 C7
 Pavilion Way
Bradmead SW8 67 B7
Bradmore Ho. E1 59 F5
 Jamaica St.
Bradmore Pk. Rd. W6 65 H4
Bradshaws Clo. SE25 95 D3
Bradstock Rd. E9 50 G6
Bradstock Rd., 99 G5
 Epsom
Bradwell Ave., Dag. 53 G2
Bradwell Clo. E18 42 F4
Bradwell Ms. N18 33 D4
 Lyndhurst Rd.
Bradwell Rd., Buck.H. 35 B1
Bradwell St. E1 59 G3
Brady Ave., Loug. 27 F2
Brady St. E1 59 E4
Braemar Ave. N22 40 E1
Braemar Ave. NW10 47 D3
Braemar Ave. SW19 84 D2
Braemar Ave., Bexh. 80 J4
Braemar Ave., 94 G3
 Th.Hth.
Braemar Ave., Wem. 46 G7
Braemar Gdns. NW9 38 D1
Braemar Gdns., Sid. 88 G3
Braemar Gdns., 103 C1
 W.Wick.
Braemar Rd. E13 60 G2
Braemar Rd. N15 41 B5
Braemar Rd., Brent. 64 G6
Braemar Rd., 99 H3
 Wor.Pk.
Braes St. N1 49 H7
Braeside, Beck. 87 A5
Braeside Ave. SW19 93 B1
Braeside Clo., Pnr. 28 G7
 The Ave.
Braeside Cres., Bexh. 80 J4
Braeside Rd. SW16 85 C7
Braesyde Clo., Belv. 71 F4
Brafferton Rd., 101 J4
 Croy.
Braganza St. SE17 20 G4
Braganza St. SE17 67 H5
Braham St. E1 13 G4
Braham St. E1 59 C6
Braid Ave. W3 56 E6
Braid Clo., Felt. 81 F2
Braidwood Rd. SE6 87 D1
Braidwood St. SE1 17 D2
Brailsford Clo., 84 H7
 Mitch.
Brailsford Rd. SW2 76 G5
Brainton Ave., Felt. 72 B7
Braintree Ave., Ilf. 44 B4
Braintree Rd., Dag. 53 G3
Braintree Rd., Ruis. 45 B4
Braintree St. E2 59 F4
Braithwaite Ave., 44 G7
 Rom.
Braithwaite Gdns., 37 F1
 Stan.
Braithwaite Rd., Enf. 25 J3

Bramah Grn. SW9 76 G1
Bramalea Clo. N6 40 A6
Bramall Clo. E15 51 F5
 Idmiston Rd.
Bramber Ct. W5 64 H4
 Sterling Pl.
Bramber Rd. N12 31 H5
Bramber Rd. W14 66 C6
Bramble Acres Clo., 100 D7
 Sutt.
Bramble Clo., Croy. 103 A4
Bramble Clo., Stan. 29 G7
Bramble Cft., Erith 71 J4
Bramble Gdns. W12 56 F7
 Wallflower St.
Bramble La., Hmptn. 81 F6
Bramblebury Rd. 70 F5
 SE18
Brambledown Clo., 96 E5
 W.Wick.
Brambledown Rd., 101 A7
 Cars.
Brambledown Rd., 102 B7
 S.Croy.
Brambledown Rd., 101 B7
 Wall.
Brambles, The, Chig. 35 F6
Brambles Clo., Islw. 64 E7
Bramblewood Clo., 100 J1
 Cars.
Bramblings, The E4 34 D4
Bramcote Ave., 93 J4
 Mitch.
Bramcote Gro. SE16 68 F5
Bramcote Rd. SW15 74 H4
Bramdean Cres. 87 G1
 SE12
Bramdean Gdns. 87 G1
 SE12
Bramerton Rd., 95 J3
 Beck.
Bramerton St. SW3 18 G5
Bramerton St. SW3 66 H6
Bramfield Ct. N4 49 J2
 Queens Dr.
Bramfield Rd. SW11 75 H6
Bramford Ct. N14 32 D2
Bramford Rd. SW18 75 F4
Bramham Gdns. SW5 18 A3
Bramham Gdns. SW5 66 E5
Bramham Gdns., 98 G4
 Chess.
Bramhope La. SE7 69 H6
Bramlands Clo. SW11 75 H3
Bramley Clo. E17 41 H2
Bramley Clo. N14 24 B5
Bramley Clo., Hayes 54 A7
 Orchard Rd.
Bramley Clo., Orp. 104 E1
Bramley Clo., 101 H5
 S.Croy.
Bramley Ct., Well. 80 B1
Bramley Cres. SW8 19 J7
Bramley Cres., Ilf. 43 D6
Bramley Gdns., Wat. 28 C5
Bramley Hill, 101 H5
 S.Croy.
Bramley Rd. N14 24 B5
Bramley Rd. W5 64 F3
Bramley Rd. W10 57 A7
Bramley Rd., Sutt. 100 G5
Bramley St. W10 57 A6
Bramley Way, Houns. 72 F5
Bramley Way, 103 B2
 W.Wick.
Brampton Clo. E5 50 E2
Brampton Gdns. N15 40 J5
 Brampton Rd.
Brampton Gro. NW4 38 H4
Brampton Gro., Har. 37 D4
Brampton Gro., Wem. 46 J1
Brampton La. NW4 38 H4
Brampton Pk. Rd. N8 40 G3
Brampton Rd. E6 61 A4
Brampton Rd. N15 40 J5
Brampton Rd. NW9 38 A4
Brampton Rd. SE2 71 C6
Brampton Rd., Bexh. 80 D3
Brampton Rd., Croy. 95 C7
Brampton Rd., Wat. 28 A3
Bramsham Gdns., 28 D5
 Wat.
Bramshaw Ri., N.Mal. 92 E6
Bramshaw Rd. E9 50 G8
Bramshill Clo., Chig. 35 H5
 Tine Rd.
Bramshill Gdns. NW5 49 B3
Bramshill Rd. NW10 56 E2
Bramshot Ave. SE7 69 G6
Bramshot Way, Wat. 28 A2
Bramston Clo., Ilf. 35 J6
Bramston Rd. NW10 56 G2

Bramwell Clo., Sun. 90 D2
Brancaster Rd. E12 52 C4
Brancaster Rd. SW16 85 E3
Brancaster Rd., Ilf. 43 G6
Brancepeth Gdns., 34 G2
 Buck.H.
Branch Hill NW3 48 F3
Branch Pl. N1 59 A1
Branch Rd. E14 59 H7
Brancker Clo., Wall. 101 E7
 Brown Clo.
Brancker Rd., Har. 37 G3
Brancroft Way, Enf. 25 H1
Brand St. SE10 69 C7
Brandlehow Rd. 75 C4
 SW15
Brandon Est. SE17 20 H6
Brandon Est. SE17 67 H6
Brandon Rd. E17 42 C3
Brandon Rd. N7 49 E7
Brandon Rd., Sthl. 63 F5
Brandon Rd., Sutt. 100 E4
Brandon St. SE17 21 A2
Brandon St. SE17 67 J4
Brandram Rd. SE13 78 E3
Brandreth Rd. E6 61 C6
Brandreth Rd. SW17 85 B2
Brandries, The, 101 D3
 Wall.
Brandville Gdns., Ilf. 43 E4
Brandy Way, Sutt. 100 D7
Brangbourne Rd., 87 E5
 Brom.
Brangton Rd. SE11 20 D4
Brangton Rd. SE11 67 F5
Brangwyn Cres. SW19 93 F2
Branksea St. SW6 66 B7
Branksome Ave. N18 33 C6
Branksome Rd. SW2 76 E4
Branksome Rd. SW19 93 D1
Branksome Way, Har. 37 H6
Branksome Way, 92 C1
 N.Mal.
Bransby Rd., Chess. 98 H7
Branscombe Gdns. 24 A1
 N21
Branscombe St. SE13 78 B3
Bransdale Clo. NW6 57 E1
 West End La.
Bransgrove Rd., Edg. 29 J7
 Merlin Cres.
Branston Cres., Orp. 104 G1
Branstone Rd., Rich. 73 J1
Brants Wk. W7 55 B4
Brantwood Ave., 73 D4
 Erith
Brantwood Ave., 73 D4
 Islw.
Brantwood Clo. E17 42 B3
Brantwood Gdns., 24 E4
 Enf.
Brantwood Gdns., 43 B4
 Ilf.
Brantwood Rd. N17 33 C6
Brantwood Rd. SE24 76 J5
Brantwood Rd., 80 H2
 Bexh.
Brasher Clo., Grnf. 46 A5
 Lilian Board Way
Brass Tally All. SE16 68 G2
 Archangel St.
Brassey Rd. NW6 48 C6
Brassey Sq. SW11 76 A3
Brassie Ave. W3 56 E6
Brasted Clo. SE26 78 E4
Brasted Clo., Bexh. 80 D5
Brathway Rd. SW18 75 D7
Bratley St. E1 9 H6
Braund Ave., Grnf. 54 H4
Braundton Ave., 88 J1
 Sid.
Braunston Dr., 55 C4
 Hayes
Bravington Pl. W9 57 C4
 Bravington Rd.
Bravington Rd. W9 57 C3
Brawne Ho. SE17 20 H6
Braxfield Rd. SE4 76 J1
Braxted Pk. SW16 85 F6
Bray NW3 48 H7
Bray Clo., Borwd. 22 C1
 Marlow Way
Bray Cres. SE16 68 G2
Bray Dr. E16 60 F7
 Bowman Ave.
Bray Pas. E16 60 F7
 Bowman Ave.
Bray Pl. SW3 18 J2
Bray Rd. SW3 66 J4
Bray Rd. NW7 23 J6
Brayards Rd. SE15 77 E2
Braybourne Dr., Islw. 64 C7
Braybrook St. W12 56 F5

Braybrooke Gdns. 86 C7
 SE19
 Fox Hill
Brayburne Ave. SW4 76 C2
Braycourt Ave., 90 B7
 Walt.
Braydon Rd. N16 41 D7
Brayfield Ter. N1 49 G7
 Lofting Rd.
Brayford Sq. E1 59 H6
 Summercourt Rd.
Brayton Gdns., Enf. 24 D4
Braywood Rd. SE9 79 G4
Brazil Clo., Croy. 94 E7
Breach La., Dag. 62 G3
Bread St. EC4 13 A5
Bread St. EC4 58 J7
Breakspears Rd. SE4 77 J3
Bream Gdns. E6 61 D3
Bream St. E3 51 A7
Breamore Clo. SW15 83 G1
Breamore Rd., Ilf. 52 J2
Bream's Bldgs. EC4 12 E3
Bream's Bldgs. EC4 58 G4
Breamwater Gdns., 82 E3
 Rich.
Brearley Clo., Edg. 30 C7
 Pavilion Way
Breasley Clo. SW15 74 H4
Brechin Pl. SW7 18 D2
Brechin Pl. SW7 66 B4
Brecknock Rd. N7 49 D5
Brecknock Rd. N19 49 C4
Brecknock Rd. Est. 49 C4
 N7
Brecon Clo., Mitch. 94 E3
Brecon Clo., Wor.Pk. 99 J2
 Cotswold Way
Brecon Rd. W6 66 B6
Brecon Rd., Enf. 25 F4
Brede Clo. E6 61 D3
Bredgar Rd. N19 49 C2
Bredhurst Clo. SE20 86 F6
Bredon Rd. SE5 76 J3
Bredon Rd., Croy. 95 C7
Breer St. SW6 75 E3
Breezers Hill E1 13 J6
Brember Rd., Har. 45 J2
Bremner Rd. SW7 14 D5
Brenchley Clo., Brom. 96 F6
Brenchley Clo., Chis. 97 D1
Brenchley Gdns. 61 B5
 SE23
Brenchley Rd., Orp. 97 H1
Brenda Rd. SW17 84 J2
Brende Gdns., 90 H4
 W.Mol.
Brendon Ave. NW10 47 E4
Brendon Gdns., Har. 45 H4
Brendon Gdns., Ilf. 43 H5
Brendon Rd. SE9 88 G2
Brendon Rd., Dag. 53 F1
Brendon St. W1 10 H3
Brendon St. W1 57 H6
Brendon Way, Enf. 25 B7
Brenley Clo., Mitch. 94 A3
Brenley Gdns. SE9 79 A4
Brent Clo., Bex. 89 E1
Brent Cres. NW10 55 J2
Brent Cross Shop. 38 J7
 Cen. NW4
Brent Grn. NW4 38 J5
Brent Grn. Wk., Wem. 47 G7
Brent Lea, Brent. 64 F7
Brent Pk. NW10 47 D5
Brent Pk. Rd. NW4 38 H7
Brent Pl., Barn. 23 D5
Brent Rd. E16 60 G5
Brent Rd. SE18 70 E7
Brent Rd., Brent. 64 F6
Brent Rd., Sthl. 63 C3
Brent St. NW4 38 J4
Brent Ter. NW2 47 J1
Brent Vw. Rd. NW9 38 G6
Brent Way N3 31 D6
Brent Way, Brent. 64 G7
Brent Way, Wem. 47 B6
Brentcot Clo. W13 55 E4
Brentfield NW10 47 B7
Brentfield Clo. NW10 47 D6
 Normans Mead
Brentfield Gdns. 39 G7
 NW2
 Hendon Way
Brentfield Rd. NW10 47 D6
Brentford Business 64 F7
 Cen., Brent.
Brentford Clo., Hayes 54 D4
Brentham Way W5 55 G4
Brenthouse Rd. E9 50 F6
Brenthurst Rd. NW10 47 F6
Brentmead Clo. W7 55 B7
Brentmead Gdns. 55 J2
 NW10

Brentmead Pl. NW11 39 A6
North Circular Rd.
Brenton St. E14 59 H6
Brentside, Brent. 64 F6
Brentside Clo. W13 55 D4
Brentside Executive 64 E6
Cen., Brent.
Brentvale Ave., Sthl. 64 A1
Brentvale Ave., 55 J1
Wem.
Brentwick Gdns., 64 H4
Brent.
Brentwood Clo. SE9 88 F1
Brentwood Ho. SE18 70 A7
Shooter's Hill Rd.
Brereton Rd. N17 33 C7
Bressenden Pl. SW1 15 E5
Bressenden Pl. SW1 67 B3
Bressey Gro. E18 42 F2
Brett Clo. N16 50 B2
Yoakley Rd.
Brett Clo., Nthlt. 54 D3
Broomcroft Ave.
Brett Ct. N9 33 F2
Brett Cres. NW10 47 D7
Brett Gdns., Dag. 53 E7
Brett Ho. Clo. SW15 75 A6
Putney Heath La.
Brett Pas. E8 50 E5
Kenmure Rd.
Brett Rd. E8 50 E5
Brettell St. SE17 21 C4
Brottonham Avo. E17 42 A1
Penrhyn Ave.
Brettenham Rd. E17 42 A2
Brettenham Rd. N18 33 D4
Brewer St. W1 11 G5
Brewer St. W1 58 C7
Brewer's Grn. SW1 15 G5
Brewers La., Rich. 73 G5
George St.
Brewery Clo., Wem. 46 D5
Brewery La., Twick. 73 C7
Brewery Rd. N7 49 E7
Brewery Rd. SE18 70 G5
Brewery Rd., Brom. 104 B1
Brewhouse La. E1 68 E1
Brewhouse Rd. SE18 70 C4
Brewhouse St. SW15 75 B3
Brewhouse Wk. SE16 68 H1
Brewhouse Yd. EC1 8 G5
Brewood Rd., Dag. 53 B6
Brewster Gdns. W10 56 J5
Brewster Ho. E14 59 J7
Brewster Rd. E10 51 B1
Brian Rd., Rom. 44 C5
Briant St. SE14 77 G1
Briants Clo., Pnr. 36 F2
Briar Ave. SW16 85 F7
Briar Clo. N2 39 E2
Briar Clo. N13 32 J3
Briar Clo., Buck.H. 35 A2
Briar Clo., Hmptn. 81 F5
Briar Clo., Islw. 73 C5
Briar Ct., Sutt. 99 J4
Briar Cres., Nthlt. 45 H6
Briar Gdns., Brom. 103 F1
Briar La., Croy. 103 B4
Briar Pas. SW16 94 E3
Pollards Cres.
Briar Pl. SW16 94 F3
Briar Rd.
Briar Rd. NW2 47 J4
Briar Rd. SW16 94 E3
Briar Rd., Har. 37 F5
Briar Rd., Twick. 82 B1
Briar Wk. SW15 74 H4
Briar Wk. W10 57 B4
Droop St.
Briar Wk., Edg. 30 C7
Briarbank Rd. W13 55 D6
Briardale Gdns. NW3 48 D3
Briarfield Ave. N3 39 E2
Briars Clo. N17 33 E7
Briarswood Way, 104 J5
Orp.
Briarwood Clo. NW9 38 C6
Briarwood Dr., 36 A2
Nthwd.
Briarwood Rd. SW4 76 D5
Briarwood Rd., 99 G6
Epsom
Briary Clo. NW3 48 H7
Fellows Rd.
Briary Ct., Sid. 89 B5
Briary Gdns., Brom. 87 H5
Briary Gro., Edg. 38 B2
Briary La. N9 33 C3
Brick Ct. EC4 12 E4
Brick Fm. Clo., Rich. 74 B1
Brick La. E1 9 G4
Brick La. E1 59 C4
Brick La. E2 9 G6

Brick La. E2 59 C3
Brick La., Enf. 25 E2
Brick La., Stan. 29 G7
Honeypot La.
Brick St. W1 15 D2
Brick St. W1 67 B1
Brickfield Clo., Brent. 64 F7
Brickfield Cotts. 70 J6
SE18
Brickfield La., Barn. 22 F6
Brickfield Rd. E3 60 B4
Brickfield Rd. SW19 84 E4
Brickfield Rd., Th.Hth. 94 H1
Brickfields, Har. 46 A2
Bricklayer's Arms 21 E1
SE1
Brickwood Clo. SE26 86 E3
Brickwood Rd., Croy.102 B2
Bride Ct. EC4 12 G4
Bride La. EC4 12 G4
Bride Pl., Croy. 102 A1
Bride St. N7 49 F6
Bridewell Pl. E1 68 E1
Brewhouse La.
Bridewell Pl. EC4 12 G4
Bridford Ms. W1 11 E1
Bridge, The, Har. 37 C4
Bridge App. NW1 49 A7
Bridge Ave. W6 65 H5
Bridge Ave. W7 55 A5
Bridge Clo., Enf. 25 E2
Bridge End E17 42 C1
Bridge Gate N21 24 J7
Prestons Rd.
Bridge Ho. Quay E14 69 C1
Bridge La. NW11 39 B4
Bridge La. SW11 75 H1
Bridge Pk. SW18 75 D5
Bridge Pl. SW1 19 E1
Bridge Pl. SW1 67 B4
Bridge Pl., Croy. 102 A1
Bridge Rd. E6 52 C7
Bridge Rd. E15 60 D1
Bridge Rd. E17 41 J7
Bridge Rd. N9 33 D3
Fore St.
Bridge Rd. N22 40 E1
Bridge Rd. NW10 47 E6
Bridge Rd., Beck. 86 J7
Bridge Rd., Bexh. 80 F3
Bridge Rd., Chess. 98 G5
Bridge Rd., Croy. 101 J3
Duppas Hill Rd.
Bridge Rd., E.Mol. 91 A5
Bridge Rd., Houns. 73 A3
Bridge Rd., Islw. 73 A3
Bridge Rd., Sthl. 63 F2
Bridge Rd., Sutt. 100 E6
Bridge Rd., Twick. 73 E6
Bridge Rd., Wall. 101 B5
Bridge Rd., Wem. 47 A3
Bridge Row, Croy. 102 A1
Cross Rd.
Bridge St. SW1 16 A4
Bridge St. SW1 67 E2
Bridge St. W4 65 D4
Bridge St., Pnr. 36 E3
Bridge St., Rich. 73 G5
Bridge Ter. E15 51 F7
Bridge Vw. W6 65 J5
Bridge Way N11 49 F7
Bridge Way NW11 39 C5
Bridge Way, Twick. 72 J7
Bridge Way, Wem. 46 H7
Bridge Wf. Rd., Islw. 73 E3
Church St.
Bridge Wks. Ind. Est., 64 E4
Uxb.
Bridgefield Rd. SE1 17 C1
Bridgefield Rd., Sutt. 100 D6
Bridgefoot SE1 20 B4
Bridgefoot SE1 67 E5
Bridgeford St. SW18 84 F3
Bridgeland Rd. E16 60 G7
Bridgeman Rd. N1 49 F7
Bridgeman Rd. W4 65 C3
Bridgeman Rd., Tedd. 82 D6
Bridgeman St. NW8 6 G2
Bridgeman St. NW8 57 H2
Bridgen Rd., Bex. 80 E6
Bridgend Rd. SW18 75 F4
Bridgenhall Rd., Enf. 25 G1
Bridgeport Pl. E1 17 J1
Bridgeport Pl. E1 68 D1
Bridges Ct. SW11 75 G3
Bridges La., Croy. 101 E4
Bridges Pl. SW6 75 C1
Bridges Rd. SW19 84 E6
Bridges Rd., Stan. 29 C5
Bridges Rd. Ms. 84 E6
SW19
Bridges Rd.

Bridgetown Clo. 86 B5
SE19
St. Kitts Ter.
Bridgeview Ct., Ilf. 35 G6
Bridgewater Clo., 97 H3
Chis.
Bridgewater Gdns., 37 J2
Edg.
Bridgewater Rd., 45 A4
Ruis.
Bridgewater Rd., 46 F6
Wem.
Bridgewater Sq. EC2 12 J1
Bridgewater St. EC2 12 J1
Bridgeway, Bark. 52 J7
Bridgeway St. NW1 7 G2
Bridgeway St. NW1 58 C2
Bridgewood Clo. 86 E7
SE20
Bridgewood Rd. 85 D7
SW16
Bridgewood Rd., 99 G3
Wor.Pk.
Bridgwater Rd. E15 60 C1
Bridle Ave., Epsom 99 D5
Bridle Clo., Kings.T. 91 G4
Bridle La. W1 11 G5
Bridle Path, Croy. 101 E3
Bridle Path, Wdf.Grn. 34 E7
Bridle Rd., Croy. 103 A3
Bridle Rd., Esher 98 E6
Bridle Rd., Pnr. 36 C6
Bridle Way, The, 101 C4
Wall.
Bridlington Rd. N9 25 E7
Bridlington Rd., Wat. 28 D3
Bridport Ave., Rom. 44 H6
Bridport Pl. N1 9 C1
Bridport Pl. N1 59 A1
Bridport Rd. N18 33 B5
Bridport Rd., Grnf. 54 H1
Bridport Rd., Th.Hth. 94 G3
Bridport Ter. SW8 76 D1
Wandsworth Rd.
Bridstow Pl. W2 57 D6
Talbot Rd.
Brief St. SE5 76 H1
Brierley, Croy. 103 B6
Brierley Ave. N9 33 F1
Brierley Clo. SE25 95 D4
Brierley Rd. E11 51 D4
Brierley Rd. SW12 85 C2
Brierly Gdns. E2 59 F2
Royston St.
Brig Ms. SE8 69 A6
Watergate St.
Brigade Clo., Har. 46 A2
Brigade St. SE3 78 F2
Royal Par.
Briggeford Clo. E5 50 D2
Geldeston Rd.
Bright Clo., Belv. 71 D4
Bright St. E14 60 B6
Brightfield Rd. SE12 78 F5
Brightling Rd. SE4 77 J6
Brightlingsea Pl. E14 59 J7
Brightman Rd. SW18 84 G1
Brighton Ave. E17 41 J5
Brighton Dr., Nthlt. 45 G6
Brighton Gro. SE14 77 H1
New Cross Rd.
Brighton Rd. E6 61 D3
Brighton Rd. N2 39 F2
Brighton Rd. N16 50 B4
Brighton Rd., 101 J5
S.Croy.
Brighton Rd., Surb. 91 F6
Brighton Ter. SW9 91 F4
Brightside, The, Enf. 25 G1
Brightside Rd. SE13 78 D6
Brightwell Cres. 84 J5
SW17
Brigstock Rd., Belv. 71 H4
Brigstock Rd., Th.Hth. 94 B4
Brill Pl. NW1 7 J2
Brill Pl. NW1 58 D2
Brim Hill N2 39 F4
Brimpsfield Clo. SE2 71 B3
Brimsdown Ave., 25 H2
Enf.
Brimsdown Ind. Est., 25 J2
Enf.
Brindle Gate, Sid. 88 H1
Pinewood Ave.
Brindley St. SE14 77 J1
Brindley Way, Brom. 87 G5
Brindley Way, Sthl. 54 H7
Brindwood Rd. E4 33 J3
Brinkburn Clo. SE2 71 A4
Brinkburn Clo., Edg. 38 B2
Brinkburn Gdns., Edg. 38 A3

Brinkley Rd., Wor.Pk. 99 H2
Brinklow Cres. SE18 70 E7
Brinklow Ho. W2 57 E5
Brinkworth Rd., Ilf. 43 B3
Brinkworth Way E9 50 J6
Brinsdale Rd. NW4 39 A3
Brinsley Rd., Har. 37 A2
Brinsley St. E1 59 E6
Watney St.
Brinsworth Clo., 82 A1
Twick.
Brinton Wk. SE1 16 G2
Brion Pl. E14 60 C5
Brisbane Ave. SW19 93 E1
Brisbane Rd. E10 51 B2
Brisbane Rd. W13 64 D2
Brisbane Rd., Ilf. 43 E7
Brisbane St. SE5 68 A7
Briscoe Clo. E11 51 F2
Briscoe Rd. SW19 84 G1
Briset Rd. SE9 79 A3
Briset St. EC1 12 G1
Briset Way N7 49 F2
Bristol Gdns. W9 6 B6
Bristol Gdns. W9 57 E4
Bristol Ms. W9 6 B6
Bristol Ms. W9 57 E4
Bristol Pk. Rd. E17 41 H4
Hervey Pk. Rd.
Bristol Rd. E7 51 J6
Bristol Rd., Grnf. 54 H1
Bristol Rd., Mord. 93 F5
Bristol Rd., Wem. 40 E6
Goodwin Rd.
Bristow Rd., Bexh. 80 E1
Bristow Rd., Croy. 101 E4
Bristow Rd., Houns. 72 H3
Britannia Clo. SW4 76 D4
Clapham Cres.
Britannia Clo., Nthlt. 54 D3
Britannia La., Twick. 72 J7
Britannia Rd. E14 69 A4
Britannia Rd. N12 31 F3
Britannia Rd. SW6 66 E7
Britannia Rd., Ilf. 52 E3
Britannia Rd., Surb. 91 J7
Britannia Row N1 58 H1
Britannia St. WC1 8 C3
Britannia St. WC1 58 F3
Britannia Wk. N1 9 B3
Britannia Way NW10 56 R4
Britannia Way SW6 75 E1
Britannia Rd.
British Gro. W4 65 F5
British Gro. Pas. W4 65 F5
British Gro. S. W4 65 F5
British Gro. Pas.
British Legion Rd. E4 34 F2
British St. E3 59 J3
Brittain Rd., Dag. 53 E3
Britten Clo. NW11 48 E1
Britten Dr., Sthl. 55 G7
Britten St. SW3 18 G4
Britten St. SW3 66 H5
Brittenden Clo., Orp. 104 H6
Britten's Ct. E1 59 E7
The Highway
Britton St. EC1 8 G5
Britton St. EC1 58 H4
Brixham Cres., Ruis. 45 A1
Brixham Gdns., Ilf. 52 H5
Brixham Rd., Well. 80 D1
Brixham St. E16 70 C1
Brixton Est., Edg. 38 B2
Brixton Hill SW2 76 E7
Brixton Hill Pl. SW2 76 E7
Brixton Hill
Brixton Oval SW2 76 G4
Brixton Rd. SW9 76 G3
Brixton Sta. Rd. SW9 76 G3
Brixton Water La. 76 G5
SW2
Broad Ct. WC2 12 A4
Broad Grn. Ave., 94 H7
Croy.
Broad La. EC2 13 D2
Broad La. EC2 59 F6
Broad La. N8 40 F5
Tottenham La.
Broad La. N15 41 C4
Broad La., Hmptn. 81 F7
Broad Lawn SE9 88 D2
Broad Oak, Wdf.Grn. 34 H5
Broad Oak Clo. E4 34 A5
Royston Ave.
Broad Sanctuary 15 J4
SW1
Broad Sanctuary 67 D2
SW1
Broad St., Dag. 53 G7
Broad St., Tedd. 82 C6
Broad St. Ave. EC2 13 D2
Broad St. Pl. EC2 13 C2
Broad Vw. NW9 38 A6

Name		
Broad Wk. N21	32	F2
Broad Wk. NW1	**7**	**C1**
Broad Wk. NW1	58	A1
Outer Circle		
Broad Wk. SE3	78	J2
Broad Wk. W1	**15**	**B1**
Broad Wk. W1	67	A1
Broad Wk., Houns.	72	D1
Broad Wk., Rich.	64	J7
Broad Wk., The W8	**14**	**C3**
Broad Wk., The W8	66	F1
Broad Wk., The,	91	C4
E.Mol.		
Broad Wk. La. NW11	39	C7
Broad Yd. EC1	**8**	**G6**
Broadbent Clo. N6	49	B1
Broadbent St. W1	**11**	**D5**
Broadberry Ct. N18	33	E6
Broadbridge Clo.	69	G7
SE3		
Broadcoombe,	102	F7
S.Croy.		
Broadcroft Ave.,	37	G2
Stan.		
Broadcroft Rd., Orp.	97	G7
Broadfield Clo. NW2	47	J3
Broadfield Ct.	29	B2
(Bushey), Wat.		
Broadfield Heights,	30	B4
Edg.		
Broadfield La. NW1	49	E7
Broadfield Rd. SE6	78	E7
Broadfield Sq., Enf.	25	E2
Broadfield Way,	34	J3
Buck.H.		
Broadfields, E.Mol.	91	A6
Broadfields, Har.	36	H1
Broadfields Ave.	24	G7
N21		
Broadfields Ave.,	30	B4
Edg.		
Broadfields La., Wat.	28	B1
Broadfields Way	47	F5
NW10		
Broadgate E13	60	J2
Broadgate Circle EC2	**13**	**D1**
Broadgate Rd. E16	61	A6
Fulmer Rd.		
Broadgates Ave.,	23	E1
Barn.		
Broadhead Strand	38	F1
NW9		
Broadheath Dr., Chis.	88	C5
Broadhinton Rd. SW4	76	B3
Broadhurst Ave.,	30	B4
Edg.		
Broadhurst Ave., Ilf.	52	J4
Broadhurst Clo. NW6	48	F6
Broadhurst Gdns.		
Broadhurst Clo.,	73	J5
Rich.		
Lwr. Gro. Rd.		
Broadhurst Gdns.	48	E6
NW6		
Broadhurst Gdns.,	35	F4
Chig.		
Broadhurst Gdns.,	45	C2
Ruis.		
Broadlands, The,	81	F3
Felt.		
Broadlands Ave.	85	E2
SW16		
Broadlands Ave.,	25	E3
Enf.		
Broadlands Clo. N6	40	A7
Broadlands Clo.	85	E2
SW16		
Broadlands Clo., Enf.	25	F3
Broadlands Rd. N6	39	J7
Broadlands Rd.,	87	H4
Brom.		
Broadlands Way,	92	F6
N.Mal.		
Broadlawns Ct., Har.	37	C1
Broadley St. NW8	**10**	**F1**
Broadley St. NW8	57	G5
Broadley Ter. NW1	**6**	**H6**
Broadley Ter. NW1	57	H4
Broadmayne SE17	**21**	**B3**
Broadmead SE6	87	A3
Broadmead Ave.,	92	G7
Wor.Pk.		
Broadmead Clo.,	81	G6
Hmptn.		
Broadmead Clo., Pnr.	28	E7
Broadmead Est.,	34	J7
Wdf.Grn.		
Broadmead Rd.,	54	E4
Hayes		
Broadmead Rd.,	54	E4
Nthlt.		
Broadmead Rd.,	34	G6
Wdf.Grn.		
Broadoaks, Surb.	99	B1
Broadoaks Way,	96	F5
Brom.		
Broadstone Pl. W1	**11**	**B2**
Broadview Rd. SW16	85	D7
Broadwalk E18	42	F3
Broadwalk, Har.	36	G5
Broadwall SE1	**16**	**F1**
Broadwall SE1	67	G1
Broadwater Gdns.	104	E4
Orp.		
Broadwater Rd. N17	41	B1
Broadwater Rd. SE28	70	F3
Broadwater Rd.	84	H4
SW17		
Broadway E15	51	D7
Broadway N20	31	F2
Broadway SW1	**15**	**H5**
Broadway SW1	67	D3
Broadway, Bark.	52	F7
Broadway, Bexh.	80	E4
Broadway, Grnf.	54	J4
Broadway, Surb.	99	B1
Broadway, The E4	34	C6
Broadway, The E13	60	H2
Broadway, The N8	40	E6
Broadway, The N9	33	D3
Broadway, The N22	40	G2
Broadway, The NW7	30	E5
Broadway, The SW19	84	D7
Broadway, The W5	55	G7
Broadway, The W7	64	B1
Broadway, The W13	64	D1
Broadway, The, Dag.	53	F2
Whalebone La. S.		
Broadway, The,	99	G5
Epsom		
Broadway, The, Har.	37	B2
Broadway, The,	27	F4
Loug.		
Broadway, The, Pnr.	28	F7
Broadway, The, Sthl.	54	D7
Broadway Ms., Stan.	29	F5
Broadway, The,	100	B6
Sutt.		
Broadway, The,	98	B1
T.Ditt.		
Hampton Ct. Way		
Broadway, The, Wem.	46	H3
East La.		
Broadway, The,	34	H6
Wdf.Grn.		
Broadway Ave.,	95	A5
Croy.		
Broadway Ave.,	73	E6
Twick.		
Broadway Clo.,	34	H6
Wdf.Grn.		
Broadway Ct. SW19	84	D6
The Bdy.		
Broadway Gdns.,	93	H4
Mitch.		
Broadway Mkt. E8	59	E1
Broadway Ms. E5	41	C7*
Broadwick St. W1	**11**	**G5**
Broadwick St. W1	58	C6
Brocas Clo. NW3	48	H7
Fellows Rd.		
Brock Pl. E3	60	B4
Brock Rd. E13	60	H5
Brock St. SE15	77	E3
Evelina Rd.		
Brockdish Ave., Bark.	52	J5
Brockenhurst, W.Mol.	90	F6
Brockenhurst Ave.,	99	E1
Wor.Pk.		
Brockenhurst Gdns.	30	E6
NW7		
Brockenhurst Gdns.,	52	F5
Ilf.		
Brockenhurst Rd.,	95	E7
Croy.		
Brockenhurst Way	94	D2
SW16		
Brocket Clo., Chig.	35	J5
Brocket Way, Chig.	35	H5
Brockham Clo. SW19	84	C5
Brockham Cres.,	103	D7
Croy.		
Brockham Dr. SW2	76	F7
Fairview Pl.		
Brockham Dr., Ilf.	43	E6
Brockham St. SE1	**17**	**A5**
Brockham St. SE1	67	J3
Brockhurst Clo., Stan.	29	C6
Brockill Cres. SE4	77	H4
Brocklebank Rd. SE7	69	H4
Brocklebank Rd.	75	F7
SW18		
Brocklehurst St. SE14	68	G7
Brocklesby Rd. SE25	95	E4
Brockley Ave., Stan.	29	H3
Brockley Clo., Stan.	29	H4
Brockley Cross SE4	77	H3
Endwell Rd.		
Brockley Footpath	77	F4
SE15		
Brockley Gdns. SE4	77	J5
Brockley Gro. SE4	77	J5
Brockley Hall Rd. SE4	77	H5
Brockley Hill, Stan.	29	F1
Brockley Ms. SE4	77	H5
Brockley Pk. SE23	77	H7
Brockley Ri. SE23	77	H7
Brockley Rd. SE4	77	J3
Brockley Vw. SE23	77	H7
Brockley Way SE4	77	G5
Brockleyside, Stan.	29	H4
Brockman Ri., Brom.	87	D4
Brocks Dr., Sutt.	100	B3
Brockshot Clo.,	64	G5
Brent.		
Brockway Clo. E11	51	F2
Brockwell Clo., Orp.	97	J4
Brockwell Pk. Gdns.	76	G7
SE24		
Brockworth Clo.	**21**	**E6**
SE15		
Brockworth Clo.	68	B6
SE15		
Broderick Gro. SE2	71	H4
Brodewater Rd.,	22	B2
Borwd.		
Brodia Rd. N16	50	B3
Brodie Rd. E4	34	C1
Brodie St. SE1	**21**	**G3**
Brodlove La. E1	59	H3
Brodrick Rd. SW17	84	H2
Brograve Gdns.,	96	B2
Beck.		
Broke Wk. E8	59	D1
Marlborough Ave.		
Broken Wf. EC4	**12**	**J5**
Brokesley St. E3	59	J3
Bromar Rd. SE5	77	B3
Bromborough Grn.,	28	C5
Wat.		
Brome Rd. SE9	79	C3
Bromefield, Stan.	37	F1
Bromehead St. E1	59	F6
Commercial Rd.		
Bromell's Rd. SW4	76	C4
Bromfelde Rd. SW4	76	D3
Bromfelde Wk. SW4	76	E2
Bromfield St. N1	**8**	**F1**
Bromfield St. N1	58	G2
Bromhall Rd., Dag.	53	B6
Bromhedge SE9	88	C3
Bromholm Rd. SE2	71	B3
Bromley Ave., Brom.	87	E7
Bromley Common	96	J4
Brom.		
Bromley Cres., Brom.	96	F3
Bromley Gdns.,	96	F3
Brom.		
Bromley Gro., Brom.	96	D2
Bromley Hall Rd. E14	60	E5
Bromley High St. E3	60	B3
Bromley Hill, Brom.	87	F7
Bromley La., Chis.	88	F7
Bromley Pl. W1	**11**	**F1**
Bromley Rd. E10	42	B6
Bromley Rd. E17	42	A2
Bromley Rd. N17	41	C1
Bromley Rd. N18	33	A3
Bromley Rd. SE6	87	B2
Bromley Rd., Beck.	96	B2
Bromley Rd. (BR1),	87	D4
Brom.		
Bromley Rd. (BR2),	96	E2
Brom.		
Bromley Rd., Chis.	97	E1
Bromley St. E1	59	H5
Brompton Arc. SW3	**14**	**J4**
Brompton Clo. SE20	95	D2
Selby Rd.		
Brompton Clo.,	72	F5
Houns.		
Brompton Gro. N2	39	H4
Brompton Pk. Cres.	**18**	**A6**
SW6		
Brompton Pk. Cres.	66	E6
SW6		
Brompton Pl. SW3	**14**	**H3**
Brompton Rd. SW3	66	H3
Brompton Rd. SW1	**14**	**H6**
Brompton Rd. SW1	66	J2
Brompton Rd. SW3	**18**	**G1**
Brompton Rd. SW3	66	H4
Brompton Rd. SW7	**14**	**H6**
Brompton Rd. SW7	66	H3
Brompton Sq. SW3	**14**	**H5**
Brompton Sq. SW3	66	H3
Brompton Ter. SE18	79	D1
Bromwich Ave. N6	49	A2
Bromyard Ave. W3	56	E7
Bromyard Ho. SE15	68	E7
Commercial Way		
Brondesbury Ct. NW2	48	A6
Brondesbury Ms.	48	D7
NW6		
Willesden La.		
Brondesbury Pk.	47	J7
NW2		
Brondesbury Pk.	48	A7
NW6		
Brondesbury Rd.	57	C2
NW6		
Brondesbury Vill.	57	C2
NW6		
Bronsart Rd. SW6	66	B7
Bronson Rd. SW20	93	A2
Bronte Clo. E7	51	G4
Bective Rd.		
Bronte Clo., Ilf.	43	D4
Bronte Ho. NW6	57	D3
Bronti Clo. SE17	**21**	**A4**
Bronti Clo. SE17	67	J5
Bronze St. SE8	69	A7
Brook Ave., Dag.	53	H7
Brook Ave., Edg.	30	B6
Brook Ave., Wem.	47	A3
Brook Clo. SW20	92	H3
Brook Clo., Chis.	97	D1
Brook Cres. E4	34	A4
Brook Cres. N9	33	E4
Brook Dr. SE11	**16**	**F6**
Brook Dr. SE11	67	G3
Brook Dr., Har.	36	J4
Brook Gdns. E4	34	B4
Brook Gdns. SW13	74	F3
Brook Gdns.,	92	C1
Kings.T.		
Brook Gate W1	**11**	**A6**
Brook Grn. W6	65	J3
Brook Ind. Est.,	63	D1
Hayes		
Brook La. SE3	78	H2
Brook La., Bex.	80	D6
Brook La., Brom.	87	G6
Brook La. N., Brent.	64	G5
Brook Mead, Epsom	99	E6
Brook Meadow N12	31	E3
Brook Ms. N. W2	**10**	**D5**
Brook Par., Chig.	35	E3
High Rd.		
Brook Pl., Barn.	23	D5
Brook Ri., Chig.	35	D3
Brook Rd. N8	40	E4
Brook Rd. N22	40	F3
Brook Rd. NW2	47	F2
Brook Rd., Borwd.	22	A1
Brook Rd., Buck.H.	34	G2
Brook Rd., Ilf.	43	H6
Brook Rd., Loug.	27	B4
Brook Rd., Surb.	98	H2
Brook Rd., Th.Hth.	94	J4
Brook Rd., Twick.	73	D6
Brook Rd. S., Brent.	64	G6
Brook St. N17	41	C2
High Rd.		
Brook St. W1	**11**	**D5**
Brook St. W1	58	A7
Brook St. W2	**10**	**F5**
Brook St. W2	57	G7
Brook St., Belv.	71	H5
Brook St., Erith	71	H6
Brook St., Kings.T.	91	H2
Brook Wk. N2	39	G1
Old Fm. Rd.		
Brook Wk., Edg.	30	D6
Brook Way, Chig.	35	D3
Brookbank Ave. W7	55	A5
Brookbank Rd. SE13	78	A3
Brookdale N11	32	C4
Brookdale Rd. E17	42	A3
Brookdale Rd. SE6	78	B6
Brookdale Rd., Bex.	80	E6
Brookdene Rd. SE18	70	J4
Brooke Ave., Har.	45	J3
Brooke Rd. E5	50	D3
Brooke Rd. E17	42	C4
Brooke Rd. N16	50	C3
Brooke St. EC1	**12**	**E2**
Brooke St. EC1	58	G5
Brookehowse Rd.	87	A2
SE6		
Brookend Rd., Sid.	88	H1
Brooke's Ct. EC1	**12**	**E1**
Brookfield N6	49	A3
Brookfield Ave. E17	42	C4
Brookfield Ave. NW7	30	H6
Brookfield Ave. W5	55	G4
Brookfield Ave.,	100	H4
Sutt.		
Brookfield Clo. NW7	30	H6
Brookfield Ct., Grnf.	54	J3
Brookfield Ct., Har.	37	G5
Brookfield Cres. NW7	30	H6

Brookfield Cres., Har. 37 H5
Brookfield Gdns., 98 C6
  Esher
Brookfield Pk. NW5 49 B3
Brookfield Path, 34 E6
  Wdf.Grn.
Brookfield Rd. E9 50 H6
Brookfield Rd. N9 33 D3
Brookfield Rd. W4 65 D2
Brookfields, Enf. 25 G4
Brookfields Ave., 93 H5
  Mitch.
Brookhill Clo. SE18 70 E5
Brookhill Clo., Barn. 23 H5
Brookhill Rd. SE18 70 E4
Brookhill Rd., Barn. 23 G5
Brookhouse Gdns. E4 34 E4
Brooking Rd. E7 51 G5
Brookland Clo. NW11 39 E4
Brookland Garth 39 E4
  NW11
Brookland Hill NW11 39 E4
Brookland Ri. NW11 39 D4
Brooklands Ave. 84 E2
  SW19
Brooklands Ave., Sid. 88 G2
Brooklands Dr., Grnf. 55 F1
Brooklands Pk. SE3 78 G3
Brooklands Rd., 98 C1
  T.Ditt.
Brooklands St. SW8 76 D1
Brooklea Clo. NW9 38 E1
Brooklyn Ave., Loug. 27 B4 [defective line]
Brooklyn Ave., Loug. 27 B4
Brooklyn Gro. SE25 95 E4
Brooklyn Rd. SE25 95 E4
Brooklyn Rd., Brom. 97 A5
Brookmead Ave. 97 C5
  Brom.
Brookmead Rd., 94 C6
  Croy.
Brookmill Rd. SE8 78 A1
Brooks Ave. E6 61 C4
Brooks Clo. SE9 88 D2
Brooks Ct. E15 51 B5
  Clays La.
Brooks La. W4 65 A6
Brook's Ms. W1 11 D5
Brook's Ms. W1 58 B7
Brooks Rd. E13 60 G1
Brooks Rd. W4 65 A5
Brooksbank St. E9 50 F6
Brooksby Ms. N1 49 G7
  Brooksby St.
Brooksby St. N1 49 G7
Brooksby's Wk. E9 50 G5
Brookscroft Rd. E17 42 B1
Brookshill, Har. 29 A5
Brookshill Ave., Har. 29 A5
Brookshill Dr., Har. 29 A5
Brookside N21 24 F6
Brookside, Barn. 23 H6
Brookside, Cars. 101 A5
Brookside, Ilf. 35 F6
Brookside, Orp. 97 J7
Brookside Clo., Barn. 23 B6
Brookside Clo., Felt. 81 A3
  Sycamore Clo.
Brookside Clo., Har. 37 G5
Brookside Clo. 45 E4
  (Kenton), Har.
Brookside Cres., 99 G1
  Wor.Pk.
  Green La.
Brookside Rd. N9 33 E4
Brookside Rd. N19 49 C2
  Junction Rd.
Brookside Rd. NW11 39 B6
Brookside Rd., 54 C7
  Hayes
Brookside S., Barn. 24 A7
Brookside Wk. N3 39 A3
Brookside Wk. N12 31 D6
Brookside Wk. NW4 39 B4
Brookside Wk. NW11 39 B4
Brookside Way, 95 G6
  Croy.
Brooksville Ave. NW6 57 H2
Brookvale, Erith 80 H1
Brookview Rd. SW16 85 C5
Brookville Rd. SW6 66 C7
Brookway SE3 78 G3
Brookwood Ave. 74 F3
  SW13
Brookwood Clo., 96 F4
  Brom.
Brookwood Rd. 84 C1
  SW18
Brookwood Rd., 72 H1
  Houns.
Broom Clo., Brom. 97 B6
Broom Clo., Tedd. 82 G7

Broom Gdns., Croy. 103 A3
Broom Lock, Tedd. 82 F6
Broom Mead, Bexh. 80 G5
Broom Pk., Tedd. 82 G7
Broom Rd., Croy. 103 A3
Broom Rd., Tedd. 82 E5
Broom Water, Tedd. 82 F6
Broom Water W., 82 F5
  Tedd.
Broomcroft Ave., 54 C3
  Nthlt.
Broome Rd., Hmptn. 79 F7
Broome Way SE5 67 J7
Broomfield E17 41 J7
Broomfield, Sun. 90 A1
Broomfield Ave. N13 32 F5
Broomfield Clo., 27 C6
  Loug.
Broomfield La. N13 32 E4
Broomfield Pl. W13 64 E1
  Broomfield Rd.
Broomfield Rd. N13 32 E5
Broomfield Rd. W13 64 E1
Broomfield Rd., Beck. 95 H4
Broomfield Rd., 80 G5
  Bexh.
Broomfield Rd., Rich. 73 J1
Broomfield Rd., Rom. 44 E7
Broomfield Rd., Surb. 98 J1
Broomfield Rd., 82 F6
  Tedd.
  Melbourne Rd.
Broomfield St. E14 99 A6 [defective line]
Broomgrove Gdns., 38 A1
  Edg.
Broomgrove Rd. SW9 76 F2
Broomhill Ri., Bexh. 80 G5
Broomhill Rd. SW18 75 D5
Broomhill Rd., Ilf. 53 A2
Broomhill Rd., 34 G6
  Wdf.Grn.
Broomhill Wk., 34 F7
  Wdf.Grn.
Broomhouse La. SW6 75 D2
Broomhouse Rd. 75 D2
  SW6
Broomloan La., Sutt. 100 D2
Broomsleigh St. NW6 48 C5
Broomwood Rd. 75 J6
  SW11
Broseley Gro. SE26 86 H5
Broster Gdns. SE25 95 C3
Brough Clo. SW8 67 E7
  Kenchester Clo.
Brougham Rd. E8 59 D1
Brougham Rd. W3 56 C6
Broughinge Rd., 22 A2
  Borwd.
Broughton Ave. N3 39 B3
Broughton Ave., 82 E3
  Rich.
Broughton Dr. SW9 76 G4
Broughton Gdns. N6 40 C6
Broughton Rd. SW6 75 E2
Broughton Rd. W13 55 E7
Broughton Rd., Orp. 104 J2
Broughton Rd., 94 G6
  Th.Hth.
Broughton St. SW8 76 A2
Brouncker Rd. W3 65 C2
Browells La., Felt. 81 B2
Brown Clo., Wall. 101 E7
Brown Hart Gdns. 11 C5
W1
Brown Hart Gdns. W1 58 A7
Brown St. W1 10 J3
Brown St. W1 57 J6
Brownfield St. E14 60 B6
Brownhill Rd. SE6 78 B7
Browning Ave. W7 55 C6
Browning Ave., Sutt. 100 H4
Browning Ave., 99 H1
  Wor.Pk.
Browning Clo. W9 6 D6
Browning Clo., 81 F4
  Hmptn.
Browning Clo., Well. 79 H1
Browning Est. SE17 21 A3
Browning Est. SE17 67 J5
Browning Ho. W12 56 J6
  Wood La.
Browning Ms. W1 11 C2
Browning Rd. E11 42 F7
Browning Rd. E12 52 C6
Browning St. SE17 21 A3
Browning St. SE17 67 J5
Browning Way, 72 D1
  Houns.
Brownlea Gdns., Ilf. 53 A2
Brownlow Ms. WC1 8 D6
Brownlow Ms. WC1 58 F4
Brownlow Rd. E7 51 H4
  Woodford Rd.

Brownlow Rd. E8 59 C1
Brownlow Rd. N3 31 E7
Brownlow Rd. N11 32 E6
Brownlow Rd. NW10 47 E7
Brownlow Rd. W13 64 D1
Brownlow Rd., 22 A4
  Borwd.
Brownlow Rd., Croy. 102 B4
Brownlow St. WC1 10 D2
Brown's Bldgs. EC3 13 E4
Browns La. NW5 49 B5
Browns Rd. E17 42 A3
Browns Rd., Surb. 91 J7
Brownspring Dr. SE9 88 E4
Brownswell Rd. N2 39 G2
Brownswood Rd. N4 49 H3
Broxash Rd. SW11 76 A6
Broxbourne Ave. E18 42 H4
Broxbourne Rd. E7 51 G3
Broxbourne Rd., 104 J1
  Orp.
Broxholm Rd. SE27 85 G3
Broxted Rd. SE6 86 J2
Broxwood Way NW8 57 H1
Bruce Castle Rd. N17 41 C1
Bruce Clo. W10 57 B5
  Ladbroke Gro.
Bruce Clo., Well. 80 B1
Bruce Gdns. N20 31 J3
  Balfour Gro.
Bruce Gro. N17 41 B1
Bruce Hall Ms. SW17 85 A4
  Brudenell Rd.
Bruce Rd. E3 60 B3
Bruce Rd. NW10 47 D7
Bruce Rd. SE25 95 A4
Bruce Rd., Barn. 23 B3
  St. Albans Rd.
Bruce Rd., Har. 37 B2
Bruce Rd., Mitch. 85 A7
Bruckner St. W10 57 C3
Brudenell Rd. SW17 84 J3
Bruffs Meadow, Nthlt. 45 E6
Bruges Pl. NW1 49 C7
  Randolph St.
Brumfield Rd., Epsom 99 C5
Brummell Clo., Bexh. 80 J3
Brundley Way, Brom. 87 G5
Brune St. E1 13 F2
Brune St. E1 59 F2
Brunel Clo. SE19 86 C6
Brunel Clo., Nthlt. 54 F3
Brunel Est. W2 57 D5
Brunel Pl., Sthl. 54 H6
Brunel Rd. SE16 68 F2
Brunel Rd. W3 56 E5
Brunel Rd., Wdf.Grn. 35 C5
Brunel St. E16 60 F6
  Victoria Dock Rd.
Brunel Wk. N15 41 B4
Brunel Wk., Twick. 72 G7
  Stephenson Rd.
Brunner Clo. NW11 39 E5
Brunner Rd. E17 41 H5
Brunner Rd. W5 55 G4
Bruno Pl., Wem. 47 C2
Brunswick Ave. N11 32 A3
Brunswick Cen. WC1 8 A4
Brunswick Clo., 80 D4
  Bexh.
Brunswick Clo., Pnr. 36 E6
Brunswick Clo., T.Ditt. 98 C1
Brunswick Clo., 82 A3
  Twick.
Brunswick Ct. SE1 17 E3
Brunswick Ct. SE1 68 B2
Brunswick Ct., Barn. 23 G5
  Henry Rd.
Brunswick Cres. N11 32 A3
Brunswick Gdns. W5 55 H4
Brunswick Gdns. W8 66 D1
Brunswick Gdns., Ilf. 35 F7
Brunswick Gro. N11 32 A3
Brunswick Ind. Pk. 32 B4
  N11
Brunswick Ms. SW16 85 D6
  Potters La.
Brunswick Ms. W1 11 A3
Brunswick Pk. SE5 77 A1
Brunswick Pk. Gdns. 32 A2
  N11
Brunswick Pk. Rd. 32 A2
  N11
Brunswick Pl. N1 9 C4
Brunswick Pl. N1 59 A3
Brunswick Pl. SE19 86 D7
Brunswick Quay 63 H3
  SE16
Brunswick Rd. E10 51 C1
Brunswick Rd. E14 60 C6
Brunswick Rd. N15 41 B4
Brunswick Rd. W5 55 G4
Brunswick Rd., Bexh. 80 D4

Brunswick Rd., 92 A1
  Kings.T.
Brunswick Rd., Sutt. 100 E4
Brunswick Sq. N17 33 C6
Brunswick Sq. WC1 8 B5
Brunswick Sq. WC1 58 E4
Brunswick St. E17 42 C5
Brunswick Vill. SE5 77 B1
Brunswick Way N11 32 B4
Brunton Pl. E14 59 H6
Brushfield St. E1 13 E1
Brushfield St. E1 59 B5
Brussels Rd. SW11 75 G4
Bruton Clo., Chis. 88 C7
  Bullers Wd. Dr.
Bruton La. W1 11 E6
Bruton La. W1 58 B7
Bruton Pl. W1 11 E6
Bruton Pl. W1 58 B7
Bruton Pl., Mord. 93 F4
Bruton St. W1 11 E6
Bruton St. W1 58 B7
Bruton Way W13 55 D5
Bryan Ave. NW10 47 H7
Bryan Clo., Sun. 81 A7
Bryan Rd. SE16 68 J2
Bryanston Ave., 81 H1
  Twick.
Bryanston Clo., Sthl. 63 F4
Bryanston Ms. E. W1 10 J2
Bryanston Ms. W. W1 10 J2
Bryanston Pl. W1 10 J2
Bryanston Sq. W1 10 J2
Bryanston Sq. W1 57 J5
Bryanston St. W1 10 J4
Bryanston St. W1 57 J6
Bryanstone Rd. N8 40 D5
Bryant Clo., Barn. 23 C5
Bryant Ct. E2 9 F1
Bryant Rd., Nthlt. 54 C3
Bryant St. E15 51 D7
Bryantwood Rd. N7 49 G5
Bryce Rd., Dag. 53 C4
Brycedale Cres. N14 32 C4
Bryden Clo. SE26 86 H5
Brydges Pl. WC2 12 A6
Brydges Rd. E15 51 D5
Brydon Wk. N1 58 E1
  Outram Pl.
Bryett Rd. N7 49 E3
Brymay Clo. E3 60 A4
Bryn-y-Mawr Rd., 25 C4
  Enf.
Brynmaer Rd. SW11 75 J1
Bryony Rd. W12 56 G7
Buchan Rd. SE15 77 F3
Buchanan Ct., Borwd. 22 C2
  Banks Rd.
Buchanan Gdns. 56 H2
  NW10
Bucharest Rd. SW18 75 F7
Buck Hill Wk. W2 10 F6
Buck La. NW9 38 D4
Buck St. NW1 49 B7
Buck Wk. E17 42 D4
  Foresters Dr.
Buckden Clo. SE12 78 F6
  Upwood Rd.
Buckfast Rd., Mord. 93 E4
Buckfast St. E2 9 J4
Buckfast St. E2 59 D3
Buckhold Rd. SW18 75 D6
Buckhurst Ave., 100 H1
  Cars.
Buckhurst St. E1 59 E4
Buckhurst Way, 35 A4
  Buck.H.
Buckingham Arc. 12 B6
WC2
Buckingham Ave. 23 F7
  N20
Buckingham Ave., 72 B6
  Felt.
Buckingham Ave., 55 D1
  Grnf.
Buckingham Ave., 94 G1
  Th.Hth.
Buckingham Ave., 79 H4
  Well.
Buckingham Ave., 90 H3
  W.Mol.
Buckingham Clo. W5 55 F5
Buckingham Clo., Enf. 25 B2
Buckingham Clo., 81 F5
  Hmptn.
Buckingham Clo., 97 H7
  Orp.
Buckingham Ct. NW4 38 G3
Buckingham Dr., 88 E5
  Chis.
Buckingham Gdns., 29 H7
  Edg.

Buckingham Gdns., 94 G2
Th.Hth.
Buckingham Gdns., 90 H2
W.Mol.
Buckingham Ave.
Buckingham Gate 15 F4
SW1
Buckingham Gate 67 B3
SW1
Buckingham La. SE23 77 H2
Buckingham Ms. 56 F2
NW10
Buckingham Rd.
Buckingham Ms. 15 F5
SW1
Buckingham Palace 19 D2
Rd. SW1
Buckingham Palace 67 B4
Rd. SW1
Buckingham Pl. SW1 15 F5
Buckingham Rd. E10 51 B3
Buckingham Rd. E11 42 J5
Buckingham Rd. E15 51 F5
Buckingham Rd. E18 42 F1
Buckingham Rd. N1 50 B6
Buckingham Rd. N22 40 E1
Buckingham Rd. 56 F2
NW10
Buckingham Rd., 22 D4
Borwd.
Buckingham Rd., 29 J7
Edg.
Buckingham Rd., 81 F4
Hmptn.
Buckingham Rd., Har. 37 A5
Buckingham Rd., Ilf. 52 G2
Buckingham Rd., 91 J4
Kings.T.
Buckingham Rd., 94 E5
Mitch.
Buckingham Rd., 82 G2
Rich.
Buckingham St. WC2 12 B6
Buckland Cres. NW3 48 G7
Buckland Ri., Pnr. 36 C1
Buckland Rd. E10 51 C2
Buckland Rd., Chess. 98 A5
Buckland Rd., Orp. 104 H4
Buckland St. N1 9 C2
Buckland St. N1 59 A2
Buckland Wk., Mord. 93 F4
Buckland Way, 99 J1
Wor.Pk.
Bucklands Rd., Tedd. 82 F6
Buckle St. E1 13 G3
Buckleigh Ave. SW20 93 C3
Buckleigh Rd. SW16 85 D6
Buckleigh Way SE19 95 C1
Buckler Gdns. SE9 88 C3
Southold Rd.
Bucklers All. SW6 66 D6
Haldane Rd.
Bucklers Way, Cars. 100 J3
Bucklersbury EC4 13 B4
Bucklersbury EC4 59 A6
Buckles Ct., Belv. 71 D3
Fendyke Rd.
Buckley Rd. NW6 48 C7
Buckley St. SE1 16 E2
Buckley St. SE1 75 H4
SW11
Bucknall St. WC2 11 J3
Bucknall St. WC2 58 D6
Buckner Rd. SW2 76 F4
Buckrell Rd. E4 34 D2
Buckstone Clo. SE23 77 F6
Buckstone Rd. N18 33 D5
Buckters Rents SE16 68 H1
Buckthorne Rd. SE4 77 H6
Budd Clo. N12 31 E4
Buddings Circ., Wem. 47 C3
Budd's All., Twick. 73 F5
Arlington Clo.
Budge Row EC4 13 B5
Budge's Wk. W2 14 C1
Budge's Wk. W2 57 G7
Budich Ct., Ilf. 53 A2
Budleigh Cres., Well. 80 C1
Budoch Dr., Ilf. 53 A2
Buer Rd. SW6 75 B2
Bugsby's Way SE7 69 G4
Bugsby's Way SE10 69 G4
Buiganak Rd., Th.Hth. 94 J4
Bulinga St. SW1 20 A2
Bulinga St. SW1 67 D4
Bull All., Well. 80 B3
Welling High St.
Bull Inn Ct. WC2 12 B6
Bull La. N18 33 B5
Bull La., Chis. 88 G7
Bull La., Dag. 53 H3
Bull Rd. E15 60 F2

Bull Wf. La. EC4 13 A5
Bull Yd. SE15 77 D1
Peckham High St.
Bullards Pl. E2 59 G3
Bullbanks Rd., Belv. 71 J4
Bullen St. SW11 75 H2
Buller Clo. SE15 68 D7
Buller Rd. N17 41 D2
Buller Rd. N22 40 G2
Buller Rd. NW10 57 A3
Chamberlayne Rd.
Buller Rd., Bark. 52 H7
Buller Rd., Th.Hth. 95 A2
Bullers Clo., Sid. 89 E5
Bullers Wd. Dr., Chis. 88 C7
Bullescroft Rd., Edg. 30 A3
Bullhead Rd., Borwd. 22 C2
Bullied Way SW1 19 E2
Bullivant St. E14 60 C6
Bull's All. SW14 74 D2
Bulls Bri. Ind. Est., 63 B3
Sthl.
Bulls Bri. Rd., Sthl. 63 B3
Bulls Gdns. SW3 18 H1
Bull's Head Pas. EC3 13 D4
Bullsbrook Rd., 63 C1
Hayes
Bulmer Gdns., Har. 37 G7
Bulmer Ms. W11 57 D7
Kensington Pk. Rd.
Bulmer Pl. W11 66 D1
Bulow Ct. SW6 75 E2
Houns.
Bulstrode Ave., 72 F2
Houns.
Bulstrode Gdns., 72 F3
Houns.
Bulstrode Pl. W1 11 C2
Bulstrode Rd., Houns. 72 G3
Bulstrode St. W1 11 C3
Bulstrode St. W1 58 A6
Bulwer Ct. Rd. E11 51 D1
Bulwer Gdns., Barn. 23 F4
Bulwer Rd.
Bulwer Rd. E11 42 D7
Bulwer Rd. N18 33 B4
Bulwer Rd., Barn. 23 E4
Bulwer St. W12 65 J1
Bunces La., Wdf.Grn. 34 F7
Bungalow Rd. SE25 95 B4
Bungalows, The 85 B7
SW16
Bungalows, The, 101 B5
Wall.
Bunhill Row EC1 9 B5
Bunhill Row EC1 59 A4
Bunhouse Pl. SW1 19 B3
Bunhouse Pl. SW1 67 A5
Bunkers Hill NW11 39 F7
Bunkers Hill, Belv. 71 G4
Bunkers Hill, Sid. 89 F3
Bunning Way N7 49 E7
Bunns La. NW7 30 E6
Bunsen St. E3 59 H2
Kenilworth Rd.
Bunting Clo., Mitch. 93 J5
Buntingbridge Rd., 43 G5
Ilf.
Bunton St. SE18 70 D3
Creton St.
Bunyan Rd. E17 41 H3
Buonaparte Ms. SW1 19 H3
Burbage Clo. SE1 17 B6
Burbage Clo. SE1 68 A3
Burbage Rd. SE21 77 A7
Burbage Rd. SE24 76 J6
Burberry Clo., N.Mal. 92 E2
Burbridge Way N17 41 C2
Burcham St. E14 60 B6
Burcharbro Rd. SE2 71 D6
Burchell Rd. E10 51 B1
Burchell Rd. SE15 77 E1
Burchett Way, Rom. 44 F6
Burcote Rd. SW18 75 G7
Burden Clo., Brent. 64 F5
Burden Way E11 51 H2
Brading Cres.
Burdenshott Ave., 74 B4
Rich.
Burder Clo. N1 50 B6
Burder Rd. N1 50 B6
Balls Pond Rd.
Burdett Ave. SW20 92 G1
Burdett Clo., Sid. 89 E5
Burdett Ms. W2 10 A3
Burdett Rd. E3 59 H4
Burdett Rd. E14 59 J5
Burdett Rd., Croy. 95 A6
Burdett Rd., Rich. 73 J2
Burdett St. SE1 16 E5
Burdetts Rd., Dag. 62 F1
Burdock Clo., Croy. 102 G1
Burdock Rd. N17 41 D3
Burdon La., Sutt. 100 B7

Burfield Clo. SW17 84 G4
Burford Clo., Dag. 53 C3
Burford Clo., Ilf. 43 F4
Burford Gdns. N13 32 F3
Burford Rd. E6 61 B3
Burford Rd. E15 51 D7
Burford Rd. SE6 86 J2
Burford Rd., Brent. 64 B4
Burford Rd., Brom. 97 B4
Burford Rd., Sutt. 100 B2
Burford Rd., Wor.Pk. 92 F7
Burford Wk. SW6 66 E7
Cambria Rd.
Burford Way, Croy. 103 C6
Burges Ct. E6 52 E7
Burges Rd. E6 52 B7
Burgess Ave. NW9 38 D6
Burgess Clo., Felt. 81 E4
Burgess Hill NW2 48 D4
Burgess Rd. E15 51 E4
Burgess Rd., Sutt. 100 B2
Burgess St. E14 60 A5
Burgh St. N1 8 H1
Burgh St. N1 58 H2
Burghill Rd. SE26 86 H4
Burghley Ave., 22 C5
Borwd.
Burghley Ave., N.Mal. 92 D1
Burghley Pl., Mitch. 93 J5
Burghley Rd. E11 51 E1
Burghley Rd. N8 40 G3
Burghley Rd. NW5 49 B4
Burghley Rd. SW19 84 A4
Burghley Twr. W3 56 F7
Burgon St. EC4 12 H4
Burgos Gro. SE10 78 B1
Burgoyne Rd. N4 40 H6
Burgoyne Rd. SE25 95 C4
Burgoyne Rd. SW9 76 F3
Burham Clo. SE20 86 F7
Maple Rd.
Burhill Gro., Pnr. 36 E2
Burke Clo. SW15 74 E4
Burke St. E16 60 H6
Burland Rd. SW11 75 J5
Burleigh Ave., Sid. 79 J5
Burleigh Ave., Wall. 101 A3
Burleigh Gdns. N14 32 C1
Burleigh Ho. W10 57 A5
St. Charles Sq.
Burleigh Pl. SW15 75 A5
Burleigh Pl., Mitch 93 J5
Burleigh Rd., Enf. 25 B7
Burleigh Rd., Sutt. 100 B1
Burleigh St. WC2 12 B5
Burleigh Wk. SE6 87 C1
Muirkirk Rd.
Burley Clo. E4 34 A5
Burley Clo. SW16 94 D2
Burley Rd. E16 60 J5
Burlington Arc. W1 11 F6
Burlington Ave., Rich. 74 A1
Burlington Ave., 44 H6
Rom.
Burlington Clo. E6 61 B6
Northumberland Rd.
Burlington Clo. W9 57 C4
Burlington Clo., 104 E2
Orp.
Burlington Gdns. W1 11 F6
Burlington Gdns. W1 58 C7
Burlington Gdns. W3 65 C1
Burlington Gdns. W4 65 C5
Burlington Gdns., 44 E7
Rom.
Burlington La. W4 65 D7
Burlington Ms. W3 65 C1
Burlington Pl. SW6 75 B2
Burlington Rd.
Burlington Pl., 34 H3
Wdf.Grn.
Burlington Ri., Barn. 31 H1
Burlington Rd. N10 40 A2
Tetherdown
Burlington Rd. N17 41 D1
Burlington Rd. SW6 75 B2
Burlington Rd. W4 65 C5
Burlington Rd., Enf. 25 A1
Burlington Rd., Islw. 73 A1
Burlington Rd., 92 F4
N.Mal.
Burlington Rd., 94 J2
Th.Hth.
Burma Ms. N16 50 A4
Burma Rd. N16 50 A4
Burmester Rd SW17 84 F3
Burn Side N9 33 F3
Burnaby Cres. W4 65 C6
Burnaby Gdns. W4 65 B6
Burnaby St. SW10 66 F7
Burnbrae Clo. N12 31 E6
Burnbury Rd. SW12 85 C1

Burncroft Ave., Enf. 25 F2
Burne St. NW1 10 G1
Burne St. NW1 57 H5
Burnell Ave., Rich. 82 F5
Burnell Ave., Well. 80 A2
Burnell Gdns., Stan. 37 G1
Burnell Rd., Sutt. 100 E4
Burnell Wk. SE1 21 G3
Burnels Ave. E6 61 D3
Burness Clo. N7 49 F6
Roman Way
Burnett Clo. E9 50 F5
Burney Ave., Surb. 91 J5
Burney Dr., Loug. 27 E2
Burney St. SE10 69 C7
Burnfoot Ave. SW6 75 B1
Burnham NW3 48 H7
Burnham Clo. SE1 21 G2
Burnham Ct. NW4 38 J4
Burnham Cres. E11 42 J4
Burnham Dr., 100 A2
Wor.Pk.
Burnham Gdns., 95 C7
Croy.
Burnham Gdns., 72 B1
Houns.
Burnham Rd. E4 33 J5
Burnham Rd., Dag. 53 B7
Burnham Rd., Mord. 93 E5
Burnham St. E2 59 F3
Burnham St., 92 A1
Kings.T.
Burnham Way W13 64 E4
Burnhill Clo. SE15 68 D1
Burnhill Rd., Beck. 96 A2
Burnley Clo., Wat. 28 C5
Burnley Rd. NW10 47 F5
Burnley Rd. SW9 76 F2
Burns Ave., Felt. 72 A6
Burns Ave., Sid. 80 A6
Burns Ave., Sthl. 54 G7
Burns Clo. SW19 84 G6
North Rd.
Burns Clo., Well. 79 J1
Burns Rd. NW10 56 F1
Burns Rd. SW11 75 J2
Burns Rd. W13 64 E2
Burns Rd., Wem. 55 H2
Burns Way, Houns. 72 D2
Burnsall St. SW3 18 H3
Burnsall St. SW3 66 H5
Burnside Clo. SE16 68 G1
Burnside Clo., Barn. 23 D3
Burnside Clo., 73 D6
Twick.
Burnside Cres., Wem. 55 G1
Burnside Rd., Dag. 53 C2
Burnt Ash Hill SE12 78 F6
Burnt Ash La., 78 F5
Brom.
Burnt Ash Rd. SE12 78 F5
Burnt Oak Bdy., Edg. 30 B7
Burnt Oak Flds., Edg. 38 C1
Burnt Oak La., Sid. 89 A2
Burnthwaite Rd. SW6 66 C7
Burntwood Clo. 84 G1
SW18
Burntwood Gra. Rd. 84 G1
SW18
Burntwood La. SW17 84 F3
Buross St. E1 59 E6
Commercial Rd.
Burr Clo. E1 17 H1
Burr Clo., Bexh. 80 F3
Burr Rd. SW18 84 D1
Burrage Gro. SE18 70 F4
Burrage Pl. SE18 70 E5
Burrage Rd. SE18 70 F4
Burrard Rd. E16 60 H6
Burrard Rd. NW6 48 D5
Burrell Clo., Croy. 95 H6
Burrell Clo., Edg. 30 B2
Burrell Row, Beck. 96 A2
High St.
Burrell St. SE1 16 G1
Burrell St. SE1 67 H1
Burrell Twr. E10 42 A7
Burrells Wf. Sq. E14 69 B5
Burritt Rd., Kings.T. 92 A2
Burroughs, The NW4 38 H4
Burroughs Gdns. 38 H4
NW4
Burrow Clo., Chig. 35 J5
Burrow Rd.
Burrow Grn., Chig. 35 J5
Burrow Rd., Chig. 35 J5
Burrow Wk. SE21 76 J7
Rosendale Rd.
Burrows Ms. SE1 16 G3
Burrows Rd. NW10 56 J3
Bursdon Clo., Sid. 88 J2
Bursland Rd., Enf. 25 G4

Burslem St. E1 13 J4
Burslem St. E1 59 D6
Burstock Rd. SW15 75 B4
Burston Rd. SW15 75 A5
Burstow Rd. SW20 93 B1
Burt Rd. E16 69 J1
Burtenshaw Rd., 91 D7
T.Ditt.
Burtley Clo. N4 49 J1
Burton Clo. NW7 31 A4
Burton Clo., Chess. 98 G7
Burton Gdns., Houns. 72 F1
Burton Gro. SE17 21 B4
Burton La. SW9 76 G2
Burton Ms. SW1 19 C2
Burton Pl. WC1 7 J4
Burton Rd. E18 42 H3
Burton Rd. NW6 48 C7
Burton Rd. SW9 76 H2
Burton Rd., Kings.T. 82 H7
Burton Rd., Loug. 27 F4
Burton St. WC1 7 J4
Burton St. WC1 58 D3
Burtonhole La. NW7 30 J5
Burtons Rd., Hmptn. 81 H4
Burtwell La. SE27 86 A4
Burwash Ho. SE1 17 C4
Burwash Rd. SE18 70 G5
Burwell Ave., Grnf. 46 B6
Burwell Clo. E1 59 E6
Bigland St.
Burwell Rd. E10 50 H1
Burwell Wk. E3 80 A4
Burwood Ave., Brom.103 H2
Burwood Ave., Pnr. 36 B5
Burwood Clo., Surb. 99 A1
Burwood Pl. W2 10 H3
Burwood Pl. W2 57 H6
Bury Clo. SE16 68 G1
Rotherhithe St.
Bury Ct. EC3 13 E3
Bury Gro., Mord. 93 E5
Bury Pl. WC1 12 A2
Bury Pl. WC1 58 E5
Bury Rd. E4 26 E4
Bury Rd. N22 40 G3
Bury Rd., Dag. 53 H5
Bury St. EC3 13 E4
Bury St. EC3 59 B6
Bury St. N9 25 C7
Bury St. SW1 15 G1
Bury St. SW1 67 C1
Bury St. W. N9 25 A7
Bury Wk. SW3 18 G2
Bury Wk. SW3 66 H4
Busbridge Ho. E14 60 A5
Brabazon St.
Busby Ms. NW5 49 D6
Busby Pl. NW5 49 D6
Busby St. E2 9 G5
Bush Clo., Ilf. 43 G5
Bush Cotts. SW18 75 D5
Putney Bri. Rd.
Bush Ct. W12 66 A2
Bush Gro. NW9 38 C7
Bush Gro., Stan. 29 G7
Bush Hill N21 24 J7
Bush Hill Rd. N21 25 A6
Bush Hill Rd., Har. 37 J6
Bush Ind. Est. NW10 56 D4
Bush La. EC4 13 B5
Bush Rd. E8 59 E1
Bush Rd. E11 42 F7
Bush Rd. SE8 68 G4
Bush Rd., Buck.H. 35 A4
Bush Rd., Rich. 64 J6
Bushbaby Clo. SE1 17 D6
Bushberry Rd. E9 50 H6
Bushell Clo. SW2 85 F2
Bushell Grn. 29 A2
(Bushey), Wat.
Bushell St. E1 17 J2
Bushell Way, Chis. 88 D5
Bushey Ave. E18 42 F3
Bushey Ave., Orp. 97 G7
Bushey Ct. SW20 92 H3
Bushey Hill Rd. SE5 77 B1
Bushey La., Sutt. 100 D3
Bushey Lees, Sid. 79 J6
Fen Gro.
Bushey Rd. E13 60 J2
Bushey Rd. N15 41 B6
Bushey Rd. SW20 92 H3
Bushey Rd., Croy. 103 A2
Bushey Rd., Sutt. 100 D4
Bushey Way, Beck. 96 D6
Bushfield Clo., Edg. 30 B2
Bushfield Cres., 30 B2
Edg.
Bushfields, Loug. 48 D5
Bushgrove Rd., Dag. 53 D4
Bushmoor Cres. SE18 70 F7
Bushnell Rd. SW17 85 B2

Bushway, Dag. 53 D4
Bushwood E11 51 F1
Bushwood Dr. SE1 21 G2
Bushwood Dr. SE1 68 C4
Bushwood Rd., Rich. 65 A6
Bushy Pk. Gdns., 82 A5
Tedd.
Bushy Pk. Rd., Tedd. 82 E7
Bushy Rd., Tedd. 82 C6
Butcher Row E1 59 G7
Butcher Row E14 59 G7
Butchers Rd. E16 60 G6
Bute Ave., Rich. 82 H2
Bute Ct., Wall. 101 C5
Bute Rd.
Bute Gdns. W6 66 A4
Bute Gdns., Wall. 101 C5
Bute Gdns. W., Wall. 101 C5
Bute Rd., Croy. 101 G1
Bute Rd., Ilf. 43 E5
Bute Rd., Wall. 101 C5
Bute St. SW7 18 E1
Bute St. SW7 66 G4
Bute Wk. N1 50 A6
Marquess Rd.
Butler Ave., Har. 37 A7
Butler Pl. SW1 15 H5
Butler Rd. NW10 47 F7
Curzon Cres.
Butler Rd., Dag. 53 B4
Butler Rd., Har. 36 J7
Butler St. E2 59 F3
Butler St., Uxb.
Butter Hill, Cars. 101 A3
Butter Hill, Wall. 101 A3
Butterfield Clo. SE16 68 E2
Wilson Gro.
Butterfield Clo., 73 C6
Twick.
Rugby Rd.
Butterfield Sq. E6 61 C6
Guildford Rd.
Butterfields E17 42 C5
Butterfly La. SE9 79 E6
Butteridges Clo., Dag. 62 H1
Mord.
Buttermere Clo., 93 A6
Mord.
Buttermere Dr. 75 B5
SW15
Buttermere Wk. E8 50 C6
Butterwick W6 65 J4
Butterworth Gdns., 34 G5
Wdf.Grn.
Harts Gro.
Buttesland St. N1 9 C3
Buttesland St. N1 59 A3
Buttfield Clo., Dag. 53 H6
Buttmarsh Clo. SE18 70 E5
Butts, The, Brent. 64 F6
Butts, The, Sun. 90 C3
Elizabeth Gdns.
Butts Cotts., Felt. 81 F3
Butts Cres., Felt. 81 G3
Butts Piece, Nthlt. 54 B2
Longhook Gdns.
Butts Rd., Brom. 87 E5
Buttsbury Rd., Ilf. 52 F5
Buxted Clo. E8 50 C7
Buxted Rd. N12 31 H5
Buxton Clo., Wdf.Grn. 35 A6
Buxton Ct. N1 9 A3
Buxton Cres., Sutt. 100 B4
Buxton Dr. E11 42 E4
Buxton Dr., N.Mal. 92 D2
Buxton Gdns. W3 56 B7
Buxton Path, Wat. 28 C3
Buxton Rd. E4 26 D7
Buxton Rd. E6 61 B3
Buxton Rd. E15 51 E5
Buxton Rd. E17 41 H4
Buxton Rd. N19 49 D1
Buxton Rd. NW2 47 H6
Buxton Rd. SW14 74 E3
Buxton Rd., Ilf. 43 H6
Buxton Rd., Th.Hth. 94 H5
Buxton St. E1 9 G6
Buxton St. E1 59 C4
Buzzard Creek Ind. 61 J5
Est., Bark.
By the Wd., Wat. 28 D2
Byam St. SW6 75 F2
Byards Cft. SW16 94 D1
Byatt Wk., Hmptn. 81 E6
Victors Dr.
Bycroft Rd., Sthl. 54 G4
Bycroft St. SE20 86 G7
Parish La.
Bycullah Ave., Enf. 24 H3
Bycullah Rd., Enf. 24 H2
Bye, The W3 56 E6
Bye Way, The, Har. 37 C1
Bye Ways, Twick. 81 H3
Byegrove Rd. SW19 84 G6

Byeway, The SW14 74 C3
Byeway, The, Epsom 99 F4
Byeways, The, Surb. 92 A5
Byfeld Gdns. SW13 74 G1
Byfield Rd., Islw. 73 D3
Byford Clo. E15 51 E7
Bygrove, Croy. 103 B6
Bygrove St. E14 60 B6
Byland Clo. N21 24 F7
Byland Clo. SE2 71 B3
Finchale Rd.
Bylands Clo. SE16 68 G1
Rotherhithe St.
Byne Rd. SE26 86 F6
Byne Rd., Cars. 100 H2
Bynes Rd., S.Croy. 102 A7
Byng Pl. WC1 7 H6
Byng Pl. WC1 58 D4
Byng Rd., Barn. 23 A3
Byng St. E14 69 A2
Bynon Ave., Bexh. 80 F3
Byre, The N14 24 B6
Farm La.
Byre Rd. N14 24 A6
Farm La.
Byrne Rd. SW12 85 B1
Byron Ave. E12 52 B6
Byron Ave. E18 42 F3
Byron Ave. NW9 38 B4
Byron Ave., Borwd. 22 A5
Byron Ave., Houns. 72 A2
Byron Ave., N.Mal. 92 G5
Byron Ave. E., Sutt. 100 G4
Byron Clo. E8 59 D1
Byron Clo. SE28 71 C1
Byron Clo., Hmptn. 81 F4
Byron Ct. W9 57 D4
Lanhill Rd.
Byron Ct., Enf. 24 I12
Bycullah Rd.
Byron Dr. N2 39 G6
Byron Gdns., Sutt. 100 G4
Byron Hill Rd., Har. 46 A1
Byron Ho., Beck. 87 B6
Byron Ms. W9 57 D4
Shirland Rd.
Byron Rd. E10 51 B1
Byron Rd. E17 42 A3
Byron Rd. NW2 47 H2
Byron Rd. NW7 30 G5
Byron Rd. W5 64 J1
Byron Rd., Har. 37 C2
Byron Rd., 37 B6
(Wealdstone), Har.
Byron Rd., Wem. 46 F2
Byron St. E14 60 C6
St. Leonards Rd.
Byron Way, Nthlt. 54 E3
Bysouth Clo., Ilf. 43 E1
Bythorn St. SW9 76 F4
Byton Rd. SW17 84 J6
Byward Ave., Felt. 72 C6
Byward St. EC3 13 E6
Byward St. EC3 59 B7
Bywater Pl. SE16 60 H1
Bywater St. SW3 18 J3
Bywater St. SW3 66 J5
Bywell Pl. W1 11 F2
Bywood Ave., Croy. 95 F6
Byworth Wk. N19 49 D1
Courtauld Rd.

C

C.I. Twr., N.Mal. 92 E3
Cabbell St. NW1 10 G2
Cabbell St. NW1 57 H5
Cabinet Way E4 33 J6
Cable Pl. SE10 78 C1
Diamond Ter.
Cable St. E1 13 J5
Cable St. E1 59 D7
Cabot Sq. E14 69 A1
Cabot Way E6 61 A1
Parr Rd.
Cabul Rd. SW11 75 H2
Cactus Wk. W12 56 F7
Du Cane Rd.
Cadbury Way SE16 17 G6
Caddington Clo., 23 H5
Barn.
Caddington Rd. NW2 48 B3
Caddis Clo., Stan. 29 C7
Daventer Dr.
Cade Rd. SE10 78 D1
Cadell Clo. E2 9 G2
Cadet Dr. SE1 21 G3
Cadet Dr. SE1 68 C5
Cadet Pl. SE10 69 E5
Cadiz Rd., Dag. 53 J7

Cadiz St. SE17 21 A4
Cadiz St. SE17 67 J5
Cadley Ter. SE23 86 F2
Cadmer Clo., N.Mal. 92 E4
Cadogan Clo., Beck. 96 D1
Albemarle Rd.
Cadogan Clo., Har. 45 H4
Cadogan Clo., Tedd. 82 B5
Cadogan Ct., Sutt. 100 E6
Cadogan Gdns. E18 42 H3
Cadogan Gdns. N3 39 E1
Cadogan Gdns. N21 24 G5
Cadogan Gdns. SW3 19 A1
Cadogan Gdns. SW3 66 J4
Cadogan Gate SW1 19 A1
Cadogan Gate SW1 66 J4
Cadogan La. SW1 15 B6
Cadogan La. SW1 67 A3
Cadogan Pl. SW1 15 A5
Cadogan Pl. SW1 66 J3
Cadogan Rd., Surb. 91 G5
Cadogan Sq. SW1 15 A6
Cadogan Sq. SW1 66 J3
Cadogan St. SW3 18 J2
Cadogan St. SW3 66 J4
Cadogan Ter. E9 50 J6
Cadoxton Ave. N15 41 C6
Cadwallon Rd. SE9 88 E2
Caedmon Rd. N7 49 F4
Caerleon Clo., Sid. 89 C5
Caerleon Ter. SE2 71 B4
Blithdale Rd.
Caernarvon Clo., 94 E2
Mitch.
Caernarvon Dr., Ilf. 43 D1
Caesars Wk., Mitch. 93 J5
Cage Rd. E16 60 E5
Malmesbury Rd.
Cahill St. EC1 9 A6
Cahir St. E14 69 B4
Caird St. W10 57 B3
Cairn Ave. W5 64 G1
Cairn Way, Stan. 29 C6
Cairndale Clo., Brom. 87 F7
Cairnfield Ave. NW2 47 E3
Cairngorm Clo., 82 D5
Tedd.
Vicarage Rd.
Cairns Ave., Wdf.Grn. 35 B6
Cairns Rd. SW11 75 H5
Cairo New Rd., Croy. 101 H2
Cairo Rd. E17 42 A4
Caishowe Rd., 22 B1
Borwd.
Caistor Ms. SW12 76 B7
Caistor Rd.
Caistor Pk. Rd. E15 60 F1
Caistor Rd. SW12 76 B7
Caithness Gdns., Sid. 79 J6
Caithness Rd. W14 66 A3
Caithness Rd., Mitch. 85 B7
Calabria Rd. N5 49 H6
Calais Gate SE5 76 H1
Calais St.
Calais St. SE5 76 H1
Calbourne Rd. SW12 75 J7
Calcott Wk. SE9 88 B4
Caldbeck Ave., 99 G2
Wor.Pk.
Caldecot Rd. SE5 76 J2
Caldecott Way E5 50 G3
Calder Ave., Grnf. 55 C2
Calder Clo., Enf. 25 B3
Calder Gdns., Edg. 38 A3
Calder Rd., Mord. 93 F5
Calderon Pl. W10 56 J5
St. Quintin Gdns.
Calderon Rd. E11 51 C4
Caldervale Rd. SW4 76 D5
Calderwood St. SE18 70 D4
Caldicot Grn. NW9 38 E6
Snowdon Dr.
Caldwell Rd., Wat. 28 D4
Caldwell St. SW9 67 F7
Caldy Rd., Belv. 71 H3
Caldy Wk. N1 49 J6
Marquess Est.
Cale St. SW3 18 G3
Cale St. SW3 66 H5
Caleb St. SE1 16 J3
Caledon Rd. E6 61 B1
Caledon Rd., Wall. 101 A4
Caledonia St. N1 8 B2
Caledonia St. N1 58 E2
Caledonian Clo., Ilf. 53 B1
Caledonian Rd. N1 8 B2
Caledonian Rd. N1 58 E2
Caledonian Rd. N7 49 F4
Caledonian Wf. Rd. 69 D4
Caletock Way SE10 69 F5
Calico Row SW11 75 F3
York Pl.

Calidore Clo. SW2 76 F6
Endymion Rd.
California La. 29 A1
(Bushey), Wat.
California Rd., N.Mal. 92 C3
Callaby Ter. N1 50 A6
Wakeham St.
Callaghan Clo. SE13 78 E4
Glenton Rd.
Callander Rd. SE6 87 B2
Callard Ave. N13 32 H5
Callcott Rd. NW6 48 C7
Callcott St. W8 66 D1
Hillgate Pl.
Callendar Rd. SW7 14 E5
Callendar Rd. SW7 66 G3
Callingham Clo. E14 59 J5
Wallwood St.
Callis Rd. E17 41 J6
Callow St. SW3 18 D5
Callow St. SW3 66 G6
Calmington Rd. SE5 21 E4
Calmington Rd. SE5 68 B5
Calmont Rd., Brom. 87 D6
Calne Ave., Ilf. 43 E1
Calonne Rd. SW19 84 A4
Calshot St. N1 8 C1
Calshot St. N1 58 F2
Calshot Way, Enf. 24 H3
Calthorpe Gdns., Edg. 29 H5
Jesmond Way
Calthorpe Gdns., 100 F3
Sutt.
Calthorpe St. WC1 8 D5
Calthorpe St. WC1 58 F4
Calton Ave. SE21 77 B6
Calton Rd., Barn. 23 F6
Calverley Cres., Dag. 53 G2
Calverley Gdns., Har. 37 G7
Calverley Gro. N19 49 D1
Calverley Rd., Epsom 99 G6
Calvert Ave. E2 9 E4
Calvert Ave. E2 59 B3
Calvert Clo., Belv. 71 G4
Calvert Clo., Sid. 89 E6
Calvert Rd. SE10 69 F5
Calvert Rd., Barn. 23 A2
Calvert St. NW1 58 A1
Chalcot Rd.
Calverton SE5 21 D5
Calverton Rd. E6 61 D1
Calvert's Bldgs. SE1 17 B2
Calvin St. E1 9 F6
Calvin St. E1 59 C4
Calydon Rd. SE7 69 H5
Calypso Way SE16 68 J4
Cam Rd. E15 90 A1
Camac Rd., Twick. 82 A1
Cambalt Rd. SW15 75 A5
Camberley Ave. 92 H2
SW20
Camberley Ave., Enf. 25 B4
Camberley Clo., Sutt.100 A3
Cambert Way SE3 78 H4
Camberwell Ch. St. 77 A1
SE5
Camberwell Glebe 77 B1
SE5
Camberwell Grn. SE5 77 A1
Camberwell Gro. SE5 77 A1
**Camberwell New Rd. 20 F7
SE5**
Camberwell New Rd. 67 J6
SE5
*Camberwell Pas. SE5 76 J1
Camberwell Grn.*
Camberwell Rd. SE5 21 A6
Camberwell Rd. SE5 67 J6
Camberwell Sta. Rd. 76 J1
SE5
Cambeys Rd., Dag. 53 H5
Camborne Ave. W13 64 E2
Camborne Ms. W11 57 B6
St. Marks Rd.
Camborne Rd. SW18 75 D7
Camborne Rd., Croy. 95 D7
Camborne Rd., Mord. 93 A5
Camborne Rd., Sid. 89 C3
Camborne Rd., Sutt. 100 D7
Camborne Rd., Well. 79 J3
Camborne Way, 72 G1
Houns.
Cambourne Ave. N9 25 G7
Cambray Rd. SW12 85 C1
Cambray Rd., Orp. 97 J7
Cambria Clo., Houns. 72 G3
Cambria Clo., Sid. 88 G1
Cambria Ct., Felt. 72 B7
Hounslow Rd.
Cambria Rd. SE5 76 J3
Cambria St. SW6 66 E7
Cambrian Ave., Ilf. 43 H5

Cambrian Clo. SE27 85 H3
Cambrian Rd. E10 42 A7
Cambrian Rd., Rich. 73 J6
Cambridge Ave. NW6 57 D2
Cambridge Ave., 46 C5
Grnf.
Cambridge Ave., 92 E2
N.Mal.
Cambridge Ave., 79 J4
Well.
Cambridge Barracks 70 C4
Rd. SE18
Cambridge Circ. WC2 11 J4
Cambridge Circ. WC2 58 D6
Cambridge Clo., 92 H1
SW20
Cambridge Clo., 72 E4
Houns.
Cambridge Cotts., 65 A6
Rich.
Cambridge Cres. E2 59 E2
Cambridge Cres., 82 D5
Tedd.
Cambridge Dr. SE12 78 G5
Cambridge Dr., Ruis. 45 D2
Cambridge Gdns. 40 A1
N10
Cambridge Gdns. 33 A7
N17
Great Cambridge Rd.
Cambridge Gdns. 25 A7
N21
Cambridge Gdns. 32 G5
N21
Cambridge Gdns. 57 D2
NW6
Cambridge Gdns. 57 A6
W10
Cambridge Gdns. 25 D2
Enf.
Cambridge Gdns., 92 A2
Kings.T.
**Cambridge Gate NW1 7 E5
Cambridge Gate Ms. 7 E5
NW1**
Cambridge Grn. SE9 88 E1
Cambridge Gro. SE20 95 E1
Cambridge Gro. W6 65 H4
Cambridge Gro. Rd., 92 A3
Kings.T.
Cambridge Heath Rd. 59 E4
E1
Cambridge Heath Rd. 59 F4
E2
Cambridge Mans. 75 J1
SW11
Cambridge Rd.
Cambridge Par., Enf. 25 D1
Great Cambridge Rd.
Cambridge Pk. E11 42 G7
Cambridge Pk., 73 F6
Twick.
Cambridge Pk. Rd. 42 F7
E11
Cambridge Pl. W8 14 B4
Cambridge Pl. W8 66 E2
Cambridge Rd. E4 34 D1
Cambridge Rd. E11 42 F6
Cambridge Rd. NW6 57 D3
Cambridge Rd. SE20 95 E3
Cambridge Rd. SW11 75 J1
Cambridge Rd. SW13 74 F2
Cambridge Rd. SW20 92 H1
Cambridge Rd. W7 64 C2
Cambridge Rd., Bark. 52 F7
Cambridge Rd., 87 G7
Brom.
Cambridge Rd., Cars.100 H6
Cambridge Rd., 81 F7
Hmptn.
Cambridge Rd., Har. 36 G5
Cambridge Rd., 72 E4
Houns.
Cambridge Rd., Ilf. 52 H1
Cambridge Rd., 92 A2
Kings.T.
Cambridge Rd., 94 B3
Mitch.
Cambridge Rd., 92 D4
N.Mal.
Cambridge Rd., Rich. 65 A7
Cambridge Rd., Sid. 88 H4
Cambridge Rd., Sthl. 63 F1
Cambridge Rd., Tedd. 82 C4
Cambridge Rd., 73 G6
Twick.
Cambridge Rd., Walt. 90 B6
Cambridge Rd., 90 F4
W.Mol.
Cambridge Rd. Est., 92 A2
Kings.T.
Cambridge Rd. N. 65 B5
W4

Cambridge Row 70 E5
SE18
Cambridge Sq. W2 10 G3
Cambridge Sq. W2 57 H6
Cambridge St. SW1 19 E3
Cambridge St. SW1 67 B4
Cambridge Ter. N13 32 G5
Cambridge Ter. NW1 7 D4
**Cambridge Ter. Ms. 7 E4
NW1**
Cambus Clo., Hayes 54 E5
Cambus Rd. E16 55 G5
Camdale Rd. SE18 70 J7
Camden Ave., Felt. 81 J2
Camden Ave., Hayes 54 D7
Camden Clo., Chis. 97 F1
Camden Est. SE15 77 C1
Camden Gdns. NW1 49 B7
Kentish Town Rd.
Camden Gdns., Sutt. 100 E5
Camden Gdns., 94 H3
Th.Hth.
Camden Gro., Chis. 88 E6
Camden High St. 58 B1
NW1
Camden Hill Rd. 86 B6
SE19
Camden La. N7 49 D6
Camden Lock Pl. 49 B7
NW1
Chalk Fm. Rd.
Camden Ms. NW1 49 C7
Camden Pk. Rd. NW1 49 D6
Camden Pk. Rd., 88 C7
Chis.
Camden Pas. N1 58 H1
Camden Rd. E11 42 H6
Camden Rd. E17 41 J6
Camden Rd. N7 49 E4
Camden Rd. NW1 49 C7
Camden Rd., Bex. 89 E1
Camden Rd., Cars. 100 J4
Camden Rd., Sutt. 100 D5
Camden Row SE3 78 E2
Camden Sq. NW1 49 D6
Camden Sq. SE15 77 C1
Exeter Rd.
Camden St. NW1 49 C7
Camden Ter. NW1 49 D6
North Vill.
Camden Wk. N1 58 H1
Camden Way, Chis. 88 C7
Camden Way, Th.Hth. 94 H3
Camdenhurst St. E14 59 H6
Camel Rd. E16 70 A1
Camelford Wk. W11 57 B6
Lancaster Rd.
Camellia Pl., Twick. 73 H7
Camellia St. SW8 67 E7
Camelot Clo. SE28 70 G2
Camelot Clo. SW19 84 D4
Camelot St. SE15 68 E7
Green Hundred Rd.
Camera Pl. SW10 18 A5
Camera Pl. SW10 66 G6
Cameron Clo. N18 33 E4
Cameron Clo. N20 31 H2
Myddelton Pk.
Cameron Pl. E1 59 E6
Varden St.
Cameron Rd. SE6 86 J2
Cameron Rd., Brom. 96 G4
Cameron Rd., Croy. 94 H6
Cameron Rd., Ilf. 52 H1
Cameron Sq., Mitch. 93 H1
Camerton Clo. E8 58 C6
Buttermere Wk.
Camilla Rd. SE16 68 E4
Camille Clo. SE25 95 D3
Camlan Rd., Brom. 87 F4
Camlet St. E2 9 F5
Camlet St. E2 59 C4
Camlet Way, Barn. 23 D2
Camley St. NW1 7 J1
Camley St. NW1 49 D7
*Kings.T.
Church Rd.*
Camm Gdns., T.Ditt. 90 F1
Camomile Ave., 93 J1
Mitch.
Camomile St. EC3 13 D3
Camomile St. EC3 59 B6
Camp Rd. SW19 83 H5
Camp Vw. SW19 83 H5
Campana Rd. SW6 75 D1
Campbell Ave., Ilf. 43 E4
Campbell Clo. SE18 79 D1
Moordown
Campbell Clo. SW16 85 D5
Campbell Clo., Ruis. 36 A6
Campbell Clo., Twick. 82 A2
Campbell Ct. N17 41 C1

Campbell Cft., Edg. 30 A5
Campbell Rd. E3 60 A3
Campbell Rd. E6 61 B1
Campbell Rd. E15 51 F4
Trevelyan Rd.
Campbell Rd. E17 41 J4
Campbell Rd. N17 41 C1
Campbell Rd. W7 55 B7
Campbell Rd., Croy. 94 H7
Campbell Rd., E.Mol. 91 C3
Hampton Ct. Rd.
Campbell Rd., Twick. 82 A1
Campbell Wk. N1 58 E1
Outram Pl.
Campdale Rd. N7 49 D3
Campden Cres., Dag. 53 B4
Campden Cres., 46 E3
Wem.
Campden Gro. W8 66 D2
Campden Hill W8 66 D2
Campden Hill Gdns. 66 D1
W8
Campden Hill Pl. W11 66 C1
Holland Pk. Ave.
Campden Hill Rd. W8 66 D1
Campden Hill Sq. W8 66 C1
Campden Ho. Clo. 66 D2
W8
Hornton St.
Campden Rd., 102 B5
S.Croy.
Campden St. W8 66 D1
Campen Clo. SW19 84 B2
Queensmere Rd.
Camperdown St. E1 13 G4
Campfield Rd. SE9 79 A7
Campion Clo. E6 61 C7
Campion Clo., Croy. 102 B4
Campion Clo., Har. 37 J6
Campion Pl. SE28 71 B1
Campion Rd. SW15 74 J4
Campion Rd., Islw. 73 C1
Campion Ter. NW2 48 A4
Camplin Rd., Har. 37 H5
Camplin St. SE14 68 G7
Campsbourne, The 40 E4
N8
Rectory Gdns.
Campsbourne Rd. N8 40 E3
Campsey Gdns., Dag. 53 B7
Campsey Rd., Dag. 53 B7
Campsfield Rd. N8 40 E3
Campsbourne Rd.
Campshill Pl. SE13 78 C5
Campshill Rd.
Campshill Rd. SE13 78 C5
Campus Rd. E17 41 J6
Camrose Ave., Edg. 37 J2
Camrose Ave., Erith 71 H6
Camrose Ave., Felt. 81 B4
Camrose Clo., Croy. 95 H7
Camrose Clo., Mord. 93 D4
Camrose St. SE2 71 A5
Canada Ave. N18 32 J6
Canada Cres. W3 56 C4
Canada Est. SE16 68 F3
Canada Gdns. SE13 78 C5
Monument Gdns.
Canada Rd. W3 56 C5
Canada Sq. E14 69 B1
Canada St. SE16 68 G2
Canada Way W12 56 H7
Canada Yd. S. SE16 68 G3
Canadian Ave. SE6 87 B1
Canal App. SE8 68 H5
Canal Clo. E1 59 H4
Canal Gro. SE15 21 J5
Canal Gro. SE15 68 D6
Canal Head SE15 77 D1
Peckham High St.
Canal Rd. E3 59 H4
Canal St. SE5 21 B6
Canal St. SE5 68 A6
Canal Wk. N1 59 A1
Canal Wk. SE26 86 F5
Canal Way NW1 58 A1
Regents Pk.
Canal Way W10 57 A4
Canal Way, Wem. 55 J1
Canal Way Wk. W10 57 B4
Kensal Rd.
Canary Wf. E14 69 A1
Canberra Clo. NW4 38 G3
Canberra Dr., Nthlt. 54 C3
Canberra Rd. E6 61 C1
Barking Rd.
Canberra Rd. SE7 69 J6
Canberra Rd., Bexh. 71 D6
Canbury Ave., 91 J1
Kings.T.
Canbury Ms. SE26 86 D3
Wells Pk. Rd.

Canbury Pk. Rd., 91 H1
Kings.T.
Canbury Pas., 91 G1
Kings.T.
Cancell Rd. SW9 76 G1
Candahar Rd. SW11 75 H2
Candler St. N15 41 A6
Candover St. W1 11 F2
Candy St. E3 59 J1
Cane Clo., Wall. 101 E7
Kingsford Ave.
Caney Ms. NW2 48 A2
Claremont Rd.
Canfield Dr., Ruis. 45 B5
Canfield Gdns. NW6 48 E7
Canfield Pl. NW6 48 F6
Canfield Gdns.
Canfield Rd., 35 B7
Wdf.Grn.
Canford Ave., Nthlt. 54 E1
Canford Clo., Enf. 24 G2
Canford Gdns., 92 E6
N.Mal.
Canford Rd. SW11 76 A5
Canham Rd. SE25 95 B3
Canham Rd. W3 65 E2
Canmore Gdns. 85 C7
SW16
Cann Hall Rd. E11 51 E4
Canning Pas. N22 40 F1
Canning Cross SE5 77 B2
Canning Pas. W8 14 C5
Canning Pl. W8 66 F3
Canning Pl. Ms. W8 14 C5
Canning Rd. E15 60 E2
Canning Rd. E17 41 H4
Canning Rd. N5 49 H3
Canning Rd., Croy. 102 C2
Canning Rd., Har. 37 B3
Cannington Rd., Dag. 53 C6
Cannizaro Rd. SW19 83 J5
Cannon Clo. SW20 92 J3
Cannon Clo., Hmptn. 81 H6
Hanworth Rd.
Cannon Dr. E14 60 A7
Cannon Hill N14 32 D3
Cannon Hill NW6 48 D5
Cannon Hill La. 93 B3
SW20
Cannon La. NW3 48 G3
Cannon La., Pnr. 36 E5
Cannon Pl. NW3 48 F3
Cannon Pl. SE7 70 B5
Cannon Rd. N14 32 E3
Cannon Rd., Bexh. 80 E1
Cannon St. EC4 12 J4
Cannon St. EC4 58 J6
Cannon St. Rd. E1 59 E6
Cannon Way, W.Mol. 90 G4
Cannonbury Ave., 36 D6
Pnr.
Canon Ave., Rom. 44 C5
Canon Beck Rd. SE16 68 F2
Canon Mohan Clo. 24 B6
N14
Farm La.
Canon Rd., Brom. 96 J3
Canon Row SW1 16 A3
Canon Row SW1 67 E2
Canon St. N1 58 J1
Canon Trd. Est., 47 B4
The, Wem.
Canonbie Rd. SE23 77 F7
Canonbury Cres. N1 49 J7
Canonbury Gro. N1 49 J7
Canonbury La. N1 49 H7
Canonbury Pk. N. N1 49 J6
Canonbury Pk. S. N1 49 J6
Canonbury Pl. N1 49 H6
Canonbury Rd. N1 49 H6
Canonbury Rd., Enf. 25 B1
Canonbury Sq. N1 49 H7
Canonbury St. N1 49 J7
Canonbury Vill. N1 49 H7
Canonbury St. N1 58 J1
New N. Rd.
Canons Clo. N2 39 G7
Canons Clo., Edg. 29 J6
Canons Cor., Edg. 29 H4
Canons Dr., Edg. 29 H6
Canons Wk., Croy. 102 G3
Canonsleigh Rd., 53 B7
Dag.
Canopus Way, Nthwd.28 A4
Canrobert St. E2 59 J3
Cantelowes Rd. NW1 49 D6
Canterbury Ave., Ilf. 43 B7
Canterbury Ave., Sid. 80 D2
Canterbury Clo. E6 61 C6
Harper Rd.
Canterbury Clo., 96 B1
Beck.

Canterbury Clo., 35 J3
Chig.
Canterbury Clo., 54 H6
Grnf.
Canterbury Cres. 76 G3
SW9
Canterbury Gro. 85 G4
SE27
Canterbury Pl. SE17 20 H2
Canterbury Pl. SE17 67 H4
Canterbury Rd. E10 42 C7
Canterbury Rd. NW6 57 C2
Canterbury Rd., 22 A2
Borwd.
Canterbury Rd., Croy. 94 G7
Canterbury Rd., Felt. 81 E3
Canterbury Rd., Har. 36 H5
Canterbury Rd., 93 E7
Mord.
Canterbury Ter. NW6 57 D2
Cantley Gdns. SE19 95 C1
Cantley Gdns., Ilf. 43 F6
Cantley Rd. W7 64 D3
Canton St. E14 60 A6
Cantrell Rd. E3 59 J4
Cantwell Rd. SE18 70 E7
Canute Gdns. SE16 68 G4
Canvey St. SE1 16 H1
Cape Clo., Bark. 52 F6
North St.
Cape Rd. N17 41 D3
High Cross Rd.
Cape Yd. E1 17 J1
Capel Ave., Wall. 101 F5
Capel Clo. N20 31 F3
Capel Clo., Brom. 104 C1
Capel Ct. EC2 13 C4
Capel Ct. SE20 95 F1
Melvin Rd.
Capel Gdns., Ilf. 52 J4
Capel Gdns., Pnr. 36 F4
Capel Pt. E7 51 H4
Capel Rd. E7 51 H4
Capel Rd. E12 52 A4
Capel Rd., Barn. 23 H6
Capener's Clo. SW1 15 B4
Capern Rd. SW18 84 F1
Cargill Rd.
Capital Interchange 65 A5
Way, Brent.
Capitol Ind. Est. NW9 38 C3
Capitol Way NW9 38 C3
Capland St. NW8 6 F5
Capland St. NW8 57 G4
Caple Rd. NW10 56 F2
Capper St. WC1 7 G6
Capper St. WC1 58 C4
Caprea Clo., Hayes 54 D5
Triandra Way
Capri Rd., Croy. 102 C1
Capstan Clo., Rom. 44 B6
Capstan Ride, Enf. 24 G2
Crofton Way
Capstan Rd. SE8 68 J4
Capstan Sq. E14 69 C2
Capstan Way SE16 68 H1
Capstone Rd., Brom. 87 F4
Capthorne Ave., Har. 45 E1
Capuchin Clo., Stan. 29 E6
Capworth St. E10 51 A1
Caradoc Clo. W2 57 D6
Caradoc St. SE10 69 E5
Caradon Way N15 41 A4
Caravel Ms. SE8 69 A6
Watergate St.
Caravelle Gdns., 54 D3
Nthlt.
Javelin Way
Carberry Rd. SE19 86 B6
Carbery Ave. W3 64 J2
Carbis Clo. E4 34 D1
Carbis Rd. E14 59 J6
Carbuncle Pas. Way 41 D2
N17
Carburton St. W1 11 E1
Carburton St. W1 58 B5
Cardale St. E14 69 C3
Plevna St.
Carden Rd. SE15 77 E3
Cardiff Rd. W7 64 D3
Cardiff Rd., Enf. 25 E4
Cardiff St. SE18 70 H7
Cardigan Gdns., Ilf. 53 A2
Cardigan Rd. E3 59 J2
Cardigan Rd. SW13 74 G2
Cardigan Rd. SW19 84 F6
Cardigan Rd., Rich. 73 H6
Cardigan St. SE11 20 E3
Cardigan St. SE11 67 G5
Cardigan Wk. N1 49 J7
Ashby Gro.
Cardinal Ave., 22 B3
Borwd.

Cardinal Ave., 82 H5
Kings.T.
Cardinal Ave., Mord. 93 B6
Cardinal Bourne St. 17 C6
SE1
Cardinal Bourne St. 68 A3
SE1
Cardinal Clo., Chis. 97 G1
Cardinal Clo., Mord. 93 B6
Cardinal Clo., 99 G4
Wor.Pk.
Cardinal Cres., 92 C2
N.Mal.
Cardinal Dr., Ilf. 35 F6
Cardinal Pl. SW15 75 A4
Cardinal Rd., Felt. 81 B1
Cardinal Rd., Ruis. 45 D1
Cardinal Way, Har. 37 B3
Wolseley Rd.
Cardinals Wk., 81 J7
Hmptn.
Cardinals Way N19 49 D1
Cardine Ms. SE15 68 E7
Cardington Sq., 72 D4
Houns.
Cardington St. NW1 7 G3
Cardington St. NW1 58 C3
Cardozo Rd. N7 49 E5
Cardrew Ave. N12 31 G5
Cardrew Clo. N12 31 G5
Cardross St. W6 65 H3
Cardwell Rd. N7 49 E4
Cardwell Rd. N7 49 E4
Carew Clo. N7 49 F2
Carew Rd. N17 41 D2
Carew Rd. W13 64 F2
Carew Rd., Mitch. 94 A2
Carew Rd., Th.Hth. 94 H3
Carew Rd., Wall. 101 C6
Carew St. SE5 76 J2
Carey Ct., Bexh. 80 J5
Carey Gdns. SW8 76 C1
Carey La. EC2 12 J3
Carey Pl. SW1 19 H2
Carey Rd., Dag. 53 E4
Carey St. WC2 12 D4
Carey St. WC2 58 F6
Carey Way, Wem. 47 C4
Fourth Way
Carfax Pl. SW4 76 D4
Holwood Pl.
Carfree Clo. N1 49 G7
Bewdley St.
Cargill Rd. SW18 84 E1
Cargreen Rd. SE25 95 C4
Carholme Rd. SE23 86 J1
Carisbrook Clo., 37 G2
Stan.
Carisbrooke Ave., 89 D1
Bex.
Carisbrooke Gdns. 21 G7
SE15
Carisbrooke Rd. E17 41 H4
Carisbrooke Rd., 96 J4
Brom.
Carisbrooke Rd., 94 D4
Mitch.
Carker's La. NW5 49 B5
Carleton Ave., Wall. 101 D7
Carleton Clo., Esher 98 A1
Carleton Rd. N7 49 D5
Carlile Clo. E3 59 J2
Carlingford Gdns., 84 J7
Mitch.
Carlingford Rd. N15 40 H3
Carlingford Rd. NW3 48 G4
Carlingford Rd., 93 A6
Mord.
Carlisle Ave. EC3 13 F4
Carlisle Ave. W3 56 E6
Carlisle Clo., Kings.T. 92 A1
Carlisle Gdns., Har. 37 G7
Carlisle Gdns., Ilf. 52 C6
Carlisle La. SE1 18 D6
Carlisle La. SE1 67 F3
Carlisle Ms. NW8 10 F1
Carlisle Ms. NW8 57 G5
Carlisle Pl. N11 32 B4
Carlisle Pl. SW1 15 F6
Carlisle Pl. SW1 67 C3
Carlisle Rd. E10 51 A1
Carlisle Rd. N4 40 G7
Carlisle Rd. NW6 57 B1
Carlisle Rd. NW9 38 C3
Carlisle Rd., 81 H7
Hmptn.
Carlisle Rd., Sutt. 100 C5
Carlisle St. W1 11 H4
Carlisle Wk. E8 50 C6
Laurel St.
Carlisle Way SW17 85 A5
Carlos Pl. W1 11 C5

Carlos Pl. W1 58 A7
Carlow St. NW1 7 F1
Carlton Ave. N14 24 D5
Carlton Ave., Felt. 72 C6
Carlton Ave., Har. 37 E5
Carlton Ave., S.Croy. 102 B7
Carlton Ave. E., 46 G2
Wem.
Carlton Ave. W., 46 E2
Wem.
Carlton Clo. NW3 48 D2
Carlton Clo., Borwd. 22 D4
Carlton Clo., Chess. 98 G6
Carlton Clo., Edg. 30 A5
Carlton Ct. SW9 76 H1
Carlton Ct., Ilf. 43 G3
Carlton Cres., Sutt. 100 B4
Carlton Dr. SW15 75 A5
Carlton Dr., Ilf. 43 G3
Carlton Gdns. SW1 15 H2
Carlton Gdns. SW1 67 D1
Carlton Gdns. W5 55 F6
Carlton Gro. SE15 77 E1
Carlton Hill NW8 6 B1
Carlton Hill NW8 57 E2
Carlton Ho. Ter. SW1 15 H2
Carlton Ho. Ter. SW1 67 D1
Carlton Pk. Ave. 93 A2
SW20
Carlton Rd. E11 51 F1
Carlton Rd. E12 52 A4
Carlton Rd. E17 41 H1
Carlton Rd. N11 32 A5
Carlton Rd. SW14 74 C3
Carlton Rd. W4 65 D2
Carlton Rd. W5 55 F7
Carlton Rd., Erith 71 H6
Carlton Rd., N.Mal. 92 E2
Carlton Rd., Sid. 88 J5
Carlton Rd., S.Croy. 102 A6
Carlton Rd., Well. 80 B7
Carlton Rd., Well. 80 B3
Carlton Sq. E1 59 G4
Argyle Rd.
Carlton St. SW1 11 H6
Carlton Ter. E11 42 H5
Carlton Ter. N18 33 A3
Carlton Ter. SE26 86 F3
Carlton Twr. Pl. SW1 15 A5
Carlton Twr. Pl. SW1 66 J3
Carlton Vale NW6 57 D2
Carlwell St. SW17 84 H5
Carlyle Ave., Brom. 97 A3
Carlyle Ave., Sthl. 54 F7
Carlyle Clo. N2 39 F6
Carlyle Clo. NW10 56 D1
Carlyle Clo., W.Mol. 90 H2
Carlyle Gdns., Sthl. 54 F7
Carlyle Pl. SW15 75 A4
Carlyle Rd. E12 52 B4
Carlyle Rd. SE28 62 B7
Carlyle Rd. W5 64 F4
Carlyle Rd., Croy. 102 D2
Carlyle Sq. SW3 18 F4
Carlyle Sq. SW3 66 G5
Carlyon Ave., Har. 45 F4
Carlyon Clo., Wem. 55 H1
Carlyon Rd., Hayes 54 C5
Carlyon Rd., Wem. 55 H2
Carmalt Gdns. SW15 74 J4
Carmarthen Gdn. 38 E6
NW9
Snowdon Dr.
Carmel Ct. W8 14 A3
Carmelite Clo., Har. 36 J1
Carmelite Rd., Har. 36 J1
Carmelite St. EC4 12 F5
Carmelite St. EC4 58 G7
Carmelite Wk., Har. 36 J1
Carmelite Way, Har. 36 J2
Hampden Rd.
Carmen St. E14 60 B6
Carmichael Clo. 75 G3
SW11
Darien Rd.
Carmichael Clo., 45 A4
Ruis.
Carmichael Rd. SE25 95 D4
Carminia Rd. SW17 85 B2
Carnaby St. W1 11 F4
Carnaby St. W1 58 C6
Carnac St. SE27 86 A4
Carnanton Rd. E17 42 D7
Carnarvon Ave., Enf. 25 C3
Carnarvon Rd. E10 42 C6
Carnarvon Rd. E15 51 F6
Carnarvon Rd. E18 42 F2
Carnarvon Rd., Barn. 23 B3
Carnation St. SE2 71 B5
Carnbrook Rd. SE3 79 A3
Carnecke Gdns. SE9 79 B5

Carnegie Clo., Surb. 98 J2
Fullers Ave.
Carnegie Pl. SW19 84 A3
Carnegie St. N1 58 F1
Carnforth Clo., Epsom 99 B6
Carnforth Rd. SW16 85 D7
Carnie Lo. SW17 85 B3
Manville Rd.
Carnoustie Dr. N1 49 F7
Carnwath Rd. SW6 75 D3
Carol St. NW1 58 C1
Carolina Rd., Th.Hth. 94 H2
Caroline Clo. N10 40 B2
Alexandra Pk. Rd.
Caroline Clo. SW16 85 F4
Caroline Clo. W2 10 B6
Caroline Clo., Croy. 102 B4
Brownlow Rd.
Caroline Clo., Islw. 64 B7
Caroline Ct., Stan. 29 D6
The Chase
Caroline Gdns. E2 9 E3
Caroline Gdns. SE15 68 E7
Caroline Pl. SW11 76 A2
Caroline Pl. W2 10 B5
Caroline Pl. W2 57 E7
Caroline Pl. Ms. W2 10 B6
Caroline Rd. SW19 84 C7
Caroline St. E1 59 G6
Caroline Ter. SW1 19 B2
Caroline Ter. SW1 67 A4
Caroline Wk. W6 66 B6
Laundry Rd.
Carpenders Ave., Wat. 28 E3
Carpenter Gdns. N21 32 H2
Carpenter St. W1 11 D6
Carpenters Ct., Twick. 82 B2
Carpenters Pl. SW4 76 D4
Carpenters Rd. E15 51 A6
Carr Rd. E17 41 J2
Carr Rd., Nthlt. 45 G6
Carr St. E14 59 H5
Carrara Wk. SW9 76 G4
Somerleyton Rd.
Carriage Dr. E. SW11 19 C7
Carriage Dr. E. SW11 67 A7
Carriage Dr. N. SW11 19 C6
Carriage Dr. N. SW11 66 J7
Carriage Dr. S. SW11 75 J1
Carriage Dr. W. SW11 66 J7
Carrick Dr., Ilf. 43 F1
Carrick Gdns. N17 33 B7
Flexmere Rd.
Carrick Ms. SE8 69 A6
Watergate St.
Carrill Way, Belv. 71 D4
Carrington Ave., Borwd. 22 B5
Carrington Ave., Houns. 72 H5
Carrington Clo., Barn. 22 G5
Carrington Clo., Borwd. 22 C5
Carrington Clo., Croy. 95 H7
Carrington Gdns. E7 51 H4
Woodford Rd.
Carrington Rd., Rich. 74 A4
Carrington Sq., Har. 28 J7
Carrington St. W1 15 D2
Carrol Clo. NW5 49 B4
Carroll Clo. E15 51 F5
Carroll Hill, Loug. 27 C3
Carron Clo. E14 60 B6
Carronade Pl. SE28 70 F3
Carroun Rd. SW8 20 C7
Carroun Rd. SW8 67 F7
Carrow Rd., Dag. 53 B7
Carroway La., Grnf. 55 A3
Cowgate Rd.
Carrs La. N21 24 J5
Carshalton Gro., Sutt. 100 G4
Carshalton Pk. Rd., Cars. 100 J6
Carshalton Pl., Cars. 101 A4
Carshalton Rd., Cars. 100 H5
Carshalton Rd., Mitch. 94 A4
Carshalton Rd., Sutt. 100 F5
Carslake Rd. SW15 74 J6
Carson Rd. E16 60 G4
Carson Rd. SE21 85 J2
Carson Rd., Barn. 23 J4
Carstairs Rd. SE6 87 C3
Carston Clo. SE12 78 F5
Carswell Clo., Ilf. 43 A4
Roding La. S.
Carswell Rd. SE6 78 C7
Cart La. E4 26 D7
Carter La. EC4 12 H4
Carter La. EC4 58 H6
Carter Pl. SE17 21 A4
Carter Pl. SE17 67 J5
Carter Rd. E13 60 H1
Carter Rd. SW19 84 G6
Carter St. SE17 20 J5
Carter St. SE17 67 J6
Carteret St. SW1 15 H4
Carteret St. SW1 67 D2
Carteret Way SE8 68 H4
Carterhatch Rd., Enf. 25 F1
Carters Clo., Wor.Pk. 100 A2
Carters Hill Clo. SE9 87 J1
Carters La. SE23 86 H2
Carters Yd. SW18 75 D5
Wandsworth High St.
Carthew Rd. W6 65 H3
Carthew Vill. W6 65 H3
Carthusian St. EC1 12 J1
Carthusian St. EC1 58 J5
Cartier Circle E14 69 B1
Carting La. WC2 12 B6
Carting La. WC2 58 E7
Cartmel Clo. N17 33 E7
Heybourne Rd.
Cartmel Rd., Bexh. 80 G1
Cartmell Gdns., Mord. 93 F5
Carton St. W1 11 A3
Cartwright Gdns. WC1 8 A4
Cartwright Gdns. WC1 58 E3
Cartwright Rd., Dag. 53 E7
Cartwright St. E1 13 G6
Cartwright St. E1 59 C7
Carver Rd. SE24 76 J6
Carville Cres., Brent. 64 H4
Cary Rd. E11 51 E4
Carysfort Rd. N8 40 D5
Carysfort Rd. N16 50 A3
Cascade Ave. N10 40 C4
Cascade Clo., Buck.H. 35 A2
Cascade Rd.
Cascade Rd., Buck.H. 35 A2
Casella Rd. SE14 68 G7
Casewick Rd. SE27 85 G5
Casimir Rd. E5 50 E3
Casino Ave. SE24 77 A5
Caspian St. SE5 21 B7
Caspian St. SE5 68 A7
Caspian Wk. E16 61 A6
King George Ave.
Casselden Rd. NW10 47 D7
Cassidy Rd. SW6 66 D7
Cassilda Rd. SE2 71 A4
Cassilis Rd., Twick. 73 E5
Cassiobury Rd. E17 41 H5
Cassland Rd. E9 50 G7
Cassland Rd., Th.Hth. 95 A4
Casslee Rd. SE6 77 J7
Casson St. E1 13 H2
Casson St. E1 59 D5
Castalia Sq. E14 69 C2
Plevna St.
Castell Rd., Loug. 27 F1
Castellain Rd. W9 6 A5
Castellain Rd. W9 57 E4
Castellane Clo., Stan. 29 C7
Daventer Dr.
Castello Ave. SW15 74 J5
Castelnau SW13 74 G1
Castelnau Pl. SW13 65 H6
Castelnau
Castelnau Row SW13 65 H6
Lonsdale Rd.
Casterbridge NW6 57 E1
Casterbridge Rd. SE3 78 G3
Casterton St. E8 50 E6
Wilton Way
Castile Rd. SE18 70 D4
Castillon Rd. SE6 87 E2
Castlands Rd. SE6 86 J2
Castle Ave. E4 34 D5
Castle Baynard St. EC4 12 H5
Castle Clo. E9 50 H5
Swinnerton St.
Castle Clo. SW19 84 A3
Castle Clo., Brom. 96 E3
Castle Ct. EC3 13 C4
Castle Dr., Ilf. 43 B6
Castle La. SW1 15 F5
Castle La. SW1 67 C3
Castle Ms. N12 31 F5
Castle Rd.
Castle Ms. NW1 49 B6
Castle Rd.
Castle Par., Epsom 99 G7
Ewell Bypass
Castle Pl. NW1 49 B6
Castle Rd.
Castle Pl. W4 65 E4
Windmill Rd.
Castle Pt. E6 60 J2
Castle Rd. N12 31 F5
Castle Rd. NW1 49 B6
Castle Rd., Dag. 62 B1
Castle Rd., Enf. 25 H1
Castle Rd., Islw. 73 C2
Castle Rd., Nthlt. 45 H6
Castle Rd., Sthl. 63 F3
Castle St. E6 60 J2
Castle St., Kings.T. 91 H2
Castle Wk., Sun. 90 C3
Elizabeth Gdns.
Castle Way SW19 84 A3
Castle Way, Felt. 81 C4
Castle Yd. N6 40 A7
North Rd.
Castle Yd. SE1 16 H1
Castle Yd., Rich. 73 G5
Hill St.
Castlebar Hill W5 55 E5
Castlebar Ms. W5 55 F5
Castlebar Pk. W5 55 E4
Castlebar Rd. W5 55 F6
Castlecombe Dr. SW19 75 A7
Castlecombe Rd. SE9 88 B4
Castledine Rd. SE20 86 E7
Castleford Ave. SE9 88 E1
Castlegate, Rich. 73 J3
Castlehaven Rd. NW1 49 B7
Castleleigh Ct., Enf. 25 A5
Castlemaine Ave., S.Croy. 102 C5
Castlemaine Twr. SW11 75 J2
Castlereagh St. W1 10 H3
Castleton Ave., Wem. 46 H4
Castleton Rd. E17 42 D2
Castleton Rd. SE9 88 A4
Castleton Rd., Ilf. 53 A1
Castleton Rd., Mitch. 94 D4
Castleton Rd., Ruis. 45 D1
Castletown Rd. W14 66 B5
Castleview Gdns., Ilf. 43 B6
Castlewood Dr. SE9 79 C2
Castlewood Rd. N15 41 D6
Castlewood Rd. N16 41 D7
Castlewood Rd., Barn. 23 G3
Castor La. E14 60 B7
Cat Hill, Barn. 23 J5
Caterham Ave., Ilf. 43 C2
Caterham Rd. SE13 78 C3
Catesby St. SE17 21 C2
Catesby St. SE17 68 A4
Catford Bdy. SE6 78 B7
Catford Hill SE6 86 J1
Catford Ms. SE6 78 B7
Holbeach Rd.
Catford Rd. SE6 78 A7
Cathall Rd. E11 51 D2
Cathay St. SE16 68 E2
Cathcart Dr., Orp. 104 H2
Cathcart Hill N19 49 C3
Cathcart Rd. SW10 18 B5
Cathcart Rd. SW10 66 E6
Cathcart St. NW5 49 B6
Cathedral Pl. EC4 12 J4
Cathedral St. SE1 17 B1
Cathedral St. SE1 68 A1
Catherall Rd. N5 49 J3
Catherine Ct. N14 24 C5
Conisbee Rd.
Catherine Gdns., Houns. 73 A4
Catherine Griffiths Ct. EC1 8 F5
Catherine Gro. SE10 78 B1
Catherine Pl. SW1 15 F5
Catherine Pl. SW1 67 C3
Catherine Rd., Surb. 91 G5
Catherine St. WC2 12 C5
Catherine St. WC2 58 F7
Catherine Wheel All. E1 13 E2
Catherine Wheel Rd., Brent. 64 G7
Catherine Wheel Yd. SW1 15 F2
Cathles Rd. SW12 76 B6
Cathnor Hill Ct. W12 65 H3
Cathnor Rd. W12 65 H2
Catlin St. SE16 21 J4
Catlin St. SE16 68 D5
Catling Clo. SE23 86 F3
Catlins La., Pnr. 36 B3
Cato Rd. SW4 76 D3
Cato St. W1 10 H2
Cator La., Beck. 95 J1
Rectory Grn.
Cator Rd. SE26 86 G6
Cator Rd., Cars. 100 J5
Cator St. SE15 68 C6
Cattistock Rd. SE9 88 B5
Catton St. WC1 12 C2
Catton St. WC1 58 F5
Caulfield Rd. E6 61 B1
Caulfield Rd. SE15 77 E2
Causeway, The N2 39 H4
Causeway, The SW18 75 E5
Causeway, The SW19 83 J5
Causeway, The, Cars. 101 A3
Causeway, The, Chess. 98 H4
Causeway, The, Esher 98 C7
Causeway, The, Felt. 72 A4
Causeway, The, Tedd. 82 C6
Broad St.
Causeyware Rd. N9 25 E7
Causton Rd. N6 40 B7
Causton St. SW1 19 J2
Causton St. SW1 67 D4
Cautley Ave. SW4 76 C5
Cavalier Clo., Rom. 44 D4
Cavalry Cres., Houns. 72 D4
Cavalry Gdns. SW15 75 C5
Upper Richmond Rd.
Cavaye Pl. SW10 18 D4
Cave Rd. E13 60 H2
Cave Rd., Rich. 82 F4
Cavell Dr., Enf. 24 G2
Cavell Rd. N17 33 A7
Cavell St. E1 59 E5
Cavendish Ave. N3 39 D2
Cavendish Ave. NW8 6 F2
Cavendish Ave. NW8 57 G2
Cavendish Ave. W13 55 D5
Cavendish Ave., Erith 71 J7
Cavendish Ave., Har. 46 A4
Cavendish Ave., N.Mal. 92 G5
Cavendish Ave., Ruis. 45 B5
Cavendish Ave., Sid. 80 A7
Cavendish Ave., Well. 79 J3
Cavendish Ave., Wdf.Grn. 42 H1
Cavendish Clo. N18 33 E5
Cavendish Rd.
Cavendish Clo. NW6 48 C7
Cavendish Rd.
Cavendish Clo. NW8 6 F3
Cavendish Clo. NW8 57 G3
Cavendish Ct. EC3 13 E3
Cavendish Cres., Borwd. 22 A4
Cavendish Dr. E11 51 D1
Cavendish Dr., Edg. 29 J6
Cavendish Dr., Esher 98 B5
Cavendish Gdns., Bark. 52 H5
Cavendish Gdns., Ilf. 52 D1
Cavendish Gdns., Rom. 44 E5
Cavendish Ms. N. W1 11 E1
Cavendish Ms. S. W1 11 E2
Cavendish Pl. W1 11 E3
Cavendish Pl. W1 58 B6
Cavendish Rd. E4 34 C7
Cavendish Rd. N4 40 G6
Cavendish Rd. N18 33 E5
Cavendish Rd. NW6 48 B7
Cavendish Rd. SW12 76 B6
Cavendish Rd. SW19 84 G7
Cavendish Rd. W4 74 C1
Cavendish Rd., Barn. 22 J3
Cavendish Rd., Croy. 101 H1
Cavendish Rd., N.Mal. 92 E5
Cavendish Rd., Sutt. 100 F7
Cavendish Sq. W1 11 E3
Cavendish Sq. W1 58 B6
Cavendish St. N1 9 B2
Cavendish St. N1 59 A2
Cavendish Ter., Felt. 81 A2
High St.
Cavendish Way, W.Wick. 103 B1
Cavenham Gdns., Ilf. 52 G3

Name	Pg	Grid
Caverleigh Way, Wor.Pk.	99	G1
Caversham Ave. N13	32	G3
Caversham Ave., Sutt.	100	B2
Caversham Ms. SW3	18	J5
Caversham Rd. N15	49	J4
Caversham Rd. NW5	49	C6
Caversham Rd., Kings.T.	91	J2
Caversham St. SW3	18	J5
Caverswall St. W12	56	J6
Caveside Clo., Chis.	97	D1
Cawdor Cres. W7	64	D4
Cawnpore St. SE19	86	B5
Caxton Gro. E3	60	A3
Caxton Ms., Brent.	64	G6
The Butts		
Caxton Rd. N22	40	F2
Caxton Rd. SW19	84	
		F5
Caxton Rd. W12	66	A1
Caxton Rd., Sthl.	63	D3
Caxton St. SW1	15	G5
Caxton St. SW1	67	C3
Caxton St. N. E16	60	F7
Victoria Dock Rd.		
Caygill Clo., Brom.	96	F4
Cayley Clo., Wall.	101	E7
Brabazon Ave.		
Cayton Pl. EC1	9	B4
Cayton Rd., Grnf.	55	B2
Cayton St. EC1	9	B4
Cazenove Rd. E17	42	A1
Cazenove Rd. N16	50	C2
Cearns Ho. E6	61	A1
Cecil Ave., Bark.	52	G7
Cecil Ave., Enf.	25	C4
Cecil Ave., Wem.	46	J5
Cecil Clo., Chess.	98	G4
Cecil Ct. WC2	12	A6
Cecil Ct., Barn.	23	A3
Cecil Pk., Pnr.	36	E4
Cecil Pl., Mitch.	93	J5
Cecil Rd. E11	51	E3
Cecil Rd. E13	60	G1
Cecil Rd. E17	42	A1
Cecil Rd. N10	40	B2
Cecil Rd. N14	32	C1
Cecil Rd. NW9	38	D3
Cecil Rd. NW10	56	E1
Cecil Rd. SW19	84	E7
Cecil Rd. W3	56	C5
Cecil Rd., Croy.	94	E6
Cecil Rd., Enf.	24	J4
Cecil Rd., Har.	37	B3
Cecil Rd., Houns.	72	J2
Cecil Rd., Ilf.	52	E4
Cecil Rd., Rom.	44	D7
Cecil Rd., Sutt.	100	C6
Cecil Way, Brom.	103	G1
Cecile Pk. N8	40	E6
Cecilia Clo. N2	39	F3
Cecilia Rd. E8	50	C5
Cedar Ave., Barn.	23	H7
Cedar Ave., Enf.	25	F2
Cedar Ave., Hayes	54	A6
Acacia Ave.		
Cedar Ave., Rom.	44	E5
Cedar Ave., Ruis.	45	C6
Cedar Ave., Sid.	80	A7
Cedar Ave., Twick.	72	H6
Cedar Clo. SE21	85	J1
Cedar Clo. SW15	83	D4
Cedar Clo., Borwd.	22	B4
Cedar Clo., Brom.	104	B3
Cedar Clo., Buck.H.	35	A2
Cedar Clo., Cars.	100	J6
Cedar Clo., E.Mol.	91	B4
Cedar Rd.		
Cedar Clo., Rom.	44	J4
Cedar Copse, Brom.	97	C2
Cedar Ct. E8	50	C7
Cedar Ct. N1	49	J7
Essex Rd.		
Cedar Ct. SE9	79	B6
Cedar Ct. SW19	84	A3
Cedar Cres., Brom.	104	B3
Cedar Dr. N2	39	H4
Cedar Dr., Pnr.	28	G7
Cedar Gdns., Sutt.	100	F6
Cedar Gro. W5	64	H3
Cedar Gro., Bex.	80	C6
Cedar Gro., Sthl.	54	G5
Cedar Heights, Rich.	82	H1
Cedar Ho., Croy.	103	B6
Cedar Lawn Ave., Barn.	23	B5
Cedar Mt. SE9	88	A1
Cedar Pk. Gdns., Rom.	44	D7
Cedar Ri. N14	24	A7
Cedar Rd. N17	41	C1
Cedar Rd. NW2	47	J4
Cedar Rd., Brom.	96	J2
Cedar Rd., Croy.	102	A2
Cedar Rd., E.Mol.	80	B4
Cedar Rd., Houns.	72	C2
Cedar Rd., Rom.	44	J4
Cedar Rd., Sutt.	100	F6
Cedar Rd., Tedd.	62	C5
Cedar Ter., Rich.	73	H4
Cedar Tree Gro. SE27	85	H5
Cedar Vista, Rich.	73	H1
Kew Rd.		
Cedar Way NW1	49	D7
Cedarcroft Rd., Chess.	91	J6
Cedarhurst Dr. SE9	78	J5
Cedarne Rd. SW6	66	E7
Cedars, The, Buck.H.	34	G1
Cedars, The, Tedd.	82	C6
Adelaide Rd.		
Cedars Ave. E17	42	A5
Cedars Ave., Mitch.	94	A4
Cedars Clo. NW4	39	A3
Cedars Ct. N9	33	B2
Church St.		
Cedars Ms. SW4	76	B4
Cedars Rd.		
Cedars Rd. E15	51	E6
Cedars Rd. N9	33	D2
Church St.		
Cedars Rd. N21	32	H2
Cedars Rd. SW4	76	B3
Cedars Rd. SW13	74	F2
Cedars Rd. W4	65	C6
Cedars Rd., Beck.	95	H2
Cedars Rd., Croy.	101	E3
Cedars Rd., Kings.T.	91	F1
Cedars Rd., Mord.	93	D4
Cedarville Gdns. SW16	85	F6
Cedra Ct. N16	50	D1
Cedric Rd. SE9	88	F3
Celadon Clo., Enf.	25	H3
Celandine Clo. E14	60	A5
Celandine Dr. SE28	71	B1
Celandine Way E15	60	E3
Celbridge Ms. W2	10	B3
Celestial Gdns. SE13	78	D4
Celia Rd. N19	49	C4
Celtic Ave., Brom.	96	E3
Celtic St. E14	60	B5
Cemetery La. SE7	70	B6
Cemetery Rd. E7	51	F4
Cemetery Rd. N17	33	B7
Cemetery Rd. SE2	71	B7
Cenacle Clo. NW3	48	D3
Centaur St. SE1	16	D5
Centaur St. SE1	67	F3
Centaurs Business Pk., Islw.	64	D6
Centenary Rd., Enf.	25	J4
Centenary Trd. Est., Enf.	25	J4
Central Ave. E11	51	D2
Central Ave. N2	39	G2
Central Ave. N9	33	B3
Central Ave. SW11	149	E7
Central Ave., Enf.	25	E2
Central Ave., Houns.	72	J4
Central Ave., Pnr.	36	F6
Central Ave., Wall.	101	E5
Central Ave., Well.	79	J2
Central Ave., W.Mol.	90	F4
Central Gdns., Mord.	93	F5
Central Hill SE19	86	A5
Central Mkts. EC1	12	H2
Central Mkts. EC1	58	J5
Central Pk. Ave., Dag.	53	H3
Central Pk. Est., Houns.	72	D1
Central Pk. Rd. E6	61	A2
Central Pl. SE25	95	E4
Portland Rd.		
Central Rd., Mord.	93	D6
Central Rd., Wem.	46	E5
Central Rd., Wor.Pk.	99	G1
Central Sq. NW11	39	D5
Central Sq., W.Mol.	90	F4
Central St. EC1	8	J3
Central St. EC1	111	J3
Central Way SE28	71	A1
Central Way, Cars.	100	H7
Central Way, Felt.	72	A5
Centre Ave. W3	66	D1
Centre Ave. W10	56	J3
Harrow Rd.		
Centre Common Rd., Chis.	88	F6
Centre Rd. E7	51	G2
Centre Rd. E11	51	G2
Centre Rd., Dag.	62	H2
Centre St. E2	59	E2
Centre Way E17	34	C7
Centre Way N9	33	F2
Centreway NW7	30	G7
Centreway, Ilf.	52	F2
Centric Clo. NW1	58	B1
Oval Rd.		
Centurion Clo. N7	49	F7
Centurion Way, Erith	71	G3
Century Rd. E17	41	H3
Cephas Ave. E1	59	F4
Cephas St. E1	59	F4
Ceres Rd. SE18	70	J4
Cerise Rd. SE15	77	D1
Cerne Clo., Hayes	54	C7
Cerne Rd., Mord.	93	F6
Cerney Ms. W2	10	E5
Cervantes Ct. W2	10	B4
Cester St. E2	59	D1
Whiston Rd.		
Ceylon Rd. W14	66	A3
Chadacre Ave., Ilf.	43	C3
Chadacre Rd., Epsom	99	H6
Chadbourn St. E14	60	B5
Chadd Dr., Brom.	97	B3
Chadd Grn. E13	60	G1
Chadville Gdns., Rom.	44	D5
Chadway, Dag.	53	C1
Chadwell Ave., Rom.	44	B7
Chadwell Heath La., Rom.	44	A4
Chadwell St. EC1	8	F3
Chadwick Ave. E4	34	D4
Chadwick Clo., Tedd.	82	D6
Chadwick Rd. E11	42	E7
Chadwick Rd. NW10	56	F1
Chadwick Rd. SE15	77	C2
Chadwick Rd., Ilf.	52	E3
Chadwick St. SW1	15	H6
Chadwick St. SW1	67	D3
Chadwick Way SE28	62	D7
Chadwin Ms. E13	60	H5
Chadwin Rd. E13	60	H5
Chadworth Way, Esher	98	A5
Chaffinch Ave., Croy.	95	G6
Chaffinch Clo. N9	33	G1
Chaffinch Clo., Croy.	95	G5
Chaffinch Clo., Surb.	99	A3
Chaffinch Rd., Beck.	95	H1
Chafford Way, Rom.	44	C4
Chagford St. NW1	6	J6
Chagford St. NW1	57	J4
Chailey Ave., Enf.	25	C2
Chailey Clo., Houns.	72	D1
Springwell Rd.		
Chailey St. E5	50	F3
Chalcombe Rd. SE2	71	B3
Chalcot Clo., Sutt.	100	D7
Chalcot Cres. NW1	57	J1
Chalcot Gdns. NW3	48	J6
Chalcot Rd. NW1	49	A7
Chalcot Sq. NW1	49	A7
Chalcott Gdns., Surb.	98	F1
Chalcroft Rd. SE13	78	E5
Chaldon Path, Th.Hth.	94	H4
Chaldon Rd. SW6	66	B7
Chale Rd. SW2	76	E6
Chalet Est. NW7	30	G4
Chalfont Ave., Wem.	47	B6
Chalfont Ct. NW9	38	F3
Chalfont Grn. N9	33	B3
Chalfont Rd. N9	33	B3
Chalfont Rd. SE25	95	C3
Chalfont Rd., Hayes	63	A2
Chalfont Way W13	64	E3
Chalford Clo., W.Mol.	90	G4
Chalford Rd. SE21	86	A3
Chalford Wk., Wdf.Grn.	43	A1
Chalgrove Ave., Mord.	93	D5
Chalgrove Cres., Ilf.	43	B2
Chalgrove Gdns. N3	39	B3
Chalgrove Rd. E9	50	F6
Morning La.		
Chalgrove Rd. N17	41	E1
Chalgrove Rd., Sutt.	100	G7
Chalice Clo., Wall.	101	D6
Lavender Vale		
Chalk Cres. SE12	87	H3
Chalk Fm. Rd. NW1	49	A7
Chalk Hill Rd. W6	66	A4
Shortlands		
Chalk La., Barn.	23	J3
Chalk Pit Way, Sutt.	100	F5
Chalk Rd. E13	60	H5
Chalkenden Clo. SE20	86	E7
Chalkhill Rd., Wem.	47	A3
Chalklands, The, Wem.	47	C3
The Leadings		
Chalkstone Clo., Well.	80	A1
Chalkwell Pk. Ave., Enf.	25	B4
Challice Way SW2	85	F1
Challin St. SE20	95	F1
Challis Rd., Brent.	64	G5
Challoner Clo. N2	39	G2
Challoner Cres. W14	66	C5
Challoner St.		
Challoner St. W14	66	C5
Challoners Clo., E.Mol.	91	A4
Chalmers Wk. SE17	20	H6
Chalmers Way, Felt.	72	A5
Chalsey Rd. SE4	77	J4
Chalton Dr. N2	39	F6
Chalton St. NW1	7	G1
Chalton St. NW1	58	C2
Chamber St. E1	13	G5
Chamber St. E1	59	C7
Chamberlain Clo. SE28	70	C3
Broadwater Rd.		
Chamberlain Cotts. SE5	77	A1
Camberwell Gro.		
Chamberlain Cres., W.Wick.	103	B1
Chamberlain La., Pnr.	26	A1
Chamberlain Rd. N2	39	D3
Chamberlain Rd. N9	33	D3
Chamberlain Rd. W13	64	D2
Midhurst Rd.		
Chamberlain St. NW1	48	J7
Regents Pk. Rd.		
Chamberlain Wk., Felt.	81	E4
Burgess Clo.		
Chamberlain Way, Pnr.	36	B3
Chamberlain Way, Surb.	91	H7
Chamberlayne Rd. NW10	56	J1
Chambers Gdns. N2	39	G1
Chambers La. NW10	47	H1
Chambers Rd. N7	49	E4
Chambers St. SE16	17	H4
Chambers St. SE16	68	D2
Chambord St. E2	9	G4
Chambord St. E2	59	C3
Champion Cres. SE26	86	H4
Champion Gro. SE5	77	A3
Champion Hill SE5	77	A3
Champion Hill Est. SE5	77	B3
Champion Pk. SE5	77	A2
Champion Rd. SE26	86	H4
Champness Clo. SE27	86	A4
Rommany Rd.		
Champneys Clo., Sutt.	100	C7
Chance St. E1	9	F5
Chance St. E1	59	C4
Chance St. E2	59	C4
Chancel St. SE1	16	G2
Chancel St. SE1	67	H1
Chancellor Gro. SE21	85	J2
Chancellor Pas. E14	69	A1
South Colonnade		
Chancellors Rd. W6	65	J5
Chancellors St. W6	65	J5
Chancelot Rd. SE2	71	B4
Chancery La. WC2	12	E3
Chancery La. WC2	58	G6
Chancery La., Beck.	96	B2
Chanctonbury Clo. SE9	88	E3
Chanctonbury Gdns., Sutt.	100	E7
Chanctonbury Way N12	31	D4
Chandler Ave. E16	60	G5
Chandler Clo., Hmptn.	90	G1
Chandler Rd., Loug.	27	E1
Chandler St. E1	68	E1
Wapping La.		
Chandlers Ms. E14	69	A2
Chandlers Way SW2	76	G7
Chandos Ave. E17	42	A2
Chandos Ave. N14	32	C3
Chandos Ave. N20	31	F1
Chandos Ave. W5	64	G4
Chandos Clo., Buck.H.	34	H2
Chandos Cres., Edg.	29	J7

Chandos Pl. WC2	12	A6
Chandos Pl. WC2	58	E7
Chandos Rd. E15	51	D5
Chandos Rd. N2	39	G2
Chandos Rd. N17	41	B2
Chandos Rd. NW2	47	J5
Chandos Rd. NW10	56	E4
Chandos Rd., Har.	36	J5
Chandos Rd., Pnr.	36	D7
Chandos St. W1	11	E2
Chandos St. N2	58	B5
Chandos Way NW11	48	E1
Change All. EC3	13	C4
Channel Clo., Houns.	72	G1
Channelsea Rd. E15	60	D1
Chant Sq. E15	51	D7
Chant St. E15	51	D7
Chantrey Rd. SW9	76	F3
Chantry Clo., Har.	37	J5
Chantry Clo., Sid.	89	E5
Ellenborough Rd.		
Chantry La., Brom.	97	A5
Bromley Common		
Chantry Pl., Har.	36	H1
Chantry Pt. W9	57	C4
Chantry Rd., Chess.	98	J5
Chantry Rd., Har.	36	H1
Chantry St. N1	58	H1
Chapel Ct. N2	39	H3
Chapel Ct. SE1	17	B3
Chapel Fm. Rd. SE9	88	C3
Chapel Ho. St. E14	69	B5
Chapel La., Chig.	35	J3
Chapel La., Pnr.	36	D3
Chapel La., Rom.	44	D7
Chapel Mkt. N1	8	E1
Chapel Mkt. N1	58	G2
Chapel Path E11	42	H6
Chapel Pl. EC2	9	D4
Chapel Pl. N1	8	F1
Chapel Pl. N17	33	C7
White Hart La.		
Chapel Pl. W1	11	D4
Chapel Pl. W1	58	B6
Chapel Rd. SE27	85	H4
Chapel Rd. W13	64	E1
Chapel Rd., Bexh.	80	G4
Chapel Rd., Houns.	72	H3
Chapel Rd., Ilf.	52	D3
Chapel Rd., Twick.	73	E7
Orleans Rd.		
Chapel Side W2	10	A5
Chapel Side W2	57	E7
Chapel Stones N17	41	C1
Kings Rd.		
Chapel St. E15	51	D7
Chapel St. NW1	10	G2
Chapel St. NW1	57	H5
Chapel St. SW1	15	C4
Chapel St. SW1	67	A3
Chapel St., Enf.	25	A3
Chapel Ter., Loug.	27	B7
Forest Rd.		
Chapel Vw., S.Croy.	102	F6
Chapel Wk. NW4	38	H4
Chapel Wk., Croy.	101	J2
Wellesley Rd.		
Chapel Way N7	49	F3
Sussex Way		
Chapelmount Rd., Wdf.Grn.	35	C6
Chaplin Clo. SE1	16	F3
Chaplin Clo. Sid.	67	G2
Chaplin Rd. E15	60	E1
Chaplin Rd. N17	41	C3
Chaplin Rd. NW2	47	G6
Chaplin Rd., Dag.	53	E7
Chaplin Rd., Wem.	46	F6
Chapman Cres., Har.	37	H5
Chapman Rd. E9	50	J6
Chapman Rd., Belv.	71	G5
Chapman Rd., Croy.	101	G1
Chapman St. E1	59	F7
Chapman's La. SE2	71	C4
Chapmans La., Belv.	71	D4
Chapmans Pk. Ind. Est. NW10	47	F6
Chapone Pl. W1	11	H4
Chapter Clo. W4	65	C3
Beaumont Rd.		
Chapter Ho. Ct. EC4	12	H4
Chapter Rd. NW2	47	G5
Chapter Rd. SE17	20	H4
Chapter Rd. SE17	67	H5
Chapter St. SW1	19	H2
Chapter St. SW1	67	D4
Chapter Way, Hmptn.	81	G4
Chara Pl. W4	65	D6
Charcroft Gdns., Enf.	25	F3
Chardin Rd. W4	65	E4
Elliott Rd.		
Chardmore Rd. N16	50	D1

Chardwell Clo. E6	61	B6
Northumberland Rd.		
Charecroft Way W12	66	A2
Charfield Ct. W9	6	A6
Charford Rd. E16	60	G5
Chargeable La. E13	60	F4
Chargeable St. E16	60	F4
Chargrove Clo. SE16	68	G2
Marlow Way		
Charing Clo., Orp.	104	J4
Charing Cross WC2	16	A1
Charing Cross Rd. WC2	11	J4
Charing Cross Rd. WC2	58	D6
Charlbert St. NW8	6	G1
Charlbert St. NW8	57	H2
Charlbury Ave., Stan.	29	G5
Charlbury Gdns., Ilf.	52	J2
Charlbury Gro. W5	55	F6
Charldane Rd. SE9	88	E3
Charlecote Gro. SE26	88	E3
Charlecote Rd., Dag.	53	E3
Charlemont Rd. E6	61	C3
Charles Barry Clo. SW4	76	C3
Charles Burton Ct. E5	50	H5
Ashenden Rd.		
Charles Clo., Sid.	89	B4
Charles Cres., Har.	37	A7
Charles Dickens Ho. E2	59	E3
Charles Grinling Wk. SE18	70	D4
Charles Ho. N17	33	C7
Charles La. NW8	6	G1
Charles Pl. NW1	7	G4
Charles Rd. E7	51	J7
Lens Rd.		
Charles Rd. SW19	93	D1
Charles Rd. W13	55	D6
Charles Rd., Rom.	44	D7
Charles II St. SW1	15	H1
Charles II St. SW1	67	D1
Charles Sevright Dr. NW7	31	A5
Charles Sq. N1	9	C4
Charles St. E16	70	A1
Charles St. SW13	74	E2
Charles St. W1	15	D1
Charles St. W1	67	B1
Charles St., Croy.	101	J3
Charles St., Enf.	25	C5
Charles St., Houns.	72	D2
Charlesfield SE9	87	J3
Charleston Clo., Felt.	81	A3
Charleston St. SE17	21	A2
Charleston St. SE17	67	J4
Charleville Circ. SE26	86	D5
Charleville Rd. W14	66	B5
Charlieville Rd., Erith	71	J7
Northumberland Pk.		
Charlmont Rd. SW17	84	J6
Charlotte Despard Ave. SW11	76	A1
Charlotte Ms. W1	11	G1
Charlotte Ms. W14	66	B4
Munden St.		
Charlotte Pl. NW9	38	C5
Uphill Dr.		
Charlotte Pl. SW1	19	F2
Charlotte Pl. W1	11	G2
Charlotte Rd. EC2	9	D4
Charlotte Rd. EC2	59	B4
Charlotte Rd. SW13	74	F1
Charlotte Rd., Dag.	53	H6
Charlotte Rd., Wall.	101	C6
Charlotte Row SW4	76	C3
North St.		
Charlotte Sq., Rich.	73	J6
Greville Rd.		
Charlotte St. W1	11	G1
Charlotte St. W1	58	C5
Charlotte Ter. N1	58	F1
Charlton Ch. La. SE7	69	J5
Charlton Cres., Bark.	61	J2
Charlton Dene SE7	69	J7
Charlton Kings Rd. NW5	49	D5
Charlton La. SE7	70	A5
Charlton Pk. La. SE7	70	A7
Charlton Pk. Rd. SE7	70	A6
Charlton Pl. N1	8	G1
Charlton Pl. N1	58	H2
Charlton Rd. N9	33	G1
Charlton Rd. NW10	56	E1
Charlton Rd. SE3	69	H7
Charlton Rd. SE7	69	J6
Charlton Rd., Har.	37	G5
Charlton Rd., Wem.	46	J1
Charlton Way SE3	78	E1

Charlwood Clo., Har.	29	B7
Kelvin Cres.		
Charlwood Pl. SW1	19	G2
Charlwood Pl. SW1	67	C4
Charlwood Rd. SW15	75	A4
Charlwood Sq., Mitch.	93	G3
Charlwood St. SW1	19	G3
Charlwood St. SW1	67	C5
Charlwood Ter. SW15	75	A4
Cardinal Pl.		
Charmian Ave., Stan.	37	G3
Charminster Ave. SW19	93	D2
Charminster Ct., Surb.	91	G6
Charminster Rd. SE9	88	A4
Charminster Rd., Wor.Pk.	100	A1
Charmouth Rd., Well.	80	B1
Charnock Rd. E5	50	E3
Charnwood Ave. SW19	93	D2
Charnwood Clo., N.Mal.	92	E4
Charnwood Dr. E18	42	H3
Charnwood Gdns. E14	69	A4
Charnwood Pl. N20	31	F3
Charnwood Rd. SE25	95	A5
Charnwood St. E5	50	E2
Charrington Rd., Croy.	101	H2
Drayton Rd.		
Charrington St. NW1	7	H1
Charrington St. NW1	58	D2
Charsley Rd. SE6	87	B2
Chart Clo., Brom.	96	E1
Chart Clo., Croy.	95	F6
Stockbury Rd.		
Chart St. N1	9	C3
Chart St. N1	59	A3
Charter Ave., Ilf.	52	G1
Charter Ct., N.Mal.	92	E3
Charter Cres., Houns.	72	E4
Charter Dr., Bex.	60	F7
Charter Rd., Kings.T.	92	B3
Charter Rd., The, Wdf.Grn.	34	E6
Charter Sq., Kings.T.	92	B2
Charter Way N3	39	C4
Charter Way N14	24	C6
Charterhouse Ave., Wem.	46	F4
Charterhouse Bldgs. EC1	8	H6
Charterhouse Sq. EC1	12	H1
Charterhouse Sq. EC1	58	H5
Charterhouse St. EC1	12	G2
Charterhouse St. EC1	58	G5
Charteris Rd. N4	49	G1
Charteris Rd. NW6	57	C1
Charteris Rd., Wdf.Grn.	34	H7
Charters Clo. SE19	86	B5
Chartfield Ave. SW15	74	H5
Chartfield Sq. SW15	75	A5
Chartfield Ave.		
Chartham Gro. SE27	85	G3
Royal Circ.		
Chartham Rd. SE25	95	E3
Chartley Ave. NW2	47	E3
Chartley Ave., Stan.	29	C6
Charton Clo., Belv.	71	F6
Chartridge Clo., Barn.	22	G5
Chartwell Clo. SE9	88	F2
Chartwell Dr., Orp.	104	G5
Chartwell Pl., Sutt.	100	C3
Chartwell Way SE20	95	E1
Charwood SW16	85	G4
Chase, The E12	52	A4
Chase, The SW4	76	B3
Chase, The SW16	85	F7
Chase, The SW20	93	B1
Chase, The, Bexh.	80	H3
Chase, The, Brom.	96	H3
Chase, The, Chig.	35	F4
Chase, The, Edg.	38	B1
Chase, The, Pnr.	36	F4
Chase, The, (Eastcote), Pnr.	36	C6
Chase, The, Rom. (Chadwell Heath)	44	E6
Chase, The, Stan.	29	D5
Chase, The, Sun.	90	B1
Chase, The, Wall.	101	E5
Chase Ct. Gdns., Enf.	24	J3

Chase Gdns. E4	34	A4
Chase Gdns., Twick.	73	A6
Chase Grn., Enf.	24	J3
Chase Grn. Ave., Enf.	24	H2
Chase Hill, Enf.	24	J3
Chase La., Ilf.	43	G5
Chase Ridings, Enf.	24	G2
Chase Rd. N14	24	C5
Chase Rd. NW10	56	D4
Chase Rd. W3	56	D4
Chase Side N14	24	A5
Chase Side, Enf.	24	J3
Chase Side Ave. SW20	93	B2
Chase Side Ave., Enf.	24	J2
Chase Side Cres., Enf.	24	J1
Chase Way N14	32	B2
Chasefield Rd. SW17	84	J4
Chaseley Dr. W4	74	B1
Wellesley Rd.		
Chaseley St. E14	59	H6
Chasemore Gdns., Croy.	101	H5
Thorneloe Gdns.		
Chaseville Pk. Rd. N21	24	E5
Chasewood Ave., Enf.	24	H2
Chatfield Rd. SW11	75	F3
Chatfield Rd., Croy.	101	H1
Chatham Ave., Brom.	96	F7
Chatham Clo. NW11	39	D5
Chatham Clo., Sutt.	93	C7
Chatham Pl. E9	50	F6
Chatham Rd. E17	41	H3
Chatham Rd. E18	42	F2
Grove Hill		
Chatham Rd. SW11	75	J6
Chatham Rd., Kings.T.	92	A2
Chatham Rd., Orp.	104	F5
Chatham St. SE17	21	B1
Chatham St. SE17	68	A4
Chatsfield Pl. W5	55	H6
Chatsworth Ave. NW4	38	J2
Chatsworth Ave. SW20	93	B1
Chatsworth Ave., Brom.	87	H5
Chatsworth Ave., Sid.	89	A1
Chatsworth Ave., Wem.	46	J5
Chatsworth Clo. NW4	38	J2
Chatsworth Clo., Borwd.	22	A3
Chatsworth Clo., W.Wick.	103	F2
Chatsworth Ct. W8	66	D4
Pembroke Rd.		
Chatsworth Cres., Houns.	73	A4
Chatsworth Dr., Enf.	25	D7
Chatsworth Est. E5	50	G4
Elderfield Rd.		
Chatsworth Gdns. W3	65	H1
Chatsworth Gdns., Har.	45	H1
Chatsworth Gdns., N.Mal.	92	F5
Chatsworth Pl., Mitch.	93	J3
Chatsworth Pl., Tedd.	82	D4
Chatsworth Ri. W5	55	J4
Chatsworth Rd. E5	50	F3
Chatsworth Rd. E15	51	F5
Chatsworth Rd. NW2	48	A6
Chatsworth Rd. W4	65	C6
Chatsworth Rd. W5	55	J4
Chatsworth Rd., Croy.	102	A4
Chatsworth Rd., Hayes	54	B4
Chatsworth Rd., Sutt.	100	A5
Chatsworth Way SE27	85	H3
Chatterton Rd. N4	49	H3
Chatterton Rd., Brom.	97	A4
Chatto Rd. SW11	75	J5
Chaucer Ave., Hayes	54	A5
Chaucer Ave., Houns.	72	B2
Chaucer Ave., Rich.	74	A3
Chaucer Clo. N11	32	C5
Chaucer Ct. N16	50	B4
Chaucer Dr. SE1	21	G2
Chaucer Dr. SE1	68	C4
Chaucer Gdns., Sutt.	100	D3
Chaucer Grn., Croy.	95	F7

Chaucer Rd. E7 51 G6
Chaucer Rd. E11 42 G6
Chaucer Rd. E17 42 C2
Chaucer Rd. SE24 76 G5
Chaucer Rd. W3 65 C1
Chaucer Rd., Sid. 89 C1
Chaucer Rd., Sutt. 100 D4
Chaucer Rd., Well. 79 J1
Chaucer Way SW19 84 G6
Chauncey Clo. N9 33 D3
Chaundrye Clo. SE9 79 B6
Chauntler Rd. E16 60 H7
Victoria Dock Rd.
Cheam Common Rd., 99 H2
Wor.Pk.
Cheam Mans., Sutt. 100 B7
Cheam Pk. Way, 100 B6
Sutt.
Cheam Rd. (SM1), 100 C6
Sutt.
Cheam St. SE15 77 E3
Evelina Rd.
Cheapside EC2 12 J4
Cheapside EC2 58 J6
Cheddar Waye, Hayes 54 B6
Cheddington Rd. N18 33 B3
Chedworth Clo. E16 60 F6
Hallsville Rd.
Cheeseman Clo., 81 E6
Hmptn.
Cheesemans Ter. 66 C5
W14
Chelford Rd., Brom. 87 D5
Chelmer Cres., Bark. 62 B2
Chelmer Rd. E9 50 G5
Chelmsford Clo. E6 61 C6
Guildford Rd.
Chelmsford Clo. W6 66 A6
Chelmsford Gdns., Ilf. 43 B7
Chelmsford Rd. E11 51 D1
Chelmsford Rd. E17 42 A6
Chelmsford Rd. E18 42 F1
Chelmsford Rd. N14 24 C7
Chelmsford Sq. 56 J1
NW10
Chelsea Bri. SW1 19 D5
Chelsea Bri. SW1 67 B6
Chelsea Bri. SW8 19 D5
Chelsea Bri. SW8 67 B6
Chelsea Bri. Rd. SW1 19 D5
Choloa Bri. Rd. SW1 67 A5
Chelsea Cloisters 18 H2
SW3
Chelsea Clo. NW10 56 D1
Winchelsea Rd.
Chelsea Clo., Edg. 38 A2
Chelsea Clo., Hmptn. 81 J6
Chelsea Embk. SW1 18 H6
Chelsea Embk. SW3 66 H6
Chelsea Gdns., Sutt. 100 B4
Chelsea Harbour Dr. 75 F1
SW10
Chelsea Manor Gdns. 18 H4
SW3
Chelsea Manor Gdns. 66 H5
SW3
Chelsea Manor St. 18 H4
SW3
Chelsea Manor St. 66 H5
SW3
Chelsea Pk. Gdns. 18 E5
SW3
Chelsea Pk. Gdns. 66 G6
SW3
Chelsea Sq. SW3 18 F3
Chelsea Sq. SW3 66 G5
Chelsea Wf. SW10 66 G7
Lots Rd.
Chelsfield Ave. N9 25 G7
Chelsfield Gdns. 86 F3
SE26
Chelsham Rd. SW4 76 D3
Chelsham Rd., 102 A6
S.Croy.
Chelston App., Ruis. 45 A2
Chelston Rd., Ruis. 45 A1
Chelsworth Dr. SE18 70 G6
Cheltenham Ave., 73 D7
Twick.
Cheltenham Clo., 92 C3
N.Mal.
Northcote Rd.
Cheltenham Clo., 45 H6
Nthlt.
Cheltenham Gdns. E6 61 B2
Cheltenham Gdns., 27 B6
Loug.
Cheltenham Pl. W3 58 B7
Cheltenham Pl., Har. 37 H4
Cheltenham Rd. E10 36 A6
Cheltenham Rd. SE15 77 F4
Cheltenham Ter. 19 A3
SW3

Cheltenham Ter. 66 J5
SW3
Chelverton Rd. SW15 75 A4
Chelwood Clo. E4 26 B6
Chelwood Gdns., 74 A2
Rich.
Chelwood Wk. SE4 77 H4
Chenappa Clo. E13 60 G3
Chenduit Way, Stan. 29 C5
Cheney Rd. NW1 8 A2
Cheney Rd. NW1 58 E2
Cheney Row E17 41 J7
Cheney St., Pnr. 36 C5
Cheneys Rd. E11 51 G3
Chenies, The, Orp. 97 H6
Chenies Ms. WC1 7 H6
Chenies Pl. NW1 7 J1
Chenies Pl. NW1 58 D2
Chenies St. WC1 7 H6
Chenies St. WC1 11 H1
Cheniston Gdns. W8 14 A5
Cheniston Gdns. W8 66 E3
Chepstow Clo. SW15 75 B6
Lytton Gro.
Chepstow Cres. W11 57 D7
Chepstow Cres., Ilf. 43 H6
Chepstow Gdns., 54 F6
Sthl.
Chepstow Pl. W2 57 D6
Chepstow Ri., Croy. 102 B3
Chepstow Rd. W2 57 D6
Chepstow Rd. W7 64 D3
Chepstow Rd., Croy. 102 B3
Chepstow Vill. W11 57 C7
Chepstow Way SE15 68 C7
Exeter Rd.
Chequer St. EC1 9 A6
Chequers Clo., Orp. 97 J4
Chequers Gdns. N13 32 H5
Chequers La., Dag. 62 F5
Chequers Rd., Loug. 27 D5
Chequers Way N13 32 H5
Cherbury Clo. SE28 62 D6
Cherbury St. N1 9 C2
Cherbury St. N1 59 A2
Cherchefelle Ms., 29 E5
Stan.
Cherimoya Gdns., 90 H3
W.Mol.
Kelvinbrook
Cherington Rd. W7 64 C1
Cheriton Ave., Brom. 96 F5
Cheriton Ave., Ilf. 43 C2
Cheriton Clo. W5 55 F5
Cheriton Dr. SE18 70 G7
Cheriton Sq. SW17 83 A2
Cherry Clo. SW2 76 G7
Tulse Hill
Cherry Clo. W5 64 G3
Cherry Clo., Cars. 100 J2
Cherry Clo., Mord. 93 B4
Cherry Cres., Brent. 64 E7
Cherry Gdn. St. SE16 68 E2
Cherry Gdns., Dag. 53 F5
Cherry Garth, Brent. 64 G5
Cherry Gro., Hayes 63 B1
Cherry Hill, Barn. 23 E6
Cherry Hill Gdns., 101 F4
Croy.
Cherry Laurel Wk. 76 F6
SW2
Beechdale Rd.
Cherry Orchard 102 A2
Gdns., Croy.
Oval Rd.
Cherry Orchard 90 F3
Gdns., W.Mol.
Cherry Orchard Rd., 104 B2
Brom.
Cherry Orchard Rd., 102 A2
Croy.
Cherry Orchard Rd., 90 F3
W.Mol.
Cherry Tree Clo., 46 C4
Wem.
Cherry Tree Ct. NW9 38 E1
Cherry Tree Dr. 85 E3
SW16
Cherry Tree Ri., 34 J4
Buck.H.
Cherry Tree Rd. E15 51 E4
Wingfield Rd.
Cherry Tree Rd. N2 39 J4
Cherry Tree Wk., 95 J4
Beck.
Cherry Tree Wk. 103 F4
W.Wick.
Cherry Tree Way, 29 E6
Stan.
Cherry Wk., Brom. 103 G1
Cherry Way, Epsom 99 D6
Cherry Wd. Way W5 56 A5

Hanger Vale La.
Cherrycot Hill, Orp. 104 G4
Cherrycot Ri., Orp. 104 F4
Cherrycroft Gdns., 28 F7
Pnr.
Westfield Pk.
Cherrydown Ave. E4 33 J3
Cherrydown Clo. E4 33 J3
Cherrydown Rd., Sid. 89 D2
Cherrydown Wk., 44 H2
Rom.
Cherrywood Clo., 83 A7
Kings.T.
Cherrywood Dr. 75 A5
SW15
Cherrywood La., 93 B4
Mord.
Cherston Gdns., 27 D4
Loug.
Cherston Rd.
Cherston Rd., Loug. 27 D4
Chertsey Dr., Sutt. 100 B2
Chertsey Rd. E11 51 D2
Chertsey Rd., Ilf. 52 G4
Chertsey Rd., Twick. 73 C6
Chervil Clo., Felt. 81 A3
Chervil Ms. SE28 71 B1
Cherwell Ct., Epsom 99 C4
Cheryls Clo. SW6 75 E1
Cheseman St. SE26 86 E3
Chesfield Rd., 82 H7
Kings.T.
Chesham Ave., Orp. 97 E6
Chesham Clo. SW1 15 B6
Chesham Cres. SE20 95 F2
Chesham Ms. SW1 15 B5
Chesham Ms. SW1 67 A3
Chesham Pl. SW1 15 B6
Chesham Pl. SW1 67 A3
Chesham Rd. SE20 95 F2
Chesham Rd. SW19 84 G5
Chesham Rd., 92 A2
Kings.T.
Chesham St. NW10 47 D3
Chesham St. SW1 15 B6
Chesham St. SW1 67 A3
Chesham Ter. W13 64 E2
Cheshire Clo. SE4 77 J2
Cheshire Clo., Mitch. 94 E3
Cheshire Gdns., 00 GG
Chess.
Cheshire Rd. N22 32 F6
Cheshire St. E2 9 G5
Cheshire St. E2 59 C4
Chesholm Rd. N16 50 B3
Cheshunt Rd. E7 51 H6
Cheshunt Rd., Belv. 71 G5
Chesilton Rd. SW6 75 C1
Chesley Gdns. E6 61 A2
Chesney Cres., 103 C7
Croy.
Chesney St. SW11 76 A1
Chesnut Est. N17 41 C3
Chesnut Gro. N17 41 C3
Chesnut Rd.
Chesnut Rd. N17 41 C3
Chessington Ave. N3 39 B3
Chessington Ave., 71 E7
Bexh.
Chessington Clo., 99 C6
Epsom
Chessington Ct., Pnr. 36 F4
Chessington Hall 98 G7
Gdns., Chess.
Chessington Hill Pk., 99 A5
Chess.
Chessington Lo. N3 39 C3
Chessington Rd., 99 B6
Epsom
Chessington Way, 103 B2
W.Wick.
Chesson Rd. W14 66 C6
Chesswood Way, Pnr. 36 D2
Chester Ave., Rich. 73 J6
Chester Ave., 81 F1
Twick.
Chester Clo. SW1 15 D4
Chester Clo. SW1 67 B2
Chester Clo. SW13 74 H3
Chester Clo., Loug. 27 F1
Chester Clo., Sutt. 100 D2
Broomloan La.
Chester Clo. N. NW1 7 E3
Chester Clo. S. NW1 7 E4
Chester Cotts. SW1 19 B2
Chester Ct. NW1 7 E3
Chester Ct. SE5 68 A7
Ridley Rd.
Chester Cres. E8 50 C6
Chester Dr., Har. 36 F6
Chester Gdns. W13 55 E6

Chester Gdns., Enf. 25 E6
Chester Gdns., Mord. 93 F6
Chester Gate NW1 7 D4
Chester Gate NW1 58 B3
Chester Grn., Loug. 27 F1
Chester Ms. SW1 15 D5
Chester Ms. SW1 67 B3
Chester Path, Loug. 27 F1
Chester Pl. NW1 7 D3
Chester Rd. E7 52 A7
Chester Rd. E11 42 H6
Chester Rd. E16 60 E4
Chester Rd. E17 41 G5
Chester Rd. N9 33 E1
Chester Rd. N17 41 A3
Chester Rd. N19 49 B2
Chester Rd. NW1 7 C4
Chester Rd. NW1 58 A3
Chester Rd. SW19 83 J6
Chester Rd., Borwd. 22 C3
Chester Rd., Chig. 35 D2
Chester Rd., Houns. 72 B3
Chester Rd., Ilf. 52 J1
Chester Rd., Loug. 27 E2
Chester Rd., Sid. 79 H5
Chester Row SW1 19 B2
Chester Row SW1 67 A4
Chester Sq. SW1 19 C1
Chester Sq. SW1 67 A4
Chester Sq. Ms. SW1 15 D6
Chester St. E2 9 J5
Chester St. E2 59 D4
Chester St. SW1 15 C5
Chester St. SW1 67 A3
Chester Ter. NW1 7 D3
Chester Way SE11 20 F2
Chester Way SE11 67 G4
Chesterfield Dr., 98 D2
Esher
Chesterfield Gdns. 40 H5
N4
Chesterfield Gdns. 69 D7
SE10
Crooms Hill
Chesterfield Gdns. 15 D1
W1
Chesterfield Gdns. 67 B1
W1
Chesterfield Gro. 77 C5
SE22
Chesterfield Hill W1 15 D1
Chesterfield Hill W1 67 B1
Chesterfield Rd. E10 42 C6
Chesterfield Rd. N3 31 D6
Chesterfield Rd. W4 65 C6
Chesterfield Rd., 23 A5
Barn.
Chesterfield Rd., 99 D5
Epsom
Chesterfield St. W1 15 D1
Chesterfield St. W1 67 B1
Chesterfield Wk. 78 D1
SE10
Chesterfield Way 68 F7
SE15
Chesterfield Way, 63 A2
Hayes
Chesterford Gdns. 48 E4
NW3
Chesterford Ho. SE18 70 A7
Shooter's Hill Rd.
Chesterford Rd. E12 52 C5
Chesters, The, N.Mal. 92 E1
Chesterton Clo. 75 D5
SW18
Ericson Clo.
Chesterton Clo., Grnf. 54 H2
Chesterton Rd. E13 60 G3
Chesterton Rd. W10 57 A5
Chesterton Ter. E13 60 G3
Chesterton Ter., 92 A2
Kings.T.
Chesthunte Rd. N17 40 J1
Chestnut All. SW6 66 C6
Lillie Rd.
Chestnut Ave. E7 51 H4
Chestnut Ave. N8 40 E5
Chestnut Ave. SW14 74 D3
Thornton Rd.
Chestnut Ave., Brent. 64 G4
Chestnut Ave., 35 A3
Buck.H.
Chestnut Ave., E.Mol. 91 G3
Chestnut Ave., Edg. 29 H6
Chestnut Ave., 99 E4
Epsom
Chestnut Ave., Esher 91 A7
Chestnut Ave., 81 G7
Hmptn.
Chestnut Ave., Tedd. 91 C2
Chestnut Ave., Wem. 46 E5
Chestnut Ave., 103 E5
W.Wick.

Chestnut Ave. N. E17 42 C4
Chestnut Ave. S. E17 42 C4
Chestnut Clo. N14 24 C5
Chestnut Clo. N16 50 A2
  Lordship Gro.
Chestnut Clo. SE6 87 C5
Chestnut Clo. SW16 85 G4
Chestnut Clo., 35 A3
  Buck.H.
Chestnut Clo., Cars. 100 J1
Chestnut Ct. SW6 66 C6
  North End Rd.
Chestnut Dr. E11 42 G6
Chestnut Dr., Bexh. 80 D3
Chestnut Dr., Har. 29 C7
Chestnut Dr., Pnr. 36 D6
Chestnut Gro. SW12 76 A7
Chestnut Gro. W5 64 G3
Chestnut Gro., Barn. 23 J5
Chestnut Gro., Ilf. 35 H6
Chestnut Gro., Islw. 73 D4
Chestnut Gro., Mitch. 94 D5
Chestnut Gro., N.Mal. 92 D3
Chestnut Gro., 102 E7
  S.Croy.
Chestnut Gro., Wem. 46 E5
Chestnut La. N20 31 B1
Chestnut Ri. SE18 70 H5
Chestnut Rd. SE27 85 H3
Chestnut Rd. SW20 93 A2
Chestnut Rd., 82 H7
  Kings.T.
Chestnut Rd., 82 B2
  Twick.
Chestnut Wk., 34 G5
  Wdf.Grn.
Chestnut Way, Felt. 81 B3
Cheston Ave., Croy. 102 H2
Chettle Clo. SE1 17 B5
Chettle Ct. N8 40 G6
Chetwode Rd. SW17 84 J3
Chetwynd Ave., Barn. 31 J1
Chetwynd Rd. NW5 49 B4
Cheval Pl. SW7 14 H5
Cheval Pl. SW7 66 H3
Cheval St. E14 69 A3
Chevening Rd., Wrom. 96 G3
  Marina Clo.
Chevening Rd. NW6 57 A2
Chevening Rd. SE10 69 F5
Chevening Rd. SE19 86 A6
Chevenings, The, 89 C3
  Sid.
Cheverton Rd. N19 49 D1
Chevet St. E9 50 H5
  Kenworthy Rd.
Cheviot Clo., Enf. 25 A2
Cheviot Gdns. NW2 48 A2
Cheviot Gate NW2 48 B2
Cheviot Rd. SE27 85 G5
Cheviot Way, Ilf. 43 H4
Chevron Clo. E16 60 G6
  Butchers Rd.
Chewton Rd. E17 41 H4
Cheyne Ave. E18 42 F3
Cheyne Ave., Twick. 81 F1
Cheyne La. NW4 38 J6
  Cheyne Wk.
Cheyne Clo., Brom. 104 B3
  Cedar Cres.
Cheyne Ct. SW3 18 J5
Cheyne Gdns. SW3 18 H5
Cheyne Gdns. SW3 66 H6
Cheyne Hill, Surb. 91 J4
Cheyne Ms. SW3 18 H6
Cheyne Pl. SW3 18 J5
Cheyne Row SW3 18 G6
Cheyne Row SW3 66 H6
Cheyne Wk. N21 24 H5
Cheyne Wk. NW4 38 J6
Cheyne Wk. SW3 18 H6
Cheyne Wk. SW3 66 H6
Cheyne Wk. SW10 18 E7
Cheyne Wk. SW10 66 G5
Cheyne Wk., Croy. 102 D2
Cheyneys Ave., Edg. 29 G6
Chichele Gdns., 102 C4
  Croy.
  Brownlow Rd.
Chichele Rd. NW2 48 A5
Chicheley Gdns., 28 J7
  Har.
Chicheley Rd., Har. 28 J7
Chicheley St. SE1 16 D3
Chicheley St. SE1 67 F2
Chichester Clo. E6 61 B6
Chichester Clo. SE3 87 J1
Chichester Clo., 81 F6
  Hmptn.
  Maple Clo.
Chichester Ct., Stan. 37 H3
Chichester Gdns., Ilf. 43 B7
Chichester Ms. SE27 85 G4

Chichester Rents 12 E3
  WC2
Chichester Rd. E11 51 E3
Chichester Rd. N9 33 D2
Chichester Rd. NW6 57 D2
Chichester Rd. W2 10 B1
Chichester Rd. W2 57 E5
Chichester Rd., 102 B3
  Croy.
Chichester St. SW1 19 G4
Chichester St. SW1 67 C5
Chichester Way E14 69 D4
Chichester Way, Felt. 72 C7
Chicksand St. E1 13 G2
Chicksand St. E1 59 C5
Chiddingfold N12 31 D3
Chiddingstone Ave., 71 F7
  Bexh.
Chiddingstone St. 75 D2
  SW6
Chieveley Rd., 80 H4
  Bexh.
Chignell Pl. W13 64 D1
  The Bdy.
Chigwell Hill E1 59 E7
  Pennington St.
Chigwell Hurst Ct., 36 D2
  Pnr.
Chigwell La., Loug. 27 F4
Chigwell Pk. Dr., 35 D3
  Chig.
Chigwell Ri., Chig. 35 D2
Chigwell Rd. E18 42 H3
Chigwell Rd., 35 A7
  Wdf.Grn.
Chilcot Clo. E14 60 B6
  Grundy St.
Childebert Rd. SW17 85 B2
Childeric Rd. SE14 68 H7
Childerley St. SW6 75 A1
  Fulham Palace Rd.
Childers, The, 35 C5
  Wdf.Grn.
Childers St. SE8 68 H6
Childs La. SE19 86 B6
  Westow St.
Child's Pl. SW5 66 D4
Child's St. SW5 66 D4
Child's Wk. SW5 66 D4
  Child's Pl.
Childs Way NW11 39 C5
Chilham Clo., Grnf. 55 D2
Chilham Rd. SE9 88 B4
Chilham Way, Brom. 96 G2
Chillerton Rd. SW17 85 A5
Chillingworth Gdns., 82 C3
  Twick.
  Tower Rd.
Chillingworth Rd. N7 49 G5
  Liverpool Rd.
Chilmark Gdns., 92 F7
  N.Mal.
Chilmark Rd. SW16 94 D2
Chiltern Ave., 81 G1
  Twick.
Chiltern Clo., Croy. 102 B3
Chiltern Clo., Wor.Pk. 99 J2
  Cotswold Way
Chiltern Dene, Enf. 24 F4
Chiltern Dr., Surb. 92 A6
Chiltern Gdns. NW2 48 A3
Chiltern Gdns., Brom. 66 A4
Chiltern Rd. E3 60 A4
  Knapp Rd.
Chiltern Rd., Ilf. 43 H4
Chiltern Rd., Pnr. 36 C5
Chiltern St. W1 11 B1
Chiltern St. W1 58 C5
Chiltern Way, 34 G3
  Wdf.Grn.
Chilthorne Clo. SE6 77 J7
  Ravensbourne Pk. Cres.
Chilton Ave. W5 64 G4
Chilton Gro. SE8 68 G4
Chilton Rd., Edg. 30 A6
  Manor Pk. Cres.
Chilton Rd., Rich. 74 A3
Chilton St. E2 9 G5
Chilton St. E2 59 C4
Chiltonian Ind. Est. 78 F6
  SE12
Chiltons, The E18 42 G2
  Grove Hill
Chilver St. SE10 69 F5
Chilwell Gdns., Wat. 28 C4
Chilworth Ct. SW19 84 A1
Chilworth Gdns., 100 F3
  Sutt.
Chilworth Ms. W2 10 E4
Chilworth Ms. W2 57 G6
Chilworth St. W2 10 D4
Chilworth St. W2 57 F6
Chimes Ave. N13 32 G5

Chinbrook Cres. 87 H3
  SE12
  Chinbrook Rd.
Chinbrook Est. SE9 88 A3
Chinbrook Rd. SE12 87 H3
Chinchilla Dr., 72 C2
  Houns.
Chine, The N10 40 C4
Chine, The N21 24 H6
Ching St. WC2 12 A4
Chingdale Rd. E4 34 E3
Chingford Ave. E4 34 A3
Chingford Hall Est. 33 J6
  E4
Chingford Ind. Est. 33 H5
  E4
Chingford La., 34 E4
  Wdf.Grn.
Chingford Mt. Rd. 34 A4
  E4
Chingford Rd. E4 34 A6
Chingford Rd. E17 42 B1
Chingley Clo., Brom. 87 E6
Chinnor Cres., Grnf. 54 H2
Chip St. SW4 76 D3
  Stonhouse St.
Chipka St. E14 69 C2
Chipley St. SE14 68 H6
  Nynehead St.
Chipmunk Gro., Nthlt. 54 E3
  Argus Way
Chippendale St. E5 50 G3
Chippenham Ave., 47 B5
  Wem.
Chippenham Gdns. 57 D3
  NW6
Chippenham Ms. W9 57 D4
Chippenham Rd. W9 57 D4
Chipping Clo., Barn. 23 B3
  St. Albans Rd.
Chipstead Ave., 94 H4
  Th.Hth.
Chipstead Clo. SE19 86 C7
Chipstead Gdns. NW2 47 H2
Chipstead St. SW6 75 D1
Chirk Clo., Hayes 54 E4
  Braunston Clo.
Chisenhale Rd. E3 59 H2
Chisholm Rd., Croy. 102 B2
Chisholm Rd., Rich. 73 J6
Chisledon Wk. E9 50 J6
  Trowbridge Est.
Chislehurst Ave. N12 31 F7
Chislehurst Rd., 97 A2
  Brom.
Chislehurst Rd., Chis. 97 C1
Chislehurst Rd., Orp. 97 H6
Chislehurst Rd., 73 H5
  Rich.
Chislehurst Rd., Sid. 89 A5
Chislet Clo., Beck. 87 A7
  Abbey La.
Chisley Rd. N15 41 B6
Chiswell Sq. SE3 78 H2
  Brook La.
Chiswell St. EC1 13 B1
Chiswell St. EC1 59 A5
Chiswick Bri. SW14 74 C2
Chiswick Bri. W4 74 C2
Chiswick Clo., Croy. 101 F3
Chiswick Common 65 D4
  Rd. W4
Chiswick Ct., Pnr. 36 F3
Chiswick Gdns. W4 74 C1
  Hartington Rd.
Chiswick High Rd. 65 A5
  W4
Chiswick Ho. Grds. 65 D6
  W4
Chiswick La. W4 65 E5
Chiswick La. S. W4 65 F5
Chiswick Mall W4 65 F6
Chiswick Mall W6 65 G5
Chiswick Quay W4 74 C1
Chiswick Rd. N9 33 D2
Chiswick Rd. W4 65 C4
Chiswick Sq. W4 65 E6
  Hogarth Roundabout
Chiswick Staithe W4 74 C1
Chiswick Vill. W4 65 B6
Chiswick Wf. W4 65 F6
Chitty St. W1 11 G1
Chitty St. W1 58 C5
Chitty's La., Dag. 53 D7
Chivalry Rd. SW11 75 H5
Chivers Rd. E4 34 B4
Choats Manor Way, 62 B4
  Bark.
  Renwick Rd.
Choats Rd., Dag. 62 E3
Chobham Gdns. 84 A2
  SW19

Chobham Rd. E15 51 D5
Cholmeley Cres. N6 40 B7
Cholmeley Pk. N6 49 B1
Cholmley Gdns. NW6 48 D5
  Fortune Grn. Rd.
Cholmley Rd., 91 E6
  T.Ditt.
Cholmondeley Ave. 56 G2
  NW10
Cholmondeley Wk., 73 F5
  Rich.
Choppins Ct. E1 68 E1
  Wapping La.
Chopwell Clo. E15 51 D7
  Bryant St.
Chorleywood Cres., 97 J2
  Orp.
Choumert Gro. SE15 77 D2
Choumert Rd. SE15 77 C3
Choumert Sq. SE15 77 D2
Chrisp St. E14 60 B5
Christ Ch. Rd. SW14 74 B5
Christ Ch. Rd., Beck. 96 A2
  Fairfield Rd.
Christchurch Ave. 31 F6
  N12
Christchurch Ave. 57 A1
  NW6
Christchurch Ave., 37 C4
  Har.
Christchurch Ave., 82 D5
  Tedd.
Christchurch Ave., 46 H6
  Wem.
Christchurch Clo. 84 G7
  SW19
Christchurch Gdns., 37 D4
  Har.
Christchurch Grn., 46 H6
  Wem.
Christchurch Hill 48 G3
  NW3
Christchurch Ind. 37 C4
  Cen., Har.
Christchurch La., 23 B2
  Barn.
Christchurch Pk., 100 F7
  Sutt.
Christchurch Pas. 48 G3
  NW3
  Christchurch Hill Rd.
Christchurch Pas., 23 B3
  Barn.
  Christchurch La.
Christchurch Rd. N8 40 C4
Christchurch Rd. 85 F1
  SW2
Christchurch Rd. 93 G1
  SW19
Christchurch Rd., Ilf. 52 E1
Christchurch Rd., 88 J4
  Sid.
Christchurch Rd., 91 J7
  Surb.
Christchurch Sq. E9 59 F1
  Victoria Pk. Rd.
Christchurch St. SW3 18 J5
Christchurch St. SW3 66 J6
Christchurch Ter. 18 J5
  SW3
Christchurch Way 69 E5
  SE10
Christian Ct. SE16 68 J1
Christian Flds. SW16 85 G7
Christian St. E1 13 J3
Christian St. E1 59 D6
Christie Gdns., Rom. 44 B6
Christie Rd. E9 50 H6
Christina Ct. N4 49 H1
  Adolphus Rd.
Christina St. EC2 9 D5
Christopher Ave. W7 64 D3
Christopher Clo. 68 G2
  SE16
Christopher Clo., Sid. 79 J5
Christopher Gdns., 53 D5
  Dag.
  Wren Rd.
Christopher Pl. NW1 7 J4
Christopher Rd., 63 B4
  Sthl.
Christopher St. EC2 9 C6
Christopher St. EC2 59 A4
Christopher's Ms. 66 B1
  W11
  Penzance St.
Chryssell Rd. SW9 67 G7
Chubworthy St. SE14 68 H6
Chudleigh Cres., 52 H4
  Ilf.
Chudleigh Gdns., 100 F3
  Sutt.
Chudleigh Rd. NW6 48 A7

Chudleigh Rd. SE4 77 J5
Chudleigh Rd., 73 B6
Twick.
Chudleigh St. E1 59 G6
Chudleigh Way, Ruis. 45 A1
Chulsa Rd. SE26 86 E5
Chumleigh St. SE5 21 D5
Chumleigh St. SE5 68 B6
Chumleigh Wk., Surb. 91 J4
Church All., Croy. 94 H7
Handcroft Rd.
Church App. SE21 86 A3
Church Ave. E4 34 D6
Church Ave. NW1 49 B6
Kentish Town Rd.
Church Ave. SW14 74 D3
Church Ave., Beck. 96 A1
Church Ave., Nthlt. 45 F7
Church Ave., Pnr. 36 E6
Church Ave., Sid. 89 A5
Church Ave., Sthl. 63 E3
Church Clo. N20 31 H3
Church Clo. W8 14 A3
Church Clo., Edg. 30 C5
Church Clo., Loug. 27 C2
Church Ct., Rich. 73 G5
George St.
Church Cres. E9 50 G7
Church Cres. N3 39 C1
Church Cres. N10 40 B4
Church Cres. N20 31 H3
Church Dr. NW9 47 D1
Church Dri., Har. 36 T6
Church Dr., W.Wick. 103 E3
Church Elm La., Dag. 53 G6
Church End E11 42 B4
Church End NW4 38 H3
Church Fm. La., 100 B6
Sutt.
Church Gdns. W5 64 G2
Church Gdns., Wem. 46 D4
Church Gate SW6 75 B3
Church Gro. SE13 78 B4
Church Gro., 91 F1
Kings.T.
Church Hill E17 42 A4
Church Hill N21 24 F7
Church Hill SE18 70 C3
Church Hill SW19 84 C5
Church Hill, Cars. 100 J5
Church Hill, Har. 46 B1
Church Hill, Loug. 27 C3
Church Hill Rd. E17 42 B4
Church Hill Rd., Barn. 23 H6
Church Hill Rd., 91 H5
Surb.
Church Hill Rd., 100 A4
Sutt.
Church Hyde SE18 70 H6
Old Mill Rd.
Church La. E11 51 E1
Church La. E17 42 B4
Church La. N2 39 F3
Church La. N8 40 F4
Church La. N9 33 D2
Church La. N17 41 B1
Church La. NW9 38 C6
Church La. SW17 85 B5
Church La. SW19 93 C1
Church La. W5 64 F2
Church La., Brom. 104 B1
Church La., Chess. 98 J6
Church La., Chis. 97 F1
Church La., Dag. 53 H6
Church La., Enf. 25 A3
Church La., Har. 37 C1
Church La., Loug. 27 C3
Church La., Pnr. 36 E3
Church La., Tedd. 82 C5
Church La., T.Ditt. 91 C6
Church La., Twick. 82 D1
Church La., Wall. 101 D3
Church Manor Est. 67 G7
SW9
Vassall Rd.
Church Manorway 71 A5
SE2
Church Meadow, 98 F2
Surb.
Church Mt. N2 39 G5
Church Pas., Barn. 23 C4
Wood St.
Church Pas., Surb. 91 H5
Adelaide Rd.
Church Path E11 42 G5
Church Path N5 49 H5
Church Path N12 31 F5
Church Path N17 33 B7
White Hart La.
Church Path N20 31 F4
Church Path NW10 47 E7
Church Path SW14 74 D3
North Worple Way

Church Path SW19 93 C2
Church Path W4 65 C3
Church Path W7 64 B1
Station Rd.
Church Path, Croy. 101 J2
Keeley Rd.
Church Path, Mitch. 93 H3
Church Path, Sthl. 63 F3
Church Pl. SW1 11 G6
Church Pl. W5 64 G2
Church Pl., Mitch. 93 H3
Church Pl., Twick. 82 E1
Church St.
Church Ri. SE23 86 G2
Church Ri., Chess. 98 J6
Church Rd. E10 51 A1
Church Rd. E12 52 B5
Church Rd. E17 41 H2
Church Rd. N6 40 A6
Church Rd. N17 41 B1
Church Rd. NW4 38 H4
Church Rd. NW10 47 E7
Church Rd. SE19 95 B1
Church Rd. SW13 74 F2
Church Rd. (Merton) 93 G1
SW19
Church Rd. 84 B5
(Wimbledon) SW19
Church Rd. W3 65 C1
Church Rd. W7 55 A7
Church Rd., Bark. 52 F6
Church Rd., Bexh. 80 F3
Church Rd., Brom. 96 G2
Church Rd. 96 E3
(Shortlands), Brom.
Church Rd., Buck.H. 34 H1
Church Rd., Croy. 101 H2
Church Rd., E.Mol. 91 A4
Church Rd., Enf. 25 F6
Church Rd. 99 D7
(West Ewell), Epsom
Church Rd., Erith 71 J5
Church Rd., Esher 98 C6
Church Rd., Felt. 81 D5
Church Rd., Houns. 63 B5
Church Rd., Ilf. 43 H6
Church Rd., Islw. 73 A1
Church Rd., Kes. 104 A7
Church Rd., 91 J2
Kings.T.
Church Rd., Loug. 26 G3
Church Rd., Mitch. 93 G3
Church Rd., Nthlt. 54 D2
Church Rd. 104 F5
(Farnborough), Orp.
Church Rd., Rich. 73 H4
Church Rd. (Ham), 82 E4
Rich.
Church Rd., Sid. 89 A4
Church Rd., Sthl. 63 F3
Church Rd., Stan. 29 E5
Church Rd., Surb. 98 F1
Church Rd., Sutt. 100 B6
Church Rd., Tedd. 82 B4
Church Rd., Wall. 101 C3
Church Rd., Well. 80 B2
Church Rd., Wor.Pk. 99 E2
Church Row NW3 48 F4
Church Row, Chis. 97 F1
Church St. E15 60 E1
Church St. E16 70 E1
Church St. N9 33 C2
Church St. NW8 10 F1
Church St. NW8 57 G5
Church St. W2 10 F1
Church St. W2 57 G5
Church St. W4 65 F6
Church St., Croy. 101 H3
Church St., Dag. 53 H6
Church St., Enf. 24 J3
Church St., Hmptn. 90 J2
Church St., Islw. 73 E3
Church St., Kings.T. 91 G2
Church St., Sun. 90 A3
Church St., Sutt. 100 E5
High St.
Church St., Twick. 82 D1
Church St. Est. NW8 6 F6
Church St. Est. NW8 57 G4
Church St. N. E15 60 E1
Church St. Pas. E15 60 E1
Church St.
Church Stretton Rd., 72 J5
Houns.
Church Ter. NW4 38 H3
Church Ter. SE13 78 E3
Church Ter. SW8 76 D2
Church Ter., Rich. 73 G5
Church Vale N2 39 J3
Church Vale SE23 86 F2
Church Wk. N16 50 A4
Church Wk. NW2 48 C3
Church Wk. NW4 38 J3

Church Wk. NW9 47 D2
Church Wk. SW13 74 G1
Church Wk. SW15 74 H5
St. Margarets Cres.
Church Wk. SW16 94 C2
Church Wk. SW20 92 J3
Church Wk., Brent. 64 F6
Church Wk., Rich. 73 G5
Red Lion St.
Church Wk., T.Ditt. 91 C6
Church Way N20 31 G3
Church Way, Barn. 23 J4
Mount Pleasant
Church Way, Edg. 30 A6
Station Rd.
Church Yd. Row 20 H1
SE11
Churchbury Clo., Enf. 25 B2
Churchbury La., Enf. 25 A3
Churchbury Rd. SE9 79 A7
Churchbury Rd., Enf. 25 A2
Churchcroft Clo. 76 A7
SW12
Endlesham Rd.
Churchdown, Brom. 87 E4
Churchfield Ave. N12 31 F6
Churchfield Clo., 36 J4
Har.
Churchfield Rd. W3 65 C1
Churchfield Rd. W7 64 B2
Churchfield Rd. W13 64 E1
Churchfield Rd., 80 A3
Well.
Churchfields E18 42 G1
Churchfields SE10 69 C6
Roan St.
Churchfields, Loug. 27 B4
Churchfields, W.Mol. 90 G3
Churchfields Ave., 81 F3
Felt.
Churchfields Rd., 95 G2
Beck.
Churchill Ave., Har. 37 E6
Churchill Ct. W5 55 J4
Churchill Ct., Nthlt. 45 G5
Churchill Gdns. W3 56 A6
Churchill Gdns. Est. 19 F4
SW1
Churchill Gdns. Est. 67 C5
SW1
Churchill Gdns. Rd. 19 E4
SW1
Churchill Gdns. Rd. 67 B5
SW1
Churchill Ms., 34 F6
Wdf.Grn.
High Rd.
Churchill Pl. E14 69 B1
Churchill Rd. E16 60 J6
Churchill Rd. NW2 47 H6
Churchill Rd. NW5 49 B4
Churchill Rd., Edg. 29 J6
Churchill Ter. E4 34 A4
Churchill Wk. E9 50 F5
Churchill Way, Brom. 96 G3
Ethelbert Rd.
Churchill Way, Sun. 81 A5
Churchley Rd. SE26 86 E4
Churchmead Clo., 23 H6
Barn.
Churchmead Rd. 47 G6
NW10
Churchmore Rd. 94 C1
SW16
Churchview Rd., 82 A1
Twick.
Churchway NW1 7 J3
Churchway NW1 58 D3
Churchwell Path E9 50 F6
Morning La.
Churston Ave. E13 60 H1
Churston Clo. SW2 85 H1
Tulse Hill
Churston Dr., Mord. 93 A5
Churston Gdns. N11 32 C6
Churton Pl. SW1 19 G2
Churton St. SW1 19 G2
Churton St. SW1 67 C4
Chusan Pl. E14 59 J6
Commercial Rd.
Chyngton Clo., Sid. 88 J3
Cibber Rd. SE23 86 G2
Cicada Rd. SW18 75 F6
Cicely Rd. SE15 77 D1
Cinderford Way, 87 E4
Brom.
Cinema Par. W5 55 J4
Ashbourne Rd.
Cinnamon Row SW11 75 F3
Cinnamon St. E1 68 E1
Cintra Pk. SE19 86 C7
Circle, The NW2 47 E3
Circle, The NW7 30 D5

Circle Gdns. SW19 93 G3
Circuits, The, Pnr. 36 C4
Circular Rd. N17 41 C3
Circular Way SE18 70 C6
Circus Ms. W1 10 J1
Circus Pl. EC2 13 C2
Circus Rd. NW8 6 E3
Circus Rd. NW8 57 G3
Circus Rd. SE10 69 C7
Cirencester St. W2 10 A1
Cirencester St. W2 57 E5
Cissbury Ring N. 31 C5
N12
Cissbury Ring S. 31 C5
N12
Cissbury Rd. N15 41 A5
Citadel Pl. SE11 20 C3
Citizen Rd. N7 49 G3
City Gdn. Row N1 8 H2
City Gdn. Row N1 58 H2
City Rd. EC1 8 G2
City Rd. EC1 58 H2
Civic Way, Ilf. 43 F4
Clabon Ms. SW1 14 J6
Clabon Ms. SW1 66 J3
Clack St. SE16 68 F2
Clacton Rd. E6 61 A3
Clacton Rd. E17 41 H6
Clacton Rd. N17 41 C2
Sperling Rd.
Claigmar Gdns. N3 39 E1
Claire Ct. N12 31 F3
Claire Ct., Pnr. 28 F7
Westfield Pk.
Claire Ct., Wat. 29 A1
Claire Pl. E14 69 A3
Clairvale Rd., 72 D1
Houns.
Clairview Rd. SW16 85 B5
Clairvilla Gdns. W7 64 B1
Clairville Pl. SE23 86 G3
Clamp Hill, Stan. 29 A4
Clancarty Rd. SW6 75 D2
Clandon Clo. W3 65 B2
Avenue Rd.
Clandon Clo., Epsom 99 F6
Clandon Gdns. N3 39 D3
Clandon Rd., Ilf. 52 H2
Clandon St. SE8 78 A2
Clanfield Way SE15 21 E7
Clanricarde Gdns. 57 D7
W2
Clap La., Dag. 53 H3
Clapham Common 75 J4
N. Side SW4
Clapham Common 76 B6
S. Side SW4
Clapham Common 75 J4
W. Side SW4
Clapham Cres. SW4 76 D4
Clapham High St. 76 D4
SW4
Clapham Junct. Est. 75 H4
SW11
Clapham Manor St. 76 C3
SW4
Clapham Pk. Est. 76 D6
SW4
Clapham Pk. Rd. SW4 76 D4
Clapham Rd. SW9 76 E3
Clapham Rd. SW9 76 D3
SW4
Claps Gate La., Bark. 61 E4
Clapton Common E5 41 C7
Clapton Pas. E5 50 F5
Lwr. Clapton Rd.
Clapton Sq. E5 50 F5
Clapton Ter. N16 50 D1
Oldhill St.
Clapton Way E5 50 D4
Clara Pl. SE18 70 D4
Clare Gdns. N2 39 F3
Thomas More Way
Clare Cor. SE9 79 E7
Clare Gdns. E7 51 G4
Clare Gdns. W11 57 B6
Westbourne Pk. Rd.
Clare Gdns., Bark. 52 J6
Clare Gdns., Stan. 29 F5
Clare La. N1 49 J7
Clare Lawn Ave. 74 D5
SW14
Clare Mkt. WC2 12 C4
Clare Ms. SW6 66 E7
Waterford Rd.
Clare Pl. SW15 74 F6
Minstead Gdns.
Clare Rd. E11 42 D6
Clare Rd. NW10 47 G7
Clare Rd. SE14 77 J2
Clare Rd., Grnf. 46 A6
Clare Rd., Houns. 72 F3
Clare St. E2 59 E2

Clare Way, Bexh. 80 E1
Claredale St. E2 9 J2
Claredale St. E2 59 E2
Claremont Ave., Har. 37 H5
Claremont Ave., 92 H5
N.Mal.
Claremont Ave., Sun. 90 B1
Claremont Clo. E16 70 D1
Claremont Clo. N1 8 E2
Claremont Clo. N1 58 G2
Claremont Clo. SW2 85 F1
Garden La.
Claremont Gdns., Ilf. 52 H2
Claremont Gdns., 65 H1
Surb.
Claremont Gro. W4 65 E7
Edensor Gdns.
Claremont Gro., 34 J6
Wdf.Grn.
Claremont Pk. N3 39 B1
Claremont Rd. E7 51 H5
Claremont Rd. E11 51 D3
Claremont Rd. E17 41 H2
Claremont Rd. N6 40 B7
Claremont Rd. NW2 38 J7
Claremont Rd. W9 57 C2
Claremont Rd. W13 55 D5
Claremont Rd., Brom. 97 B4
Claremont Rd., 102 D1
Croy.
Claremont Rd., 98 B7
Esher
Claremont Rd., Har. 37 B2
Claremont Rd., Surb. 91 H6
Claremont Rd., 82 C5
Tedd.
Claremont Rd., 73 E6
Twick.
Claremont Sq. N1 8 E2
Claremont Sq. N1 58 G2
Claremont St. E16 70 D1
Claremont St. N18 33 D6
Claremont St. SE10 69 B6
Claremont Way NW2 47 J1
Clarence Ave. SW4 76 D7
Clarence Ave., Brom. 97 B4
Clarence Ave., Ilf. 43 D6
Clarence Ave., 92 C2
N.Mal.
Clarence Cres. SW4 76 D7
Clarence Cres., Sid. 89 B3
Clarence Gdns. NW1 7 E4
Clarence Gdns. NW1 58 B3
Clarence La. SW15 74 E6
Clarence Ms. E5 50 E5
Clarence Pas. NW1 8 A2
Clarence Pl. E5 50 E5
Clarence Rd. E5 50 E4
Clarence Rd. E12 52 A5
Clarence Rd. E16 60 F4
Clarence Rd. E17 41 G2
Clarence Rd. N15 40 J5
Clarence Rd. N22 32 E7
Clarence Rd. NW6 48 C7
Clarence Rd. SE9 88 B2
Clarence Rd. SW19 84 E6
Clarence Rd. W4 65 A5
Clarence Rd., Bexh. 80 E4
Clarence Rd., Brom. 97 A3
Clarence Rd., Croy. 95 A7
Clarence Rd., Enf. 25 E5
Clarence Rd., Rich. 73 J1
Clarence Rd., Sid. 89 B3
Clarence Rd., Sutt. 100 E4
Clarence Rd., Tedd. 82 C6
Clarence Rd., Wall. 101 B5
Clarence St.,
Kings.T. 91 H2
Clarence St., Rich. 73 H4
Clarence St., Sthl. 63 D3
Clarence Ter. NW1 7 A5
Clarence Ter., 72 H4
Houns.
Clarence Wk. SW4 76 E2
Clarence Way NW1 49 B7
Clarence Way Est. 49 B7
NW1
Clarendon Clo. W2 10 G5
Clarendon Cres. W11 57 B7
Clarendon Rd.
Clarendon Cres., 82 A3
Twick.
Clarendon Cross W11 57 B7
Portland Rd.
Clarendon Dr. SW15 74 D1
Clarendon Gdns. 38 G3
NW4
Clarendon Gdns. W9 6 D5
Clarendon Gdns. W9 57 F4
Clarendon Gdns., 52 C1
Ilf.
Clarendon Gdns., 46 G3
Wem.

Clarendon Gro. NW1 7 H3
Clarendon Gro., 93 J3
Mitch.
Clarendon Ms. W2 10 G5
Clarendon Ms., 22 A3
Borwd.
Clarendon Rd.
Clarendon Pl. W2 10 G5
Clarendon Pl. W2 57 H7
Clarendon Ri. SE13 78 C3
Clarendon Rd. E11 51 D1
Clarendon Rd. E17 42 B6
Clarendon Rd. E18 42 G3
Clarendon Rd. N8 40 F3
Clarendon Rd. N15 40 H4
Clarendon Rd. N18 33 D6
Clarendon Rd. N22 40 F2
Clarendon Rd. SW19 84 H7
Clarendon Rd. W5 55 H4
Clarendon Rd. W11 57 B7
Clarendon Rd., 22 A3
Borwd.
Clarendon Rd., 101 H2
Croy.
Clarendon Rd., Har. 37 B6
Clarendon Rd., 101 C6
Wall.
Clarendon St. SW1 19 E3
Clarendon St. SW1 67 B5
Clarendon Ter. W9 6 D5
Clarendon Wk. W11 57 B6
Lancaster Rd.
Clarendon Way N21 24 J6
Clarendon Way, 97 J3
Chis.
Clarens St. SE6 86 J2
Claret Gdns. SE25 95 B4
Clareville Gro. SW7 18 D2
Clareville Gro. SW7 66 F4
Clareville Rd., Orp. 104 F2
Clareville St. SW7 18 D2
Clareville St. SW7 66 F4
Clarewood Wk. SW9 76 G4
Somerleyton Rd.
Clarges Ms. W1 15 D1
Clarges Ms. W1 67 B1
Clarges St. W1 15 E1
Clarges St. W1 67 B1
Claribel Rd. SW9 76 H2
Claridge Rd., Dag. 53 D1
Clarissa Rd., Rom. 44 D7
Clarissa St. E8 59 C1
Clark St. E1 59 E5
Clark Way, Houns. 63 D7
Clarke Path N16 50 D1
Braydon Rd.
Clarkes Ave., 100 A1
Wor.Pk.
Clarke's Ms. W1 11 C1
Clarks Pl. EC2 13 D3
Clarks Pl. EC2 59 B6
Clarks Rd., Ilf. 52 G2
Clarkson Rd. E16 60 F6
Clarkson St. E2 59 E3
Clarksons, The, 61 F2
Bark.
Claude Rd. E10 51 C2
Claude Rd. E13 60 H1
Claude Rd. SE15 77 E2
Claude St. E14 69 A4
Claudia Jones Way 76 E6
SW2
Claudia Pl. SW19 84 B1
Claughton Rd. E13 60 J2
Clauson Ave., Nthlt. 45 H5
Clave St. E1 68 E1
Cinnamon St.
Clavell St. SE10 69 C6
Claverdale Rd. SW2 76 F7
Clavering Ave. SW13 65 H6
Clavering Clo., 82 D4
Twick.
Clavering Rd. E12 52 A1
Claverings Ind. Est. 33 G2
N9
Claverley Gro. N3 39 E1
Claverley Vill. N3 31 E7
Claverley Gro.
Claverton St. SW1 19 G4
Claverton St. SW1 67 C5
Claxton Gro. W6 66 A5
Clay Ave., Mitch. 94 B2
Clay La., Edg. 30 A2
Clay La., The, Loug. 29 A7
Clay St. W1 11 A2
Claybank Gro. SE13 78 B3
Algernon Rd.
Claybourne Ms. SE19 86 B7
Church Rd.
Claybridge SE12 87 J4
Claybrook Clo. N2 39 G3
Long La.
Claybrook Rd. W6 66 A6

Claybury Bdy., Ilf. 43 B3
Claybury Rd., 35 B7
Wdf.Grn.
Claydon Dr., Croy. 101 E4
Clayfarm Rd. SE9 88 F2
Claygate Cres., 103 C6
Croy.
Claygate La., Esher 98 D3
Claygate La., T.Ditt. 98 D1
Claygate Lo. Clo., 98 B7
Esher
Claygate Rd. W13 64 E3
Clayhall Ave., Ilf. 43 B3
Clayhill, Surb. 92 A5
Clayhill Cres. SE9 88 A4
Claylands Pl. SW8 20 E7
Claylands Pl. SW8 67 G7
Claylands Rd. SW8 20 D6
Claylands Rd. SW8 67 F6
Claymill Ho. SE18 70 F5
Claymore Clo., 93 D7
Mord.
Claypole Rd. E15 60 C2
Clayponds Ave., 64 H4
Brent.
Clayponds Gdns. W5 64 G4
Clayponds La., 64 H5
Brent.
Clays La. E15 51 B5
Clays La., Loug. 27 D1
Clays La. Clo. E15 51 B5
Clayside, Chig. 35 F5
Clayton Ave., Wem. 46 H7
Clayton Clo. E6 61 C6
Brandreth Rd.
Clayton Cres., Brent. 64 G5
Clayton Fld. NW9 30 E7
Clayton Rd. SE15 77 D1
Clayton Rd., Chess. 98 H4
Clayton Rd., Islw. 73 B3
Clayton Rd., Rom. 53 J1
Clayton St. SE11 20 E5
Clayton St. SE11 67 G6
Claywood Clo., Orp. 97 H7
Clayworth Clo., Sid. 80 B6
Cleanthus Clo. SE18 79 E1
Cleanthus Rd.
Cleanthus Rd. SE18 79 E1
Clearbrook Way E1 59 G6
West Arbour St.
Clearwater Dr. W9 6 B6
Clearwater Dr. W9 57 E4
Cleave Ave., Orp. 104 H6
Cleaveland Rd., 91 G5
Surb.
Cleaver Sq. SE11 20 F3
Cleaver Sq. SE11 67 G5
Cleaver St. SE11 20 F3
Cleaver St. SE11 67 G5
Cleaverholme Clo. 95 E6
SE25
Cleeve Hill SE23 86 E1
Cleeve Pk. Gdns., 89 B2
Sid.
Clegg St. E1 68 E1
Prusom St.
Clegg St. E13 60 G2
Cleland Path, Loug. 27 E1
Clem Attlee Ct. SW6 66 C6
Clematis St. W12 56 G7
Clemence St. E14 59 J5
Clement Clo. NW6 47 J7
Clement Clo. W4 65 D4
Acton La.
Clement Rd. SW19 84 B5
Clement Rd., Beck. 95 G2
Clementhorpe Rd., 53 C6
Dag.
Clementina Rd. E10 50 J1
Clementine Clo. W13 64 E2
Balfour Rd.
Clements Ave. E16 60 G7
Clements Ct., 72 D4
Houns.
Clement's Inn WC2 12 D4
Clement's Inn WC2 58 F6
Clement's Inn Pas. 12 D4
WC2
Clements La. EC4 13 C5
Clements La. EC4 59 A7
Clements La., Ilf. 52 E3
Clements Pl., 64 G5
Brent.
Clements Rd. E6 52 B7
Clements Rd. SE16 17 J6
Clements Rd. SE16 68 D3
Clements Rd., Ilf. 52 E3
Clendon Way SE18 70 G4
Polthorne Gro.
Clenham St. SE1 17 A3
Clensham La., Sutt. 100 D2
Clenston Ms. W1 10 J3
Clephane Rd. N1 49 J6

Clere St. EC2 9 C5
Clerkenwell Clo. EC1 8 F5
Clerkenwell Clo. EC1 58 G4
Clerkenwell Grn. EC1 8 F6
Clerkenwell Grn. EC1 58 G4
Clerkenwell Rd. EC1 8 E6
Clerkenwell Rd. EC1 58 G4
Clerks Piece, Loug. 27 C3
Clermont Rd. E9 59 F1
Cleve Rd. NW6 48 D7
Cleve Rd., Sid. 89 D3
Clevedon Clo. N16 50 C3
Smalley Clo.
Clevedon Gdns., 72 B1
Houns.
Clevedon Rd. SE20 95 G1
Clevedon Rd., 92 A2
Kings.T.
Clevedon Rd., 73 G6
Twick.
Cleveland Ave. SW20 93 C2
Cleveland Ave. W4 65 F4
Cleveland Ave., 81 F7
Hmptn.
Cleveland Cres., 22 C3
Borwd.
Cleveland Gdns. N4 40 J5
Cleveland Gdns. 48 A2
NW2
Cleveland Gdns. 74 F2
SW13
Cleveland Gdns. W2 10 C4
Cleveland Gdns. W2 57 F6
Cleveland Gdns., 99 E2
Wor.Pk.
Cleveland Gro. E1 59 F4
Cleveland Way
Cleveland Ms. W1 11 F1
Cleveland Pk. Ave. 42 A4
E17
Cleveland Pk. Cres. 42 A4
E17
Cleveland Pl. SW1 15 G1
Cleveland Ri., Mord. 93 A7
Cleveland Rd. E18 42 G1
Cleveland Rd. N1 50 A7
Cleveland Rd. N9 25 E7
Cleveland Rd. SW13 74 F2
Cleveland Rd. W4 65 C3
Antrobus Rd.
Cleveland Rd. W13 55 D5
Cleveland Rd., Ilf. 52 E3
Cleveland Rd., Islw. 73 D4
Cleveland Rd., 92 E4
N.Mal.
Cleveland Rd., Well. 79 J2
Cleveland Rd., 99 E2
Wor.Pk.
Cleveland Row SW1 15 F2
Cleveland Sq. W2 10 C4
Cleveland Sq. W2 57 F6
Cleveland St. W1 7 E6
Cleveland St. W1 57 F5
Cleveland Ter. W2 10 C4
Cleveland Ter. W2 57 F6
Cleveland Way E1 59 F4
Cleveley Clo. SE7 70 A4
Cleveley Cres. W5 55 H2
Cleveleys Rd. E5 50 E3
Cleverly Est. W12 65 G1
Cleves Rd. E6 61 A1
Cleves Rd., Rich. 82 F3
Cleves Wk., Ilf. 35 F7
Cleves Way, Hmptn. 80 F7
Cleves Way, Ruis. 45 D1
Clewer Cres., Har. 37 A1
Clichy Est. E1 59 F5
Clifden Rd. E5 50 F5
Clifden Rd., Brent. 64 G6
Clifden Rd., Twick. 82 C1
Cliff Rd. NW1 49 D6
Cliff Ter. SE8 78 A2
Cliff Vill. NW1 49 D6
Cliff Wk. E16 60 F5
Cliffe Rd., S.Croy. 102 A5
Cliffe Wk. SW14 74 B3
Clifford Ave., Chis. 88 C6
Clifford Ave., Ilf. 43 E1
Clifford Ave., Wall. 101 C4
Clifford Clo., 54 E1
Nthlt.
Clifford Dr. SW9 76 H4
Clifford Gdns. NW10 57 G1
Clifford Rd. E16 60 F4
Clifford Rd. E17 42 C2
Clifford Rd. N9 25 F6
Clifford Rd. SE25 95 D4
Clifford Rd., Barn. 23 E3
Clifford Rd., 72 D3
Houns.
Clifford Rd., Rich. 82 G2
Clifford Rd., Wem. 55 G1

Clifford St. W1 11 F6
Clifford Way NW10 58 C7
Clifford Way NW10 47 F4
Clifford's Inn Pas. 12 E4
EC4
Cliffview Rd. SE13 78 A3
Clifton Ave. E17 41 G3
Clifton Ave. N3 39 C1
Clifton Ave. W12 65 F2
Clifton Ave., Felt. 81 C3
Clifton Ave., Stan. 37 E2
Clifton Ave., Wem. 46 A6
Clifton Clo., Orp. 104 F5
Clifton Ct. NW8 6 E5
Clifton Cres. SE15 68 E7
Clifton Est. SE15 77 E1
Consort Rd.
Clifton Gdns. N15 41 C6
Clifton Gdns. NW11 39 C6
Clifton Gdns. W4 55 D4
Chiswick High Rd.
Clifton Gdns. W9 6 C6
Clifton Gdns. W9 57 F4
Clifton Gdns., Enf. 24 E4
Clifton Gro. E8 50 D6
Clifton Hill NW8 6 B1
Clifton Hill NW8 57 E2
Clifton Pk. Ave. 92 J2
SW20
Clifton Pl. SE16 68 F2
Canon Beck Rd.
Clifton Pl. W2 10 F4
Clifton Pl. W2 57 G6
Clifton Ri. SE14 68 H7
Clifton Rd. E7 52 A6
Clifton Rd. E16 60 E5
Clifton Rd. N3 39 F1
Clifton Rd. N8 40 D6
Clifton Rd. N22 40 C1
Clifton Rd. NW10 56 G2
Clifton Rd. SE25 95 A4
Clifton Rd. SW19 84 A6
Clifton Rd. W9 6 D5
Clifton Rd. W9 57 F4
Clifton Rd., Grnf. 54 J4
Clifton Rd., Har. 37 J5
Clifton Rd., Ilf. 43 G6
Clifton Rd., Islw. 73 A2
Clifton Rd., Kings.T. 82 J7
Clifton Rd., Loug. 27 B4
Clifton Rd., Sid. 89 H4
Clifton Rd., Sthl. 63 E4
Clifton Rd., Tedd. 82 B4
Clifton Rd., Wall. 101 B5
Clifton Rd., Well. 80 C3
Clifton St. EC2 13 D1
Clifton St. EC2 59 B5
Clifton Ter. N4 49 G2
Clifton Vill. W9 10 B1
Clifton Vill. W9 57 F5
Clifton Wk. E6 61 B5
Tollgate Rd.
Clifton Way SE15 68 F7
Clifton Way, Borwd. 22 C4
Clifton Way, Wem. 55 H1
Clinch Ct. E16 60 G5
Brent Rd.
Cline Rd. N11 32 C6
Clinger Ct. N1 59 B1
Pitfield St.
Clink St. SE1 17 B1
Clink St. SE1 67 J1
Clinton Ave., E.Mol. 90 J4
Clinton Ave., Well. 80 A4
Clinton Cres., Ilf. 35 H3
Clinton Rd. E3 59 H3
Clinton Rd. E7 51 G4
Clinton Rd. N15 41 A4
Clipper Clo. SE16 68 G2
Kinburn St.
Clipper Way SE13 78 C4
Clippesby Clo., 98 J6
Chess.
Clipstone Ms. W1 7 F6
Clipstone Rd. 58 C5
Clipstone Rd., 72 G3
Houns.
Clipstone St. W1 11 E1
Clipstone St. W1 58 B5
Clissold Clo. N2 39 J3
Clissold Ct. N4 49 J2
Clissold Cres. N16 50 A4
Clissold Rd. N16 50 A4
Clitheroe Ave., Har. 45 G1
Clitheroe Gdns., Wat. 28 D3
Clitheroe Rd. SW9 76 E2
Clitherow Ave. W7 64 D3
Clitherow Pas., 64 E5
Brent.
Clitherow Rd.
Clitherow Rd., Brent. 64 E5
Clitterhouse Cres. 47 J1
NW2

Clitterhouse Rd. 47 J1
NW2
Clive Ave. N18 33 D6
Claremont St.
Clive Ct. W9 6 D5
Clive Pas. SE21 86 A3
Clive Rd.
Clive Rd. SE21 86 A3
Clive Rd. SW19 84 H6
Clive Rd., Belv. 71 G4
Clive Rd., Enf. 25 D4
Clive Rd., Felt. 72 A6
Clive Rd., Twick. 82 C4
Clive Way, Enf. 25 D4
Cliveden Clo. N12 31 F4
Woodside Ave.
Cliveden Pl. SW1 19 B1
Cliveden Pl. SW1 67 A4
Cliveden Rd. SW19 93 C1
Clivedon Ct. W13 55 E5
Clivedon Rd. E4 34 E5
Clivesdale Dr., 63 A1
Hayes
Cloak La. EC4 13 B5
Cloak La. EC4 58 J7
Clock Ho. Rd., Beck. 95 H3
Clock Twr. Ms. N1 58 J1
Arlington Ave.
Clock Twr. Pl. N7 49 E6
Clock Twr. Rd., Islw. 73 C3
Clockhouse Ave., 61 F1
Bark.
Clockhouse Clo. 83 J3
SW19
Cloister Gdns. SE25 95 E6
Cloister Gdns., Edg. 30 C5
Cloister Rd. NW2 48 C3
Cloister Rd. W3 56 C5
Cloisters, The SW9 76 G1
Cloisters Ave., 97 C5
Brom.
Cloisters Mall, 91 G2
Kings.T.
Union St.
Clonard Way, Pnr. 28 G6
Clonbrock Rd. N16 50 B4
Cloncurry St. SW6 75 A2
Clonmel Clo., Har. 46 A2
Clonmel Rd., Tedd. 82 A4
Clonmell Rd. N17 41 A3
Clonmore St. SW18 84 C1
Cloonmore Ave., 104 J4
Orp.
Clorane Gdns. NW3 48 D3
Close, The E4 34 C7
Beech Hall Rd.
Close, The N14 32 D2
Close, The N20 31 C2
Close, The, Barn. 23 J6
Close, The, Beck. 95 H4
Close, The, Bex. 80 G6
Close, The, Har. 36 J2
Harrow Vw.
Close, The, Islw. 73 A2
Close, The, Mitch. 93 J4
Close, The, N.Mal. 92 C2
Close, The, Orp. 97 H6
Close, The 36 C7
(Eastcote), Pnr.
Close, The 36 F7
(Rayners La.), Pnr.
Close, The, Rich. 74 B3
Close, The, Rom. 44 E4
Close, The, Sid. 89 B4
Close, The, Sutt. 93 C3
Close, The 47 C3
(Barnhill Rd.), Wem.
Close, The 46 H6
(Lyon Pk. Ave.), Wem.
Cloth Ct. EC1 12 H2
Cloth Fair
Cloth Fair EC1 12 H2
Cloth Fair EC1 58 H5
Cloth St. EC1 12 J1
Clothworkers Rd. 70 G7
SE18
Cloudesdale Rd. 85 B2
SW17
Cloudesley Pl. N1 58 G1
Cloudesley Rd. N1 58 G1
Cloudesley Rd., 80 F1
Bexh.
Cloudesley Sq. N1 58 G1
Cloudesley St. N1 58 G1
Clouston Clo., Wall. 101 E5
Clova Rd. E7 51 F6
Clove Cres. E14 60 D7
Clove Hitch Quay 75 F3
SW11
Cotton Row
Clove St. E13 60 G4
Barking Rd.
Clovelly Ave. NW9 38 F4

Clovelly Clo., Pnr. 36 B3
Clovelly Gdns. SE19 95 C1
Clovelly Gdns., Enf. 35 C5
Clovelly Gdns., 44 H1
Rom.
Clovelly Rd. N8 40 D2
Clovelly Rd. W4 65 D4
Clovelly Rd. W5 64 F2
Clovelly Rd., Bexh. 71 E6
Clovelly Rd., 72 F2
Houns.
Clovelly Way E1 59 F6
Jamaica St.
Clovelly Way, Har. 45 F2
Clovelly Way, Orp. 97 J6
Clover Clo. E11 51 D2
Clover Ms. SW3 19 A5
Clover Way, Wall. 101 A1
Cloverdale Gdns., 79 J6
Sid.
Cloverleys (Park 27 A5
Hill), Loug.
Clowders Rd. SE6 86 J3
Clowser Clo., Sutt. 100 F5
Turnpike La.
Cloyster Wd., Edg. 29 G7
Cloysters Clo. E1 17 H1
Club Gdns. Rd., 96 G7
Brom.
Club Row E1 9 F5
Club Row E1 59 C4
Club Row E2 9 F5
Club Row E2 59 C4
Clunbury Ave., Sthl. 63 F5
Clunbury St. N1 9 C2
Clunbury St. N1 59 A2
Cluny Ms. SW5 66 D4
Cluny Pl. SE1 17 D5
Cluny Pl. SE1 17 D5
Cluse Pl. N1 8 J1
Clutton St. E14 60 B5
Clydach Rd., Enf. 25 C4
Clyde Circ. N15 41 B4
Clyde Pl. E10 42 B7
Clyde Rd. N15 41 B4
Clyde Rd. N22 40 D1
Clyde Rd., Croy. 102 C2
Clyde Rd., Sutt. 100 D5
Clyde Rd., Wall. 101 C6
Clyde St. SE8 68 J6
Clyde Ter. SE23 86 F2
Clyde Vale SE23 86 F2
Clydesdale, Enf. 25 G4
Clydesdale Ave., 37 G3
Stan.
Clydesdale Clo., 22 D5
Borwd.
Clydesdale Gdns., 74 B4
Rich.
Clydesdale Rd. W11 57 C6
Clymping Dene, 72 B7
Felt.
Clyston St. SW8 76 C2
Coach & Horses Yd. 11 F5
W1
Coach Ho. La. N5 49 H4
Highbury Hill
Coach Ho. La. SW19 84 A4
Coach Ho. Ms. SE20 86 E7
Coach Ho. Ms. SE23 77 F6
Coal Wf. Rd. W12 66 A2
Shepherds Bush Rd.
Coaldale Wk. SE21 76 J7
Lairdale Clo.
Coalecroft Rd. SW15 74 J4
Coate St. E2 9 J2
Coate St. E2 59 D2
Coates Hill Rd., 97 D2
Brom.
Coates Wk., Brent. 64 H5
Burford Rd.
Cobb St. E1 13 F2
Cobb St. E1 59 C4
Cobbett Rd. SE9 79 B3
Cobbett Rd., Twick. 81 G1
Cobbett St. SW8 67 F7
Cobbetts Ave., Ilf. 43 A5
Cobblers Wk., E.Mol. 91 J1
Cobblers Wk., 90 J1
Hmptn.
High St.
Cobblers Wk. 91 D1
Kings.T.
Cobblers Wk., Tedd. 82 A7
Cobblestone Pl., 101 J1
Croy.
Oakfield Rd.
Cobbold Est. NW10 57 F6
Cobbold Rd. E11 51 F3
Cobbold Rd. NW10 47 F6
Cobbold Rd. W12 65 F2
Cobb's Rd., Houns. 72 F4
Cobden Rd. E11 51 E3

Cobden Rd. SE25 95 D5
Cobden Rd., Orp. 104 G4
Cobham Ave., N.Mal. 92 G5
Cobham Clo. SW11 75 H6
Cobham Clo., Brom. 97 B7
Cobham Clo., Wall. 101 E6
Cobham Ho., Bark. 61 F1
St. Margarets
Cobham Pl., Bexh. 80 E5
Cobham Rd. E17 42 C1
Cobham Rd. N22 40 H3
Cobham Rd., Houns. 63 C7
Cobham Rd., Ilf. 52 H2
Cobham Rd., 92 A2
Kings.T.
Cobland Rd. SE12 87 J4
Coborn Rd. E3 59 J3
Coborn St. E3 59 J3
Cobourg Rd. SE5 21 F5
Cobourg Rd. SE5 68 C6
Cobourg St. NW1 7 G4
Cobourg St. NW1 58 C3
Coburg Clo. SW1 19 G1
Coburg Cres. SW2 85 F1
Coburg Gdns., Ilf. 43 A2
Coburg Rd. N22 40 F3
Cochrane Ms. NW8 6 F2
Cochrane Rd. SW19 84 C7
Cochrane St. NW8 6 F2
Cochrane St. NW8 57 G2
Cock Hill E1 13 E2
Cock La. EC1 12 G2
Cock La. EC1 59 H6
Cockayne Way SE8 68 H4
Windlass Pl.
Cockfosters Rd., Enf. 23 J3
Cockpit Steps SW1 15 J4
Cockpit Yd. WC1 12 D1
Cocks Cres., N.Mal. 92 F4
Cocksett Ave., Orp. 104 H6
Cockspur Ct. SW1 15 J1
Cockspur St. SW1 15 J1
Cockspur St. SW1 67 D1
Cocksure La., Sid. 89 G3
Code St. E1 9 G6
Code St. E1 59 C4
Codicote Ter. N4 49 J2
Green Las.
Codling Clo. E1 17 J1
Codling Way, Wem. 46 G4
Codrington Hill SE23 77 H7
Codrington Ms. W11 57 B6
Blenheim Cres.
Cody Clo., Har. 37 G3
Cody Clo., Wall. 101 D7
Alcock Clo.
Cody Rd. E16 60 E4
Coe Ave. SE25 95 D6
Coe's All., Barn. 23 B4
Wood St.
Cofers Circ., Wem. 47 B3
Cogan Ave. E17 41 H1
Coin St. SE1 16 E1
Coin St. SE1 67 G1
Coity Rd. NW5 49 A6
Coke St. E1 13 H3
Coke St. E1 59 D6
Cokers La. SE21 86 A1
Perifield
Colas Ms. NW6 57 D1
Birchington Rd.
Colbeck Ms. SW7 18 B2
Colbeck Rd. SW7 66 E4
Colbeck Rd., Har. 36 J7
Colberg Pl. N16 41 B7
Colborne Way, 99 J3
Wor.Pk.
Colburn Ave., Pnr. 28 E6
Colburn Way, Sutt. 100 G3
Colby Rd. SE19 86 B5
Colchester Ave. E12 52 C3
Colchester Dr., Pnr. 36 D5
Colchester Rd. E10 42 C7
Colchester Rd. E17 42 A6
Colchester Rd., Edg. 30 C7
Colchester Rd., 36 A2
Nthwd.
Colchester St. E1 13 G3
Cold Blow La. SE14 68 G7
Cold Blows, Mitch. 94 A3
Cold Harbour E14 69 C2
Coldbath Sq. EC1 8 E5
Coldbath St. SE13 78 B7
Coldershaw Rd. W13 64 D7
Coldfall Ave. N10 39 J2
Coldharbour La. SE5 76 J3
Coldharbour La. SW9 76 J3
Coldharbour Pl. SE5 76 J2
Denmark Hill
Coldharbour Rd., 101 G5
Croy.
Coldharbour Way, 101 G5
Croy.

Coldstream Gdns. 75 C6
SW18
Cole Clo. SE28 71 B1
Cole Gdns., Houns. 63 A7
Cole Pk. Gdns., 73 D6
Twick.
Cole Pk. Rd., Twick. 73 D7
Cole Pk. Vw., Twick. 73 D6
Cole Rd., Twick. 73 D6
Cole St. SE1 **17 A4**
Cole St. SE1 67 J2
Colebeck Ms. N1 49 H6
Colebert Ave. E1 59 F4
Colebrook Clo. SW15 75 A7
West Hill
Colebrook Gdns., 27 E2
Loug.
Colebrook Ho. E14 60 B6
Brabazon St.
Colebrook La., Loug. 27 E2
Colebrook Rd. SW16 94 E1
Colebrook Way N11 32 B5
Colebrooke Ave. W13 55 E6
Colebrooke Dr. E11 42 H7
Colebrooke Pl. N1 58 H1
St. Peters St.
Colebrooke Ri., 96 E2
Brom.
Colebrooke Row N1 8 G2
Colebrooke Row N1 58 H2
Coleby Path SE5 68 A7
Harris St.
Coledale Dr., Stan. 37 F1
Coleford Rd. SW18 75 F5
Colegrave Rd. E15 21 G6
Colegrove Rd. SE15 68 C6
Coleherne Ct. SW5 18 B4
Coleherne Ct. SW5 66 C5
Coleherne Ms. SW10 18 A4
Coleherne Ms. SW10 66 C5
Coleherne Rd. SW10 18 A4
Coleherne Rd. SW10 66 C5
Colehill Gdns. SW6 75 B2
Fulham Palace Rd.
Colehill La. SW6 75 B1
Coleman Clo. SE25 95 D2
Warminster Rd.
Coleman Flds. N1 58 J1
Coleman Rd. SE5 21 D7
Coleman Rd. SE5 68 B7
Coleman Rd., Belv. 71 G4
Coleman Rd., Dag. 53 E6
Coleman St. EC2 13 B3
Coleman St. EC2 59 A6
Colemans Heath SE9 88 D3
Colenso Rd. E5 50 F4
Colenso Rd., Ilf. 52 H1
Colepits Wd. Rd. SE9 79 G5
Coleraine Rd. N8 40 G3
Coleraine Rd. SE3 69 F6
Coleridge Ave. E12 52 B6
Coleridge Ave., 100 H4
Sutt.
Coleridge Clo. SW8 76 B2
Coleridge Gdns. 48 F7
NW6
Fairhazel Gdns.
Coleridge La. N8 40 E6
Coleridge Rd.
Coleridge Rd. E17 41 J4
Coleridge Rd. N4 49 G2
Coleridge Rd. N8 40 D6
Coleridge Rd. N12 31 F5
Coleridge Rd., Croy. 95 F6
Coleridge Sq. W13 55 D6
Coleridge Wk. NW11 39 D4
Coleridge Way, 54 A6
Hayes
Coles Grn., Har. 45 H2
Coles Grn., Loug. 27 D1
Coles Grn. 28 J1
(Bushey), Wat.
Coles Grn. Ct. NW2 47 G2
Coles Grn. Rd. NW2 47 G1
Colesburg Rd., Beck. 95 J3
Coleshill Rd., Tedd. 82 B6
Colestown St. SW11 75 H2
Colet Clo. N13 32 H6
Colet Gdns. W14 66 A5
Coley St. WC1 8 D6
Coley St. WC1 58 F4
Colfe Rd. SE23 86 H1
Colin Clo. NW9 38 E4
Colin Clo., Croy. 102 J3
Colin Clo., W.Wick. 103 F3
Colin Cres. NW9 38 F4
Colin Dr. NW9 38 F5
Colin Gdns. NW9 38 F5
Colin Pk. Rd. NW9 38 E3
Colin Rd. NW10 47 G6
Colina Ms. N15 40 H5
Harringay Rd.

Colina Rd. N15 40 H5
Colindale Ave. NW9 38 D3
Colindale Business 38 C3
Pk. NW9
Colindeep Gdns. 38 G5
NW4
Colindeep La. NW9 38 E3
Colinette Rd. SW15 74 J4
Colinton Rd., Ilf. 53 B2
Coliston Rd. SW18 75 D7
Collage Clo., Twick. 82 B1
Meadway
Collamore Ave. 84 H1
SW18
Collapit Clo., Har. 36 H6
Collard Ave., Loug. 27 F2
College App. SE10 69 C6
College Ave., Har. 37 B1
College Clo. E9 50 F5
Median Rd.
College Clo. N18 33 C5
College Clo., Har. 29 B7
College Clo., Twick. 82 A1
Meadway
College Cres. NW3 48 G6
College Cross N1 49 G7
College Dr., Ruis. 36 A7
College Gdns. E4 26 B7
College Gdns. N18 33 C5
College Gdns. SE21 86 B1
College Gdns. SW17 84 H2
College Gdns., Enf. 25 A1
College Gdns., Ilf. 43 B5
College Gdns., 92 F5
N.Mal.
College Grn. SE19 86 B7
College Gro. NW1 58 D1
St. Pancras Way
College Hill EC4 13 A5
College Hill Rd., Har. 29 B7
College La. NW5 49 B4
College Ms. SW1 16 A5
College Ms. SW18 75 E5
St. Ann's Hill
College Pk. Clo. 78 D4
SE13
College Pl. E17 42 H2
College Pl. NW1 58 C1
College Pl. SW10 66 F7
Hortensia Rd.
College Pt. E15 51 F6
Wolffe Gdns.
College Rd. E17 42 C5
College Rd. N17 33 C6
College Rd. N21 32 A2
College Rd. NW10 56 J2
College Rd. SE19 86 C5
College Rd. SE21 77 B7
College Rd. SW19 84 G6
College Rd. W13 55 E6
College Rd., Brom. 96 G1
College Rd., Croy. 102 A2
College Rd., Enf. 25 A1
College Rd., Har. 37 B6
(Harrow on the Hill)
College Rd., Har. 37 B1
(Harrow Weald)
College Rd., Islw. 73 C1
College Rd., Wem. 46 G1
College Row E9 50 G5
Homerton High St.
College Slip, Brom. 96 G1
College Ter. E3 59 J3
College Ter. N3 39 C2
Hendon La.
College Vw. SE9 88 A1
College Wk., Kings.T. 91 H2
Grange Rd.
College Yd. NW5 49 B4
College La.
Collent St. E9 50 F6
Colless Rd. N15 41 C5
Collett Rd. SE16 17 J6
Collett Rd. SE16 68 D3
Collett Way, Sthl. 63 H1
Collier Clo., Epsom 99 A6
Collier Dr., Edg. 38 A2
Collier Row Rd., 44 G1
Rom.
Collier St. N1 8 C2
Collier St. N1 58 F2
Colliers Shaw, Kes. 104 A5
Colliers Water La., 94 G5
Th.Hth.
Collindale Ave., 71 H6
Erith
Collindale Ave., 89 A1
Sid.
Collingbourne Rd. 65 H1
W12
Collingham Gdns. 18 B2
SW5

Collingham Gdns. 66 E4
SW5
Collingham Pl. SW5 18 A2
Collingham Pl. SW5 66 E4
Collingham Rd. SW5 18 B1
Collingham Rd. SW5 66 E4
Collings Clo. N22 32 F6
Whittington Rd.
Collingtree Rd. 86 F4
SE26
Collingwood Ave. 40 A3
N10
Collingwood Ave., 99 C1
Surb.
Collingwood Clo. 95 E1
SE20
Collingwood Clo., 72 G7
Twick.
Collingwood Rd. E17 42 A6
Collingwood Rd. N15 41 B4
Collingwood Rd., 93 H2
Mitch.
Collingwood Rd., 100 C3
Sutt.
Collingwood St. E1 59 E4
Collins Ave., Stan. 37 H2
Collins Dr., Ruis. 45 C2
Collins Rd. N5 49 J4
Collins Sq. SE3 78 F2
Tranquil Vale
Collins St. SE3 78 E2
Collin's Yd. N1 58 H1
Islington Grn.
Collinson St. SE1 16 J4
Collinson Wk. SE1 16 J4
Collinwood Ave., 25 F3
Enf.
Collinwood Gdns., 43 C5
Ilf.
Colls Rd. SE15 77 F1
Collyer Ave., Croy. 101 E4
Collyer Pl. SE15 77 D1
Peckham High St.
Collyer Rd., Croy. 101 E4
Colman Rd. E16 60 J5
Colmar Clo. E1 59 G4
Alderney Rd.
Colmer Pl., Har. 29 A7
Colmer Rd. SW16 94 E1
Colmore Ms. SE15 77 E1
Colmore Rd., Enf. 25 F4
Colnbrook St. SE1 16 G6
Colnbrook St. SE1 67 H3
Colne Ct., Epsom 99 C4
Colne Ho., Bark. 52 E6
Colne Rd. E5 50 H4
Colne Rd. N21 24 J7
Colne Rd., Twick. 82 B1
Colne St. E13 60 G3
Grange Rd.
Colney Hatch La. N10 32 A7
Colney Hatch La. N11 31 J6
Cologne Rd. SW11 75 G4
Colomb St. SE10 69 E5
Colombo Rd., Ilf. 52 F1
Colombo St. SE1 16 G2
Colombo St. SE1 67 H1
Colonial Ave., 72 J5
Twick.
Colonnade WC1 8 B6
Colonnade WC1 58 E4
Colonnade Wk. SW1 19 D2
Colonnades, The W2 10 B3
Colson Gdns., Loug. 27 E4
Colson Rd.
Colson Path, Loug. 27 D4
Colson Rd., Croy. 102 B2
Colson Rd., Loug. 27 D4
Colson Way SW16 85 C4
Colsterworth Rd. 41 C4
N15
Colston Ave., Cars. 100 H4
Colston Clo., Cars. 100 J4
West St.
Colston Rd. E7 52 A6
Colston Rd. SW14 74 C4
Coltness Cres. SE2 71 B5
Colton Rd. N17 40 J3
Colton Rd., Har. 37 B5
Columbia Ave., Edg. 38 B1
Columbia Ave., Ruis. 45 B1
Columbia Ave., 92 F7
Wor.Pk.
Columbia Ctyd. E14 69 A1
West India Ave.
Columbia Rd. E2 9 F3
Columbia Rd. E2 59 C3
Columbia Rd. E13 60 F4
Columbia Sq. SW14 74 C4
Upper Richmond Rd.
Columbine Ave. E6 61 B5
Columbine Ave., 101 H7
S.Croy.

Columbine Way 78 C2
SE13
Columbus Gdns., 36 A1
Nthwd.
Colva Wk. N19 49 B2
Chester Rd.
Colvestone Cres. E8 50 C5
Colview Ct. SE9 88 A1
Mottingham La.
Colville Est. N1 59 B1
Colville Gdns. W11 57 C6
Colville Hos. W11 57 C6
Colville Ms. W11 57 C6
Lonsdale Rd.
Colville Pl. W1 11 G2
Colville Rd. E11 51 C3
Colville Rd. E17 41 H2
Colville Rd. N9 33 F1
Colville Rd. W3 65 B3
Colville Rd. W11 57 C6
Colville Sq. W11 57 C6
Colville Ter. W11 57 C6
Colvin Clo. SE26 86 F5
Colvin Gdns. E4 34 C3
Colvin Gdns. E11 42 H4
Colvin Gdns., Ilf. 43 F1
Colvin Rd. E6 52 B7
Colvin Rd., Th.Hth. 94 G5
Colwell Rd. SE22 77 C5
Colwick Clo. N6 40 D7
Colwith Rd. W6 65 J6
Colwood Gdns. 84 G7
SW19
Colworth Gro. SE17 21 A2
Colworth Rd. E11 42 E6
Colworth Rd., Croy. 102 D3
Colwyn Ave., Grnf. 55 C2
Colwyn Cres., 72 J1
Houns.
Colwyn Grn. NW9 38 C6
Snowdon Dr.
Colwyn Rd. NW2 47 H3
Colyer Clo. SE9 88 E2
Colyer Clo. N1 58 D7
Colyton Clo., Well. 80 D1
Colyton Clo., Wem. 46 F6
Bridgewater Rd.
Colyton Rd. SE22 77 E5
Colyton Way N18 33 D5
Combe Ave. SE3 69 F7
Combe Lea, Brom. 97 B3
Combe St. SE7 69 J6
Elliscombe Rd.
Combe Ms. SE3 69 F7
Combedale Rd. SE10 69 G5
Combemartin Rd. 75 B7
SW18
Comber Clo. NW2 47 H2
Comber Gro. SE5 67 J7
Combermere Rd. 76 F3
SW9
Combermere Rd., 93 E5
Mord.
Comberton Rd. E5 50 E2
Combeside SE18 70 J7
Combwell Cres. SE2 71 A3
Comely Bank Rd. E17 42 C5
Comeragh Ms. W14 66 B5
Comeragh Rd.
Comeragh Rd. W14 66 B5
Comerford Rd. SE4 77 H4
Comet Pl. SE8 69 A7
Comet St. SE8 69 A7
Commerce Rd. N22 40 F1
Commerce Rd., 64 C7
Brent.
Commerce Way, 101 F2
Croy.
Commercial Rd. E1 13 H3
Commercial Rd. E1 59 D6
Commercial Rd. E14 59 H6
Commercial Rd. N17 33 B6
Commercial Rd. N18 33 B5
Commercial St. E1 9 F6
Commercial St. E1 59 C4
Commercial Way 56 B2
NW10
Commercial Way 68 C7
SE15
Commerell St. SE10 69 E5
Commodity Quay E1 13 G6
Commodore Sq. 75 F1
SW10
Commodore St. E1 59 H4
Common, The W5 55 H7
Common, The, Rich. 82 G3
Common, The, Sthl. 63 C4
Common, The, Stan. 29 B2
Common La., Esher 98 D7
Common Rd. SW13 74 G3
Common Rd., Esher 98 D6
Common Rd., Stan. 29 A3
Commondale SW15 74 J3

Commonside, Kes.	103	J4
Commonside E., Mitch.	94	A3
Commonside W., Mitch.	93	J3
Commonwealth Ave. W12	56	H7
Commonwealth Rd. N17	33	D7
Commonwealth Way SE2	71	B5
Community Clo., Houns.	72	B1
Community Rd. E15	51	D5
Community Rd., Grnf.	54	J1
Como Rd. SE23	86	H2
Compass Hill, Rich.	73	G6
Compayne Gdns. NW6	48	E7
Compton Ave. E6	61	A2
Compton Ave. N1	49	H6
Compton Ave. N6	39	H7
Compton Clo. NW1	**7**	**E4**
Compton Clo. W13	55	D6
Compton Clo., Edg. *Pavilion Way*	30	C7
Compton Ct. SE19 *Victoria Cres.*	86	B5
Compton Cres. N17	32	J7
Compton Cres. W4	65	C6
Compton Cres., Chess.	98	H6
Compton Cres., Nthlt.	54	D1
Compton Pas. EC1	**8**	**H5**
Compton Pl. WC1	**8**	**A5**
Compton Pl., Wat.	28	E3
Compton Ri., Pnr.	36	E5
Compton Rd. N1	49	H6
Compton Rd. N21	32	G1
Compton Rd. NW10	57	A3
Compton Rd. SW19	84	C6
Compton Rd., Croy.	102	E1
Compton St. EC1	**8**	**G5**
Compton St. EC1	58	H4
Compton Ter. N1	49	H6
Comreddy Rd., Enf.	24	H1
Comus Pl. SE17	**21**	**D2**
Comus Pl. SE17	68	B4
Comyn Rd. SW11	75	H4
Comyns, The (Bushey), Wat.	28	J1
Comyns Clo. E16	60	F5
Comyns Rd., Dag.	53	G7
Conant Ms. E1	**13**	**H5**
Concanon Rd. SW2	76	A4
Concert Hall App. SE1	**16**	**D2**
Concert Hall App. SE1	67	F1
Concord Clo., Nthlt. *Britannia Clo.*	54	D3
Concord Rd. W3	56	B4
Concord Rd., Enf.	25	E5
Concorde Clo., Houns. *Lampton Rd.*	72	H2
Concorde Dr. E6	61	C5
Concourse, The NW9 *Long Mead*	38	F1
Condell Rd. SW8	76	C1
Conder St. E14	59	H6
Conderton Rd. SE5	76	J3
Condover Cres. SE18	70	E7
Condray Pl. SW11	66	H7
Conduit Ct. WC2	**12**	**A5**
Conduit La. N18	33	F5
Conduit La., Croy.	102	D5
Conduit La., S.Croy.	102	D5
Conduit Ms. W2	**10**	**E4**
Conduit Pas. W2	57	G6
Conduit Pas. W2	**10**	**E4**
Conduit Pl. W2	**10**	**E4**
Conduit Pl. W2	57	G6
Conduit Rd. SE18	70	E5
Conduit St. W1	**11**	**E5**
Conduit St. W1	58	B7
Conduit Way NW10	47	C7
Conewood St. N5	49	H3
Coney Acre SE21	69	J1
Coney Burrows E4	34	E2 *Wyemead Cres.*
Coney Hill Rd., W.Wick.	103	E2
Coney Way SW8	**20**	**D6**
Coney Way SW8	76	D6
Conference Clo. E4	34	C2 *Greenbank Clo.*
Conference Rd. SE2	71	C4
Congleton Gro. SE18	70	F5

Congo Rd. SE18	70	G5
Congress Rd. SE2	71	C4
Congreve Rd. SE9	79	C3
Congreve St. SE17	**21**	**D2**
Congreve St. SE17	68	B4
Congreve Wk. E16 *Fulmer Rd.*	61	A5
Conical Cor., Enf.	24	J2
Conifer Clo., Orp.	104	G4
Conifer Gdns. SW16	85	E3
Conifer Gdns., Enf.	25	A6
Conifer Gdns., Sutt.	100	E3
Conifer Way, Hayes	54	A7
Conifer Way, Wem.	46	F3
Conifers Clo., Tedd.	82	F7
Coniger Rd. SW6	75	D2
Coningham Ms. W12 *Percy Rd.*	65	G1
Coningham Rd. W12	65	H1
Coningsby Cotts. W5 *Coningsby Rd.*	64	G2
Coningsby Gdns. E4	34	B6
Coningsby Rd. N4	40	H7
Coningsby Rd. W5	64	G2
Conington Rd. SE13	78	B2
Conisbee Ct. N14	24	C5
Conisborough Cres. SE6	87	C3
Coniscliffe Rd. N13	32	J3
Coniston Ave., Bark.	52	H7
Coniston Ave., Grnf.	55	F2
Coniston Ave., Well.	79	H3
Coniston Clo. N20	31	F3
Coniston Clo. SW13 *Lonsdale Rd.*	65	F7
Coniston Clo. SW20	93	A6
Coniston Clo. W4	65	C7
Coniston Clo., Bark. *Coniston Ave.*	52	H7
Coniston Clo., Bexh.	80	J1
Coniston Gdns. N9	33	F1
Coniston Gdns. NW9	38	D5
Coniston Gdns., Ilf.	43	B4
Coniston Gdns., Pnr.	36	A4
Coniston Gdns., Sutt.	100	G6
Coniston Gdns., Wem.	46	F1
Coniston Ho. SE5	**20**	**J7**
Coniston Rd. N10	40	B2
Coniston Rd. N17	33	D6
Coniston Rd., Bexh.	80	J1
Coniston Rd., Brom.	87	D6
Coniston Rd., Croy.	95	D7
Coniston Rd., Twick.	72	H6
Coniston Wk. E9 *Clifden Rd.*	50	F5
Coniston Way, Chess.	98	H3
Conistone Way N7	49	E7
Conlan St. W10	57	B4
Conley Rd. NW10	47	E6
Conley St. SE10 *Pelton Rd.*	69	E5
Connaught Ave. E4	26	D7
Connaught Ave. SW14	74	C3
Connaught Ave., Barn.	31	J1
Connaught Ave., Enf.	25	B2
Connaught Ave., Houns.	72	E5
Connaught Ave., Loug.	27	A4
Connaught Clo. E10	50	H2
Connaught Clo. W2	**10**	**G4**
Connaught Clo., Enf.	25	B2
Connaught Clo., Sutt.	100	G6
Connaught Crossing E16	61	A7
Connaught Dr. NW11	39	D4
Connaught Gdns. N10	40	B5
Connaught Gdns. N13	32	H4
Connaught Gdns., Mord.	93	F4
Connaught Hill, Loug.	27	A4
Connaught La., Ilf.	52	G2
Connaught Rd.		
Connaught Ms. W2	**10**	**J4**
Connaught Ms., Ilf.	52	G2
Connaught Rd.		
Connaught Pl. W2	**10**	**J4**
Connaught Pl. W2	57	J7

Connaught Rd. E4	26	E7
Connaught Rd. E11	51	D1
Connaught Rd. E16	70	A1
Connaught Crossing		
Connaught Rd. E17	42	A5
Connaught Rd. N4	40	G7
Connaught Rd. NW10	56	E1
Connaught Rd. SE18	70	D5
Connaught Rd. W13	55	E7
Connaught Rd., Barn.	40	A6
Connaught Rd., Har.	37	C1
Connaught Rd., Ilf.	52	G2
Connaught Rd., N.Mal.	92	E4
Connaught Rd., Rich.	73	J5 *Albert Rd.*
Connaught Rd., Sutt.	100	G2
Connaught Rd., Tedd.	82	A5
Connaught Sq. W2	**10**	**J4**
Connaught Sq. W2	57	J6
Connaught St. W2	**10**	**H4**
Connaught St. W2	57	H6
Connaught Way N13	32	H4
Connell Cres. W5	55	J4
Connemara Clo., Borwd. *Percheron Rd.*	22	D6
Connington Cres. E4	34	D3
Connor Clo. E11	50	F1
Connor St. E9 *Lauriston Rd.*	59	G1
Conolly Rd. W7	64	B1
Conrad Dr., Wor.Pk.	99	J1
Conrad Ho. N16	50	B5
Cons St. SE1	**16**	**F3**
Consfield Ave., N.Mal.	92	G4
Consort Ms., Islw.	73	A5
Consort Rd. SE15	77	E1
Constable Clo. NW11	39	E6
Constable Cres. N15	41	D5
Constable Gdns., Edg.	38	A1
Constable Gdns., Islw.	73	A5
Constable Wk. SE21	86	C3 *Ferrings*
Constance Cres., Brom.	96	F7
Constance Rd., Croy.	94	H7
Constance Rd., Enf.	25	B6
Constance Rd., Sutt.	100	F4
Constance Rd., Twick.	72	H7
Constance St. E16 *Albert Rd.*	70	B1
Constantine Rd. NW3	48	H4
Constitution Hill SW1	**15**	**D3**
Constitution Hill SW1	67	B2
Constitution Ri. SE18	79	D1
Consul Ave., Dag.	62	J4
Content St. SE17	**21**	**A2**
Content St. SE17	67	J4
Contessa Clo., Orp.	104	H5
Convair Wk., Nthlt. *Kittiwake Rd.*	54	D3
Convent Gdns. W5	64	F4
Convent Gdns. W11 *Kensington Pk. Rd.*	57	C6
Convent Hill SE19	69	J6
Convent Way, Sthl.	63	C4
Conway Clo., Stan.	29	B6
Conway Cres., Grnf.	55	B2
Conway Cres., Rom.	44	E6
Conway Dr., Sutt.	100	E6
Conway Gdns., Mitch.		
Conway Gdns., Wem.	37	F7
Conway Gro. W3	56	D5
Conway Ms. W1	**7**	**F6**
Conway Rd. N14	32	E3
Conway Rd. N15	40	H5
Conway Rd. NW2	47	J2
Conway Rd. SE18	70	G4
Conway Rd. SW20	92	J1
Conway Rd., Felt.	81	D5
Conway Rd., Houns.	72	F7
Conway St. E13	60	G4
Conway St. W1	**7**	**F6**
Conway St. W1	58	C4
Conway Wk., Hmptn.	81	F6 *Fearnley Cres.*
Conybeare NW3	48	H7 *King Henry's Rd.*
Conyer St. E3	59	H2

Conyers Clo., Wdf.Grn.	34	E6
Conyers Rd. SW16	85	D5
Conyers Way, Loug.	27	E3
Cooden Clo., Brom.	87	H7
Cooderidge Clo. N17	33	C6 *Brantwood Rd.*
Cookes Clo. E11	51	F2
Cookes La., Sutt.	100	B6
Cookham Cres. SE16	68	G2 *Marlow Way*
Cookham Dene Clo., Chis.	97	G1
Cookham Rd., Sid.	89	G7
Cookhill Rd. SE2	71	B2
Cooks Clo., Rom.	44	J1
Cook's Rd. E15	60	B2
Cooks Rd. SE17	**20**	**G5**
Cooks Rd. SE17	67	H6
Cool Oak La. NW9	47	E1
Coolfin Rd. E16	60	G6
Coolgardie Ave. E4	34	D5
Coolgardie Ave., Chig.	35	D3
Coolhurst Rd. N8	40	D6
Coomassie Rd. W9	57	C4 *Bravington Rd.*
Coombe Ave., Croy.	102	B4
Coombe Bank, Kings.T.	92	E1
Coombe Clo., Edg.	37	J2
Coombe Clo., Houns.	72	G4
Coombe Cres., Hmptn.	81	E7
Coombe Dr., Kings.T.	83	D7
Coombe Dr., Ruis.	45	B1
Coombe End, Kings.T.	83	D7
Coombe Gdns. SW20	92	G2
Coombe Gdns., N.Mal.	92	F4
Coombe Heights, Kings.T.	83	E7
Coombe Hill Glade, Kings.T.	83	E7
Coombe Hill Rd., Kings.T.	83	E7
Coombe Ho. Chase, N.Mal.	92	D1
Coombe La. SW20	92	F1
Coombe La., Croy.	102	E5
Coombe La. W., Kings.T.	92	B1
Coombe Lea, Brom.	97	B3
Coombe Neville, Kings.T.	83	D7
Coombe Pk., Kings.T.	83	D5
Coombe Ridings, Kings.T.	83	C5
Coombe Ri., Kings.T.	92	C1
Coombe Rd. N22	40	G2
Coombe Rd. NW10	47	D3
Coombe Rd. SE26	86	E4
Coombe Rd. W4	65	E5
Coombe Rd. W13	64	E3 *Northcroft Rd.*
Coombe Rd., Croy.	101	J4
Coombe Rd., Hmptn.	81	F6
Coombe Rd., Kings.T.	92	A1
Coombe Rd., N.Mal.	92	E2
Coombe Rd., Sutt.	100	E3
Coombe Wk., Sutt.	100	E3
Coombe Wd. Rd., Kings.T.	83	C5
Coombefield Clo., N.Mal.	92	E5
Coombehurst Clo., Barn.	23	J2
Coomber Way, Croy.	94	D7
Coombes Rd., Dag.	62	F1
Coombewood Dr., Rom.	44	G6
Coombs St. N1	**8**	**H2**
Coombs St. N1	58	H2
Coomer Ms. SW6	66	C6 *Coomer Pl.*
Coomer Pl. SW6	66	C6
Coomer Rd. SW6	66	C6 *Coomer Pl.*
Cooms Wk., Edg.	38	C1 *East Rd.*
Cooper Ave. E17	41	H1
Cooper Clo. SE1	16	F4
Cooper Ct. E15	51	B5 *Clays La.*
Cooper Cres., Cars.	100	J3
Cooper Rd. NW10	47	G5
Cooper Rd., Croy.	101	H4

Cooper St. E16 60 F5
Lawrence St.
Coopers Clo. E1 59 F4
Coopers Cres., 22 C1
Borwd.
Coopers La. E10 51 B1
Coopers La. NW1 7 J2
Coopers La. NW1 58 D2
Cooper's La. E12 87 H2
Coopers Rd. SE1 21 G4
Coopers Rd. SE1 68 C5
Cooper's Row EC3 13 F5
Cooper's Yd. SE19 86 B6
Westow Hill
Coopersale Clo., 34 J7
Wdf.Grn.
Navestock Cres.
Coopersale Rd. E9 50 G5
Coote Gdns., Dag. 53 F3
Nicholas Rd.
Coote Rd., Bexh. 80 F1
Coote Rd., Dag. 53 F3
Cope Pl. W8 66 D3
Cope St. SE16 68 G4
Copeland Dr. E14 69 A4
Copeland Rd. E17 42 B5
Copeland Rd. SE15 77 D2
Copeman Clo. SE26 86 F5
Copenhagen Gdns. 65 D2
W4
Copenhagen Pl. E14 59 J6
Copenhagen St. N1 58 E1
Copers Cope Rd., 86 J7
Beck.
Copford Clo., 35 B6
Wdf.Grn.
Popham St.
Copinger Wk., Edg. 38 B1
North Rd.
Copland Ave., Wem. 46 G5
Copland Clo., Wem. 46 F5
Copland Rd., Wem. 46 H6
Copleston Ms. SE15 77 C2
Copleston Pas. SE15 77 C2
Copleston Rd. SE15 77 C3
Copley Clo. SE17 20 H6
Copley Clo. W7 55 C4
Copley Dene, Brom. 97 A4
Copley Pk. SW16 85 F6
Copley Rd., Stan. 29 F5
Copley St. E1 59 G5
Stepney Grn.
Copnor Way SE15 21 E7
Copped Hall SE21 86 A2
Glazebrook Clo.
Coppelia Rd. SE3 78 F4
Coppen Rd., Dag. 44 F7
Copper Beech Clo., 43 D1
Ilf.
Copper Beech Ct., 27 D1
Loug.
Copper Beeches, 73 A1
Islw.
Eversley Cres.
Copper Clo. SE19 86 C7
Copper Mead Clo. 47 J3
NW2
Copper Mill Dr., Islw. 73 C2
Copper Mill La. 84 F4
SW17
Copperas St. SE8 69 B6
Copperbeech Clo. 48 G5
NW3
Akenside Rd.
Copperdale Rd., 63 A2
Hayes
Copperfield, Chig. 35 G5
Copperfield App., 35 G6
Chig.
Copperfield Ms. N18 33 B5
Copperfield Rd. E3 59 H4
Copperfield Rd. 62 C6
SE28
Copperfield St. SE1 16 H3
Copperfield St. SE1 67 H2
Copperfield Way, 88 F6
Chis.
Copperfield Way, 36 F4
Pnr.
Coppergate Clo., 96 H1
Brom.
Coppermill La. E17 41 F6
Coppetts Clo. N12 31 J7
North Circular Rd.
Coppetts Rd. N10 31 J7
Coppice, The, Enf. 24 H4
Coppice Clo. SW20 92 J3
Coppice Clo., Stan. 29 C6
Coppice Dr. SW15 74 G6
Coppice Wk. N20 31 D3
Coppice Way E18 42 F4
Coppies Gro. N11 32 B4

Copping Clo., Croy. 102 B4
Tipton Dr.
Coppins, The, Croy. 103 B6
Coppins, The, Har. 29 B6
Coppock Clo. SW11 75 H2
Coppsfield, W.Mol. 90 G3
Hurst Rd.
Copse, The E4 34 F1
Copse Ave., W.Wick. 103 B3
Copse Clo. SE7 69 H6
Copse Glade, Surb. 98 G1
Copse Hill SW20 92 G1
Copse Hill, Sutt. 100 E7
Coptefield Dr., Belv. 71 D3
Copthall Ave. EC2 13 C3
Copthall Ave. EC2 59 A6
Copthall Bldgs. EC2 13 C3
Copthall Ct. EC2 13 B3
Copthall Ct. EC2 13 C3
Copthall Ct. EC2 59 A6
Copthall Dr. NW7 30 G7
Copthall Gdns. NW7 30 G7
Copthall Gdns., 82 C1
Twick.
Copthorne Ave. 76 D7
SW12
Copthorne Ave., 104 C2
Brom.
Copthorne Ave., Ilf. 35 E6
Coptic St. WC1 12 A2
Coptic St. WC1 58 E5
Copwood Clo. N12 31 G4
Coral Clo., Rom. 44 C3
Coral Row SW11 75 F3
Gartons Way
Coral St. SE1 16 F4
Coral St. SE1 67 G2
Coraline Clo., 54 F3
Sthl.
Coralline Wk. SE2 71 C2
Coram St. WC1 8 A6
Coram St. WC1 58 E4
Coran Clo. N9 25 G7
Corban Rd., Houns. 72 G3
Corbar Clo., Barn. 23 G1
Corbet Clo., Wall. 101 A1
Corbet Ct. EC3 13 C4
Corbet Pl. E1 13 F1
Corbett Gro. N22 32 E7
Bounds Grn. Rd.
Corbett Ho., Wat. 28 C3
Corbett Rd. E11 42 J6
Corbett Rd. E17 42 F4
Corbetts La. SE16 68 F4
Rotherhithe New Rd.
Corbetts Pas. SE16 68 F4
Rotherhithe New Rd.
Corbicum E11 42 E7
Corbiere Ct. SW19 84 A6
Thornton Rd.
Corbiere Ho. N1 59 B1
Corbins La., Har. 45 H3
Corbridge Cres. E2 59 E2
Corby Cres., Enf. 24 E4
Corby Rd. NW10 56 D2
Corby Way E3 60 A4
Knapp Rd.
Corbylands Rd., Sid. 79 H7
Corbyn St. N4 49 E1
Cord Way E14 69 A3
Mellish St.
Cordelia St. E14 60 B6
Cording St. E14 60 B5
Chrisp St.
Cordova Rd. E3 59 H3
Cordwainers Wk. E13 60 G2
Clegg St.
Cordwell Rd. SE13 78 E5
Corelli Rd. SE3 79 B1
Corfe Ave., Har. 45 G4
Corfe Twr. W3 65 C2
Corfield Rd. N21 25 J3
Corfield St. E2 59 H4
Corfton Rd. W5 65 G7
Coriander Ave. E14 60 D6
Corinium Clo., 46 J4
Wem.
Corinne Rd. N19 49 C4
Cork Sq. E1 68 E1
Smeaton St.
Cork St. W1 11 F6
Cork St. W1 58 C7
Cork St. Ms. W1 11 F6
Cork Tree Way E4 33 H5
Corker Wk. N7 49 F2
Corkran Rd., Surb. 91 G7
Corkscrew Hill, 103 C7
W.Wick.
Corlett St. NW1 10 G1
Cormont Rd. SE5 76 H1
Cornbury Rd., Edg. 37 G7
Cornelia St. N7 49 F6
Cornell Clo., Sid. 89 E6
Corner Grn. SE3 78 G2

Corner Ho. St. WC2 16 A1
Corner Mead NW9 30 F7
Corney Rd. W4 65 E6
Cornflower La., 102 G1
Croy.
Cornflower Ter. 77 E6
SE22
Cornford Clo., Brom. 96 G5
Cornford Gro. SW12 85 B2
Cornhill EC3 13 C4
Cornhill EC3 59 A6
Cornish Clo. N9 25 E7
Cornish Gro. SE20 95 E1
Cornish Ho. SE17 20 G6
Cornish Ho., Brent. 64 J5
Cornmill La. SE13 78 C3
Cornmow Dr. NW10 47 G4
Cornshaw Rd., Dag. 53 D1
Cornthwaite Rd. E5 50 F3
Cornwall Ave. E2 59 F3
Cornwall Ave. N3 31 D7
Cornwall Ave. N22 40 E1
Cornwall Ave., Esher 98 C7
The Causeway
Cornwall Ave., Sthl. 54 F5
Cornwall Ave., Well. 79 H3
Cornwall Clo., Bark. 52 J6
Cornwall Cres. W11 57 B6
Cornwall Dr., Orp. 89 C7
Cornwall Gdns. 47 H6
NW10
Cornwall Gdns. SW7 14 B6
Cornwall Gdns. SW7 66 E3
Cornwall Gdns. Wk. 14 B6
SW7
Cornwall Gro. W4 65 E5
Cornwall Ms. S. SW7 14 C6
Cornwall Ms. S. SW7 66 F3
Cornwall Ms. W. SW7 14 B6
Cornwall Rd. N4 40 G7
Cornwall Rd. N15 41 A5
Cornwall Rd. N18 33 D5
Fairfield Rd.
Cornwall Rd. SE1 16 E1
Cornwall Rd. SE1 67 G1
Cornwall Rd., Croy. 101 H2
Cornwall Rd., Har. 36 J6
Cornwall Rd., Pnr. 28 F7
Cornwall Rd., Sutt. 100 C7
Cornwall Rd., 73 D7
Twick.
Cornwall St. E1 59 E7
Watney St.
Cornwall Ter. NW1 7 A6
Cornwall Ter. Ms. 7 A6
NW1
Cornwallis Ave. N9 33 E2
Cornwallis Ave. SE9 88 G2
Cornwallis Gro. N9 33 E2
Cornwallis Rd. E17 41 G4
Cornwallis Rd. N9 33 E2
Cornwallis Rd. N19 49 E2
Cornwallis Rd., Dag. 53 D4
Cornwallis Wk. SE9 79 C3
Cornwood Clo. N2 39 G5
Cornwood Dr. E1 59 F6
Cornworthy Rd., Dag. 53 C5
Corona Rd. SE12 78 G7
Coronation Ave. N16 50 C3
Victorian Rd.
Coronation Clo., Bex. 80 D6
Coronation Clo., Ilf. 43 F4
Coronation Rd. E13 60 J3
Coronation Rd. 55 J3
NW10
Coronation Wk., 81 G1
Twick.
Coronet St. N1 9 D4
Coronet St. N1 59 B3
Corporation Ave., 72 E4
Houns.
Corporation Row EC1 8 F5
Corporation Row EC1 58 G4
Corporation St. E15 60 E2
Corporation St. N7 49 E5
Corrance Rd. SW2 76 E4
Corri Ave. N14 32 D4
Corrib Dr., Sutt. 100 H5
Corringham Ct. 39 E7
NW11
Corringham Rd.
Corringham Rd. 39 D7
NW11
Corringham Rd., 47 A2
Wem.
Corringway NW11 39 E7
Corringway W5 55 J5
Corscombe Clo., 83 C5
Kings.T.
Corsehill St. SW16 85 C6
Corsham St. N1 9 C4
Corsham St. N1 59 A3
Corsica St. N5 49 H6

Corsley Way E9 50 J6
Trowbridge Est.
Cortayne Rd. SW6 75 C2
Cortis Rd. SW15 74 H6
Cortis Ter. SW15 74 H6
Corunna Rd. SW8 76 D1
Corunna Ter. SW8 76 C1
Corvette Sq. SE10 69 D6
Feathers Pl.
Coryton Path W9 57 C4
Ashmore Rd.
Cosbycote Ave. SE24 76 J5
Cosdach Ave., Wall. 101 D7
Cosedge Cres., 101 G5
Croy.
Cosgrove Clo. N21 32 J2
Cosgrove Clo., 54 E4
Hayes
Kingsash Dr.
Cosmo Pl. WC1 12 B1
Cosmur Clo. W12 65 F3
Cossall Wk. SE15 77 E1
Cosser St. SE1 16 E5
Cosser St. SE1 67 G3
Costa St. SE15 77 D2
Coston Wk. SE4 77 G4
Frendsbury Rd.
Costons Ave., Grnf. 55 A3
Costons La., Grnf. 55 A3
Cosway St. NW1 10 H1
Cosway St. NW1 57 H5
Cotall St. E14 60 A6
Coteford Clo., Loug. 27 E2
Coteford Clo., Pnr. 36 A5
Coteford St. SW17 84 J4
Cotelands, Croy. 102 B3
Cotesbach Rd. E5 50 F3
Cotesmore Gdns., 53 C4
Dag.
Cotford Rd., Th.Hth. 94 J3
Cotham St. SE17 21 A2
Cotherstone Rd. SW2 85 F1
Cotleigh Ave., Bex. 89 D2
Cotleigh Rd. NW6 48 D7
Cotman Clo. NW11 39 F6
Cotman Clo. SW15 74 J6
Westleigh Ave.
Cotman Gdns., Edg. 38 A2
Cotmans Clo., Hayes 63 A1
Coton Rd., Well. 80 A3
Cotsford Ave., N.Mal. 92 C5
Cotswold Clo., 83 B6
Kings.T.
Cotswold Gdns. E6 61 A3
Cotswold Gdns. NW2 48 A2
Cotswold Gdns., 43 D2
Ilf.
Cotswold Gate NW2 48 B1
Cotswold Gdns.
Cotswold Ms. SW11 75 G1
Battersea High St.
Cotswold Ri., Orp. 97 J3
Cotswold Rd., 81 G6
Hmptn.
Cotswold St. SE27 85 H4
Norwood High St.
Cotswold Way, Enf. 24 F3
Cotswold Way, 99 J2
Wor.Pk.
Cottage Ave., Brom. 104 B3
Cottage Fld. Clo., 89 C1
Sid.
Cottage Grn. SE5 21 C7
Cottage Gro. SE5 68 A7
Cottage Gro. SW9 91 G6
Cottage Gro., Surb. 91 G6
Cottage Homes NW7 30 G4
Cottage Homes
Chalet Est. NW7
Cottage Pl. SW3 14 G6
Cottage Pl. SW3 66 H3
Cottage Rd., Epsom 99 D7
Cottage St. E14 60 B7
Cottage Wk. SE15 68 C7
Sumner St.
Cottenham Dr. NW9 38 F3
Cottenham Dr. SW20 83 H7
Cottenham Pk. Rd. 92 H1
SW20
Cottenham Pl. SW20 83 H7
Cottenham Rd. E17 41 J4
Cotterill Rd., Surb. 98 H2
Cottesbrook St. 68 H7
SE14
Nynehead St.
Cottesmore Ave., Ilf. 43 D2
Cottesmore Gdns. 14 B5
W8
Cottesmore Gdns. 66 E3
W8
Cottimore Cres., 90 B7
Walt.
Cottimore La., Walt. 90 B7

Cottimore Ter., Walt. 90 B7
Cottingham Chase, 45 A3
Ruis.
Cottingham Rd. SE20 86 G7
Cottingham Rd. SW8 20 D7
Cottingham Rd. SW8 67 F7
**Cottington Clo. 20 G2
SE11**
Cottington Clo. 67 H4
SE11
Cottington Rd., Felt. 81 D4
Cottington St. SE11 20 F3
Cottle St. SE16 67 H6
St. Marychurch St.
Cotton Ave. W3 56 D6
Cotton Hill, Brom. 87 D4
Cotton Row SW11 75 G3
Cotton St. E14 60 C7
Cottongrass Clo., 102 G1
Croy.
Cornflower La.
Cottons Gdns. E2 9 E3
Cottons La. SE1 17 C1
Couchmore Ave., 98 B2
Esher
Couchmore Ave., Ilf. 43 C2
Coulgate St. SE4 77 H3
Coulson Clo., Dag. 44 C7
Coulson St. SW3 18 J3
Coulson St. SW3 66 J5
Coulter Rd. W6 65 H3
Coultree Clo., Hayes 54 E4
Rosymede Rd.
Councillor St. SE5 67 J7
Counter Ct. SE1 17 B2
Counter St. SE1 17 D2
Countess Rd. NW5 49 C5
Countisbury Ave., 25 C7
Enf.
Country Way, Felt. 81 B6
Country Way, Sun. 81 A7
County Gdns., Bark. 61 H2
River Rd.
County Gate SE9 88 F3
County Gate, Barn. 23 E6
County Gro. SE5 76 J1
County Rd. E6 61 E5
County Rd., Th.Hth. 94 H2
County St. SE1 17 A6
County St. SE1 67 J3
Coupland Pl. SE18 70 F5
Courcy Rd. N8 40 G3
Courland Gro. SW8 76 D2
Courland St. SW8 76 D1
Course, The SE9 88 D3
Court, The, Ruis. 45 E4
Court Ave., Belv. 71 F5
Court Clo., Har. 37 G3
Court Clo., Twick. 81 H3
Court Clo., Wall. 101 D7
Court Clo. Ave., 81 H3
Twick.
Court Cres., Chess. 98 G5
Court Downs Rd., 96 B2
Beck.
Court Dri., Croy. 101 F4
Court Dri., Stan. 29 H4
Court Dri., Sutt. 100 H4
Court Fm. Ave., 99 D5
Epsom
Court Fm. Rd. SE9 88 A2
Court Fm. Rd., Nthlt. 45 G7
Court Ho. Gdns. N3 31 D6
Court La. SE21 77 B6
Court La. Gdns. SE21 77 B7
Court Mead, Nthlt. 54 F3
Court Rd. SE9 79 C6
Court Rd. SE25 95 C2
Court Rd., Sthl. 63 F4
Court St. E1 59 E5
Durward St.
Court St., Brom. 96 G2
Court Way NW9 38 E4
Court Way W3 56 C5
Court Way, Ilf. 43 F3
Court Way, Twick. 73 C7
Court Yd. SE9 79 C6
Courtauld Clo. SE28 71 A1
Pitfield Cres.
Courtauld Rd. N19 49 D1
Courtenay Ave. N6 39 J7
Courtenay Ave., Har. 28 J7
Courtenay Dri., Beck. 96 J2
Courtenay Gdns., 36 J2
Har.
Courtenay Ms. E17 41 H5
Courtenay Pl. E17 41 H5
Courtenay Ms.
Courtenay Rd. E11 51 F3
Courtenay Rd. E17 41 G4
Courtenay Rd. SE20 86 G7
Courtenay Rd., 99 J3
Wor.Pk.

Courtenay Sq. SE11 20 E4
Courtenay St. SE11 20 E3
Courtenay St. SE11 67 G5
Courtens Ms., Stan. 29 F7
Courtfield W5 55 F5
Courtfield Ave., Har. 37 C5
Courtfield Cres., Har. 37 C5
**Courtfield Gdns. 18 B2
SW5**
Courtfield Gdns. 66 E4
SW5
Courtfield Gdns. 55 D6
W13
Courtfield Ms. SW5 18 B2
Courtfield Ri., 103 D3
W.Wick.
Courtfield Rd. SW7 18 C1
Courtfield Rd. SW7 66 F4
Courthill Rd. SE13 78 C4
Courthope Rd. NW3 48 J4
Courthope Rd. SW19 84 B5
Courthope Rd., Grnf. 55 A2
Courthope Vill. 84 B7
SW19
Courthouse Rd. N12 31 E6
Courtland Ave. E4 34 F2
Courtland Ave. NW7 30 D3
Courtland Ave. SW16 85 F7
Courtland Ave., Ilf. 52 C2
Courtland Dr., Chig. 35 E3
Courtland Gro. SE28 62 D7
Courtland Rd. E6 61 B1
Harrow Rd.
Courtlands, Rich. 74 A5
Courtlands Ave. 78 H5
SE12
Courtlands Ave., 103 E1
Brom.
Courtlands Ave., 81 F6
Hmptn.
Courtlands Ave., 74 B2
Rich.
Courtlands Dr., 99 E6
Epsom
Courtlands Rd., Surb. 92 A7
Courtleet Dr., Erith 80 H1
Courtleigh Gdns. 39 B4
NW11
Courtman Rd. N17 32 J7
Courtmead Clo. SE24 76 J6
Courtnell St. W2 57 D6
Courtney Clo. SE19 86 B6
Courtney Cres., 100 J7
Cars.
Courtney Pl., Croy. 101 G3
Courtney Rd.
Courtney Rd. N7 49 G5
Bryantwood Rd.
Courtney Rd. SW19 84 H7
Courtney Rd., Croy. 101 G3
Courtrai Rd. SE23 77 H6
Courtside N8 40 D6
Courtway, Wdf.Grn. 34 J5
Courtway, The, Wat. 28 E2
Courtyard, The E1 59 E7
Courtyard, The N1 49 F7
Barnsbury Ter.
Cousin La. EC4 13 B6
Couthurst Rd. SE3 69 H6
Coutts Ave., Chess. 98 H5
Coutts Cres. NW5 49 A3
Coval Gdns. SW14 74 B4
Coval La. SW14 74 B4
Coval Rd. SW14 74 B4
Covelees Wall E6 61 E6
Warwall
Covent Gdn. WC2 12 B5
Covent Gdn. WC2 58 E7
Coventry Clo. E6 61 C6
Harper Rd.
Coventry Clo. NW6 57 D1
Kilburn High Rd.
Coventry Cross E3 60 C4
Gillender St.
Coventry Rd. E1 59 E4
Coventry Rd. E2 59 E4
Coventry Rd. SE25 95 D4
Coventry Rd., Ilf. 52 E2
Coventry St. W1 11 H6
Coventry St. W1 58 D7
Coverack Clo. N14 24 C6
Coverack Clo., Croy. 95 H7
Coverdale Clo., Stan. 29 E5
Coverdale Gdns., 102 C3
Croy.
Park Hill Ri.
Coverdale Rd. NW2 48 A7
Coverdale Rd. W12 65 H2
Coverdales, The, 61 G2
Bark.
Coverley Clo. E1 13 J1
Coverley Clo. E1 59 D5
Covert, The, Orp. 97 H6

Covert Rd., Chig. 35 J6
Covert Way, Barn. 23 F2
Coverton Rd. SW17 84 H5
Covington Gdns. 85 H7
SW16
Covington Way 85 F6
SW16
Cow La., Grnf. 55 A2
Oldfield La. S.
Cow Leaze E6 61 D6
Downings
Cowan Clo. E6 61 B5
Oliver Gdns.
Cowbridge La., Bark. 52 E7
Cowbridge Rd., Har. 37 J4
Cowcross St. EC1 12 G1
Cowcross St. EC1 58 H5
Cowden Rd., Orp. 97 J7
Cowden St. SE6 87 A4
Cowdenbeath Path 58 F1
N1
Bingfield St.
Cowdrey Clo., Enf. 25 B2
Cowdrey Rd. SW19 84 E5
Cowdry Rd. E9 50 H6
Wick Rd.
Cowen Ave., Har. 45 J2
Cowgate Rd., Grnf. 55 A2
Cowick Rd. SW17 84 J4
Cowings Mead, 45 E6
Nthlt.
Cowland Ave., Enf. 25 F4
Kings.T.
Cowley La. E11 51 E3
Cathall Rd.
Cowley Pl. NW4 38 J5
Cowley Rd. E11 42 H5
Cowley Rd. SW9 76 G1
Cowley Rd. SW14 74 E3
Cowley Rd. W3 65 F1
Cowley Rd., Ilf. 43 C7
Cowley St. SW1 16 A5
Cowling Clo. W11 66 B1
Wilsham St.
Cowper Ave. E6 52 B7
Cowper Ave., Sutt. 100 G6
Cowper Clo., Brom. 97 A4
Cowper Clo., Well. 80 A5
Cowper Gdns. N14 24 B6
Cowper Gdns., 101 C6
Wall.
Cowper Rd. N14 32 B1
Cowper Rd. N16 50 B5
Cowper Rd. N18 33 D5
Cowper Rd. SW19 84 F6
Cowper Rd. W3 65 D1
Cowper Rd. W7 55 C7
Cowper Rd., Belv. 71 G4
Cowper Rd., Islw. 73 D5
Cowper Rd., Brom. 97 A4
Cowper Rd., Kings.T. 82 J5
Cowper St. EC2 9 C5
Cowper St. EC2 58 A3
Cowper Ter. W10 57 A5
St. Marks Rd.
Cowslip Rd. E18 42 H2
Cowthorpe Rd. SW8 76 D1
Cox La., Chess. 98 H4
Cox La., Epsom 99 B4
Coxmount Rd. SE7 70 A5
Cox's Wk. SE21 86 D1
Coxson Pl. SE1 17 F4
Coxwell Rd. SE18 70 G5
Coxwell Rd. SE19 86 B7
Crab Hill, Beck. 87 D7
Crabtree Ave., Rom. 44 D4
Crabtree Ave., Wem. 55 H2
Crabtree Ct. E15 51 B5
Clays La.
Crabtree La. SW6 66 A7
Crabtree Manorway 71 J2
N., Belv.
Crabtree Manorway 71 J3
S., Belv.
Crabtree Wk. SE15 77 C1
Crace St. NW1 7 H3
Lidford St.
Craddock Rd., Enf. 25 C3
Craddock St. NW5 49 A6
Prince of Wales Rd.
Cradley Rd. SE9 88 G1
Craig Gdns. E18 42 F2
Craig Pk. Rd. N18 33 E5
Craig Rd., Rich. 82 F4
Craigen Ave., Croy. 102 E1
Craigerne Rd. SE3 69 H7
Craigholm SE18 70 D2
Craigmuir Pk., Wem. 55 J1
Craignair Rd. SW2 76 G2
Craignish Ave. SW16 94 F2
Craigs Ct. SW1 16 A1
Craigton Rd. SE9 79 D4
Craigweil Clo., Stan. 29 G5

Craigweil Dr., Stan. 29 G5
Craigwell Ave., Felt. 81 A3
Craik Ct. NW6 57 C2
Carlton Vale
Crail Row SE17 21 C2
Cramer St. W1 11 C2
Cramond Clo. W6 66 B6
Crampton Rd. SE20 86 F6
Crampton St. SE17 20 J3
Crampton St. SE17 67 J4
Cranberry Clo., Nthlt. 54 D2
Parkfield Ave.
Cranborne Ave., 63 G4
Sthl.
Cranborne Rd., Bark. 61 G1
Cranborne Waye, 54 B6
Hayes
Cranbourn All. WC2 11 J5
Cranbourn St. WC2 11 J5
Cranbourn St. WC2 58 D7
Cranbourne Ave. E11 42 H4
Cranbourne Ave., 99 A3
Surb.
Cranbourne Clo. 94 E3
SW16
Cranbourne Dr., Pnr. 36 D5
Cranbourne Gdns. 39 B5
NW11
Cranbourne Gdns., 43 F3
Ilf.
Cranbourne Rd. E12 52 B5
High St.
Cranbourne Rd. N10 40 B2
Cranbrook Clo., 96 G6
Brom.
Cranbrook Dr., 81 H1
Twick.
Cranbrook Est. E2 59 G2
Cranbrook Ms. E17 41 J5
Cranbrook Pk. N22 40 F1
Cranbrook Pt. E16 69 G1
Cranbrook Ri., Ilf. 43 C6
Cranbrook Rd. SE8 78 A1
Cranbrook Rd. SW19 84 B7
Cranbrook Rd. W4 65 E5
Cranbrook Rd., 23 G6
Barn.
Cranbrook Rd., Bexh. 80 F1
Cranbrook Rd., 72 F4
Houns.
Cranbrook Rd., Ilf. 43 D5
Cranbrook Rd., 94 J2
Th.Hth.
Cranbrook St. E2 59 G2
Roman Rd.
Cranbury Rd. SW6 75 E2
Crane Ave. W3 56 C7
Crane Ave., Islw. 73 D5
Crane Clo., Dag. 53 G6
Crane Ct. EC4 12 F4
Crane Ct., Epsom 99 C4
Crane Gro. N7 49 G6
Crane Mead SE16 68 G4
Crane Pk. Rd., 81 H2
Twick.
Crane Rd., Twick. 82 B1
Crane St. SE10 69 D5
Park Row
Crane Way, Twick. 72 J7
Cranebrook, Twick. 81 J2
Manor Rd.
Craneford Clo., 73 C7
Twick.
Craneford Way, 73 B7
Twick.
Cranes Dr., Surb. 91 H4
Cranes Pk.
Cranes Pk., Surb. 91 H4
Cranes Pk. Ave., 91 H4
Surb.
Cranes Pk. Cres., 91 J4
Surb.
Cranes Way, Borwd. 22 C5
Craneswater Pk., 63 F5
Sthl.
Cranfield Clo. SE27 85 J3
Dunelm Gro.
Cranfield Dr. NW9 30 E7
Cranfield Rd. SE4 77 J3
Cranfield Row SE1 16 F5
Cranford Ave. N13 32 E5
Cranford Clo. SW20 83 H7
Cranford Cotts. E1 59 G7
Cranford St.
Cranford La. 63 B7
(Heston), Houns.
Cranford St. E1 59 G7
Cranford Way N8 40 F5
Cranhurst Rd. NW2 47 J5
Cranleigh Clo. SE20 95 E2
Cranleigh Clo., Bex. 80 H5
Cranleigh Gdns. N21 24 G5

Cranleigh Gdns. SE25 — 95 B3
Cranleigh Gdns., Bark. — 52 G7
Cranleigh Gdns., Har. — 37 H5
Cranleigh Gdns., Kings.T. — 82 J6
Cranleigh Gdns., Loug. — 27 C6
Cranleigh Gdns., Sthl. — 54 F6
Cranleigh Gdns., Sutt. — 100 E2
Cranleigh Ms. SW11 — 75 H2
Cranleigh Rd. N15 — 40 J5
Cranleigh Rd. SW19 — 93 C3
Cranleigh St. NW1 — **7 G2**
Cranleigh St. NW1 — 58 C2
Cranley Dene Ct. N10 — 40 B4
Cranley Dr., Ilf. — 43 F7
Cranley Gdns. N10 — 40 B4
Cranley Gdns. N13 — 32 F3
Cranley Gdns. SW7 — **18 D3**
Cranley Gdns. SW7 — 66 F5
Cranley Gdns., Wall. — 101 C7
Cranley Ms. SW7 — **18 D3**
Cranley Ms. SW7 — 66 F5
Cranley Pl. SW7 — **18 E2**
Cranley Pl. SW7 — 66 G4
Cranley Rd. E13 — 60 H5
Cranley Rd., Ilf. — 43 F6
Cranmer Ave. W13 — 64 E3
Cranmer Clo., Mord. — 93 A6
Cranmer Clo., Ruis. — 45 D1
Cranmer Clo., Stan. — 29 F7
Cranmer Ct. SW3 — **18 H2**
Cranmer Ct. SW4 — 76 D3
Cranmer Ct., Hmptn. — 81 H5
  Cranmer Rd.
Cranmer Fm. Clo., Mitch. — 93 J4
Cranmer Gdns., Dag. — 53 J4
Cranmer Rd. E7 — 51 H4
Cranmer Rd. SW9 — **20 F7**
Cranmer Rd. SW9 — 67 G7
Cranmer Rd., Croy. — 101 H3
Cranmer Rd., Edg. — 30 B3
Cranmer Rd., Hmptn. — 81 H5
Cranmer Rd., Kings.T. — 82 H5
Cranmer Rd., Mitch. — 93 J4
Cranmer Ter. SW17 — 84 G5
Cranmore Ave., Islw. — 63 J7
Cranmore Rd., Brom. — 87 F3
Cranmore Rd., Chis. — 88 C5
Cranmore Way N10 — 40 C4
Cranston Clo., Houns. — 72 E2
Cranston Est. N1 — **9 C2**
Cranston Est. N1 — 59 A2
Cranston Gdns. E4 — 34 B5
Cranston Rd. SE23 — 86 H1
Cranswick Rd. SE16 — 88 J5
Crantock Rd. SE6 — 87 B2
Cranwell Clo. E3 — 60 B4
Cranwich Ave. N21 — 25 A7
Cranwich Rd. N16 — 41 A7
Cranwood St. EC1 — **9 C4**
Cranwood St. EC1 — 59 A3
Cranworth Cres. E4 — 34 D1
Cranworth Gdns. SW9 — 76 G1
Craster Rd. SW2 — 78 A7
Crathie Rd. SE12 — 78 H6
Crathorn St. SE13 — 78 C3
  Loampit Vale
Cravan Ave., Felt. — 81 A2
Craven Ave. W5 — 55 F7
Craven Ave., Sthl. — 54 F5
Craven Clo., Hayes — 54 A6
Craven Gdns. SW19 — 84 D5
Craven Gdns., Bark. — 61 H2
Craven Gdns., Ilf. — 43 G2
Craven Hill W2 — **10 D5**
Craven Hill W2 — 57 F7
Craven Hill Gdns. W2 — **10 C5**
Craven Hill Gdns. W2 — 57 F7
Craven Hill Ms. W2 — **10 D5**
Craven Hill Ms. W2 — 57 F7
Craven Ms. SW11 — 76 A3
  Taybridge Rd.
Craven Pk. NW10 — 56 E1
Craven Pk. Ms. NW10 — 56 E1
Craven Pk. Rd. N15 — 41 C6
Craven Pk. Rd. NW10 — 56 E1
Craven Pas. WC2 — **16 A1**
Craven Rd. NW10 — 56 D1

Craven Rd. W2 — **10 D5**
Craven Rd. W2 — 57 F6
Craven Rd. W5 — 55 F7
Craven Rd., Croy. — 102 E1
Craven Rd., Kings.T. — 91 J1
Craven St. WC2 — **16 A1**
Craven St. WC2 — 67 E1
Craven Ter. W2 — **10 D5**
Craven Ter. W2 — 57 F7
Craven Wk. N16 — 41 D7
Crawford Ave., Wem. — 46 G5
Crawford Clo., Islw. — 73 B2
Crawford Est. SE5 — 76 J2
Crawford Gdns. N13 — 32 H3
Crawford Gdns., Nthlt. — 54 F3
Crawford Ms. W1 — **10 J2**
Crawford Pas. EC1 — **8 E6**
Crawford Pl. W1 — **10 H3**
Crawford Pl. W1 — 57 H6
Crawford Rd. SE5 — 76 J1
Crawford St. W1 — **10 H2**
Crawford St. W1 — 57 J5
Crawley Rd. E10 — 51 B1
Crawley Rd. N22 — 40 J2
Crawley Rd., Enf. — 25 B7
Crawshaw Ct. SW9 — 76 G1
  Eythorne Rd.
Crawthew Gro. SE22 — 77 C4
Cray Rd., Belv. — 71 G6
Cray Rd., Sid. — 89 C7
Craybrooke Rd., Sid. — 89 B4
Craybury End SE9 — 88 F2
Crayford Clo. E6 — 61 B5
  Neatscourt Rd.
Crayford Rd. N7 — 49 D4
Crayke Hill, Chess. — 98 H7
Crealock Gro., Wdf.Grn. — 34 F5
Crealock St. SW18 — 75 E6
Creasy Est. SE1 — **17 D6**
Crebor St. SE22 — 77 D6
Credenhall Dr., Brom. — 104 C1
  Lwr. Gravel Rd.
Credenhill St. SW16 — 85 C6
Crediton Hill NW6 — 48 E5
Crediton Rd. E16 — 60 G6
  Pacific Rd.
Crediton Rd. NW10 — 57 A1
Crediton Way, Esher — 98 D5
Credon Rd. E13 — 60 J2
Credon Rd. SE16 — 68 E5
Creechurch La. EC3 — **13 E4**
Creechurch La. EC3 — 59 B6
Creechurch Pl. EC3 — **13 E4**
Creed La. EC4 — **12 H4**
Creek Rd., The, Sun. — 90 A5
Creek Rd. SE8 — 69 A6
Creek Rd. SE10 — 69 B6
Creek Rd., Bark. — 61 J3
Creek Rd., E.Mol. — 91 B4
Creekside SE8 — 69 B7
Creeland Gro. SE6 — 86 J1
  Catford Hill
Crefeld Clo. W6 — 66 A6
Creffield Rd. W3 — 55 J7
Creffield Rd. W5 — 55 J7
Creighton Ave. E6 — 61 A2
Creighton Ave. N2 — 39 H3
Creighton Ave. N10 — 39 J2
Creighton Rd. N17 — 33 B7
Creighton Rd. NW6 — 57 A2
Creighton Rd. W5 — 64 G3
Cremer St. E2 — **9 F2**
Cremer St. E2 — 59 C2
Cremorne Est. SW10 — **18 E7**
Cremorne Rd. SW10 — **18 D7**
Cremorne Rd. SW10 — 66 F7
Crescent, The E17 — 41 H5
Crescent, The EC3 — **13 F5**
Crescent, The N11 — 32 A4
Crescent, The NW2 — 47 H3
Crescent, The SW13 — 74 F2
Crescent, The SW19 — 84 D3
Crescent, The W3 — 56 E6
Crescent, The, Barn. — 23 E3
Crescent, The, Beck. — 96 A1
Crescent, The, Bex. — 80 C7
Crescent, The, Croy. — 95 A5
Crescent, The, Har. — 67 E5
Crescent, The, Ilf. — 43 D6
Crescent, The, Loug. — 27 A5
Crescent, The, N.Mal. — 92 C2
Crescent, The, Sid. — 88 J4
Crescent, The, Sthl. — 63 F2
Crescent, The, Surb. — 91 H5
Crescent, The, Sutt. — 100 G5
Crescent, The (Aldenham), Wat. — 28 H2

Crescent, The, Wem. — 46 D2
Crescent, The, W.Mol. — 90 G4
Crescent, The, W.Wick. — 96 E6
Crescent Dr., Orp. — 97 E6
Crescent Gdns. SW19 — 84 D3
Crescent Gdns., Ruis. — 36 B7
Crescent Gro. SW4 — 76 D4
Crescent Gro., Mitch. — 93 H4
Crescent La. SW4 — 76 C4
Crescent Pl. SW3 — **18 G1**
Crescent Pl. SW3 — 66 H4
Crescent Ri., Barn. — 23 H5
Crescent Rd. E4 — 26 E7
Crescent Rd. E6 — 60 J1
Crescent Rd. E10 — 51 B2
Crescent Rd. E13 — 60 J7
Crescent Rd. E18 — 42 J2
Crescent Rd. N3 — 39 C1
Crescent Rd. N8 — 40 D6
Crescent Rd. N9 — 33 D1
Crescent Rd. N11 — 31 J4
Crescent Rd. N15 — 40 H3
  Carlingford Rd.
Crescent Rd. N22 — 40 D1
Crescent Rd. SE18 — 70 E5
Crescent Rd. SW20 — 93 A1
Crescent Rd., Barn. — 23 G4
Crescent Rd., Beck. — 96 B2
Crescent Rd., Brom. — 87 G7
Crescent Rd., Dag. — 53 H3
Crescent Rd., Enf. — 24 H4
Crescent Rd., Kings.T. — 82 A1
Crescent Rd., Sid. — 88 J3
Crescent Row EC1 — **8 J6**
Crescent Stables SW15 — 75 B4
  Upper Richmond Rd.
Crescent St. N1 — 49 F7
Crescent Vw., Loug. — 27 A5
Crescent Way N12 — 31 H6
Crescent Way SE4 — 78 A3
Crescent Way SW16 — 85 F6
Crescent Way, Orp. — 104 H5
Crescent W., Barn. — 23 F1
Crescent Wd. Rd. SE26 — 86 D3
Cresford Rd. SW6 — 75 E1
Crespigny Rd. NW4 — 38 H6
Cressage Clo., Sthl. — 54 G4
Cresset Rd. E9 — 50 F6
Cresset St. SW4 — 76 D3
Cressfield Clo. NW5 — 49 A5
Cressida Rd. N19 — 49 C1
Cressingham Gro., Sutt. — 100 F4
Cressingham Rd. SE13 — 78 C3
Cressingham Rd., Edg. — 30 D6
Cressington Clo. N16 — 50 B5
  Wordsworth Rd.
Cresswell Gdns. SW5 — **18 C3**
Cresswell Gdns. SW5 — 66 F5
Cresswell Pk. SE3 — 78 F3
Cresswell Pl. SW10 — **18 C3**
Cresswell Pl. SW10 — 66 F5
Cresswell Rd. SE25 — 95 D4
Cresswell Rd., Felt. — 81 E4
Cresswell Rd., Twick. — 73 G6
Cresswell Way N21 — 24 G7
Cressy Ct. E1 — 59 F5
  Cressy Pl.
Cressy Ct. W6 — 65 H3
Cressy Pl. E1 — 59 F5
Cressy Rd. NW3 — 48 J5
Crest, The N13 — 32 G4
Crest, The NW4 — 38 J5
Crest, The, Surb. — 92 A5
Crest Gdns., Ruis. — 45 C3
Crest Rd. NW2 — 47 F3
Crest Rd., Brom. — 96 F7
Crest Rd., S.Croy. — 102 E7
Crest Vw., Pnr. — 36 D4
Crest Vw. Dr., Orp. — 97 E5
Crestbrook Ave. N13 — 32 H3
Crestfield St. WC1 — **8 B3**
Crestfield St. WC1 — 58 E3
Creston Way, Wor.Pk. — 100 A1
Crestway SW15 — 74 G6
Crestwood Way, Houns. — 72 F5
Creswick Rd. W3 — 56 B7
Creswick Wk. E3 — 60 A3
  Malmesbury Rd.

Creswick Wk. NW11 — 39 C4
Creton St. SE18 — 70 D3
Crewdson Rd. SW9 — 67 G7
Crewe Pl. NW10 — 56 F3
Crews St. E14 — 69 A4
Crewys Rd. NW2 — 48 C2
Crewys Rd. SE15 — 77 E2
Crichton Ave., Wall. — 101 D5
Crichton Rd., Cars. — 100 J7
Cricket Grn., Mitch. — 93 J3
Cricket Grd. Rd., Chis. — 97 E1
Cricket La., Beck. — 86 H5
Cricketers Arms Rd., Enf. — 24 J2
Cricketers Clo. N14 — 24 C7
Cricketers Clo., Chess. — 98 G4
Cricketers Ct. SE11 — **20 G2**
Cricketfield Rd. E5 — 50 E4
Cricklade Ave. SW2 — 85 E2
Cricklewood Bdy. NW2 — 47 J3
Cricklewood La. NW2 — 48 A4
Cricklewood Trd. Est. NW2 — 48 B3
Cridland St. E15 — 60 F1
  Church St.
Crieff Ct., Tedd. — 82 F7
Crieff Rd. SW18 — 75 F6
Criffel Ave. SW2 — 84 J1
Crimscott St. SE1 — **17 E6**
Crimscott St. SE1 — 68 B3
Crimsworth Rd. SW8 — 76 D1
Crinan St. N1 — **8 B1**
Crinan St. N1 — 58 E2
Cringle St. SW8 — **19 F7**
Cringle St. SW8 — 67 C7
Cripplegate St. EC2 — **12 A1**
Crisp Rd. W6 — 65 J5
Crispe Ho., Bark. — 61 G2
  Dovehouse Mead
Crispen Rd., Felt. — 81 E4
Crispian Clo. NW10 — 47 E4
Crispin Cres., Croy. — 101 D2
Crispin Rd., Edg. — 30 C6
Crispin St. E1 — **13 F2**
Crispin St. E1 — 59 C5
Cristowe Rd. SW6 — 75 C2
Criterion Ms. N19 — 49 D2
  St. Johns Vill.
Crockerton Rd. SW17 — 84 J2
Crockham Way SE9 — 88 D4
Crocus Clo., Croy. — 102 G1
  Cornflower La.
Crocus Fld., Barn. — 23 C6
Croft, The NW10 — 56 F2
Croft, The W5 — 55 H5
Croft, The, Barn. — 23 B4
Croft, The, Houns. — 63 E6
Croft, The, Loug. — 27 D2
Croft, The, Ruis. — 45 C4
Croft, The, Wem. — 46 F5
Croft Ave., W.Wick. — 103 C1
Croft Clo. NW7 — 30 E3
Croft Clo., Belv. — 71 F5
Croft Clo., Chis. — 88 C4
Croft Gdns. W7 — 64 D2
Croft Lo. Clo., Wdf.Grn. — 34 H6
Croft Rd. SW16 — 94 G1
Croft Rd. SW19 — 84 F7
Croft Rd., Brom. — 87 G6
Croft Rd., Enf. — 25 H1
Croft Rd., Sutt. — 100 H5
Croft St. SE8 — 68 H4
Croft Way NW3 — 48 D4
  Ferncroft Ave.
Croft Way, Sid. — 88 H3
Croftdown Rd. NW5 — 49 A3
Crofters Clo., Islw. — 73 A5
  Ploughmans End
Crofters Way NW1 — 58 D1
Crofton Ave. W4 — 65 C2
Crofton Ave., Bex. — 80 D7
Crofton Ave., Orp. — 104 F2
Crofton La., Orp. — 104 G2
Crofton Pk. Rd. SE4 — 77 J6
Crofton Rd. E13 — 60 H4
Crofton Rd. SE5 — 77 B1
Crofton Rd., Orp. — 104 D3
Crofton Ter. E5 — 50 H5
  Studley Clo.
Crofton Ter., Rich. — 73 J4
Crofton Way, Barn. — 23 E6
  Wycherley Cres.
Croftongate Way SE4 — 77 H5
Crofts Rd., Har. — 37 D6
Crofts St. E1 — **13 H6**

Crofts St. E1 59 D7
Croftway NW3 48 D4
Croftway, Rich. 82 E3
Crogsland Rd. NW1 49 A7
Croham Clo., 102 B7
  S.Croy.
Croham Manor Rd., 102 B7
  S.Croy.
Croham Mt., S.Croy. 102 B7
  S.Croy.
Croham Pk. Ave., 102 B5
  S.Croy.
Croham Rd., S.Croy. 102 A6
Croham Valley Rd., 102 C6
  S.Croy.
Croindene Rd. SW16 94 E1
Cromartie Rd. N19 40 D7
Crombie Clo., Ilf. 43 C5
Crombie Rd., Sid. 88 G1
Cromer Rd. E10 42 D6
  James La.
Cromer Rd. N17 41 D2
Cromer Rd. SE25 95 E3
Cromer Rd. SW17 85 A6
Cromer Rd., Barn. 23 F4
Cromer Rd., Rom. 44 J6
Cromer Rd. Rom. 44 E6
  (Chadwell Heath)
Cromer St., Wdf.Grn. 34 G4
Cromer St. WC1 8 B4
Cromer St. WC1 58 E3
Cromer Ter. E8 50 D5
  Ferncliff Rd.
Cromer Vill Rd 75 C6
  SW18
Cromford Clo., Orp. 104 H3
Cromford Path E5 50 G4
  Overbury St.
Cromford Rd. SW18 75 D5
Cromford Way, 92 D1
  N.Mal.
Cromlix Clo., Chis. 97 C2
Crompton St. W2 6 E6
Crompton St. W2 57 G4
Cromwell Ave. N6 49 B1
Cromwell Ave. W6 65 H4
Cromwell Ave., 96 H3
  Brom.
Cromwell Ave., 92 F5
  N.Mal.
Cromwell Clo. N2 39 G4
Cromwell Clo. W3 65 C1
  High St.
Cromwell Clo., 96 H4
  Brom.
Cromwell Cres. SW5 66 D4
Cromwell Gdns. SW7 14 F6
Cromwell Gdns. SW7 66 G3
Cromwell Gro. W6 65 J3
Cromwell Ind. Est. 50 H1
  E10
Cromwell Ms. SW7 18 F1
Cromwell Ms. SW7 66 G4
Cromwell Pl. N6 49 B1
  Cromwell Pl.
Cromwell Pl. SW7 18 F1
Cromwell Pl. SW7 66 G4
Cromwell Pl. SW14 74 C3
Cromwell Pl. W3 65 C1
  Grove Pl.
Cromwell Rd. E7 51 J7
Cromwell Rd. E17 42 C5
Cromwell Rd. N3 39 F2
Cromwell Rd. N10 32 A7
Cromwell Rd. SW5 66 E4
Cromwell Rd. SW7 18 E1
Cromwell Rd. SW7 66 E4
Cromwell Rd. SW9 76 H1
Cromwell Rd. SW19 84 D5
Cromwell Rd., Beck. 95 H2
Cromwell Rd., Croy. 95 A7
Cromwell Rd., Felt. 81 B1
Cromwell Rd., 72 G4
  Houns.
Cromwell Rd., 91 H1
  Kings.T.
Cromwell Rd., Tedd. 82 D6
Cromwell Rd., Wem. 55 H2
Cromwell Rd., 99 D3
  Wor.Pk.
Cromwell Rd., 72 G4
  Houns.
Crondace Rd. SW6 75 D1
Crondall St. N1 9 D2
Crondall St. N1 59 A2
Crook Log, Bexh. 80 D3
Crooke Rd. SE8 68 H5
Crooked Billet SW19 83 J4
  Woodhayes Rd.
Crooked Billet 34 A7
  Roundabout E17
Crooked Usage N3 39 B3
Crookham Rd. SW6 75 C1
Crookston Rd. SE9 79 D3

Croombs Rd. E16 60 J5
Crooms Hill SE10 69 C7
Crooms Hill Gro. 69 C7
  SE10
Cropley St. N1 9 B1
Cropley St. N1 59 A2
Croppath Rd., Dag. 53 G4
Cropthorne Ct. W9 6 D4
Crosby Clo., Felt. 81 E4
Crosby Ct. SE1 17 B3
Crosby Rd. E7 51 G6
Crosby Rd., Dag. 62 H2
Crosby Row SE1 17 B3
Crosby Row SE1 68 A2
Crosby Sq. EC3 13 D4
Crosby Wk. E8 50 C6
  Laurel La.
Crosby Wk. SW2 76 G7
Crosland Pl. SW11 76 A3
  Taybridge Rd.
Cross Ave. SE10 69 D6
Cross Deep, Twick. 82 C3
Cross Deep Gdns. 82 C2
  Twick.
Cross Keys Clo. W1 11 C2
Cross Keys Sq. EC1 12 J2
Cross Lances Rd., 72 H4
  Houns.
Cross La. EC3 13 D6
Cross La. N8 40 F5
Cross La., Bex. 80 F7
Cross Rd. E4 34 E1
Cross Rd. N11 32 B6
Cross Rd. N22 32 G7
Cross Rd. SE5 77 B2
Cross Rd. SW19 84 D7
Cross Rd., Brom. 104 B2
Cross Rd., Croy. 102 A1
Cross Rd., Enf. 25 C4
Cross Rd., Felt. 81 C4
Cross Rd., Har. 37 A4
Cross Rd., Har. 45 H3
  (South Harrow)
Cross Rd., Har. 37 D2
  (Wealdstone)
Cross Rd., Kings.T. 82 J7
Cross Rd., Rom. 44 G4
Cross Rd., Rom. 44 C7
  (Chadwell Heath)
Cross Rd., Sid. 89 B4
  Sidcup Hill
Cross Rd., Sutt. 100 G5
Cross Rd., Wdf.Grn. 35 G2
Cross Rds., Loug. 26 H2
Cross St. N1 58 H1
Cross St. SW13 74 E2
Cross St., Hmptn. 81 J5
Cross Way, Pnr. 36 B2
Cross Way, The, Har. 37 B2
Crossbow Rd., Chig. 35 J5
Crossbrook Rd. SE3 79 B2
Crossfield Rd. N17 40 J3
Crossfield Rd. NW3 48 G6
Crossfield St. SE8 69 A7
Crossfields, Loug. 27 E5
Crossford St. SW9 76 E2
Crossgate, Edg. 30 A3
Crossgate, Grnf. 46 E6
Crossland Rd., 94 H5
  Th.Hth.
Crosslands Ave. W5 64 J1
Crosslands Ave., 63 F5
  Sthl.
Crosslands Rd., 99 D1
  Epsom
Crosslet St. SE17 21 C1
Crossley St. N7 49 G6
Crossmead SE8 88 C1
Crossmead Ave., 54 G3
  Grnf.
Crossmount Ho. SE5 21 A7
Crossness Rd., 61 J3
  Bark.
Crossthwaite Ave. 77 A4
  SE5
Crosswall EC3 13 F5
Crosswall EC3 59 C7
Crossway N12 31 G6
Crossway N16 50 B5
Crossway NW9 38 F4
Crossway SE28 62 C6
Crossway SW20 92 J4
Crossway, Dag. 53 C3
Crossway, Enf. 25 B7
Crossway, Hayes 63 A1
Crossway, Orp. 75 J1
Crossway, Ruis. 45 C4
Crossway, Wdf.Grn. 34 J4
Crossway, The N22 32 H7
Crossway, The SE9 88 A2
Crossway, The W13 55 D4
Crossways N21 24 J6
Crossways, S.Croy. 102 H7

Crossways, The, 63 F7
  Houns.
Crossways, The, 47 A2
  Wem.
Crossways Rd., Beck. 96 A4
Crossways Rd., 94 B3
  Mitch.
Croston St. E8 59 D1
Crothall Clo. N13 32 F3
Crouch Ave., Bark. 62 B2
Crouch Clo., Beck. 87 A6
Crouch Cft. SE9 88 D3
Crouch End Hill N8 40 D6
Crouch Hall Rd. N8 40 D6
Crouch Hill N4 40 E7
Crouch Hill N8 40 E6
Crouch Rd. NW10 47 D7
Crouchman Clo. 86 C3
  SE26
Crow La., Rom. 44 F7
Crowborough Path, 28 D4
  Wat.
  Prestwick Rd.
Crowborough Rd. 85 A6
  SW17
Crowden Way SE28 62 C7
Crowder St. E1 59 E7
Crowfoot Clo. SW9 76 G2
Crowland Gdns. N14 24 E7
Crowland Rd. N15 41 C5
Crowland Rd., 95 A4
  Th.Hth.
Crowland Ter. N1 50 A7
Crowland Wk., Mord. 93 E6
Crowlands Ave., 44 H6
  Rom.
Crowley Cres., Croy. 101 D4
Crowline Wk. N1 50 A6
  Clephane Rd.
Crowmarsh Gdns. 77 F7
  SE23
  Tyson Rd.
Crown Arc., Kings.T. 91 G2
  Union St.
Crown Clo. E3 60 A1
Crown Clo. NW6 48 E6
  Lymington Rd.
Crown Clo. NW7 30 F2
Crown Clo., Walt. 90 C7
Crown Ct. EC2 13 A4
Crown Ct. SE12 78 H6
Crown Ct. WC2 12 B4
Crown Ct., Brom. 97 A5
  Victoria Rd.
Crown Dale SE19 85 H6
Crown Hill, Croy. 101 J2
Crown La. N14 32 C1
Crown La. SW16 85 G5
Crown La., Brom. 97 A5
Crown La., Chis. 97 F1
Crown La., Mord. 93 D3
Crown La. Gdns. 85 G5
  SW16
  Crown La.
Crown La. Spur, 97 A6
  Brom.
Crown Ms. W6 65 G4
Crown Office Row 12 E5
  EC4
Crown Pas. SW1 15 G2
Crown Pl. NW5 49 B6
  Kentish Town Rd.
Crown Pt. Par. SE19 85 H6
  Beulah Hill
Crown Rd. N10 32 A7
Crown Rd. N17 33 D7
Crown Rd., Borwd. 22 A1
Crown Rd., Enf. 25 E4
Crown Rd., Ilf. 43 G4
Crown Rd., Mord. 93 D4
Crown Rd., N.Mal. 92 C1
Crown Rd., Sutt. 100 D4
Crown Rd., Twick. 73 E6
Crown St. SE5 21 A7
Crown St. SE5 67 J7
Crown St. W3 65 B1
Crown St., Dag. 53 J6
Crown St., Har. 46 A1
Crown Ter., Rich. 73 J4
Crown Wk., Wem. 46 H4
Crown Wds. La. SE9 79 F2
Crown Wds. La. 79 E2
  SE18
Crown Wds. Way 79 G5
  SE9
Crown Yd., Houns. 72 J3
  High St.
Crowndale Rd. NW1 7 G1
Crowndale Rd. NW1 58 C2
Crownfield Ave., Ilf. 43 H6
Crownfield Rd. E15 51 D1
Crownhill Rd. NW10 56 F1

Crownhill Rd., 35 B7
  Wdf.Grn.
Crownmead Way, 44 H4
  Rom.
Crownstone Rd. SW2 76 G5
Crowntree Clo., Islw. 64 C6
Crows Rd. E15 60 D3
Crowshott Ave., 37 F2
  Stan.
Crowther Ave., 64 H4
  Brent.
Crowther Rd. SE25 95 D4
Crowthorne Clo. 84 C1
  SW18
Crowthorne Rd. W10 57 A6
Croxden Clo., Edg. 37 J3
Croxden Wk., Mord. 93 F6
Croxford Gdns. N22 32 H7
Croxley Rd. W9 57 C3
Croxted Clo. SE21 76 J7
Croxted Rd. SE21 76 J7
Croxted Rd. SE24 76 J7
Croyde Ave., Grnf. 54 J3
Croyde Clo., Sid. 79 G7
Croydon Flyover, 101 H4
  The, Croy.
  Duppas Hill Rd.
Croydon Gro., Croy. 101 H1
Croydon Rd. E13 60 F4
Croydon Rd. SE20 95 E2
Croydon Rd., Beck. 95 H3
Croydon Rd., Brom. 103 J3
Croydon Rd., Kes. 104 C3
Croydon Rd., Mitch. 94 C4
Croydon Rd., Wall. 101 B4
Croydon Rd., 103 E3
  W.Wick.
Croyland Rd. N9 33 D1
Croylands Dr., 91 H7
  Surb.
Croysdale Ave., Sun. 90 A3
Crozier Ter. E9 50 G5
Crucible Clo., Rom. 44 B6
Crucifix La. SE1 17 D3
Crucifix La. SE1 68 B2
Cruden Ho. SE17 20 G6
Cruden St. N1 58 H1
Cruikshank Rd. E15 51 E4
Cruikshank St. WC1 8 E3
Cruikshank St. WC1 58 G3
Crummock Gdns. 38 E5
  NW9
Crumpsall St. SE2 71 C4
Crundale Ave. NW9 38 A5
Crunden Rd., 102 A7
  S.Croy.
Crusader Gdns., 102 B3
  Croy.
  Cotelands
Crusoe Rd., Mitch. 84 J7
Crutched Friars EC3 13 E5
Crutched Friars EC3 59 B7
Crutchley Rd. SE6 87 E2
Crystal Ct. SE19 86 C5
  College Rd.
Crystal Palace Par. 86 C6
  SE19
Crystal Palace Pk. 86 D5
  Rd. SE26
Crystal Palace Rd. 77 C6
  SE22
Crystal Palace Sta. 86 D7
  Rd. SE19
  Anerley Rd.
Crystal Ter. SE19 86 A6
Crystal Vw. Ct., 87 D4
  Brom.
  Winlaton Rd.
Crystal Way, Dag. 53 C1
Crystal Way, Har. 37 C5
Cuba Dr., Enf. 25 F2
Cuba St. E14 69 A2
Cubitt Steps E14 69 A1
  Cabot Sq.
Cubitt St. WC1 8 D4
Cubitt St. WC1 58 F3
Cubitt St., Croy. 101 F5
Cubitt Ter. SW4 76 C3
Cubitts Yd. WC2 12 B5
Cuckoo Ave. W7 55 B4
Cuckoo Dene W7 55 A5
Cuckoo Hall La. N9 25 F7
Cuckoo Hill, Pnr. 36 C3
Cuckoo Hill Dr., Pnr. 36 C3
Cuckoo Hill Rd., Pnr. 36 C4
Cuckoo La. W7 55 B7
Cudas Clo., Epsom 99 F4
Cuddington Ave., 99 F3
  Wor.Pk.
Cudham St. SE6 78 C7
Cudworth St. E1 59 E4
Cuff Cres. SE9 79 A6

Cuff Pt. E2   9 F3
Culford Gdns. SW3   19 A2
Culford Gdns. SW3   66 J4
Culford Gro. N1   50 B6
Culford Ms. N1   50 B6
Southgate Rd.
Culford Rd. N1   50 B7
Culgaith Gdns., Enf.   24 E4
Cullen Way NW10   56 C4
Culling Rd. SE16   68 F3
Lwr. Rd.
Cullington Clo., Har.   37 D4
Cullingworth Rd.   47 G5
NW10
Culloden Rd., Enf.   24 H2
Culloden St. E14   60 C6
Cullum St. EC3   **13 D5**
Culmington Rd. W13   64 F1
Culmington Rd.,   101 J7
S.Croy.
Culmore Cross SW12   85 B1
Culmore Rd. SE15   68 E7
Culmstock Rd. SW11   76 A5
Culpeper Clo., Ilf.   35 E6
Culross Clo. N15   40 J4
Culross St. W1   **11 B6**
Culross St. W1   58 A7
Culsac Rd., Surb.   98 H2
Culver Gro., Stan.   37 F2
Culverden Rd. SW12   85 C2
Culverden Rd., Wat.   28 B3
Culverhouse Gdns.   85 F3
SW16
Culverlands Clo.,   29 E4
Stan.
Culverley Rd. SE6   87 B1
Culvers Ave., Cars.   100 H2
Culvers Retreat,   100 J1
Cars.
Culvers Way, Cars.   100 J3
Culverstone Clo.,   96 F6
Brom.
Culvert Pl. SW11   76 A2
Culvert Rd. N15   41 B5
Culvert Rd. SW11   75 J1
Culworth St. NW8   **6 G2**
Cumberland Ave.   56 B3
NW10
Cumberland Ave.,   79 H3
Well.
Cumberland Clo. E8   50 C6
Cumberland Clo.   84 A7
SW20
Lansdowne Rd.
Cumberland Clo.,   73 E6
Twick.
Westmorland Clo.
Cumberland Cres.   66 B4
W14
Cumberland Dr.,   71 E7
Bexh.
Cumberland Dr.,   98 J3
Chess.
Cumberland Dr.,   98 D2
Esher
Cumberland Gdns.   39 A2
NW4
Cumberland Gdns.   **8 D3**
WC1
Cumberland Gate W1 10 J5
Cumberland Gate W1 57 J7
Cumberland Mkt.   **7 E3**
NW1
Cumberland Mkt.   58 B3
NW1
Cumberland Mkt.   **7 E3**
Est. NW1
Cumberland Mills   69 D5
Sq. E14
Saunders Ness Rd.
Cumberland Pk. W3   56 C7
Cumberland Pl. NW1 7 D3
Cumberland Pl. SE6   87 F1
Cumberland Pl.,   104 C1
Sun.
Cumberland Rd. E12   52 A4
Cumberland Rd. E13   60 H5
Cumberland Rd. E17   41 H2
Cumberland Rd. N9   33 F1
Cumberland Rd. N22   40 F2
Cumberland Rd.   95 E6
SE25
Cumberland Rd.   74 F1
SW13
Cumberland Rd. W3   56 C7
Cumberland Rd. W7   64 C2
Cumberland Rd.,   96 E4
Brom.
Cumberland Rd., Har.   36 H5
Cumberland Rd.,   65 A7
Rich.
Cumberland Rd.,   37 J3
Stan.

Cumberland St. SW1   19 E3
Cumberland St. SW1   67 B5
Cumberland Ter. NW1 7 D2
Cumberland Ter. Ms.   **7 D2**
NW1
Cumberlow Ave.   95 C3
SE25
Cumberton Rd. N17   41 A1
Cumbrae Gdns.,   98 F1
Surb.
Cumbrian Gdns.   48 A2
NW2
Cumming St. N1   **8 D2**
Cumming St. N1   58 F2
Cumnor Gdns.,   99 G6
Epsom
Cumnor Rd., Sutt.   100 F6
Cunard Pl. EC3   **13 E4**
Cunard Rd. NW10   56 D3
Cunard Wk. SE16   68 G4
Trident Way
Cundy Rd. E16   60 J6
Cundy St. SW1   **19 C2**
Cundy St. SW1   67 A4
Cundy St. Est. SW1   **19 C2**
Cunliffe Rd.,   99 F4
Wor.Pk.
Cunliffe St. SW16   85 C6
Cunningham Clo.,   44 C5
Rom.
Chadwell Heath La.
Cunningham Clo.,   103 B2
W.Wick.
Cunningham Pk.,   36 J5
Har.
Cunningham Pl. NW8 6 E5
Cunningham Pl. NW8 57 G4
Cunningham Rd. N15 41 D4
Cunnington St. W4   65 C4
Cupar Rd. SW11   76 B1
Cupola Clo., Brom.   87 H5
Cureton St. SW1   **19 J2**
Cureton St. SW1   67 D4
Curfew Ho., Bark.   61 F1
St. Ann's
Curlew Clo. SE28   62 D7
Curlew Ct., Surb.   98 J3
Curlew St. SE1   **17 F3**
Curlew St. SE1   68 C2
Curnick's La. SE27   85 J4
Chapel Rd.
Curnock Est. NW1   58 C1
Plender St.
Curran Ave., Sid.   79 J5
Curran Ave., Wall.   101 A3
Currey Rd., Grnf.   45 J6
Curricle St. W3   65 E1
Currie Hill Clo.   84 C4
SW19
Curry Ri. NW7   31 A6
Cursitor St. EC4   **12 E3**
Cursitor St. EC4   58 G6
Curtain Rd. EC2   **9 E4**
Curtain Rd. EC2   59 B3
Curthwaite Gdns.,   24 D4
Enf.
Curtis Dr. W3   56 D6
Curtis Fld. Rd.   85 F4
SW16
Curtis La., Wem.   46 H5
Station Gro.
Curtis Rd., Epsom   99 C4
Curtis Rd., Houns.   72 E7
Curtis St. SE1   **21 F1**
Curtis St. SE1   68 C4
Curtis Way SE1   **21 F1**
Curtis Way SE1   68 C4
Curtis Way SE28   62 B7
Tawney Rd.
Curve, The W12   56 G7
Curwen Ave. E7   51 H4
Woodford Rd.
Curwen Rd. W12   65 G2
Curzon Ave., Enf.   25 G5
Curzon Ave., Stan.   37 D1
Curzon Clo., Orp.   104 G4
Curzon Cres. NW10 47 E7
Curzon Cres., Bark.   61 J2
Curzon Gate W1   **15 C2**
Curzon Pl. W1   **15 C2**
Curzon Pl., Pnr.   36 C5
Curzon Rd. N10   40 B2
Curzon Rd. W5   55 E4
Curzon Rd., Th.Hth.   94 G6
Curzon St. W1   **15 C2**
Curzon St. W1   67 A1
Cusack Clo., Twick.   82 C4
Waldegrave Rd.
Cut, The SE1   **16 F3**
Cut, The SE1   67 G2
Cutcombe Rd. SE5   76 J2
Cuthbert Gdns. SE25 95 B3
Cuthbert Rd. E17   42 C3

Cuthbert Rd. N18   33 D5
Fairfield Rd.
Cuthbert Rd., Croy.   101 H2
Cuthbert St. W2   **10 E1**
Cuthbert St. W2   57 G4
Cutler St. E1   13 E3
Cutler St. E1   59 B6
Cutlers Gdns. E1   **13 E3**
Cutthroat All., Rich.   82 F2
Ham St.
Cuxton Clo., Bexh.   80 E5
Cyclamen Clo.,   81 G6
Hmptn.
Gresham Rd.
Cyclamen Way,   99 C5
Epsom
Cyclops Ms. E14   69 A4
Cygnet Ave., Felt.   72 C7
Cygnet Clo. NW10   47 D5
Cygnet Clo., Borwd.   22 C1
Cygnet St. E1   **9 G5**
Cygnets, The, Felt.   81 A4
Cymbeline Ct., Har.   37 C6
Cynthia St. N1   **8 D2**
Cynthia St. N1   58 F2
Cyntra Pl. E8   50 E7
Mare St.
Cypress Ave., Twick.   72 J7
Cypress Gro., Ilf.   35 H6
Cypress Pl. W1   **7 G6**
Cypress Rd. SE25   95 B2
Cypress Rd., Har.   37 A2
Cyprus Ave. N3   39 B2
Cyprus Gdns. N3   39 B2
Cyprus Pl. E2   59 F2
Cyprus Pl. E6   61 D7
Cyprus Rd. N3   39 C2
Cyprus Rd. N9   33 C2
Cyprus St. E2   59 F2
Cyrena Rd. SE22   77 C6
Cyril Mans. SW11   75 J1
Cyril Rd., Bexh.   80 E2
Cyrus St. EC1   **8 H5**
Cyrus St. EC1   58 H4
Czar St. SE8   69 A6

D

Dabbs Hill La., Nthlt. 45 G5
Dabin Cres. SE10   78 C1
Dacca St. SE8   68 J6
Dace Rd. E3   60 A1
Dacre Ave., Ilf.   43 D2
Dacre Clo., Chig.   35 F4
Dacre Clo., Grnf.   64 H2
Dacre Gdns. SE13   78 E4
Dacre Gdns., Borwd. 22 D5
Dacre Gdns., Chig.   35 F4
Dacre Pk. SE13   78 E3
Dacre Pl. SE13   78 E3
Dacre Rd. E11   51 F1
Dacre Rd. E13   60 H1
Dacre Rd., Croy.   94 E7
Dacre St. SW1   **15 H5**
Dacre St. SW1   67 D3
Dacres Rd. SE23   86 G3
Dade Way, Sthl.   63 F5
Daerwood Clo.,   104 C1
Brom.
Daffodil Pl.,   81 G6
Hmptn.
Primrose La.
Daffodil St. W12   56 F7
Dafforne Rd. SW17   84 J3
Dagenham Ave., Dag. 62 E1
Dagenham Rd. E10   50 J1
Dagenham Rd., Dag. 53 H4
Dagmar Ave., Wem. 46 A4
Dagmar Gdns.   57 A2
NW10
Dagmar Pas. N1   58 H1
Cross St.
Dagmar Rd. N4   40 G7
Dagmar Rd. N15   41 A4
Cornwall Rd.
Dagmar Rd. N22   40 D1
Dagmar Rd. SE5   77 B1
Dagmar Rd. SE25   95 B5
Dagmar Rd., Dag.   53 J7
Dagmar Rd.,   91 J1
Kings.T.
Dagmar Rd., Sthl.   63 E3
Dagmar Ter. N1   58 H1
Dagnall Pk. SE25   95 B6
Dagnall Rd. SE25   95 B5
Dagnall St. SW11   75 J2
Dagnan Rd. SW12   76 B7
Dagonet Gdns.,   87 G3
Brom.
Shroffold Rd.
Dagonet Rd., Brom.   87 G3

Dahlia Gdns., Mitch.   94 B4
Dahlia Rd. SE2   71 B4
Dahomey Rd. SW16   85 C6
Daimler Way, Wall.   101 E7
Daines Clo. E12   52 C3
Colchester Ave.
Dainford Clo.,   87 D5
Brom.
Dainton Clo., Brom.   96 H1
Daintry Clo., Har.   37 D4
Daintry Way E9   50 J6
Eastway
Dairsie Rd. SE9   79 D3
Dairy Clo., Th.Hth.   94 J2
Dairy La. SE18   70 C4
Rideout St.
Dairy Ms. SW9   76 E3
Dairy Wk. SW19   84 B4
Daisy Clo., Croy.   102 G1
Primrose La.
Daisy La. SW6   75 D3
Daisy Rd. E18   42 H2
Dakota Gdns., Nthlt.   54 E3
Argus Way
Dalberg Rd. SW2   76 G5
Dalberg Way SE2   71 D3
Lanridge Rd.
Dalby Rd. SW18   75 F4
Dalby St. NW5   49 B6
Dalcross Rd.,   72 E2
Houns.
Dale, The, Kes.   104 A4
Dale Ave., Edg.   37 J1
Dale Ave., Houns.   72 E3
Dale Clo. SE3   78 G3
Dale Clo., Barn.   23 E6
Dale Clo., Pnr.   36 B1
Dale Gdns.,   34 H4
Wdf.Grn.
Dale Grn. Rd. N11   32 B3
Dale Gro. N12   31 F5
Dale Pk. Ave., Cars.   100 J2
Dale Pk. Rd. SE19   94 J1
Dale Rd. NW5   49 A5
Grafton Rd.
Dale Rd. SE17   **20 H6**
Dale Rd. SE17   67 H6
Dale Rd., Grnf.   54 H5
Dale Rd., Sutt.   100 C4
Dale Row W11   57 B6
St. Marks Rd.
Dale St. W4   65 E5
Dale Vw. Ave. E4   34 C2
Dale Vw. Cres. E4   34 C2
Dale Vw. Gdns. E4   34 D3
Dale Wd. Rd., Orp.   97 H7
Dalebury Rd. SW17   84 H2
Daleham Gdns. NW3 48 G5
Daleham Ms. NW3   48 G6
Dalehead NW1   **7 F2**
Dalehead NW1   58 C2
Dales Path, Borwd.   22 D5
Farriers Way
Dales Rd., Borwd.   22 D5
Daleside Gdns.,   35 F3
Chig.
Daleside Rd. SW16   85 B5
Daleside Rd., Epsom 99 B8
Daleview Rd. N15   41 B6
Dalewood Gdns.,   99 H2
Wor.Pk.
Daley St. E9   50 G6
Daley Thompson   76 B3
Way SW8
Dalgarno Gdns. W10 56 J5
Dalgarno Gdns. Est.   56 J4
W10
Dalgarno Way W10   56 J4
Dalgleish St. E14   59 H6
Daling Way E3   59 H2
Dalkeith Gro., Stan.   29 G5
Dalkeith Rd. SE21   85 J1
Dalkeith Rd., Ilf.   52 F3
Dallas Rd. NW4   38 G7
Dallas Rd. SE26   86 E4
Dallas Rd. W5   55 J5
Dallas Rd., Sutt.   100 B6
Dallin Rd. SE18   70 E7
Dallin Rd., Bexh.   80 D4
Dalling Rd. W6   65 H4
Dallinger Rd. SE12   78 F6
Dallington St. EC1   **8 H5**
Dallington St. EC1   58 H4
Dalmain Rd. SE23   86 G1
Dalmally Rd., Croy.   95 C7
Dalmeny Ave. N7   49 D4
Dalmeny Ave. SW16 94 H1
Dalmeny Clo., Wem. 46 F6
Dalmeny Cres.,   73 A4
Houns.
Dalmeny Rd. N7   49 D3
Dalmeny Rd., Barn.   23 F6
Dalmeny Rd., Cars.   101 A7

Dalmeny Rd., Erith 80 H1
Dalmeny Rd., Wor.Pk. 99 H3
Dalmeyer Rd. NW10 47 F6
Dalmore Ave., Esher 98 C6
Dalmore Rd. SE21 85 J2
Dalrymple Rd. SE4 77 H4
Dalston Gdns., Stan. 37 H1
Dalston La. E8 50 C6
Dalton Ave., Mitch. 93 H2
Dalton Clo., Orp. 104 H3
Dalton Rd., Har. 37 A2
Athelstone Rd.
Dalton St. SE27 85 H2
Dalwood St. SE5 77 B1
Daly Ct. E15 51 C5
Clays La.
Dalyell Rd. SW9 76 F3
Dame St. N1 8 J1
Damer Ter. SW10 66 F7
Tadema Rd.
Dames Rd. E7 51 G3
Damien St. E1 59 E6
Damon Clo., Sid. 89 B3
Damsonwood Clo., Sthl. 63 G3
Dan Leno Wk. SW6 66 E7
Britannia Rd.
Danbrook Rd. SW16 94 E1
Danbury Clo., Rom. 44 D3
Danbury Ms., Wall. 101 D1
Danbury Rd., Loug. 27 B7
Danbury St. N1 8 H1
Danbury St. N1 58 H2
Danbury Way, Wdf.Grn. 34 J6
Danby St. SE15 77 C3
Dancer Rd. SW6 75 C1
Dancer Rd., Rich. 74 A3
Dando Cres. SE3 78 H3
Dandridge Clo. SE10 69 F5
Dane Clo., Bex. 80 G7
Dane Clo., Orp. 104 G5
Dane Pl. E3 59 H2
Roman Rd.
Dane Rd. N18 33 F4
Dane Rd. SW19 93 F1
Dane Rd. W13 64 F1
Dane Rd., Ilf. 52 F5
Dane Rd., Sthl. 54 E7
Dane St. WC1 12 C2
Danebury, Croy. 103 B6
Danebury Ave. SW15 74 G6
Daneby Rd. SE6 87 B3
Danecourt Gdns., Croy. 102 C3
Danecroft Rd. SE24 76 J5
Danehill Wk., Sid. 89 A3
Hatherley Rd.
Danehurst Gdns., Ilf. 43 B5
Danehurst St. SW6 75 B1
Daneland, Barn. 23 J5
Danemead Gro., Nthlt. 45 H5
Danemere St. SW15 74 J3
Danes Gate, Har. 37 B3
Danes Rd., Rom. 44 J7
Danesbury Rd., Felt. 81 B1
Danescombe SE12 87 G1
Winn Rd.
Danescourt Cres., Sutt. 100 F2
Danescroft NW4 39 A5
Danescroft Ave. NW4 39 A5
Danescroft Gdns. NW4 39 A5
Danesdale Rd. E9 50 H6
Danesfield SE5 21 D5
Daneswood Ave. SE6 87 C3
Danethorpe Rd., Wem. 46 G6
Danetree Clo., Epsom 99 C7
Danetree Rd., Epsom 99 C7
Danette Gdns., Dag. 53 F2
Daneville Rd. SE5 77 A1
Dangan Rd. E11 42 G6
Daniel Bolt Clo. E14 60 B5
Uamvar St.
Daniel Clo. N18 33 F4
Daniel Clo. SW17 87 H6
Daniel Gdns. SE15 21 F7
Daniel Gdns. SE15 68 C7
Daniel Pl. NW4 38 H6
Daniel Rd. W5 55 J7
Daniels Rd. SE15 77 F3
Dansey Pl. W1 11 H5
Dansington Rd., Well. 80 A4

Danson Mead, Well. 80 C3
Danson Rd., Bex. 80 D5
Danson Rd., Bexh. 80 D5
Dante Pl. SE11 20 H2
Dante Rd. SE11 20 G1
Dante Rd. SE11 67 H4
Danube St. SW3 18 H3
Danvers Rd. N8 40 D4
Danvers St. SW3 18 F6
Danvers St. SW3 66 G6
Danziger Way, Borwd. 22 C1
Daphne Gdns. E4 34 C3
Gunners Gro.
Daphne St. SW18 75 F6
Daplyn St. E1 13 H1
D'Arblay St. W1 11 G4
D'Arblay St. W1 58 C6
Darby Cres., Sun. 90 C2
Darby Gdns., Sun. 90 C2
Darcy Ave., Wall. 101 C4
Darcy Clo. N20 31 G2
D'Arcy Dr., Har. 37 G4
Darcy Gdns., Dag. 62 F1
D'Arcy Gdns., Har. 37 H4
Darcy Rd. SW16 94 E2
D'Arcy Rd., Sutt. 100 A4
Dare Gdns., Dag. 53 E3
Grafton Rd.
Darell Rd., Rich. 74 A3
Darenth Rd. N16 41 C7
Darenth Rd., Well. 80 A1
Darfield Rd. SE4 77 J5
Darfield Way W10 57 A6
Darfur St. SW15 75 A3
Dargate Clo. SE19 86 C7
Chipstead Clo.
Darien Rd. SW11 75 G3
Darlan Rd. SW6 66 C3
Darlaston Rd. SW19 84 A7
Darley Clo., Croy. 95 H6
Darley Dr., N.Mal. 92 D2
Darley Gdns., Mord. 93 F6
Darley Rd. N9 33 C1
Darley Rd. SW11 75 J6
Darling Rd. SE4 78 A3
Darling Row E1 59 E4
Darlington Rd. SE27 85 H5
Darmaine Clo., S.Croy. 101 J7
Churchill St.
Darnley Ho. E14 59 H6
Camdenhurst St.
Darnley Rd. E9 50 F6
Darnley Rd., Wdf.Grn. 42 G1
Darnley Ter. W11 68 A1
St. James Gdns.
Darrell Rd. SE22 77 D5
Darren Clo. N4 40 F7
Darrick Wd. Rd., Orp. 104 G2
Darris Clo., Hayes 54 E4
Darsley Dr. SW8 76 E1
Dart St. W10 57 B3
Dartford Ave. N9 25 F6
Dartford Rd., Bex. 89 J1
Dartford St. SE17 21 A5
Dartford St. SE17 67 J6
Dartmoor Wk. E14 69 A4
Charnwood Gdns.
Dartmouth Clo. W11 57 D6
Dartmouth Gro. SE10 79 C1
Dartmouth Hill SE10 79 C1
Dartmouth Pk. Ave. NW5 49 B3
Dartmouth Pk. Hill N19 49 B1
Dartmouth Pk. Hill NW5 49 C3
Dartmouth Pk. Rd. NW5 49 B4
Dartmouth Pl. SE23 86 F2
Dartmouth Rd.
Dartmouth Rd. W4 65 E6
Dartmouth Rd. E16 60 G6
Fords Pk. Rd.
Dartmouth Rd. NW2 48 A6
Dartmouth Rd. NW4 38 G6
Dartmouth Rd. SE23 86 F2
Dartmouth Rd. SE26 86 E3
Dartmouth Rd., Brom. 96 G7
Dartmouth Rd., Ruis. 45 A3
Dartmouth Row SE10 78 C1
Dartmouth St. SW1 15 A4
Dartmouth St. SW1 67 D2
Dartnell Rd., Croy. 96 B7
Dartrey Wk. SW10 18 E7
Darville Rd. N16 50 C3
Darwell Clo. E6 61 D2
Darwin Clo. N11 32 B3

Darwin Clo., Orp. 104 G5
Darwin Dr., Sthl. 54 H6
Darwin Gdns., Wat. 28 C5
Barnhurst Path
Darwin Rd. N22 40 H1
Darwin Rd. W5 64 F5
Darwin Rd., Well. 79 J3
Darwin St. SE17 21 C1
Darwin St. SE17 68 A4
Daryngton Dr., Grnf. 55 A2
Dashwood Clo., Bexh. 80 G5
Dashwood Rd. N8 40 F6
Dassett Rd. SE27 85 H5
Datchelor Pl. SE5 77 A1
Datchet Rd. SE6 86 J3
Datchworth Ct. N4 49 J3
Queens Dr.
Date St. SE17 21 A4
Date St. SE17 68 A4
Daubeney Gdns. N17 32 J7
Daubeney Rd. E5 50 H4
Daubeney Rd. N17 32 J7
Daubeney Twr. SE8 68 J4
Dault Rd. SW18 75 F6
Davema Clo., Chis. 97 D1
Davenant Rd. N19 49 D2
Davenant Rd., Croy. 101 H4
Duppas Hill Rd.
Davenant St. E1 13 J2
Davenant St. E1 59 D5
Davenport Clo., Tedd. 82 D6
Davenport Rd. SE6 78 C6
Davenport Rd., Sid. 89 D2
Daventer Dr., Stan. 29 C7
Daventry Ave. E17 42 A5
Daventry St. NW1 10 G1
Daventry St. NW1 57 H5
Davern Clo. SE10 69 H4
Davey Clo. N7 49 F6
Davey Rd. E9 51 A7
White Post La.
Davey St. SE15 21 G6
Davey St. SE15 68 C6
David Ave., Grnf. 55 B3
David Ms. W1 11 B1
David Rd., Dag. 53 E2
David St. E15 51 D6
Davidge St. SE1 16 H4
Davidge St. SE1 67 H2
Davids Rd. SE23 86 F1
Davids Way, Ilf. 35 H7
Davidson Gdns. SW8 67 E7
Davidson La., Har. 37 C7
Grove Hill
Davidson Rd., Croy. 102 B1
Davies Clo., Croy. 95 C6
Davies La. E11 51 E2
Davies Ms. W1 11 D5
Davies St. W1 11 D5
Davies St. W1 58 B7
Davington Gdns., Dag. 53 B5
Davington Rd., Dag. 53 B6
Davinia Clo., Wdf.Grn. 35 C6
Deacon Way
Davis Rd. W3 65 F1
Davis Rd., Chess. 99 A4
Davis St. E13 60 H2
Davisville Rd. W12 65 G2
Dawes Ave., Islw. 73 D5
Dawes Ho. SE17 21 B2
Dawes Rd. SW6 66 B7
Dawes St. SE17 21 C3
Dawes St. SE17 68 A5
Dawlish Ave. N13 32 E4
Dawlish Ave. SW18 84 E2
Dawlish Dr., Ilf. 52 H4
Dawlish Dr., Pnr. 36 E5
Dawlish Dr., Ruis. 45 A2
Dawlish Rd. E10 51 C1
Dawlish Rd. N17 41 D3
Dawlish Rd. NW2 48 A6
Dawn Clo., Houns. 72 E3
Dawnay Gdns. SW18 84 G2
Dawnay Rd. SW18 84 F2
Dawpool Rd. NW2 47 F2
Daws Hill E4 26 C2
Daws La. NW7 30 F5
Dawson Clo. SE18 70 F4
Dawson Gdns., Bark. 52 J7
Dawson Ave.
Dawson Heights Est. SE22 77 D7
Dawson Pl. W2 57 D7
Dawson Rd. NW2 47 J5
Dawson Rd., Kings.T. 91 J3

Dawson St. E2 9 G2
Dawson St. E2 59 C2
Dax Ct., Sun. 90 C3
Thames Rd.
Daybrook Rd. SW19 93 E2
Daylesford Ave. SW15 74 G4
Daymer Gdns., Pnr. 36 B4
Days La., Sid. 79 H7
Daysbrook Rd. SW2 85 F2
Dayton Gro. SE15 77 F1
De Beauvoir Cres. N1 59 B1
De Beauvoir Est. N1 59 A1
De Beauvoir Rd. N1 59 B1
De Beauvoir Sq. N1 50 B7
De Bohun Ave. N14 24 B6
De Crespigny Pk. SE5 77 A2
De Frene Rd. SE26 86 G4
De Havilland Rd., Edg. 38 A2
De Havilland Rd., Wall. 101 E7
De Laune St. SE17 20 G4
De Laune St. SE17 67 H5
De Luci Rd., Erith 71 J5
De Lucy St. SE2 71 B4
De Montfort Rd. SW16 85 E3
De Morgan Rd. SW6 75 E3
De Quincey Rd. N17 41 A1
De Vere Cotts. W8 14 C5
De Vere Gdns. W8 14 C4
De Vere Gdns. W8 66 F2
De Vere Gdns., Ilf. 52 C2
De Vere Ms. W8 14 C5
De Walden St. W1 11 C2
Deacon Ms. N1 12 C1
Deacon Rd. NW2 47 G5
Deacon Rd., Kings.T. 91 J1
Deacon Way SE17 20 J1
Deacon Way SE17 67 J4
Deacon Way, Wdf.Grn. 35 C7
Deacons Clo., Borwd. 22 A4
Deacons Clo., Pnr. 36 B2
Deacons Leas, Orp. 104 G4
Deacons Wk., Hmptn. 81 F4
Bishops Gro.
Deal Porters Way SE16 68 F3
Deal Rd. SW17 85 A6
Deal St. E1 13 H1
Deal St. E1 59 D5
Deal Wk. SW9 67 G7
Mandela St.
Deal's Gateway SE10 78 B1
Deptford Bri.
Dealtry Rd. SW15 74 J4
Dean Bradley St. SW1 16 A6
Dean Bradley St. SW1 67 E3
Dean Clo. E9 50 F5
Dean Clo. SE16 68 G1
Surrey Water Rd.
Dean Ct., Wem. 46 E3
Dean Dr., Stan. 37 H2
Dean Farrar St. SW1 15 J5
Dean Farrar St. SW1 67 D3
Dean Gdns. E17 42 D4
Dean Rd. NW2 47 J6
Dean Rd., Croy. 102 A4
Dean Rd., Hmptn. 81 F5
Dean Rd., Houns. 72 H5
Dean Ryle St. SW1 20 A1
Dean Ryle St. SW1 67 E4
Dean Stanley St. SW1 16 A6
Dean Stanley St. SW1 67 E3
Dean St. E7 51 G5
Dean St. W1 11 H3
Dean St. W1 58 D6
Dean Trench St. SW1 16 A6
Dean Wk., Edg. 30 C6
Deansbrook Rd.
Dean Way, Sthl. 63 H2
Deancross St. E1 59 F6
Deane Ave., Ruis. 45 B5
Deane Cft. Rd., Pnr. 36 C5
Deane Way, Ruis. 36 B6
Deanery Clo. N2 39 H4
Deanery Ms. W1 15 C1
Deanery Rd. E15 51 E6
Deanery St. W1 15 C1
Deanery St. W1 67 A1
Deanhill Rd. SW14 74 B4
Deans Bldgs. SE17 21 C2
Deans Bldgs. SE17 68 A4

Deans Clo. W4 65 B6
Dean's Clo., Croy. 102 C3
Deans Clo., Edg. 30 C6
Dean's Ct. EC4 12 H4
Deans Dr. N13 32 H6
Deans Dr., Edg. 30 D5
Dean's Gate Clo. 86 G3
SE23
Deans La., Edg. 30 C6
Deans Ms. W1 11 E3
Dean's Pl. SW1 19 H3
Dean's Pl. SW1 67 D5
Deans Rd. W7 64 C1
Deans Rd., Sutt. 100 E3
Deans Way, Edg. 30 C5
Dean's Yd. SW1 15 J5
Deansbrook Clo., 30 C6
Edg.
Deansbrook Rd., 30 B7
Edg.
Deanscroft Ave. NW9 47 C2
Deansway N2 39 G4
Deansway N9 33 B3
Dearn Gdns., Mitch. 93 H3
Dearne Clo., Stan. 29 D5
Deason St. E15 60 C1
High St.
Debden Clo., 35 A7
Wdf.Grn.
Debden Ind. Group, 27 G4
Loug.
Debnams Rd. SE16 68 F4
Rotherhithe New Rd.
Deborah Clo., Islw. 73 B1
DeBurgh Rd. SW19 84 F7
Decima St. SE1 17 D5
Decima St. SE1 68 B3
Deck Clo. SE16 68 G2
Thame Rd.
Decoy Ave. NW11 39 B5
Dee Rd., Rich. 73 J4
Dee St. E14 60 C6
Deeley Rd. SW8 76 D1
Deena Clo. W3 55 J6
Deepdale SW19 84 A4
Deepdale Ave. 96 F4
Brom.
Deepdene W5 55 J4
Deepdene Ave., 102 C5
Croy.
Deepdene Clo. E11 42 G4
Deepdene Ct. N21 24 H6
Deepdene Gdns. 76 F7
SW2
Deepdene Path, 27 D4
Loug.
Deepdene Rd. SE5 77 A4
Deepdene Rd., Loug. 27 D4
Deepdene Rd., Well. 80 A3
Deepwell Clo., Islw. 73 D1
Deepwood La., Grnf. 55 A3
Cowgate Rd.
Deer Pk. Clo., 83 B7
Kings.T.
Deer Pk. Gdns. 93 G3
Mitch.
Deer Pk. Rd. SW19 93 E2
Deer Pk. Way, 103 E2
W.Wick.
Deerbrook Rd. SE24 85 H1
Deerdale Rd. SE24 76 J4
Deerhurst Clo., Felt. 81 A4
Deerhurst Rd. NW2 48 A6
Deerhurst Rd. SW16 85 F5
Deerings Dr., Pnr. 36 A5
Deerleap Gro. E4 26 B5
Deeside Rd. SW17 84 G3
Defiance Wk. SE18 70 C3
Antelope Rd.
Defiant Way, Wall. 101 E7
Defoe Ave., Rich. 65 A4
Defoe Clo. SW17 84 A6
Defoe Rd. N16 50 B2
Degema Rd., Chis. 88 E5
Dehar Cres. NW9 38 F7
Dekker Rd. SE21 77 B6
Delacourt Rd. SE3 69 H7
Old Dover Rd.
Delafield Rd. SE7 69 H5
Delaford Rd. SE16 68 G5
Delaford St. SW6 66 B7
Delamere Cres. 95 F6
Croy.
Delamere Gdns. NW7 30 D6
Delamere Rd. SW20 93 A1
Delamere Rd. W5 64 H1
Delamere Rd., 22 B3
Borwd.
Delamere Rd., Hayes 54 D7
Delamere Ter. W2 10 B1
Delamere Ter. W2 57 E5
Delancey Pas. NW1 58 B1
Delancey St.

Delancey St. NW1 58 B1
Delaware Rd. W9 6 A5
Delaware Rd. W9 57 E4
Delawyk Cres. SE24 76 J6
Delcombe Ave., 99 J1
Wor.Pk.
Delft Way SE22 77 B5
East Dulwich Gro.
Delhi Rd., Enf. 25 C7
Delhi St. N1 58 E1
Delia St. SW18 75 E7
Dell, The SE2 71 A5
Dell, The SE19 95 C1
Dell, The, Brent. 64 F6
Dell, The, Felt. 72 B7
Harlington Rd. W.
Dell, The, Pnr. 36 D2
Dell, The, Wem. 46 E5
Dell, The, Wdf.Grn. 34 H3
Dell Clo. E15 60 D7
Dell Clo., Wall. 101 C4
Dell Clo., Wdf.Grn. 34 H3
Dell La., Epsom 99 G5
Dell Rd., Epsom 99 G6
Dell Wk., N.Mal. 92 E2
Dell Way W13 55 F6
Della Path E5 50 E3
Napoleon Rd.
Dellbow Rd., Felt. 72 B5
Central Way
Dellfield Clo., Beck. 87 C7
Foxgrove Rd.
Dellors Clo., Barn. 23 A5
Dellow Clo., Ilf. 43 G7
Dellow St. E1 59 E7
Dell's Ms. SW1 19 G2
Dellwood Gdns., Ilf. 43 D3
Delmare Clo. SW9 76 F4
Brighton Ter.
Delme Cres. SE3 78 H2
Delmey Clo., Croy. 102 C3
Radcliffe Rd.
Deloraine St. SE8 78 A1
Delorme St. W6 66 A6
Delta Clo., Wor.Pk. 99 F3
Delta Ct. NW2 47 G2
Delta Gain, Wat. 28 D2
Delta Gro., Nthlt. 54 D3
Delta Rd., Wor.Pk. 99 E3
Delta St. E2 9 H3
Delvan Clo. SE18 70 D7
Ordnance Rd.
Delvers Mead, Dag. 53 J4
Delverton Rd. SE17 20 H4
Delverton Rd. SE17 67 H5
Delvino Rd. SW6 75 D1
Demesne Rd., Wall. 101 D4
Demeta Clo., Wem. 47 C3
Dempster Clo., 91 F7
Surb.
Dempster Rd. SW18 75 F5
Den Clo., Beck. 96 D3
Den Rd., Brom. 96 D3
Denberry Dr., Sid. 89 B3
Denbigh Clo. NW10 47 E7
Denbigh Clo. W11 57 C7
Denbigh Clo., Chis. 88 C6
Denbigh Clo., Sutt. 100 C5
Denbigh Gdns. 73 J5
Rich.
Denbigh Ms. SW1 19 F2
Denbigh Pl. SW1 19 F3
Denbigh Pl. SW1 67 C5
Denbigh Rd. E6 61 A3
Denbigh Rd. W11 57 C7
Denbigh Rd. W13 55 E7
Denbigh Rd., Houns. 72 H2
Denbigh Rd., Sthl. 54 F6
Denbigh St. SW1 19 F2
Denbigh St. SW1 67 C4
Denbigh Ter. W11 57 C7
Denbridge Rd., 97 C2
Brom.
Dendy St. SW12 85 A1
Dene, The W13 55 E5
Dene, The, Croy. 102 G4
Dene, The, Wem. 46 H4
Dene, The, W.Mol. 90 F5
Dene Ave., Houns. 72 F3
Dene Ave., Sid. 80 B7
Dene Clo. SE4 77 H3
Dene Clo., Brom. 103 F1
Dene Clo., Wor.Pk. 99 F2
Dene Gdns., Stan. 29 F5
Dene Gdns., T.Ditt. 98 D2
Dene Rd., Buck.H. 35 A1
Denehurst Gdns. 38 J6
NW4
Denehurst Gdns. W3 65 B3
Denehurst Gdns., 74 A4
Rich.
Denehurst Gdns., 73 A7
Twick.

Denehurst Gdns., 34 H4
Wdf.Grn.
Denewood, Barn. 23 F5
Denewood Rd. N6 39 J6
Dengie Wk. N1 58 J1
Basire St.
Denham Clo., Well. 80 C3
Park Vw. Rd.
Denham Cres., 93 J4
Mitch.
Denham Dr., Esher 98 D5
Denham Dr., Ilf. 40 F6
Denham Rd. N20 31 J3
Denham Rd., Felt. 72 C6
Denham St. SE10 69 G5
Denham Way, Bark. 61 H1
Denham Way, Borwd. 22 C1
Denholme Rd. W9 57 C3
Denison Clo. N2 39 F3
Denison Rd. SW19 84 G6
Denison Rd. W5 55 F4
Deniston Ave., Bex. 89 E1
Denleigh Gdns. N21 32 G1
Denleigh Gdns., 91 B6
T.Ditt.
Denman Dr. NW11 39 D5
Denman Dr. N. NW11 39 D5
Denman Dr. S. NW11 39 D5
Denman Rd. SE15 77 C1
Denman St. W1 11 H6
Denmark Ave. SW19 84 B7
Denmark Ct., Mord. 93 D5
Denmark Gdns., 100 J3
Cars.
Denmark Gro. N1 8 E1
Denmark Gro. N1 58 G2
Denmark Hill SE5 77 A1
Denmark Hill Dr. 38 F4
NW9
Denmark Hill Est. 77 A4
SE5
Denmark Pl. WC2 11 J3
Denmark Rd. N8 40 G4
Denmark Rd. NW6 57 C2
Denmark Rd. SE5 76 J1
Denmark Rd. SE25 95 D5
Denmark Rd. SW19 84 A6
Denmark Rd. W13 55 E7
Denmark Rd., Brom. 96 H1
Denmark Rd., Cars. 100 J3
Denmark St. E11 51 E3
Denmark St. E13 60 H5
Denmark St. N17 41 E1
Denmark St. WC2 11 J3
Denmark St. WC2 58 D6
Denmark Wk. SE27 85 J4
Denmead Ho. SW15 74 F6
Highcliffe Dr.
Denmead Rd., Croy. 101 H1
Denmead Way SE15 68 C7
Pentridge St.
Dennan Rd., Surb. 98 J1
Denne Ter. E8 59 C1
Denner Rd. E4 34 A2
Dennett Rd., Croy. 101 G1
Dennett's Gro. SE14 77 G2
Dennetts Rd.
Dennetts Rd. SE14 77 F1
Denning Ave., Croy. 101 G4
Denning Clo. NW8 6 D3
Denning Clo. NW8 57 F3
Denning Clo., 81 F6
Hmptn.
Denning Rd. NW3 48 G4
Dennington Clo. E5 50 E2
Detmold Rd.
Dennington Pk. Rd. 48 D6
NW6
Denningtons, The, 99 E2
Wor.Pk.
Dennis Ave., Wem. 46 J5
Dennis Gdns., Stan. 29 F5
Dennis La., Stan. 29 E3
Dennis Pk. Cres. 93 B1
SW20
Dennis Reeve Clo., 93 J1
Mitch.
Dennis Rd., E.Mol. 90 J4
Dennis Way SW4 76 D3
Gauden Rd.
Dennison Pt. E15 51 C7
Denny Clo. E6 61 B5
Linton Gdns.
Denny Cres. SE11 20 F3
Denny Gdns., Dag. 53 B7
Canonsleigh Rd.
Denny Rd. N9 33 E1
Denny St. SE11 20 F3
Denny St. SE11 67 G5
Densham Rd. E15 60 E1

Densole Clo., Beck. 95 H1
Kings Hall Rd.
Densworth Gro. N9 33 F2
Denton Clo., Barn. 22 J5
Denton Rd. N8 40 F5
Denton Rd. N18 33 B4
Denton Rd., Twick. 73 G6
Denton Rd., Well. 71 C7
Denton St. SW18 75 E6
Denton Way E5 50 G3
Dents Rd. SW11 75 J6
Denver Clo., Orp. 97 H6
Denver Rd. N16 50 B1
Denyer St. SW3 18 H2
Denyer St. SW3 66 H4
Denzil Rd. NW10 47 F5
Deodar Rd. SW15 75 B4
Deodara Clo. N20 31 H3
Depot App. N3 39 E1
Depot Rd., Houns. 73 A3
Deptford Bri. SE8 78 A1
Deptford Bdy. SE8 78 A1
Deptford Ch. St. 69 A6
SE8
Deptford Ferry Rd. 69 A4
E14
Deptford Grn. SE8 69 A6
Deptford High St. 69 A6
SE8
Deptford Strand SE8 68 J4
Deptford Wf. SE8 68 J4
Derby Ave. N12 31 F5
Derby Ave., Har. 37 A1
Derby Ave., Rom. 44 J6
Derby Ct. E5 50 G4
Overbury St.
Derby Est., Houns. 72 G4
Derby Gate SW1 16 A3
Derby Hill SE23 86 F2
Derby Hill Cres. 86 F2
SE23
Derby Rd. E7 52 A7
Derby Rd. E9 59 G1
Derby Rd. E18 42 F1
Derby Rd. N18 33 F5
Derby Rd. SW14 74 B4
Derby Rd. SW19 84 D7
Russell Rd.
Derby Rd., Croy. 101 H2
Derby Rd., Enf. 25 E5
Derby Rd., Grnf. 54 H1
Derby Rd., Houns. 72 H4
Derby Rd., Surb. 99 A1
Derby Rd., Sutt. 100 C6
Derby St. W1 15 C2
Derbyshire St. E2 9 J4
Derbyshire St. E2 59 D3
Dereham Pl. EC2 9 E4
Dereham Rd., Bark. 52 G6
Derek Ave., Epsom 99 A6
Derek Ave., Wall. 101 B3
Derek Ave., Wem. 47 B7
Derek Clo., Epsom 99 B5
Dericote St. E8 59 D1
Derifall Clo. E6 61 C5
Dering Pl., Croy. 101 J4
Dering Rd., Croy. 101 J4
Dering St. W1 11 D4
Dering St. W1 58 B6
Derinton Rd. SW17 84 J4
Derley Rd., Sthl. 63 C3
Dermody Gdns. SE13 78 D5
Dermody Rd. SE13 78 D5
Deronda Rd. SE24 85 H1
Deroy Clo., Cars. 100 J6
Derrick Gdns. SE7 69 A4
Anchor & Hope La.
Derrick Rd., Beck. 95 J3
Derry Rd., Croy. 101 E3
Derry St. W8 14 A4
Derry St. W8 66 E2
Dersingham Ave. 52 C4
E12
Dersingham Rd. 48 B3
NW2
Derwent Ave. N18 33 A5
Derwent Ave. NW7 30 D6
Derwent Ave. NW9 38 E5
Derwent Ave. SW15 83 E4
Derwent Ave., Barn. 31 J1
Derwent Ave., Pnr. 28 E6
Derwent Clo., Esher 98 B6
Derwent Cres. N20 31 F3
Derwent Cres., Bexh. 80 G2
Derwent Cres., Stan. 37 F2
Derwent Dr., Orp. 97 G7
Derwent Gdns., Ilf. 43 B4
Derwent Gdns., Wem. 37 F7
Derwent Gro. SE22 77 C4
Derwent Ri. NW9 38 E6
Derwent Rd. N13 32 F4
Derwent Rd. SE20 95 D2
Derwent Rd. SW20 93 A6

Derwent Rd. W5 64 F3
Derwent Rd., Sthl. 54 F6
Derwent Rd., Twick. 72 H6
Derwent St. SE10 69 E5
Derwent Wk., Wall. 101 B7
Derwent Yd. W5 64 F3
 Northfield Ave.
Derwentwater Rd. 65 C1
 W3
Desborough St. W2 10 A1
Desenfans Rd. SE21 77 B6
Desford Rd. E16 60 E4
Desmond St. SE14 68 H6
Despard Rd. N19 49 C1
Detling Rd., Brom. 87 G5
Detmold Rd. E5 50 F2
Devalls Clo. E6 61 D7
Devana End, Cars. 100 J3
Devas Rd. SW20 92 J1
Devas St. E3 60 B4
Devenay Rd. E15 51 F7
Devenish Rd. SE2 71 A2
Deventer Cres. SE22 77 B5
 East Dulwich Gro.
Deverell St. SE1 17 B6
Deverell St. SE1 68 A3
Devereux Ct. WC2 12 E4
Devereux Rd. SW11 75 J6
Deverill Ct. SE20 95 F1
Devizes St. N1 59 A1
 Poole St.
Devon Ave., Twick. 81 J1
Devon Clo. N17 41 C3
Devon Clo., Buck.H. 34 H2
Devon Clo., Grnf. 55 F1
Devon Gdns. N4 40 H6
Devon Ri. N2 39 G4
Devon Rd., Bark. 61 H1
Devon St. SE15 68 E6
Devon Way, Chess. 98 F5
Devon Way, Epsom 99 B5
Devon Waye, Houns. 63 F7
Devoncroft Gdns. 73 D7
 Twick.
Devonia Gdns. N18 32 J6
Devonia Rd. N1 8 H1
Devonia Rd. N1 58 H2
Devonport Gdns., Ilf. 43 C6
Devonport Ms. W12 65 H1
 Devonport Rd.
Devonport Rd. W12 65 H2
Devonport St. E1 59 G6
Devons Est. E3 60 B3
Devons Rd. E3 60 A5
Devonshire Ave., 100 F7
 Sutt.
Devonshire Clo. E15 51 E4
Devonshire Clo. N13 32 G4
 Devonshire Rd.
Devonshire Clo. W1 11 C1
Devonshire Clo. W1 58 B5
Devonshire Cres. 31 A7
 NW7
Devonshire Dr. SE10 69 B7
Devonshire Dr., 98 G2
 Surb.
Devonshire Gdns. 32 J6
 N17
Devonshire Gdns. 24 J7
 N21
Devonshire Gdns. 65 C7
 W4
Devonshire Gro. 68 E6
 SE15
Devonshire Hill La. 32 H6
 N17
Devonshire Ms. W4 65 E5
 Glebe St.
Devonshire Ms. N. 11 D1
 W1
Devonshire Ms. S. 11 D1
 W1
Devonshire Ms. S. 58 B5
 W1
Devonshire Ms. W. 7 D6
 W1
Devonshire Ms. W. 58 A4
 W1
Devonshire Pas. W4 65 E5
 Duke Rd.
Devonshire Pl. NW2 48 D3
Devonshire Pl. W1 7 C6
Devonshire Pl. W1 58 A4
Devonshire Pl. W4 65 E5
Devonshire Pl. Ms. 7 C6
 W1
Devonshire Rd. E15 51 E4
 Janson Rd.
Devonshire Rd. E16 60 H6
Devonshire Rd. E17 42 A6
Devonshire Rd. N9 33 F1
Devonshire Rd. N13 32 F4
Devonshire Rd. N17 32 J6

Devonshire Rd. NW7 31 A7
 Barking Rd.
Devonshire Rd. SE9 88 B2
Devonshire Rd. SE23 86 F1
Devonshire Rd. 84 H7
 SW19
Devonshire Rd. W4 65 E5
Devonshire Rd. W5 64 F3
Devonshire Rd., 80 E4
 Bexh.
Devonshire Rd., 101 A4
 Cars.
Devonshire Rd., 95 A7
 Croy.
Devonshire Rd., Felt. 81 E3
Devonshire Rd., Har. 37 A6
Devonshire Rd., Ilf. 43 G7
Devonshire Rd. 36 C6
 (Eastcote), Pnr.
Devonshire Rd. 36 F1
 (Hatch End), Pnr.
Devonshire Rd., Sthl. 54 G5
Devonshire Rd., 100 F7
 Sutt.
Devonshire Row EC2 13 E2
Devonshire Row Ms. 7 E6
 W1
Devonshire Sq. EC2 13 E2
Devonshire Sq., 96 H4
 Brom.
Devonshire St. W1 11 C1
Devonshire St. W1 58 B5
Devonshire St. W4 65 E5
Devonshire Ter. W2 10 D4
Devonshire Ter. W2 57 F6
Devonshire Way, 102 H2
 Croy.
Devonshire Way, 54 B6
 Hayes
Dewar St. SE15 77 D3
Dewberry Gdns. E6 61 B5
Dewberry St. E14 60 C5
Dewey Rd. N1 8 E1
Dewey Rd. N1 58 G2
Dewey Rd., Dag. 53 H6
Dewey St. SW17 84 J5
Dewhurst Rd. W14 66 A3
Dewsbury Clo., Pnr. 36 E6
Dewsbury Ct. W4 65 C4
 Chiswick Rd.
Dewsbury Gdns., 99 G3
 Wor.Pk.
Dewsbury Rd. NW10 47 G5
Dewsbury Ter. NW1 58 B1
 Camden High St.
Dexter Rd., Barn. 23 A6
Deyncourt Rd. N17 40 J1
Deynecourt Gdns. 35 J1
 E11
D'Eynsford Rd. SE5 77 A1
Diadem Ct. W1 14 H1
Dial Wk., The W8 14 B3
Diameter Rd., Orp. 97 E7
Diamond Clo., Dag. 53 C1
Diamond Rd., Ruis. 45 D4
Diamond St. SE15 68 B7
Diamond Ter. SE10 78 C1
Diana Clo. E18 42 H1
Diana Gdns., Surb. 98 J2
Diana Ho. SW13 74 F1
Diana Pl. NW1 7 E5
Diana Pl. NW1 58 B4
Diana Pl. E17 41 J3
Dianna Way, Barn. 23 H5
Dianthus Clo. SE2 71 B5
 Carnation St.
Dibden St. N1 58 J1
Dibdin Clo., Sutt. 100 D3
Dibdin Rd., Sutt. 100 D3
Dicey Ave. NW2 47 J4
Dickens Ave. N3 39 F1
Dickens Clo., Rich. 83 H2
Dickens Dr., Chis. 88 F6
Dickens Est. SE1 17 H4
Dickens Est. SE1 68 C2
Dickens Est. SE16 17 H5
Dickens Est. SE16 68 C2
Dickens La. N18 33 B5
Dickens Ri., Chig. 35 E3
Dickens Rd. E6 61 A2
Dickens Sq. SE1 17 A5
Dickens St. SW8 76 B2
Dickenson Rd. N8 40 E7
Dickenson Rd., Felt. 81 D5
Dickensons La. SE25 95 D5
Dickensons Pl. SE25 95 D6
Dickerage La., N.Mal. 92 C3
Dickerage Rd., 92 C1
 Kings.T.
Dickerage Rd., 92 C1
 N.Mal.
Dickson Fold, Pnr. 36 D4
Dickson Rd. SE9 79 B3

Didsbury Clo. E6 61 C1
 Barking Rd.
Digby Cres. N4 49 J2
Digby Gdns., Dag. 62 G1
Digby Pl., Croy. 102 C3
Digby Rd. E9 50 G5
Digby Rd., Bark. 52 J7
Digby St. E2 59 F3
Dighton Ct. SE5 20 J6
Dighton Rd. SW18 75 F5
Digswell St. N7 49 G6
 Holloway Rd.
Dilhorne Clo. SE12 87 H3
Dilke St. SW3 19 A5
Dilke St. SW3 66 J6
Dillwyn Clo. SE26 86 H4
Dilston Clo., Nthlt. 54 C3
 Yeading La.
Dilston Gro. SE16 68 F4
 Abbeyfield Rd.
Dilton Gdns. SW15 83 H1
Dimes Pl. W6 65 H4
 King St.
Dimmock Dr., Grnf. 46 A5
Dimond Clo. E7 51 G4
Dimsdale Dr. NW9 47 C1
Dimsdale Dr., Enf. 25 D6
Dimsdale Wk. E13 60 G1
 Stratford Rd.
Dingle Clo., Barn. 22 F6
Dingle Gdns. E14 60 A7
Dingley La. SW16 85 D2
Dingley Pl. EC1 12 A1
Dingley Pl. EC1 58 J3
Dingley Rd. EC1 8 J4
Dingley Rd. EC1 58 J3
Dingonhill Clo. 54 B7
 Hayes
Dingwall Ave., 101 J2
 Croy.
Dingwall Gdns. 39 D6
 NW11
Dingwall Pl., Croy. 102 A2
 Dingwall Rd.
Dingwall Rd. SW18 75 F7
Dingwall Rd., Croy. 102 A1
Dinmont St. E2 59 E2
 Coate St.
Dinsdale Gdns. SE25 95 B5
Dinsdale Gdns., 23 E5
 Barn.
Dinsdale Rd. SE3 69 F6
Dinsmore Rd. SW12 76 B7
Dinton Rd. SW19 84 G6
Dinton Rd., Kings.T. 82 J7
Diploma Ave. N2 39 H4
Dirleton Rd. E15 60 F1
Disbrowe Rd. W6 66 B6
Discovery Wk. E1 68 E1
 Waterman Way
Dishforth La. NW9 38 E1
Disney Pl. SE1 17 A3
Disney St. SE1 17 A3
Dison Clo., Enf. 25 G1
Disraeli Clo. SE28 71 C1
Disraeli Rd. E7 51 G6
Disraeli Rd. NW10 56 D2
Disraeli Rd. SW15 75 B4
Disraeli Rd. W5 64 G1
Diss St. E2 9 F3
Diss St. E2 59 C3
Distaff La. EC4 12 J5
Distaff La. EC4 58 J7
Distillery La. W6 65 J5
 Fulham Palace Rd.
Distillery Rd. W6 65 J5
Distin St. SE11 20 E2
District Rd., Wem. 46 E5
Ditch All. SE10 78 B1
Ditchburn St. E14 60 C7
Ditchfield Rd., 54 E4
 Hayes
Dittisham Rd. SE9 88 B4
Ditton Clo., T.Ditt. 91 D7
Ditton Gra. Clo., 98 G1
 Surb.
Ditton Gra. Dr., 98 G1
 Surb.
Ditton Hill, Surb. 98 F1
Ditton Hill Rd., 98 F1
 Surb.
Ditton Lawn, T.Ditt. 98 D1
Ditton Reach, 91 E6
 T.Ditt.
Ditton Rd., Bexh. 80 D5
Ditton Rd., Sthl. 63 F5
Ditton Rd., Surb. 98 G2
Divis Way SW15 74 H6
 Dover Pk. Dr.
Dixon Clark Ct. N1 49 H6
 Canonbury Rd.
Dixon Clo. E6 61 C6
 Brandreth Rd.

Dixon Pl., W.Wick. 103 B1
Dixon Rd. SE14 77 H1
Dixon Rd. SE25 95 B3
Dixons All. SE16 68 E2
 West La.
Dobbin Clo., Har. 37 D2
Dobell Rd. SE9 79 C5
Dobree Ave. NW10 47 H7
Dobson Clo. NW6 48 G7
Dock Hill Ave. SE16 68 G2
Dock Rd. E16 60 F7
Dock Rd., Brent. 64 G7
Dock St. E1 13 H5
Dock St. E1 59 D7
Dockers Tanner Rd. 69 A4
 E14
Dockhead SE1 17 G4
Dockhead St. E16 70 D1
Dockley Rd. SE16 17 H6
Dockley Rd. SE16 68 D3
Dockwell Clo., Felt. 72 A4
Doctor Johnson Ave. 85 B3
 SW17
Doctors Clo. SE26 86 F5
Docwra's Bldgs. N1 50 B6
Dod St. E14 60 A6
Dodbrooke Rd. SE27 85 G3
Doddington Gro. 20 G5
 SE17
Doddington Gro. 67 H6
 SE17
Doddington Pl. SE17 67 H6
Dodsley Pl. N9 33 F3
Dodson St. SE1 16 F4
Dodson St. SE1 67 G2
Doel Clo. SW19 84 F7
Dog Kennel Hill 77 B3
 SE22
Dog Kennel Hill 77 B3
 Est. SE22
Dog La. NW10 47 E4
Doggets Clo., Barn. 23 H5
Doggett Rd. SE6 78 A7
Doherty Rd. E13 60 G4
Dolben St. SE1 16 H2
Dolben St. SE1 67 H1
Dolby Ct. EC4 58 J7
 Garlick Hill
Dolby Rd. SW6 75 C2
Dolland St. SE11 20 D4
Dolland St. SE11 67 F5
Dollis Ave. N3 39 C1
Dollis Brook Wk., 23 B6
 Barn.
 Alan Dr.
Dollis Cres., Ruis. 45 C1
Dollis Hill Ave. NW2 47 H3
Dollis Hill Est. NW2 47 G3
Dollis Hill La. NW2 47 F4
Dollis Pk. N3 39 C1
Dollis Rd. N3 39 B1
Dollis Rd. NW7 31 B7
Dollis Valley Grn.Wk. 31 F2
 N20
 Totteridge La.
Dollis Valley Grn.Wk., 23 B6
 Barn.
 Leeside
Dollis Valley Way, 23 C5
 Barn.
Dolman Rd. W4 65 D4
Dolman St. SW4 76 F4
Dolphin Clo. SE16 68 G2
 Kinburn St.
Dolphin Clo. SE28 62 D6
Dolphin Clo., Surb. 91 G6
Dolphin Ct. NW11 39 B6
Dolphin La. E14 60 B7
Dolphin Rd., Nthlt. 54 F1
Dolphin Sq. SW1 19 G4
Dolphin Sq. SW1 65 C5
Dolphin Sq. W4 65 E7
Dolphin St., Kings.T. 91 H1
 Wood St.
Dombey St. WC1 12 C1
Dombey St. WC1 58 F5
Dome Hill Pk. SE26 86 C4
Domett Clo. SE5 77 A4
Domfe Pl. E5 50 F4
 Rushmore Rd.
Domingo St. EC1 8 J5
Dominion Rd., Croy. 95 C1
Dominion Rd., Sthl. 63 E3
Dominion St. EC2 13 C1
Domonic Dr. SE9 88 E4
Domville Clo. N20 31 G2
Don Phelan Clo. SE5 77 A1
Donald Dr., Rom. 44 C5
Donald Rd. E13 60 H1
Donald Rd., Croy. 94 F6
Donaldson Rd. NW6 57 C1

Donaldson Rd. SE18 79 D1
Doncaster Dr., 45 F5
Nthlt.
Doncaster Gdns. N4 40 J6
Stanhope Gdns.
Doncaster Gdns., 45 F5
Nthlt.
Doncaster Grn., Mald. 28 C5
Doncaster Rd. N9 25 E7
Doncel Ct. E4 26 D7
Donegal St. N1 8 D2
Donegal St. N1 8 D2
Doneraile St. SW6 75 A2
Dongola Rd. E13 60 H3
Dongola Rd. N17 41 B3
Dongola Rd. W. E13 60 H3
Balaam St.
Donington Ave., Ilf. 43 F5
Donkey All. SE22 77 D7
Donkey La., Enf. 25 D2
Donne Ct. SE24 76 J6
Burbage Rd.
Donne Pl. SW3 18 H1
Donne Pl. SW3 66 H4
Donne Pl., Mitch. 94 B4
Donne Rd., Dag. 53 C2
Donnefield Ave., 29 H7
Edg.
Donnington Rd. 47 H7
NW10
Donnington Rd., 37 F5
Har.
Donnington Rd., 99 G2
Wor.Pk.
Donnybrook Rd. 85 C7
SW16
Donovan Ave. N10 40 B3
Doon St. SE1 16 E1
Doone Clo., Tedd. 82 D6
Dora Rd. SW19 84 D5
Dora St. E14 59 J6
Doral Way, Cars. 100 J5
Doran Gro. SE18 70 H7
Doran Mans. N2 39 J5
Great N. Rd.
Doran Wk. E15 51 C7
Dorchester Ave. N13 32 J4
Dorchester Ave., 89 D1
Bex.
Dorchester Ave., Har. 36 J6
Dorchester Clo., 45 H5
Nthlt.
Dorchester Clo., Orp. 89 A7
Grovelands Rd.
Dorchester Ct. N14 24 B7
Dorchester Ct. SE24 76 J5
Dorchester Dr. SE24 76 J5
Dorchester Gdns. E4 34 A4
Dorchester Gdns. 39 D4
NW11
Dorchester Gro. W4 65 E5
Dorchester Ms., 92 D4
N.Mal.
Elm Rd.
Dorchester Rd., 93 E7
Mord.
Dorchester Rd., 45 H5
Nthlt.
Dorchester Rd., 99 J1
Wor.Pk.
Dorchester Way, Har. 37 J6
Dorchester Way, 54 B6
Hayes
Dorcis Ave., Bexh. 80 E2
Dordrecht Rd. W3 65 E1
Dore Ave. E12 52 D5
Dore Gdns., Mord. 93 E7
Doreen Ave. NW9 47 D1
Dorell Clo., Sthl. 54 F5
Doria Rd. SW6 75 C2
Doric Way NW1 7 H3
Doric Way NW1 58 D3
Dorien Rd. SW20 93 A2
Doris Ave., Erith 80 J1
Doris Rd. E7 51 G7
Dorking Clo. SE8 68 J6
Dorking Clo., 100 A2
Wor.Pk.
Dorlcote Rd. SW18 75 H7
Dorma Trd. Est. E10 50 G1
Dorman Pl. N9 25 H3
Balham Rd.
Dorman Wk. NW10 47 D5
Garden Way
Dorman Way NW8 57 G1
Dormay St. SW18 75 E5
Dormer Clo. E15 51 F6
Dormer Clo., Barn. 23 A5
Dormers Ave., Sthl. 54 G6
Dormers Ri., Sthl. 54 H7
Dormers Wells La., 54 G6
Sthl.
Dornberg Clo. SE3 69 G7

Dornberg Rd. SE3 69 H7
Banchory Rd.
Dorncliffe Rd. SW6 75 B2
Dorney NW3 48 H7
Dorney Ri., Orp. 97 J4
Dorney Way, Houns. 72 E5
Dornfell St. SW6 48 C5
Dornton Rd. SW12 85 B2
Dornton Rd., 102 A5
S.Croy.
Dorothy Ave., Wem. 46 H7
Dorothy Evans Clo., 80 H4
Bexh.
Dorothy Gdns., Dag. 53 B4
Dorothy Rd. SW11 75 J3
Dorrell Pl. SW9 76 G4
Brixton Rd.
Dorrington Ct. SE25 95 B2
Dorrington Pt. E3 60 B3
Bromley High St.
Dorrington St. EC1 12 E1
Dorrington St. EC1 58 G5
Dorrit Ms. N18 33 B5
Dorrit Way, Chis. 88 F6
Dors Clo. NW9 47 D1
Dorset Ave., Sthl. 63 G4
Dorset Ave., Well. 79 J4
Dorset Bldgs. EC4 12 G4
Dorset Clo. NW1 10 J1
Dorset Dr., Edg. 29 J6
Dorset Est. E2 9 G3
Dorset Est. E2 59 C3
Dorset Gdns., 94 F4
Mitch.
Dorset Ms. SW1 15 D5
Dorset Pl. E15 51 D6
Dorset Pl. SW1 19 H3
Dorset Ri. EC4 12 G4
Dorset Ri. EC4 58 H6
Dorset Rd. E7 51 J7
Dorset Rd. N15 41 A4
Dorset Rd. N22 40 E1
Dorset Rd. SW8 20 B7
Dorset Rd. SW8 67 E7
Dorset Rd. SW19 93 D1
Dorset Rd. W5 64 B3
Dorset Rd., Beck. 95 G3
Dorset Rd., Har. 36 J6
Dorset Rd., Mitch. 93 H2
Dorset Sq. NW1 6 J6
Dorset Sq. NW1 57 J4
Dorset St. W1 11 A2
Dorset St. W1 57 J5
Dorset Way, Twick. 82 A1
Dorset Waye, Houns. 63 F7
Dorville Cres. W6 65 H3
Dorville Rd. SE12 78 F5
Dothill Rd. SE18 70 G7
Douai Gro., Hmptn. 90 J1
Doubleday Rd., 27 F3
Loug.
Doughty Ms. WC1 8 C6
Doughty Ms. WC1 58 F4
Doughty St. WC1 8 C5
Doughty St. WC1 58 F4
Douglas Ave. E17 42 A1
Douglas Ave., 92 H4
N.Mal.
Douglas Ave., Wem. 46 H7
Douglas Clo., Stan. 29 D5
Douglas Clo., Wall. 101 E6
Douglas Cres., 54 C4
Hayes
Douglas Dr., Croy. 103 A3
Douglas Pl. E14 69 C5
Manchester Rd.
Douglas Rd. E4 26 E7
Douglas Rd. E16 60 G5
Douglas Rd. N1 49 J7
Douglas Rd. N22 40 G1
Douglas Rd. NW6 57 C1
Douglas Rd., Houns. 72 H3
Douglas Rd., Ilf. 44 A7
Douglas Rd., 92 B2
Kings.T.
Douglas Rd., Surb. 98 J2
Douglas Rd., Well. 80 B1
Douglas St. SW1 19 H2
Douglas St. SW1 67 D4
Douglas Way SE8 68 J7
Doulton Ms. NW6 48 E6
Lymington Rd.
Dounesforth Gdns. 84 E1
SW18
Douro Pl. W8 14 B5
Douro Pl. W8 66 E3
Douro St. E3 60 A2
Douthwaite Sq. E1 17 J1
Dove App. E6 61 B5
Dove Clo., Nthlt. 54 D4
Wayfarer Rd.
Dove Ct. EC2 13 B4

Dove Ho. Gdns. E4 34 A2
Dove Ms. SW5 18 C2
Dove Ms. SW5 66 F4
Dove Pk., Pnr. 28 G7
Dove Rd. N1 50 A6
Dove Row E2 59 D1
Dove Wk. SW1 19 B3
Dovecote Ave. N22 40 G1
Dovecott Gdns. 74 D3
SW14
North Worple Way
Dovedale Ave., Har. 37 F6
Dovedale Ave., Ilf. 43 D2
Dovedale Clo., 80 A1
Well.
Dovedale Rd. SE22 77 E5
Dovedon Clo. N14 32 E2
Dovehouse Mead, 61 G2
Bark.
Dovehouse St. SW3 18 G3
Dovehouse St. SW3 66 G5
Dover Clo., Rom. 41 J1
Dover Ct. Est. N1 50 A6
Dover Rd.
Dover Ho. Rd. SW15 74 G4
Dover Pk. Dr. SW15 74 H6
Dover Rd. E12 51 J2
Dover Rd. N9 33 F2
Dover Rd. SE19 86 A6
Dover Rd., Rom. 44 E6
Dover St. W1 11 E6
Dover St. W1 58 B7
Dover Yd. W1 15 E1
Dovercourt Ave., 94 G5
Th.Hth.
Dovercourt Gdns., 29 H5
Stan.
Dovercourt La., 100 F3
Sutt.
Dovercourt Rd. SE21 77 B6
Dovercourt Rd. SE22 77 B6
Doverfield Rd. SW2 76 E6
Doveridge Gdns. N13 32 H4
Doves Clo., Brom. 104 B2
Doveton Rd., 102 A5
S.Croy.
Doveton St. E1 59 F4
Malcolm Rd.
Dowanhill Rd. SE6 87 D1
Dowdeswell Clo. 74 E4
SW15
Dowding Pl., Stan. 29 D6
Dowgate Hill EC4 13 B5
Dowgate Hill EC4 59 A4
Dowland St. W10 57 B3
Dowlas St. SE5 21 D7
Dowlas St. SE5 68 B7
Dowlerville Rd., 104 J6
Orp.
Dowman Clo. SW19 93 E1
Nelson Gro. Rd.
Down Clo., Nthlt. 54 B2
Down End SE18 70 E7
Moordown
Down Hall Rd., 91 G1
Kings.T.
Down Pl. W6 65 H4
Down Rd., Tedd. 82 E6
Down St. W1 15 D2
Down St. W1 67 B1
Down St., W.Mol. 90 G5
Down St. Ms. W1 15 D2
Down Way, Nthlt. 54 B3
Downage NW4 38 J3
Downalong (Bushey), 29 A1
Wat.
Downbarns Rd., 45 D3
Ruis.
Downderry Rd., 87 D5
Brom.
Downe Clo., Well. 71 C7
Downe Rd., Mitch. 93 J2
Downers Cotts. SW4 76 C4
The Pavement
Downes Clo., Twick. 73 E6
St. Margarets Rd.
Downes Ct. N21 32 G1
Downfield, Wor.Pk. 99 F1
Downfield Clo. W9 6 A6
Downfield Clo. W9 58 D4
Downham Rd. N1 50 A7
Downham Way, 87 D5
Brom.
Downhills Ave. N17 41 A3
Downhills Pk. Rd. 40 J3
N17
Downhills Way N17 40 J2
Downhurst Ave. NW7 36 J5
Downing Dr., Grnf. 55 A1
Downing Rd., Dag. 62 F1

Downing St. SW1 16 A3
Downing St. SW1 67 E2
Downings E6 61 D6
Downland Clo. N20 31 F1
Downsway Clo. SE9 88 B2
Downman Rd. SE9 79 B3
Downs, The SW20 84 A7
Downs Ave., Chis. 88 C5
Downs Ave., Pnr. 36 F6
Downs Bri. Rd., 96 D1
Beck.
Downs Hill, Beck. 87 D7
Downs Pk. Rd. E5 50 D5
Downs Pk. Rd. E8 50 C5
Downs Rd. E5 50 D4
Downs Rd., Beck. 96 B2
Downs Rd., Enf. 25 B4
Downs Rd., Th.Hth. 94 J1
Downs Vw., Islw. 73 C1
Downsbury Ms. 75 D5
SW18
Merton Rd.
Downsell Rd. E15 51 C4
Downsfield Rd. E17 41 H6
Downshall Ave., Ilf. 43 H6
Downshire Hill NW3 48 G4
Downside, Sun. 90 A1
Downside, Twick. 82 C3
Downside Clo. SW19 84 F6
Downside Cres. NW3 48 H5
Downside Cres. W13 55 D4
Downside Rd., Sutt. 100 G6
Downsview Gdns. 85 J7
SE19
Downsview Rd. SE19 85 J7
Downsway, Orp. 104 H5
Southlands Ave.
Downton Ave. SW2 85 E2
Downtown Rd. SE16 68 H2
Downway N12 31 H7
Dowrey St. N1 58 G1
Richmond Ave.
Dowsett Rd. N17 41 C2
Dowson Clo. SE5 77 A4
Doyce St. SE1 16 J3
Doyle Gdns. NW10 56 G1
Doyle Rd. SE25 95 D4
D'Oyley St. SW1 19 B1
D'Oyley St. SW1 67 A4
Doynton St. N19 49 B2
Draco St. SE17 20 J5
Draco St. SE17 67 J6
Dragmire La., Mitch. 93 G4
Dragoon Rd. SE8 68 J5
Dragor Rd. NW10 56 C4
Drake Clo. SE16 68 G2
Middleton Dr.
Drake Ct. SE19 86 C5
Drake Ct., Har. 45 F1
Drake Cres. SE28 62 C6
Drake Rd. SE4 78 A3
Drake Rd., Chess. 99 A5
Drake Rd., Croy. 94 F7
Drake Rd., Har. 45 F2
Drake Rd., Mitch. 94 A6
Drake St. WC1 12 C2
Drake St., Enf. 25 A1
Drakefell Rd. SE4 77 H3
Drakefell Rd. SE14 77 G2
Drakefield Rd. SW17 85 A3
Drakely Ct. N5 49 H4
Highbury Hill
Drakes Wk. E6 61 D2
Talbot Rd.
Drakewood Rd. 85 D7
SW16
Draper Clo., Belv. 71 F4
Drapers Rd. E15 51 D4
Drapers Rd. N17 41 C3
Drapers Rd., Enf. 24 H2
Drappers Way SE16 21 J1
Drawdock Rd. SE10 69 D1
Drawell Clo. SE18 70 H5
Drax Ave. SW20 83 G3
Draxmont SW19 84 B6
Dray Gdns. SW2 76 F5
Draycot Rd. E11 42 H6
Draycot Rd., Surb. 99 A1
Draycott Ave. SW3 18 H1
Draycott Ave. SW3 66 H4
Draycott Ave., Har. 37 G6
Draycott Clo., Har. 37 G6
Draycott Ms. SW6 75 C2
New Kings Rd.
Draycott Pl. SW3 18 J2
Draycott Pl. SW3 66 J4
Draycott Ter. SW3 19 A2
Draycott Ter. SW3 66 J4
Drayford Clo. W9 57 C4
Drayside Ms., Sthl. 63 F2
Kingston Rd.
Drayson Ms. W8 66 D2
Drayton Ave. W13 55 D7

Name	Page	Grid
Drayton Ave., Loug.	27	C6
Drayton Ave., Orp.	104	E1
Drayton Bri. Rd. W7	55	C7
Drayton Bri. Rd. W13	55	D6
Drayton Clo., Houns.	72	F5
Bramley Way		
Drayton Gdns. N21	24	H7
Drayton Gdns. SW10	**18**	**D3**
Drayton Gdns. W10	66	F6
Drayton Gdns. W13	55	D7
Drayton Grn. W13	55	D7
Drayton Grn. Rd. W13	55	E7
Drayton Gro. W13	55	D7
Drayton Pk. N5	49	G5
Drayton Rd. E11	51	D1
Drayton Rd. N17	41	B2
Drayton Rd. NW10	56	F1
Drayton Rd. W13	55	D7
Drayton Rd., Borwd.	22	A4
Drayton Rd., Croy.	101	H2
Drayton Waye, Har.	37	E6
Dreadnought St. SE10	69	E3
Dresden Clo. NW6	48	E5
Lymington Rd.		
Dresden Rd. N19	49	C1
Dressington Ave. SE4	78	A6
Drew Ave. NW7	31	B6
Drew Gdns., Grnf.	46	C6
Drew Rd. E16	70	B1
Drewstead Rd. SW16	85	D2
Driffield Rd. E3	59	H2
Drift, The, Brom.	104	A3
Drift Way, Rich.	82	J1
Driftway, The, Mitch.	94	A1
Drinkwater Rd., Har.	45	H2
Drive, The E4	26	D7
Drive, The E17	42	B3
Drive, The E18	42	B3
Drive, The N3	31	D7
Drive, The N6	39	J5
Fordington Rd.		
Drive, The N11	32	C6
Drive, The NW10	56	F1
Longstone Ave.		
Drive, The NW11	39	B7
Drive, The SW16	94	F3
Drive, The SW20	83	J7
Drive, The W3	56	C6
Drive, The, Bark.	52	J7
Drive, The, Barn.	23	B3
Drive, The, Barn., (New Barnet)	23	F6
Drive, The, Beck.	96	A2
Drive, The, Bex.	80	C6
Drive, The, Buck.H.	26	J7
Drive, The, Chis.	97	J3
Drive, The, Edg.	30	A5
Drive, The, Enf.	25	A1
Drive, The, Epsom	99	F6
Drive, The, Erith	71	H7
Drive, The, Felt.	72	C7
Drive, The, Har.	36	G7
Drive, The, Houns.	72	J2
Drive, The, Ilf.	43	B6
Drive, The, Islw.	73	A2
Drive, The, Kings.T.	83	C7
Drive, The, Loug.	27	B3
Drive, The, Mord.	93	F5
Drive, The, Orp.	104	J2
Drive, The, Rom.	44	J1
Drive, The, Sid.	89	B3
Drive, The, Surb.	91	H7
Drive, The, Th.Hth.	95	A4
Drive, The, Wem.	47	C2
Drive, The, W.Wick.	96	D7
Driveway, The, E17	42	B6
Hoe St.		
Droitwich Clo. SE26	86	D3
Dromey Gdns., Har.	29	C7
Dromore Rd. SW15	75	B6
Dronfield Gdns., Dag.	53	C5
Droop St. W10	57	B4
Drove Way, Loug.	27	E2
Drover La. SE15	68	E7
Drovers Pl. SE15	68	E7
Drovers Rd., S.Croy.	102	A5
Druce Rd. SE21	77	B6
Druid St. SE1	**17**	**E3**
Druid St. SE1	68	B2
Druids Way, Brom.	96	D4
Drum St. E1	**13**	**G3**
Drumaline Ridge, Wor.Pk.	99	E2
Drummond Cres. NW1	**7**	**H3**
Drummond Cres. NW1	58	D3
Drummond Dr., Stan.	29	C7
Drummond Gate SW1	**19**	**J3**
Drummond Gate SW1	67	D5
Drummond Pl., Twick.	73	E7
Drummond Rd. E11	42	J6
Drummond Rd. SE16	68	E3
Drummond Rd., Croy.	101	J2
Drummond St. NW1	**7**	**F5**
Drummond St. NW1	58	C4
Drummonds, The, Buck.H.	34	H2
Drury Cres., Croy.	101	G2
Drury Ind. Est.	47	C5
Drury La. WC2	**12**	**B3**
Drury La. WC2	58	E6
Drury Rd., Har.	36	J7
Drury Way NW10	47	D5
Dryad St. SW15	75	A3
Dryburgh Gdns. NW9	38	A3
Dryburgh Rd. SW15	74	F1
Dryden Ave. W7	55	C6
Dryden Clo., Ilf.	35	J6
Dryden Ct. SE11	**20**	**F2**
Dryden Rd. SW19	84	F6
Dryden Rd., Enf.	25	B6
Dryden Rd., Har.	46	C1
Dryden Rd., Well.	79	H1
Dryden St. WC2	**12**	**B4**
Dryfield Clo. NW10	47	C6
Dryfield Rd., Edg.	30	C6
Dryfield Wk. SE8	69	A6
New King St.		
Dryhill Rd., Belv.	71	F6
Dryland Ave., Orp.	104	J4
Drylands Rd. N8	40	E6
Drysdale Ave. E4	26	B7
Drysdale Pl. N1	**9**	**E3**
Drysdale St. N1	**9**	**E3**
Drysdale St. N1	59	B3
Du Burstow Ter. W7	64	B2
Du Cane Ct. SW17	85	A1
Du Cane Rd. W12	56	F6
Du Cros Dr., Stan.	29	G6
Du Cros Rd. W3	56	E1
The Vale		
Dublin Cres. E8	59	D1
Ducal St. E2	**9**	**G4**
Duchess Ms. W1	**11**	**E2**
Duchess of Bedford's Wk. W8	66	D2
Duchess St. W1	**11**	**E2**
Duchess St. W1	58	B5
Duchy St. SE1	**16**	**F1**
Duchy St. SE1	67	G1
Ducie St. SW4	50	F4
Duck La. W1	**11**	**H4**
Duck Lees La., Enf.	25	H4
Duckett Rd. N4	40	G6
Duckett St. E1	59	G4
Ducks Wk., Twick.	73	F5
Dudden Hill La. NW10	47	F4
Duddington Clo. SE9	88	A4
Dudley Ave., Har.	37	F3
Dudley Ct. NW11	39	C4
Dudley Dr., Mord.	100	E3
Dudley Dr., Ruis.	45	B5
Dudley Gdns. W13	64	E2
Dudley Gdns., Har.	46	A1
Dudley Rd. E17	42	A2
Dudley Rd. N3	39	E2
Dudley Rd. NW6	57	B2
Dudley Rd. SW19	84	D6
Dudley Rd., Har.	45	J2
Dudley Rd., Ilf.	52	E4
Dudley Rd., Kings.T.	91	J3
Dudley Rd., Rich.	73	J2
Dudley Rd., Sthl.	63	D2
Dudley Rd., Walt.	90	A6
Dudley St. W2	**10**	**E2**
Dudlington Rd. E5	50	F2
Dudmaston Ms. SW3	**18**	**F3**
Dudsbury Rd., Sid.	89	B6
Dudset La., Houns.	72	A1
Duff St. E14	60	B6
Dufferin Ave. EC1	**9**	**B6**
Dufferin St. EC1	**9**	**A6**
Dufferin St. EC1	59	A4
Duffield Clo., Har.	37	C5
Dufour's Pl. W1	**11**	**G4**
Duke Gdns., Ilf.	43	G4
Duke Humphrey Rd. SE3	78	E1
Duke of Cambridge Clo., Twick.	73	A6
Duke of Edinburgh Rd., Sutt.	100	G2
Duke of Wellington Pl. SW1	**15**	**C3**
Duke of Wellington Pl. SW1	67	A2
Duke of York St. SW1	**15**	**G1**
Duke of York St. SW1	67	C1
Duke Rd. W4	65	D5
Duke Rd., Ilf.	52	E4
Duke Shore Pl. E14	59	J7
Narrow St.		
Duke St. SW1	**15**	**G1**
Duke St. SW1	67	C1
Duke St. W1	**11**	**C3**
Duke St. W1	58	A6
Duke St., Rich.	73	G5
Duke St., Sutt.	100	G4
Duke St. Hill SE1	**17**	**C1**
Dukes Ave. N3	39	E1
Dukes Ave. N10	40	C3
Dukes Ave. W4	65	D5
Dukes Ave., Edg.	29	J6
Dukes Ave., Har.	36	F6
Dukes Ave. (Wealdstone), Har.	37	B4
Dukes Ave., Houns.	72	E4
Dukes Ave., Kings.T.	82	F4
Dukes Ave., N.Mal.	92	F3
Dukes Ave., Nthlt.	45	E7
Dukes Ave., Rich.	82	F4
Dukes Clo., Hmptn.	61	F5
Dukes Clo., Kings.T.	82	G4
Dukes Ct. E6	61	D1
Dukes Grn. Ave., Felt.	72	A5
Dukes La. W8	66	E2
Dukes Ms. N10	40	B3
Dukes Ave.		
Dukes Orchard, Bex.	89	J1
Dukes Pl. EC3	**13**	**E4**
Dukes Pl. EC3	59	B6
Dukes Rd. E6	61	D1
Dukes Rd. W3	56	A4
Duke's Rd. WC1	**7**	**J4**
Duke's Rd. WC1	58	D3
Dukes Way, W.Wick.	103	E3
Duke's Yd. W1	**11**	**C5**
Dukesthorpe Rd. SE26	86	G4
Dulas St. N4	49	F1
Everleigh St.		
Dulford St. W11	57	B7
Dulka Rd. SW11	75	J5
Dulverton Rd. SE9	88	F2
Dulverton Rd., Ruis.	45	A1
Dulwich Common SE21	86	B1
Dulwich Oaks, The SE21	86	C3
Dulwich Rd. SE24	76	G5
Dulwich Village SE21	77	B6
Dulwich Wd. Ave. SE19	86	B4
Dulwich Wd. Pk. SE19	86	B4
Dumbarton Rd. SW2	76	E6
Dumbleton Clo., Kings.T.	92	B1
Gloucester Rd.		
Dumbreck Rd. SE9	79	C4
Dumont Rd. N16	50	B3
Dumpton Pl. NW1	49	A7
Gloucester Ave.		
Dunbar Ave. SW16	94	G2
Dunbar Ave., Beck.	95	H4
Dunbar Ave., Dag.	53	G3
Dunbar Clo., Hayes	54	A5
Dunbar Ct., Sutt.	100	G5
Dunbar Gdns., Dag.	53	G5
Dunbar Rd. E7	51	G6
Dunbar Rd. N22	40	G1
Dunbar Rd., N.Mal.	92	C4
Dunbar St. SE27	85	J3
Dunblane Clo., Edg.	30	B2
Tayside Dr.		
Dunblane Rd. SE9	79	B2
Dunboyne Rd. NW3	48	J5
Dunbridge St. E2	**9**	**H5**
Dunbridge St. E2	59	D4
Duncan Clo., Barn.	34	G4
Duncan Gro. W3	56	E6
Duncan Rd. E8	59	E1
Duncan Rd., Rich.	73	H4
Duncan St. N1	**8**	**G1**
Duncan St. N1	58	H2
Duncan Ter. N1	**8**	**G2**
Duncan Ter. N1	58	H2
Duncannon St. WC2	**12**	**A6**
Duncannon St. WC2	58	E7
Dunch St. E1	59	E6
Watney St.		
Duncombe Hill SE23	77	H7
Duncombe Rd. N19	49	D1
Duncrievie Rd. SE13	78	D1
Duncroft SE18	70	H7
Dundalk Rd. SE4	77	H3
Dundas Gdns., W.Mol.	90	H3
Dundas Rd. SE15	77	F2
Dundee Rd. E13	60	H2
Dundee Rd. SE25	95	E5
Dundee St. E1	68	E1
Dundela Gdns., Wor.Pk.	99	H4
Dundonald Clo. E6	61	B6
Northumberland Rd.		
Dundonald Rd. NW10	57	A1
Dundonald Rd. SW19	84	B7
Dunedin Rd. E10	51	B3
Dunedin Rd., Ilf.	52	F1
Dunedin Way, Hayes	54	C4
Dunelm Gro. SE27	85	J4
Dunelm St. E1	59	G6
Dunfield Gdns. SE6	87	B5
Dunfield Rd. SE6	87	B5
Dunford Rd. N7	49	F4
Dungarvan Ave. SW15	74	G4
Dunheved Clo., Th.Hth.	94	G6
Dunheved Rd. N., Th.Hth.	94	G6
Dunheved Rd. S., Th.Hth.	94	G6
Dunheved Rd. W., Th.Hth.	94	G6
Dunholme Grn. N9	33	C3
Dunholme La. N9	33	C3
Dunholme Rd.		
Dunholme Rd. N9	33	C3
Dunkeld Rd. SE25	95	A4
Dunkeld Rd., Dag.	53	B2
Dunkery Rd. SE9	88	A4
Dunkirk St. SE27	85	J4
Waring St.		
Dunlace Rd. E5	50	F4
Dunleary Clo., Houns.	72	F7
Dunley Dr., Croy.	103	G7
Dunlin Ho. W13	55	C4
Dunloe Ave. N17	41	A3
Dunloe St. E2	**9**	**G2**
Dunloe St. E2	59	C2
Dunlop Pl. SE16	**17**	**G6**
Dunlop Pl. SE16	69	G1
Dunmore Pt. E2	**9**	**F4**
Dunmore Rd. NW6	57	B1
Dunmore Rd. SW20	92	J1
Dunmow Clo., Felt.	81	D4
Dunmow Clo., Loug.	27	B6
Dunmow Clo., Rom.	44	C5
Dunmow Ho., Dag.	62	B1
Dunmow Rd. E15	51	D4
Dunmow Wk. N1	58	J1
Popham St.		
Dunn Mead NW9	30	F7
Field Mead		
Dunn St. E8	50	C5
Dunnock Clo. N9	33	G1
Dunnock Clo., Borwd.	22	A4
Siskin Clo.		
Dunnock Rd. E6	61	B6
Dunns Pas. WC1	**12**	**B3**
Dunollie Pl. NW5	49	C5
Dunollie Rd.		
Dunollie Rd. NW5	49	C5
Dunoon Rd. SE23	71	F7
Dunraven Dr., Enf.	24	G2
Dunraven Rd. W12	65	G1
Dunraven St. W1	**11**	**A5**
Dunsany Rd. W14	128	A3
Dunsfold Way, Croy.	103	B7
Dunsford Way SW15	74	H6
Dover Pk. Dr.		
Dunsmore Clo., Hayes	54	E4
Kingsash Dr.		
Dunsmore Rd., Walt.	90	B6
Dunsmure Rd. N16	50	B3
Dunspring La., Ilf.	81	E6
Dunstable Ms. W1	**11**	**C1**
Dunstable Rd., Rich.	73	H4
Dunstable Rd., W.Mol.	90	H3
Dunstall Rd. SW20	83	H6
Dunstall Way, W.Mol.	90	H3
Dunstan Clo. N2	39	F3
Thomas More Way		

Dunstan Rd. NW11 48 C1
Dunstans Gro. SE22 77 E6
Dunstans Rd. SE22 77 D7
Dunster Ave., Mord. 100 A1
Dunster Clo., Barn. 23 A4
Dunster Clo., Rom. 44 J2
Dunster Ct. EC3 13 D5
Dunster Dr. NW9 47 C1
Dunster Gdns. NW6 48 C7
Dunster Way, Har. 45 E3
Dunsterville Way 17 C4
SE1
Dunston Rd. E8 59 C1
Dunston Rd. SW11 76 A3
Dunston St. E8 59 C1
Dunton Clo., Surb. 98 H1
Dunton Rd. E10 42 B7
Dunton Rd. SE1 21 F2
Dunton Rd. SE1 68 C4
Duntshill Rd. SW18 84 E1
Dunvegan Clo., 90 H4
W.Mol.
Dunvegan Rd. SE9 79 C4
Dunwich Rd., Bexh. 80 F1
Dunworth Ms. W11 57 C6
Portobello Rd.
Duplex Ride SW1 15 A4
Dupont Rd. SW20 93 A2
Dupont St. E14 59 H5
Marion St.
Duppas Ave., Croy. 101 H4
Violet La.
Duppas Hill La., 101 H4
Croy.
Duppas Hill Rd.
Duppas Hill Rd., 101 G4
Croy.
Duppas Hill Ter., 101 H3
Croy.
Duppas Rd., Croy. 101 G3
Dupree Rd. SE7 69 H5
Dura Den Clo., Beck. 87 B7
Durand Clo., Cars. 100 J1
Durand Gdns. SW9 76 F1
Durand Way NW10 47 C7
Durands Wk. SE16 68 H2
Salter Rd.
Durant St. E2 9 H3
Durant St. E2 59 D3
Durants Pk. Ave., Enf. 25 G4
Durants Rd., Enf. 25 F4
Durban Gdns., Dag. 53 J7
Durban Rd. E15 60 E3
Durban Rd. E17 41 J1
Durban Rd. N17 33 B6
Durban Rd. SE27 85 J4
Durban Rd., Beck. 95 J2
Durban Rd., Ilf. 52 H1
Durbin Rd., Chess. 98 H4
Durdans Rd., Sthl. 54 F6
Durell Gdns., Dag. 53 D5
Durell Rd., Dag. 53 D5
Durford Cres. SW15 83 H1
Durham Ave., Brom. 96 F4
Durham Ave., Houns. 63 F6
Durham Ave., 68 J7
Wdf.Grn.
Durham Clo. SW20 92 H2
Durham Hill, Brom. 87 F4
Durham Ho. St. WC2 12 B6
Durham Pl. SW3 18 J4
Durham Pl., Ilf. 52 F5
Eton Rd.
Durham Ri. SE18 70 F5
Durham Rd. E12 52 A4
Durham Rd. E16 60 E4
Durham Rd. N2 39 H3
Durham Rd. N7 49 F2
Durham Rd. N9 33 D2
Durham Rd. SW20 92 H1
Durham Rd. W5 64 G3
Durham Rd., Borwd. 22 C3
Durham Rd., Brom. 96 F2
Durham Rd., Dag. 53 J5
Durham Rd., Felt. 61 F7
Durham Rd., Har. 36 H5
Durham Rd., Sid. 89 B5
Durham Row E1 59 H5
Durham St. SE11 20 C4
Durham St. SE11 67 F5
Durham Ter. W2 10 A3
Durham Ter. W2 57 E6
Durham Wf., Brent. 64 F7
High St.
Durley Ave., Pnr. 36 E7
Durley Rd. N16 41 B7
Durlston Rd. E5 50 D2
Durlston Rd., 82 H6
Kings.T.
Durnell Way, Loug. 15 E7
Durnford St. N15 41 B5
Durnford St. SE10 69 C6
Greenwich Ch. St.

Durning Rd. SE19 86 A5
Durnsford Ave. 84 D2
SW19
Durnsford Rd. N11 40 D1
Durnsford Rd. SW19 84 D2
Durrant Way, Orp. 104 G5
Durrell Rd. SW6 75 C1
Durrington Ave. 92 J1
SW20
Durrington Pk. Rd. 92 J1
SW20
Durrington Rd. E5 50 H4
Dursley Clo. SE3 78 J2
Dursley Gdns. SE3 79 A1
Dursley Rd. SE3 78 J2
Durward St. E1 59 E5
Durweston Ms. W1 11 A1
Durweston St. W1 11 A2
Dury Rd., Barn. 23 C2
Dutch Gdns., 83 B6
Kings.T.
Windmill Ri.
Dutch Yd. SW18 75 D5
Wandsworth High St.
Duthie St. E14 60 C7
Dutton St. SE10 78 C1
Dwight Ct. SW6 75 B2
Burlington Rd.
Dye Ho. La. E3 60 A1
Dyer's Bldgs. EC1 12 E2
Dyers Hall Rd. E11 51 E2
Dyers La. SW15 74 H4
Dykes Way, Brom. 96 F3
Dylan Rd., Belv. 71 G3
Dylan Thomas Ho. 40 F4
N8
Dylways SE5 77 A4
Dymchurch Clo., Ilf. 43 D3
Dymchurch Clo., 104 H4
Orp.
Dymes Path SW19 84 A2
Queensmere Rd.
Dymock St. SW6 75 E3
Dymond Est. SW17 84 H3
Glenburnie Rd.
Dyne Rd. NW6 48 B7
Dyneley Rd. SE12 87 J4
Dynevor Rd. N16 50 C3
Dynevor Rd., Rich. 73 E5
Dynham Rd. NW6 48 D7
Dyott St. WC1 11 J3
Dyott St. WC1 58 D6
Dysart Ave., Kings.T. 82 F5
Dysart St. EC2 9 D6
Dyson Rd. E11 42 E6
Dyson Rd. E15 51 F6
Dysons Rd. N18 33 E5

E

Eade Rd. N4 40 J7
Eagans Clo. N2 39 H3
Market Pl.
Eagle Ave., Rom. 44 E6
Eagle Clo., Enf. 25 F4
Eagle Ct. EC1 12 G1
Eagle Ct. EC1 58 H5
Eagle Dr. NW9 38 E2
Eagle Hill SE19 86 A6
Eagle La. E11 42 G4
Eagle Ms. N1 50 B6
Tottenham Rd.
Eagle Pl. SW1 11 G6
Eagle Rd., Wem. 46 G7
Eagle St. WC1 12 C2
Eagle St. WC1 58 F5
Eagle Ter., Wdf.Grn. 34 H7
Eagle Wf. Rd. N1 9 A1
Eagle Wf. Rd. N1 58 J2
Eaglesfield Rd. SE18 79 E2
Ealdham Sq. SE9 78 J4
Ealing Clo., Borwd. 22 D1
Ealing Downs Ct., 55 D3
Grnf.
Perivale La.
Ealing Grn. W5 64 G1
Ealing Pk. Gdns. W5 64 F4
Ealing Rd., Brent. 64 G4
Ealing Rd., Nthlt. 54 G1
Ealing Rd., Wem. 46 H6
Ealing Village W5 55 H6
Eamont St. NW8 6 G1
Eamont St. NW8 57 H2
Eardley Cres. SW5 66 D5
Eardley Pt. SE18 70 E4
Wilmount St.
Eardley Rd. SW16 85 C5
Eardley Rd., Belv. 71 G5
Eardley Ri. SE18 70 G4
Earl Rd. SE1 21 F3
Earl Rd. SE1 68 C5
Earl Rd. SW14 74 C4
Elm Rd.

Earl St. EC2 13 C1
Earl St. EC2 59 A5
Earldom Rd. SW15 74 J4
Earle Gdns., Kings.T. 82 H7
Earlham Gro. E7 51 F5
Earlham Gro. N22 32 F1
Earlham St. WC2 11 J4
Earlham St. WC2 58 D6
Earls Ct. Gdns. SW5 18 A2
Earls Ct. Gdns. SW5 66 E4
Earls Ct. Rd. SW5 66 D4
Earls Ct. Rd. W8 66 D4
Earls Ct. Sq. SW5 18 A3
Earls Ct. Sq. SW5 66 E5
Earls Cres., Har. 37 B4
Earls Path, Loug. 26 J2
Earls Ter. W8 66 C3
Earls Wk. W8 66 D3
Earls Wk., Dag. 53 B4
Earlsdown Ho., Bark. 61 G2
Wheelers Cross
Earlsferry Way N1 49 F7
Earlsfield Rd. SW18 84 F1
Earlshall Rd. SE9 79 C4
Earlsmead, Har. 35 J4
Earlsmead Rd. N15 41 C5
Earlsmead Rd. NW10 56 J3
Earlsthorpe Ms. 76 A6
SW12
Earlsthorpe Rd. 86 G4
SE26
Earlstoke St. EC1 8 G3
Earlston Gro. E9 59 E1
Earlswood Ave., 94 G5
Th.Hth.
Earlswood Clo. SE10 69 E5
Earlswood Rd.
Earlswood Gdns., 43 D3
Ilf.
Earlswood Rd. SE10 69 E5
Early Ms. NW1 57 J1
Arlington Rd.
Earnshaw St. WC2 11 J3
Earnshaw St. WC2 58 D6
Earsby St. W14 56 B3
Easby Cres., Mord. 93 E6
Easebourne Rd., 53 C5
Dag.
Easedale Ho., Islw. 73 C5
Easley's Ms. W1 11 E3
East Acton La. W3 56 E7
East Arbour St. E1 59 G5
East Ave. E12 52 B7
East Ave. E17 42 B4
East Ave., Sthl. 54 F7
East Ave., Wall. 101 F5
East Bank N16 41 B7
East Barnet Rd., 23 G4
Barn.
East Churchfield Rd. 65 D1
W3
East Clo. W5 56 A4
East Clo., Barn. 24 A4
East Clo., Grnf. 54 J2
East Ct., Wem. 46 F2
East Cres. N11 31 J4
East Cres., Enf. 25 B5
East Cross Route E3 52 H6
East Dulwich Gro. 77 B5
SE22
East Dulwich Rd. 77 D4
SE15
East Dulwich Rd. 77 C4
SE22
East End Rd. N2 39 E3
East End Rd. N3 39 C2
East End Way, Pnr. 36 E3
East Entrance, Dag. 62 H2
Oval Rd. S.
East Ferry Rd. E14 69 B4
East Gdns. SW17 84 H6
East Glade, Pnr. 36 F3
East Ham Ind. Est. 61 A4
E6
East Ham Manor Way 61 D6
E6
East Harding St. EC4 12 F3
East Heath Rd. NW3 48 F3
East Hill SW18 75 E5
East Hill, Wem. 47 A2
East Holme, Hayes 63 H4
East India Dock Rd. 60 A6
E14
East India Dock 60 D7
Wall Rd E14
East La. SE16 17 H4
East La. SE16 68 D2
East La., Kings.T. 91 G3
East La., Wem. 46 E3
East Mascalls SE7 69 J6
Mascalls Rd.
East Mead, Ruis. 45 D3
East Mt. St. E1 59 E5

East Pk. Clo., Rom. 44 D5
East Pas. EC1 12 J1
East Pier E1 68 E1
Wapping High St.
East Pl. SE27 85 J4
Pilgrim Hill
East Poultry Ave. 12 G2
EC1
East Rd. E15 60 G1
East Rd. N1 9 C3
East Rd. N1 59 A3
East Rd. SW19 84 F6
East Rd., Barn. 24 A7
East Rd., Edg. 38 B1
East Rd., Kings.T. 91 H1
East Rd., Rom. 44 C5
(Chadwell Heath)
East Rd., Well. 80 B2
East Rochester Way 79 G4
SE9
East Rochester Way, 80 D6
Bex.
East Rochester Way, 79 H4
Sid.
East Row E11 42 G6
East Row W10 57 B4
East Sheen Ave. 74 D5
SW14
East Smithfield E1 13 G6
East Smithfield E1 59 C7
East St. SE17 21 A3
East St. SE17 67 J5
East St., Bark. 52 F7
East St., Bexh. 80 G4
East St., Brent. 64 F7
East St., Brom. 96 G2
East Surrey Gro. 68 C7
SE15
East Tenter St. E1 13 G4
East Tenter St. E1 59 C6
East Twrs., Pnr. 36 D5
East Vw. E4 34 C5
East Vw., Barn. 23 C2
East Vw., NW7 30 G7
Northway
East Wk., Barn. 24 A7
East Wk., Hayes 63 A1
East Way E11 42 H5
East Way, Brom. 96 G7
East Way, Croy. 102 H4
East Way, Hayes 63 A1
East Way, Ruis. 45 A3
East Woodside, Bex. 89 E1
Maiden Erlegh Ave.
Eastbank Rd., 81 J5
Hmptn.
Eastbourne Ave. W3 56 D6
Eastbourne Gdns. 74 C3
SW14
Eastbourne Ms. W2 10 D3
Eastbourne Ms. W2 57 F6
Eastbourne Rd. E6 61 D3
Eastbourne Rd. E15 60 E1
Eastbourne Rd. N15 41 B6
Eastbourne Rd. 85 A6
SW17
Eastbourne Rd. W4 65 C6
Eastbourne Rd., 64 G5
Brent.
Eastbourne Rd., Felt. 81 D2
Eastbourne Ter. W2 10 D3
Eastbourne Ter. W2 57 F6
Eastbournia Ave. N9 25 E3
Eastbrook Ave. N9 25 F7
Eastbrook Ave., Dag. 53 J4
Eastbrook Rd. SE3 78 H1
Eastbury Ave., Bark. 61 H1
Eastbury Ave., Enf. 25 B1
Eastbury Ct., Bark. 61 H1
Eastbury Gro. W4 65 E5
Eastbury Ho., Bark. 61 J1
Eastbury Rd. E6 61 D4
Eastbury Rd., 82 H7
Kings.T.
Eastbury Rd., Orp. 97 G6
Eastbury Sq., Bark. 61 J1
Eastbury Ter. E1 59 G4
Eastcastle St. W1 11 F3
Eastcastle St. W1 58 C6
Eastcheap EC3 13 C5
Eastcheap EC3 59 A7
Eastcombe Ave. SE7 69 H6
Eastcote, Orp. 104 J1
Eastcote Ave., Grnf. 46 D6
Eastcote Ave., Har. 45 H2
Eastcote Ave., 90 F5
W.Mol.
Eastcote High Rd., 36 A6
Pnr.
Eastcote La., Har. 45 E4
Eastcote La., Nthlt. 45 F5
Eastcote La. N., 45 F6
Nthlt.

Eastcote Rd., Har.	45	J3
Eastcote Rd., Pnr.	36	D5
Eastcote Rd., Ruis.	36	A6
Eastcote Rd., Well.	79	G2
Eastcote St. SW9	76	F2
Eastcote Vw., Pnr.	36	C4
Eastcroft Rd., Epsom	99	E7
Eastdown Pk. SE13	78	D4
Eastern Ave. E11	42	H6
Eastern Ave., Ilf.	43	A6
Eastern Ave., Pnr.	36	D7
Eastern Ave., Rom.	44	C4
Eastern Ave. W., Rom.	44	E4
Eastern Gateway Access Rd. E6	61	E7
Eastern Ind. Est., Belv.	71	F2
Eastern Ind. Est., Erith	71	F2
Eastern Rd. E13	60	H2
Eastern Rd. E17	42	C5
Eastern Rd. N2	39	J3
Eastern Rd. N22	40	E1
Eastern Rd. SE4	78	A4
Eastern Way SE28	71	A2
Eastern Way, Erith	71	E1
Easternville Gdns., Ilf.	43	F6
Eastfield Gdns., Dag.	53	G4
Eastfield Rd. E17	42	A4
Eastfield Rd. N8	40	E3
Eastfield Rd., Dag.	53	F4
Eastfields, Pnr.	36	C5
Eastfields Rd. W3	56	C5
Eastfields Rd., Mitch.	94	A2
Eastgate Clo. SE28	62	D6
Eastholm NW11	39	E4
Eastlake Rd. SE5	76	J2
Eastlands Cres. SE21	77	C6
Eastleigh Ave., Har.	45	H2
Eastleigh Clo. NW2	47	E3
Eastleigh Clo., Sutt.	100	E7
Eastleigh Rd., Bexh.	80	J2
Eastleigh Wk. SW15	74	G7
Eastman Rd. W3	65	D2
Eastmead Ave., Grnf.	54	H3
Eastmead Clo., Brom.	97	B2
Eastmearn Rd. SE21	85	J2
Eastmont Rd., Esher	98	C2
Eastmoor Pl. SE7	70	A3
Eastmoor St. SE7	70	A3
Eastney Rd., Croy.	101	H1
Eastney St. SE10	69	D5
Eastnor Rd. SE9	88	F1
Easton Gdns., Borwd.	22	D4
Easton St. WC1	8	E4
Eastry Ave., Brom.	96	F6
Eastry Rd., Erith	71	G6
Eastside Rd. NW11	39	C4
Eastview Ave. SE18	70	H7
Eastville Ave. NW11	39	C6
Eastway E9	50	J6
Eastway E10	51	A4
Eastway, Mord.	93	A5
Eastway, Wall.	101	C4
Eastwell Clo., Beck.	86	H7
Eastwood Clo. E18	42	G2
The Viaduct		
Eastwood Rd. E18	42	G2
Eastwood Rd. N10	40	A2
Eastwood Rd., Ilf.	44	A7
Eastwood St. SW16	85	C6
Eatington Rd. E10	42	D5
Eaton Clo. SW1	19	B2
Eaton Clo. SW1	67	A4
Eaton Clo., Stan.	29	E4
Eaton Dr. SW9	76	H4
Eaton Dr., Kings.T.	83	A7
Eaton Gdns., Dag.	53	E7
Eaton Gate SW1	19	B1
Eaton Gate SW1	67	A4
Eaton La. SW1	15	E6
Eaton La. SW1	67	B3
Eaton Ms. N. SW1	15	B6
Eaton Ms. N. SW1	67	A3
Eaton Ms. S. SW1	15	D6
Eaton Ms. S. SW1	67	A4
Eaton Ms. W. SW1	19	C1
Eaton Ms. W. SW1	67	A4
Eaton Pk. Rd. N13	32	G2

Eaton Pl. SW1	15	B6
Eaton Pl. SW1	67	A3
Eaton Ri. E11	42	J5
Eaton Ri. W5	55	F5
Eaton Rd. NW4	38	J5
Eaton Rd., Enf.	25	B3
Eaton Rd., Houns.	73	A4
Eaton Rd., Sid.	89	D2
Eaton Rd., Sutt.	100	G6
Eaton Row SW1	15	D6
Eaton Row SW1	67	B3
Eaton Sq. SW1	19	C1
Eaton Sq. SW1	67	A4
Eaton Ter. SW1	19	B1
Eaton Ter. SW1	67	A4
Eaton Ter. Ms. SW1	19	B1
Eaton Wk. SE15	68	C7
Sumner Est.		
Eatons Mead E4	34	A2
Eatonville Rd. SW17	84	J3
Eatonville Vill. SW17	84	J2
Eatonville Rd.		
Ebbisham Dr. SW8	20	C6
Ebbisham Dr. SW8	67	F6
Ebbisham Rd., Wor.Pk.	99	J2
Ebbsfleet Rd. NW2	48	B5
Ebdon Way SE3	78	H3
Ebenezer St. N1	9	B3
Ebenezer Wk. SW16	94	C1
Meopham Rd.		
Ebley Clo. SE15	21	F6
Ebner St. SW18	73	E5
Ebor St. E1	9	F5
Ebor St. E1	59	C4
Ebrington Rd., Har.	37	F6
Ebsworth St. SE23	77	G7
Eburne Rd. N7	49	E3
Ebury Bri. SW1	19	D3
Ebury Bri. SW1	67	A5
Ebury Bri. Est. SW1	19	D3
Ebury Bri. Est. SW1	67	B5
Ebury Bri. Rd. SW1	19	C4
Ebury Bri. Rd. SW1	67	A5
Ebury Clo., Kes.	104	B3
Ebury Ms. SE27	85	H3
Norwood Rd.		
Ebury Ms. SW1	19	D1
Ebury Ms. SW1	67	B4
Ebury Ms. E. SW1	15	D6
Ebury Sq. SW1	19	C2
Ebury Sq. SW1	67	A4
Ebury St. SW1	19	C2
Ebury St. SW1	67	A4
Eccles Rd. SW11	75	J4
Ecclesbourne Clo. N13	32	G5
Ecclesbourne Gdns. N13	32	G5
Ecclesbourne Rd. N1	49	J7
Ecclesbourne Rd., Th.Hth.	94	J5
Eccleston Bri. SW1	19	E1
Eccleston Bri. SW1	67	B4
Eccleston Clo., Barn.	23	J4
Eccleston Clo., Orp.	104	G1
Eccleston Cres., Rom.	44	A7
Eccleston Ms. SW1	15	C6
Eccleston Ms. SW1	67	A3
Eccleston Pl. SW1	19	D1
Eccleston Pl. SW1	67	B4
Eccleston Rd. W13	55	D7
Eccleston Sq. SW1	19	E2
Eccleston Sq. SW1	67	B4
Eccleston Sq. Ms. SW1	19	E2
Eccleston St. SW1	15	C6
Eccleston St. SW1	67	B4
Ecclestone Ms., Wem.	46	H5
Ecclestone Pl., Wem.	46	J5
Echo Heights E4	34	B1
Mount Echo Dr.		
Eckford St. N1	8	E1
Eckford St. N1	58	G2
Eckstein Rd. SW11	75	H4
Eclipse Rd. E13	60	H5
Ector Rd. SE6	87	E2
Edbrooke Rd. W9	57	D4
Eddiscombe Rd. SW6	75	C2
Eddy Clo., Rom.	44	H6
Eddystone Rd. SE4	77	H5
Ede Clo., Houns.	72	F3
Eden Clo. W8	66	D3
Adam & Eve Ms.		
Eden Clo., Wem.	55	G1
Eden Gro. E17	42	B5
Eden Gro. N7	49	F5
Eden Ms. SW17	84	F3
Huntspill St.		

Eden Pk. Ave., Beck.	95	H4
Eden Rd. E17	42	B5
Eden Rd. SE27	85	H5
Eden Rd., Beck.	95	H4
Eden Rd., Bex.	89	J4
Eden Rd., Croy.	102	A4
Eden St., Kings.T.	91	G2
Eden Wk., Kings.T.	91	H2
Eden St.		
Eden Way, Beck.	95	J5
Edenbridge Rd. E9	50	G7
Edenbridge Rd., Enf.	25	B6
Edencourt Rd. SW16	85	B6
Edenfield Gdns., Wor.Pk.	99	F3
Edenham Way W10	57	C5
Elkstone Rd.		
Edenhurst Ave. SW6	75	C3
Edensor Gdns. W4	65	E7
Edensor Rd. W4	65	A7
Edenvale Rd., Mitch.	85	A7
Edenvale St. SW6	75	E2
Ederline Ave. SW16	94	F3
Edgar Rd. E3	60	B3
Edgar Rd., Houns.	72	F7
Edgar Rd., Rom.	44	D7
Edgarley Ter. SW6	75	B1
Edgbaston Rd., Wat.	28	B3
Holmside Ri.		
Edge Hill SE18	70	E6
Edge Hill SW19	84	A7
Edge Hill Ct. SW19	84	A7
Edge St. W8	66	D1
Kensington Ch. St.		
Edgeborough Way, Brom.	88	A7
Edgebury, Chis.	88	E4
Edgebury Wk., Chis.	88	F4
Edgehill Ho. SW19	84	B1
Edgecombe Clo., Kings.T.	83	D7
Edgecombe Ho. SW19	84	B1
Edgecombe Rd. E11	51	F1
Harvey Rd.		
Edgecoombe, S.Croy.	102	F7
Edgecot Gro. N15	41	A5
Oulton Rd.		
Edgecote Clo. W3	65	C1
Cheltenham Pl.		
Edgefield Ave., Bark.	52	J7
Edgehill Gdns., Dag.	53	G4
Edgehill Rd. W13	55	F5
Edgehill Rd., Chis.	88	F3
Edgehill Rd., Mitch.	94	B1
Edgel St. SW18	75	E4
Ferrier St.		
Edgeley La. SW4	76	D3
Edgeley Rd.		
Edgeley Rd. SW4	76	D3
Edgepoint Clo. SE27	85	H5
Knights Hill		
Edgewood Dr., Orp.	104	J5
Edgewood Grn., Croy.	102	G1
Edgeworth Ave. NW4	38	G5
Edgeworth Clo. NW4	38	G5
Edgeworth Cres. NW4	38	G5
Edgeworth Rd. SE9	78	J4
Edgeworth Rd., Barn.	23	H4
Edgington Rd. SW16	85	D6
Edgington Way, Sid.	89	C7
Edgware Rd. NW2	47	H1
Edgware Rd. NW9	38	C2
Edgware Rd. W2	6	E6
Edgware Rd. W2	57	G4
Edgware Way, Edg.	29	J4
Edgwarebury Gdns., Edg.	30	A5
Edgwarebury La., Edg.	30	A2
Edinburgh Ct. SW20	93	A5
Edinburgh Gate SW1	14	J4
Edinburgh Gate SW1	66	J2
Edinburgh Ho. W9	6	B3
Edinburgh Ho. W9	57	E3
Edinburgh Rd. E13	60	H2
Edinburgh Rd. E17	42	A5
Edinburgh Rd. N18	33	D5
Edinburgh Rd. W7	64	C2
Edinburgh Rd., Sutt.	100	F2
Edington Rd. SE2	71	B3
Edington Rd., Enf.	25	F2
Edis St. NW1	58	A1
Edison Dr., Sthl.	54	H6
Edison Gro. SE18	70	J7
Edison Rd. N8	40	D6
Edison Rd., Brom.	96	G2

Edison Rd., Enf.	25	J2
Edison Rd., Well.	79	J1
Edith Gdns., Surb.	92	B7
Edith Gro. SW10	18	C6
Edith Gro. SW10	66	F6
Edith Rd. E6	52	A7
Edith Rd. E15	51	D5
Chandos Rd.		
Edith Rd. N11	32	D7
Edith Rd. SE25	95	A5
Edith Rd. SW19	84	E6
Edith Rd. W14	66	B4
Edith Rd., Rom.	44	D6
Edith Row SW6	75	E1
Edith St. E2	9	H1
Edith Ter. SW10	18	C7
Edith Ter. SW10	66	F7
Edith Vill. W14	66	C5
Edith Yd. SW10	18	D7
Edithna St. SW9	76	E3
Edmansons Clo. N17	41	B1
Bruce Gro.		
Edmeston Clo. E9	50	H6
Edmonds Ct., W.Mol.	90	H4
Avern Rd.		
Edmund Rd., Mitch.	93	H3
Edmund Rd., Well.	80	A3
Edmund St. SE5	21	B7
Edmund St. SE5	68	A7
Edmunds Clo., Hayes	54	C5
Edmunds Wk. N2	39	H4
Edna Rd. SW20	93	A2
Edna St. SW11	75	H1
Edric Rd. SE14	68	G7
Edrich Ho. SW4	76	E1
Edrick Rd., Edg.	30	C6
Edrick Wk., Edg.	30	C6
Edridge Rd., Croy.	101	J3
Edulf Rd., Borwd.	22	B1
Edward Ave. E4	34	B6
Edward Ave., Mord.	93	G5
Edward Clo. N9	25	C7
Edward Clo., Hmptn.	81	J5
Edward Rd.		
Edward Clo., Nthlt.	54	C2
Edward Ct. E16	60	G5
Alexandra St.		
Edward Gro., Barn.	23	G5
Edward Rd.		
Edward Ms. NW1	7	E2
Edward Pl. SE8	68	J6
Edward Rd. E17	41	G4
Edward Rd. SE20	86	G7
Edward Rd., Barn.	23	G4
Edward Rd., Brom.	87	H7
Edward Rd., Chis.	88	E5
Edward Rd., Croy.	95	B7
Edward Rd., Hmptn.	81	J5
Edward Rd., Har.	36	J3
Edward Rd., Nthlt.	54	C2
Edward Rd., Rom.	44	D6
Edward Sq. N1	58	F1
Caledonian Rd.		
Edward St. E16	60	G4
Edward St. SE8	68	J6
Edward St. SE14	68	H7
Edward Temme Ave. E15	51	F7
Edwardes Sq. W8	66	C3
Edward's Ave., Ruis.	45	B6
Edwards Clo., Wor.Pk.	100	A2
Edwards Cotts. N1	49	H6
Compton Ave.		
Edwards Dr. N11	32	D7
Gordon Way		
Edwards La. N16	50	A2
Edwards Ms. W1	11	B4
Edwards Ms. W1	58	A6
Edwards Rd., Belv.	71	G4
Edwin Ave. E6	61	D2
Edwin Clo., Bexh.	71	F6
Edwin Pl., Croy.	102	A1
Cross Rd.		
Edwin Rd., Edg.	30	D6
Edwin Rd., Twick.	82	B1
Edwin St. E1	59	F4
Edwin St. E16	60	G5
Edwina Gdns., Ilf.	43	B5
Edwin's Mead E9	50	H4
Lindisfarne Way		
Edwyn Clo., Barn.	22	J6
Eel Brook Studios SW6	66	D7
Moore Pk. Rd.		
Effie Pl. SW6	66	D7
Effie Rd. SW6	66	D7
Effingham Clo., Sutt.	100	E7
Effingham Rd. N8	40	G5
Effingham Rd. SE12	78	E5
Effingham Rd., Croy.	94	F7

Effingham Rd., Surb. 91 E7
Effort St. SW17 84 H5
Effra Par. SW2 76 G5
Effra Rd. SW2 76 G4
Effra Rd. SW19 84 D6
Egan Way SE16 68 E5
Egbert St. NW1 58 A1
Egerton Clo., Pnr. 36 A2
Egerton Cres. SW3 18 H1
Egerton Cres. SW3 66 H4
Egerton Dr. SE10 78 B1
Egerton Gdns. NW4 38 H4
Egerton Gdns. NW10 56 J1
Egerton Gdns. SW3 14 G6
Egerton Gdns. SW3 66 H4
Egerton Gdns. W13 55 E6
Egerton Gdns., Ilf. 52 J3
Egerton Gdns. Ms. 14 H6
  SW3
Egerton Gdns. Ms. 66 H3
  SW3
Egerton Pl. SW3 14 H6
Egerton Pl. SW3 66 H3
Egerton Rd. N16 41 C7
Egerton Rd. SE25 95 B3
Egerton Rd., N.Mal. 92 F4
Egerton Rd., Twick. 73 B7
Egerton Rd., Wem. 46 J7
Egerton Ter. SW3 14 H6
Egerton Ter. SW3 66 H3
Egham Clo. SW19 84 B2
  Winterfold Clo.
Egham Clo., Sutt. 100 B2
Egham Cres., Sutt. 100 A3
Egham Rd. E13 60 H5
Eglantine Rd. SW18 75 F5
Egleston Rd., Mord. 93 E6
Eglington Ct. SE17 20 J5
Eglington Rd. E4 26 D7
Eglinton Hill SE18 70 E6
Eglinton Rd. SE18 70 E6
Egliston Ms. SW15 74 J3
Egliston Rd. SW15 74 J3
Eglon Ms. NW1 48 J7
  Berkley Rd.
Egmont Ave., Surb. 98 J1
Egmont Rd., N.Mal. 92 F4
Egmont Rd., Surb. 98 J1
Egmont Rd., Sutt. 100 F7
Egmont Rd., Walt. 90 B7
Egmont St. SE14 68 G7
Egremont Rd. SE27 85 G3
Eighteenth Rd., 94 E4
  Mitch.
Eighth Ave. E12 52 C4
Eighth Ave., Hayes 63 A5
Eileen Rd. SE25 95 A5
Eisenhower Dr. E6 61 B5
Elaine Gro. NW5 49 A5
Elam Clo. SE5 76 H2
Elam St. SE5 76 H2
Eland Rd. SW11 75 J3
Eland Rd., Croy. 101 H3
Elba Pl. SE17 21 A1
Elbe St. SW6 75 F2
Elberon Ave., Croy. 94 G6
Elborough St. SW18 84 D1
Elbury Dr. E16 60 G6
Elcho St. SW11 66 H7
Elcot Ave. SE15 68 D7
Elder Ave. N8 40 E5
Elder Ct. (Bushey), 29 B2
  Wat.
Elder Oak Clo. SE20 95 E1
Elder Rd. SE27 85 J5
Elder St. E1 9 F6
Elder St. E1 59 C5
Elder Wk. N1 58 H1
  Essex Rd.
Elderberry Gro. SE27 85 J5
  Linton Gro.
Elderberry Rd. W5 64 H2
Elderfield Rd. E5 50 G4
Elderfield Wk. E11 42 H5
Elderslie Clo., 96 A5
  Beck.
Elderslie Rd. SE9 79 D5
Elderton Rd. SE26 86 H4
Eldertree Pl., Mitch. 94 C1
  Eldertree Way
Eldertree Way, 94 C1
  Mitch.
Elderwood Pl. SE27 85 J5
  Elder Rd.
Eldon Ave., Borwd. 22 A2
Eldon Ave., Croy. 102 G3
Eldon Ave., Houns. 63 G7
Eldon Gro. NW3 68 G4
Eldon Pk. SE25 95 E4
  Lincoln Rd.
Eldon Rd. E17 41 J4
Eldon Rd. N9 33 F2

Eldon Rd. N22 40 H1
Eldon Rd. W8 14 B6
Eldon Rd. W8 66 E3
Eldon St. EC2 13 C2
Eldon St. EC2 59 A5
Eldon Way NW10 56 B2
Eldonwall Trd. Est. 47 G1
  NW2
Eldred Rd., Bark. 61 H1
Eldridge Clo., Felt. 81 A1
Eleanor Clo. SE16 68 G2
Eleanor Cres. NW7 31 A4
Eleanor Gdns., Barn. 23 A5
  Chesterfield Rd.
Eleanor Gdns., Dag. 53 F3
  Nicholas Rd.
Eleanor Gro. SW13 74 E3
Eleanor Rd. E8 50 E6
Eleanor Rd. E15 51 F6
Eleanor Rd. N11 32 E6
Eleanor St. E3 60 A3
Eleanor Wk. SE18 70 C4
  Samuel Rd.
Electric Ave. SW9 76 G4
Electric La. SW9 76 G4
Electric Par., Surb. 91 G6
Elephant & Castle 20 H1
  SE1
Elephant & Castle 67 H3
  SE1
Elephant La. SE16 68 F2
Elephant Rd. SE17 20 J1
Elephant Rd. SE17 67 J4
Elers Rd. W13 64 F2
Eleven Acre Ri., 27 C3
  Loug.
Eley Est. N18 33 F4
Eley Rd. N18 33 F4
Eley's Est. N18 33 G5
  Angel La.
Elf Row E1 59 F7
Elfin Gro., Tedd. 82 C5
  Broad St.
Elfindale Rd. SE24 76 J5
Elford Clo. SE3 78 J4
Elfort Rd. N5 49 G4
Elfrida Cres. SE6 87 A4
Elfwine Rd. W7 55 B5
Elgar Ave. NW10 47 D6
  Mitchellbrook Way
Elgar Ave. SW16 94 E3
Elgar Ave. W5 64 H2
Elgar Ave., Surb. 99 A1
Elgar Clo. SE8 69 A7
  Comet St.
Elgar Clo., Buck.H. 35 A2
Elgar St. SE16 68 H2
Elgin Ave. W9 57 D4
Elgin Ave., Har. 37 E2
Elgin Cres. W11 57 B7
Elgin Est. W9 57 D4
Elgin Ms. W11 57 B6
  Ladbroke Gro.
Elgin Ms. N. W9 6 B3
Elgin Ms. S. W9 6 B3
Elgin Rd. N22 40 C2
Elgin Rd., Croy. 102 C2
Elgin Rd., Ilf. 52 H1
Elgin Rd., Sutt. 100 F3
Elgin Rd., Wall. 101 C6
Elgood Clo. W11 57 B7
  Avondale Pk. Rd.
Elham Clo., Brom. 88 A7
Elia Ms. N1 8 G2
Elia Ms. N1 58 H2
Elia St. N1 8 G2
Elia St. N1 58 H2
Elias Pl. SW8 20 E6
Elias Pl. SW8 67 G6
Elibank Rd. SE9 79 C4
Elim Est. SE1 17 D5
Elim Est. SE1 68 A3
Elim Way E13 60 F3
Eliot Bank SE23 86 E2
Eliot Cotts. SE3 78 E2
  Eliot Pl.
Eliot Dr., Har. 45 H2
Eliot Gdns. SW15 74 G4
Eliot Hill SE13 78 C2
Eliot Pk. SE13 78 C2
Eliot Pl. SE3 78 E2
Eliot Rd., Dag. 53 D4
Eliot Vale SE3 78 D2
Elizabeth Ave. N1 49 J7
Elizabeth Ave., Enf. 24 H3
Elizabeth Ave., Ilf. 52 G2
Elizabeth Blackwell 40 G1
  Ho. N22
  Progress Way
Elizabeth Bri. SW1 19 D2
Elizabeth Bri. SW1 67 B4
Elizabeth Clo. E14 60 B6
  Grundy St.

Elizabeth Clo. W9 6 D6
Elizabeth Clo., Barn. 23 A3
Elizabeth Clo., Rom. 44 H1
Elizabeth Clyde Clo. 41 B4
  N15
Elizabeth Cotts., 73 J1
  Rich.
Elizabeth Ct. SW1 19 C1
Elizabeth Est. SE17 21 B5
Elizabeth Est. SE17 68 A6
Elizabeth Fry Rd. 50 E7
  E8
  Lamb La.
Elizabeth Gdns. W3 65 F1
Elizabeth Gdns., 29 F6
  Stan.
Elizabeth Gdns., 90 C3
  Sun.
Elizabeth Ms. NW3 48 J6
Elizabeth Pl. N15 41 A4
Elizabeth Ride N9 25 E7
Elizabeth Rd. E6 61 A1
Elizabeth Rd. N15 41 B5
Elizabeth St. SW1 19 C1
Elizabeth St. SW1 67 G3
Elizabeth Ter. SE9 79 C6
Elizabeth Way SE19 86 A7
Elizabeth Way, Felt. 81 C4
Elkington Rd. E13 60 H4
Elkstone Rd. W10 57 C5
Ella Rd. N8 40 E7
Ellaline Rd. W6 66 A6
Ellanby Cres. N18 33 E4
Elland Rd. SE15 77 F4
Ellement Clo., Pnr. 36 D5
Ellen Clo., Brom. 97 A3
Ellen Ct. N9 33 F2
  Densworth Gro.
Ellen St. E1 13 J4
Ellen St. E1 59 D6
Ellenborough Pl. 74 G4
  SW15
Ellenborough Rd. 40 J1
  N22
Ellenborough Rd., 89 D5
  Sid.
Elleray Rd., Tedd. 82 C6
Ellerby St. SW6 75 A1
Ellerdale Clo. NW3 48 A4
  Ellerdale Rd.
Ellerdale Rd. NW3 48 F5
Ellerdale St. SE13 78 B4
Ellerdine Rd., 73 A4
  Houns.
Ellerker Gdns., Rich. 73 H5
Ellerman Ave., 81 F1
  Twick.
Ellerslie Gdns. 56 G1
  NW10
Ellerslie Rd. W12 65 H1
Ellerslie Sq. Ind. 76 E4
  Est. SW2
Ellerton Gdns., 53 C7
  Dag.
Ellerton Rd. SW13 74 G1
Ellerton Rd. SW18 84 G1
Ellerton Rd. SW20 83 G7
Ellerton Rd., Dag. 53 C7
Ellerton Rd., Surb. 98 J2
Ellery Rd. SE19 86 A7
Ellery St. SE15 77 E2
Ellesborough Clo., 28 C5
  Wat.
Ellesmere Ave. NW7 30 D3
Ellesmere Ave., 96 B2
  Beck.
Ellesmere Clo. E11 42 F5
Ellesmere Gdns., Ilf. 43 B5
Ellesmere Gro., 23 C5
  Barn.
Ellesmere Rd. E3 59 H2
Ellesmere Rd. NW10 47 G5
Ellesmere Rd. W4 65 D6
Ellesmere Rd., 54 J4
  Grnf.
Ellesmere Rd., 73 F6
  Twick.
Ellesmere St. E14 60 B6
Ellingfort Rd. E8 50 E7
Ellingham Rd. E15 51 D4
Ellingham Rd. W12 65 G2
Ellingham Rd., 98 G6
  Chess.
Ellington Rd. N10 40 B4
Ellington Rd., 72 H2
  Houns.
Ellington St. N7 49 G6
Elliot Ave., Ruis. 45 B2
Elliot Clo. E15 51 E7
Elliot Rd. NW4 38 H6
Elliot Rd., Stan. 29 D6
Elliott Clo., Wem. 46 J3
Elliott Rd. SW9 67 H7

Elliott Rd. W4 65 E4
Elliott Rd., Brom. 97 A4
Elliott Rd., 94 H4
  Th.Hth.
Elliott Sq. NW3 48 H7
Elliott's Pl. N1 58 H1
  St. Peters St.
Elliotts Row SE11 20 G5
Elliotts Row SE11 67 H4
Ellis Clo. SE9 88 F2
Ellis Ct. W7 55 C5
Ellis Ms. SE7 69 J6
Ellis Rd., Mitch. 93 J6
Ellis St. SW1 19 A1
Ellis St. SW1 66 J4
Elliscombe Rd. SE7 69 J5
Ellisfield Dr. SW15 74 F7
Ellison Gdns., Sthl. 63 F4
Ellison Rd. SW13 74 F2
Ellison Rd. SW16 85 D7
Ellison Rd., Sid. 88 G1
Elliston Ho. SE18 70 D4
  Wellington St.
Ellora Rd. SW16 85 D5
Ellsworth St. E2 59 E3
Ellwood Ct. W9 6 A6
Elm Ave. W5 64 H1
Elm Ave., Ruis. 45 A1
Elm Bank N14 24 E7
Elm Bank, Brom. 97 A2
Elm Bank Gdns. 74 E2
  SW13
Elm Clo. E11 42 H6
Elm Clo. N19 49 C2
  Hargrave Pk.
Elm Clo. NW4 39 A5
Elm Clo. SW20 92 J4
  Grand Dr.
Elm Clo., Buck.H. 35 A2
Elm Clo., Cars. 100 J1
Elm Clo., Har. 36 H6
Elm Clo., Hayes 54 A6
Elm Clo., Rom. 44 H1
Elm Clo., S.Croy. 102 B6
Elm Clo., Surb. 92 C7
Elm Clo., Twick. 81 H2
Elm Ct. EC4 12 E5
Elm Cres. W5 64 H1
Elm Cres., Kings.T. 91 H1
Elm Dr., Har. 36 H6
Elm Dr., Sun. 90 C2
Elm Friars Wk. NW1 49 D7
  Maiden La.
Elm Gdns. N2 39 F3
Elm Gdns., Esher 98 C6
Elm Gdns., Mitch. 94 D4
Elm Grn. W3 56 E6
Elm Gro. N8 40 E6
Elm Gro. NW2 48 A4
Elm Gro. SE15 77 C2
Elm Gro. SW19 84 B7
Elm Gro., Har. 36 G7
Elm Gro., Kings.T. 91 H1
Elm Gro., Orp. 104 J3
Elm Gro., Sutt. 100 E4
Elm Gro., Wdf.Grn. 34 F5
Elm Gro. Par., Wall. 101 A3
  Butter Hill
Elm Gro. Rd. SW13 74 G2
Elm Gro. Rd. W5 64 H2
Elm Hall Gdns. E11 42 H6
Elm La. SE6 86 J2
Elm Ms., Rich. 73 J6
  Grove Rd.
Elm Pk. SW2 76 F6
Elm Pk., Stan. 29 E5
Elm Pk. Ave. N15 41 C5
Elm Pk. Ct., Pnr. 36 C3
Elm Pk. Gdns. NW4 39 A5
Elm Pk. Gdns. SW10 18 E4
Elm Pk. Gdns. SW10 66 G5
Elm Pk. La. SW3 18 E4
Elm Pk. La. SW3 66 G5
Elm Pk. Mans. SW10 18 D5
Elm Pk. Rd. E10 50 H1
Elm Pk. Rd. N3 31 C7
Elm Pk. Rd. N21 24 J7
Elm Pk. Rd. SE25 95 C3
Elm Pk. Rd. SW3 18 E5
Elm Pk. Rd. SW3 66 G6
Elm Pk. Rd., Pnr. 36 C2
Elm Pl. SW7 18 E3
Elm Pl. SW7 66 G5
Elm Quay Ct. SW8 19 H6
Elm Quay Ct. SW8 67 D6
Elm Rd. E7 51 F6
Elm Rd. E11 51 D2
Elm Rd. E17 42 C5
Elm Rd. N22 40 H1
  Granville Rd.
Elm Rd. SW14 74 C3
Elm Rd., Barn. 23 C4
Elm Rd., Beck. 95 J2

Elm Rd., Chess. 98 H4
Elm Rd., Epsom 99 F6
Elm Rd., Esher 98 C6
Elm Rd., Kings.T. 91 J1
Elm Rd., N.Mal. 92 D3
Elm Rd., Rom. 44 H2
Elm Rd., Sid. 89 A4
Elm Rd., Th.Hth. 95 A4
Elm Rd., Wem. 46 H5
Elm Rd. W., Sutt. 93 C7
Elm Row NW3 48 F3
Elm St. WC1 8 D6
Elm St. WC1 58 F4
Elm Ter. NW2 48 D3
Elm Ter. SE9 79 D6
Elm Ter., Har. 37 A1
Elm Tree Ave., 91 A7
 Esher
Elm Tree Clo. NW8 6 E3
Elm Tree Clo. NW8 57 G3
Elm Tree Clo., 54 F2
 Nthlt.
Elm Tree Rd. NW8 6 E3
Elm Tree Rd. NW8 57 G3
Elm Wk. NW3 48 D2
Elm Wk. SW20 92 J4
Elm Wk., Orp. 104 C3
Elm Way N11 32 A6
Elm Way NW10 47 E4
Elm Way, Epsom 99 D5
Elm Way, Wor.Pk. 99 J3
Elmar Rd N15 41 A4
Elmbank Ave., Barn. 22 J4
Elmbank Way W7 55 A5
Elmbourne Dr., 71 H4
 Belv.
Elmbourne Rd. SW17 85 A3
Elmbridge Ave., 92 B5
 Surb.
Elmbridge Clo., 36 A6
 Ruis.
Elmbridge Wk. E8 50 D7
 Wilman Gro.
Elmbrook Clo., Sun. 90 B1
Elmbrook Gdns. SE9 79 B4
Elmbrook Rd., Sutt. 100 C4
Elmcourt Rd. SE27 85 H2
Elmcroft Ave. E11 42 H5
Elmcroft Ave. N9 25 E6
Elmcroft Ave. NW11 39 C7
Elmcroft Ave., Sid. 79 J7
Elmcroft Clo. E11 42 H4
Elmcroft Clo. W5 55 G6
Elmcroft Clo., 98 H3
 Chess.
Elmcroft Cres. NW11 39 A7
Elmcroft Cres., Har. 36 G3
Elmcroft Dr., 98 H3
 Chess.
Elmcroft Gdns. NW9 38 A5
Elmcroft St. E5 50 F4
Elmdale Rd. N13 32 F5
Elmdene, Surb. 99 C1
Elmdene Clo., Beck. 95 J5
Elmdene Rd. SE18 70 E5
Elmdon Rd., Houns. 72 D2
Elmer Clo., Enf. 24 F3
Elmer Gdns., Edg. 30 B7
Elmer Gdns., Islw. 73 A3
Elmer Rd. SE6 78 C7
Elmers Dr., Tedd. 82 E6
 St. Mark's Rd.
Elmers End Rd. SE20 95 F2
Elmers End Rd., 95 F3
 Beck.
Elmers Rd. SE25 95 D7
Elmerside Rd., Beck. 95 H4
Elmfield Ave. N8 40 E5
Elmfield Ave., 94 A1
 Mitch.
Elmfield Ave., 82 C5
 Tedd.
Elmfield Clo., Har. 46 B2
Elmfield Pk., Brom. 96 G3
Elmfield Rd. E4 34 C2
Elmfield Rd. E17 41 G5
Elmfield Rd. N2 39 G3
Elmfield Rd. SW17 85 A2
Elmfield Rd., Brom. 96 G3
Elmfield Rd., Sthl. 63 E3
Elmgate Ave., Felt. 81 B3
Elmgate Gdns., Edg. 30 D5
Elmgreen Clo. E15 60 E1
 Church St. N.
Elmgrove Cres., Har. 37 C5
Elmgrove Gdns., Har. 37 D5
Elmgrove Rd., Croy. 95 E7
Elmgrove Rd., Har. 37 C5
Elmhurst, Belv. 71 E6
Elmhurst Ave. N2 39 G3
Elmhurst Ave., 85 A7
 Mitch.

Elmhurst Cres. N2 39 F4
Elmhurst Dr. E18 42 G2
Elmhurst Gdns. E18 42 H1
Elmhurst Rd. E7 51 H7
Elmhurst Rd. N17 41 B2
Elmhurst Rd. SE9 88 B2
Elmhurst St. SW4 76 D3
Elmhurst Way, Loug. 27 C7
Elmington Clo., Bex. 80 H6
Elmington Est. SE5 21 C7
Elmington Est. SE5 68 A7
Elmington Rd. SE5 77 A1
Elmira St. SE13 78 B3
Elmlee Clo., Chis. 88 C6
Elmley Clo. E6 61 B5
 Northumberland Rd.
Elmley St. SE18 70 G4
Elmore Clo., Wem. 55 H2
Elmore Rd. E11 51 C3
Elmore St. N1 50 A7
Elmores, Loug. 27 D3
Elms, The SW13 74 F3
Elms Ave. N10 40 B3
Elms Ave. NW4 39 A5
Elms Ct., Wem. 46 D4
Elms Cres. SW4 76 C6
Elms Gdns., Dag. 53 F4
Elms Gdns., Wem. 46 D4
Elms La., Wem. 46 D3
Elms Ms. W2 10 E5
Elms Ms. W2 57 G7
Elms Pk. Ave., Wem. 46 D4
Elms Rd. SW4 76 C5
Elms Rd., Har. 29 B7
Elms Wk. SE3 78 F4
Elmscott Gdns. N21 24 J6
Elmscott Rd., Brom. 87 E5
Elmscroft N8 40 F5
 Tottenham La.
Elmsdale Rd. E17 41 J4
Elmshaw Rd. SW15 74 G5
Elmside, Croy. 103 B6
Elmside Rd., Wem. 47 A3
Elmsleigh Ave., 37 E4
 Har.
Elmsleigh Rd., 82 A2
 Twick.
Elmslie Clo., 35 C6
 Wdf.Grn.
Elmslie Pt. E3 59 J5
 Ackroyd Dr.
Elmstead Ave. 88 C5
 Chis.
Elmstead Ave., Wem. 46 H1
Elmstead Clo. N20 31 D2
Elmstead Clo., 99 E5
 Epsom
Elmstead Cres., 71 C6
 Well.
Elmstead Gdns., 99 G3
 Wor.Pk.
Elmstead Glade, 88 C6
 Chis.
Elmstead La., Chis. 88 B7
Elmstead Rd., Ilf. 52 H2
Elmstone Rd. SW6 75 D1
Elmsworth Ave., 72 H2
 Houns.
Elmton Way E5 50 D3
 Rendlesham Rd.
Elmtree Rd., Tedd. 82 B4
Elmwood Ave. N13 32 E5
Elmwood Ave., 22 B4
 Borwd.
Elmwood Ave., Felt. 81 A2
Elmwood Ave., Har. 37 D5
Elmwood Clo., 99 G7
 Epsom
Elmwood Clo., Wall. 101 A2
Elmwood Ct., Wem. 46 D3
Elmwood Cres. NW9 38 C4
Elmwood Dr., Bex. 80 E7
Elmwood Dr., Epsom 99 G6
Elmwood Gdns. W7 55 B6
Elmwood Rd. SE24 77 A5
Elmwood Rd. W4 65 C6
Elmwood Rd., Croy. 94 H7
Elmwood Rd., Mitch. 93 J3
Elmworth Gro. SE21 86 A2
Elnathan Ms. W9 6 B7
Elphinstone Rd. E17 41 J2
Elphinstone St. N5 49 H4
 Avenell Rd.
Elrington Rd. E8 50 D6
Elsa Rd., Well. 80 B1
Elsa St. E1 59 H5
Elsdale St. E9 59 F2
Elsden Ms. E2 59 F2
 Old Ford Rd.
Elsden Rd. N17 41 C1
Elsenham Rd. E12 52 D5
Elsenham St. SW18 84 C1
Elsham Rd. E11 51 E3

Elsham Rd. W14 66 B2
Elsham Ter. W14 66 B2
Elsie Rd. SE22 77 C4
Elsiedene Rd. N21 24 J7
Elsiemaud Rd. SE4 77 J3
Elsinore Rd. SE23 86 H1
Elsinore Way, Rich. 74 B3
 Lwr. Richmond Rd.
Elsley Rd. SW11 75 J3
Elspeth Rd. SW11 75 J4
Elspeth Rd., Wem. 46 H5
Elsrick Ave., Mord. 93 D5
 Chalgrove Ave.
Elstan Way, Croy. 96 D7
Elsted St. SE17 21 C2
Elsted St. SE17 68 A4
Elstow Clo. SE9 79 D5
Elstow Clo., Ruis. 36 D7
Elstow Gdns., Dag. 62 E1
Elstow Rd., Dag. 63 E7
Elstree Gdns. N9 33 E1
Elstree Gdns., 71 E4
 Belv.
Elstree Gdns., Ilf. 52 F5
Elstree Hill, Brom. 87 E7
Elstree Way, Borwd. 22 B3
Elswick Rd. SE13 78 B2
Elswick St. SW6 75 F2
Elsworthy, T.Ditt. 91 B6
Elsworthy Ri. NW3 48 H7
Elsworthy Rd. NW3 57 H1
Elsworthy Ter. NW3 48 H7
Eltham Grn. SE9 78 J5
Eltham Grn. Rd. SE9 78 J4
Eltham High St. SE9 79 C6
Eltham Hill SE9 79 A5
Eltham Palace Rd. 78 J6
 SE9
Eltham Pk. Gdns. 79 D4
 SE9
Eltham Rd. SE9 78 J5
Eltham Rd. SE12 78 G5
Elthiron Rd. SW6 75 D1
Elthorne Ave. W7 64 C2
Elthorne Ct., Felt. 81 C1
Elthorne Pk. Rd. W7 64 C2
Elthorne Rd. N19 49 D2
Elthorne Rd. NW9 38 D7
Elthorne Way NW9 38 D6
Elthruda Rd. SE13 78 D6
Eltisley Rd., Ilf. 52 E4
Elton Ave., Barn. 23 C5
Elton Ave., Grnf. 46 B6
Elton Ave., Wem. 46 E5
Elton Clo., 82 F7
 Kings.T.
Elton Ho. E3 59 J1
Elton Pl. N16 50 B5
Elton Rd., Kings.T. 91 J1
Eltringham St. SW18 75 F4
Elvaston Ms. SW7 14 D6
Elvaston Ms. SW7 66 F3
Elvaston Pl. SW7 14 C6
Elvaston Pl. SW7 66 F3
Elveden Pl. NW10 56 A2
Elveden Rd. NW10 56 A2
Elvendon Rd. N13 32 E6
Elver Gdns. E2 9 J2
Elverson Rd. SE8 78 B2
Elverton St. SW1 19 H1
Elverton St. SW1 67 D4
Elvington Grn., 96 F5
 Brom.
Elvington La. NW9 38 E1
Elvino Rd. SE26 86 G5
Elvis Rd. NW2 47 J6
Elwill Way, Beck. 96 C4
Elwin St. E2 9 H3
Elwin St. E2 59 D3
Elwood St. N5 49 H3
Elwyn Gdns. SE12 78 G7
Ely Clo., N.Mal. 92 F2
Ely Ct. EC1 12 F2
Ely Gdns., Borwd. 22 D5
Ely Gdns., Dag. 53 J3
Ely Gdns., Ilf. 43 B7
 Canterbury Ave.
Ely Pl. EC1 12 F2
Ely Pl., Wdf.Grn. 35 D6
Ely Rd. E10 42 C7
Ely Rd., Croy. 95 A5
Ely Rd. (TW4), 72 C3
 Houns.
Elyne Rd. N4 40 G6
Elysian Ave., Orp. 97 H6
Elysium Pl. SW6 75 C2
 Fulham Pk. Gdns.
Elysium St. SW6 75 C2
 Fulham Pk. Gdns.
Elystan Pl. SW3 18 H3
Elystan Pl. SW3 66 H5
Elystan St. SW3 18 G2

Elystan St. SW3 66 H4
Elystan Wk. N1 58 G1
 Cloudesley Rd.
Emanuel Ave. W3 56 C6
Emba St. SE16 17 J4
Emba St. SE16 68 D2
Embankment SW15 75 A2
Embankment, The, 82 D1
 Twick.
Embankment Gdns. 19 A5
 SW3
Embankment Gdns. 66 J6
 SW3
Embankment Pl. WC2 16 B1
Embankment Pl. WC2 67 E1
Embassy Ct., Sid. 89 B3
Embassy Ct., Well. 80 B3
Ember Clo., Orp. 97 F7
Ember Fm. Ave., 91 A6
 E.Mol.
Ember Fm. Way, 91 A6
 E.Mol.
Ember Gdns., 91 B7
 T.Ditt.
Ember La., E.Mol. 91 A5
Ember La., Esher 91 A7
Embercourt Rd., 91 B6
 T.Ditt.
Emberton SE5 21 D5
Embleton Rd. SE13 78 B4
Embleton Rd., Wat. 28 A3
Embleton Wk., 81 F6
 Hmptn.
 Fearnley Cres.
Embley Pt. E5 50 E4
 Tiger Way
Embry Clo., Stan. 29 D3
Embry Dr., Stan. 29 D6
Embry Way, Stan. 29 D4
Emden St. SW6 75 E1
Emerald Clo. E16 61 B6
Emerald Gdns., Dag. 53 G1
Emerald St. WC1 12 C5
Emerald St. WC1 58 F5
Emerson Gdns., Har. 37 J6
Emerson Rd., Ilf. 43 D7
Emerson St. SE1 16 J1
Emerson St. SE1 67 J1
Emerton Clo., Bexh. 80 E4
Emery Hill St. SW1 15 G6
Emery Hill St. SW1 67 C3
Emery St. SE1 16 F5
Emery St. SE1 67 F5
Emes Rd., Erith 71 J7
Emily Pl. N7 49 G4
Emlyn Gdns. W12 65 E2
Emlyn Rd. W12 65 E2
Emma Rd. E13 60 F2
Emma St. E2 59 E2
Emmanuel Rd. SW12 85 C1
Emmaus Way, Chig. 35 D5
Emmott Ave., Ilf. 43 F5
Emmott Clo. E1 59 H4
Emmott Clo. NW11 39 F6
Emms Pas., Kings.T. 91 G2
 High St.
Emperor's Gate SW7 14 B6
Emperor's Gate SW7 66 E3
Empire Ave. N18 32 J5
Empire Ct., Wem. 47 B3
Empire Rd., Grnf. 55 E1
Empire Way, Wem. 46 J4
Empire Wf. Rd. E14 69 D4
Empire Yd. N7 49 E3
 Holloway Rd.
Empress Ave. E4 34 B7
Empress Ave. E12 51 J2
Empress Ave., Ilf. 52 C2
Empress Ave., 34 F7
 Wdf.Grn.
Empress Dr., Chis. 88 E6
Empress Pl. SW6 66 D5
Empress St. SE17 21 A5
Empress St. SE17 67 J6
Empson St. E3 60 B4
Emsworth Clo. N9 33 F1
Emsworth Rd., Ilf. 43 E2
Emsworth St. SW2 85 E2
Emu Rd. SW8 76 B2
Ena Rd. SW16 94 E3
Enbrook St. W10 57 B3
End Way, Surb. 92 A7
Endale Clo., Cars. 100 J2
Endeavour Way 84 E4
 SW19
Endeavour Way, 62 A2
 Bark.
Endeavour Way, 94 D7
 Croy.
Endell St. WC2 12 A3
Endell St. WC2 58 E6
Enderby St. SE10 69 E5
Enderley Clo., Har. 37 B1
Enderley Rd., Har. 37 B1

Endersby Rd., Barn. 22 J5
Endersleigh Gdns. 38 G4
NW4
Endleigh Rd. E4 34 C2
Endlesham Rd. SW12 76 A7
Endsleigh Gdns. WC1 7 H5
Endsleigh Gdns. WC1 58 D4
Endsleigh Gdns., Ilf. 52 C2
Endsleigh Gdns., 91 F6
Surb.
Endsleigh Pl. WC1 7 J5
Endsleigh Pl. WC1 58 D4
Endsleigh Rd. W13 55 D7
Endsleigh Rd., 63 E4
Sthl.
Endsleigh St. WC1 7 J5
Endsleigh St. WC1 58 D4
Endwell Rd. SE4 77 H2
Endymion Rd. N4 40 G7
Endymion Rd. SW2 76 F6
Enfield Rd. N1 50 B7
Enfield Rd. W3 65 B2
Enfield Rd., Brent. 64 G5
Enfield Rd., Enf. 24 E4
Enfield Wk., Brent. 64 G5
Enfield Rd.
Enford St. W1 10 J1
Enford St. W1 57 J5
Engadine Clo., 102 C3
Croy.
Engadine St. SW18 84 C1
Engate St. SE13 78 C4
Engel Pk. NW7 30 J6
Engineer Clo. SE18 70 D6
Engineers Way, 47 A4
Wem.
Englands La. NW3 48 J6
Englands La., Loug. 27 D2
Englefield Clo., Croy. 94 J6
Queens Rd.
Englefield Clo., Enf. 24 G2
Chase Ridings
Englefield Clo., Orp. 97 J4
Englefield Cres., Orp. 97 J4
Englefield Rd. N1 50 A7
Engleheart Rd. SE6 78 B7
Englewood Rd. SW12 76 B4
English Grds. SE1 17 D2
English St. E3 59 J4
Enid St. SE16 17 G5
Enid St. SE16 68 C3
Enmore Ave. SE25 95 D5
Enmore Gdns. SW14 74 D5
Enmore Rd. SE25 95 D5
Enmore Rd. SW15 74 J4
Enmore Rd., Sthl. 54 G4
Ennerdale Ave., 37 F3
Stan.
Ennerdale Clo. 100 C3
(Cheam), Sutt.
Ennerdale Dr. NW9 38 E5
Ennerdale Gdns., 46 F1
Wem.
Ennerdale Ho. E3 59 J4
Ennerdale Rd., Bexh. 80 G1
Ennerdale Rd., Rich. 73 J2
Ennersdale Rd. SE13 78 D5
Ennis Rd. N4 49 G1
Ennis Rd. SE18 70 F6
Ennismore Ave. W4 65 F4
Ennismore Ave., 46 B6
Grnf.
Ennismore Gdns. 14 G5
SW7
Ennismore Gdns. 66 H2
SW7
Ennismore Gdns., 91 B6
T.Ditt.
Ennismore Gdns. Ms. 14 G5
SW7
Ennismore Gdns. Ms. 66 H3
SW7
Ennismore Ms. SW7 14 G5
Ennismore Ms. SW7 66 H3
Ennismore St. SW7 14 G5
Ennismore St. SW7 66 H3
Ensign Dr. N13 32 J3
Ensign St. E1 13 H5
Ensign St. E1 59 D7
Enslin Rd. SE9 79 D7
Ensor Ms. SW7 18 E3
Enstone Rd., Enf. 25 H3
Enterprise Clo., 101 G1
Croy.
Enterprise Way 56 G3
NW10
Enterprise Way 75 D4
SW18
Enterprise Way, 82 C5
Tedd.
Enterprize Way SE8 68 J4
Epirus Ms. SW6 66 D7
Epirus Rd.

Epirus Rd. SW6 66 C7
Epping Clo. E14 69 A4
Epping Clo., Rom. 44 H3
Epping Glade E4 26 C6
Epping New Rd., 34 G3
Buck.H.
Epping New Rd., 26 J3
Loug.
Epping Pl. N1 49 G6
Liverpool Rd.
Epping Way E4 26 B6
Epple Rd. SW6 75 C1
Epsom Clo., Bexh. 80 H3
Epsom Clo., Nthlt. 45 F5
Epsom Rd. E10 42 C6
Epsom Rd., Croy. 101 G4
Epsom Rd., Ilf. 43 J6
Epsom Rd., Mord. 93 D6
Epsom Rd., Sutt. 93 C7
Epstein Rd. SE28 71 A1
Epworth Rd., Islw. 73 E1
Epworth St. EC2 9 C6
Epworth St. EC2 59 A4
Erasmus St. SW1 19 J2
Erasmus St. SW1 67 D4
Erconwald St. W12 56 F6
Eresby Dr., Beck. 103 A1
Eresby Pl. NW6 48 D7
Eric Clo. E7 51 G4
Eric Rd. E7 51 G4
Eric Rd. NW10 47 F6
Church Rd.
Eric Rd., Rom. 44 D7
Eric St. E3 59 J4
Erica Gdns., Croy. 103 A3
Erica St. W12 56 G7
Ericcson Clo. SW18 75 D5
Eridge Rd. W4 65 D3
Erin Clo., Brom. 87 E7
Erindale SE18 70 G6
Erindale Ter. SE18 70 G6
Erith Cres., Rom. 44 J1
Erith Rd., Belv. 71 G5
Erith Rd., Bexh. 80 H4
Erith Rd., Erith 80 J1
Erlanger Rd. SE14 77 G1
Erlesmere Gdns. W13 64 D3
Ermine Clo., Houns. 72 C2
Ermine Ho. N17 33 C7
Ermine Rd. N15 41 C6
Ermine Rd. SE13 78 B4
Ermine Side, Enf. 25 D5
Ermington Rd. SE9 88 F2
Ernald Ave. E6 61 B2
Erncroft Way, 73 C6
Twick.
Ernest Ave. SE27 85 H4
Ernest Clo., Beck. 96 A5
Ernest Gdns. W4 65 B6
Ernest Gro., Beck. 95 J5
Ernest Rd., 92 B2
Kings.T.
Ernest Sq., 92 B2
Kings.T.
Ernest St. E1 59 G4
Ernle Rd. SW20 83 H7
Ernshaw Pl. SW15 75 B5
Carlton Dr.
Erpingham Rd. SW15 74 J3
Erridge Rd. SW19 93 D2
Errington Rd. W9 57 C4
Errol Gdns., Hayes 54 B4
Errol Gdns., N.Mal. 92 G4
Errol St. EC1 9 A6
Errol St. EC1 58 J4
Erskine Clo., Sutt. 100 H3
Erskine Cres. N17 41 E4
Erskine Hill NW11 39 D5
Erskine Ms. NW3 48 J7
Erskine Rd.
Erskine Rd. E17 41 J4
Erskine Rd. NW3 48 J7
Erskine Rd., Sutt. 100 G4
Erwood Rd. SE7 70 B5
Esam Way SW16 85 G5
Escot Way, Barn. 22 J5
Escott Gdns. SE9 88 B4
Escreet Gro. SE18 70 D4
Esher Ave., Rom. 44 J6
Esher Ave., Sutt. 100 A3
Esher Ave., Walt. 90 A6
Esher Bypass, 98 F4
Chess.
Esher Clo., Bex. 89 E1
Esher Gdns. SW19 84 A2
Esher Ms., Mitch. 93 J3
Esher Rd., E.Mol. 91 A6
Esher Rd., Ilf. 52 H3
Esk Rd. E13 60 G4
Eskdale Ave., Nthlt. 54 F1
Eskdale Clo., Wem. 46 G2
Eskdale Rd., Bexh. 80 G2
Eskmont Ridge SE19 86 B7

Esmar Cres. NW9 38 G7
Esme Ho. SW16 74 F4
Ludovick Wk.
Esmeralda Rd. SE1 21 J2
Esmeralda Rd. SE1 68 D4
Esmond Rd. NW6 57 C1
Esmond Rd. W4 65 D4
Esmond St. SW15 75 B4
Esparto St. SW18 75 E7
Essenden Rd., Belv. 71 G5
Essenden Rd., 102 B7
S.Croy.
Essendine Rd. W9 57 D3
Essex Ave., Islw. 73 B3
Essex Clo. E17 41 H4
Essex Clo., Mord. 93 A7
Essex Clo., Rom. 44 H4
Essex Clo., Ruis. 45 D1
Essex Ct. EC4 12 E4
Essex Ct. SW13 74 F2
Essex Gdns. N4 40 H6
Essex Gro. SE19 86 A6
Essex Ho. E14 60 B6
Giraud St.
Essex Pk. N3 31 E6
Essex Pk. Ms. W3 65 E1
Essex Pl. W4 65 C4
Essex Rd. E4 34 E1
Essex Rd. E10 42 C6
Essex Rd. E12 52 B5
Essex Rd. E17 41 H6
Essex Rd. E18 42 H2
Essex Rd. N1 58 H1
Essex Rd. NW10 47 E7
Essex Rd. W3 56 C7
Essex Rd. W4 65 D4
Belmont Rd.
Essex Rd., Bark. 52 G7
Essex Rd., Borwd. 22 A3
Essex Rd., Dag. 53 J5
Essex Rd., Enf. 25 A4
Essex Rd., Rom. 44 G4
Essex Rd., Rom. 44 C7
(Chadwell Heath)
Essex Rd. S. E11 42 D7
Essex St. E7 51 G5
Essex St. WC2 12 E5
Essex Twr. SE20 95 E1
Essex Vill. W8 66 D2
Essex Wf. E5 50 F2
Essian St. E1 59 H4
Essoldo Way, Edg. 37 J3
Estate Way E10 50 D1
Estcourt Rd. SE25 95 E6
Estcourt Rd. SW6 66 C7
Este Rd. SW11 75 H3
Estella Ave., 92 H4
N.Mal.
Estelle Rd. NW3 48 J4
Esterbrooke St. SW1 19 H2
Esterbrooke St. SW1 67 D4
Esther Clo. N21 24 G7
Esther Rd. E11 42 E7
Estreham Rd. SW16 85 D6
Estridge Clo., 72 G4
Houns.
Eswyn Rd. SW17 84 J4
Etchingham Pk. Rd. 31 E7
N3
Etchingham Rd. E15 51 C4
Eternit Wk. SW6 74 J1
Etfield Gro., Sid. 89 B5
Ethel Rd. E16 60 H6
Ethel St. SE17 21 A2
Ethelbert Clo., 96 G3
Brom.
Ethelbert Gdns., Ilf. 43 C5
Ethelbert Rd. SW20 93 A1
Ethelbert Rd., 96 G3
Brom.
Ethelbert Rd., Erith 71 J7
Hengist Rd.
Ethelbert St. SW12 85 B1
Fernlea Rd.
Ethelburga St. SW11 75 H1
Etheldene Ave. N10 40 C4
Etheridge Rd. NW2 38 J7
Etheridge Rd., 27 E2
Loug.
Etherley Rd. N15 40 J5
Etherow St. SE22 77 D6
Etherstone Grn. 85 G4
SW16
Etherstone Rd.
Etherstone Rd. SW16 85 G4
Ethnard Rd. SE15 68 E6
Ethronvi Rd., Bexh. 80 E3
Etloe Rd. E10 51 A2
Eton Ave. N12 31 F7
Eton Ave. NW3 48 G7
Eton Ave., Barn. 23 H6
Eton Ave., Houns. 63 F6

Eton Ave., N.Mal. 92 D5
Eton Ave., Wem. 46 E5
Eton College Rd. 48 J6
NW3
Eton Ct. NW3 48 G7
Eton Ave.
Eton Ct., Wem. 46 F4
Eton Ave.
Eton Garages NW3 48 H6
Lambolle Pl.
Eton Gro. NW9 38 A3
Eton Gro. SE13 78 E3
Eton Hall NW3 48 J6
Eton College Rd.
Eton Pl. NW3 49 A7
Eton Ave.
Eton Ri. NW3 48 J6
Eton College Rd.
Eton Rd. NW3 48 J7
Eton Rd., Ilf. 52 F5
Eton Rd., Rich. 73 H5
Eton Vill. NW3 48 J6
Etta St. SE8 68 H6
Ettrick St. E14 60 C6
Etwell Pl., Surb. 91 J6
Eugenia Rd. SE16 68 F4
Eureka Rd., Kings.T. 92 A2
Washington Rd.
Europa Pl. EC1 8 J4
Europe Rd. SE18 70 C3
Eustace Rd. E6 61 B3
Eustace Rd. SW6 66 D7
Eustace Rd., Rom. 44 D7
Euston Gro. NW1 7 H4
Euston Gro. NW1 58 D3
Euston Rd. NW1 7 E6
Euston Rd. NW1 58 B4
Euston Rd., Croy. 101 G1
Euston Sq. NW1 7 H4
Euston Sq. NW1 58 D3
Euston Sta. 7 H4
Colonnade NW1
Euston St. NW1 7 G4
Euston St. NW1 58 C3
Eva Rd., Rom. 44 C7
Evandale Rd. SW9 76 G2
Evangelist Rd. NW5 49 B4
Evans Clo. E8 50 C6
Buttermere Wk.
Evans Gro., Felt. 81 G2
Evans Rd. SE6 87 E2
Evanston Ave. E4 34 C7
Evanston Gdns., Ilf. 43 B6
Eve Rd. E11 51 E4
Eve Rd. E15 60 E2
Eve Rd. N17 41 B3
Eve Rd., Islw. 73 D4
Evelina Rd. SE15 77 F3
Evelina Rd. SE20 86 G7
Eveline Lowe Est. 17 H6
SE16
Eveline Lowe Est. 68 D3
SE16
Eveline Rd., Mitch. 93 J1
Evelyn Ave. NW9 38 D3
Evelyn Clo., Twick. 72 H7
Evelyn Ct. N1 9 B2
Evelyn Dennington 61 C5
Rd. E6
Evelyn Dr., Pnr. 28 D7
Evelyn Fox Ct. W10 56 J5
Evelyn Gdns. SW7 18 E4
Evelyn Gdns. SW7 66 G5
Evelyn Gdns., Rich. 73 H4
Kew Rd.
Evelyn Gro. W5 64 J1
Evelyn Gro., Sthl. 54 F6
Evelyn Rd. E17 42 C4
Evelyn Rd. SW19 84 E5
Evelyn Rd. W4 65 D3
Evelyn Rd., Barn. 23 J4
Evelyn Rd., Rich. 73 H3
Evelyn St. SE8 68 H5
Evelyn Ter., Rich. 73 H3
Evelyn Wk. N1 9 B2
Evelyn Wk. N1 59 A2
Evelyn Way, Walt. 101 D4
Evelyn Yd. W1 11 H3
Evening Hill, Beck. 87 C7
Evenwood Clo. 75 B5
SW15
Everard Ave., Brom. 103 G1
Everard Way, Wem. 46 H3
Everatt Clo. SW18 75 C6
Amerland Rd.
Everdon Rd. SW13 65 G6
Everest Pl. E14 60 C5
Everest Rd. SE9 79 C5
Everett Wk., Belv. 71 F5
Osborne Rd.
Everglade Strand 38 F1
NW9
Everilda St. N1 58 F1

Evering Rd. E5 50 D3
Evering Rd. N16 50 D3
Everington Rd. N10 39 J2
Everington St. W6 66 A6
Everitt Rd. NW10 56 D3
Everleigh St. N4 49 F1
Eversfield Gdns. 30 E6
  NW7
Eversfield Rd., 73 J2
  Rich.
Eversholt St. NW1 7 G1
Evershot Rd. N4 58 C2
Evershot Rd. N4 49 F1
Eversleigh Rd. E6 61 A1
Eversleigh Rd. N3 31 C7
Eversleigh Rd. SW11 75 J3
Eversleigh Rd., 23 F5
  Barn.
Eversley Ave., Wem. 47 A2
Eversley Clo. N21 24 F6
Eversley Cres. N21 24 F6
Eversley Cres., 73 A1
  Islw.
Eversley Mt. N21 24 F6
Eversley Pk. SW19 83 H5
Eversley Pk. Rd. 24 F6
  N21
Eversley Rd. SE7 69 H6
Eversley Rd. SE19 86 A7
Eversley Rd., Surb. 91 J4
Eversley Way, Croy. 103 A4
Everthorpe Rd. SE15 77 C3
Everton Bldgs. NW1 7 F1
Everton Dr., Stan. 37 J3
Everton Rd., Croy. 102 D1
Evesham Ave. E17 42 A2
Evesham Clo., Grnf. 54 H2
Evesham Clo., Sutt. 100 D7
Evesham Grn., Mord. 93 E6
Evesham Rd. E15 51 F7
Evesham Rd. N11 32 C5
Evesham Rd., Felt. 72 C7
  Sparrow Fm. Dr.
Evesham Rd., Mord. 93 E6
Evesham St. W11 57 A7
Evesham Wk. SE5 77 A2
  Love Wk.
Evesham Wk. SW9 76 G2
Evesham Way SW11 76 A3
Evesham Way, Ilf. 43 D3
Evry Rd., Sid. 89 C6
Ewald Rd. SW6 75 C2
Ewanrigg Ter., 34 J5
  Wdf.Grn.
Ewart Rd. N22 40 G1
Ewart Pl. E3 59 J2
Ewart Rd. SE23 77 G7
Ewe Clo. N7 49 E6
Ewell Bypass, 99 G6
  Epsom
Ewell Ct. Ave., 99 E5
  Epsom
Ewell Pk. Way, 99 G6
  Epsom
Ewell Rd., Surb. 91 H5
Ewell Rd., Surb. 91 E7
  (Long Ditton),
Ewell Rd., Sutt. 100 A7
Ewellhurst Rd., Ilf. 43 B2
Ewelme Rd. SE23 86 F1
Ewen Cres. SW2 76 G7
Ewer St. SE1 16 J2
Ewer St. SE1 67 J1
Ewhurst Ho. E1 59 F5
  Jamaica St.
Ewhurst Rd. SE4 77 J6
Exbury Rd. SE6 87 A2
Excel Ct. WC2 11 A6
Excelsior Clo., 92 A2
  Kings.T.
  Washington Rd.
Excelsior Gdns. 78 C2
  SE13
Exchange Arc. EC2 13 E1
Exchange Arc. EC2 59 B5
Exchange Ct. WC2 12 B6
Exchange Pl. EC2 13 D1
Exchange Pl. EC2 59 B5
Exchange Sq. EC2 13 D1
Exchange Sq. EC2 59 B5
Exeter Clo. E6 61 C6
  Harper Rd.
Exeter Gdns., Ilf. 52 B1
Exeter Ho. SW15 74 J6
  Putney Heath
Exeter Ms. NW6 48 E6
  West Hampstead Ms.
Exeter Rd. E16 60 G5
Exeter Rd. E17 42 A5
Exeter Rd. N9 33 F2
Exeter Rd. N14 32 B1
Exeter Rd. NW2 48 B5
Exeter Rd. SE15 77 C1

Exeter Rd., Croy. 95 B7
Exeter Rd., Dag. 53 H6
Exeter Rd., Enf. 25 G3
Exeter Rd., Felt. 81 F3
Exeter Rd., Har. 45 E2
Exeter Rd., Well. 79 J2
Exeter St. WC2 12 B5
Exeter St. WC2 58 E7
Exeter Way SE14 68 J7
Exford Gdns. SE12 87 H1
Exford Rd. SE12 87 H2
Exhibition Clo. W12 56 J7
Exhibition Rd. SW7 14 F5
Exhibition Rd. SW7 66 G2
Exmoor Clo., Ilf. 43 F1
Exmoor St. W10 57 A5
Exmouth Mkt. EC1 8 E5
Exmouth Mkt. EC1 58 G4
Exmouth Ms. NW1 7 G4
Exmouth Pl. E8 50 E7
Exmouth Rd. E17 41 J5
Exmouth Rd., Brom. 96 H3
Exmouth Rd., Ruis. 45 C3
Exmouth Rd., Well. 80 C1
Exmouth St. E1 59 F6
  Commercial Rd.
Exning Rd. E16 60 F4
Exon St. SE17 21 D2
Exon St. SE17 68 B4
Express Dr., Ilf. 53 B1
Exton Cres. NW10 47 C7
Exton Gdns., Dag. 53 C5
Exton St. SE1 16 E3
Exton St. SE1 67 G1
Eyhurst Clo. NW2 47 G2
Eylewood Rd. SE27 85 J5
Eynella Rd. SE22 77 C7
Eynham Rd. W12 56 J6
Eynsford Clo., Orp. 97 F7
Eynsford Cres., 89 C1
  Bex.
Eynsford Rd., Ilf. 52 H2
Eynsham Dr. SE2 71 A4
Eynswood Dr., Sid. 89 B5
Eyot Gdns. W6 65 F5
Eyot Grn. W4 65 F6
  Chiswick Mall
Eyre Ct. NW8 6 E1
Eyre St. Hill EC1 8 E6
Eythorne Rd. SW9 76 G1
Ezra St. E2 9 G3
Ezra St. E2 59 C3

F

Faber Gdns. NW4 38 G5
Fabian Rd. SW6 66 C7
Fabian St. E6 61 C4
Factory La. N17 41 C2
Factory La., Croy. 101 G1
Factory Pl. E14 69 B5
Factory Rd. E16 70 B1
Factory Sq. SW16 85 E6
Factory Yd. W7 64 B1
  Uxbridge Rd.
Faggs Rd., Felt. 72 A5
Fair Acres, Brom. 96 G5
Fair St. SE1 17 E3
Fair St., Houns. 72 J3
  High St.
Fairacre, N.Mal. 92 E3
Fairacres SW15 74 G5
Fairbairn Grn. SW9 76 G1
Fairbank Ave., Orp. 104 E2
Fairbanks Rd. N17 41 C3
Fairbourne Rd. N17 41 B3
Fairbridge Rd. N19 49 D2
Fairbrook Clo. N13 32 G5
Fairbrook Rd. N13 32 G6
Fairburn Clo., 22 A1
  Borwd.
Fairburn Ct. SW15 75 B5
  Mercier Rd.
Fairby Rd. SE12 78 H5
Fairchild Pl. EC2 9 E6
Fairchild St. EC2 9 E6
Fairclough St. E1 13 J4
Fairclough St. E1 59 D6
Faircross Ave., 52 F6
  Bark.
Fairdale Gdns. SW15 74 H4
Fairdale Gdns., 63 A2
  Hayes
Fairfax Gdns. SE3 78 J1
Fairfax Pl. NW6 48 F7
Fairfax Rd. N8 40 G4
Fairfax Rd. NW6 48 F7
Fairfax Rd. W4 65 E3
Fairfax Rd., Tedd. 82 D6
Fairfield Ave. NW4 38 H6
Fairfield Ave., 30 B6
  Edg.
Fairfield Ave., Twick. 81 H1

Fairfield Ave., Wat. 28 C3
Fairfield Clo. N12 31 F4
Fairfield Clo., 99 E5
  Epsom
Fairfield Clo., 84 H7
  Mitch.
Fairfield Clo., Sid. 79 J6
Fairfield Cres., Edg. 30 B6
Fairfield Ct. NW10 56 G1
Fairfield Cres., Edg. 30 B6
Fairfield Dr. SW18 75 E5
Fairfield Dr., 55 F1
  Grnf.
Fairfield Dr., Har. 36 J3
Fairfield E., 91 H2
  Kings.T.
Fairfield Gdns. N8 40 E5
  Elder Ave.
Fairfield Gro. SE7 70 A6
Fairfield Ind. 92 A3
  Est., Kings.T.
Fairfield N., 91 H2
  Kings.T.
Fairfield Path, 102 A3
  Croy.
Fairfield Pl., 91 H3
  Kings.T.
Fairfield Rd. E3 60 A2
Fairfield Rd. E17 41 H2
Fairfield Rd. N8 40 E5
Fairfield Rd. N18 33 D4
Fairfield Rd. W7 64 D3
  Southdown Ave.
Fairfield Rd., Beck. 90 A2
Fairfield Rd., Bexh. 80 F2
Fairfield Rd., 87 G7
  Brom.
Fairfield Rd., 102 B3
  Croy.
Fairfield Rd., Ilf. 52 E6
Fairfield Rd., 91 H2
  Kings.T.
Fairfield Rd., Orp. 97 G6
Fairfield Rd., 54 F6
  Sthl.
Fairfield Rd., 34 G6
  Wdf.Grn.
Fairfield S., 91 H3
  Kings.T.
Fairfield St. SW18 75 E5
Fairfield Way, 23 D5
  Barn.
Fairfield Way, 99 E5
  Epsom
Fairfield W., 91 H2
  Kings.T.
Fairfields Clo. NW9 38 C5
Fairfields Cres. NW9 38 C5
Fairfields Rd., 72 J3
  Houns.
Fairfoot Rd. E3 60 A4
Fairford Ave., 95 G5
  Croy.
Fairford Clo., 95 G5
  Croy.
Fairford Gdns., 99 F2
  Wor.Pk.
Fairgreen, Barn. 23 J3
Fairgreen E., Barn. 23 J3
Fairgreen Rd., 94 H5
  Th.Hth.
Fairhaven Ave., 95 G6
  Croy.
Fairhaven Cres., 28 A3
  Wat.
Fairhazel Gdns. NW6 48 E6
Fairholme Clo. N3 39 B4
Fairholme Gdns. N3 39 B3
Fairholme Rd. W14 66 B5
Fairholme Rd., 94 G7
  Croy.
Fairholme Rd., Har. 37 C5
Fairholme Rd., Ilf. 43 C7
Fairholme Rd., 100 C6
  Sutt.
Fairholt Clo. N16 50 B1
  Fairholt Rd.
Fairholt Rd. N16 50 A1
Fairholt St. SW7 14 H5
Fairland Rd. E15 51 F6
Fairlands Ave., 34 G2
  Buck.H.
Fairlands Ave., 100 D2
  Sutt.
Fairlands Ave., 94 F4
  Th.Hth.
Fairlands Ct. SE9 79 D6
  North Pk.
Fairlawn SE7 69 J6
Fairlawn Ave. N2 39 H4
Fairlawn Ave. W4 65 C4
Fairlawn Ave., 80 D2
  Bexh.
Fairlawn Clo. N14 24 C6

Fairlawn Clo., 98 C6
  Esher
Fairlawn Clo., 81 F4
  Felt.
Fairlawn Clo., 83 C6
  Kings.T.
Fairlawn Dr., 34 G7
  Wdf.Grn.
Fairlawn Gdns., 54 F7
  Sthl.
Fairlawn Gro. W4 65 C4
Fairlawn Pk. SE26 86 H5
Fairlawn Rd. SW19 84 C7
Fairlawns, Sun. 90 A3
Fairlawns, Twick. 73 F6
Fairlea Pl. W5 55 F5
Fairlie Gdns. SE23 77 F7
Fairlight Ave. E4 34 D2
Fairlight Ave. NW10 56 F2
Fairlight Ave., 34 G6
  Wdf.Grn.
Fairlight Clo. E4 34 D2
Fairlight Clo., 99 J4
  Wor.Pk.
Fairlight Rd. SW17 84 G4
Fairlop Gdns., Ilf. 35 F7
Fairlop Rd. E11 42 D7
Fairlop Rd., Ilf. 43 F2
Fairmead, Brom. 97 C4
Fairmead, Surb. 99 B1
Fairmead Clo., 97 C4
  Brom.
Fairmead Clo., 62 D7
  Houns.
Fairmead Clo., 92 D3
  N.Mal.
Fairmead Cres., Edg. 30 C3
Fairmead Gdns., Ilf. 43 B5
Fairmead Rd. N19 49 D3
Fairmead Rd., Croy. 101 F1
Fairmead Rd., Loug. 26 H5
Fairmead Side, 26 J5
  Loug.
Fairmile Ave. SW16 85 D5
Fairmont Clo., 71 F5
  Belv.
  Lullingstone Rd.
Fairmount Rd. SW2 76 F6
Fairoak Clo., Orp. 97 E7
Fairoak Dr. SE9 79 G5
Fairseat Clo. 29 B2
  (Bushey), Wat.
  Hive Rd.
Fairstead Wk. N1 58 J1
  Popham Rd.
Fairthorn Rd. SE7 69 G5
Fairview Ave., Wem. 46 G6
Fairview Clo. E17 41 H1
Fairview Clo., 35 H4
  Chig.
Fairview Cres., 45 G1
  Har.
Fairview Dr., Chig. 35 H4
Fairview Dr., Orp. 104 G4
Fairview Gdns., 42 H1
  Wdf.Grn.
Fairview Pl. SW2 76 F7
Fairview Rd. N15 41 C5
Fairview Rd. SW16 94 F1
Fairview Rd., Chig. 35 H4
Fairview Rd., Enf. 24 G1
Fairview Rd., Sutt. 100 G5
Fairview Way, Edg. 30 A4
Fairwater Ave., Well. 80 A4
Fairway SW20 92 J3
Fairway, Bexh. 80 E5
Fairway, Orp. 97 G5
Fairway, Wdf.Grn. 34 J5
Fairway, The N13 32 J3
Fairway, The N14 24 B6
Fairway, The NW7 30 D3
Fairway, The W3 56 E6
Fairway, The, Barn. 23 E6
Fairway, The, Brom. 97 C5
Fairway, The, 92 D1
  N.Mal.
Fairway, The, 45 J6
  Nthlt.
Fairway, The, Ruis. 45 C4
Fairway, The, Wem. 46 E3
Fairway, The, 90 H3
  W.Mol.
Fairway Ave. NW9 38 B3
Fairway Ave., 22 B2
  Borwd.
Fairway Clo. NW11 39 F7
Fairway Clo., Beck. 90 D6
Fairway Clo., Croy. 95 H5
Fairway Clo., Epsom 99 C4
Fairway Clo., 72 C5
  Houns.
Fairway Ct. NW7 30 D3
  The Fairway

Fairway Dr., Grnf. 45 H7
Fairway Est., Grnf. 45 J7
Fairway Gdns., Ilf. 52 F5
Fairways, Stan. 37 H2
Fairways, Tedd. 82 G7
Fairweather Clo. 41 B4
N15
Fairweather Rd. N16 41 D6
Fairwyn Rd. SE26 86 H4
Fakenham Clo., 45 G6
Nthlt.
Goodwood Dr.
Fakruddin St. E1 9 J6
Fakruddin St. E1 59 D4
Falcon Ave., Brom. 97 B4
Falcon Clo. SE1 16 H1
Falcon Cres., Enf. 25 G5
Falcon Gro. SW11 75 H3
Falcon Rd. W13 55 C4
Falcon La. SW11 75 H3
Falcon Rd. SW11 75 H2
Falcon Rd., Enf. 25 G5
Falcon Rd., Hmptn. 81 F7
Falcon St. E13 60 F4
Falcon Ter. SW11 75 H3
Falcon Trd. Est. 47 E4
NW10
Falcon Way E11 42 G4
Falcon Way E14 69 B4
Falcon Way NW9 38 E2
Falcon Way, Felt. 72 B5
Falcon Way, Har. 37 H6
Falconberg Ct. W1 11 J3
Falconberg Ms. W1 11 H3
Falconer Wk. N7 49 F2
Newington Barrow Way
Falconwood Ave., 79 G2
Well.
Falconwood Par., 79 H4
Well.
Falcourt Clo., Sutt. 100 E5
Falkirk Gdns., Har. 28 D5
Blackford Rd.
Falkirk Ho. W9 6 B3
Falkirk Ho. W9 57 E3
Falkirk St. N1 9 E2
Falkirk St. N1 59 B2
Falkland Ave. N3 31 D7
Falkland Ave. N11 32 A4
Falkland Pk. Ave. 95 B3
SE25
Falkland Rd. N8 40 G4
Falkland Rd. NW5 49 C5
Falkland Rd., Barn. 23 B2
Fallaize Ave., Ilf. 52 E4
Riverdene Rd.
Falloden Way NW11 39 D4
Fallow Clo., Chig. 35 J5
Fallow Ct. Ave. N12 31 F7
Fallowfield, Stan. 29 D4
Fallowfield Ct., Stan. 29 D3
Stanmore Hill
Fallsbrook Rd. SW16 85 B6
Falmer Rd. E17 42 B3
Falmer Rd. N15 40 J5
Falmer Rd., Enf. 25 B4
Falmouth Ave. E4 34 D7
Falmouth Clo. N22 32 F7
Truro Rd.
Falmouth Clo. SE12 78 F5
Falmouth Gdns., Ilf. 43 A4
Falmouth Rd. SE1 17 A6
Falmouth Rd. SE1 67 J3
Falmouth St. E15 51 D5
Fambridge Clo. SE26 86 J4
Fambridge Rd., Dag. 53 G1
Fane St. W14 66 C6
North End Rd.
Fann St. EC1 8 J6
Fann St. EC1 58 J4
Fanshaw St. N1 9 D3
Fanshaw St. N1 59 B3
Fanshawe Ave., Bark. 52 F6
Fanshawe Cres. 53 E5
Dag.
Fanshawe Rd., Rich. 82 F4
Fanthorpe St. SW15 74 J3
Faraday Ave., Sid. 89 A2
Faraday Clo. N7 49 F6
Bride St.
Faraday Rd. E15 51 F6
Faraday Rd. SW19 84 D6
Faraday Rd. W3 56 C7
Faraday Rd. W10 57 B5
Faraday Rd., Sthl. 54 H7
Faraday Rd., Well. 80 A3
Faraday Rd., W.Mol. 90 G4
Faraday Way SE18 70 A3
Faraday Way, Croy. 101 F1
Ampere Way
Fareham Rd., Felt. 72 C7
Fareham St. W1 11 H3

Farewell Pl., 93 H1
Mitch.
Faringdon Ave., 97 D7
Brom.
Faringford Rd. E15 51 E7
Farjeon Rd. SE3 79 A1
Farleigh Ave., Brom. 96 F6
Farleigh Pl. N16 50 C4
Farleigh Rd.
Farleigh Rd. N16 50 C4
Farley Dr., Ilf. 52 H1
Farley Pl. SE25 95 D4
Farley Rd. SE6 78 C7
Farley Rd., S.Croy. 102 D7
Farlington Pl. SW15 74 H7
Roehampton La.
Farlow Rd. SW15 74 J3
Farlton Rd. SW18 75 E7
Farm Ave. NW2 48 B3
Farm Ave. SW16 85 E4
Farm Ave., Har. 36 F7
Farm Ave., Wem. 46 F6
Farm Clo., Barn. 22 H5
Farm Clo., Buck.H. 34 J3
Farm Clo., Dag. 53 J7
Farm Clo., Sthl. 54 H7
Farm Clo., Sutt. 100 G7
Farm Clo., W.Wick. 103 E3
Farm Ct. NW4 38 G3
Farm Dr., Croy. 102 J2
Farm End E4 26 E5
Farm La. N14 24 A6
Farm La. SW6 66 D6
Farm La., Croy. 102 J2
Farm Pl. W8 66 D1
Uxbridge St.
Farm Rd. N21 32 J1
Farm Rd., Edg. 30 B6
Farm Rd., Houns. 81 E1
Farm Rd., Mord. 93 E5
Farm Rd., Sutt. 100 G7
Farm St. W1 11 D6
Farm St. W1 58 B7
Farm Vale, Bex. 80 H6
Farm Wk. NW11 34 J3
Farm Way, Buck.H. 34 J4
Farm Way, Wor.Pk. 99 J7
Wayfarer Rd.
Farmborough Clo., 37 A7
Har.
Pool Rd.
Farmcote Rd. SE12 87 G1
Farmdale Rd. SE10 69 G5
Farmdale Rd., Cars. 100 H7
Farmer Rd. E10 51 B1
Farmer St. W8 66 D1
Uxbridge St.
Farmers Rd. SE5 67 H7
Farmfield Rd., 87 E5
Brom.
Farmhouse Rd. 85 C7
SW16
Farmilo Rd. E17 41 J7
Farmington Ave., 100 G3
Sutt.
Farmland Wk., Chis. 88 E5
Farmlands, Enf. 24 G1
Farmlands, Pnr. 36 A4
Farmlands, The, 45 G6
Nthlt.
Moat Fm. Rd.
Farmleigh N14 24 C7
Farmstead Rd. SE6 78 B4
Farmstead Rd., Har. 37 A1
Farmway, Dag. 53 C3
Farnaby Rd. SE9 78 J4
Farnaby Rd., Brom. 87 D7
Farnan Ave. E17 42 A2
Farnan Rd. SW16 85 E5
Farnborough Ave. 41 H3
E17
Farnborough Ave. 102 G7
S.Croy.
Farnborough Clo., 47 B2
Wem.
Chalkhill Rd.
Farnborough 104 C3
Common, Orp.
Farnborough Cres. 103 F1
Brom.
Saville Row
Farnborough Hill, 104 G5
Orp.
**Farnborough Way 21 E7
SE15**
Farnborough Way, 104 E5
Orp.
Farncombe St. SE16 17 J4
Farncombe St. SE16 68 D2
Farndale Ave. N13 32 H3
Farndale Cres, 54 J3
Grnf.

Farnell Ms. SW5 18 A3
Farnell Rd., Islw. 73 A4
Farnham Clo. N20 23 F7
Farnham Gdns. 92 H2
SW20
Farnham Pl. SE1 16 H2
Farnham Rd., Ilf. 43 J7
Farnham Rd., Well. 80 C2
Farnham Royal SE11 20 D4
Farnham Royal SE11 67 F5
Farningham Rd. N17 33 D7
Farnley Rd. E4 26 E7
Farnley Rd. SE25 95 A4
Faro Clo., Brom. 97 D2
Faroe Rd. W14 66 A3
Farorna Wk., Enf. 24 G1
Farquhar Rd. SE19 86 C5
Farquhar Rd. SW19 84 D3
Farquharson Rd., 101 J1
Croy.
Farr Ave., Bark. 62 A2
Farr Rd., Enf. 25 A1
Farrance Rd., Rom. 44 E6
Farrance St. E14 60 A6
Farrans Ct., Har. 37 E7
Farrant Ave. N22 40 G2
Farrell Ho. E1 59 F6
Devonport St.
Farren Rd. SE23 86 H2
Farrer Ms. N8 40 C4
Farrer Rd.
Farrer Rd. N8 40 C4
Farrer Rd., Har. 37 H5
Farrier Clo., Sun. 90 A4
Farrier Rd., Nthlt. 54 G2
Farrier St. NW1 49 B7
Farriers Way, 22 D5
Borwd.
Farringdon La. EC1 8 F6
Farringdon La. EC1 58 G4
Farringdon Rd. EC1 8 E5
Farringdon Rd. EC1 58 G4
Farringdon St. EC4 12 G3
Farringdon St. EC4 58 H5
Farrington Pl., Chis. 88 G7
Farrins Rents SE16 68 H1
Farrow La. SE14 68 F7
Farrow Pl. SE16 68 H3
Ropemaker Rd.
Farthing All. SE1 17 H4
Farthing Flds. E1 68 E1
Raine St.
Farthing St., Orp. 104 C7
Farthings, The, 92 A1
Kings.T.
Brunswick Rd.
Farthings Clo. E4 34 E3
Farthings Clo., Pnr. 36 B6
Farwell Rd., Sid. 89 B3
Farwig La., Brom. 96 F1
Fashion St. E1 13 G2
Fashion St. E1 59 C5
Fashoda Rd., Brom. 96 J4
Fassett Rd. E8 50 D6
Fassett Rd., 91 H4
Kings.T.
Fassett Sq. E8 50 D6
Fauconberg Rd. W4 65 C6
Faulkner Clo., Dag. 44 D7
Faulkner St. SE14 77 F1
Faulkner's All. EC1 12 G1
Fauna Clo., Rom. 44 C6
Favart Rd. SW6 75 D1
Faversham Ave. E4 34 E1
Faversham Ave., 24 H6
Enf.
Faversham Rd. SE6 77 J7
Faversham Rd., 95 J2
Beck.
Faversham Rd., 93 E6
Mord.
Fawcett Clo. SW11 75 G2
Fawcett Est. E5 50 D1
Fawcett Rd. NW10 47 F7
Fawcett Rd., Croy. 101 J3
Fawcett St. SW10 18 C6
Fawcett St. SW10 66 E6
Fawcus Clo., Esher 98 C6
Dalmore Ave.
Fawe Pk. Rd. SW15 75 C4
Fawe St. E14 60 B5
Fawley Rd. NW6 48 E5
Fawn Rd. E13 60 J2
Fawn Rd., Chig. 35 J5
Fawnbrake Ave. SE24 76 H5
Fawood Ave. NW10 47 D7
Faygate Cres., 80 G5
Bexh.
Faygate Rd. SW2 85 F2
Fayland Ave. SW16 85 C5
Fearnley Cres., 81 E5
Hmptn.

Fearon St. SE10 69 G5
Featherbed La., 102 J7
Croy.
Feathers Pl. SE10 69 D6
Featherstone Ave. 86 E2
SE23
Featherstone Gdns., 22 C4
Borwd.
Featherstone Ind. 63 E2
Est., Sthl.
Featherstone Rd. 30 H6
NW7
Featherstone Rd., 63 E3
Sthl.
Featherstone St. EC1 9 B5
Featherstone St. 59 A4
EC1
Featherstone Ter., 63 E3
Sthl.
Featley Rd. SW9 76 H3
Federal Rd., Grnf. 55 F2
Federation Rd. SE2 71 B4
Fee Fm. Rd., Esher 98 C7
Felbridge Ave., 37 D1
Stan.
Felbridge Clo. SW16 85 G4
Felbridge Rd., Ilf. 52 J2
Felday Rd. SE13 78 B6
Felden Clo., Pnr. 28 E7
Felden St. SW6 75 C1
Feldman Clo. N16 50 D1
Oldhill St.
Felgate Ms. W6 65 H4
Felhampton Rd. SE9 88 E2
Felhurst Cres., 53 H4
Dag.
Felix Ave. N8 40 E6
Felix Rd. W13 55 D7
Felix Rd., Walt. 90 A6
Felix St. E2 59 E2
Hackney Rd.
Felixstowe Rd. N9 33 D3
Felixstowe Rd. N17 41 C3
Felixstowe Rd. 56 H3
NW10
Felixstowe Rd. SE2 71 B3
Fell Rd., Croy. 101 J3
Fell Wk., Edg. 38 B1
East Rd.
Fellbrigg Rd. SE22 77 C5
Fellbrigg St. E1 59 E4
Headlam St.
Fellbrook, Rich. 82 E3
Fellowes Clo., 54 D4
Hayes
Paddington Clo.
Fellowes Rd., Cars. 100 H3
Fellows Ct. E2 9 F2
Fellows Rd. NW3 48 G7
Felltram Way SE7 69 G4
Felmersham Clo. 76 D4
SW4
Haselrigge Rd.
Felmingham Rd. 95 F2
SE20
Fels Clo., Dag. 53 H3
Fels Fm. Ave., Dag. 53 J3
Felsberg Rd. SW2 76 E6
Felsham Rd. SW15 75 A3
Felspar Clo. SE18 70 J5
Felstead Ave., Ilf. 43 D1
Felstead Gdns. E14 69 C5
Ferry St.
Felstead Rd. E11 42 G7
Felstead Rd., Loug. 27 B7
Felstead St. E9 50 J6
Felsted Rd. E16 61 A6
Feltham Ave., 91 B4
E.Mol.
Feltham Rd., Mitch. 93 J3
Felthambrook Ind. 81 B3
Est., Felt.
Felthambrook Way, 81 B3
Felt.
Felthamhill Rd., 81 A4
Felt.
Felton Clo., Orp. 97 E6
Felton Lea, Sid. 88 J5
Felton Rd. W13 64 F2
Camborne Ave.
Felton Rd., Bark. 61 H2
Sutton Rd.
Felton St. N1 59 A1
Fen Ct. EC3 13 D5
Fen Gro., Sid. 79 J6
Fen St. E16 60 F7
Caxton St. N.
Fencepiece Rd., 35 F5
Chig.
Fencepiece Rd., 35 F6
Ilf.
Fenchurch Ave. EC3 13 D4
Fenchurch Ave. EC3 59 B6

Fenchurch Bldgs. EC3	13	E4
Fenchurch Pl. EC3	13	E5
Fenchurch St. EC3	13	D5
Fenchurch St. EC3	59	B7
Fendall Rd., Epsom	99	C5
Fendall St. SE1	17	E6
Fendall St. SE1	68	B3
Fendt Clo. E16	60	F7
Bowman Clo.		
Fendyke Rd., Belv.	71	D3
Fenelon Pl. W14	66	C4
Fenham Rd. SE15	68	D7
Fenman Ct. N17	41	E1
Shelbourne Rd.		
Fenman Gdns., Ilf.	53	B1
Fenn Clo., Brom.	87	G6
Fenn St. E9	50	F5
Fennel Clo., Croy.	102	G1
Primrose La.		
Fennel St. SE18	70	D6
Fenner Clo. SE16	68	E4
Layard Rd.		
Fenner Sq. SW11	75	G3
Thomas Baines Rd.		
Fenning St. SE1	17	D3
Fenstanton Ave. N12	31	G6
Fentiman Rd. SW8	20	C6
Fentiman Rd. SW8	67	E6
Fenton Clo. E8	50	C6
Laurel St.		
Fenton Clo. SW9	76	F2
Fenton Clo. Chis.	88	C6
Fenton Rd. N17	32	J7
Fentons Ave. E13	60	H2
Fenwick Clo. SE18	70	D6
Ritter St.		
Fenwick Gro. SE15	77	D3
Fenwick Pl. SW9	76	E3
Fenwick Rd. SE15	77	D3
Ferdinand Pl. NW1	49	A7
Ferdinand Rd.		
Ferdinand St. NW1	49	A7
Fergus Rd. N5	49	H5
Calabria Rd.		
Ferguson Ave., Surb.	91	J5
Ferguson Clo., Brom.	96	D3
Ferguson Dr. W3	56	D6
Ferme Pk. Rd. N4	40	F7
Ferme Pk. Rd. N8	40	E5
Fermor Rd. SE23	86	H1
Fermoy Rd. W9	57	C4
Fermoy Rd., Grnf.	54	H4
Fern Ave., Mitch.	94	D4
Fern Dene W13	55	E5
Templewood		
Fern Gro., Felt.	72	B7
Fern La., Houns.	63	F5
Fern St. E3	60	A4
Fernbank, Buck.H.	34	H1
Fernbank Ave., Walt.	90	E7
Fernbank Ave., Wem.	46	C4
Fernbrook Ave., Sid.	79	H5
Blackfen Rd.		
Fernbrook Cres. SE13	78	E6
Fernbrook Rd.		
Fernbrook Dr., Har.	36	H7
Fernbrook Rd. SE13	78	E6
Ferncliff Rd. E8	50	D5
Ferncroft Ave. N12	31	H6
Ferncroft Ave. NW3	48	D3
Ferncroft Ave., Ruis.	45	C2
Ferndale, Brom.	96	J2
Ferndale Ave. E17	42	D5
Ferndale Ave., Houns.	72	E3
Ferndale Ct. SE3	69	F7
Ferndale Rd. E7	51	H7
Ferndale Rd. E11	51	E2
Ferndale Rd. N15	41	C6
Ferndale Rd. SE25	95	E5
Ferndale Rd. SW4	76	F4
Ferndale Rd. SW9	76	E4
Ferndale Rd., Rom.	44	J2
Ferndale St. E6	61	E7
Ferndale Ter., Har.	37	C4
Ferndale Way, Orp.	104	G5
Fernden Way, Rom.	44	H6
Ferndene Rd. SE24	76	J4
Ferndown, Nthwd.	36	A2
Ferndown Ave., Orp.	104	G5
Ferndown Clo., Pnr.	28	E7
Ferndown Clo., Sutt.	100	G6
Ferndown Rd. SE9	79	A7
Ferndown Rd., Wat.	28	C3
Ferney Rd., Barn.	24	A7
Fernhall Dr., Ilf.	43	A5
Fernham Rd., Th.Hth.	94	J3
Fernhead Rd. W9	57	C3
Fernhill Ct. E17	42	D2
Fernhill Gdns., Kings.T.	82	G5
Fernhill St. E16	70	C1
Fernholme Rd. SE15	77	G5
Fernhurst Gdns., Edg.	30	A6
Fernhurst Rd. SW6	75	B1
Fernhurst Rd., Croy.	95	D7
Fernlea Rd. SW12	85	B1
Fernlea Rd., Mitch.	94	A2
Fernleigh Clo., Croy.	101	G4
Stafford Rd.		
Fernleigh Ct., Har.	36	H2
Fernleigh Ct., Wem.	46	H2
Fernleigh Rd. N21	32	G2
Ferns Rd E15	51	F6
Fernsbury St. WC1	8	E4
Fernshaw Rd. SW10	18	C6
Fernshaw Rd. SW10	66	F6
Fernside NW11	48	D2
Finchley Rd.		
Fernside, Buck.H.	34	H1
Fernside Ave. NW7	30	D3
Fernside Ave., Felt.	81	B4
Fernside Rd. SW12	84	J1
Fernthorpe Rd. SW16	85	C6
Ferntower Rd. N5	50	A5
Fernways, Ilf.	52	E4
Fernwood Ave. SW16	85	D4
Fernwood Ave., Wem.	46	F5
Bridgewater Rd.		
Fernwood Clo., Brom.	96	J2
Fernwood Cres. N20	31	J3
Ferranti Clo. SE18	70	A3
Ferraro Clo., Houns.	63	G6
Ferrers Ave., Wall.	101	D4
Ferrers Rd. SW16	85	D5
Ferrestone Rd. N8	40	F4
Ferriby Clo. N1	49	G7
Bewdley St.		
Ferrier Pt. E16	60	H5
Forty Acre La.		
Ferrier St. SW18	75	E4
Ferring Clo., Har.	45	J1
Ferrings SE21	86	B2
Ferris Ave., Croy.	102	J3
Ferris Rd. SE22	77	D4
Ferron Rd. E5	50	E3
Ferry App. SE18	70	D3
Ferry La. N17	41	E4
Ferry La. SW13	65	F6
Ferry La., Brent.	64	H6
Ferry La., Rich.	64	J6
Ferry Pl. SE18	70	D3
Woolwich High St.		
Ferry Rd. SW13	65	G7
Ferry Rd., Tedd.	82	G7
Ferry Rd., T.Ditt.	91	E6
Ferry Rd., Twick.	82	E1
Ferry Rd., W.Mol.	90	G3
Ferry Sq., Brent.	64	G6
Ferry St. E14	69	C5
Ferryhills Clo., Wat.	28	C3
Ferrymead Ave., Grnf.	54	G3
Ferrymead Dr., Grnf.	54	G3
Ferrymead Gdns., Grnf.	54	J2
Ferrymoor, Rich.	82	E3
Festing Rd. SW15	75	A3
Festival Clo., Bex.	89	D1
Fetter La. EC4	12	F4
Fetter La. EC4	58	G6
Ffinch St. SE8	69	A7
Field Clo. E4	34	B6
Field Clo., Brom.	96	J2
Field Clo., Buck.H.	34	J3
Field Clo., Chess.	98	F5
Field Clo., Houns.	72	B1
Field Ct. WC1	12	D2
Field End, Barn.	22	H4
Field End, Nthlt.	45	D6
Field End, Ruis.	45	C6
Field End, Twick.	82	C4
Field End Rd., Pnr.	36	B5
Field End Rd., Ruis.	45	F1
Field La., Brent.	64	F7
Field La., Tedd.	82	D5
Field Mead NW7	30	E7
Field Mead NW9	30	E7
Field Pl., N.Mal.	92	F6
Field Rd. E7	51	G4
Field Rd. N17	41	A3
Field Rd. W6	66	B5
Field Rd., Felt.	72	B6
Field St. WC1	8	C3
Field St. WC1	58	F3
Field Way NW10	47	C7
Twybridge Way		
Field Way, Croy.	103	B7
Field Way, Grnf.	54	H1
Fieldend Rd. SW16	94	C1
Fielders Clo., Enf.	25	B4
Woodfield Clo.		
Fielders Clo., Har.	45	J1
Fieldfare Rd. SE28	62	C7
Fieldgate La. Mitch.	93	H3
Fieldgate St. E1	13	J2
Fieldgate St. E1	59	D5
Fieldhouse Rd. SW12	85	C1
Fielding Ave., Twick.	81	J3
Fielding Ho. NW6	57	J2
Fielding Rd. W4	65	D3
Fielding Rd. W14	66	A3
Fielding St. SE17	21	A5
Fieldings, The SE23	86	F1
Fields Est. E8	50	D7
Fields Pk. Cres., Rom.	11	CE
Fieldsend Rd., Sutt.	100	B5
Fieldside Rd., Brom.	87	D5
Fieldview SW18	84	G1
Fieldway, Dag.	53	C3
Fieldway, Orp.	97	G6
Fieldway Cres. N5	49	G5
Fiennes Clo., Dag.	53	C1
Fiesta Dr., Dag.	62	J4
Fife Rd. E16	60	G5
Fife Rd. N22	32	H7
Fife Rd. SW14	74	C5
Fife Rd., Kings.T.	91	H2
Fife Ter. N1	8	D1
Fifield Path SE23	86	G3
Bampton Rd.		
Fifth Ave. E12	52	C4
Fifth Ave. W10	57	B3
Fifth Cross Rd., Twick.	82	A2
Fifth Way, Wem.	47	B4
Fig Tree Clo. NW10	56	E1
Craven Pk.		
Figges Rd., Mitch.	85	A7
Filby Rd., Chess.	98	J6
Filey Ave. N16	50	D1
Filey Clo., Sutt.	100	F7
Filey Waye, Ruis.	45	A2
Fillebrook Ave., Enf.	25	B2
Fillebrook Rd. E11	51	D1
Filmer Rd. SW6	75	B1
Filston Rd., Erith	71	H5
Riverdale Rd.		
Finborough Rd. SW10	18	A4
Finborough Rd. SW10	66	E5
Finborough Rd. SW17	84	J6
Finch Ave. SE27	86	A4
Finch Clo. NW10	47	D5
Finch Clo., Barn.	23	D5
Finch Clo.		
Finch Dr., Felt.	72	D7
Finch La. EC3	13	C4
Finchale Rd. SE2	71	A3
Finchdale Rd. SE2	71	A3
Finchdean Way SE15	68	C7
Daniel Gdns.		
Finchingfield Ave., Wdf.Grn.	34	J7
Finchley Ct. N3	31	E6
Finchley La. NW4	38	J4
Finchley Pk. N12	31	F4
Finchley Pl. NW8	6	E1
Finchley Rd. NW2	48	D3
Finchley Rd. NW3	48	E5
Finchley Rd. NW8	48	G7
Finchley Rd. NW11	39	C7
Finchley Way N3	31	D7
Finck St. SE1	67	F2
Findhorn Ave., Hayes	54	B5
Findhorn St. E14	60	C6
Findon Clo. SW18	75	D6
Wimbledon Pk. Rd.		
Findon Clo., Har.	45	H3
Findon Rd. N9	33	E1
Findon Rd. W12	65	G2
Fingal St. SE10	69	F5
Finland Quay SE16	68	H3
Finland Rd. SE4	77	H3
Finland St. SE16	68	H3
Finlay St. SW6	75	A1
Finlays Clo., Chess.	99	A5
Finnis St. E2	59	E3
Finnymore Rd., Dag.	53	E7
Finsbury Ave. EC2	13	C2
Finsbury Circ. EC2	13	C2
Finsbury Circ. EC2	59	A5
Finsbury Cotts. N22	32	E7
Clarence Rd.		
Finsbury Est. EC1	8	F4
Finsbury Est. EC1	58	G3
Finsbury Ho. N22	40	E1
Finsbury Mkt. EC2	9	D6
Finsbury Mkt. EC2	59	A5
Finsbury Pk. Ave. N4	40	J6
Finsbury Pk. Rd. N4	49	H2
Finsbury Pavement EC2	13	C1
Finsbury Pavement EC2	59	A5
Finsbury Rd. N22	40	F1
Finsbury Sq. EC2	9	C4
Finsbury Sq. EC2	59	A5
Finsbury St. EC2	13	B1
Finsbury Way, Bex.	89	F7
Finsen Rd. SE5	76	J3
Finstock Rd. W10	57	A6
Fincuane Ri. (Bushey), Wat.	28	J2
Fir Clo., Walt.	90	A7
Fir Dene, Orp.	104	C3
Fir Gro., N.Mal.	92	F6
Fir Rd., Felt.	81	D5
Fir Rd., Sutt.	100	C1
Fir Tree Clo. SW16	85	C5
Fir Tree Clo. W5	55	H6
Fir Tree Clo., Epsom	99	F4
Fir Tree Gdns., Croy.	103	A4
Fir Tree Gro., Cars.	100	J7
Fir Tree Rd., Houns.	72	E4
Fir Tree Wk., Dag.	53	J3
Wheel Fm. Dr.		
Fir Tree Wk., Enf.	25	A3
Fir Trees Clo. SE16	68	H1
Firbank Clo. E16	61	A5
Firbank Clo., Enf.	24	J4
Gladbeck Way		
Firbank Rd. SE15	77	E2
Fircroft Ave., Chess.	98	J4
Fircroft Gdns., Har.	46	B3
Fircroft Rd. SW17	84	J2
Firdene, Surb.	99	C1
Fire Bell All., Surb.	91	H6
Fire Sta. All., Barn.	23	C2
Christchurch La.		
Firecrest Dr. NW3	48	E3
Firefly Clo., Wall.	101	E7
Defiant Way		
Firhill Rd. SE6	87	A4
Firs, The N20	31	G1
Firs, The W5	55	G5
Firs Ave. N10	40	A3
Firs Ave. N11	31	J6
Firs Ave. SW14	74	C4
Firs Clo. N10	40	A3
Firs Ave.		
Firs Clo. SE23	77	G7
Firs Clo., Esher	98	B6
Firs Clo., Mitch.	94	B2
Firs Dr., Houns.	72	B1
Firs Dr., Loug.	27	D1
Firs La. N13	32	J3
Firs La. N21	32	J2
Firs Pk. Ave. N21	33	A1
Firs Pk. Gdns. N21	32	J1
Firs Wk., Wdf.Grn.	34	G5
Firsby Ave., Croy.	102	G1
Firsby Rd. N16	50	C1
Firscroft N13	32	J3
Firside Gro., Sid.	88	J1
First Ave. E12	52	B4
First Ave. E13	60	G3
First Ave. E17	42	A5
First Ave. N18	33	F4
First Ave. NW4	38	J4
First Ave. SW14	74	E3
First Ave. W3	65	F1
First Ave. W10	57	C4
First Ave., Bexh.	71	C7

First Ave., Dag. 62 H2
First Ave., Enf. 25 C5
First Ave., Rom. 44 C5
First Ave., Walt. 90 B6
First Ave., Wem. 46 G2
First Ave., W.Mol. 90 F4
First Clo., W.Mol. 90 J3
First Cross Rd., 82 B2
Twick.
First St. SW3 18 H1
First St. SW3 66 H4
First Way, Wem. 47 B4
Firstway SW20 92 J2
Firswood Ave., 99 F5
Epsom
Firth Gdns. SW6 75 B1
Firtree Ave., 94 A2
Mitch.
Firtree Clo., Orp. 104 J5
Fish St. Hill EC3 13 C6
Fish St. Hill EC3 59 A7
Fisher Clo., Croy. 102 C1
Lwr. Addiscombe Rd.
Fisher Clo., Grnf. 54 G3
Gosling Clo.
Fisher Rd., Har. 37 C2
Fisher St. E16 60 G5
Fisher St. WC1 12 C2
Fisher St. WC1 58 F5
Fisherman Dr., 82 F4
Rich.
Locksmeade Rd.
Fishermans Dr. SE16 68 G2
Fishermans Pl. W4 65 F6
Fisherman's Wk. E14 69 A1
Cabot Sq.
Fishers Ct. SE14 77 G1
Besson St.
Fishers La. W4 65 D4
Fishers Way, Belv. 71 J1
Fishersdene, Esher 98 D6
Fisherton Est. NW8 6 E5
Fisherton St. NW8 6 E5
Fisherton St. NW8 57 G4
Fisherton St. NW8 57 G4
NW8
Fishponds Rd. SW17 84 H4
Fishponds Rd., Kes. 104 A5
Fisons Ct. E16 69 G1
Fitzalan Rd. N3 39 B3
Fitzalan Rd., Esher 98 B7
Fitzalan St. SE11 20 E1
Fitzalan St. SE11 67 F4
Fitzgeorge Ave. W14 66 B4
Fitzgeorge Ave., 92 D1
N.Mal.
Fitzgerald Ave. 74 E3
SW14
Fitzgerald Clo. E11 42 G5
Fitzgerald Rd.
Fitzgerald Ho. E14 60 B6
Kerbey St.
Fitzgerald Ho., 63 B1
Hayes
Fitzgerald Rd. E11 42 G5
Fitzgerald Rd. SW14 74 D3
Fitzgerald Rd., 91 D6
T.Ditt.
Fitzhardinge St. W1 11 B3
Fitzhardinge St. W1 58 A4
Fitzhugh Gro. SW18 75 G6
Fitzhugh Gro. Est. 75 G6
SW18
Fitzjames Ave. W14 66 B4
Fitzjames Ave., 102 D2
Croy.
Fitzjohn Ave., 23 B5
Barn.
Fitzjohn's Ave. NW3 48 G5
Fitzmaurice Pl. W1 15 E1
Fitzmaurice Pl. W1 67 B1
Fitzneal St. W12 56 F6
Fitzroy Clo. N6 48 J1
Fitzroy Ct. W1 7 G6
Fitzroy Cres. W4 65 D7
Fitzroy Gdns. SE19 86 B7
Fitzroy Ms. W1 7 F6
Fitzroy Pk. N6 48 J2
Fitzroy Rd. NW1 58 A1
Fitzroy Sq. W1 7 F6
Fitzroy Sq. W1 58 C4
Fitzroy St. W1 7 F6
Fitzroy St. W1 58 C4
Fitzroy Yd. NW1 58 A1
Fitzroy Rd.
Fitzstephen Rd., 53 B5
Dag.
Fitzwarren Gdns. 49 C1
N19
Fitzwilliam Ave., 73 J2
Rich.
Fitzwilliam Rd. SW4 76 C3

Fitzwygram Clo., 81 J5
Hmptn.
Five Acre NW9 38 F1
Five Bell All. E14 59 J7
Three Colt St.
Five Elms Rd., Brom. 103 H3.
Five Elms Rd., Dag. 53 F3
Five Ways Rd. SW9 76 G2
Fiveacre Clo., 94 G6
Th.Hth.
Fladbury Rd. N15 41 A6
Fladgate Rd. E11 42 E6
Flag Clo., Croy. 102 G1
Primrose La.
Flag Wk., Pnr. 36 A6
Eastcote Rd.
Flambard Rd., Har. 37 D6
Flamborough Rd., 45 A3
Ruis.
Flamborough St. E14 59 H6
Flamingo Gdns., 54 E3
Nthlt.
Jetstar Way
Flamstead Gdns., 53 C7
Dag.
Flamstead Rd.
Flamstead Rd. SE7 70 B5
Flamstead Rd., Dag. 53 C7
Flamsted Ave., Wem. 47 A6
Flanchford Rd. W12 65 F3
Flanders Cres. SW17 84 J7
Flanders Rd. E6 61 C2
Flanders Rd. W4 65 E4
Flanders Way E9 50 G6
Flank St. E1 21 H5
Flask Wk. NW3 48 F4
Flast Cotts. NW3 48 G4
New End Sq.
Flaxen Rd. E4 34 B3
Flaxley Rd., Mord. 93 A6
Flaxman Ct. W1 11 H4
Flaxman Rd. SE5 76 H3
Flaxman Ter. WC1 7 J4
Flaxton Rd. SE18 79 G2
Flecker Clo., Stan. 29 C5
Fleece Rd., Surb. 98 F1
Fleece Wk. N7 49 E6
Manger Rd.
Fleeming Clo. E17 41 J2
Pennant Ter.
Fleeming Rd. E17 41 J2
Fleet Clo., W.Mol. 90 G5
Fleet La. EC4 12 G3
Fleet La., W.Mol. 90 F6
Fleet Rd. NW3 48 H5
Fleet Sq. WC1 8 D4
Fleet St. EC4 12 F4
Fleet St. EC4 58 G6
Fleet St. Hill E1 9 H6
Fleetside, W.Mol. 90 F4
Fleetway W. 55 E2
Business Pk., Grnf.
Fleetwood Clo. E16 61 A5
Fleetwood Clo., 98 G7
Chess.
Fleetwood Gro. W3 56 E7
East Acton La.
Fleetwood Rd. NW10 47 G5
Fleetwood Rd., 92 B3
Kings.T.
Fleetwood Sq., 92 B3
Kings.T.
Fleetwood St. N16 50 B2
*Stoke Newington
Ch. St.*
Fleetwood Way, Wat. 28 C4
Fleming Ave., Ruis. 45 B2
Fleming Ct. W2 10 E1
Fleming Ct., Croy. 101 G5
Fleming Mead 84 H7
Mitch.
Fleming Rd. SE17 20 H5
Fleming Rd. SE17 67 H6
Fleming Rd., Sthl. 54 H6
Fleming Way SE28 62 D7
Fleming Way, Islw. 73 C3
Flempton Rd. E10 50 H1
Fletcher La. E10 42 C1
Fletcher Path SE8 69 A7
New Butt La.
Fletcher Rd. W4 65 C3
Fletcher Rd., Chig. 35 J5
Fletcher St. E1 13 J5
Fletchers Clo., Brom. 96 H4
Fletching Rd. E5 50 F3
Fletching Rd. SE7 69 J6
Fletton Rd. N11 32 E7
Fleur De Lis St. E1 9 E6
Fleur de Lis St. E1 59 H5
Fleur Gates SW19 75 A7
Princes Way

Flexmere Gdns. N17 41 A1
Flexmere Rd.
Flexmere Rd. N17 41 A1
Flimwell Clo., 87 E5
Brom.
Flint Clo. E15 21 C2
Flint St. SE17 68 A4
Flintmill Cres. SE3 79 B2
Flinton St. SE17 21 E3
Flinton St. SE17 68 B5
Flitcroft St. WC2 11 J4
Flockton St. SE16 17 H4
Flodden Rd. SE5 76 J1
Flood La., Twick. 82 D1
Church La.
Flood Pas. SE18 70 C4
Samuel St.
Flood St. SW3 18 H4
Flood St. SW3 66 H5
Flood Wk. SW3 18 H5
Flood Wk. SW3 66 H6
Flora Clo. E14 60 B6
Flora Gdns. W6 65 H4
Ravenscourt Rd.
Flora Gdns., Rom. 44 C6
Flora St., Belv. 71 F5
Floral St. WC2 12 A5
Floral St. WC2 58 E7
Florence Ave., Enf. 24 J3
Florence Ave., 93 F5
Mord.
Florence Clo., Walt. 90 B7
Florence Rd.
Florence Dr., Enf. 24 J3
Florence Gdns. W4 65 C6
Florence Nightingale 50 A6
Ho. N1
Clephane Rd.
Florence Rd. E6 60 J1
Florence Rd. E13 60 F2
Florence Rd. N4 49 G1
Florence Rd. SE2 71 C3
Florence Rd. SE14 77 J1
Florence Rd. SW19 84 E6
Florence Rd. W4 65 D3
Florence Rd. W5 55 H7
Florence Rd., Beck. 95 H2
Florence Rd., Brom. 96 G1
Florence Rd., Felt. 81 B1
Florence Rd., 82 J7
Kings.T.
Florence Rd., Sthl. 63 D4
Florence Rd., Walt. 90 B7
Florence St. E16 60 F4
Florence St. N1 49 H7
Florence St. NW4 38 J4
Florence Ter. SE14 77 J1
Florfield Rd. E8 50 E6
Reading La.
Florian Ave., Sutt. 100 G4
Florian Rd. SW15 75 B4
Florida Clo. 29 A2
(Bushey), Wat.
Florida Rd., 94 H1
Th.Hth.
Florida St. E2 9 J4
Florida St. E2 59 D3
Floriston Clo., Stan. 37 E1
Floriston Gdns., 37 E1
Stan.
Floss St. SW15 75 E7
Flower & Dean Wk. 13 G2
E1
Flower La. NW7 30 F5
Flower Wk., The 14 D4
SW7
Flower Wk., The SW7 66 F2
Flowersmead SW17 85 A2
Floyd Rd. SE7 69 J5
Fludyer St. SE13 78 E4
Folair Way SE16 68 E5
Catlin Rd.
Foley Rd., Esher 98 B7
Foley St. W1 11 F2
Foley St. W1 58 C5
Folgate St. E1 13 E1
Folgate St. E1 59 B5
Foliot St. W12 56 F6
Folkestone Rd. E6 61 D2
Folkestone Rd. E17 42 B4
Folkestone Rd. N18 33 D4
Folkingham La. NW9 38 D1
Folkington Cor. N12 31 C5
Follett St. E14 60 E6
Folly La. E17 41 H1
Folly Ms. W11 57 C6
Kensington Pk. Rd.
Folly Wall E14 69 C2
Font Hills N2 39 F2
Fontaine Rd. SW16 85 F7
Fontarabia Rd. SW11 76 A4
Fontayne Ave., 35 F4
Chig.

Fontenoy Rd. SW12 85 B2
Fonteyne Gdns., 43 A2
Wdf.Grn.
Lechmere Ave.
Fonthill Clo. SE20 95 D2
Selby Rd.
Fonthill Ms. N4 49 G2
Lennox Rd.
Fonthill Rd. N4 49 F1
Fontley Way SW15 74 G7
Fontwell Clo., Har. 29 B7
Fontwell Clo., 45 G6
Nthlt.
Fontwell Dr., Brom. 97 D5
Football La., Har. 46 B1
Parkstead Rd.
Footpath, The SW15 74 G5
Foots Cray High 89 C1
St., Sid.
Foots Cray La., 89 C1
Sid.
Footscray Rd. SE9 79 D6
Footway, The SE9 79 F7
Forbes Ct. SE19 86 B5
Forbes St. E1 13 J4
Forburg Rd. N16 50 D1
Ford Clo., Har. 37 A7
Ford Clo., Th.Hth. 94 H5
Ford End, Wdf.Grn. 34 H6
Ford Rd. E3 59 H1
Ford Rd., Dag. 53 F7
Ford Sq. E1 59 H1
Ford St. E3 59 H1
Ford St. E16 60 F6
Forde Ave., Brom. 96 J3
Fordel Rd. SE6 87 D1
Fordham Clo., Barn. 23 H3
Fordham Rd., Barn. 23 G3
Fordham St. E1 13 J3
Fordham St. E1 59 D6
Fordhook Ave. W5 55 J7
Fordingley Rd. W9 57 C3
Fordington Rd. N6 39 J5
Fordmill Rd. SE6 87 A2
Fords Gro. N21 33 J2
Fords Pk. Rd. E16 60 G6
Fordwich Clo., Orp. 97 J7
Fordwych Rd. NW2 48 B4
Fordyce Rd. SE13 78 C6
Fordyke Rd., Dag. 53 F2
Fore St. EC2 13 A2
Fore St. EC2 58 J5
Fore St. N9 33 J6
Fore St. N18 33 C6
Fore St. Ave. EC2 13 B2
Foreland Ct. NW4 39 A1
Foreland St. SE18 70 G4
Plumstead Rd.
Foreman Ct. W6 65 J4
Hammersmith Bdy.
Foremark Clo., Ilf. 35 J6
Foreshore SE8 68 J4
Forest, The E4 42 E4
Forest App. E4 26 E7
Forest App. 34 G7
Wdf.Grn.
Forest Ave. E4 26 E7
Forest Ave., Chig. 35 D5
Forest Business Pk. 41 H7
E17
Forest Clo. E11 42 F5
Forest Clo., Chis. 97 D1
Forest Clo., 34 H4
Wdf.Grn.
Forest Ct. E4 34 F1
Forest Ct. E11 42 E4
Forest Cft. SE23 86 E2
Forest Cft. SE26 86 E2
Forest Dr. E12 52 A3
Forest Dr., Kes. 104 B4
Forest Dr., 34 D7
Wdf.Grn.
Forest Dr. E. E11 42 D7
Forest Dr. W. E11 42 D7
Forest Edge, 34 J4
Buck.H.
Forest Gdns. N17 41 C2
Forest Gate NW9 38 E5
Forest Glade E4 34 E4
Forest Glade E11 42 E6
Forest Gro. E8 50 C6-
Buck.H.
Forest Heights, 34 G2
Buck.H.
Forest Hill Rd. SE22 77 E5
Forest Hill Rd. SE23 77 F6
Forest Ind. Est., Ilf. 43 H1
Forest La. E7 51 G5
Forest La. E15 51 E6
Forest La., Chig. 35 D5
Forest Mt. Rd. 34 D7
Wdf.Grn.
Forest Ridge, Beck. 96 A3
Forest Ridge, Kes. 104 B4

Forest Ri. E17 42 D5
Forest Rd. E7 51 G4
Forest Rd. E8 50 C6
Forest Rd. E11 42 D7
Forest Rd. E17 41 F4
Forest Rd. N9 33 E1
Forest Rd., Felt. 81 C2
Forest Rd., Ilf. 43 H1
Forest Rd., Loug. 27 A3
Forest Rd., Rich. 65 A7
Forest Rd., Rom. 44 H3
Forest Rd., Sutt. 100 D1
Forest Rd., Wdf.Grn. 34 G3
Forest Side E4 26 F7
Forest Side E7 51 H4
  Capel Rd.
Forest Side, Buck.H. 34 H1
Forest Side, Wor.Pk. 99 F1
Forest Vw. E7 51 G5
Forest Vw. E4 26 D7
Forest Vw. E11 42 F7
Forest Vw. Ave. E10 42 D5
Forest Vw. Rd. E12 52 B4
Forest Vw. Rd. E17 42 C1
Forest Vw. Rd., Loug. 27 A4
Forest Way N19 49 C2
  Hargrave Pk.
Forest Way, Loug. 27 B3
Forest Way, Orp. 97 J5
Forest Way, Sid. 79 G7
Forest Way, Wdf.Grn. 34 H4
Forestdale N14 32 D4
Forester Rd. SE15 77 E4
Foresters Clo., Wall. 101 D7
Foresters Cres., Bexh. 80 H4
Foresters Dr. E17 42 D4
Foresters Dr., Wall. 101 D6
Forestholme Clo. SE23 86 F2
Forfar Rd. N22 40 H1
Forfar Rd. SW11 76 A1
Forge Clo., Brom. 103 G1
Forge Dr., Esher 98 D7
Forge La., Felt. 81 E6
Forge La., Sun. 90 A3
Forge La., Sutt. 100 B7
Forge Pl. NW1 49 A6
  Malden Cres.
Forman Pl. N16 50 C4
  Farleigh Rd.
Formby Ave., Stan. 37 F3
Formosa St. W9 6 B6
Formosa St. W9 57 E4
Formunt Clo. E16 60 F5
  Vincent St.
Forres Gdns. NW11 39 D6
Forrest Gdns. SW16 94 F3
Forrester Path SE26 86 F4
Forset St. W1 10 H3
Forset St. W1 57 H6
Forstal Clo., Brom. 96 G3
  Ridley Rd.
Forster Rd. E17 41 H6
Forster Rd. N17 41 C3
Forster Rd. SW2 76 E7
Forster Rd., Beck. 95 H3
Forster Rd., Croy. 94 J7
  Windmill Rd.
Forsters Clo., Rom. 44 F6
Forsters Way, Hayes 54 B6
Forston St. N1 9 B1
Forsyte Cres. SE19 95 B1
Forsyth Gdns. SE17 20 H5
Forsyth Gdns. SE17 67 H6
Forsyth Pl., Enf. 25 B5
Forsythia Clo., Ilf. 52 E5
Fort Rd. SE1 21 G2
Fort Rd. SE1 68 C4
Fort Rd., Nthlt. 45 G7
Fort St. E1 13 E2
Fort St. E1 59 B5
Fort St. E16 69 H1
Forterie Gdns., Ilf. 53 A3
Fortescue Ave. E8 50 E7
  Mentmore Ter.
Fortescue Ave., Twick. 81 J3
Fortescue Rd. SW19 84 G7
Fortescue Rd., Edg. 38 C1
Fortess Gro. NW5 49 B5
  Fortess Rd.
Fortess Rd. NW5 49 B5
Fortess Wk. NW5 49 B5
  Fortess Rd.
Forthbridge Rd. SW11 76 A4

Fortis Clo. E16 60 J6
Fortis Grn. N2 39 H4
Fortis Grn. N10 40 A3
Fortis Grn. Ave. N2 39 J3
Fortis Grn. Rd. N10 40 A3
Fortismere Ave. N10 40 A3
Fortnam Rd. N19 49 D2
Fortnums Acre, Stan. 29 C6
Fortrose Gdns. SW2 85 D1
  New Pk. Rd.
Fortuna Clo. N7 49 F6
  Vulcan Way
Fortune Gate Rd. NW10 56 E1
Fortune Grn. Rd. NW6 48 D4
Fortune St. EC1 9 A6
Fortune St. EC1 58 J4
Fortune Wk. SE28 70 G3
  Broadwater Rd.
Fortune Way NW10 56 G3
Fortunes Mead, Nthlt. 45 E6
Forty Acre La. E16 60 G5
Forty Ave., Wem. 46 J3
Forty Clo., Wem. 46 J3
Forty La., Wem. 47 B2
Forum, The, W.Mol. 90 H4
Forum Way, Edg. 30 A6
  High St.
Forumside, Edg. 30 A6
  Forum Way
Forval Clo., Mitch. 93 J6
Forward Dr., Har. 37 C4
Fosbury Ms. W2 10 B6
Foscote Ms. W9 57 D5
  Amberley Rd.
Foscote Rd. NW4 38 H5
Foskett Rd. SW6 75 C2
Foss Ave., Croy. 101 G5
Foss Rd. SW17 84 G4
Fossdene Rd. SE7 69 H5
Fossdyke Clo., Hayes 54 E5
Fosse Way W13 55 D5
Fossil Rd. SE13 78 A3
Fossington Rd., Belv. 71 D4
Fossway, Dag. 53 C2
Foster La. EC2 12 J3
Foster La. EC2 58 J6
Foster Rd. E13 60 G4
Foster Rd. W3 56 E7
Foster Rd. W4 65 D5
Foster St. NW4 38 J4
Foster Wk. NW4 38 J4
  New Brent St.
Fosters Clo. E18 42 H1
Fosters Clo., Chis. 88 C5
Fothergill Clo. E13 60 G2
Fotheringham Rd., Enf. 25 C4
Fossway, Dag. 53 C2
Foubert's Pl. W1 11 F4
Foubert's Pl. W1 58 C6
Foulden Rd. N16 50 C4
Foulden Ter. N16 50 C4
  Foulden Rd.
Foulis Ter. SW7 18 F3
Foulis Ter. SW7 66 G5
Foulser Rd. SW17 84 J3
Foulsham Rd., Th.Hth. 94 J3
Founders Ct. EC2 13 B3
Founders Gdns. SE19 85 J7
Foundry Clo. SE16 68 H1
Foundry Ms. NW1 7 G5
Fount St. SW8 78 D7
Fountain Ct. EC4 12 E5
Fountain Dr. SE19 86 C4
Fountain Pl. SW9 76 G1
Fountain Rd. SW17 84 G5
Fountain Rd., Th.Hth. 94 J2
Fountain Sq. SW1 19 D1
Fountains Ave., Felt. 81 F3
Fountains Clo., Felt. 81 F2
Fountains Cres. N14 24 E7
Fountayne Rd. N15 41 D4
Fountayne Rd. N16 50 D2
Four Seasons Cres., Sutt. 100 C2
  Kimpton Rd.
Four Seasons Ind. Est., Sthl. 63 H3
Four Wents, The E4 34 D2
  Kings Rd.
Fouracres, Enf. 25 H1
Fourland Wk., Edg. 30 C6
Fournier St. E1 13 G1
Fournier St. E1 59 C5
Fourth Ave. E12 52 C4

Fourth Ave. W10 57 B3
Fourth Ave., Rom. 53 J1
Fourth Cross Rd., Twick. 82 A2
Fourth Way, Wem. 47 C4
Fowey Ave., Ilf. 43 A5
Fowey Clo. E1 68 E1
  Kennet St.
Fowler Clo. SW11 75 G3
Fowler Rd. E7 51 G4
Fowler Rd. N1 49 H7
  Halton Rd.
Fowler Rd., Mitch. 94 A2
Fowlers Clo., Sid. 89 E5
  Thursland Rd.
Fowlers Wk. W5 55 G4
Fownes St. SW11 75 H3
Fox and Knot St. EC1 12 H1
Fox Clo. E1 59 F4
Fox Clo. E16 60 G5
Fox Hill SE19 86 C7
Fox Hill, Kes. 103 H5
Fox Hill Gdns. SE19 86 C7
Fox Hollow Dr., Bexh. 80 D3
Fox Ho. Rd., Belv. 71 H4
Fox La. N13 32 E2
Fox La. W5 55 H4
Fox La., Kes. 103 H5
Fox Rd. E16 60 F5
Foxberry Rd. SE4 77 H3
Foxborough Gdns. SE4 78 A6
Foxbourne Rd. SW17 85 A2
Foxbury Ave., Chis. 88 G6
Foxbury Clo., Brom. 87 H6
Foxbury Rd., Brom. 87 G6
Foxcombe, Croy. 103 B6
Foxcombe Clo. E6 61 A2
  Boleyn Rd.
Foxcombe Rd. SW15 83 G1
  Alton Rd.
Foxcote SE5 21 E4
Foxcroft Rd. SE18 79 E1
Foxes Dale SE3 78 G3
Foxes Dale, Brom. 96 D3
Foxfield Rd., Orp. 104 G2
Foxglove La., Chess. 99 A4
Foxglove St. W12 56 F7
Foxgrove, Wall. 101 B1
Foxgrove N14 32 E3
Foxgrove Ave., Beck. 87 B7
Foxgrove Path, Wat. 28 D5
Foxgrove Rd., Beck. 87 B7
Foxham Rd. N19 49 D3
Foxhole Rd. SE9 79 B5
Foxholt Gdns. NW10 47 C7
Foxhome Clo., Chis. 88 D6
Foxlands Cres., Dag. 53 J5
Foxlands Rd., Dag. 53 J5
Foxlees, Wem. 46 D4
Foxley Clo. E8 50 D5
  Ferncliff Rd.
Foxley Clo., Loug. 27 E2
Foxley Rd. SW9 20 F7
Foxley Rd. SW9 67 G7
Foxley Rd., Th.Hth. 94 H4
Foxley Sq. SW9 67 H7
  Cancell Rd.
Foxleys, Wat. 28 E3
Foxmead Clo., Enf. 24 F3
Foxmore St. SW11 75 J1
Fox's Path, Mitch. 93 H2
Foxwell St. SE4 77 H3
Foxwood Clo., Felt. 81 B3
Foxwood Rd. SE3 78 F4
Foyle Rd. N17 41 D1
Foyle Rd. SE3 69 F6
Framfield Clo. N12 31 D3
Framfield Ct., Enf. 25 B6
Framfield Rd. N5 49 H5
Framfield Rd. W7 55 C6
Framfield Rd., Mitch. 85 A7
Framlingham Clo. E5 50 F2
  Detmold Rd.
Framlingham Cres. SE9 88 B4
Frampton Clo., Sutt. 100 D7
Frampton Pk. Est. E9 50 F7
Frampton Pk. Rd. E9 50 F6
Frampton Rd., Houns. 72 E5
Frampton St. NW8 7 D6
Frampton St. NW8 57 G4
Francemary Rd. SE4 78 A5
Frances Rd. E4 34 A6

Frances St. SE18 70 C4
Franche Ct. Rd. SW17 84 F3
Francis Ave., Bexh. 80 G2
Francis Ave., Felt. 81 A3
Francis Ave., Ilf. 52 G2
Francis Barber Clo. SW16 85 F4
  Valley Rd.
Francis Chichester Way SW11 76 A1
Francis Clo. E14 69 D4
  Saunders Ness Rd.
Francis Clo., Epsom 99 D4
Francis Gro. SW19 84 C6
Francis Rd. E10 51 C1
Francis Rd. N2 39 J4
  Lynmouth Rd.
Francis Rd., Croy. 94 H6
Francis Rd., Grnf. 55 E2
Francis Rd., Har. 37 D5
Francis Rd., Houns. 72 D2
Francis Rd., Ilf. 52 G2
Francis Rd., Pnr. 36 C5
Francis Rd., Wall. 101 C6
Francis St. E15 51 E5
Francis St. SW1 **19** **F1**
Francis St. SW1 67 C4
Francis St., Ilf. 52 G2
Francis Ter. N19 49 C3
  Junction Rd.
Franciscan Rd. SW17 84 J5
Francklyn Gdns., Edg. 30 A3
Franconia Rd. SW4 76 D5
Frank Bailey Wk. E12 52 D5
  Gainsborough Ave.
Frank Dixon Clo. SE21 86 B1
Frank Dixon Way SE21 86 B1
Frank St. E13 60 G4
Frank Trowell Ct., Felt. 81 A1
Frankfurt Rd. SE24 76 J5
Frankham St. SE8 69 A7
Frankland Clo. SE16 68 F4
Frankland Clo., Wdf.Grn. 34 A5
Frankland Rd. E4 34 A5
Frankland Rd. SW7 **14** **E6**
Frankland Rd. SW7 66 G3
Franklin Clo. N20 23 F7
Franklin Clo. SE27 85 H3
Franklin Clo., Kings.T. 92 A3
Franklin Cres., Mitch. 94 C4
Franklin Ho. NW9 38 F7
Franklin Pas. SE9 79 B3
  Phineas Pett Rd.
Franklin Rd. SE20 86 F7
Franklin Rd., Bexh. 80 E7
Franklin Sq. W14 66 C5
  Marchbank Rd.
Franklin St. E3 60 B3
  Leonard St.
Franklin St. N15 41 B6
Franklin Way, Croy. 101 E1
Franklins Ms., Har. 45 J2
Franklin's Row SW3 **19** **A3**
Franklin's Row SW3 67 G2
Franklyn Gdns., Ilf. 35 G3
Franklyn Rd. NW10 47 F7
Franklyn Rd., Walt. 90 A6
Franks Ave., N.Mal. 92 C3
Frankswood Ave., Orp. 97 E5
Franlaw Cres. N13 32 J4
Fransfield Gro. SE26 86 E3
Frant Clo. SE20 86 F7
Frant Rd., Th.Hth. 94 H5
Franthorne Way SE6 87 B2
Fraser Clo. E6 61 B6
  Linton Gdns.
Fraser Clo., Bex. 89 J1
  Dartford Rd.
Fraser Ho., Brent. 56 A5
Fraser Rd. E17 42 B5
Fraser Rd. N9 33 E3
Fraser Rd., Erith 71 J5
Fraser Rd., Grnf. 55 E1
Fraser St. W4 65 E5
Frating Cres., Wdf.Grn. 34 H6
Frazer Ave., Ruis. 45 G5
Frazier St. SE1 **16** **E4**
Frazier St. SE1 67 G2
Frean St. SE16 **17** **H5**
Frean St. SE16 68 D3

Fred Wigg Twr. E11 51 F2
Freda Corbett Clo. 21 H7
SE15
Frederic Ms. SW1 **15 A4**
Frederic St. E17 41 H5
Frederica Rd. E4 26 D7
Frederica St. N7 49 F7
Caledonian Rd.
Frederick Clo. W2 **10 H5**
Frederick Clo. W2 57 H7
Frederick Clo., 100 C4
Sutt.
Frederick Cres. SW9 67 H7
Frederick Gdns., 100 C5
Sutt.
Frederick Rd. SE18 70 E5
Frederick Rd. SE17 **20 H5**
Frederick Rd., 100 C5
Sutt.
Frederick St. WC1 **8 C4**
Frederick St. WC1 58 F3
Frederick Ter. E8 59 C1
Haggerston Rd.
Frederick's Pl. EC2 **13 B4**
Fredericks Pl. N12 31 F4
Frederick's Row EC1 **8 G3**
Freedom Clo. E17 41 H4
Freedom St. SW11 75 J2
Freegrove Rd. N7 49 E5
Freeland Pk. NW4 39 B2
Freeland Rd. W5 55 J7
Freelands Gro., 96 H1
Brom.
Freelands Rd., 96 H1
Brom.
Freeling St. N1 49 F7
Caledonian Rd.
Freeman Clo., 45 E7
Nthlt.
Freeman Rd., Mord. 93 G5
Freemantle Ave., 25 G5
Enf.
Freemasons Rd. E16 60 H5
Freemasons Rd., 102 B1
Croy.
Freesia Clo., Orp. 104 J5
Briarswood Way
Freethorpe Clo. 95 B1
SE19
Freke Rd. SW11 76 A3
Fremantle Rd., Belv. 71 G4
Fremantle Rd., Ilf. 43 F2
Fremantle St. SE17 **21 D3**
Fremantle St. SE17 68 B5
Fremont St. E9 59 F7
French Ordinary Ct. 59 B7
EC3
Crutched Friars
French Pl. E1 **9 E5**
French St., Sun. 90 C2
Frendsbury Rd. SE4 77 H4
Frensham Clo., 54 F4
Sthl.
Frensham Dr. SW15 83 F3
Frensham Dr., Croy. 103 C7
Frensham Rd. SE9 88 G2
Frensham St. SE15 **21 J6**
Frensham St. SE15 68 D6
Frere St. SW11 75 H2
Fresh Wf. Rd., 61 E1
Bark.
Freshfield Clo. SE13 78 D4
Marischal Rd.
Freshfield Dr. N14 24 B7
Freshfields, Croy. 95 J7
Freshford St. SW18 84 F3
Freshwater Clo. 85 A6
SW17
Freshwater Rd. 85 A6
SW17
Freshwater Rd., Dag. 53 D1
Freshwell Ave., 44 C4
Rom.
Freshwood Clo., 96 B1
Beck.
Freston Gdns., Barn. 23 J5
Freston Pk. N3 39 C2
Freston Rd. W10 57 A7
Freston Rd. W11 57 A7
Freta Rd., Bexh. 80 F5
Frewin Rd. SW18 84 G1
Friar Ms. SE27 85 H3
Prioress Rd.
Friar Rd., Hayes 54 D4
Friar St. EC4 **12 H4**
Friars, The, Chig. 35 H4
Friars Ave. N20 31 H3
Friars Ave. SW15 83 F3
Friars Clo. N2 39 G4
Friars Clo., Nthlt. 54 D3
Broomcroft Ave.
Friars Gdns. W3 56 D6
St. Dunstans Ave.

Friars Gate Clo., 34 G4
Wdf.Grn.
Friars La., Rich. 73 G5
Friars Mead E14 69 C3
Friars Ms. SE9 79 D5
Friars Pl. La. W3 56 D7
Friars Rd. E6 61 A1
Friars Stile Rd., Rich. 73 H6
Friars Wk. N14 24 B7
Friars Wk. SE2 71 D5
Friars Way W3 56 D6
Friary Clo. N12 31 H5
Friary Ct. SW1 **15 G2**
Friary Est. SE15 **21 J6**
Friary Est. SE15 68 D6
Friary La., 34 G4
Wdf.Grn.
Friary Rd. N12 31 G4
Friary Rd. SE15 68 D7
Friary Rd. W3 56 C6
Friary Way N12 31 H4
Friday Hill E4 34 E2
Friday Hill E. E4 34 E3
Friday Hill W. E4 34 E2
Friday Rd., Mitch. 84 J7
Friday St. EC4 **12 J5**
Friday St. EC4 58 J7
Frideswide Pl. NW5 49 C5
Islip St.
Friend St. EC1 **8 G3**
Friend St. EC1 58 H3
Friendly St. SE8 78 A2
Friendly St. Ms. SE8 78 A2
Friendship St.
Friends Rd., Croy. 102 A3
Friendship Wk., 54 D3
Nthlt.
Wayfarer Rd.
Friern Barnet La. 31 J4
N11
Friern Barnet La. 31 F2
N20
Friern Barnet Rd. 31 J5
N11
Friern Ct. N20 31 G3
Friern Mt. Dr. N20 23 F7
Friern Pk. N12 31 F5
Friern Rd. SE22 77 D7
Friern Watch Ave. 31 F4
N12
Frigate Ms. SE8 69 A6
Watergate St.
Frimley Clo. SW19 84 B2
Frimley Clo., Croy. 103 C7
Frimley Ct., Sid. 89 C5
Frimley Cres., 103 C7
Croy.
Frimley Gdns., 93 H3
Mitch.
Frimley Rd., Chess. 98 G5
Frimley Rd., Ilf. 52 H3
Frimley Way E1 59 G4
Frimley Way, Wall. 101 E5
Frinton Dr., 34 D7
Wdf.Grn.
Frinton Ms., Ilf. 43 D6
Bramley Cres.
Frinton Rd. E6 61 A3
Frinton Rd. N15 41 B6
Frinton Rd. SW17 85 A6
Frinton Rd., Sid. 89 E2
Friston Path, Chig. 35 H5
Manford Way
Friston St. SW6 75 E2
Friswell Pl., Bexh. 80 G4
Frith Ct. NW7 31 B7
Frith La. NW7 31 B7
Frith Rd. E11 51 C4
Frith Rd., Croy. 101 J2
Frith St. W1 **11 H4**
Frith St. W1 58 D6
Fritham Clo., 92 E6
N.Mal.
Frithville Gdns. 65 J1
W12
Frizlands La., Dag. 53 H4
Frobisher Clo., Pnr. 36 D7
Frobisher Pas. E14 69 A1
North Colonnade
Frobisher Rd. E6 61 C6
Frobisher Rd. N8 40 G4
Frobisher St. SE10 69 E6
Froghall La., Chig. 35 G4
Frogley Rd. SE22 77 C4
Frogmore SW18 75 D5
Frogmore, 100 A3
Sutt.
Frogmore Gdns., 100 B4
Sutt.
Frognal NW3 48 F5
Frognal Ave., Har. 37 C4

Frognal Ave., Sid. 89 A5
Frognal Clo. NW3 48 F5
Frognal
Frognal Ct. NW3 48 F6
Frognal Gdns. NW3 48 F5
Frognal La. NW3 48 E5
Frognal Par. NW3 48 F6
Frognal Ct.
Frognal Pl., Sid. 89 A6
Frognal Ri. NW3 48 F5
Frognal Way NW3 48 F4
Froissart Rd. SE9 79 A5
Frome Rd. N15 40 H3
Westbury Ave.
Frome St. N1 **8 J1**
Frome St. N1 58 J2
Fromondes Rd., 100 B5
Sutt.
Frostic Wk. E1 **13 H2**
Froude St. SW8 76 B2
Frowyk Cres. NW9 38 A5
Fry Rd. E6 52 A7
Fry Rd. NW10 56 F1
Fryatt Rd. N17 33 A7
Fryatt St. E14 60 E6
Orchard Pl.
Fryent Clo. NW9 38 A5
Fryent Cres. NW9 38 E6
Fryent Flds. NW9 38 E6
Fryent Gro. NW9 38 E6
Fryent Way NW9 38 A5
Frye's Bldgs. N1 **8 F1**
Frying Pan All. E1 **13 F2**
Fryston Ave., Croy. 102 D2
Fuchsia St. SE2 71 B5
Fulbeck Dr. NW9 38 E1
Fulbeck Way, Har. 36 J2
Fulbourne Rd. E17 42 C1
Fulbourne St. E1 59 E5
Durward St.
Fulbrook Ms. N19 49 C4
Junction Rd.
Fulbrook Rd. N19 49 C4
Junction Rd.
Fulbrooks Ave., 99 F1
Wor.Pk.
Fulford Gro., Wat. 28 B2
Fulford Rd., Epsom 93 F7
Fulford St. SE16 68 E2
Paradise St.
Fulham Bdy. SW6 66 D7
Fulham Clo. SW6 66 D7
Fulham Rd.
Fulham High St. SW6 75 B2
Fulham Palace Rd. 66 A6
SW6
Fulham Palace Rd. 65 J5
W6
Fulham Pk. Gdns. 75 C2
SW6
Fulham Pk. Rd. SW6 75 C2
Fulham Rd. SW3 **18 E4**
Fulham Rd. SW3 66 G5
Fulham Rd. SW6 75 B2
Fulham Rd. SW10 **18 E4**
Fulham Rd. SW10 66 G5
Fuller Clo., Orp. 104 J5
Fuller Rd., Dag. 53 B3
Fuller St. E2 **9 H5**
Fuller St. NW4 38 J4
Fullers Ave., Surb. 98 J2
Fullers Ave., 34 F7
Wdf.Grn.
Fullers Rd. E18 42 F1
Fullers Way N., 98 J3
Surb.
Fullers Way S., 98 H4
Chess.
Fullers Wd., Croy. 103 A5
Fullerton Rd. SW18 75 F5
Fullerton Rd., 101 J2
Croy.
Fullwell Ave., Ilf. 43 C1
Fullwoods Ms. N1 **9 C3**
Fulmar Ct., Surb. 91 J6
Fulmead St. SW6 75 E2
Fulmer Clo., Hmptn. 81 E5
Fulmer Rd. E16 61 A5
Fulmer Way W13 64 E3
Fulready Rd. E10 42 G5
Fulstone Clo., 72 F4
Houns.
Fulthorp Rd. SE3 78 F2
Fulton Ms. W2 **10 C5**
Fulton Rd., Wem. 47 A3
Fulwell Pk. Ave., 81 H5
Twick.
Fulwell Rd., Tedd. 82 A4
Fulwood Ave., Wem. 55 J2
Fulwood Gdns., 73 C6
Twick.
Fulwood Pl. WC1 **12 D2**
Fulwood Wk. SW19 84 B1
Furber St. W6 65 H3

Furham Feild, Pnr. 28 G7
Furley Rd. SE15 68 D7
Furlong Clo., Wall. 101 A1
Furlong Rd. N7 49 G6
Furmage St. SW18 75 E7
Furneaux Ave. SE27 85 H5
Furness Rd. NW10 56 G2
Furness Rd. SW6 75 E2
Furness Rd., Har. 36 H7
Furness Rd., Mord. 93 E7
Furnival St. EC4 **12 E3**
Furnival St. EC4 58 G6
Furrow La. E9 50 F5
Fursby Ave. N3 31 D6
Further Acre NW9 38 F2
Further Grn. Rd. 78 E7
SE6
Furtherfield Clo., 94 G6
Croy.
Furze Clo., Wat. 28 C5
Furze Fm. Clo., Rom. 44 E2
Furze Rd., Th.Hth. 94 J3
Furze St. E3 60 A5
Furzedown Dr. SW17 85 B5
Furzedown Rd. SW17 85 B5
Furzefield Clo., 88 E6
Chis.
Furzefield Rd. SE3 69 H7
Furzehill Rd., 22 A3
Borwd.
Furzewood, Sun. 90 A1
Fyfield Clo., Brom. 96 D4
Fyfield Rd. E17 42 D3
Fyfield Rd. SW9 76 G3
Fyfield Rd., Enf. 25 B3
Fyfield Rd., 34 J7
Wdf.Grn.
Fynes St. SW1 **19 H1**
Fynes St. SW1 67 D4

G

Gable Clo. SE26 86 E4
Lawrie Pk. Ave.
Gable Clo., Pnr. 28 G7
Gable Clo. SE26 86 E5
Lawrie Pk. Ave.
Gables Clo. SE5 77 B1
Gables Clo. SE12 87 G1
Gabriel Clo., Felt. 81 D4
Gabriel St. SE23 77 G7
Gabrielle Clo., Wem. 46 J3
Gabrielle Ct. NW3 48 G6
Gaddesden Ave., 46 J6
Wem.
Gade Clo., Hayes 63 B1
Gadesden Rd., 99 C6
Epsom
Gadsbury Clo. NW9 38 F6
Gadwall Clo. E16 60 H6
Freemasons Rd.
Gadwall Way SE28 70 G2
Goldfinch Rd.
Gage Rd. E16 60 E5
Malmesbury Rd.
Gage St. WC1 **12 B1**
Gainford St. N1 58 G1
Richmond Ave.
Gainsborough Ave. 52 D5
E12
Gainsborough Clo., 87 A7
Beck.
Gainsborough Clo., 98 B1
Esher
Lime Tree Ave.
Gainsborough Ct. 31 E5
N12
Gainsborough Gdns. 48 G3
NW3
Gainsborough Gdns. 39 C7
NW11
Gainsborough Gdns. 37 J2
Edg.
Gainsborough Gdns. 46 B5
Grnf.
Gainsborough Gdns. 73 A5
Islw.
Gainsborough Ms. 86 E3
SE26
Panmure Rd.
Gainsborough Rd. 42 E7
E11
Gainsborough Rd. 60 E3
E15
Gainsborough Rd. 31 E5
N12
Gainsborough Rd. W4 65 F4
Gainsborough Rd., 53 B4
Dag.
Gainsborough Rd. 92 D6
N.Mal.
Gainsborough Rd., 73 J2
Rich.

Gainsborough Rd., Wdf.Grn. 35 B6
Gainsborough Sq., Bexh. 80 D3
Regency Way
Gainsford Rd. E17 41 J4
Gainsford St. SE1 17 F3
Gainsford St. SE1 68 C2
Gairloch Rd. SE5 77 B2
Gaisford St. NW5 49 C6
Gaitskell Rd. SE9 88 F1
Galahad Rd., Brom. 87 G3
Galata Rd. SW13 65 G7
Galatea Sq. SE15 77 E3
Scylla Rd.
Galbraith St. E14 69 C3
Galdana Ave., Barn. 23 F3
Gale Clo., Hmptn. 81 E6
Stewart La.
Gale Clo., Mitch. 93 G3
Gale St. E3 60 A5
Gale St., Dag. 53 C5
Galeborough Ave., Wdf.Grn. 34 D7
Galen Pl. WC1 12 B2
Galena Rd. W6 65 H4
Gales Gdns. E2 59 E3
Gales Way, Wdf.Grn. 35 B7
Galesbury Rd. SW18 75 F6
Galgate Clo. SW19 84 B1
Gallants Fm. Rd., Barn. 23 H7
Galleon Clo. SE16 68 G2
Kinburn St.
Gallery Gdns., Nthlt. 54 D2
Gallery Rd. SE21 86 A1
Galleywall Rd. SE16 68 E4
Gallia Rd. N5 49 H5
Galliard Clo. N9 25 F6
Galliard Rd. N9 33 D1
Gallions Clo., Bark. 62 A3
Gallions Rd. SE7 69 H4
Gallon Clo. SE7 69 J4
Gallop, The, S.Croy. 102 E7
Gallosson Rd. SE18 70 H4
Galloway Rd. W12 65 G1
Gallus Clo. N21 24 F6
Gallus Sq. SE3 78 H3
Galpins Rd., Th.Hth. 94 E5
Galsworthy Ave., Rom. 44 B7
Galsworthy Clo. SE28 71 B1
Galsworthy Cres. SE3 78 J1
Merriman Rd.
Galsworthy Rd. NW2 48 B4
Galsworthy Rd., Kings.T. 83 B7
Galsworthy Ter. N16 50 B3
Hawksley Rd.
Galton St. W10 57 B3
Galva Clo., Barn. 24 A4
Galvani Way, Croy. 101 F1
Ampere Way
Galveston Rd. SW15 75 C5
Galway St. EC1 9 A4
Galway St. EC1 58 J3
Gambetta St. SW8 76 B2
Gambia St. SE1 16 H2
Gambole Rd. SW17 84 H4
Games Rd., Barn. 23 J3
Gamlen Rd. SW15 75 A4
Gander Grn. La., Sutt. 100 B2
Gandhi Clo. E17 42 A6
Gane Clo., Wall. 101 E7
Kingsford Ave.
Ganton St. W1 11 F5
Ganton Wk., Wat. 28 E4
Woodhall La.
Gantshill Cres., Ilf. 43 D5
Gantshill Cross, Ilf. 43 D6
Eastern Ave.
Gap Rd. SW19 84 D5
Garage Rd. W3 56 A6
Garbutt Pl. W1 11 C1
Gard St. EC1 8 H3
Garden Ave., Bexh. 80 G3
Garden Ave., Mitch. 85 B7
Garden City, Edg. 30 A6
Garden Clo. E4 34 A5
Garden Clo. SE12 87 H3
Garden Clo. SW15 74 H7
Garden Clo., Barn. 22 H4
Garden Clo., Hmptn. 81 F5
Garden Clo., Nthlt. 54 E1
Garden Clo., Wall. 101 E5
Garden Ct. EC4 12 E5

Garden Ct. SE15 77 C1
Sumner Est.
Garden Ct., Rich. 73 J1
Lichfield Rd.
Garden Ct., W.Mol. 90 H4
Avern Rd.
Garden La. SW2 85 F1
Garden La., Brom. 87 H6
Garden Ms. W2 57 D7
Linden Gdns.
Garden Rd. NW8 6 D3
Garden Rd. NW8 57 F3
Garden Rd. SE20 95 F1
Garden Rd., Brom. 87 H7
Garden Rd., Rich. 74 A3
Garden Rd., Walt. 90 B6
Garden Row SE1 16 G6
Garden Row SE1 67 H3
Garden St. E1 59 G5
Garden Ter. SW1 19 H3
Garden Wk. EC2 9 D4
Garden Wk., Beck. 95 J1
Hayne Rd.
Garden Way NW10 47 C6
Gardeners La. EC4 12 J5
Gardeners Rd. E3 59 G2
Gardeners Rd., Croy. 101 H1
Gardenia Rd., Enf. 25 B6
Gardenia Way, Wdf.Grn. 34 H5
Harts Gro.
Gardens, The SE22 77 D4
Gardens, The, Beck. 96 C1
Gardens, The, Har. 36 C5
Gardens, The, Pnr. 36 F6
Gardiner Ave. NW2 47 J5
Gardiner Clo. E11 42 H6
Gardner Gro., Felt. 81 F2
Gardner Rd. E13 60 H4
Gardnor Rd. NW3 48 G4
Flask Wk.
Garendon Gdns., Mord. 93 E7
Garendon Rd., Mord. 93 D7
Gareth Clo., Wor.Pk. 100 A2
Burnham Dr.
Gareth Gro., Brom. 87 G4
Garfield Rd. E4 34 D1
Garfield Rd. E13 60 H4
Garfield Rd. SW11 76 A3
Garfield Rd. SW19 84 F5
Garfield Rd., Enf. 25 F4
Garfield Rd., Twick. 82 E1
York St.
Garford St. E14 60 A7
Gargery Wk. SE28 62 C7
Garibaldi St. SE18 70 H4
Garland Rd. SE18 70 G7
Garland Rd., Stan. 37 H1
Garlands Ct., Croy. 102 A4
Chatsworth Rd.
Garlick Hill EC4 13 A5
Garlick Hill EC4 58 J7
Garlies Rd. SE23 86 H3
Garlinge Rd. NW2 48 C6
Garman Rd. N17 33 F7
Garnault Ms. EC1 8 F4
Garnault Pl. EC1 8 F4
Garner Rd. E17 42 C1
Garner St. E2 9 J2
Garnet Rd. NW10 47 E6
Garnet Rd., Th.Hth. 94 J4
Garnet St. E1 59 F7
Garnet Wk. E6 61 B5
Kingfisher St.
Garnet Way E17 41 H1
McEntee Ave.
Garnett Clo. SE9 79 C3
Garnett Rd. NW3 48 F5
Garnham St. N16 50 C2
Garnies Clo. SE15 21 F7
Garrads Rd. SW16 85 D3
Garrard Clo., Bexh. 80 G3
Garrard Clo., Chis. 88 E5
Garrard Wk. NW10 47 E6
Garnet Rd.
Garratt Clo., Croy. 101 E4
Garratt La. SW17 84 G4
Garratt La. SW18 75 F5
Garratt Rd., Edg. 30 A7
Garratt Ter. SW17 84 H4
Garratts Rd. W3 56 D5
Jenner Ave.
Garrett St. EC1 9 A5
Garrick Ave. NW11 39 B6
Garrick Clo. SW18 75 F4
Garrick Clo. W5 65 H4
Garrick Clo., Islw. 73 D3
Byfield Rd.
Garrick Clo., Islw. 73 D3
Byfield Rd.

Garrick Clo., Rich. 73 G5
The Grn.
Garrick Cres., Croy. 102 B2
Garrick Dr. NW4 38 J2
Garrick Dr. SE28 70 G3
Broadwater Rd.
Garrick Gdns., W.Mol. 90 G3
Garrick Pk. NW4 39 A2
Garrick Rd. NW9 38 F6
Garrick Rd., Grnf. 54 H4
Garrick Rd., Rich. 74 A2
Garrick St. WC2 12 A5
Garrick St. WC2 58 E7
Garrick Way NW4 39 A4
Garrison Clo. SE18 70 D7
Red Lion La.
Garrison La., Chess. 98 G7
Garside Clo. SE28 70 G3
Goosander Way
Garside Clo., Hmptn. 81 H6
Garsington Ms. SE4 77 J3
Garth, The, Hmptn. 81 H6
Uxbridge Rd.
Garth, The, Har. 37 J6
Garth Clo. W4 65 D5
Garth Clo., Kings.T. 82 J5
Garth Clo., Mord. 93 A7
Garth Clo., Ruis. 45 D1
Garth Ct. W4 65 D5
Garth Rd.
Garth Rd. NW2 48 C2
Garth Rd. W4 65 D6
Garth Rd., Kings.T. 82 J5
Garth Rd., Mord. 92 J6
Garth Rd. Ind. Est., Mord. 93 A7
Garthland Dr., Barn. 22 H5
Garthorne Rd. SE23 77 G7
Garthside, Rich. 82 H5
Garthway N12 31 H6
Gartmoor Gdns. SW19 84 C1
Gartmore Rd., Ilf. 52 J2
Garton Pl. SW18 75 F6
Gartons Clo., Enf. 25 F4
Gartons Way SW11 75 F3
Garvary Rd. E16 60 H4
Garway Rd. W2 10 A4
Garway Rd. W2 57 E6
Gascoigne Gdns., Wdf.Grn. 34 E7
Gascoigne Pl. E2 9 F3
Gascoigne Pl. E2 59 C3
Gascoigne Rd., Bark. 61 F1
Gascony Ave. NW6 48 D7
Gascoyne Rd. E9 50 G7
Gaselee St. E14 60 C7
Gasholder Pl. SE11 20 D4
Gaskarth Rd. SW12 76 B6
Gaskarth Rd., Edg. 38 C1
Gaskell Rd. N6 39 J6
Gaskell St. SW4 76 E2
Gaskin St. N1 58 H1
Gaspar Clo. SW5 18 B1
Gaspar Ms. SW5 18 B1
Gassiot Rd. SW17 84 J4
Gassiot Way, Sutt. 100 G3
Gastein Rd. W6 66 A6
Gaston Bell Clo., Rich. 73 J3
Gaston Rd., Mitch. 94 A3
Gataker St. SE16 68 E3
Gatcombe Rd. N19 49 D3
Gate Clo., Borwd. 22 C1
Gate Ms. SW7 14 H4
Gate Ms. SW7 66 H2
Gate St. WC2 12 C3
Gateforth St. NW8 6 G6
Gatehouse Clo., Kings.T. 83 C7
Gateley Rd. SW9 76 F3
Gates Grn. Rd., Kes. 103 H4
Gates Grn. Rd., W.Wick. 103 F3
Gatesborough St. EC2 9 D5
Gateside Rd. SW17 84 J3
Gatestone Rd. SE19 86 B6
Gateway SE17 21 A5
Gateway SE17 67 J6
Gateway Ind. Est. NW10 56 F3

Gateway Ms. E8 50 C5
Shacklewell La.
Gateways, The SW3 18 H2
Gatfield Gro., Felt. 81 G2
Gathorne Rd. N22 40 G2
Gathorne St. E2 59 G2
Mace St.
Gatley Ave., Epsom 99 B5
Gatliff Rd. SW1 19 D4
Gatliff Rd. SW1 67 B5
Gatling Rd. SE2 71 A5
Gatting Clo., Edg. 30 C7
Pavilion Way
Gatton Rd. SW17 84 H4
Gattons Way, Sid. 89 F4
Gatward Clo. N21 24 H6
Gatward Grn. N9 33 C2
Gatwick Rd. SW18 75 C7
Gauden Clo. SW4 76 D3
Gauden Rd. SW4 76 D2
Gaunt St. SE1 16 H5
Gaunt St. SE1 67 J3
Gauntlet Clo., Nthlt. 45 E7
Gauntlett Ct., Wem. 46 E5
Gauntlett Rd., Sutt. 100 G5
Gautrey Rd. SE15 77 F2
Gautrey Sq. E6 61 C6
Truesdale Rd.
Gavel St. SE17 21 C1
Gaverick St. E14 69 A4
Gawsworth Clo. E15 79 H7
SE12
Gavestone Rd. SE12 78 H7
Gaviller Pl. E5 50 E4
Clarence Rd.
Gavin St. SE18 70 H4
Gavina Clo., Mord. 93 G5
Gawber St. E2 59 F3
Gawsworth Clo. E15 51 E5
Ash Rd.
Gawthorne Ave. NW7 31 B5
Lane App.
Gay Clo. NW2 47 H5
Gay Gdns., Dag. 53 J4
Gay Rd. E15 60 D2
Gay St. SW15 75 A3
Waterman St.
Gaydon Ho. W2 10 A1
Gaydon Ho. W2 57 E5
Gaydon La. NW9 38 E1
Gayfere Rd., Epsom 99 G5
Gayfere Rd., Ilf. 43 C3
Gayfere St. SW1 16 A6
Gayfere St. SW1 67 E3
Gayford Rd. W12 65 F2
Gayhurst SE17 21 C5
Gayhurst Rd. E8 50 D7
Gaylor Rd., Nthlt. 45 F5
Gaynes Hill Rd., Wdf.Grn. 35 B6
Gaynesford Rd. SE23 86 G2
Gaynesford Rd., Cars. 100 J7
Gaysham Ave., Ilf. 43 D5
Gaysham Hall, Ilf. 43 E3
Gayton Ct., Har. 37 C6
Gayton Cres. NW3 48 G4
Gayton Rd. NW3 48 G4
Gayton Rd. SE2 71 C3
Florence Rd.
Gayton Rd., Har. 37 C6
Gayville Rd. SW11 75 J6
Gaywood Clo. SW2 85 F1
Gaywood Est. SE1 16 H6
Gaywood Rd. E17 42 A3
Gaywood St. SE1 16 H6
Gaza St. SE17 20 G4
Geariesville Gdns., Ilf. 43 E4
Geary Rd. NW10 47 G5
Geary St. N7 49 F5
GEC Est., Wem. 46 G3
Gedeney Rd. N17 40 J1
Gedling Pl. SE1 17 G5
Gedling Pl. SE1 68 C3
Gee St. EC1 8 J5
Gee St. EC1 58 J4
Geere Rd. E15 60 F1
Gees Ct. W1 11 C4
Geffrye Ct. N1 9 E2
Geffrye St. E2 9 E2
Geffrye St. E2 59 C2
Geldart Rd. SE15 68 E7
Geldeston Rd. E5 50 D2
Gellatly Rd. SE14 77 F2
Gelston Pt. E1 59 E6
Gemini Gro., Nthlt. 54 E3
Javelin Way
General Gordon Pl. SE18 70 E4

General Wolfe Rd.	78	D1
SE10		
Genesta Rd. SE18	70	E6
Geneva Dr. SW9	76	G4
Geneva Gdns., Rom.	44	E5
Geneva Rd.,	91	H4
Kings.T.		
Geneva Rd., Th.Hth.	94	A5
Genever Clo. E4	34	A5
Genista Rd. N18	33	E5
Genoa Ave. SW15	74	J5
Genoa Rd. SE20	95	F1
Genotin Rd., Enf.	25	A3
Genotin Ter., Enf.	25	A3
Genotin Rd.		
Gentian Row SE13	78	C1
Sparta St.		
Gentlemans Row,	24	J3
Enf.		
Gentry Gdns. E13	60	G4
Whitwell Rd.		
Geoffrey Clo. SE5	76	J2
Geoffrey Gdns. E6	61	B2
Geoffrey Rd. SE4	77	J3
George Beard Rd.	68	J4
SE8		
George Comberton	52	D5
Wk. E12		
Gainsborough Ave.		
George Ct. WC2	**12**	**B6**
George Cres. N10	32	A7
George Downing Est.	50	C2
N16		
Cazenove Rd.		
George Fifth Way,	55	E1
Grnf.		
George V Ave., Pnr.	36	F1
George V Clo., Pnr.	36	G3
George V Ave.		
George Gros. Rd.	95	D1
SE20		
George Inn Yd. SE1	**17**	**B2**
George La. E18	42	G2
George La. SE13	78	C6
George La., Brom.	103	H1
George Lansbury Ho.	40	G1
N22		
Progress Way		
George Loveless Ho.	**9**	**G3**
E2		
George Ms. NW1	**7**	**F4**
George Rd. E4	34	A6
George Rd.,	83	B7
Kings.T.		
George Rd., N.Mal.	92	F4
George Row SE16	**17**	**H4**
George Sq. SW19	93	C3
Mostyn Rd.		
George St. E16	60	F6
George St. EC4	**13**	**B4**
George St. W1	**10**	**J3**
George St. W1	57	J6
George St. W7	64	B1
The Bdy.		
George St., Bark.	52	F7
George St., Croy.	101	J2
George St., Houns.	72	F2
George St., Rich.	73	G5
George St., Sthl.	63	E4
George St., Sutt.	100	E5
George Wyver Clo.	75	B7
SW19		
Beaumont Rd.		
George Yd. EC3	**13**	**C4**
George Yd. W1	**11**	**C5**
George Yd. W1	58	A7
Georges Rd. N7	49	F5
Georges Rd., Brom.	97	C3
Georges Sq. SW6	66	C6
North End Rd.		
Georgetown Clo.	86	A5
SE19		
St. Kitts Ter.		
Georgette Pl. SE10	69	C7
King George St.		
Georgeville Gdns.,	43	E4
Ilf.		
Georgia Rd., N.Mal.	92	C4
Georgia Rd., Th.Hth.	94	H1
Georgian Clo.,	115	J1
Brom.		
Georgian Clo., Stan.	29	D7
Georgian Ct., Wem.	47	A6
Georgian Way, Har.	46	A2
Georgiana St. NW1	58	C1
Georgina Gdns. E2	**9**	**G3**
Geraint Rd., Brom.	87	G4
Gerald Ms. SW1	**19**	**C1**
Gerald Rd. E16	60	F4
Gerald Rd. SW1	**19**	**C1**
Gerald Rd. SW1	67	A4
Gerald Rd., Dag.	53	F2
Geraldine Rd. SW18	75	F5
Geraldine Rd. W4	65	A6
Geraldine St. SE11	**16**	**G6**
Geraldine St. SE11	67	H3
Gerard Ave., Houns.	72	G7
Redfern Ave.		
Gerard Rd. SW13	74	F1
Gerard Rd., Har.	37	D6
Gerards Clo. SE16	68	F5
Gerda Rd. SE9	88	F2
Gillett St.		
Germander Way E15	60	E3
Gernon Rd. E3	59	H2
Geron Way NW2	47	H2
Gerrard Gdns., Pnr.	36	A5
Gerrard Pl. W1	**11**	**J5**
Gerrard Rd. N1	**8**	**G1**
Gerrard Rd. N1	58	H2
Gerrard St. W1	**11**	**J5**
Gerrard St. W1	58	D7
Gerrards Clo. N14	24	C5
Gerridge St. SE1	**16**	**F5**
Gerridge St. SE1	67	G3
Gerry Raffles Sq.	51	D6
E15		
Salway Rd.		
Gertrude Rd., Belv.	71	G4
Gertrude St. SW10	**18**	**D6**
Gertrude St. SW10	66	F6
Gervase Clo., Wem.	47	C3
Gervase Rd., Edg.	38	C1
Gervase St. SE15	68	E7
Ghent St. SE6	87	A2
Ghent Way E8	50	C6
Giant Tree Hill	29	A1
(Bushey), Wat.		
Gibbard Ms. SW19	84	A5
Gibbins Rd. E15	51	C7
Gibbon Rd. SE15	77	F2
Gibbon Rd. W3	56	E7
Gibbon Rd.,	91	H1
Kings.T.		
Gibbon Wk. SW15	74	G4
Swinburne Rd.		
Gibbons Rd. NW10	47	E6
Gibbs Ave. SE19	86	A5
Gibbs Clo. SE19	86	A5
Gibbs Couch, Wat.	28	D3
Gibbs Grn. W14	66	C5
Gibbs Grn., Edg.	30	C5
Gibbs Rd. N18	33	F4
Gibbs Sq. SE19	86	A5
Gibraltar Wk. E2	**9**	**G4**
Gibraltar Wk. E2	59	C3
Gibson Clo. E1	59	F4
Colebert Ave.		
Gibson Clo., Chess.	98	F6
Gibson Clo., Islw.	73	A3
Gibson Gdns. N16	50	C2
Northwold Rd.		
Gibson Rd. SE11	**20**	**D2**
Gibson Rd. SE11	67	F4
Gibson Rd., Dag.	53	C1
Gibson Rd., Sutt.	100	E5
Gibson Sq. N1	58	G1
Gibson St. SE10	69	E5
Gibson's Hill SW16	85	G7
Gideon Clo., Belv.	71	H4
Gideon Rd. SW11	76	A3
Giesbach Rd. N19	49	C2
Giffard Rd. N18	33	B5
Giffin St. SE8	69	A7
Gifford Gdns. W7	55	A5
Gifford St. N1	49	E7
Gift La. E15	60	F1
Giggs Hill Gdns.,	98	D1
T.Ditt.		
Giggs Hill Rd.,	91	D7
T.Ditt.		
Gilbert Gro., Edg.	38	D1
Gilbert Ho. SE8	69	A6
McMillan St.		
Gilbert Pl. WC1	**12**	**A2**
Gilbert Rd. SE11	**20**	**F2**
Gilbert Rd. SE11	67	G4
Gilbert Rd. SW19	84	F7
Gilbert Rd., Belv.	71	G3
Gilbert Rd., Brom.	87	G7
Gilbert Rd., Pnr.	36	D4
Gilbert St. E15	51	E4
Gilbert St. W1	**11**	**C4**
Gilbert St. W1	58	A6
Gilbert St., Houns.	72	J3
High St.		
Gilbey Rd. SW17	84	H4
Gilbourne Rd. SE18	70	J6
Gilda Ave., Enf.	25	H5
Gilda Cres. N16	50	D1
Gildea St. W1	**11**	**E2**
Gilden Cres. NW5	49	A5
Gilders Rd., Chess.	98	J7
Giles Coppice SE19	86	C4
Gilkes Cres. SE21	77	B6
Gilkes Pl. SE21	77	B6
Gill Ave. E16	60	G6
Gill St. E14	59	J7
Gillan Grn.,	28	J2
(Bushey), Wat.		
Gillender St. E3	60	C4
Gillender St. E14	60	C4
Gillespie Rd. N5	49	G3
Gillett Ave. E6	61	B2
Gillett Pl. N16	50	B5
Gillett St.		
Gillett Rd., Th.Hth.	95	A4
Gillett St. N16	50	B5
Gillfoot NW1	**7**	**F2**
Gillham Ter. N17	33	D6
Gillian Pk. Rd.,	100	C1
Sutt.		
Gillian St. SE13	78	B5
Gillies St. NW5	49	A5
Gilling Ct. NW3	48	H6
Gillingham Ms. SW1	19	F1
Gillingham Rd. NW2	48	B3
Gillingham Row SW1	19	F1
Gillingham St. SW1	**19**	**E1**
Gillingham St. SW1	67	C4
Gillison Wk. SE16	**17**	**J5**
Gillman Dr. E15	60	F1
Gillum Clo., Barn.	31	J1
Gilmore Rd. SE13	78	D4
Gilpin Ave. SW14	74	D4
Gilpin Clo., Mitch.	93	H2
Gilpin Cres. N18	33	C5
Gilpin Cres., Twick.	72	H7
Gilpin Rd. E5	50	H4
Gilsland Rd.,	95	A4
Th.Hth.		
Gilstead Ho., Bark.	62	B2
Gilstead Rd. SW6	75	E2
Gilston Rd. SW10	66	F5
Gilton Rd. SE6	87	E3
Giltspur St. EC1	**12**	**H3**
Giltspur St. EC1	58	H6
Gilwell La. E4	26	D4
Gippeswyck Clo.,	36	D1
Pnr.		
Uxbridge Rd.		
Gipsy Hill SE19	86	B5
Gipsy La. SW15	74	G3
Gipsy Rd. SE27	85	J4
Gipsy Rd., Well.	80	D1
Gipsy Rd. Gdns.	85	J4
SE27		
Giralda Clo. E16	61	A5
Fulmer Rd.		
Giraud St. E14	60	B6
Girdlers Rd. W14	66	A4
Girdlestone Wk. N19	49	C2
Girdwood Rd. SW18	75	B7
Girling Way, Felt.	72	A3
Gironde Rd. SW6	66	C7
Girton Ave. NW9	38	A3
Girton Clo., Nthlt.	45	J6
Girton Gdns., Croy.	103	A3
Girton Rd. SE26	86	G5
Girton Rd., Nthlt.	45	J6
Girton Vill. W10	57	A6
Cambridge Gdns.		
Gisburn Rd. N8	40	F4
Gissing Wk. N1	49	G7
Lofting Rd.		
Given Wilson Wk.	60	F2
E13		
Gladbeck Way, Enf.	24	H5
Gladding Rd. E12	52	A4
Glade, The N21	24	F6
Glade, The SE7	69	J7
Glade, The, Brom.	92	A1
Glade, The, Croy.	95	G5
Glade, The, Enf.	24	G2
Stride Rd.		
Glade, The, Epsom	97	J6
Glade, The, Ilf.	43	C1
Glade, The, W.Wick.	103	B3
Glade, The,	34	H3
Wdf.Grn.		
Glade Clo., Surb.	98	G2
Glade Ct., Ilf.	43	C1
The Glade		
Glade Gdns., Croy.	95	H7
Glade La., Sthl.	63	H2
Glades Shop. Cen.,	96	G2
The, Brom.		
Gladeside N21	24	F7
Gladeside, Croy.	95	G7
Gladeside Clo.,	98	G7
Chess.		
Leatherhead Rd.		
Gladesmore Rd. N15	41	C6
Gladeswood Rd.,	71	H4
Belv.		
Gladiator St. SE23	77	H7
Glading Ter. N16	50	C3
Gladioli Clo., Hmptn.	81	G6
Gresham Rd.		
Gladsdale Dr., Pnr.	36	B4
Gladsmuir Rd. N19	49	C1
Gladsmuir Rd.,	23	B2
Barn.		
Gladstone Ave. E12	52	B7
Gladstone Ave. N22	40	G2
Gladstone Ave.,	72	A6
Felt.		
Gladstone Ave.,	73	A7
Twick.		
Gladstone Ms. SE20	86	F7
Gladstone Pk. Gdns.	47	H4
NW2		
Gladstone Pl. E3	59	J2
Roman Rd.		
Gladstone Pl.,	23	A4
Barn.		
Gladstone Rd. SW19	84	D7
Gladstone Rd. W4	65	D3
Acton La.		
Gladstone Rd.,	34	H1
Buck.H.		
Gladstone Rd.,	95	A7
Croy.		
Gladstone Rd.,	92	A3
Kings.T.		
Gladstone Rd., Orp.	104	F5
Gladstone Rd.,	63	E2
Sthl.		
Gladstone Rd.,	98	G2
Surb.		
Gladstone St. SE1	**16**	**G5**
Gladstone St. SE1	67	H3
Gladstone Ter. SE27	85	J4
Gladstone Ter. SW8	76	B1
Gladstone Way, Har.	37	B3
Gladwell Rd. N8	40	F6
Gladwell Rd., Brom.	87	G6
Gladwyn Rd. SW15	75	A3
Gladys Rd. NW6	48	D7
Glaisher St. SE10	69	C7
Straightsmouth		
Glamis Pl. E1	59	F7
Glamis Rd. E1	59	F7
Glamis Way, Nthlt.	45	J6
Glamorgan Clo.,	94	E3
Mitch.		
Glamorgan Rd.,	82	F7
Kings.T.		
Glanfield Rd.,	95	J4
Beck.		
Glanleam Rd., Stan.	29	G4
Glanville Rd. SW2	76	E5
Glanville Rd.,	96	H3
Brom.		
Glasbrook Ave.,	81	F1
Twick.		
Glasbrook Rd. SE9	79	A7
Glaserton Rd. N16	41	B7
Glasford St. SW17	84	J6
Glasgow Ho. W9	**6**	**B2**
Glasgow Ho. W9	57	E2
Glasgow Rd. E13	60	H2
Glasgow Rd. N18	33	E5
Aberdeen Rd.		
Glasgow Ter. SW1	**19**	**F4**
Glasgow Ter. SW1	67	C5
Glass St. E2	59	E4
Coventry Rd.		
Glass Yd. SE18	70	D3
Glassbrook Rd. W13	55	D7
Glasshill St. SE1	**16**	**H3**
Glasshill St. SE1	67	H2
Glasshouse All. EC4	**12**	**F4**
Glasshouse Flds. E1	59	G7
Glasshouse St. W1	**11**	**G6**
Glasshouse St. W1	58	C7
Glasshouse Wk.	**20**	**B3**
SE11		
Glasshouse Wk.	67	G6
SE11		
Glasshouse Yd. EC1	**13**	**J6**
Glasslyn Rd. N8	40	D5
Glassmill La.,	96	F2
Brom.		
Glastonbury Ave.,	35	A7
Wdf.Grn.		
Glastonbury Rd. N9	33	D1
Glastonbury Rd.,	93	D7
Mord.		
Glastonbury St. NW6	48	C5
Glaucus St. E3	60	B5
Glazbury Rd. W14	66	B4
Glazebrook Clo.	86	A2
SE21		
Glazebrook Rd.,	82	C7
Tedd.		
Glebe, The SE3	78	E3
Glebe, The SW16	85	D4
Glebe, The, Chis.	97	F1

Glebe, The, Wor.Pk. 99 F1
Glebe Ave., Enf. 24 H3
Glebe Ave., Har. 37 H3
Glebe Ave., Mitch. 93 H2
Glebe Ave., Ruis. 45 B6
Glebe Ave., Wdf.Grn. 34 G6
Glebe Clo. W4 65 E5
  Glebe St.
Glebe Ct. W7 55 A7
Glebe Ct., Mitch. 93 J3
Glebe Ct., Stan. 29 F5
  Glebe Rd.
Glebe Cres. NW4 38 J4
Glebe Cres., Har. 37 H3
Glebe Gdns., N.Mal. 92 E7
Glebe Ho. Dr., 103 H1
  Brom.
Glebe Hyrst SE19 86 C4
  Giles Coppice
Glebe La., Barn. 22 G5
Glebe La., Har. 37 H4
Glebe Path, Mitch. 93 H3
Glebe Pl. SW3 18 G5
Glebe Pl. SW3 66 H6
Glebe Rd. E8 50 C7
  Middleton Rd.
Glebe Rd. N3 39 F1
Glebe Rd. N8 40 F4
Glebe Rd. NW10 47 F6
Glebe Rd. SW13 74 G2
Glebe Rd., Brom. 96 G1
Glebe Rd., Cars. 100 J6
Glebe Rd., Dag. 53 H6
Glebe Rd., Stan. 29 F5
Glebe Side, Twick. 73 C7
Glebe St. W4 65 E5
  Bow Rd.
Glebe Way, Felt. 81 G3
Glebe Way, W.Wick. 103 C2
Glebelands, W.Mol. 90 H5
Glebelands Ave. E18 42 G2
Glebelands Ave., Ilf. 43 G7
Glebelands Clo. SE5 77 B6
  Grove Hill Rd.
Glebelands Rd., Felt. 72 A7
Glebeway, Wdf.Grn. 34 J5
Gledhow Gdns. SW5 18 C2
Gledhow Gdns. SW5 66 F4
Gledstanes Rd. W14 66 B5
Gleed Ave. 29 A2
  (Bushey), Wat.
Gleeson Dr., Orp. 104 J5
Glegg Pl. SW15 75 A4
Glen, The, Brom. 96 E2
Glen, The, Croy. 102 G3
Glen, The, Enf. 24 H4
Glen, The, Orp. 104 C3
Glen, The, Pnr. 36 B5
Glen, The 36 E7
  (Eastcote), Pnr.
Glen, The, Sthl. 63 F5
Glen, The, Wem. 46 G4
Glen Albyn Rd. 84 A2
  SW19
Glen Cres., 34 H6
  Wdf.Grn.
Glen Gdns., Croy. 101 H3
Glen Mill, Hmptn. 81 F5
Glen Ri., Wdf.Grn. 34 H6
Glen Rd. E13 60 J4
Glen Rd. E17 41 J5
Glen Rd., Chess. 98 H3
Glen Wk., Islw. 73 A5
Glena Mt., Sutt. 100 F4
Glenaffric Ave. E14 69 D4
Glenalmond Rd., 37 H4
  Har.
Glenalvon Way SE18 70 B4
Glenarm Rd. E5 50 F5
Glenavon Clo., 98 D6
  Esher
Glenavon Rd. E15 51 E7
Glenbarr Clo. SE9 79 E3
  Dumbreck Rd.
Glenbow Rd., Brom. 87 E6
Glenbrook N., Enf. 24 F4
Glenbrook Rd. NW6 48 D5
Glenbrook S., Enf. 24 F4
Glenbuck Ct., Surb. 91 G6
  Glenbuck Rd.
Glenbuck Rd., Surb. 91 G6
Glenburnie Rd. 84 H3
  SW17
Glencairn Dr. W5 55 F4
Glencairn Rd. SW16 85 E7
Glencairne Clo. E16 61 A5
Glencoe Ave., Ilf. 43 G7
Glencoe Dr., Dag. 53 G4
Glencoe Rd., Hayes 54 D4
Glencourse Grn., 28 D4
  Wat.
  Caldwell Rd.

Glendale Ave. N22 32 G7
Glendale Ave., Edg. 30 A4
Glendale Ave., Rom. 44 C7
Glendale Clo. SE9 79 D3
  Dumbreck Rd.
Glendale Dr. SW19 84 C5
Glendale Gdns. 46 G1
  Wem.
Glendale Ms., Beck. 96 B1
Glendale Rd., Erith 71 J4
Glendale Way SE28 62 C7
Glendall St. SW9 76 F4
Glendarvon St. 75 A3
  SW15
Glendevon Clo., Edg. 30 B3
  Tayside Dr.
Glendish Rd. N17 41 D1
Glendor Gdns. NW7 30 D4
Glendower Gdns. 74 D3
  SW14
  Glendower Rd.
Glendower Pl. SW7 18 E1
Glendower Pl. SW7 66 G4
Glendower Rd. E4 34 D1
Glendower Rd. SW14 74 D3
Glendown Rd. SE2 71 A5
Glendun Rd. W3 56 E7
Gleneagle Rd. SW16 85 D5
  Ambleside Ave.
Gleneagle Rd. SW16 85 D6
Gleneagles, Stan. 29 E6
Gleneagles Clo., 104 G1
  Orp.
Gleneagles Clo. 29 E6
  Stan.
Gleneagles Clo., 28 D4
  Wat.
Gleneagles Twr., 54 J6
  Sthl.
Gleneldon Ms. SW16 85 E4
Gleneldon Rd. SW16 85 E4
Glenelg Rd. SW2 76 E5
Glenesk Rd. SE9 79 D3
Glenfarg Rd. SE6 87 D1
Glenfield Rd. SW12 85 C1
Glenfield Rd. W13 64 E2
Glenfield Ter. W13 64 E1
Glenfinlas Way SE5 20 H7
Glenfinlas Way SE5 77 H7
Glenforth St. SE10 69 F5
Glengall Causeway 69 A3
  E14
  Ferry Rd.
Glengall Gro. E14 69 C3
Glengall Rd. NW6 57 C1
Glengall Rd. SE15 21 G5
Glengall Rd. SE15 68 C5
Glengall Rd., Bexh. 80 E3
Glengall Rd., Edg. 30 B1
Glengall Rd., 34 G6
  Wdf.Grn.
Glengall Ter. SE15 21 G5
Glengall Ter. SE15 68 C5
Glengarnock Ave. 69 C4
  E14
Glengarry Rd. SE22 77 B5
Glenham Dr., Ilf. 43 E5
Glenhaven Ave., 22 A3
  Borwd.
Glenhead Clo. SE9 79 E3
  Dumbreck Rd.
Glenhill Clo. N3 39 D2
Glenhouse Rd. SE9 79 D5
Glenhurst Ave. NW5 49 A4
Glenhurst Ave., Bex. 89 F1
Glenhurst Ct. SE19 86 C5
Glenhurst Ri. SE19 85 J7
Glenhurst Rd. N12 31 G5
Glenhurst Rd., 64 F6
  Brent.
Glenilla Rd. NW3 48 H6
Glenister Ho., 63 B1
  Hayes
Glenister Pk. Rd. 85 D7
  SW16
Glenister Rd. SE10 69 F5
Glenister St. E16 70 D1
Glenlea Rd. SE9 79 D5
Glenloch Rd. NW3 48 H6
Glenloch Rd., Enf. 25 F2
Glenluce Rd. SE3 69 H6
Glenlyon Rd. SE9 79 D5
Glenmere Ave. NW7 30 G7
Glenmore Rd. NW3 48 H6
Glenmore Rd., Well. 70 J7
Glenmore Way, Bark. 62 A3
Glenmount Path 70 F5
  SE18
  Raglan Rd.
Glennie Rd. SE27 85 G3
Glenny Rd., Bark. 52 F6
Glenorchy Clo., 54 E5
  Hayes

Glenparke Rd. E7 51 H6
Glenrosa St. SW6 75 F2
Glenrose Ct., Sid. 89 B5
Glenroy St. W12 56 J6
Glensdale Rd. SE4 77 J3
Glenshiel Rd. SE9 79 D5
Glenside, Chig. 35 E6
Glentanner Way 84 G3
  SW17
  Aboyne Rd.
Glentham Gdns. 65 H6
  SW13
  Glentham Rd.
Glentham Rd. SW13 65 G6
Glenthorne Ave., 102 E1
  Croy.
Glenthorne Clo., 100 D1
  Sutt.
Glenthorne Gdns., 43 D3
  Ilf.
Glenthorne Gdns., 100 D1
  Sutt.
Glenthorne Rd. E17 41 H5
Glenthorne Rd. N11 31 J5
Glenthorne Rd. W6 65 H4
Glenthorne Rd., 91 J4
  Kings.T.
Glenthorpe Rd., 93 A5
  Mord.
Glenton Rd. SE13 78 E4
Glentrammon Ave., 104 J6
  Orp.
Glentrammon Clo., 104 J5
  Orp.
Glentrammon Gdns.,104 J6
  Orp.
Glentrammon Rd., 104 J6
  Orp.
Glentworth St. NW1 7 A6
Glenure Rd. SE9 79 D5
Glenview SE2 71 D6
Glenview Rd., Brom. 97 A2
Glenville Gro. SE8 68 J7
Glenville Ms. SW18 75 E7
Glenville Rd., 92 A1
  Kings.T.
Glenwood Ave. NW9 47 E1
Glenwood Clo., Har. 37 C5
Glenwood Gdns., 43 D5
  Ilf.
Glenwood Gro. NW9 47 C1
Glenwood Rd. N15 40 H5
Glenwood Rd. NW7 30 E3
Glenwood Rd. SE6 86 J1
Glenwood Rd., 99 G6
  Epsom
Glenwood Rd., 73 A3
  Houns.
Glenwood Way, 95 G6
  Croy.
Glenworth Ave. E14 69 D4
Gliddon Rd. W14 66 B4
Glimpsing Grn., 71 E3
  Erith
Global App. E3 60 B2
  Hancock Rd.
Globe Pond Rd. SE16 68 H1
Globe Rd. E1 59 G4
Globe Rd. E2 59 F3
Globe Rd. E15 51 F5
Globe Rd., Wdf.Grn. 34 J6
Globe Robe Wk. E14 69 C4
  East Ferry Rd.
Globe St. SE1 17 B4
Globe St. SE1 68 A2
Globe Ter. E2 59 F3
  Globe Rd.
Globe Yd. W1 11 D4
Gloster Rd., N.Mal. 92 E4
Gloucester Ave. NW1 49 A7
Gloucester Ave., 88 H2
  Sid.
Gloucester Ave., 79 J4
  Well.
Gloucester Circ. 69 C7
  SE10
Gloucester Clo. 47 D7
  NW10
Gloucester Clo., 98 D1
  T.Ditt.
Gloucester Ct. EC3 13 E6
Gloucester Ct., 65 A7
  Rich.
Gloucester Cres. 58 B1
  NW1
Gloucester Dr. N4 49 H2
Gloucester Dr. NW11 39 D4
Gloucester Gdns. 39 C7
  NW11
Gloucester Gdns. W2 10 B3
Gloucester Gdns., 24 A4
  Barn.

Gloucester Gdns., 43 B7
  Ilf.
Gloucester Gdns., 100 E2
  Sutt.
Gloucester Gate NW1 7 D1
Gloucester Gate NW1 58 B2
Gloucester Gate Ms. 7 D1
  NW1
Gloucester Gro., 38 D1
  Edg.
Gloucester Gro. Est. 68 B6
  SE15
Gloucester Ho. N7 49 E3
Gloucester Ho. NW6 57 D2
Gloucester Ms. W2 10 D4
Gloucester Ms. W2 57 F6
Gloucester Ms. W. 10 C4
  W2
Gloucester Par., Sid. 80 A5
Gloucester Pl. NW1 6 J5
Gloucester Pl. NW1 7 A6
Gloucester Pl. W1 11 A1
Gloucester Pl. W1 7 J5
Gloucester Pl. Ms. 11 A2
  W1
Gloucester Rd. E10 42 A7
Gloucester Rd. E11 42 H5
Gloucester Rd. E12 52 C3
Gloucester Rd. E17 41 G2
Gloucester Rd. N17 41 A3
Gloucester Rd. N18 33 C5
Gloucester Rd. SW7 14 C5
Gloucester Rd. SW7 66 F5
Gloucester Rd. W3 65 C2
Gloucester Rd. W5 64 F2
Gloucester Rd., 23 E5
  Barn.
Gloucester Rd., 71 F5
  Belv.
Gloucester Rd., 102 A1
  Croy.
Gloucester Rd., 81 C1
  Felt.
Gloucester Rd., 81 H7
  Hmptn.
Gloucester Rd., Har. 36 H5
Gloucester Rd., 72 E4
  Houns.
Gloucester Rd., 92 A2
  Kings.T.
Gloucester Rd., Rich. 65 A7
Gloucester Rd., Tedd. 82 B5
Gloucester Rd., 81 J1
  Twick.
Gloucester Sq. E2 59 D1
  Whiston Rd.
Gloucester Sq. W2 10 F4
Gloucester Sq. W2 57 G6
Gloucester St. SW1 19 F4
Gloucester St. SW1 67 C5
Gloucester Ter. W2 10 B3
Gloucester Ter. W2 57 E6
Gloucester Wk. W8 66 D2
Gloucester Way EC1 8 F4
Gloucester Way EC1 58 G3
Glover Dr. N18 33 F6
Glover Rd., Pnr. 36 D6
Gloxinia Wk., 81 G6
  Hmptn.
  The Ave.
Glycena Rd. SW11 75 J3
Glyn Ave., Barn. 23 G4
Glyn Clo. SE25 95 B2
Glyn Ct. SW16 85 G3
Glyn Dr., Sid. 89 B4
Glyn Rd. E5 50 G4
Glyn Rd., Enf. 25 F4
Glyn Rd., Wor.Pk. 100 A2
Glyn St. SE11 20 C4
Glynde Ms. SW3 14 H6
Glynde Rd., Bexh. 80 D3
Glynde St. SE4 77 J6
Glyndebourne Pk., 104 C3
  Orp.
Glyndon Rd. SE18 70 F4
Glynfield Rd. NW10 47 E7
Glynne Rd. N22 40 G2
Glynwood Dr. SE23 86 F3
Goat La., Surb. 98 E2
Goat La., Mitch. 93 J7
Goat St. SE1 17 F3
Goat Wf., Brent. 64 H6
Goaters All. SW6 66 C7
  Dawes Rd.
Godalming Ave., 101 E5
  Wall.
Godalming Rd. E14 60 B5
Godbold Rd. E15 60 E3
Goddard Rd., Beck. 95 G4
Godfrey Ave., Nthlt. 54 E1
Godfrey Ave., Twick. 73 A7
Godfrey Hill SE18 70 B4
Godfrey Rd. SE18 70 C4

Godfrey St. E15 60 C2
Abbey La.
Godfrey St. SW3 **18 H3**
Godfrey St. SW3 66 H5
Godfrey Way, Houns. 72 F7
Goding St. SE11 **20 B4**
Goding St. SE11 67 E5
Godley Rd. SW18 84 G1
Godliman St. EC4 **12 J4**
Godliman St. EC4 58 J6
Godman Rd. SE15 77 E2
Godolphin Clo. N13 32 H6
Godolphin Pl. W3 56 D7
Vyner Rd.
Godolphin Rd. W12 65 H1
Godson Rd., Croy. 101 G3
Godson St. N1 **8 E1**
Godstone Rd., Sutt. 100 F4
Godstone Rd., 73 D6
Twick.
Godstow Rd. SE2 71 B2
Godwin Clo. N1 **9 A1**
Godwin Clo., Epsom 99 C6
Godwin Ct. NW1 **7 G1**
Godwin Rd. E7 51 H4
Godwin Rd., Brom. 96 J3
Goffers Rd. SE3 78 E2
Goidel, Clo., Wall. 101 D4
Golborne Gdns. W10 57 C4
Golborne Rd.
Golborne Ms. W10 57 B5
Portobello Rd.
Golborne Rd. W10 57 B5
Gold Hill, Edg. 30 D6
Gold La., Edg. 30 D6
Golda Clo., Barn. 23 A6
Goldbeaters Gro., 30 E6
Edg.
Goldcliff Clo., Mord. 93 D7
Goldcrest Clo. SE28 62 C7
Sheerwater Rd.
Goldcrest Clo. E16 61 A5
Maplin Rd.
Goldcrest Ms. W5 55 G5
Montpelier Ave.
Goldcrest Way 28 J1
(Bushey), Wat.
Golden Ct., Rich. 73 G5
George St.
Golden La. EC1 **8 J6**
Golden La. EC1 8 J6
Golden La. Est. EC1 **8 J6**
Golden Manor W7 55 B7
Golden Plover Clo. 60 H6
E16
Maplin Rd.
Golden Sq. W1 **11 G5**
Golden Sq. W1 58 C7
Golden Yd. NW3 48 F4
Heath St.
Golders Clo., Edg. 30 B5
Golders Gdns. NW11 39 B7
Golders Grn. Cres. 39 C7
NW11
Golders Grn. Rd. 39 B6
NW11
Golders Manor Dr. 39 A6
NW11
Golders Pk. Clo. 48 D1
NW11
Golders Ri. NW4 39 A5
Golders Way NW11 39 C7
Goldfinch Rd. SE28 70 G3
Goldfinch Way, 22 A4
Borwd.
Siskin Clo.
Goldhawk Ms. W12 65 H2
Devonport Rd.
Goldhawk Rd. W6 65 F4
Goldhawk Rd. W12 65 G3
Goldhaze Clo., 35 A7
Wdf.Grn.
Goldhurst Ter. NW6 48 E7
Golding St. E1 **13 J4**
Golding St. E1 59 D6
Goldingham Ave., 27 F2
Loug.
Goldings Ri., Loug. 27 D1
Goldings Rd., Loug. 27 D1
Goldington Cres. **7 H1**
NW1
Goldington Cres. 58 D2
NW1
Goldington Cres. 58 D2
Gdns. NW1
Goldington St. NW1 **7 H1**
Goldington St. NW1 58 D2
Goldman Clo. E2 **9 H5**
Goldman Clo. E2 59 D4
Goldney Rd. W9 57 D4
Goldsborough Cres. 34 B2
E4
Goldsborough Rd. 76 D1
SW8

Goldsdown Clo., 25 H2
Enf.
Goldsdown Rd., Enf. 25 G2
Goldsmid St. SE18 70 H5
Sladedale Rd.
Goldsmith Ave. E12 52 B6
Goldsmith Ave. NW9 38 E5
Goldsmith Ave. W3 56 D7
Goldsmith Ave., 44 G7
Rom.
Goldsmith Clo. W3 65 E1
East Acton La.
Goldsmith Clo., 45 H1
Har.
Goldsmith La. NW9 38 B4
Goldsmith Rd. E10 51 A1
Goldsmith Rd. E17 41 G2
Goldsmith Rd. N11 31 J5
Goldsmith Rd. SE15 77 D1
Goldsmith Rd. W3 65 D1
Goldsmith St. EC2 **13 A3**
Goldsmith's Row E2 **9 J1**
Goldsmith's Row E2 59 D2
Goldsmith's Sq. E2 **9 J1**
Goldsmith's Sq. E2 59 D2
Goldsworthy Gdns. 68 F4
SE16
Goldwell Rd., 94 F4
Th.Hth.
Goldwin Clo. SE14 77 F1
Golf Clo., Stan. 29 F7
Golf Club Dr., 83 D7
Kings.T.
Golf Rd. W5 55 J6
Boileau Rd.
Golf Rd., Brom. 97 D3
Golf Side, Twick. 82 A3
Golfe Rd., Ilf. 52 G3
Golfside Clo. N20 31 H3
Golfside Clo., 92 E2
N.Mal.
Goliath Clo., Wall. 101 E7
Avro Way
Gollogly Ter. SE7 69 J5
Gomer Gdns., Tedd. 82 D6
Gomer Pl., Tedd. 82 D6
Gomm Rd. SE16 68 F3
Gomshall Ave., 101 E5
Wall.
Gondar Gdns. NW6 48 C5
Gonson Pl. SE8 69 A6
Gonson St. SE8 69 B6
Gonston Clo. SW19 84 B2
Bodicott Clo.
Gonville Cres., 45 H6
Nthlt.
Gonville Rd., 94 F5
Th.Hth.
Gonville St. SW6 75 B3
Putney Bri. App.
Goodall Rd. E11 51 C3
Gooden Ct., Har. 46 B3
Goodenough Rd. 84 C7
SW19
Goodge Pl. W1 **11 G2**
Goodge St. W1 **11 G2**
Goodge St. W1 58 C5
Goodhall St. NW10 56 E3
Goodhart Pl. E14 59 H7
Goodhart Way, 91 F7
W.Wick.
Goodhew Rd., Croy. 95 D6
Gooding Clo., 92 C4
N.Mal.
Goodinge Clo. N7 49 E6
Goodman Cres. SW2 85 D2
Goodman Rd. E10 42 C7
Goodmans Ct., Wem. 46 G4
Goodman's Flds. E1 **13 H4**
Goodman's Stile E1 **13 H3**
Goodman's Stile E1 59 D6
Goodmans Yd. E1 **13 F5**
Goodmayes Ave. 53 A1
Ilf.
Goodmayes La., Ilf. 53 A2
Goodmayes Rd., Ilf. 53 A1
Goodrich Rd. SE22 77 C6
Goods Way NW1 **8 A1**
Goodson Rd. NW10 47 E7
Goodway Gdns. E14 60 D6
Goodwin Clo., 93 G3
Mitch.
Goodwin Dr., Sid. 89 D3
Goodwin Gdns., 101 H6
Croy.
Goodwin Rd. N9 33 F1
Goodwin Rd. W12 65 G2
Goodwin Rd., Croy. 101 H5
Goodwin St. N4 49 G2
Fonthill Rd.
Goodwins Ct. WC2 **12 A5**

Goodwood Clo., 93 D4
Mord.
Goodwood Clo., 29 F5
Stan.
Marsh La.
Goodwood Dr., 45 G6
Nthlt.
Goodwood Path, 22 A3
Borwd.
Stratfield Rd.
Goodwood Rd. SE14 68 H7
Goodwyn Ave. NW7 30 E5
Goodwyns Vale N10 40 A1
Goodyers Gdns. NW4 39 A5
Goosander Way 70 G3
SE28
Goose Sq. E6 61 C6
Harper Rd.
Gooseacre La., Har. 37 G5
Gooseley La. E6 61 D3
Goossens Clo., 100 F5
Sutt.
Turnpike La.
Gophir La. EC4 **13 B5**
Gopsall St. N1 59 A1
Gordon Ave. E4 34 E6
Gordon Ave. SW14 74 E4
Gordon Ave., Stan. 29 C7
Gordon Ave., Twick. 73 D5
Gordon Clo. E17 42 A6
Gordon Clo. N19 49 C1
Highgate Hill
Gordon Ct. W12 56 H6
Gordon Cres., Croy. 102 B1
Gordon Cres., Hayes 63 A3
Gordon Gdns., Edg. 38 B2
Gordon Gro. SE5 76 H2
Gordon Hill, Enf. 24 J1
Gordon Ho. Rd. NW5 49 A4
Gordon Pl. W8 66 D2
Gordon Rd. E4 26 E7
Gordon Rd. E11 42 G6
Gordon Rd. E15 51 C4
Gordon Rd. E18 42 H1
Gordon Rd. N3 31 C7
Gordon Rd. N9 33 E2
Gordon Rd. N11 32 D7
Gordon Rd. SE15 77 E2
Gordon Rd. W4 65 B6
Gordon Rd. W5 55 F7
Gordon Rd. W13 55 E7
Gordon Rd., Bark. 61 H1
Gordon Rd., Beck. 95 J3
Gordon Rd., Belv. 71 J4
Gordon Rd., Cars. 100 J6
Gordon Rd., Enf. 25 A1
Gordon Rd., Esher 98 B7
Gordon Rd., Har. 37 B3
Gordon Rd., Houns. 72 J4
Gordon Rd., Ilf. 52 G3
Gordon Rd., 91 J1
Kings.T.
Gordon Rd., Rich. 73 J2
Gordon Rd., Rom. 44 F6
Gordon Rd., Sid. 79 H5
Gordon Rd., Sthl. 63 E4
Gordon Rd., Surb. 91 J7
Gordon Sq. WC1 **7 H5**
Gordon Sq. WC1 58 C4
Gordon St. E13 60 G3
Grange Rd.
Gordon St. WC1 **7 H5**
Gordon St. WC1 58 D4
Gordon Way, Barn. 23 C4
Gordonbrock Rd. SE4 78 A5
Gordondale Rd. 84 D2
SW19
Gore Ct. NW9 38 A5
Gore Rd. E9 59 F1
Gore Rd. SW20 92 J2
Gore St. SW7 **14 D5**
Gore St. SW7 66 F3
Gorefield Rd. NW6 57 D2
Goresbrook Rd., 62 B1
Dag.
Gorham Pl. W11 57 B7
Mary Pl.
Goring Clo., Rom. 44 J1
Goring Rd. N11 32 E6
Goring St. EC3 **13 E3**
Goring St. EC3 59 B6
Goring Way, Grnf. 54 J2
Gorleston Rd. N15 41 A5
Gorleston St. W14 66 B4
Gorman Rd. SE18 70 C4
Gorringe Pk. Ave., 84 J7
Mitch.
Gorse Ri. SW17 85 A5
Gorse Rd., Croy. 103 A3
Gorst Rd. NW10 56 C4
Gorst Rd. SW11 75 J6
Gorsuch Pl. E2 **9 F3**
Gorsuch St. E2 **9 F3**

Gorsuch St. E2 59 C3
Gosberton Rd. SW12 84 J1
Gosbury Hill, 98 H4
Chess.
Gosfield Rd., Dag. 53 G2
Gosfield St. W1 **11 F1**
Gosfield St. W1 58 C5
Gosford Gdns., Ilf. 43 C5
Gosforth La., Wat. 28 A3
Gosforth Path, Wat. 28 A3
Gosforth La.
Goslett Yd. WC2 **11 J4**
Gosling Clo., Grnf. 54 G3
Gosling Way SW9 76 G1
Gospatrick Rd. N17 32 J7
Gospel Oak Est. NW5 48 J5
Gosport Rd. E17 41 J5
Gosport Way SE15 **21 F7**
Gossage Rd. SE18 70 G5
Ancona Rd.
Gosset St. E2 **9 G4**
Gosset St. E2 59 C3
Gosshill Rd., Chis. 97 D2
Gossington Clo., 88 E4
Chis.
Beechwood Ri.
Gosterwood St. SE8 68 H6
Gostling Rd., 81 G1
Twick.
Goston Gdns. 94 G3
Th.Hth.
Goswell Rd. EC1 **8 G2**
Goswell Rd. EC1 58 H2
Gothic Rd., Twick. 82 A2
Goudhurst Rd., 87 E5
Brom.
Gough Rd. E15 51 F4
Gough Rd., Enf. 25 E2
Gough Sq. EC4 **12 F3**
Gough St. WC1 8 D5
Gough St. WC1 58 F4
Gough Wk. E14 60 A3
Saracen St.
Gould Ct. SE19 86 B5
Gould Rd., Twick. 82 B1
Gould Ter. E8 50 E5
Kenmure Rd.
Goulston St. E1 **13 F3**
Goulston St. E1 59 C6
Goulton Rd. E5 50 E4
Gourley Pl. N15 41 B5
Gourley St.
Gourley St. N15 41 B5
Gourock Rd. SE9 79 D5
Govan St. E2 59 D1
Whiston Rd.
Govier Clo. E15 51 E7
Gowan Ave. SW6 75 B1
Gowan Rd. NW10 47 H6
Gower Ct. WC1 **7 H5**
Gower Ms. WC1 **11 J2**
Gower Ms. WC1 58 D5
Gower Pl. WC1 **7 G5**
Gower Pl. WC1 58 C4
Gower Rd. E7 51 G6
Gower Rd., Islw. 64 C6
Gower St. WC1 **7 H6**
Gower St. WC1 58 C4
Gower's Wk. E1 **13 H3**
Gower's Wk. E1 59 D6
Gowland Pl., Beck. 95 J2
Gowlett Rd. SE15 77 D3
Gowrie Rd. SW11 76 A3
Graburn Way, E.Mol. 91 A3
Grace Ave., Bexh. 80 F2
Grace Clo. SE9 88 A3
Grace Clo., Borwd. 22 D1
Grace Clo., Edg. 30 C7
Pavilion Way
Grace Clo., Ilf. 35 J6
Grace Jones Clo. E8 50 D6
Parkholme Rd.
Grace Rd., Croy. 94 J6
Grace St. E3 60 B3
Gracechurch St. EC3 **13 C5**
Gracechurch St. EC3 59 A7
Gracedale Rd. SW16 85 B5
Gracefield Gdns. 85 E3
SW16
Grace's All. E1 **13 H5**
Graces Ms. SE5 77 A2
Graces Rd. SE5 77 B2
Gradient, The SE26 86 D4
Graeme Rd., Enf. 25 A2
Graemesdyke Ave. 74 B3
SW14
Grafton Clo. W13 55 D6
Grafton Clo., 81 E1
Houns.
Grafton Clo., 99 E3
Wor.Pk.
Grafton Cres. NW1 49 B6
Grafton Gdns. N4 40 J6

Grafton Gdns., Dag.	53	E2
Grafton Ho. E3	60	A3
Wellington Way		
Grafton Ms. W1	7	F6
Grafton Pk. Rd.,	99	E2
Wor.Pk.		
Grafton Pl. NW1	7	H4
Grafton Pl. NW1	58	D3
Grafton Rd. NW5	49	A5
Grafton Rd. W3	56	C7
Grafton Rd., Croy.	101	G1
Grafton Rd., Dag.	53	E1
Grafton Rd., Enf.	24	F3
Grafton Rd., Har.	36	J5
Grafton Rd., N.Mal.	92	E3
Grafton Rd.,	99	D4
Wor.Pk.		
Grafton Sq. SW4	76	C3
Grafton St. W1	11	E6
Grafton St. W1	58	B7
Grafton Ter. NW5	48	J5
Grafton Way W1	7	F6
Grafton Way W1	58	C4
Grafton Way WC1	7	G6
Grafton Way WC1	58	C4
Grafton Way, W.Mol.	90	F4
Grafton Yd. NW5	49	B6
Graftons, The NW2	48	D3
Hermitage La.		
Graham Ave. W13	64	E2
Graham Ave., Mitch.	94	A1
Graham Clo., Croy.	103	A2
Graham Gdns., Surb.	98	H1
Graham Rd. E8	50	D6
Graham Rd. E13	60	G3
Graham Rd. N15	40	H3
Graham Rd. NW4	38	H6
Graham Rd. SW19	84	C7
Graham Rd. W4	65	D3
Graham Rd., Bexh.	80	G4
Graham Rd., Hmptn.	81	G4
Graham Rd., Har.	37	B3
Graham Rd., Mitch.	94	A1
Graham St. N1	8	H2
Graham St. N1	58	H2
Graham Ter. SW1	19	B2
Graham Ter. SW1	67	A4
Grahame Pk. Est.	30	F7
NW9		
Grahame Pk. Way	30	F7
NW7		
Grahame Pk. Way	38	F2
NW9		
Grainger Clo., Nthlt.	45	J5
Lancaster Rd.		
Grainger Rd. N22	40	J1
Grainger Rd., Islw.	73	C2
Gramer Clo. E11	51	D2
Grampian Clo., Orp.	97	J6
Cotswold Ri.		
Grampian Clo., NW2	48	B1
Granard Ave. SW15	74	H5
Granard Rd. SW12	75	J7
Granary Clo. N9	25	F7
Turin Rd.		
Granary St. NW1	58	D1
Granby Bldgs. SE11	20	C2
Granby Rd. SE9	79	C2
Granby St. E2	9	H5
Granby St. E2	59	C4
Granby Ter. NW1	7	F2
Granby Ter. NW1	58	C2
Grand Ave. EC1	12	H1
Grand Ave. N10	40	A4
Grand Ave., Surb.	92	B5
Grand Ave., Wem.	47	A5
Grand Ave. E., Wem.	47	A6
Victoria Ave.		
Grand Depot Rd.	70	D5
SE18		
Grand Dr. SW20	92	J2
Grand Par. Ms. SW15	75	B5
Upper Richmond Rd.		
Grand Union Cres.	59	D1
E8		
Grand Union Ind.	56	B2
Est. NW10		
Grand Wk. E1	59	H4
Solebay St.		
Granden Rd. SW16	94	E2
Grandison Rd. SW11	75	J5
Grandison Rd.,	99	J2
Wor.Pk.		
Granfield St. SW11	75	G1
Grange, The N2	39	G2
Central Ave.		
Grange, The N20	31	F1
Grange, The SE1	17	F5
Grange, The SE1	68	C3
Grange, The SW19	84	A6
Grange, The, Croy.	102	J2
Grange, The, Wem.	47	A7
Grange, The,	99	D3
Wor.Pk.		
Grange Ave. N12	31	F5
Grange Ave. N20	23	B7
Grange Ave. SE25	95	B2
Grange Ave., Barn.	31	H1
Grange Ave., Stan.	37	E2
Grange Ave., Twick.	82	B2
Grange Ave.,	34	G6
Wdf.Grn.		
Grange Clo., Edg.	30	C5
Grange Clo., Houns.	63	F6
Grange Clo., Sid.	89	A3
Grange Clo., W.Mol.	90	H4
Grange Clo.,	34	G7
Wdf.Grn.		
Grange Ct. E8	50	C7
Grange Ct. WC2	12	D4
Grange Ct., Chig.	35	F2
Grange Ct., Loug.	27	A5
Grange Ct., Nthlt.	54	C2
Grange Cres. SE28	62	C6
Grange Cres., Chig.	35	G5
Grange Dr., Chis.	88	B6
Grange Fm. Clo.,	45	J2
Har.		
Grange Gdns. N14	32	D1
Grange Gdns. NW3	48	E3
Grange Gdns. SE25	95	B2
Grange Gdns., Pnr.	36	E3
Grange Gro. N1	49	J6
Grange Hill SE25	95	B2
Grange Hill, Edg.	30	C5
Grange Ho., Bark.	61	G1
St. Margarets		
Grange La. SE21	86	C2
Grange Mans.,	99	F7
Epsom		
Grange Ms. SE10	69	D7
Crooms Hill		
Grange Pk. W5	64	H1
Grange Pk. Ave. N21	24	J6
Grange Pk. Pl. SW20	83	H7
Grange Pk. Rd. E10	51	B1
Grange Pk. Rd.,	95	A4
Th.Hth.		
Grange Pl. NW6	48	D7
Grange Pl. SE16	17	H6
Grange Pl. SE16	68	D3
Grange Rd. E10	51	A1
Grange Rd. E13	60	F3
Grange Rd. E17	41	H5
Grange Rd. N6	40	A6
Grange Rd. N17	33	D6
Grange Rd. N18	33	D6
Grange Rd. NW10	47	H6
Grange Rd. SE1	17	E6
Grange Rd. SE1	68	B3
Grange Rd. SE19	95	A2
Grange Rd. SE25	95	A3
Grange Rd. SW13	74	G1
Grange Rd. W4	65	B5
Grange Rd. W5	64	G1
Grange Rd., Chess.	98	H3
Grange Rd., Edg.	30	D6
Grange Rd.	37	D6
(Greenhill), Har.		
Grange Rd.	46	A2
(Roxeth), Har.		
Grange Rd., Ilf.	52	E4
Grange Rd.,	91	H3
Kings.T.		
Grange Rd., Orp.	104	F2
Grange Rd., Sthl.	63	E2
Grange Rd., Sutt.	100	D7
Grange Rd., Th.Hth.	95	A4
Grange Rd., W.Mol.	90	H4
Grange Vale, Sutt.	100	E7
Grange Vw. Rd. N20	31	F1
Chandos Ave.		
Grange Wk. SE1	17	E5
Grange Wk. SE1	68	B3
Grange Way N12	31	E4
Grange Yd. SE1	17	F6
Grange Yd. SE1	68	C3
Grangecliffe Gdns.	95	B2
SE25		
Grangecourt Rd. N16	50	B1
Grangehill Pl. SE9	79	C3
Westmount Rd.		
Grangehill Rd. SE9	79	C4
Grangemill Rd. SE6	87	A3
Grangemill Way SE6	87	A2
Grangeway NW6	48	D7
Messina Ave.		
Grangeway, Wdf.Grn.	34	J4
Grangeway, The N21	24	H6
Grangeway Gdns.,	43	B5
Ilf.		
Grangewood, Bex.	89	F1
Hurst Rd.		
Grangewood Clo.,	36	A5
Pnr.		
Grangewood La.,	86	J6
Beck.		
Grangewood St. E6	61	A1
Granham Gdns. N9	33	C2
Granite St. SE18	70	J5
Granleigh Rd. E11	51	E2
Gransden Ave. E8	50	E7
Gransden Rd. W12	65	F2
Wendell Rd.		
Grant Clo. N14	24	C7
Grant Pl., Croy.	102	C1
Grant Rd. SW11	75	G4
Grant Rd., Croy.	102	C1
Grant St. E13	60	G3
Grant St. N1	8	E1
Grant Way, Islw.	64	D7
Grantbridge St. N1	8	H1
Grantbridge St. N1	58	H2
Grantchester Clo.,	46	C3
Har.		
Grantham Clo., Edg.	29	H3
Grantham Gdns.,	44	F6
Rom.		
Grantham Grn.,	22	C5
Borwd.		
Grantham Pl. W1	15	D2
Grantham Rd. E12	52	D4
Grantham Rd. SW9	76	E3
Grantham Rd. W4	65	E7
Grantley Rd.,	72	C2
Houns.		
Grantley St. E1	59	G3
Grantock Rd. E17	42	D1
Granton Rd. SW16	94	C1
Granton Rd., Ilf.	53	A1
Granton Rd., Sid.	89	C6
Grants Clo. NW7	30	J7
Grantully Rd. W9	6	A4
Grantully Rd. W9	57	E3
Granville Ave. N9	33	F3
Granville Ave., Felt.	81	A2
Granville Ave.,	72	G5
Houns.		
Granville Clo.,	102	B2
Croy.		
Granville Ct. N1	59	A1
Granville Gdns.	94	F1
SW16		
Granville Gdns. W5	64	J1
Granville Gro. SE13	78	C3
Granville Ms., Sid.	89	A4
Granville Pk. SE13	78	C3
Granville Pl.	31	F7
(North Finchley) N12		
High Rd.		
Granville Pl. W1	11	B4
Granville Pl. W1	58	A6
Granville Rd. E17	42	B6
Granville Rd. E18	42	H2
Granville Rd. N4	40	F6
Granville Rd. N12	31	E6
Granville Rd. N13	32	F6
Russell Rd.		
Granville Rd. N22	40	H1
Granville Rd. NW2	48	C2
Granville Rd. NW6	57	D2
Granville Rd. SW18	75	C7
Granville Rd. SW19	84	D7
Russell Rd.		
Granville Rd., Barn.	22	J4
Granville Rd., Ilf.	52	D4
Granville Rd., Sid.	89	A4
Granville Rd., Well.	80	C3
Granville Sq. SE15	21	E7
Granville Sq. WC1	8	D4
Granville Sq. WC1	58	F3
Granville St. WC1	8	D4
Granville St. WC1	58	F3
Grape St. WC2	12	A3
Graphite Sq. SE11	20	C3
Grasdene Rd. SE18	71	A7
Grasmere Ave.	83	D4
SW15		
Grasmere Ave.	93	D3
SW19		
Grasmere Ave. W3	56	D7
Grasmere Ave.,	72	H6
Houns.		
Grasmere Ave., Orp.	104	E3
Grasmere Ave.,	37	F7
Wem.		
Grasmere Clo.,	27	C2
Loug.		
Grasmere Ct. N22	32	F6
Palmerston Rd.		
Grasmere Gdns.,	37	D2
Har.		
Grasmere Gdns., Ilf.	43	C5
Grasmere Gdns.,	104	E3
Orp.		
Grasmere Rd. E13	60	G2
Grasmere Rd. N10	40	B1
Grasmere Rd. N17	33	D6
Grasmere Rd. SE25	95	E6
Grasmere Rd. SW16	95	F5
Grasmere Rd., Bexh.	80	J1
Grasmere Rd., Brom.	96	F1
Grasmere Rd., Orp.	104	E3
Grass Pk. N3	39	C1
Grassington Rd.,	89	A4
Sid.		
Grassmount SE23	86	E2
Grassway, Wall.	101	C4
Grasvenor Ave.,	23	E6
Barn.		
Grately Way SE15	21	F7
Gratton Rd. W14	66	B3
Gratton Ter. NW2	48	A3
Gravel Hill N3	39	C2
Gravel Hill, Bexh.	80	H5
Gravel Hill, Croy.	102	G6
Gravel Hill,	80	H5
Bexh.		
Gravel La. E1	13	F3
Gravel La., Chig.	27	J4
Gravel Pit La. SE9	79	F5
Gravel Rd., Brom.	104	B3
Gravel Rd., Twick.	82	B1
Graveley Ave.,	22	C4
Borwd.		
Gravelly Ride SW19	83	F4
Gravelwood Clo.,	88	F3
Chis.		
Graveney Gro. SE20	86	F7
Graveney Rd. SW17	84	H4
Gravesend Rd. W12	56	G7
Gray Ave., Dag.	53	F1
Gray St. SE1	16	F4
Grayham Cres.,	92	D4
N.Mal.		
Grayham Rd., N.Mal.	92	D4
Grayland Clo.,	97	A1
Brom.		
Grayling Rd. N16	50	A2
Gray's Inn Pl. WC1	12	D2
Gray's Inn Pl. WC1	8	B3
Gray's Inn Rd. WC1	58	E3
Gray's Inn Sq. WC1	12	E1
Gray's Yd. W1	11	C3
Grayscroft Rd. SW16	95	D7
Grayshott Rd. SW11	76	A2
Grayswood Gdns.	92	H2
SW20		
Farnham Gdns.		
Graywood Ct. N12	31	F7
Grazebrook Rd. N16	50	A2
Grazeley Clo., Bexh.	80	J5
Grazeley Ct. SE19	86	B4
Gipsy Hill		
Great Bell All. EC2	13	B3
Great Brownings	86	C4
SE21		
Great Bushey Dr.	31	E1
N20		
Great Cambridge Rd.	33	A3
N9		
Great Cambridge Rd.	33	A7
N17		
Great Cambridge Rd.	33	A4
N18		
Great Cambridge	25	D3
Rd., Enf.		
Great Castle St. W1	11	E3
Great Castle St. W1	58	B6
Great Cen. Ave.,	45	C5
Ruis.		
Great Cen. St. NW1	10	J1
Great Cen. St. NW1	57	J5
Great Cen. Way	47	C4
NW10		
Great Chapel St. W1	11	H3
Great Chapel St. W1	58	D6
Great Chertsey Rd.	74	C2
W4		
Great Chertsey Rd.,	81	G3
Felt.		
Great Chertsey Rd.,	81	J1
Twick.		
Great Ch. La. W6	46	A5
Great College St.	16	A5
SW1		
Great College St.	67	E3
SW1		
Great Cross Ave.	69	E7
SE10		
Great Cumberland	10	J4
Ms. W1		
Great Cumberland	11	A3
Pl. W1		
Great Cumberland	57	J6
Pl. W1		
Great Dover St. SE1	17	B4
Great Dover St. SE1	68	A2
Great Eastern Rd.	51	D7
E15		

Name	Page	Grid
Great Eastern St. EC2	9	D4
Great Eastern St. EC2	59	B3
Great Eastern Wk. EC2	13	D2
Great Elms Rd., Brom.	96	J4
Great Fld. NW9	38	E1
Great George St. SW1	15	J4
Warrender Rd.		
Great George St. SW1	67	D2
Great Guildford St. SE1	16	J2
Great Guildford St. SE1	67	J1
Great Harry Dr. SE9	88	D3
Great James St. WC1	12	C1
Great James St. WC1	58	F5
Great Marlborough St. W1	11	F4
Great Marlborough St. W1	58	C6
Great Maze Pond SE1	17	C3
Great Maze Pond SE1	68	A1
Great New St. EC4	12	F3
Great Newport St. WC2	11	J5
Great N. Rd. N2	39	H4
Great N. Rd. N6	39	J5
Great N. Rd., Barn.	23	C2
Great N. Way NW4	38	H1
Great Oaks, Chig.	35	F4
Great Ormond St. WC1	12	B1
Great Ormond St. WC1	58	E5
Great Owl Rd., Chig.	35	D3
Great Percy St. WC1	8	D3
Great Percy St. WC1	58	F3
Great Peter St. SW1	15	H6
Great Peter St. SW1	67	D3
Great Portland St. W1	11	E1
Great Portland St. W1	58	B4
Great Pulteney St. W1	11	G5
Great Pulteney St. W1	58	C7
Great Queen St. WC2	12	B4
Great Queen St. WC2	58	E6
Great Russell St. WC1	11	J3
Great Russell St. WC1	58	D6
Great St. Helens EC3	13	D3
Great St. Thomas Apostle EC4	13	A5
Great Scotland Yd. SW1	16	A1
Great Scotland Yd. SW1	67	E1
Great Smith St. SW1	15	J5
Great Smith St. SW1	67	D3
Great Spilmans SE22	77	B5
Great Strand NW9	38	F1
Great Suffolk St. SE1	16	H2
Great Suffolk St. SE1	67	H1
Great Sutton St. EC1	8	H6
Great Sutton St. EC1	58	H4
Great Swan All. EC2	13	B3
Great Thrift, Orp.	97	F4
Great Titchfield St. W1	11	F1
Great Titchfield St. W1	58	C5
Great Twr. St. EC3	13	D5
Great Twr. St. EC3	59	B7
Great Trinity La. EC4	13	A5
Great Turnstile WC1	12	D2
Great W. Rd. W4	65	B5
Great W. Rd. W6	65	G5
Great W. Rd., Brent.	65	B5
Great W. Rd., Houns.	72	E2
Great W. Rd., Islw.	64	A7
Great Western Ind. Pk., Sthl.	63	H2
Great Western Rd. W9	57	C5
Great Western Rd. W11	57	C5
Great Winchester St. EC2	13	C3
Great Winchester St. EC2	59	A6
Great Windmill St. W1	11	H5
Great Windmill St. W1	58	D7
Great Yd. SE1	17	E3
Greatdown Rd. W7	55	C4
Greatfield Ave. E6	61	C4
Greatfield Clo. N19	49	C4
Warrender Rd.		
Greatfield Clo. SE4	78	A4
Greatfields Rd., Bark.	61	G1
Greatham Wk. SW15	83	G1
Bessborough Rd.		
Greatorex St. E1	13	H1
Greatorex St. E1	59	D5
Greatwood, Chis.	88	D7
Greaves Pl. SW17	84	H4
Grebe Clo. E17	33	H7
Banbury Rd.		
Grecian Cres. SE19	85	H6
Gredo Ho., Bark.	62	B3
Greek Ct. W1	11	J4
Greek St. W1	11	J4
Greek St. W1	58	D6
Greek Yd. WC2	12	A5
Green, The E4	34	C1
Green, The E11	42	H6
Green, The E15	51	E6
Green, The N9	33	D2
Green, The N14	32	D3
Green, The N21	24	G7
Green, The SW19	84	A5
Green, The W3	56	E6
Green, The, Bexh.	80	G1
Green, The, Brom.	96	G7
Green, The, Cars.	101	A4
Green, The, Esher	98	C6
Green, The, Felt.	81	B2
Green, The, Houns.	63	G6
Heston Rd.		
Green, The, Mord.	93	B4
Green, The, N.Mal.	92	C3
Green, The, Orp.	89	B7
The Ave.		
Green, The, Rich.	73	G5
Green, The, Sid.	89	A4
Green, The, Sthl.	63	E3
Green, The, Sutt.	100	E3
Green, The, Twick.	82	B2
Green, The, Well.	79	H4
Green, The, Wem.	46	D2
Green, The, Wdf.Grn.	34	G5
Green Acres, Croy.	102	C3
Green Arbour Ct. EC1	12	G3
Green Ave. NW7	30	D4
Green Ave. W13	64	E3
Green Bank E1	68	E1
Green Bank N12	31	E4
Green Clo. NW9	38	C6
Green Clo. NW11	39	F7
Green Clo., Brom.	96	E3
Green Clo., Cars.	100	J2
Green Clo., Felt.	81	E5
Green Dale SE22	77	B5
Green Dale Clo. SE22	77	B5
Green Dale		
Green Dragon Ct. SE1	17	B1
Green Dragon La. N21	24	G5
Green Dragon La., Brent.	64	H5
Green Dragon Yd. E1	13	H2
Green Dr., Sthl.	63	G1
Green End N21	32	H2
Green End, Chess.	98	H4
Green Gdns., Orp.	104	F5
Green Hill, Buck.H.	34	J1
Green Hundred Rd. SE15	21	J6
Green Hundred Rd. SE15	68	D6
Green La. E4	26	D3
Green La. NW4	39	A4
Green La. SE9	88	E1
Green La. SE20	86	G7
Green La. SW16	85	F7
Green La. W7	64	B2
Green La., Chig.	35	F1
Green La., Chis.	88	E3
Green La., Dag.	53	D2
Green La., Edg.	29	J4
Green La., Felt.	81	E5
Green La., Har.	46	B4
South Vale		
Green La., Houns.	72	B3
Green La., Ilf.	52	F2
Green La., Mord.	93	D6
Green La., N.Mal.	92	C5
Green La., Stan.	29	E4
Green La., Th.Hth.	94	H1
Green La., Wat.	28	C1
Green La., W.Mol.	90	H5
Green La., Wor.Pk.	99	G1
Green La. Gdns., Th.Hth.	94	H2
Green Las. N4	40	H7
Green Las. N8	40	H3
Green Las. N13	32	F6
Green Las. N16	49	J3
Green Las. N21	32	F4
Green Lawns, Ruis.	45	C1
Green Man Gdns. W13	55	D7
Green Man La. W13	55	D7
Green Man La., Felt.	72	A4
Green Moor Link N21	24	H7
Green Pt. E15	51	E6
Green Pond Clo. E17	41	H3
Green Pond Rd. E17	41	H3
Green Ride, Loug.	26	G5
Green Rd. N14	24	B6
Green Rd. N20	31	F3
Green Shield Ind. Est. E16	69	G1
Green St. E7	51	H6
Green St. E13	51	J7
Green St. W1	11	A5
Green St. W1	57	J7
Green St., Enf.	25	F2
Green Vale W5	55	J6
Green Vale, Bexh.	80	D5
Green Verges, Stan.	29	G7
Green Vw., Chess.	98	J7
Green Wk. NW4	39	A5
Green Wk. SE1	17	D6
Green Wk., Hmptn.	81	F6
Orpwood Clo.		
Green Wk., Sthl.	63	G5
Green Wk., Wdf.Grn.	35	B6
Green Wk., The E4	34	C1
Green Way SE9	79	A5
Green Way, Brom.	97	B6
Green Way, Sun.	90	A4
Green Wrythe Cres., Cars.	100	H1
Green Wrythe La., Cars.	93	G6
Greenacre Gdns. E17	42	C4
Greenacre Sq. SE16	68	G2
Fishermans Dr.		
Greenacre Wk. N14	32	E3
Greenacres SE9	79	D6
Greenacres (Bushey), Wat.	29	A2
Greenacres Dr., Stan.	29	E6
Greenaway Gdns. NW3	48	E4
Greenbank Ave., Wem.	46	D5
Greenbank Clo. E4	34	C2
Greenbank Cres. NW4	39	B4
Greenbay Rd. SE7	70	A7
Greenberry St. NW8	6	G2
Greenberry St. NW8	57	H2
Greenbrook Ave., Barn.	23	F1
Greencoat Pl. SW1	19	G1
Greencoat Pl. SW1	67	C4
Greencoat Row SW1	15	G6
Greencourt Ave., Croy.	102	E2
Greencourt Ave., Edg.	38	B1
Greencourt Gdns., Croy.	102	E1
Greencourt Rd., Orp.	97	G5
Greencrest Pl. NW2	47	H3
Dollis Hill La.		
Greencroft Ave., Ruis.	45	C2
Greencroft Clo. E6	61	B5
Neatscourt Rd.		
Greencroft Gdns. NW6	48	E7
Greencroft Gdns., Enf.	25	B3
Greencroft Rd., Houns.	72	F1
Greenend Rd. W4	65	E2
Greenfarm Clo., Orp.	104	J5
Greenfell St. SE10	69	E3
Greenfield Ave., Surb.	92	B7
Greenfield Ave., Wat.	28	D2
Greenfield Gdns. NW2	48	B2
Greenfield Gdns., Dag.	62	D1
Greenfield Gdns., Orp.	97	G7
Greenfield Rd. E1	13	J2
Greenfield Rd. E1	59	D5
Greenfield Rd. N15	41	B5
Greenfield Rd., Dag.	53	C7
Greenfield Way, Har.	36	H3
Greenfields, Loug.	27	D4
Greenfields Clo., Loug.	27	D4
Greenford Ave. W7	55	B4
Greenford Ave., Sthl.	54	F7
Greenford Gdns., Grnf.	54	H3
Greenford Rd., Grnf.	54	J4
Greenford Rd., Har.	46	C4
Greenford Rd., Sthl.	54	J6
Greenford Rd., Sutt.	100	E4
Greengate, Grnf.	46	E6
Greengate St. E13	60	H2
Greenhalgh Wk. N2	39	F4
Greenham Clo. SE1	16	E4
Greenham Clo. SE1	67	G2
Greenham Rd. N10	40	A2
Greenheys Dr. E18	42	F3
Greenhill NW3	48	G4
Hampstead High St.		
Greenhill SE18	70	C5
Greenhill, Sutt.	100	F2
Greenhill, Wem.	47	B2
Greenhill Gdns., Nthlt.	54	F2
Greenhill Gro. E12	52	B4
Greenhill Pk. NW10	56	E1
Greenhill Pk., Barn.	23	E5
Greenhill Rd. NW10	56	E1
Greenhill Rd., Har.	37	B6
Greenhill Ter. SE18	70	C5
Greenhill Ter., Nthlt.	54	F2
Greenhill Way, Har.	37	B6
Greenhill Way, S.Croy.	102	G4
Greenhill Way, Wem.	47	B2
Greenhill's Rents EC1	12	G1
Greenhills Ter. N1	50	A6
Baxter Rd.		
Greenhithe Clo., Sid.	79	H7
Greenholm Rd. SE9	79	E5
Greenhurst Rd. SE27	85	G5
Greening St. SE2	71	C4
Greenland Cres., Sthl.	63	C3
Greenland Pl. NW1	58	B1
Greenland Rd.		
Greenland Quay SE16	68	G4
Greenland Rd. NW1	58	B1
Greenland Rd., Barn.	22	J5
Greenland St. NW1	58	B1
Camden High St.		
Greenlaw Gdns., N.Mal.	92	F7
Greenlaw St. SE18	70	D3
Greenlea Trd. Pk. SW19	93	G1
Greenleaf Clo. SW2	76	G7
Tulse Hill		
Greenleaf Rd. E6	60	J1
Redclyffe Rd.		
Greenleaf Rd. E17	41	J3
Greenleafe Dr., Ilf.	43	E3
Greenman St. N1	49	J7
Greenmoor Rd., Enf.	25	F2
Greenoak Way SW19	84	A4
Greenock Rd. SW16	94	D1
Greenock Rd. W3	65	B3
Greens Clo., The, Loug.	27	D2
Green's Ct. W1	11	H5
Green's End SE18	70	E4
Greenside, Bex.	89	E1
Greenside, Dag.	53	C1
Greenside Clo. N20	31	G2
Greenside Rd. W12	65	G3
Greenside Rd., Croy.	94	G7
Greenstead Ave., Wdf.Grn.	34	J7
Greenstead Clo., Wdf.Grn.	34	J6
Greenstead Gdns.		

Greenstead Gdns. SW15	74	G5
Greenstead Gdns., Wdf.Grn.	34	J6
Greensted Rd., Loug.	27	B7
Greenstone Ms. E11	42	G6
Greenvale Rd. SE9	79	C4
Greenview Ave., Beck.	95	H6
Greenview Ave., Croy.	95	H6
Greenway N14	32	E2
Greenway N20	31	D2
Greenway SW20	92	J4
Greenway, Chis.	88	D5
Greenway, Dag.	53	C2
Greenway, Har.	37	H5
Greenway, Hayes	54	A3
Greenway, Pnr.	36	B2
Greenway, Wall.	101	C4
Greenway, Wdf.Grn.	34	J5
Greenway, The NW9	38	D2
Greenway, The, Har.	37	B1
Greenway, The, Houns.	72	F4
Greenway, The, Pnr.	36	B4
Greenway Ave. E17	42	D4
Greenway Clo. N4	49	J2
Greenway Clo. N11	32	A6
Greenway Clo. N20	31	D2
Greenway Clo. NW9	38	D2
Greenway Gdns. NW9	38	D2
Greenway Gdns., Croy.	102	J3
Greenway Gdns., Grnf.	54	G3
Greenway Gdns., Har.	37	B2
Greenways, Beck.	96	A2
Greenways, Esher	98	B4
Greenways, The, Twick.	73	D6
Greenwell St. W1	**7**	**E6**
Greenwell St. W1	58	B4
Greenwich Ch. St. SE10	69	C6
Greenwich Cres. E6	61	B5
Swan App.		
Greenwich High Rd. SE10	78	B1
Greenwich Ind. Est. SE7	69	H4
Greenwich Mkt. SE10	69	C6
Greenwich Pk. SE10	69	D7
Greenwich Pk. St. SE10	69	D5
Greenwich S. St. SE10	78	B1
Greenwich Vw. Pl. E14	69	B3
Greenwood Ave., Dag.	53	H4
Greenwood Ave., Enf.	25	H2
Greenwood Clo., Mord.	93	B4
Greenwood Clo., Orp.	97	H6
Greenwood Clo., Sid.	89	A2
Hurst Rd.		
Greenwood Clo., T.Ditt.	98	D1
Greenwood Ct. SW1	**19**	**G4**
Greenwood Dr. E4	34	C5
Avril Way		
Greenwood Gdns. N13	32	H3
Greenwood Gdns., Ilf.	35	F7
Greenwood La., Hmptn.	81	H5
Greenwood Pk., Kings.T.	83	E7
Greenwood Pl. NW5	49	B5
Highgate Rd.		
Greenwood Rd. E8	50	D6
Greenwood Rd. E13	60	F2
Maud Rd.		
Greenwood Rd., Croy.	94	H7
Greenwood Rd., Islw.	73	C3
Greenwood Rd., Mitch.	94	D3
Greenwood Rd., T.Ditt.	98	D1
Greenwood Ter. NW10	56	D1
Greenwood Rd., Har.	36	J1
Greet St. SE1	**16**	**F2**
Greet St. SE1	67	G1

Gregor Ms. SE3	69	G7
Gregory Cres. SE9	79	A7
Gregory Pl. W8	**14**	**A3**
Gregory Pl. W8	66	E2
Gregory Rd., Rom.	44	D4
Gregory Rd., Sthl.	63	G3
Gregson Clo., Borwd.	22	C1
Greig Clo. N8	40	E5
Greig Ter. SE17	**20**	**H5**
Grena Gdns., Rich.	73	J4
Grena Rd., Rich.	73	J4
Grenaby Ave., Croy.	95	A7
Grenaby Rd., Croy.	95	A7
Grenada Rd. SE7	69	J7
Grenade St. E14	59	J7
Grenadier St. E16	70	D1
Grendon Gdns., Wem.	47	A2
Grendon St. NW8	**6**	**G5**
Grendon St. NW8	57	H4
Grenfell Gdns., Har.	37	H7
Grenfell Rd. W11	57	A7
Grenfell Rd., Mitch.	84	J6
Grenfell Twr. W11	57	A7
Grenfell Wk. W11	57	A7
Grennell Clo., Sutt.	100	G2
Grennell Rd., Sutt.	100	F3
Grenoble Gdns. N13	32	G6
Grenville Clo. N3	39	C1
Grenville Clo., Surb.	99	C1
Grenville Gdns., Wdf.Grn.	42	J1
Grenville Ms. SW7	**18**	**D1**
Grenville Ms. SW7	66	F4
Grenville Ms., Hmptn.	81	H5
Grenville Pl. NW7	30	D5
Grenville Pl. SW7	**14**	**C6**
Grenville Pl. SW7	66	F3
Grenville Rd. N19	49	E1
Grenville St. WC1	**18**	**D1**
Grenville St. WC1	58	E4
Gresham Ave. N20	31	J4
Gresham Clo., Bex.	80	E6
Gresham Dr., Rom.	44	B5
Gresham Gdns. NW11	88	B1
Gresham Rd. E6	61	C2
Gresham Rd. E16	60	H6
Gresham Rd. NW10	47	D5
Gresham Rd. SE25	95	D4
Gresham Rd. SW9	76	G3
Gresham Rd., Beck.	95	H2
Gresham Rd., Edg.	29	J6
Gresham Rd., Hmptn.	81	G6
Gresham Rd., Houns.	72	J1
Gresham St. EC2	**13**	**A3**
Gresham St. EC2	58	J6
Gresham Way SW19	84	D3
Gresley Clo. N15	41	A4
Clinton Rd.		
Gresley Rd. N19	49	C1
Gresse St. W1	**11**	**H3**
Gresse St. W1	58	D5
Gressenhall Rd. SW18	75	C6
Gresswell Clo., Sid.	89	A
Greswell St. SW6	75	A1
Gretton Rd. N17	33	B7
Greville Clo., Twick.	73	F7
Greville Hall NW6	**6**	**B1**
Greville Hall NW6	57	E2
Greville Pl. NW6	**6**	**B1**
Greville Pl. NW6	57	E2
Greville Rd. E17	42	C4
Greville Rd. NW6	**6**	**A1**
Greville Rd. NW6	57	E2
Greville Rd., Rich.	73	J6
Greville St. EC1	**12**	**F2**
Greville St. EC1	58	G5
Grey Clo. NW11	39	F6
Grey Eagle St. E1	**9**	**G6**
Grey Eagle St. E1	59	C5
Greycoat Pl. SW1	**15**	**H6**
Greycoat Pl. SW1	67	D3
Greycoat St. SW1	**15**	**H6**
Greycoat St. SW1	67	D3
Greycot Rd., Beck.	87	A5
Greyfell Clo., Stan.	29	E5
Coverdale Clo.		
Greyfriars Pas. EC1	**12**	**H3**
Greyhound Hill NW4	38	G3
Greyhound La. SW16	85	D6
Greyhound Rd. N17	41	B3
Greyhound Rd. NW10	56	H3
Greyhound Rd. W6	66	A6
Greyhound Rd. W14	66	B6

Greyhound Rd., Sutt.	100	F5
Greyhound Ter. SW16	94	C1
Greys Pk. Clo., Kes.	104	A5
Greystead Rd. SE23	77	F7
Greystoke Ave., Pnr.	36	G3
Greystoke Gdns. W5	55	H4
Greystoke Gdns., Enf.	24	D4
Greystoke Pk. Ter. W5	55	G3
Greystoke Pl. EC4	**12**	**E3**
Greystone Gdns., Har.	37	F6
Greystone Gdns., Ilf.	43	F2
Greyswood St. SW16	85	B6
Grierson Rd. SE23	77	G7
Griffin Clo. NW10	47	H5
Griffin Manor Way SE28	70	G3
Griffin Rd. N17	41	B2
Griffin Rd. SE18	70	G5
Griffin Way, Sun.	90	A2
Griffith Clo., Dag.	53	C1
Gibson Rd.		
Griffiths Clo., Wor.Pk.	99	H2
Griffiths Rd. SW19	84	D7
Griggs App., Ilf.	52	F2
Griggs Pl. SE1	**17**	**E5**
Griggs Rd. E10	42	C6
Grilse Clo. N9	33	E4
Parr Clo.		
Grimsby St. E2	**9**	**G6**
Grimsdyke Cres., Barn.	22	J3
Grimsdyke Rd., Pnr.	28	E7
Grimsel Path SE5	**20**	**H7**
Grimshaw Clo. N6	40	A7
Grimston Rd. SW6	75	C2
Grimwade Ave., Croy.	102	D3
Grimwood Rd., Twick.	73	C7
Grindal St. SE1	**16**	**E4**
Grindall Clo., Croy.	101	H4
Hillside Rd.		
Grinling Pl. SE8	69	A6
Grinstead Rd. SE8	68	H5
Grittleton Ave., Wem.	47	B6
Grittleton Rd. W9	57	D4
Grizedale Ter. SE23	86	E2
Grocer's Hall Ct. EC2	**13**	**B4**
Grogan Clo., Hmptn.	81	F6
Groom Cres. SW18	75	G7
Groom Pl. SW1	**15**	**C5**
Groom Pl. SW1	67	A3
Groombridge Clo., Well.	80	A5
Groombridge Rd. E9	50	G7
Groomfield Clo. SW17	85	A4
Grooms Dr., Pnr.	36	A5
Grosmont Rd. SE18	70	J6
Grosse Way SW15	74	H6
Grosvenor Ave. N5	49	J5
Grosvenor Ave. SW14	74	E3
Grosvenor Ave., Cars.	100	J6
Grosvenor Ave., Har.	36	H6
Grosvenor Ave., Rich.	73	H5
Grosvenor Rd.		
Grosvenor Clo., Loug.	24	E1
Grosvenor Cotts. SW1	**19**	**B1**
Grosvenor Ct. N14	24	C7
Grosvenor Cres. NW9	38	A4
Grosvenor Cres. SW1	**15**	**C4**
Grosvenor Cres. SW1	67	A2
Grosvenor Cres. Ms. SW1	**15**	**B4**
Grosvenor Cres. Ms. SW1	67	A2
Grosvenor Dr., Loug.	27	E2
Grosvenor Est. SW1	**19**	**J1**
Grosvenor Est. SW1	67	D4
Grosvenor Gdns. E6	61	A3
Grosvenor Gdns. N10	40	C3
Grosvenor Gdns. N14	24	D4
Grosvenor Gdns. NW2	47	J5
Grosvenor Gdns. NW11	39	C6
Grosvenor Gdns. SW1	**15**	**E6**

Grosvenor Gdns. SW1	67	B3
Grosvenor Gdns. SW14	74	E3
Grosvenor Gdns., Kings.T.	82	G6
Grosvenor Gdns., Wall.	101	C7
Grosvenor Gdns., Wdf.Grn.	34	G6
Grosvenor Gdns. Ms. E. SW1	**15**	**E5**
Grosvenor Gdns. Ms. N. SW1	**15**	**D6**
Grosvenor Gdns. Ms. S. SW1	**15**	**E6**
Grosvenor Gate W1	11	A6
Grosvenor Hill SW19	84	B6
Grosvenor Hill W1	**11**	**D5**
Grosvenor Hill W1	58	B7
Grosvenor Pk. SE5	20	J6
Grosvenor Pk. SE5	67	J7
Grosvenor Pk. Rd. E17	42	A5
Grosvenor Path, Loug.	27	E1
Grosvenor Pl. SW1	**15**	**C4**
Grosvenor Pl. SW1	67	A2
Grosvenor Ri. E. E17	42	B5
Grosvenor Rd. E6	61	A1
Grosvenor Rd. E7	51	H6
Grosvenor Rd. E10	51	C1
Grosvenor Rd. E11	42	G5
Grosvenor Rd. N3	31	C7
Grosvenor Rd. N9	33	E1
Grosvenor Rd. N10	40	B1
Grosvenor Rd. SE25	95	D4
Grosvenor Rd. SW1	**19**	**F5**
Grosvenor Rd. SW1	67	D6
Grosvenor Rd. W4	65	B5
Grosvenor Rd. W7	64	D1
Grosvenor Rd., Belv.	71	G6
Grosvenor Rd., Bexh.	80	D5
Grosvenor Rd., Borwd.	22	A3
Grosvenor Rd., Brent.	64	G6
Grosvenor Rd., Dag.	53	E3
Grosvenor Rd., Houns.	72	F3
Grosvenor Rd., Ilf.	52	F3
Grosvenor Rd., Orp.	97	H6
Grosvenor Rd., Rich.	73	H5
Grosvenor Rd., Sthl.	63	F3
Grosvenor Rd., Twick.	73	D7
Grosvenor Rd., Wall.	101	B6
Grosvenor Rd., W.Wick.	103	B1
Grosvenor Sq. W1	**11**	**C5**
Grosvenor Sq. W1	58	A7
Grosvenor St. W1	**11**	**D5**
Grosvenor St. W1	58	B7
Grosvenor Ter. SE5	**20**	**J6**
Grosvenor Ter. SE5	67	J6
Grosvenor Wf. Rd. E14	69	D4
Grote's Bldgs. SE3	78	E2
Grote's Pl. SE3	78	E2
Groton Rd. SW18	84	E2
Grotto Pas. W1	**11**	**C1**
Grotto Rd., Twick.	82	C2
Grove, The E15	51	E6
Grove, The N3	39	D1
Grove, The N4	40	F7
Grove, The N6	49	A1
Grove, The N8	40	D5
Grove, The N13	32	G5
Grove, The N14	24	C5
Grove, The NW9	38	D5
Grove, The NW11	39	B7
Grove, The W5	64	G1
Grove, The, Bexh.	80	B4
Grove, The, Edg.	30	B4
Grove, The, Enf.	22	J2
Grove, The, Grnf.	54	J6
Grove, The, Islw.	73	B1
Grove, The, Sid.	89	E5
Grove, The, Tedd.	82	E4
Grove, The, Twick.	73	E6
Bridge Rd.		
Grove, The, Walt.	90	B7
Grove, The, W.Wick.	103	B3
Grove Ave. N3	31	D7
Grove Ave. N10	40	C2
Grove Ave. W7	55	B6
Grove Ave., Pnr.	36	E5
Grove Ave., Sutt.	100	D6
Grove Rd.		

Grove Ave., Twick. 82 C1
Grove Clo. SE23 86 H1
Grove Clo., Brom. 103 G2
Grove Clo., Felt. 81 A3
Grove Clo., 91 J4
Kings.T.
Grove Cotts. SW3 18 H5
Grove Ct. SE3 78 G1
Grove Ct., E.Mol. 91 A5
Walton Rd.
Grove Cres. E18 42 F2
Grove Cres. NW9 38 C4
Grove Cres. SE5 77 B2
Grove Cres., Felt. 81 E4
Grove Cres., 91 H3
Kings.T.
Grove Cres., Walt. 90 B7
Grove Cres. Rd. E15 51 D6
Grove End E18 42 F2
Grove End Hill
Grove End La., 98 A1
Esher
Grove End Rd. NW8 6 E3
Grove End Rd. NW8 57 G2
Grove Footpath, 91 H4
Surb.
Grove Gdns. E15 51 E6
Grove Gdns. NW4 38 G5
Grove Gdns. NW8 6 H4
Grove Gdns., Dag. 53 J3
Grove Gdns., Tedd. 82 D4
Grove Grn. Rd. E11 51 C3
Grove Hall Ct. NW8 6 D3
Grove Hill E18 42 F2
Grove Hill, Har. 37 B7
Grove Hill Rd. SE5 77 B3
Grove Hill Rd., Har. 37 B7
Grove Ho. Rd. N8 40 E4
Grove La. SE5 77 B2
Grove La., Chig. 35 J3
Grove La., Kings.T. 91 H4
Grove Mkt. Pl. SE9 79 C6
Grove Ms. W6 65 J3
Grove Ms. W11 57 C6
Portobello Rd.
Grove Pk. E11 42 H6
Grove Pk. NW9 38 C4
Grove Pk. SE5 77 B2
Grove Pk. Ave. E4 34 B7
Grove Pk. Bri. W4 65 C7
Grove Pk. Gdns. W4 65 C7
Grove Pk. Ms. W4 65 C7
Grove Pk. Rd. N15 41 B4
Grove Pk. Rd. SE9 87 J3
Grove Pk. Rd. W4 65 B7
Grove Pk. Ter. W4 65 B7
Grove Pas. E2 59 E2
The Oval
Grove Pas., Tedd. 82 D5
Grove Pl. NW3 48 G4
Christchurch Hill
Grove Pl. W3 65 C1
Grove Pl., Bark. 61 F1
Clockhouse Ave.
Grove Rd. E3 59 G1
Grove Rd. E4 34 C4
Grove Rd. E17 42 F7
Grove Rd. E18 42 F2
Grove Rd. N11 32 B5
Grove Rd. N12 31 G5
Grove Rd. N15 41 B5
Grove Rd. NW2 47 J6
Grove Rd. SW13 74 F2
Grove Rd. SW19 84 F7
Grove Rd. W3 65 C1
Grove Rd. W5 55 G7
Grove Rd., Barn. 23 H3
Grove Rd., Belv. 71 F6
Grove Rd., Bexh. 80 J4
Grove Rd., Borwd. 22 A1
Grove Rd., Brent. 64 F5
Grove Rd., E.Mol. 91 A4
Grove Rd., Edg. 30 A6
Grove Rd., Houns. 72 G4
Grove Rd., Islw. 73 B1
Grove Rd., Mitch. 94 A3
Grove Rd., Pnr. 36 F5
Grove Rd., Rich. 73 J6
Grove Rd., Rom. 44 B7
Grove Rd., Surb. 95 G5
Grove Rd., Sutt. 100 D6
Grove Rd., Th.Hth. 94 G4
Grove Rd., Twick. 82 A3
Grove St. N18 33 C5
Grove St. SE8 68 J4
Grove Ter. NW5 49 B3
Grove Ter., Tedd. 82 D4
Grove Vale SE22 77 B4
Grove Vale, Chis. 88 D6
Grove Vill. E14 60 B7
Grove Way, Esher 90 J7
Grovebury Ct. N14 24 D7

Grovebury Rd. SE2 71 B2
Grovedale Rd. N19 49 D2
Groveland Ave. 85 F7
SW16
Groveland Ct. EC4 13 A4
Groveland Rd., 95 J3
Beck.
Groveland Way, 92 C5
N.Mal.
Grovelands, W.Mol. 90 G4
Grovelands Clo. SE5 77 B2
Grovelands Clo., 45 H3
Har.
Grovelands Ct. N14 24 D7
Grovelands Rd. N13 32 F4
Grovelands Rd. N15 41 D6
Grovelands Rd., 89 A7
Orp.
Groveside Clo. W3 56 B6
Groveside Clo., 100 H2
Cars.
Groveside Rd. E4 34 E2
Groveway SW9 76 F1
Groveway, Dag. 53 D4
Groveway, Wem. 47 C5
Grovewood, Rich. 73 J1
Sandycombe Rd.
Grummant Rd. SE15 77 C1
Grundy St. E14 60 B6
Gruneisen Rd. N3 31 E7
Gubyon Ave. SE24 76 H5
Guerin Sq. E3 59 J3

Guernsey Clo., 72 G1
Houns.
Guernsey Gro. SE24 76 J7
Guernsey Rd. E11 51 D1
Guibal Rd. SE12 78 H7
Guild Rd. SE7 70 A5
Guildersfield Rd. 85 E7
SW16
Guildford Gro. SE10 78 B1
Guildford Rd. E6 61 C6
Guildford Rd. E17 42 C1
Guildford Rd. SW8 76 E1
Guildford Rd., 95 A6
Croy.
Guildford Rd., Ilf. 52 H2
Guildford Way, 101 E5
Wall.
Guildhall Bldgs. EC2 13 B3
Guildhouse St. SW1 19 F1
Guildhouse St. SW1 67 C4
Guildown Ave. N12 31 E4
Guildsway E17 41 J1
Guilford Ave., Surb. 91 J5
Guilford Pl. WC1 8 C6
Guilford Pl. WC1 58 F4
Guilford St. WC1 8 B6
Guilford St. WC1 58 E4
Guilsborough Clo. 47 E7
NW10
Guinness Bldgs. SE1 17 D6
Guinness Bldgs. SE1 68 B4
Guinness Clo. E9 50 H7
Guinness Sq. SE1 21 D1
Guinness Trust 20 G3
Bldgs. SE11
Guinness Trust 67 H5
Bldgs. SE11
Guinness Trust 18 J2
Bldgs. SW3
Guinness Trust Est. 50 B1
N16
Guinness Trust Est. 76 H4
SW9
Guion Rd. SW6 75 C2
Gull Clo., Wall. 101 E7
Gulland Wk. N1 49 J6
Marquess Rd.
Gulliver Clo., Nthlt. 54 F1
Gulliver Rd., Sid. 88 H2
Gulliver St. SE16 68 J3
Gumleigh Rd. W5 64 F4
Gumley Gdns., Islw. 73 D3
Gumping Rd., Orp. 104 F1
Gun St. E1 13 F2
Gun St. E1 59 C5
Gundulph Rd., Brom. 96 J3
Gunmakers La. E3 59 H1
Gunner La. SE18 70 D5
Gunners Gro. E4 34 C3
Gunners Rd. SW18 84 G2
Gunnersbury Ave. 65 A3
W3
Gunnersbury Ave. 64 J1
W5
Gunnersbury Clo. W4 65 B5
Grange Rd.
Gunnersbury Ct. W3 65 B2
Bollo La.
Gunnersbury Cres. 65 A2
W3

Gunnersbury Dr. W5 64 J2
Gunnersbury Gdns. 65 A2
W3
Gunnersbury La. W3 65 A3
Gunnersbury Ms. W4 65 B5
Chiswick High Rd.
Gunnersbury Pk. W3 64 J4
Gunnersbury Pk. W5 64 J4
Gunning St. SE18 70 H4
Gunpowder Sq. EC4 12 F3
Gunpowder Sq. EC4 58 G6
Gunstor Rd. N16 50 B4
Gunter Gro. SW10 66 F6
Gunter Gro., Edg. 38 D1
Gunterstone Rd. W14 66 B4
Gunthorpe St. E1 59 C5
Gunton Rd. E5 50 E2
Gunton Rd. SW17 85 A6
Gunwhale Clo. SE16 68 G1
Gurdon Rd. SE7 69 G5
Gurnell Gro. W13 55 C4
Gurney Clo. E15 51 E5
Gurney Rd.
Gurney Clo. E17 41 G1
Gurney Clo., Bark. 52 E6
Gurney Cres., Croy. 101 F1
Gurney Dr. N2 39 F4
Gurney Rd. E15 51 E5
Gurney Rd., Cars. 101 A3
Gurney Rd., Nthlt. 54 B3
Guthrie St. SW3 17 C3
Gutter La. EC2 13 A3
Gutter La. EC2 58 J6
Guy Rd., Wall. 101 D3
Guy St. SE1 17 C3
Guy St. SE1 68 A2
Guyatt Gdns., Mitch. 94 A2
Ormerod Gdns.
Guyscliff Rd. SE13 86 C5
Gwalior Rd. SW15 75 A3
Felsham Rd.
Gwendolen Ave. 75 A4
SW15
Gwendolen Clo. 75 A5
SW15
Gwendoline Ave. E13 60 H1
Gwendwr Rd. W14 66 B5
Gwillim Clo., Sid. 80 A5
Gwydor Rd., Beck. 95 G4
Gwydyr Rd., Brom. 96 F3
Gwyn Clo. SW6 66 F7
Gwynne Ave., Croy. 95 G7
Gwynne Pk. Ave., 35 C6
Wdf.Grn.
Gwynne Pl. WC1 8 D4
Gwynne Rd. SW11 75 G2
Gylcote Clo. SE5 77 A4
Gyles Pk., Stan. 29 F7
Gyllyngdune Gdns., 52 J3
Ilf.

H

Ha-Ha Rd. SE18 70 C6
Haarlem Rd. W14 66 A3
Haberdasher Pl. N1 9 C3
Haberdasher St. N1 9 C3
Haberdasher St. N1 59 E3
Habgood Rd., Loug. 27 B3
Haccombe Rd. SW19 84 F6
Hackbridge Grn., 101 A2
Wall.
Hackbridge Pk. 101 A2
Gdns., Cars.
Hackbridge Rd., 101 A2
Wall.
Hackford Rd. SW9 76 F1
Hackforth Clo., 22 H5
Barn.
Hackington Cres., 87 A6
Beck.
Hackney Clo., 22 D5
Borwd.
Hackney Gro. E8 50 E6
Reading La.
Hackney Rd. E2 9 F3
Hackney Rd. E2 59 C5
Hadden Rd. SE28 70 H3
Hadden Way, Grnf. 46 A6
Haddington Rd., 87 D4
Brom.
Haddo St. SE10 70 B6
Haddon Clo., Borwd. 22 A2
Haddon Clo., Enf. 25 D6
Haddon Clo., N.Mal. 92 F5
Haddon Gro., Sid. 79 J7
Haddon Rd., Sutt. 100 E4
Haddonfield SE8 68 A4
Hadleigh Clo. E1 59 F4
Mantus Rd.
Hadleigh Rd. N9 25 E7

Hadleigh St. E2 59 F3
Hadleigh Wk. E6 61 B6
Dunnock Rd.
Hadley Clo. N21 24 G6
Hadley Common, 23 D2
Barn.
Hadley Gdns. W4 65 D5
Hadley Gdns., Sthl. 63 F5
Hadley Grn., Barn. 23 C2
Hadley Grn. Rd., 23 C2
Barn.
Hadley Grn. W., 23 B2
Barn.
Hadley Gro., Barn. 23 B2
Hadley Highstone, 23 C1
Barn.
Hadley Ridge, Barn. 23 C3
Hadley Rd., Barn. 23 E3
Hadley Rd., Belv. 71 F4
Hadley Rd., Mitch. 94 D4
Hadley St. NW1 49 B6
Hadley Way N21 24 G6
Hadlow Pl. SE19 86 D7
Hadlow Rd., Sid. 89 A4
Hadlow Rd., Well. 71 C7
Hadrian Clo., Wall. 101 E7
De Havilland Rd.
Hadrian Est. E2 9 J2
Hadrian St. SE10 69 E5
Hadrians Ride, Enf. 25 C5
Hadyn Pk. Rd. W12 65 G2
Hafer Rd. SW11 75 J4
Hafton Rd. SE6 87 E1
Haggard Rd., Twick. 73 D7
Haggerston Rd. E8 50 C7
Hague St. E2 9 J4
Haig Rd., Stan. 29 F5
Haig Rd. E. E13 60 J3
Haig Rd. W. E13 60 J3
Haigville Gdns., Ilf. 43 E4
Hailes Clo. SW19 84 F6
North Rd.
Hailey Rd., Erith 71 G2
Haileybury Ave., 25 C6
Enf.
Hailsham Ave. SW2 85 F2
Hailsham Clo., 91 G7
Surb.
Hailsham Dr., Har. 37 A3
Hailsham Rd. SW17 85 A4
Hailsham Ter. N18 32 J5
Haimo Rd. SE9 79 A5
Hainault Clo. E17 42 D4
Hainault Gore, Rom. 44 E5
Hainault Rd., 35 F4
Chig.
Hainault Rd. E11 51 C1
Hainault Rd., Chig. 35 E3
Hainault Rd., Rom. 44 B1
Hainault Rd., Rom. 44 F6
Hainault Rd., Rom. 44 J2
Hainault St. SE9 88 E1
Hainault St., Ilf. 52 F2
Hainford Clo. SE4 77 G4
Haining Clo. W4 65 A5
Wellesley Rd.
Hainthorpe Rd. SE27 85 H3
Hainton Path E1 59 E6
Commercial Rd.
Halberd Ms. E5 50 E2
Knightland Rd.
Halbutt Gdns., Dag. 53 F3
Halbutt St., Dag. 53 F4
Halcomb St. N1 59 B1
Halcot Ave., Bexh. 80 H5
Halcrow St. E1 59 E5
Haldan Rd. E4 34 C6
Haldane Pl. SW18 84 E1
Haldane Rd. E6 61 A3
Haldane Rd. SE28 62 D7
Haldane Rd. SW6 66 C7
Haldane Rd., Sthl. 54 J7
Haldon Clo., Chig. 35 H5
Haldon Rd. SW18 75 C5
Hale, The E4 34 D7
Hale, The N17 41 D3
Hale Clo. E4 34 C3
Hale Clo., Edg. 30 C5
Hale Clo., Orp. 104 F4
Hale Dr. NW7 30 C6
Hale End Clo., Ruis. 36 A6
Hale End Rd. E4 34 D6
Hale End Rd. E17 42 D1
Hale End Rd., 34 D7
Wdf.Grn.
Hale Gdns. N17 41 D3
Hale Gdns. W3 65 A1
Hale Gro. Gdns. NW7 30 D5
Hale La. NW7 30 D5
Hale La., Edg. 30 D5
Hale Path SE27 85 H4
Hale Rd. E6 61 B4

Hale Rd. N17 41 D3
Hale St. E14 60 B7
Hale Wk. W7 55 B5
  Benham Rd.
Halefield Rd. N17 41 D1
Hales St. SE8 69 A7
Halesowen Rd., 93 E7
  Mord.
Halesworth Clo. E5 50 F2
  Theydon Rd.
Halesworth Rd. SE13 78 B3
Haley Rd. NW4 38 J6
Half Acre, Brent. 64 G6
Half Acre Rd. W7 64 B1
Half Moon Ct. EC1 12 J2
Half Moon Cres. N1 8 D1
Half Moon Cres. N1 58 F2
Half Moon La. SE24 76 J6
Half Moon Pas. E1 13 G4
Half Moon St. W1 15 E1
Half Moon St. W1 67 B1
Halford Rd. E10 42 D5
Halford Rd. SW6 66 D6
Halford Rd., Rich. 73 H5
Halfway St., Sid. 79 G7
Haliburton Rd., 73 D5
  Twick.
Haliday Wk. N1 50 A6
  Mildmay St.
Halidon Clo. E9 50 F5
  Urswick Rd.
Halifax Rd., Enf. 24 J2
Halifax Rd., Grnf. 51 H1
Halifax St. SE26 86 E4
Halifield Dr., Belv. 71 E3
Haling Gro., 101 J7
  S.Croy.
Haling Pk. Gdns., 101 H6
  S.Croy.
Haling Pk. Rd., 101 H6
  S.Croy.
Haling Rd., S.Croy. 102 A6
Halkin Arc. SW1 15 B5
Halkin Ms. SW1 15 B5
Halkin Pl. SW1 15 B5
Halkin Pl. SW1 67 A3
Halkin St. SW1 15 C4
Halkin St. SW1 67 A2
Hall, The SE3 78 G3
Hall Ave. N18 33 A6
  Weir Hall Ave.
Hall Clo. W5 55 H5
Hall Ct., Tedd. 82 C5
  Teddington Pk.
Hall Dr. SE26 86 F5
Hall Dr. W7 55 B6
Hall Fm. Clo., Stan. 29 E4
Hall Fm. Dr., Twick. 73 A7
Hall Gdns. E4 33 J4
Hall Gate NW8 6 D3
Hall La. E4 33 H5
Hall La. NW4 38 G1
Hall Oak Wk. NW6 48 C6
  Maygrove Rd.
Hall Pl. W2 6 E6
Hall Pl. W2 57 G4
Hall Pl. Cres., Bex. 80 J5
Hall Rd. E6 61 C1
Hall Rd. E15 51 D4
Hall Rd. NW8 6 D4
Hall Rd. NW8 57 F3
Hall Rd., Islw. 73 A5
Hall Rd., Rom. 44 C6
Hall St. EC1 8 H3
Hall St. EC1 58 H3
Hall St. N12 31 F5
Hall Vw. SE9 88 A2
Hallam Clo., Chis. 88 C5
Hallam Gdns., Pnr. 28 E7
Hallam Ms. W1 11 E1
Hallam Rd. N15 40 H4
Hallam St. W1 7 E6
Hallam St. W1 58 B5
Halley Gdns. SE13 78 D4
Halley Rd. E7 51 J6
Halley Rd. E12 52 A6
Halley St. E14 59 H5
Hallfield Est. W2 10 C4
Halliards, The, Walt. 90 A6
  Felix Rd.
Halliford St. N1 49 J7
Hallingbury Ct. E17 42 B3
Halliwell Rd. SW2 76 F6
Halliwick Rd. N10 40 A1
Hallmead Rd., Sutt. 100 E3
Hallowell Ave., 101 E4
  Croy.
Hallowell Clo., 94 A3
  Mitch.
Hallowes Cres., Wat. 28 A3
  Hayling Rd.
Hallsville Rd. E16 60 F6
Hallswelle Rd. NW11 39 C5

Hallywell Cres. E6 61 C5
Halons Rd. SE9 79 D7
Halpin Pl. SE17 21 C2
Halsbrook Rd. SE3 78 J3
Halsbury Clo., 29 E4
  Stan.
Halsbury Rd. W12 65 G1
Halsbury Rd. E., 45 J4
  Nthlt.
Halsbury Rd. W., 45 H5
  Nthlt.
Halsend, Hayes 63 B1
Halsey Ms. SW3 18 J1
Halsey St. SW3 18 J1
Halsey St. SW3 66 J4
Halsham Cres., Bark. 52 J6
Halsmere Rd. SE5 76 H1
Halstead Ct. N1 9 C2
Halstead Gdns. N21 33 A1
Halstead Rd. E11 42 G5
Halstead Rd. N21 33 A1
Halstead Rd., Enf. 25 B4
Halston Clo. SW11 75 J6
Halstow Rd. NW10 57 A3
Halstow Rd. SE10 69 G5
Halsway, Hayes 63 A2
Halt Robin La., Belv. 71 H4
  Halt Robin Rd.
Halt Robin Rd., 71 G4
  Belv.
Halter Clo., Borwd. 22 D5
  Clydesdale Clo.
Halton Cross St. N1 50 H1
Halton Rd. N1 49 H7
Ham, The, Brent. 64 F7
Ham Clo., Rich. 82 F3
Ham Fm. Rd., Rich. 82 G4
Ham Gate Ave., 82 H4
  Rich.
Ham Pk. Rd. E7 51 G7
Ham Pk. Rd. E15 51 F7
Ham Ridings, Rich. 82 J5
Ham St., Rich. 82 E1
Ham Vw., Croy. 95 H6
Ham Yd. W1 11 H5
Hambalt Rd. SW4 75 H5
Hamble Ct., 82 G7
  Kings.T.
Hamble St. SW6 75 E3
Hambleden Pl. SE21 86 B1
Hambledon Gdns. 95 C3
  SE25
Hambledon Rd. 75 C7
  SW18
Hambledown Rd., 79 G7
  Sid.
Hambleton Clo., 99 J2
  Wor.Pk.
  Cotswold Way
Hambridge Way 76 G7
  SW2
Hambro Ave., Brom. 103 G1
Hambro Rd. SW16 85 D6
Hambrook Rd. SE25 95 E3
Hambrough Rd., 63 E1
  Sthl.
Hamden Cres., Dag. 53 H3
Hamelin St. E14 60 C6
  St. Leonards Rd.
Hameway E6 61 D4
Hamfrith Rd. E15 51 F6
Hamilton Ave. N9 25 D7
Hamilton Ave., Ilf. 37 A4
Hamilton Ave., 99 A2
  Surb.
Hamilton Ave., 100 B1
  Sutt.
Hamilton Clo. N17 41 C3
Hamilton Clo. NW8 6 E4
Hamilton Clo. NW8 57 G3
Hamilton Clo. SE16 68 H2
  Somerford Way
Hamilton Clo., Barn. 23 H4
Hamilton Clo., Stan. 29 C2
Hamilton Ct. W5 55 J7
Hamilton Ct. W9 6 C3
Hamilton Cres. N13 32 G4
Hamilton Cres., Har. 45 F3
Hamilton Cres., 72 H5
  Houns.
Hamilton Gdns. NW8 6 D3
Hamilton Gdns. NW8 57 F3
Hamilton La. N5 49 H4
  Hamilton Pk.
Hamilton Ms. W1 15 D3
Hamilton Pk. N5 49 H4
Hamilton Pk. W. N5 49 H4
Hamilton Pl. W1 15 C2
Hamilton Pl. W1 67 A1
Hamilton Pl., Sun. 81 B7
Hamilton Rd. E15 60 E3
Hamilton Rd. E17 41 H2

Hamilton Rd. N2 39 F3
Hamilton Rd. N9 25 D7
Hamilton Rd. NW10 47 G5
Hamilton Rd. NW11 39 A7
Hamilton Rd. SE27 86 A4
Hamilton Rd. SW19 84 E7
Hamilton Rd. W4 65 E2
Hamilton Rd. W5 55 H7
Hamilton Rd., Barn. 23 H4
Hamilton Rd., Bexh. 80 E2
Hamilton Rd., Brent. 64 G6
Hamilton Rd., Har. 37 B5
Hamilton Rd., Hayes 54 B7
Hamilton Rd., Ilf. 52 E4
Hamilton Rd., Sid. 89 A4
Hamilton Rd., Sthl. 63 F1
Hamilton Rd., 95 A3
  Th.Hth.
Hamilton Rd., 82 B1
  Twick.
Hamilton Rd., Wat. 28 B3
Hamilton Sq. SE1 17 C3
Hamilton St. SE8 69 A6
  Deptford High St.
Hamilton Ter. NW8 6 B2
Hamilton Ter. NW8 57 E2
Hamilton Way N3 31 D6
Hamilton Way N13 32 H4
Hamlea Clo. SE12 78 G5
Hamlet, The SE5 77 A3
Hamlet Clo. SE13 78 E4
  Old Rd.
Hamlet Gdns. W6 65 G4
Hamlet Rd. SE19 86 C7
Hamlet Sq. NW2 48 B3
  Cricklewood Trd. Est.
Hamlet Way SE1 17 C3
  The Vale
Hamlets Way E3 59 J4
Hamlin Cres., Pnr. 36 C5
Hamlyn Clo., Edg. 29 H3
Hamlyn Gdns. SE19 86 E7
Hammelton Grn. 76 H1
  SW9
  Cromwell Rd.
Hammelton Rd., 96 F1
  Brom.
Hammers La. NW7 30 G5
Hammersmith Bri. 65 H5
  SW13
Hammersmith Bri. 65 J5
  Rd. W6
Hammersmith Bdy. 65 J4
  W6
Hammersmith 65 J5
  Flyover W6
Hammersmith Gro. 65 J2
  W6
Hammersmith Rd. 66 A4
  W6
Hammersmith Rd. 66 B4
  W14
Hammersmith Ter. 65 G5
  W6
Hammet Clo., Hayes 54 D7
  Willow Tree La.
Hammett St. EC3 13 F5
Hammond Ave., 94 B2
  Mitch.
Hammond Clo., Barn. 23 B5
Hammond Clo., Grnf. 46 A5
  Lilian Board Way
Hammond Clo., 90 G1
  Hmptn.
Hammond Rd., Enf. 25 C2
Hammond Rd., Sthl. 63 E3
Hammond St. NW5 49 C6
Hammond Way SE28 62 B7
  Oriole Way
Hamonde Clo., Edg. 30 B2
Hampden Ave., Beck. 95 H2
Hampden Clo. NW1 7 J2
Hampden Gurney St. 10 J4
  W1
Hampden La. N17 41 C1
Hampden Rd. N8 40 G4
Hampden Rd. N10 32 A7
Hampden Rd. N17 41 D1
Hampden Rd. N19 49 D2
  Holloway Rd.
Hampden Rd., Beck. 95 H2
Hampden Rd., Har. 36 J1
Hampden Rd., 92 A3
  Kings.T.
Hampden Way N14 32 B2
Hampshire Clo. N18 33 E5
Hampshire Hog La. 65 H4
  W6
  King St.
Hampshire Rd. N22 32 F7
Hampshire St. NW5 49 D6
  Torriano Ave.

Hampson Way SW8 76 F1
Hampstead Clo. SE28 71 B1
Hampstead Gdns. 39 D6
  NW11
Hampstead Grn. NW3 48 H5
Hampstead Gro. NW3 48 F3
Hampstead High St. 48 F4
  NW3
Hampstead Hill 48 G4
  Gdns. NW3
Hampstead La. N6 39 G7
Hampstead La. NW3 48 E7
Hampstead Rd. NW1 7 F2
Hampstead Rd. NW1 58 C2
Hampstead Sq. NW3 48 F3
Hampstead Way 39 C5
  NW11
Hampton Clo. NW6 57 D3
Hampton Clo. SW20 83 J7
Hampton Ct. N1 49 H6
  Upper St.
Hampton Ct. Ave., 91 A5
  E.Mol.
Hampton Ct. Palace, 91 B3
  E.Mol.
Hampton Ct. Par., 91 B4
  E.Mol.
  Creek Rd.
Hampton Ct. Rd., 91 C3
  E.Mol.
Hampton Ct. Rd., 90 J2
  Hmptn.
Hampton Ct. Rd., 91 F3
  Kings.T.
Hampton Ct. Way, 91 B6
  E.Mol.
Hampton Ct. Way, 98 B2
  T.Ditt.
Hampton Fm. Ind. 81 E3
  Est., Felt.
Hampton La., Felt. 81 A4
Hampton Mead, 27 E3
  Loug.
Hampton Ri., Har. 37 H6
Hampton Rd. E4 33 J5
Hampton Rd. E7 51 H5
Hampton Rd. E11 51 D1
Hampton Rd., Croy. 94 J6
Hampton Rd., Ilf. 52 E6
Hampton Rd., Tedd. 82 A5
Hampton Rd., Twick. 82 A3
Hampton Rd., 99 G2
  Wor.Pk.
Hampton Rd. E., Felt. 81 F3
Hampton Rd. W., 81 E2
  Felt.
Hampton St. SE1 20 H2
Hampton St. SE1 67 J4
Hampton St. SE17 20 H2
Hampton St. SE17 67 H4
Hamshades Clo., 88 J3
  Sid.
Hanah Ct. SW19 84 A7
Hanameel St. E16 69 H1
Hanbury Ms. N1 58 J1
  Mary St.
Hanbury Rd. N17 41 E2
Hanbury Rd. W3 65 B2
Hanbury St. E1 13 G1
Hanbury St. E1 59 C5
Hancock Ct., Borwd. 22 C2
  Banks Rd.
Hancock Rd. E3 60 C3
Hancock Rd. SE19 86 A6
Hand Ct. WC1 12 D2
Handa Wk. N1 50 A6
  Clephane Rd.
Handcroft Rd., Croy. 94 H7
Handel Clo., Edg. 29 J6
Handel Pl. NW10 47 D6
  Mitchellbrook Way
Handel St. WC1 8 A5
Handel St. WC1 58 E4
Handel Way, Edg. 30 A7
Handen Rd. SE12 78 E5
Handforth Rd. SW9 20 E7
Handforth Rd. SW9 67 G1
Handforth Rd., Ilf. 52 E3
  Winston Way
Handley Rd. E9 59 F1
Handowe Clo. NW4 38 G4
Hands Wk. E16 60 G6
  Butchers Rd.
Handside Clo., 100 A1
  Wor.Pk.
  Carters Clo.
Handsworth Ave. E4 34 D6
Handsworth Rd. N17 41 A3
Handsworth Way, 28 A3
  Wat.
Handtrough Way, 61 E2
  Bark.
  Fresh Wf. Rd.

Hanford Clo. SW18 84 D1
Hanford Row SW19 83 J6
Hangar Ruding, Wat. 28 F3
Hanger Grn. W5 56 A4
Hanger La. W5 55 H2
Hanger Vale La. W3 55 J6
Hanger Vale La. W5 55 J6
Hanger Vw. Way W3 56 A6
Hankey Pl. SE1 17 C4
Hankey Pl. SE1 68 A2
Hankins La. NW7 30 E2
Hanley Rd. N4 49 E1
Hanmer Wk. N7 49 F2
Newington Barrow Way
Hannah Clo. NW10 47 C4
Hannah Mary Way SE1 21 J2
Hannah Ms., Wall. 101 C7
Hannay Wk. SW16 85 D2
Dingley La.
Hannell Rd. SW6 66 B7
Hannen Rd. SE27 85 H3
Norwood High St.
Hannibal Rd. E1 59 F5
Hannibal Way, Croy. 101 F5
Hannington Rd. SW4 76 B3
Hanover Ave., Felt. 81 A1
Hanover Clo., Rich. 65 A7
Hanover Clo., Sutt. 100 B4
Hanover Ct. W12 65 G1
Uxbridge Rd.
Hanover Dr., Chis. 88 F4
Hanover Gdns. SE11 20 E6
Hanover Gdns. SE11 67 G6
Hanover Gdns., Ilf. 35 F7
Hanover Gate NW1 6 H4
Hanover Gate NW1 57 H3
Hanover Pk. SE15 77 D1
Hanover Pl. WC2 12 B4
Hanover Rd. N15 41 C4
Hanover Rd. NW10 47 J7
Hanover Rd. SW19 84 F7
Hanover Sq. W1 11 E4
Hanover Sq. W1 58 B6
Hanover St. W1 11 E4
Hanover St. W1 58 B6
Hanover St., Croy. 101 H3
Abbey Rd.
Hanover Ter. NW1 6 H4
Hanover Ter. NW1 57 H3
Hanover Ter., Islw. 73 D1
Hanover Ter. Ms. NW1 6 H4
Hanover Way, Bexh. 80 D3
Hanover W. Ind. Est. NW10 56 D3
Acton La.
Hanover Yd. N1 8 H1
Hans Cres. SW1 14 J5
Hans Cres. SW1 66 J3
Hans Pl. SW1 15 A5
Hans Pl. SW1 66 J3
Hans Rd. SW3 14 J5
Hans Rd. SW3 66 J3
Hans St. SW1 15 A6
Hansard Ms. W14 66 A2
Holland Rd.
Hansart Way, Enf. 24 G1
The Ridgeway
Hanselin Clo., Stan. 29 C5
Chenduit Way
Hansha Dr., Edg. 38 D1
Hansler Gro., E.Mol. 91 A5
Hansler Rd. SE22 77 C5
Hansol Rd., Bexh. 80 E5
Hanson Clo. SW12 76 B7
Hanson Clo., Loug. 27 F2
Hanson Dr.
Hanson Dr., Loug. 27 F2
Hanson Gdns., Sthl. 63 E2
Hanson Grn., Loug. 27 F2
Hanson Dr.
Hanson St. W1 11 F1
Hanson St. W1 58 C5
Hanway Pl. W1 11 H3
Hanway Rd. W7 55 A6
Hanway St. W1 11 H3
Hanway St. W1 58 D6
Hanworth Rd., Felt. 81 B1
Hanworth Rd., Hmptn. 81 F4
Hanworth Rd. (TW3), Houns. 72 H4
Hanworth Rd. (TW4), Houns. 81 E1
Hanworth Rd., Sun. 81 A7
Hanworth Ter., Houns. 72 H4
Hanworth Trd. Est., Felt. 81 E3
Hapgood Clo., Grnf. 46 A5
Harben Rd. NW6 48 F7
Harberson Rd. E15 60 F1
Harberson Rd. SW12 85 B1
Harberton Rd. N19 49 C1
Harbet Rd. N18 33 G5
Harbet Rd. W2 10 F2
Harbet Rd. W2 57 G5
Harbex Clo., Bex. 80 H7
Harbinger Rd. E14 69 B4
Harbledown Rd. SW6 75 D1
Harbord Clo. SE5 77 A2
De Crespigny Pk.
Harbord St. SW6 75 A1
Harborne Clo., Wat. 28 C5
Anglesey Rd.
Harborough Ave., Sid. 79 H7
Harborough Rd. SW16 85 F4
Harbour Ave. SW10 75 F1
Harbour Ex. Sq. E14 69 B2
Harbour Rd. SE5 76 J3
Harbridge Ave. SW15 74 F7
Harbut Rd. SW11 75 G4
Harcombe Rd. N16 50 B3
Harcourt Ave. E12 52 C4
Harcourt Ave., Edg. 30 C3
Harcourt Ave., Sid. 80 C6
Harcourt Ave., Wall. 101 B4
Harcourt Clo., Islw. 73 D3
Harcourt Fld., Wall. 101 B4
Harcourt Rd. E15 60 F2
Harcourt Rd. N22 40 D1
Harcourt Rd. SE4 77 H4
Harcourt Rd. SW19 84 D7
Russell Rd.
Harcourt Rd., Bexh. 80 E4
Harcourt Rd., Th.Hth. 94 F6
Harcourt Rd., Wall. 101 B4
Harcourt St. W1 10 H2
Harcourt St. W1 57 H5
Harcourt Ter. SW10 18 B4
Harcourt Ter. SW10 66 E5
Hardcastle Clo., Croy. 95 C6
Hardcourts Clo., W.Wick. 103 B3
Hardel Ri. SW2 85 H1
Hardel Wk. SW2 76 G7
Papworth Way
Hardens Manorway SE7 70 A3
Harders Rd. SE15 77 E2
Hardess St. SE24 76 J3
Herne Hill Rd.
Hardie Clo. NW10 47 D5
Hardie Rd., Dag. 53 J3
Harding Clo. SE17 20 J6
Harding Ho., Hayes 54 A6
Harding Rd., Bexh. 80 F2
Hardinge Rd. N18 33 B5
Hardinge Rd. NW10 56 H1
Hardinge St. E1 59 F6
Hardings La. SE20 86 G6
Hardman Rd. SE7 69 H5
Hardman Rd., Kings.T. 91 H2
Hardwick Clo., Stan. 29 F5
Hardwick Grn. W13 55 E5
Hardwick St. EC1 8 F4
Hardwick St. EC1 58 G3
Hardwicke Ave., Houns. 72 G1
Hardwicke Rd. N13 32 E6
Hardwicke Rd. W4 65 C4
Hardwicke Rd., Rich. 82 F4
Hardwicke St., Bark. 61 F1
Hardwicks Way SW18 75 D5
Buckhold Rd.
Hardwidge St. SE1 17 D3
Hardy Ave., Ruis. 45 B5
Hardy Clo. SE16 68 G2
Middleton Dr.
Hardy Clo., Pnr. 36 D7
Hardy Rd. SE3 69 F6
Hardy Rd. SW19 84 E7
Hardy Way, Enf. 24 G1
Hare & Billet Rd. SE3 78 D1
Hare Ct. EC4 12 E4
Hare La., Esher 98 A5
Hare Marsh E2 9 H5
Hare Pl. EC4 12 F4
Hare Row E2 59 E2
Hare St. SE18 70 D3
Hare Wk. N1 9 E2
Hare Wk. N1 59 B2
Harecastle Clo., Hayes 54 E4
Braunston Dr.
Harecourt Rd. N1 49 J6
Haredale Rd. SE24 76 J4
Haredon Clo. SE23 77 F7
Harefield, Esher 98 B3
Harefield Clo., Enf. 24 G1
Harefield Ms. SE4 77 J3
Harefield Rd. N8 40 D5
Harefield Rd. SE4 77 J3
Harefield Rd. SW16 85 F7
Harefield Rd., Sid. 89 D2
Haresfield Rd., Dag. 53 G6
Harewood Ave. NW1 6 H6
Harewood Ave. NW1 57 H4
Harewood Ave., Nthlt. 45 E7
Harewood Clo., Nthlt. 45 F7
Harewood Dr., Ilf. 43 C2
Harewood Pl. W1 11 E4
Harewood Rd. SW19 84 H6
Harewood Rd., Islw. 64 C7
Harewood Rd., S.Croy. 102 B6
Harewood Rd., Wat. 28 B2
Harewood Row NW1 10 H1
Harewood Ter., Sthl. 63 F4
Harfield Gdns. SE5 77 B3
Harfield Rd., Sun. 90 D2
Harford Clo. E4 26 B7
Harford Rd. E4 26 B7
Harford St. E1 59 H4
Harford Wk. N2 39 G4
Hargood Clo., Har. 37 H6
Hargood Rd. SE3 78 J1
Hargrave Pk. N19 49 C2
Hargrave Pl. N7 49 D5
Brecknock Rd.
Hargrave Rd. N19 49 C2
Hargwyne St. SW9 76 F3
Haringey Pk. N8 40 E6
Haringey Pas. N4 40 H5
Warham Rd.
Haringey Pas. N8 40 H4
Haringey Rd. N8 40 E4
Harington Ter. N9 33 A3
Harington Ter. N18 33 A3
Harkett Clo., Har. 37 C2
Byron Rd.
Harkett Ct., Har. 37 C2
Harland Ave., Croy. 102 C3
Harland Ave., Sid. 88 G3
Harland Rd. SE12 87 G1
Harlech Gdns., Houns. 63 C6
Harlech Rd. N14 32 E3
Harlech Twr. W3 65 C2
Harlequin Ave., Brent. 64 D6
Harlequin Clo., Islw. 73 B5
Harlequin Rd., Tedd. 82 E7
Harlescott Rd. SE15 77 G4
Harlesden Gdns. NW10 56 F1
Harlesden La. NW10 56 G1
Harlesden Rd. NW10 56 G1
Harleston Clo. E5 50 F2
Theydon Rd.
Harley Clo., Wem. 46 G6
Harley Ct. E11 42 G7
Harley Cres., Har. 37 A4
Harley Gdns. SW10 18 D4
Harley Gdns. SW10 66 F5
Harley Gdns., Orp. 104 H4
Harley Gro. E3 59 J3
Harley Pl. W1 11 D2
Harley Pl. W1 58 B5
Harley Rd. NW3 48 G7
Harley Rd. NW10 56 E2
Harley Rd., Har. 37 A4
Harley St. W1 7 D6
Harley St. W1 58 B5
Harleyford, Brom. 96 J1
Harleyford Rd. SE11 20 C5
Harleyford Rd. SE11 67 F6
Harleyford St. SE11 20 E6
Harleyford St. SE11 67 G6
Harlington Rd., Bexh. 80 E3
Harlington Rd. E., Felt. 72 B7
Harlington Rd. W., Felt. 72 B6
Harlow Rd. N13 33 A3
Harlyn Dr., Pnr. 36 B3
Harman Ave., Wdf.Grn. 34 F6
Harman Clo. E4 34 D4
Harman Clo. NW2 48 B3
Harman Dr. NW2 48 B3
Harman Dr., Sid. 79 J6
Harman Rd., Enf. 25 C5
Harmony Clo. NW11 39 B5
Harmood Gro. NW1 49 B7
Clarence Way
Harmood Pl. NW1 49 B7
Harmood St.
Harmood St. NW1 49 B6
Harmsworth St. SE17 20 G4
Harmsworth St. SE17 67 H5
Harmsworth Way N20 31 C1
Harnage Rd., Brent. 64 E7
Harness Rd. SE28 71 A2
Harold Ave., Belv. 71 F5
Harold Est. SE1 17 E6
Harold Est. SE1 68 B3
Harold Gibbons Ct. SE7 69 J6
Victoria Way
Harold Pl. SE11 20 E4
Harold Rd. E4 34 C4
Harold Rd. E11 51 E1
Harold Rd. E13 60 H1
Harold Rd. N8 40 F5
Harold Rd. N15 41 C5
Harold Rd. NW10 56 D3
Harold Rd. SE19 86 A7
Harold Rd., Sutt. 100 G4
Harold Rd., Wdf.Grn. 42 G1
Haroldstone Rd. E17 41 G5
Harp All. EC4 12 G3
Harp Island Clo. NW10 47 D2
Harp La. EC3 13 D6
Harp Rd. W7 55 B4
Harpenden Rd. E12 51 J2
Harpenden Rd. SE27 85 H2
Harper Rd. E6 61 C6
Harper Rd. SE1 17 A5
Harper Rd. SE1 67 J3
Harpley Sq. E1 59 F3
Harpour Rd., Bark. 52 F6
Harpsden St. SW11 76 A1
Harpur Ms. WC1 12 C1
Harpur St. WC1 12 C1
Harpur St. WC1 58 F5
Harraden Rd. SE3 78 J1
Harrier Ms. SE28 70 G3
Harrier Rd. NW9 38 E2
Harrier Way E6 61 C5
Harriers Clo. W5 55 H7
Harries Rd., Hayes 54 C4
Harriet Clo. E8 59 D1
Harriet Gdns., Croy. 102 D2
Harriet St. SW1 15 A4
Harriet Wk. SW1 15 A4
Harriet Wk. SW1 66 J2
Harringay Gdns. N8 40 H4
Harringay Rd. N15 40 H5
Harrington Clo., Croy. 101 E2
Harrington Gdns. SW7 18 B2
Harrington Gdns. SW7 66 F4
Harrington Hill E5 50 E1
Harrington Rd. E11 51 E1
Harrington Rd. SE25 95 D4
Harrington Rd. SW7 18 F1
Harrington Rd. SW7 66 G4
Harrington Sq. NW1 7 F2
Harrington Sq. NW1 58 C2
Harrington St. NW1 7 F2
Harrington St. NW1 58 C3
Harrington Way SE18 70 A3
Harriott Clo. SE10 69 F4
Harris Clo., Enf. 24 H1
Harris Clo., Houns. 72 G1
Harris Rd., Bexh. 80 E1
Harris Rd., Dag. 53 F5
Harris St. E17 41 J7
Harris St. SE5 68 A7
Harrison Rd., Dag. 53 H6
Harrison St. WC1 8 B4
Harrison St. WC1 58 E3
Harrisons Ri., Croy. 101 H3
Harrogate Rd., Wat. 28 C3
Harrold Rd., Dag. 53 B5
Harrow Ave., Enf. 25 C6
Harrow Clo., Chess. 98 G7
Harrow Dr. N9 33 C1
Harrow Flds. Gdns., Har. 46 B3
Harrow La. E14 60 C7
Harrow Manorway SE2 71 C3
Harrow Pk., Har. 46 B2
Harrow Pas., Kings.T. 91 G2
Market Pl.
Harrow Pl. E1 13 F3
Harrow Pl. E1 59 B6

Harrow Rd. E6 61 B1
Harrow Rd. E11 51 E3
Harrow Rd. NW10 56 H3
Harrow Rd. W2 57 D5
Harrow Rd. W9 57 C4
Harrow Rd. W10 57 B4
Harrow Rd., Bark. 61 H1
Harrow Rd., Cars. 100 H5
Harrow Rd., Ilf. 52 F4
Harrow Rd., Wem. 46 C4
Harrow Vw., Har. 36 J1
Harrow Vw., Hayes 54 A6
Harrow Vw. Rd. W5 55 E4
Harrow Way, Wat. 28 E3
Harrow Weald Pk., 29 A6
  Har.
Harroway Rd. SW11 75 G2
Harrowby St. W1 10 H3
Harrowby St. W1 57 H6
Harrowdene Clo., 46 G4
  Wem.
Harrowdene Gdns., 82 D6
  Tedd.
Harrowdene Rd., 46 G5
  Wem.
Harrowes Meade, 30 A3
  Edg.
Harrowgate Rd. E9 50 H6
Hart Cres., Chig. 35 J5
Hart Gro. W5 65 A1
Hart Gro., Sthl. 54 G5
Hart St. EC3 13 E5
Harte Rd., Houns. 72 F2
Hartfield Ave., 22 A6
  Borwd.
Hartfield Ave., 54 B2
  Nthlt.
Hartfield Clo., 22 A5
  Borwd.
Hartfield Cres. 84 C7
  SW19
Hartfield Cres., 103 G3
  W.Wick.
Hartfield Gro. SE20 95 F1
Hartfield Rd. SW19 84 C6
Hartfield Rd., 98 G5
  Chess.
Hartfield Rd., 103 G4
  W.Wick.
Hartfield Ter. E3 60 A2
Hartford Ave., Har. 37 D3
Hartford Rd., Bex. 80 G6
Hartford Rd., Epsom 99 A6
Hartforde Rd., 22 A2
  Borwd.
Hartham Clo. N7 49 E5
Hartham Clo., Islw. 73 D1
Hartham Rd. N7 49 E5
Hartham Rd. N17 41 C2
Hartham Rd., Islw. 73 C1
Harting Rd. SE9 88 B4
Hartington Clo., 46 B4
  Har.
Hartington Ct. W4 65 B7
Hartington Rd. E16 60 H6
Hartington Rd. E17 41 H6
Hartington Rd. SW8 76 E1
Hartington Rd. W4 65 B7
Hartington Rd. W13 55 E7
Hartington Rd., 63 E3
  Sthl.
Hartington Rd., 73 E7
  Twick.
Hartismere Rd. SW6 66 C7
Hartlake Rd. E9 50 G6
Hartland Clo., Edg. 30 A2
Hartland Dr., Edg. 30 A2
Hartland Dr., Ruis. 45 B3
Hartland Rd. E15 51 F7
Hartland Rd. N11 31 J5
Hartland Rd. NW1 49 B7
Hartland Rd. NW6 57 C2
Hartland Rd., 81 H4
  Hmptn.
Hartland Rd., Islw. 73 D3
Hartland Rd., Mord. 93 D7
Hartland Way, Croy. 102 H2
Hartland Way, Mord. 93 C7
Hartlands Clo., 80 F6
  Bex.
Hartley Ave. E6 61 B1
Hartley Ave. NW7 30 F5
Hartley Clo. NW7 30 F5
Hartley Clo., Brom. 97 C2
Hartley Clo. E11 51 F1
Hartley Rd., Croy. 94 H7
Hartley Rd., Well. 71 C7
Hartley St. E2 59 F3
Hartnoll St. N7 49 F5
  Eden Gro.
Harton Clo., Brom. 97 A1
Harton Rd. N9 33 E2
Harton St. SE8 78 A1

Harts Gro., 34 G5
  Wdf.Grn.
Harts La. SE14 68 H7
Harts La., Bark. 52 E6
Hartsbourne Ave. 28 J2
  (Bushey), Wat.
Hartsbourne Clo. 29 A2
  (Bushey), Wat.
Hartsbourne Rd. 29 A2
  (Bushey), Wat.
Hartswood Grn. 29 A2
  (Bushey), Wat.
Hartswood Rd. W12 65 F2
Hartsworth Clo. E13 60 F2
Hartville Rd. SE18 70 H4
Hartwell Dr. E4 34 C6
Hartwell St. E8 50 C6
  Dalston La.
Harvard Hill W4 65 B5
  Wolseley Gdns.
Harvard La. W4 65 B5
  Harvard Rd.
Harvard Rd. SE13 78 C5
Harvard Rd. W4 65 B5
Harvard Rd., Islw. 73 B1
Harvel Cres. SE2 71 G5
Harvest Bank Rd., 103 F3
  W.Wick.
Harvest La. E2 59 E2
Harvest La., T.Ditt. 91 D6
Harvest Rd., Felt. 91 A4
Harvesters Clo., 73 A5
  Islw.
Harvey Gdns. E11 51 F1
  Harvey Rd.
Harvey Gdns. SE7 69 J5
Harvey Gdns., Loug. 27 E3
Harvey Ho., Brent. 64 H5
Harvey Pt. E16 60 H5
  Fife Rd.
Harvey Rd. E11 51 E1
Harvey Rd. N8 40 F5
Harvey Rd. SE5 77 A1
Harvey Rd., Houns. 72 F7
Harvey Rd., Ilf. 52 E5
Harvey Rd., Nthlt. 45 C7
Harvey Rd., Walt. 90 A7
Harvey St. N1 59 A1
Harvill Rd., Sid. 89 D5
Harvington Wk. E8 50 D7
  Wilman Gro.
Harvist Est. N7 49 G4
Harvist Rd. NW6 57 A2
Harwater Dr., Loug. 27 C2
Harwell Pas. N2 39 J4
Harwich La. EC2 13 E1
Harwich La. EC2 59 B5
Harwood Ave., Brom. 96 H2
Harwood Ave., 93 H3
  Mitch.
Harwood Ave., Wem. 46 G4
  Harwodene Rd.
Harwood Rd. SW6 66 D7
Harwood Ter. SW6 75 E1
Harwoods Yd. N21 24 G7
  Wades Hill
Hascombe Ter. SE5 77 A2
Haselbury Rd. N9 33 B3
Haselbury Rd. N18 33 B4
Haseley End SE23 77 F7
  Tyson Rd.
Haselrigge Rd. SW4 76 D4
Haseltine Rd. SE26 86 J4
Haselwood Dr., Enf. 24 H4
Haskard Rd., Dag. 53 D4
Haskell Ho. NW10 56 D1
Hasker St. SW3 13 H1
Hasker St. SW3 66 H4
Haslam Ave., Sutt. 100 B1
Haslam Clo. N1 49 G7
Haslemere Ave. NW4 39 A6
Haslemere Ave. 84 E2
  SW18
Haslemere Ave. W7 64 D3
Haslemere Ave. W13 64 D3
Haslemere Ave., 31 J1
  Barn.
Haslemere Ave., 72 C2
  Houns.
Haslemere Ave., 93 G2
  Mitch.
Haslemere Clo., 81 F5
  Hmptn.
Haslemere Clo., 101 E5
  Wall.
  Stafford Rd.
Haslemere Gdns. N3 39 C3
Haslemere Heathrow 72 B2
  Est., Houns.

Haslemere Rd. N8 40 D7
Haslemere Rd. N21 32 H2
Haslemere Rd., 80 F2
  Bexh.
Haslemere Rd., Ilf. 52 J2
Haslemere Rd., 94 H5
  Th.Hth.
Hasler Clo. SE28 62 B7
Hasluck Gdns., 23 E6
  Barn.
Hassard St. E2 9 G2
Hassendean Rd. SE3 69 H6
Hassett Rd. E9 50 G6
Hassock Wd., Kes. 104 A4
Hassocks Clo. SE26 86 E3
Hassocks Rd. SW16 94 C1
Hassop Rd. NW2 48 A4
Hassop Wk. SE9 88 B4
Hasted Rd. SE7 70 A5
Hastings Ave., Ilf. 43 F4
Hastings Clo. SE15 68 D7
Hastings Clo., 23 F4
  Barn.
  Leicester Rd.
Hastings Ho. SE18 70 C4
  Cardwell Rd.
Hastings Rd. N11 32 C5
Hastings Rd. N17 41 A3
Hastings Rd. W13 55 E7
Hastings Rd., Brom. 104 B1
Hastings Rd., Croy. 102 C1
Hastings St. WC1 8 A4
Hastings St. WC1 58 E3
Hastings St. NW8 6 F6
  Kingsash Dr.
Hat and Mitre Ct. EC1 8 H6
Hatch, The, Enf. 25 G1
Hatch Gro., Rom. 44 E4
Hatch La. E4 34 D4
Hatch Pl., Kings.T. 82 J5
Hatch Rd. SW16 94 E2
Hatch Side, Chig. 35 D5
Hatcham Pk. Ms. 77 G1
  SE14
  Hatcham Pk. Rd.
Hatcham Pk. Rd. 77 G1
  SE14
Hatcham Rd. SE15 68 F6
Hatchard Rd. N19 49 D2
Hatchcroft NW4 38 H3
Hatchwood Clo., 34 F4
  Wdf.Grn.
  Sunset Ave.
Hatcliffe Clo. SE3 78 F3
Hatcliffe St. SE10 69 F5
  Woolwich Rd.
Hatfield Clo. SE14 68 G7
Hatfield Clo., Ilf. 43 E3
Hatfield Clo., 93 G4
  Mitch.
Hatfield Mead, 93 D5
  Mord.
  Central Rd.
Hatfield Rd. E15 51 E5
Hatfield Rd. W4 65 D2
Hatfield Rd. W13 64 D1
Hatfield Rd., Dag. 53 E6
Hatfields SE1 16 F1
Hatfields SE1 67 G1
Hatfields, Loug. 27 E3
Hathaway Clo., 104 C1
  Brom.
Hathaway Clo., 29 D5
  Stan.
Hathaway Cres., E12 52 C6
Hathaway Gdns. 55 C5
  W13
Hathaway Gdns., 44 D5
  Rom.
Hathaway Rd., Croy. 94 H7
Hatherleigh Clo., 98 G5
  Chess.
Hatherleigh Clo., 93 D4
  Mord.
Hatherleigh Rd., 45 A2
  Ruis.
Hatherley Cres., Sid. 89 A2
Hatherley Gdns. E6 61 A2
Hatherley Gdns. N8 40 E6
Hatherley Gro. W2 10 A3
Hatherley Gro. W2 57 E6
Hatherley Ms. E17 42 A4
Hatherley Rd. E17 41 J4
Hatherley Rd., 73 J1
  Rich.
Hatherley Rd., Sid. 89 A4
Hatherley St. SW1 19 G2
Hathern Gdns. SE9 88 D4
Hatherop Rd., 81 F7
  Hmptn.
Hathorne Clo. SE15 77 E2
Hathway St. SE15 77 F2
  Gibbon Rd.

Hathway Ter. SE14 77 F2
  Gibbon Rd.
Hatley Ave., Ilf. 43 F4
Hatley Clo. N11 31 J5
Hatley Rd. N4 49 F2
Hatteraick St. SE16 68 F2
  Church St.
Hattersfield Clo., 71 F4
  Belv.
Hatton Clo. SE18 70 G7
Hatton Ct. E5 50 H4
  Gilpin Rd.
Hatton Gdn. EC1 12 F1
Hatton Gdn. EC1 58 G5
Hatton Gdns., Mitch. 93 J5
Hatton Grn., Felt. 72 A4
Hatton Ho. E1 13 J5
Hatton Pl. EC1 58 G5
Hatton Rd., Croy. 101 G1
Hatton Row NW8 6 F6
Hatton St. NW8 6 F6
Hatton Wall EC1 12 E1
Hatton Wall EC1 58 G5
Haunch of Venison 11 D4
  Yd. W1
Havana Rd. SW19 84 D2
Havannah St. E14 69 A2
Havant Rd. E17 42 C3
Havant Way SE15 21 F7
Havelock Pl., Har. 37 B6
Havelock Rd. N17 41 D2
Havelock Rd. SW19 84 F5
Havelock Rd., Belv. 71 F4
Havelock Rd., Brom. 96 J4
Havelock Rd., Croy. 102 C2
Havelock Rd., Har. 37 B3
Havelock Rd., Sthl. 63 E3
Havelock St. N1 58 E1
Havelock St., Ilf. 52 E2
Havelock Ter. SW8 67 B7
Havelock Wk. SE23 86 F1
Haven, The, Rich. 74 A3
Haven Clo. SE9 88 C3
Haven Clo. SW19 84 A3
Havon Clo., Sid. 89 C6
Haven Grn. W5 55 G6
Haven Grn. Ct. W5 55 G6
Haven La. W5 55 H6
Haven Pl. W5 55 G7
  The Bdy.
Haven St. NW1 49 B7
  Castlehaven Rd.
Havenhurst Ri., Enf. 24 G2
Havenwood, Wem. 47 B3
Haverfield Gdns., 65 A7
  Rich.
Haverfield Rd. E3 59 H3
Haverford Way, Edg. 37 J1
Haverhill Rd. E4 34 C1
Haverhill Rd. SW12 85 C1
Havering Gdns., 44 C5
  Rom.
Havering St. E1 59 G6
  Devonport St.
Havering Way, Bark. 62 B3
Haversfield Est., 64 H5
  Brent.
Haversham Clo., 73 G6
  Twick.
Haversham Pl. SE19 85 H7
  Biggin Hill
Haverstock Hill NW3 48 J6
Haverstock Rd. NW5 49 A5
Haverstock St. N1 8 H2
Haverstock St. N1 58 H2
Haverthwaite Rd., 104 G3
  Orp.
Havil St. SE5 68 B7
Hawarden Gro. SE24 76 J7
Hawarden Hill NW2 47 G3
Hawarden Rd. E17 41 G4
Hawbridge Rd. E11 51 D1
Hawes Clo., W.Wick. 103 C1
Hawes Rd. N18 33 E6
Hawes Rd., Brom. 96 H1
Hawes St. N1 49 H7
Hawes St. N1 73 C5
Haweswater Ho., 73 C5
  Islw.
Hawgood St. E3 60 A5
Hawkdene E4 26 B6
Hawke Pk. Rd. N22 40 H3
Hawke Pl. SE16 68 G2
  Middleton Dr.
Hawke Rd. SE19 86 A6
Hawker Clo., Wall. 101 E7
  Kingsford Ave.
Hawkes Rd., Mitch. 93 H1
Hawkesbury Rd. 74 H5
  SW15
Hawkesfield Rd. 86 H2
  SE23
Hawkesley Clo., 82 D4
  Twick.

Hawkewood Rd., 90 A3
Sun.
Hawkhurst Gdns., 98 H4
Chess.
Hawkhurst Rd. SW16 94 D1
Hawkhurst Way, 92 D5
N.Mal.
Hawkhurst Way, 103 B2
W.Wick.
Hawkins Clo., Borwd. 22 C2
Banks Rd.
Hawkins Clo., Har. 37 A7
Hawkins Rd., Tedd. 82 E6
Hawkley Gdns. SE27 85 H2
Hawkridge Clo., Rom. 44 C6
Hawks Ms. SE10 69 C7
Luton Pl.
Hawks Rd., Kings.T. 91 J2
Hawksbrook La., 96 B6
Beck.
Hawkshaw Clo. SW2 76 E7
Tierney Rd.
Hawkshead Clo., 87 E7
Brom.
Hawkshead Rd. 47 F7
NW10
Hawkshead Rd. W4 65 E2
Hawkslade Rd. SE15 77 G5
Hawksley Rd. N16 50 A3
Hawksmoor Clo. E6 61 B6
Allhallows Rd.
Hawksmoor Ms. E1 59 E7
Cable St.
Hawksmoor St. W6 66 A6
Hawksmouth E4 26 B7
Hawkstone Rd. SE16 68 F4
Hawkwell Wk. N1 58 J1
Basire St.
Hawkwood Cres. E4 26 B6
Hawkwood La., Chis. 97 F1
Hawkwood Mt. E5 50 E1
Hawlands Dr., Pnr. 36 E7
Hawley Clo., Hmptn. 81 F6
Hawley Cres. NW1 49 B7
Hawley Ms. NW1 49 B7
Hawley Rd.
Hawley Rd. N1 49 B7
Hawley St. NW1 49 B7
Hawstead Rd. SE6 78 B6
Hawsted, Buck.H. 26 H7
Hawthorn Ave. N13 32 E5
Hawthorn Ave., 101 A7
Cars.
Hawthorn Ave., Rich. 73 H2
Kew Rd.
Hawthorn Ave., 94 H1
Th.Hth.
Hawthorn Clo., 81 G5
Hmptn.
Hawthorn Clo., 63 B7
Houns.
Hawthorn Clo., Orp. 97 G6
Hawthorn Ct., Rich. 74 B1
Hawthorn Cres. 85 A5
SW17
Hawthorn Dr., Har. 36 G6
Hawthorn Dr., 103 E4
W.Wick.
Hawthorn Gdns. W5 64 G3
Hawthorn Gro. SE20 86 E7
Hawthorn Gro., 22 F6
Barn.
Hawthorn Hatch, 64 E7
Brent.
Hawthorn Ms. NW7 39 B1
Holders Hill Rd.
Hawthorn Pl., Erith 71 J5
Hawthorn Rd. N8 40 D3
Hawthorn Rd. N18 33 C6
Hawthorn Rd. NW10 47 G7
Hawthorn Rd., Bexh. 80 F4
Hawthorn Rd., 64 E7
Brent.
Hawthorn Rd., 35 A4
Buck.H.
Hawthorn Rd., Sutt. 100 H5
Hawthorn Rd., Wall. 101 B7
Hawthorn Wk. W10 57 B4
Droop St.
Hawthorn Way N9 33 B2
Hawthorndene Clo., 103 F2
Brom.
Hawthorndene Rd., 103 F2
Brom.
Hawthorne Ave., 37 D6
Har.
Hawthorne Ave., 93 G2
Mitch.
Hawthorne Ave., 36 B7
Ruis.
Hawthorne Clo. N1 50 B6
Hawthorne Clo., 97 C3
Brom.

Hawthorne Clo., 100 E2
Sutt.
Aultone Way
Hawthorne Fm. Ave., 54 E1
Nthlt.
Hawthorne Gro. NW9 38 C7
Hawthorne Rd. E17 42 A3
Hawthorne Rd., 97 C3
Brom.
Hawthornes Cen., 37 C4
Har.
Hawthorns, Wdf.Grn. 34 G3
Hawthorns, The, 99 F6
Epsom
Ewell Bypass
Hawthorns, The, 27 D4
Loug.
Hawtrey Ave., Nthlt. 54 D2
Hawtrey Dr., Ruis. 36 A7
Hawtrey Rd. NW3 48 H7
Haxted Rd., Brom. 96 H1
North Rd.
Hay Clo. E15 51 E7
Hay Clo., Borwd. 22 C2
Banks Rd.
Hay Currie St. E14 60 B6
Hay Hill W1 11 E6
Hay Hill W1 58 B7
Hay La. NW9 38 C4
Hay St. E2 59 D1
Haycroft Gdns. 56 G1
NW10
Haycroft Rd. SW2 76 E5
Haycroft Rd., Surb. 98 G3
Hayday Rd. E16 60 G5
Hayden Way, Rom. 44 J2
Haydens Pl. W11 57 C6
Portobello Rd.
Haydns Ms. W3 56 C6
Emanuel Ave.
Haydock Ave., Nthlt. 45 G6
Haydock Grn., Nthlt. 45 G6
Haydock Ave.
Haydon Clo. NW9 38 C4
Haydon Clo., Enf. 25 B6
Mortimer Dr.
Haydon Dr., Pnr. 36 B4
Haydon Pk. Rd. 84 D5
SW19
Haydon Rd., Dag. 53 C2
Haydon St. EC3 13 F5
Haydon Wk. E1 13 G5
Haydons Rd. SW19 84 E5
Hayes Chase, 96 D6
W.Wick.
Hayes Clo., Brom. 103 G2
Hayes Ct. SW2 85 E1
Hayes Cres. NW11 39 C5
Hayes Cres., Sutt. 100 A4
Hayes Gdns., Brom. 103 G2
Hayes Hill, Brom. 103 E1
Hayes Hill Rd. 103 F1
Brom.
Hayes La., Beck. 96 C3
Hayes La., Brom. 96 G5
Hayes Mead Rd., 103 E1
Brom.
Hayes Pl. NW1 6 H6
Hayes Rd., Brom. 96 G4
Hayes Rd., Sthl. 63 B4
Hayes St., Brom. 103 H1
Hayes Way, Beck. 96 C4
Hayes Wd. Ave., 103 H1
Brom.
Hayesford Pk. Dr., 96 F5
Brom.
Hayfield Pas. E1 59 F4
Stepney Grn.
Hayfield Yd. E1 59 F4
Mile End Rd.
Haygarth Pl. SW19 84 A5
Haygreen Clo., 83 B6
Kings.T.
Kingsnympton Pk.
Hayland Clo. NW9 38 D4
Hayles St. SE11 20 G1
Hayles St. SE11 67 H4
Haylett Gdns., 91 G4
Kings.T.
Anglesea Rd.
Hayling Ave., Felt. 81 A3
Hayman St. N1 49 H7
Cross St.
Haymarket SW1 11 H6
Haymarket SW1 58 D7
Haymarket Arc. SW1 11 H6
Haymer Gdns., 99 G3
Wor.Pk.
Haymerle Rd. SE15 21 H6
Haymerle Rd. SE15 68 D6
Haymill Clo., Grnf. 55 C3
Hayne Rd., Beck. 95 J2
Hayne St. EC1 12 H1

Haynes Clo. N17 33 E7
Haynes Clo. SE3 78 E3
Haynes La. SE19 86 B6
Haynes Rd., Wem. 46 H7
Haynt Wk. SW20 93 B3
Hay's La. SE1 17 D2
Hay's Ms. W1 15 D1
Hay's Ms. W1 67 B1
Haysleigh Gdns. 95 D2
SE20
Hayter Rd. SW2 76 E5
Hayton Clo. E8 50 C6
Buttermere Wk.
Hayward Clo. SW19 84 E7
Hayward Gdns. 74 J6
SW15
Hayward Rd. N20 31 F2
Hayward's Pl. EC1 8 G6
Haywood Clo., Pnr. 36 D2
Haywood Ri., Orp. 104 H4
Haywood Rd., Brom. 97 A4
Hayworth Clo., Enf. 25 H2
Green St.
Hazel Bank, Surb. 99 C1
Hazel Clo. N13 33 A3
Hazel Clo. N19 49 C2
Hargrave Pk.
Hazel Clo. SE15 77 D2
Copeland Rd.
Hazel Clo., Brent. 64 E7
Hazel Clo., Croy. 102 G1
Primrose La.
Hazel Clo., Mitch. 94 D4
Hazel Clo., Twick. 72 J7
Hazel Gdns., Edg. 30 B4
Hazel Gro. SE26 86 G4
Hazel Gro., Orp. 104 E2
Hazel Gro., Rom. 44 E3
Hazel Gro., Wem. 55 H1
Carlyon Rd.
Hazel Gro. Est. 86 G4
SE26
Hazel La., Rich. 82 H2
Hazel Mead, Barn. 22 H5
Hazel Rd. E15 51 E5
Wingfield Rd.
Hazel Rd. NW10 56 H3
Hazel Wk., Brom. 97 D6
Hazel Way E4 33 J6
Hazel Way SE1 21 F1
Hazelbank Rd. SE6 87 D2
Hazelbourne Rd. 76 B6
SW12
Hazelbrouck Gdns., 35 G7
Ilf.
Hazelbury Clo. SW19 93 D2
Hazelbury Grn. N9 33 B3
Hazelbury La. N9 33 B3
Hazelcroft, Pnr. 28 H6
Hazeldean Rd. NW10 47 D7
Hazeldene Dr., Pnr. 36 C3
Hazeldene Rd., Ilf. 53 B2
Hazeldene Rd., 80 C2
Well.
Hazeldon Rd. SE4 77 H5
Hazeleigh Gdns., 35 B1
Wdf.Grn.
Hazelgreen Clo. N21 32 H1
Hazelhurst, Beck. 96 D1
Hazelhurst Rd. SW17 84 F4
Hazell Cres., Rom. 44 H1
Hazellville Rd. N19 40 D7
Hazelmere Clo., 54 F2
Nthlt.
Hazelmere Dr., 54 F2
Nthlt.
Hazelmere Rd. NW6 57 C1
Hazelmere Rd., 54 F2
Nthlt.
Hazelmere Rd., Orp. 97 F4
Hazelmere Wk., 54 F2
Nthlt.
Hazelmere Way, 96 G6
Brom.
Hazeltree La., Nthlt. 54 E3
Hazelwood, Loug. 27 A5
Hazelwood Ave., 93 E4
Mord.
Hazelwood Clo. W5 64 H2
Hazelwood Clo., 36 H4
Har.
Hazelwood Ct. NW10 47 E3
Neasden La. N.
Hazelwood Cres. N13 32 G4
Hazelwood Cres. W10 57 B4
Hazelwood Cft., 91 H6
Surb.
Hazelwood Dr., Pnr. 36 B2
Hazelwood La. N13 32 G4
Hazelwood Pk. Clo., 35 H5
Chig.

Hazelwood Rd. E17 41 H5
Hazelwood Rd., Enf. 25 C6
Hazlebury Rd. SW6 75 E2
Hazledean Rd., 102 A2
Croy.
Hazledene Rd. W4 65 C6
Hazlemere Gdns., 99 G1
Wor.Pk.
Hazlewell Rd. SW15 74 H5
Hazlitt Ms. W14 66 B3
Hazlitt Rd.
Hazlitt Rd. W14 66 B3
Head St. E1 59 G6
Headcorn Pl., 94 F4
Th.Hth.
Headcorn Rd.
Headcorn Rd. N17 33 C7
Headcorn Rd., Brom. 87 G5
Headcorn Rd., 94 F4
Th.Hth.
Headfort Pl. SW1 15 C4
Headfort Pl. SW1 67 A2
Headingley Clo., Ilf. 35 J6
Headington Rd. 84 F2
SW18
Headlam Rd. SW4 76 D6
Headlam St. E1 59 E4
Headley App., Ilf. 43 E5
Headley Ave., Wall. 101 F5
Headley Clo., Epsom 99 A6
Headley Ct. SE26 86 F5
Headley Dr., Croy. 103 B7
Headley Dr., Ilf. 43 E6
Head's Ms. W11 57 D6
Artesian Rd.
Headstone Dr., Har. 37 B3
Headstone Gdns., 36 J4
Har.
Headstone La., Har. 28 H7
Headstone Rd., Har. 37 B5
Headway Clo., Rich. 82 F4
Locksmeade Rd.
Heald St. SE14 77 J1
Healey Dr., Orp. 104 J4
Healey St. NW1 49 B6
Heanor Ct. E5 50 G3
Pedro St.
Hearn Ri., Nthlt. 54 D1
Hearn St. EC2 9 E6
Hearn St. EC2 59 B4
Hearne Rd. W4 65 A6
Hearn's Bldgs. SE17 21 C2
Hearnville Rd. SW12 85 A1
Heath, The W7 64 B1
Lwr. Boston Rd.
Heath Ave., Bexh. 71 D6
Heath Brow NW3 48 F3
North End Way
Heath Clo. NW11 39 E7
Heath Clo. W5 55 J4
Heath Ct., Houns. 72 F4
Heath Dr. NW3 48 E4
Heath Dr. SW20 92 J4
Heath Gdns., Twick. 82 C1
Heath Gro. SE20 86 F7
Maple Rd.
Heath Hurst Rd. NW3 48 H4
Heath La. SE3 78 D2
Heath Mead SW19 84 A3
Heath Pk. Dr., 97 B3
Brom.
Heath Ri. SW15 75 A6
Heath Ri., Brom. 96 F6
Heath Rd. SW8 76 B2
Heath Rd., Bex. 89 J1
Heath Rd., Har. 36 J7
Heath Rd., Houns. 72 H4
Heath Rd., Rom. 44 D7
Heath Rd., Th.Hth. 94 J3
Heath Rd., Twick. 82 C1
Heath Side NW3 48 G4
Heath Side, Orp. 104 F1
Heath St. NW3 48 F3
Heath Vw. N2 39 F4
Heath Vw. Clo. N2 39 F4
Heath Vill. SE18 70 J5
Heath Way, Erith 80 J1
Heatham Pk., Twick. 73 C7
Heathbourne Rd. 29 B3
(Bushey), Wat.
Heathcock Ct. WC2 58 E7
Strand
Heathcote Ave., 43 C2
Ilf.
Heathcote Gro. E4 34 C3
Heathcote Rd., 73 E6
Twick.
Heathcote St. WC1 8 C5
Heathcote St. WC1 58 F4
Heathcroft NW11 48 E1
Heathcroft W5 55 J4
Heathdale Ave., 72 E3
Houns.

Heathdene Dr., Belv. 71 H4
Heathdene Rd. SW16 85 F7
Heathdene Rd., 101 A7
Wall.
Heathedge SE26 86 E2
Heather Clo. E6 61 E6
Heather Clo. SW8 76 B3
Heather Clo., 90 F1
Hmptn.
Heather Clo., Islw. 73 A5
Harvesters Clo.
Heather Dr., Enf. 24 H2
Chasewood Ave.
Heather Gdns. NW11 39 B6
Heather Gdns., 100 D6
Sutt.
Heather Pk. Dr., 47 A7
Wem.
Heather Rd. NW2 47 F2
Heather Rd. SE12 87 G2
Heather Wk. W10 57 B4
Droop St.
Heather Wk., Edg. 30 B5
Heather Way, Stan. 29 C6
Heatherbank, Chis. 97 D2
Heatherbank, Chis. 97 D2
Heatherdale Clo., 83 B7
Kings.T.
Heatherdene Clo. 39 F1
N12
Bow La.
Heatherdene Clo., 93 H4
Mitch.
Heatherlands, Sun. 81 A6
Heatherley Dr., Ilf. 43 B3
Heatherset Gdns. 85 F7
SW16
Heatherside Rd., 99 D7
Epsom
Heatherside Rd., 89 D3
Sid.
Wren Rd.
Heatherwood Clo. 51 J2
E12
Heathfield E4 34 C3
Heathfield, Chis. 88 F6
Heathfield Ave. 75 G7
SW18
Heathfield Rd.
Heathfield Clo. E16 61 A5
Heathfield Clo., Kes. 103 J5
Heathfield Dr., 93 H1
Mitch.
Heathfield Gdns. 39 A6
NW11
Heathfield Gdns. 75 G6
SW18
Heathfield Rd.
Heathfield Gdns. W4 65 C5
Heathfield La., Chis. 88 E6
Heathfield N., Twick. 73 C7
Heathfield Pk. NW2 47 J6
Heathfield Rd. SW18 75 F6
Heathfield Rd. W3 65 B2
Heathfield Rd., 80 F4
Bexh.
Heathfield Rd., 87 F7
Brom.
Heathfield Rd., 102 A4
Croy.
Heathfield Rd., Kes. 103 J5
Heathfield S., 73 C7
Twick.
Heathfield Sq. SW18 75 G7
Heathfield St. W11 57 B7
Portland Rd.
Heathfield Ter. SE18 70 H6
Heathfield Ter. W4 65 C5
Houns.
Heathfields Ct., 72 E5
Frampton Rd.
Heathgate NW11 39 E6
Heathland Rd. N16 50 B1
Heathlands Clo., 82 C1
Twick.
Heathlands Way, 72 E5
Houns.
Frampton Rd.
Heathlee Rd. SE3 78 F4
Heathly End, Chis. 88 F6
Heathmans Rd. SW6 75 C1
Heathrow 72 B3
International Trd. Est.,
Houns.
Heaths Clo., Enf. 25 B2
Heathside, Esher 98 B3
Heathside, Houns. 72 F7
Heathside Ave., 80 E2
Bexh.
Heathside Clo., 98 B3
Esher
Heathstan Rd. W12 56 G6
Heathview Ct. SW19 84 A2

Heathview Dr. SE2 71 D6
Heathview Gdns. 74 J7
SW15
Heathview Rd., 94 G4
Th.Hth.
Heathville Rd. N19 40 E7
Heathwall St. SW11 75 J3
Heathway SE3 69 G7
Heathway, Croy. 102 J3
Heathway, Dag. 53 F3
Heathway, Wdf.Grn. 34 J4
Heathwood Gdns. 70 B4
SE7
Heaton Rd. SE15 77 D3
Heaton Rd., Mitch. 85 A7
Heaver Rd. SW11 75 G3
Wye St.
Heavitree Rd. SE18 70 G5
Hebden Ct. E2 59 C1
Laburnum St.
Hebdon Rd. SW17 84 H3
Heber Rd. NW2 48 A5
Heber Rd. SE22 77 C6
Hebron Rd. W6 65 H3
Hecham Clo. E17 41 H2
Heckfield Pl. SW6 66 D7
Fulham Rd.
Heckford St. E1 59 G7
The Highway
Hector St. SE18 70 H4
Heddington Gro. N7 49 F5
Heddon Clo., Islw. 73 D4
Heddon Ct. Ave. 23 J6
Barn.
Heddon Rd., Barn. 23 J5
Heddon St. W1 11 F5
Heddon St. W1 58 C7
Hedge Hill, Enf. 24 H1
Hedge La. N13 32 H3
Hedge Wk. SE6 87 B5
Lushington Rd.
Hedgeley, Ilf. 43 C4
Hedgeley St. SE12 78 F5
Hedgemans Rd., 53 D7
Dag.
Hedgemans Way, 53 E6
Dag.
Hedgerley Gdns., 54 J2
Grnf.
Hedgers Gro. E9 50 H6
Hedgewood Gdns., 43 D4
Ilf.
Hedingham Clo. N1 49 J7
Popham Rd.
Hedingham Rd., Dag. 53 B5
Hedley Rd., Twick. 72 G7
Hedley Row N5 50 A5
Poets Rd.
Heenan Clo., Bark. 52 F6
Glenny Rd.
Heene Rd., Enf. 25 A1
Heigham Rd. E6 52 B7
Heighton Gdns., 101 H5
Croy.
Heights, The SE7 69 J5
Heights, The, Beck. 87 C7
Heights, The, Loug. 27 C2
Heights, The, Nthlt. 45 F5
Heights Clo. SW20 83 H7
Heiron St. SE17 20 H6
Heiron St. SE17 67 H6
Helby Rd. SW4 76 D6
Helder Gro. SE12 78 F7
Helder St., S.Croy. 102 A6
Heldmann Clo., 73 A4
Houns.
Helen Ave., Felt. 72 B7
Helen Clo. N2 39 F3
Thomas More Way
Helen Clo., W.Mol. 90 H4
Helen St. SE18 70 E4
Wilmount St.
Helena Clo., Wall. 101 E7
Kingsford Ave.
Helena Pl. E9 59 F1
Fremont St.
Helena Rd. E13 60 F2
Helena Rd. E17 42 A5
Helena Rd. NW10 41 H7
Helena Rd. W5 55 G5
Helens Pl. E2 59 F3
Roman Rd.
Helenslea Ave. NW11 48 C1
Helix Gdns. SW2 76 F6
Helix Rd.
Helix Rd. SW2 76 F6
Hellings St. E1 17 J2
Helme Clo. SW19 84 C5
Helmet Row EC1 9 A5
Helmet Row EC1 58 J4
Helmsdale Clo., 54 E4
Hayes
Berrydale Rd.

Helmsdale Rd. SW16 94 D1
Helmsley Pl. E8 50 E7
Helston Clo., Pnr. 28 F7
Helvetia St. SE6 86 J2
Hemans St. SW8 67 D7
Hemberton Rd. SW9 76 E3
Hemery Rd., Grnf. 46 A5
Lilian Board Way
Heming Rd., Edg. 30 B7
Hemingford Rd. N1 58 H1
Hemingford Rd., 99 J4
Sutt.
Hemington Ave. N11 31 J5
Hemlock Rd. W12 56 F7
Hemming Clo., 90 G1
Hmptn.
Chandler Clo.
Hemming St. E1 9 J6
Hemming St. E1 59 D4
Hemp Wk. SE17 21 C1
Hempstead Clo., 34 G2
Buck.H.
Hempstead Rd. E17 42 D2
Hemsby Rd., Chess. 98 J6
Hemstal Rd. NW6 48 D7
Hemswell Dr. NW9 38 E1
Fulham Rd.
Hemsworth Ct. N1 9 D1
Hemsworth St. N1 9 D1
Hemsworth St. N1 59 B2
Hemus Pl. SW3 18 H4
Hen & Chicken Ct. 58 G6
EC4
Fleet St.
Henbury Way, Wat. 28 D3
Henchman St. W12 56 F6
Hendale Ave. NW4 38 G3
Henderson Clo. 47 C6
NW10
Henderson Dr. NW8 6 E5
Henderson Rd. E7 51 J6
Henderson Rd. N9 33 E1
Henderson Rd. 75 H7
SW18
Henderson Rd., 95 A6
Croy.
Henderson Rd., 54 A3
Hayes
Hendham Rd. SW17 84 H2
Hendon Ave. N3 39 B1
Hendon La. N3 39 B3
Hendon Pk. Row 39 C6
NW11
Hendon Rd. N9 33 D2
Hendon Way NW2 39 A7
Hendon Way NW4 38 H6
Hendon Wd. La. 22 F7
NW7
Hendre Rd. SE1 21 E2
Hendren Clo., Grnf. 46 A5
Dimmock Dr.
Hendrick Ave. SW12 75 J7
Heneage La. EC3 13 E4
Heneage St. E1 13 G1
Heneage St. E1 59 C5
Henfield Clo. N19 49 C1
Henfield Clo., Bex. 80 G6
Henfield Rd. SW19 93 C1
Hengelo Gdns., 93 G4
Mitch.
Hengist Rd. SE12 78 H7
Hengist Rd., Erith 71 H7
Hengist Way, Brom. 96 D4
Hengrave Rd. SE23 77 F7
Hengrove Ct., Bex. 89 E1
Hurst Rd.
Henley Ave., Sutt. 100 B3
Henley Clo., Grnf. 54 J2
Henley Clo., Islw. 73 C1
Henley Ct. N14 24 C7
Henley Dr. SE1 21 G1
Henley Dr. SE1 68 C4
Henley Dr., Kings.T. 83 F7
Henley Gdns., Pnr. 26 B5
Henley Gdns., Rom. 44 E5
Henley Rd. E16 70 C2
Henley Rd. N18 33 B4
Henley Rd. NW10 56 J1
Henley Rd., Ilf. 52 F4
Henley St. SW11 76 A2
Henley Way, Felt. 81 D5
Conway Rd.
Hennel Clo. SE23 86 F3
Henniker Gdns. E6 61 A3
Henniker Ms. SW3 18 E5
Henniker Pt. E15 51 E5
Henniker Rd. E15 51 D5
Henning St. SW11 75 H1
Henningham Rd. N17 41 A1
Henrietta Ms. WC1 8 B5
Henrietta Pl. W1 11 D3
Henrietta St. E15 51 C5
Henrietta St. WC2 12 B5

Henrietta St. WC2 58 E7
Henriques St. E1 13 J3
Henriques St. E1 59 D6
Henry Cooper Way 88 A3
SE9
Henry Darlot Dr. 31 A5
NW7
Henry Dickens Ct. 57 A7
W11
Henry Jackson Rd. 75 A3
SW15
Henry Rd. E6 61 B2
Henry Rd. N4 49 J1
Henry Rd., Barn. 23 G5
Henry St., Brom. 96 H1
Henry's Ave., 34 F5
Wdf.Grn.
Henry's Wk., Ilf. 35 G7
Henryson Rd. SE4 78 A5
Hensford Gdns. SE26 86 E4
Wells Pk. Rd.
Henshall St. N1 50 A6
Henshaw St. SE17 21 B1
Henshaw St. SE17 68 A4
Henshawe Rd., Dag. 53 D3
Henshill Pt. E3 60 B3
Bromley High St.
Henslowe Rd. SE22 77 D5
Henson Ave. NW2 47 J5
Henson Clo., Orp. 104 E2
Henson Path, Har. 37 C3
Brancker Rd.
Henson Pl., Nthlt. 54 C1
Henstridge Pl. NW8 57 H2
Henty Clo. SW11 66 H7
Henty Wk. SW15 74 H5
Henville Rd., Brom. 96 J1
Henwick Rd. SE9 79 A3
Henwood Rd. SE16 68 F3
Gomm Rd.
Henwood Side, 35 C6
Wdf.Grn.
Love La.
Hepburn Gdns., 103 E1
Brom.
Hepburn Ms. SW11 75 J5
Webbs Rd.
Hepple Clo., Islw. 73 E2
Hepplestone Clo. 74 H6
SW15
Dover Pk. Dr.
Hepscott Rd. E9 51 A6
Hepworth Ct., Bark. 53 A5
Hepworth Gdns., 53 A5
Bark.
Hepworth Rd. SW16 85 E7
Hepworth Wk. NW3 48 H5
Haverstock Rd.
Heracles Clo., Wall. 101 E1
Gull Clo.
Herald Gdns., Wall. 101 B3
Herald St. E2 59 E4
Three Colts La.
Herald's Ct. SE11 20 G2
Herald's Pl. SE11 20 F1
Herbal Hill EC1 8 F6
Herbal Hill EC1 58 G4
Herbert Cres. SW1 15 A5
Herbert Gdns. NW10 56 H1
Herbert Gdns. W4 65 B6
Magnolia Rd.
Herbert Gdns., Rom. 44 D7
Herbert Pl. SE18 70 E4
Plumstead Common
Rd.
Herbert Rd. E12 52 B4
Herbert Rd. E17 41 J7
Herbert Rd. N11 32 E7
Herbert Rd. N15 41 C5
Herbert Rd. NW9 38 G6
Herbert Rd. SE18 70 D7
Herbert Rd. SW19 84 C7
Herbert Rd., Bexh. 80 E2
Herbert Rd., Brom. 97 A5
Herbert Rd., Ilf. 52 H2
Herbert Rd., Kings.T. 91 J3
Herbert Rd., Sthl. 63 F1
Herbert St. E13 60 G2
Herbert St. NW5 49 A6
Herbert Ter. SE18 70 E6
Herbert Rd.
Herbrand St. WC1 8 A5
Herbrand St. WC1 58 E4
Hercules Pl. N7 49 E3
Hercules St.
Hercules Rd. SE1 16 D6
Hercules Rd. SE1 67 F3
Hercules St. N7 49 E3
Hercules Twr. SE13 68 H6
Milton Ct. Rd.
Hereford Ave., Barn. 31 J1
Hereford Gdns., Ilf. 43 B7
Hereford Gdns., Pnr. 36 E5

Hereford Gdns., | 81 | J1
Twick.
Hereford Ho. NW6 | 57 | D2
Hereford Ms. W2 | 57 | D6
Hereford Rd.
Hereford Pl. SE14 | 68 | J7
Hereford Retreat | **21** | **H7**
SE15
Hereford Rd. E11 | 42 | H5
Hereford Rd. W2 | 57 | D6
Hereford Rd. W3 | 56 | B7
Hereford Rd. W5 | 64 | F3
Hereford Rd., Felt. | 81 | C1
Hereford Sq. SW7 | **18** | **D2**
Hereford St. SW7 | 66 | F4
Hereford St. E2 | 59 | D4
Hereford Way, | 98 | F5
Chess.
Herent Dr., Ilf. | 43 | B4
Hereward Gdns. N13 | 32 | G5
Hereward Grn., | 27 | F1
Loug.
Hereward Rd. SW17 | 84 | H4
Herga Ct., Har. | 46 | B3
Herga Rd., Har. | 37 | C4
Heriot Ave. E4 | 34 | A2
Heriot Rd. NW4 | 38 | J5
Heriots Clo., Stan. | 29 | D4
Heritage Hill, Kes. | 103 | J5
Heritage Vw., Har. | 46 | C3
Herlwyn Gdns. | 84 | J4
SW17
Hermes Pt. W9 | 57 | D4
Harrow Rd.
Hermes St. N1 | **8** | **E2**
Hermes Wk., Nthlt. | 54 | G2
Hotspur Rd.
Hermes Way, Wall. | 101 | D7
Herminston Ave. N8 | 40 | E5
Hermit Pl. NW6 | 57 | E1
Belsize Rd.
Hermit Rd. E16 | 60 | F4
Hermit St. EC1 | **8** | **G3**
Hermit St. EC1 | 58 | H3
Hermitage, The SE23 | 86 | F1
Hermitage, The | 74 | F1
SW13
Hermitage, The, | 73 | H5
Rich.
Hermitage Clo. E18 | 42 | F4
Hermitage Clo., Enf. | 24 | H2
Hermitage Clo., | 98 | D6
Esher
Hermitage Ct. E18 | 42 | F4
Hermitage Ct. NW2 | 48 | D3
Hermitage La.
Hermitage Gdns. | 48 | D3
NW2
Hermitage Gdns. | 85 | J7
SE19
Hermitage La. N18 | 33 | A5
Great Cambridge Rd.
Hermitage La. NW2 | 48 | D3
Hermitage La. SE25 | 95 | D6
Hermitage La. SW16 | 85 | F7
Hermitage La., Croy. | 95 | D6
Hermitage Path | 94 | E1
SW16
Hermitage Rd. N4 | 40 | H7
Hermitage Rd. N15 | 40 | H7
Hermitage Rd. SE19 | 85 | J7
Hermitage St. W2 | **10** | **E2**
Hermitage Wk. E18 | 42 | F4
Hermitage Wall E1 | **17** | **J2**
Hermitage Wall E1 | 68 | D1
Hermitage Way, | 37 | D1
Stan.
Hermon Gro., Hayes | 63 | A1
Hermon Hill E11 | 42 | H3
Hermon Hill E18 | 42 | H3
Herndon Rd. SW18 | 75 | F5
Herne Clo. NW10 | 47 | D5
North Circular Rd.
Herne Hill SE24 | 76 | J5
Herne Hill Rd. SE24 | 76 | J3
Herne Ms. N18 | 33 | D4
Lyndhurst Rd.
Herne Pl. SE24 | 76 | H5
Herne Rd., Surb. | 95 | F2
Heron Clo. E17 | 41 | J2
Heron Clo. NW10 | 46 | E6
Heron Clo., Buck.H. | 34 | G1
Heron Ct., Brom. | 96 | B4
Heron Cres., Sid. | 88 | H3
Heron Hill, Belv. | 71 | F5
Heron Ms., Ilf. | 52 | E2
Balfour Rd.
Heron Pl. SE16 | 66 | H1
Heron Quay E14 | 69 | A1
Heron Rd. SE24 | 76 | J4
Heron Rd., Croy. | 102 | B2
Tunstall Rd.
Heron Rd., Twick. | 73 | D4

Herondale Ave. | 84 | G1
SW18
Herongate Rd. E12 | 51 | J2
Herons, The E11 | 42 | F6
Heron's Pl., Islw. | 73 | E3
Herons Ri., Barn. | 23 | H4
Heronsforde W13 | 55 | F6
Heronsgate, Edg. | 30 | A5
Heronslea Dr., Stan. | 29 | H5
Heronway, Wdf.Grn. | 34 | J4
Herrick Rd. N5 | 49 | J3
Herrick St. SW1 | **19** | **J2**
Herrick St. SW1 | 67 | D4
Herries St. W10 | 57 | B2
Herringham Rd. SE7 | 69 | J3
Herrongate Clo., | 25 | C2
Enf.
Hersant Clo. NW10 | 56 | G1
Herschell Rd. SE23 | 77 | H7
Hersham Clo. SW15 | 74 | G7
Hertford Ave. SW14 | 74 | D5
Hertford Clo., Barn. | 23 | G3
Hertford Pl. W1 | **7** | **F6**
Hertford Rd. N1 | 59 | B1
Hertford Rd. N2 | 39 | H3
Hertford Rd. N9 | 33 | D2
Hertford Rd., Bark. | 52 | E7
Hertford Rd., Barn. | 23 | F3
Hertford Rd., Enf. | 25 | F2
Hertford Rd., Ilf. | 43 | H6
Hertford St. W1 | **15** | **C2**
Hertford St. W1 | 67 | A1
Hertford Wk., Belv. | 71 | G5
Hertford Way, Mitch. | 94 | E4
Hertslet Rd. N7 | 49 | F3
Hertsmere Rd. E14 | 60 | A7
Hervey Clo. N3 | 39 | D1
Hervey Pk. Rd. E17 | 41 | H4
Hervey Rd. SE3 | 78 | H1
Hesa Rd., Hayes | 54 | A6
Hesketh Pl. W11 | 57 | B7
Hesketh Rd. E7 | 51 | G3
Heslop Rd. SW12 | 84 | J1
Hesper Ms. SW5 | **18** | **A3**
Hesper Ms. SW5 | 66 | E5
Hesperus Cres. E14 | 69 | B4
Hessel Rd. W13 | 64 | D2
Hessel St. E1 | 59 | H6
Hester Rd. N18 | 33 | D5
Hester Rd. SW11 | 66 | H7
Hestercombe Ave. | 75 | B2
SW6
Heston Ave., Houns. | 63 | E6
Heston Gra. La., | 63 | F6
Houns.
Heston Ind. Cen., | 63 | C6
Houns.
Heston Ind. Mall, | 63 | F7
Houns.
Heston Rd., Houns. | 63 | G6
Heston St. SE14 | 78 | A1
Heswell Grn., Wat. | 28 | A3
Fairhaven Cres.
Hetherington Rd. | 76 | E4
SW4
Hetley Gdns. SE19 | 86 | C7
Fox Hill
Hetley Rd. W12 | 65 | H1
Heton Gdns. NW4 | 38 | G4
Hevelius Clo. SE10 | 69 | F5
Hever Cft. SE9 | 88 | D4
Hever Gdns., Brom. | 97 | D2
Heverham Rd. SE18 | 70 | H4
Heversham Rd., | 80 | G2
Bexh.
Hewer St. W10 | 57 | A5
Hewett Clo., Stan. | 29 | E4
Hewett Rd., Dag. | 53 | C5
Hewett St. EC2 | **9** | **E6**
Hewish Rd. N18 | 33 | B4
Hewitt Ave. N22 | 40 | H2
Hewitt Rd. N8 | 40 | G5
Hewlett Rd. E3 | 59 | H2
Hexagon, The N6 | 48 | J1
Hexal Rd. SE6 | 87 | E3
Hexham Gdns., Islw. | 64 | D7
Hexham Rd. SE27 | 85 | J2
Hexham Rd., Barn. | 23 | E4
Hexham Rd., Mord. | 100 | E1
Heybourne Rd. N17 | 33 | E7
Heybridge Ave. | 85 | E7
SW16
Heybridge Dr., Ilf. | 43 | G2
Heybridge Way E10 | 41 | H7
Heyford Ave. SW8 | 20 | B7
Heyford Ave. SW8 | 67 | E7
Heyford Ave. SW20 | 93 | C3
Heyford Rd., Mitch. | 93 | H2
Heygate St. SE17 | **20** | **J2**
Heygate St. SE17 | 67 | J4
Heylyn Sq. E3 | 59 | J3
Malmesbury Rd.
Heynes Rd., Dag. | 53 | C4

Heysham Dr., Wat. | 28 | C5
Heysham La. NW3 | 48 | E3
Heysham Rd. N15 | 41 | A6
Heythorp St. SW18 | 84 | C1
Heywood Ave. NW9 | 38 | E1
Heyworth Rd. E5 | 50 | E4
Heyworth Rd. E15 | 51 | F4
Hibbert Rd. E17 | 41 | J7
Hibbert Rd., Har. | 37 | C2
Hibbert St. SW11 | 75 | F3
Hibernia Gdns., | 72 | G4
Houns.
Hibernia Rd., Houns. | 72 | G4
Hichisson Rd. SE15 | 77 | F5
Hickin Clo. SE7 | 70 | A4
Hickin St. E14 | 69 | C3
Plevna St.
Hickling Rd., Ilf. | 52 | E5
Hickman Ave. E4 | 34 | C6
Hickman Clo. E16 | 61 | A5
Hickman Rd., Rom. | 44 | C7
Hickmore Wk. SW4 | 76 | C3
Hickory Clo. N9 | 25 | D7
Hicks Ave., Grnf. | 55 | A2
Hicks Clo. SW11 | 75 | H3
Hicks St. SE8 | 68 | H5
Hidcote Gdns. SW20 | 92 | H3
Hide Pl. SW1 | **19** | **H2**
Hide Pl. SW1 | 67 | D4
Hide Rd., Har. | 36 | J4
Hides St. N7 | 49 | F6
Sheringham Rd.
Higgins Wk., Hmptn. | 81 | E6
Abbott Clo.
High Beech, S.Croy. | 102 | B7
High Beech Rd., | 27 | B4
Loug.
High Beeches, Sid. | 89 | E5
High Bri. SE10 | 69 | D5
Eastney St.
High Broom Cres., | 96 | B7
W.Wick.
High Cedar Dr. SW20 | 83 | H7
High Coombe Pl., | 83 | D7
Kings.T.
High Cross Cen. N15 | 41 | D4
High Cross Rd. N17 | 41 | D3
High Dr., N.Mal. | 92 | C1
High Elms, Chig. | 35 | H4
High Elms, Wdf.Grn. | 34 | G5
High Foleys, Esher | 98 | E7
High Gables, Loug. | 27 | A2
High Gro. SE18 | 70 | G7
High Gro., Brom. | 96 | J1
High Hill Est. E5 | 50 | E1
Mount Pleasant La.
High Holborn WC1 | **12** | **A3**
High Holborn WC1 | 58 | E6
High La. W7 | 55 | A5
High Lawns, Har. | 46 | B3
High Level Dr. SE26 | 86 | D4
High Mead, Chig. | 35 | F2
High Mead, Har. | 37 | B5
High Meadow, W.Wick. | 103 | D2
High Meadow Clo., | 36 | B4
Pnr.
Daymer Gdns.
High Meadow Cres. | 38 | D5
NW9
High Meadows, Chig. | 35 | G5
High Meads Rd. E16 | 61 | A6
Aleston Beck Rd.
High Mt. NW4 | 38 | G6
High Pk. Ave., Rich. | 74 | A1
High Pk. Rd., Rich. | 74 | A1
High Path SW19 | 93 | E1
High Pt. N6 | 48 | A7
High Pt. SE9 | 88 | E3
High Rd. E18 | 42 | G1
High Rd. N2 | 39 | G1
High Rd. N11 | 32 | B5
High Rd. N12 | 31 | F4
High Rd. N15 | 41 | C3
High Rd. N17 | 41 | C3
High Rd. N20 | 31 | F2
High Rd. N22 | 32 | F6
High Rd. | 47 | F6
(Willesden) NW10
High Rd., Buck.H. | 34 | H3
High Rd., Chig. | 35 | D5
High Rd. (Harrow | 52 | F7
Weald), Har.
High Rd., Ilf. | 52 | F7
High Rd., Loug. | 26 | J6
High Rd., Rom. | 53 | A1
High Rd. (Bushey), | 29 | A1
Wat.
High Rd., Wem. | 46 | H5
High Rd., Wdf.Grn. | 34 | F6
High Rd. Leyton E10 | 42 | B6
High Rd. Leyton E15 | 51 | C4
High Rd. | 51 | E4
Leytonstone E11

High Rd. | 51 | E4
Leytonstone E15
High Silver, Loug. | 27 | A4
High St. E11 | 42 | G5
High St. E13 | 60 | G2
High St. E15 | 60 | C2
High St. E17 | 41 | H5
High St. N8 | 40 | E4
High St. N14 | 32 | D2
High St. | 32 | D1
(Southgate) N14
High St. NW7 | 30 | H4
Wills Gro.
High St. | 56 | F2
(Harlesden) NW10
High St. SE20 | 86 | F7
High St. (South | 95 | C4
Norwood) SE25
High St. SW6 | 75 | B3
High St. SW19 | 84 | G7
(Colliers Wd.)
High St. SW19 | 84 | A5
(Wimbledon)
High St. W3 | 65 | B1
High St. W5 | 55 | G7
High St., Barn. | 23 | B3
High St., Beck. | 96 | A2
High St., Brent. | 64 | H6
High St., Brom. | 96 | G2
High St., Cars. | 100 | J4
High St., Chis. | 88 | E6
High St., Croy. | 101 | J3
High St., Edg. | 30 | A6
High St., Enf. | 25 | F4
(Ponders End),
High St. | 98 | C6
(Claygate), Esher
High St., Hmptn. | 90 | H1
High St., Har. | 37 | B2
High St. | 46 | B1
(Wealdstone), Har.
High St., Houns. | 72 | H3
High St. | 63 | A7
(Cranford), Houns.
High St., Ilf. | 43 | F3
High St., Kings.T. | 91 | G3
High St., Kings.T. | 91 | F1
(Hampton Wick)
High St., N.Mal. | 92 | E4
High St., Orp. | 104 | E5
(Farnborough)
High St., Orp. | 104 | J7
(Green St.Grn.)
High St., Pnr. | 36 | E3
High St., Sthl. | 63 | F1
High St., Sutt. | 100 | E4
High St. (Cheam) | 100 | B6
Sutt.
High St., Tedd. | 82 | C5
High St., T.Ditt. | 91 | D7
High St., Th.Hth. | 94 | J4
High St. (Whitton), | 72 | J7
Twick.
High St., Wem. | 46 | J4
High St., W.Mol. | 90 | G4
High St., W.Wick. | 103 | B1
High St. Ms. SW19 | 84 | B5
High St. N. E6 | 52 | B7
High St. N. E12 | 52 | B5
High St. S. E6 | 61 | C2
High Timber St. EC4 | **12** | **J5**
High Timber St. EC4 | 58 | J7
High Tor Clo., Brom. | 87 | H7
Babbacombe Rd.
High Tree Ct. W7 | 55 | B7
High Trees SW2 | 85 | G1
High Trees, Barn. | 23 | H5
High Trees, Croy. | 102 | H1
High Vw., Pnr. | 36 | C3
High Vw. Clo. SE19 | 95 | C2
High Vw. Clo., Loug. | 26 | B3
High Vw. Rd. E18 | 42 | F3
High Vw. Rd., Sid. | 89 | B4
High Worple, Har. | 36 | E7
Higham Hill Rd. E17 | 41 | H1
Higham Pl. E17 | 41 | H3
Higham Rd. N17 | 41 | A3
Higham Rd., | 34 | G6
Wdf.Grn.
Higham Sta. Ave. E4 | 34 | A6
Higham St. E17 | 41 | H3
Highams Lo. | 41 | G3
Business Cen. E17
Highams Pk. Ind. | 34 | C6
Est. E4
Highbanks Clo., Well. | 71 | B7
Highbanks Rd., Pnr. | 28 | G6
Highbarrow Rd., | 95 | D7
Croy.
Highbridge Rd., Bark. | 61 | E1
Highbrook Rd. SE3 | 79 | A3
Highbury Ave., | 94 | G2
Th.Hth.

Highbury Clo., N.Mal.	92	C4
Highbury Clo., W.Wick.	103	B2
Highbury Cor. N5	49	H6
Highbury Cres. N5	49	H5
Highbury Est. N5	49	J5
Highbury Gdns., Ilf.	52	F2
Highbury Gra. N5	49	J4
Highbury Gro. N5	49	H6
Highbury Hill N5	49	G3
Highbury Ms. N7	49	G6
Highbury New Pk.		
Highbury New Pk. N5	49	J5
Highbury Pk. N5	49	H4
Highbury Pk. Ms. N5	49	J4
Highbury Gra.		
Highbury Pl. N5	49	H5
Highbury Quad. N5	49	J3
Highbury Rd. SW19	84	B5
Highbury Sta. Rd. N1	49	G6
Highbury Ter. N5	49	H5
Highbury Ter. Ms. N5	49	H5
Highclere Rd., N.Mal.	92	D3
Highclere St. SE26	86	H4
Highcliffe Dr. SW15	74	F6
Highcliffe Gdns., Ilf.	43	B5
Highcombe SE7	69	H6
Highcombe Clo. SE9	89	A1
Highcroft NW9	38	E5
Highcroft Ave., Wem.	56	A1
Highcroft Gdns. NW11	39	C6
Highcroft Rd. N19	40	E7
Highcross Way SW15	83	G1
Highdaun Dr. SW16	94	F4
Highdown, Wor.Pk.	99	E2
Highdown Rd. SW15	74	H6
Highfield, Felt.	81	A1
Highfield Ave. NW9	38	C5
Highfield Ave. NW11	39	A7
Highfield Ave., Erith	71	H6
Highfield Ave., Grnf.	46	B5
Highfield Ave., Orp.	104	J5
Highfield Ave., Pnr.	36	F5
Highfield Ave., Wem.	46	H3
Highfield Clo. NW9	38	C5
Highfield Clo., Surb.	98	F1
Highfield Dr. N14	24	C6
Highfield Dr., Brom.	96	E4
Highfield Dr., Epsom	99	F7
Highfield Dr., W.Wick.	103	B2
Highfield Gdns. NW11	39	B6
Highfield Hill SE19	86	A7
Highfield Rd. N21	32	H2
Highfield Rd. NW11	39	B6
Highfield Rd. W3	56	B5
Highfield Rd., Bexh.	80	F5
Highfield Rd., Brom.	97	C4
Highfield Rd., Chis.	97	J3
Highfield Rd., Felt.	81	A1
Highfield Rd., Islw.	73	C1
Highfield Rd., Surb.	92	C7
Highfield Rd., Sutt.	100	H5
Highfield Rd., Wdf.Grn.	35	B7
Highfields Gro. N6	48	J1
Highgate Ave. N6	40	B7
Highgate Clo. N6	40	A7
Highgate High St. N6	49	A1
Highgate Hill N19	49	B1
Highgate Rd. NW5	49	B4
Highgate Wk. SE23	86	F2
Highgate W. Hill N6	49	A1
Highgrove Clo., Chis.	97	B1
Highgrove Rd., Dag.	53	C5
Highgrove Way, Ruis.	36	A6
Highland Ave. W7	55	B6

Highland Ave., Dag.	53	J3
Highland Ave., Loug.	27	B6
Highland Cotts., Wall.	101	B4
Highland Ct. E18	42	H1
Highland Cft., Beck.	87	B5
Highland Rd. SE19	86	B6
Highland Rd., Bexh.	80	G5
Highland Rd., Brom.	96	F1
Highlands, Wat.	28	C1
Highlands, The, Edg.	38	B2
Highlands Ave. W3	56	C7
Highlands Clo. N4	40	E7
Mount Vw. Rd.		
Highlands Clo., Houns.	72	H1
Highlands Gdns., Ilf.	52	C1
Highlands Heath SW15	74	J7
Highlands Rd., Barn.	23	D5
Highlea Clo. NW9	38	E1
Highlever Rd. W10	56	J5
Highmead SE18	70	J7
Highmead Cres., Wem.	46	J7
Highmore Rd. SE3	69	E7
Highshore Rd. SE15	77	C2
Hightone Ave. E11	42	G6
Highview Ave., Edg.	30	C4
Highview Ave., Wall.	101	F5
Highview Gdns. N3	39	B4
Highview Gdns. N11	32	C5
Highview Gdns., Edg.	30	C5
Highview Ho., Rom.	44	E4
Highview Rd. SE19	86	A6
Highview Rd. W13	55	D5
Highway, The E1	13	J6
Highway, The E1	59	D7
Highway, The E14	59	G7
Highway, The, Stan.	37	C1
Highwood, Brom.	96	D3
Highwood Ave. N12	31	F4
Highwood Clo., Orp.	104	F2
Highwood Dr., Orp.	104	F2
Highwood Gdns., Ilf.	43	C5
Highwood Gro. NW7	30	D5
Highwood Hill NW7	30	F2
Highwood La., Loug.	27	D5
Highwood Rd. N19	49	E3
Highworth Rd. N11	32	D6
Hilary Ave., Mitch.	94	A3
Hilary Clo. SW6	18	A7
Hilary Clo. SW6	66	E7
Hilary Clo., Erith	80	H1
Hilary Rd. W12	56	F6
Hilbert Rd., Sutt.	100	A3
Hilborough Way, Orp.	104	G5
Hilda Rd. E6	52	A7
Hilda Rd. E16	60	E4
Hilda Ter. SW9	76	G2
Hilda Vale Clo., Orp.	104	E4
Hilda Vale Rd., Orp.	104	D4
Hildenborough Gdns., Brom.	87	E6
Hildenlea Pl., Brom.	96	E2
Hildreth St. SW12	85	B1
Hildyard Rd. SW6	66	D6
Hiley Rd. NW10	56	J3
Hilgrove Rd. NW6	48	F7
Hiliary Gdns., Stan.	37	F2
Hill Brow, Brom.	97	A1
Hill Clo. NW2	47	H3
Hill Clo. NW11	39	D6
Hill Clo., Barn.	22	J5
Hill Clo., Chis.	88	E5
Hill Clo., Har.	46	B3
Hill Clo., Stan.	29	E4
Hill Ct., Nthlt.	45	G5
Hill Cres. N20	31	E2
Hill Cres., Har.	89	J1
Hill Cres., Har.	37	D5
Hill Cres., Surb.	91	J5
Hill Cres., Wor.Pk.	99	J2
Hill Crest, Sid.	80	A7
Hill Crest Gdns. N3	39	B4
Hill Dr. NW9	47	C1
Hill Dr. SW16	94	F3
Hill End, Orp.	104	J2
The App.		
Hill Fm. Rd. W10	56	J5

Hill Ho. Ave., Stan.	29	C7
Hill Ho. Clo. N21	24	G7
Hill Ho. Rd. SW16	85	F5
Hill Path SW16	85	F5
Valley Rd.		
Hill Ri. N9	25	E6
Hill Ri. NW11	39	E4
Hill Ri. SE23	86	E1
London Rd.		
Hill Ri., Esher	98	E2
Hill Ri., Grnf.	45	J7
Hill Ri., Rich.	73	G5
Hill Ri. N10	39	J1
Hill Rd. NW8	**6**	**D3**
Hill Rd. NW8	57	F2
Hill Rd., Cars.	100	H6
Hill Rd., Har.	37	D5
Hill Rd., Mitch.	94	B1
Hill Rd., Pnr.	36	E6
Hill Rd., Sutt.	100	E5
Hill Rd., Wem.	46	E3
Hill St. W1	**15**	**C1**
Hill St. W1	58	A7
Hill St., Rich.	73	G5
Hill Top NW11	39	E4
Hill Top, Loug.	27	D2
Hill Top Clo., Loug.	27	D3
Hill Top Vw., Wdf.Grn.	35	C6
Hill Vw. Cres., Orp.	104	J1
Hill Vw. Dr., Well.	79	H3
Hill Vw. Gdns. NW9	38	D5
Hill Vw. Rd., Esher	98	D7
Hill Vw. Rd., Orp.	104	J1
Hill Vw. Rd., Twick.	82	D1
Hillary Ri., Barn.	23	D4
Hillary Rd., Sthl.	63	G3
Hillbeck Clo. SE15	68	F7
Hillbeck Way, Grnf.	55	A1
Hillborne Clo., Hayes	84	A5
Hillborough Clo. SW19	84	F7
Hillbrook Rd. SW17	84	J3
Hillbrow, N.Mal.	92	F3
Hillbrow Rd., Brom.	87	E7
Hillbury Ave., Har.	37	E5
Hillbury Rd. SW17	85	B3
Hillcote Ave. SW16	85	G7
Hillcourt Ave. N12	31	E6
Hillcourt Est. N16	50	A1
Hillcourt Rd. SE22	77	E6
Hillcrest N6	40	A7
Hillcrest N21	24	G7
Hillcrest Ave. NW11	39	B5
Hillcrest Ave., Edg.	30	B4
Hillcrest Ave., Pnr.	36	D4
Hillcrest Clo. SE26	86	D4
Hillcrest Clo., Beck.	95	J5
Hillcrest Gdns. NW2	47	G3
Hillcrest Gdns., Esher	98	C3
Hillcrest Rd. E17	42	D2
Hillcrest Rd. E18	42	F2
Hillcrest Rd. W3	65	A1
Hillcrest Rd. W5	55	H5
Hillcrest Rd., Brom.	87	G4
Hillcrest Rd., Loug.	27	A6
Hillcrest Vw., Beck.	95	J6
Hillcroft, Loug.	27	D7
Hillcroft Ave., Pnr.	36	F6
Hillcroft Cres. W5	55	G6
Hillcroft Cres., Ruis.	45	D3
Hillcroft Cres., Wat.	28	A1
Hillcroft Cres., Wem.	46	J4
Hillcroft Rd. E6	61	E5
Hillcroome Rd., Sutt.	100	G6
Hillcross Ave., Mord.	93	A6
Hilldale Rd., Sutt.	100	C4
Hilldown Rd. SW16	85	E7
Hilldown Rd., Brom.	103	E1
Hilldrop Cres. N7	49	D5
Hilldrop Est. N7	49	D5
Hilldrop La. N7	49	D5
Hilldrop Rd. N7	49	D5
Hilldrop Rd., Brom.	87	G6
Hilldend SE18	79	E1
Hillersdon Ave. SW13	74	G2

Hillersdon Ave., Edg.	29	J5
Hillery Clo. SE17	**21**	**C2**
Hillfield Ave. N8	40	E5
Hillfield Ave. NW9	38	E5
Hillfield Ave., Mord.	93	H6
Hillfield Ave., Wem.	46	H7
Hillfield Clo., Har.	36	J4
Hillfield Ct. NW3	48	H5
Hillfield Pk. N10	40	B3
Hillfield Pk. N21	32	G2
Hillfield Pk. Ms. N10	40	B4
Hillfield Rd. NW6	48	C5
Hillfield Rd., Hmptn.	81	F7
Hillfoot Ave., Rom.	44	J1
Hillfoot Rd., Rom.	44	J1
Hillgate Pl. SW12	76	B7
Hillgate Pl. W8	66	D1
Hillgate St. W8	66	D1
Hilliards Ct. E1	68	E1
Prusom St.		
Hilliards St. E1	68	F1
Wapping High St.		
Hillier Clo., Barn.	23	E6
Hillier Gdns., Croy.	101	G5
Crowley Cres.		
Hillier Rd. SW11	75	J6
Hilliers La., Croy.	101	E3
Hillingdon Rd., Bexh.	80	J2
Hillingdon St. SE5	20	G7
Hillingdon St. SE5	67	H6
Hillingdon St. SE17	**20**	**A6**
Hillingdon St. SE17	67	H6
Hillington Gdns., Wdf.Grn.	43	A2
Hillman St. E8	50	E6
Hillmarton Rd. N7	49	E5
Hillmead Dr. SW9	76	H4
Hillmont Rd., Esher	98	B3
Hillmore Gro. SE26	86	G5
Hillreach SE18	70	C5
Hillrise Rd. N19	40	E7
Hills Ms. W5	55	H7
Hills Pl. W1	**11**	**F4**
Hills Rd., Buck.H.	34	H1
Hillsborough Grn., Wat.	28	A3
Ashburnham Dr.		
Hillsborough Rd. SE22	77	B5
Hillside NW9	38	D4
Hillside NW10	47	C7
Hillside SW19	84	A6
Hillside, Barn.	23	F5
Hillside Ave. N11	31	J6
Hillside Ave., Borwd.	22	B4
Hillside Ave., Wem.	46	J4
Hillside Ave., Wdf.Grn.	34	J5
Hillside Clo. NW8	**6**	**B2**
Hillside Clo. NW8	57	E2
Hillside Clo., Mord.	93	B4
Hillside Clo., Wdf.Grn.	34	J5
Hillside Cres., Har.	45	J1
Hillside Cres., Nthwd.	36	A1
Hillside Dr., Edg.	30	A6
Hillside Est. N15	41	C6
Hillside Gdns. E17	42	D3
Hillside Gdns. N6	40	A6
Hillside Gdns. SW2	85	G2
Hillside Gdns., Barn.	23	B4
Hillside Gdns., Edg.	29	J4
Hillside Gdns., Har.	37	H7
Hillside Gdns., Nthwd.	28	A7
Hillside Gdns., Wall.	101	C1
Hillside Gro. N14	24	D7
Hillside Gro. NW7	30	G7
Hillside La., Brom.	103	G2
Hillside Pas. SW2	85	F2
Hillside Ri., Nthwd.	28	A7
Hillside Rd. N15	41	B6
Hillside Rd. SW2	85	F2
Hillside Rd. W5	55	H5
Hillside Rd., Brom.	96	F3
Hillside Rd., Croy.	101	H5

Hillside Rd., Nthwd. 28 A7
Hillside Rd., Sthl. 54 G4
Hillside Rd., Surb. 91 J4
Hillside Rd., Sutt. 100 C7
Hillsleigh Rd. W8 66 C1
Hillstowe St. E5 50 F3
Hilltop, Sutt. 93 C7
Hilltop Gdns. NW4 38 H1
Great N. Way
Hilltop Gdns., Orp. 104 H2
Hilltop Rd. NW6 48 D7
Hilltop Way, Stan. 29 D3
Hillview SW20 83 H7
Hillview, Mitch. 94 E4
Hillview, Har. 37 H5
Hillview Clo., Pnr. 28 F6
Hillview Cres., Ilf. 43 C6
Hillview Gdns. NW4 39 A4
Hillview Gdns., Har. 36 G3
Hillview Rd. NW7 31 A4
Hillview Rd., Chis. 88 D5
Hillview Rd., Pnr. 28 F7
Hillview Rd., Sutt. 100 F3
Hillway N6 49 A1
Hillway NW9 38 E7
Hillworth Rd. SW2 76 G7
Hilly Flds. Cres. SE4 78 A3
Hillyard Rd. W7 55 B5
Hillyard St. SW9 76 G1
Hillyfields E17 41 H3
Hillyfields, Loug. 27 D2
Hilsea St. E5 50 F4
Hilton Ave. N12 31 G5
Hilversum Cres. 77 B5
SE22
East Dulwich Gro.
Himley Rd. SW17 84 H5
Hinchcliffe Clo., 101 F7
Wall.
Roe Way
Hinchley Clo., 98 C3
Esher
Hinchley Dr., Esher 98 C3
Hinchley Way, Esher 98 D3
Hinckler Clo., Wall. 101 E7
Kingsfield Ave.
Hinckley Rd. SE15 77 D4
Hind Clo., Chig. 35 J5
Hind Ct. EC4 **12 F4**
Hind Gro. E14 60 A6
Hinde Ms. W1 58 A6
Marylebone La.
Hinde St. W1 **11 C3**
Hinde St. W1 58 A6
Hindes Rd., Har. 37 A5
Hindhead Clo. N16 50 B1
East Bank
Hindhead Gdns., 54 E1
Nthlt.
Hindhead Grn., Wat. 28 C3
Hindhead Way, Wall. 101 E5
Hindmans Rd. SE22 77 D5
Hindmans Way, Dag. 62 F4
Hindmarsh Clo. E1 **13 J5**
Hindrey Rd. E5 50 E5
Hindsley's Path SE22 86 F2
Hinkler Rd., Har. 37 G3
Hinksey Path SE2 71 D2
Hinstock Rd. SE18 70 F6
Hinton Ave., Houns. 72 D4
Hinton Clo. SE9 88 B1
Hinton Rd. N18 33 B4
Hinton Rd. SE24 76 H3
Hinton Rd., Wall. 101 C6
Hippodrome Ms. 57 B7
W11
Portland Rd.
Hippodrome Pl. W11 57 B7
Hiroshima Wk. SE7 69 H3
Hiscocks Ho. NW10 47 C7
Hitcham Rd. E17 41 J7
Hitchin Sq. E3 59 H2
Hither Grn. La. SE13 78 C5
Hitherbroom Rd., 63 A1
Hayes
Hitherfield Rd. 85 F2
SW16
Hitherfield Rd., Dag. 53 E2
Hitherlands SE12 85 B2
Hitherwell Dr., 37 A1
Har.
Hitherwood Dr. SE19 86 C4
Hive Clo. (Bushey), 29 A2
Wat.
Hive Rd. (Bushey), 29 A2
Wat.
Hoadly Rd. SW16 85 D3
Hobart Clo. N20 31 H2
Hobart Clo., Hayes 54 D4
Hobart Dr., Hayes 54 D4
Hobart Gdns., 95 A3
Th.Hth.
Hobart La., Hayes 54 D4

Hobart Pl. SW1 **15 D5**
Hobart Pl. SW1 67 B3
Hobart Rd., Rich. 73 J6
Chisholm Rd.
Hobart Rd., Dag. 53 D4
Hobart Rd., Hayes 54 D4
Hobart Rd., Ilf. 43 F2
Hobart Rd., Wor.Pk. 99 H3
Hobbayne Rd. W7 55 A6
Hobbes Wk. SW15 74 H5
Hobbs Grn. N2 39 F3
Hobbs Rd. SE27 85 J4
Hobday St. E14 60 B5
Hobill Wk., Surb. 91 J6
Hoblands End, Chis. 88 H6
Hobury St. SW10 **18 D6**
Hobury St. SW10 66 F6
Hocker St. E2 **9 F4**
Hockett Clo. SE8 68 J4
Carteret Way
Hockley Ave. E6 61 B2
Hocroft Ave. NW2 48 C3
Hocroft Rd. NW2 48 C4
Hocroft Wk. NW2 48 C3
Hodder Dr., Grnf. 55 C2
Hoddesdon Rd., 71 G5
Belv.
Hodford Rd. NW11 48 C1
Hodgkin Clo. SE28 62 D7
Fleming Way
Hodnet Gro. SE16 68 G4
Hawkstone Rd.
Hodson Clo., Har. 45 F3
Hoe, The, Wat. 28 D2
Hoe St. E17 42 A5
Hofland Rd. W14 66 A3
Hogan Way E5 50 D2
Geldeston Rd.
Hogans Ms. W2 **10 E1**
Hogarth Clo. E16 61 A5
Hogarth Clo. W5 55 H5
Hogarth Ct. EC3 **13 E5**
Hogarth Ct. SE19 86 C4
Fountain Dr.
Hogarth Cres. SW19 93 G1
Hogarth Cres., 94 J7
Croy.
Hogarth Gdns., 63 G7
Houns.
Hogarth Hill NW11 39 C4
Hogarth La. W4 66 E6
Hogarth Pl. SW5 **18 A2**
Hogarth Reach, 27 C5
Loug.
Hogarth Rd. SW5 **18 A2**
Hogarth Rd. SW5 66 E4
Hogarth Rd., Edg. 38 A2
Hogarth Roundabout 65 E6
W4
Hogarth Way, 90 J1
Hmptn.
Hogshead Pas. E1 59 E7
Pennington St.
Hogsmill Way, 99 C5
Epsom
Holbeach Gdns., 79 H6
Sid.
Holbeach Ms. SW12 85 B1
Harberson Rd.
Holbeach Rd. SE6 78 A7
Holbeck Row SE15 68 D7
Holbein Ms. SW1 **19 B3**
Holbein Ms. SW1 67 A5
Holbein Pl. SW1 **19 B2**
Holbein Pl. SW1 67 A4
Holberton Gdns. 56 H3
NW10
Holborn EC1 **12 E2**
Holborn EC1 58 G5
Holborn Circ. EC1 **12 F2**
Holborn Pl. WC1 **12 C2**
Holborn Rd. E13 60 H4
Holborn Viaduct EC1 **12 F2**
Holborn Viaduct EC1 58 G5
Holbrook Clo. N19 49 B1
Dartmouth Pk. Hill
Holbrook Clo., Enf. 25 C1
Holbrook La., Chis. 88 G7
Holbrook Rd. E15 60 F2
Holbrook Way, Brom. 97 C6
Holbrooke Ct. N7 49 E3
Holbrooke Pl., Rich. 73 G5
Hill Ri.
Holburne Clo. SE3 78 J1
Holburne Gdns. SE3 79 A1
Holburne Rd. SE3 78 J1
Holcombe Hill NW7 30 G3
Highwood Hill
Holcombe Rd. N17 41 C3
Holcombe Rd., Ilf. 43 D7
Holcombe St. W6 65 H5
Holcote Clo., Belv. 71 E3
Blakemore Way

Holcroft Rd. E9 50 F7
Holden Ave. N12 31 E5
Holden Ave. NW9 47 C1
Holden Clo., Dag. 53 B3
Holden Pt. E15 51 D6
Waddington Rd.
Holden Rd. N12 31 E5
Holden St. SW11 76 A2
Holdenby Rd. SE4 77 H5
Holdenhurst Ave. 31 E7
N12
Holderness Way 85 H5
SE27
Holdernesse Rd. 84 J3
SW17
Holders Hill Ave. 39 A2
NW4
Holders Hill Circ. 31 B7
NW7
Dollis Rd.
Holders Hill Cres. 39 A2
NW4
Holders Hill Dr. 39 A3
NW4
Holders Hill Gdns. 39 B2
NW4
Holders Hill Rd. 39 A2
NW4
Holders Hill Rd. 39 B1
NW7
Holdgate St. SE7 70 A3
Westmoor St.
Holford Pl. WC1 **8 D3**
Holford Rd. NW3 48 F3
Holford St. WC1 **8 E3**
Holford St. WC1 58 G3
Holgate Ave. SW11 75 G3
Holgate Gdns., Dag. 53 G6
Holgate Rd., Dag. 53 G5
Holland Ave. SW20 92 F1
Holland Ave., Sutt. 100 D7
Holland Clo., Barn. 23 G7
Holland Clo., Brom. 103 F2
Holland Clo., Stan. 29 E5
Holland Dr. SE23 86 H3
Holland Gdns. W14 66 B3
Holland Gro. SW9 67 G7
Holland Pk. W11 66 B1
Holland Pk. Ave. 66 B1
W11
Holland Pk. Ave., 43 H6
Ilf.
Holland Pk. Gdns. 66 B2
W14
Holland Pk. Ms. W11 66 C1
Holland Pk. Rd. W14 66 C3
Holland Pl. W8 66 C2
Holland Pt. E6 61 C1
Holland Rd. E15 60 E3
Holland Rd. NW10 56 G1
Holland Rd. SE25 95 D5
Holland Rd., Wem. 46 G6
Holland St. SE1 **16 H1**
Holland St. SE1 67 H1
Holland St. W8 66 D2
Holland Vill. Rd. 66 B2
W14
Holland Wk. N19 49 D1
Duncombe Rd.
Holland Wk. W8 66 C2
Holland Wk., Stan. 29 D5
Holland Way, Brom. 103 F2
Hollands, The, 81 D4
Felt.
Hollands, The, 99 F1
Wor.Pk.
Hollar Rd. N16 50 C3
*Stoke Newington
High St.*
Hollen St. W1 **11 G3**
Hollen St. W1 58 D6
Holles Clo., Hmptn. 81 G5
Holles St. W1 **11 E3**
Holles St. W1 58 B6
Holley Rd. W3 65 E2
Hollickwood Ave. 31 J6
N12
Holliday Sq. SW11 75 C7
Fowler Clo.
Hollidge Way, Dag. 53 H6
Hollies, The E11 42 G5
Hollies, The N20 31 G1
Hollies Ave., Sid. 88 J2
Hollies Clo. SW16 85 G6
Hollies Clo., 82 C2
Twick.
Hollies End NW7 30 H5
Hollies Rd. W5 64 F4
Hollies Way SW12 76 A7
Bracken Ave.
Holligrave Rd., 96 G1
Brom.

Hollingbourne Ave., 71 F7
Bexh.
Hollingbourne Gdns. 55 E5
W13
Hollingbourne Rd. 76 J5
SE24
Hollingsworth Rd., 102 E6
Croy.
Hollington Cres., 92 F6
N.Mal.
Hollington Rd. E6 61 C3
Hollington Rd. N17 41 D2
Hollingworth Rd., 97 E7
Orp.
Hollman Gdns. SW16 85 H6
Hollow, The, 34 F4
Wdf.Grn.
Hollow Wk., Rich. 64 H7
Kew Rd.
Holloway Rd. E6 61 C3
Holloway Rd. E11 51 E3
Holloway Rd. N7 49 F3
Holloway Rd. N19 49 C2
Holloway St., 72 H3
Houns.
Hollowfield Wk., 45 E6
Nthlt.
Hollows, The, Brent. 64 J6
Kew Bri. Rd.
Holly Ave., Stan. 37 H2
Holly Bush Hill NW3 48 F4
Holly Bush La., 81 F7
Hmptn.
Holly Bush Steps 48 F4
NW3
Heath St.
Holly Bush Vale NW3 48 F4
Heath St.
Holly Clo. NW10 47 E7
Holly Clo., Buck.H. 35 A3
Holly Clo., Felt. 81 E5
Holly Clo., Wall. 101 B7
Holly Cres., Beck. 95 J5
Holly Cres., 34 D7
Wdf.Grn.
Holly Dr. E4 26 B7
Holly Fm. Rd., Sthl. 63 E5
Holly Gro. NW9 38 C7
Holly Gro. SE15 77 C2
Holly Gro., Pnr. 36 E1
Holly Hedge Ter. 78 D5
SE13
Holly Hill N21 24 F6
Holly Hill NW3 48 F4
Holly Hill Rd., Belv. 71 H5
Holly Hill Rd., 71 J5
Erith
Holly Lo. Gdns. N6 49 A1
Holly Ms. SW10 **18 D4**
Holly Mt. NW3 48 F4
Holly Bush Hill
Holly Pk. N3 39 C3
Holly Pk. N4 40 E7
Holly Pk. Est. N4 40 F7
Blythwood Rd.
Holly Pk. Gdns. N3 39 D3
Holly Pk. Rd. N11 32 A5
Holly Pk. Rd. W7 64 C1
Holly Rd. E11 42 F7
Holly Rd. W4 65 D4
Dolman Rd.
Holly Rd., Hmptn. 81 J6
Holly Rd., Houns. 72 H4
Holly Rd., Twick. 82 D1
Holly St. E8 50 C6
Holly St. Est. E8 50 C7
Holly Ter. N20 31 F2
Holly Vw. Clo. NW4 38 G6
Holly Wk. NW3 48 F4
Holly Wk., Enf. 24 J3
Gentlemans Row
Holly Wk., Rich. 73 H2
Holly Way, Mitch. 94 D4
Hollybank Clo., 81 G5
Hmptn.
Hollyberry La. NW3 48 F4
Holly Wk.
Hollybrake Clo., 88 G7
Chis.
Hollybush Clo. E11 42 G5
Hollybush Clo., 37 B1
Har.
Hollybush Gdns. E2 59 E3
Hollybush Hill E11 42 F7
Hollybush Pl. E2 59 E3
Bethnal Grn. Rd.
Hollybush Rd., 82 H5
Kings.T.
Hollybush St. E13 60 H3
Hollybush Wk. SW9 76 H4
Hollycroft Ave. NW3 48 D3
Hollycroft Ave., 46 J2
Wem.

Hollydale Dr., Brom. 104 C3
Hollydale Rd. SE15 77 F1
Hollydene SE15 77 E1
Hollydown Way E11 51 D3
Hollyfield Ave. N11 31 J5
Hollyfield Rd., 91 J7
Surb.
Hollymead, Cars. 100 J3
Hollymount Clo. 78 C1
SE10
Hollytree Clo. SW19 84 A1
Hollywood Gdns., 54 B6
Hayes
Hollywood Ms. SW10 18 C5
Hollywood Rd. E4 33 H5
Hollywood Rd. SW10 18 C5
Hollywood Rd. SW10 66 F6
Hollywood Way, 34 D7
Wdf.Grn.
Holm Oak Clo. SW15 75 C6
West Hill
Holm Oak Ms. SW4 76 E5
King's Ave.
Holm Wk. SE3 78 G2
Blackheath Pk.
Holman Rd. SW11 75 G2
Holman Rd., Epsom 99 C5
Holmbridge Gdns., 25 G4
Enf.
Holmbrook Dr. NW4 39 A5
Holmbury Ct. SW17 84 J3
Holmbury Ct. SW19 84 H7
Cavendish Rd
Holmbury Gro., 102 J7
Croy.
Holmbury Pk., Brom. 88 B7
Holmbury Vw. E5 50 E1
Holmbush Rd. SW15 75 B6
Holmcote Gdns. N5 49 J5
Holmcroft Way, 97 C5
Brom.
Holmdale Gdns. NW4 39 A5
Holmdale Rd. NW6 48 D5
Holmdale Rd., Chis. 88 F5
Holmdale Ter. N15 41 B7
Holmdene Ave. NW7 30 G6
Holmdene Ave. SE24 76 J5
Holmdene Ave., Har. 36 H3
Holmdene Clo., 96 C2
Beck.
Holme Lacey Rd. 78 F6
SE12
Holme Rd. E6 61 B1
Holme Way, Stan. 29 C6
Holmead Rd. SW6 66 E7
Holmebury Clo. 29 B2
(Bushey), Wat.
Holmefield Ct. NW3 44 H3
Holmes Ave. E17 41 J4
Holmes Ave. NW7 31 B5
Holmes Pl. SW10 18 D5
Holmes Rd. NW5 49 B6
Holmes Rd. SW19 84 F7
Holmes Rd., Twick. 82 C2
Holmes Ter. SE1 16 E3
Holmes Ter. SE1 67 G2
Holmesdale Ave. 74 B3
SW14
Holmesdale Clo. 95 C3
SE25
Holmesdale Rd. N6 40 B7
Holmesdale Rd. SE25 95 A5
Holmesdale Rd., 80 D2
Bexh.
Holmesdale Rd., 95 A5
Croy.
Holmesdale Rd., 73 J1
Rich.
Holmesdale Rd., 82 F7
Tedd.
Holmesley Rd. SE23 77 H6
Holmewood Gdns. 76 F7
SW2
Holmewood Rd. 95 B3
SE25
Holmewood Rd. SW2 76 E7
Holmfield Ave. NW4 39 A5
Holmhurst Rd., 71 H5
Belv.
Holmleigh Rd. N16 50 B1
Holms St. E2 9 H1
Holmshaw Clo. SE26 86 H4
Holmside Ri., Wat. 28 B3
Holmside Rd. SW12 76 A6
Holmsley Clo., 92 F6
N.Mal.
Holmstall Ave., Edg. 38 C3
Holmwood Clo., Har. 36 J3
Holmwood Clo., 45 H6
Nthlt.
Holmwood Gdns. N3 39 D2
Holmwood Gdns., 101 B6
Wall.

Holmwood Gro. NW7 30 D5
Holmwood Rd., 98 G5
Chess.
Holmwood Rd., Ilf. 52 H2
Holmwood Vill. SE7 69 G5
Holne Chase N2 39 F6
Holne Chase, Mord. 93 C6
Holness Rd. E15 51 F6
Holroyd Rd. SW15 74 J4
Holstein Way, Erith 71 D3
Holstock Rd., Ilf. 52 F2
Holsworth Clo., Har. 36 J5
Holsworthy Sq. WC1 8 D6
Holsworthy Way, 98 F5
Chess.
Holt, The, Ilf. 35 F6
Holt, The, Wall. 101 C4
Holt Clo. N10 40 A4
Holt Clo. SE28 62 B7
Holt Clo., Chig. 35 J5
Holt Ct. E15 51 C5
Clays La.
Holt Rd. E16 70 B1
Holt Rd., Wem. 46 E3
Holt Way, Chig. 35 J5
Holton St. E1 59 G4
Holtwhite Ave., Enf. 24 J2
Holtwhites Hill, Enf. 24 H1
Holwell Pl., Pnr. 36 E4
Holwood Pk. Ave., 104 C4
Orp.
Holwood Pl. SW4 76 D4
Holybourne Ave. 74 G7
SW15
Holyhead Clo. E3 60 A3
Holyoak Rd. SE11 20 G1
Holyoak Rd. SE11 67 H4
Holyoake Ct. SE16 68 J2
Bryan Rd.
Holyoake Wk. N2 39 F3
Holyoake Wk. W5 55 F4
Holyport Rd. SW6 65 J7
Holyrood Ave., Har. 45 E4
Holyrood Gdns., 38 B3
Edg.
Holyrood Rd., Barn. 23 F6
Holyrood St. SE1 17 D2
Holywell Clo. SE3 69 G6
Holywell La. EC2 9 E5
Holywell La. EC2 59 B4
Holywell Row EC2 9 D6
Holywell Row EC2 59 B4
Home Clo., Cars. 100 J2
Home Clo., Nthlt. 54 F3
Home Ct., Felt. 81 A1
Home Fm. Clo., 91 C7
T.Ditt.
Home Gdns., Dag. 53 J3
Home Lea, Orp. 104 J5
Home Mead, Stan. 37 F1
Home Pk. Rd. SW19 84 C4
Home Pk. Wk., 91 G4
Kings.T.
Home Rd. SW11 75 H2
Homecroft Gdns., 27 E4
Loug.
Homecroft Rd. N22 40 H1
Homecroft Rd. SE26 86 F5
Homefarm Rd. W7 55 B6
Homefield Ave., Ilf. 43 H5
Homefield Clo. NW10 47 C6
Homefield Gdns. N2 39 G3
Homefield Gdns., 93 F2
Mitch.
Homefield Pk., Sutt. 100 E6
Homefield Rd. SW19 84 A6
Homefield Rd. W4 65 F5
Homefield Rd., 96 J1
Brom.
Homefield Rd., Edg. 30 D6
Homefield Rd., Wall. 90 E7
Homefield Rd., Wem. 46 D4
Homefield St. N1 10 D2
Homelands Dr. SE19 86 B7
Homeleigh Rd. SE15 77 G5
Homemead SW12 85 B2
Homemead Rd., 97 C5
Brom.
Homemead Rd., 95 F6
Croy.
Homer Clo., Bexh. 80 J1
Homer Dr. E14 69 A4
Homer Rd. E9 50 H6
Homer Rd., Croy. 95 G6
Homer Row W1 10 H2
Homer Row W1 57 H5
Homer St. W1 10 H2
Homer St. W1 57 H5
Homersham Rd., 92 A2
Kings.T.
Homerton Gro. E9 50 G5
Homerton High St. 50 F5
E9

Homerton Rd. E9 50 H5
Homerton Row E9 50 F5
Homerton Ter. E9 50 F6
Morning La.
Homesdale Clo. E11 42 G5
Homesdale Rd., 96 J4
Brom.
Homesdale Rd., Orp. 97 H7
Homesfield NW11 39 D5
Homestall Rd. SE22 77 F5
Homestead, The N11 32 B4
Homestead Gdns., 98 B5
Esher
Homestead Paddock 24 B5
N14
Homestead Pk. NW2 47 F3
Homestead Rd. SW6 66 C7
Homestead Rd., Dag. 53 F2
Homewillow Clo. N21 24 H6
Homewood Clo., 81 F6
Hmptn.
Fearnley Cres.
Homewood Cres., 88 H6
Chis.
Honduras St. EC1 8 J5
Honey La. EC2 13 A4
Honeybourne Rd. 48 E5
NW6
Honeybourne Way, 104 G1
Orp.
Honeybrook Rd. 76 C7
SW12
Honeyden Rd., Sid. 98 G1
Honeyman Clo. NW6 48 A7
Honeypot Clo. NW9 37 J4
Honeypot La. NW9 38 A5
Honeypot La., Stan. 37 G3
Honeysett Rd. N17 41 C2
Reform Row
Honeysuckle Gdns., 102 G1
Croy.
Primrose La.
Honeywell Rd. SW11 75 H6
Honeywood Rd. 56 F2
NW10
Honeywood Rd., 73 D4
Islw.
Honeywood Wk., 100 J4
Cars.
Honister Clo., Stan. 37 E1
Honister Gdns., 37 E1
Stan.
Honister Pl., Stan. 37 E1
Honiton Rd. NW6 57 C2
Honiton Rd., Well. 79 J2
Honley Rd. SE6 78 B7
Honor Oak Pk. SE23 77 G6
Honor Oak Ri. SE23 77 F6
Honor Oak Rd. SE23 77 G3
Hood Ave. N14 24 B6
Hood Ave. SW14 74 C5
Hood Clo., Croy. 101 H1
Parsons Mead
Hood Ct. EC4 12 F4
Hood Rd. SW20 83 F7
Hood Wk., Rom. 44 H1
Hoodcote Gdns. N21 24 H7
Hook, The, Barn. 23 G6
Hook Fm. Rd., Brom. 91 H5
Hook Ri. N., Surb. 99 A3
Hook Ri. S., Surb. 99 A3
Hook Rd., Chess. 98 G5
Hook Rd., Epsom 99 C7
Hook Rd., Surb. 98 H3
Hook Wk., Edg. 30 C6
Hookers Rd. E17 41 G3
Hooking Grn., Har. 36 H5
Woods End
Hooks Hall Dr., Dag. 53 J3
Hooks Way SE22 86 D1
Dulwich Common
Hookstone Way, 35 A7
Wdf.Grn.
Hoop La. NW11 39 J1
Hooper Rd. E16 60 G6
Hooper St. E1 13 H4
Hooper St. E1 59 H7
Hooper's Ct. SW3 14 J4
Hop Gdns. WC2 12 A6
Hope Clo. SE12 87 H3
Hope Clo., Sutt. 100 F5
Hope Clo., Wdf.Grn. 34 J6
West Gro.
Hope Pk., Brom. 77 F7
Hope St. SW11 75 G3
Hopedale Rd. SE7 69 H6
Hopefield Ave. NW6 57 B2
Hopetown St. E1 13 G2
Hopewell St. SE5 68 A7
Hopewell Yd. SE5 68 A7

Hopgood St. W12 65 J1
Macfarlane Rd.
Hopkins St. W1 11 G4
Hopkinsons Pl. NW1 58 A1
Fitzroy Rd.
Hoppers Rd. N13 32 G2
Hoppers Rd. N21 32 G2
Hoppett Rd. E4 34 E2
Hopping La. N1 49 H6
St. Mary's Gro.
Hoppingwood Ave., 92 E3
N.Mal.
Hopton Gdns. SE1 16 H1
Hopton Gdns., 92 G6
N.Mal.
Hopton Rd. SW16 85 E5
Hopton St. SE1 16 H1
Hopton St. SE1 67 H1
Hopwood Rd. SE17 21 C5
Hopwood Rd. SE17 68 A6
Hopwood Wk. E8 50 D7
Wilman Gro.
Horace Ave., Rom. 53 J1
Horace Rd. E7 51 H4
Horace Rd., Ilf. 43 F3
Horace Rd., 91 J3
Kings.T.
Horatio Pl. SW19 84 D7
Kingston Rd.
Horatio St. E2 9 G2
Horatio St. E2 59 D2
Horatius Way, Croy. 101 F5
Horbury Cres. W11 57 D7
Horbury Ms. W11 57 C7
Ladbroke Rd.
Horder Rd. SW6 75 B1
Hordle Prom. E. 21 G7
SE15
Hordle Prom. N. 21 F7
SE15
Hordle Prom. S. 68 C7
SE15
Pentridge St.
Hordle Prom. W. 21 E7
SE15
Horizon Way SE7 69 H4
Horley Clo., Bexh. 80 G5
Horley Rd. SE9 88 B4
Hormead Rd. W9 57 C4
Horn La. SE10 69 G4
Horn La. W3 65 C1
Horn La., Bexh. 80 J2
Horn La., Wdf.Grn. 34 G6
Horn Pk. Clo. SE12 78 H5
Horn Pk. La. SE12 78 H5
Hornbeam Clo. SE11 20 E1
Hornbeam Clo., 22 A1
Borwd.
Hornbeam Clo., 35 A3
Buck.H.
Hornbeam Rd.
Hornbeam Clo., 45 F5
Nthlt.
Hornbeam Cres., 64 E7
Brent.
Hornbeam Gro. E4 34 E3
Hornbeam La. E4 26 E5
Hornbeam La., Bexh. 80 J2
Hornbeam Rd., 35 A3
Buck.H.
Hornbeam Rd., 54 C5
Hayes
Hornbeam Ter., 100 H1
Cars.
Hornbeam Twr. E11 51 D3
Hornbeam Wk., Rich. 82 J2
Hornbeam Way, 97 D6
Brom.
Hornbeams Ri. N11 32 A6
Hornblower Clo. 68 H4
SE16
Greenland Quay
Hornbuckle Clo., 46 A2
Har.
Hornby Clo. NW3 48 G7
Horncastle Clo. 78 G7
SE12
Horncastle Rd. SE12 78 G7
Horndean Clo. SW15 83 G1
Bessborough Rd.
Horndon Clo., Rom. 44 J1
Horndon Grn., Rom. 44 J1
Horndon Rd., Rom. 44 J1
Horne Way SW15 74 J2
Horner La., Mitch. 93 G2
Hornfair Rd. SE7 69 J6
Horniman Dr. SE23 86 E1
Horning Clo. SE9 88 B4
Horns End, Pnr. 36 C4
Horns Rd., Ilf. 43 G6
Hornsey La. N6 49 B1
Hornsey La. Est. 40 D7
N19

Hornsey La. Gdns. N6	40	C7
Hornsey Pk. Rd. N8	40	F3
Hornsey Ri. N19	40	D7
Hornsey Ri. Gdns. N19	40	D7
Hornsey Rd. N7	49	F3
Hornsey Rd. N19	49	E1
Hornsey St. N7	49	F5
Hornshay St. SE15	68	F6
Hornton St. W8	66	D2
Horsa Clo., Wall.	101	E7
Kingsford Ave.		
Horsa Rd. SE12	78	J7
Horsa Rd., Erith	71	H7
Horse and Dolphin Yd. W1	**11**	**J5**
Horse Fair, Kings.T.	91	G2
Wood St.		
Horse Guards Ave. SW1	**16**	**A2**
Horse Guards Ave. SW1	67	E1
Horse Guards Rd. SW1	**15**	**J2**
Horse Guards Rd. SW1	67	D1
Horse Leaze E6	61	D6
Horse Ride SW1	**15**	**H2**
Horse Rd. E7	51	H3
Centre Rd.		
Horse Shoe Cres., Nthlt.	54	G2
Horse Shoe Yd. W1	**11**	**E5**
Horsebridges Clo., Dag.	62	E1
Horsecroft Rd., Edg.	30	D7
Horseferry Pl. SE10	69	C6
Horseferry Rd. E14	59	G7
Horseferry Rd. SW1	**15**	**H6**
Horseferry Rd. SW1	67	D4
Horsell Rd. N5	49	G5
Horselydown La. SE1	**17**	**F3**
Horselydown La. SE1	68	C2
Horsenden Ave., Grnf.	46	B5
Horsenden Cres., Grnf.	46	C5
Horsenden La. N., Grnf.	46	C6
Horsenden La. S., Grnf.	55	D1
Horseshoe Clo. E14	69	C5
Ferry St.		
Horseshoe Clo. NW2	47	H2
Horseshoe Grn., Sutt.	100	E2
Aultone Way		
Horseshoe La. N20	31	A1
Horsfeld Gdns. SE9	79	A5
Horsfeld Rd. SE9	79	A5
Horsford Rd. SW2	76	F5
Horsham Ave. N12	31	H5
Horsham Rd., Bexh.	80	G6
Horsley Dr., Croy.	103	C7
Horsley Rd. E4	34	C2
Horsley Rd., Brom.	96	H1
Palace Rd.		
Horsley St. SE17	**21**	**B5**
Horsley St. SE17	68	A6
Horsmonden Clo., Orp.	97	J7
Horsmonden Rd. SE4	77	J5
Hortensia Rd. SW10	**18**	**C7**
Hortensia Rd. SW10	66	F7
Horticultural Pl. W4	65	D5
Heathfield Ter.		
Horton Ave. NW2	48	B4
Horton Rd. E8	50	E6
Horton St. SE13	78	B3
Hortus Rd. E4	34	C2
Hortus Rd., Sthl.	63	F2
Hosack Rd. SW17	84	J1
Hoser Ave. SE12	87	G2
Hosier La. EC1	**12**	**G2**
Hosier La. EC1	58	H5
Hoskins Clo. E16	60	J6
Hoskins St. SE10	69	D5
Hospital Bri. Rd., Twick.	72	H7
Hospital La., Islw.	73	C5
Hospital Rd. E9	50	G5
Homerton Row		
Hospital Rd., Houns.	72	G3
Hotham Clo., W.Mol.	90	G3
Garrick Gdns.		
Hotham Rd. SW15	74	J3
Hotham Rd. SW19	84	F7
Hotham Rd. Ms. SW19	84	F7
Haydons Rd.		

Hotham St. E15	60	E1
Hothfield Pl. SE16	68	F3
Lwr. Rd.		
Hotspur Rd., Nthlt.	54	G2
Hotspur St. SE11	**20**	**E3**
Hotspur St. SE11	67	G5
Houblon Rd., Rich.	73	H5
Houghton Clo. E8	50	C6
Buttermere Wk.		
Houghton Clo., Hmptn.	81	E6
Houghton Rd. N15	41	C5
West Grn. Rd.		
Houghton St. WC2	**12**	**D4**
Houlder Cres., Croy.	101	H6
Houndsden Rd. N21	24	F6
Houndsditch EC3	**13**	**E3**
Houndsditch EC3	59	B6
Houndsfield Rd. N9	25	E7
Hounslow Ave., Houns.	72	H5
Hounslow Gdns., Houns.	72	H5
Hounslow Rd. (Feltham), Felt.	81	B1
Hounslow Rd. (Hanworth), Felt.	81	D4
Hounslow Rd., Twick.	72	H6
Houseman Way SE5	68	A7
Benhill Rd.		
Houston Pl., Esher	98	B1
Lime Tree Ave.		
Houston Rd. SE23	86	H2
Hove Ave. E17	41	J5
Hove Gdns., Sutt.	100	E1
Hoveden Rd. NW2	48	B5
Hoveton Rd. SE28	62	C6
Howard Ave., Bex.	89	C1
Howard Clo. N11	32	A2
Howard Clo. NW2	48	B4
Howard Clo. W3	56	B6
Howard Clo., Hmptn.	81	J6
Howard Dr., Borwd.	22	J6
Howard Ms. N5	49	H4
Hamilton Pk.		
Howard Pl. SW1	**15**	**F6**
Howard Rd. E6	61	C2
Howard Rd. E11	51	E3
Howard Rd. E17	42	A3
Howard Rd. N15	41	B6
Howard Rd. N16	50	A4
Howard Rd. NW2	48	A4
Howard Rd. SE20	95	F1
Howard Rd. SE25	95	D5
Howard Rd., Bark.	61	G1
Howard Rd., Brom.	87	G7
Howard Rd., Ilf.	52	E4
Howard Rd., Islw.	73	C3
Howard Rd., N.Mal.	92	E3
Howard Rd., Sthl.	54	H6
Howard Rd., Surb.	91	J6
Howard St., T.Ditt.	91	J6
Howard Wk. N2	39	F4
Howards Clo., Pnr.	36	B2
Howards Crest Clo., Beck.	96	C2
Howards La. SW15	74	H5
Howards Rd. E13	60	G3
Howarth Ct. E15	51	C5
Taylor Ct.		
Howarth Rd. SE2	71	A5
Howberry Clo., Edg.	29	G6
Howberry Rd., Edg.	29	G6
Howberry Rd., Stan.	29	G6
Howberry Rd., Th.Hth.	95	A1
Howbury Rd. SE15	77	F3
Howcroft Cres. N3	31	D7
Howcroft La., Grnf.	55	A3
Cowgate Rd.		
Howden Clo. SE28	62	D7
Howden Rd. SE25	95	C2
Howden St. SE15	77	D3
Howe Clo., Rom.	44	G1
Howell Clo., Rom.	44	D5
Howell Wk. SE1	**20**	**H2**
Howes Clo. N3	39	D3
Howgate Rd. SW14	74	D3
Howick Pl. SW1	**15**	**G6**
Howick Pl. SW1	67	C3
Howie St. SW11	67	H7
Howitt Rd. NW3	48	H6
Howland Ms. E. W1	**11**	**F1**
Howland St. W1	**11**	**F1**
Howland St. W1	58	C5
Howland Way SE16	68	H2
Howletts Rd. SE24	76	J6
Howley Pl. W2	**10**	**D1**
Howley Pl. W2	57	F5
Howley Rd., Croy.	101	H3
Hows St. E2	**9**	**F1**

Hows St. E2	59	C2
Howsman Rd. SW13	65	G6
Howson Rd. SE4	77	H4
Howson Ter., Rich.	73	H6
Howton Pl. (Bushey), Wat.	29	A1
Hoxton Mkt. N1	**9**	**D4**
Hoxton Sq. N1	**9**	**D4**
Hoxton Sq. N1	59	B3
Hoxton St. N1	59	B1
Hoy St. E16	60	F6
Hoylake Gdns., Mitch.	94	C3
Hoylake Gdns., Ruis.	45	B1
Hoylake Gdns., Wat.	28	D4
Hoylake Rd. W3	56	E6
Hoyland Clo. SE15	68	E7
Commercial Way		
Hoyle Rd. SW17	84	H5
Hubbard Rd. SE27	85	J4
Hubbard St. E15	60	E1
Hubert Gro. SW9	76	E3
Hubert Rd. E6	61	A3
Huddart St. E3	59	J5
Huddleston Rd. N7	49	C3
Huddlestone Rd. E7	51	F4
Huddlestone Rd. NW2	47	H6
Hudson Ct. SW19	84	E7
Hudson Pl. SE18	70	F5
Hudson Rd., Bexh.	80	F2
Hudson's Pl. SW1	**19**	**F1**
Huggin Ct. EC4	**13**	**A5**
Huggin Hill EC4	**13**	**A5**
Hugh Ms. SW1	**19**	**E2**
Hugh Pl. SW1	**19**	**H1**
Hugh St. SW1	**19**	**E2**
Hugh St. SW1	67	B4
Hughan Rd. E15	51	D5
Hughenden Ave., Har.	37	E5
Hughenden Gdns., Nthlt.	54	C3
Hughenden Rd., Wor.Pk.	92	G7
Hughenden Ter. E15	51	C4
Westdown Rd.		
Hughes Rd., Hayes	54	A7
Hughes Wk., Croy.	94	J7
St. Saviours Rd.		
Hugo Rd. N19	49	C4
Hugo Rd. SW6	75	F3
Huguenot Pl. SW18	75	F5
Huguenot Sq. SE15	77	E3
Scylla Rd.		
Hull Clo. SE16	68	G2
Hull St. EC1	**11**	**J4**
Hullbridge Ms. N1	59	A1
Sherborne St.		
Hulse Ave., Bark.	52	G6
Hulse Ave., Rom.	44	H1
Humber Rd. NW2	47	H2
Humber Rd. SE3	69	F6
Humberstone Rd. E13	60	J3
Humberton Clo. E9	50	H5
Marsh Hill		
Humbolt Rd. W6	66	B6
Hume Pl. E16	60	H5
Hume Way, Ruis.	36	A6
Humes Ave. W7	64	B3
Humphrey Clo., Ilf.	43	C1
Humphrey St. SE1	**21**	**F3**
Humphrey St. SE1	68	C5
Humphries Clo., Dag.	53	F4
Hundred Acre NW9	38	F2
Hungerdown E4	34	C1
Hungerford Bri. SE1	**16**	**C2**
Hungerford Bri. SE1	67	E1
Hungerford Bri. WC2	**16**	**C2**
Hungerford Bri. WC2	67	E1
Hungerford La. WC2	**16**	**B1**
Hungerford Rd. N7	49	D6
Hungerford St. E1	59	E6
Commercial Rd.		
Hunsdon Clo., Dag.	53	E6
Hunsdon Rd. SE14	68	G7
Hunslett St. E2	59	F2
Royston St.		
Hunston Rd., Mord.	100	E1
Hunt, Rd., Sthl.	63	G3
Hunt St. W11	66	A1
Hunt Way SE22	86	D1
Dulwich Common		
Hunter Clo. SE1	**17**	**C6**
Hunter Clo., Borwd.	22	C5
Hunter Ho., Felt.	81	A1
Hunter Rd. SW20	92	J1
Hunter Rd., Ilf.	52	E5
Hunter Rd., Th.Hth.	95	A3
Hunter St. WC1	**8**	**B5**

Hunter St. WC1	58	E4
Hunter Wk. E13	60	G1
Stratford Rd.		
Hunter Wk., Borwd.	22	C5
Ashley Dr.		
Huntercrombe Gdns., Wat.	28	C5
Hunters, The, Beck.	96	C1
Hunters Clo. SW12	85	A1
Balham Pk. Rd.		
Hunters Ct., Rich.	73	G5
Friars La.		
Hunters Gro., Har.	37	F4
Hunters Gro., Hayes	63	A1
Hunters Gro., Orp.	104	F4
State Fm. Ave.		
Hunters Hall Rd., Dag.	53	G4
Hunters Hill, Ruis.	45	C3
Hunters Meadow SE19	86	B4
Dulwich Wd. Ave.		
Hunters Rd., Chess.	98	H3
Hunters Sq., Dag.	53	G4
Hunters Way, Croy.	102	B4
Brownlow Rd.		
Hunters Way, Enf.	24	G1
Hunting Gate Clo., Enf.	24	G3
Hunting Gate Dr., Chess.	98	H7
Hunting Gate Ms., Sutt.	100	E3
Hunting Gate Ms., Twick.	82	B1
Colne Rd.		
Huntingdon Clo., Mitch.	94	E4
Huntingdon Gdns. W4	65	C7
Huntingdon Gdns., Wor.Pk.	99	J3
Huntingdon Rd. N2	39	H3
Huntingdon Rd. N9	33	F1
Huntingdon St. E16	60	F6
Huntingdon St. N1	49	F7
Huntingfield, Croy.	102	J7
Huntingfield Rd. SW15	74	G4
Huntings Rd., Dag.	53	G6
Huntley Dr. N3	31	D6
Huntley St. WC1	**7**	**G6**
Huntley St. WC1	58	C4
Huntley Way SW20	92	G2
Huntly Rd. SE25	95	B4
Hunton St. E1	**9**	**H6**
Hunton St. E1	59	D5
Hunt's Clo. SE3	78	G2
Hunt's Ct. WC2	**11**	**J6**
Hunts La. E15	60	C2
Hunts Mead, Enf.	25	G3
Hunts Slip Rd. SE21	86	B3
Huntsman St. SE17	**21**	**C2**
Huntsman St. SE17	68	B4
Huntsmans Clo., Felt.	81	B4
Huntsmead Clo., Chis.	88	C7
Huntsmoor Rd., Epsom	99	D5
Huntspill St. SW17	84	F3
Huntsworth Ms. NW1	**6**	**J6**
Marlow Way		
Hurley Cres. SE16	68	G2
Hurley Rd., Grnf.	54	H6
Hurlingham Ct. SW6	75	C3
Hurlingham Gdns. SW6	75	C3
Hurlingham Rd. SW6	75	C2
Hurlingham Rd., Bexh.	71	F7
Hurlingham Sq. SW6	75	E3
Peterborough Rd.		
Hurlock St. N5	49	H3
Hurlstone Rd. SE25	95	A5
Hurn Ct. Rd., Houns.	72	D2
Renfrew Rd.		
Huron Rd. SW17	85	A2
Hurren Clo. SE3	78	E3
Hurry Clo. E15	51	E7
Hurst Ave. E4	34	A4
Hurst Ave. N6	40	C6
Hurst Clo. E4	34	A3
Hurst Clo. NW11	39	E6
Hurst Clo., Brom.	103	F1
Hurst Clo., Chess.	99	A5
Hurst Clo., Nthlt.	45	F6
Hurst Est. SE2	71	D3
Hurst La. SE2	71	D5
Hurst La., E.Mol.	90	J4
Hurst Ri., Barn.	23	D3
Hurst Rd. E17	42	B3

Hurst Rd. N21 32 G1
Hurst Rd., Bex. 89 C1
Hurst Rd., Buck.H. 35 A1
Hurst Rd., Croy. 102 A5
Hurst Rd., E.Mol. 90 G3
Hurst Rd., Erith 80 J1
Hurst Rd., Sid. 89 A2
Hurst Rd., Walt. 90 C5
Hurst Rd., W.Mol. 90 G3
Hurst Springs, Bex. 89 E1
Hurst St. SE24 76 H6
Hurst Vw. Rd., 102 B7
S.Croy.
Hurst Way, S.Croy. 102 B6
Hurstbourne, Esher 98 C6
Hurstbourne Gdns., 52 H6
Bark.
Hurstbourne Rd. 86 H1
SE23
Hurstcourt Rd., Sutt. 100 E1
Hurstdene Ave., 103 F1
Brom.
Hurstdene Gdns. N15 41 B7
Hurstfield, Brom. 96 G5
Hurstfield Rd., 90 G3
W.Mol.
Hurstfield Gdns., 43 C1
Ilf.
Hurstmead Ct., Edg. 30 B4
Hurstway Wk. W11 57 A7
Whitchurch Rd.
Hurstwood Ave. E18 42 H4
Hurstwood Ave. 89 F1
Bex.
Hurstwood Dr., 97 C3
Brom.
Hurstwood Rd. NW11 39 B4
Hurtwood Rd., Walt. 90 F7
Huson Clo. NW3 48 H7
Husseywell Cres., 103 G1
Brom.
Hutchings St. E14 69 A2
Hutchings Wk. NW11 39 E4
Hutchins Clo. E15 51 C7
Gibbins Rd.
Hutchinson Ter., 46 G3
Wem.
Hutton Clo., Grnf. 46 A5
Mary Peters Dr.
Hutton Clo., 34 H6
Wdf.Grn.
Hutton Gdns., Har. 28 J7
Hutton Wk.
Hutton Gro. N12 31 E5
Hutton La., Har. 28 J7
Hutton Row, Edg. 30 C7
Pavilion Way
Hutton St. EC4 12 F4
Hutton Wk., Har. 28 J7
Huxbear St. SE4 77 J5
Huxley Clo., Nthlt. 54 E1
Huxley Dr., Rom. 44 B7
Huxley Gdns. NW10 55 J3
Huxley Par. N18 32 J5
Huxley Pl. N13 32 H3
Huxley Rd. E10 51 C2
Huxley Rd. N18 33 A4
Huxley Rd., Well. 79 J3
Huxley Sayze, Nthlt. 32 J5
Huxley St. W10 57 B3
Hyacinth Clo., 81 G6
Hmptn.
Gresham Rd.
Hyacinth Ct., Pnr. 36 C3
Tulip Ct.
Hyacinth Rd. SW15 83 G1
Hycliffe Gdns., 35 F4
Chig.
Hyde, The NW9 38 E4
Hyde Clo. E13 60 G1
Pelly Rd.
Hyde Clo., Barn. 23 C3
Hyde Ct. N20 31 G3
Hyde Cres. NW9 38 E5
Hyde La. SW11 75 H1
Battersea Bri. Rd.
Hyde Pk. W2 14 G1
Hyde Pk. W2 66 H1
Hyde Pk. Ave. N21 33 J2
Hyde Pk. Cor. W1 15 C3
Hyde Pk. Cor. W1 67 A2
Hyde Pk. Cres. W2 10 G4
Hyde Pk. Cres. W2 57 H6
Hyde Pk. Gdns. N21 32 J1
Hyde Pk. Ave.
Hyde Pk. Gdns. W2 10 F5
Hyde Pk. Gdns. W2 66 G3
Hyde Pk. Gdns. Ms. 10 F5
W2
Hyde Pk. Gate SW7 14 D4
Hyde Pk. Gate SW7 66 F2
Hyde Pk. Gate Ms. 14 D4
SW7

Hyde Pk. Pl. W2 10 H5
Hyde Pk. Sq. W2 10 G4
Hyde Pk. Sq. W2 57 H6
Hyde Pk. Sq. Ms. W2 10 G4
Hyde Pk. St. W2 10 G4
Hyde Pk. St. W2 57 H6
Hyde Rd. N1 59 B1
Hyde Rd., Bexh. 80 F2
Hyde Rd., Rich. 73 J5
Albert Rd.
Hyde St. SE8 69 A6
Deptford High St.
Hyde Vale SE10 78 D1
Hyde Way N9 33 C2
Hydefield Clo. N21 33 A1
Hydefield Ct. N9 33 B2
Hydes Pl. N1 49 H7
Compton Ave.
Hydeside Gdns. N9 33 C2
Hydethorpe Ave. N9 33 C2
Hydethorpe Rd. 85 C1
SW12
Hylands Rd. E17 42 D2
Hylton St. SE18 70 J4
Hyndewood SE23 86 G3
Hyndman St. SE15 68 E6
Hynton Rd., Dag. 53 C2
Hyrst Dene, S.Croy. 101 H4
Hyson Rd. SE16 68 E4
Galleywall Rd.
Hythe Ave., Bexh. 71 E7
Hythe Clo. N18 33 D4
Hythe Rd. NW10 56 G4
Hythe Rd., Th.Hth. 95 A2
Hyver Hill NW7 22 D6

I

Ibbetson Path, 27 E3
Loug.
Ibbotson Ave. E16 60 F6
Ibbott St. E1 59 F4
Mantus Rd.
Iberian Ave., Wall. 101 D4
Ibis La. W4 74 C1
Ibscott Clo., Dag. 53 J6
Ibsley Gdns. SW15 83 G1
Ibsley Way, Barn. 23 H5
Iceland Rd. E3 60 A1
Ickburgh Est. E5 50 E3
Ickburgh Rd.
Ickburgh Rd. E5 50 E3
Ickleton Rd. SE9 88 B4
Icknield Dr., Ilf. 43 E5
Ickworth Pk. Rd. E17 41 H4
Ida Rd. N15 41 A5
Ida St. E14 60 C6
Iden Clo., Brom. 96 E3
Idlecombe Rd. SW17 85 A6
Idmiston Rd. E15 51 F5
Idmiston Rd. SE27 85 J3
Idmiston Rd., 92 F7
Wor.Pk.
Idmiston Sq., 99 F1
Wor.Pk.
Idol La. EC3 13 D6
Idonia St. SE8 69 A7
Iffley Rd. W6 65 H3
Ifield Rd. SW10 18 B5
Ifield Rd. SW10 66 E6
Ightham Rd., Erith 71 G7
Ikea Twr. NW10 47 D5
Ilbert St. W10 57 A3
Ilchester Gdns. W2 10 A5
Ilchester Gdns. W2 57 E7
Ilchester Pl. W14 66 C3
Ilchester Rd., Dag. 53 B5
Ildersly Gro. SE21 86 A2
Ilderton Rd. SE15 68 F7
Ilderton Rd. SE16 68 E5
Ilex Clo., Sun. 90 C2
Oakington Dr.
Ilex Ho. N4 40 F7
Ilex Rd. NW10 47 F6
Ilex Way SW16 85 G5
Ilford Hill, Ilf. 52 D3
Ilford La., Ilf. 52 E3
Ilfracombe Gdns., 44 B7
Rom.
Ilfracombe Rd., 87 F3
Brom.
Iliffe St. SE17 20 H3
Iliffe St. SE17 67 H5
Iliffe Yd. SE17 20 H3
Ilkeston Ct. E5 50 G4
Overbury St.
Ilkley Clo. SE19 86 A6
Ilkley Rd. E16 60 J5
Ilkley Rd., Wat. 28 D5
Illingworth Clo., 93 G3
Mitch.
Illingworth Way, 25 B4
Enf.

Ilmington Rd., Har. 37 G6
Ilminster Gdns. 75 H4
SW11
Imber Clo. N14 24 C7
Imber Clo., Esher 98 A1
Ember La.
Imber Ct. Ind. Est., 91 A6
E.Mol.
Imber Gro., Esher 91 A7
Imber Pk. Rd., 98 A1
Esher
Imber St. N1 59 A1
Imperial Ave. N16 50 C3
Victorian Rd.
Imperial Clo., Har. 36 G6
Imperial College 14 E5
Rd. SW7
Imperial College 66 G3
Rd. SW7
Imperial Dr., Har. 36 G7
Imperial Gdns., 94 B3
Mitch.
Imperial Ms. E6 60 J2
Central Pk. Rd.
Imperial Rd. N22 40 E1
Imperial Rd. SW6 75 E1
Imperial Sq. SW6 75 E1
Imperial St. E3 60 C3
Imperial Way, Chis. 88 F3
Imperial Way, Croy. 101 G6
Imperial Way, Har. 37 H6
Inca Dr. SE9 74 D2
Inchmery Rd. SE6 97 D2
Inchwood, Croy. 103 B4
Independent Pl. E8 50 C5
Downs Pk. Rd.
Independents Rd. 78 F3
SE3
Blackheath Village
Inderwick Rd. N8 40 F5
Indescon Ct. E14 69 A2
India St. EC3 13 F4
India Way W12 56 H7
Indus Rd. SE7 69 J7
Industry Ter. SW9 76 G3
Canterbury Cres.
Ingal Rd. E13 60 G4
Ingate Pl. SW8 76 B1
Ingatestone Rd. E12 51 J1
Ingatestone Rd. 95 E5
SE25
Ingatestone Rd., 34 H7
Wdf.Grn.
Ingelow Rd. SW8 76 B2
Ingersoll Rd. W12 65 H1
Ingestre Pl. W1 11 G4
Ingestre Rd. E7 51 G4
Ingestre Rd. NW5 49 B4
Ingham Rd. NW6 48 D4
Ingle Clo., Pnr. 36 D2
Inglebert St. EC1 8 E3
Ingleborough St. 76 G2
SW9
Ingleby Clo., Dag. 53 H6
Ingleby Dr., Har. 46 A3
Ingleby Rd. N7 49 E3
Ingleby Rd., Dag. 53 H6
Ingleby Rd., Ilf. 52 C2
Ingleby Way, Chis. 88 D5
Ingledew Rd. SE18 70 G5
Inglehurst Gdns., 43 C5
Ilf.
Inglemere Rd. SE23 86 G3
Inglemere Rd., 84 J7
Mitch.
Inglesham Wk. E9 50 J6
Trowbridge Est.
Ingleside Clo., 87 A7
Beck.
Ingleside Gro. SE3 69 F6
Inglethorpe St. SW6 75 A1
Ingleton Ave., 80 A5
Well.
Ingleton Rd. N18 33 D6
Ingleton St. SW9 76 G2
Ingleway N12 31 G6
Inglewood Clo. E14 69 A4
Inglewood Clo., Ilf. 35 J6
Inglewood Copse, 97 D2
Brom.
Inglewood Rd. NW6 48 D5
Inglis Barracks NW7 31 B5
Inglis Rd. W5 55 J7
Inglis Rd., Croy. 102 C1
Inglis St. SE5 76 H1
Ingram Ave. NW11 39 F7
Ingram Clo. SE11 20 D1
Ingram Clo., Stan. 29 F5
Ingram Rd. N2 39 H4
Ingram Rd., Th.Hth. 94 J1
Ingram Way, Grnf. 46 A1
Ingrave Ho., Dag. 62 B1
Ingrave St. SW11 75 G3

Ingress St. W4 65 E5
Devonshire Rd.
Inigo Jones Rd. SE7 70 B7
Inigo Pl. WC2 12 A5
Inkerman Rd. NW5 49 B6
Inks Grn. E4 34 B5
Inman Rd. NW10 56 E1
Inman Rd. SW18 75 F7
Inmans Row, 34 G4
Wdf.Grn.
Inner Circle NW1 7 B4
Inner Circle NW1 58 A3
Inner Pk. Rd. SW19 84 A1
Inner Temple La. 12 E4
EC4
Innes Clo. SW20 93 B2
Innes Gdns. SW15 74 H6
Innes Yd., Croy. 101 J3
High St.
Inniskilling Rd. E13 60 J2
Inskip Clo. E10 51 B2
Inskip Rd., Dag. 53 D1
Institute Pl. E8 50 E5
Amhurst Rd.
Instone Clo., Wall. 101 E7
De Havilland Rd.
Insurance St. WC1 8 E4
Integer Gdns. E11 42 D7
Forest Rd.
International Ave., 63 C5
Houns.
International Trd. 63 B3
Est., Cthl.
Inver Clo. E5 50 F2
Theydon Rd.
Inver Ct. W2 10 B4
Inveraray Pl. SE18 70 G6
Old Mill Rd.
Inverclyde Gdns., 44 D4
Rom.
Inveresk Gdns., 99 F3
Wor.Pk.
Inverforth Clo. NW3 48 F2
North End Way
Inverforth Rd. N11 32 B5
Invermore Pl. SE18 70 F4
Inverness Ave., Enf. 25 B1
Inverness Dr., Ilf. 35 H6
Inverness Gdns. W8 14 A2
Inverness Ms. W2 10 B5
Inverness Pl. W2 10 B5
Inverness Pl. W2 57 E7
Inverness Rd. N18 33 E5
Inverness Rd., 72 F4
Houns.
Inverness Rd., Sthl. 63 E4
Inverness Rd., 100 A1
Wor.Pk.
Inverness St. NW1 58 B1
Inverness Ter. W2 10 B5
Inverness Ter. W2 57 E6
Inverton Rd. SE15 77 G4
Invicta Clo., Chis. 88 D5
Invicta Gro., 54 F3
Nthlt.
Invicta Rd. SE3 69 G7
Inville Rd. SE17 21 C4
Inville Rd. SE17 68 A5
Inwood Ave., Houns. 72 J3
Inwood Clo., Croy. 102 H2
Inwood Rd., Houns. 72 H4
Inworth St. SW11 75 H2
Inworth St. N1 58 J1
Popham St.
Ion Sq. E2 9 H2
Iona Clo. SE6 78 A7
Ipswich Rd. SW17 85 A6
Ireland Pl. N22 32 E7
Whittington Rd.
Ireland Row E14 59 J6
Commercial Rd.
Ireland Yd. EC4 12 H4
Irene Rd. SW6 75 D1
Irene Rd., Orp. 97 J7
Iris Ave., Bex. 80 E6
Iris Clo., Croy. 102 G1
Primrose La.
Iris Clo., Surb. 91 J7
Iris Ct., Pnr. 36 C3
Iris Cres., Bexh. 71 F6
Iris Rd., Epsom 99 B5
Iris Way E4 33 J6
Irkdale Ave., Enf. 25 C1
Iron Mill Pl. SW18 75 E6
Garratt La.
Iron Mill Rd. SW18 75 E6
Ironmonger La. EC2 13 B4
Ironmonger Pas. EC1 9 A4
Ironmonger Row EC1 9 A4
Ironmonger Row EC1 58 J3
Ironmongers Pl. E14 69 A4
Spindrift Ave.

Ironside Clo. SE16　68 G2
　Kinburn St.
Irvine Ave., Har.　37 D3
Irvine Clo. N20　31 H2
Irving Ave., Orp.　97 J7
Irving Ave., Nthlt.　54 D1
Irving Gro. SW9　76 F2
Irving Rd. W14　66 A3
Irving St. WC2　**11 J6**
Irving St. WC2　58 D7
Irving Way NW9　38 F5
Irwin Ave. SE18　70 H7
Irwin Gdns. NW10　56 H1
Isabel St. SW9　76 F1
Isabella Clo. N14　24 C7
　Old Fm. Ave.
Isabella Dr., Orp.　104 F4
Isabella Rd. E9　50 F5
Isabella St. SE1　**16 G2**
Isabella St. SE1　67 H1
Isambard Ms. E14　69 C3
Isambard Pl. SE16　68 F1
　Rotherhithe St.
Isel Way SE22　77 B5
　East Dulwich Gro.
Isham Rd. SW16　94 E2
Isis Clo. SW15　74 J4
Isis St. SW18　84 F2
Isla Rd. SE18　70 F6
Island Fm. Ave.,　90 F5
　W.Mol.
Island Fm. Rd.,　90 F5
　W.Mol.
Island Rd., Mitch.　84 J7
Island Row E14　59 H6
　Commercial Rd.
Islay Gdns., Houns.　72 D5
Islay Wk. N1　49 J6
　Douglas Rd.
Isledon Rd. N7　49 G3
Islehurst Clo.,　97 D1
　Chis.
Islington High St.　58 H1
　N1
Islington High St.　**8 G1**
　N1
Islington High St.　58 H2
　N1
Islington Pk. Ms.　49 G7
　N1
　Islington Pk. St.
Islington Pk. St.　49 G7
　N1
Islip Gdns., Edg.　30 D7
Islip Gdns., Nthlt.　45 E7
Islip Manor Rd.,　45 E7
　Nthlt.
Islip St. NW5　49 C5
Ismailia Rd. E7　51 H7
Isom Clo. E13　60 J4
　Belgrave Rd.
Ivanhoe Dr., Har.　37 D3
Ivanhoe Rd. SE5　77 C3
Ivanhoe Rd., Houns.　72 D3
Ivatt Pl. W14　66 C5
Ivatt Way N17　40 H3
Ive Fm. Clo. E10　51 A2
Ive Fm. La. E10　51 A2
Iveagh Ave. NW10　56 A2
Iveagh Clo. E9　59 G1
Iveagh Clo. NW10　56 A2
Ivedon Rd., Well.　80 C2
Iveley Rd. SW4　76 C2
Ivere Dr., Barn.　23 E6
Iverhurst Clo., Bexh.　80 D3
Iverna Ct. W8　66 D3
Iverna Gdns. W8　66 D3
Ivers Way, Croy.　103 B7
Iverson Rd. NW6　48 C6
Ives Rd. E16　60 E5
Ives St. SW3　**18 H1**
Ives St. SW3　66 H4
Ivestor Ter. SE23　77 F7
Ivimey St. E2　**9 J3**
Ivimey St. E2　59 D3
Ivinghoe Clo., Enf.　25 B1
Ivinghoe Rd., Dag.　53 B5
Ivor Gro. SE9　88 E1
Ivor Pl. NW1　**6 J6**
Ivor Pl. NW1　57 J4
Ivor St. NW1　49 C7
Ivory Sq. SW11　75 F3
　Gartons Way
Ivorydown, Brom.　87 G4
Ivy Clo., Har.　45 F4
Ivy Clo., Pnr.　36 C7
Ivy Clo., Sun.　90 C2
Ivy Cotts. E14　60 B7
　Grove Vill.
Ivy Cres. W4　65 C4
　Bollo La.
Ivy Gdns. N8　40 E6
Ivy Gdns., Mitch.　94 D3
Ivy La., Houns.　72 F4

Ivy Rd. E16　60 G6
　Pacific Rd.
Ivy Rd. E17　42 A6
Ivy Rd. N14　24 C7
Ivy Rd. NW2　47 J4
Ivy Rd. SE4　72 H4
Ivy Rd., Houns.　72 H4
Ivy Rd., Surb.　99 A2
Ivy St. N1　**9 D1**
Ivy St. N1　59 B2
Ivy Wk., Dag.　53 E6
Ivybridge Clo.,　73 D7
　Twick.
Ivybridge Est.,　73 C5
　Islw.
Ivybridge La. WC2　**12 B6**
Ivychurch Clo. SE20　86 F7
　Laurel Gro.
Ivychurch La. SE17　**21 E3**
Ivydale Rd. SE15　77 G3
Ivydale Rd., Cars.　100 J2
Ivyday Gro. SW16　85 F3
Ivydene, W.Mol.　90 F5
Ivydene Clo., Sutt.　100 F4
Ivyhouse Rd., Dag.　53 D6
Ivymount Rd. SE27　85 G3
Ixworth Pl. SW3　**18 G3**
Ixworth Pl. SW3　66 H4
Izane Rd., Bexh.　80 F4

J

Jack Cornwell St.　52 D4
　E12
Jack Walker Ct. N5　49 H4
Jackass La., Kes.　103 H5
Jacklin Grn.,　34 G4
　Wdf.Grn.
Jackman Ms. NW10　47 E3
Jackman St. E8　59 E1
Jackson Rd. N7　49 F4
Jackson Rd., Bark.　61 G1
Jackson Rd., Barn.　23 G6
Jackson Rd., Brom.　104 B2
Jackson St. SE18　70 D6
Jackson Way, Sthl.　63 H2
Jacksons La. N6　40 A7
Jacksons Pl., Croy.　102 A1
　Cross Rd.
Jacob St. SE1　**17 H3**
Jacob St. SE1　68 C2
Jacobs Clo., Dag.　53 H4
Jacobs Ho. E14　60 J3
Jacob's Well Ms. W1　**11 C3**
Jacqueline Clo.,　54 F1
　Nthlt.
　Canford Ave.
Jade Clo. E16　61 A6
Jade Clo., Dag.　53 C1
Jaffray Pl. SE27　85 H4
　Chapel Rd.
Jaffray Rd., Brom.　97 A4
Jaggard Way SW12　75 J7
Jago Clo. SE18　70 F6
Jago Wk. SE5　68 A7
　Lomond Gro.
Jamaica Rd. SE1　**17 G4**
Jamaica Rd. SE1　68 C2
Jamaica Rd. SE16　**17 H5**
Jamaica Rd. SE16　68 D3
Jamaica Rd.,　94 H6
　Th.Hth.
Jamaica St. E1　59 F5
James Ave. NW2　47 J5
James Ave., Dag.　53 F1
James Bedford Clo.,　36 C2
　Pnr.
James Boswell Clo.　85 G4
　SW16
　Curtis Fld. Rd.
James Clo. NW11　39 B6
　Woodlands
James Collins Clo.　57 C4
　W9
　Fermoy Rd.
James Ct. N1　49 J7
　Morton Rd.
James Dudson Ct.　47 C7
　NW10
James Gdns. N22　32 H7
James Hammett Ho.　**9 G3**
　E2
James La. E10　42 D7
James La. E11　42 D6
James Newman St.　88 D3
　SE9
　Great Harry Dr.
James Sinclair Pt.　60 J1
　E13
James St. W1　**11 C3**
James St. W1　58 A6
James St. WC2　**12 B5**
James St., Bark.　52 F7

James St., Enf.　25 C5
James St., Houns.　73 A3
James Yd. E4　34 D6
　Larkshall Rd.
Jameson St. W8　66 D1
James's Cotts.,　65 A7
　Rich.
　Kew Rd.
Jamestown Rd. NW1　58 B1
Jamieson Ho.,　72 F6
　Houns.
Jane St. E1　59 E6
　Commercial Rd.
Janet St. E14　69 A3
Janeway Pl. SE16　68 E2
　Janeway St.
Janeway St. SE16　**17 J4**
Janeway St. SE16　68 D2
Janice Ms., Ilf.　52 E3
　Oakfield Rd.
Jansen Wk. SW11　75 G4
　Hope St.
Janson Clo. E15　51 E5
　Janson Rd.
Janson Clo. NW10　47 E3
Janson Rd. E15　51 E5
Jansons Rd. N15　41 B3
Japan Cres. N4　40 F7
Japan Rd., Rom.　44 D6
Jarrett Clo. SW2　85 H1
Jarrow Clo., Mord.　93 E5
Jarrow Rd. N17　41 E4
Jarrow Rd. SE16　68 F4
Jarrow Rd., Rom.　44 C6
Jarrow Way E9　50 J5
Jarvis Clo., Barn.　23 A5
Jarvis Rd. SE22　77 B4
　Melbourne Gro.
Jarvis Rd., S.Croy.　102 A6
Jasmin Rd., Epsom　99 B6
Jasmine Clo., Ilf.　52 E5
Jasmine Clo., Orp.　104 E2
Jasmine Gdns.,　103 A3
　Croy.
Jasmine Gdns., Har.　45 G2
Jasmine Gro. SE20　95 E1
Jasmine Way, E.Mol.　91 B4
　Hampton Ct. way
Jason Ct. W1　58 A6
　Marylebone La.
Jason Wk. SE9　88 D4
Jasper Pas. SE19　86 C6
Jasper Rd. E16　61 A6
Jasper Rd. SE19　86 C6
Jasper Wk. N1　**9 B3**
Javelin Way, Nthlt.　54 D3
Jay Gdns., Chis.　88 C4
Jay Ms. SW7　**14 D4**
Jay Ms. SW7　66 F2
Jaycroft, Enf.　24 G1
　The Ridgeway
Jebb Ave. SW2　76 E6
Jebb St. E3　60 A2
Jedburgh Rd. E13　60 A3
Jedburgh St. SW11　76 A4
Jeddo Rd. W12　65 F2
Jefferies Ho. NW10　47 D7
Jefferson Clo. W13　64 E3
Jefferson Clo., Ilf.　43 E5
Jeffreys Pl. NW1　49 C7
　Jeffreys St.
Jeffreys Rd. SW4　76 E2
Jeffreys Rd., Enf.　45 C7
Jeffreys St. NW1　49 C7
Jeffreys Wk. SW4　76 E2
Jeffs Clo., Hmptn.　81 H6
　Uxbridge Rd.
Jeffs Rd., Sutt.　100 C4
Jeken Rd. SE9　78 J4
Jelf Rd. SW2　76 G5
Jellicoe Gdns.,　29 C6
　Stan.
Jellicoe Rd. E13　60 G4
　Jutland Rd.
Jellicoe Rd. N17　33 A7
Jengar Clo., Sutt.　100 E4
Jenkins La. E6　61 D2
Jenkins La., Bark.　61 E2
Jenkins Rd. E13　60 H4
Jenner Ave. W3　56 D5
Jenner Ho. SE3　69 E6
Jenner Pl. SW13　65 H6
Jenner Rd. N16　50 C2
Jennett Rd., Croy.　101 G3
Jennifer Rd., Brom.　87 F3
Jennings Rd. SE22　77 C6
Jennings Way, Barn.　22 J3
Jenningtree Way,　71 J2
　Erith
Jenny Hammond　51 F3
　Clo. E11
　Newcomen Rd.
Jenson Way SE19　86 C7

James St., Hmptn.　80 E1
Jephson Rd. E7　51 J7
Jephson St. SE5　77 A1
　Grove La.
Jephtha Rd. SW18　75 D6
Jeppos La., Mitch.　93 J4
Jerdan Pl. SW6　66 D7
　Fulham Bdy.
Jeremiah St. E14　60 B6
Jeremys Grn. N18　33 E4
Jermyn St. SW1　**15 G1**
Jermyn St. SW1　67 C1
Jerningham Ave.,　43 E2
　Ilf.
Jerningham Rd. SE14　77 H2
Jerome Cres. NW8　**6 G5**
Jerome Cres. NW8　57 H4
Jerome St. E1　**9 F6**
Jerrard St. N1　**9 E2**
Jerrard St. SE13　78 B3
Jersey Ave., Stan.　37 E2
Jersey Dr., Orp.　97 G6
Jersey Par., Houns.　72 H1
Jersey Rd. E11　51 D1
Jersey Rd. E16　60 J6
Jersey Rd. SW17　85 B6
Jersey Rd. W7　64 D2
Jersey Rd., Houns.　72 H1
Jersey Rd., Ilf.　52 E4
Jersey Rd., Islw.　64 A7
Jersey St. E2　59 E3
　Bethnal Grn. Rd.
Jerusalem Pas. EC1　**8 G6**
Jervis Ct. W1　**11 E4**
Jerviston Gdns.　85 G5
　SW16
Jesmond Ave., Wem.　46 J6
Jesmond Rd., Croy.　95 C7
Jesmond Way, Stan.　29 H5
Jessam Ave. E5　50 E1
Jessamine Rd. W7　64 B1
Jesse Rd. E10　51 C1
Jessel Dr., Loug.　27 F1
Jessica Rd. SW18　75 F6
Jessop Ave., Sthl.　63 F4
Jessops Way, Croy.　94 C6
Jessup Clo. SE18　70 F4
Jetstar Way, Nthlt.　54 E3
Jevington Way SE12　87 H1
Jewel Rd. E17　42 A3
Jewry St. EC3　**13 F4**
Jewry St. EC3　59 C6
Jew's Row SW18　75 E4
Jews Wk. SE26　86 E4
Jeymer Ave. NW2　47 H5
Jeymer Dr., Grnf.　54 J1
Jeypore Rd. SW18　75 F7
Jillian Clo., Hmptn.　81 G7
Jim Bradley Clo.　70 D4
　SE18
　John Wilson St.
Joan Cres. SE9　79 A7
Joan Gdns., Dag.　53 E2
Joan Rd., Dag.　53 E1
Joan St. SE1　**16 G2**
Joan St. SE1　67 H1
Jocelyn Rd., Rich.　73 H3
Jockey's Flds. WC1　**12 D1**
Jockey's Flds. WC1　58 F5
Jodrell Rd. E3　59 J1
Joel St., Nthwd.　36 A3
Joel St., Pnr.　36 A3
Johanna St. SE1　**12 E4**
John Adam St. WC2　**12 B6**
John Adam St. WC2　58 E7
John Aird Ct. W2　**10 D1**
John Ashby Clo.　76 E6
　SW2
John Barnes Wk. E15　51 F6
John Bradshaw Rd.　32 D1
　N14
John Burns Dr.,　52 H7
　Bark.
John Campbell Rd.　50 B5
　N16
John Carpenter St.　**12 F5**
　EC4
John Carpenter St.　58 H7
　EC4
John Cornwall VC　52 D4
　Ho. E12
John Felton Rd.　**17 H4**
　SE16
John Felton Rd.　68 D2
　SE16
John Fisher St. E1　**13 H5**
John Fisher St. E1　59 D7
John Gooch Dr.,　24 H1
　Enf.
John Groom's Est.,　30 C4
　Edg.
John Islip St. SW1　**19 J3**

Name	Page	Grid
John Islip St. SW1	67	D5
John Keats Ho. N22	32	F7
John McKenna Wk.	**17**	**J5**
SE16		
John Newton Ct.,	80	B3
Well.		
Danson La.		
John Parker Clo.,	53	H7
Dag.		
John Parker Sq.	75	G3
SW11		
Thomas Baines Rd.		
John Penn St. SE13	78	B1
John Perrin Pl.,	37	H7
Har.		
John Princes St. W1	**11**	**E3**
John Princes St. W1	58	B6
John Rennie Wk. E1	68	E1
Wine Clo.		
John Roll Way SE16	**17**	**J5**
John Roll Way SE16	68	D3
John Ruskin St. SE5	**20**	**H7**
John Ruskin St. SE5	67	H7
John Spencer Sq. N1	49	H6
John St. E15	60	F1
John St. SE25	95	D4
John St. WC1	**8**	**D6**
John St. WC1	58	F4
John St., Enf.	25	C5
John St., Houns.	72	E2
John Walsh Twr. E11	51	F2
John Wilson St.	70	D3
SE18		
John Woolley Clo.	78	D4
SE13		
Johns Ave. NW4	38	J4
Johns La., Mord.	93	F5
John's Ms. WC1	**8**	**D6**
John's Ms. WC1	58	F4
John's Pl. E1	59	E6
Damien St.		
Johns Ter., Croy.	102	B1
Johnson Clo. E8	59	D1
Johnson Rd., Brom.	97	A5
Johnson Rd., Croy.	95	A7
Johnson Rd., Houns.	63	C7
Johnson St. E1	59	F7
Cable St.		
Johnson St., Sthl.	63	C3
Johnsons Clo.,	100	H3
Cars.		
Johnson's Ct. EC4	58	G6
Fleet St.		
Johnsons Dr.,	90	J1
Hmptn.		
Johnson's Pl. SW1	**19**	**F4**
Johnson's Pl. SW1	67	C5
Johnsons Way NW10	56	B4
Johnston Rd.,	34	G5
Wdf.Grn.		
Johnston Ter. NW2	48	A3
Campion Ter.		
Johnstone Rd. E6	61	C3
Joiner St. SE1	**17**	**C2**
Joiner's Arms Yd.	77	A1
SE5		
Denmark Hill		
Jollys La., Har.	46	A1
Lwr. Rd.		
Jolly's La., Hayes	54	D5
Jonathan St. SE11	**20**	**C3**
Jonathan St. SE11	67	F5
Jones Rd. E13	60	H4
Holborn Rd.		
Jones St. W1	**11**	**D6**
Jonquil Gdns.,	81	F6
Hmptn.		
Partridge Rd.		
Jonson Clo., Hayes	54	A5
Jonson Clo., Mitch.	94	B4
Joram Way SE16	68	E5
Egan Way		
Jordan Clo., Dag.	53	H4
Muggeridge Rd.		
Jordan Clo., Har.	45	F3
Hamilton Cres.		
Jordan Rd., Grnf.	55	E1
Jordans Clo., Islw.	73	B1
Joseph Ave. W3	56	D6
Joseph Powell Clo.	76	B6
SW12		
Hazelbourne Rd.		
Joseph St. E3	59	J4
Josephine Ave. SW2	76	F5
Joshua St. E14	60	C6
St. Leonards St.		
Joubert St. SW11	75	J2
Jowett St. SE15	68	C7
Joyce Ave. N18	33	C5
Joyce Dawson Way	62	A7
SE28		
Thamesmere Dr.		
Joyce Page Clo. SE7	70	A6
Lansdowne La.		
Joydon Dr., Rom.	44	B6
Joyners Clo., Dag.	53	F4
Jubb Powell Ho. N15	41	B6
Jubilee Ave. E4	34	C6
Jubilee Ave., Rom.	44	H5
Jubilee Ave.,	72	J7
Twick.		
Jubilee Clo. NW9	38	D6
Jubilee Clo., Pnr.	36	C2
Jubilee Clo., Rom.	44	H5
Jubilee Cres. E14	69	C3
Jubilee Cres. N9	33	D1
Jubilee Dr., Ruis.	45	D4
Jubilee Gdns.,	54	G6
Sthl.		
Jubilee Pl. SW3	**18**	**H3**
Jubilee Pl. SW3	66	H5
Jubilee Rd., Grnf.	55	E1
Jubilee Rd., Sutt.	100	A7
Jubilee St. E1	59	F6
Jubilee Way SW19	93	E1
Jubilee Way, Chess.	99	A4
Jubilee Way, Sid.	89	A2
Judd St. WC1	**8**	**A4**
Judd St. WC1	58	E3
Jude St. E16	60	F6
Judge Wk., Esher	98	B6
Juer St. SW11	66	H7
Julia Gdns., Bark.	62	D2
Julia St. NW5	49	A4
Oak Village		
Julian Ave. W3	56	R7
Julian Clo., Barn.	23	E3
Julian Hill, Har.	86	B2
Julian Pl. E14	69	B5
Julien Rd. W5	64	F4
Junction App. SE13	78	C3
Loampit Vale		
Junction App. SW11	75	H3
Junction Ave. W10	56	J3
Harrow Rd.		
Junction Ms. W2	**10**	**G3**
Junction Pl. W2	**10**	**F3**
Junction Rd. E13	60	H2
Junction Rd. N9	33	D1
Junction Rd. N17	41	D3
Junction Rd. N19	49	C4
Junction Rd. W5	64	G4
Junction Rd., Har.	37	B6
Junction Rd.,	102	A5
S.Croy.		
Junction Rd. E.,	44	E7
Rom.		
Kenneth Rd.		
Junction Rd. W.,	44	E7
Rom.		
Junction Wf. N1	**8**	**J2**
Junction Wf. N1	58	J2
Juniper Clo., Wem.	47	A5
Juniper Gdns. SW16	94	C1
Leonard Rd.		
Juniper La. E6	61	B5
Juniper Rd., Ilf.	52	E4
Juniper St. E1	59	F7
Juno Way SE14	68	G6
Jupiter Way N7	49	F6
Jupp Rd. E15	51	D7
Jupp Rd. W. E15	60	C1
Justice Wk. SW3	**18**	**G6**
Justin Clo., Brent.	64	G7
Justin Rd. E4	33	J6
Jute La., Enf.	25	H2
Jutland Clo. N19	49	E5
Sussex Way		
Jutland Rd. E13	60	G4
Jutland Rd. SE6	78	C7
Jutsums Ave., Rom.	44	H6
Jutsums La., Rom.	44	H6
Juxon Clo., Har.	36	H1
Augustine Rd.		
Juxon St. SE11	**20**	**D1**
Juxon St. SE11	67	F4

K

Name	Page	Grid
Kaduna Clo., Pnr.	36	B5
Kale Rd., Erith	71	E2
Kambala Rd. SW11	75	G3
Kangley Bri. Rd.	86	J4
SE26		
Karen Ct. SE4	77	J2
Wickham Rd.		
Karen Ct., Brom.	96	F1
Blyth Rd.		
Karoline Gdns.,	55	A2
Grnf.		
Oldfield La. N.		
Kashgar Rd. SE18	70	J4
Kashmir Rd. SE7	70	B6
Kassala Rd. SW11	75	J1
Katella Trd. Est.,	61	H3
Bark.		
Kates Clo., Barn.	22	G5
Katharine St.,	101	J3
Croy.		
Katherine Gdns. SE9	79	A4
Katherine Gdns., Ilf.	35	F7
Katherine Rd. E6	52	A7
Katherine Rd. E7	51	J6
Katherine Rd.,	82	D1
Twick.		
London Rd.		
Katherine Sq. W11	66	B1
Wilsham St.		
Kathleen Ave. W3	56	C5
Kathleen Ave., Wem.	46	H7
Kathleen Rd. SW11	75	J3
Kay Rd. SW9	76	E2
Kay St. E2	**9**	**J1**
Kay St. E2	59	D2
Kay St. E15	51	D7
Kay St., Well.	80	B7
Kayemoor Rd., Sutt.	100	H7
Kean St. WC2	**12**	**C4**
Kean St. WC2	58	F6
Keats Clo. E11	42	H5
Nightingale La.		
Keats Clo. NW3	48	H4
Keats Gro.		
Keats Clo. SE1	**21**	**F2**
Keats Clo. SW19	84	G6
North Rd.		
Keats Clo., Chig.	35	F6
Keats Clo., Hayes	54	A5
Keats Gro. NW3	48	H4
Keats Pl. EC2	**13**	**B2**
Keats Rd., Belv.	71	J3
Keats Rd., Well.	79	H1
Keats Way, Croy.	95	F6
Keats Way, Grnf.	54	H5
Keble Clo., Nthlt.	45	J5
Keble Clo., Wor.Pk.	97	F1
Keble St. SW17	84	F4
Kechill Gdns.,	96	G7
Brom.		
Kedelston Ct. E5	50	G4
Redwald Rd.		
Kedleston Dr., Orp.	97	J6
Kedleston Wk. E2	59	E3
Middleton St.		
Keedonwood Rd.,	87	E5
Brom.		
Keel Clo. SE16	68	G1
Keeley Rd., Croy.	101	J2
Keeley St. WC2	**12**	**C4**
Keeley St. WC2	58	F6
Keeling Rd. SE9	79	A5
Keely Clo., Barn.	23	H5
Keemor Clo. SE18	70	D7
Llanover Rd.		
Keens Rd., Croy.	101	J4
Keens Yd. N1	49	H6
St. Pauls Rd.		
Keep, The SE3	78	G2
Keep, The Kings.T.	82	A6
Keetons Rd. SE16	68	E3
Keevil Dr. SW19	75	A7
Keighley Clo. N7	49	E5
Penn Rd.		
Keightley Dr. SE9	88	F1
Keildon Rd. SW11	75	J4
Keir Hardie Est. E5	50	E1
Springfield		
Keir Hardie Ho. W6	65	J6
Lochaline St.		
Keir Hardie Way,	53	A7
Bark.		
Keir Hardie Way,	54	A3
Hayes		
Keith Connor Clo.	76	B3
SW8		
Daley Thompson		
Way		
Keith Gro. W12	65	G2
Keith Rd. E17	41	J1
Keith Rd., Bark.	61	G2
Kelbrook Rd. SE3	79	B2
Kelby Path SE9	88	E3
Kelceda Clo. NW2	47	G2
Kelfield Gdns. W10	56	J6
Kell St. SE1	**16**	**H5**
Kelland Clo. N8	40	D5
Palace Rd.		
Kelland Rd. E13	60	G4
Kellaway Rd. SE3	78	J2
Kellerton Rd. SE13	78	E5
Kellett Rd. SW2	76	G4
Kelling Gdns.,	94	H7
Croy.		
Kellino St. SW17	84	J4
Kellner Rd. SE28	70	J3
Kelly Ct., Borwd.	22	C2
Banks Rd.		
Kelly Rd. NW7	31	B6
Kelly St. NW1	49	B6
Kelly Way, Rom.	44	E5
Kelman Clo. SW4	76	D2
Kelmore Rd. SE22	77	D4
Kelmscott Clo. E17	41	J2
Kelmscott Gdns. W12	65	G3
Kelmscott Rd. SW11	75	H5
Kelross Pas. N5	49	J4
Kelross Rd.		
Kelross Rd. N5	49	J4
Kelsall Clo. SE3	78	H2
Kelsey La., Beck.	96	A3
Kelsey Pk. Ave.,	96	B2
Beck.		
Kelsey Pk. Rd., Beck.	96	A2
Kelsey St. E2	**9**	**J5**
Kelsey St. E2	59	D4
Kelsey Way, Beck.	96	A3
Kelshall Ct. N4	49	J2
Brownswood Rd.		
Kelsie Way, Ilf.	35	H6
Kelso Pl. W8	**14**	**B5**
Kelso Pl. W8	66	E3
Kelso Rd., Cars.	93	F7
Kelson Ho. E14	69	C3
Kelston Rd., Ilf.	43	E2
Kelvedon Clo.,	83	A6
Kings.T.		
Kelvedon Rd. SW6	66	C7
Kelvedon Way,	35	C6
Wdf.Grn.		
Kelvin Ave. N13	32	F6
Kelvin Ave., Tedd.	93	D6
Kelvin Ave., Epsom	99	A6
Kelvin Cres., Har.	29	B7
Kelvin Dr., Twick.	73	E6
Kelvin Gdns., Sthl.	54	G6
Kelvin Gro. SE26	86	E3
Kelvin Gro., Chess.	98	H3
Kelvin Ind. Est., Grnf.	45	H7
Kelvin Par., Orp.	104	H1
Kelvin Rd. N5	49	H4
Kelvin Rd., Well.	80	A3
Kelvinbrook, W.Mol.	90	H3
Kelvington Clo.,	95	H7
Croy.		
Kelvington Rd. SE15	77	G5
Kember St. N1	49	F7
Carnoustie Dr.		
Kemble Dr., Brom.	104	B3
Kemble Rd. N17	41	D1
Kemble Rd. SE23	86	G1
Kemble Rd., Croy.	101	G3
Kemble St. WC2	**12**	**C4**
Kemble St. WC2	58	F6
Kemerton Rd. SE5	76	J3
Kemerton Rd., Beck.	96	B2
Kemerton Rd., Croy.	95	C7
Kemeys St. E9	50	H5
Kemnal Rd., Chis.	88	F7
Kemp Gdns., Croy.	94	J6
St. Saviours Rd.		
Kemp Rd., Dag.	53	D1
Kempe Rd. NW6	57	A2
Kempis Way SE22	77	B5
East Dulwich Gro.		
Kemplay Rd. NW3	48	G4
Kemp's Ct. W1	**11**	**G4**
Kemps Dr. E14	60	A7
Morant St.		
Kemps Gdns. SE13	78	C5
Thornford Rd.		
Kempsford Gdns.	66	D5
SW5		
Kempsford Rd. SE11	**20**	**G2**
Kempsford Rd. SE11	67	G4
Kempshott Rd. SW16	85	G7
Kempson Rd. SW6	75	D1
Kempt St. SE18	70	D6
Kempthorne Rd. SE8	68	H1
Kempton Ave.,	45	G6
Nthlt.		
Kempton Ave. SW1	90	B1
Kempton Clo., Erith	71	J6
Kempton Ct., Sun.	90	B1
Kempton Rd. E6	61	C1
Kempton Rd., Hmptn.	90	F2
Kempton Wk., Croy.	95	H6
Kemsing Clo., Bex.	80	E7
Kemsing Clo., Brom.	103	F2
Bourne Way		
Kemsing Clo.,	94	J4
Th.Hth.		
Kemsing Rd. SE10	69	G5
Ken Way, Wem.	47	C2
Kenbury St. SE5	76	J2
Kenchester Clo. SW8	67	E7
Kencot Way, Erith	71	F2
Kendal Ave. N18	33	A4
Kendal Ave. W3	56	A4
Kendal Ave., Bark.	61	H7
Kendal Clo. SW9	**20**	**G7**
Kendal Clo. SW9	67	H7

Kendal Clo., 34 F2
 Wdf.Grn.
Kendal Gdns. N18 33 A4
Kendal Gdns., Sutt. 100 F2
Kendal Par. N18 33 A4
 Great Cambridge Rd.
Kendal Rd. NW15 75 C5
 Upper Richmond Rd.
Kendal Rd. NW10 47 G4
Kendal St. W2 10 H4
Kendal St. W2 57 H6
Kendale Rd., Brom. 87 E5
Kendall Ave., Beck. 95 H2
Kendall Pl. W1 11 B2
Kendall Rd., Beck. 95 H2
Kendall Rd., Islw. 73 D2
Kender St. SE14 77 F1
Kendoa Rd. SW4 76 D4
Kendon Clo. E11 42 H5
 The Ave.
Kendra Hall Rd., 101 H7
 S.Croy.
Kendrey Gdns., 73 B6
 Twick.
Kendrick Ms. SW7 18 E1
Kendrick Pl. SW7 18 E2
Kendrick Pl. SW7 66 G4
Kenelm Clo., Har. 46 D3
Kenerne Dr., Barn. 23 B5
Kenilford Rd. SW12 76 B7
Kenilworth Ave. E17 42 A2
Kenilworth Ave. 84 D5
 SW19
Kenilworth Ave., 45 F4
 Har.
Kenilworth Clo., 22 C3
 Borwd.
Kenilworth Ct. SW15 75 A3
Kenilworth Cres., 25 B1
 Enf.
Kenilworth Dr., 22 C3
 Borwd.
Kenilworth Gdns. 79 E2
 SE18
Kenilworth Gdns., 52 J2
 Ilf.
Kenilworth Gdns., 27 C5
 Loug.
Kenilworth Gdns., 54 F3
 Sthl.
Kenilworth Gdns., 28 C5
 Wat.
Kenilworth Rd. E3 59 H2
Kenilworth Rd. NW6 47 C6
Kenilworth Rd. SE20 95 G1
Kenilworth Rd. W5 64 H1
Kenilworth Rd., 30 C3
 Edg.
Kenilworth Rd., 99 G5
 Epsom
Kenilworth Rd., Orp. 97 F6
Kenley Ave. NW9 38 E1
Kenley Clo., Bex. 80 G7
Kenley Clo., Chis. 97 H3
Kenley Gdns., 94 H4
 Th.Hth.
Kenley Rd. SW19 93 C2
Kenley Rd., Kings.T. 92 B2
Kenley Rd., Twick. 73 D6
Kenley Wk. W11 57 B7
 Princedale Rd.
Kenley Wk., Sutt. 100 A4
Kenlor Rd. SW17 84 G5
Kenmare Dr., Mitch. 84 J7
Kenmare Gdns. N13 32 J4
Kenmare Rd., 94 G6
 Th.Hth.
Kenmere Gdns., 56 A1
 Wem.
Kenmere Rd., Well. 80 C2
Kenmont Gdns. 56 H3
 NW10
Kenmore Ave., Har. 37 D4
Kenmore Clo., Rich. 65 A7
 Kent Rd.
Kenmore Gdns., Edg. 38 B2
Kenmore Rd., Har. 37 G3
Kenmure Rd. E8 50 E5
Kennard Rd. E15 51 D7
Kennard Rd. N11 31 J5
Kennard St. E16 70 C1
Kennard St. SW11 76 A1
Kennedy Ave., Enf. 25 F4
Kennedy Clo. E13 60 G2
Kennedy Clo., Orp. 104 G1
Kennedy Path W7 55 C4
 Harp Rd.
Kennedy Rd. W7 55 B5
Kennedy Rd., Bark. 61 H1
Kennet Clo. SW11 75 G4
 Maysoule Rd.
Kennet Rd. W9 57 C4
Kennet Rd., Islw. 73 C3

Kennet Sq., Mitch. 93 H1
Kennet St. E1 17 J1
Kennet St. E1 68 D1
Kennet Wf. La. EC4 13 A5
Kenneth Ave., Ilf. 52 E4
Kenneth Cres. NW2 47 H5
Kenneth Gdns., 29 D6
 Stan.
Kenneth More Rd., 52 E3
 Ilf.
 Oakfield Rd.
Kenneth Rd., Rom. 44 D7
Kenneth Robbins Ho. 33 E7
 N17
Kennett Dr., Hayes 54 E5
Kenning St. SE16 68 F2
 Railway Ave.
Kenning Ter. N1 59 B1
Kenninghall Rd. E5 50 D3
Kenninghall Rd. N18 33 F5
Kennings Way SE11 20 G3
Kennings Way SE11 67 G5
Kennington Grn. 20 E4
 SE11
Kennington Gro. 20 D5
 SE11
Kennington La. SE11 20 C4
Kennington La. SE11 67 E5
Kennington Oval 20 D5
 SE11
Kennington Oval 67 F6
 SE11
Kennington Pk. Est. 20 E6
 SE11
Kennington Pk. 20 G5
 Gdns. SE11
Kennington Pk. Pl. 20 F5
 SE11
Kennington Pk. Pl. 67 G6
 SE11
Kennington Pk. Rd. 20 F5
 SE11
Kennington Pk. Rd. 67 G6
 SE11
Kennington Rd. SE1 16 E5
Kennington Rd. SE1 67 G3
Kennington Rd. SE11 20 E1
Kennington Rd. SE11 67 G3
Kenny Rd. NW7 31 B5
Kenrick Pl. W1 11 B2
Kensal Rd. W10 57 A4
Kensington Ave. E12 52 B6
Kensington Ave., 94 G1
 Th.Hth.
Kensington Ch. Ct. 14 A4
 W8
Kensington Ch. Ct. 66 E2
 W8
Kensington Ch. St. 66 D1
 W8
Kensington Ch. St. 66 D1
 W8
Kensington Ch. Wk. 14 A3
 W8
Kensington Ch. Wk. 66 E2
 W8
Kensington Ct. W8 14 B4
Kensington Ct. W8 66 E2
Kensington Ct. Ms. 14 B4
 W8
Kensington Ct. Pl. 14 B5
 W8
Kensington Ct. Pl. 66 E3
 W8
Kensington Dr., 43 A2
 Wdf.Grn.
Kensington Gdns., 52 C1
 Ilf.
Kensington Gdns. 10 A4
 Sq. W2
Kensington Gdns. 57 E6
 Sq. W2
Kensington Gate W8 14 C5
Kensington Gate W8 66 F3
Kensington Gore 14 E4
 SW7
Kensington Gore 66 F2
 SW7
Kensington Hall 66 C5
 Gdns. W14
 Beaumont Ave.
Kensington High St. 66 D3
 W8
Kensington High St. 66 C3
 W14
Kensington Mall W8 66 D1
Kensington Palace 14 A1
 Gdns. W8
Kensington Palace 66 E1
 Gdns. W8
Kensington Pk. 57 C7
 Gdns. W11
Kensington Pk. Ms. 57 C6
 W11
 Kensington Pk. Rd.

Kensington Pk. Rd. 57 C6
 W11
Kensington Pl. W8 66 D1
Kensington Rd. SW7 14 C4
Kensington Rd. SW7 66 F2
Kensington Rd. W8 14 B4
Kensington Rd. W8 66 E1
Kensington Rd., 54 G3
 Nthlt.
Kensington Rd., 44 J6
 Rom.
Kensington Sq. W8 14 A4
Kensington Sq. W8 66 E2
Kensington Ter., 102 A7
 S.Croy.
 Sanderstead Rd.
Kent Ave. W13 55 E5
Kent Ave., Dag. 62 G4
Kent Ave., Well. 79 J5
Kent Clo., Mitch. 94 E4
Kent Clo., Orp. 104 H6
Kent Dr., Barn. 24 A4
Kent Dr., Tedd. 82 B5
Kent Gdns. W13 55 E5
Kent Gate Way, 102 J6
 Croy.
Kent Ho. La., Beck. 86 H5
Kent Ho. Rd. SE26 86 H5
Kent Ho. Rd., Beck. 86 G7
Kent Pas. NW1 6 A5
Kent Rd. N21 33 A1
Kent Rd. W4 65 C3
Kent Rd., Dag. 53 H5
Kent Rd., E.Mol. 90 J4
Kent Rd., Kings.T. 91 G3
Kent Rd., Rich. 65 A7
Kent Rd., W.Wick. 103 B1
Kent St. E2 9 G1
Kent St. E2 59 C2
Kent St. E13 60 H3
Kent Ter. NW1 6 H4
Kent Ter. NW1 57 H3
Kent Twrs. SE20 86 E7
Kent Vw. Gdns., 52 H2
 Ilf.
Kent Wk. SW9 76 H4
 Moorland Rd.
Kent Way SE15 77 C1
 Sumner Est.
Kent Way, Surb. 98 H3
Kent Yd. SW7 14 H4
Kentford Way, 54 E1
 Nthlt.
Kentish Bldgs. SE1 17 B3
Kentish Rd., Belv. 71 G4
Kentish Town Rd. 49 B7
 NW1
Kentish Town Rd. 49 B6
 NW5
Kentish Way, Brom. 96 G2
Kentmere Rd. SE18 70 H4
Kenton Ave., Har. 37 C7
Kenton Ave., Sthl. 54 G7
Kenton Ave., Sun. 90 D2
Kenton Gdns., Har. 37 F5
Kenton La., Har. 29 C6
Kenton Pk. Ave., 37 G4
 Har.
Kenton Pk. Clo., Har. 37 F4
Kenton Pk. Cres., 37 G4
 Har.
Kenton Pk. Rd., Har. 37 F4
Kenton Rd. E9 50 G6
Kenton Rd., Har. 37 C7
Kenton St. WC1 8 A5
Kenton St. WC1 58 E4
Kents Pas., Hmptn. 90 F1
Kentwoode Grn. SW13 65 G7
Kenver Ave. N12 31 G6
Kenward Rd. SE9 78 F5
Kenway, Rom. 44 J2
Kenway Rd. SW5 18 A2
Kenway Rd. SW5 66 E4
Kenwood Ave. N14 24 D5
Kenwood Ave. SE14 77 G1
 Besson St.
Kenwood Clo. NW3 48 G1
Kenwood Dr., Beck. 96 C3
Kenwood Gdns. E18 42 H3
Kenwood Gdns., Ilf. 53 E4
Kenwood Rd. N6 39 J6
Kenwood Rd. N9 33 D1
Kenworthy Rd. E9 50 H5
Kenwyn Dr. NW2 47 E3
Kenwyn Rd. SW4 76 D4
Kenwyn Rd. SW20 92 J1
Kenya Rd. SE7 70 A7
Kenyngton Dr., Sun. 81 A5
Kenyngton Pl., Har. 37 F5
Kenyon St. SW6 75 A1
Keogh Rd. E15 51 E6
Kepler Rd. SW4 76 E4

Keppel Rd. E6 52 C7
Keppel Rd., Dag. 53 E4
Keppel Row SE1 16 J2
Keppel St. WC1 11 J1
Keppel St. WC1 58 D5
Kerbela St. E2 9 H5
Kerbey St. E14 60 B6
Kerfield Cres. SE5 77 A1
 Grove La.
Kerfield Pl. SE5 77 A1
Kerri Clo., Barn. 22 J4
Kerridge Ct. N1 50 B6
 Kingsbury Rd.
Kerrison Pl. W5 64 G1
Kerrison Rd. E15 60 D1
Kerrison Rd. SW11 75 H3
Kerrison Rd. W5 64 G1
Kerry Ave., Stan. 29 G4
Kerry Clo. E16 60 H6
Kerry Ct., Stan. 29 G4
Kerry Path SE14 68 J2
 Edward St.
Kersey Gdns. SE9 88 B4
Kersfield Rd. SW15 75 A6
Kershaw Clo. SW18 75 G6
 Westover Rd.
Kershaw Rd., Dag. 53 G3
Kersley Ms. SW11 75 J2
Kersley Rd. N16 50 B2
Kersley St. SW11 75 J2
Kerswell Clo. N15 41 B5
Kerwick Clo. N7 49 F7
 Sutterton St.
Keslake Rd. NW6 57 A2
Kessock Clo. N17 41 E5
Kesteven Clo., Ilf. 35 J6
Keston Ave., Kes. 103 J5
Keston Clo. N18 33 A3
Keston Clo., Well. 71 C7
Keston Gdns., Kes. 103 J4
Keston Pk. Clo., 104 C3
 Kes.
Keston Rd. N17 41 A3
Keston Rd. SE15 77 D3
Keston Rd., Th.Hth. 94 F6
Kestrel Ave. E6 61 B5
 Swan App.
Kestrel Ave. SE24 76 H5
Kestrel Clo. NW9 38 E2
Kestrel Clo. NW10 47 D5
Kestrel Ho. EC1 8 J3
Kestrel Ho. W13 55 C4
Keswick Ave. SW15 83 E5
Keswick Ave. SW19 93 D2
Keswick Clo., Sutt. 100 F4
Keswick Gdns., Ilf. 43 B5
Keswick Gdns., Wem. 46 H4
Keswick Ms. W5 64 H1
Keswick Rd. SW15 75 B5
Keswick Rd., Bexh. 80 G2
Keswick Rd., Orp. 104 J1
Keswick Rd., Twick. 72 J6
Keswick Rd., 103 E2
 W.Wick.
Kett Gdns. SW2 76 F5
Kettering St. SW16 85 C6
Kettlebaston Rd. 50 J1
 E10
Kevan Ho. SE5 67 J7
 Wyndham Rd.
Kevelioc Rd. N17 40 J1
Kevin Clo., Houns. 72 C2
Kevington Clo., 97 J4
 Orp.
Kevington Dr., Chis. 97 H4
Kew Bri., Brent. 64 J6
Kew Bri., Rich. 64 J6
Kew Bri. Ct. W4 65 A5
Kew Bri. Rd., Brent. 64 J6
Kew Cres., Sutt. 100 B3
Kew Foot Rd., Rich. 73 H4
Kew Gdns. Rd., Rich. 64 J7
Kew Grn., Rich. 64 J6
Kew Meadows Path, 74 B1
 Rich.
Kew Palace, Rich. 64 H7
Kew Rd., Rich. 73 H4
Keybridge Ho. SW8 20 B6
Keybridge Ho. SW8 67 E6
Keyes Rd. NW2 48 A5
Keymer Rd. SW2 85 F2
Keynes Clo. N2 39 J4
Keynsham Ave., 34 E4
 Wdf.Grn.
Keynsham Gdns. SE9 79 B5
Keynsham Rd. SE9 79 A5
Keynsham Rd., 100 E1
 Mord.
Keynsham Wk., 100 E1
 Mord.
 Hunston Rd.
Keyse Rd. SE1 17 F6

Keysham Ave., 72 A1
Houns.
The Ave.
Keystone Cres. N1 8 B2
Keywood Dr., Sun. 81 A6
Keyworth Pl. SE1 16 H5
Keyworth St. SE1 16 H5
Keyworth St. SE1 67 H3
Kezia St. SE8 68 H5
Trundleys Rd.
Khama Rd. SW17 84 H4
Khartoum Rd. E13 60 H3
Khartoum Rd. SW17 84 G4
Khartoum Rd., Ilf. 52 E5
Khyber Rd. SW11 75 H2
Kibworth St. SW8 67 F7
Kidbrooke Gdns. SE3 78 G2
Kidbrooke Gro. SE3 78 G1
Kidbrooke La. SE9 79 B4
Kidbrooke Pk. Clo. SE3 78 H1
Kidbrooke Pk. Rd. SE3 78 H1
Kidbrooke Way SE3 78 H2
Kidd Pl. SE7 70 B5
Kidderminster Pl., Croy. 101 H1
Kidderminster Rd.
Kidderminster Rd., Croy. 101 H1
Kidderpore Ave. NW3 48 D4
Kidderpore Gdns. NW3 48 D4
Kidlington Way NW9 38 E2
Kidron Way E9 59 F1
Clermont Rd.
Kielder Clo., Ilf. 35 J6
Kiffen St. EC2 9 C5
Kilberry Clo., Islw. 73 A1
Kilburn Bldgs. NW6 57 E1
Kilburn High Rd.
Kilburn Gate NW6 6 A1
Kilburn High Rd. NW6 48 C7
Kilburn La. W9 57 A3
Kilburn La. W10 57 A3
Kilburn Pk. Rd. NW6 57 D3
Kilburn Pl. NW6 57 D1
Kilburn Priory NW6 57 E1
Kilburn Sq. NW6 57 D1
Kilburn High Rd.
Kilburn Vale NW6 57 E1
Belsize Rd.
Kildare Clo., Ruis. 45 C1
Kildare Gdns. W2 57 D6
Kildare Rd. E16 60 G5
Kildare Ter. W2 57 D6
Kildare Wk. E14 60 A6
Farrance St.
Kildoran Rd. SW2 76 E5
Kildowan Rd., Ilf. 53 A1
Kilgour Rd. SE23 77 H6
Kilkie St. SW6 75 F2
Killarney Rd. SW18 75 F6
Killearn Rd. SE6 87 D1
Killester Gdns., Wor.Pk. 99 H4
Killick St. N1 8 C1
Killick St. N1 58 F2
Killieser Ave. SW2 85 E1
Killip Clo. E16 60 F6
Killowen Ave., Nthlt. 45 J5
Killowen Rd. E9 50 G6
Killyon Rd. SW8 76 C2
Killyon Ter. SW8 76 C2
Killyon Rd.
Kilmaine Rd. SW6 66 B7
Kilmarnock Gdns., Dag. 53 C3
Lindsey Rd.
Kilmarnock Rd., Wat. 28 D4
Kilmarsh Rd. W6 65 J4
Kilmartin Ave. SW16 94 F3
Kilmartin Rd., Ilf. 53 A2
Kilmeston Way SE15 21 G7
Kilmington Rd. SW13 65 G6
Kilmorey Gdns., Twick. 73 E4
Kilmorey Rd., Twick. 73 E4
Kilmorie Rd. SE23 86 H1
Kiln Pl. NW5 49 A4
Kilner St. E14 60 A5
Kilnside, Esher 98 D7
Kilpatrick Way, Hayes 54 E5
Kilravock St. W10 57 B3
Kilsby Wk., Dag. 53 B6
Rugby Rd.
Kilsha Rd., Walt. 90 B6

Kimbell Gdns. SW6 75 B1
Kimber Rd. SW18 75 D7
Kimberley Ave. E6 61 B2
Kimberley Ave. SE15 77 E2
Kimberley Ave., Ilf. 43 G7
Kimberley Ave., Rom. 44 J6
Kimberley Dr., Sid. 89 D2
Kimberley Gdns. N4 40 H5
Kimberley Gdns., Enf. 25 C3
Kimberley Rd. E4 34 E1
Kimberley Rd. E11 51 D2
Kimberley Rd. E16 60 F4
Kimberley Rd. E17 41 J1
Kimberley Rd. N17 41 D5
Kimberley Rd. N18 33 E6
Kimberley Rd. NW6 57 B1
Kimberley Rd. SW9 76 H2
Kimberley Rd., Beck. 95 G2
Kimberley Rd., Croy. 94 H6
Kimberley Way E4 34 E1
Kimble Rd. SW19 84 G6
Kimbolton Clo. SE12 78 F6
Kimbolton Grn., Borwd. 22 C4
Kimbolton Row SW3 18 G2
Kimmeridge Gdns. SE9 88 B4
Kimmeridge Rd. SE9 88 B4
Kimpton Ind. Est., Sutt. 100 C2
Kimpton Rd. SE5 77 A1
Kimpton Rd., Sutt. 100 C3
Kinburn St. SE16 68 G2
Kincaid Rd. SE15 68 E7
Kincardine Gdns. W9 57 C4
Harrow Rd.
Kinch Gro., Har. 37 J7
Kinder Clo. SE28 62 D7
Kinder St. E1 59 E6
Cannon St. Rd.
Kinfauns Rd. SW2 85 G2
Kinfauns Rd., Ilf. 53 A1
King Alfred Ave. SE6 87 A4
King & Queen St. SE17 21 A3
King & Queen St. SE17 67 J5
King Arthur Clo. SE15 68 F7
King Charles Cres., Surb. 91 J7
King Charles Rd., Surb. 91 J5
King Charles St. SW1 16 A3
King Charles St. SW1 67 D2
King Charles Wk. SW19 84 B1
Princes Way
King David La. E1 59 F7
King Edward Dr., Chess. 98 H3
Kelvin Gro.
King Edward Ms. SW13 74 G1
King Edward Rd. E10 51 C1
King Edward Rd. E17 41 H3
King Edward Rd., Barn. 23 D4
King Edward St. EC1 12 J3
King Edward St. EC1 58 J6
King Edward Wk. SE1 16 F5
King Edward Wk. SE1 67 G3
King Edwards Gdns. W3 65 A1
King Edwards Gro., Tedd. 82 E6
King Edwards Rd. E9 59 E1
King Edwards Rd. N9 25 E7
King Edwards Rd., Bark. 61 G1
King Edward's Rd., Enf. 25 G4
King Gdns., Croy. 101 H5
King George Ave. E16 61 A6
King George Ave., Ilf. 43 G5
King George Clo., Rom. 44 J3
King George VI Ave., Mitch. 93 J4
King George Sq., Rich. 73 J6

King George St. SE10 69 C7
King Georges Dr., Sthl. 54 F5
King Harolds Way, Bexh. 71 D7
King Henry Ms., Orp. 104 J5
Osgood Ave.
King Henry St. N16 50 B5
King Henry's Rd. NW3 48 H7
King Henrys Rd., Kings.T. 92 B3
King Henry's Wk. N1 50 B6
King James St. SE1 16 H4
King James St. SE1 67 H2
King John Ct. EC2 9 E5
King John St. E1 59 G5
King John's Wk. SE9 88 A1
King Sq. EC1 8 J4
King Stairs Clo. SE16 68 E2
Elephant La.
King St. E13 60 G4
King St. EC2 13 A4
King St. EC2 58 J6
King St. N2 39 G3
King St. SW1 15 G2
King St. SW1 67 C1
King St. W3 65 B1
King St. W6 65 G4
King St. WC2 13 A5
King St. WC2 58 E7
King St., Rich. 73 G5
King St., Sthl. 63 E3
King St., Twick. 82 D1
King William IV Gdns. SE20 86 F6
St. Johns Rd.
King William La. SE10 69 E5
Orlop St.
King William St. EC4 13 C6
King William St. EC4 59 A7
King William St. SW12 69 C6
King William Wk. SE10
Kingcup Clo., Croy. 102 G1
Primrose La.
Kingdon Rd. NW6 48 D6
Kingfield Rd. W5 55 G4
Kingfield St. E14 69 C4
Kingfisher Clo. SE28 62 C7
Kingfisher Ct. SW19 84 B2
Queensmere Rd.
Kingfisher Dr., Rich. 82 E4
Kingfisher Rd. E6 61 B5
Kingfisher Way NW10 47 D6
Kingham Clo. SW18 75 F7
Kingham Clo. W11 66 B2
Kinghorn St. EC1 12 J2
Kinglake Est. SE17 21 E3
Kinglake St. SE17 21 D4
Kinglake St. SE17 68 B5
Kingly Ct. W1 11 G5
Kingly St. W1 11 F5
Kingly St. W1 58 C7
Kings Arbour, Sthl. 63 E5
Ringway
Kings Arms Ct. E1 13 H2
Kings Arms Yd. EC2 13 B3
Kings Ave. N10 40 A3
Kings Ave. N21 32 H1
King's Ave. SW4 76 E5
King's Ave. SW12 85 D1
Kings Ave. W5 55 G6
Kings Ave., Brom. 87 F6
Kings Ave., Buck.H. 35 A2
Kings Ave., Cars. 100 H7
Kings Ave., Grnf. 54 H6
Kings Ave., Houns. 72 H1
Kings Ave., N.Mal. 92 E4
Kings Ave., Rom. 44 F6
Kings Ave., Wdf.Grn.
Kings Bench St. SE1 16 H3
Kings Bench Wk. EC4 12 F4
Kings Chase, E.Mol. 90 J3
Kings Clo. E10 42 B7
Kings Clo. NW4 39 A4
Kings College Rd. NW3 48 H7
Kings Ct. E13 60 H1
Kings Ct. W6 65 G4
King St.
Kings Ct., Wem. 47 B2
Kings Cres. N4 49 J3
Kings Cres. Est. N4 49 J2
King's Cross Rd. WC1 8 C3

King's Cross Rd. WC1 58 F3
Kings Dr., Edg. 29 J4
Kings Dr., Surb. 92 A7
Kings Dr., Tedd. 82 A5
Kings Dr., T.Ditt. 91 E6
Kings Dr., Wem. 47 B2
Kings Fm. Ave., Rich. 74 A4
Kings Gdns. NW6 48 D7
West End La.
Kings Gdns., Ilf. 52 G1
King's Garth Ms. SE23 86 F2
London Rd.
Kings Grn., Loug. 27 B3
Kings Gro. SE15 77 E1
Kings Hall Rd., Beck. 86 H7
Kings Head Hill E4 26 B7
Kings Head Yd. SE1 17 B2
Kings Highway SE18 70 H6
Kings Hill, Loug. 27 B2
Kings Keep, Kings.T. 91 H4
Beaufort Rd.
Kings La., Sutt. 100 G6
Kings Mead Pk., Esher 98 B7
Kings Ms. SW4 76 E5
King's Ave.
King's Ms. WC1 8 D6
King's Ms. WC1 60 F1
Kings Ms., Chig. 35 F2
Kings Orchard SE9 79 B6
Kings Paddock, Hmptn. 90 J1
King's Pas. E11 42 E7
Kings Pas., Kings.T. 91 G2
Kings Pl. SE1 16 J4
Kings Pl. W4 65 C4
Chiswick High Rd.
Kings Pl., Buck.H. 35 A2
King's Reach Twr. SE1 16 F1
Kings Ride Gate, Rich. 74 A4
Kings Rd. E4 34 D1
Kings Rd. E6 60 J1
Kings Rd. E11 42 E7
Kings Rd. N17 41 C1
Kings Rd. N18 33 D5
Kings Rd. N22 40 F1
Kings Rd. NW10 47 F7
Kings Rd. SE25 95 D3
King's Rd. SW1 19 C1
King's Rd. SW1 67 A4
King's Rd. SW3 18 F5
King's Rd. SW3 66 E4
King's Rd. SW6 66 E7
King's Rd. SW10 66 E7
Kings Rd. SW14 74 D3
Kings Rd. SW19 84 D6
Kings Rd. W5 55 G5
Kings Rd., Bark. 52 F7
North St.
Kings Rd., Barn. 22 J3
Kings Rd., Felt. 81 C1
Kings Rd., Har. 85 F7
Kings Rd., Kings.T. 82 H7
Kings Rd., Mitch. 94 A3
Kings Rd., Orp. 104 J4
Kings Rd., Rich. 73 J6
Kings Rd., Surb. 98 F1
Kings Rd., Tedd. 82 A5
Kings Rd., Twick. 73 E6
King's Scholars' Pas. SW1 15 F6
Kings Ter. NW1 58 C1
Plender St.
Kings Wk., Kings.T. 91 G1
Kings Way, Har. 37 B4
Kingsand Rd. SE12 87 G2
Kingsash Dr., Hayes 54 F5
Kingsbridge Ave. W3 64 J2
Kingsbridge Cres., Sthl. 54 F5
Kingsbridge Rd. W10 56 J4
Kingsbridge Rd., Bark. 61 G2
Kingsbridge Rd., Mord. 93 A7
Kingsbridge Rd., Sthl. 63 F4
Kingsbridge Rd., Walt. 90 B7
Kingsbury Circ. NW9 38 A5
Kingsbury Rd. N1 50 B6
Kingsbury Rd. NW9 38 A5
Kingsbury Ter. N1 50 B6
Kingsbury Trd. Est. NW9 38 D6

Kingsclere Clo. SW15 74 G7
Kingscliffe Gdns. SW19 84 C1
Kingscote Rd. W4 65 D3
Kingscote Rd., Croy. 95 E7
Kingscote Rd., N.Mal. 92 D3
Kingscote St. EC4 12 G5
Kingscourt Rd. SW16 85 D3
Kingscroft Rd. NW2 48 C6
Kingsdale Gdns. W11 66 A1
Kingsdale Rd. SE18 70 J6
Kingsdale Rd. SE20 86 G7
Kingsdown Ave. W3 56 E7
Kingsdown Ave. W13 64 E2
Kingsdown Clo. W10 57 H4
Kingsdown Rd. E11 51 E3
Kingsdown Rd. N19 49 E3
Kingsdown Rd., Sutt. 100 B5
Kingsdown Way, Brom. 96 G7
Kingsdowne Rd., Surb. 91 H7
Kingsfield Ave., Har. 36 H4
Kingsfield Ho. SE9 88 A3
Kingsfield Rd., Har. 37 A7
Kingsford Ave., Wall. 101 E7
Kingsford St. NW5 48 J5
Kingsgate, Wem. 47 C3
Kingsgate Ave. N3 39 D3
Kingsgate Clo. Bexh. 80 E1
Kingsgate Pl. NW6 48 D7
Kingsgate Rd. NW6 48 D7
Kingsgate Rd., Kings.T. 91 H1
Kingsground SE9 79 B7
Kingshill Ave., Har. 37 E4
Kingshill Ave., Nthlt. 54 A3
Kingshill Ave., Wor.Pk. 92 G7
Kingshill Dr., Har. 37 E2
Kingshold Rd. E9 50 F7
Kingsholm Gdns. SE9 79 A4
Kingshurst Rd. SE12 78 G7
Kingsland NW8 57 H1
Broxwood Way
Kingsland Grn. E8 50 B6
Kingsland High St. E8 50 C6
Kingsland Pas. E8 50 B6
Kingsland Grn.
Kingsland Rd. E2 9 E3
Kingsland Rd. E2 59 B3
Kingsland Rd. E8 59 B1
Kingsland Rd. E13 60 J3
Kingslawn Clo. SW15 74 H5
Howards La.
Kingsleigh Pl., Mitch. 93 J3
Whitford Gdns.
Kingsleigh Wk., Brom. 96 F4
Stamford Dr.
Kingsley Ave. W13 55 D6
Kingsley Ave., Houns. 72 J2
Kingsley Ave., Sthl. 54 G7
Kingsley Ave., Sutt. 100 G4
Kingsley Clo. N2 39 F5
Kingsley Clo., Dag. 53 H4
Kingsley Ct., Edg. 30 B2
Kingsley Dr., Wor.Pk. 99 F2
Badgers Copse
Kingsley Gdns. E4 34 A5
Kingsley Ms. W8 14 B6
Kingsley Pl. N6 40 A7
Kingsley Rd. E7 51 G7
Kingsley Rd. E17 42 C2
Kingsley Rd. N13 32 G4
Kingsley Rd. NW6 57 C1
Kingsley Rd. SW19 84 E5
Kingsley Rd., Croy. 101 G1
Kingsley Rd., Har. 45 J4
Kingsley Rd., Houns. 72 H1
Kingsley Rd., Ilf. 43 F1
Kingsley Rd., Loug. 27 G3
Kingsley Rd., Orp. 104 F4
Kingsley Rd., Pnr. 36 F4
Kingsley St. SW11 75 J3
Kingsley Way N2 39 F5

Kingsley Wd. Dr. SE9 88 C3
Kingslyn Cres. SE19 95 B1
Kingsman Par. SE18 70 C3
Woolwich Ch. St.
Kingsman St. SE18 70 C3
Kingsmead, Barn. 23 D4
Kingsmead, Rich. 73 J6
Kingsmead Ave. N9 33 E1
Kingsmead Ave. NW9 38 D7
Kingsmead Ave., Mitch. 94 C3
Kingsmead Ave., Sun. 90 C2
Kingsmead Ave., Surb. 99 A2
Kingsmead Ave., Wor.Pk. 99 H2
Kingsmead Clo., Epsom 99 D7
Kingsmead Clo. Sid. 89 A2
Kingsmead Clo. Tedd. 82 E6
Kingsmead Dr., Nthlt. 45 F7
Kingsmead Rd. SW2 85 G2
Kingsmead Way E9 50 H4
Kingsmere Clo. SW15 75 B3
Weimar St.
Kingsmere Pk. NW9 47 B1
Kingsmere Rd. SW19 84 A2
Kingsmill Gdns. Dag. 53 F5
Kingsmill Rd., Dag. 53 F5
Kingsmill Ter. NW8 6 F1
Kingsmill Ter. NW8 57 G2
Kingsnympton Pk., Kings.T. 83 B7
Kingspark Ct. E18 42 G3
Kingsridge SW19 84 B2
Kingsthorpe Rd. SE26 86 G4
Kingston Ave., Sutt. 100 B3
Kingston Bri., Kings.T. 91 G2
Kingston Bypass SW15 83 E4
Kingston Bypass SW20 83 E6
Kingston Bypass, Esher 98 B2
Kingston Bypass, N.Mal. 92 G4
Kingston Bypass, Surb. 98 E3
Kingston Clo., Nthlt. 45 F7
Kingston Clo., Rom. 44 E3
Kingston Clo., Tedd. 82 E6
Kingston Ct. N4 40 J6
Wiltshire Gdns.
Kingston Cres., Beck. 95 J1
Kingston Gdns., Croy. 101 E3
Wandle Rd.
Kingston Hall Rd., Kings.T. 91 G3
Kingston Hill, Kings.T. 92 A1
Kingston Hill Ave., Rom. 44 E3
Kingston La., Tedd. 82 D5
Kingston Pk. Est., Kings.T. 83 B6
Kingston Pl., Har. 29 C7
Richmond Gdns.
Kingston Rd. N9 33 D2
Kingston Rd. SW15 83 G2
Kingston Rd. SW19 93 B2
Kingston Rd. SW20 92 J2
Kingston Rd., Barn. 23 G5
Kingston Rd., Epsom 99 E4
Kingston Rd., Ilf. 52 E4
Kingston Rd., Kings.T. 92 B3
Kingston Rd., N.Mal. 92 D4
Kingston Rd., Sthl. 63 F2
Kingston Rd., Surb. 99 B2
Kingston Rd., Tedd. 82 E5
Kingston Rd., Wor.Pk. 99 C3
Kingston Sq. SE19 86 A5
Kingston Vale SW15 83 D4
Kingston St. NW1 58 A1
Kingswater Pl. SW11 16 H7
Battersea Ch. Rd.
Kingsway N12 31 F6
Kingsway SW14 74 B3
Kingsway WC2 12 C3

Kingsway WC2 58 F6
Kingsway, Croy. 101 F5
Kingsway, Enf. 25 E5
Kingsway, N.Mal. 92 J4
Kingsway, W.Wick. 103 E3
Kingsway, Wdf.Grn. 34 J5
Kingsway Business Pk., Hmptn. 90 F1
Kingsway Cres., Har. 36 J4
Kingsway Ind. Est. N18 33 G6
Kingsway Rd., Sutt. 100 B6
Kingswear Rd. NW5 49 B3
Kingswear Rd., Ruis. 45 A2
Kingswood Ave. NW6 57 B1
Kingswood Ave., Belv. 71 F4
Kingswood Ave., Brom. 96 E3
Kingswood Ave., Hmptn. 81 H6
Kingswood Ave., Houns. 72 F1
Kingswood Ave., Th.Hth. 94 G5
Kingswood Clo. N20 23 F7
Kingswood Clo. SW8 67 E7
Kenchester Clo.
Kingswood Clo., Enf. 25 B5
Kingswood Clo., N.Mal. 92 F6
Motspur Pk.
Kingswood Clo., Orp. 97 G7
Kingswood Clo., Surb. 91 H7
Kingswood Clo., Wey. 98 A7
Kingswood Dr. SE19 86 B4
Kingswood Dr., Cars. 100 J1
Kingswood Est. SE21 86 B4
Bowen Dr.
Kingswood Pk. N3 39 C2
Kingswood Pl. SE13 78 E4
Kingswood Rd. SE20 86 F6
Kingswood Rd. SW2 76 G6
Kingswood Rd. SW19 84 C7
Kingswood Rd. W4 65 C3
Kingswood Rd., Brom. 96 D4
Kingswood Rd., Ilf. 53 A1
Kingswood Way, Wall. 101 E5
Kingsworth Clo. Beck. 95 H5
Shirley Cres.
Kingsworthy Clo., Kings.T. 91 J3
Kingthorpe Rd. NW10 47 D7
Kingthorpe Ter. NW10 47 D6
Kingwood Rd. SW6 66 B7
Kinlet Rd. SE18 79 F1
Kinloch Dr. NW9 38 D7
Kinloch St. N7 49 F3
Hornsey Rd.
Kinloss Gdns. N3 39 C3
Kinloss Rd., Cars. 93 F7
Kinnaird Ave. W4 65 C7
Kinnaird Ave., Brom. 87 F6
Kinnaird Clo., Brom. 87 F6
Kinnaird Way, Wdf.Grn. 35 C6
Kinnear Rd. W12 65 F2
Kinnerton Pl. N. SW1 15 A4
Kinnerton Pl. S. SW1 15 A4
Kinnerton St. SW1 15 B4
Kinnerton St. SW1 67 A2
Kinnerton Yd. SW1 15 B4
Kinnoul Rd. W6 66 B6
Kinross Ave., Wor.Pk. 99 G2
Kinross Clo., Edg. 30 B2
Tayside Dr.
Kinross Clo., Har. 37 H5
Kinsale Rd. SE15 77 D3
Kintore Way SE1 21 E7
Kintyre Clo. SW16 94 F2
Kinveachy Gdns. SE7 70 B5
Kinver Rd. SE26 86 F4
Kipling Dr. SW19 84 G6

Kipling Est. SE1 17 C4
Kipling Est. SE1 68 A2
Kipling Pl., Stan. 29 C6
Uxbridge Rd.
Kipling Rd., Bexh. 80 E1
Kipling St. SE1 17 C4
Kipling St. SE1 68 A2
Kipling Ter. N9 33 A3
Kippington Dr. SE9 88 A1
Kirby Clo., Epsom 99 F5
Kirby Clo., Ilf. 35 H6
Kirby Clo., Loug. 27 B7
Kirby Est. SE16 68 E3
Kirby Gro. SE1 17 D3
Kirby Gro. SE1 68 B2
Kirby St. EC1 12 F1
Kirby Way, Walt. 90 C6
Kirchen Rd. W13 55 E7
Kirk La. SE18 70 F6
Kirk Ri., Sutt. 100 E3
Kirk Rd. E17 41 J3
Kirkcaldy Grn., Wat. 28 C3
Trevose Way
Kirkdale SE26 86 F4
Kirkdale Rd. E11 51 E1
Kirkham Rd. E6 61 B6
Kirkham St. SE18 70 H6
Kirkland Ave., Ilf. 43 D2
Kirkland Clo., Sid. 79 H6
Kirkland Wk. E8 50 C6
Laurel St.
Kirkleas Rd., Surb. 98 H1
Kirklees Rd., Dag. 53 C5
Kirklees Rd., Th.Hth. 94 G5
Kirkley Rd. SW19 93 D1
Kirkman Pl. W1 11 H2
Kirkmichael Rd. E14 60 C6
Dee St.
Kirks Pl. E14 59 J5
Rhodeswell Rd.
Kirkside Rd. SE3 69 G6
Kirkstall Ave. N17 41 A4
Kirkstall Gdns. SW2 85 D1
Kirkstall Rd. SW2 85 D1
Kirkstead Ct. E5 50 H3
Mandeville St.
Kirksted Rd., Mord. 100 E1
Kirkstone Way, Brom. 87 G6
Kirkton Rd. N15 41 B4
Kirkwall Pl. E2 59 F3
Kirkwood Rd. SE15 77 E2
Kirn Rd. W13 55 E7
Kirchen Rd.
Kirtley Rd. SE26 86 H4
Kirtling St. SW8 19 F7
Kirtling St. SW8 67 C7
Kirton Clo. W4 65 D4
Dolman Rd.
Kirton Gdns. E2 9 G4
Kirton Rd. E13 60 J2
Kirton Wk., Edg. 30 C7
Kirwyn Way SE5 20 H7
Kirwyn Way SE5 67 H7
Kitcat Ter. E3 60 A2
Kitchener Rd. E7 51 H6
Kitchener Rd. E17 42 B1
Kitchener Rd. N2 39 H3
Kitchener Rd. N17 41 A3
Kitchener Rd., Dag. 53 H6
Kitchener Rd., Th.Hth. 95 A3
Kitley Gdns. SE19 95 C1
Kitson Rd. SE5 21 A7
Kitson Rd. SE5 68 A7
Kitson Rd. SW13 74 G1
Kittiwake Rd., Nthlt. 54 D3
Kitto Rd. SE14 77 G2
Kiver Rd. N19 49 D2
Klea Ave. SW4 76 C6
Knapdale Clo. SE23 86 J2
Knapmill Rd. SE6 87 A2
Knapmill Way SE6 87 B2
Knapp Clo. NW10 47 E6
Knapp Rd. E3 60 A4
Knapton Ms. SW17 85 A6
Seely Rd.
Knaresborough Pl. SW5 18 A1
Knaresborough Pl. SW5 66 E4
Knatchbull Rd. NW10 56 J1
Knatchbull Rd. SE5 76 H2
Knebworth Ave. E17 42 A1
Knebworth Path, Borwd. 22 H2
Knebworth Rd. N16 50 B4
Nevill Rd.

Kneller Rd. SE4 77 H4
Kneller Rd., N.Mal. 92 E7
Kneller Rd., Twick. 72 J6
Knighten St. E1 17 J2
Knightland Rd. E5 50 E2
Knighton Clo., 101 H7
S.Croy.
Knighton Clo., 34 H4
Wdf.Grn.
Knighton Dr., 34 H4
Wdf.Grn.
Knighton La., 34 H2
Buck.H.
Knighton Pk. Rd. 86 G5
SE26
Knighton Rd. E7 51 G3
Knighton Rd., Rom. 44 J6
Knightrider Ct. EC4 58 J7
Knightrider St.
Knightrider St. EC4 12 H5
Knights Arc. SW1 14 J4
Knights Ave. W5 64 H2
Knights Clo. E9 50 F5
Churchill Wk.
Knights Ct., 91 H3
Kings.T.
Knights Ct., Rom. 44 E6
Knights Hill SE27 85 H5
Knights Hill Sq. SE27 85 H4
Knights Hill
Knights La. N9 33 D3
Knights Pk., 91 H3
Kings.T.
Knights Rd. E16 69 G2
Knights Rd., Stan. 29 F4
Knights Wk. SE11 20 G2
Knights Way, Ilf. 35 F6
Knightsbridge SW1 15 A3
Knightsbridge SW1 66 J2
Knightsbridge SW7 14 H4
Knightsbridge SW7 66 H2
Knightsbridge Grn. 14 J4
SW1
Knightsbridge Grn. 66 J2
SW1
Knightswood Clo., 30 C2
Edg.
Knightwood Cres., 92 E6
N.Mal.
Knivet Rd. SW6 66 D6
Knobs Hill Rd. E15 60 B1
Knockholt Rd. SE9 79 A5
Knole, The SE9 88 D4
Stockbury Rd.
Knole Clo., Croy. 95 F6
Knole Gate, Sid. 88 H3
Knoll Dr. N14 24 A7
Knoll Ri., Orp. 104 J1
Knoll Rd. SW18 75 F5
Knoll Rd., Bex. 80 G7
Knoll Rd., Sid. 89 B5
Knollmead, Surb. 99 C1
Knolls Clo., 99 H3
Wor.Pk.
Knollys Clo. SW16 85 G3
Knollys Rd. SW16 85 F3
Knottisford St. E2 59 F3
Knotts Grn. Rd. E10 42 B6
Knowle Ave., Bexh. 71 E7
Knowle Clo. SW9 76 G3
Knowle Rd., Brom. 104 B2
Knowle Rd., Twick. 82 B1
Knowles Hill Cres. 78 D5
SE13
Knowles Wk. SW4 76 C3
Knowlton Grn., 96 F5
Brom.
Knowsley Ave., Sthl. 48 H3
Knowsley Rd. SW11 75 J2
Knox Rd. E7 51 F6
Knox St. W1 10 J1
Knox St. W1 57 J5
Knoyle St. SE14 68 H6
Chubworthy St.
Kohat Rd. SW19 84 E5
Kossuth St. SE10 69 E5
Kotree Way SE1 21 J2
Kramer Ms. SW5 66 D5
Kempsford Gdns.
Kreisel Wk., Rich. 64 B3
Kuala Gdns. SW16 94 F1
Kuhn Way E7 50 H5
Brooking Rd.
Kydbrook Clo., Orp. 97 F7
Kylemore Clo. E6 61 A2
Parr Rd.
Kylemore Rd. NW6 48 D7
Kymberley Rd., Har. 37 B6

Kynance Gdns., 37 F1
Stan.
Kynance Ms. SW7 14 B6
Kynance Pl. SW7 14 C6
Kynance Pl. SW7 66 F3
Kynaston Ave. N16 50 C3
Dynevor Rd.
Kynaston Ave., 94 J5
Th.Hth.
Kynaston Clo., Har. 29 A7
Kynaston Cres., 94 J5
Th.Hth.
Kynaston Rd. N16 50 B3
Kynaston Rd., Brom. 87 G5
Kynaston Rd., Enf. 25 A1
Kynaston Rd., 94 J5
Th.Hth.
Kynaston Wd., Har. 29 A7
Kynnersley Clo., 100 J3
Cars.
William St.
Kynock Rd. N18 33 F4
Kyrle Rd. SW11 75 J6
Kyverdale Rd. N16 41 C7

L

La Tourne Gdns., 104 F3
Orp.
Laburnham Ct., Stan. 29 F4
Laburnum Ave. N9 33 B2
Laburnum Ave. N17 33 A7
Laburnum Ave. 100 H2
Sutt.
Laburnum Clo. E4 33 J4
Laburnum Clo. N11 32 A6
Laburnum Clo. SE15 68 F7
Clifton Way
Laburnum Clo. E2 59 C1
Laburnum St.
Laburnum Cres., 90 B1
Sun.
Batavia Rd.
Laburnum Gdns. N21 32 J2
Laburnum Gro.
Laburnum Gdns., 102 G1
Croy.
Primrose La.
Laburnum Gro. N21 32 J2
Laburnum Gro. NW9 38 C7
Laburnum Gro., 72 F4
Houns.
Laburnum Gro., 92 D2
N.Mal.
Laburnum Gro., 54 F4
Sthl.
Laburnum Ho., Dag. 53 G2
Laburnum Rd. SW19 84 F7
Laburnum Rd., 94 A2
Mitch.
Laburnum St. E2 59 C1
Laburnum Way, 97 D7
Brom.
Laceback Clo., Sid. 79 J7
Lacey Clo. N9 33 D2
Lacey Dr., Edg. 29 H4
Lacey Dr., Hmptn. 90 F1
Lacey Wk. E3 60 A2
Lackington St. EC2 13 C1
Lackington St. EC2 59 A5
Lacock Clo. SW19 84 A5
Lacon Rd. SE22 77 D4
Lacy Rd. SW15 75 A4
Ladas Rd. SE27 85 J4
Ladbroke Cres. W11 57 B6
Ladbroke Gro.
Ladbroke Gdns. W11 57 C7
Ladbroke Gro. W10 57 A4
Ladbroke Gro. W11 57 B6
Ladbroke Ms. W11 66 B1
Ladbroke Rd.
Ladbroke Rd. W11 66 C1
Ladbroke Rd., Enf. 25 C6
Ladbroke Sq. W11 57 C7
Ladbroke Ter. W11 57 C7
Ladbroke Wk. W11 66 C1
Ladbrook Clo., Pnr. 36 F5
Ladbrook Rd. SE25 95 A3
Ladbrooke Cres., 89 D3
Sid.
Ladderstile Ride, 83 C5
Kings.T.
Ladderswood Way 32 C5
N11
Lady Booth Rd., 91 J1
Kings.T.
Lady Hay, Wor.Pk. 99 F2
Lady Margaret Rd. 49 C4
N19
Lady Margaret Rd. 49 C5
NW5
Lady Margaret Rd., 54 F5
Sthl.

Lady Somerset Rd. 49 B4
NW5
Ladybower Ct. E5 50 H4
Gilpin Rd.
Ladycroft Gdns., 104 F5
Orp.
Ladycroft Rd. SE13 78 B3
Ladycroft Wk., 37 G1
Stan.
Ladycroft Way, Orp. 104 F5
Ladyfield Clo., 27 E4
Loug.
Ladyfields, Loug. 27 E4
Ladysmith Ave. E6 61 B2
Ladysmith Ave., Ilf. 43 G7
Ladysmith Rd. E16 60 F3
Ladysmith Rd. N17 41 D2
Ladysmith Rd. N18 33 E5
Ladysmith Rd. SE9 79 D6
Ladysmith Rd., Enf. 25 B3
Ladysmith Rd., Har. 37 B2
Ladywell Rd. SE13 78 B5
Plaistow Gro.
Ladywell Ave., Orp. 97 H5
Ladywood Rd., Surb. 99 A2
Lafone Ave., Felt. 81 C1
Alfred Rd.
Lafone St. SE1 17 F3
Lafone St. SE1 68 C2
Lagado Ms. SE16 68 G1
Lagonda Ave., Ilf. 35 J6
Laing Clo., Ilf. 25 C6
Laing Dean, Nthlt. 54 C1
Laings Ave., Mitch. 93 J2
Lainlock Pl., Houns. 72 H1
Spring Gro. Rd.
Lainson St. SW18 75 D7
Laird Ho. SE5 67 J7
Redcar St.
Lairdale Clo. SE21 85 J1
Lairs Clo. N7 49 E6
Manger Rd.
Laitwood Rd. SW12 85 B1
Lake, The (Bushey), 28 J1
Wat.
Lake Ave., Brom. 87 G6
Lake Dr. (Bushey), 28 J2
Wat.
Lake Gdns., Dag. 53 G5
Lake Gdns., Rich. 82 E2
Lake Gdns., Wall. 101 B3
Lake Ho. Rd. E11 51 G3
Lake Rd. SW19 84 C5
Lake Rd., Croy. 102 J2
Lake Rd., Rom. 44 D4
Lake Vw., Edg. 29 J5
Lakedale Rd. SE18 70 H5
Lakefield Rd. N22 40 H2
Lakehall Gdns., 94 H5
Th.Hth.
Lakehall Rd., 94 H5
Th.Hth.
Lakehurst Rd., 99 E5
Epsom
Lakeland Clo., Har. 29 A6
Lakenheath N14 24 C5
Laker Pl. SW15 75 B6
Lakes Rd., Kes. 103 J5
Lakeside N3 39 E2
Lakeside W13 55 F6
Edgehill Rd.
Lakeside, Beck. 96 B3
Lakeside, Enf. 24 D4
Lakeside, Wall. 101 B3
Derek Ave.
Lakeside Ave., Ilf. 43 A4
Lakeside Clo. SE25 95 D2
Lakeside Clo., Sid. 80 C5
Lakeside Ct. N4 49 H2
Lakeside Cres., 23 J5
Barn.
Lakeside Dr., Brom. 104 B3
Lakeside Rd. N13 32 F4
Lakeside Rd. W14 66 A3
Lakeside Way, Wem. 47 A4
Lakeswood Rd., Orp. 97 E5
Lakeview Ct. SW19 84 B2
Victoria Dr.
Lakeview Rd. SE27 85 G5
Lakeview Rd., Well. 80 B4
Lakis Clo. NW3 48 F4
Flask Wk.
Laleham Ave. NW7 30 D3
Laleham Rd. SE6 78 C7
Lalor St. SW6 75 B2
Lamb La. E8 50 E7
Lamb St. E1 13 F1
Lamb St. E1 59 C5
Lamb Wk. SE1 17 D4
Lambarde Ave. SE9 88 D4
Lamberhurst Rd. 85 G4
SE27

Lamberhurst Rd., 53 E1
Dag.
Lambert Ave., Rich. 74 A3
Lambert Rd. E16 60 H6
Lambert Rd. N12 31 F5
Lambert Rd. SW2 76 E5
Lambert St. N1 49 G7
Lambert Way N12 31 F5
Woodhouse Rd.
Lamberts Pl., Croy. 102 A1
Lamberts Rd., Surb. 91 H5
Lambeth Bri. SE1 20 B5
Lambeth Bri. SE1 67 E4
Lambeth Bri. SW1 20 B5
Lambeth Bri. SW1 67 E4
Lambeth High St. 20 C1
SE1
Lambeth High St. 67 F4
SE1
Lambeth Hill EC4 12 A5
Lambeth Hill EC4 58 J7
Lambeth Palace Rd. 16 C6
SE1
Lambeth Palace Rd. 67 F3
SE1
Lambeth Rd. SE1 16 E6
Lambeth Rd. SE1 67 F3
Lambeth Rd., Croy. 94 G7
Lambeth Wk. SE11 20 D1
Lambeth Wk. SE11 67 F4
Lamble St. NW5 49 A5
Lambley Rd., Dag. 53 B6
Lambolle Pl. NW3 48 H6
Lambolle Rd. NW3 48 H6
Lambourn Clo. W7 64 C2
Lambourn Rd. SW4 76 B3
Lambourne Ave. 84 C4
SW19
Lambourne Gdns. E4 34 A2
Lambourne Gdns., 52 J7
Bark.
Lambourne Rd.
Lambourne Gdns., 25 C2
Enf.
Lambourne Gro., 92 B2
Kings.T.
Kenley Rd.
Lambourne Pl. SE3 78 H1
Shooter's Hill Rd.
Lambourne Rd. E11 42 D7
Lambourne Rd., 52 H7
Bark.
Lambourne Rd., Ilf. 35 J4
Chig.
Lambourne Rd., Ilf. 52 H7
Lambrook Ter. SW6 75 B1
Lamb's Bldgs. EC1 9 B6
Lambs Conduit Pas. 12 C1
WC1
Lamb's Conduit St. 8 C6
WC1
Lamb's Conduit St. 58 F4
WC1
Lambs Meadow, 43 A2
Wdf.Grn.
Lambs Ms. N1 58 H1
Colebrooke Row
Lamb's Pas. EC1 13 B1
Lamb's Pas. EC1 59 A5
Lambs Ter. N9 33 A2
Lambs Wk., Enf. 24 J2
Lambscroft Ave. SE9 87 J3
Lambton Pl. W11 57 C9
Westbourne Gro.
Lambton Rd. N19 49 E1
Lambton Rd. SW20 92 J1
Lamerock Rd., Brom. 87 F4
Lamerton Rd., Ilf. 43 E2
Lamerton St. SE8 69 A6
Lamford Clo. N17 33 A7
Lamington St. W6 65 H4
Lamlash St. SE11 20 G1
Lammas Ave., Mitch. 94 A2
Lammas Grn. SE26 86 E3
Lammas Pk. Gdns. 64 F1
W5
Lammas Pk. Rd. W5 64 F1
Lammas Rd. E9 50 G7
Lammas Rd. E10 50 H2
Lea Bri. Rd.
Lammas Rd., Rich. 82 F4
Lammermoor Rd. 76 B7
SW12
Lamont Rd. SW10 18 D6
Lamont Rd. SW10 66 F6
Lamont Rd. Pas. 18 E6
SW10
Lamorbey Clo., Sid. 88 J1
Lamorna Gro., Stan. 37 G1
Lampard Gro. N16 50 C1
Lampern Sq. E2 9 J3
Lampeter Sq. W6 66 B6
Humbolt Rd.

..mplighter Clo. E1	59	F4
Cleveland Way		
Lampmead Rd. SE12	78	F5
Lamport Clo. SE18	70	C4
Lampton Ave.,	72	H1
Houns.		
Lampton Ho. Clo.	84	A4
SW19		
Lampton Pk. Rd.,	72	H2
Houns.		
Lampton Rd., Houns.	72	H2
Lanacre Ave. NW9	38	D1
Lanark Clo. W5	55	F5
Lanark Pl. W9	6	D5
Lanark Pl. W9	57	F4
Lanark Rd. W9	6	B2
Lanark Rd. W9	57	E2
Lanark Sq. E14	69	B3
Lanbury Rd. SE15	77	G4
Lancashire Ct. W1	11	E5
Lancaster Ave. E18	42	H4
Lancaster Ave. SE27	85	H2
Lancaster Ave. SW19	84	A5
Lancaster Ave.,	52	H7
Bark.		
Lancaster Ave.,	94	C5
Mitch.		
Lancaster Clo. N1	50	B7
Hertford Rd.		
Lancaster Clo. N17	33	D7
Park La.		
Lancaster Clo. SE27	85	H2
Lancaster Clo.,	96	F4
Brom.		
Lancaster Clo.,	82	G5
Kings.T.		
Lancaster Cotts.,Rich.	73	H6
Lancaster Pk.		
Lancaster Ct. SW6	66	C7
Lancaster Ct. W2	10	D6
Lancaster Ct.,	90	A7
Walt.		
Lancaster Dr. E14	69	C1
Prestons Rd.		
Lancaster Dr. NW3	48	H6
Lancaster Gdns.	84	B5
SW19		
Lancaster Gdns. W13	64	E2
Lancaster Gdns.,	82	G5
Kings.T.		
Lancaster Gate W2	10	D6
Lancaster Gate W2	57	F7
Lancaster Gro. NW3	48	G6
Lancaster Ms. W2	10	D5
Lancaster Ms. W2	57	F7
Lancaster Ms., Rich.	73	H6
Richmond Hill		
Lancaster Pk., Rich.	73	H5
Lancaster Pl. SW19	84	A5
Lancaster Rd.		
Lancaster Pl. WC2	12	C5
Lancaster Pl. WC2	58	F7
Lancaster Pl.,	72	C2
Houns.		
Lancaster Pl., Ilf.	52	F5
Staines Rd.		
Lancaster Pl.,	73	D6
Twick.		
Lancaster Rd. E7	51	G7
Lancaster Rd. E11	51	C3
Lancaster Rd. E17	41	G2
Lancaster Rd. N4	40	F7
Lancaster Rd. N11	32	D6
Lancaster Rd. N18	33	C5
Lancaster Rd. NW10	47	G5
Lancaster Rd. SE25	95	C2
Lancaster Rd. SW19	84	A5
Lancaster Rd. W11	57	B6
Lancaster Rd.,	23	G5
Barn.		
Lancaster Rd., Enf.	25	A1
Lancaster Rd., Har.	36	G5
Lancaster Rd., Nthlt.	45	J4
Lancaster Rd., Sthl.	54	E7
Lancaster St. SE1	16	H4
Lancaster St. SE1	67	H2
Lancaster Ter. W2	10	E5
Lancaster Ter. W2	57	G7
Lancaster Wk. W2	14	D1
Lancaster Wk. W2	66	G1
Lance Rd., Har.	36	A7
Lancefield St. W10	57	C3
Lancell St. N16	50	B2
Stoke Newington		
Ch. St.		
Lancelot Ave., Wem.	46	G4
Lancelot Cres., Wem.	46	G4
Lancelot Gdns.,	24	A7
Barn.		
Lancelot Pl. SW7	14	J4
Lancelot Pl. SW7	66	J2
Lancelot Rd., Ilf.	35	H6
Lancelot Rd., Well.	80	A4

Lancelot Rd., Wem.	46	G4
Lancer Sq. W8	14	A3
Lancey Clo. SE7	70	A4
Cleveley Clo.		
Lanchester Rd. N6	39	J5
Lancing Gdns. N9	33	C1
Lancing Rd. W13	55	E7
Drayton Grn. Rd.		
Lancing Rd., Croy.	94	F6
Lancing Rd., Ilf.	43	G6
Lancing St. NW1	7	H4
Lancresse Ct. N1	59	B1
Landcroft Rd. SE22	77	C5
Landells Rd. SE22	77	C6
Landford Rd. SW15	74	J3
Landgrove Rd. SW19	84	D5
Landmann Way SE14	68	G6
Landon Pl. SW1	14	J5
Landon Pl. SW1	66	J3
Landon Wk. E14	60	B7
Cottage St.		
Landons Clo. E14	69	C1
Landor Rd. SW9	76	E3
Landor Wk. W12	65	G2
Landport Way SE15	21	G7
Landra Gdns. N21	24	H6
Landridge Rd. SW6	75	C2
Landrock Rd. N8	40	E6
Landscape Rd.,	34	H7
Wdf.Grn.		
Landseer Ave. E12	52	D5
Landseer Clo. SW19	93	F1
Brangwyn Cres.		
Landseer Clo., Edg.	38	A2
Landseer Rd. N19	49	E3
Landseer Rd., Enf.	25	D5
Landseer Rd.,	92	D7
N.Mal.		
Landseer Rd., Sutt.	100	D6
Landstead Rd. SE18	70	G7
Lane, The NW8	6	C2
Lane, The SE3	78	G3
Lane App. NW7	31	B5
Lane Clo. NW2	47	H3
Lane End, Bexh.	80	H3
Lanercost Clo. SW2	85	G2
Lanercost Gdns. N14	24	E7
Lanercost Rd. SW2	85	G2
Lanesborough Pl.	15	C3
SW1		
Laneside, Chis.	88	E5
Laneside, Edg.	30	C5
Laneside Ave., Dag.	44	F7
Laneway Rd. SW15	74	H5
Sunnymead Rd.		
Lanfranc Rd. E3	59	H2
Lanfrey Pl. W14	66	C5
North End Rd.		
Lang St. E1	59	F4
Langbourne Ave. N6	49	A2
Langbourne Way,	98	D6
Esher		
Langbrook Rd. SE3	79	A3
Langcroft Rd.	100	J3
Cars.		
Langdale Ave.,	93	J3
Mitch.		
Langdale Clo. SE17	20	J5
Langdale Clo. SE17	67	J6
Langdale Clo. SW14	74	B4
Clifford Ave.		
Langdale Cres.,	71	G7
Bexh.		
Langdale Gdns.,	55	E3
Grnf.		
Langdale Rd. SE10	69	C7
Langdale Rd.,	94	G4
Th.Hth.		
Langdale St. E1	59	E6
Burslem St.		
Langdon Ct. NW10	56	E1
Langdon Cres. E6	61	D2
Langdon Dr. NW9	47	C1
Langdon Pk. Rd. N6	40	C7
Langdon Pl. SW14	74	C3
Rosemary La.		
Langdon Rd. E6	61	D1
Langdon Rd., Brom.	96	H3
Langdon Rd., Mord.	93	F5
Langdon Shaw, Sid.	88	J5
Langdon Wk., Mord.	93	F5
Langdon Way		
SE1	21	J2
Langford Clo. E8	50	D5
Langford Clo. N15	41	B6
Langford Clo. NW8	6	D1
Langford Ct. NW8	6	D2
Langford Cres.,	23	J4
Barn.		
Langford Grn. SE5	77	B3
Langford Pl. NW8	6	D1
Langford Pl., Sid.	89	A3

Langford Rd. SW6	75	E2
Gilstead Rd.		
Langford Rd., Barn.	23	H4
Langford Rd.,	34	J6
Wdf.Grn.		
Langfords, Buck.H.	35	A2
Langham Dr., Rom.	44	B6
Langham Gdns. N21	24	G5
Langham Gdns. W13	55	E7
Langham Gdns., Edg.	30	C7
Langham Gdns.,	82	F4
Rich.		
Langham Gdns.,	46	F2
Wem.		
Langham Ho. Clo.,	82	G4
Rich.		
Langham Pl. N15	40	H3
Langham Pl. W1	11	E2
Langham Pl. W1	58	B5
Langham Rd. N15	40	H3
Langham Rd. SW20	92	J1
Langham Rd., Edg.	30	C6
Langham Rd., Tedd.	82	E5
Langham St. W1	11	E2
Langham St. W1	58	B5
Langhedge Clo. N18	33	C6
Langhedge La.		
Langhedge La. N18	33	C5
Langhedge La. Ind.	33	C6
Est. N18		
Langholm Clo. SW12	76	D7
King's Ave.		
Langholme (Bushey)	28	J1
Wat.		
Langhorne Rd., Dag.	63	G7
Langland Cres.,	37	G2
Stan.		
Langland Dr., Pnr.	28	E7
Langland Gdns. NW3	48	E5
Langland Gdns.,	102	J2
Croy.		
Langler Rd. NW10	56	J2
Langley Ave., Ruis.	45	B2
Langley Ave., Surb.	98	G1
Langley Ave.,	100	A1
Wor.Pk.		
Langley Ct. SE9	79	D6
Langley Ct. WC2	12	A4
Langley Cres. E11	42	H7
Langley Cres., Dag.	62	D7
Langley Cres., Edg.	30	C3
Langley Dr. E11	42	H7
Langley Dr. W3	65	B2
Langley Gdns.	96	J4
Brom.		
Langley Gdns., Dag.	63	D7
Langley Gdns., Orp.	97	E6
Langley Gro., N.Mal.	92	E2
Langley La. SW8	20	B5
Langley La. SW8	67	E6
Langley Meadow,	27	G2
Loug.		
Langley Pk. NW7	30	E6
Langley Pk. Rd.,	100	F5
Sutt.		
Langley Rd. SW19	93	C1
Langley Rd., Beck.	95	H4
Langley Rd., Islw.	73	C2
Langley Rd., Surb.	91	H7
Langley Rd., Well.	71	C6
Langley St. WC2	12	A4
Langley St. WC2	58	E6
Langley Way,	103	D1
W.Wick.		
Langmead St. SE27	85	H4
Beadman St.		
Langmore Ct., Bexh.	80	D3
Regency Way		
Langroyd Rd. SW17	84	J2
Langside Ave. SW15	74	G4
Langside Cres. N14	32	D3
Langston Rd., Loug.	27	F5
Langthorn Ct. EC2	13	C3
Langthorne Rd. E11	51	C3
Langthorne St. SW6	75	A1
Langton Ave. E6	61	D3
Langton Ave. N20	23	F1
Langton Clo. WC1	8	D5
Langton Ri. SE23	77	F7
Langton Rd. NW2	47	J3
Langton Rd. SW9	76	A7
Langton Rd., Har.	28	J7
Langton Rd., W.Mol.	90	J5
Langton St. SW10	18	D6
Langton St. SW10	66	B6
Langton Way SE3	78	F1
Langton Way, Croy.	102	B3
Langtry Rd. NW8	57	F1
Langtry Rd., Nthlt.	54	D2
Langtry Wk. NW8	48	F7
Alexandra Pl.		

Langwood Chase,	82	F6
Tedd.		
Langworth Dr.,	54	A6
Hayes		
Lanhill Rd. W9	57	D4
Lanier Rd. SE13	78	C6
Lankaster Gdns. N2	39	G1
Lankers Dr., Har.	36	F6
Lanrick Rd. E14	60	D6
Lanridge Rd. SE2	71	D3
Lansbury Ave. N18	33	A5
Lansbury Ave., Bark.	53	A7
Lansbury Ave., Felt.	72	B6
Lansbury Ave., Rom.	44	E5
Lansbury Clo. NW10	47	C5
Lansbury Est. E14	60	B6
Lansbury Gdns. E14	60	C6
Lansbury Rd., Enf.	25	G1
Lansbury Way N18	33	B5
Lansbury Ave.		
Lansdell Rd., Mitch.	94	A2
Lansdown Rd. E7	51	J7
Lansdown Rd., Sid.	89	B3
Lansdowne Ave.,	71	C7
Bexh.		
Lansdowne Ave.,	104	E1
Orp.		
Lansdowne Clo.	84	A7
SW20		
Lansdowne Clo.,	82	C1
Twick.		
Lion Rd.		
Lansdowne Ct.,	99	G2
Wor.Pk.		
Lansdowne Cres.	57	C7
W11		
Lansdowne Dr. E8	50	D6
Lansdowne Gdns.	76	E1
SW8		
Lansdowne Gro.	47	E4
NW10		
Lansdowne Hill SE27	85	H3
Lansdowne La. SE7	70	A5
Lansdowne Ms. SE7	70	A5
Lansdowne Ms. W11	66	C1
Lansdowne Rd.		
Lansdowne Pl. SE1	17	C5
Lansdowne Pl. SE19	86	F7
Lansdowne Ri. W11	57	B7
Lansdowne Rd. E4	34	A2
Lansdowne Rd. E11	51	F2
Lansdowne Rd. E17	42	A6
Lansdowne Rd. E18	42	G3
Lansdowne Rd. N3	31	C7
Lansdowne Rd. N10	40	C2
Lansdowne Rd. N17	41	D1
Lansdowne Rd.	83	J7
SW20		
Lansdowne Rd. W11	57	B7
Lansdowne Rd.,	87	G7
Brom.		
Lansdowne Rd.,	101	J2
Croy.		
Lansdowne Rd.,	99	C7
Epsom		
Lansdowne Rd., Har.	37	B7
Lansdowne Rd.,	72	H3
Houns.		
Lansdowne Rd., Ilf.	52	J1
Lansdowne Rd.,	29	F6
Stan.		
Lansdowne Row W1	15	E1
Lansdowne Ter. WC1	8	E4
Lansdowne Ter. WC1	58	E4
Lansdowne Wk. W11	66	C1
Lansdowne Way	76	D1
SW8		
Lansdowne Wd. Clo.	85	H3
SE27		
Lansfield Ave. N18	33	D4
Lant St. SE1	16	J3
Lant St. SE1	67	J2
Lantern Clo. SW15	74	G4
Lantern Clo., Wem.	46	G5
Lanterns Ct. E14	69	A2
Lanvanor Rd. SE15	77	F2
Lapford Clo. W9	57	C4
Lapse Wd. Wk. SE23	86	E2
Lapstone Gdns.,	37	F6
Har.		
Lapwing Ct., Surb.	99	A3
Chaffinch Clo.		
Lara Clo. SE13	78	C6
Lara Clo., Chess.	98	H7
Larbert Rd. SW16	85	C7
Larch Ave. W3	65	E1
Larch Clo. N11	32	A7
Larch Clo. N19	49	C2
Bredgar Rd.		
Larch Clo. SE8	68	J6
Clyde St.		

Larch Clo. SW12 85 B1
Larch Cres., Epsom 99 B6
Larch Cres., Hayes 54 C4
Larch Dr. W4 65 A5
Gunnersbury Ave.
Larch Gro., Sid. 88 J1
Larch Ms. N19 49 C2
Bredgar Rd.
Larch Rd. NW2 47 J4
Larch Tree Way, 103 A3
Croy.
Larch Way, Brom. 97 D7
Larchdene, Orp. 104 D2
Larches, The N13 32 J3
Larches Ave. SW14 74 D4
Larchwood Rd. SE9 88 E2
Larcom St. SE17 **21 A2**
Larcom St. SE17 67 J4
Larcombe Clo., 102 C4
Croy.
Larden Rd. W3 65 E1
Largewood Ave., 98 J2
Surb.
Larissa St. SE17 **21 C3**
Lark Row E2 59 F1
Larkbere Rd. SE26 86 H4
Larken Dr. 28 J1
(Bushey), Wat.
Larkfield Ave., Har. 37 E3
Larkfield Clo., 103 F2
Brom.
Larkfield Rd., Rich. 73 H4
Larkfield Rd., Sid. 00 J0
Larkhall Ct., Rom. 44 J2
Larkhall La. SW4 76 D2
Larkhall Ri. SW4 76 C3
Larkhill Ter. SE18 70 D7
Larks Gro., Bark. 52 H7
Larksfield Gro., 25 E1
Enf.
Larkshall Cres. E4 34 C4
Larkshall Rd. E4 34 C5
Larkspur Clo. E6 61 B5
Larkspur Clo. N17 33 A7
Fryatt Rd.
Larkspur Way, 99 B5
Epsom
Larkswood Ct. E4 34 D5
Larkswood Ri., Pnr. 36 C4
Larkswood Rd. E4 34 A4
Larkway Clo. NW9 38 D4
Larnach Rd. W6 66 A6
Larpent Ave. SW15 74 J5
Larwood Clo., Grnf. 46 A5
Lascelles Ave., 34 A7
Har.
Lascelles Clo. E11 51 D2
Lascotts Rd. N22 32 F6
Lassa Rd. SE9 79 B5
Lassell St. SE10 69 D5
Lasterton St. E8 50 E6
Wilton Way
Latchett Rd. E18 42 H1
Latchingdon Ct. E17 41 G4
Latchingdon Gdns., 35 B6
Wdf.Grn.
Latchmere La., 82 H5
Kings.T.
Latchmere Pas. SW11 75 H2
Cabul Rd.
Latchmere Rd. SW11 75 J2
Latchmere Rd., 82 H7
Kings.T.
Latchmere St. SW11 75 J2
Lateward Rd., 64 G6
Brent.
Latham Clo. E6 61 B6
Oliver Gdns.
Latham Clo., Twick. 73 D7
Latham Ho. E1 59 G6
Latham Rd., Bexh. 80 G5
Latham Rd., Twick. 73 C7
Lathams Way, Croy. 101 F1
Lathkill Clo., Enf. 25 C7
Lathom Rd. E6 52 B7
Latimer SE17 **21 D4**
Latimer Ave. E6 61 C1
Latimer Clo., Pnr. 36 C1
Latimer Clo., 99 H4
Wor.Pk.
Latimer Gdns., Pnr. 36 C1
Latimer Pl. W10 56 J6
Latimer Rd. E7 51 H4
Latimer Rd. N15 41 B6
Latimer Rd. SW19 84 E6
Latimer Rd. W10 56 J5
Latimer Rd., Barn. 23 E3
Latimer Rd., Croy. 101 H3
Abbey Rd.
Latimer Rd., Tedd. 82 C5
Latimer St. E1 59 G5
Stepney Way

Latona Rd. SE15 **21 H6**
Latona Rd. SE15 68 D6
Latton Clo., Walt. 90 E7
Latymer Ct. W6 66 A4
Latymer Rd. N9 33 C2
Latymer Way N9 33 A2
Laud St. SE11 **20 C3**
Laud St., Croy. 101 J3
Lauder Clo., Nthlt. 54 D2
Lauderdale Dr., 82 G3
Rich.
Lauderdale Rd. W9 **6 A4**
Lauderdale Rd. W9 57 E3
Laughton Ct., 22 D2
Borwd.
Banks Rd.
Laughton Rd., Nthlt. 54 D1
Launcelot St. SE1 **16 E4**
Launceston Gdns., 55 F1
Grnf.
Launceston Pl. W8 14 C5
Launceston Pl. W8 66 F3
Launceston Rd., 55 F1
Grnf.
Launch St. E14 69 C3
Laundry La. N1 58 J1
Greenman St.
Laundry Rd. W6 66 B6
Laura Clo. E11 42 J5
Laura Clo., Enf. 25 B5
Lauradale Rd. N2 39 J4
Laurel Ave., Twick. 82 C1
Laurel Bank Gdns. 75 C2
SW6
New Kings Rd.
Laurel Bank Rd., 24 J1
Enf.
Laurel Clo. N19 49 C2
Hargrave Pk.
Laurel Clo., Ilf. 35 F6
Laurel Clo., Sid. 89 A3
Laurel Cres., Croy. 103 A3
Laurel Dr. N21 24 G7
Laurel Gdns. E4 26 B7
Laurel Gdns. NW7 30 D3
Laurel Gdns. W7 64 B1
Laurel Gdns., 72 E4
Houns.
Laurel Gro. SE20 86 E7
Laurel Gro. SE26 86 G4
Laurel Pk., Har. 29 C7
Laurel Rd. SW13 74 G2
Laurel Rd. SW20 92 H1
Laurel Rd., Hmptn. 82 A5
Laurel St. E8 50 C6
Laurel Vw. N12 31 E3
Laurel Way E18 42 F4
Laurel Way N20 31 D3
Laurence Ms. W12 65 G2
Askew Rd.
Laurence Pountney **13 B5**
Hill EC4
Laurence Pountney **13 B5**
La. EC4
Laurie Gro. SE14 77 H1
Laurie Rd. W7 55 B5
Laurier Rd. NW5 49 B3
Laurier Rd., Croy. 95 C7
Laurimel Clo., 29 E6
Stan.
September Way
Laurino Pl. 28 J2
(Bushey), Wat.
Lauriston Rd. E9 59 G1
Lauriston Rd. SW19 84 A6
Lausanne Rd. N8 40 G4
Lausanne Rd. SE15 77 F1
Lavell St. N16 50 A4
Lavender Ave. NW9 47 C1
Lavender Ave., 93 H1
Mitch.
Lavender Ave., 99 J3
Wor.Pk.
Lavender Clo. SW3 **18 F6**
Lavender Clo., 101 B4
Cars.
Lavender Clo., 90 H3
W.Mol.
Molesham Way
Lavender Gdns. 75 J4
SW11
Lavender Gdns., 24 H1
Enf.
Lavender Gro. E8 50 D7
Lavender Gro., 93 H1
Mitch.
Lavender Hill SW11 75 J4
Lavender Hill, Enf. 24 G1
Lavender Pl., Ilf. 52 E5
Lavender Rd. SE16 68 H1

Lavender Rd. SW11 75 G3
Lavender Rd., Cars. 101 A4
Lavender Rd., Croy. 94 F6
Lavender Rd., Enf. 25 A1
Lavender Rd., 99 B5
Epsom
Lavender Rd., Sutt. 100 G4
Lavender St. E15 51 E6
Manbey Gro.
Lavender Sweep 75 J4
SW11
Lavender Ter. SW11 75 H3
Falcon Rd.
Lavender Vale, 101 D6
Wall.
Lavender Wk. SW11 75 J4
Lavender Wk., 94 A3
Mitch.
Lavengro Rd. SE27 85 J2
Lavenham Rd. SW18 84 C2
Lavernock Rd., 80 G2
Bexh.
Laverock St. N16 50 B3
Laverstoke Gdns. 74 F7
SW15
Laverton Ms. SW5 **18 B2**
Laverton Pl. SW5 **18 B2**
Laverton Pl. SW5 66 E4
Lavidge Rd. SE9 88 B2
Lavina Gro. N1 **8 C1**
Lavington Rd. W13 64 E7
Lavington Rd., 101 F6
Croy.
Lavington St. SE1 16 H2
Lavington St. SE1 67 H1
Law St. SE1 **17 C5**
Law St. SE1 68 A3
Lawdons Gdns., 101 H4
Croy.
Lawford Rd. N1 50 B7
Lawford Rd. NW5 49 C6
Lawford Rd. W4 65 C7
Lawless St. E14 60 B7
Lawley Rd. N14 24 B7
Lawley St. E5 50 F4
Lawn Clo. N9 25 C7
Lawn Clo., Brom. 87 H6
Lawn Clo., N.Mal. 92 E2
Lawn Cres., Rich. 74 A2
Lawn Fm. Gro., Rom. 44 D7
Lawn Gdns. W7 64 B1
Lawn Ho. Clo. E14 69 C2
Lawn La. SW8 20 B6
Lawn La. SW8 67 E6
Lawn Pl. SE15 77 C1
Sumner Est.
Lawn Rd. NW3 48 J5
Lawn Rd., Beck. 86 J7
Lawn Ter. SE3 78 E3
Lawnfield NW6 48 A7
Coverdale Rd.
Lawns, The E4 34 A5
Lawns, The SE3 78 E3
Lee Ter.
Lawns, The SW19 95 A1
Lawns, The, Pnr. 28 H7
Lawns, The, Sid. 89 B4
Lawns, The, Sutt. 100 B7
Lawnside SE3 78 F1
Lawrence Ave. E12 52 D4
Lawrence Ave. E17 41 G1
Lawrence Ave. N13 32 H4
Lawrence Ave. NW7 30 E4
Lawrence Ave., 92 D6
N.Mal.
Lawrence Bldgs. N16 50 C3
Lawrence Campe 31 G3
Clo. N20
Friern Barnet La.
Lawrence Clo. E3 60 A3
Lawrence Clo. N15 41 B3
Lawrence Rd.
Lawrence Ct. NW7 30 E5
Lawrence Cres., 53 H3
Dag.
Lawrence Cres., 38 A2
Edg.
Lawrence Est., 72 C4
Houns.
Lawrence Gdns. NW7 30 F3
Lawrence Hill E4 34 A2
Lawrence La. EC2 **13 D4**
Lawrence Pl. N1 58 E1
Outram Pl.
Lawrence Rd. E6 61 B1
Lawrence Rd. E13 60 H1
Lawrence Rd. N15 41 B4
Lawrence Rd. N18 33 E4
Lawrence Rd. SE25 95 C4
Lawrence Rd. W5 64 G4

Lawrence Rd., 81 F7
Hmptn.
Lawrence Rd., 72 C4
Houns.
Lawrence Rd., Pnr. 36 D6
Lawrence Rd., Rich. 82 F4
Lawrence Rd., 103 G4
W.Wick.
Lawrence St. E16 60 F5
Lawrence St. NW7 30 F5
Lawrence St. SW3 **18 G6**
Lawrence St. SW3 66 H6
Lawrence Weaver 93 E6
Clo., Mord.
Green La.
Lawrie Pk. Ave. 86 E5
SE26
Lawrie Pk. Cres. 86 E5
SE26
Lawrie Pk. Gdns. 86 E4
SE26
Lawrie Pk. Rd. SE26 86 E6
Lawson Clo. E16 60 J5
Lawson Clo. SW19 84 A3
Lawson Est. SE1 17 B6
Lawson Gdns., Pnr. 36 B3
Lawson Rd., Enf. 25 F1
Lawson Rd., Sthl. 54 F4
Lawton Rd. E3 59 H3
Lawton Rd. E10 51 D1
Lawton Rd., Barn. 23 G3
Lawton Rd., Loug. 27 E2
Laxcon Clo. NW10 47 C5
Laxey Rd., Orp. 104 J6
Laxley Clo. SE5 **20 H7**
Laxley Clo. SE5 67 H7
Laxton Pl. NW1 **7 E5**
Layard Rd. SE16 68 E4
Layard Rd., Enf. 25 C1
Layard Rd., Th.Hth. 95 A2
Layard Sq. SE16 68 E4
Laycock St. N1 49 G6
Layer Gdns. W3 56 A7
Layfield Clo. NW4 38 H7
Layfield Cres. NW4 38 H7
Layfield Rd. NW4 38 H7
Layhams Rd., Kes. 103 F5
Layhams Rd., 103 D3
W.Wick.
Laymarsh Clo., Belv. 71 F3
Laymead Clo., Nthlt. 45 E6
Laystall St. EC1 **8 E6**
Laystall St. EC1 58 G4
Layton Cres., Croy. 101 G5
Layton Rd. N1 **8 F1**
Layton Rd. N1 58 G2
Layton Rd., Brent. 64 G5
Layton Rd., Houns. 72 H4
Laytons Bldgs. SE1 **17 B3**
Layzell Wk. SE9 88 A1
Mottingham La.
Lazar Wk. N7 49 F2
Briset Way
Le May Ave. SE12 87 H3
Lea Bri. Rd. E5 50 E3
Lea Bri. Rd. E10 42 A7
Lea Bri. Rd. E17 42 D5
Lea Gdns., Wem. 46 J4
Lea Hall Rd. E10 51 A1
Lea Pk. Way N9 33 G5
Lea Rd., Beck. 96 A2
Fairfield Rd.
Lea Rd., Enf. 25 A1
Lea Rd., Sthl. 63 E4
Lea Side Ind. Est., 25 J3
Enf.
Lea Valley Rd. E4 26 A6
Lea Valley Rd., 25 G5
Enf.
Lea Valley Viaduct 33 G5
E4
Lea Valley Viaduct 33 G5
N18
Lea Vw. Hos. E5 50 E1
Springfield
Leabank Clo., Har. 46 B3
Leabank Sq. E9 51 A6
Leabank Vw. N15 41 D6
Leabourne Rd. N16 41 A6
Leacroft Ave. SW12 75 J7
Leadale Ave. E4 33 J2
Leadale Rd. N15 41 D6
Leadale Rd. N16 41 D6
Leadenhall Mkt. EC3 **13 D4**
Leadenhall Pl. EC3 **13 D4**
Leadenhall St. EC3 **13 D4**
Leadenhall St. EC3 59 B6
Leader Ave. E12 52 D5
Leadings, The, Wem. 47 C3
Leaf Clo., T.Ditt. 91 B5
Leaf Gro. SE27 85 G5
Leafield Clo. SW16 85 H6
Leafield La., Sid. 89 F4

...d Rd. SW20	93	C3	
...eld Rd., Sutt.	100	D2	
...fy Gro., Kes.	103	J5	
...eafy Oak Rd. SE12	87	J4	
Leafy Way, Croy.	102	C2	
Leagrave St. E5	50	F3	
Leahurst Rd. SE13	78	D5	
Leake Ct. SE1	**16**	**D3**	
Leake St. SE1	**16**	**D3**	
Leake St. SE1	67	F2	
Lealand Rd. N15	41	C6	
Leamington Ave. E17	42	A5	
Leamington Ave., Brom.	87	J5	
Leamington Ave., Mord.	93	B4	
Leamington Ave., Orp.	104	H4	
Leamington Clo. E12	52	C5	
Leamington Clo., Brom.	87	J5	
Leamington Clo., Houns.	72	C3	
Leamington Cres., Har.	45	E3	
Leamington Gdns., Ilf.	52	J2	
Leamington Pk. W3	56	D5	
Leamington Rd., Sthl.	63	D4	
Leamington Rd. Vill. W11	57	C5	
Leamore St. W6	65	H4	
Leamouth Rd. E6	61	B6	
Leamouth Rd. E14	60	D6	
Leander Ct. SE8	78	A1	
Leander Rd. SW2	76	F7	
Leander Rd., Nthlt.	54	G2	
Leander Rd., Th.Hth.	94	F4	
Learoyd Gdns. E6	61	D7	
Leas Clo., Chess.	98	J7	
Leas Dale SE9	88	D3	
Leas Grn., Chis.	88	J6	
Leaside Ave. N10	40	A3	
Leaside Rd. E5	50	F1	
Leasowes Rd. E10	51	A1	
Leather Bottle La., Belv.	71	F4	
St. Augustine's Rd.			
Leather Clo., Mitch.	94	A2	
Leather Gdns. E15	60	E1	
Leather La. EC1	**12**	**E1**	
Leather La. EC1	58	G5	
Leatherbottle Grn., Erith	71	F3	
Leatherdale St. E1	59	F4	
Portelet Rd.			
Leatherhead Clo. N16	50	B1	
Leathermarket St. SE1	**17**	**D4**	
Leathermarket St. SE1	68	B2	
Leathersellers Clo., Barn.	23	B4	
The Ave.			
Leathsail Rd., Har.	45	H3	
Leathwaite Rd. SW11	75	J4	
Leathwell Rd. SE8	78	B2	
Leaveland Clo., Beck.	96	A4	
Leaver Gdns., Grnf.	55	A2	
Leavesden Rd., Stan.	29	D6	
Leaway E10	50	G1	
Lebanon Ave., Felt.	81	D5	
Lebanon Ct., Twick.	73	E7	
Lebanon Gdns. SW18	75	D5	
Lebanon Pk., Twick.	73	E7	
Lebanon Rd. SW18	75	D5	
Lebanon Rd., Croy.	102	B1	
Lebrun Sq. SE3	78	H3	
Lechmere App., Wdf.Grn.	42	J2	
Lechmere Ave., Chig.	35	F4	
Lechmere Ave., Wdf.Grn.	43	A5	
Lechmere Rd. NW2	47	H6	
Leckford Rd. SW18	84	F2	
Leckwith Ave., Bexh.	71	E6	
Lecky St. SW7	**18**	**E3**	
Lecky St. SW7	66	G5	
Leconfield Ave. SW13	74	F3	
Leconfield Rd. N5	50	A4	
Leda Ave., Enf.	25	G1	
Ledbury Est. SE15	68	E7	
Ledbury Ms. N. W11	57	D7	
Ledbury Rd.			
Ledbury Ms. W. W11	57	D7	
Ledbury Rd.			
Ledbury Pl., Croy.	101	J4	
Ledbury Rd.			
Ledbury Rd. W11	57	C6	
Ledbury Rd., Croy.	101	J4	
Ledbury St. SE15	**21**	**J7**	
Ledbury St. SE15	68	D7	
Ledrington Rd. SE19	86	D6	
Anerley Rd.			
Ledway Dr., Wem.	37	J7	
Lee Ave., Rom.	44	E6	
Lee Bri. SE13	78	C3	
Lee Ch. St. SE13	78	E4	
Lee Clo. E17	41	G1	
Lee Conservancy Rd. E9	50	J5	
Lee Grn. SE12	78	F5	
Lee Gro., Chig.	35	D2	
Lee High Rd. SE12	78	F4	
Lee High Rd. SE13	78	D4	
Lee Pk. SE3	78	F4	
Lee Pk. Way N9	33	H3	
Lee Pk. Way N18	33	H3	
Lee Rd. NW7	31	A7	
Lee Rd. SE3	78	F3	
Lee Rd. SW19	93	E1	
Lee Rd., Enf.	25	D6	
Lee Rd., Grnf.	55	F1	
Lee St. E8	59	C1	
Lee Ter. SE3	78	E3	
Lee Valley Trd. Est. N18	33	G5	
Leechcroft Ave., Sid.	79	J5	
Leechcroft Rd., Wall.	101	A3	
Leecroft Rd., Barn.	23	B5	
Leeds Pl. N4	49	F2	
Tollington Pk.			
Leeds Rd., Ilf.	52	G1	
Leeds St. N18	33	D5	
Leefern Rd. W12	65	G2	
Leegate SE12	78	F5	
Leeke St. WC1	**8**	**C3**	
Leeke St. WC1	58	F3	
Leeland Rd. W13	64	D1	
Leeland Ter. W13	64	D1	
Leeland Way NW10	47	F4	
Leerdam Dr. E14	69	C3	
Lees, The W1	102	J2	
Lees Pl. W1	**11**	**B5**	
Lees Pl. W1	58	A7	
Leeside, Barn.	23	B5	
Leeside Cres. NW11	39	B6	
Leeside Rd. N17	33	E6	
Leeson Rd. SE24	76	G4	
Leesons Hill, Chis.	97	H3	
Leesons Way, Orp.	97	J2	
Leeward Gdns. SW19	84	C5	
Leeway SE8	68	J5	
Leeway Clo., Pnr.	28	F7	
Woodridings Clo.			
Lefevre Wk. E3	59	J1	
Old Ford Rd.			
Lefroy Rd. W12	65	F2	
Legard Rd. N5	49	H3	
Legatt Rd. SE9	79	A5	
Leggatt Rd. E15	60	C2	
Legge St. SE13	78	C5	
Leghorn Rd. NW10	56	F2	
Leghorn Rd. SE18	70	G5	
Legion Clo. N1	49	G7	
Legion Ct., Mord.	93	D6	
Legion Rd., Grnf.	54	J1	
Legion Way N12	31	H7	
Downway			
Legon Ave., Rom.	53	J1	
Legrace Ave., Houns.	72	D2	
Leicester Ave., Mitch.	94	E4	
Leicester Clo., Wor.Pk.	99	J4	
Leicester Ct. WC2	**11**	**J5**	
Leicester Gdns., Ilf.	43	H7	
Leicester Pl. WC2	**11**	**J5**	
Leicester Rd. E11	42	H5	
Leicester Rd. N2	39	H3	
Leicester Rd. NW10	47	D7	
Leicester Rd., Barn.	23	E5	
Leicester Rd., Croy.	95	B7	
Leicester Sq. WC2	**11**	**J6**	
Leicester Sq. WC2	58	D7	
Leicester St. WC2	**11**	**J5**	
Leigh Ave., Ilf.	43	A4	
Leigh Clo., N.Mal.	92	D4	
Leigh Ct., Borwd.	22	D2	
Banks Rd.			
Leigh Ct., Har.	46	B1	
Leigh Cres., Croy.	103	B7	
Leigh Gdns. NW10	56	J2	
Leigh Hunt St. SE1	**16**	**J3**	
Leigh Orchard Clo. SW16	85	F3	
Leigh Pl., Well.	80	A2	
Leigh Rd. E6	52	D6	
Leigh Rd. E10	42	C7	
Leigh Rd. N5	49	H4	
Leigh Rd., Houns.	73	A4	
Leigh Rodd, Wat.	28	F3	
Leigh St. WC1	**8**	**A5**	
Leigh St. WC1	58	E4	
Leigham Ave. SW16	85	E3	
Leigham Ct. Rd. SW16	85	E2	
Leigham Dr., Islw.	64	B7	
Leigham Vale SW2	85	G2	
Leigham Vale SW16	85	F3	
Leighton Ave. E12	52	D5	
Leighton Ave., Pnr.	36	E3	
Leighton Clo., Edg.	38	A2	
Leighton Cres. NW5	49	C5	
Leighton Gro.			
Leighton Gdns. NW10	56	H2	
Leighton Gro. NW5	49	C5	
Leighton Pl. NW5	49	C5	
Leighton Rd. NW5	49	C5	
Leighton Rd. W13	64	D2	
Leighton Rd., Enf.	25	C5	
Leighton Rd., Har.	37	A2	
Leighton St. E., Croy.	101	H1	
Leighton St. W., Croy.	101	H1	
Leinster Ave. SW14	74	C3	
Leinster Gdns. W2	**10**	**C4**	
Leinster Gdns. W2	57	F6	
Leinster Ms. W2	**10**	**C6**	
Leinster Ms. W2	57	F7	
Leinster Pl. W2	**10**	**B4**	
Leinster Pl. W2	57	F6	
Leinster Rd. N10	40	B4	
Leinster Rd. NW6	57	D3	
Stafford Rd.			
Leinster Sq. W2	57	D6	
Leinster Ter. W2	**10**	**C5**	
Leinster Ter. W2	57	F7	
Leith Clo. NW9	47	D1	
Leith Rd. N22	40	H1	
Leith Yd. NW6	57	D1	
Quex Rd.			
Leithcote Gdns. SW16	85	F4	
Leithcote Path SW16	85	F3	
Lela Ave., Houns.	72	C2	
Lelitia Clo. E8	59	D1	
Pownall Rd.			
Leman St. E1	**13**	**G4**	
Leman St. E1	59	C6	
Lemark Clo., Stan.	29	F5	
Lemmon Rd. SE10	69	E6	
Lemna Rd. E11	42	E7	
Lemonwell Ct. SE9	79	F5	
Lemsford Clo. N15	41	D5	
Lemsford Ct. N4	49	J2	
Brownswood Rd.			
Lemsford Ct., Borwd.	22	C4	
Lemuel St. SW18	75	E6	
St. Ann's Hill			
Lena Gdns. W6	65	J3	
Lena Kennedy Clo. E4	34	C6	
Lenanton Steps E14	69	A2	
Manilla St.			
Lendal Ter. SW4	76	D3	
Lenelby Rd., Surb.	99	A1	
Lenham Rd. SE12	78	F4	
Lenham Rd., Bexh.	71	F6	
Lenham Rd., Sutt.	100	E4	
Lenham Rd., Th.Hth.	95	A2	
Lennard Ave., W.Wick.	103	E2	
Lennard Clo., W.Wick.	103	E2	
Lennard Rd. SE20	86	G6	
Lennard Rd., Beck.	86	H7	
Lennard Rd., Brom.	104	C1	
Lennard Rd., Croy.	101	J1	
Lennon Rd. NW2	47	J6	
Lennox Gdns. NW10	47	F4	
Lennox Gdns. SW1	**14**	**J6**	
Lennox Gdns. SW1	66	D3	
Lennox Gdns., Croy.	101	H4	
Lennox Gdns., Ilf.	52	C7	
Lennox Gdns. Ms. SW1	**14**	**J6**	
Lennox Gdns. Ms. SW1	66	J3	
Lennox Rd. E17	41	J6	
Lennox Rd. N4	49	F2	
Lenor Clo., Bexh.	80	E4	
Lens Rd. E7	51	J7	
Lensbury Way SE2	71	C3	
Lenthall Pl. SW7	**18**	**C1**	
Lenthall Rd. E8	50	C7	
Lenthall Rd., Loug.	27	G4	
Lenthorp Rd. SE10	69	F4	
Lentmead Rd., Brom.	87	F3	
Lenton Ri., Rich.	73	H3	
Evelyn Ter.			
Lenton St. SE18	70	G4	
Lenville Way SE16	**21**	**A4**	
Leo St. SE15	68	E7	
Leo Yd. EC1	**8**	**H6**	
Leof Cres. SE6	87	B5	
Leominster Rd., Mord.	93	F6	
Leominster Wk., Mord.	93	F6	
Leonard Ave., Mord.	93	F5	
Leonard Rd. E4	34	A6	
Leonard Rd. E7	51	G4	
Leonard Rd. N9	33	C3	
Leonard Rd. SW16	94	C1	
Leonard Rd., Sthl.	63	D3	
Leonard Robbins Path SE28	62	B7	
Tawney Rd.			
Leonard St. E16	70	B1	
Leonard St. EC2	**9**	**C5**	
Leonard St. EC2	59	A4	
Leontine Clo. SE15	68	D7	
Leopards Ct. EC1	**12**	**E1**	
Leopold Ave. SW19	84	C5	
Leopold Ms. E9	59	F1	
Fremont St.			
Leopold Rd. E17	42	A5	
Leopold Rd. N2	39	G3	
Leopold Rd. N18	33	E5	
Leopold Rd. NW10	47	E7	
Leopold Rd. SW19	84	C4	
Leopold Rd. W5	64	J1	
Leopold St. E3	59	J5	
Lepe Clo., Brom.	87	E4	
Winlaton Rd.			
Leppoc Rd. SW4	76	D5	
Leroy St. SE1	**17**	**D6**	
Leroy St. SE1	68	B4	
Lescombe Clo. SE23	86	H3	
Lescombe Rd. SE23	86	H3	
Lesley Clo., Bex.	77	J7	
Leslie Gdns., Sutt.	100	D6	
Leslie Gro., Croy.	102	A1	
Leslie Pk. Rd., Croy.	102	B1	
Leslie Rd. E11	51	C4	
Leslie Rd. E16	60	H6	
Leslie Rd. N2	39	G3	
Leslie Smith Sq. SE18	70	D6	
Nightingale La.			
Lessar Ave. SW4	76	B5	
Lessing St. SE23	77	H7	
Lessingham Ave. SW17	84	J4	
Lessingham Ave., Ilf.	43	D3	
Lessington Ave., Rom.	44	J6	
Lessness Ave., Bexh.	71	D7	
Lessness Pk., Belv.	71	F5	
Lessness Rd., Belv.	71	G5	
Stapley Rd.			
Lessness Rd., Mord.	93	F6	
Lester Ave. E15	60	E4	
Leswin Pl. N16	50	C3	
Leswin Rd.			
Leswin Rd. N16	50	C3	
Letchford Gdns. NW10	56	G3	
Letchford Ms. NW10	56	G3	
Letchford Gdns.			
Letchford Ter. Har.	36	H1	
Letchworth Clo., Brom.	96	G5	
Letchworth Clo., Wat.	28	D5	
Letchworth Dr., Brom.	96	G5	
Letchworth St. SW17	84	J4	
Lethbridge Clo. SE13	78	C1	
Lett Rd. E15	51	D7	
Letterstone Rd. SW6	66	C7	
Varna Rd.			
Lettice St. SW6	75	C1	
Lettsom St. SE5	77	B2	
Lettsom Wk. E13	60	G2	
Hunter Way.			
Leucha Rd. E17	41	H5	
Levana Clo. SW19	84	B1	
Levehurst Way SW4	76	E2	
Leven Clo., Wat.	28	D5	
Benton Rd.			

Leven Rd. E14	60	C5
Levendale Rd. SE23	86	H2
Lever St. EC1	**8**	**H4**
Lever St. EC1	58	H3
Leverett St. SW3	**18**	**H1**
Leverholme Gdns. SE9	88	D3
Leverson St. SW16	85	C6
Leverton Pl. NW5	49	C5
Leverton St.		
Leverton St. NW5	49	C5
Levett Gdns., Ilf.	52	J4
Levett Rd., Bark.	52	H6
Levine Gdns., Bark.	62	D2
Lewes Rd. N12	31	H5
Lewes Rd., Brom.	97	A2
Lewesdon Clo. SW19	84	A1
Leweston Pl. N16	41	C7
Lewey Ho. E3	59	J4
Lewgars Ave. NW9	38	C6
Lewin Rd. SW14	74	D3
Lewin Rd. SW16	85	D6
Lewin Rd., Bexh.	80	E5
Lewis Ave. E17	42	A1
Lewis Cres. NW10	47	C5
Lewis Gdns. N2	39	G2
Lewis Gro. SE13	78	C3
Lewis Rd., Mitch.	93	G2
Lewis Rd., Rich.	73	G5
Red Lion St.		
Lewis Rd., Sid.	89	C3
Lewis Rd., Sthl.	63	F2
Lewis Rd., Sutt.	100	E4
Lewis Rd., Well.	80	C3
Lewis St. NW1	49	B6
Lewisham High St. SE13	78	C4
Lewisham Hill SE13	78	C2
Lewisham Pk. SE13	78	C5
Lewisham Rd. SE13	78	B1
Lewisham St. SW1	**15**	**J4**
Lewisham Way SE4	78	A2
Lewisham Way SE14	77	J1
Lexden Dr., Rom.	44	B6
Lexden Rd. W3	65	B1
Lexden Rd., Mitch.	94	D4
Lexham Gdns. W8	**14**	**A6**
Lexham Gdns. W8	66	D4
Lexham Gdns. Ms. W8	**14**	**B6**
Lexham Ho., Bark.	61	G1
St. Margarets		
Lexham Ms. W8	66	D4
Lexham Wk. W8	**14**	**B6**
Lexington St. W1	11	G5
Lexington St. W1	58	C7
Lexington Way, Barn.	23	A4
Lexton Gdns. SW12	85	D1
Ley St., Ilf.	52	E2
Leyborne Ave. W13	64	E2
Leyborne Pk., Rich.	74	A1
Leybourne Clo., Brom.	96	G6
Leybourne Rd. E11	51	F1
Leybourne Rd. NW1	49	B7
Leybourne Rd. NW9	38	A5
Leybourne Rd. NW1	49	B7
Hawley St.		
Leybridge Ct. SE12	78	G5
Leyburn Clo. E17	42	C4
Leyburn Gdns., Croy.	102	C2
Leyburn Gro. N18	33	D6
Leyburn Rd. N18	33	D6
Leycroft Clo., Loug.	27	D5
Leyden St. E1	**13**	**F2**
Leydon Clo. SE16	68	G1
Lagado Ms.		
Leyes Rd. E16	60	J6
Leyfield, Wor.Pk.	99	E1
Leyland Ave., Enf.	25	H2
Leyland Gdns., Wdf.Grn.	34	J5
Leyland Rd. SE12	78	F5
Leylang Rd. SE14	68	G7
Leys, The N2	39	F4
Leys, The, Har.	37	H6
Leys Ave., Dag.	62	J1
Leys Clo., Dag.	53	J7
Leys Clo., Har.	37	A5
Leys Gdns., Barn.	24	A5
Leys Rd. E., Enf.	25	H1
Leys Rd. W., Enf.	25	H1
Leysdown Ave., Bexh.	80	J4
Leysdown Rd. SE9	88	B2
Leysfield Rd. W12	65	G3
Leyspring Rd. E11	51	F1
Leyswood Dr., Ilf.	43	H5
Leythe Rd. W3	65	C2

Leyton Business Cen. E10	51	A2
Leyton Gra. E10	51	B1
Leyton Gra. Est. E10	51	A1
Leyton Grn. Rd. E10	42	C6
Leyton Ind. Village E10	41	G7
Leyton Pk. Rd. E10	51	C3
Leyton Rd. E15	51	D5
Leyton Rd. E19	84	F7
Leyton Way E11	42	E7
Leytonstone Rd. E15	51	E6
Leywick St. E15	60	E2
Lezayre Rd., Orp.	104	J6
Liardet St. SE14	68	H6
Liberia Rd. N5	49	H6
Liberty Ave. SW19	93	F1
Liberty Ms. SW12	76	B6
Liberty St. SW9	76	F1
Libra Rd. E3	59	J1
Libra Rd. E13	60	G2
Library Pl. E1	59	E7
Cable St.		
Library St. SE1	**16**	**G4**
Library St. SE1	67	H2
Lichfield Gdns., Rich.	73	H4
Lichfield Gro. N3	39	D1
Lichfield Rd. E3	59	H3
Lichfield Rd. E6	61	A3
Lichfield Rd. N9	33	D2
Winchester Rd.		
Lichfield Rd. NW2	48	B4
Lichfield Rd., Dag.	53	B4
Lichfield Rd., Houns.	72	C3
Lichfield Rd., Nthwd.	36	A3
Lichfield Rd., Rich.	73	J1
Lichfield Rd., Wdf.Grn.	34	E4
Lichlade Clo., Orp.	104	J4
Lidbury Rd. NW7	31	B6
Lidcote Gdns. SW9	76	G2
Liddell Clo., Har.	37	G3
Liddell Gdns. NW10	56	J2
Liddell Rd. NW6	48	D6
Lidding Rd., Har.	37	G5
Liddington Rd. E15	60	F1
Liddon Rd. E13	60	H3
Liddon Rd., Brom.	96	J3
Liden Clo. E17	50	J1
Hitcham Rd.		
Lidfield Rd. N16	50	A4
Lidiard Rd. SW18	84	F2
Lidlington Pl. NW1	**7**	**G2**
Lidlington Pl. NW1	58	C2
Lidyard Rd. N19	49	C1
Liffler Rd. SE18	70	H5
Lifford St. SW15	75	A4
Liffords Pl. SW13	74	F2
Lightcliffe Rd. N13	32	G4
Lightermans Rd. E14	69	A2
Lightfoot Rd. N8	40	E5
Lightley Clo., Wem.	46	J7
Stanley Ave.		
Ligonier St. E2	**9**	**F5**
Lilac Clo. E4	33	J6
Lilac Gdns. W5	64	G3
Lilac Gdns., Croy.	103	A3
Lilac Pl. SE11	**20**	**C2**
Lilac Pl. SE11	67	F4
Lilac St. W12	56	G7
Lilburne Gdns. SE9	79	B5
Lilburne Rd. SE9	79	B5
Lilburne Wk. NW10	47	C6
Pitfield Way		
Lile Cres. W7	55	B5
Lilestone St. NW8	**6**	**E6**
Lilestone St. NW8	7	G5
Lilestone St. NW8	57	H4
Lilford Rd. SE5	76	H2
Lilian Barker Clo. SE12	78	G5
Lilian Board Way, Grnf.	46	A5
Lilian Clo. N16	50	B3
Barbauld Rd.		
Lilian Gdns., Wdf.Grn.	42	H1
Lilian Rd. SW16	94	C1
Lillechurch Rd., Dag.	53	B6
Lilleshall Rd. SW3	93	G5
Lilley La. NW7	30	D5
Lillian Ave. W3	65	A2
Lillian Rd. SW13	65	G6
Lillie Rd. SW6	66	A6
Lillie Yd. SW6	66	A6
Lillieshall Rd. SW4	76	B3
Lillington Gdns. Est. SW1	**19**	**G2**
Lilliput Ave., Nthlt.	54	E1

Lily Clo. W14	66	A4
Gliddon Rd.		
Lily Gdns., Wem.	55	F2
Lily Pl. EC1	**12**	**F1**
Lily Pl. EC1	58	G5
Lily Rd. E17	42	A6
Lilyville Rd. SW6	75	C1
Limbourne Ave., Dag.	44	F7
Limburg Rd. SW11	75	J4
Lime Clo. E1	**17**	**J1**
Lime Clo. E1	68	D1
Lime Clo., Brom.	97	B4
Lime Clo., Buck.H.	35	A3
Lime Clo., Cars.	100	J2
Lime Clo., Har.	37	D2
Lime Clo., Rom.	44	J4
Lime Ct., Mitch.	93	G2
Lime Cres., Sun.	90	C2
Lime Gro. N20	31	C1
Lime Gro. W12	65	J2
Lime Gro., Ilf.	35	J6
Lime Gro., N.Mal.	92	D3
Lime Gro., Orp.	104	E2
Lime Gro., Ruis.	36	B6
Lime Gro., Sid.	79	J6
Lime Gro., Twick.	73	C6
Lime Rd., Rich.	73	J4
St. Mary's Gro.		
Lime Row, Erith	71	F3
Northwood Pl.		
Lime St. E17	41	H4
Lime St. EC3	**12**	**D6**
Lime St. EC3	59	B7
Lime St. Pas. EC3	**13**	**D5**
Lime Tree Ave., Esher	98	A1
Lime Tree Ave., T.Ditt.	98	B1
Lime Tree Gro., Croy.	102	J3
Lime Tree Pl., Mitch.	94	B1
Lime Tree Rd., Houns.	72	H1
Lime Tree Wk. (Bushey), Wat.	29	B1
Lime Tree Wk., W.Wick.	103	F4
Lime Wk. E15	60	E1
Church St. N.		
Limecroft Clo., Epsom	99	D7
Limedene Clo., Pnr.	36	D1
Limeharbour E14	69	B3
Limehouse Causeway E14	59	J7
Limehouse Flds. Est. E14	59	H5
Limerick Clo. SW12	76	C7
Limerston St. SW10	**18**	**D5**
Limerston St. SW10	66	F6
Limes, The W2	57	D7
Linden Gdns.		
Limes, The, Brom.	104	B2
Oakley Rd.		
Limes Ave. E11	42	H4
Limes Ave. N12	31	F4
Limes Ave. NW7	30	E6
Limes Ave. NW11	39	B7
Limes Ave. SE20	86	E7
Limes Ave. SW13	74	F2
Limes Ave., Cars.	100	J1
Limes Ave., Chig.	35	F5
Limes Ave., Croy.	101	G3
Limes Ave., The N11	32	B5
Limes Gdns. SW18	75	D6
Limes Gro. SE13	78	C4
Limes Pl., Croy.	95	A7
Limes Rd., Beck.	90	B2
Limes Rd., Croy.	95	A6
Limes Wk. SE15	77	E4
Limes Wk. W5	64	G2
Chestnut Gro.		
Limesdale Gdns., Edg.	38	C2
Limesfield Rd. SW14	74	E3
White Hart La.		
Limesford Rd. SE15	77	G4
Limestone Wk., Erith	71	D3
Alsike Rd.		
Limetree Clo. SW2	85	F1
Limetree Wk. SW17	85	A5
Church La.		
Limewood Clo. W13	55	E6
St. Stephens Rd.		
Limewood Ct., Ilf.	43	C5
Beehive La.		
Limewood Rd., Erith	71	J7
Limpsfield Ave. SW19	84	A2
Limpsfield Ave., Th.Hth.	94	F5

Linacre Rd. NW2	47	H6
Linberry Wk. SE8	68	H4
Carteret Way		
Linchmere Rd. SE12	78	F7
Lincoln Ave. N14	32	C3
Lincoln Ave. SW19	84	A3
Lincoln Ave., Twick.	81	H2
Lincoln Clo. SE25	95	D6
Woodside Grn.		
Lincoln Clo., Grnf.	54	J1
Lincoln Clo., Har.	36	F5
Lincoln Ct. N16	41	A7
Lincoln Ct., Borwd.	22	D5
Lincoln Cres., Enf.	25	B5
Lincoln Dr., Wat.	28	C3
Lincoln Gdns., Ilf.	43	B7
Lincoln Grn. Rd., Orp.	97	J5
Lincoln Ms. NW6	57	C1
Willesden La.		
Lincoln Ms. SE21	86	A2
Lincoln Rd. E7	52	A6
Lincoln Rd. E13	60	H4
Lincoln Rd. E18	42	G1
Grove Rd.		
Lincoln Rd. N2	39	H3
Lincoln Rd. SE25	95	E2
Lincoln Rd., Enf.	25	B4
Lincoln Rd., Felt.	81	F3
Lincoln Rd., Har.	36	F5
Lincoln Rd., Mitch.	94	E5
Lincoln Rd., N.Mal.	92	C3
Lincoln Rd., Sid.	89	B5
Lincoln Rd., Wem.	46	G6
Lincoln Rd., Wor.Pk.	99	H1
Lincoln St. E11	51	E2
Lincoln St. SW3	**31**	**J2**
Lincoln St. SW3	66	J4
Lincoln Way, Enf.	25	F5
Lincolns, The NW7	30	E5
Lincoln's Inn Flds. WC2	**12**	**C3**
Lincoln's Inn Flds. WC2	58	F6
Lincombe Rd., Brom.	87	F3
Lind Rd., Sutt.	100	F5
Lind St. SE8	74	A1
Lindal Cres., Enf.	24	E5
Lindal Rd. SE4	77	J5
Lindales, The N17	33	C6
Brantwood Rd.		
Lindbergh Rd., Wall.	101	E7
Linden Ave. NW10	57	A2
Linden Ave., Enf.	25	D1
Linden Ave., Houns.	72	H5
Linden Ave., Ruis.	45	A1
Linden Ave., Th.Hth.	94	H4
Linden Ave., Wem.	46	J5
Linden Clo. N14	24	C6
Linden Clo., Ruis.	45	A1
Linden Clo., Stan.	29	C5
Linden Clo., T.Ditt.	91	C7
Linden Ct. W12	65	J1
Linden Cres., Grnf.	46	C6
Linden Cres., Kings.T.	91	J2
Linden Cres., Wdf.Grn.	34	H6
Linden Gdns. W2	57	D7
Linden Gdns. W4	65	E5
Linden Gdns., Enf.	25	D1
Linden Gro. SE15	77	E3
Linden Gro. SE26	86	F6
Linden Gro., N.Mal.	92	E3
Linden Gro., Tedd.	82	C5
Waldegrave Rd.		
Linden Lawns, Wem.	46	J4
Linden Lea N2	39	F5
Linden Leas, W.Wick.	103	D2
Linden Ms. W2	57	D7
Linden Rd. N10	40	B4
Linden Rd. N11	31	J2
Linden Rd. N15	40	J4
Linden Rd., Hmptn.	81	G7
Linden Way N14	24	C6
Lindenfield, Chis.	97	E2
Lindens, The N12	31	G5
Lindens, The W4	74	C1
Hartington Rd.		
Lindens, The, Croy.	103	C6
Lindens, The, Loug.	27	C5
Lindeth Clo., Stan.	29	C6
Old Ch. La.		
Lindfield Gdns. NW3	48	F5
Lindfield Rd. W5	55	F4
Lindfield Rd., Croy.	95	C6
Lindfield St. E14	60	A6

Lindisfarne Rd. 83 G7
SW20
Lindisfarne Rd., 53 C3
Dag.
Lindisfarne Way E9 50 H4
Lindley Est. SE15 21 H7
Lindley Rd. E10 51 B2
Lindley St. E1 59 F5
Lindo St. SE15 77 F2
Selden Rd.
Lindore Rd. SW11 75 J4
Lindores Rd., Cars. 94 D5
Lindrop St. SW6 75 F2
Lindsay Clo., 98 H1
Chess.
Lindsay Dr., Har. 37 H6
Lindsay Rd., Hmptn. 81 H4
Lindsay Rd., 99 H2
Wor.Pk.
Lindsay Sq. SW1 19 J4
Lindsay Sq. SW1 67 D5
Lindsell St. SE10 78 C1
Lindsey Clo., Brom. 97 A3
Lindsey Clo., Mitch. 94 E4
Lindsey Ms. N1 49 J7
Lindsey Rd., Dag. 53 C4
Lindsey St. EC1 12 H1
Lindsey St. EC1 58 H5
Lindum Rd., Tedd. 82 F7
Lindway SE27 85 H5
Lindwood Clo. E6 61 B5
Northumberland Rd.
Linford Rd. E17 42 C3
Linford St. SW8 76 C1
Ling Rd. E16 60 G5
Ling Rd., Erith 71 J6
Lingards Rd. SE13 78 C4
Lingey Clo., Sid. 88 J2
Lingfield Ave., 91 H4
Kings.T.
Lingfield Clo., 25 B6
Enf.
Lingfield Cres. SE9 79 G4
Lingfield Gdns. N9 25 E7
Lingfield Rd. SW19 84 A6
Lingfield Rd., 99 J3
Wor.Pk.
Lingham St. SW9 76 E2
Lingholm Way, Barn. 23 A4
Lingmere Clo., 35 F2
Chig.
Lingrove Gdns., 34 H2
Buck.H.
Beech La.
Lings Coppice SE21 86 A2
Lingwell Rd. SW17 84 H3
Lingwood Gdns., 64 B7
Islw.
Lingwood Rd. E5 41 D7
Linhope St. NW1 6 J5
Linhope St. NW1 57 J4
Link, The W3 56 B6
Link, The, Enf. 25 H1
Link, The, Nthlt. 45 F5
Eastcote La.
Link, The, Pnr. 36 C7
Link, The, Wem. 46 F1
Nathans Rd.
Link La., Wall. 101 D6
Link Rd. N11 32 A4
Link Rd., Dag. 62 H2
Link Rd., Wall. 101 A1
Link St. E9 50 F5
Link Way, Brom. 97 B7
Link Way, Dag. 53 C4
Link Way, Pnr. 36 D1
Linkfield, Brom. 97 B7
Linkfield, W.Mol. 90 H3
Linkfield Rd., 73 C2
Islw.
Linklea Clo. NW9 30 E7
Links, The E17 41 H4
Links Ave., Mord. 93 D4
Links Dr. N20 31 D1
Links Gdns. SW16 85 G7
Links Rd. NW2 47 F2
Links Rd. SW17 85 A6
Links Rd. W3 56 A6
Links Rd., W.Wick. 103 C1
Links Rd., Wdf.Grn. 34 G5
Links Side, Enf. 24 F3
Links Vw. N3 31 C7
Links Vw. Clo., 29 D6
Stan.
Links Vw. Rd., 103 A3
Croy.
Links Vw. Rd., 81 J5
Hmptn.
Links Way, Beck. 96 A6
Linkside N12 31 C6
Linkside, Chig. 35 F5
Linkside, N.Mal. 92 E2
Linkside Clo., 24 F3

Linkside Gdns., Enf. 24 F3
Linksway NW4 39 A2
Linkway NW4 40 J7
Linkway SW20 92 H3
Linkway, Rich. 82 E3
Linkway, The, Barn. 23 E6
Linkwood Wk. NW1 49 D7
Maiden La.
Linley Cres., Rom. 44 H3
Linley Rd. N17 41 B2
Linnell Clo. NW11 39 E6
Linnell Dr. NW11 39 E6
Linnell Rd. N18 33 D5
Fairfield Rd.
Linnell Rd. SE5 77 B2
Linnet Clo. N9 33 G1
Linnet Clo. SE28 62 C7
Linnet Ms. SW12 76 A7
Linnett Clo. E4 34 C4
Linom Rd. SW4 76 E4
Linscott Rd. SE5 50 F4
Linsdell Rd., Bark. 61 F1
Linsey St. SE16 21 H1
Linsey St. SE16 68 D4
Linslade Clo., 72 E5
Houns.
Frampton Rd.
Linslade Clo., Pnr. 36 B3
Linstead Ct. SE9 79 H6
Linstead St. NW6 48 D7
Linstead Way SW18 75 B7
Linster Gro., 22 C5
Borwd.
Lintaine Clo. W6 66 B6
Moylan Rd.
Linthorpe Ave., 46 F6
Wem.
Linthorpe Rd. N16 41 B7
Linthorpe Rd., 23 H3
Barn.
Linton Clo., Well. 80 B1
Anthony Rd.
Linton Gdns. E6 61 B6
Linton Gro. SE27 85 H5
Linton Rd., Bark. 52 F7
Linton St. N1 58 J1
Lintons, The, Bark. 52 F7
Linver Rd. SW6 75 C2
Linwood Clo. E6 61 B5
Northumberland Rd.
Linwood Gro. SE5 77 C2
Linwood Way SE15 21 F7
Linzee Rd. N8 40 E4
Lion Ave., Twick. 82 C1
Lion Rd.
Lion Clo. SE4 78 A6
Lion Ct., Borwd. 22 C1
Lion Gate Gdns., 73 J3
Rich.
Lion Pk. Ave., 99 A4
Chess.
Lion Rd. E6 61 C5
Lion Rd. N9 33 D2
Lion Rd., Bexh. 80 F4
Lion Rd., Croy. 94 J5
Lion Rd., Twick. 82 C1
Lion Way, Brent. 64 G7
Lion Wf. Rd., Islw. 73 E3
Lionel Gdns. SE9 79 A5
Lionel Ms. W10 57 B5
Telford Rd.
Lionel Rd. SE9 79 A5
Lionel Rd., Brent. 64 H3
Lions Clo. SE9 87 J3
Liphook Cres. SE23 77 F7
Liphook Rd., Wat. 28 D4
Lippitts Hill, 26 E1
Loug.
Lipton Clo. SE28 62 C7
Aisher Rd.
Lipton Rd. E1 59 G6
Bower Rd.
Lisbon Ave., Twick. 81 J2
Lisburne Rd. NW3 48 J4
Lisford St. SE15 77 C1
Lisgar Ter. W14 66 C4
Liskeard Clo., 28 F6
Chis.
Liskeard Gdns. SE3 78 G1
Lisle St. WC2 11 J5
Lisle St. WC2 58 D7
Wellesley Rd.
Lismore Circ. NW5 49 A5
Lismore Clo., Islw. 73 D2
Lismore Rd. N17 41 A3
Lismore Rd., 102 B6
S.Croy.
Lismore Wk. N1 49 J6
Clephane Rd.
Liss Way SE15 21 G7
Lissenden Gdns. 49 A4
NW5
Lisson Grn. Est. NW8 6 G4

Lisson Grn. Est. NW8 57 H3
Lisson Gro. NW1 6 H6
Lisson Gro. NW1 57 H4
Lisson Gro. NW8 6 F5
Lisson Gro. NW8 57 G4
Lisson St. NW1 10 G1
Lisson St. NW1 57 H5
Lister Clo. W3 56 D5
Lister Clo., Mitch. 93 H1
Lister Gdns. N18 32 J5
Lister Ho. SE3 69 E6
Lister Ms. N7 49 F4
Lister Rd. E11 51 E1
Lister St. E13 60 G3
Sewell St.
Lister Wk. SE28 62 D7
Haldane Rd.
Liston Rd. N17 41 D1
Liston Rd. SW4 76 C3
Liston Way, 67 G7
Wdf.Grn.
Listowel Clo. SW9 51 E6
Mandela St.
Listowel Rd., Dag. 53 G3
Listria Pk. N16 50 E2
Litchfield Ave. E15 51 E6
Litchfield Ave., 93 C7
Mord.
Litchfield Gdns. 47 G6
NW10
Litchfield Rd., Sutt. 100 F4
Litchfield St. WC2 11 J5
Litchfield St. WC2 58 D7
Litchfield Way NW11 39 E5
Lithos Rd. NW3 48 F7
Little Acre, Beck. 96 A3
Little Albany St. 7 F4
NW1
Little Argyll St. W1 11 F4
Little Birches, Sid. 88 H2
Little Boltons, The 18 B3
SW10
Little Boltons, The 65 B5
SW10
Little Bornes SE21 86 B4
Little Britain EC1 12 H2
Little Britain EC1 58 H5
Little Brownings 86 E2
SE23
Little Bury St. N9 33 A1
Little Cedars N12 31 F4
Woodside Ave.
Little Chester St. 15 D5
SW1
Little Chester St. 67 B3
SW1
Little College St. 16 A5
SW1
Little Ct., W.Wick. 103 E2
Little Dean's Yd. 16 A5
SW1
Little Dimocks SW12 85 B2
Little Dorrit Ct. 17 A3
SE1
Little Dorrit Ct. SE1 67 J2
Little Dragons, 27 A4
Loug.
Little Ealing La. W5 64 F4
Little Edward St. 7 E3
NW1
Little Essex St. WC2 12 E5
Little Ferry Rd., 82 E1
Twick.
Ferry Rd.
Little Friday Rd. E4 34 E2
Little Gearies, Ilf. 43 E4
Little George St. 16 A4
SW1
Little Gra., Grnf. 55 D3
Perivale La.
Little Grn., Rich. 73 G4
Little Grn. St. NW5 49 B4
College La.
Little Halliards, Walt. 90 A6
Felix Rd.
Little Heath SE7 70 B5
Little Heath, Rom. 44 B4
Little Heath Rd., 80 E1
Bexh.
Little Ilford La. E12 52 C4
Little Marlborough 11 F4
St. W1
Little Moss La., Pnr. 36 E2
Little New St. EC4 12 F3
Little Newport St. 11 J5
WC2
Little Newport St. 58 D7
WC2
Little Orchard Clo., 36 E2
Pnr.
Barrow Pt. La.
Little Oxhey La., 28 D5
Wat.

Little Pk. Dr., Felt. 81 D2
Little Pk. Gdns., 24 J3
Enf.
Little Plucketts 34 J1
Way, Buck.H.
Little Portland St. 11 E3
W1
Little Portland St. 58 C1
W1
Little Queens Rd., 82 C6
Tedd.
Little Redlands, 97 B2
Brom.
Little Rd., Croy. 102 B1
Lwr. Addiscombe Rd.
Little Russell St. 12 A2
WC1
Little Russell St. 58 E5
WC1
Little St. James's 15 F2
St. SW1
Little St. James's St. 67 C1
SW1
Little St. Leonards 74 C3
SW14
Little Sanctuary SW1 15 J4
Little Smith St. SW1 15 J5
Little Somerset St. 13 F4
E1
Little Strand NW9 38 F2
Little Thrift, Orp. 97 F4
Little Titchfield St. 11 F2
W1
Little Trinity La. 13 A5
EC4
Little Turnstile WC1 12 C2
Littlebrook Clo., 95 G6
Croy.
Littlebury Rd. SW4 76 D3
Littlecombe SE7 69 H6
Littlecombe Clo. 75 A6
SW15
Littlecote Clo. 75 A7
SW19
Littlecroft SE9 79 D3
Littledale SE2 71 A6
Littlefield Clo. N19 49 C4
Junction Rd.
Littlefield Clo., 91 H2
Kings.T.
Fairfield W.
Littlefield Rd., 30 C7
Edg.
Littlegrove, Barn. 23 H6
Littleheath Rd., 102 E7
S.Croy.
Littlejohn Rd. W7 55 C6
Littlemead, Esher 98 A4
Littlemede SE9 88 C3
Littlemoor Rd., 52 D1
Ilf.
Littlemore Rd. SE2 71 A2
Littlers Clo. SW19 93 G1
Runnymede
Littlestone Clo., 87 A6
Beck.
Abbey La.
Littleton Ave. E4 34 F1
Littleton Cres., 46 C2
Har.
Littleton Rd., Har. 46 C2
Littleton St. SW18 84 F2
Littlewood SE13 78 C5
Littlewood Clo. W13 64 E3
Littleworth Ave. 98 A5
Esher
Littleworth Common 98 A3
Rd., Esher
Littleworth La. 98 A4
Esher
Littleworth Pl., 98 A4
Esher
Littleworth Rd., 98 A5
Esher
Livermere Rd. E8 59 C1
Liverpool Gro. SE17 21 B4
Liverpool Gro. SE17 68 A5
Liverpool Rd. E10 42 C6
Liverpool Rd. E16 60 E5
Liverpool Rd. N1 49 G7
Liverpool Rd. N7 49 G5
Liverpool Rd. W5 64 G2
Liverpool Rd., 83 A7
Kings.T.
Liverpool Rd., 94 J3
Th.Hth.
Liverpool St. EC2 13 D2
Liverpool St. EC2 59 B5
Livesey Pl. SE15 21 J5
Livingstone College 42 C6
Twrs. E10
Livingstone Pl. E14 69 C5
Ferry St.

Livingstone Rd. E15 60 C1
Livingstone Rd. E17 42 B6
Livingstone Rd. N13 32 E6
Livingstone Rd. 75 G3
SW11
Winstanley Rd.
Livingstone Rd., 72 J4
Houns.
Livingstone Rd., 54 D7
Sthl.
Livingstone Rd., 94 J2
Th.Hth.
Livingstone Wk. 75 G3
SW11
Livonia St. W1 11 G4
Lizard St. EC1 9 A4
Lizard St. EC1 58 J3
Lizban St. SE3 69 H7
Llanelly Rd. NW2 48 C2
Llanover Rd. SE18 70 D6
Llanover Rd., Wem. 46 G3
Llanthony Rd., 93 G6
Mord.
Llanvanor Rd. NW2 48 C2
Llewellyn St. SE16 17 J4
Lloyd Ave. SW16 94 E1
Lloyd Baker St. WC1 8 D4
Lloyd Baker St. WC1 58 F3
Lloyd Ct., Pnr. 36 D5
Lloyd Pk. Ave., 102 C4
Croy.
Lloyd Rd. E6 61 C1
Lloyd Rd. E17 41 G4
Lloyd Rd., Dag. 53 F6
Lloyd Rd., Wor.Pk. 99 J3
Lloyd Sq. WC1 8 E3
Lloyd Sq. WC1 58 G3
Lloyd St. WC1 8 E3
Lloyd St. WC1 58 G3
Lloyd's Ave. EC3 13 E4
Lloyd's Ave. EC3 59 B6
Lloyds Pl. SE3 78 E2
Lloyd's Row EC1 8 G4
Lloyds Way, Beck. 95 H5
Loampit Hill SE13 78 A2
Loampit Vale SE13 78 B3
Loanda Clo. E8 59 C1
Clarissa St.
Loats Rd. SW2 76 E6
Lobelia Clo. E6 61 B5
Sorrell Gdns.
Locarno Rd. W3 65 C1
High St.
Locarno Rd., Grnf. 54 J4
Lochaber Rd. SE13 78 F4
Lochaline St. W6 65 J6
Lochan Clo., Hayes 54 E4
Lochinvar St. SW12 76 B7
Lochmere Clo., 71 H6
Erith
Lochnagar St. E14 60 C5
Lock Chase SE3 78 E3
Lock Rd., Rich. 82 F4
Lockesfield Pl. E14 69 B5
Lockesley Dr., Orp. 97 J6
Lockesley Sq., 91 G6
Surb.
Locket Rd., Har. 37 B3
Lockfield Ave., 25 H2
Enf.
Lockhart Clo. N7 49 F6
Lockhart St. E3 59 J4
Lockhurst St. E5 50 G4
Lockie Pl. SE25 89 D3
Lockington Rd. SW8 76 B1
Lockmead Rd. N15 41 D6
Lockmead Rd. SE13 78 C3
Locks La., Mitch. 93 J1
Lockside E14 59 H7
Northey St.
Locksley Est. E14 59 J6
Locksley St. E14 59 J5
Locksmeade Rd., 82 F4
Rich.
Lockwood Clo. SE26 86 G4
Lockwood Ind. Pk. 41 E3
N17
Lockwood Sq. SE16 68 E3
Lockwood Way E17 41 G2
Lockwood Way, 99 A5
Chess.
Lockyer Est. SE1 17 C3
Lockyer St. SE1 17 C4
Loddiges Rd. E9 50 F7
Loder St. SE15 68 F7
Lodge Ave. SW14 74 E3
Lodge Ave., Croy. 101 G3
Lodge Ave., Dag. 62 A1
Lodge Ave., Har. 37 H4
Lodge Clo. N18 32 J5
Lodge Clo., Edg. 29 J6
Lodge Clo., Islw. 73 E1
Lodge Clo., Wall. 101 A1

Lodge Ct., Wem. 46 H5
Lodge Dr. N13 32 G4
Lodge Gdns., Beck. 95 J5
Lodge Hill, Ilf. 43 B4
Lodge Hill, Well. 71 B7
Lodge La. N12 31 F5
Lodge La., Bex. 80 D6
Lodge La., Croy. 103 A6
Lodge Pl., Sutt. 100 E5
Lodge Rd. NW4 38 J4
Lodge Rd. NW8 6 F4
Lodge Rd. NW8 57 G3
Lodge Rd., Brom. 87 H7
Lodge Rd., Croy. 94 H6
Lodge Rd., Wall. 101 B5
Lodge Vill., 34 F7
Wdf.Grn.
Lodgehill Pk. Clo., 45 H2
Har.
Lodore Gdns. NW9 38 E5
Lodore St. E14 60 C6
Loftie St. SE16 17 J4
Loftie St. SE16 68 D2
Lofting Rd. N1 49 F7
Loftus Rd. W12 65 H1
Logan Clo., Enf. 25 G1
Logan Clo., Houns. 72 F3
Logan Ms. W8 66 D4
Logan Pl. W8 66 D4
Logan Rd. N9 33 E2
Logan Rd., Wem. 46 H2
Loggetts, The SE21 86 A3
Logs Hill, Chis. 86 A7
Logs Hill Clo., 97 B1
Chis.
Lolesworth Clo. E1 13 G2
Lollard St. SE11 20 D1
Lollard St. SE11 67 G4
Loman St. SE1 16 H3
Loman St. SE1 67 H2
Lomas Clo., Croy. 103 C7
Lomas St. E8 50 C7
Lomas St. E1 13 J1
Lomas St. E1 59 D5
Lombard Ave., Enf. 25 F1
Lombard Ave., Ilf. 52 H1
Lombard Business 93 E2
Pk. SW19
Lombard St. EC3 13 C5
Lombard La. EC4 12 F4
Lombard Rd. N11 32 B5
Lombard Rd. SW11 75 G2
Lombard Rd. SW19 93 E2
Lombard St. EC3 13 C4
Lombard St. EC3 59 A6
Lombard Wall SE7 69 H3
Lombardy Pl. W2 10 A6
Lomond Clo. N15 41 B5
Lomond Clo., Wem. 46 J7
Lomond Gdns., 102 H7
S.Croy.
Lomond Gro. SE5 21 B7
Lomond Gro. SE5 68 A7
Lomond Ho. SE5 77 A1
Camberwell Grn.
Loncroft Rd. SE5 21 E5
Loncroft Rd. SE5 68 B6
Londesborough Rd. 50 B4
N16
London Bri. EC4 17 C1
London Bri. EC4 59 A7
London Bri. SE1 17 C1
London Bri. SE1 68 A1
London Bri. St. SE1 17 C2
London Bri. St. SE1 68 A1
London Flds. E8 50 E7
London Flds. E. 50 E7
Side E8
London Flds. W. 50 D7
Side E8
London Ind. Pk. E6 61 E5
London La. E8 50 E1
London La., Brom. 87 F7
London Ms. W2 10 F4
London Rd. E13 60 G2
London Rd. SE1 16 G5
London Rd. SE1 67 H3
London Rd. SE23 86 E1
London Rd. SW16 94 F1
London Rd. SW17 84 J7
London Rd., Bark. 52 E7
London Rd., Brom. 87 F7
London Rd., Croy. 94 G5
London Rd., Enf. 25 A4
London Rd., Epsom 99 G7
London Rd., Har. 46 B2
London Rd., Houns. 72 J3
London Rd., Islw. 73 C2
London Rd., 91 J2
Kings.T.
London Rd., Mitch. 93 H4
London Rd. Mitch. 94 A7
(Mitcham Junct.)

London Rd., Mord. 93 D5
London Rd., Rom. 44 G6
London Rd., Stan. 29 F5
London Rd., Sutt. 99 J4
London Rd., Th.Hth. 94 G5
London Rd., Twick. 73 D7
London Rd., Wall. 101 B4
London Rd., Wem. 46 H5
London Stile W4 65 A5
Wellesley Rd.
London St. EC3 13 E5
London St. W2 10 E3
London St. W2 57 G6
London Wall EC2 13 A2
London Wall EC2 58 J5
Long Acre WC2 12 A5
Long Acre WC2 58 E7
Long Ct. WC2 11 J6
Long Deacon Rd. E4 34 E1
Long Dr. W3 56 E6
Long Dr., Grnf. 54 H1
Long Dr., Ruis. 45 D4
Long Elmes, Har. 36 H1
Long Fld. NW9 30 E7
Long Grn., Chig. 35 H4
Long Hedges, Houns. 72 G1
Great W. Rd.
Long La. EC1 12 H1
Long La. EC1 58 H5
Long La. N2 39 F2
Long La. N3 31 E7
Long La. SE1 17 B4
Long La. SE1 68 A2
Long La., Bexh. 71 D7
Long La., Croy. 95 E6
Long Levs E4 34 B6
Long Mark Rd. E16 61 A5
Long Mead NW9 38 F1
Long Meadow NW5 49 D5
Torriano Ave.
Long Meadow Clo., 96 C7
W.Wick.
Long Pond Rd. SE3 78 E1
Long Reach Ct., 61 G2
Bark.
Long Reach Rd., 61 J4
Bark.
Long Rd. SW4 76 B4
Long St. E2 9 F3
Long St. E2 59 C3
Long Wk. SE1 17 E5
Long Wk. SE18 70 E6
Long Wk. SW13 74 E2
The Ter.
Long Wk., N.Mal. 92 C3
Long Yd. WC1 8 C6
Long Yd. WC1 58 F4
Longacre Pl., Cars. 101 A6
Beddington Gdns.
Longacre Rd. E17 42 D1
Longbeach Rd. SW11 75 J3
Longberrys NW2 48 C3
Longboat Row, Sthl. 54 F6
Longbridge Rd., 52 G6
Bark.
Longbridge Rd., 53 A4
Dag.
Longbridge Way 78 C5
SE13
Longcliffe Path, 28 A3
Wat.
Gosforth La.
Longcroft SE9 88 C3
Longcroft Ri., Loug. 27 D5
Longcrofte Rd., 29 G7
Edg.
Longdon Wd. Ave., 104 B3
Kes.
Longdown Rd. SE6 87 A4
Longfellow Rd. E17 41 J4
Longfellow Rd., 99 G1
Wor.Pk.
Longfellow Way SE1 21 G2
Longfield, Brom. 96 F1
Longfield, Loug. 26 J5
Longfield Ave. E17 41 H4
Longfield Ave. NW7 30 G7
Longfield Ave. W5 55 F7
Longfield Ave., 101 A1
Wall.
Longfield Ave., 46 H1
Wem.
Longfield Cres. 86 F3
SE26
Longfield Dr. SW14 74 B5
Longfield Dr., 84 H7
Mitch.
Longfield Est. SE1 21 G2
Longfield Est. SE1 68 C3
Longfield St. W5 55 F6
Longfield St. SW18 75 D7
Longfield Wk. W5 55 F6

Longford Ave., 54 G7
Sthl.
Longford Clo., 81 G4
Hmptn.
Longford Ct. E5 50 G4
Pedro St.
Longford Ct. NW4 39 A4
Longford Ct., Epsom 99 C4
Longford Gdns., 54 D7
Hayes
Longford Gdns., 100 F3
Sutt.
Longford Rd., 81 G1
Twick.
Longford St. NW1 7 E5
Longford St. NW1 58 B4
Longford Wk. SW2 76 G7
Papworth Way
Longhayes Ave., 44 D4
Rom.
Longheath Gdns., 95 F6
Croy.
Longhedge Ho. SE26 86 C4
Longhedge St. SW11 76 A2
Longhill Rd. SE6 87 D2
Longhook Gdns., 54 A2
Nthlt.
Longhope Clo. SE15 21 F6
Longhope Clo. SE15 68 B6
Longhurst Rd. SE13 78 D5
Longhurst Rd., 95 E6
Croy.
Longland Ct. SE1 21 H3
Longland Dr. N20 31 E3
Longlands Ct. W11 57 C7
Portobello Rd.
Longlands Ct., Mitch. 94 A1
Summerhill Way
Longlands Pk. 88 H3
Cres., Sid.
Longlands Rd., Sid. 88 H3
Longleat Ho., Enf. 25 B5
Longleigh La. SE2 71 C6
Longleigh La., 71 C6
Bexh.
Longlents Ho. NW10 56 D1
Shrewsbury Cres.
Longley Ave., Wem. 55 J1
Longley Rd. SW17 84 H6
Longley Rd., Croy. 94 H6
Longley Rd., Har. 36 J5
Longley St. SE1 21 H1
Longley St. SE1 68 D4
Longley Way NW2 47 J3
Longmead, Chis. 97 D2
Longmead Dr., Sid. 89 D2
Longmead Rd. SW17 84 J5
Longmead Rd., 91 B7
T.Ditt.
Longmeadow Rd., 88 H7
Sid.
Longmoor Pt. SW15 83 H1
Norley Vale
Longmoore St. SW1 19 F2
Longmore St. SW1 67 C4
Longmore Ave., 23 F6
Barn.
Longnor Rd. E1 59 G3
Longridge La. 54 H6
Sthl.
Longridge Rd. SW5 66 D4
Longs Ct., Rich. 73 J4
Crown Ter.
Longshaw Rd. E4 34 D3
Longshore SE8 68 J4
Longstaff Cres. 75 D6
SW18
Longstaff Rd. SW18 75 D6
Longstone Ave. 47 F7
NW10
Longstone Rd. SW17 85 B5
Longthornton Rd. 94 C2
SW16
Longton Ave. SE26 86 D4
Longton Gro. SE26 86 E4
Longville Rd. SE11 20 H1
Longwood Dr. SW15 74 G6
Longwood Gdns., 43 C4
Ilf.
Loning, The NW9 38 E4
Lonsdale Ave. E6 61 A4
Lonsdale Ave., Rom. 44 J6
Lonsdale Ave., Wem. 46 H5
Lonsdale Clo. E6 61 B4
Lonsdale Ave.
Lonsdale Clo. SE9 88 A3
Lonsdale Clo., Pnr. 36 E1
Uxbridge Rd.
Lonsdale Cres., Ilf. 43 E6
Lonsdale Dr., Enf. 24 D4
Lonsdale Gdns., 94 F4
Th.Hth.

Lonsdale Ms., Rich. 74 A1
Lonsdale Pl. N1 49 G7
Barnsbury La.
Lonsdale Rd. E11 42 F7
Lonsdale Rd. NW6 57 C1
Lonsdale Rd. SE25 95 E4
Lonsdale Rd. SW13 74 F1
Lonsdale Rd. W4 65 F4
Lonsdale Rd. W11 57 C6
Lonsdale Rd., Bexh. 80 F2
Lonsdale Rd., Sthl. 63 D3
Lonsdale Sq. N1 58 G1
Loobert Rd. N15 41 B3
Looe Gdns., Ilf. 43 E3
Loop Rd., Chis. 88 F6
Lopen Rd. N18 33 B4
Loraine Clo., Enf. 25 F5
Loraine Rd. N7 49 F4
Loraine Rd. W4 65 B6
Lord Ave., Ilf. 43 C4
Lord Chancellor 92 C1
Wk., Kings.T.
Lord Gdns., Ilf. 43 B4
Lord Hills Bri. W2 10 B2
Lord Hills Rd. W2 10 B1
Lord Hills Rd. W2 57 E5
Lord Holland La. 76 G1
SW9
Myatts Flds. S.
Lord Napier Pl. W6 65 G5
Upper Mall
Lord N. St. SW1 16 A6
Lord N. St. SW1 67 E3
Lord Roberts Ms. 66 E7
SW6
Moore Pk. Rd.
Lord Roberts Ter. 70 D5
SE18
Lord St. E16 70 B1
Lord Warwick St. 70 C3
SE18
Lorden Wk. E2 9 H4
Lord's Clo. SE21 85 J2
Lords Clo., Felt. 81 E2
Lord's Vw. NW8 6 F4
Lordship Gro. N16 50 A2
Lordship La. N17 40 J1
Lordship La. N22 40 G2
Lordship La. SE22 77 C6
Lordship La. Est. 86 D1
SE22
Lordship Pk. N16 49 J2
Lordship Pk. Ms. 49 J2
N16
Allerton Rd.
Lordship Pl. SW3 18 G6
Lordship Rd. N16 50 A1
Lordship Rd., 45 E7
Nthlt.
Lordship Ter. N16 50 A2
Lordsmead Rd. N17 41 B1
Lorenzo St. WC1 8 C2
Lorenzo St. WC1 58 F3
Loretto Gdns., Har. 37 H4
Lorian Clo. N12 31 E4
Loring Rd. N20 31 H2
Loring Rd., Islw. 73 C2
Loris Rd. W6 65 J3
Lorn Rd. SW9 76 F2
Lorne Ave., Croy. 95 G7
Lorne Clo. NW8 6 H4
Lorne Gdns. E11 42 J4
Lorne Gdns. W11 66 A2
Lorne Gdns., Croy. 95 G7
Lorne Rd. E7 51 H4
Lorne Rd. E17 42 A5
Lorne Rd. N4 49 F1
Lorne Rd., Har. 37 C2
Lorne Rd., Rich. 73 J5
Albert Rd.
Lorraine Rd., Har. 29 B7
Lorrimore Rd. SE17 20 H5
Lorrimore Rd. SE17 67 H6
Lorrimore Sq. SE17 20 H5
Lorrimore Sq. SE17 67 H6
Losberne Way SE16 21 J4
Loseberry Rd., 98 A5
Esher
Lothair Rd. W5 64 G2
Lothair Rd. N. N4 40 H6
Lothair Rd. S. N4 40 G7
Lothbury EC2 13 B3
Lothbury EC2 59 A6
Lothian Ave., Hayes 54 B5
Lothian Clo., Wem. 46 D4
Lothian Rd. SW9 76 H1
Lothrop St. W10 57 B3
Lots Rd. SW10 66 F7
Loubet St. SW17 84 J6
Loudoun Ave., Ilf. 43 E5
Loudoun Rd. NW8 57 F1
Loudwater Clo., 90 A4
Sun.

Loudwater Rd., Sun. 90 A4
Lough Rd. N7 49 F5
Loughborough Est. 76 H2
SW9
Loughborough Rd.
Loughborough Pk. 76 H4
SW9
Loughborough Rd. 76 G2
SW9
Loughborough St. 20 D4
SE11
Loughborough St. 67 F5
SE11
Loughton Way, 35 A1
Buck.H.
Louisa Gdns. E1 59 G4
Louisa St.
Louisa Ho. SW15 74 F4
Arabella Dr.
Louisa St. E1 59 G4
Louise Rd. E15 51 E6
Louisville Rd. SW17 85 A3
Louvaine Rd. SW11 75 G4
Lovage App. E6 61 B5
Lovat Clo. NW2 47 F3
Lovat La. EC3 13 D6
Lovat Wk., Houns. 63 E7
Cranford La.
Lovatt Clo., Edg. 30 B6
Love La. EC2 13 A3
Love La. EC2 58 J6
Love La. N17 33 C7
Love La. SE18 70 E4
Love La. SE25 95 E3
Love La., Bex. 80 F6
Love La., Mitch. 93 H3
Love La., Mord. 93 D7
Love La., Pnr. 36 E3
Love La., Surb. 98 F2
Love La., Sutt. 100 B6
Love La., Wdf.Grn. 35 C6
Love Wk. SE5 77 A4
Lovegrove St. SE1 21 J5
Lovegrove St. SE1 68 D5
Lovegrove Wk. E14 69 C1
Lovekyn Clo., 91 J2
Kings.T.
Queen Elizabeth Rd.
Lovel Ave., Well. 80 A2
Lovelace Ave., 97 D6
Brom.
Lovelace Gdns., 53 A4
Bark.
Lovelace Gdns., 91 G7
Surb.
Lovelace Grn. SE9 79 C3
Lovelace Rd. SE21 85 J2
Lovelace Rd., Barn. 23 H7
Lovelace Rd., Surb. 91 F7
Lovelinch Clo. SE15 68 F6
Lovell Ho. E8 59 D1
Lovell Pl. SE16 68 H3
Ropemaker Rd.
Lovell Rd., Rich. 82 F3
Lovell Rd., Sthl. 54 H6
Loveridge Ms. NW6 48 C6
Loveridge Rd.
Loveridge Rd. NW6 48 C6
Lovers Wk. N3 31 D7
Lovers Wk. NW7 31 D7
Lovers Wk. SE10 69 E7
Lover's Wk. W1 15 B1
Lover's Wk. W1 67 A1
Lovett Dr., Cars. 93 F7
Lovett Way NW10 47 C5
Lovibonds Ave., 104 E3
Orp.
Low Cross Wd. La. 86 C3
SE21
Low Hall Clo. E4 26 A7
Low Hall La. E17 41 H6
Lowbrook Rd., Ilf. 52 E4
Lowden Rd. N9 33 E1
Lowden Rd. SE24 76 H4
Lowden Rd., Sthl. 54 E7
Lowe Ave. E16 60 G5
Charford Rd.
Lowell St. E14 59 H6
Lwr. Addiscombe 102 B1
Rd., Croy.
Lwr. Addison Gdns. 66 B2
W14
Lwr. Alderton Hall 27 D5
La., Loug.
Lwr. Belgrave St. 15 D6
SW1
Lwr. Belgrave St. 67 B3
SW1
Lwr. Boston Rd. W7 64 B1
Lwr. Broad St., 62 G1
Dag.
Lwr. Camden, Chis. 88 C7

Lwr. Clapton Rd. E5 50 F5
Lwr. Clarendon Wk. 57 B6
W11
Lancaster Rd.
Lwr. Common S. 74 H3
SW15
Lwr. Coombe St., 101 J4
Croy.
Lwr. Downs Rd. 93 A1
SW20
Lwr. Drayton Pl., 101 H2
Croy.
Drayton Rd.
Lwr. George St., 73 G5
Rich.
George St.
Lwr. Gravel Rd., 104 B1
Brom.
Lwr. Grn. W., Mitch. 93 H3
Lwr. Grosvenor Pl. 15 D5
SW1
Lwr. Grosvenor Pl. 67 B3
SW1
Lwr. Gro. Rd., 73 J6
Rich.
Lwr. Hall La. E4 33 H5
Lwr. Ham Rd., 82 G6
Kings.T.
Lwr. Hampton Rd., 90 C3
Sun.
Lwr. James St. W1 11 G5
Lwr. John St. W1 11 G5
Lwr. Kenwood Ave., 24 D5
Enf.
Lwr. Lea Crossing 60 E7
E14
Lwr. Maidstone Rd. 32 C6
N11
Telford Rd.
Lwr. Mall W6 65 H5
Lwr. Mardyke Ave., 62 J2
Rain.
Lwr. Marsh SE1 16 E4
Lwr. Marsh SE1 67 F2
Lwr. Marsh La., 91 J4
Kings.T.
Lwr. Merton Ri. NW3 48 H7
Lwr. Morden La., 93 A6
Mord.
Lwr. Mortlake Rd., 73 H4
Rich.
Lwr. Pk. Rd. N11 32 C5
Lwr. Pk. Rd., Belv. 71 G3
Lwr. Pk. Rd., Loug. 27 A5
Lwr. Queens Rd., 35 A2
Buck.H.
Lwr. Richmond Rd. 74 B3
SW14
Lwr. Richmond Rd. 74 H3
SW15
Lwr. Richmond Rd., 74 A3
Rich.
Lwr. Rd. SE8 68 G4
Lwr. Rd. SE16 68 F3
Lwr. Rd., Belv. 71 H3
Lwr. Rd., Har. 46 A1
Lwr. Rd., Loug. 27 D1
Lwr. Rd., Sutt. 100 F4
Lwr. Robert St. WC2 12 B6
Lwr. Sloane St. SW1 19 B2
Lwr. Sloane St. SW1 67 A4
Lwr. Sq., Islw. 73 E3
Lwr. Strand NW9 38 F2
Lwr. Sunbury Rd., 90 F2
Hmptn.
Lwr. Sydenham Ind. 86 J5
Est. SE26
Lwr. Tail, Wat. 28 E3
Lwr. Talbot Wk. W11 57 B6
Lancaster Rd.
Lwr. Teddington 82 G7
Rd., Kings.T.
Lwr. Ter. NW3 48 F3
Lwr. Thames St. EC3 13 C6
Lwr. Thames St. EC3 59 A3
Lwr. Wd. Rd., Esher 98 D6
Lowestoft Clo. E5 50 F2
Theydon Rd.
Loweswater Clo., 46 G2
Wem.
Lowfield Rd. NW6 48 D7
Lowfield Rd. W3 56 C6
Lowick Rd., Har. 37 B4
Lowlands Gdns., 44 H6
Rom.
Lowlands Rd., Har. 37 B6
Lowlands Rd., Pnr. 36 C6
Lowman Rd. N7 49 F4
Lowndes Clo. SW1 15 C6
Lowndes Clo. SW1 67 A3
Lowndes Pl. SW1 15 B6
Lowndes Pl. SW1 67 A3
Lowndes Sq. SW1 15 A4

Lowndes Sq. SW1 66 J3
Lowndes St. SW1 15 A5
Lowndes St. SW1 66 J3
Lowood Ct. SE19 86 C5
Lowood St. E1 59 E7
Dellow St.
Lowry Cres., Mitch. 93 H2
Lowshoe La., Rom. 44 G1
Lowth Rd. SE5 76 J2
Lowther Dr., Enf. 24 F4
Lowther Gdns., SW7 14 E4
Lowther Hill SE23 77 H7
Lowther Rd. E17 41 H2
Lowther Rd. N7 49 G5
Mackenzie Rd.
Lowther Rd. SW13 74 F1
Lowther Rd., 91 J1
Kings.T.
Lowther Rd., Stan. 37 J3
Loxford Ave. E6 61 A2
Loxford La., Ilf. 52 F5
Loxford Rd., Bark. 52 E6
Loxham Rd. E4 34 A7
Loxham St. WC1 8 B4
Loxley Clo. SE26 86 G5
Loxley Rd. SW18 84 G1
Loxley Rd., Hmptn. 81 F4
Loxton Rd. SE23 86 G1
Loxwood Rd. N17 41 B3
Lubbock Rd., Chis. 88 C7
Lubbock St. SE14 68 F7
Lucan Pl. SW3 18 G2
Lucan Pl. SW3 66 H4
Lucan Rd., Barn. 20 C3
Lucas Ave. E13 60 H1
Lucas Ave., Har. 45 G2
Lucas Ct., Har. 45 G2
Lucas Rd. SE20 86 F6
Lucas Sq. NW11 39 D6
Hampstead Way
Lucas St. SE8 78 A1
Lucerne Clo. N13 32 E3
Lucerne Ct., Erith 71 E3
Middle Way
Lucerne Gro. E17 42 D4
Lucerne Ms. W8 66 D1
Kensington Mall
Lucerne Rd. N5 49 H4
Lucerne Rd., Orp. 104 J1
Lucerne Rd., 94 H5
Th.Hth.
Lucey Rd. SE16 17 H6
Lucey Rd. SE16 68 D3
Lucey Way SE16 17 J6
Lucien Rd. SW17 85 A4
Lucien Rd. SW19 84 E2
Lucknow St. SE18 70 H7
Lucorn Clo. SE12 78 F6
Luctons Ave., 34 J1
Buck.H.
Lucy Cres. W3 56 C5
Lucy Gdns., Dag. 53 E3
Grafton Rd.
Luddesdon Rd., 71 G6
Erith
Ludford Clo. NW9 38 E2
Ludford Clo., Croy. 101 H4
Warrington Rd.
Ludgate Bdy. EC4 12 G4
Ludgate Bdy. EC4 58 H6
Ludgate Circ. EC4 12 G4
Ludgate Ct. EC4 12 G4
Ludgate Hill EC4 12 G4
Ludgate Hill EC4 58 H6
Ludgate Sq. EC4 12 H4
Ludham Clo. SE28 62 C6
Rollesby Way
Ludlow Clo., Brom. 96 G3
Ludlow Clo., Har. 45 F4
Ludlow Mead, Wat. 28 B3
Ludlow Rd. W5 56 F3
Ludlow Rd., Felt. 81 A4
Ludlow St. EC1 8 A5
Ludlow Way N2 39 F4
Ludovick Wk. SW15 74 F4
Ludwick Ms. SE14 68 H7
Luffield Rd. SE2 71 B3
Luffman Rd. SE12 87 H3
Lugard Rd. SE15 77 E2
Lugg App. E12 52 D3
Romford Rd.
Luke Ho. E1 59 E6
Luke St. EC2 9 D5
Luke St. EC2 59 B4
Lukin Cres. E4 34 D3
Lukin St. E1 59 F6
Lullingstone Clo., 89 B7
Orp.
Lullingstone Cres.
Lullingstone Cres., 89 A7
Orp.
Lullingstone Rd., 71 F6
Belv.

Entry	Page	Grid
Lullington Garth N12	31	C5
Lullington Garth, Borwd.	22	B5
Lullington Garth, Brom.	87	E7
Lullington Rd. SE20	86	D7
Lullington Rd., Dag.	53	E7
Lulot Gdns. N19	49	B2
Dartmouth Pk. Hill		
Lulworth SE17	21	B3
Lulworth Ave., Houns.	63	H7
Lulworth Ave., Wem.	37	F7
Lulworth Clo., Har.	45	F3
Lulworth Cres., Mitch.	93	H2
Lulworth Dr., Pnr.	36	D7
Lulworth Gdns., Har.	45	E2
Lulworth Rd. SE9	88	B2
Lulworth Rd. SE15	77	E2
Lulworth Rd., Well.	79	J2
Lulworth Waye, Hayes	54	B6
Lumley Clo., Belv.	71	G6
Lumley Ct. WC2	12	B6
Lumley Gdns., Sutt.	100	B5
Lumley Rd., Sutt.	100	B6
Lumley St. W1	11	C4
Lumley St. W1	58	A6
Luna Rd., Th.Hth.	94	J3
Lunar Ho., Croy.	101	J1
Lundin Wk., Wat.	28	D4
Woodhall La.		
Lundy Wk. N1	49	J6
Marquess Est.		
Lunham Rd. SE19	86	B6
Lupin Clo. SW2	85	H2
Palace Rd.		
Lupin Clo., Croy.	102	G1
Primrose La.		
Lupton Clo. SE12	87	H4
Lupton St. NW5	49	C4
Lupus St. SW1	19	E4
Lupus St. SW1	67	B5
Luralda Gdns. E14	69	C5
Saunders Ness Rd.		
Lurgan Ave. W6	66	A6
Lurline Gdns. SW11	76	A1
Luscombe Ct., Brom.	96	E2
Luscombe Way SW8	20	A7
Luscombe Way SW8	67	E7
Lushes Rd., Loug.	27	E5
Lushington Rd. NW10	56	H2
Lushington Rd. SE6	87	B5
Lushington Ter. E8	50	D5
Wayland Ave.		
Luther Clo., Edg.	30	C2
Luther King Clo. E17	41	H6
Luther Rd., Tedd.	82	C5
Luton Pl. SE10	69	C7
Luton Rd. E17	41	J3
Luton Rd., Sid.	89	C3
Luton St. NW8	6	F4
Luton St. NW8	57	G4
Lutton Ter. NW3	48	G4
Flask Wk.		
Luttrell Ave. SW15	74	H5
Lutwyche Rd. SE6	86	J2
Luxborough La., Chig.	35	B3
Luxborough St. W1	7	B6
Luxborough St. W1	58	A5
Luxemburg Gdns. W6	66	A4
Luxfield Rd. SE9	88	B1
Luxford St. SE16	68	A3
Luxmore Gdns. SE4	77	J1
Luxmore St.		
Luxmore St. SE4	77	J1
Luxor St. SE5	76	J3
Lyal Rd. E3	59	H2
Lyall Ave. SE21	86	B3
Lyall Ms. SW1	15	B6
Lyall Ms. SW1	67	A3
Lyall Ms. W. SW1	15	B6
Lyall St. SW1	15	B6
Lyall St. SW1	67	A3
Lycett Pl. W12	65	G2
Becklow Rd.		
Lyconby Gdns., Croy.	95	H7
Lydd Clo., Sid.	88	H3
Lydd Rd., Bexh.	71	F7
Lydden Ct. SE9	79	H6
Lydden Gro. SW18	75	E7
Lydden Rd. SW18	75	E7
Lydeard Rd. E6	52	C7
Lydford Rd. N15	41	A5
Lydford Rd. NW2	47	J6
Lydford Rd. W9	57	C4
Lydney Clo. SE15	21	E7
Lydney Clo. SW19	84	B2
Princes Way		
Lydon Rd. SW4	76	C3
Lydstep Rd., Chis.	88	D4
Lyford Rd. SW18	75	G7
Lygon Pl. SW1	15	D6
Lyham Clo. SW2	76	E6
Lyham Rd. SW2	76	E5
Lyme Fm. Rd. SE12	78	G4
Lyme Rd., Well.	80	B1
Lyme St. NW1	49	C7
Lyme Ter. NW1	49	C7
Royal College St.		
Lymer Ave. SE19	86	C5
Lymescote Gdns., Sutt.	100	D2
Lyminge Clo., Sid.	88	J4
Lyminge Gdns. SW18	84	H1
Lymington Ave. N22	40	G2
Lymington Clo. SW16	94	D2
Lymington Gdns., Epsom	99	F5
Lymington Rd. NW6	48	E6
Lymington Rd., Dag.	53	D1
Lympstone Gdns. SE15	21	J7
Lympstone Gdns. SE15	68	D7
Lynbridge Gdns. N13	32	H4
Lynbrook Clo. SE15	21	E7
Lynch Wk. SE8	68	J6
Prince St.		
Lynchen Clo., Houns.	72	A1
The Ave.		
Lyncott Cres. SW4	76	B4
Lyncroft Ave., Pnr.	36	E5
Lyncroft Gdns. NW6	48	D5
Lyncroft Gdns. W13	64	F2
Lyncroft Gdns., Houns.	72	J5
Lyndale NW2	48	C4
Lyndale Ave. NW2	48	C3
Lyndale Clo. SE3	69	F6
Lyndhurst Ave. N12	31	J6
Lyndhurst Ave. NW7	30	E6
Lyndhurst Ave. SW16	94	D2
Lyndhurst Ave., Pnr.	36	B1
Lyndhurst Ave., Sthl.	63	H1
Lyndhurst Ave., Sun.	90	A3
Lyndhurst Ave., Surb.	99	B1
Lyndhurst Ave., Twick.	81	F1
Lyndhurst Clo. NW10	47	D3
Lyndhurst Clo., Bexh.	80	H3
Lyndhurst Clo., Croy.	102	C3
Lyndhurst Clo., Orp.	104	E4
Lyndhurst Dr. E10	42	C7
Lyndhurst Dr., N.Mal.	92	E6
Lyndhurst Gdns. N3	39	B1
Lyndhurst Gdns. NW3	48	G5
Lyndhurst Gdns., Bark.	52	H6
Lyndhurst Gdns., Enf.	25	B4
Lyndhurst Gdns., Ilf.	43	G6
Lyndhurst Gdns., Pnr.	36	B1
Lyndhurst Gro. SE15	77	B2
Lyndhurst Ri., Chig.	35	D4
Lyndhurst Rd. E4	34	C7
Lyndhurst Rd. N18	33	D4
Lyndhurst Rd. N22	32	F6
Lyndhurst Rd. NW3	48	G5
Lyndhurst Rd., Bexh.	80	H3
Lyndhurst Rd., Grnf.	54	H4
Lyndhurst Rd., Th.Hth.	94	G4
Lyndhurst Sq. SE15	77	C1
Lyndhurst Ter. NW3	48	G5
Lyndhurst Way SE15	77	C1
Lyndhurst Way, Sutt.	100	D7
Lyndon Ave., Pnr.	28	E6
Lyndon Ave., Sid.	79	J5
Lyndon Ave., Wall.	101	A3
Lyndon Rd., Belv.	71	G4
Lyne Cres. E17	41	J1
Lyneham Wk. E5	50	H5
Ashenden Rd.		
Lynett Rd., Dag.	53	D2
Lynette Ave. SW4	76	B6
Lynford Clo., Edg.	38	C1
Lynford Gdns., Edg.	30	B3
Lynford Gdns., Ilf.	52	J2
Lynmere Rd., Well.	80	B2
Lynmouth Ave., Enf.	25	C6
Lynmouth Ave., Mord.	93	A7
Lynmouth Dr., Ruis.	45	B2
Lynmouth Gdns., Grnf.	55	E1
Lynmouth Gdns., Houns.	72	D1
Lynmouth Rd. E17	41	H6
Lynmouth Rd. N2	39	J4
Lynmouth Rd. N16	50	C1
Lynmouth Rd., Grnf.	55	E1
Lynn Clo., Har.	37	A2
Lynn Ms. E11	51	E2
Lynn Rd.		
Lynn Rd. E11	51	E2
Lynn Rd. SW12	76	B7
Lynn Rd., Ilf.	43	G7
Lynn Rd., Enf.	25	A1
Lynne Way, Nthlt.	54	D2
Lynsted Clo., Bexh.	80	H5
Lynsted Clo., Brom.	96	J2
Lynsted Ct., Beck.	95	H2
Churchfields Rd.		
Lynsted Gdns. SE9	79	A3
Lynton Ave. N12	31	G4
Lynton Ave. NW9	38	D4
Lynton Ave. W13	55	D6
Lynton Ave., Rom.	44	G1
Lynton Clo., Chess.	98	H4
Lynton Clo., Islw.	73	C4
Lynton Cres., Ilf.	43	E6
Lynton Est. SE1	21	H2
Lynton Gdns. N11	32	D6
Lynton Gdns., Enf.	25	F7
Lynton Mead N20	31	D3
Lynton Rd. E4	34	B6
Lynton Rd. N8	40	D5
Lynton Rd. NW6	57	C2
Lynton Rd. SE1	21	E2
Lynton Rd. W3	56	A7
Lynton Rd., Croy.	94	G6
Lynton Rd., Har.	45	E2
Lynton Rd., N.Mal.	92	D5
Lynwood Clo. E18	42	J1
Lynwood Clo., Har.	45	E3
Lynwood Dr., Wor.Pk.	99	G2
Lynwood Gdns., Croy.	101	F4
Lynwood Gdns., Sthl.	54	E7
Lynwood Gro. N21	32	G1
Lynwood Gro., Orp.	97	H7
Lynwood Rd. SW17	84	J3
Lynwood Rd. W5	55	H4
Lynwood Rd., T.Ditt.	98	C2
Lyon Ind. Est., Bark.	61	H2
Lyon Meade, Stan.	37	F1
Lyon Pk. Ave., Wem.	46	H6
Lyon Rd. SW19	93	F1
Lyon Rd., Har.	37	C6
Lyon St. N1	49	F7
Caledonian Rd.		
Lyon Way, Grnf.	55	B1
Lyons Pl. NW8	6	E6
Lyons Pl. NW8	57	G4
Lyons Wk. W14	66	B4
Lyonsdown Ave., Barn.	23	F6
Lyonsdown Rd., Barn.	23	E6
Lyoth Rd., Orp.	104	F2
Lyric Dr., Grnf.	54	H4
Lyric Rd. SW13	74	F1
Lysander Gro. N19	49	D1
Lysander Rd., Croy.	101	F6
Lysander Way, Orp.	104	F3
Lysia St. SW6	66	A7
Lysias Rd. SW12	76	B6
Lysons Wk. SW15	74	G5
Swinburne Rd.		
Lytchet Rd., Brom.	87	H7
Lytchet Way, Enf.	25	F1
Lytchgate Clo., S.Croy.	102	B7
Lyte St. E2	59	F2
Bishops Way		
Lytham Ave., Wat.	28	D5
Lytham Gro. W5	55	J3
Lytham St. SE17	21	B4
Lytham St. SE17	68	A5
Lytton Clo. NW3	48	H7
Hawtrey Rd.		
Lyttelton Rd. E10	51	B3
Lyttelton Rd. N8	40	G3
Lytton Ave. N13	32	G2
Lytton Clo. N2	39	F6
Lytton Clo., Loug.	27	G3
Lytton Clo., Nthlt.	45	F7
Lytton Gdns., Wall.	101	D4
Lytton Gro. SW15	75	A5
Lytton Rd. E11	42	E7
Lytton Rd., Barn.	23	F4
Lytton Rd., Pnr.	28	E7
Lytton Strachey Path SE28	62	B7
Titmuss Ave.		
Lyveden Rd. SE3	69	H7
Lyveden Rd. SW17	84	H6

M

Entry	Page	Grid
Maberley Cres. SE19	86	D7
Maberley Rd. SE19	95	C1
Maberley Rd., Beck.	95	G3
Mabledon Pl. WC1	7	J4
Mabledon Pl. WC1	58	D3
Mablethorpe Rd. SW6	66	B7
Mabley St. E9	50	H5
Macaret Clo. N20	23	F7
Macarthur Ter. SE7	70	A6
Macaulay Ave., Esher	98	B2
Macaulay Ct. SW4	76	B3
Macaulay Rd. E6	61	A2
Macaulay Rd. SW4	76	B3
Macaulay Sq. SW4	76	B4
Macaulay Way SE28	62	B7
Booth Clo.		
Macaulay Ms. SE13	78	C1
Macbean St. SE18	70	E3
Macbeth St. W6	65	H5
Macclesfield Bri. NW1	6	H1
Macclesfield Bri. NW1	57	H2
Macclesfield Rd. EC1	8	J3
Macclesfield Rd. EC1	58	J3
Macclesfield Rd. SE25	95	E5
Macclesfield St. W1	11	J5
Macdonald Ave., Dag.	53	H3
Macdonald Rd. E7	51	G4
Macdonald Rd. E17	42	C2
Macdonald Rd. N11	31	J5
Macdonald Rd. N19	49	C2
Macduff Rd. SW11	76	A1
Mace Clo. E1	68	E1
Kennet St.		
Mace St. E2	59	G2
MacFarlane La., Islw.	65	J1
Macfarlane Rd. W12	65	J1
Macfarren Pl. NW1	7	C6
Macgregor Rd. E16	60	J5
Machell Rd. SE15	77	F3
Mackay Rd. SW4	76	B3
Mackennal St. NW8	6	H1
Mackennal St. NW8	57	H2
Mackenzie Rd. N7	49	F6
Mackenzie Rd., Beck.	95	F2
Mackenzie Wk. E14	69	A1
Cabot Sq.		
Mackeson Rd. NW3	48	J4
Mackie Rd. SW2	76	G7
Mackintosh La. E9	50	G6
High St.		
Macklin St. WC2	12	B3
Macklin St. WC2	58	E6
Mackrow Wk. E14	60	C7
Poplar High St.		
Macks Rd. SE16	21	J1
Macks Rd. SE16	68	D4
Mackworth St. NW1	7	F3
Mackworth St. NW1	58	C3
Maclaren Ms. SW15	74	J4
Clarendon Dr.		
Maclean Rd. SE23	77	H6
Macleod St. SE17	21	A4
Macleod St. SE17	67	J5
Maclise Rd. W14	66	B3
Macoma Rd. SE18	70	G6
Macoma Ter. SE18	70	G6
Maconochies Rd. E14	69	B5
Macquarie Way E14	69	B4

Macready Pl. N7 49 E4
  Walters Rd.
Macroom Rd. W9 57 C3
Mada Rd., Orp. 104 E2
Maddams St. E3 60 B4
Maddison Clo., Tedd. 82 C6
Maddox Way SE17 20 H6
Maddocks Clo., Sid. 89 D5
Maddox St. W1 11 E5
Maddox St. W1 58 B7
Madeira Ave., Brom. 87 E7
Madeira Gro., 34 J6
  Wdf.Grn.
Madeira Rd. E11 51 D1
Madeira Rd. N13 32 H4
Madeira Rd. SW16 85 E5
Madeira Rd., Mitch. 93 J4
Madeley Rd. W5 56 H6
Madeline Rd. SE20 86 D7
Madison Cres., 71 C7
  Bexh.
Madison Gdns., 71 C7
  Bexh.
Madison Gdns., 96 F3
  Brom.
Madras Pl. N7 49 G6
Madras Rd., Ilf. 52 E4
Madrid Rd. SW13 74 G1
Madrigal La. SE5 67 H7
Madron St. SE17 21 E3
Madron St. SE17 68 B5
Mafeking Ave. E6 61 B2
Mafeking Ave., 64 H6
  Brent.
Mafeking Ave., Ilf. 43 G7
Mafeking Rd. E16 60 F4
Mafeking Rd. N17 41 D2
Mafeking Rd., Enf. 25 C3
Magdala Ave. N19 49 B2
Magdala Rd., Islw. 73 D3
Magdala Rd., 102 A7
  S.Croy.
  Napier Rd.
Magdalen Pas. E1 13 G5
Magdalen Rd. SW18 84 F1
Magdalen St. SE1 17 D2
Magdalen St. SE1 68 B1
Magdalene Clo. SE15 77 E2
  Heaton Rd.
Magdalene Gdns. E6 61 D4
Magee St. SE11 20 E5
Magee St. SE11 67 G6
Maggie Blake's 17 F2
  Cause SE1
Magnin Clo. E8 59 D1
  Wilde Clo.
Magnolia Clo., 83 B6
  Kings.T.
Magnolia Ct., Har. 37 J7
Magnolia Ct., Rich. 74 B1
  West Hall Rd.
Magnolia Pl. SW4 76 E5
Magnolia Pl. W5 55 H5
  Montpelier Rd.
Magnolia Rd. W4 65 B6
Magnolia Way, 99 C5
  Epsom
Magpie All. EC4 12 F4
Magpie Clo. NW9 38 E2
  Eagle Dr.
Magpie Clo., Enf. 25 D1
Magpie Hall Clo., 97 B6
  Brom.
Magpie Hall La., 97 B7
  Brom.
Magpie Hall Rd. 29 B2
  (Bushey), Wat.
Magri Wk. E1 59 F5
  Ashfield St.
Maguire Dr., Rich. 82 F4
Maguire St. SE1 17 G3
Maguire St. SE1 68 C2
Mahatma Gandhi 46 J5
  Ho., Wem.
Mahlon Ave., Ruis. 45 B5
Mahogany Clo. SE16 68 H1
Mahon Clo., Enf. 25 C1
Maida Ave. E4 26 B7
Maida Ave. W2 10 D1
Maida Ave. W2 57 F5
Maida Rd., Belv. 71 G3
Maida Vale W9 6 A1
Maida Vale W9 57 E2
Maida Way E4 26 B7
Maiden Erlegh Ave., 89 E1
  Bex.
Maiden La. NW1 49 D7
Maiden La. SE1 17 A1
Maiden La. WC2 12 B5
Maiden La. WC2 58 E7
Maiden Rd. E15 51 E7
Maidenstone Hill 78 C1
  SE10

Maidstone Ave., 44 J2
  Rom.
Maidstone Bldgs. 17 B2
  SE1
Maidstone Ho. E14 60 B6
  Carmen St.
Maidstone Rd. N11 32 C6
Maidstone Rd., Sid. 89 D6
Mail Coach Yd. N1 9 E3
Main Ave., Enf. 25 C5
Main Rd., Sid. 88 H3
Main St., Felt. 81 D5
Mainridge Rd., 88 E1
  Chis.
Maisemore St. SE15 21 H7
Maitland Clo. SE10 69 B7
Maitland Clo., 72 F3
  Houns.
Maitland Pk. Est. 48 J6
  NW3
Maitland Pk. Rd. 48 J6
  NW3
Maitland Pk. Vill. 48 J6
  NW3
Maitland Rd. E15 51 F6
Maitland Rd. SE26 86 G6
Maize Row E14 59 J6
  Oak La.
Majendie Rd. SE18 70 G5
Majestic Way, Mitch. 93 J2
Major Rd. E15 51 D5
Major Rd. SE16 17 J5
Makepeace Ave. N6 49 A2
Makepeace Rd., 54 E1
  Nthlt.
Makins St. SW3 18 H2
Makins St. SW3 66 G6
Malabar St. E14 69 A2
Malam Gdns. E14 60 B7
  Wades Pl.
Malbrook Rd. SW15 74 H1
Malcolm Ct., Stan. 29 F5
Malcolm Cres. NW4 38 G6
Malcolm Dr., Surb. 95 G1
Malcolm Pl. E2 59 F4
Malcolm Rd. E1 59 F4
Malcolm Rd. SE20 86 F7
Malcolm Rd. SE25 95 D6
Malcolm Rd. SW19 84 B6
Malcolm Way E11 42 G5
Malden Ave. SE25 95 E3
Malden Ave., Grnf. 46 B5
Malden Cres. NW1 49 A6
Malden Grn. Ave., 99 F1
  Wor.Pk.
Malden Hill, N.Mal. 92 F3
Malden Hill Gdns., 92 F3
  N.Mal.
Malden Pk., N.Mal. 92 F6
Malden Pl. NW5 49 A5
  Grafton Ter.
Malden Rd. NW5 48 J5
Malden Rd., Borwd. 22 A3
Malden Rd., N.Mal. 92 E5
Malden Rd., Sutt. 99 J4
Malden Rd., Wor.Pk. 92 F7
Malden Way, N.Mal. 92 D6
Maldon Clo. E15 51 D5
  Maryland St.
Maldon Clo. N1 58 J1
Maldon Clo. SE5 77 B3
Maldon Rd. N9 33 C3
Maldon Rd. W3 56 C7
Maldon Rd., Rom. 44 J7
Maldon Rd., Wall. 101 B5
Maldon Wk., 34 J6
  Wdf.Grn.
Malet Pl. WC1 7 H6
Malet Pl. WC1 58 D4
Malet St. WC1 7 H6
Malet St. WC1 58 D4
Maley Ave. SE27 85 H2
Malford Ct. E18 42 G2
Malford Gro. E18 42 F4
Malfort Rd. SE5 77 B3
Malham Rd. SE23 86 G1
Malins Clo., Barn. 22 H5
Mall, The E15 51 D7
  Broadway
Mall, The N14 32 E3
Mall, The SW1 15 G3
Mall, The SW1 67 C1
Mall, The SW14 74 C5
Mall, The W5 55 H7
Mall, The, Brom. 96 G3
  High St.
Mall, The, Croy. 101 J1
  Poplar Wk.
Mall, The, Har. 37 J6
Mall, The, Surb. 91 G5
Mall Rd. W6 65 H5
Mallams Ms. SW9 76 H3
  St. James's Cres.

Mallard Clo. E9 50 J6
Mallard Clo., Barn. 23 G6
  The Hook
Mallard Clo., 72 G7
  Twick.
  Stephenson Rd.
Mallard Pl., Twick. 82 E3
Mallard Pt. E3 60 B3
  Rainhill Way
Mallard Wk. SE18 70 G3
  Goosander Way
Mallard Wk., Sid. 89 C6
  Cray Rd.
Mallard Way NW9 38 C7
Mallards Rd., 34 H7
  Wdf.Grn.
Mallet Dr., Nthlt. 45 F5
Mallet Rd. SE13 78 D6
Malling Clo., Croy. 95 F6
Malling Gdns., 93 F6
  Mord.
Malling Way, Brom. 96 F7
Mallinson Rd. SW11 75 H5
Mallinson Rd., 101 D3
  Croy.
Mallord St. SW3 18 F5
Mallord St. SW3 66 G6
Mallory Clo. SE4 77 H4
Mallory Gdns., 24 A7
  Barn.
Mallory St. NW8 6 G6
Mallory St. NW8 57 H4
Mallow Clo., Croy. 102 G1
  Marigold Way
Mallow Mead NW7 31 B7
Mallow St. EC1 9 B5
Malmains Clo., 96 D4
  Beck.
Malmains Way, 96 C4
  Beck.
Malmesbury Rd. E3 59 J3
Malmesbury Rd. E16 60 E5
Malmesbury Rd. E18 42 F1
Malmesbury Rd., 93 F7
  Mord.
Malmesbury Ter. E16 60 F5
Malpas Dr., Pnr. 36 D5
Malpas Rd. E8 50 E6
Malpas Rd. SE4 77 J2
Malpas Rd., Dag. 53 D6
Malt St. SE1 21 H5
Malt St. SE1 68 D6
Malta Rd. E10 51 A1
Malta St. EC1 8 H5
Maltby Rd., Chess. 99 A6
Maltby St. SE1 17 F4
Maltby St. SE1 68 C3
Malthouse Dr., 81 D5
  Felt.
Malting Ho. E14 59 J7
  Oak La.
Maltings, The, Orp. 104 J1
Maltings Clo. SW13 74 E2
  Cleveland Gdns.
Maltings Ms., Sid. 89 A3
  Station Rd.
Maltings Pl. SW6 75 E1
Malton Ms. W10 57 B6
  Cambridge Gdns.
Malton Rd. W10 57 B6
  St. Marks Rd.
Malton St. SE18 70 H6
Maltravers St. WC2 12 D5
Malva Clo. SW18 75 E5
  St. Ann's Hill
Malvern Ave. E4 34 D7
Malvern Ave., Bexh. 71 E7
Malvern Ave., Har. 45 E3
Malvern Clo. SE20 95 D2
  Derwent Rd.
Malvern Clo. W10 57 C5
Malvern Clo., 94 C3
  Mitch.
Malvern Clo., Surb. 98 H1
Malvern Ct. SE14 68 F7
  Avonley Rd.
Malvern Ct. SW7 18 F1
Malvern Ct. SW7 66 G4
Malvern Dr., Felt. 81 D5
Malvern Dr., Ilf. 52 J4
Malvern Dr., 34 J5
  Wdf.Grn.
Malvern Gdns. NW2 43 B2
Malvern Gdns. NW6 57 C2
Malvern Gdns., Har. 37 H4
Malvern Gdns., 27 C6
  Loug.
Malvern Ms. NW6 57 D3
  Malvern Rd.
Malvern Pl. NW6 57 C3
Malvern Rd. E6 61 B1
Malvern Rd. E8 50 D7
Malvern Rd. E11 51 E2

Malvern Rd. N8 40 F3
Malvern Rd. N17 41 D3
Malvern Rd. NW6 57 D3
Malvern Rd., Hmptn. 81 G7
Malvern Rd., Surb. 98 H2
Malvern Rd., 94 H4
  Th.Hth.
Malvern Ter. N1 58 G1
Malvern Ter. N9 33 C1
Malvern Way W13 55 E5
  Templewood
Malwood Rd. SE12 76 B6
Malyons Rd. SE13 78 B6
Malyons Ter. SE13 78 B5
Managers St. E14 69 C1
  Prestons Rd.
Manaton Clo. SE15 77 E3
Manaton Cres., 54 G6
  Sthl.
Manbey Gro. E15 51 E6
Manbey Pk. Rd. E15 51 E6
Manbey Rd. E15 51 E6
Manbey St. E15 51 E6
Manborough Ave. E6 61 C3
Manbre Rd. W6 65 J6
Manchester Dr. W10 57 B4
Manchester Gro. E14 69 C5
Manchester Ms. W1 11 B2
Manchester Rd. E14 69 C5
Manchester Rd. N15 41 A6
Manchester Rd., 94 J3
  Th.Hth.
Manchester Sq. W1 11 B3
Manchester Sq. W1 58 A6
Manchester St. W1 11 B2
Manchester St. W1 58 A5
Manchester Way, 53 H4
  Dag.
Manchuria Rd. SW11 76 A6
Manciple St. SE1 17 C4
Manciple St. SE1 68 A2
Mandalay Rd. SW4 76 C5
Mandarin St. E14 60 A7
  Salter St.
Mandela Clo. NW10 47 C7
Mandela Rd. E16 60 G6
Mandela St. NW1 58 C1
Mandela St. SW9 67 G7
Mandela Way SE1 21 E1
Mandela Way SE1 68 B4
Mandeville Clo. SE3 69 F7
  Vanbrugh Pk.
Mandeville Clo. 93 B1
  SW20
Mandeville Ct. E4 33 H4
Mandeville Dr., 98 G1
  Surb.
Mandeville Pl. W1 11 C3
Mandeville Pl. W1 58 A6
Mandeville Rd. N14 32 B2
Mandeville Rd., 73 D2
  Islw.
Mandeville Rd., 45 F7
  Nthlt.
Mandeville St. E5 50 H3
Mandrake Rd. SW17 84 J2
Mandrell Rd. SW2 76 E5
Manette St. W1 11 J4
Manette St. W1 58 D6
Manford Way, Chig. 35 H4
Manfred Rd. SW15 75 C5
Manger Rd. N7 49 E6
Mangold Way, Erith 71 E3
Manhattan Ct., 54 D3
  Nthlt.
Manilla St. E14 69 A2
Manister Rd. SE2 71 A3
Manley Ct. N16 50 C3
  Stoke Newington
  High St.
Manley St. NW1 58 A1
Mannin Rd., Rom. 44 B7
Manning Gdns., Har. 37 G7
Manning Rd. E17 41 H5
  Southcote Rd.
Manning Rd., Dag. 53 G6
Manningford Clo. EC1 8 G3
Manningtree Clo. 84 B1
  SW19
Manningtree Rd., 45 B4
  Ruis.
Manningtree St. E1 13 H3
Mannock Dr., Loug. 27 F2
Mannock Rd. N22 40 H3
Manns Clo., Islw. 73 C5
Manns Rd., Edg. 30 A6
Manoel Rd., Twick. 81 J2
Manor Ave. SE4 77 J2
Manor Ave., Houns. 72 D3
Manor Ave., Nthlt. 45 F7
Manor Clo. NW7 30 D5
  Manor Dr.
Manor Clo. NW9 38 B5

Manor Clo. SE28 62 C7
Manor Clo., Barn. 23 B4
Manor Clo., Wor.Pk. 99 E1
Manor Cotts. App. 39 F2
N2
Manor Ct. N2 39 J5
Manor Ct. SW6 75 E1
Bagley's La.
Manor Ct., Twick. 81 J2
Manor Ct., Wem. 46 H5
Manor Ct. Rd. W7 55 B7
Manor Cres., Surb. 92 A6
Manor Dr. N14 24 B7
Manor Dr. N20 31 H3
Manor Dr. NW7 30 D5
Manor Dr., Epsom 99 E6
Manor Dr., Esher 98 C3
Manor Dr., Felt. 81 D5
Manor Dr., Sun. 90 A2
Manor Dr., Surb. 91 J6
Manor Dr., Wem. 46 J4
Manor Dr., The, 99 E1
Wor.Pk.
Manor Dr. N., 92 D6
N.Mal.
Manor Dr. N., 99 E1
Wor.Pk.
Manor Est. SE16 68 E4
Manor Fm. Dr. E4 34 E3
Manor Fm. Rd., 94 G2
Th.Hth.
Manor Fm. Rd., 55 G1
Wem.
Manor Flds. SW15 75 A6
Manor Gdns. N7 49 E3
Manor Gdns. SW20 93 C2
Manor Gdns. W3 65 A4
Manor Gdns., Hmptn. 81 H7
Manor Gdns., Rich. 73 J4
Manor Gdns., Ruis. 45 C5
Manor Gdns., 102 C6
S.Croy.
Manor Gdns., Sun. 90 A1
Manor Gro. SE15 68 F6
Manor Gro., Beck. 96 B2
Manor Gro., Rich. 74 A4
Manor Hall Ave. NW4 38 J2
Manor Hall Dr. NW4 39 A2
Manor Ho. Dr. NW6 48 A7
Manor Ho. Way, 73 E3
Islw.
Manor La. SE12 78 E6
Manor La. SE13 78 E5
Manor La., Felt. 81 A2
Manor La., Sun. 90 A2
Manor La., Sutt. 100 F5
Manor La. Ter. SE13 78 E4
Manor Ms. NW6 57 D2
Cambridge Ave.
Manor Ms. SE4 77 J2
Manor Mt. SE23 86 F1
Manor Pk. SE13 78 D5
Manor Pk., Chis. 97 G2
Manor Pk., Rich. 73 J4
Manor Pk. Clo., 103 B1
W.Wick.
Manor Pk. Cres., 30 A6
Edg.
Manor Pk. Dr., Har. 36 H3
Manor Pk. Gdns., 30 A5
Edg.
Manor Pk. Rd. E12 52 A4
Manor Pk. Rd. N2 39 F3
Manor Pk. Rd. NW10 56 F1
Manor Pk. Rd., 97 F1
Chis.
Manor Pk. Rd., 100 F5
Sutt.
Manor Pk. Rd., 103 B1
W.Wick.
Manor Pl. SE17 20 J3
Manor Pl. SE17 67 H5
Manor Pl., Chis. 97 G2
Manor Pl., Felt. 81 A1
Manor Pl., Mitch. 94 C3
Manor Pl., Sutt. 100 E5
Manor Rd. E10 42 H4
Manor Rd. E15 60 E2
Manor Rd. E16 60 E4
Manor Rd. E17 41 H2
Manor Rd. N16 50 A2
Manor Rd. N17 41 D1
Manor Rd. N22 32 E6
Manor Rd. SE25 95 D4
Manor Rd. SW20 93 C2
Manor Rd. W13 55 D7
Manor Rd., Bark. 52 J6
Manor Rd., Beck. 96 A2
Manor Rd., Bex. 89 H1
Manor Rd., Chig. 35 D6
Manor Rd., Dag. 53 J6

Manor Rd., E.Mol. 91 A4
Manor Rd., Enf. 24 J2
Manor Rd., Har. 37 D6
Manor Rd., Hayes 54 A6
Manor Rd., Loug. 26 H6
Manor Rd. (High 26 H1
Beach), Loug.
Manor Rd., Mitch. 94 C4
Manor Rd., Rich. 73 J3
Manor Rd., Rom. 44 D6
(Chadwell Heath)
Manor Rd., Sid. 89 A3
Manor Rd., Sutt. 100 C7
Manor Rd., Tedd. 82 D5
Manor Rd., Twick. 81 J2
Manor Rd., Wall. 101 B4
Manor Rd., W.Wick. 103 B2
Manor Rd., Wdf.Grn. 35 C6
Manor Rd. N., Esher 98 C3
Manor Rd. N., 98 D2
T.Ditt.
Manor Rd. N., Wall. 101 B4
Manor Rd. S., Esher 98 B4
Manor Sq., Dag. 53 C2
Manor Vale, Brent. 64 F5
Manor Vw. N3 39 E2
Manor Way E4 34 D4
Manor Way NW9 38 E4
Manor Way SE3 78 F4
Manor Way, Beck. 96 A2
Manor Way, Bex. 89 G1
Manor Way, Borwd. 22 C2
Manor Way, Brom. 97 B6
Manor Way, Har. 36 H4
Manor Way, Mitch. 94 C3
Manor Way, S.Croy. 102 B6
Manor Way, Sthl. 63 D4
Manor Way, Wor.Pk. 99 E1
Manor Way, The, 101 B4
Wall.
Manorbrook SE3 78 G4
Manordene Clo., 98 D1
T.Ditt.
Manordene Rd. SE28 62 C6
Manorgate Rd., 87 A1
Kings.T.
Manorhall Gdns. E10 51 A1
Manorside, Barn. 23 B4
Manorside Clo. SE2 71 C4
Manorway, Enf. 25 B7
Manorway, Wdf.Grn. 34 J5
Manresa Rd. SW3 18 G4
Manresa Rd. SW3 66 H5
Mansard Beeches 85 A5
SW17
Mansard Clo., Pnr. 36 D3
Manse Rd. N16 50 C3
Mansel Gro. E17 42 A1
Mansel Rd. SW19 84 B6
Mansell Rd. W3 65 D2
Mansell Rd., Grnf. 54 H5
Mansell St. E1 13 G4
Mansell St. E1 59 C6
Mansergh Clo. SE18 70 B7
Mansfield Ave. N15 41 A4
Mansfield Ave., 23 J6
Barn.
Mansfield Ave., 45 B1
Ruis.
Mansfield Clo. N9 25 D6
Mansfield Hill E4 34 B1
Mansfield Ms. W1 11 D2
New End
Mansfield Rd. E11 42 H6
Mansfield Rd. E17 41 J4
Mansfield Rd. NW3 48 J5
Mansfield Rd. W3 56 B4
Mansfield Rd., 98 F5
Chess.
Mansfield Rd., Ilf. 52 D2
Mansfield Rd., 102 A6
S.Croy.
Mansfield St. W1 11 D2
Mansfield St. W1 58 B5
Mansford St. E2 59 D2
Manship Rd., Mitch. 85 A7
Mansion Gdns. NW3 48 E3
Mansion Ho. Pl. EC4 13 B4
Manson Ms. SW7 18 E2
Manson Ms. SW7 66 F4
Manson Pl. SW7 18 E2
Manson Pl. SW7 66 G4
Mansted Gdns., Rom. 44 C7
Manston Ave., Sthl. 63 G4
Manston Clo. SE20 95 F1
Garden Rd.
Manstone Rd. NW2 48 B5
Manthorp Rd. SE18 70 F5
Mantilla Rd. SW17 85 A4
Mantle Rd. SE4 77 H3
Mantlet Clo. SW16 85 C7

Manton Ave. W7 64 C2
Manton Rd. SE2 71 A4
Mantua St. SW11 75 G3
Mantus Clo. E1 59 F4
Mantus Rd.
Mantus Rd. E1 59 F4
Manus Way N20 31 F2
Blakeney Clo.
Manville Gdns. SW17 85 B2
Manville Rd. SW17 85 A2
Manwood Rd. SE4 77 J5
Manwood St. E16 70 C1
Manygates SW12 85 B2
Mape St. E2 59 E4
Mapesbury Rd. NW2 48 B7
Maple Ave. E4 33 J5
Maple Ave. W3 65 E1
Maple Ave., Har. 45 H2
Maple Clo. N16 41 D6
Maple Clo. SW4 94 B1
Maple Clo., Buck.H. 35 A3
Maple Clo., Hmptn. 81 F6
Maple Clo., Hayes 54 D3
Maple Clo., Ilf. 35 H5
Maple Clo., Mitch. 94 B1
Maple Clo., Orp. 97 G5
Maple Clo., Ruis. 36 B6
Maple Ct., N.Mal. 92 D3
Maple Cres., Sid. 80 A6
Maple Gate, Loug. 27 D2
Maple Gro. NW9 38 C7
Maple Gro. W5 64 F3
Maple Gro., Sthl. 54 F5
Maple Ind. Est., 81 A3
Felt.
Maple Leaf Dr., 88 J1
Sid.
Maple Leaf Sq. SE16 68 G2
St. Elmos Rd.
Maple Ms. NW6 6 A1
Maple Ms. SW16 85 F5
Maple Pl. W1 7 G6
Maple Rd. E11 42 E6
Maple Rd. SE20 95 E1
Maple Rd., Hayes 54 C3
Maple Rd., Surb. 91 G6
Maple St. W1 11 F1
Maple St. W1 58 C5
Maple St., Rom. 44 J4
Maple Wk. W10 57 A4
Droop St.
Maple Way, Felt. 81 A3
Maplecroft Clo. E6 61 B6
Allhallows Rd.
Mapledale Ave., 102 D2
Croy.
Mapledene, Chis. 88 F5
Kemnal Rd.
Mapledene Rd. E8 50 D7
Maplehurst Clo., 91 H4
Kings.T.
Mapleleafe Gdns., 43 E3
Ilf.
Maples Pl. E1 59 E5
Raven Row
Maplestead Rd. SW2 76 F7
Maplestead Rd., 62 B1
Dag.
Maplethorpe Rd., 94 G4
Th.Hth.
Mapleton Clo., 96 G6
Brom.
Mapleton Cres. SW18 75 E6
Mapleton Rd. E4 34 C3
Mapleton Rd. SW18 75 D6
Mapleton Rd., Enf. 25 E2
Maplin Clo. N21 24 F6
Maplin Rd. E16 60 G6
Maplin St. E3 59 J3
Maran Way, Erith 71 D2
Marban Rd. W9 57 C3
Marble Arch W1 10 J5
Marble Arch W1 57 J7
Marble Clo. W3 65 B1
Marble Hill Clo., 73 E7
Twick.
Marble Hill Gdns., 73 E7
Twick.
Marble Quay E1 17 H1
Marble Quay E1 68 D1
Marbrook Ct. SE12 87 J3
Marcellina Way, 104 H3
Orp.
March Rd., Twick. 73 D7
Marchant Rd. E11 51 D2
Marchbank Rd. W14 66 C6
Marchmont Rd., 73 J5
Rich.
Marchmont Rd., 101 C7
Wall.
Marchmont St. WC1 8 A5
Marchmont St. WC1 58 E4

Marchside Clo., 72 D1
Houns.
Springwell Rd.
Marchwood Clo. SE5 68 B7
Marchwood Cres. 55 F6
W5
Marcia Rd. SE1 21 E2
Marcia Rd. SE1 68 B4
Marcilly Rd. SW18 75 G5
Marco Rd. W6 65 H3
Marcon Pl. E8 50 E5
Marconi Way, Sthl. 54 H6
Marcourt Lawns W5 55 H4
Marcus Ct. E15 60 E1
Marcus Garvey Way 76 G4
SE24
Marcus St. E15 60 E1
Marcus St. SW18 75 E6
Marcus Ter. SW18 75 E6
Mardale Dr. NW9 38 D5
Mardell Rd., Croy. 95 G5
Marden Ave., Brom. 96 F6
Marden Cres., Bex. 80 J5
Marden Cres., Croy. 94 F6
Marden Rd. N17 41 B3
Marden Rd., Croy. 94 F6
Marden Sq. SE16 68 E3
Marder Rd. W13 64 D2
Mardon St. E14 59 H5
Mare St. E8 59 E1
Marechal Niel Ave., 88 G3
Sid.
Maresa Flds. Croy. 100 D9
Maresfield Gdns. 48 F5
NW3
Marfleet Clo., 100 H2
Cars.
Margaret Ave. E4 26 B6
Margaret Bondfield 53 A7
Ave., Bark.
Margaret Bldgs. N16 50 C1
Margaret Rd.
Margaret Ct. W1 11 F3
Margaret Rd. N16 50 C1
Margaret Rd., Barn. 23 G4
Margaret Rd., Bex. 80 D6
Margaret St. W1 11 E3
Margaret St. W1 58 B6
Margaret Way, Ilf. 35 D6
Margaretta Ter. SW3 18 G5
Margaretta Ter. SW3 66 H6
Margaretting Rd. 51 J1
E12
Margate Rd. SW2 76 E5
Margeholes, Wat. 22 E1
Margery Pk. Rd. E7 51 G6
Margery Rd., Dag. 53 D3
Margery St. WC1 8 E4
Margery St. WC1 58 G3
Margin Dr. SW19 84 A5
Margravine Gdns. 66 A5
W6
Margravine Rd. W6 66 A5
Marham Gdns. 84 H1
SW18
Marham Gdns., 93 F6
Mord.
Maria Ter. E1 59 G4
Maria Theresa Clo., 92 D5
N.Mal.
Marian Clo., Hayes 54 D4
Marian Ct., Sutt. 100 E5
Marian Pl. E2 59 E2
Marian Rd. SW16 94 C1
Marian Sq. E2 9 J1
Marian St. E2 59 E2
Hackney Rd.
Marian Way NW10 47 F7
Maricas Ave., Har. 29 A7
Marie Lloyd Gdns. 40 E7
N19
Hornsey Ri. Gdns.
Marie Lloyd Wk. E8 50 D6
Forest Rd.
Marigold All. SE1 12 G6
Marigold Rd. N17 33 F7
Marigold St. SE16 68 E2
Marigold Way, Croy. 102 G1
Marina App., Hayes 54 E5
Marina Ave., N.Mal. 92 H5
Marina Clo., Brom. 96 G3
Marina Dr., Well. 79 H2
Marina Gdns., Rom. 44 H5
Marina Way, Tedd. 82 G7
Fairways
Marine Dr. SE18 70 C4
Marine St. SE16 17 H5
Marinefield Rd. SW6 75 E3
Mariner Gdns., 82 F3
Rich.
Mariner Rd. E12 52 C4
Dersingham Ave.
Mariners Ms. E14 69 D4

Marion Clo., Ilf. 35 G7
Marion Gro., Wdf.Grn. 34 E5
Marion Rd. NW7 30 G5
Marion Rd., Th.Hth. 94 J5
Marischal Rd. SE13 78 D3
Maritime St. E3 59 J4
Marius Pas. SW17 85 A2
Marius Rd.
Marius Rd. SW17 85 A2
Marjorams Ave., Loug. 27 C2
Marjorie Gro. SW11 75 J4
Mark Ave. E4 26 B6
Mark Clo., Bexh. 80 E1
Mark Clo., Sthl. 63 H1
Longford Ave.
Mark La. EC3 13 E5
Mark La. EC3 59 B7
Mark Rd. N22 40 H2
Mark St. E15 51 E7
West Ham La.
Mark St. EC2 9 D5
Markab Rd., Nthwd. 28 A5
Atria Rd.
Marke Clo., Kes. 104 B4
Markeston Grn., Wat. 28 D4
Market Ct. W1 11 F3
Market Est. N7 49 E6
Clock Twr. Pl.
Market Hill SE18 70 D3
Market La., Edg. 38 C1
Market Ms. W1 15 D2
Market Par. SE15 77 D2
Rye La.
Market Pl. N2 39 H3
Market Pl. NW11 39 F4
Market Pl. SE16 21 J1
Market Pl. W1 11 F3
Market Pl. W3 65 C1
Market Pl., Bexh. 80 G4
Market Pl., Brent. 64 G7
Lion Way
Market Pl., Enf. 25 A3
The Town
Market Pl., Kings.T. 91 G2
Market Rd. N7 49 E6
Market Rd., Rich. 74 A3
Market Sq. E14 60 B6
Chrisp St.
Market Sq. N9 33 D2
New Rd.
Market Sq., Brom. 96 G2
Market St. E6 61 C2
Market St. SE18 70 D4
Market Way E14 60 B6
Kerbey St.
Markfield Gdns. E4 26 B7
Markfield Rd. N15 41 D4
Markham Pl. SW3 18 J3
Markham Sq. SW3 18 J3
Markham St. SW3 66 J5
Markham St. SW3 18 H3
Markham St. SW3 66 H5
Markhole Clo., Hmptn. 81 F7
Priory Rd.
Markhouse Ave. E17 41 H6
Markhouse Rd. E17 41 J5
Markmanor Ave. E17 41 H7
Marks Rd., Rom. 44 J5
Marksbury Ave., Rich. 74 A3
Markway, The, Sun. 90 C2
Markwell Clo. SE26 86 E4
Taylors La.
Markyate Rd., Dag. 53 B5
Marl Rd. SW18 75 E4
Marlands Rd., Ilf. 43 B3
Marlborough Ave. E8 59 D1
Marlborough Ave. N14 32 C3
Marlborough Ave., Edg. 30 B3
Marlborough Bldgs. SW3 18 H1
Marlborough Bldgs. SW3 66 H4
Marlborough Clo. SE17 20 J2
Marlborough Clo. SW19 84 H7
Marlborough Clo., Orp. 97 J7
Aylesham Rd.
Marlborough Ct. W8 66 D4
Marlborough Cres. W4 65 D3
Marlborough Dr., Ilf. 43 B3
Marlborough Gdns. N20 31 J3

Marlborough Gate Ho. W2 10 E5
Marlborough Gro. SE1 21 H4
Marlborough Gro. SE1 68 D5
Marlborough Hill NW8 57 F1
Marlborough Hill, Har. 37 A4
Marlborough La. SE7 69 J6
Marlborough Pk. Ave., Sid. 89 A1
Marlborough Pl. NW8 6 C2
Marlborough Pl. NW8 57 F2
Marlborough Rd. E4 34 A6
Marlborough Rd. E7 51 J7
Marlborough Rd. E15 51 E4
Borthwick Rd.
Marlborough Rd. E18 42 G3
Marlborough Rd. N9 33 G1
Marlborough Rd. N19 49 D2
Marlborough Rd. N22 32 E7
Marlborough Rd. SW1 15 G2
Marlborough Rd. SW1 67 C1
Marlborough Rd. SW19 84 H6
Marlborough Rd. W4 65 C5
Marlborough Rd. W5 64 G2
Marlborough Rd., Bexh. 80 D3
Marlborough Rd., Brom. 96 J4
Marlborough Rd., Dag. 53 B4
Marlborough Rd., Felt. 81 D2
Marlborough Rd., Hmptn. 81 G6
Marlborough Rd., Islw. 73 E1
Marlborough Rd., Rich. 73 H6
Marlborough Rd., Rom. 44 G4
Marlborough Rd., S.Croy. 101 J7
Marlborough Rd., Sthl. 63 C3
Marlborough Rd., Sutt. 100 D3
Marlborough St. SW3 18 G2
Marlborough St. SW3 66 H4
Marlborough Yd. N19 49 D2
Marlborough Rd.
Marler Rd. SE23 86 H1
Marlescroft Way, Loug. 27 E5
Marley Ave., Bexh. 71 D6
Marley Clo., Grnf. 54 G3
Marley Wk. NW2 47 J5
Lennon Rd.
Marlingdene Clo., Hmptn. 81 G6
Marlings Clo., Chis. 97 H4
Marlings Pk. Ave., Chis. 97 H4
Marloes Clo., Wem. 46 G4
Marloes Rd. W8 14 A6
Marloes Rd. W8 66 E3
Marlow Clo. SE20 95 E3
Marlow Ct. NW6 48 A7
Marlow Ct. NW9 38 E3
Marlow Cres., Twick. 73 C6
Marlow Dr., Sutt. 100 A2
Marlow Rd. E6 61 C3
Marlow Rd. SE20 95 E3
Marlow Rd., Sthl. 63 F3
Marlow Way SE16 68 G2
Marlowe Clo., Chis. 88 G6
Marlowe Clo., Ilf. 43 F1
Marlowe Gdns. SE9 79 D6
Marlowe Rd. E17 42 C4
Marlowe Sq., Mitch. 94 C3
Tamworth La.
Marlowe Way, Croy. 101 E2
Marlowes, The NW8 57 G1
Marlton St. SE10 69 F5
Woolwich Rd.
Marmadon Rd. SE18 70 J4
Marmion App. E4 34 A4
Marmion Ave. E4 33 J4
Marmion Clo. E4 33 J4
Marmion Ms. SW11 76 A3
Taybridge Rd.

Marmion Rd. SW11 76 A4
Marmont Rd. SE15 77 D1
Marmora Rd. SE22 77 F6
Marmot Rd., Houns. 72 D3
Marne Ave. N11 32 A4
Marne Ave., Well. 80 A3
Marne St. W10 57 B3
Marnell Way, Houns. 72 D3
Marney Rd. SW11 76 A4
Marnham Ave. NW2 48 B4
Marnham Cres., Grnf. 54 H3
Marnock Rd. SE4 77 J5
Maroon St. E14 59 H5
Maroons Way SE6 87 A5
Marquess Est. N1 49 A6
Marquess Rd. N1 50 A6
Marquis Clo., Wem. 46 J7
Marquis Rd. N4 49 F1
Marquis Rd. N22 32 F6
Marquis Rd. NW1 49 D6
Marrick Clo. SW15 74 G4
Marriot Rd., Barn. 23 A3
Marriots Clo. NW9 38 F6
Marriott Rd. E15 60 E1
Marriott Rd. N4 49 F1
Marriott Rd. N10 39 J1
Marryat Pl. SW19 84 B4
Marryat Rd. SW19 84 B3
Marsala Rd. SE13 78 B4
Marsden Rd. N9 33 E2
Marsden Rd. SE15 77 C3
Marsden St. NW5 49 A6
Marsden Way, Orp. 104 H3
Marsh Ave., Mitch. 93 J2
Marsh Clo. NW7 30 F3
Marsh Ct. SW19 93 F1
Marsh Dr. NW9 38 F6
Marsh Fm. Rd., Twick. 82 C1
Marsh Grn. Rd., Dag. 62 G1
Marsh Hill E9 50 H5
Marsh La. E10 51 A2
Marsh La. N17 41 E1
Marsh La. NW7 30 D4
Marsh La., Stan. 29 F5
Marsh La., Pnr. 36 E4
Marsh Rd., Wem. 55 G3
Marsh St. E14 69 B4
Harbinger Rd.
Marsh Wall E14 69 A1
Marshall Clo. SW18 75 F6
Allfarthing La.
Marshall Clo., Har. 37 A7
Bowen Rd.
Marshall Clo., Houns. 72 F5
Marshall Path SE28 62 B7
Attlee Rd.
Marshall Rd. N17 41 A1
Marshall St. W1 11 G4
Marshall St. W1 58 C6
Marshalls Clo. N11 32 B4
Marshall's Gro. SE18 70 B4
Marshalls Pl. SE16 17 G6
Marshall's Rd., Sutt. 100 E4
Marshalsea Rd. SE1 17 A3
Marshalsea Rd. SE1 67 J2
Marsham Clo., Chis. 88 E5
Marsham St. SW1 15 J6
Marsham St. SW1 67 D3
Marshbrook Clo. SE3 79 A3
Marshfield St. E14 69 C3
Marshgate La. E15 51 B7
Marshgate Path SE18 70 F4
Ton Cribb Rd.
Marsland Clo. SE17 20 H4
Marsland Clo. SE17 67 H5
Marston Ave., Chess. 98 H6
Marston Ave., Dag. 53 G2
Fairfax Rd.
Marston Clo. NW6 48 F7
Marston Clo., Dag. 53 G2
Marston Rd., Ilf. 43 B1
Marston Rd., Tedd. 82 E5
Kingston Rd.
Marston Way SE19 85 H7
Marsworth Ave., Pnr. 36 D1
Marsworth Clo., Hayes 54 E5
Mart St. WC2 12 B5
Martaban Rd. N16 50 C2
Martel Pl. E8 50 D1
Dalston La.
Martell Rd. SE21 86 A3
Martello St. E8 50 E7
Martello Ter. E8 50 E7

Marten Rd. E17 42 A2
Martens Ave., Bexh. 80 H4
Martens Clo., Bexh. 80 J4
Martha Ct. E2 59 E2
Cambridge Heath Rd.
Martha Rd. E15 51 E6
Martha St. E1 59 E6
Martham Clo. SE28 62 D7
Marthorne Cres., Har. 37 A2
Martin Bowes Rd. SE9 79 C3
Martin Clo. N9 33 G1
Martin Cres., Croy. 101 G1
Martin Dale Ind. Est., Enf. 25 E3
Martin Dene, Bexh. 80 F5
Martin Dr., Nthlt. 45 F5
Martin Gdns., Dag. 53 C4
Martin Gro., Mord. 93 D3
Martin La. EC4 13 C5
Martin Ri., Bexh. 80 F5
Martin Rd., Dag. 53 C4
Martin Way SW20 93 A2
Martin Way, Mord. 93 D3
Martinbridge Trd. Est., Enf. 25 D4
Martindale SW14 74 C5
Martindale Rd. SW12 76 B7
Martindale Rd., Houns. 72 E4
Martineau Clo., Esher 98 A4
Martineau Est. E1 59 F7
Martineau Rd. N5 49 H4
Martineau St. E1 59 F7
Lukin St.
Martingale Clo., Sun. 90 A4
Martingales Clo., Rich. 82 G3
Martins Mt., Barn. 23 D4
Martins Rd., Brom. 96 E2
Martins Wk. N10 39 J1
Coppetts Rd.
Martinsfield Clo., Chig. 35 H4
Martlet Gro., Nthlt. 54 D3
Javelin Way
Martlett Ct. WC2 12 B4
Martley Dr., Ilf. 43 E5
Martock Clo., Har. 37 D4
Marton Clo. SE6 86 A3
Marton Rd. N16 50 B2
Martys Yd. NW3 48 G4
Hampstead High St.
Marvell Ave., Hayes 54 A5
Marvels Clo. SE12 87 H2
Marvels La. SE12 87 H2
Marville Rd. SW6 66 C7
Marvin St. E8 50 E6
Sylvester Rd.
Marwell Clo., W.Wick. 103 F2
Deer Pk. Way
Marwood Clo., Well. 80 B3
Marwood Way SE16 68 E5
Catlin St.
Mary Adelaide Clo. SW15 83 E4
Mary Ann Gdns. SE8 69 A6
Mary Clo., Stan. 37 J4
Mary Datchelor Clo. SE5 77 A1
Mary Datchelor Pl. SE5 77 A1
Mary Gardener Dr. SE9 88 C2
Mary Grn. NW8 57 E1
Mary Macarthur Ho. W6 66 B6
Field Rd.
Mary Peters Dr., Grnf. 46 A5
Mary Pl. W11 57 B7
Mary Rose Clo., Hmptn. 90 G1
Ashley Rd.
Mary Rose Mall E6 61 D5
Frobisher Rd.
Mary Rose Way N20 31 G1
Mary Seacole Clo. E8 59 C1
Clarissa St.
Mary St. E16 60 F5
Barking Rd.
Mary St. N1 58 J1
Mary Ter. NW1 58 B1
Arlington Rd.
Maryatt Ave., Har. 45 H2
Marybank SE18 70 C4
Maryland Pk. E15 51 E5
Maryland Rd. E15 51 D5

Maryland Rd. N22 32 F6
Maryland Rd., 94 H1
  Th.Hth.
Maryland Sq. E15 51 E5
Maryland St. E15 51 D5
Maryland Wk. N1 58 J1
  Popham St.
Maryland Way, Sun. 90 A2
Marylands Rd. W9 57 D4
Marylebone Flyover 10 G2
  NW1
Marylebone Flyover 10 F2
  W2
Marylebone High St. 11 C1
  W1
Marylebone High St. 58 A5
  W1
Marylebone La. W1 11 C3
Marylebone La. W1 58 A6
Marylebone Ms. W1 11 D2
Marylebone Ms. W1 58 B5
Marylebone Pas. W1 11 C3
Marylebone Pas. W1 58 A5
Marylebone Rd. NW1 11 A1
Marylebone Rd. NW1 57 H5
Marylebone St. W1 11 C2
Marylebone St. W1 58 A5
Marylee Way SE11 20 D3
Marylee Way SE11 67 F4
Maryon Gro. SE7 70 B4
Maryon Ms. NW3 48 H4
  South End Rd.
Maryon Rd. SE7 70 B4
Maryon Rd. SE18 70 R4
Mary's Clo. N17 41 C1
  Kemble Rd.
Mary's Ter., Twick. 73 D7
Masbro Rd. W14 66 A3
Mascalls Ct. SE7 69 J6
  Victoria Way
Mascalls Rd. SE7 69 J6
Mascotte Rd. SW15 75 A4
Mascotts Clo. NW2 47 H3
Masefield Ave., 22 B5
  Borwd.
Masefield Ave., 54 G7
  Sthl.
Masefield Ave., 29 C5
  Stan.
Masefield Cres. N14 24 C5
Masefield Gdns. E6 61 D4
Masefield La., 54 B4
  Hayes
Masefield Rd., 81 F4
  Hmptn.
  Wordsworth Rd.
Masefield Vw., Orp. 104 F3
Mashie Rd. W3 56 E6
Maskall Clo. SW2 85 G1
Maskani Wk. SW16 85 C7
  Bates Cres.
Maskell Rd. SW17 84 F3
Maskelyn Clo. SW11 75 H1
Mason Bradbear Ct. 50 A6
  N1
  St. Pauls Rd.
Mason Clo. E16 60 G7
Mason Clo. SE16 21 J3
Mason Clo., Bexh. 80 H3
Mason Clo., Borwd. 22 D2
  Banks Rd.
Mason Clo., Hmptn. 90 F1
Mason Rd., Wdf.Grn. 34 E4
Mason St. SE17 21 C1
Mason St. SE17 68 A4
Masons Arms Ms. W1 11 E5
Masons Ave. EC2 13 B3
Masons Ave., Croy. 101 J3
Masons Ave., Har. 37 C4
Masons Ct., Wem. 47 A2
Masons Grn. La. W3 56 A4
  Dukes Rd.
Masons Hill SE18 70 E4
Masons Hill, Brom. 96 G3
Mason's Pl. EC1 8 J3
Mason's Pl. EC1 58 J3
Masons Pl., Mitch. 93 J1
Mason's Yd. SW1 15 G1
Mason's Yd. SW19 84 A5
  High St.
Massey Clo. N11 32 B5
  Grove Rd.
Massie Rd. E8 50 D6
  Graham Rd.
Massinger St. SE17 21 D2
Massingham St. E1 59 G4
Masson Ave., Ruis. 45 C6
Mast Ho. Ter. E14 69 A4
Master Gunner Pl. 70 B7
  SE18
Masterman Ho. SE5 21 B7
Masterman Rd. E6 61 B3
Masters St. E1 59 G5
Mastmaker Rd. E14 69 A2

Maswell Pk. Cres., 72 J5
  Houns.
Maswell Pk. Rd., 72 H5
  Houns.
Matcham Rd. E11 51 E3
Matchless Dr. SE18 70 D7
  Red Lion La.
Matfield Clo., 96 G5
  Brom.
Matfield Rd., Belv. 71 G6
Matham Gro. SE22 77 C4
Matham Rd., E.Mol. 91 A5
Matheson Rd. W14 66 C4
Mathews Pk. Ave. 51 F6
  E15
Matilda St. N1 58 F1
Matlock Clo. SE24 76 J4
Matlock Ct. SE5 77 A4
  Denmark Hill Est.
Matlock Cres., 100 B4
  Sutt.
Matlock Cres., Wat. 28 C3
Matlock Gdns., 100 B4
  Sutt.
Matlock Pl., Sutt. 100 B4
Matlock Rd. E10 42 C6
Matlock St. E14 59 H6
Matlock Way, N.Mal. 92 D1
Matrimony Pl. SW8 76 C2
  Wandsworth Rd.
Matthew Clo. W10 57 A4
Matthew Ct., Mitch. 94 D5
Matthew Parker St. 16 J4
  SW1
Matthew Parker St. 67 D2
  SW1
Matthews Ave. E6 61 D2
Matthews Dr., Grnf. 46 A5
Matthews St. SW11 75 J2
Matthews Yd. WC2 12 A4
Matthias Rd. N16 50 A5
Mattingley Way SE15 68 C7
  Daniel Gdns.
Mattison Rd. N4 40 G6
Mattock La. W5 64 F1
Mattock La. W13 64 E1
Maud Gdns. E13 60 F1
Maud Gdns., Bark. 61 J2
Maud Rd. E10 51 C3
Maud Rd. E13 60 F2
Maud St. E16 60 F5
Maude Rd. E17 41 H5
Maude Rd. SE5 77 B1
Maude Ter. E17 41 H4
Maudlins Grn. E1 17 H1
Maudslay Rd. SE9 79 C3
Maudsley Ho., 64 H5
  Brent.
Mauleverer Rd. SW2 76 B3
Maundeby Wk. 47 E6
  NW10
  Neasden La.
Maunder Rd. W7 64 B1
Maunsel St. SW1 19 H1
Maunsel St. SW1 67 D4
Maurice Ave. N22 40 H2
Maurice Brown Clo. 31 A5
  NW7
Maurice St. W12 56 H6
Maurice Wk. NW11 39 F4
Maurier Clo., 54 C1
  Nthlt.
Mauritius Rd. SE10 69 E4
Maury Rd. N16 50 D2
Mavelstone Clo., 97 B1
  Brom.
Mavelstone Rd., 97 A1
  Brom.
Maverton Rd. E3 60 A1
Mavis Ave., Epsom 99 E5
Mavis Clo., Epsom 99 E5
Mavis Wk. E6 61 B5
  Tollgate Rd.
Mawbey Est. SE1 21 H4
Mawbey Pl. SE1 68 C5
Mawbey Pl. SE1 21 G4
Mawbey Rd. SE1 68 C5
Mawbey St. SW8 21 G4
Mawbey St. SW8 67 E7
Mawney Clo., Rom. 44 H2
Mawney Rd., Rom. 44 H2
Mawson Clo. SW20 93 B2
Mawson La. W4 65 F6
  Great W. Rd.
Maxey Gdns., Dag. 53 E4
Maxey Rd. SE18 70 F4
Maxey Rd., Dag. 53 E4
Maxfield Clo. N20 23 F7
Maxilla Gdns. W10 57 A6
  Cambridge Gdns.
Maxilla Wk. W10 57 A6
  Bartle Rd.
Maxim Rd. N21 24 G6

Maxted Pk., Har. 37 B7
Maxted Rd. SE15 77 C3
Maxwell Gdns., Orp. 104 J3
Maxwell Rd. SW6 66 E7
Maxwell Rd., Borwd. 22 B3
Maxwell Rd., Well. 80 A3
Maxwelton Ave. NW7 30 D5
Maxwelton Clo. NW7 30 D5
May Clo., Chess. 98 J6
May Ct. SW19 93 E1
May Gdns., Wem. 55 F3
May Rd. E4 34 A6
May Rd. E13 60 G2
May Rd., Twick. 82 B1
May St. W14 66 C5
  North End Rd.
May Tree La., Stan. 29 C7
May Wk. E13 60 H2
  Queens Rd. W.
Maya Rd. N2 39 F4
Mayall Rd. SE24 76 H5
Maybank Ave. E18 42 H2
Maybank Ave., Wem. 46 C5
Maybank Gdns., Pnr. 36 A5
Maybank Rd. E18 42 H1
Maybells 62 D2
  Commercial Est.,
  Bark.
Mayberry Pl., Surb. 91 J7
Maybourne Clo. 86 E5
  SE26
Maybrook Meadow 53 A5
  Est., Bark.
Maybury Clo., Orp. 97 E5
Maybury Gdns. 47 H6
  NW10
Maybury Ms. N6 40 C7
Maybury Rd. E13 60 J4
Maybury Rd., Bark. 61 J2
Maybury St. SW17 84 H5
Maychurch Clo., 29 G7
  Stan.
Maycroft, Pnr. 36 B2
Maycross Ave., 93 C3
  Mord.
Mayday Gdns. SE3 79 B2
Mayday Rd., Th.Hth. 94 H6
Mayerne Rd. SE9 79 A5
Mayes Rd. N22 40 F2
Mayesbrook Rd., 61 J1
  Bark.
Mayesbrook Rd., 53 B3
  Dag.
Mayesbrook Rd., Ilf. 53 A3
Mayesford Rd., Rom. 44 C7
Mayeswood Rd. 87 J3
  SE12
Mayfair Ave., Bexh. 80 D1
Mayfair Ave., Ilf. 52 C2
Mayfair Ave., Rom. 44 D6
Mayfair Ave., 72 J7
  Twick.
Mayfair Ave., 99 F1
  Wor.Pk.
Mayfair Clo., Beck. 96 B1
Mayfair Clo., Surb. 98 H1
Mayfair Gdns. N17 32 J6
Mayfair Gdns., 34 G7
  Wdf.Grn.
Mayfair Ms. NW1 48 J7
  Regents Pk. Rd.
Mayfair Pl. W1 15 E1
Mayfair Pl. W1 67 B1
Mayfair Ter. N14 24 D7
Mayfield, Bexh. 80 F3
Mayfield Ave. N12 31 H4
Mayfield Ave. N14 32 C2
Mayfield Ave. W4 65 E4
Mayfield Ave. W13 64 E3
Mayfield Ave., Har. 37 E5
Mayfield Ave., Orp. 97 J7
Mayfield Ave., 34 G6
  Wdf.Grn.
Mayfield Clo. E8 50 C6
  Forest Rd.
Mayfield Clo. SW4 76 D5
Mayfield Clo., 98 E1
  T.Ditt.
Mayfield Cres. N9 25 E6
Mayfield Cres., 94 F4
  Th.Hth.
Mayfield Dr., Pnr. 36 F4
Mayfield Gdns. NW4 39 A6
Mayfield Gdns. W7 55 A6
Mayfield Rd. E4 34 C2
Mayfield Rd. E8 50 C7
Mayfield Rd. E13 60 F4
Mayfield Rd. E17 41 H2
Mayfield Rd. N8 40 F5
Mayfield Rd. SW19 93 C1
Mayfield Rd. W3 56 B7
Mayfield Rd. W12 65 E2
Mayfield Rd., Belv. 71 J4

Mayfield Rd., Brom. 97 B5
Mayfield Rd., Dag. 53 C1
Mayfield Rd., Enf. 25 G2
Mayfield Rd., Sutt. 100 G6
Mayfield Rd., 94 F4
  Th.Hth.
Mayfields, Wem. 47 A2
Mayfields Clo., 47 A2
  Wem.
Mayflower Clo. SE16 68 G4
  Greenland Quay
Mayflower Ct. SE16 68 F2
  St. Marychurch St.
Mayflower Rd. SW9 76 E3
Mayflower St. SE16 68 F2
  St. Marychurch St.
Mayfly Gdns., Nthlt. 54 D3
  Ruislip Rd.
Mayford Clo. SW12 75 J7
Mayford Clo., Beck. 95 G3
Mayford Rd. SW12 75 J7
Maygood St. N1 8 E1
Maygood St. N1 58 F2
Maygrove Rd. NW6 48 C6
Mayhew Clo. E4 34 A3
Mayhill Rd. SE7 69 H6
Mayhill Rd., Barn. 23 B5
Maylands Dr., Sid. 89 D3
Maylands Rd., Wat. 28 C4
Maynard Clo. SW6 66 E7
  Cambria St.
Maynard Rd. E17 42 C5
  Garnet St.
Maynards Quay E1 59 F7
  Garnet St.
Mayo Rd. NW10 47 E6
Mayo Rd., Croy. 95 A5
Mayola Rd. E5 50 F4
Mayow Rd. SE23 86 G3
Mayow Rd. SE26 86 G4
Mayplace Clo., 80 H3
  Bexh.
Mayplace La. SE18 70 E7
Mayplace Rd. E., 80 H3
  Bexh.
Mayplace Rd. W., 80 G4
  Bexh.
Maypole Cres., Ilf. 35 G7
Mayroyd Ave., Surb. 99 A2
Mays Ct. WC2 12 A6
Mays Hill Rd., 96 E2
  Brom.
Mays La. E4 34 D2
Mays La., Barn. 22 G7
Mays Rd., Tedd. 82 A5
Maysoule Rd. SW11 75 G4
Mayswood Gdns., 53 J6
  Dag.
Mayton St. N7 49 F3
Maytree Clo., Edg. 30 C3
Maytree Wk. SW2 85 G2
Mayville Est. N16 50 B5
  Woodville Rd.
Mayville Rd. E11 51 E2
Mayville Rd., Ilf. 52 E5
Maywood Clo., Beck. 87 B7
Maze Hill SE3 69 E7
Maze Hill SE10 69 E6
Maze Rd., Rich. 65 A7
Mazenod Ave. NW6 48 D7
McAdam Dr., Enf. 24 H2
  Rowantree Rd.
McAuley Clo. SE1 16 E5
McAuley Clo. SE1 67 G3
McAuley Clo. SE9 79 E5
McCall Clo. SW4 76 E2
  Jeffreys Rd.
McCall Cres. SE7 70 B6
McCarthy Rd., Felt. 81 D5
McCoid Way SE1 16 J4
McCrone Ms. NW3 48 G6
  Belsize La.
McCullum Rd. E3 59 J2
  Wrights Rd.
McDermott Clo. 75 H3
  SW11
McDermott Rd. SE15 77 D3
McDonough Clo., 98 H4
  Chess.
McDowall Rd. SE5 76 J1
McDowell Clo. E16 60 F5
McEntee Ave. E17 41 H1
McEwan Way E15 60 D1
McGrath Rd. E15 51 F5
McGregor Rd. W11 57 C5
McIntosh Clo., 101 F7
  Wall.
McKay Rd. SW20 83 H7
McKellar Clo. 28 J2
  (Bushey), Wat.
McKerrell Rd. SE15 77 D1
McLeod Rd. SE2 71 A4
McLeod's Ms. SW7 18 B1
McLeod's Ms. SW7 66 E4

McMillan St. SE8 69 A6
McNeil Rd. SE5 77 B2
Mead, The N2 39 F2
Mead, The W13 55 E5
Mead, The, Beck. 96 C1
Mead, The, Stan. 37 F1
Mead, The, Wall. 101 D6
Mead, The, Wat. 28 E2
Mead, The, W.Wick. 103 D1
Mead Clo., Har. 37 A1
Mead Ct. NW9 38 C5
Mead Cres. E4 34 C4
Mead Cres., Sutt. 100 H4
Mead Gro., Rom. 44 D3
Mead Path SW17 84 F4
Mead Pl. E9 50 F6
Mead Pl., Croy. 101 H1
Mead Plat NW10 47 C6
Mead Rd., Chis. 88 F6
Mead Rd., Edg. 30 A6
Mead Rd., Rich. 82 F3
Mead Row SE1 16 E5
Mead Way, Brom. 96 E6
Mead Way, Croy. 102 H2
Meadcroft Rd. SE11 20 G6
Meadcroft Rd. SE11 67 H6
Meade Clo. W4 65 A6
Meadfield, Edg. 30 B2
Meadfield Grn., Edg. 30 B2
Meadfoot Rd. SW16 85 C7
Meadgate Ave., Wdf.Grn. 35 B5
Meadlands Dr., Rich. 82 G2
Meadow, The, Chis. 88 F6
Meadow Ave., Croy. 95 G6
Meadow Bank N21 24 F6
Meadow Clo. E4 34 B1
Mount Echo Ave.
Meadow Clo. SE6 87 A5
Meadow Clo. SW20 92 J4
Meadow Clo., Barn. 23 C6
Meadow Clo., Chis. 88 E5
Meadow Clo., Esher 98 C3
Meadow Clo., Houns. 72 G6
Meadow Clo., Nthlt. 54 G2
Meadow Clo., Rich. 82 H1
Meadow Clo., Sutt. 100 E2
Aultone Way
Meadow Dr. N10 40 A3
Meadow Dr. NW4 38 J2
Meadow Gdns., Edg. 30 B6
Meadow Garth NW10 47 C6
Meadow Hill, N.Mal. 92 E6
Meadow Ms. SW8 20 C6
Meadow Ms. SW8 67 F6
Meadow Pl. SW8 20 B7
Meadow Pl. SW8 67 E7
Meadow Pl. W4 65 E7
Edensor Rd.
Meadow Rd. SW8 20 C6
Meadow Rd. SW8 67 F7
Meadow Rd. SW19 84 F7
Meadow Rd., Bark. 52 J7
Meadow Rd., Borwd. 22 B2
Meadow Rd., Brom. 96 E1
Meadow Rd., Dag. 53 F6
Meadow Rd., Esher 98 B5
Meadow Rd., Felt. 81 E2
Meadow Rd., Loug. 27 B5
Meadow Rd., Pnr. 36 D4
Meadow Rd., Rom. 53 J1
Meadow Rd., Sthl. 54 F7
Meadow Rd., Sutt. 100 H5
Meadow Row SE1 16 J6
Meadow Row SE1 67 J3
Meadow Stile, Croy. 101 J3
High St.
Meadow Vw., Sid. 80 B7
Meadow Vw. Rd., Th.Hth. 94 H5
Meadow Wk. E18 42 G4
Meadow Wk., Dag. 53 F6
Meadow Wk., Epsom 99 E6
Meadow Wk., Wall. 101 B3
Meadow Way NW9 38 D5
Meadow Way, Chess. 98 H5
Meadow Way, Chig. 35 F3
Meadow Way, Orp. 104 D3
Meadow Way, Ruis. 36 B6
Meadow Way, Wem. 46 G4
Meadow Way, The, Har. 37 B1
Meadow Waye, Houns. 63 E6
Meadowbank NW3 48 J7
Meadowbank SE3 78 F3
Meadowbank, Surb. 91 J6
Meadowbank Clo. SW6 65 J7
Meadowbank Gdns., Houns. 72 A1
Meadowbank Rd. NW9 38 D7
Meadowcourt Rd. SE3 78 F4
Meadowcroft, Brom. 97 C3
Meadowcroft Rd. N13 32 G2
Meadows Clo. E10 51 A2
Meadows End, Sun. 90 A1
Meadowside SE9 78 J4
Meadowsweet Clo. E16 61 A5
Monarch Dr.
Meadowview Rd. SE6 87 A4
Meadowview Rd., Bex. 80 E6
Meads, The, Edg. 30 D6
Meads, The, Sutt. 100 B3
Meads La., Ilf. 43 H7
Meads Rd. N22 40 H2
Meads Rd., Enf. 25 H1
Meadvale Rd. W5 55 E4
Meadvale Rd., Croy. 95 C7
Meadway N14 32 D2
Meadway NW11 39 E6
Meadway SW20 92 J4
Meadway, Barn. 23 C4
Meadway, Beck. 96 C1
Meadway, Ilf. 52 H4
Meadway, Surb. 99 C1
Meadway, Twick. 82 A1
Meadway, Wdf.Grn. 34 J5
Meadway, The SE3 78 D2
Heath La.
Meadway, The, Buck.H. 35 A1
Meadway, The, Loug. 27 C6
Meadway Clo. NW11 39 E6
Meadway Clo., Barn. 23 D4
Meadway Clo., Pnr. 28 H6
Highbanks Rd.
Meadway Ct. NW11 39 E6
Meadway Gate NW11 39 D6
Meaford Way SE20 86 E7
Meakin Est. SE1 17 D5
Meakin Est. SE1 68 B3
Meanley Rd. E12 52 B4
Meard St. W1 11 H4
Meard St. W1 58 D6
Meath Rd. E15 60 F2
Meath Rd., Ilf. 52 F3
Meath St. SW11 76 B1
Mechanics Path SE8 69 A7
Deptford High St.
Mecklenburgh Pl. WC1 8 C5
Mecklenburgh Pl. WC1 58 F4
Mecklenburgh Sq. WC1 8 C5
Mecklenburgh Sq. WC1 58 F4
Mecklenburgh St. WC1 8 C5
Medburn St. NW1 7 H1
Medburn St. NW1 58 D2
Medcroft Gdns. SW14 74 C4
Medebourne Clo. SE3 78 G3
Medesenge Way N13 32 H6
Medfield St. SW15 74 G7
Medhurst Clo. E3 59 H2
Arbery Rd.
Medhurst Rd. E3 59 H2
Arbery Rd.
Median Rd. E5 50 F5
Medina Ave., Esher 98 B3
Medina Gro. N7 49 G3
Medina Rd.
Medina Rd. N7 49 G3
Medland Clo., Wall. 101 A1
Medlar Clo., Nthlt. 54 E2
Parkfield Ave.
Medlar St. SE5 76 J1
Medley Rd. NW6 48 D6
Medora Rd. SW2 76 F7
Medusa Rd. SE6 78 B6
Medway Bldgs. E3 59 H2
Medway Rd.
Medway Clo., Croy. 95 F6
Medway Clo., Ilf. 52 F5
Loxford La.
Medway Dr., Grnf. 55 C2
Medway Gdns., Wem. 46 D4
Medway Ms. E3 59 H2
Medway Rd.
Medway Par., Grnf. 55 C2
Medway Rd. E3 59 H2
Medway St. SW1 15 J6
Medway St. SW1 67 D3
Medwin St. SW4 76 F4
Meerbrook Rd. SE3 78 J3
Meeson Rd. E15 60 F1
Meeson St. E5 50 H4
Meeting Flds. Path E9 50 F6
Homerton Ter.
Meeting Ho. La. SE15 77 E1
Meetinghouse All. E1 68 E1
Chandler St.
Mehetabel Rd. E9 50 F6
Melancholy Wk., Rich. 55 F3
Melanda Clo., Chis. 88 C5
Melanie Clo., Bexh. 80 E1
Melba Way SE13 78 B1
Melbourne Ave. N13 32 F6
Melbourne Ave. W13 64 D1
Melbourne Ave., Pnr. 36 H3
Melbourne Clo., Orp. 97 H7
Melbourne Clo., Wall. 101 C5
Melbourne Rd.
Melbourne Ct. E5 50 H4
Daubeney Rd.
Melbourne Ct. SE20 86 D7
Melbourne Gdns., Rom. 44 E5
Melbourne Gro. SE22 77 B4
Melbourne Ho., Hayes 54 C4
Melbourne Ms. SE6 78 C7
Melbourne Ms. SW9 76 G1
Melbourne Pl. WC2 12 D4
Melbourne Pl. WC2 58 F7
Melbourne Rd. E6 61 C1
Melbourne Rd. E10 42 B7
Melbourne Rd. E17 41 H4
Melbourne Rd. SW19 93 D1
Melbourne Rd., Ilf. 52 E1
Melbourne Rd., Tedd. 82 F6
Melbourne Rd., Wall. 101 B5
Melbourne Sq. SW9 76 G1
Melbourne Ms.
Melbourne Ter. SW6 66 E7
Waterford Rd.
Melbourne Way, Enf. 25 C6
Melbury Ave., Sthl. 63 H3
Melbury Clo., Chis. 88 B6
Melbury Clo., Esher 98 E6
Melbury Ct. W8 66 C3
Melbury Dr. SE5 68 B7
Sedgmoor Pl.
Melbury Gdns. SW20 92 H1
Melbury Rd. W14 66 C3
Melbury Rd., Har. 37 J5
Melbury Ter. NW1 6 H6
Melbury Ter. NW1 57 H4
Melcombe Gdns., Har. 37 J6
Melcombe Pl. NW1 10 J1
Melcombe Pl. NW1 57 J5
Melcombe St. NW1 7 A6
Melcombe St. NW1 57 J4
Meldon Clo. SW6 75 E1
Bagley's La.
Meldrum Rd., Ilf. 53 A2
Melfield Gdns. SE6 87 B4
Melford Ave., Bark. 52 H6
Melford Rd. E6 61 C4
Melford Rd. E11 51 E2
Melford Rd. E17 41 H4
Melford Rd. SE22 77 D7
Melford Rd., Ilf. 52 G2
Melfort Ave., Th.Hth. 94 H3
Melfort Rd., Th.Hth. 94 H3
Melgund Rd. N5 49 G5
Melina Pl. NW8 6 E4
Melina Pl. NW8 57 G3
Melina Rd. W12 65 H2
Melior Pl. SE1 17 D3
Melior St. SE1 17 D3
Melior St. SE1 68 A2
Meliot Rd. SE6 87 D2
Mell St. SE10 69 E5
Trafalgar Rd.
Meller Clo., Croy. 101 E3
Melling St. SE18 70 H6
Mellish Clo., Bark. 61 J1
Mellish Gdns., Wdf.Grn. 34 G5
Harts Gro.
Mellish St. E14 69 A3
Mellison Rd. SW17 84 H5
Mellitus St. W12 56 F6
Mellor Clo., Walt. 90 F7
Mellows Rd., Ilf. 43 C3
Mellows Rd., Wall. 101 D5
Mells Cres. SE9 88 C4
Melody Rd. SW18 75 F5
Melon Rd. SE15 77 D1
Melrose Ave. N22 40 H1
Melrose Ave. NW2 47 H5
Melrose Ave. SW16 94 F3
Melrose Ave. SW19 84 C2
Melrose Ave., Borwd. 22 B5
Melrose Ave., Grnf. 54 H2
Melrose Ave., Mitch. 85 B7
Melrose Ave., Twick. 72 H7
Melrose Clo. SE12 87 G1
Melrose Clo., Grnf. 54 H2
Melrose Clo., Hayes 54 A5
Melrose Cres., Orp. 104 G4
Melrose Dr., Sthl. 63 G1
Melrose Gdns. W6 65 J3
Melrose Gdns., Edg. 38 B2
Melrose Gdns., N.Mal. 92 D3
Melrose Rd. SW13 74 F2
Melrose Rd. SW18 75 C6
Melrose Rd. SW19 93 D2
Melrose Rd. W3 65 C3
Stanley Rd.
Melrose Rd., Pnr. 36 F4
Melrose Ter. W6 65 J2
Melsa Rd., Mord. 93 F6
Meltham Way SE16 68 E5
Egan Way
Melthorne Dr., Ruis. 45 C3
Melthorpe Gdns. SE3 79 A1
Melton Clo., Ruis. 45 C1
Melton Ct. SW7 18 F2
Melton Ct. SW7 66 G4
Melton St. NW1 7 G4
Melton St. NW1 58 C3
Melville Ave. SW20 83 G7
Melville Ave., Grnf. 46 C5
Melville Ave., S.Croy. 102 C5
Melville Gdns. N13 32 G5
Melville Rd. E17 41 J3
Melville Rd. NW10 47 D7
Melville Rd. SW13 74 G1
Melville Rd., Sid. 89 C2
Melville Vill. Rd. W3 65 D1
High St.
Melvin Rd. SE20 95 F1
Melyn Clo. N7 49 C4
Anson Rd.
Memel Ct. EC1 8 J6
Memel St. EC1 8 J6
Memorial Ave. E15 60 E3
Memorial Clo., Houns. 63 F6
Mendip Clo. SE26 86 F4
Mendip Clo. SW19 84 B2
Queensmere Rd.
Mendip Clo., Wor.Pk. 99 J2
Cotswold Way
Mendip Dr. NW2 48 B2
Mendip Rd. SW11 75 F3
Mendip Rd., Ilf. 43 H5
Mendora Rd. SW6 66 B7
Menelik Rd. NW2 48 B4
Menlo Gdns. SE19 86 A7
Menotti St. E2 9 J5
Mentmore Clo., Har. 37 F6
Mentmore Ter. E8 50 E7
Meon Ct., Islw. 73 B2
Meon Rd. W3 65 C2
Meopham Rd., Mitch. 94 C1
Mepham Cres., Har. 28 J7
Mepham Gdns., Har. 28 J7
Mepham St. SE1 16 E2
Mepham St. SE1 67 F1
Mera Dr., Bexh. 80 G4
Merantun Way SW19 93 F1
Merbury Clo. SE13 78 D5
Merbury Rd. SE28 70 H2
Mercator Rd. SE13 78 D4
Mercer Clo., T.Ditt. 91 C7
Mercer St. WC2 12 A4
Mercer St. WC2 58 E6
Merceron St. E1 59 E4
Mercers Clo. SE10 69 F4
Mercers Pl. W6 65 J4
Mercers Rd. N19 49 D3
Merchant St. E3 59 J3
Merchiston Rd. SE6 87 D2
Merchland Rd. SE9 88 F1
Mercia Gro. SE13 78 C4
Mercier Rd. SW15 75 B5

Mercury Cen. Ind. 72 A5
Est., Felt.
Mercury Way SE14 68 G6
Mercy Ter. SE13 78 B4
Mere Clo. SW15 75 A7
Mere Clo., Orp. 104 D2
Mere End, Croy. 95 G7
Mere Side, Orp. 104 D2
Merebank La., Croy. 101 F5
Meredith Ave. NW2 47 J5
Meredith Clo., Pnr. 28 D7
Meredith St. E13 60 G3
Meredith St. EC1 **8 G4**
Meredyth Rd. SW13 74 G2
Meretone Clo. SE4 77 H4
Merevale Cres., 93 F6
Mord.
Mereway Rd., Twick. 82 A1
Merewood Clo., 97 D2
Brom.
Merewood Rd., Bexh. 80 J2
Mereworth Clo., 96 F5
Brom.
Mereworth Dr. SE18 70 E7
Meriden Clo., Brom. 88 A7
Meriden Clo., Ilf. 43 F1
Meridian Gate E14 69 C2
Meridian Rd. SE7 70 A7
Meridian Trd. Est. 69 H4
SE7
Meridian Way N9 33 G2
Meridian Way N18 33 F6
Meridian Way, Enf. 25 G6
Merifield Rd. SE9 78 J4
Merino Pl., Sid. 80 A6
Blackfen Rd.
Merivale Rd. SW15 75 B4
Merivale Rd., Har. 36 J7
Merlewood Dr., Chis. 97 C1
Morley Ct. NW9 47 C1
Merlin Clo., Croy. 102 B4
Minster Dr.
Merlin Clo., Nthlt. 54 C3
Merlin Cres., Edg. 37 J1
Merlin Gdns., Brom. 87 G3
Merlin Gro., Beck. 95 J4
Merlin Gro., Ilf. 35 E6
Merlin Rd. E12 52 A2
Merlin Rd., Well. 80 A4
Merlin Rd. N., Well. 80 A4
Merlin St. WC1 **8 E4**
Merlins Ave., Har. 45 F3
Mermaid Ct. SE1 **17 B3**
Mermaid Ct. SE1 68 A2
Mermaid Ct. SE16 68 J1
Merredene St. SW2 76 F6
Merrick Rd., Sthl. 63 F2
Merrick Sq. SE1 **17 B5**
Merrick Sq. SE1 67 J3
Merridene N21 24 H6
Merrielands Cres., 62 F1
Dag.
Merrilands Rd., 99 J1
Wor.Pk.
Merrilees Rd., Sid. 88 H1
Merrilyn Clo., 98 D6
Esher
Merriman Rd. SE3 78 J1
Merrington Rd. SW6 66 D6
Merrion Ave., Stan. 29 G5
Merritt Rd. SE4 77 J5
Merrivale N14 24 D6
Merrivale Ave., Ilf. 43 A4
Merrow St. SE17 **21 B4**
Merrow St. SE17 67 J6
Merrow Wk. SE17 **21 C3**
Merrow Way, Croy. 103 C6
Merry Hill Mt. 28 H1
(Bushey), Wat.
Merrydown Way, 97 B1
Chis.
Merryfield SE3 78 F2
Merryfield Gdns., 29 F5
Stan.
Merryhill Clo. E4 26 B7
Merryhills Ct. N14 24 C5
Merryhills Dr., Enf. 24 D4
Mersea Ho., Bark. 52 E6
Mersey Rd. E17 41 J3
Mersham Dr. NW9 38 A5
Mersham Pl. SE20 95 E1
Mersham Rd., 95 A3
Th.Hth.
Merten Rd., Rom. 44 E7
Merthyr Ter. SW13 65 H6
Merton Ave. W4 65 F4
Merton Ave., Nthlt. 45 J5
Merton Hall Rd. 93 B1
SW20
Merton Hall Rd. 84 B7
SW19
Merton High St. 84 F7
SW19

Merton Ind. Pk. 93 F1
SW19
Merton La. N6 48 J2
Merton Mans. SW20 93 A2
Merton Ri. NW3 48 H7
Merton Rd. E17 42 C5
Merton Rd. SE25 95 D5
Merton Rd. SW18 75 D5
Merton Rd. SW19 84 E7
Merton Rd., Bark. 52 J7
Merton Rd., Har. 45 J1
Merton Rd., Ilf. 43 J7
Merton Way, W.Mol. 90 H4
Merttins Rd. SE15 77 G5
Mervan Rd. SW2 76 G4
Mervyn Ave. SE9 88 F3
Mervyn Rd. W13 64 D3
Messaline Ave. W3 56 C6
Messent Rd. SE9 78 J5
Messeter Pl. SE9 79 D6
Messina Ave. NW6 48 D7
Metcalfe Wk., Felt. 81 E4
Gabriel Clo.
Meteor St. SW11 76 A4
Meteor Way, Wall. 101 E7
Metheringham Way 38 E1
NW9
Methley St. SE11 **29 F4**
Methley St. SE11 67 G5
Methuen Clo., Edg. 30 A7
Methuen Pk. N10 40 B2
Methuen Rd., Belv. 71 H4
Methuen Rd., Edg. 30 A7
Methwold Rd. W10 57 A5
Metro Ind. Cen., 73 B2
Islw.
Metropolitan Cen., 54 H1
The, Grnf.
Mews, The N1 50 J1
St. Paul St.
Mews, The, Ilf. 43 A5
Mews, The, Twick. 73 E6
Bridge Rd.
Mews Pl., Wdf.Grn. 34 G4
Mews St. E1 **17 H1**
Mews St. E1 68 D1
Mexfield Rd. SW15 75 C5
Meyer Rd., Erith 71 J6
Meymott St. SE1 **16 G2**
Meymott St. SE1 67 H2
Meynell Cres. E9 50 G7
Meynell Gdns. E9 50 G7
Meynell Rd. E9 50 G7
Meyrick Rd. NW10 47 G6
Meyrick Rd. SW11 75 G3
Miall Wk. SE26 86 H4
Micawber St. N1 **9 A3**
Micawber St. N1 68 J3
Michael Faraday Ho. **21 C4**
SE17
Michael Gaynor Clo. 64 C1
W7
Michael Rd. E11 51 E1
Michael Rd. SE25 95 B3
Michael Rd. SW6 75 E1
Michaels Clo. SE13 78 E4
Micheldever Rd. 78 E6
SE12
Michelham Gdns., 82 D3
Twick.
Michels Row, Rich. 73 H4
Kew Foot Rd.
Michigan Ave. E12 52 C4
Michleham Down 31 C4
N12
Mickleham Clo., Orp. 97 J2
Mickleham Gdns., 100 B6
Sutt.
Mickleham Rd., Orp. 97 J1
Mickleham Way, 103 D7
Croy.
Micklethwaite Rd. 66 D6
SW6
Middle Dene NW7 30 D3
Middle Fld. NW8 57 G1
Middle Grn. Clo., 91 J6
Surb.
Alpha Rd.
Middle La. N8 40 E5
Middle La., Tedd. 92 C6
Middle La. Ms. N8 40 E5
Middle La.
Middle Pk. Ave. SE9 79 A6
Middle Path, Har. 46 A1
Middle Rd. E13 60 G2
London Rd.
Middle Rd. SW16 94 C2
Middle Rd., Barn. 23 H6
Middle Rd., Har. 46 A2
Middle Row W10 57 B4
Middle St. EC1 **12 J1**

Middle Temple La. **12 E4**
EC4
Middle Temple La. 58 G6
EC4
Middle Way SW16 94 D2
Middle Way, Erith 71 E3
Middle Way, Hayes 54 D4
Douglas Cres.
Middle Way, The, 37 C2
Har.
Middle Yd. SE1 **17 D1**
Middlefield Gdns., 43 E6
Ilf.
Middlefield W13 55 E5
Middleham Gdns. 33 D6
N18
Middleham Rd. N18 33 D6
Middlesborough Rd. 33 D6
N18
Middlesex Business 63 F2
Cen., The, Sthl.
Middlesex Ct. W4 65 F4
British Gro.
Middlesex Pas. EC1 **12 H2**
Middlesex Rd., 94 E4
Mitch.
Middlesex St. E1 **13 E2**
Middlesex St. E1 59 B5
Middlesex Wf. E5 50 F2
Middleton Ave. E4 33 J4
Middleton Ave., 55 A2
Grnf.
Middleton Ave., 99 C5
Sid.
Middleton Bldgs. W1 **11 F2**
Middleton Clo. E4 33 J3
Middleton Dr. SE16 68 G2
Middleton Dr., Pnr. 36 A3
Middleton Gdns., 43 E6
Ilf.
Middleton Gro. N7 49 E5
Middleton Ms. N7 49 E5
Middleton Gro.
Middleton Rd. E8 50 C7
Middleton Rd. NW11 39 D7
Middleton Rd., 93 G7
Cars.
Middleton Rd., 93 E6
Mord.
Middleton St. E2 59 E3
Middleton Way SE13 78 D4
Middleway NW11 39 E5
Midfield Ave., 80 J3
Bexh.
Midford Pl. W1 **7 G6**
Midholm NW11 39 E4
Midholm, Wem. 47 A1
Midholm Clo. NW11 39 E4
Midhope Rd., Croy. 102 H2
Midhope St. WC1 **8 B4**
Midhurst Ave. N10 40 A3
Midhurst Ave., 94 G7
Croy.
Midhurst Hill, 80 G6
Bexh.
Midhurst Rd. W13 64 D2
Midland Pl. E14 69 C5
Ferry St.
Midland Rd. E10 42 C7
Midland Rd. NW1 **7 J2**
Midland Rd. NW1 58 D2
Midland Ter. NW2 48 A3
Midland Ter. NW10 56 E4
Midleton Rd., 92 C2
N.Mal.
Midlothian Rd. E3 59 H5
Midmoor Rd. SW12 85 C1
Midmoor Rd. SW19 93 A1
Midship Clo. SE16 68 G1
Surrey Water Rd.
Midstrath Rd. NW10 47 E4
Midsummer Ave., 72 F4
Houns.
Midway, Sutt. 93 C7
Midwood Clo. NW2 47 H3
Miers Clo. E6 61 D1
Mighell Ave., Ilf. 43 A5
Milborne Gro. SW10 **18 D4**
Milborne Gro. SW10 66 F5
Milborne St. E9 50 F6
Milborough Cres. 78 E6
SE12
Milcote St. SE1 **16 G4**
Milcote St. SE1 67 H2
Mildenhall Rd. E5 50 F4
Mildmay Ave. N1 50 A6
Mildmay Gro. N1 50 A5
Mildmay Pk. N1 50 A5
Mildmay Rd. N1 50 A5
Mildmay Rd., Ilf. 52 E3
Winston Way
Mildmay Rd., Rom. 44 J5
Mildmay St. N1 50 A6

Mildred Ave., 22 A7
Borwd.
Mildred Ave., Nthlt. 45 H5
Mile End, The E17 41 G1
Mile End Pl. E1 59 G4
Mile End Rd. E1 59 F5
Mile End Rd. E3 59 H4
Mile Rd., Wall. 101 B1
Miles Pl. NW1 **10 G1**
Miles Pl., Surb. 91 G4
Villiers Ave.
Miles Rd. N8 40 E3
Miles Rd., Mitch. 93 G3
Miles St. SW8 **20 A6**
Miles St. SW8 67 E6
Miles Way N20 31 H2
Milespit Hill NW7 30 H5
Milestone Clo., 100 G6
Sutt.
Milestone Rd. SE19 86 C6
Milfoil St. W12 57 G7
Milford Clo. SE2 71 E6
Milford Gdns., Edg. 30 A7
Milford Gdns., Wem. 46 G4
Milford Gdns., Croy. 100 F4
Milford La. WC2 **12 E5**
Milford La. WC2 58 F7
Milford Ms. SW16 85 F3
Milford Rd. W13 64 E1
Milford Rd., Sthl. 54 G7
Milford Way SE15 77 C1
Sumner Est.
Mill Ct. E10 70 E1
Milk St. EC2 **13 A3**
Milk St., Brom. 87 H6
Milk Yd. E1 59 F7
Milkwell Gdns., 34 H7
Wdf.Grn.
Milkwell Yd. SE5 76 J1
Milkwood Rd. SE24 76 H5
Mill Clo., Cars. 101 A2
Mill Cor., Barn. 23 C1
Mill Ct. E10 51 C3
Mill Fm. Clo., Pnr. 36 C2
Mill Fm. Cres., 81 E1
Houns.
Mill Gdns. SE26 86 E4
Mill Grn. Rd., Mitch. 93 J7
Mill Hill SW13 74 G2
Mill Hill Rd.
Mill Hill Circ. NW7 30 F5
Watford Way
Mill Hill Gro. W3 65 B1
Mill Hill Rd.
Mill Hill Rd. SW13 74 G2
Mill Hill Rd. W3 65 B2
Mill La. E4 26 B3
Mill La. NW6 48 B5
Mill La. SE18 70 D5
Mill La., Cars. 100 J4
Mill La., Croy. 101 G3
Mill La., Rom. 44 E6
(Chadwell Heath),
Mill La., Wdf.Grn. 34 F5
Mill Mead Ind. Cen. 41 E2
N17
Mill Mead Rd. N17 41 E3
Mill Pl. E14 59 J6
East India Dock Rd.
Mill Pl., Chis. 97 E1
Mill Pl., Kings.T. 91 J3
Mill Plat, Islw. 73 D2
Mill Plat Ave., Islw. 73 D2
Mill Ridge, Edg. 29 J5
Mill Rd. E16 69 H1
Mill Rd. SE13 78 C3
Loampit Vale
Mill Rd. SW19 84 F7
Mill Rd., Erith 71 J7
Mill Rd., Ilf. 52 D3
Mill Rd., Twick. 81 J2
Mill Row N1 59 B1
Mill Shot Clo. SW6 74 J1
Mill St. SE1 **17 G4**
Mill St. SE1 68 C2
Mill St. W1 **11 F5**
Mill St. W1 58 C7
Mill St., Kings.T. 91 H3
Mill Trd. Est., The 56 C3
NW10
Mill Vale, Brom. 96 F2
Mill Vw. Gdns., 102 G3
Croy.
Mill Way, Felt. 72 B5
Mill Yd. E1 **13 H5**
Millais Ave. E12 52 D5
Millais Gdns., Edg. 38 A2
Millais Rd. E11 51 C4
Millais Rd., Enf. 25 C5
Millais Rd., N.Mal. 92 E7
Millais Way, Epsom 99 C4
Millard Clo. N16 50 B5
Boleyn Rd.

Millard Ter., Dag.   53 G6
  Church Elm La.
Millbank SW1   **16 A5**
Millbank SW1   67 E4
Millbank Twr. SW1 **20 A2**
Millbank Twr. SW1   67 E4
Millbank Way SE12   78 G5
Millbourne Rd.,   81 E4
  Felt.
Millbrook Ave., Well. 79 G4
Millbrook Gdns.   44 F6
  (Chadwell Heath)
  Rom.
Millbrook Rd. N9   33 E1
Millbrook Rd. SW9   76 H3
Millender Wk. SE16   68 F4
Miller Clo., Pnr.   36 C2
Miller Rd. SW19   84 G6
Miller Rd., Croy.   101 F1
Miller St. NW1   **7 F1**
Miller St. NW1   58 C2
Millers Ave. E8   50 C5
Millers Clo. NW7   30 G4
Millers Ct. W4   65 F5
  Chiswick Mall
Millers Grn. Clo., Enf. 24 H3
Millers Ter. E8   50 C5
Millers Way W6   65 J2
Millet Rd., Grnf.   54 H3
Millfield Est. E17   41 H1
Millfield La. N6   48 J2
Millfield Pl. N6   49 A2
Millfield Rd., Edg.   38 C2
Millfield Rd.,   81 E1
  Houns.
Millfields Rd. E5   50 F4
Millgrove St. SW11   76 H4
Millharbour E14   69 B3
Millhaven Clo.,   44 B6
  Rom.
Millhouse Pl. SE27   85 H4
Millicent Rd. E10   50 J1
Milligan St. E14   59 J7
  Three Colt St.
Milling Rd., Edg.   30 D7
Millman Ms. WC1   **8 C6**
Millman Ms. WC1   58 F4
Millman St. WC1   **8 C6**
Millman St. WC1   58 F4
Millmark Gro. SE14   77 H2
Millmarsh La., Enf.   25 H2
Millpond Est. SE16   68 E2
  West La.
Mills Ct. EC2   **9 D5**
Mills Gro. E14   60 C5
  Dewberry St.
Mills Gro. NW4   39 A3
Mills Row W4   65 D4
  Bridge St.
Millside, Cars.   100 J2
Millside Pl., Islw.   73 E2
Millsmead Way,   27 C2
  Loug.
Millson Clo. N20   31 G2
Millstream Rd. SE1 **17 F4**
Millstream Rd. SE1   68 C2
Millwall Dock Rd.   69 A3
  E14
Millway NW7   30 E5
Millway Gdns., Nthlt. 45 F6
Millwell Cres., Chig. 35 G5
Millwood Rd.,   73 J1
  Houns.
Millwood St. W10   57 B5
  St. Charles Sq.
Milman Clo., Pnr.   36 D3
Milman Rd. NW6   57 A2
Milmans St. SW10   **18 E6**
Milmans St. SW10   66 G6
Milne Feild, Pnr.   28 G7
Milne Gdns. SE9   79 B5
Milner Dr., Twick.   73 A7
Milner Pl. N1   58 G1
Milner Pl., Cars.   101 A4
  High St.
Milner Rd. E15   60 E3
Milner Rd. SW19   93 E1
Milner Rd., Dag.   53 C2
Milner Rd.,   91 G3
  Kings.T.
Milner Rd., Mord.   93 G5
Milner Rd., Th.Hth.   95 A3
Milner Sq. N1   49 H7
Milner St. SW3   **18 J1**
Milner St. SW3   58 C3
Milnthorpe Rd. W4   65 D6
Milo Rd. SE22   77 C6
Milroy Wk. SE1   **16 G1**
Milson Rd. W14   66 A3
Milton Ave. E6   52 A7
Milton Ave. N6   40 C7
Milton Ave. NW9   38 C3
Milton Ave. NW10   56 C1

Milton Ave., Barn.   23 C5
Milton Ave., Croy.   95 A7
Milton Ave., Sutt.   100 G3
Milton Clo. N2   39 F5
Milton Clo. SE1   **21 F2**
Milton Clo. SE1   68 C4
Milton Clo., Hayes   54 A6
Milton Clo., Sutt.   100 G3
Milton Ct. EC2   **13 B1**
Milton Ct. Rd. SE14   68 H6
Milton Cres., Ilf.   43 F7
Milton Dr., Borwd.   22 B5
Milton Gro. N11   32 C5
Milton Gro. N16   50 A4
Milton Pk. N6   40 C7
Milton Pl. N7   49 G5
  Georges Rd.
Milton Rd. E17   42 A4
Milton Rd. N6   40 C7
Milton Rd. N15   40 H4
Milton Rd. NW7   30 G5
Milton Rd. NW9   38 G7
  West Hendon Bdy.
Milton Rd. SE24   76 H6
Milton Rd. SW14   74 D3
Milton Rd. SW19   84 F6
Milton Rd. W3   65 D1
Milton Rd. W7   55 C7
Milton Rd., Belv.   71 G4
Milton Rd., Croy.   102 A1
Milton Rd., Hmptn.   81 G7
Milton Rd., Har.   37 B4
Milton Rd., Mitch.   85 A7
Milton Rd., Sutt.   100 D3
Milton St. EC2   **13 B1**
Milton St. EC2   59 A5
Milverton Gdns., Ilf. 52 J2
Milverton Rd. NW6   47 J7
Milverton St. SE11 **20 F4**
Milverton St. SE11   67 G5
Milverton Way SE9   88 D4
Milward St. E1   59 E5
  Stepney Way
Milward Wk. SE18   70 D6
  Spearman St.
Mimosa Rd., Hayes   54 C5
Mimosa St. SW6   75 C1
Mina Rd. SE17   21 E4
Mina Rd. SE17   68 B5
Mina Rd. SW19   93 D1
Minard Rd. SE6   78 E7
Minchenden Cres.   32 C3
  N14
Mincing La. EC3   **13 D5**
Mincing La. EC3   59 B7
Minden Rd. SE20   95 E1
Minden Rd., Sutt.   100 C2
Minehead Rd. SW16   85 F5
Minehead Rd., Har.   45 G3
Minera Ms. SW1   **19 C1**
Minera Ms. SW1   67 A4
Mineral St. SE18   70 H4
Minerva Clo. SW9   67 G7
Minerva Clo., Sid.   88 H3
Minerva Rd. E4   34 B7
Minerva Rd. NW10   56 C3
Minerva Rd.,   91 J2
  Kings.T.
Minerva St. E2   59 E2
Minet Ave. NW10   56 E2
Minet Dr., Hayes   63 A1
Minet Gdns. NW10   56 E2
Minet Gdns., Hayes   63 A1
Minet Rd. SW9   76 H2
Minford Gdns. W14   66 A2
Ming St. E14   60 A7
Mingard Wk. N7   49 F2
  Hornsey Rd.
Ministry Way SE9   88 C2
Miniver Pl. EC4   58 J7
  Garlick Hill
Mink Ct., Houns.   72 C2
Minniedale, Surb.   91 J5
Minnow Wk. SE17   **21 E2**
Minories EC3   **13 F4**
Minories EC3   59 C6
Minshull Pl., Beck.   87 A7
Minshull St. SW8   76 D1
  Wandsworth Rd.
Minson Rd. E9   59 G1
Minstead Gdns.   74 F7
  SW15
Minstead Way,   92 E6
  N.Mal.
Minster Ave., Sutt.   100 D2
  Burford Rd.
Minster Dr., Croy.   102 B4
Minster Gdns.,   90 F5
  W.Mol.
  Molesey Ave.
Minster Rd. NW2   48 B5

Minster Rd., Brom.   87 H7
Minster Wk. N8   40 E4
  Lightfoot Rd.
Minstrel Gdns., Surb. 91 J5
Mint Rd., Wall.   101 B4
Mint St. SE1   **16 J3**
Mint Wk., Croy.   101 J3
  High St.
Mintern Clo. N13   32 H3
Mintern St. N1   **9 C1**
Mintern St. N1   59 A2
Minterne Ave.,   63 G4
  Sthl.
Minterne Rd., Har.   37 J5
Minterne Way, Hayes   54 C6
Minton Ms. NW6   48 E6
  Lymington Rd.
Mirabel Rd. SW6   66 C7
Miranda Ct. W3   55 J6
  Queens Dr.
Miranda Rd. N19   49 C1
Mirfield St. SE7   70 A3
Miriam Rd. SE18   70 H5
Missenden Gdns.,   93 F6
  Mord.
Mission Gro. E17   41 H5
Mission Pl. SE15   77 D1
Mistletoe Clo.,   102 G1
  Croy.
  Marigold Way
Mitcham Gdn. Vill.,   94 A5
  Mitch.
Mitcham Ind. Est.,   94 A1
  Mitch.
Mitcham La. SW16   85 B6
Mitcham Pk., Mitch.   93 H4
Mitcham Rd. E6   61 B3
Mitcham Rd. SW17   84 J5
Mitcham Rd., Croy.   94 G5
Mitcham Rd., Ilf.   43 J7
Mitchell Clo. SE2   71 C7
Mitchell Clo., Belv.   71 J3
  Lwr. Rd.
Mitchell Rd. N13   32 H5
Mitchell Rd., Orp.   107 J4
Mitchell St. EC1   **8 J5**
Mitchell St. EC1   58 J4
Mitchell Wk. E6   61 B5
  Oliver Gdns.
Mitchell Way NW10   47 C6
Mitchell Way, Brom.   96 G1
Mitchellbrook Way   47 D6
  NW10
Mitchison Rd. N1   50 A6
Mitchley Rd. N17   41 D3
Mitford Rd. N19   49 E2
Mitre, The E14   59 J7
  Three Colt St.
Mitre Clo., Brom.   96 F2
  Beckenham La.
Mitre Clo., Sutt.   100 F7
Mitre Ct. EC2   **13 A3**
Mitre Ct. EC4   **12 F4**
Mitre Rd. E15   60 E2
Mitre Rd. SE1   **16 F3**
Mitre Rd. SE1   67 G2
Mitre Sq. EC3   **13 E4**
Mitre St. EC3   **13 E4**
Mitre St. EC3   59 B6
Mitre Way NW10   56 H4
Moat, The, N.Mal.   92 E1
Moat Clo., Orp.   104 J6
Moat Cres. N3   39 E3
Moat Cft., Well.   80 C3
Moat Dr. E13   60 J2
  Boundary Rd.
Moat Dr., Har.   36 J4
Moat Fm. Rd., Nthlt.   45 F6
Moat Pl. SW9   76 F3
Moat Pl. W3   56 B6
Moatside, Enf.   25 F4
Moatside, Felt.   81 C4
Moberley Rd. SW4   76 D7
Modbury Gdns. NW5   49 A6
  Queens Cres.
Modder Pl. SW15   75 A4
  Cardinal Pl.
Model Fm. Clo. SE9   88 B3
Modling Ho. E2   59 G3
  Mace St.
Moelwyn Hughes Ct.   49 D5
  N7
  Hilldrop Cres.
Moelyn Ms., Har.   37 D5
Moffat Gdns.,   93 G3
  Mitch.
Moffat Rd. N13   32 E6
Moffat Rd. SW17   84 H4
Moffat Rd., Th.Hth.   94 J2
Mogden La., Islw.   73 B5
Moiety Rd. E14   69 A2
Moira Clo. N17   41 B2
Moira Rd. SE9   79 C4

Moland Mead SE16   68 G5
  Crane Mead
Molasses Row SW11   75 F3
  Cinnamon Row
Mole Ct., Epsom   99 C4
Molember Ct.,   91 B5
  E.Mol.
Molember Rd.,   91 A5
  E.Mol.
Molescroft SE9   88 F3
Molesey Ave.,   90 F5
  W.Mol.
Molesey Dr., Sutt.   100 B2
Molesey Pk. Ave.,   90 H5
  W.Mol.
Molesey Pk. Clo.,   90 J5
  E.Mol.
Molesey Pk. Rd.,   90 H5
  E.Mol.
Molesey Pk. Rd.,   90 H5
  W.Mol.
Molesey Rd., W.Mol.   90 G5
Molesey Rd., W.Mol.   90 G5
Molesford Rd. SW6   75 D1
Molesham Clo.,   90 H3
  W.Mol.
Molesham Way,   90 H3
  W.Mol.
Molesworth St. SE13   78 C4
Molineaux Pl., Tedd.   82 D5
Mollison Dr., Wall.   101 D7
Mollison Way, Edg.   37 J2
Molly Huggins Clo.   76 C7
  SW12
Molyneux St. W1   **10 H2**
Molyneux St. W1   57 H5
Mona Rd. SE15   77 F2
Mona St. E16   60 F5
Monarch Clo.,   103 F4
  W.Wick.
Monarch Dr. E16   61 A5
Monarch Ms. SW16   85 G5
Monarch Rd., Belv.   71 G3
Monastery Gdns.,   25 A2
  Enf.
Monaveen Gdns.,   90 G3
  W.Mol.
Monck St. SW1   **15 J6**
Monck St. SW1   67 D3
Monclar Rd. SE5   77 A4
Moncorvo Clo. SW7   **14 G4**
Moncrieff Clo. E6   61 B6
  Linton Gdns.
Moncrieff St. SE15   77 D2
Monega Rd. E7   51 J6
Monega Rd. E12   52 A6
Monfitchet Rd.   61 E6
  E16
  Warwall
Monier Rd. E3   51 A7
Monivea Rd., Beck.   86 J7
Monk Dr. E16   60 G6
Monk Pas. E16   60 G7
  Monk Dr.
Monk St. SE18   70 D4
Monkchester Clo.,   27 D1
  Loug.
Monkfrith Ave. N14   24 B6
Monkfrith Clo. N14   24 B7
Monkfrith Way N14   24 A7
Monkhams Ave.,   34 G5
  Wdf.Grn.
Monkhams Dr.,   34 H5
  Wdf.Grn.
Monkhams La.,   34 H3
  Buck.H.
Monkhams La.,   34 G5
  Wdf.Grn.
Monkleigh Rd.,   93 B3
  Mord.
Monks Ave., Barn.   23 F6
Monks Ave., W.Mol.   90 F5
Monks Clo. SE2   71 D4
Monks Clo., Enf.   24 J2
Monks Clo., Har.   45 H2
Monks Clo., Ruis.   45 D4
Monks Dr. W3   56 A5
Monks Orchard Rd.,   103 A1
  Beck.
Monks Pk., Wem.   47 B6
Monks Pk. Gdns.,   47 B7
  Wem.
Monks Rd., Enf.   24 J2
Monks Way NW11   39 C4
  Hurstwood Rd.
Monks Way, Beck.   96 A6
Monks Way, Orp.   104 F1
Monksdene Gdns.,   100 E3
  Sutt.
Monksgrove, Loug.   27 D5
Monksmead, Borwd.   22 C2
Monkswell Ct. N10   40 A1
  Pembroke Rd.
Monkswood Gdns.,   22 D5
  Borwd.

Monkswood Gdns., 43 D3 Ilf.
Monkton Rd., Well. 79 J2
Monkton St. SE11 20 F1
Monkton St. SE11 67 G4
Monkville Ave. NW11 39 C4
Monkwell Sq. EC2 13 A2
Monmouth Ave. E18 42 H3
Monmouth Ave., 82 F7 Kings.T.
Monmouth Clo., 94 E4 Mitch.
Recreation Way
Monmouth Clo., 80 A4 Well.
Monmouth Gro. W5 64 H4
Sterling Pl.
Monmouth Pl. W2 10 A4
Monmouth Pl. W2 57 D6
Monmouth Rd.
Monmouth Rd. E6 61 C3
Monmouth Rd. N9 33 E2
Monmouth Rd. W2 57 D6
Monmouth Rd., Dag. 53 F5
Monmouth St. WC2 12 A5
Monmouth St. WC2 58 E6
Monnery Rd. N19 49 C3
Monnow Rd. SE1 21 H2
Monnow Rd. SE1 68 D5
Mono La., Felt. 81 B2
Monoux Gro. E17 42 A1
Monro Gdns., Har. 29 B7
Monroe Cres., Enf. 15 E1
Monroe Dr. SW14 74 B5
Mons Way, Brom. 97 B6
Monsal Ct. E5 50 G4
Redwald Rd.
Monsell Rd. N4 49 H3
Monson Rd. NW10 56 G2
Monson Rd. SE14 68 G7
Montacute Rd. SE6 77 J7
Montacute Rd., 93 F6 Mord.
Montagu Cres. N18 33 E4
Montagu Gdns. N18 33 E4
Montagu Gdns., 101 C4 Wall.
Montagu Mans. W1 11 A1
Montagu Ms. N. W1 11 A2
Montagu Ms. N. W1 57 J5
Montagu Ms. S. W1 11 A3
Montagu Ms. W. W1 11 A3
Montagu Pl. W1 10 J2
Montagu Pl. W1 57 J5
Montagu Rd. N9 33 F3
Montagu Rd. N18 33 E5
Montagu Rd. NW4 38 G6
Montagu Row W1 11 A2
Montagu Sq. W1 11 A2
Montagu Sq. W1 57 J5
Montagu St. W1 11 A3
Montagu St. W1 57 J6
Montague Ave. SE4 77 J4
Montague Ave. W7 64 C1
Montague Clo. SE1 17 B1
Montague Clo. SE1 68 A1
Montague Clo., 90 A7 Walt.
Montague Gdns. W3 56 A7
Montague Pl. WC1 11 J1
Montague Pl. WC1 58 D5
Montague Rd. E8 50 D5
Montague Rd. E11 51 F3
Montague Rd. N8 40 F5
Montague Rd. N15 41 D4
Montague Rd. SW19 84 E7
Montague Rd. W7 64 C2
Montague Rd. W13 55 E6
Montague Rd., Croy. 101 H1
Montague Rd., 72 H3 Houns.
Montague Rd., Rich. 73 H6
Montague Rd., Sthl. 63 E4
Montague Rd. Ind. 33 F4 Est. N18
Montague Sq. SE15 68 F7
Clifton Way
Montague St. EC1 12 J2
Montague St. EC1 58 J5
Montague St. WC1 12 A1
Montague St. WC1 58 E5
Montague Waye, 63 E3 Sthl.
Montalt Rd., 34 F5 Wdf.Grn.
Montana Rd. SW17 85 A4
Montana Rd. SW20 92 J1
Montbelle Rd. SE9 88 E3
Montcalm Clo., 96 G6 Brom.
Montcalm Clo., 54 B3 Hayes
Ayles Rd.

Montcalm Rd. SE7 70 A7
Montclare St. E2 9 F5
Monteagle Ave., 52 F6 Bark.
Monteagle Way E5 50 D3
Rendlesham Rd.
Monteagle Way SE15 77 E3
Montefiore St. SW8 76 B2
Monteith Rd. E3 59 J1
Montem Rd. SE23 77 J7
Montem Rd., N.Mal. 92 E4
Montem St. N4 49 F1
Thorpedale Rd.
Montenotte Rd. N8 40 C5
Monterey Clo., Bex. 89 J2
Montford Pl. SE11 20 E4
Montford Pl. SE11 67 G5
Montfort Rd., Sun. 90 A4
Montfort Gdns., Ilf. 35 F6
Montfort Pl. SW19 84 A1
Montgolfier Wk. 54 E3 Nthlt.
Jetstar Way
Montgomery Ave., 98 B3 Esher
Montgomery Clo., 94 E4 Mitch.
Montgomery Clo., 79 J6 Sid.
Montgomery Rd. W4 65 C4
Montgomery Rd., 29 J6 Edg.
Montholme Rd. 73 J6 SW11
Monthope Rd. E1 13 H2
Stephen's Rd.
Montolieu Gdns. 74 H5 SW15
Montpelier Ave. W5 55 F4
Montpelier Ave., 80 D7 Bex.
Montpelier Gdns. E6 61 A3
Montpelier Gdns., 44 C7 Rom.
Montpelier Gro. NW5 49 C5
Montpelier Ms. SW7 14 H5
Montpelier Pl. SW7 14 H5
Montpelier Pl. SW7 66 H3
Montpelier Ri. NW11 39 B7
Montpelier Ri., 46 G1 Wem.
Montpelier Rd. N3 39 F1
Montpelier Rd. SE15 77 E1
Montpelier Rd. W5 55 G5
Montpelier Rd., 100 F4 Sutt.
Montpelier Row SE3 78 F2
Montpelier Row, 74 D7 Twick.
Montpelier Sq. SW7 14 H5
Montpelier Sq. SW7 66 H2
Montpelier St. SW7 14 H4
Montpelier St. SW7 66 H3
Montpelier Ter. SW7 14 H4
Montpelier Vale SE3 78 F2
Montpelier Wk. SW7 14 G5
Montpelier Wk. SW7 66 H3
Montpelier Way 39 B7 NW11
Montrave Rd. SE20 86 F7
Montreal Pl. WC2 12 C5
Montreal Pl. WC2 58 F7
Montreal Rd., Ilf. 43 F7
Montrell Rd. SW2 85 E1
Montrose Ave. NW6 57 B2
Montrose Ave., Sid. 80 A7
Montrose Ave., 72 H7 Twick.
Montrose Ave., 79 G3 Well.
Montrose Clo., 79 J3 Well.
Montrose Clo., 34 G4 Wdf.Grn.
Montrose Ct. SW7 14 F4
Montrose Ct. SW7 66 G2
Montrose Cres. N12 31 F6
Montrose Cres., 46 H6 Wem.
Montrose Gdns., 93 J3 Mitch.
Montrose Gdns., 100 D2 Sutt.
Montrose Pl. SW1 15 C4
Montrose Pl. SW1 67 A2
Montrose Rd., Har. 37 B2
Montrose Way SE23 86 G1
Montserrat Ave., 34 D7 Wdf.Grn.
Montserrat Clo. 86 A5 SE19
Montserrat Rd. SW15 75 B4
Monument Gdns. 78 C5 SE13

Monument St. EC3 13 C5
Monument St. EC3 59 A7
Monument Way N17 41 C3
Monza St. E1 59 F7
Moodkee St. SE16 88 F3
Moody St. E1 59 G3
Moon La., Barn. 23 C3
Moon St. N1 58 H1
Moor La. EC2 13 B2
Moor La. EC2 59 A5
Moor La., Chess. 98 H4
Moor Mead Rd., 73 D6 Twick.
Moor Pl. EC2 13 B2
Moor St. W1 11 J4
Moorcroft Rd. SW16 85 E3
Moorcroft Way, Pnr. 36 E5
Moordown SE18 79 D1
Moore Clo. SW14 74 C3
Little St. Leonards
Moore Clo., Mitch. 94 B2
Moore Cres., Dag. 62 B1
Moore Pk. Rd. SW6 66 E7
Moore Rd. SE19 85 J6
Moore St. SW3 18 J1
Moore St. SW3 66 J4
Moore Wk. E7 51 G4
Stracey Rd.
Moore Way SE22 86 D1
Lordship La.
Moorefield Rd. N17 41 C3
Moorehead Way SE3 78 H3
Moorend Rd., 87 F7 Brom.
Moorey Clo. E15 60 F1
Stephen's Rd.
Moorfield Ave. W5 55 G4
Moorfield Rd., 98 H5 Chess.
Moorfield Rd., Enf. 25 F1
Moorfields EC2 13 B2
Moorfields EC2 59 A5
Moorgate EC2 13 B2
Moorgate EC2 59 A5
Moorgate Pl. EC2 13 B3
Moorhouse Rd. W2 57 D6
Moorhouse Rd., Har. 37 G3
Moorland Clo., Rom. 44 H1
Moorland Clo., 72 G7 Twick.
Telford Rd.
Moorland Rd. SW9 76 H4
Moorlands Ave. NW7 30 H6
Moorlands Est. SW9 76 G4
Moormead Dr., 99 E5 Epsom
Moorside Rd., Brom. 87 E3
Moortown Rd., Wat. 28 C4
Moot Ct. NW9 38 A5
Mora Rd. NW2 47 J4
Mora St. EC1 9 A4
Mora St. EC1 58 J3
Morant Pl. N.22 40 F1
Commerce Rd.
Morant St. E14 60 A7
Morat St. SW9 76 G1
Moravian Pl. SW10 18 F6
Moravian St. E2 59 F3
Moray Ms. N7 49 F2
Durham Rd.
Moray Rd. N4 49 F2
Mordaunt Gdns., 53 E7 Dag.
Mordaunt Ho. NW10 56 D1
Mordaunt Rd. NW10 56 D1
Mordaunt St. SW9 76 D1
Morden Clo. SE13 78 C2
Morden Ct., Mord. 93 E4
Morden Gdns., Grnf. 46 C5
Morden Gdns., 93 G4 Mitch.
Morden Hall Rd., 93 E3 Mord.
Morden Hill SE13 78 C2
Morden La. SE13 78 C1
Morden Rd. SE3 78 E2
Morden Rd. SW19 93 E1
Morden Rd., Mitch. 93 F4
Morden Rd., Rom. 44 E7
Morden Rd. Ms. SE3 78 G2
Morden St. SE13 78 B1
Morden Way, Sutt. 93 D7
Morden Wf. Rd. SE10 69 E3
Mordon Rd., Ilf. 43 J7
Mordred Rd. SE6 87 E2
More Clo. E16 60 F6
More Clo. W14 64 A4
Morecambe Clo. E1 59 G5
Morecambe Gdns., 79 B5 Stan.
Morecambe St. SE17 21 A2
Morecambe St. SE17 67 J4
Morecambe Ter. N18 33 A4

Morecombe Clo., 83 B7 Kings.T.
Moree Way N18 33 D4
Moreland Clo. NW11 48 E1
Moreland St. EC1 8 H3
Moreland St. EC1 58 H3
Moreland Way E4 34 B3
Morella Rd. SW12 75 J7
Moremead Rd. SE6 86 J4
Morena St. SE6 78 B7
Moresby Ave., Surb. 92 B7
Moresby Rd. E5 50 E1
Moresby Wk. SW8 76 B2
Moreton Ave., Islw. 73 B1
Moreton Clo. E5 50 F2
Moreton Clo. N15 41 A6
Moreton Clo. NW7 30 J6
Moreton Gdns., 35 B5 Wdf.Grn.
Moreton Pl. SW1 19 G3
Moreton Pl. SW1 67 C5
Moreton Rd. N15 41 A6
Moreton Rd., 102 A5 S.Croy.
Moreton Rd., 99 G2 Wor.Pk.
Moreton St. SW1 19 G3
Moreton St. SW1 67 C5
Moreton Ter. SW1 19 G3
Moreton Ter. SW1 67 C5
Moreton Ter. Ms. N. 19 G3 SW1
Moreton Ter. Ms. S. 19 G3 SW1
Moreton Twr. W3 65 B1
Morford Clo., Ruis. 36 B7
Morford Way, Ruis. 36 B7
Morgan Ave. E17 42 D4
Morgan Clo., Dag. 53 G7
Morgan Rd. N7 49 G5
Morgan Rd. W10 57 C5
Morgan Rd., Brom. 87 G7
Morgan St. E3 59 H3
Morgan St. E16 60 F5
Morgan Way, 35 B6 Wdf.Grn.
Morgans La. SE1 17 D2
Morgans La. SE1 68 B1
Moriatti Clo. N7 49 E4
Morie St. SW18 75 E4
Morieux Rd. E10 50 J1
Moring Rd. SW17 85 A4
Morkyns Wk. SE21 86 B3
Morland Ave., Croy. 102 B1
Morland Clo., 81 F5 Hmptn.
Morland Clo., 93 H3 Mitch.
Morland Gdns. 47 D7 NW10
Morland Gdns., 63 H1 Sthl.
Morland Ms. N1 49 G7
Lofting Rd.
Morland Rd. E17 41 G5
Morland Rd. SE20 86 G6
Morland Rd., Croy. 102 B1
Morland Rd., Dag. 53 G7
Morland Rd., Har. 37 H5
Morland Rd., Ilf. 52 E2
Morland Rd., Sutt. 100 F5
Morley Ave. E4 34 D7
Morley Ave. N18 33 D4
Morley Ave. N22 40 G2
Morley Clo., Orp. 104 E2
Morley Clo., Ruis. 45 C2
Morley Cres., Edg. 30 C2
Morley Cres. E., 37 F2 Stan.
Morley Cres. W., 37 F3 Stan.
Morley Rd. E10 51 C1
Morley Rd. E15 60 F2
Morley Rd. SE13 78 C4
Morley Rd., Bark. 61 G1
Morley Rd., Chis. 97 F1
Morley Rd., Rom. 44 E5
Morley Rd., Twick. 73 G6
Morley St. SE1 16 F5
Morley St. SE1 67 G3
Morna Rd. SE5 76 J2
Morning La. E9 50 F6
Morningside Rd., 99 H2 Wor.Pk.
Mornington Ave. 66 C4 W14
Mornington Ave., 96 J3 Brom.
Mornington Ave., 43 D7 Ilf.
Mornington Clo., 34 G4 Wdf.Grn.

Mornington Ct., Bex. 89 J1
Mornington Cres. **7** **F1**
NW1
Mornington Cres. 58 C2
NW1
Mornington Cres., 72 B1
Houns.
Mornington Gro. E3 60 A3
Mornington Ms. SE5 76 J1
Mornington Pl. NW1 **7** **E1**
Mornington Rd. E4 26 D7
Mornington Rd. E11 51 F1
Mornington Rd. SE8 68 J7
Mornington Rd., 54 H5
Grnf.
Mornington Rd., 27 F3
Loug.
Mornington Rd., 34 F4
Wdf.Grn.
Mornington St. NW1 **7** **E1**
Mornington St. NW1 58 B2
Mornington Ter. NW1 58 B2
Mornington Wk., 82 F4
Rich.
Morocco St. SE1 **17** **D4**
Morocco St. SE1 68 B2
Morpeth Gro. E9 59 G1
Morpeth Rd. E9 59 F1
Morpeth St. E2 59 G3
Morpeth Ter. SW1 **15** **F6**
Morpeth Ter. SW1 67 C3
Morpeth Wk. N17 33 E7
West Rd.
Morrab Gdns., Ilf. 52 J3
Morrell Clo., Barn. 23 F3
Galdana Ave.
Morris Ave. E12 52 C5
Morris Clo., Orp. 104 H3
Morris Gdns. SW18 75 D7
Morris Pl. N4 49 G2
Morris Rd. E14 60 B5
Morris Rd. E15 51 D4
Morris Rd., Dag. 53 F2
Morris Rd., Islw. 73 C3
Morris St. E1 59 E6
Morrish Rd. SW2 76 E7
Morrison Ave. N17 41 B3
Morrison Rd., Bark. 62 E2
Morrison Rd., Hayes 54 B3
Morrison St. SW11 76 A3
Morriston Clo., 28 C5
Wat.
Morse Clo. E13 60 G3
Morshead Rd. W9 57 D3
Morson Rd., Enf. 25 F7
Morston Gdns. SE9 88 C4
Morten Clo. SW4 76 D6
Morteyne Rd. N17 41 A1
Mortham St. E15 60 E1
Mortimer Clo. NW2 48 C3
Mortimer Clo. SW16 85 D2
Mortimer Cres. NW6 57 E1
Mortimer Cres., 99 D3
Wor.Pk.
Mortimer Dr., Enf. 25 B5
Mortimer Est. NW6 57 E1
Mortimer Mkt. WC1 **7** **G6**
Mortimer Pl. NW6 57 E1
Mortimer Rd. E6 61 C3
Mortimer Rd. N1 50 B7
Mortimer Rd. NW10 56 J3
Mortimer Rd. W13 55 F6
Mortimer Rd., 93 J1
Mitch.
Mortimer Sq. W11 57 A7
St. Anns Rd.
Mortimer St. W1 **11** **F3**
Mortimer St. W1 58 C6
Mortimer Ter. NW5 49 B4
Gordon Ho. Rd.
Mortlake Clo., 101 E3
Croy.
Richmond Rd.
Mortlake Dr., 93 H1
Mitch.
Mortlake High St. 74 D3
SW14
Mortlake Rd. E16 60 H6
Mortlake Rd., Ilf. 52 E3
Mortlake Rd., Rich. 65 A7
Mortlock Clo. SE15 77 E2
Kirkwood Rd.
Morton Cres. N14 32 D4
Morton Gdns., Wall. 101 C5
Morton Ms. SW5 **18** **A2**
Morton Pl. SE1 **16** **E6**
Morton Rd. E15 51 F7
Morton Rd. N1 49 J7
Morton Rd., Mord. 93 G6
Morton Way N14 32 C3
Morval Rd. SW2 76 G5
Morvale Clo., Belv. 71 F4
Morven Rd. SW17 84 J3

Morville St. E3 60 A2
Morwell St. WC1 **11** **J2**
Moscow Pl. W2 **10** **A5**
Moscow Rd. W2 **10** **A5**
Moscow Rd. W2 57 E7
Moselle Ave. N22 40 G2
Moselle Clo. N8 40 F3
Miles Rd.
Moselle Ho. N17 33 C7
Moselle Pl. N17 33 C7
High Rd.
Moselle St. N17 33 C7
Moss Clo. E1 **13** **J2**
Moss Clo., Pnr. 36 F2
Moss Gdns., S.Croy. 102 G7
Warren Ave.
Moss Hall Cres. N12 31 E6
Moss Hall Gro. N12 31 E6
Moss La., Pnr. 36 E1
Moss Rd., Dag. 53 G7
Mossborough Clo. 31 E6
N12
Mossbury Rd. SW11 75 H3
Mossdown Clo., 71 G4
Belv.
Mossford Ct., Ilf. 43 E3
Mossford Grn., Ilf. 43 E3
Mossford La., Ilf. 43 E2
Mossford St. E3 59 J4
Mossington Gdns. 68 F4
SE16
Abbeyfield Rd.
Mosslea Rd. SE20 86 F6
Mosslea Rd., Brom. 97 A5
Mosslea Rd., Orp. 104 F3
Mossop St. SW3 **18** **H1**
Mossop St. SW3 66 H4
Mossville Gdns., 93 C3
Mord.
Mostyn Ave., Wem. 46 J5
Mostyn Gdns. NW10 57 A3
Mostyn Gro. E3 60 A2
Mostyn Rd. SW9 76 G1
Mostyn Rd. SW19 93 C1
Mostyn Rd., Edg. 30 D7
Mosul Way, Brom. 97 B6
Motcomb St. SW1 **15** **A5**
Motcomb St. SW1 67 A3
Motley St. SW8 76 C2
St. Rule St.
Motspur Pk., N.Mal. 92 F6
Mott St., Loug. 26 E1
Mottingham Gdns. 88 A1
SE9
Mottingham La. SE9 87 J1
Mottingham La. SE12 87 J1
Mottingham Rd. N9 25 G6
Mottingham Rd. SE9 88 B2
Mottisfont Rd. SE2 71 A3
Moulins Rd. E9 59 F7
Moulton Ave., 72 E2
Houns.
Mound, The SE9 88 D3
Moundfield Rd. N16 41 D6
Mount, The N20 31 F2
Mount, The NW3 48 F4
Heath St.
Mount, The W3 65 B1
High St.
Mount, The N.Mal. 92 F3
Mount, The, Wem. 47 B2
Mount, The, Wor.Pk. 99 H4
Mount Adon Pk. 77 D7
SE22
Mount Angelus Rd. 74 F7
SW15
Laverstoke Gdns.
Mount Ararat Rd., 73 H5
Rich.
Mount Ash Rd. SE26 86 E3
Mount Ave. E4 34 A3
Mount Ave. W5 55 F5
Mount Ave., Sthl. 54 G6
Mount Clo. W5 55 F5
Mount Clo., Barn. 24 A4
Mount Clo., Brom. 97 B1
Mount Cor., Felt. 81 D2
Mount Ct. SW15 75 B3
Weimar St.
Mount Ct., W.Wick. 103 E2
Mount Culver Ave., 89 D6
Sid.
Mount Dr., Bexh. 80 E5
Mount Dr., Har. 36 F5
Mount Dr., Wem. 47 C2
Mount Echo Ave. E4 34 B2
Mount Echo Dr. E4 34 B1
Mount Ephraim La. 85 D3
SW16
Mount Ephraim Rd. 85 D3
SW16
Mount Est., The E5 50 E2
Mount Pleasant

Mount Gdns. SE26 86 E3
Mount Gro., Edg. 30 C3
Mount Ms., Hmptn. 90 H1
Mount Mills EC1 **8** **H4**
Mount Nod Rd. SW16 85 F3
Mount Pk. Ave., Har. 46 A2
Mount Pk. Cres. W5 55 G5
Mount Pk. Rd. W5 55 G5
Mount Pk. Rd., Har. 46 A3
Mount Pk. Rd., Pnr. 36 A5
Mount Pleasant SE27 85 J4
Mount Pleasant WC1 **8** **E6**
Mount Pleasant WC1 58 G4
Mount Pleasant, 23 H4
Barn.
Mount Pleasant, 45 C2
Ruis.
Mount Pleasant, 55 H1
Wem.
Mount Pleasant 40 F7
Cres. N4
Mount Pleasant Hill 50 E2
E5
Mount Pleasant La. 50 E2
E5
Mount Pleasant Rd. 41 H2
E17
Mount Pleasant Rd. 41 B1
N17
Mount Pleasant Rd. 47 J7
NW10
Mount Pleasant Rd. 78 C6
SE13
Mount Pleasant Rd. 55 F4
W5
Mount Pleasant Rd., 35 G4
Chig.
Mount Pleasant Rd., 92 C3
N.Mal.
Mount Pleasant 40 F7
Vill. N4
Mount Pleasant Wk., 80 J5
Bex.
Mount Rd. NW2 47 H3
Mount Rd. NW4 38 G6
Mount Rd. SE19 86 A6
Mount Rd. SW19 84 D2
Mount Rd., Barn. 23 H5
Mount Rd., Bexh. 80 D5
Mount Rd., Chess. 98 J5
Mount Rd., Dag. 53 F1
Mount Rd., Felt. 81 E3
Mount Rd., Ilf. 52 E5
Mount Rd., Mitch. 93 G2
Mount Rd., N.Mal. 92 D3
Mount Row W1 **11** **D6**
Mount Row W1 58 B7
Mount Sq., The NW3 48 F3
Heath St.
Mount Stewart Ave., 37 G6
Har.
Mount St. W1 **11** **B6**
Mount St. W1 58 A7
Mount Ter. E1 59 E5
New Rd.
Mount Vernon NW3 48 F4
Mount Vw. NW7 30 D3
Mount Vw. W5 55 G4
Mount Vw. Rd. E4 26 C7
Mount Vw. Rd. N4 40 E7
Mount Vw. Rd. NW9 38 D5
Mount Vill. SE27 85 H3
Mountacre Clo. SE26 86 C4
Mountague Pl. E14 60 C7
Mountbatten Clo. 70 H6
SE18
Mountbatten Clo. 86 B5
SE19
Mountbatten Ct., 35 A2
Buck.H.
Mountbatten Ms. 84 F1
SW18
Inman Rd.
Mountbel Rd., Stan. 37 D1
Mountcombe Clo., 91 H7
Surb.
Mountearl Gdns. 85 F3
SW16
Mountfield Rd. E6 61 D2
Mountfield Rd. N3 39 C3
Mountfield Rd. W5 55 G5
Mountford St. E1 **13** **H3**
Mountfort Cres. N1 49 G7
Barnsbury Rd.
Mountfort Ter. N1 49 G7
Barnsbury Sq.
Mountgrove Rd. N5 49 H3
Mounthurst Rd., 96 F7
Brom.
Mountington Pk. 37 G6
Clo., Har.
Mountjoy Clo. SE2 71 B2
Mounts Pond Rd. SE3 78 D2

Mountsfield Ct. 78 E6
SE13
Mountside, Felt. 81 E3
Mountside, Stan. 37 C1
Mountview Cr. N8 40 H4
Green Las.
Mountview Rd., 98 E7
Esher
Mountwood, W.Mol. 90 G3
Movers La., Bark. 61 G1
Mowatt Clo. N19 49 D1
Mowbray Rd. NW6 48 B7
Mowbray Rd. SE19 95 C1
Mowbray Rd., Barn. 23 F4
Mowbray Rd., Edg. 30 A4
Mowbray Rd., Rich. 82 F3
Mowbrays Clo., Rom. 44 J1
Mowbrays Rd., Rom. 44 J2
Mowbray Gdns., 27 F3
Loug.
Mowlem St. E2 59 E2
Mowlem Trd. Est. 33 F7
N17
Mowll St. SW9 67 G7
Moxon Clo. E13 60 F2
Whitelegg Rd.
Moxon St. W1 **11** **B2**
Moxon St. W1 58 A5
Moxon St., Barn. 23 C3
Moye Clo. E2 **9** **J1**
Moye Clo. E2 59 D1
Dove Row
Moyers Rd. E10 42 C7
Moylan Rd. W6 66 B6
Moyne Pl. NW10 56 A2
Moyser Rd. SW16 85 B5
Mozart St. W10 57 C3
Mozart Ter. SW1 **19** **C2**
Muchelney Rd., 93 F6
Mord.
Mud La. W5 55 G5
Mudlarks Way SE7 69 H3
Mudlarks Way SE10 69 F3
Muggeridge Rd., 53 H4
Dag.
Muir Rd. E5 50 D4
Muir St. E16 70 C1
Tate Rd.
Muirdown Ave. 74 D4
SW14
Muirfield W3 56 E6
Muirfield Clo., 28 C5
Wat.
Muirfield Cres. E14 69 B3
Millharbour
Muirfield Grn., 28 C4
Wat.
Muirfield Rd., Wat. 28 B4
Muirkirk Rd. SE6 87 C1
Mulberry Clo. E4 34 A2
Mulberry Clo. NW3 48 G4
Hampstead High St.
Mulberry Clo. NW4 38 J3
Mulberry Clo. SE7 70 A6
Mulberry Clo. SE22 77 D6
Mulberry Clo. SW16 85 C4
Mulberry Clo., Barn. 23 G4
Mulberry Clo., 54 E2
Nthlt.
Parkfield Ave.
Mulberry Ct., Bark. 52 J7
Westrow Dr.
Mulberry Cres., 64 E7
Brent.
Mulberry La., Croy. 102 C1
Mulberry Ms., Wall. 101 C6
Ross Rd.
Mulberry Pl. W6 65 G5
Chiswick Mall
Mulberry St. E1 **13** **H3**
Mulberry Wk. SW3 **18** **F5**
Mulberry Wk. SW3 66 G6
Mulberry Way E18 42 H2
Mulberry Way, Belv. 71 J2
Mulberry Way, Ilf. 43 F4
Mulgrave Rd. NW10 47 F4
Mulgrave Rd. SW6 66 C6
Mulgrave Rd. W5 55 G4
Mulgrave Rd., Croy. 102 A3
Mulgrave Rd., Har. 46 D2
Mulgrave Rd., Sutt. 100 C7
Mulholland Clo., 94 B2
Mitch.
Mulkern Rd. N19 49 D1
Mull Wk. N1 49 J6
Clephane Rd.
Muller Rd. SW4 76 D6
Mullet Gdns. E2 **9** **J3**
Mullins Path SW14 74 D3
Mullion Clo., Har. 36 H1
Mullion Wk., Wat. 28 D4
Ormskirk Rd.
Mulready St. NW8 **6** **G6**

Multon Rd. SW18	75	G7
Mulvaney Way SE1	**17**	**C4**
Mulvaney Way SE1	68	A2
Mumford Ct. EC2	**13**	**A3**
Mumford Rd. SE24	76	H5
Railton Rd.		
Muncaster Rd. SW11	75	J5
Muncies Ms. SE6	87	C2
Mund St. W14	66	C5
Mundania Rd. SE22	77	E6
Munday Rd. E16	60	G6
Munden St. W14	66	B4
Mundesley Clo., Wat.	28	C4
Mundford Rd. E5	50	F2
Mundon Gdns., Ilf.	52	G1
Mundy St. N1	**9**	**E3**
Mundy St. N1	59	B3
Mungo Pk. Clo. (Bushey), Wat.	28	J2
Munnery Way, Orp.	104	D2
Munnings Gdns., Islw.	73	A5
Munro Dr. N11	32	C6
Munro Ms. W10	57	B5
Munro Ter. SW10	**18**	**E7**
Munro Ter. SW10	66	G6
Munster Ave., Houns.	72	E4
Munster Rd., Tedd.	82	F6
Munster Gdns. N13	32	H4
Munster Rd. SW6	66	B7
Munster Rd., Tedd.	93	E6
Munster Sq. NW1	**7**	**E4**
Munster Sq. NW1	58	B3
Munton Rd. SE17	**21**	**A1**
Munton Rd. SE17	67	J4
Murchison Ave., Bex.	89	D1
Murchison Rd. E10	51	C2
Murdock Clo. E16	60	F6
Rogers Rd.		
Murdock St. SE15	68	E6
Murfett Clo. SW19	84	B2
Muriel St. N1	58	F1
Murillo Rd. SE13	78	D4
Murphy St. SE1	**16**	**E4**
Murphy St. SE1	67	G2
Murray Ave., Brom.	96	H3
Murray Ave., Houns.	72	H5
Murray Cres., Pnr.	36	D1
Murray Gro. N1	**9**	**A2**
Murray Gro. N1	58	J2
Murray Ms. NW1	49	D7
Murray Rd. SW19	84	A6
Murray Rd. W5	64	G4
Murray Rd., Rich.	82	E2
Murray Sq. E16	60	G6
Murray St. NW1	49	D7
Murray Ter. NW3	48	G4
Flask Wk.		
Mursell Est. SW8	76	F1
Murtwell Dr., Chig.	35	F6
Musard Rd. W6	66	B6
Musbury St. E1	59	F6
Muscal W6	66	A6
Muscatel Pl. SE5	77	B1
Dalwood St.		
Muschamp Rd. SE15	77	C3
Muschamp Rd., Cars.	100	H2
Muscovy St. EC3	**13**	**E5**
Museum Pas. E2	59	E3
Victoria Pk. Sq.		
Museum St. WC1	**12**	**A2**
Museum St. WC1	58	E5
Musgrave Clo., Barn.	23	F1
Musgrave Cres. SW6	66	D7
Musgrave Rd., Islw.	73	C1
Musgrove Rd. SE14	77	G1
Musjid Rd. SW11	75	G2
Kambala Rd.		
Musquash Way, Houns.	72	C2
Muston Rd. E5	50	E2
Mustow Pl. SW6	75	C2
Munster Rd.		
Muswell Ave. N10	40	B3
Muswell Hill N10	40	B3
Muswell Hill Bdy. N10	40	B3
Muswell Hill Pl. N10	40	B4
Muswell Hill Rd. N6	40	A6
Muswell Hill Rd. N10	40	A5
Muswell Ms. N10	40	B3
Muswell Rd.		
Muswell Rd. N10	40	B3
Mutrix Rd. NW6	57	D1
Mutton Pl. NW1	49	B6
Harmood St.		
Muybridge Rd., N.Mal.	92	C2
Myatt Rd. SW9	76	H1
Myatt's Flds. N. SW9	76	G1
Eythorne Rd.		
Myatt's Flds. S. SW9	76	G2
Mycenae Rd. SE3	69	G7
Myddelton Clo., Enf.	25	C1
Myddelton Ave.		
Myddelton Gdns. N21	24	H7
Myddelton Pk. N20	31	G3
Myddelton Pas. EC1	**8**	**F3**
Myddelton Rd. N8	40	E4
Myddelton Sq. EC1	**8**	**F3**
Myddelton Sq. EC1	58	G3
Myddelton St. EC1	**8**	**F4**
Myddelton St. EC1	58	G3
Myddleton Rd. N22	32	E7
Myers La. SE14	68	G6
Mylis Clo. SE26	86	E4
Mylne St. EC1	**8**	**E3**
Mylne St. EC1	58	G2
Myra St. SE2	71	A4
Myrdle St. E1	**13**	**J3**
Myrdle St. E1	59	D5
Myrna Clo., Mitch.	84	H7
Myron Pl. SE13	78	C3
Myrtle Ave., Ruis.	36	A7
Myrtle Clo., Barn.	31	J1
Myrtle Gdns. W7	64	B1
Myrtle Gro., N.Mal.	92	C2
Myrtle Rd. E6	61	B1
Myrtle Rd. E17	41	H6
Myrtle Rd. N13	32	J3
Myrtle Rd. W3	65	C1
Myrtle Rd., Croy.	103	A3
Myrtle Rd., Hmptn.	81	J6
Myrtle Rd., Houns.	72	J2
Myrtle Rd., Ilf.	52	E2
Myrtle Rd., Sutt.	100	F5
Myrtle Wk. N1	**9**	**D2**
Myrtle Wk. N1	59	B2
Myrtleberry Clo. E8	50	C6
Beechwood Rd.		
Myrtledene Rd. SE2	71	A5
Mysore Rd. SW11	75	J3
Myton Rd. SE21	86	A3

N

Nadine St. SE7	69	J5
Nagasaki Wk. SE7	69	J3
Nagle Clo. E17	42	D2
Nag's Head Ct. EC1	**9**	**J6**
Nags Head La., Well.	80	B3
Nags Head Rd., Enf.	25	F4
Nairn Grn., Wat.	28	A3
Nairn Rd., Ruis.	45	C6
Nairn St. E14	60	C5
Nairne Gro. SE24	77	A5
Naish Ct. N1	58	E1
Nallhead Rd., Felt.	81	C5
Namton Dr., Th.Hth.	94	F4
Nan Clark's La. NW7	30	F2
Nankin St. E14	60	A6
Nansen Rd. SW11	76	A4
Nant Rd. NW2	48	C2
Nant St. E2	59	E3
Cambridge Heath Rd.		
Nantes Clo. SW18	75	F4
Nantes Pas. E1	**13**	**F1**
Napier Ave. E14	69	A5
Napier Ave. SW6	75	C3
Napier Clo. SE8	68	J7
Amersham Vale		
Napier Clo. W14	66	C3
Napier Rd.		
Napier Ct. SW6	75	C3
Ranelagh Gdns.		
Napier Gro. N1	58	J2
Napier Pl. W14	66	C3
Napier Rd. E11	61	D1
Napier Rd. E11	51	E4
Napier Rd. E15	60	E2
Napier Rd. N17	41	B3
Napier Rd. NW10	56	H3
Napier Rd. SE25	95	E4
Napier Rd. W14	66	B3
Napier Rd., Belv.	71	F4
Napier Rd., Brom.	96	H4
Napier Rd., Enf.	25	G5
Napier Rd., Islw.	73	D4
Napier Rd., S.Croy.	102	A7
Napier Rd., Wem.	46	G5
Napier Ter. N1	49	H6
Napoleon Rd. E5	50	E3
Napoleon Rd., Twick.	73	E7
Napton Clo., Hayes	54	E4
Kingsash Dr.		
Narbonne Ave. SW4	76	C5
Narborough St. SW6	75	E2
Narcissus Rd. NW6	48	D5
Naresby Fold, Stan.	29	F6
Narford Rd. E5	50	D3
Narrow St. E14	59	H7
Narrow Way, Brom.	97	B6
Nascot St. W12	56	J6
Naseby Clo. NW6	48	F7
Fairfax Rd.		
Naseby Clo., Islw.	73	B1
Naseby Rd. SE19	86	G3
Naseby Rd., Dag.	53	G3
Naseby Rd., Ilf.	43	C1
Nash Grn., Brom.	87	G6
Nash La., Kes.	103	G7
Nash Pl. E14	69	B1
South Colonnade		
Nash Rd. N9	33	F2
Nash Rd. SE4	77	H4
Nash Rd., Rom.	44	D4
Nash St. NW1	**7**	**E3**
Nasmyth St. W6	65	H3
Nassau Path SE28	71	C1
Disraeli Clo.		
Nassau Rd. SW13	74	F1
Nassau St. W1	**11**	**F2**
Nassau St. W1	58	C5
Nassington Rd. NW3	48	H4
Natal Rd. N11	32	E6
Natal Rd. SW16	85	D6
Natal Rd., Ilf.	62	H3
Natal Rd., Th.Hth.	95	A3
Nathan Way SE28	70	H3
Nathaniel Clo. E1	**13**	**G2**
Thrawl St.		
Nathans Rd., Wem.	46	F1
Naval Row E14	60	C7
Naval Wk., Brom.	96	G3
High St.		
Navarino Gro. E8	50	D6
Navarino Rd. E8	50	D6
Navarre Rd. E6	61	B2
Navarre St. E2	**9**	**F5**
Navarre St. E2	59	C4
Navenby Wk. E3	60	A4
Rounton Rd.		
Navestock Clo. E4	34	C3
Mapleton Rd.		
Navestock Cres., Wdf.Grn.	42	J1
Navestock Ho., Bark.	62	B2
Navy St. SW4	76	D3
Naylor Gro., Enf.	25	G5
South St.		
Naylor Rd. N20	31	F2
Naylor Rd. SE15	68	E7
Nazrul St. E2	**9**	**F3**
Nazrul St. E2	59	C3
Neagle Clo., Pot.B.	22	C1
Neal Ave., Sthl.	54	F3
Neal Clo., Nthwd.	36	A1
Neal St. WC2	**12**	**A4**
Neal St. WC2	58	E1
Nealden St. SW9	76	F3
Neale Clo. N2	39	F3
Neal's Yd. WC2	**12**	**A4**
Near Acre NW9	38	F1
Neasden Clo. NW10	47	E5
Neasden La. NW10	47	E4
Neasden La. N. NW10	47	D3
Neasham Rd., Dag.	53	B5
Neate St. SE5	**21**	**D6**
Neate St. SE5	68	B6
Neath Gdns., Mord.	93	F6
Neathouse Pl. SW1	**19**	**F1**
Neatscourt Rd. E6	61	A5
Nebraska St. SE1	**17**	**B4**
Neckinger SE16	**17**	**G5**
Neckinger SE16	68	C3
Neckinger Est. SE16	**17**	**G5**
Neckinger Est. SE16	68	C3
Neckinger St. SE1	**17**	**G5**
Neckinger St. SE1	68	C3
Nectarine Way SE13	78	B2
Needham Rd. W11	57	D6
Westbourne Gro.		
Needham Ter. NW2	48	A3
Needleman St. SE16	68	G3
Neeld Cres. NW4	38	H5
Neeld Cres., Wem.	47	A5
Nelgarde Rd. SE6	78	A6
Nella Rd. W6	66	A6
Nelldale Rd. SE16	68	F4
Nello James Gdns. SE27	86	A4
Nelson Clo., Croy.	101	H1
Nelson Clo., Rom.	44	H1
Nelson Gdns. E2	**9**	**J3**
Nelson Gdns. E2	59	D3
Nelson Gdns., Houns.	72	G6
Nelson Gro. Rd. SW19	93	E1
Nelson Mandela Clo. N10	40	A2
Nelson Mandela Rd. SE3	78	J3
Nelson Pas. EC1	**9**	**A4**
Nelson Pas. EC1	58	J3
Nelson Pl. N1	**8**	**H2**
Nelson Pl. N1	58	H2
Nelson Pl. W3	65	B1
Steyne Rd.		
Nelson Pl., Sid.	89	A4
Nelson Rd. E4	34	A6
Nelson Rd. E11	42	G4
Nelson Rd. N8	40	F5
Nelson Rd. N9	33	E2
Nelson Rd. N15	41	B4
Nelson Rd. SE10	69	C6
Nelson Rd. SW19	84	E7
Nelson Rd., Belv.	71	F5
Nelson Rd., Brom.	96	J4
Nelson Rd., Enf.	25	G6
Nelson Rd., Har.	46	A1
Nelson Rd., Houns.	72	G6
Nelson Rd., N.Mal.	92	D5
Nelson Rd., Sid.	89	A4
Nelson Rd., Stan.	29	F6
Nelson Rd., Twick.	72	H7
Nelson Sq. SE1	**16**	**G3**
Nelson Sq. SE1	67	H2
Nelson St. E1	59	E6
Nelson St. E6	61	C2
Nelson St. E16	60	F7
Huntingdon St.		
Nelson Ter. N1	**8**	**H2**
Nelson Ter. N1	58	H2
Nelson Trd. Est. SW19	93	E1
Nelson Wk. SE16	68	H1
Rotherhithe St.		
Nelson's Row SW4	76	D4
Nemoure Rd. W3	56	C7
Nene Gdns., Felt.	81	F2
Nepaul Rd. SW11	75	H2
Afghan Rd.		
Nepean St. SW15	74	G6
Neptune Rd., Har.	37	A6
Neptune St. SE16	68	F3
Nesbit Clo. SE3	78	E3
Hurren Clo.		
Nesbit Rd. SE9	79	A4
Nesbitt Sq. SE19	86	B7
Coxwell Rd.		
Nesbitts All., Barn.	23	C3
Bath Pl.		
Nesham St. E1	**17**	**H1**
Nesham St. E1	68	D1
Ness St. SE16	**17**	**H5**
Nesta Rd., Wdf.Grn.	34	E6
Nestor Ave. N21	24	H6
Nether Clo. N3	31	D7
Nether St. N3	39	D1
Nether St. N12	31	E6
Netheravon Rd. W7	64	C1
Netheravon Rd. N. W4	65	F4
Netheravon Rd. S. W4	65	F5
Netherbury Rd. W5	64	G3
Netherby Gdns., Enf.	24	E4
Netherby Rd. SE23	77	F7
Nethercourt Ave. N3	31	D6
Netherfield Gdns., Bark.	52	G6
Netherfield Rd. N12	31	E5
Netherfield Rd. SW17	85	A3
Netherford Rd. SW4	76	C2
Netherhall Gdns. NW3	48	F6
Netherhall Way NW3	48	F5
Netherhall Gdns.		
Netherlands Rd., Barn.	23	G6
Netherleigh Clo. N6	49	C1
Netherton Gro. SW10	**18**	**D6**
Netherton Gro. SW10	66	G6
Netherton Rd., Twick.	73	D5
Netherwood N2	39	G2
Netherwood Pl. W14	66	A3
Netherwood Rd.		
Netherwood Rd. W14	66	A3
Netherwood St. NW6	48	C7
Netley Clo., Croy.	103	C7
Netley Clo., Sutt.	100	A5
Netley Dr., Walt.	90	F7
Netley Gdns., Mord.	93	F7
Netley Rd. E17	41	J5
Netley Rd., Brent.	64	H6
Netley Rd., Ilf.	43	G5

Street	Page	Grid
Netley Rd., Mord.	93	F7
Netley St. NW1	7	F4
Nettleden Ave., Wem.	47	A6
Nettlefold Pl. SE27	85	H3
Nettleton Rd. SE14	77	G1
Nettlewood Rd. SW16	85	D7
Neuchatel Rd. SE6	86	J2
Nevada Clo., N.Mal.	92	C4
Georgia Rd.		
Nevada St. SE10	69	C6
Nevern Pl. SW5	66	D4
Nevern Rd. SW5	66	D4
Nevern Sq. SW5	66	D4
Nevill Rd. N16	50	B3
Neville Ave., N.Mal.	92	D1
Neville Clo. E11	51	F3
Neville Clo. NW1	7	J2
Neville Clo. NW6	57	C2
Neville Clo. SE15	68	D7
Neville Clo. W3	65	C2
Acton La.		
Neville Clo., Houns.	72	H2
Neville Clo., Sid.	88	J4
Neville Dr. N2	39	F6
Neville Gdns., Dag.	53	D3
Neville Gill Clo. SW18	75	E6
Neville Pl. N22	40	F1
Neville Rd. E7	51	G7
Neville Rd. NW6	57	C2
Neville Rd. W5	55	G4
Neville Rd., Croy.	95	A7
Neville Rd., Dag.	53	D2
Neville Rd., Ilf.	43	F1
Neville Rd., Kings.T.	92	A2
Neville Rd., Rich.	82	F2
Neville St. SW7	18	E3
Neville St. SW7	66	G5
Neville Ter. SW7	18	E3
Neville Ter. SW7	66	G5
Neville Wk., Cars.	93	H7
Green Wrythe La.		
Nevilles Ct. NW2	47	G3
Nevin Dr. E4	34	B1
Nevis Rd. SW17	85	A2
New Ash Clo. N2	39	G3
Oakridge Dr.		
New Barn St. E13	60	G4
New Barns Ave., Mitch.	94	D4
New Barns Way, Chig.	35	E3
New Bond St. W1	11	D4
New Bond St. W1	58	B6
New Brent St. NW4	38	J5
New Bri., Erith	71	J4
New Bri. St. EC4	12	G4
New Bri. St. EC4	58	H6
New Broad St. EC2	13	D2
New Bdy. W5	55	F7
New Burlington Ms. W1	11	F5
New Burlington Pl. W1	11	F5
New Burlington St. W1	11	F5
New Burlington St. W1	58	C7
New Butt La. SE8	69	A7
New Cavendish St. W1	11	C2
New Cavendish St. W1	58	A5
New Change EC4	12	J4
New Change EC4	58	J6
New Chapel Sq., Felt.	81	B1
New Charles St. EC1	8	H3
New Ch. Rd. SE5	21	B7
New Ch. Rd. SE5	68	A7
New City Rd. E13	60	J3
New Clo. SW19	93	F3
New Clo., Felt.	81	E5
New College Ms. N1	49	G7
Islington Pk. St.		
New Compton St. WC2	11	J4
New Compton St. WC2	58	D6
New Ct. EC4	12	E5
New Covent Gdn. Mkt. SW8	67	D7
New Coventry St. W1	11	J6
New Crane Pl. E1	68	F1
Garnet St.		
New Cross Rd. SE14	68	F7
New End NW3	48	F4
New End Sq. NW3	48	G4
New Fm. Ave., Brom.	96	G4
New Fetter La. EC4	12	F3
New Fetter La. EC4	58	G6
New Forest La., Chig.	35	D6
New Goulston St. E1	13	F3
New Heston Rd., Houns.	63	F7
New Horizon Ct., Brent.	64	D6
New Inn Bdy. EC2	9	E5
New Inn Pas. EC2	12	D4
New Inn St. EC2	9	E5
New Inn Yd. EC2	9	E5
New Inn Yd. EC2	59	B4
New James Ct. SE15	77	E3
Nunhead La.		
New Kent Rd. SE1	16	J6
New Kent Rd. SE1	67	J3
New King St. SE8	69	A6
New Kings Rd. SW6	75	C2
New London St. EC3	13	E5
New Lydenburgh St. SE7	69	J3
New Mt. St. E15	51	D7
New N. Pl. EC2	9	D6
New N. Rd. N1	9	B1
New N. Rd. N1	49	J7
New N. Rd., Ilf.	35	G7
New N. St. WC1	12	C1
New N. St. WC1	58	F5
New Oak Rd. N2	39	F2
New Orleans Wk. N19	40	D7
New Oxford St. WC1	11	J3
New Oxford St. WC1	58	D6
New Pk. Ave. N13	32	J3
New Pk. Clo., Nthlt.	45	E6
New Pk. Ct. SW2	76	E7
New Pk. Rd. SW2	85	D1
New Pl. Sq. SE16	68	E3
New Plaistow Rd. E15	60	E1
New Priory Ct. NW6	48	D7
Mazenod Ave.		
New Quebec St. W1	11	A4
New Quebec St. W1	57	J6
New Ride SW7	14	G3
New River Cres. N13	32	H4
New River Wk. N1	49	J6
Arran Wk.		
New Rd. E1	59	E5
New Rd. E4	34	B4
New Rd. N8	40	E5
New Rd. N9	33	D3
New Rd. N17	41	C1
New Rd. N22	40	J1
New Rd. NW7	31	B7
New Rd. NW7 (Barnet Gate)	22	F7
New Rd. SE2	71	D4
New Rd., Brent.	64	G5
New Rd., Dag.	62	G1
New Rd. (East Bedfont), Felt.	81	B1
New Rd. (Hanworth), Felt.	81	E5
New Rd., Har.	46	C4
New Rd., Houns.	72	H4
Station Rd.		
New Rd., Ilf.	52	H2
New Rd., Kings.T.	83	A7
New Rd., Mitch.	101	A1
New Rd., Rain.	62	J2
New Rd., Rich.	82	F4
New Rd., Well.	80	B2
New Rd., W.Mol.	90	G3
New Row WC2	12	A5
New Row WC2	58	E7
New Spring Gdns. Wk. SE11	20	B4
New Sq. WC2	12	D3
New Sq. WC2	58	F6
New St. EC2	13	E2
New St. EC2	59	B5
New St. Hill, Brom.	87	H5
New St. Sq. EC4	12	F3
New Trinity Rd. N2	39	E6
New Turnstile WC1	12	C2
New Union Clo. E14	69	C3
New Union St. EC2	13	B2
New Union St. EC2	59	A5
New Wanstead E11	42	F6
New Way Rd. NW9	38	E4
New Wf. Rd. N1	8	B1
New Wf. Rd. N1	58	E2
New Zealand Way NW12	56	H7
India Way		
Newark Cres. NW10	56	D3
Newark Grn., Borwd.	22	D3
Newark Knok E6	61	D5
Newark Rd., S.Croy.	102	A6
Newark St. E1	59	E5
Newark Way NW4	38	G4
Newbiggin Path, Wat.	28	C4
Newbolt Ave., Sutt.	99	J5
Newbolt Rd., Stan.	29	C5
Newborough Grn., N.Mal.	92	D4
Newburgh Rd. W3	65	C1
Newburgh St. W1	11	F4
Newburgh St. W1	58	C6
Newburn St. SE11	20	D4
Newburn St. SE11	67	F5
Newbury Clo., Nthlt.	45	F6
Newbury Gdns., Epsom	99	F4
Newbury Ho. N22	40	E1
Newbury Ms. NW5	47	H6
Malden Rd.		
Newbury Rd. E4	34	C6
Newbury Rd., Brom.	96	G3
Newbury Rd., Ilf.	43	H6
Newbury St. EC1	12	J1
Newbury Way, Nthlt.	45	F6
Newby Clo., Enf.	25	B2
Newby Pl. E14	60	C7
Newby St. SW8	76	B3
Newcastle Clo. EC4	12	G3
Newcastle Pl. W2	10	F2
Newcastle Pl. W2	57	C5
Newcastle Row EC1	11	G3
Newcombe Gdns. SW16	85	E4
Newcombe Pk. NW7	30	E5
Newcombe Pk., Wem.	55	J1
Newcombe St. W8	66	D1
Kensington Pl.		
Newcomen Rd. E11	51	F3
Newcomen Rd. SW11	75	G3
Newcomen St. SE1	13	B3
Newcomen St. SE1	68	A2
Newcourt St. NW8	6	G2
Newcourt St. NW8	57	H2
Newdales Clo. N9	33	D2
Balham Rd.		
Newdene Ave., Nthlt.	54	D2
Newell St. E14	59	J6
Newent Clo. SE15	21	D7
Newent Clo. SE15	68	B7
Newent Clo., Cars.	100	J1
Newfield Clo., Hmptn.	90	G1
Percy Rd.		
Newfield Ri. NW2	47	H3
Newgale Gdns., Edg.	37	J1
Newgate, Croy.	101	J1
Newgate Clo., Felt.	81	E2
Newgate St. E4	34	F3
Newgate St. EC1	12	H3
Newgate St. EC1	58	H6
Newham Way E6	61	D4
Newham Way E16	60	F5
Newhams Clo., Brom.	97	C3
Newhams Row SE1	17	E4
Newhaven Gdns. SE9	79	A4
Newhaven Rd. SE25	95	A5
Newhouse Ave., Rom.	44	D3
Newhouse Clo., N.Mal.	92	E7
Newhouse Wk., Mord.	93	F7
Newick Clo., Bex.	80	H6
Newick Rd. E5	50	E3
Newing Grn., Brom.	88	A7
Newington Barrow Way N7	49	F3
Newington Butts SE1	20	H2
Newington Butts SE1	67	H4
Newington Butts SE11	20	H2
Newington Butts SE11	67	H4
Newington Causeway SE1	16	H6
Newington Causeway SE1	67	H4
Newington Grn. N1	50	A5
Newington Grn. N16	50	A5
Newington Grn. Rd. N1	50	A5
Newington Way N7	49	F2
Hornsey Rd.		
Newland Clo., Pnr.	28	E6
Newland Ct., Wem.	47	A2
Forty Ave.		
Newland Dr., Enf.	25	E1
Newland Gdns. W13	64	D2
Newland Rd. N8	40	E3
Newland St. E16	70	B1
Newlands, The, Wall.	101	C7
Newlands Ave., T.Ditt.	98	B1
Newlands Clo., Edg.	29	H3
Newlands Clo., Sthl.	63	E5
Newlands Ct. SE9	79	D6
Newlands Pk. SE26	86	G5
Newlands Pl., Barn.	23	A5
Newlands Quay E1	59	F7
Newlands Rd. SW16	94	E2
Newlands Rd., Wdf.Grn.	34	F2
Newlands Way, Chess.	98	F5
Newling Clo. E6	61	C6
Porter Rd.		
Newlyn Gdns., Har.	36	F7
Newlyn Rd. N17	41	C1
Newlyn Rd., Barn.	23	C4
Newlyn Rd., Well.	79	J2
Newman Pas. W1	11	G2
Newman Rd. E13	60	H3
Newman Rd. E17	41	G5
Southcote Rd.		
Newman Rd., Brom.	96	G1
Newman Rd., Croy.	101	F1
Newman Rd., Hayes	54	B7
Newman St. W1	11	G2
Newman St. W1	58	C5
Newman Yd. W1	11	G3
Newmans Clo., Loug.	27	E3
Newman's Ct. EC3	13	C4
Newmans La., Loug.	27	D3
Newmans La., Surb.	91	G6
Newman's Row WC2	12	D2
Newmans Way, Barn.	23	F1
Newmarket Ave. Nthlt.	45	H5
Newmarket Grn. SE9	79	A7
Newminster Rd., Mord.	93	F6
Newnes Path SW15	74	H4
Putney Pk. La.		
Newnham Ave., Ruis.	45	C1
Newnham Clo., Loug.	27	A6
Newnham Clo., Nthlt.	45	J5
Newnham Clo., Th.Hth.	94	J2
Newnham Gdns., Nthlt.	45	J5
Newnham Ms. N22	40	F1
Newnham Rd.		
Newnham Rd. N22	40	F1
Newnham Ter. SE1	16	E5
Newnham Way, Har.	37	H5
Newnhams Clo., Brom.	97	C3
Newnton Clo. N4	47	A7
Newpiece, Loug.	27	E3
Newport Ave. E13	60	H4
Palmer Rd.		
Newport Ct. WC2	11	J5
Newport Mead, Wat.	28	D4
Kilmarnock Rd.		
Newport Ct. WC2	11	J5
Newport Pl. WC2	58	D7
Newport Rd. E10	51	C2
Newport Rd. E17	41	H4
Newport Rd. SW13	74	G1
Newport St. SE11	20	C2
Newport St. SE11	67	F4
Newquay Cres., Har.	45	E2
Newquay Gdns., Wat.	28	B2
Fulford Gro.		
Newquay Rd. SE6	87	B2
Newry Rd., Twick.	73	D5
Newsam Ave. N15	41	A5
Newstead Ave., Orp.	104	G3
Newstead Rd. SE12	78	F7
Newstead Wk., Cars.	93	F7
Newstead Way SW19	84	A4
Newton Ave. N10	40	A1
Newton Ave. W3	65	C2
Newton Cres., Borwd.	22	C4
Newton Gro. W4	65	E4
Newton Rd. E15	51	E5
Newton Rd. N15	41	C5
Newton Rd. NW2	47	B4
Newton Rd. SW19	84	B7
Newton Rd., Har.	37	B2
Newton Rd., Islw.	73	C2
Newton Rd., Well.	80	A3
Newton Rd., Wem.	46	J7
Newton St. WC2	12	B3
Newton St. WC2	58	E8
Newton Wk., Edg.	38	B1
North Rd.		
Newton Way N18	32	J5

Newtons Yd. SW18 75 E5
Wandsworth High St.
Newtown St. SW11 76 B1
Strasburg Rd.
Niagara Ave. W5 64 F4
Nibthwaite Rd., 37 B5
Har.
Nichol Clo. N14 32 D1
Nichol La., Brom. 87 G7
Nicholas Clo., Grnf. 54 H2
Nicholas Gdns. W5 64 G2
Nicholas La. EC4 13 C5
Nicholas Rd. E1 59 F4
Nicholas Rd., Croy. 101 E4
Nicholas Rd., Dag. 53 F2
Nicholay Rd. N19 49 D1
Calverley Gro.
Nicholes Rd., 72 G3
Houns.
Nicholl St. E2 59 D1
Nichollsfield Wk. 49 F5
N7
Hillmarton Rd.
Nichols Grn. W5 55 H5
Montpelier Rd.
Nicholson Dr. 28 J1
(Bushey), Wat.
Nicholson Rd., 102 C1
Croy.
Nicholson St. SE1 16 G2
Nicholson St. SE1 67 H1
Nickelby Clo. SE28 62 C6
Nical Clo., Twick. 73 C6
Cassilis Rd.
Nicola Clo., Har. 37 A2
Nicola Clo., S.Croy. 101 J6
Nicola Ms., Ilf. 35 E7
Nicoll Pl. NW4 38 H6
Nicoll Rd. NW10 56 E1
Nicoll Way, Borwd. 22 D5
Nicosia Rd. SW18 75 H7
Niederwald Rd. SE26 86 H4
Nigel Clo., Nthlt. 54 E1
Church Rd.
Nigel Ms., Ilf. 52 E4
Nigel Playfair Ave. 65 H4
W6
King St.
Nigel Rd. E7 51 J5
Nigel Rd. SE15 77 D3
Nigeria Rd. SE7 69 J7
Nightingale Ave. E4 34 E5
Nightingale Clo. E4 34 E4
Nightingale Clo. W4 65 C6
Grove Pk. Ter.
Nightingale Clo., 101 A2
Cars.
Nightingale Clo., 36 C5
Pnr.
Nightingale Dr. 99 B6
Epsom
Nightingale Est. E5 50 D3
Nightingale Gro. 78 D5
SE13
Nightingale La. E11 42 H5
Nightingale La. N6 39 H7
Nightingale La. N8 40 E4
Nightingale La. SW4 76 J7
Nightingale La. 75 J7
SW12
Nightingale La., 96 J2
Brom.
Nightingale La., 73 H7
Rich.
Nightingale Pl. 70 D6
SE18
Nightingale Rd. E5 50 E3
Nightingale Rd. N9 25 F6
Nightingale Rd. N22 40 E1
Nightingale Rd. 56 F2
NW10
Nightingale Rd. W7 64 C1
Nightingale Rd., 100 J3
Cars.
Nightingale Rd., 81 G5
Hmptn.
Nightingale Rd., 97 F6
Orp.
Nightingale Rd., 90 B7
Walt.
Nightingale Rd., 90 H5
W.Mol.
Nightingale Sq. 76 A7
SW12
Nightingale Vale 70 D6
SE18
Nightingale Wk. SW4 76 B6
Nightingale Way E6 61 B5
Nile Path SE18 70 D6
Jackson St.
Nile Rd. E13 60 J2
Nile St. N1 9 A3
Nile St. N1 59 A3

Nile Ter. SE15 21 G4
Nile Ter. SE15 68 C5
Nimegen Way SE22 77 B5
East Dulwich Gro.
Nimrod Clo., Nthlt. 54 D3
Britannia Clo.
Nimrod Rd. SW16 85 B6
Nine Acres Clo. E12 52 B5
Nine Elms La. SW8 19 G7
Nine Elms La. SW8 67 C7
Nineteenth Rd., 94 E4
Mitch.
Ninhams Wd., Orp. 104 D4
Ninth Ave., Hayes 54 A7
Nisbet Ho. E9 50 G5
Homerton High St.
Nithdale Rd. SE18 70 E7
Niton Clo., Barn. 23 A6
Niton Rd., Rich. 74 A3
Niton St. SW6 66 A7
Niven Clo., Borwd. 22 C1
Nobel Rd. N18 33 F4
Noble St. EC2 12 J3
Noble St. EC2 58 J6
Noel Pk. Rd. N22 40 G2
Noel Rd. E6 61 B4
Noel Rd. N1 8 H1
Noel Rd. N1 58 H2
Noel Rd. W3 56 A6
Noel Sq., Dag. 53 C4
Noel St. W1 11 G4
Noel St. W1 58 C6
Nolan Way E5 50 D4
Nolton Pl., Edg. 37 J1
Nonsuch Clo., Ilf. 35 E6
Nora Gdns. NW4 39 A4
Nora Ter., Har. 46 B1
Norbiton Ave. 92 A1
Kings.T.
Norbiton Common 92 B3
Rd., Kings.T.
Norbiton Rd. E14 59 J6
Norbreck Gdns. 55 J3
NW10
North Circular Rd.
Norbreck Par. NW10 55 J3
North Circular Rd.
Norbroke St. W12 56 F7
Norburn St. W10 57 B5
Chesterton Rd.
Norbury Ave. SW16 94 F1
Norbury Ave., 73 A4
Houns.
Norbury Ave., 94 G2
Th.Hth.
Norbury Clo. SW16 94 G1
Norbury Ct. E5 50 H4
Norbury Ct. Rd. 94 E3
SW16
Norbury Cres. SW16 94 F1
Norbury Cross SW16 94 E3
Norbury Gdns., Rom. 44 D5
Norbury Gro. NW7 30 E3
Norbury Hill SW16 85 G7
Norbury Ri. SW16 94 E3
Norbury Rd. E4 34 A5
Norbury Rd., 94 J2
Th.Hth.
Norcombe Gdns., 37 F6
Har.
Norcott Clo., Hayes 54 C4
Willow Tree La.
Norcott Rd. N16 50 D2
Norcroft Gdns. SE22 77 D7
Norcutt Rd., Twick. 82 B1
Norfield Rd. Dart. 89 J4
Norfolk Ave. N13 32 H6
Norfolk Ave. N15 41 C6
Norfolk Clo. N2 39 H3
Park Rd.
Norfolk Clo. N13 32 H6
Norfolk Clo., Barn. 24 A4
Norfolk Clo., Twick. 73 E6
Cassilis Rd.
Norfolk Cres. W2 10 G3
Norfolk Cres. W2 57 H6
Norfolk Cres., Sid. 79 H7
Norfolk Gdns., Bexh. 80 F1
Norfolk Gdns., 22 D4
Borwd.
Norfolk Ho. SE3 69 E6
Norfolk Ho. 85 D3
SW16
Norfolk Pl. W2 10 F3
Norfolk Pl. W2 57 G6
Norfolk Pl., Well. 80 A2
Norfolk Rd. E6 61 C1
Norfolk Rd. E17 41 G2
Norfolk Rd. NW8 57 G1
Norfolk Rd. NW10 47 E7
Norfolk Rd. SW19 84 H7
Norfolk Rd., Bark. 52 H7
Norfolk Rd., Barn. 23 D3

Norfolk Rd., Dag. 53 H5
Norfolk Rd., Enf. 25 E6
Norfolk Rd., Esher 98 B5
Norfolk Rd., Felt. 81 C1
Norfolk Rd., Har. 36 H5
Norfolk Rd., Ilf. 52 H1
Norfolk Rd., Th.Hth. 94 J3
Norfolk Row SE1 20 C1
Norfolk Row SE1 67 F3
Norfolk Sq. W2 10 F4
Norfolk Sq. Ms. W2 10 F4
Norfolk Ter. W6 66 B5
Field Rd.
Norgrove St. SW12 85 A1
Norhyrst Ave. SE25 95 C3
Norland Pl. W11 66 B1
Norland Rd. W11 66 A1
Norland Sq. W11 66 B1
Norlands Cres., Chis. 97 E1
Norley Vale SW15 83 G1
Norlington Rd. E10 51 C1
Norlington Rd. E11 51 D1
Norman Ave. N22 40 H1
Norman Ave., Felt. 81 E2
Norman Ave., Sthl. 54 E7
Norman Ave., Twick. 73 E7
Norman Clo., Orp. 104 F3
Norman Clo., Rom. 44 H2
Norman Ct., Ilf. 43 G7
Norman Cres., 63 D7
Houns.
Norman Cres., Pnr. 36 C1
Norman Gro. E3 59 H2
Norman Rd. E6 61 C4
Norman Rd. E11 51 D2
Norman Rd. N15 41 C5
Norman Rd. SE10 69 B7
Norman Rd. SW19 84 F7
Norman Rd., Belv. 71 H3
Norman Rd., Ilf. 52 E5
Norman Rd., Sutt. 100 D5
Norman Rd., Th.Hth. 94 H5
Norman St. EC1 8 J4
Norman Way N14 32 E2
Norman Way W3 56 B5
Normanby Clo. SW15 75 C5
Manfred Rd.
Normanby Rd. NW10 47 F4
Normand Gdns. W14 66 B6
Greyhound Rd.
Normand Ms. W14 66 B6
Normand Rd.
Normand Rd. W14 66 C6
Normandy Ave., 23 C5
Barn.
Normandy Rd. SW9 76 G1
Normandy Ter. E16 60 H6
Normanhurst Ave., 80 D1
Bexh.
Normanhurst Dr., 73 E5
Twick.
St. Margarets Rd.
Normanhurst Rd. 85 F2
SW2
Normans Clo. NW10 47 D6
Normans Mead 47 D6
NW10
Normansfield Ave., 82 F7
Tedd.
Normanshire Ave. E4 34 C4
Normanshire Dr.
Normanshire Dr. E4 34 A4
Normanton Ave. 84 D2
SW19
Normanton Pk. E4 34 E3
Normanton Rd., 102 B5
S.Croy.
Normanton St. SE23 85 G5
Normington Clo. 85 G5
SW16
Norrice Lea N2 39 G5
Norris St. SW1 11 H6
Norroy Rd. SW15 75 A4
Norrys Clo., Barn. 23 J4
Norrys Rd., Barn. 23 J4
Norseman Clo., Ilf. 53 B1
Norseman Way, Grnf. 54 H1
Olympic Way
Norstead Pl. SW15 83 G2
North Access Rd. 41 G6
E17
North Acre NW9 38 E1
North Acton Rd. 56 D2
NW10
North Audley St. W1 11 B4
North Audley St. W1 58 A7
North Ave. N18 33 H2
North Ave. W13 55 E5
North Ave., Cars. 101 A7
North Ave., Har. 36 H6

North Ave., Hayes 54 A7
North Ave., Rich. 73 G1
Sandycombe Rd.
North Ave., Sthl. 54 F7
North Bank NW8 6 G4
North Bank NW8 57 H3
North Birkbeck Rd. 51 D3
E11
North Branch Ave. 56 J3
W10
Harrow Rd.
North Carriage Dr. 10 G5
W2
North Carriage Dr. 57 H7
W2
E4
North Circular Rd. 33 J7
N2
North Circular Rd. 42 H1
E18
North Circular Rd. 39 C4
N3
North Circular Rd. 39 G1
N12
North Circular Rd. 32 G5
N13
North Circular Rd. 47 E3
NW2
North Circular Rd. 47 E4
NW10
North Circular Rd. 39 A6
NW11
North Clo., Barn. 22 J5
North Clo., Bexh. 80 D4
North Clo., Dag. 62 G1
North Clo., Mord. 93 B4
North Colonnade E14 69 A1
North Common Rd. 55 H7
W5
North Countess Rd. 41 J2
E17
North Ct. W1 11 G1
North Cray Rd. 89 G2
Bex.
North Cray Rd., 89 E6
Sid.
North Cres. N3 39 C2
North Cres. WC1 11 H1
North Cross Rd. 77 C5
SE22
North Cross Rd., Ilf. 43 F4
North Dene NW7 30 D3
North Dene, Houns. 72 H1
North Dr. SW16 85 C4
North Dr., Houns. 72 J2
North Dr., Orp. 104 H4
North End NW3 48 F2
North End, Buck.H. 26 J7
North End, Croy. 101 J2
North End Ave. NW3 48 F2
North End Cres. W14 66 C4
North End Ho. W14 66 B4
North End Rd. NW11 48 D1
North End Rd. SW6 66 C6
North End Rd. W14 66 B4
North End Rd., Wem. 47 A3
North End Way NW3 48 F2
North Eyot Gdns. W6 65 F5
St. Peters Sq.
North Feltham Trd. 72 B5
Est., Felt.
North Gdns. SW19 84 G7
North Glade, The, 80 F7
Bex.
Camden Rd.
North Gower St. NW1 7 G4
North Gower St. NW1 58 C3
North Grn. NW9 30 E7
Clayton Fld.
North Gro. N6 40 A7
North Gro. N15 41 A5
North Hill N6 39 J6
North Hill Ave. N6 39 J6
North Hyde Gdns., 63 A4
Hayes
North Hyde La. 63 E6
Houns.
North Hyde Rd., Sthl. 63 D5
North La., Tedd. 82 C6
North Lo. Clo. SW15 75 A5
Westleigh Ave.
North Mall N9 33 E2
St. Martins Rd.
North Ms. WC1 8 D6
North Ms. WC1 58 F4
North Par., Chess. 98 H5
North Pas. SW18 79 D6
North Pk. SE9 79 D6
North Peckham Est. 21 F7
SE15
North Peckham Est. 68 B7
SE15

North Pl., Mitch. 84 J7
North Pl., Tedd. 82 C6
North Pole La., Kes. 103 F6
North Pole Rd. W10 56 J5
North Ride W2 **10 G6**
North Ride W2 66 H1
North Rd. N6 40 A7
North Rd. N7 49 E6
North Rd. N9 33 E1
North Rd. SE18 70 H4
North Rd. SW19 84 F6
North Rd. W5 64 G3
North Rd., Belv. 71 H3
North Rd., Brent. 64 H6
North Rd., Brom. 96 H1
North Rd., Edg. 38 B1
North Rd., Ilf. 52 H2
North Rd., Rich. 74 A3
North Rd., Rom. 44 E5
North Rd., Sthl. 54 G6
North Rd., Surb. 91 G6
North Rd., W.Wick. 103 B1
North Row W1 **11 A5**
North Row W1 57 J7
North Several SE3 78 D2
Orchard Dr.
North Sq. N9 33 E2
St. Martins Rd.
North Sq. NW11 39 D5
North St. E13 60 H2
North St. NW4 38 J5
North St. SW4 76 C3
North St., Bark. 52 E6
North St., Bexh. 80 G4
North St., Brom. 96 G1
North St., Cars. 100 J3
North St., Islw. 73 D3
North St. Pas. E13 60 H2
North St.
North Tenter St. E1 **13 G4**
North Tenter St. E1 59 C6
North Ter. SW3 **14 G6**
North Verbena Gdns. 65 G5
W6
St. Peters Sq.
North Vw. SW19 83 J5
North Vw. W5 55 F4
North Vw., Pnr. 36 C7
North Vw. Cres. 47 F4
NW10
North Vw. Dr., 43 A2
Wdf.Grn.
North Vw. Rd. N8 40 D3
North Vill. NW1 49 D6
North Wk. W2 **10 C6**
North Wk., Croy. 103 B6
North Way N9 33 G2
North Way N11 32 C6
North Way NW9 38 B3
North Way, Mord. 93 B3
North Way, Pnr. 36 C3
North Wf. Rd. W2 **10 E2**
North Wf. Rd. W2 57 G5
North Woolwich Rd. 69 G1
E16
North Worple Way 74 D3
SW14
Northall Rd., Bexh. 80 J2
Northampton Pk. N1 49 J6
Northampton Rd. EC1 **8 F5**
Northampton Rd. 58 G4
EC1
Northampton Rd., 102 D2
Croy.
Northampton Rd., 25 H4
Enf.
Northampton Sq. EC1 **8 G4**
Northampton Sq. EC1 58 H3
Northampton St. N1 49 J7
Northanger Rd. 85 E6
SW16
Northbank Rd. E17 42 C2
Northborough Rd. 94 D3
SW16
Northbourne, Brom. 96 G7
Northbourne Rd. 76 D4
SW4
Northbrook Rd. N22 32 E7
Northbrook Rd. SE13 78 D5
Northbrook Rd., 23 B6
Barn.
Northbrook Rd., 95 A5
Croy.
Northbrook Rd., 52 D2
Ilf.
Northburgh St. EC1 **8 H6**
Northburgh St. EC1 58 H4
Northchurch SE17 **21 C3**
Northchurch Rd. N1 50 A7
Northchurch Rd., 47 A6
Wem.

Northchurch Ter. N1 50 B7
Northcliffe Clo., 99 E3
Wor.Pk.
Northcliffe Dr. N20 31 C1
Northcote Ave. W5 55 H7
Northcote Ave., 73 D5
Islw.
Northcote Ave., 54 E7
Sthl.
Northcote Ave., 92 A7
Surb.
Northcote Ms. SW11 75 H4
Northcote Rd.
Northcote Rd. E17 41 H4
Northcote Rd. NW10 47 E7
Northcote Rd. SW11 75 H5
Northcote Rd., Croy. 95 A6
Northcote Rd., Sid. 88 H4
Northcote Rd., 73 D5
N.Mal.
Northcote Rd., 92 D3
Twick.
Northcott Ave. N22 40 E1
Northcroft Rd. W13 64 E2
Northcroft Rd., 99 D7
Epsom
Northdene, Chig. 35 G5
Northdene Gdns. N15 41 C6
Northdown Gdns., 43 H5
Ilf.
Northdown Rd., 80 B2
Well.
Northdown St. N1 **8 B1**
Northdown St. N1 58 E2
Northern Ave. N9 33 B2
Northern Relief Rd. 52 E7
Bark.
Northern Rd. E13 60 H2
Northern Service 23 B3
Rd., Barn.
Northernhay Wk., 93 B4
Mord.
Northey St. E14 59 H7
Northfield, Loug. 27 A4
Northfield Ave. W5 64 E1
Northfield Ave. W13 64 E1
Northfield Ave., 36 D4
Pnr.
Northfield Clo., 97 B1
Brom.
Northfield Cres., 100 B4
Sutt.
Northfield Gdns., 53 F4
Dag.
Northfield Rd.
Northfield Path, 53 F4
Dag.
Connor Rd.
Northfield Rd. E6 52 C7
Northfield Rd. N16 41 B7
Northfield Rd. W13 64 E2
Northfield Rd., 23 H3
Barn.
Northfield Rd., 22 B1
Borwd.
Northfield Rd., Dag. 53 F4
Northfield Rd., 25 E5
Enf.
Northfield Rd., 63 D7
Houns.
Northfields SW18 75 D4
Northfields Ind. Est., 56 A1
Wem.
Northfields Rd. W3 56 B5
Northgate Dr. NW9 38 E6
Northiam N12 31 D4
Northiam St. E9 59 E1
Northington St. WC1 **8 D6**
Northington St. WC1 58 F4
Northlands Ave., 104 H4
Orp.
Northlands St. SE5 76 J2
Northolm, Edg. 30 D4
Northolme Gdns., 38 A1
Edg.
Northolme Ri., Orp. 104 H2
Northolme Rd. N5 49 J4
Northolt Ave., Ruis. 45 B5
Northolt Gdns., 46 C5
Grnf.
Northolt Ind. Est., 45 H7
Nthlt.
Northolt Rd., Har. 45 H4
Northover, Brom. 87 F3
Northport St. N1 59 A1
Northside Rd., 96 G1
Brom.
Mitchell Way
Northspur Rd., 100 D3
Sutt.
Northstead Rd. SW2 85 G2
Northumberland All. **13 E4**
EC3

Northumberland All. 59 B6
EC3
Northumberland Ave. 51 J1
E12
Northumberland Ave. 16 A1
WC2
Northumberland Ave. 67 E1
WC2
Northumberland 25 E1
Ave., Enf.
Northumberland 73 C1
Ave., Islw.
Northumberland 79 G4
Ave., Well.
Northumberland 71 J7
Clo., Erith
Northumberland 33 C3
Gdns. N9
Northumberland 64 D7
Gdns., Islw.
Northumberland Ave.
Northumberland 94 D5
Gdns., Mitch.
Northumberland Gro. 33 E7
N17
Northumberland Pk. 33 C7
N17
Northumberland Pk., 71 J7
Erith
Northumberland Pl. 57 D6
W2
Northumberland Pl., 73 G6
Rich.
Northumberland Rd. 61 B6
E6
Northumberland Rd. 42 A7
E17
Northumberland Rd., 23 F6
Barn.
Northumberland Rd., 36 F5
Har.
Northumberland Row,82 B1
Twick.
Colne Rd.
Northumberland St. **16 A1**
WC2
Northumberland St. 67 E1
WC2
Northumberland 80 J1
Way, Erith
Northumbria St. E14 60 A6
Northway NW7 30 G7
Northway NW11 39 E5
Northway, Wall. 101 C4
Northway Circ. NW7 30 D4
Northway Cres. NW7 30 D4
Northway Rd. SE5 76 J3
Northway Rd., Croy. 95 C6
Northwest Pl. N1 **8 F1**
Northwick Ave., 37 D6
Har.
Northwick Circle, 37 F6
Har.
Northwick Clo. NW8 **6 E5**
Northwick Pk. Rd., 37 C6
Har.
Northwick Rd., Wat. 28 C4
Northwick Rd., Wem. 55 G1
Northwick Ter. NW8 **6 E5**
Northwick Ter. NW8 57 G4
Northwick Wk., Har. 37 C7
Peterborough Rd.
Northwold Est. E5 50 D2
Northwold Rd. E5 50 D2
Northwold Rd. N16 50 C2
Northwood Gdns. 31 G5
N12
Northwood Gdns., 46 C5
Grnf.
Northwood Gdns., 43 D4
Ilf.
Northwood Hall N6 40 C7
Northwood Ho. SE27 86 A4
Northwood Pl., 71 F3
Erith
Northwood Rd. N6 40 B7
Northwood Rd. SE23 86 J1
Northwood Rd., 101 A6
Cars.
Northwood Rd., 94 H2
Th.Hth.
Northwood Way 86 A6
SE19
Roman Ri.
Norton Ave., Surb. 92 B7
Norton Clo. E4 34 A5
Norton Clo., Borwd. 22 A1
Norton Clo., Enf. 25 E2
Brick La.
Norton Folgate E1 **13 E1**
Norton Folgate E1 59 B5
Norton Gdns. SW16 94 E2
Norton Rd. E10 50 J1

Norton Rd., Wem. 46 G6
Norval Rd., Wem. 46 E2
Norway Gate SE16 68 H3
Norway Pl. E14 59 J6
East India Dock Rd.
Norway St. SE10 69 B6
Norwich Ho. E14 60 B6
Cordelia St.
Norwich Ms., Ilf. 53 A1
Ashgrove Rd.
Norwich Pl., Bexh. 80 G4
Norwich Rd. E7 51 G5
Norwich Rd., Dag. 62 G2
Norwich Rd., Grnf. 54 H1
Norwich Rd., Th.Hth. 94 J3
Norwich St. EC4 **12 E3**
Norwich St. EC4 58 G6
Norwich Wk., Edg. 30 C7
Norwood Ave., Wem. 55 J1
Norwood Clo., Sthl. 63 G4
Norwood Dr., Har. 36 F6
Norwood Gdns., 54 C4
Hayes
Norwood Gdns., 63 F4
Sthl.
Norwood Grn. Rd., 63 G4
Sthl.
Norwood High St. 85 H3
SE27
Norwood Pk. Rd. 85 J5
SE27
Norwood Rd. SE24 85 H1
Norwood Rd. SE27 85 H2
Norwood Rd., Sthl. 63 F4
Notley St. SE5 **21 B7**
Notley St. SE5 68 A7
Notre Dame Est. SW4 76 C4
Notson Rd. SE25 95 E4
Belfast Rd.
Notting Barn Rd. 57 A4
W10
Notting Hill Gate 66 D1
W11
Nottingham Ave. E16 60 J5
Nottingham Ct. WC2 12 A4
Nottingham Pl. W1 **7 B6**
Nottingham Pl. W1 58 A5
Nottingham Rd. E10 42 C6
Nottingham Rd. 84 J1
SW17
Nottingham Rd., 73 C2
Islw.
Nottingham Rd., 101 J4
S.Croy.
Nottingham St. W1 **11 B1**
Nottingham St. W1 58 A5
Nottingham Ter. NW1 7 B6
Nova Ms., Sutt. 93 B7
Nova Rd., Croy. 101 H1
Novar Clo., Orp. 97 J7
Novar Rd. SE9 88 F1
Novello St. SW6 75 D1
Nowell Rd. SW13 65 G6
Nower Hill, Pnr. 36 F4
Noyna Rd. SW17 84 J3
Nuding Clo. SE13 78 A3
Nugent Rd. N19 49 E1
Nugent Rd. SE25 95 C3
Nugent Ter. NW8 **6 E5**
Nugent Ter. NW8 57 F2
Nugents Ct., Pnr. 36 E1
St. Thomas' Dr.
Nugents Pk., Pnr. 36 E1
Nun Ct. EC2 **13 B3**
Nuneaton Rd., Dag. 53 D7
Nunhead Cres. SE15 77 E3
Nunhead Grn. SE15 77 E3
Nunhead Gro. SE15 77 E3
Nunhead La. SE15 77 E3
Nunhead Pas. SE15 77 D3
Peckham Rye
Nunnington Clo. SE9 88 B3
Nunns Rd., Enf. 24 J2
Nupton Dr., Barn. 22 J5
Nursery Ave. N3 39 F2
Nursery Ave., Bexh. 80 F3
Nursery Ave., Croy. 102 G2
Nursery Clo. SW15 75 A4
Nursery Clo., Croy. 102 G2
Nursery Clo., Enf. 25 G1
Nursery Clo., Felt. 72 B7
Nursery Clo., Orp. 97 J7
Nursery Clo., Rom. 44 D6
Nursery Clo., 34 H5
Wdf.Grn.
Nursery Ct. N17 33 C7
Nursery St.
Nursery Gdns., Enf. 25 G1
Nursery La. E7 51 G6
Nursery La. W10 56 J5
Nursery Rd. E9 50 F6
Morning La.
Nursery Rd. N2 39 G1

Name	Page	Grid
Nursery Rd. N14	24	C7
Nursery Rd. SW9	76	F4
Nursery Rd. (Merton) SW19	93	E2
Nursery Rd. (Wimbledon) SW19 *Worple Rd.*	84	B7
Nursery Rd., Loug.	26	J5
Nursery Rd. (High Beach), Loug.	26	H1
Nursery Rd., Pnr.	36	C3
Nursery Rd., Sutt.	100	F4
Nursery Rd., Th.Hth.	95	A4
Nursery Row, Barn. *St. Albans Rd.*	23	B3
Nursery St. N17	33	C7
Nursery Wk. NW4	38	H3
Nurstead Rd., Erith	71	G7
Nutbourne St. W10	57	B3
Nutbrook St. SE15	77	D3
Nutbrowne Rd., Dag.	62	F1
Nutcroft Rd. SE15	68	E7
Nutfield Clo. N18	33	D6
Nutfield Clo., Cars.	100	H3
Nutfield Gdns., Ilf.	52	J2
Nutfield Gdns., Nthlt.	54	C2
Nutfield Rd. E15	51	C4
Nutfield Rd. NW2	47	G2
Nutfield Rd. SE22	77	C5
Nutfield Rd., Th.Hth.	94	H4
Nutfield Way, Orp.	104	D2
Nutford Pl. W1	**10**	**H3**
Nutford Pl. W1	57	H6
Nuthatch Gdns. SE28	70	G2
Nuthurst Ave. SW2	85	F2
Nutley Ter. NW3	48	F6
Nutmead Clo., Bex.	89	J1
Nutmeg La. E14	60	D6
Nutt Gro., Edg.	29	G2
Nutt St. SE15	**21**	**G7**
Nutt St. SE15	68	C7
Nuttall St. N1	**9**	**E1**
Nuttall St. N1	59	B2
Nutter La. E11	42	J6
Nutwell St. SW17	84	H5
Nuxley Rd., Belv.	71	F6
Nyanza St. SE18	70	G6
Nye Bevan Est. E5	50	G3
Nylands Ave., Rich.	74	A1
Nymans Gdns. SW20 *Hidcote Gdns.*	92	H3
Nynehead St. SE14	68	H7
Nyon Gro. SE6	86	J2
Nyssa Clo., Wdf.Grn. *Gwynne Pk. Ave.*	35	C7
Nyton Clo. N19 *Courtauld Rd.*	49	E1

O

Name	Page	Grid
Oak Ave. N8	40	E4
Oak Ave. N10	32	B7
Oak Ave. N17	33	A7
Oak Ave., Croy.	103	A1
Oak Ave., Enf.	24	F1
Oak Ave., Hmptn.	81	E5
Oak Ave., Houns.	63	E7
Oak Bank, Croy.	103	C6
Oak Clo. N14	24	B7
Oak Clo., Sutt.	100	F2
Oak Cottage Clo. SE6	87	F1
Oak Cres. E16	60	E5
Oak Dene W13 *The Dene*	55	E5
Oak Gdns., Croy.	103	A2
Oak Gdns., Edg.	38	C2
Oak Gro. NW2	48	A4
Oak Gro., Ruis.	36	B7
Oak Gro., Sun.	81	B7
Oak Gro., W.Wick.	103	C2
Oak Gro. Rd. SE20	95	F2
Oak Hall Rd. E11	42	H6
Oak Hill, Wdf.Grn.	34	D7
Oak Hill Ave. NW3	48	E4
Oak Hill Clo., Wdf.Grn.	34	D7
Oak Hill Ct. SW19	84	A7
Oak Hill Cres., Wdf.Grn.	34	D7
Oak Hill Gdns., Wdf.Grn.	42	E1
Oak Hill Pk. NW3	48	E4
Oak Hill Pk. Ms. NW3	48	F4
Oak Hill Way NW3	48	F4
Oak La. E14	59	J7
Oak La. N2	39	G2
Oak La. N11	32	D6
Oak La., Islw.	73	B4
Oak La., Twick.	73	D7
Oak La., Wdf.Grn.	34	F4
Oak Lo. Ave., Chig.	35	G5
Oak Lo. Clo., Stan. *Dennis La.*	29	C7
Oak Lo. Dr., W.Wick.	96	B7
Oak Manor Dr., Wem. *Oakington Manor Dr.*	46	J5
Oak Pk. Gdns. SW19	75	A7
Oak Pl. SW18 *East Hill*	75	E5
Oak Ri., Buck.H.	35	A3
Oak Rd. W5 *The Bdy.*	55	G7
Oak Rd. Erith (Northumberland Heath),	71	J7
Oak Rd., N.Mal.	92	D2
Oak Row SW16	94	C2
Oak St., Rom.	44	J5
Oak Tree Clo. W5 *Pinewood Gro.*	55	F6
Oak Tree Clo., Stan.	29	E7
Oak Tree Dell NW9	38	C5
Oak Tree Dr. N20	31	E1
Oak Tree Gdns., Brom.	87	H5
Oak Tree Rd. NW8	**6**	**F4**
Oak Tree Rd. NW8	57	H3
Oak Village NW5	49	A4
Oak Way N14	24	B7
Oak Way W3	65	E1
Oak Way, Croy.	95	G6
Oakapple Ct. SE12	87	G2
Oakbank Ave., Walt.	90	F7
Oakbank Gro. SE24	76	J4
Oakbrook Clo., Brom.	87	H4
Oakbury Rd. SW6	75	E2
Oakcombe Clo., N.Mal. *Traps La.*	92	E1
Oakcroft Clo., Pnr.	36	B2
Oakcroft Rd. SE13	78	D2
Oakcroft Rd., Chess.	98	J4
Oakcroft Vill., Chess.	98	J4
Oakdale N14	32	B1
Oakdale Ave., Har.	37	H5
Oakdale Ave., Nthwd.	36	A2
Oakdale Clo., Wat.	28	C4
Oakdale Ct. E4	34	C5
Oakdale Rd. E7	51	H7
Oakdale Rd. E11	51	D2
Oakdale Rd. E18	42	H2
Oakdale Rd. N4	40	J6
Oakdale Rd. SE15	77	F3
Oakdale Rd. SW16	85	E5
Oakdale Rd., Wat.	28	C3
Oakden St. SE11	**20**	**F1**
Oakden St. SE11	67	G4
Oakdene SE15 *Carlton Gro.*	77	E1
Oakdene Ave., Chis.	88	D5
Oakdene Ave., Erith	71	J6
Oakdene Ave., T.Ditt.	98	D1
Oakdene Clo., Pnr.	28	F7
Oakdene Dr., Surb.	92	C7
Oakdene Ms., Sutt.	100	C1
Oakdene Pk. N3	31	C7
Oakdene Rd., Orp.	97	J5
Oake Ct. SW15	75	B5
Oaken Dr., Esher	98	C6
Oaken La., Esher	98	B4
Oakenshaw Clo., Surb.	91	H7
Oakes Clo. E6 *Savage Gdns.*	61	C6
Oakeshott Ave. N6	49	A2
Oakey La. SE1	**16**	**E5**
Oakfield E4	34	B5
Oakfield Ave., Har.	37	E3
Oakfield Clo., N.Mal. *Blakes La.*	92	F5
Oakfield Ct. N8	40	E7
Oakfield Ct. NW2 *Hendon Way*	39	A7
Oakfield Gdns. N18	33	B4
Oakfield Gdns. SE19	86	C5
Oakfield Gdns., Beck.	96	A5
Oakfield Gdns., Cars.	100	H1
Oakfield Gdns., Grnf.	55	A4
Oakfield La., Kes.	103	J4
Oakfield Rd. E6	61	B1
Oakfield Rd. E17	41	H2
Oakfield Rd. N3	39	E1
Oakfield Rd. N4	40	G6
Oakfield Rd. N14	32	E3
Oakfield Rd. SE20	95	E1
Oakfield Rd. SW19	84	A3
Oakfield Rd., Croy.	101	J1
Oakfield Rd., Ilf.	52	E2
Oakfield St. SW10	**18**	**C5**
Oakfield St. SW10	66	F6
Oakfields Rd. NW11	39	B6
Oakford Rd. NW5	49	C4
Oakham Clo. SE6 *Rutland Wk.*	86	J2
Oakham Dr., Brom.	96	F4
Oakhampton Rd. NW7	31	A7
Oakhill, Esher	98	D6
Oakhill, Surb.	91	H7
Oakhill Ave., Pnr.	36	E2
Oakhill Ct. E11 *Eastern Ave.*	42	H6
Oakhill Ct. SW19 *Edge Hill*	84	A7
Oakhill Cres., Surb.	91	H7
Oakhill Dr., Surb.	91	H7
Oakhill Gro., Surb. *Glenbuck Rd.*	91	H6
Oakhill Path, Surb.	91	H6
Oakhill Pl. SW15 *Oakhill Rd.*	75	D5
Oakhill Rd. SW15	75	C5
Oakhill Rd. SW16	94	E2
Oakhill Rd., Beck.	96	C2
Oakhill Rd., Orp.	104	J1
Oakhill Rd., Surb.	91	H6
Oakhill Rd., Sutt.	100	F3
Oakhouse Rd., Bexh.	100	G5
Oakhurst Ave., Barn.	23	H7
Oakhurst Ave., Bexh.	71	E7
Oakhurst Clo. E17	42	E4
Oakhurst Clo., Ilf.	43	F1
Oakhurst Clo., Tedd.	82	B5
Oakhurst Gdns. E4	34	F1
Oakhurst Gdns. E17	42	E4
Oakhurst Gdns., Bexh.	71	E7
Oakhurst Gro. SE22	77	D4
Oakhurst Rd., Epsom	99	C6
Oakington Ave., Har.	36	G7
Oakington Ave., Wem.	46	J3
Oakington Dr., Sun.	90	C2
Oakington Manor Dr., Wem.	47	A5
Oakington Rd. W9	57	D4
Oakland Way, Epsom	99	D6
Oaklands N21	32	F2
Oaklands, Twick.	75	J2
Oaklands Ave. N9	25	E6
Oaklands Ave., Esher	98	A1
Oaklands Ave., Islw.	64	C6
Oaklands Ave., Sid.	79	J7
Oaklands Ave., Th.Hth.	94	G4
Oaklands Ave., Wat.	28	B1
Oaklands Ave., W.Wick.	103	B3
Oaklands Clo., Bexh.	80	F5
Oaklands Clo., Chess.	98	F4
Oaklands Clo., Orp.	97	H6
Oaklands Ct., Wem.	46	G5
Oaklands Est. SW4	76	C6
Oaklands Gro. W12	65	G1
Oaklands La., Barn.	22	H4
Oaklands Pk. Ave., Ilf. *High Rd.*	52	G2
Oaklands Pl. SW4 *St. Alphonsus Rd.*	76	C4
Oaklands Rd. N20	23	C7
Oaklands Rd. NW2	48	A4
Oaklands Rd. SW14	74	D3
Oaklands Rd. W7	64	C2
Oaklands Rd., Bexh.	80	F4
Oaklands Rd., Brom.	87	E7
Oaklands Way, Wall.	101	D7
Oaklea Pas., Kings.T.	91	G3
Oakleafe Gdns., Ilf.	43	E3
Oakleigh Ave. N20	31	G2
Oakleigh Ave., Edg.	38	B2
Oakleigh Ave., Surb.	99	A1
Oakleigh Clo. N20	31	J3
Oakleigh Ct., Barn. *Church Hill Rd.*	23	H6
Oakleigh Ct., Edg.	38	C2
Oakleigh Cres. N20	31	H2
Oakleigh Gdns. N20	31	F1
Oakleigh Gdns., Edg.	29	J5
Oakleigh Gdns., Orp.	104	H4
Oakleigh Ms. N20	31	F2
Oakleigh Pk. Ave., Chis.	97	D2
Oakleigh Pk. N. N20	31	G1
Oakleigh Pk. S. N20	23	H7
Oakleigh Rd., Pnr.	28	F6
Oakleigh Rd. N. N20	31	H2
Oakleigh Rd. S. N11	32	A3
Oakleigh Way, Mitch.	94	B1
Oakleigh Way, Surb.	99	A1
Oakley Ave. W5	56	A7
Oakley Ave., Bark.	52	J7
Oakley Ave., Croy.	101	F4
Oakley Clo. E4 *Mapleton Rd.*	34	C3
Oakley Clo. E6 *Northumberland Rd.*	61	B6
Oakley Clo. W7	55	B7
Oakley Clo., Islw.	73	A1
Oakley Cres. EC1	**8**	**H2**
Oakley Dr. SE9	88	G1
Oakley Dr., Brom.	104	B3
Oakley Gdns. N8	40	F5
Oakley Gdns. SW3	**18**	**H5**
Oakley Gdns. SW3	66	H6
Oakley Pl., Bex.	80	C7
Oakley Pl. SE1	**21**	**F4**
Oakley Pl. SE1	68	C5
Oakley Rd. N1	50	A7
Oakley Rd. SE25	95	E5
Oakley Rd., Brom.	104	B3
Oakley Rd., Har.	37	B6
Oakley Sq. NW1	**7**	**G1**
Oakley Sq. NW1	58	C2
Oakley St. SW3	**18**	**G5**
Oakley St. SW3	66	H6
Oakley Wk. W6 *Greyhound Rd.*	66	A6
Oakmead Ave., Brom.	96	G6
Oakmead Gdns., Edg.	30	D4
Oakmead Pl., Mitch.	93	H1
Oakmead Rd. SW12	85	H1
Oakmead Rd., Croy.	95	F6
Oakmeade, Pnr.	28	G6
Oakmere Rd. SE2	71	A6
Oakmoor Way, Chig.	35	H5
Oakmount Pl., Orp.	104	G1
Oakridge Dr. N2	39	G3
Oakridge Rd., Brom.	87	D4
Oaks, The N12	31	E4
Oaks, The SE18	70	F5
Oaks, The, Wdf.Grn.	34	E7
Oaks Ave. SE19	86	B5
Oaks Ave., Felt.	81	E2
Oaks Ave., Rom.	44	J2
Oaks Ave., Wor.Pk.	99	H3
Oaks Gro. E4	34	E2
Oaks La., Croy.	102	F3
Oaks La., Ilf.	43	H5
Oaks Rd., Croy.	102	E5
Oaks Way, Cars.	100	J7
Oaks Way, Surb.	98	G2
Oaksford Ave. SE26	86	E3
Oakshade Rd., Brom.	87	D4
Oakshaw Rd. SW18	75	E7
Oakthorpe Rd. N13	32	G5
Oaktree Ave. N13	25	H4
Oakview Gdns. N2	39	G4
Oakview Gro., Croy.	102	H1
Oakview Rd. SE6	87	B5
Oakway SW20	92	J4
Oakway, Brom.	96	D2
Oakway Clo., Bex.	80	E6
Oakways SE9	79	E6
Oakwood Ave. N14	24	D7
Oakwood Ave., Beck.	96	C2
Oakwood Ave., Borwd.	22	B4
Oakwood Ave., Brom.	96	H3
Oakwood Ave., Mitch.	93	G2
Oakwood Ave., Sthl.	54	G7
Oakwood Clo. N14	24	C6
Oakwood Clo., Chis.	88	C6
Oakwood Clo., Wdf.Grn. *Green Wk.*	35	B6
Oakwood Ct. W14	66	C3
Oakwood Cres. N21	24	E6
Oakwood Cres., Grnf.	46	D6
Oakwood Dr. SE19	86	A6
Oakwood Dr., Edg.	30	C6

Oakwood Gdns., Ilf. 52 J2
Oakwood Gdns., Orp.104 F2
Oakwood Gdns., 100 D2
Sutt.
Oakwood Hill, Loug. 27 C6
Oakwood Hill Ind. 27 E5
Est. (Oakwood Hill),
Loug.
Oakwood La. W14 66 C3
Oakwood Pk. Rd. N14 24 D7
Oakwood Pl., Croy. 94 G6
Oakwood Rd. NW11 39 D4
Oakwood Rd. SW20 92 G1
Oakwood Rd., Croy. 94 G6
Oakwood Rd., Orp. 104 F2
Oakwood Rd., Pnr. 36 B2
Oakwood Vw. N14 24 D5
Oakworth Rd. W10 56 J5
Oat La. EC2 13 A3
Oat La. EC2 58 J6
Oates Clo., Brom. 96 D3
Oatfield Rd., Orp. 104 J1
Oatland Ri. E17 41 H2
Oatlands Rd., Enf. 25 F1
Oban Ho., Bark. 61 G2
Wheelers Cross
Oban Rd. E13 68 J3
Oban Rd. SE25 95 A4
Oban St. E14 60 D6
Oberstein Rd. SW11 75 G4
Oborne Clo. SE24 76 H5
Observatory Gdns. 66 D2
W8
Observatory Rd. 74 C4
SW14
Occupation La. SE18 79 E1
Occupation La. W5 64 G4
Occupation Rd. SE17 20 J3
Occupation Rd. SE17 67 J5
Occupation Rd. W13 64 E2
Ocean St. E1 59 G4
Ocean St. E1 59 G5
Ockenden Rd. N1 50 A6
Ockham Dr., Orp. 89 A7
Ockley Rd. SW16 85 E4
Ockley Rd., Croy. 94 F7
Octagon Arc. EC2 13 D2
Octagon Arc. EC2 58 G5
Octavia Clo., 93 H5
Mitch.
Octavia Rd., Islw. 73 C3
Octavia St. SW11 75 H1
Octavia Way SE28 62 B7
Booth Clo.
Octavius St. SE8 69 A7
Odard Rd., W.Mol. 90 G4
Down St.
Oddesey Rd., Borwd. 22 B1
Odessa Rd. E7 51 F4
Odessa Rd. NW10 56 G2
Odessa St. SE16 68 J2
Odger St. SW11 75 J2
Odhams Wk. WC2 12 A4
Odyssey Business 45 B5
Pk., Ruis.
Offas Mead E9 50 H4
Lindisfarne Way
Offenbach Ho. E2 59 G2
Mace St.
Offenham Rd. SE9 88 C4
Offerton Rd. SW4 76 C3
Offham Slope N12 31 C5
Offley Rd. SW9 20 E7
Offley Rd. SW9 67 G7
Offord Clo. N17 33 D7
Offord Rd. N1 49 F7
Offord St. N1 49 F7
Ogilby St. SE18 70 C4
Oglander Rd. SE15 77 C4
Ogle St. W1 11 F1
Ogle St. W1 58 C5
Oglethorpe Rd., 53 F3
Dag.
Ohio Rd. E13 60 F4
Okeburn Rd. SW17 85 A5
Okehampton Clo. N1231 G5
Okehampton Cres., 80 B1
Well.
Okehampton Rd. 56 J1
NW10
Olaf St. W11 57 A7
Old Bailey EC4 12 H4
Old Bailey EC4 58 H6
Old Barge Ho. All. 15 F2
SE1
Old Barn Clo., Sutt. 100 B7
Old Barrack Yd. SW1 15 B4
Old Barrowfield E15 60 E1
New Plaistow Rd.
Old Bethnal Grn. 9 J3
Rd. E2
Old Bethnal Grn. 59 D3
Rd. E2

Old Bond St. W1 58 C7
Old Brewers Yd. 12 A4
WC2
Old Brewery Ms. 48 G4
NW3
Hampstead High St.
Old Bri. Clo., Nthlt. 54 G2
Old Bri. St., Kings.T. 91 G2
Old Broad St. EC2 13 C4
Old Broad St. EC2 59 A6
Old Bromley Rd., 87 D5
Brom.
Old Brompton Rd. 66 E5
SW5
Old Brompton Rd. 18 D3
SW7
Old Brompton Rd. 66 E5
SW7
Old Bldgs. WC2 12 E3
Old Burlington St. 11 F5
W1
Old Burlington St. 58 C7
W1
Old Castle St. E1 13 F3
Old Castle St. E1 59 C6
Old Cavendish St. 11 D3
W1
Old Cavendish St. 58 B6
W1
Old Chelsea Ms. SW3 18 F6
Old Ch. La. NW9 47 D2
Old Ch. La., Grnf. 55 D3
Perivale La.
Old Ch. La., Stan. 29 E5
Old Ch. Rd. E1 59 G6
Old Ch. Rd. E4 34 A4
Old Ch. St. SW3 18 F4
Old Ch. St. SW3 66 G5
Old Claygate La., 98 D6
Esher
Old Compton St. W1 11 H5
Old Compton St. W1 58 D7
Old Cote Dr., 63 G6
Houns.
Old Ct. Pl. W8 14 A3
Old Ct. Pl. W8 66 E2
Old Deer Pk. Gdns., 73 H3
Rich.
Old Devonshire Rd. 76 B7
SW12
Old Dock Clo., 65 A6
Rich.
Watcombe Cotts.
Old Dover Rd. SE3 69 G7
Old Fm. Ave. N14 24 C7
Old Fm. Ave., Sid. 88 G1
Old Fm. Clo., 72 F4
Houns.
Old Fm. Pas., 90 J1
Hmptn.
Old Fm. Rd. N2 39 G1
Old Fm. Rd., Hmptn. 81 F6
Old Fm. Rd. E., 89 A2
Sid.
Old Fm. Rd. W., 88 J2
Sid.
Old Fish St. Hill EC4 12 J5
Old Fold Clo., Barn. 23 C1
Old Fold La.
Old Fold La., Barn. 23 C1
Old Fold Vw., Barn. 22 J3
Old Ford Rd. E2 59 F2
Old Ford Rd. E3 59 G2
Old Forge Clo., 29 D4
Stan.
Old Forge Ms. W12 65 H2
Goodwin Rd.
Old Forge Way, Sid. 89 B4
Old Fox Footpath, 102 B7
S.Croy.
Essenden Rd.
Old Gloucester St. 12 B1
WC1
Old Gloucester St. 58 E5
WC1
Old Hall Clo., Pnr. 36 E1
Old Hall Dr., Pnr. 36 E1
Old Hill, Chis. 97 D1
Old Hill, Orp. 104 G6
Old Homesdale Rd., 96 J4
Brom.
Old Ho. Clo. SW19 84 B5
Old Ho. Gdns., 73 F6
Twick.
Old Jamaica Rd. 17 H5
SE16
Old Jamaica Rd. 68 D3
SE16
Old James St. SE15 77 C4
Old Jewry EC2 13 B4
Old Jewry EC2 59 A6
Old Kent Rd. SE1 21 D1
Old Kent Rd. SE1 68 B4

Old Kent Rd. SE15 21 J5
Old Kent Rd. SE15 68 E6
Old Kenton La. NW9 38 B5
Old Kingston Rd., 99 C3
Wor.Pk.
Old Lo. Pl., Twick. 73 E6
St. Margarets Rd.
Old Lo. Way, Stan. 29 D5
Old Maidstone Rd., 89 F7
Sid.
Old Malden La., 99 D3
Wor.Pk.
Old Manor Dr., Islw. 72 J6
Old Manor Way, 88 C5
Chis.
Old Manor Rd. SW5 18 A2
Old Marylebone Rd. 10 H2
NW1
Old Marylebone Rd. 57 H5
NW1
Old Ms., Har. 37 B5
Hindes Rd.
Old Mill Ct. E18 42 J3
Old Mill La. W6 65 D5
Old Mill Rd. SE18 70 G6
Old Montague St. E1 13 H2
Old Montague St. E1 59 D5
Old Nichol St. E2 9 F5
Old Nichol St. E2 59 H4
Old N. St. WC1 12 C1
Old Oak Common La. 56 E4
NW10
Old Oak Common La. 56 E5
W3
Old Oak La. NW10 56 F3
Old Oak Rd. W3 56 F7
Old Orchard, Sun. 96 C2
Old Orchard, The 48 J4
NW3
Nassington Rd.
Old Palace La., 73 F5
Rich.
Old Palace Rd., 101 H3
Croy.
Old Palace Ter., Rich. 73 G5
King St.
Old Palace Yd. SW1 16 A5
Old Palace Yd. SW1 67 E3
Old Palace Yd., 73 G5
Rich.
Old Paradise St. 20 C1
SE11
Old Paradise St. 67 F4
SE11
Old Pk. Ave. SW12 76 A6
Old Pk. Ave., Enf. 24 J4
Old Pk. Gro., Enf. 24 J4
Old Pk. La. W1 15 C2
Old Pk. La. W1 67 A1
Old Pk. Ms., Houns. 63 F7
Old Pk. Ridings N21 24 H6
Old Pk. Rd. N13 32 F4
Old Pk. Rd. SE2 71 A5
Old Pk. Rd., Enf. 24 H4
Old Pk. Rd., S., Enf. 24 H4
Old Pk. Vw., Enf. 24 G3
Old Perry St., 88 H6
Chis.
Old Pl. N1 58 G1
Liverpool Rd.
Old Pye St. SW1 15 H5
Old Pye St. SW1 67 H3
Old Quebec St. W1 11 A4
Old Quebec St. W1 57 J6
Old Queen St. SW1 15 J4
Old Queen St. SW1 67 D2
Old Rectory Gdns., 30 A6
Edg.
Old Redding, Har. 28 H5
Old Rd. SE13 78 E4
Old Rd., Enf. 25 H1
Old Rope Wk., Sun. 90 B3
The Ave.
Old Ruislip Rd., 54 C2
Nthlt.
Old Savill's Cotts., 35 F4
Chig.
The Chase
Old Sch. Clo. SW19 93 D2
Old Sch. Clo., 95 G2
Beck.
Old Seacoal La. EC4 12 G4
Old Sch. Clo., Pnr. 36 D1
Old S. Lambeth Rd. 20 B7
SW8
Old S. Lambeth Rd. 67 E7
Old Sq. N1 58 G1
Liverpool Rd.
Old Sq. WC2 12 D3
Old Sq. WC2 58 F6
Old Sta. Rd., Loug. 27 B5
Old St. E13 60 H2

Old St. EC1 8 J6
Old St. EC1 58 J4
Old Swan Yd., Cars. 100 J4
Old Town SW4 76 C3
Old Town, Croy. 101 H3
Old Tram Yd. SE18 70 H4
Lakedale Rd.
Old Woolwich Rd. 69 D5
SE10
Old York Rd. SW18 75 E5
Oldberry Rd., Edg. 30 D6
Oldborough Rd., 46 F2
Wem.
Oldbury Pl. W1 11 C1
Oldbury Pl. W1 58 A5
Oldbury Rd., Enf. 25 D2
Oldfield Circ., Nthlt. 45 J6
Currey Rd.
Oldfield Clo., 97 C4
Brom.
Oldfield Clo., 46 B5
Grnf.
Oldfield Clo., 29 D5
Stan.
Oldfield Fm. Gdns., 55 A1
Grnf.
Oldfield Gro. SE16 68 G4
Oldfield La. N., 55 A2
Grnf.
Oldfield La. S., 54 J3
Grnf.
Oldfield Ms. N6 40 C7
Oldfield Pk., Brom. 97 D4
Oldfield Rd. N16 50 B3
Oldfield Rd. NW10 47 F7
Oldfield Rd. SW19 84 B6
Oldfield Rd. W3 65 F2
Valetta Rd.
Oldfield Rd., Bexh. 80 E2
Oldfield Rd., Brom. 97 B4
Oldfield Rd., 90 F1
Hmptn.
Oldfields Rd., Sutt. 100 C3
Oldham Ter. W3 65 C1
Oldhill St. N16 50 D1
Oldridge Rd. SW12 76 A7
Oldstead Rd., Brom. 87 D4
Oleander Clo., Orp. 104 G5
O'Leary Sq. E1 59 F5
Oley Pl. E1 59 G5
Redman's Rd.
Olga St. E3 59 H2
Conyer St.
Olinda Rd. N16 41 C6
Oliphant St. W10 57 A3
Olive Rd. E13 60 J3
Olive Rd. NW2 47 J4
Olive Rd. SW19 84 F7
Norman Rd.
Olive Rd. W5 64 G3
Oliver Ave. SE25 95 C3
Oliver Clo. E10 51 A2
Oliver Clo. W4 65 B6
Oliver Gdns. E6 61 B6
Oliver Goldsmith 77 D1
Est. SE15
Goldsmith Rd.
Oliver Gro. SE25 95 C4
Oliver Rd. E10 51 B2
Oliver Rd. E17 42 C5
Oliver Rd., N.Mal. 92 C2
Oliver Rd., Sutt. 100 G4
Olivers Yd. EC1 9 C5
Olivette St. SW15 75 A3
Felsham Rd.
Ollards Gro., Loug. 27 A4
Ollerton Grn. E3 59 J1
Ollerton Rd. N11 32 D5
Olley Clo., Wall. 101 E6
Ollgar Clo. W12 65 F1
Olliffe St. E14 69 C3
Olmar St. SE1 21 H5
Olmar St. SE1 68 D6
Olney Rd. SE17 20 J5
Olney Rd. SE17 67 H6
Olron Cres., Bexh. 80 D5
Olven Rd. SE18 70 F6
Olveston Wk., Cars. 93 G6
Olwen Ms., Pnr. 36 D2
Olyffe Ave., Well. 80 A1
Olyffe Dr., Beck. 96 C1
Olympia Ms. W2 10 B6
Olympia Way W14 66 B3
Olympic Ind. Est., 47 B4
Wem.
Olympic Way, Grnf. 54 H1
Olympic Way, Wem. 47 A3
Olympus Sq. E5 50 D4
Nolan Way
Oman Ave. NW2 47 H4
O'Meara St. SE1 17 A2
O'Meara St. SE1 67 J1
Omega Pl. N1 8 B2

Omega St. SE14 78 A1
Ommaney Rd. SE14 77 G1
On The Hill, Wat. 28 E2
Ondine Rd. SE15 77 C4
One Tree Clo. SE23 77 F6
Onega Gate SE16 68 H3
Ongar Clo., Rom. 44 C5
Ongar Rd. SW6 66 D6
Onra Rd. E17 42 A7
Onslow Ave., Rich. 73 H5
Onslow Clo. E4 34 D2
Onslow Clo., T.Ditt. 98 B1
Onslow Cres., Chis. 97 E1
Onslow Dr., Sid. 89 D3
Onslow Gdns. E18 42 H3
Onslow Gdns. N10 40 B5
Onslow Gdns. N21 24 G5
Onslow Gdns. SW7 18 E3
Onslow Gdns. SW7 66 G5
Onslow Gdns., T.Ditt. 98 B1
Onslow Gdns., Wall. 101 C6
Onslow Ms. E. SW7 18 E2
Onslow Ms. W. SW7 18 E2
Onslow Rd., Croy. 101 G1
Onslow Rd., N.Mal. 92 G4
Onslow Rd., Rich. 73 H5
Onslow Sq. SW7 18 F2
Onslow Sq. SW7 66 G4
Onslow St. EC1 8 F6
Onslow Way, T.Ditt. 98 B1
Ontario St. SE1 16 H6
Opal Clo. E16 61 A6
Opal Ms., Ilf. 52 E2
Ley St.
Opal St. SE11 20 G3
Opal St. SE11 67 H4
Openshaw Rd. SE2 71 B4
Openview SW18 84 F1
Ophelia Gdns. NW2 48 B3
The Vale
Ophir Ter. SE15 77 D1
Opossum Way, Houns. 72 C2
Oppenheim Rd. SE13 78 C2
Oppidans Ms. NW3 48 J7
Meadowbank
Oppidans Rd. NW3 48 J7
Orange Ct. E1 17 J2
Orange Hill Rd., Edg. 30 C7
Orange Pl. SE16 68 F3
Lwr. Rd.
Orange St. WC2 11 J6
Orange St. WC2 58 D7
Orange Yd. W1 11 J4
Orangery, The, Rich. 82 F2
Orangery La. SE9 79 C5
Oratory La. SW3 18 F3
Orb St. SE17 21 B2
Orb St. SE17 68 A4
Orbain Rd. SW6 66 B7
Orbel St. SW11 75 H1
Orchard, The N14 24 B5
Orchard, The N21 25 A6
Orchard, The NW11 39 D5
Orchard, The SE3 78 D2
Orchard, The W4 65 D4
Orchard, The W5 55 G5
Orchard, The, Epsom 99 F7
Orchard, The, Houns. 72 J2
Orchard Ave. N3 39 D3
Orchard Ave. N14 24 C6
Orchard Ave. N20 31 G2
Orchard Ave., Belv. 71 E6
Orchard Ave., Croy. 102 H2
Orchard Ave., Houns. 63 E7
Orchard Ave., Mitch. 101 A1
Orchard Ave., N.Mal. 92 E2
Orchard Ave., Sthl. 63 E1
Orchard Ave., T.Ditt. 98 D1
Orchard Clo. E4 34 A4
Chingford Mt. Rd.
Orchard Clo. E11 42 H4
Orchard Clo. NW2 47 G3
Orchard Clo. SE23 77 F6
Brenchley Gdns.
Orchard Clo. SW20 92 J4
Grand Dr.
Orchard Clo. W10 57 B5
Orchard Clo., Bexh. 80 E1
Orchard Clo., Edg. 29 H6
Orchard Clo., Epsom 99 B6
Orchard Clo., Nthlt. 45 J5
Orchard Clo., Surb. 91 E7
Orchard Clo. (Bushey), Wat. 29 A1
Orchard Clo., Wem. 55 H1
Orchard Ct., Islw. 73 A1
Orchard Ct., Twick. 82 A2
Orchard Ct., Wor.Pk. 99 G1
Orchard Cres., Edg. 30 C5
Orchard Cres., Enf. 25 C1
Orchard Dr. SE3 78 E2
Orchard Dr., Edg. 29 J5
Orchard Gdns., Chess. 98 H4
Orchard Gdns., Sutt. 100 D5
Orchard Gate NW9 38 E4
Orchard Gate, Esher 98 A1
Orchard Gate, Grnf. 46 E5
Orchard Grn., Orp. 104 H2
Orchard Gro. SE20 86 D7
Orchard Gro., Croy. 95 H7
Orchard Gro., Edg. 38 A1
Orchard Gro., Har. 37 J5
Orchard Gro., Orp. 104 J2
Orchard Hill SE13 78 B2
Coldbath St.
Orchard Hill, Cars. 100 J5
Orchard La., E.Mol. 91 A6
Orchard La., Wdf.Grn. 34 J4
Orchard Ms. N1 50 A7
Southgate Gro.
Orchard Pl. E14 60 E7
Orchard Pl. N17 33 C7
Orchard Ri., Croy. 102 H1
Orchard Ri., Kings.T. 92 C1
Orchard Ri., Rich. 74 B4
Orchard Ri. E., Sid. 79 H5
Orchard Ri. W., Sid. 79 H5
Orchard Rd. N6 40 B7
Orchard Rd. SE3 78 E2
Eliot Pl.
Orchard Rd. SE18 70 G4
Orchard Rd., Barn. 23 B4
Orchard Rd., Belv. 71 G4
Orchard Rd., Brent. 64 F6
Orchard Rd., Brom. 96 J1
Orchard Rd., Chess. 98 H4
Orchard Rd., Dag. 62 G1
Orchard Rd., Enf. 25 F5
Orchard Rd., Hmptn. 81 F7
Orchard Rd., Houns. 72 F5
Orchard Rd., Kings.T. 91 H2
Orchard Rd., Mitch. 101 A1
Orchard Rd. Orp. (Farnborough) 104 E5
Orchard Rd., Rich. 74 A3
Orchard Rd., Rom. 44 H2
Orchard Rd., Sid. 88 H4
Orchard Rd., Sun. 81 B7
Hanworth Rd.
Orchard Rd., Sutt. 100 D4
Orchard Rd., Twick. 73 D5
Orchard Rd., Well. 80 B3
Orchard Sq. W14 66 C5
Sun Rd.
Orchard St. E17 41 H4
Orchard St. W1 11 B4
Orchard St. W1 58 A6
Orchard Ter., Enf. 25 D6
Great Cambridge Rd.
Orchard Way, Beck. 95 H5
Orchard Way, Croy. 102 H1
Orchard Way, Enf. 25 B3
Orchard Way, Sutt. 100 G4
Orchardleigh Ave., Enf. 25 F2
Orchardmede N21 25 A6
Orchardson St. NW8 6 E6
Orchardson St. NW8 57 G4
Orchid Clo. E6 61 B5
Orchid Rd. N14 24 C7
Orchid St. W12 56 G7
Orde Hall St. WC1 12 C1
Orde Hall St. WC1 58 F5
Ordell Rd. E3 59 J2
Ordnance Clo., Felt. 81 A3
Ordnance Cres. SE10 69 E2
Ordnance Hill NW8 57 G1
Ordnance Ms. NW8 6 F1
Ordnance Rd. E16 60 F5
Ordnance Rd. SE18 70 D6
Oregano Dr. E14 60 D6
Oregon Ave. E12 52 C4
Oregon Clo., N.Mal. 92 C4
Georgia Rd.
Oregon Sq., Orp. 104 G1
Orestes Ms. NW6 48 D5
Aldred Rd.
Orford Ct. SE27 85 H2
Orford Gdns., Twick. 82 C2
Orford Rd. E17 42 A5
Orford Rd. E18 42 H3
Organ La. E4 34 C2
Oriel Clo., Mitch. 94 D4
Oriel Ct. NW3 48 F4
Heath St.
Oriel Gdns., Ilf. 43 C3
Oriel Pl. NW3 48 F4
Heath St.
Oriel Rd. E9 50 G6
Oriel Way, Nthlt. 45 H7
Orient Ind. Pk. E10 51 A2
Orient St. SE11 20 G1
Orient Way E5 50 G3
Oriental Rd. E16 70 A1
Oriental St. E14 60 A7
Morant St.
Oriole Way SE28 62 B7
Orissa Rd. SE18 70 H5
Orkney St. SW11 76 A2
Orlando Rd. SW4 76 C3
Orleans Rd. SE19 86 A6
Orleans Rd., Twick. 73 E7
Orleston Ms. N7 49 G6
Orleston Rd. N7 49 G6
Orley Fm. Rd., Har. 46 B3
Orlop St. SE10 69 E5
Ormanton Rd. SE26 86 D4
Orme Ct. W2 10 A6
Orme Ct. W2 57 E7
Orme Ct. Ms. W2 10 B6
Orme La. W2 10 A6
Orme La. W2 57 E7
Orme Rd., Kings.T. 92 B2
Orme Sq. W2 10 A6
Ormeley Rd. SW12 76 B7
Ormerod Gdns., Mitch. 94 A2
Ormesby Clo. SE28 62 D7
Wroxham Rd.
Ormesby Way, Har. 37 J6
Ormiston Gro. W12 65 H1
Ormiston Rd. SE10 69 G5
Ormond Ave., Hmptn. 90 H1
Ormond Clo. WC1 12 B1
Ormond Cres., Hmptn. 90 H1
Ormond Dr., Hmptn. 81 H7
Ormond Ms. WC1 8 B6
Ormond Rd. N19 49 E1
Ormond Rd., Rich. 73 G5
Ormond Yd. SW1 15 G1
Ormonde Ave., Orp. 104 F2
Ormonde Gate SW3 19 A4
Ormonde Gate SW3 66 J5
Ormonde Pl. SW1 19 B2
Ormonde Ri., Buck.H. 34 J1
Ormonde Rd. SW14 74 C3
Ormonde Ter. NW8 57 J1
Ormsby Gdns., Grnf. 54 J2
Ormsby Pl. N16 50 C3
Victorian Gro.
Ormsby Pt. SE18 70 E4
Troy Ct.
Ormsby St. E2 9 F2
Ormsby St. E2 59 C2
Ormside St. SE15 68 F6
Ormskirk Rd., Wat. 28 D4
Ornan Rd. NW3 48 H5
Oronsay Wk. N1 49 J6
Marquess Est.
Orpen Wk. N16 50 B3
Orpheus St. SE5 77 A1
Orpington Gdns. N18 33 B3
Orpington Rd. N21 32 G1
Orpington Rd., Chis. 97 H3
Orpwood Clo., Hmptn. 81 F6
Orsett St. SE11 20 D3
Orsett St. SE11 67 F5
Orsett Ter. W2 10 B3
Orsett Ter. W2 57 E6
Orsett Ter., Wdf.Grn. 34 J7
Orsman Rd. N1 59 B1
Orton St. E1 17 H2
Orville Rd. SW11 75 G2
Orwell Ct. N5 49 J4
Orwell Rd. E13 60 J1
Osbaldeston Rd. N16 50 D2
Osbert St. SW1 19 H2
Osberton Rd. SE12 78 G5
Osborn Clo. E8 59 D1
Osborn Gdns. NW7 31 A7
Osborn La. SE23 77 H7
Osborn St. E1 13 G2
Osborn St. E1 59 C5
Osborn Ter. SE3 78 F4
Lee Rd.
Osborne Clo., Beck. 95 H4
Osborne Clo., Felt. 81 D5
Osborne Gdns., Th.Hth. 94 J2
Osborne Gro. E17 41 J4
Osborne Gro. N4 49 G1
Osborne Ms. E17 41 J4
Osborne Gro.
Osborne Pl., Sutt. 100 G5
Osborne Rd. E7 51 H5
Osborne Rd. E9 50 J6
Osborne Rd. E10 51 B3
Osborne Rd. N4 49 G1
Osborne Rd. N13 32 G3
Osborne Rd. NW2 47 H6
Osborne Rd. W3 65 B2
Osborne Rd., Belv. 71 F5
Osborne Rd., Buck.H. 34 H1
Osborne Rd., Dag. 53 F5
Osborne Rd., Enf. 25 H2
Osborne Rd., Houns. 72 F3
Osborne Rd., Kings.T. 82 H7
Osborne Rd., Sthl. 54 J6
Osborne Rd., Th.Hth. 94 J2
Osborne Sq., Dag. 53 F4
Oscar St. SE8 78 A1
Oseney Cres. NW5 49 C6
Osgood Ave., Orp. 104 J5
Osgood Gdns., Orp. 104 J5
O'Shea Gro. E3 59 J1
Osidge La. N14 32 A1
Osier St. E1 59 F4
Osier Way E10 51 B3
Osier Way, Mitch. 93 H5
Osiers Rd. SW18 75 D4
Oslac Rd. SE6 87 B5
Oslo Sq. SE16 68 H3
Norway Gate
Osman Clo. N15 41 A6
Tewkesbury Rd.
Osman Rd. N9 33 D3
Osman Rd. W6 65 J3
Batoum Gdns.
Osmond Clo., Har. 45 J2
Osmond Gdns., Wall. 101 C5
Osmund St. W12 56 F6
Braybrook St.
Osnaburgh St. NW1 7 E5
Osnaburgh St. NW1 58 B4
Osnaburgh Ter. NW1 7 E5
Osney Wk., Cars. 93 G6
Osprey Clo. E6 61 B5
Dove App.
Osprey Clo. E11 42 G4
Osprey Ms., Enf. 25 E5
Ospringe Clo. SE20 86 F7
Ospringe Ct. SE9 79 G6
Ospringe Rd. NW5 49 C4
Osric Path N1 9 D2
Ossian Rd. N4 40 F7
Ossington Bldgs. W1 11 B1
Ossington St. W2 10 A6
Ossington St. W2 57 E7
Ossory Rd. SE1 21 H5
Ossory Rd. SE1 68 D6
Ossulston St. NW1 7 H2
Ossulston St. NW1 58 D2
Ossulton Pl. N2 39 F3
East End Rd.
Ossulton Way N2 39 F4
Ostade Rd. SW2 76 F7
Osten Ms. SW7 14 B6
Osterley Ave., Islw. 64 A7
Osterley Ct., Islw. 73 A1
Osterley Cres., Islw. 73 B1
Osterley Gdns., Th.Hth. 94 J2
Osterley Ho. E14 60 B6
Giraud St.
Osterley La., Islw. 63 J5
Osterley La., Sthl. 63 G5
Osterley Pk. Rd., Sthl. 63 F3
Osterley Pk. Vw. Rd. W7 64 B2
Osterley Rd. N16 50 B4
Osterley Rd., Islw. 64 B7
Ostliffe Rd. N13 32 H5
Oswald Rd., Sthl. 63 E1
Oswald St. E5 50 G3
Oswalds Mead E9 50 H4
Lindisfarne Way
Osward Pl. N9 33 E2
Osward Rd. SW17 84 J2
Oswell Ho. E1 68 E1
Penang St.
Oswin St. SE11 20 H1
Oswin St. SE11 67 H4
Oswyth Rd. SE5 77 B2

Otford Clo., Bex. 80 H6
  Southwold Rd.
Otford Clo., Brom. 97 D3
Otford Cres. SE4 77 J6
Othello Clo. SE11 20 G3
Otis St. E3 60 C3
Otley App., Ilf. 43 E6
Otley Dr., Ilf. 43 E6
Otley Rd. E16 60 J6
Otley Ter. E5 50 C3
Otley Way, Wat. 28 C3
Ottaway St. E5 50 D3
  Stellman Clo.
Otter Rd., Grnf. 54 J4
Otterbourne Rd. E4 34 D3
Otterbourne Rd., 101 H2
  Croy.
Otterburn Gdns., 64 D7
  Islw.
Otterburn Ho. SE5 20 J7
Otterburn St. SW17 84 J6
Otterden Clo., Orp. 104 H4
  Southfleet Rd.
Otterden St. SE6 87 A4
Otto Clo. SE26 86 E3
Otto St. SE17 20 G6
Otto St. SE17 67 H6
Oulton Clo. E5 50 F2
  Mundford Rd.
Oulton Clo. SE28 62 C6
  Rollesby Way
Oulton Cres., Bark. 52 J6
Oulton Rd. N15 41 A5
Oulton Way, Wat. 28 E4
Ouseley Rd. SW12 84 J1
Outer Circle NW1 6 J1
Outer Circle NW1 57 H3
Outgate Rd. NW10 47 F7
Outram Pl. N1 58 E1
Outram Rd. E6 61 B1
Outram Rd. N22 40 D1
Outram Rd., 102 C2
  Croy.
Outwich St. EC3 13 E3
Outwich St. EC3 59 B6
Oval, The E2 59 E2
Oval, The, Sid. 80 A7
Oval Pl. SW8 20 C7
Oval Rd. NW1 67 F7
Oval Rd., Croy. 102 A2
Oval Rd. N., Dag. 62 H1
Oval Rd. S., Dag. 62 H2
Oval Way SE11 20 D4
Oval Way SE11 67 F5
Overbrae, Beck. 87 A6
Overbrook Wk., Edg. 30 A7
  Edg.
Overbury Ave., 96 B3
  Beck.
Overbury Rd. N15 41 A6
Overbury St. E5 50 G4
Overcliff Rd. SE13 78 A3
Overcourt Clo., Sid. 80 B6
Overdale Ave., 92 C2
  N.Mal.
Overdale Rd. W5 64 F3
Overdown Rd. SE6 87 A4
Overhill Rd. SE22 77 D7
Overhill Way, Beck. 96 C5
Overlea Rd. E5 41 D7
Overmead, Sid. 79 G7
Oversley Ho. W2 57 D5
Overstand Clo., 96 A5
  Beck.
Overstone Gdns., 95 J7
  Croy.
Overstone Rd. W6 65 J3
Overton Clo. NW10 47 C6
Overton Clo., Islw. 73 C1
  Avenue Rd.
Overton Ct. E11 42 G7
Overton Dr. E11 42 G7
Overton Dr., Rom. 44 C7
Overton Rd. E10 50 H1
Overton Rd. N14 24 E5
Overton Rd. SE2 71 C3
Overton Rd. SW9 76 G2
Overton Rd., Sutt. 100 D6
Overton Rd. E. SE2 71 D3
Overtons Yd., Croy. 101 J3
Ovesdon Ave., Har. 45 F1
Ovett Clo. SE19 86 B6
Ovex Clo. E14 69 C2
**Ovington Gdns. 14 H6
  SW3**
Ovington Gdns. SW3 66 H3
Ovington Ms. SW3 66 H3
Ovington Ms. SW3 14 H6
Ovington Sq. SW3 14 H6
Ovington Sq. SW3 66 H3
Ovington St. SW3 14 H6
Ovington St. SW3 66 H4

Owen Clo. SE28 71 C1
Owen Clo., Hayes 54 B3
Owen Gdns., 35 B6
  Wdf.Grn.
Owen Rd. N13 32 J4
Owen Rd., Hayes 54 B3
Owen St. EC1 8 F2
Owen Wk. SE20 95 D1
  Sycamore Gro.
Owen Waters Ho., 43 D1
  Ilf.
Owen Way NW10 47 C5
Owenite St. SE2 71 B4
Owen's Ct. EC1 8 G3
Owen's Row EC1 8 G3
Owens Way SE23 77 H7
Owgan Clo. SE5 68 A7
  Benhill Rd.
Oxberry Ave. SW6 75 B2
Oxenden St. SW1 11 H6
Oxendon St. SW1 58 D7
Oxenford St. SE15 77 C3
Oxenholme NW1 7 G2
Oxenholme NW1 58 C2
Oxenpark Ave., 46 H1
  Wem.
Oxestalls Rd. SE8 68 H5
Oxford Ave. SW20 93 B2
Oxford Ave., Houns. 63 G5
**Oxford Circ. Ave. 11 F4
  W1**
Oxford Clo. N9 33 E2
Oxford Clo., Mitch. 94 C3
Oxford Ct. EC4 13 B5
Oxford Ct. W3 56 A6
  Queens Dr.
Oxford Ct., Felt. 81 D4
  Oxford Way
Oxford Cres., 92 D6
  N.Mal.
Oxford Dr., Ruis. 45 C2
Oxford Gdns. N20 31 G1
Oxford Gdns. N21 24 J7
Oxford Gdns. W4 65 A5
Oxford Gdns. W10 57 A6
Oxford Gate W6 66 A4
Oxford Ms., Bex. 80 G7
  Bexley High St.
Oxford Rd. E15 51 D6
Oxford Rd. N4 49 G1
Oxford Rd. N9 33 E2
Oxford Rd. NW6 57 D2
Oxford Rd. SE19 86 A6
Oxford Rd. SW15 75 B4
Oxford Rd. W5 55 G7
Oxford Rd., Cars. 100 H6
Oxford Rd., Enf. 25 E5
Oxford Rd., Har. 36 J6
Oxford Rd., Har. 37 C3
  (Wealdstone)
Oxford Rd., Ilf. 52 F5
Oxford Rd., Sid. 80 B5
Oxford Rd., Tedd. 82 A5
Oxford Rd., Wall. 101 C5
Oxford Rd., 35 A5
  Wdf.Grn.
Oxford Rd. N. W4 65 B5
Oxford Rd. S. W4 65 A5
Oxford Sq. W2 10 H4
Oxford Sq. W2 57 H6
Oxford St. W1 11 B4
Oxford St. W1 57 H6
Oxford Wk., Sthl. 63 F1
Oxford Way, Felt. 81 D4
Oxgate Gdns. NW2 47 H3
Oxgate La. NW2 47 H2
Oxhawth Cres., 97 D5
  Brom.
Oxhey Dr., Nthwd. 28 B4
Oxhey Dr., Wat. 28 C3
Oxhey La., Wat. 28 E1
Oxhey Ridge Clo., 28 A5
  Nthwd.
Oxleas E6 61 E6
Oxleas Clo., Well. 79 E2
Oxleay Ct., Har. 45 G1
Oxleay Rd., Har. 45 G1
Oxleigh Clo., 92 E5
  N.Mal.
Oxley Clo. SE1 21 G3
Oxley Clo. SE1 68 C5
Oxleys Rd. NW2 47 H3
Oxlip Clo., Croy. 102 G1
  Marigold Way
Oxlow La., Dag. 53 F4
Oxonian St. SE22 77 C4
Oxted Clo., Mitch. 93 G3
Oxtoby Way SW16 94 D1
Oyster Catchers 60 H6
  Clo. E16
Oyster Row E1 59 F6
  Lukin St.

Ozalins Way E16 60 G6

P

Pace Pl. E1 59 E6
  Bigland St.
Pacific Rd. E16 60 G6
Packington Rd. W3 65 C3
Packington Sq. N1 58 J1
Packington St. N1 58 H1
Packmores Rd. SE9 79 G5
Padbury SE17 21 D4
Padbury Ct. E2 9 G4
Paddenswick Rd. W6 65 G3
Paddington Clo., 54 D4
  Hayes
Paddington Grn. W2 10 F1
Paddington Grn. W2 57 G5
Paddington St. W1 11 B1
Paddington St. W1 58 A5
Paddock Clo. SE3 78 G3
Paddock Clo. SE26 86 G4
Paddock Clo., Nthlt. 54 G2
Paddock Clo., 99 E1
  Wor.Pk.
Paddock Gdns. SE19 86 B6
  Westow St.
Paddock Rd. NW2 47 G3
Paddock Rd., Bexh. 80 E4
Paddock Rd., Ruis. 45 D3
Paddock Way, Chis. 88 G7
Paddocks, The, 23 J3
  Barn.
Paddocks, The, Wem. 47 B2
Paddocks Clo., Har. 45 H4
Padfield Rd. SE5 76 J3
Padnall Rd., Rom. 44 D3
Padstow Rd., Enf. 24 H2
Padua Rd. SE20 95 F1
Pagden St. SW8 76 B1
Page Clo., Dag. 53 E5
Page Clo., Hmptn. 81 E6
Page Clo., Har. 37 J6
Page Cres., Croy. 101 G5
Page Grn. Rd. N15 41 D5
Page Grn. Ter. N15 41 C5
Page Heath La., 97 A3
  Brom.
Page Heath Vill., 97 A3
  Brom.
Page Meadow NW7 30 G7
Page St. NW7 30 G6
Page St. NW7 19 J1
Page St. SW1 67 D4
Pageant Ave. NW9 38 E1
Pageant Wk., Croy. 102 B3
Pagehurst Rd., 95 E7
  Croy.
Pages Hill N10 40 A2
Pages La. N10 40 A2
Pages Wk. SE1 21 D1
Pages Wk. SE1 68 B4
Pages Yd. W4 65 E6
  Church St.
Paget Ave., Sutt. 100 G3
Paget Clo., Hmptn. 82 A4
Paget Gdns., Chis. 97 E1
Paget La., Islw. 73 A3
Paget Pl., Kings.T. 83 C6
Paget Ri. SE18 70 D6
Paget Rd. N16 50 A1
Paget Rd., Ilf. 52 E4
Paget St. EC1 8 G3
Paget Ter. SE18 70 D6
Pagitts Gro., Barn. 23 E1
Pagnell St. SE14 68 J7
Pagoda Ave., Rich. 73 J3
Pagoda Gdns. SE3 78 D2
Paignton Rd. N15 41 B6
Paignton Rd., Ruis. 45 A3
Paines Clo., Pnr. 36 E2
Paines La., Pnr. 36 E1
Pains Clo., Mitch. 94 B2
Painters Rd., Ilf. 43 J3
Paisley Rd. N22 40 H1
Paisley Rd., Cars. 100 G1
Pakeman St. N7 49 F3
Pakenham Clo. SW12 85 A1
  Balham Pk. Rd.
Pakenham St. WC1 8 D4
Pakenham St. WC1 58 F3
Palace Ave. W8 14 B2
Palace Ave. W8 66 E1
Palace Ct. NW3 48 E5
Palace Ct. W2 10 A5
Palace Ct. W2 57 E7
Palace Ct., Brom. 96 H1
  Palace Gro.
Palace Ct., Har. 37 H6
Palace Ct. Gdns. N10 40 C3
Palace Gdn. Ms. W8 66 D1
Palace Gdns., 35 A1
  Buck.H.

Palace Gdns. Ter. 66 D1
  W8
Palace Gate W8 14 C4
Palace Gate W8 66 F2
Palace Gates Rd. 40 D2
  N22
Palace Grn. W8 14 A2
Palace Grn. W8 66 E2
Palace Grn., Croy. 102 J7
Palace Gro. SE19 86 C7
Palace Gro., Brom. 96 H1
Palace Ms. E17 41 J4
Palace Ms. SW1 19 C2
Palace Ms. SW6 66 C7
  Hartismere Rd.
Palace Pl. SW1 15 F5
Palace Rd. N8 40 D5
Palace Rd. N11 32 D7
Palace Rd. SE19 86 C7
Palace Rd. SW2 85 F1
Palace Rd., Brom. 96 H1
Palace Rd., E.Mol. 91 A3
Palace Rd., 91 G4
  Kings.T.
Palace Rd., Ruis. 45 E4
Palace Rd. Est. SW2 85 F1
Palace Sq. SE19 86 C7
Palace St. SW1 15 F5
Palace St. SW1 67 C3
Palace Vw. SE12 87 G2
Palace Vw., Brom. 96 H3
Palace Vw., Croy. 102 J4
Palace Vw. Rd. E4 34 B5
Palamos Rd. E10 51 A1
Palatine Ave. N16 50 C4
  Stoke Newington Rd.
Palatine Rd. N16 50 B4
Palermo Rd. NW10 56 G2
Palestine Gro. SW19 93 G1
Palewell Common Dr. 74 D5
  SW14
Palewell Pk. SW14 74 D5
Paley Gdns., Loug. 27 E3
Palfrey Pl. SW8 67 F7
Palgrave Ave., Sthl. 54 G7
Palgrave Rd. W12 65 F3
Palissy St. E2 9 F4
Pall Mall SW1 15 G2
Pall Mall SW1 67 C1
Pall Mall E. SW1 15 J1
Pall Mall E. SW1 67 D1
Pall Mall Pl. SW1 15 G2
Pallant Way, Orp. 104 D3
Pallet Way SE18 79 B1
Palliser Rd. W14 66 B5
Palm Ave., Sid. 89 D6
Palm Gro. W5 64 H3
Palm Rd., Rom. 44 J3
Palmar Cres., Bexh. 80 G3
Palmar Rd., Bexh. 80 G2
Palmeira Rd., Bexh. 80 D3
Palmer Ave., Sutt. 99 J4
Palmer Clo., Houns. 72 G1
Palmer Clo., W.Wick. 103 D3
Palmer Cres., 91 H3
  Kings.T.
Palmer Gdns., Barn. 23 A5
Palmer Pl. N7 49 G5
Palmer Rd. E13 60 H4
Palmer Rd., Dag. 52 D1
Palmer St. SW1 15 H5
Palmer St. SW1 67 D3
Palmers Gro., 90 C3
  W.Mol.
Palmers La., Enf. 25 F1
Palmers Pas. SW14 74 C3
  Palmers Rd.
Palmers Rd. E2 59 G2
Palmers Rd. N11 32 C5
Palmers Rd. SW14 74 C3
Palmers Rd. SW16 94 F2
Palmers Rd., Borwd. 22 B1
Palmerston Cres. 32 F5
  N13
Palmerston Cres. 70 F6
  SE18
Palmerston Gro. 84 D7
  SW19
Palmerston Rd. E7 51 H5
Palmerston Rd. E17 41 J3
Palmerston Rd. N22 32 F7
Palmerston Rd. NW6 48 C7
Palmerston Rd. 74 C4
  SW14
Palmerston Rd. 84 D7
  SW19
Palmerston Rd. W3 65 C3
Palmerston Rd., 34 H2
  Buck.H.
Palmerston Rd., 100 J4
  Cars.
Palmerston Rd., 37 B3
  Har.

Name	Page	Grid
Palmerston Rd., Orp.	104	F4
Palmerston Rd., Sutt.	100	F4
Vernon Rd.		
Palmerston Rd., Th.Hth.	95	A5
Palmerston Rd., Twick.	73	B6
Palmerston Way SW8	67	B7
Bradmead		
Pamber St. W10	57	A6
Pamela Gdns., Pnr.	36	B5
Pamela Wk. E8	59	D1
Marlborough Ave.		
Pams Way, Epsom	99	D5
Pancras La. EC4	13	A4
Pancras Rd. NW1	7	H1
Pancras Rd. NW1	58	D2
Pandora Rd. NW6	48	D6
Panfield Ms., Ilf.	43	D6
Cranbrook Rd.		
Panfield Rd. SE2	71	A3
Pangbourne Ave. W10	56	J5
Pangbourne Dr., Stan.	29	G5
Pankhurst Clo. SE14	68	G7
Briant St.		
Pankhurst Rd., Walt.	90	C7
Panmuir Rd. SW20	92	H1
Panmure Clo. N5	49	H4
Panmure Rd. SE26	86	E3
Pannard Pl., Sthl.	54	H7
Pansy Gdns. W12	56	G7
Pantiles, The NW11	39	C5
Willifield Way		
Pantiles, The, Bexh.	71	F7
Pantiles, The, Brom.	97	B3
Panton St. SW1	11	H6
Panyer All. EC4	12	J3
Papillons Wk. SE3	78	G3
Papworth Gdns. N7	49	F5
Chillingworth Rd.		
Papworth Way SW2	76	G7
Parade, The SW11	19	A7
Parade, The W12	66	J7
Parade, The, Esher	98	B6
Parade, The, Wat.	28	E3
Parade Ms. SE27	85	H2
Norwood Rd.		
Paradise Pas. N7	49	G5
Sheringham Rd.		
Paradise Rd. SW4	76	E2
Paradise Rd., Rich.	73	H5
Paradise Row E2	59	E3
Bethnal Grn. Rd.		
Paradise St. SE16	68	G2
Paradise Wk. SW3	19	A5
Paradise Wk. SW3	66	J6
Paragon, The SE3	78	F2
Paragon Gro., Surb.	91	J6
Paragon Ms. SE1	21	C1
Paragon Pl. SE3	78	F2
Paragon Pl., Surb.	91	J6
Berrylands Rd.		
Paragon Rd. E9	50	F6
Parbury Ri., Chess.	98	H6
Parbury Rd. SE23	77	H6
Parchmore Rd., Th.Hth.	94	H2
Parchmore Way, Th.Hth.	94	H3
Pardon St. EC1	8	H5
Pardoner St. SE1	17	C5
Pardoner St. SE1	68	A3
Parfett St. E1	13	J2
Parfett St. E1	59	D5
Parfitt Clo. NW3	48	F2
North End		
Parfrey St. W6	65	J6
Parham Dr., Ilf.	43	E6
Paris Gdn. SE1	16	G1
Paris Gdn. SE1	67	H1
Parish Gate Dr., Sid.	79	H6
Parish La. SE20	86	G6
Parish Ms. SE20	86	G7
Park, The N6	40	A6
Park, The NW11	48	E1
Park, The SE19	86	B7
Park, The SE23	86	E1
Park Hill		
Park, The W5	64	G1
Park, The, Cars.	100	J5
Park, The, Sid.	89	A4
Park App., Well.	80	B4
Park Ave. E6	61	D1
Park Ave. E15	51	E6
Park Ave. N3	39	E1
Park Ave. N13	32	G3
Park Ave. N18	33	D4
Park Ave. N22	40	E2
Park Ave. NW2	47	H6
Park Ave. NW10	55	J2
Park Ave. NW11	48	E1
Park Ave. SW14	74	D4
Park Ave., Bark.	52	F6
Park Ave., Barn.	23	F5
Park Ave., Brom.	87	F7
Park Ave., Cars.	101	A6
Park Ave., Chis.	97	H3
Park Ave., Enf.	25	A5
Park Ave., Houns.	72	H6
Park Ave., Ilf.	52	D1
Park Ave., Mitch.	85	B7
Park Ave., Orp.	104	C3
(Farnborough)		
Park Ave., Sthl.	63	F2
Park Ave., W.Wick.	103	C2
Park Ave., Wdf.Grn.	34	H5
Park Ave. E., Epsom	99	G6
Park Ave. Ms., Mitch.	85	B7
Park Ave.		
Park Ave. N. N8	40	D3
Park Ave. N. NW10	47	H5
Park Ave. Rd. N17	33	E7
Park Ave. S. N8	40	D4
Park Ave. W., Epsom	99	G6
Park Chase, Wem.	46	J4
Park Clo. E9	59	F1
Skipworth Rd.		
Park Clo. NW10	55	J3
Park Clo. SW1	14	J4
Park Clo. W4	65	D5
Park Clo. W14	66	C3
Park Clo., Cars.	100	J6
Park Clo., Hmptn.	90	J1
Park Clo., Har.	37	B1
Park Clo., Houns.	72	J5
Park Ct. SE26	86	E6
Park Ct., Kings.T.	91	F1
Park Ct., Wem.	46	H5
Park Cres. N3	31	E7
Park Cres. W1	7	D6
Park Cres. W1	58	B4
Park Cres., Enf.	25	A4
Park Cres., Erith	71	J6
Park Cres., Twick.	82	A1
Park Cres. Ms. E. W1	7	E6
Park Cres. Ms. W. W1	7	D6
Park Cft., Edg.	38	C1
Park Dale N11	32	D6
Bounds Grn. Rd.		
Park Dr. N21	24	J6
Park Dr. NW11	48	E1
Park Dr. SE7	70	B6
Park Dr. SW14	74	D4
Park Dr. W3	65	A3
Park Dr., Dag.	53	J3
Park Dr., Har.	36	G7
Park Dr., Har.	29	B6
(Harrow Weald)		
Uxbridge Rd.		
Park Dr. Clo. SE7	70	B5
Park End NW3	48	H4
South Hill Pk.		
Park End, Brom.	96	F1
Park Fm. Clo. N2	39	F3
Park Fm. Clo., Pnr.	36	B5
Field End Rd.		
Park Fm. Rd., Brom.	97	A1
Park Fm. Rd., Kings.T.	82	H7
Park Gdn. N2	39	G3
Park Gdns. NW9	38	B3
Park Gdns., Kings.T.	82	J5
Park Gate N2	39	G3
Park Gate N21	24	F7
Park Gate W5	55	G5
Mount Ave.		
Park Gate Clo., Kings.T.	83	B6
Warboys App.		
Park Gate Clo., Kings.T.	83	B6
Warboys App.		
Park Gro. E15	60	G1
Park Gro. N11	32	D7
Park Gro., Bexh.	80	J4
Park Gro., Brom.	96	H1
Park Gro., Edg.	29	J5
Park Gro. Rd. E11	51	E2
Park Hall Rd. N2	39	H4
Park Hall Rd. SE21	86	A3
Park Hill SE23	86	E2
Park Hill SW4	76	D5
Park Hill W5	55	G5
Park Hill, Brom.	97	B4
Park Hill, Cars.	100	H6
Park Hill, Loug.	27	A5
Park Hill, Rich.	73	J6
Park Hill Clo., Cars.	100	H5
Park Hill Ct. SW17	84	J3
Beeches Rd.		
Park Hill Ri., Croy.	102	B2
Park Hill Rd., Brom.	96	E2
Park Hill Rd., Croy.	102	B2
Park Hill Rd., Sid.	88	H3
Park Hill Rd., Wall.	101	B6
Park Ho. N21	24	F7
Park Ho. Gdns., Twick.	73	F6
Park La. E15	60	D1
High St.		
Park La. N9	33	B3
Park La. N17	33	C7
Park La. N18	33	B4
Sheldon Rd.		
Park La. W1	11	A5
Park La. W1	57	J7
Park La., Cars.	101	A4
Park La., Croy.	102	A3
Park La., Har.	63	A7
Park La. (Cranford), Houns.	72	A7
Park La., Rich.	73	G4
Park La., Rom.	44	D6
Park La., Stan.	29	D3
Park La., Sutt.	100	B6
Park La., Tedd.	82	C6
Park La., Wem.	46	H5
Park La. Clo. N17	33	D7
Park Lawns, Wem.	46	J4
Park Mead, Har.	45	H3
Park Mead, Sid.	80	B5
Park Ms. SE24	76	J6
Croxted Rd.		
Park Ms., E.Mol.	90	J4
Park Ms., Hmptn.	81	J5
Park Rd.		
Park Par. NW10	56	F2
Park Pl. E14	69	A1
Park Pl. SW1	15	F2
Park Pl. SW1	67	C1
Park Pl. W3	65	A4
Park Pl. W5	64	G1
Park Pl., Hmptn.	81	J6
Park Pl., Wem.	46	J4
Park Pl. Vill. W2	10	D1
Park Pl. Vill. W2	57	F5
Park Ridings N8	32	D6
Park Ri. SE23	86	H1
Park Ri., Har.	37	B1
Park Ri. Rd. SE23	86	J1
Park Rd. E6	60	J1
Park Rd. E10	51	A1
Park Rd. E12	51	H1
Park Rd. E15	60	G1
Park Rd. E17	41	J5
Park Rd. N2	39	G3
Park Rd. N8	40	C4
Park Rd. N11	32	D7
Park Rd. N14	24	D7
Park Rd. N15	40	H4
Park Rd. N18	33	C4
Park Rd. NW1	6	J5
Park Rd. NW1	57	J4
Park Rd. NW4	38	G7
Park Rd. NW8	6	G3
Park Rd. NW8	57	H3
Park Rd. NW9	38	D7
Park Rd. NW10	56	E1
Park Rd. SE25	95	B4
Park Rd. SW19	84	G7
Park Rd. W4	65	C7
Park Rd. W7	55	C7
Park Rd., Barn.	23	C4
Park Rd. (New Barnet), Barn.	23	G4
Park Rd., Beck.	86	J7
Park Rd., Brom.	96	H1
Park Rd., Chis.	88	E6
Park Rd., E.Mol.	90	J4
Park Rd., Felt.	81	D4
Park Rd., Hmptn.	81	H4
Park Rd., Houns.	72	H5
Park Rd., Ilf.	52	G3
Park Rd., Islw.	73	E1
Park Rd., Kings.T.	82	J5
Park Rd., Kings.T. (Hampton Wick)	91	F1
Park Rd., N.Mal.	92	D4
Park Rd., Rich.	73	J6
Park Rd., Sun.	81	B7
Park Rd., Surb.	91	J6
Park Rd., Sutt.	100	B6
Park Rd., Tedd.	82	C7
Park Rd., Twick.	73	F6
Park Rd., Wall.	101	B5
Park Rd. (Hackbridge), Wall.	101	B2
Park Rd., Wem.	46	H6
Park Rd. E. W3	65	B2
Park Rd. N. W3	65	B2
Park Rd. N. W4	65	D5
Park Rd. W., Kings.T.	91	F1
Park Row SE10	69	D6
Park Royal Rd. NW10	56	C4
Park Royal Rd. W3	56	C4
Park Side, Sutt.	100	B6
Park Sq. E. NW1	7	D5
Park Sq. E. NW1	58	B4
Park Sq. Ms. NW1	7	D6
Park Sq. Ms. NW1	58	B4
Park Sq. W. NW1	7	D5
Park Sq. W. NW1	58	B4
Park St. SE1	16	J1
Park St. SE1	67	J1
Park St. W1	11	B5
Park St. W1	58	A7
Park St., Croy.	101	J2
Park St., Tedd.	82	B6
Park Ter., Wor.Pk.	99	G1
Park Vw. N21	24	F7
Park Vw. W3	56	C5
Park Vw., N.Mal.	92	F3
Park Vw., Pnr.	36	F1
Park Vw., Wem.	47	B5
Park Vw. Ct., Ilf.	43	H6
Brancaster Rd.		
Park Vw. Cres. N11	32	B4
Park Vw. Est. E2	59	G2
Park Vw. Gdns. NW4	39	A6
Park Vw. Gdns., Bark.	61	H2
River Rd.		
Park Vw. Gdns., Ilf.	43	C4
Woodford Ave.		
Park Vw. Rd. N3	39	E1
Park Vw. Rd. N17	41	D3
Park Vw. Rd. NW10	47	F4
Park Vw. Rd. W5	55	H5
Park Vw. Rd., Pnr.	28	B7
Park Vw. Rd., Sthl.	63	G1
Park Vw. Rd., Well.	80	B3
Park Village E. NW1	7	D1
Park Village E. NW1	58	B2
Park Village W. NW1	7	D1
Park Village W. NW1	58	B2
Park Vill., Rom.	44	D6
Park Vista SE10	69	D6
Park Wk. N6	40	A7
Park Wk. SW10	18	D5
Park Wk. SW10	66	F6
Park Way N20	31	J4
Park Way NW11	39	B5
Park Way, Edg.	38	B1
Park Way, Enf.	24	G2
Park Way, Felt.	72	B7
Park Way, Ilf.	52	J3
Park Way, Ruis.	45	A1
Park Way, W.Mol.	90	H3
Park W. W2	10	F4
Park W. Pl. W2	10	H3
Parkcroft Rd. SE12	78	F7
Parkdale Cres., Wor.Pk.	99	D3
Parkdale Rd. SE18	70	H5
Parke Rd. SW13	74	G1
Parke Rd., Sun.	90	A4
Parker Clo. E16	70	B1
Parker Ms. WC2	12	B3
Parker Rd., Croy.	101	J4
Parker St. E16	70	B1
Parker St. WC2	12	B3
Parker St. WC2	56	E6
Parkers Row SE1	17	G4
Parkfield Ave. SW14	74	E4
Parkfield Ave., Felt.	81	A3
Parkfield Ave., Har.	36	J2
Parkfield Ave., Nthlt.	54	D2
Parkfield Clo., Edg.	30	B6
Parkfield Clo., Nthlt.	54	E2
Parkfield Cres., Felt.	81	A3
Parkfield Cres., Har.	36	J2
Parkfield Cres., Ruis.	45	E3
Parkfield Dr., Nthlt.	54	D2
Parkfield Gdns., Har.	36	H3

Parkfield Rd. NW10 47 G7
Parkfield Rd. SE14 77 J1
Parkfield Rd., Felt. 81 A3
Parkfield Rd., Har. 45 J3
Parkfield Rd., 54 E2
 Nthlt.
Parkfield St. N1 8 F1
Parkfield St. N1 58 G2
Parkfield Way, 97 C6
 Brom.
Parkfields SW15 74 J4
Parkfields, Croy. 102 J1
Parkfields Ave. NW9 47 D1
Parkfields Ave. 92 H2
 SW20
Parkfields Rd., 82 J5
 Kings.T.
Parkgate SE3 78 F3
Parkgate Ave., Barn. 23 F1
Parkgate Cres., 23 F1
 Barn.
Parkgate Gdns. SW14 74 D5
Parkgate Rd. SW11 66 H7
Parkgate Rd., Wall. 101 A5
Parkham St. SW11 75 G1
Parkhill Rd. E4 34 C1
Parkhill Rd. NW3 48 J5
Parkhill Rd., Bex. 80 F7
Parkhill Wk. NW3 48 J5
Parkholme Rd. E8 50 D6
Parkhouse St. SE5 21 C7
Parkhouse St. SE5 68 A7
Parkhurst Gdns., 80 G7
 Bex.
Parkhurst Rd. E12 52 D4
Parkhurst Rd. E17 41 H4
Parkhurst Rd. N7 49 E4
Parkhurst Rd. N11 32 A4
Parkhurst Rd. N17 41 D2
Parkhurst Rd. N22 32 F6
Parkhurst Rd., Bex. 80 G7
Parkhurst Rd., Sutt. 100 G4
Parkland Clo., 35 F3
 Chig.
Parkland Gdns. SW19 84 A1
Parkland Rd. N22 40 F2
Parkland Rd., 34 G7
 Wdf.Grn.
Parkland Wk. N4 40 G7
Parkland Wk. N6 40 C7
Parkland Wk. N10 40 A4
 Cranley Gdns.
Parklands, Chig. 35 F3
Parklands, Surb. 91 J5
Parklands Clo. SW14 74 C5
Parklands Ct., 72 D2
 Houns.
Parklands Dr. N3 39 B3
Parklands Rd. SW16 85 B5
Parklands Way, 99 E2
 Wor.Pk.
Parklea Clo. NW9 38 E1
Parkleigh Rd. SW19 93 E2
Parkleys, Rich. 82 G4
Parkmead SW15 74 H6
Parkmead, Loug. 27 D5
Parkmead Gdns. NW7 30 H6
Parkmore Clo., 34 G4
 Wdf.Grn.
Parkshot, Rich. 73 H4
Parkside N3 39 F1
Parkside NW2 47 G3
Parkside NW7 30 G6
Parkside SE3 69 F7
Parkside SW19 84 A4
Parkside, Buck.H. 34 H2
Parkside, Hmptn. 82 A5
Parkside, Sid. 89 B2
Parkside Ave. SW19 84 A5
Parkside Ave., 97 B4
 Brom.
Parkside Cres., 92 C6
 Surb.
Parkside Dr., Edg. 30 A3
Parkside Est. E9 59 F1
 Rutland Rd.
Parkside Gdns. SW19 84 A4
Parkside Gdns., 31 J1
 Barn.
Parkside Ho., Dag. 53 J3
Parkside Rd. SW11 76 A1
Parkside Rd., Belv. 71 H4
Parkside Rd., 72 H5
 Houns.
Parkside Ter. N18 33 A4
 Great Cambridge Rd.
Parkside Way, Har. 36 H4
Parkstead Rd. SW15 74 G5
Parkstone Ave. N18 33 C5
Parkstone Rd. E17 42 C3
Parkstone Rd. SE15 77 D2
 Rye La.

Parkthorne Clo., 36 H6
 Har.
Parkthorne Dr., 36 G6
 Har.
Parkthorne Rd. SW12 76 D7
Parkview Rd. SE9 88 E1
Parkview Rd., Croy. 102 D1
Parkville Rd. SW6 66 C7
Parkway N14 32 E2
Parkway NW1 58 B1
Parkway SW20 93 A4
Parkway, Erith 71 E3
Parkway, Wdf.Grn. 34 J3
Parkway, The, Hayes 54 E3
Parkway, The 63 A6
 (Cranford), Houns.
Parkway Trd. Est., 63 C6
 Houns.
Parkwood N20 31 J3
Parkwood, Beck. 96 A1
Parkwood Gro., Sun. 90 A3
Parkwood Ms. N6 40 B6
Parkwood Rd. SW19 84 C5
Parkwood Rd., Bex. 80 F7
Parkwood Rd., Islw. 73 C1
Parliament Hill NW3 48 H4
Parliament Ms. SW14 74 C2
 Thames Bank
Parliament Sq. SW1 16 A4
Parliament Sq. SW1 67 E2
Parliament St. SW1 16 A4
Parliament St. SW1 67 E2
Parma Cres. SW11 75 J4
Parmiter St. E2 59 E2
Parnell Clo., Edg. 30 B4
Parnell Rd. E3 59 J1
Parnham St. E14 59 H6
 Blount St.
Parolles Rd. N19 49 C1
Paroma Rd., Belv. 71 G3
Parr Clo. N9 33 E4
Parr Ct., Felt. 81 C4
Parr Rd. E6 61 A1
Parr Rd., Stan. 37 G1
Parr St. N1 9 B1
Parr St. N1 59 A2
Parrs Pl., Hmptn. 81 F7
Parry Ave. E6 61 C6
Parry Clo., Epsom 61 C6
Parry Pl. SE18 70 E4
Parry Rd. SE25 95 B3
Parry Rd. W10 57 B3
 Dart St.
Parry St. SW8 20 A5
Parry St. SW8 67 E6
Parsifal Rd. NW6 48 D5
Parsloes Ave., Dag. 53 D4
Parson St. NW4 38 J4
Parsonage Gdns., 24 J2
 Enf.
Parsonage La., Enf. 25 A2
Parsonage La., Sid. 89 F4
Parsonage 71 G6
 Manorway, Belv.
Parsonage St. E14 69 C4
Parsons Cres., Edg. 30 A3
Parsons Grn. SW6 75 D2
Parsons Grn. La. 75 D1
 SW6
Parsons Gro., Edg. 30 A3
Parson's Ho. W2 6 E6
Parson's Mead, 101 H1
 Croy.
Parsons Mead, 90 J3
 E.Mol.
Parsons Rd. E13 60 J2
 Old St.
Parthenia Rd. SW6 75 D1
Partingdale La. NW7 31 A5
Partington Clo. N19 49 D1
 Fulmer Rd.
Partridge Clo. E16 61 A5
Partridge Clo. 28 H1
 (Bushey), Wat.
Partridge Dr., Orp. 104 F3
Partridge Grn. SE9 88 D3
Partridge Rd., 81 F6
 Hmptn.
Partridge Rd., Sid. 88 H3
Partridge Sq. E6 61 B5
 Nightingale Way
Partridge Way N22 40 E1
Parvin St. SW8 76 D1
Pasadena Clo., 63 A2
 Hayes
Pascal St. SW8 19 J7
Pascal St. SW8 67 H7
Pascoe Rd. SE13 78 D5
Pasley Clo. SE17 20 J4
Pasquier Rd. E17 41 H1
Passey Pl. SE9 79 C6
Passfield Dr. E14 60 B5
 St. Leonards Rd.

Passfield Path SE28 62 B7
 Booth Clo.
Passing All. EC1 8 G6
Passmore Gdns. N11 32 D6
Passmore St. SW1 19 B2
Passmore St. SW1 67 A5
Pasteur Clo. NW9 38 E2
Pasteur Gdns. N18 32 H5
Paston Clo. E5 50 G3
 Caldecott Way
Pastor St. SE11 20 H1
Pastor St. SE11 67 H4
Pasture Clo., Wem. 46 E3
Pasture Rd. SE6 87 E1
Pasture Rd., Dag. 53 F4
Pasture Rd., Wem. 46 E2
Pastures, The N20 31 C1
Patcham Ter. SW8 76 B1
Pater St. W8 66 D3
Paternoster Row EC4 12 J4
Paternoster Sq. EC4 12 H3
Path, The SW19 93 E1
Pathfield Rd. SW16 85 D6
Pathway, The, Wat. 28 D1
 Anthony Clo.
Patience Rd. SW11 75 H2
Patio Clo. SW4 76 D6
Patmore Est. SW8 76 C1
Patmore St. SW8 76 C1
Patmos Rd. SW9 67 H7
Paton Clo. E3 60 A3
Paton St. EC1 8 J4
Patricia Ct., Chis. 97 G1
 Manor Pk. Rd.
Patricia Ct., Well. 71 B7
Patrick Connolly 60 B3
 Gdns. E3
 Talwin St.
Patrick Pas. SW11 75 H2
Patrick Rd. E13 60 J3
Patriot Sq. E2 59 E2
Patrol Pl. SE6 78 B6
Patshull Pl. NW5 49 C6
 Patshull Rd.
Patshull Rd. NW5 49 C6
Patten All., Rich. 73 G5
 The Hermitage
Patten Rd. SW18 75 H7
Pattenden Rd. SE6 86 J1
Patterdale Clo., 87 F1
 Brom.
Patterdale Rd. SE15 68 F7
Patterson Ct. SE19 86 C7
Patterson Rd. SE19 86 C6
Pattison Pt. E16 60 G5
 Fife Rd.
Pattison Rd. NW2 48 D3
Pattison Wk. SE18 70 F5
 Sandbach Pl.
Paul Clo. E15 51 E7
 Paul St.
Paul Gdns., Croy. 102 C2
Paul St. E15 60 E1
Paul St. EC2 9 C6
Paul St. EC2 59 A4
Paulet Rd. SE5 76 H2
Paulhan Rd., Har. 37 F4
Paulin Dr. N21 24 G7
Pauline Cres., 81 J1
 Twick.
Paultons Sq. SW3 18 F5
Paultons Sq. SW3 66 G6
Paultons St. SW3 18 F6
Paultons St. SW3 66 G6
Pauntley St. N19 49 C1
Paved Ct., Rich. 73 G5
 King St.
Paveley Dr. SW11 75 H7
Paveley St. NW8 6 H4
Paveley St. NW8 57 H3
Pavement, The SW4 76 C4
Pavement, The W5 64 H3
 Popes La.
Pavement Ms., Rom. 44 D7
 Clarissa Rd.
Pavement Sq., Croy. 102 D1
Pavet Clo., Dag. 53 H6
Pavilion Rd. SW1 15 A4
Pavilion Rd. SW1 66 J3
Pavilion Rd., Ilf. 43 C7
Pavilion St. SW1 15 A6
Pavilion Ter., 91 C4
 E.Mol.
Pavilion Ter., Ilf. 43 H6
 Southdown Cres.
Pavilion Way, Edg. 30 B7
Pavilion Way, Ruis. 45 C2
Pawleyne Clo. SE20 86 F7
Pawsey Clo. E13 60 G1
 Plashet Rd.
Pawson's Rd., Croy. 94 J6
Paxford Rd., Wem. 46 E2

Paxton Clo., Rich. 73 J2
Paxton Clo., Walt. 90 C7
 Shaw Dr.
Paxton Pl. SE27 86 B4
Paxton Rd. N17 33 C7
Paxton Rd. SE23 86 H3
Paxton Rd. W4 65 E6
Paxton Rd., Brom. 87 G7
Paxton Ter. SW1 19 E5
Paxton Ter. SW1 67 B6
Payne Rd. E3 60 B2
Payne St. SE8 68 J6
Paynell Ct. SE3 78 E3
 Lawn Ter.
Paynes Wk. W6 66 B6
 Ancill Clo.
Paynesfield Ave. 74 D3
 SW14
Peabody Ave. SW1 19 D4
Peabody Clo. SE10 78 B1
 Devonshire Dr.
Peabody Dws. WC1 8 A5
Peabody Est. EC1 9 A6
Peabody Est. N17 41 B1
Peabody Est. SE1 16 F2
Peabody Est. SE24 76 J7
Peabody Est. SW3 18 H5
Peabody Est. W6 65 J5
Peabody Est. W10 56 J4
 Dalgarno Gdns.
Peabody Hill SE21 85 H1
Peabody Hill Est. 85 H1
 SE21
Peabody Sq. SE1 16 G4
Peabody Sq. SE1 67 H2
Peabody Yd. N1 58 J1
 Greenman St.
Peace Clo. N14 24 B5
Peace Gro., Wem. 47 B2
Peach Rd. W10 57 A3
Peaches Clo., Sutt. 100 B7
Peachum Rd. SE3 69 F6
Peacock St. SE17 20 H2
 Sophia Rd.
Peacock Yd. SE17 20 H2
Peak, The SE26 86 F3
Peak Hill SE26 86 F4
Peak Hill Ave. SE26 86 F4
Peak Hill Gdns. 86 F4
 SE26
Peaketon Ave., Ilf. 43 A4
Peal Gdns. W13 55 D4
 Ruislip Rd. E.
Peall Rd., Croy. 94 F6
Pear Clo. NW9 38 D4
Pear Clo. SE14 68 H7
 Southerngate Way
Pear Pl. SE1 16 E3
Pear Tree Ct. EC1 8 F6
Pear Tree Ct. EC1 58 G4
Pear Tree St. EC1 8 H5
Pear Tree St. EC1 58 H4
Pearce Rd., W.Mol. 90 H3
Pearcefield Ave. 86 F1
 SE23
Pearcroft Rd. E11 51 D2
Peardon St. SW8 76 B2
Peareswood Gdns., 37 G1
 Stan.
Pearfield Rd. SE23 86 H3
Pearl Clo. E6 61 D6
Pearl Rd. E17 42 A3
Pearl St. E1 68 E1
 Penang St.
Pearman St. SE1 16 F5
Pearman St. SE1 67 G3
Pears Rd., Houns. 72 J3
Pearscroft Ct. SW6 75 E1
Pearscroft Rd. SW6 75 E1
Pearson St. E2 9 F1
Pearson St. E2 59 C2
Pearsons Ave. SE14 78 A1
 Tanners Hill
Peartree Clo., Mitch. 93 H2
Peartree Gdns. 53 B4
 Dag.
Peartree Gdns. 44 H2
 Rom.
Peartree La. E1 59 F7
 Glamis Rd.
Peartree Rd., Enf. 25 B3
Peary Pl. E2 59 F3
 Kirkwall Pl.
Peatfield Clo., 88 H3
 Sid.
 Woodside Rd.
Pebworth Rd., Har. 46 D2
Peckarmans Wk. 86 C3
 SE26
Peckett Sq. N5 49 J4
 Highbury Gra.
Peckford Pl. SW9 76 G2

Peckham Gro. SE15 21 E7
Peckham Gro. SE15 68 B7
Peckham High St. 77 D1
  SE15
Peckham Hill St. 21 H7
  SE15
Peckham Hill St. 68 D7
  SE15
Peckham Pk. Rd. 68 D7
  SE15
Peckham Rd. SE5 77 B1
Peckham Rd. SE15 77 C1
Peckham Rye SE15 77 D3
Peckham Rye SE22 77 D4
Peckwater St. NW5 49 C5
Pedlars Wk. N7 49 E6
Pedley Rd., Dag. 53 C1
Pedley St. E1 9 G6
Pedley St. E1 59 D4
Pedro St. E5 50 G3
Pedworth Gdns. SE16 68 F4
  Rotherhithe New Rd.
Peek Cres. SW19 84 A5
Peel Clo. E4 34 B2
Peel Clo. N9 33 D3
  Plevna Rd.
Peel Dr. NW9 38 F3
Peel Dr., Ilf. 43 B3
Peel Gro. E2 59 F2
Peel Pas. W8 66 D1
  Peel St.
Peel Pl., Ilf. 43 B2
Peel Prec. NW6 57 D3
Peel Rd. E18 42 F1
Peel Rd. NW6 57 C3
Peel Rd., Har. 37 C3
Peel Rd., Orp. 104 F5
Peel Rd., Wem. 46 G3
Peel St. W8 66 D1
Peerless St. EC1 9 B4
Peerless St. EC1 59 A3
Pegamoid Rd. N18 33 F3
Pegasus Ct., Kings.T. 91 G3
Pegasus Pl. SE11 20 E5
Pegg Rd., Houns. 63 D7
Pegley Gdns. SE12 87 G2
Pegwell St. SE18 70 H7
Pekin Clo. E14 60 A6
  Pekin St.
Pekin St. E14 60 A6
Peldon Ct., Rich. 73 J4
Peldon Wk. N1 58 H1
  Britannia Row
Pelham Ave., Bark. 61 J1
Pelham Clo. SE5 77 B3
Pelham Cres. SW7 18 G2
Pelham Cres. SW7 66 H4
Pelham Pl. SW7 18 G1
Pelham Pl. SW7 66 H4
Pelham Rd. E18 42 H3
Pelham Rd. N15 41 C4
Pelham Rd. N22 40 G2
Pelham Rd. SW19 84 D7
Pelham Rd., Beck. 95 F2
Pelham Rd., Bexh. 80 G3
Pelham Rd., Ilf. 52 G2
Pelham St. SW7 18 F1
Pelham St. SW7 66 G4
Pelican Est. SE15 77 C1
Pelican Pas. E1 59 F4
  Cambridge Heath Rd.
Pelican Wk. SW9 76 H4
  Loughborough Pk.
Pelier St. SE17 21 A5
Pelinore Rd. SE6 87 E2
Pellant Rd. SW6 66 B7
Pellatt Gro. N22 40 G1
Pellatt Rd. SE22 77 C5
Pellerin Rd. N16 50 B5
Pelling St. E14 60 A6
Pellipar Clo. N13 32 G3
Pellipar Gdns. SE18 70 C5
Pelly Rd. E13 60 G1
Pelter St. E2 9 F3
Pelter St. E2 59 C3
Pelton Rd. SE10 69 E5
Pembar Ave. E17 41 H3
Pember Rd. NW10 57 A3
Pemberton Gdns. 49 C3
  N19
Pemberton Gdns., 44 E5
  Rom.
Pemberton Ho. SE26 86 D4
  High Level Dr.
Pemberton Pl. E8 50 E7
  Mare St.
Pemberton Rd. N4 40 G5
Pemberton Rd., 90 J4
  E.Mol.
Pemberton Row EC4 12 F2
Pemberton Ter. N19 49 C3
Pembridge Ave., 81 F1
  Twick.

Pembridge Cres. 57 D7
  W11
Pembridge Gdns. 57 D7
  W2
Pembridge Ms. W11 57 D7
Pembridge Pl. W2 57 D7
Pembridge Rd. W11 57 D7
Pembridge Sq. W2 57 D7
Pembridge Vill. W11 57 D7
Pembroke Ave., Har. 37 D3
Pembroke Ave., 92 B5
  Surb.
Pembroke Clo. SW1 15 C4
Pembroke Clo. SW1 67 A2
Pembroke Gdns. W8 66 C4
Pembroke Gdns., 53 H3
  Dag.
Pembroke Gdns. Clo. 66 C3
  W8
Pembroke Ms. E3 59 H3
  Morgan St.
Pembroke Ms. N10 40 A1
  Pembroke Rd.
Pembroke Ms. W8 66 D3
  Earls Wk.
Pembroke Pl. W8 66 D3
Pembroke Pl., Edg. 30 A7
Pembroke Pl., Islw. 73 B2
  Clifton Rd.
Pembroke Rd. E6 61 C5
Pembroke Rd. E17 42 B5
Pembroke Rd. N8 40 E4
Pembroke Rd. N10 40 A1
Pembroke Rd. N13 32 J3
Pembroke Rd. N15 41 C5
Pembroke Rd. SE25 95 B4
Pembroke Rd. W8 66 D4
Pembroke Rd., Brom. 96 J2
Pembroke Rd., Erith 71 J5
Pembroke Rd., Grnf. 54 H3
Pembroke Rd., Ilf. 52 J1
Pembroke Rd., 94 A2
  Mitch.
Pembroke Rd., Wem. 46 G3
Pembroke Sq. W8 66 D3
Pembroke St. N1 49 E7
Pembroke Studios 66 C3
  W8
Pembroke Vill. W8 66 D4
Pembroke Vill., Rich. 73 G4
Pembroke Wk. W8 66 D4
Pembury Ave., 99 G1
  Wor.Pk.
Pembury Clo., Brom. 96 F7
Pembury Cres., Sid. 89 E3
Pembury Pl. E5 50 E5
Pembury Rd. E5 50 E5
Pembury Rd. N17 41 C1
Pembury Rd. SE25 95 D4
Pembury Rd., Bexh. 71 E7
Pemdevon Rd., Croy. 94 G7
Pemell Clo. E1 59 F4
  Colebert Ave.
Pempath Pl., Wem. 46 G2
  Shepperton Rd.
Penally Pl. N1 59 A1
Penang St. E1 68 E1
Penarth St. SE15 68 E6
Penates, Esher 98 A4
Penberth Rd. SE6 87 C1
Penbury Rd., Sthl. 63 F4
Pencombe Ms. W11 57 C7
  Denbigh Rd.
Pencraig Way SE15 68 E6
Penda Rd., Erith 71 H7
Pendarves Rd. SW20 92 J1
Penda's Mead E9 50 H4
  Lindisfarne Way
Pendennis Rd. N17 41 A3
Pendennis Rd. SW16 85 E4
Penderel Rd., 72 G5
  Houns.
Penderry Ri. SE6 87 D2
Penderyn Way N7 49 D4
Pendle Rd. SW16 85 B6
Pendlestone Rd. E17 42 B5
Pendragon Rd., 87 F3
  Brom.
Pendragon Wk. NW9 38 E6
Pendrell Rd. SE4 77 H2
Pendrell St. SE18 70 G6
Pendula Dr., Hayes 54 D4
Penerley Rd. SE6 87 B1
Penfold Clo., Croy. 101 G3
  Epsom Rd.
Penfold La., Bex. 89 D1
  Carisbrooke Ave.
Penfold Pl. NW1 10 G1
Penfold Pl. NW1 57 H5
Penfold Rd. N9 33 G1
Penfold St. NW1 10 G1
Penfold St. NW1 57 H5
Penfold St. NW8 6 F6

Penfold St. NW8 57 J4
Penford Gdns. SE9 79 A3
Penford St. SE5 76 H2
Pengarth Rd., Bex. 80 D5
Penge Ho. SW11 75 G3
  Wye St.
Penge La. SE20 86 F7
Penge Rd. E13 60 J1
Penge Rd. SE20 95 D3
Penge Rd. SE25 95 D3
Penhall Rd. SE7 70 A4
Penhill Rd., Bex. 80 C6
Penhurst Rd., Ilf. 35 E7
Penifather La., Grnf. 55 A3
Penistone Rd. SW16 85 E7
Penketh Dr., Har. 46 A3
Penmon Rd. SE2 71 A3
Penn Clo., Grnf. 54 H2
Penn Clo., Har. 37 F4
Penn Gdns., Chis. 97 E2
Penn La., Bex. 80 D6
Penn Rd. N7 49 E5
Penn St. N1 59 A1
Pennack Rd. SE15 21 G6
Pennack Rd. SE15 68 C6
Pennant Ms. W8 18 A1
Pennant Ms. W8 66 E4
Pennant Ter. E17 41 J2
Pennard Rd. W12 65 J2
Pennards, The, Sun. 90 C2
Penner Clo. SW19 84 B2
  Victoria Dr.
Pennethorne Clo. E9 59 F1
  Victoria Pk. Rd.
Pennethorne Rd. 68 E7
  SE15
Pennine Dr. NW2 48 A2
Pennine La. NW2 48 B2
  Pennine Dr.
Pennington Clo. 86 A4
  SE27
  Hamilton Rd.
Pennington St. E1 13 J6
Pennington St. E1 59 D7
Penny Rd. NW10 56 B3
Pennyfields E14 60 A7
Pennymoor Wk. W9 57 C3
  Ashmore Rd.
Pennyroyal Ave. E6 61 D6
Penpoll Rd. E8 50 E6
Penpool La., Well. 80 B3
Penrhyn Ave. E17 41 J1
Penrhyn Cres. E17 42 A1
Penrhyn Cres. SW14 74 C4
Penrhyn Gro. E17 42 A1
Penrhyn Rd., 91 H4
  Kings.T.
Penrith Clo. SW15 75 B5
Penrith Clo., Beck. 96 B1
  Albemarle Rd.
Penrith Pl. SE27 85 H2
  Harpenden Rd.
Penrith Rd. N15 41 A5
Penrith Rd., Ilf. 35 J6
Penrith Rd., N.Mal. 92 D4
Penrith Rd., 94 J2
  Th.Hth.
Penrith St. SW16 85 C6
Penrose Ave., Wat. 28 D2
Penrose Gro. SE17 20 J4
Penrose Ho. SE17 20 J4
Penrose St. SE17 20 J4
Penrose St. SE17 67 J5
Penry St. SE1 21 E2
Penryn St. NW1 7 H1
Penryn St. NW1 58 D2
Pensbury Pl. SW8 76 C2
Pensbury St. SW8 76 C2
Penscroft Gdns., 22 D4
  Borwd.
Pensford Ave., 74 A2
  Rich.
Penshurst Ave., 80 A6
  Sid.
Penshurst Gdns., 30 B5
  Edg.
Penshurst Grn., 95 F6
  Brom.
Penshurst Rd. E9 50 G7
Penshurst Rd. N17 33 C7
Penshurst Rd., 80 F1
  Bexh.
Penshurst Rd., 94 H5
  Th.Hth.
Penshurst Wk., 96 F5
  Brom.
  Hayesford Pk. Dr.
Penshurst Way, 100 D7
  Sutt.
Penstock Footpath 40 E3
  N22

Pentelowe Gdns., 72 A6
  Felt.
Pentire Rd. E17 42 D1
Pentland Clo. NW11 48 B2
Pentland Gdns. SW18 75 F6
  St. Ann's Hill
Pentland Pl., 54 E1
  Nthlt.
Pentland St. SW18 75 F6
Pentlands Clo., 94 B3
  Mitch.
Pentlow St. SW15 74 J3
Pentlow Way, 27 B7
  Buck.H.
Pentney Rd. E4 34 D3
Pentney Rd. SW12 85 C1
Pentney Rd. SW19 93 B1
  Midmoor Rd.
Penton Gro. N1 8 E2
Penton Pl. SE17 20 H3
Penton Pl. SE17 67 H5
Penton Ri. WC1 8 D3
Penton Ri. WC1 58 F3
Penton St. N1 8 E2
Penton St. N1 58 G2
Pentonville Rd. N1 8 C2
Pentonville Rd. N1 58 F2
Pentridge St. SE15 68 C7
Pentyre Ave. N18 33 H3
Penwerris Ave., 63 J7
  Islw.
Penwith Rd. SW18 84 D2
Penwortham Rd. 85 B6
  SW16
Penylan Pl., Edg. 30 A7
Penywern Rd. SW5 66 D5
Penzance Pl. W11 66 B1
Penzance St. W11 66 B1
Peony Gdns. W12 56 G7
Peploe Rd. NW6 57 A2
Pepper All., Loug. 26 F2
Pepper Clo. E6 61 C5
Pepper St. E14 69 B3
Pepper St. SE1 16 J3
Peppermint Clo., 94 E7
  Croy.
Pepys Cres., Barn. 22 J5
Pepys Ri., Orp. 104 J1
Pepys Rd. SE14 77 G1
Pepys Rd. SW20 92 J2
Pepys St. EC3 13 E5
Pepys St. EC3 59 B7
Perceval Ave. NW3 48 H5
Perch St. E8 50 C4
Percheron Rd., 22 D6
  Borwd.
Percival Ct. N17 33 C7
  High Rd.
Percival Ct., 45 G5
  Nthlt.
Percival Gdns., Rom. 44 C6
Percival Rd. SW14 74 C4
Percival Rd., Enf. 25 C4
Percival Rd., Orp. 104 E2
Percival St. EC1 8 G5
Percival St. EC1 58 H4
Percival Way, Epsom 99 C4
Percy Circ. WC1 8 D3
Percy Circ. WC1 58 F3
Percy Gdns., Enf. 25 G5
Percy Gdns., Islw. 73 D3
Percy Gdns., 99 E1
  Wor.Pk.
Percy Ms. W1 11 H2
Percy Pas. W1 11 G2
Percy Rd. E11 42 E7
Percy Rd. E16 60 E5
Percy Rd. N12 31 F5
Percy Rd. N21 24 J7
Percy Rd. NW6 57 D3
  Stafford Rd.
Percy Rd. SE20 95 G1
Percy Rd. SE25 95 D5
Percy Rd. W12 65 G2
Percy Rd., Bexh. 80 E2
Percy Rd., Dag. 62 F4
Percy Rd., Hmptn. 81 G7
Percy Rd., Ilf. 44 A7
Percy Rd., Islw. 73 D4
Percy Rd., Mitch. 94 A7
Percy Rd., Rom. 44 H3
Percy Rd., Twick. 81 H1
Percy St. W1 11 H2
Percy St. W1 58 D5
Percy Way, Twick. 81 J1
Percy Yd. WC1 8 D3
Peregrine Clo. NW10 47 D5
Peregrine Ct. SW16 85 F4
  Leithcote Gdns.
Peregrine Gdns., 102 H2
  Croy.
Peregrine Ho. EC1 8 H3
Peregrine Ho. EC1 58 H3

Peregrine Way SW19 83 J7
Perham Rd. W14 66 B5
Peridot St. E6 61 B5
Perifield SE21 85 J1
Perimeade Rd., Grnf. 55 F2
Periton Rd. SE9 79 A4
Perivale Gdns. W13 55 E4
  Bellevue Rd.
Perivale Gra., 55 D3
  Grnf.
Perivale Ind. Pk., 55 D1
  Grnf.
Perivale La., Grnf. 55 D3
Perivale New 55 E2
  Business Cen., Grnf.
Perkins Clo., Wem. 46 E5
Perkin's Rents SW1 15 H5
Perkin's Rents SW1 67 D3
Perkins Rd., Ilf. 43 G5
Perks Clo. SE3 78 E3
  Hurren Clo.
Perpins Rd. SE9 79 G6
Perran Rd. SW2 85 H2
  Christchurch Rd.
Perran Wk., Brent. 64 H5
  Burford Rd.
Perren St. NW5 49 B6
  Ryland Rd.
Perrers Rd. W6 56 D6
Perrin Rd., Wem. 46 D4
Perrins Ct. NW3 48 F4
  Hampstead High St.
Perrins La. NW3 48 F4
Perrin's Wk. NW3 48 F4
Perry Ave. W3 56 D6
Perry Ct. N15 41 B6
  Albert Rd.
Perry Gdns. N9 33 B3
  Deansway
Perry Garth, Nthlt. 54 C1
Perry Hall Rd., 97 J6
  Orp.
Perry Hill SE6 86 J3
Perry How, Wor.Pk. 99 F1
Perry Mead, Enf. 24 H2
Perry Ri. SE23 86 H3
Perry St., Chis. 88 G6
Perry St. Gdns., Chis. 88 H6
  Perry St.
Perry Vale SE23 86 F3
Perryfield Way NW9 38 F6
Perryfield Way, 82 E2
  Rich.
Perryman Ho., Bark. 61 F1
Perrymans Fm. Rd., 43 G6
  Ilf.
Perrymead St. SW6 75 D1
Perryn Rd. SE16 68 E3
  Drummond Rd.
Perryn Rd. W3 65 D1
Perrys Pl. W1 11 H3
Persant Rd. SE6 87 E3
Perseverance Pl. 67 G7
  SW9
  Mandela St.
Perseverance Pl., 73 H3
  Rich.
  Shaftesbury Rd.
Pershore Clo., Ilf. 43 E5
Pershore Gro., Cars. 93 G6
Pert Clo. N10 32 B6
Perth Ave. NW9 38 D7
Perth Ave., Hayes 54 C4
Perth Clo. SW20 92 G2
Perth Rd. E10 50 H1
Perth Rd. E13 60 H2
Perth Rd. N4 49 G1
Perth Rd. N22 40 H1
Perth Rd., Bark. 61 G1
Perth Rd., Beck. 96 C2
Perth Rd., Ilf. 43 D6
Perth Ter., Ilf. 43 F7
Perwell Ave., Har. 45 F1
Perwell Ct., Har. 45 F1
Peter Ave. NW10 47 H7
Peter St. W1 11 H5
Peter St. W1 58 D7
Peterboat Clo. SE10 69 E4
  Tunnel Ave.
Peterborough Gdns., 43 B7
  Ilf.
Peterborough Ms. 75 D2
  SW6
Peterborough Rd. 42 C5
  E10
Peterborough Rd. 75 D2
  SW6
Peterborough Rd., 93 H6
  Cars.
Peterborough Rd., 46 B1
  Har.
Peterborough Vill. 75 E1
  SW6

Peterchurch Ho. 68 E6
  SE15
  Commercial Way
Petergate SW11 75 F4
Peters Clo., Dag. 53 D1
Peters Clo., Stan. 29 G6
Peters Clo., Well. 79 H2
Peters Hill EC4 12 J5
Peters La. EC1 12 G1
Peters Path SE26 86 E4
Petersfield Clo. 32 J5
  N18
Petersfield Ri. 83 H1
  SW15
Petersfield Rd. W3 65 C2
Petersham Clo., 82 G2
  Rich.
Petersham Clo., 100 C5
  Sutt.
Petersham Dr., Orp. 97 J2
Petersham Gdns., 97 J2
  Orp.
Petersham La. SW7 14 C5
Petersham La. SW7 66 F3
Petersham Ms. SW7 14 C6
Petersham Ms. SW7 66 F3
Petersham Pl. SW7 14 C5
Petersham Pl. SW7 66 F3
Petersham Rd., 73 G6
  Rich.
Peterstone Rd. SE2 71 B3
Peterstow Clo. SW19 84 B2
Peterwood Way, 101 F2
  Croy.
Petherton Rd. N5 49 J5
Petley Rd. W6 65 J6
Peto Pl. NW1 7 E5
Peto Pl. NW1 58 B4
Peto St. N. E16 60 F7
  Victoria Dock Rd.
Petrie Clo. NW2 48 B6
Pett St. SE18 70 B4
Petticoat Sq. E1 13 F3
Pettits Pl., Dag. 53 G5
Pettits Rd., Dag. 53 G5
Pettiward Clo. SW15 74 J4
Pettman Cres. SE28 70 G3
Petts Hill, Nthlt. 45 H5
Pettsgrove Ave., 46 F5
  Wem.
Petty France SW1 15 G5
Petty France SW1 67 C3
Petworth Clo., 45 F7
  Nthlt.
Petworth Gdns. 92 H3
  SW20
  Hidcote Gdns.
Petworth Rd. N12 31 H5
Petworth Rd., Bexh. 80 G5
Petworth St. SW11 75 H1
Petyt Pl. SW3 18 G6
Petyward SW3 18 H2
Petyward SW3 66 H4
Pevel Ho., Dag. 53 G2
Pevensey Ave. N11 32 D5
Pevensey Ave., Enf. 25 A2
Pevensey Clo., 63 J7
  Islw.
Pevensey Rd. E7 51 F4
Pevensey Rd. SW17 84 G4
Pevensey Rd., Felt. 81 E1
Peverel St. E13 32 B5
Peveret Clo. N11 32 B5
  Woodland Rd.
Peveril Dr., Tedd. 81 E5
Pewsey Clo. E4 34 A5
Peyton Pl. SE10 69 C7
Pheasant Clo. E16 60 H6
  Maplin Rd.
Phelp St. SE17 21 B5
Phelp St. SE17 68 A6
Phene St. SW3 18 H5
Phene St. SW3 66 H6
Philbeach Gdns. SW5 66 D5
Philchurch Pl. E1 13 J4
Philip Gdns., Croy. 102 J2
Philip La. N15 41 A4
Philip St. E13 60 G4
Philip Wk. SE15 77 E3
Philpot Path SE9 79 C6
  Court Yd.
Philippa Gdns. SE9 79 A5
Phillimore Gdns. 56 J1
  NW10
Phillimore Gdns. W8 66 D2
Phillimore Gdns. 66 D3
  Clo. W8
  Phillimore Gdns.
Phillimore Pl. W8 66 D2
Phillimore Wk. W8 66 D3
Phillipp St. N1 59 B1
Philpot La. EC3 13 D5
Philpot Path, Ilf. 52 F3
  Sunnyside Rd.

Philpot Sq. SW6 75 E3
  Peterborough Rd.
Philpot St. E1 59 E6
Phipp St. EC2 9 D5
Phipp St. EC2 59 B4
Phipps Bri. Rd. 93 F2
  SW19
Phipps Bri. Rd., 93 F2
  Mitch.
Phipp's Ms. SW1 15 D6
Phoebeth Rd. SE4 78 A5
Phoenix Clo. E8 59 C1
  Stean St.
Phoenix Clo., 103 D2
  W.Wick.
Phoenix Dr., Kes. 104 A3
Phoenix Pk., Brent. 64 G5
Phoenix Pl. WC1 8 D5
Phoenix Pl. WC1 58 F4
Phoenix Rd. NW1 7 H3
Phoenix Rd. NW1 58 D3
Phoenix Rd. SE20 86 E6
Phoenix St. WC2 11 J4
Phoenix Way, Houns. 63 C6
Phyllis Ave., 92 H5
  N.Mal.
Physic Pl. SW3 18 J4
Picardy Manorway, 71 H3
  Belv.
Picardy Rd., Belv. 71 G5
Picardy St., Belv. 71 G3
Piccadilly W1 15 E2
Piccadilly W1 67 B1
Piccadilly Arc. SW1 15 F1
Piccadilly Circ. W1 11 H6
Piccadilly Circ. W1 58 C7
Piccadilly Pl. W1 11 G6
Pickard St. EC1 8 H3
Pickering Ave. E6 61 D3
  Vicarage La.
Pickering Ms. W2 10 B3
Pickering Pl. SW1 15 G2
Pickering St. N1 58 H1
  Essex Rd.
Pickets Clo. 29 A1
  (Bushey), Wat.
Pickets St. SW12 76 B7
Pickett Cft., Stan. 37 G1
Picketts Lock La. N9 33 F2
Pickford Clo., 80 E2
  Bexh.
Pickford La., Bexh. 80 E4
Pickford Rd., Bexh. 80 E4
Pickford Wf. N1 8 J2
Pickford Wf. N1 58 J2
Pickhurst Grn., 96 F7
  Brom.
Pickhurst La., 96 F7
  Brom.
Pickhurst La., 96 E5
  W.Wick.
Pickhurst Mead, 96 F7
  Brom.
Pickhurst Pk., 96 E5
  Brom.
Pickhurst Ri., 96 C7
  W.Wick.
Pickwick Clo., 72 E5
  Houns.
  Dorney Way
Pickwick Ms. N18 33 B5
Pickwick Pl., Har. 37 B7
Pickwick Rd. SE21 77 A7
Pickwick St. SE1 16 J4
Pickwick Way, Chis. 88 F6
Pickworth Clo. SW8 67 E7
  Kenchester Clo.
Picton Pl. W1 11 C4
Picton St. SE5 68 A6
Piedmont Rd. SE18 70 G5
Pier Head E1 68 E1
  Wapping High St.
Pier Rd. E16 70 D2
Pier Rd., Felt. 72 B5
Pier St. E14 69 C4
Pier Ter. SW18 75 F4
  Jew's Row
Pier Way SE28 70 G3
Piermont Pl., Brom. 92 B2
Piermont Rd. SE22 77 E5
Pierrepoint Rd. W3 56 B7
Pierrepoint Row N1 8 G1
Pigeon La., Hmptn. 81 G4
Piggott St. E14 60 A6
Pike Clo., Brom. 87 H5
Pike Rd. NW7 30 D4
  Ellesmere Ave.
Pikes End, Pnr. 36 B4
Pikestone Clo., 54 E4
  Hayes
  Berrydale Rd.

Pilgrim Hill SE27 85 J4
Pilgrim St. EC4 12 G4
Pilgrim St. EC4 58 H6
Pilgrimage St. SE1 17 B4
Pilgrimage St. SE1 68 A2
Pilgrims Clo. N13 32 F4
Pilgrims Clo., 45 J5
  Nthlt.
Pilgrims Ct. SE3 78 G1
Pilgrim's La. NW3 48 G4
Pilgrims Pl. NW3 48 G4
  Hampstead High St.
Pilgrims Ri., Barn. 23 H5
Pilgrims Way N19 49 D1
Pilgrims Way, 102 C6
  S.Croy.
  Bench Fld.
Pilgrim's Way, Wem. 47 B1
Pilkington Rd. SE15 77 E2
Pilkington Rd., 104 F2
  Orp.
Pilot Ind. Est. 56 D4
  NW10
Pilsdon Clo. SW19 84 A1
  Inner Pk. Rd.
Piltdown Rd., Wat. 28 D4
Pimlico Rd. SW1 19 B3
Pimlico Rd. SW1 67 A5
Pimlico Wk. N1 9 D3
Pinchbeck Rd., Orp. 104 J6
Pinchin St. E1 13 J6
Pinchin St. E1 59 D7
Pincott Rd. SW19 84 F7
Pincott Rd., Bexh. 80 G5
Pindar St. EC2 13 D1
Pindar St. EC2 59 B5
Pindock Ms. W9 6 B6
Pine Ave. E15 51 D5
Pine Ave., W.Wick. 103 B1
Pine Clo. N14 24 C7
Pine Clo. N19 49 C2
  Hargrave Pk.
Pine Clo., Stan. 29 E4
Pine Coombe, Croy. 102 G4
Pine Gdns., Ruis. 45 B1
Pine Gdns., Surb. 92 A6
Pine Glade, Orp. 104 C4
Pine Gro. N4 49 E2
Pine Gro. N20 31 C1
Pine Gro. SW19 84 C5
Pine Rd. N11 32 A2
Pine Rd. NW2 47 J4
Pine St. EC1 8 E5
Pine St. EC1 58 G4
Pine Tree Clo., 72 B1
  Houns.
Pine Wk., Surb. 92 A6
Pine Wd., Sun. 90 A1
Pineapple Ct. SW1 15 F5
Pinecrest Gdns., 104 E4
  Orp.
Pinedene SE15 77 E1
  Meeting Ho. La.
Pinefield Clo. E14 60 A7
Pinelands Clo. SE3 69 F7
  St. John's Pk.
Pines, The N14 24 C5
Pines, The, Sun. 90 A3
Pines, The, 34 G3
  Wdf.Grn.
Pines Rd., Brom. 97 B2
Pinewood Ave., Pnr. 28 H6
Pinewood Ave., Sid. 88 H1
Pinewood Clo., 22 D1
  Borwd.
Pinewood Clo., 102 H3
  Croy.
Pinewood Clo., Orp. 104 G1
Pinewood Clo., Pnr. 28 H6
Pinewood Dr., Orp. 104 H5
Pinewood Gro. W5 55 F6
Pinewood Rd. SE2 71 D6
Pinewood Rd., Brom. 96 G4
Pinewood Rd., Felt. 81 B3
Pinfold Rd. SW16 85 E4
Pinkcoat Clo., 81 B3
  Felt.
  Tanglewood Way
Pinkerton Pl. SW16 85 D4
  Riggindale Rd.
Pinkham Way N11 32 A7
Pinley Gdns., Dag. 62 B1
  Stamford Rd.
Pinnacle Hill, 80 H3
  Bexh.
Pinnacle Hill N., 80 H3
  Bexh.
Pinnell Rd. SE9 79 A4
Pinnell Rd. SE9 79 A4
Pinner Ct., Pnr. 36 G4
Pinner Grn., Pnr. 36 C2
Pinner Gro., Pnr. 36 E4
Pinner Hill, Pnr. 28 B7

Pinner Hill Rd., Pnr.	36	C1
Pinner Pk. Ave., Har.	36	H3
Pinner Pk. Gdns., Har.	36	J2
Pinner Rd., Har.	36	H5
Pinner Rd., Pnr.	36	F4
Pinner Vw., Har.	36	J4
Pintail Clo. E6	61	B5
Swan App.		
Pintail Rd., Wdf.Grn.	34	H7
Pinto Clo., Borwd.	22	D6
Percheron Rd.		
Pinto Way SE3	78	H4
Pioneer Way W12	56	H6
Du Cane Rd.		
Piper Clo. N7	49	F5
Piper Rd., Kings.T.	92	A3
Pipers Gdns., Croy.	95	H7
Pipers Grn. NW9	38	C5
Pipers Grn. La., Edg.	29	H3
Pipewell Rd., Cars.	93	H6
Pippin Clo., Croy.	102	J1
Piquet Rd. SE20	95	F2
Pirbright Cres., Croy.	103	C6
Pirbright Rd. SW18	84	C1
Pirie St. SE5	77	A3
Denmark Hill		
Pirie St. E16	69	H1
Pitcairn Clo., Rom.	44	G4
Pitcairn Rd., Mitch.	84	J7
Pitchford St. E15	51	D7
Pitfield Cres. SE28	71	A1
Pitfield Est. N1	**9**	**D3**
Pitfield St. N1	**9**	**D4**
Pitfield St. N1	59	B3
Pitfield Way NW10	47	C6
Pitfield Way, Enf.	25	F1
Pitfold Clo. SE12	78	G6
Pitfold Rd. SE12	78	G6
Pitlake, Croy.	101	H2
Pitman St. SE5	20	J7
Pitman St. SE5	67	J7
Pitsea Pl. E1	59	G6
Pitsea St.		
Pitsea St. E1	59	G6
Pitshanger La. W5	55	E4
Pitshanger Pk. W13	55	D4
Pitt Cres. SW19	84	E4
Pitt Rd., Har.	45	J2
Pitt Rd., Orp.	104	F4
Pitt Rd., Th.Hth.	94	J5
Pitt St. SE15	68	C7
Pitt St. W8	66	D2
Pittman Gdns., Ilf.	52	F5
Pitt's Head Ms. W1	**15**	**C2**
Pitt's Head Ms. W1	67	A1
Pittsmead Ave., Brom.	96	G7
Pittville Gdns. SE25	95	D3
Pixfield Ct., Brom.	96	F2
Beckenham La.		
Pixley St. E14	59	J6
Place Fm. Ave., Orp.	104	G1
Plaistow Gro. E15	60	F1
Plaistow Gro., Brom.	87	H7
Plaistow La., Brom.	87	G7
Plaistow Pk. Rd. E13	60	H2
Plaistow Rd. E15	60	F1
Plane St. SE26	86	E3
Plane Tree Cres., Felt.	81	B3
Plane Tree Wk. SE19	86	B6
Central Hill		
Plantagenet Clo., Wor.Pk.	99	D4
Plantagenet Gdns., Rom.	44	D7
Broomfield Rd.		
Plantagenet Pl., Rom.	44	D7
Broomfield Rd.		
Plantagenet Rd., Barn.	23	F4
Plantain Pl. SE1	**17**	**B3**
Plantation, The SE3	78	G2
Plasel Ct. E13	60	G1
Plashet Rd.		
Plashet Gro. E6	60	J1
Plashet Rd. E13	60	G1
Plassy Rd. SE6	78	B7
Platina St. EC2	**9**	**C5**
Plato Rd. SW2	76	E4
Platt, The SW15	75	A3
Platt St. NW1	**7**	**H1**
Platt St. NW1	58	D2
Platt's La. NW3	48	D4
Platts Rd., Enf.	25	F1
Plawsfield Rd., Beck.	95	G1
Plaxtol Clo., Brom.	96	J1
Plaxtol Rd., Erith	71	G6
Playfield Ave., Rom.	44	J1
Playfield Cres. SE22	77	C5
Playfield Rd., Edg.	38	C2
Playford Rd. N4	49	F2
Playgreen Way SE6	87	A3
Playground Clo., Beck.	95	G2
Churchfields Rd.		
Playhouse Yd. EC4	12	G4
Plaza W., Houns.	72	H1
Pleasance, The SW15	74	H4
Pleasance Rd. SW15	74	H5
Pleasant Gro., Croy.	102	J3
Pleasant Pl. N1	49	H7
Pleasant Rd., Kings.T.	92	C3
Pleasant Row NW1	58	B1
Camden High St.		
Pleasant Way, Wem.	55	F2
Plender St. NW1	58	C1
Plender St. Est. NW1	58	C1
Plender St.		
Pleshey Rd. N7	49	D4
Plevna Cres. N15	41	B6
Plevna Rd. N9	33	D3
Plevna Rd., Hmptn.	90	H1
Plevna St. E14	69	C3
Pleydell Ave. SE19	86	C7
Pleydell Ave. W6	65	F4
Pleydell Ct. EC4	58	G6
Fleet St.		
Pleydell St. EC4	**12**	**F4**
Plimsoll Clo. E14	60	B6
Grundy St.		
Plimsoll Rd. N4	49	G3
Plough Ct. EC3	**13**	**C5**
Plough La. SE22	77	C6
Plough La. SW17	84	F4
Plough La. SW19	84	E5
Plough La., Wall.	101	E4
Plough La. Clo., Wall.	101	E5
Plough Pl. EC4	**12**	**F3**
Plough Rd. SW11	75	G3
Plough Ter. SW11	75	G4
Plough Way SE16	68	G4
Plough Yd. EC2	**9**	**E6**
Plough Yd. EC2	59	B4
Ploughmans Clo. NW1	58	D1
Crofters Way		
Ploughmans End, Islw.	73	A5
Plover Way SE16	68	H3
Plowman Clo. N18	33	A5
Plowman Way, Dag.	53	C1
Plum Garth, Brent.	64	G4
Plum La. SE18	70	E7
Plumbers Row E1	**13**	**J2**
Plumbers Row E1	59	D5
Plumbridge St. SE10	78	C1
Blackheath Hill		
Plummer La., Mitch.	93	J2
Plummer Rd. SW4	76	D7
Plumpton Clo., Nthlt.	45	G6
Plumpton Way, Cars.	100	H3
Plumstead Common Rd. SE18	70	E6
Plumstead High St. SE18	70	G4
Plumstead Rd. SE18	70	E4
Plumtree Clo., Wall.	101	D7
Plumtree Ct. EC4	**12**	**G3**
Plumtree Mead, Loug.	27	D3
Plymouth Rd. E16	60	G5
Plymouth Rd., Brom.	96	H1
Plymouth Wf. E14	69	D4
Plympton Ave. NW6	48	C7
Plympton Clo., Belv.	71	E3
Halifield Dr.		
Plympton Pl. NW8	**6**	**G6**
Plympton Rd. NW6	48	C7
Plympton St. NW8	**6**	**G6**
Plympton St. NW8	57	H4
Plymstock Rd., Well.	71	C7
Pocklington Clo. NW9	38	E2
Pocock St. SE1	16	G3
Pocock St. SE1	67	H2
Podmore Rd. SW18	75	F4
Poets Rd. N5	50	A5
Poets Way, Har.	37	B4
Blawith Rd.		
Point Clo. SE10	78	C1
Point Hill		
Point Hill SE10	69	C7
Point Pleasant SW18	75	D4
Pointalls Clo. N3	39	F2
Pointer Clo. SE28	62	D6
Pointers Clo. E14	69	B5
Pointers Cotts., Rich.	82	F2
Poland St. W1	11	G3
Poland St. W1	58	C6
Pole Cat All., Brom.	103	F2
Pole Hill Rd. E4	26	C7
Polebrook Rd. SE3	78	J3
Polecroft La. SE6	86	J2
Polesden Gdns. SW20	92	H2
Polesworth Ho. W2	57	D5
Polesworth Rd., Dag.	53	D7
Pollard Clo. E16	60	G7
Pollard Clo. N7	49	F4
Pollard Rd. N20	31	H2
Pollard Rd., Mord.	85	G5
Pollard Row E2	**9**	**J3**
Pollard Row E2	59	D3
Pollard St. E2	**9**	**J3**
Pollard St. E2	59	D3
Pollard Wk., Sid.	89	C6
Evry Rd.		
Pollards Clo., Loug.	26	J5
Pollards Cres. SW16	94	E3
Pollards Hill E. SW16	94	F3
Pollards Hill N. SW16	94	E3
Pollards Hill S. SW16	94	E3
Pollards Hill W. SW16	94	E3
Pollards Wd. Rd. SW16	94	E2
Pollen St. W1	11	F4
Pollitt Dr. NW8	6	F5
Polperro Clo., Orp.	97	J6
Cotswold Ri.		
Polsted Rd. SE6	77	J7
Polthorne Gro. SE18	70	F4
Polworth Rd. SW16	85	E5
Polygon, The SW4	76	C4
Old Town		
Polygon Rd. NW1	7	H2
Polygon Rd. NW1	58	D2
Polytechnic St. SE18	70	D4
Pomell Way E1	13	G3
Pomeroy St. SE14	77	F1
Pomfret Rd. SE5	76	H3
Flaxman Rd.		
Pond Clo. SE3	78	F2
Pond Cottage La., W.Wick.	103	A1
Pond Cotts. SE21	86	B1
Pond Hill Gdns., Sutt.	100	B6
Pond Mead SE21	77	A6
Pond Pl. SW3	**18**	**G2**
Pond Pl. SW3	66	H4
Pond Rd. E15	60	E2
Pond Rd. SE3	78	F2
Pond Sq. N6	49	A1
South Gro.		
Pond St. NW3	48	H5
Pond Way, Tedd.	82	F6
Holmesdale Rd.		
Ponder St. N7	49	F7
Ponders End Ind. Est., Enf.	25	J4
Pondfield Rd., Brom.	103	E1
Pondfield Rd., Dag.	53	H5
Pondfield Rd., Orp.	104	E3
Pondwood Ri., Orp.	97	H1
Ponler St. E1	59	E6
Ponsard Rd. NW10	56	H3
Ponsford St. E9	51	F5
Ponsonby Pl. SW1	**19**	**J3**
Ponsonby Pl. SW1	67	D5
Ponsonby Rd. SW15	74	H7
Ponsonby Ter. SW1	**19**	**J3**
Ponsonby Ter. SW1	67	D5
Pont St. SW1	**14**	**J6**
Pont St. SW1	66	J3
Pont St. Ms. SW1	**14**	**J6**
Pont St. Ms. SW1	66	J3
Pontefract Rd., Brom.	87	F5
Ponton Rd. SW8	**19**	**J6**
Ponton Rd. SW8	67	D6
Pontypool Pl. SE1	**16**	**G3**
Pool Clo., Beck.	87	A5
Pool Clo., W.Mol.	90	F5
Pool Rd., Har.	37	A7
Pool Rd., W.Mol.	90	F5
Poole Ct. E1	72	E2
Vicarage Fm. Rd.		
Poole Rd. E9	50	G6
Poole Rd., Epsom	99	D6
Poole St. N1	59	A1
Pooles Bldgs. EC1	**8**	**E6**
Pooles La. SW10	66	F7
Lots Rd.		
Pooles La., Dag.	62	E2
Pooles Pk. N4	49	G2
Seven Sisters Rd.		
Poolmans St. SE16	68	G2
Poolsford Rd. NW9	38	E4
Poonah St. E1	59	F6
Hardinge St.		
Pope Clo. SW19	84	G6
Shelley Way		
Pope Rd., Brom.	97	A5
Pope St. SE1	**17**	**E4**
Pope St. SE1	68	B2
Popes Ave., Twick.	82	B2
Popes Dr. N3	39	D1
Popes Gro., Croy.	102	J3
Popes Gro., Twick.	82	B2
Pope's Head All. EC3	59	A6
Cornhill		
Popes La. W5	64	G3
Popes Rd. SW9	76	G3
Popham Clo., Felt.	81	F3
Popham Rd. N1	58	J1
Popham St. N1	58	J1
Poplar Ave., Mitch.	93	J1
Poplar Ave., Orp.	104	E2
Poplar Ave., Sthl.	63	H3
Poplar Bath St. E14	60	B7
Lawless St.		
Poplar Clo., Pnr.	36	D1
Poplar Ct. SW19	84	D5
Poplar Cres., Epsom	99	C6
Poplar Fm. Clo., Epsom	99	C6
Poplar Gdns., N.Mal.	92	D2
Poplar Gro. N11	32	A6
Poplar Gro. W6	65	J2
Poplar Gro., N.Mal.	92	D3
Poplar Gro., Wem.	47	C3
Poplar High St. E14	60	B7
Poplar Mt., Belv.	71	H4
Poplar Pl. SE28	62	C7
Poplar Pl. W2	**10**	**A5**
Poplar Pl. W2	57	E7
Poplar Pl., Hayes	54	A7
Central Ave.		
Poplar Rd. SE24	76	J4
Poplar Rd. SW19	93	D2
Poplar Rd., Sutt.	100	C1
Poplar Rd. S. SW19	93	D3
Poplar St., Rom.	44	J4
Poplar Wk. SE24	76	J4
Poplar Wk., Croy.	101	J2
Poplar Way, Felt.	81	A3
Poplar Way, Ilf.	43	F4
Poplars, The N14	24	B5
Poplars Ave. NW2	47	J6
Poplars Rd. E17	42	B6
Poppins Ct. EC4	**12**	**G4**
Poppleton Rd. E11	42	E6
Poppy Clo., Wall.	101	A1
Poppy La., Croy.	95	F7
Porch Way N20	31	J3
Porchester Gdns. W2	10	B5
Porchester Gdns. W2	57	E7
Porchester Gdns. Ms. W2	10	B4
Porchester Mead, Beck.	87	A6
Porchester Pl. W2	**10**	**B3**
Porchester Pl. W2	**10**	**H4**
Porchester Pl. W2	57	H6
Porchester Rd. W2	**10**	**B3**
Porchester Rd. W2	57	E5
Porchester Rd., Kings.T.	92	B2
Porchester Sq. W2	**10**	**B3**
Porchester Sq. W2	57	E6
Porchester Ter. W2	**10**	**C5**
Porchester Ter. W2	57	F7
Porchester Ter. N. W2	**10**	**B3**
Porchester Ter. N. W2	57	E6
Porcupine Clo. SE9	88	B2
Porden Rd. SW2	76	F4

Porlock Ave., Har. 45 J1
Porlock Rd. W10 57 A4
  Ladbroke Gro.
Porlock Rd., Enf. 25 C7
Porlock St. SE1 17 C3
Porlock St. SE1 68 A2
Porrington Clo., 97 D1
  Chis.
Port Cres. E13 60 H4
  Jenkins Rd.
Portal Clo. SE27 85 G3
Portal Clo., Ruis. 45 A4
Portbury Clo. SE15 77 D1
  Clayton Rd.
Portchester Clo. SE5 77 A4
Portcullis Lo. Rd., 25 A3
  Enf.
Portelet Rd. E1 59 G3
Porten Rd. W14 66 B3
Porter Rd. E6 61 C6
Porter St. SE1 17 A1
Porter St. W1 11 A1
Porters Ave., Dag. 53 B6
Porters Wk. E1 59 E7
  Pennington St.
Portersfield Rd., 25 B4
  Enf.
Porteus Rd. W2 10 D1
Porteus Rd. W2 57 A4
Portgate Clo. W9 57 C4
Porthcawe Rd. SE26 86 H4
Porthkerry Ave., 80 A4
  Well.
Portia Way E3 59 J4
Portinscale Rd. 75 B5
  SW15
Portland Ave. N16 41 C7
Portland Ave., 92 F7
  N.Mal.
Portland Ave., Sid. 80 A6
Portland Clo., Rom. 44 E5
Portland Cres. SE9 88 B2
Portland Cres., 54 H4
  Grnf.
Portland Cres., Stan. 37 G2
Portland Gdns. N4 40 H6
Portland Gro. SW8 76 F1
Portland Ms. W1 11 G4
Portland Pl. W1 7 D6
Portland Pl. W1 58 B5
Portland Ri. N4 49 H1
Portland Ri. Est. 49 J1
  N4
Portland Rd. N15 41 C4
Portland Rd. SE9 88 B2
Portland Rd. SE25 95 D4
Portland Rd. W11 57 B7
Portland Rd., Brom. 88 J2
Portland Rd., 91 H3
  Kings.T.
Portland Rd., 93 H2
  Mitch.
Portland Rd., Sthl. 63 F3
Portland Sq. E1 68 E1
  Vinegar Rd.
Portland St. SE17 21 B3
Portland St. SE17 68 A5
Portland Ter., 73 G4
  Rich.
Portland Wk. SE15 21 C5
Portland Wk. SE17 21 C5
Portman Ave. SW14 74 D3
Portman Clo. W1 11 A3
Portman Clo. W1 57 J6
Portman Clo., Bexh. 80 D3
  Queen Anne's Gate
Portman Dr., 43 A2
  Wdf.Grn.
Portman Gdns. NW9 38 D2
Portman Ms. S. W1 11 B4
Portman Ms. S. W1 59 F3
Portman Pl. E2 59 F3
Portman Rd., 91 J2
  Kings.T.
Portman Sq. W1 11 B3
Portman Sq. W1 58 A6
Portman St. W1 11 B4
Portman St. W1 58 A6
Portmeadow Wk. SE2 71 D2
Portmeers Clo. E17 41 J6
  Lennox Rd.
Portnall Rd. W9 57 C2
Portobello Ct. SE15 57 C7
  Westbourne Gro.
Portobello Ms. W11 57 D7
  Portobello Rd.
Portobello Rd. W10 57 B5
Portobello Rd. W11 57 C6
Porton Ct., Surb. 91 F6
Portpool La. EC1 12 E1
Portpool La. EC1 58 D5
Portree Clo. N22 32 F7
  Nightingale Rd.

Portree St. E14 60 D6
Portsdown Ave. 39 C6
  NW11
Portsdown Ms. 39 C6
  NW11
Portsea Ms. W2 10 H4
Portsea Pl. W2 10 H4
Portslade Rd. SW8 76 C2
Portsmouth Ave., 91 D7
  T.Ditt.
Portsmouth Rd. 74 H7
  SW15
Portsmouth Rd., 91 G4
  Kings.T.
Portsmouth Rd., 91 F6
  Surb.
Portsmouth Rd., 98 B2
  T.Ditt.
Portsmouth St. WC2 12 C4
Portsoken St. E1 13 F5
Portsoken St. E1 59 C7
Portswood Pl. SW15 74 F7
  Danebury Ave.
Portugal Gdns., 81 J2
  Twick.
  Fulwell Pk. Ave.
Portugal St. WC2 12 C4
Portugal St. WC2 58 F6
Portway E15 60 F1
Portway Gdns. SE18 70 A7
  Shooter's Hill Rd.
Post La., Twick. 82 A1
Post Office App. E7 51 H6
Post Office Ct. EC3 13 C4
Post Office Way SW8 19 H7
Post Office Way SW8 67 D7
Postern Grn., Enf. 24 G2
Postway Ms., Ilf. 52 E3
  Clements Rd.
Potier St. SE1 17 C6
Potier St. SE1 68 A3
Pott St. E2 59 E3
Potter Clo., Mitch. 94 B2
Potter St., Nthwd. 36 A1
Potter St., Pnr. 36 B1
Potter St. Hill, Pnr. 28 B6
Potterne Clo. SW19 75 A7
  Castlecombe Dr.
Potters Clo., Croy. 102 H1
Potters Clo., Loug. 27 B2
Potters Gro., 92 C4
  N.Mal.
Potters Heights 28 B7
  Clo., Pnr.
Potters La. SW16 85 D6
Potters La., Barn. 23 D4
Potters La., Borwd. 22 C1
Potters Rd., Barn. 23 E4
Pottery La. W11 57 B7
  Portland Rd.
Pottery Rd., Bex. 89 J2
Pottery Rd., Brent. 64 H6
Pottery St. SE16 68 E2
Poulett Gdns., 82 C1
  Twick.
Poulett Rd. E6 61 C2
Poulner Way SE15 68 C7
  Daniel Gdns.
Poulters Wd., Kes. 104 A5
Poulton Ave., Sutt. 100 G3
Poulton Clo. E8 50 E5
  Spurstowe Ter.
Poultry EC2 13 B4
Poultry EC2 59 A6
Pound Clo., Orp. 104 G2
Pound Clo., Surb. 98 F1
Pound Ct. Dr., Orp. 104 G2
Pound La. NW10 47 G6
Pound Pk. Rd. SE7 70 A4
Pound Pl. SE9 79 D6
Pound St., Cars. 100 J5
Poundfield Rd., 27 D5
  Loug.
Pountney Rd. SW11 76 A3
Poverest Rd., Orp. 97 J5
Powder Mill La., 72 F7
  Twick.
Powell Clo., Edg. 29 J6
Powell Clo., Wall. 101 D7
  Hermes Way
Powell Gdns., Dag. 53 G4
Powell Rd. E5 50 E3
Powell Rd., Buck.H. 26 J7
Powell's Wk. W4 65 E6
Power Rd. W4 65 A4
Powers Ct., Twick. 73 G7
Powerscroft Rd. E5 50 F4
Powerscroft Rd., 89 C6
  Sid.
Powis Gdns. NW11 39 C7
Powis Gdns. W11 57 C6
Powis Ms. W11 57 C6
  Westbourne Pk. Rd.

Powis Pl. WC1 8 B6
Powis Pl. WC1 58 B6
Powis Rd. E3 60 B3
Powis Sq. W11 57 C6
Powis St. SE18 70 D3
Powis Ter. W11 57 C6
Powlett Pl. NW1 49 B6
  Harmood St.
Pownall Gdns., 72 H4
  Houns.
Pownall Rd. E8 59 D1
Pownall Rd., Houns. 72 H4
Powster Rd., Brom. 87 H5
Powys Clo., Bexh. 71 D6
Powys La. N13 32 E4
Powys La. N14 32 E4
Poynders Ct. SW4 76 C6
  Poynders Rd.
Poynders Gdns. SW4 76 C7
Poynders Rd. SW4 76 C6
Poynings Rd. N19 49 C3
Poynings Way N12 31 D5
Poyntell Cres., Chis. 97 G1
Poynter Rd., Enf. 25 D5
Poynton Rd. N17 41 D2
Poyntz Rd. SW11 75 J2
Poyser St. E2 59 E2
Praed Ms. W2 10 F3
Praed St. W2 10 F3
Praed St. W2 57 G6
Pragel St. E13 60 H2
Pragnell Rd. SE12 87 H2
Prague Pl. SW2 76 E5
Prah Rd. N4 49 G2
Prairie St. SW8 76 H2
Pratt Ms. NW1 58 C1
  Pratt St.
Pratt St. NW1 58 C1
Pratt Wk. SE11 20 D1
Pratt Wk. SE11 67 F4
Pratts Pas., Kings.T. 91 H2
  Eden St.
Prayle Gro. NW2 48 A1
Prebend Gdns. W4 65 F4
Prebend Gdns. W6 65 F4
Prebend St. N1 58 J1
Precinct, The, 90 H3
  W.Mol.
  Victoria Ave.
Precinct Rd., Hayes 54 A7
Precincts, The, 93 E6
  Mord.
  Green La.
Precincts, The, 93 F5
  Mord.
Premier Cor. W9 57 C2
  Kilburn La.
Prendergast Rd. SE3 78 E3
Prentis Rd. SW16 85 D4
Prentiss Ct. SE7 70 A4
Presburg Rd., 92 E5
  N.Mal.
Prescelly Pl., Edg. 37 J1
Prescot St. E1 13 G5
Prescot St. E1 59 C7
Prescott Ave., Orp. 97 E6
Prescott Clo. SW16 85 E7
Prescott Grn., 27 F3
  Loug.
Prescott Ho. SE17 20 H6
Prescott Pl. SW4 76 D3
President Dr. E1 68 E1
  Waterman Way
President St. EC1 8 J3
Press Rd. NW10 47 D3
Prestbury Rd. E7 51 J7
Prestbury Sq. SE9 88 C4
Prested Rd. SW11 75 H4
  St. Johns Hill
Preston Ave. E4 34 D6
Preston Clo. SE1 21 D1
Preston Clo., 82 B3
  Twick.
Preston Dr. E11 42 J5
Preston Dr., Bexh. 80 D1
Preston Dr., Epsom 99 E6
Preston Gdns. NW10 47 E6
  Church Rd.
Preston Gdns., Ilf. 43 B6
Preston Hill, Har. 37 H7
Preston Pl. NW2 47 G6
Preston Rd. E11 42 E6
Preston Rd. SE19 85 H6
Preston Rd. SW20 83 F7
Preston Rd., Har. 37 H7
Preston Rd., Wem. 46 H2
Preston Waye, Har. 46 H1
Prestons Rd. E14 69 C2
Prestons Rd., Brom. 103 G3
Prestwick Clo., 63 E5
  Sthl.
  Ringway

Prestwick Rd., Wat. 28 C1
Prestwood Ave., 37 E4
  Har.
Prestwood Clo. SE18 71 A7
Prestwood Clo., 37 E4
  Har.
Prestwood Gdns., 94 J7
  Croy.
Prestwood St. N1 9 A2
Pretoria Ave. E17 41 H4
Pretoria Clo. N17 33 C7
  Pretoria Rd.
Pretoria Cres. E4 34 C1
Pretoria Rd. E4 34 C1
Pretoria Rd. E11 51 D1
Pretoria Rd. E16 60 F4
Pretoria Rd. N17 33 C7
Pretoria Rd. SW16 85 B6
Pretoria Rd., Ilf. 52 E5
Pretoria Rd., Rom. 44 J4
Pretoria Rd. N. N18 33 C6
Prevost Rd. N11 32 A2
Price Clo. NW7 31 B6
Price Clo. SW17 84 J3
Price Rd., Croy. 101 H4
Price Way, Hmptn. 81 E6
  Victors Dr.
Price's St. SE1 16 H2
Price's St. SE1 67 H1
Pricklers Hill, 23 E6
  Barn.
Prickley Wd., Brom. 103 F1
Priddy's Yd., Croy. 101 J2
  Crown Rd.
Prideaux Pl. W3 56 D7
  Friars Pl. La.
Prideaux Pl. WC1 8 D3
Prideaux Pl. WC1 58 F3
Prideaux Rd. SW9 76 E3
Pridham Rd., 95 A4
  Th.Hth.
Priest Ct. EC2 12 J3
Priest Pk. Ave., Har. 45 G2
Priestfield Rd. 86 H3
  SE23
Priestlands Pk. 88 J3
  Rd., Sid.
  Ravensdale Rd.
Priestley Clo. N16 41 C7
Priestley Gdns., 44 B6
  Rom.
Priestley Rd., 94 A2
  Mitch.
Priestley Way E17 41 G3
Priestley Way NW2 47 G1
Priests Bri. SW14 74 E3
Prima Rd. SW9 20 E7
Prima Rd. SW9 67 G2
Primrose Ave., Enf. 25 A1
Primrose Ave., Rom. 44 A7
Primrose Clo. SE6 87 C5
Primrose Clo., Har. 45 F3
Primrose Clo., 94 B7
  Wall.
Primrose Gdns. NW3 48 H6
Primrose Gdns., 45 C5
  Ruis.
Primrose Hill EC4 12 F4
Primrose Hill Ct. 48 J7
  NW3
Primrose Hill Rd. 48 J7
  NW3
Primrose Hill 58 A1
  Studios NW1
  Fitzroy Rd.
Primrose La., Croy. 102 F1
Primrose Ms. NW1 48 J7
  Sharpleshall St.
Primrose Rd. E10 51 B1
Primrose Rd. E18 42 H1
Primrose St. EC2 13 D1
Primrose St. EC2 59 B5
Primrose Way, Wem. 55 G2
Primula St. W12 56 G6
Prince Albert Rd. 6 H2
  NW1
Prince Albert Rd. 58 A1
  NW1
Prince Albert Rd. 6 H2
  NW8
Prince Albert Rd. 57 H3
  NW8
Prince Arthur Ms. 48 F4
  NW3
  Perrins La.
Prince Arthur Rd. 48 F5
  NW3
Prince Charles Dr. 38 J7
  NW4
Prince Charles Rd. 78 F2
  SE3
Prince Charles Way, 101 B3
  Wall.

Name	Ref
Prince Consort Dr., Chis.	97 G1
Prince Consort Rd. SW7	14 E5
Prince Consort Rd. SW7	66 F3
Prince Edward Rd. E9	50 J6
Prince George Ave. N14	24 C4
Prince George Duke of Kent Ct., Chis.	88 G7
Holbrook La.	
Prince George Rd. N16	50 B4
Prince George's Ave. SW20	92 J2
Prince George's Rd. SW19	93 G1
Prince Henry Rd. SE7	70 A7
Prince Imperial Rd. SE18	79 C1
Prince Imperial Rd. Chis.	88 E7
Prince John Rd. SE9	79 B5
Prince of Orange La. SE10	69 C7
Greenwich High Rd.	
Prince of Wales Clo. NW4	38 H4
Church Ter.	
Prince of Wales Dr SW8	67 B7
Prince of Wales Dr. SW11	75 H1
Prince of Wales Gate SW7	14 G4
Prince of Wales Gate SW7	66 H2
Prince of Wales Pas. NW1	7 F4
Prince of Wales Rd. E16	60 J6
Prince of Wales Rd. NW5	49 A6
Prince of Wales Rd. SE3	78 F1
Prince of Wales Rd., Sutt.	100 G2
Prince of Wales Ter. W4	65 E5
Prince of Wales Ter. W8	14 B4
Prince Regent La. E13	60 H3
Prince Regent La. E16	60 J5
Prince Regent Rd., Houns.	72 J3
Prince Rd. SE25	95 B5
Prince Rupert Rd. SE9	79 C4
Prince St. SE8	68 J6
Princedale Rd. W11	66 B1
Princelet St. E1	13 G1
Princelet St. E1	59 C5
Prince's Ave. SW1	15 G1
Princes Ave. N3	39 D1
Princes Ave. N10	40 B3
Princes Ave. N13	32 G5
Princes Ave. N22	40 D1
Princes Ave. NW9	38 A4
Princes Ave. W3	65 A3
Princes Ave., Cars.	100 J7
Princes Ave., Grnf.	54 H6
Princes Ave., Orp.	97 H5
Princes Ave., Surb.	99 A1
Princes Ave., Wdf.Grn.	34 H4
Princes Clo. N4	39 A4
Princes Clo. SW4	76 C3
Old Town	
Princes Clo., Edg.	30 A5
Princes Clo., Sid.	89 D3
Princes Clo., Tedd.	82 A4
Princes Ct. E1	59 E7
Princes Ct., Wem.	46 H5
Princes Dr., Har.	37 B3
Princes Gdns. SW7	14 F5
Princes Gdns. SW7	66 G3
Princes Gdns. W3	56 A5
Princes Gdns. W5	55 H3
Princes Gate SW7	14 F4
Princes Gate SW7	66 H2
Princes Gate Ct. SW7	14 F4
Princes Gate Ms. SW7	14 F5
Princes Gate Ms. SW7	66 G3
Princes La. N10	40 B3
Princes Ms. W2	10 A5
Princes Ms. W2	57 D7
Hereford Rd.	
Princes Pk. Ave. NW11	39 B6
Princes Pl. SW1	15 G1
Princes Pl. W11	66 B1
Princes Plain, Brom.	97 B7
Princes Ri. SE13	78 C2
Princes Rd. N18	33 F4
Princes Rd. SE20	86 G6
Princes Rd. SW14	74 D3
Princes Rd. SW19	84 D6
Princes Rd. W13	64 E1
Broomfield Rd.	
Princes Rd., Buck.H.	34 J2
Princes Rd., Ilf.	43 G4
Princes Rd., Kings.T.	92 A1
Princes Rd., Rich.	73 J5
Princes Rd. (Kew), Rich.	73 J1
Princes Rd., Tedd.	82 A4
Princes Sq. W2	10 A5
Princes Sq. W2	57 E7
Princes St. EC2	13 B4
Princes St. EC2	59 A6
Princes St. N17	33 B6
Queen St.	
Princes St. W1	11 E4
Princes St. W1	58 B6
Princes St., Bexh.	80 F4
Princes St., Rich.	73 H5
Sheen Rd.	
Princes St., Sutt.	100 G4
Princes Ter. E13	60 H1
Princes Way SW19	75 A7
Princes Way, Buck.H.	34 J2
Princes Way, Croy.	101 F5
Princes Way, Ruis.	45 G4
Princes Way, W.Wick.	103 F4
Princes Yd. W11	66 B1
Princedale Rd.	
Princess Ave., Wem.	46 H2
Princess Ct. SE16	68 J3
Princess Cres. N4	49 H2
Princess May Rd. N16	50 B4
Princess Ms. NW3	48 G6
Belsize Cres.	
Princess Rd. NW1	58 A1
Princess Rd. NW6	57 D2
Princess Rd., Croy.	94 J6
Princess St. SE1	16 H6
Princess St. SE1	67 H3
Princesses Wk., Rich.	64 H7
Kew Rd.	
Princethorpe Ho. W2	10 A1
Princethorpe Ho. W2	57 E5
Princethorpe Rd. SE26	86 G4
Princeton St. WC1	12 C2
Princeton St. WC1	58 F5
Pringle Gdns. SW16	85 C4
Printer St. EC4	12 F3
Printing Ho. Yd. E2	9 E4
Priolo Rd. SE7	69 J5
Prior Ave., Sutt.	100 H7
Prior Bolton St. N1	49 H6
Prior Rd., Ilf.	52 D3
Prior St. SE10	69 C7
Prioress Rd. SE27	85 H3
Prioress St. SE1	17 C6
Prioress St. SE1	68 A3
Priors Cft. E17	41 H2
Priors Fld., Nthlt.	45 E6
Arnold Rd.	
Priors Gdns., Ruis.	45 C5
Priors Mead, Enf.	25 B1
Priory, The SE3	78 F4
Priory Ave. E4	33 J3
Priory Ave. E17	42 A5
Priory Ave. N8	40 D4
Priory Ave. W4	65 E4
Priory Ave., Orp.	97 G6
Priory Ave., Sutt.	100 A4
Priory Ave., Wem.	46 C4
Priory Clo. E4	33 J3
Priory Clo. E18	42 G1
Priory Clo. N3	39 C1
Church Cres.	
Priory Clo., Beck.	95 H3
Priory Clo., Chis.	97 C1
Priory Clo., Hmptn.	90 F1
Priory Gdns.	
Priory Clo., Hayes	54 B7
Priory Clo., Stan.	29 C3
Priory Clo., Sun.	81 A7
Priory Clo. (Sudbury), Wem.	46 C4
Priory Ct. E17	41 J2
Priory Ct. SW8	76 D1
Priory Ct. (Bushey), Wat.	28 J1
Sparrows Herne	
Priory Ct. Est. E17	41 J2
Priory Cres. SE19	85 J7
Priory Cres., Sutt.	100 A4
Priory Cres., Wem.	46 D3
Priory Dr. SE2	71 D5
Priory Dr., Stan.	29 C3
Priory Fld. Dr., Edg.	30 B4
Priory Gdns. N6	40 B6
Priory Gdns. SW13	74 F3
Priory Gdns. W4	65 E4
Priory Gdns. W5	55 H3
Hanger La.	
Priory Gdns., Hmptn.	81 F7
Priory Gdns., Wem.	46 D4
Priory Grn. Est. N1	8 D1
Priory Grn. Est. N1	58 F2
Priory Gro. SW8	76 E1
Priory Hill, Wem.	46 D4
Priory La. SW15	74 F2
Priory La., Rich.	65 A7
Forest Rd.	
Priory La., W.Mol.	99 G1
Priory Ms. SW8	76 E1
Priory Pk. SE3	78 F3
Priory Pk. Rd. NW6	57 C1
Priory Pk. Rd., Wem.	46 D4
Priory Rd. E6	61 A1
Priory Rd. N8	40 C4
Priory Rd. NW6	57 E1
Priory Rd. SW19	84 G7
Priory Rd. W4	65 D3
Priory Rd., Bark.	52 G7
Priory Rd., Chess.	98 H3
Priory Rd., Croy.	94 G7
Priory Rd., Hmptn.	81 F7
Priory Rd., Houns.	72 J5
Priory Rd., Loug.	27 E8
Priory Rd., Rich.	65 A7
Priory Rd., Sutt.	100 A4
Priory St. E3	60 B3
Leonard St.	
Priory Ter. NW6	57 E1
Priory Ter., Sun.	81 A7
Priory Clo.	
Priory Wk. SW10	18 D4
Priory Wk. SW10	66 F5
Priory Way, Har.	36 H4
Pritchard's Rd. E2	59 D2
Priter Rd. SE16	17 J6
Priter Rd. SE16	68 D3
Private Rd., Enf.	25 A5
Probert Rd. SW2	76 D1
Probyn Rd. SW2	85 H2
Procter St. WC1	12 C2
Procter St. WC1	58 F5
Proctors Clo., Felt.	81 A1
Progress Business Pk., The, Croy.	101 F2
Progress Way N22	40 G1
Progress Way, Croy.	101 F2
Progress Way, Enf.	25 D5
Promenade, The W4	74 E1
Promenade App. Rd. W4	65 E7
Prospect Clo. SE26	86 E4
Prospect Clo., Belv.	71 G4
Prospect Clo., Houns.	72 F1
Prospect Clo., Ruis.	36 D7
Prospect Cotts. SW18	75 D4
Point Pleasant	
Prospect Cres., Twick.	72 J6
Prospect Hill E17	42 B4
Prospect Pl. E1	21 E1
Prospect Pl. N2	39 G4
Prospect Pl. N17	41 B1
Church Rd.	
Prospect Pl. NW2	48 C3
Ridge Rd.	
Prospect Pl. NW3	48 F4
Holly Wk.	
Prospect Pl., Brom.	96 H3
Prospect Pl., Rom.	44 J2
Prospect Ring N2	39 G3
Prospect Rd. NW2	48 C3
Prospect Rd., Barn.	23 D5
Prospect Rd., Surb.	91 F6
Prospect Rd., Wdf.Grn.	34 J6
Prospect St. SE16	68 E2
Jamaica Rd.	
Prospect Vale SE18	70 B4
Prospero Rd. N19	49 C1
Prothero Gdns. NW4	38 H5
Prothero Ho. NW10	47 D7
Prothero Rd. SW6	66 B7
Prout Gro. NW10	47 E4
Prout Rd. E5	50 F4
Providence Ct. W1	11 C5
Providence Ct. W1	58 A7
Providence Pl. N1	58 H1
Upper St.	
Providence Pl., Rom.	44 F2
Providence Row N1	8 C2
Providence Yd. E2	9 H3
Provident Ind. Est. Hayes	63 A2
Provost Est. N1	9 B3
Provost Est. N1	59 A2
Provost Rd. NW3	48 J7
Provost St. N1	9 B2
Provost St. N1	59 A2
Prowse Ave. (Bushey), Wat.	28 J2
Prowse Pl. NW1	49 B7
Bonny St.	
Pruden Clo. N14	32 C2
Prudent Pas. EC2	10 D6
Prusom St. E1	68 E1
Pryors, The NW3	48 G3
Pudding La. EC3	13 C6
Pudding La. EC3	59 A7
Pudding La., Chig.	27 H6
Pudding Mill La. E15	60 B1
Puddle Dock EC4	12 H5
Pulborough Rd. SW18	75 C7
Pulborough Way, Houns.	72 C4
Pulford Rd. N15	41 A6
Pulham Ave. N2	39 F4
Puller Rd., Barn.	23 B2
Pulleyns Ave. E6	61 B3
Pullman Ct. SW2	85 E1
Pullman Gdns. SW15	74 J6
Pulross Rd. SW9	76 F3
Pulteney Clo. E3	59 J1
Pulteney Rd. E18	42 H3
Pulteney Ter. N1	58 F1
Pulton Pl. SW6	66 D7
Puma Ct. E1	13 F1
Pump All., Brent.	64 G7
Pump Clo., Nthlt.	54 G2
Union Rd.	
Pump Ct. EC4	12 E4
Pump Hill, Loug.	27 C2
Pump La. SE14	68 F7
Farrow La.	
Pump Pail N., Croy.	101 J3
Old Town	
Pump Pail S., Croy.	101 J3
Southbridge Rd.	
Pumping Sta. Rd. W4	65 E7
Pundersons Gdns. E2	59 E3
Purbeck Ave., N.Mal.	92 F6
Purbeck Dr. NW2	48 A2
Purbrook Est. SE1	17 E4
Purbrook St. SE1	17 E5
Purcell Cres. SW6	66 A7
Purcell Rd., Grnf.	54 H5
Purcell St. N1	9 D1
Purcell St. N1	59 B2
Purcells Ave., Edg.	30 A5
Purchese St. NW1	7 J1
Purchese St. NW1	58 D2
Purdy St. E3	60 B4
Purex Rd., Grnf.	55 A1
Purland Clo., Dag.	53 F1
Purland Rd. SE28	70 J2
Purleigh Ave., Wdf.Grn.	35 B6
Purley Ave. NW2	48 B2
Purley Clo., Ilf.	43 D2
Purley Pl. N1	49 H7
Islington Pk. St.	
Purley Rd. N9	33 A3
Purley Rd., S.Croy.	102 A7
Purley Way, Croy.	94 F7
Purneys Rd. SE9	79 A4
Purrett Rd. SE18	70 J5
Purser's Cross Rd. SW6	75 C1
Pursewardens Clo. W13	64 F1
Pursley Rd. NW7	30 H7
Purves Rd. NW10	56 H2

Puteaux Ho. E2 59 G2
Mace St.
Putney Bri. SW6 75 B3
Putney Bri. SW15 75 B3
Putney Bri. App. 75 B3
SW6
Putney Bri. Rd. 75 B4
SW15
Putney Bri. Rd. 75 D5
SW18
Putney Common 74 J3
SW15
Putney Heath SW15 74 H7
Putney Heath La. 75 A6
SW15
Putney High St. 75 A4
SW15
Putney Hill SW15 75 A6
Putney Pk. Ave. 74 G4
SW15
Putney Pk. La. SW15 74 H4
Puttenham Clo., 28 D2
Wat.
Pycroft Way N9 33 D3
Pyecombe Cor. N12 31 C4
Pylbrook Rd., Sutt. 100 D3
Pylon Way, Croy. 101 E1
Pym Clo., Barn. 23 G5
Pymers Mead SE21 85 J1
Pymmes Clo. N13 32 F5
Pymmes Clo. N17 41 E1
Pymmes Gdns. N. N9 33 C3
Pymmes Gdns. S. N9 33 C3
Pymmes Grn. Rd. N13 32 E6
Pymmes Rd. N13 32 E6
Pymms Brook Dr., 23 H4
Barn.
Pyne Rd., Surb. 99 A1
Pynham Clo. SE2 71 B3
Pynnacles Clo., 29 E5
Stan.
Pyrland Rd. N5 50 A5
Pyrland Rd., Rich. 73 J6
Pyrles Grn., Loug. 27 E1
Pyrles La., Loug. 27 E2
Pyrmont Gro. SE27 85 H3
Pyrmont Rd. W4 65 A6
Pytchley Cres. SE19 85 J6
Pytchley Rd. SE22 77 B3

Q

Quadrant, The SE24 76 J5
Herne Hill
Quadrant, The SW20 93 B1
Quadrant, The, Bexh. 71 D7
Quadrant, The, 73 H4
Rich.
Quadrant, The, 100 F6
Sutt.
Quadrant Arc. W1 11 G6
Quadrant Gro. NW5 48 J5
Quadrant Rd., Rich. 73 G4
Quadrant Rd., 94 H4
Th.Hth.
Quaggy Wk. SE3 78 G4
Quainton St. NW10 47 D3
Quaker La., Sthl. 63 G3
Quaker St. E1 9 F6
Quaker St. E1 59 C4
Quakers Course NW9 38 F1
Quakers La., Islw. 73 D1
Quakers Wk. N21 25 A6
Quality Ct. WC2 12 E3
Quantock Dr., 99 J2
Wor.Pk.
Cotswold Way
Quantock Gdns. NW2 48 A2
Quarley Way SE15 21 F7
Quarr Rd., Cars. 93 G6
Quarrendon St. SW6 75 D2
Quarry Rd., 100 C6
Sutt.
Quarry Ri., Sutt. 100 C6
Quarry Rd. SW18 75 F6
Quarry Way SE16 68 G2
Quarter Mile La. 51 B4
E10
Quarterdeck, The 69 A2
E14
Quay W., Tedd. 82 E5
Quebec Ms. W1 11 A4
Quebec Rd., Hayes 54 C7
Quebec Rd., Ilf. 73 E7
Quebec Way SE16 68 G2
Queen Adelaide Rd. 86 F6
SE20
Queen Alexandra's 84 C5
Ct. SW19
Queen Anne Ave. 41 C5
N15
Suffield Rd.
Queen Anne Ave., 96 F3
Brom.

Queen Anne Clo., 98 B7
Esher
Queen Anne Ms. W1 11 E2
Queen Anne Rd. E9 50 G6
Queen Anne St. W1 11 D3
Queen Anne St. W1 58 B5
Queen Anne's Clo., 82 A3
Twick.
Queen Anne's Gdns. 65 E3
W4
Queen Annes Gdns. 64 H2
W5
Queen Annes Gdns., 25 B6
Enf.
Queen Anne's Gdns., 93 J3
Mitch.
Queen Anne's Gate 15 H4
SW1
Queen Anne's Gate 67 D2
SW1
Queen Anne's Gate, 80 D3
Bexh.
Queen Annes Gro. 65 E3
W4
Queen Annes Gro. 64 H2
W5
Queen Annes Gro., 25 A7
Enf.
Queen Annes Pl., 25 B6
Enf.
Queen Anne's Wk. 8 B6
WC1
Queen Caroline Est. 65 J5
W6
Queen Caroline St. 65 J5
W6
Queen Elizabeth 93 D4
Gdns., Mord.
Queen Elizabeth Rd. 41 H3
E17
Queen Elizabeth 91 J2
Rd., Kings.T.
Queen Elizabeth St. 17 F3
SE1
Queen Elizabeth St. 68 C2
SE1
Queen Elizabeth Wk. 74 G1
SW13
Queen Elizabeth 101 D4
Wk., Wall.
Queen Elizabeths 50 A2
Clo. N16
Queen Elizabeths 32 D1
Dr. N14
Queen Elizabeths 50 A2
Wk. N16
Queen Margarets 50 B5
Gro. N1
Queen Mary Ave., 93 A5
Mord.
Queen Mary Rd. 85 H6
SE19
Queen Mary's Ave., 100 J7
Cars.
Queen of Denmark 68 J3
Ct. SE16
Queen Sq. WC1 12 B1
Queen Sq. WC1 58 E4
Queen Sq. Pl. WC1 8 B6
Queen St. EC4 13 A5
Queen St. EC4 58 J7
Queen St. N17 33 B6
Queen St. W1 15 D3
Queen St. W1 67 B1
Queen St., Bexh. 80 F3
Queen St., Croy. 101 J3
Church Rd.
Queen St. Pl. EC4 13 A6
Queen Victoria 46 G7
Ave., Wem.
Queen Victoria St. 12 H5
EC4
Queen Victoria St. 58 H7
EC4
Queenborough 88 G6
Gdns., Chis.
Queenborough 43 D4
Gdns., Ilf.
Queenhithe EC4 13 A5
Queenhithe EC4 58 J7
Queens Ave., Sutt. 100 A7
Queens Ave. N3 31 F7
Queens Ave. N10 40 A3
Queens Ave. N20 31 G2
Queen's Ave. N21 32 H1
Queens Ave., Felt. 81 C4
Queens Ave., Grnf. 54 H6
Queens Ave., Stan. 37 E3
Queens Ave., 34 H5
Wdf.Grn.
Queen's Circ. SW8 67 B7
Queenstown Rd.
Queens Clo., Edg. 30 A5

Queens Clo., Wall. 101 B5
Queens Rd.
Queens Club Gdns. 66 B6
W14
Queens Ct. SE23 86 F2
Queens Ct., Rich. 73 J6
Queens Cres. NW5 49 A6
Queens Cres., Rich. 73 J5
Queens Dr. E10 42 A7
Queens Dr. N4 49 H2
Queens Dr. W3 55 J6
Queens Dr., Surb. 92 A7
Queens Dr., T.Ditt. 91 D7
Queen's Elm Sq. 18 F4
SW3
Queens Gdns. NW4 38 J5
Queens Gdns. W2 10 C5
Queens Gdns. W2 57 F6
Queens Gdns. W5 55 F5
Queen's Gdns., 72 E1
Houns.
Queen's Gate SW7 14 D4
Queen's Gate SW7 66 F3
Queen's Gate Gdns. 14 D6
SW7
Queen's Gate Gdns. 66 F3
SW7
Queens Gate Gdns. 74 H4
SW15
Upper Richmond Rd.
Queen's Gate Ms. 14 D4
SW7
Queen's Gate Ms. 66 F3
SW7
Queen's Gate Pl. 14 D6
SW7
Queen's Gate Pl. 66 F3
SW7
Queen's Gate Pl. 14 D6
Ms. SW7
Queen's Gate Pl. 66 F3
Ms. SW7
Queen's Gate Ter. 14 C5
SW7
Queen's Gate Ter. 66 F3
SW7
Queen's Gro. NW8 57 G1
Queen's Gro. Ms. 57 G1
NW8
Queen's Gro.
Queens Gro. Rd. E4 34 D1
Queen's Head St. N1 58 H1
Queen's Head Yd. SE1 17 B2
Queens Ho., Tedd. 82 C6
Queens La. N10 40 A3
Queens Mkt. E13 60 J1
Green St.
Queens Ms. W2 10 A5
Queens Par. N11 31 J5
Colney Hatch La.
Queens Par. W5 55 J6
Queens Pk. Ct. W10 57 A3
Queens Pk. Gdns., 81 A3
Felt.
Vernon Rd.
Queens Pas., Chis. 88 E6
High St.
Queens Pl., Mord. 93 D4
Queen's Prom., 91 G3
Kings.T.
Portsmouth Rd.
Queens Reach, 91 B4
E.Mol.
Queens Ride SW13 74 G3
Queen's Ride, Rich. 83 B1
Queens Ri., Rich. 73 J6
Queens Rd. E11 42 D7
Queens Rd. E13 60 H1
Queen's Rd. E17 41 J6
Queens Rd. N3 39 F1
Queens Rd. N9 33 E3
Queen's Rd. N11 32 E7
Queens Rd. NW4 38 J5
Queens Rd. SE14 77 E1
Queens Rd. SE15 77 E1
Queens Rd. SW14 74 D3
Queens Rd. SW19 84 C6
Queens Rd. W5 55 H6
Queens Rd., Bark. 52 F6
Queens Rd., Barn. 23 A3
Queens Rd., Beck. 95 H2
Queens Rd., Brom. 96 G2
Queens Rd., Buck.H. 34 A2
Queens Rd., Chis. 88 E6
Queens Rd., Croy. 94 H6
Queens Rd., Enf. 25 B4
Queens Rd., Felt. 81 B1
Queens Rd., Hmptn. 81 H4
Queens Rd., Houns. 72 H3
Queens Rd., Ilf. 52 F6
Queens Rd., 83 A7
Kings.T.
Queens Rd., Loug. 27 B3

Queens Rd., Mitch. 93 G2
Queens Rd., Mord. 93 D4
Queens Rd., N.Mal. 92 F4
Queens Rd., Rich. 73 J6
Queens Rd., Sthl. 63 D2
Queens Rd., Tedd. 82 B6
Queens Rd., T.Ditt. 91 C5
Queens Rd., Twick. 73 C7
Queens Rd., Wall. 101 B5
Queen's Rd., Well. 80 B2
Queen's Row SE17 21 B5
Queen's Row SE17 68 A6
Queens Ter. E13 60 H1
Queens Ter. NW8 57 G1
Queens Ter., Islw. 73 D4
Queens Ter. Cotts. 64 B2
W7
Boston Rd.
Queens Wk. E4 34 D1
The Grn. Wk.
Queens Wk. NW9 47 C2
Queen's Wk. SW1 15 F2
Queens Wk. SW1 67 C1
Queens Wk. W5 55 F4
Queens Wk., Har. 37 B4
Queens Wk., Ruis. 45 D3
Queens Way NW4 38 J5
Queensway, Felt. 81 C4
Queens Well Ave. 31 H4
N20
Queen's Wd. Rd. N10 40 B6
Queens Yd. WC1 7 G6
Queensberry Ms. W. 18 E1
SW7
Queensberry Pl. SW7 18 E1
Queensberry Pl. SW7 66 G4
Queensberry Way 18 E1
SW7
Queensborough Ms. 10 C5
W2
Queensborough Pas. 10 C5
W2
Queensborough 10 C5
Studios W2
Queensborough Ter. 10 B5
W2
Queensborough Ter. 57 E5
W2
Queensbridge Pk., 73 B5
Islw.
Queensbridge Rd. E2 9 G2
Queensbridge Rd. E2 50 C7
Queensbridge Rd. E8 50 C7
Queensbury Rd. NW9 38 D7
Queensbury Rd., 55 J2
Wem.
Queensbury Sta. 37 J3
Par., Edg.
Queensbury St. N1 49 J7
Queenscourt, Wem. 46 H4
Queenscroft Rd. SE9 79 H4
Queensdale Cres. 66 A1
W11
Queensdale Pl. W11 66 B1
Queensdale Rd. W11 66 A1
Queensdale Wk. W11 66 B1
Queensdown Rd. E5 50 E4
Queensgate Gdns., 97 G1
Chis.
Queensgate Pl. NW6 48 D7
Queensland Ave. N18 32 J6
Queensland Ave. 93 E1
SW19
Queensland Pl. N7 49 G4
Queensland Rd.
Queensland Rd. N7 49 G4
Queensmead NW8 57 G1
Queensmead Rd., 96 F2
Brom.
Queensmere Clo. 84 A2
SW19
Queensmere Rd. 84 A2
SW19
Queensmill Rd. SW6 66 A4
Queensthorpe Rd. 86 G4
SE26
Queenstown Rd. 19 D6
SW8
Queenstown Rd. 67 B6
SW8
Queensville Rd. 76 D7
SW12
Queensway W2 10 B4
Queensway W2 57 E6
Queensway, Croy. 101 F6
Queensway, Enf. 25 E4
Queensway, Orp. 97 F5
Queensway, Sun. 90 B2
Queensway, 103 E3
W.Wick.
Queenswood Ave. 42 C1
E17

Name	Page	Grid
Queenswood Ave., Hmptn.	81	H6
Queenswood Ave., Houns.	72	F2
Queenswood Ave., Th.Hth.	94	G5
Queenswood Ave., Wall.	101	D4
Queenswood Gdns. E11	51	H1
Queenswood Pk. N3	39	B2
Queenswood Rd. SE23	86	G3
Queenswood Rd., Sid.	79	J5
Quemerford Rd. N7	49	F5
Quentin Pl. SE13	78	E3
Quentin Rd. SE13	78	E3
Quernmore Clo., Brom.	87	G6
Quernmore Rd. N4	40	G6
Quernmore Rd., Brom.	87	G6
Querrin St. SW6	75	F2
Quex Ms. NW6	57	D1
Quex Rd.		
Quex Rd. NW6	57	D1
Quick Rd. W4	65	E5
Quick St. N1	**8**	**H2**
Quick St. N1	58	H2
Quicks Rd. SW19	84	E7
Quickswood NW3	48	H7
King Henry's Rd		
Quiet Nook, Kes.	104	A3
Croydon Rd.		
Quill La. SW15	75	A4
Quilp St. SE1	**16**	**J3**
Quilter St. E2	**9**	**H3**
Quilter St. E2	59	D3
Quinta Dr., Barn.	22	H5
Quintin Ave. SW20	93	C1
Quinton Clo., Beck.	96	C3
Quinton Clo., Wall.	101	B4
Quinton Rd., T.Ditt.	98	D1
Quinton St. SW18	84	F2
Quixley St. E14	60	D7
Quorn Rd. SE22	77	B4

R

Name	Page	Grid
Rabbit Row W8	66	D1
Kensington Mall		
Rabbits Rd. E12	52	B4
Rabournmead Dr., Nthlt.	45	E5
Raby Rd., N.Mal.	92	D4
Raby St. E14	59	H6
Salmon La.		
Raccoon Way, Houns.	72	C2
Rachel Pt. E5	50	D4
Muir Rd.		
Rackham Ms. SW16	85	C6
Westcote Rd.		
Racton Rd. SW6	66	D6
Radbourne Ave. W5	64	F4
Radbourne Clo. E5	50	G4
Overbury St.		
Radbourne Cres. E17	42	D2
Radbourne Rd. SW12	76	C7
Radcliffe Ave. NW10	56	G2
Radcliffe Ave., Enf.	24	J1
Radcliffe Gdns., Cars.	100	H7
Radcliffe Rd. N21	32	H1
Radcliffe Rd., Croy.	102	C2
Radcliffe Rd., Har.	37	D2
Radcliffe Sq. SW15	75	A6
Radcliffe Way, Nthlt.	54	D3
Radcot Pt. SE23	86	G3
Radcot St. SE11	**20**	**F4**
Raddington Rd. W10	57	B5
Radfield Way, Sid.	79	G7
Radford St. SE13	78	C5
Radford Way, Bark.	60	A3
Radipole Rd. SW6	75	C1
Radland Rd. E16	60	F6
Radlet Ave. SE26	86	E3
Radlett Clo. E7	51	F6
Radlett Pl. NW8	57	H1
Radley Ave., Ilf.	52	J4
Radley Ct. SE16	68	G2
Thame Rd.		
Radley Gdns., Har.	37	H4
Radley Ms. W8	66	D3
Radley Rd. N17	41	B2
Radleys La. E18	42	G2
Radleys Mead, Dag.	53	H6
Radlix Rd. E10	51	A1
Radnor Ave., Har.	37	B5
Radnor Ave., Well.	80	B5
Radnor Clo., Chis.	88	H6
Homewood Cres.		
Radnor Clo., Mitch.	94	E4
Radnor Cres. SE18	71	A7
Radnor Cres., Ilf.	43	C5
Radnor Gdns., Enf.	25	B1
Radnor Gdns., Twick.	82	C2
Radnor Ms. W2	**10**	**F4**
Radnor Pl. W2	**10**	**G4**
Radnor Pl. W2	57	H6
Radnor Rd. NW6	57	B1
Radnor Rd. SE15	**21**	**H7**
Radnor Rd. SE15	68	D7
Radnor Rd., Har.	37	A5
Radnor Rd., Twick.	82	C1
Radnor St. EC1	**9**	**A4**
Radnor St. EC1	58	J3
Radnor Ter. W14	66	C4
Radnor Wk. E14	69	A4
Barnsdale Ave.		
Radnor Wk. SW3	**18**	**H4**
Radnor Wk. SW3	66	H5
Radnor Wk., Croy.	95	H6
Radnor Way NW10	56	B4
Radstock Ave., Har.	37	D3
Radstock St. SW11	66	H7
Raebarn Gdns., Barn.	22	H5
Raeburn Ave., Surb.	99	B1
Raeburn Clo. NW11	39	F6
Raeburn Clo., King's.T.	82	G7
Raeburn Rd., Edg.	38	A2
Raeburn Rd., Sid.	79	H6
Raeburn St. SW2	76	E4
Rafford Way, Brom.	96	H2
Raft Rd. SW18	75	D4
North Pas.		
Raggleswood, Chis.	97	D1
Raglan Clo., Houns.	72	E5
Vickers Way		
Raglan Ct. SE12	78	G5
Raglan Ct., S.Croy.	101	H5
Raglan Ct., Wem.	46	J4
Raglan Gdns., Wat.	28	B1
Raglan Rd. E17	42	C5
Raglan Rd. SE18	70	F5
Raglan Rd., Belv.	71	F5
Raglan Rd., Brom.	96	J4
Raglan Rd., Enf.	25	B7
Raglan St. NW5	49	B6
Raglan Ter., Har.	45	H4
Raglan Way, Nthlt.	45	J6
Ragley Clo. W3	65	C2
Avenue Rd.		
Raider Clo., Rom.	44	G1
Railey Ms. NW5	49	C5
Railshead Rd., Twick.	73	E4
Railton Rd. SE24	76	G4
Railway App. SE1	**17**	**C2**
Railway App. SE1	68	A1
Railway App., Har.	37	C4
Railway App., Twick.	73	D7
Railway App., Wall.	101	B6
Railway Ave. SE16	68	F2
Railway Ms. E3	60	A3
Wellington Way		
Railway Ms. W10	57	B6
Ladbroke Gro.		
Railway Pas., Tedd.	82	D6
Victoria Rd.		
Railway Pl., Belv.	71	G3
Railway Ri. SE22	77	B4
Grove Vale		
Railway Rd., Tedd.	82	C4
Railway Side SW13	74	E3
Railway St. N1	**8**	**B2**
Railway St. N1	58	E2
Railway St., Rom.	53	C1
Railway Ter. SE13	78	B5
Ladywell Rd.		
Railway Ter., Felt.	81	A1
Rainborough Clo. NW10	47	C6
Rainbow Ave. E14	69	B5
Rainbow St. SE5	**21**	**D7**
Rainbow St. SE5	68	B7
Raine St. E1	68	E1
Rainham Clo. SE9	79	G6
Rainham Clo. SW11	75	H6
Rainham Rd. NW10	56	J3
Rainham Rd. N., Dag.	53	G2
Rainham Rd. S., Dag.	53	H4
Rainhill Way E3	60	A3
Rainsborough Ave. SE8	68	H4
Rainsford Clo., Stan.	29	F5
Rainsford Rd. NW10	56	B2
Rainsford St. W2	**10**	**G3**
Rainton Rd. SE7	69	G5
Rainville Rd. W6	65	J6
Raisins Hill, Pnr.	36	C3
Raith Ave. N14	32	D3
Raleana Rd. E14	69	C1
Raleigh Ave., Hayes	54	B5
Raleigh Ave., Wall.	101	D4
Raleigh Clo. NW4	38	J5
Raleigh Clo., Pnr.	36	D7
Raleigh Ct., Wall.	101	B6
Raleigh Dr. N20	31	H3
Raleigh Dr., Esher	98	A5
Raleigh Dr., Surb.	99	C1
Raleigh Gdns. SW2	76	F6
Brixton Hill		
Raleigh Gdns., Mitch.	93	J3
Raleigh Ms., Orp.	104	J5
Osgood Ave.		
Raleigh Rd. N8	40	G4
Raleigh Rd. SE20	86	G7
Raleigh Rd., Enf.	24	A5
Raleigh Rd., Rich.	73	J3
Raleigh Rd., Sthl.	63	E5
Raleigh St. N1	58	H1
Raleigh Way N14	32	D1
Raleigh Way, Felt.	81	C4
Ralph Ct. W2	**10**	**B3**
Ralph Perring Ct., Beck.	96	A4
Ralston Way, Wat.	28	D2
Ram Pas., Kings.T.	91	G2
High St.		
Ram Pl. E9	50	F6
Chatham Pl.		
Ram St. SW18	75	E5
Rama Ct., Har.	46	B2
Ramac Ind. Est. SE7	69	G4
Ramac Way SE7	69	H5
Rambler Clo. SW16	85	C4
Ramillies Clo. SW2	76	F6
Ramillies Pl. W1	**11**	**F4**
Ramillies Pl. W1	58	C6
Ramillies Rd. NW7	30	E2
Ramillies Rd. W4	65	D4
Ramillies Rd., Sid.	80	B6
Ramillies St. W1	**11**	**F4**
Rampart St. E1	9	G5
Commercial Rd.		
Rampayne St. SW1	**19**	**H3**
Rampayne St. SW1	67	D5
Rampton Clo. E4	34	A3
Rams Gro., Rom.	44	E4
Ramsay Pl., Har.	46	B1
West St.		
Ramsay Rd. E7	51	E4
Ramsay Rd. W3	65	C2
Ramscroft Clo. N9	25	B7
Ramsdale Rd. SW17	85	A5
Ramsden Rd. N11	31	J5
Ramsden Rd. SW12	76	A6
Ramsey Clo. NW9	38	F6
West Hendon Bdy.		
Ramsey Clo., Grnf.	46	A5
Ramsey Ho., Wem.	46	H6
Ramsey Rd., Th.Hth.	94	F6
Ramsey St. E2	**9**	**J5**
Ramsey St. E2	59	D4
Ramsey Wk. N1	50	A6
Marquess Est.		
Ramsey Way N14	24	C7
Ramsgate Clo. E16	50	C6
Dalston La.		
Ramsgate St. E8	50	C6
Ramsgill App., Ilf.	43	J4
Ramsgill Dr., Ilf.	43	J5
Ramulis Dr., Hayes	54	D4
Ramus Wd. Ave., Orp.	104	H5
Rancliffe Gdns. SE9	79	B4
Rancliffe Rd. E6	67	B2
Randall Ave. NW2	47	E2
Randall Clo. SW11	75	H1
Randall Clo., Erith	71	J6
Randall Pl. SE10	69	C7
Randall Rd. SE11	**20**	**C2**
Randall Rd. SE11	67	F5
Randall Row SE11	**20**	**C2**
Randell's Rd. N1	58	E1
Randle Rd., Rich.	82	F4
Randlesdown Rd. SE6	87	A4
Randolph App. E16	60	A6
Baxter Rd.		
Randolph Ave. W9	**6**	**A2**
Randolph Ave. W9	57	E2
Randolph Clo., Bexh.	80	J3
Randolph Clo., Kings.T.	83	C5
Randolph Cres. W9	**6**	**C6**
Randolph Cres. W9	57	F4
Randolph Gdns. NW6	**6**	**A2**
Randolph Gdns. NW6	57	E2
Randolph Gro., Rom.	44	C5
Donald Dr.		
Randolph Ho., Croy.	101	J1
Randolph Ms. W9	**6**	**D6**
Randolph Ms. W9	57	F4
Randolph Rd. E17	42	B5
Randolph Rd. W9	**6**	**C6**
Randolph Rd. W9	57	F4
Randolph Rd., Sthl.	63	F2
Randolph St. NW1	49	F5?
Randon Clo., Har.	36	H2
Ranelagh Ave. SW6	75	C3
Ranelagh Ave. SW13	74	G2
Ranelagh Clo., Edg.	30	A4
Ranelagh Dr., Edg.	30	A4
Ranelagh Dr., Twick.	73	E4
Ranelagh Gdns. E11	42	J5
Ranelagh Gdns. SW6	75	C3
Ranelagh Gdns. W4	65	C7
Grove Pk. Gdns.		
Ranelagh Gdns. W6	65	F3
Ranelagh Gdns., Ilf.	52	C1
Ranelagh Gro. SW1	**19**	**C3**
Ranelagh Gro. SW1	67	A5
Ranelagh Ms. W5	64	G2
Ranelagh Rd.		
Ranelagh Pl., N.Mal.	92	E5
Rodney Rd.		
Ranelagh Rd. E6	61	D1
Ranelagh Rd. E11	51	E4
Ranelagh Rd. E15	60	E1
Ranelagh Rd. N17	41	B3
Ranelagh Rd. N22	40	F1
Ranelagh Rd. NW10	56	F2
Ranelagh Rd. W5	64	G2
Ranelagh Rd., Sthl.	63	D1
Ranelagh Rd., Wem.	46	G6
Ranfurly Rd., Sutt.	100	D2
Rangefield Rd., Brom.	87	E5
Rangemoor Rd. N15	41	C5
Rangers Rd. E4	26	E7
Rangers Rd., Loug.	26	G7
Rangers Sq. SE10	78	D1
Rangeworth Pl., Sid.	88	J3
Priestlands Pk. Rd.		
Rankin Clo. NW9	38	E3
Ranleigh Gdns., Bexh.	71	F7
Ranmere St. SW12	85	B1
Ormeley Rd.		
Ranmoor Clo., Har.	37	A4
Ranmoor Gdns., Har.	37	A4
Ranmore Ave., Croy.	102	C3
Rannoch Rd. W6	65	J6
Rannock Ave. NW9	38	D7
Ranskill Rd., Borwd.	22	A1
Ransom Rd. SE7	69	J5
Harvey Gdns.		
Ransom Wk. SE7	69	J5
Woolwich Rd.		
Ranston St. NW1	**10**	**G1**
Ranulf Rd. NW2	48	C4
Ranwell Clo. E3	59	J1
Beale Rd.		
Ranwell St. E3	59	J1
Ranworth Rd. N9	33	F2
Ranyard Clo., Chess.	98	J3
Raphael St. SW7	**14**	**J4**
Raphael St. SW7	66	J2
Rashleigh St. SW8	76	B2
Peardon St.		
Rasper Rd. N20	31	F2
Rastell Ave. SW2	85	D2
Ratcliff Rd. E7	51	J5
Ratcliffe Cross St. E1	59	G6
Ratcliffe La. E14	59	H6
Ratcliffe Orchard E1	59	G6
Rathbone Mkt. E16	60	F5
Barking Rd.		
Rathbone Pl. W1	**11**	**H2**
Rathbone Pl. W1	58	D5
Rathbone Pl. E5	50	D4
Nolan Way		
Rathbone St. E16	60	F5
Rathbone St. W1	**11**	**G2**
Rathbone St. W1	58	C5
Rathcoole Ave. N8	40	F5
Rathcoole Gdns. N8	40	F5
Rathfern Rd. SE6	86	J1
Rathgar Ave. W13	64	E1
Rathgar Clo. N3	39	C2

Rathgar Rd. SW9 76 H3
Coldharbour La.
Rathlin Wk. N1 49 J6
Marquess Est.
Rathmell Dr. SW4 76 D6
Rathmore Rd. SE7 69 H5
Rattray Rd. SW2 76 G4
Raul Rd. SE15 77 D1
Raveley St. NW5 49 C4
Raven Clo. NW9 38 E2
Eagle Dr.
Raven Ct. E5 50 D3
Stellman Clo.
Raven Rd. E18 42 J2
Raven Row E1 59 E5
Ravenet St. SW11 76 B1
Strasburg St.
Ravenfield Rd. SW17 84 J3
Ravenhill Rd. E13 60 J2
Ravenna Rd. SW15 75 A5
Ravenor Pk. Rd., 54 H3
Grnf.
Ravens Clo., Brom. 96 F2
Ravens Clo., Enf. 25 B2
Ravens Ms. SE12 78 G5
Ravens Way
Ravens Way SE12 78 G5
Ravensbourne Ave., 87 D3
Brom.
Ravensbourne Gdns. 55 E5
W13
Ravensbourne Gdns., 43 D1
Ilf.
Ravensbourne Pk. 78 A7
SE6
Ravensbourne Pk. 77 J7
Cres. SE6
Ravensbourne Pl. 78 B2
SE13
Ravensbourne Rd. 86 J1
SE6
Ravensbourne Rd., 96 G3
Brom.
Ravensbourne Rd., 73 F6
Twick.
Ravensbury Ave., 93 F5
Mord.
Ravensbury Gro., 93 G4
Mitch.
Ravensbury La., 93 G4
Mitch.
Ravensbury Path, 93 G4
Mitch.
Ravensbury Rd. 84 D2
SW18
Ravensbury Rd., 97 J3
Orp.
Ravensbury Ter. 84 E1
SW18
Ravenscar Rd., 87 E4
Brom.
Ravenscar Rd., 98 J2
Surb.
Ravenscourt Ave. W6 65 G4
Ravenscourt Gdns. 65 G4
W6
Ravenscourt Pk. W6 65 G3
Ravenscourt Pl. W6 65 H4
Ravenscourt Rd. W6 65 H4
Ravenscourt Sq. W6 65 G3
Ravenscraig Rd. N11 32 B4
Ravenscroft Ave. 39 C7
NW11
Ravenscroft Ave., 46 H1
Wem.
Ravenscroft Clo. 60 G5
E16
Ravenscroft Cres. 88 C3
SE9
Ravenscroft Pk. 23 A4
Barn.
Ravenscroft Rd. E16 60 G5
Ravenscroft Rd. W4 65 C4
Ravenscroft Rd., 95 F2
Beck.
Ravenscroft St. E2 9 G2
Ravenscroft St. E2 59 C2
Ravensdale Ave. N12 31 F4
Ravensdale Gdns. 86 A7
SE19
Ravensdale Rd. N16 41 C7
Ravensdale Rd., 72 E3
Houns.
Ravensdon St. SE11 20 F4
Ravensdon St. SE11 67 G5
Ravensfield Clo. 53 D4
Dag.
Ravensfield Gdns., 99 E5
Epsom
Ravenshaw St. NW6 48 C5
Ravenshill, Chis. 97 E1
Ravenshurst Ave. 38 J4
NW4

Ravenside Clo. N18 33 G5
Ravenslea Rd. SW12 75 J7
Ravensmead Rd., 87 D7
Brom.
Ravensmede Way 65 F4
W4
Ravenstone SE17 21 E4
Ravenstone Rd. N8 40 G3
Ravenstone Rd. NW9 38 F6
West Hendon Bdy.
Ravenstone St. 85 A1
SW12
Ravenswood, Bex. 89 E1
Ravenswood Ave., 98 J2
Surb.
Ravenswood Ave., 103 C1
W.Wick.
Ravenswood Ct., 83 B6
Kings.T.
Ravenswood Cres. 45 F2
Har.
Ravenswood Cres., 103 C1
W.Wick.
Ravenswood Gdns., 73 B1
Islw.
Ravenswood Pk., 28 A6
Nthwd.
Ravenswood Rd. E17 42 C4
Ravenswood Rd. 76 B7
SW12
Ravenswood Rd., 101 H3
Croy.
Ravensworth Rd. 56 H3
NW10
Ravensworth Rd. 88 C3
SE9
Ravent Rd. SE11 20 D1
Ravent Rd. SE11 67 F4
Ravey St. EC2 9 D5
Ravine Gro. SE18 70 H6
Rawlings Clo., Orp. 104 J5
Rawlings St. SW3 18 J1
Rawlings St. SW3 66 J4
Rawlins Clo. N3 39 B3
Rawlins Clo., 102 H7
S.Croy.
Rawnsley Ave., 93 G5
Mitch.
Rawreth Wk. N1 58 J1
Basire St.
Rawson St. SW11 76 A1
Strasburg Rd.
Rawsthorne Clo. E16 70 C1
Kennard St.
Rawstone Wk. E13 60 G2
Grasmere Rd.
Rawstorne Pl. EC1 8 G3
Rawstorne St. EC1 8 G3
Rawstorne St. EC1 58 H3
Ray Gdns., Bark. 62 A2
Ray Gdns., Stan. 29 E5
Ray Lo. Rd., 34 J6
Wdf.Grn.
Ray Rd., W.Mol. 90 H5
Ray St. EC1 8 F6
Ray St. EC1 58 G4
Ray St. Bri. EC1 8 F6
Ray Wk. N7 49 F2
Andover Rd.
Raydean Rd., Barn. 23 E5
Raydon St. N19 49 B2
Raydons Gdns., Dag. 53 E5
Raydons Rd., Dag. 53 E5
Rayfield Clo., 96 B7
Brom.
Rayford Ave. SE12 78 F7
Rayleas Clo. SE18 79 E1
Rayleigh Ave., 82 B6
Tedd.
Rayleigh Clo. N13 33 A3
Rayleigh Rd.
Rayleigh Ct., 91 J2
Kings.T.
Rayleigh Ri., 102 B6
S.Croy.
Rayleigh Rd. N13 32 J3
Rayleigh Rd. SW19 93 C1
Rayleigh Rd., 34 J6
Wdf.Grn.
Raymead NW4 38 J4
Raymead Ave., 94 G5
Th.Hth.
Raymere Gdns. SE18 70 G7
Raymond Ave. E18 42 F3
Raymond Ave. W13 64 D3
Raymond Bldgs. 12 D1
WC1
Raymond Clo. SE26 86 F5
Raymond Rd. E13 51 J7
Raymond Rd. SW19 84 B6
Raymond Rd., Beck. 95 H4
Raymond Rd., Ilf. 43 G7
Raymond Way, Esher 98 D6

Raymouth Rd. SE16 68 E4
Rayne Ct. E18 42 F4
Rayner Twr. E10 42 A7
Rayners Clo., Wem. 46 G5
Rayners Ct., Har. 45 G1
Rayners Cres. 54 B3
Rayners Gdns., 54 B2
Nthlt.
Rayners La., Har. 45 G1
Rayners La., Pnr. 36 F5
Rayners Rd. SW15 75 B5
Raynes Ave. E11 42 J7
Raynham Ave. N18 33 D6
Raynham Rd. N18 33 D5
Raynham Rd. W6 65 H4
Raynham Ter. N18 33 D5
Raynor Clo., Sthl. 63 F1
Raynor Pl. N1 58 J1
Elizabeth Ave.
Raynton Clo., Har. 45 E1
Rays Ave. N18 33 F4
Rays Rd. N18 33 F4
Rays Rd., W.Wick. 96 C7
Raywood St. SW8 76 B1
Gladstone Ter.
Reachview Clo. NW1 49 C7
Baynes St.
Reade Wk. NW10 47 E7
Denbigh Clo.
Reading La. E8 50 E6
Reading Rd., Nthlt. 45 H5
Reading Rd., Sutt. 100 F5
Reading Way NW7 31 A5
Reads Clo., Ilf. 52 E3
Chapel Rd.
Reapers Clo. NW1 58 D1
Crofters Way
Reardon Path E1 68 E1
Reardon St. E1 68 E1
Reaston St. SE14 68 F7
Rebecca Ter. SE16 68 F3
Gomm Rd.
Reckitt Rd. W4 65 E5
Record St. SE15 68 F6
Recovery St. SW17 84 H5
Recreation Ave., 44 J5
Rom.
Recreation Rd. SE26 86 G4
Recreation Rd., 96 F2
Brom.
Recreation Rd., Sid. 88 J3
Recreation Rd., 63 E4
Sthl.
Recreation Way, 94 E3
Mitch.
Rector St. N1 58 J1
Rectory Clo. E4 34 A3
Rectory Clo. N3 39 C2
Rectory Clo. SW20 92 J3
Rectory Clo., Sid. 89 B4
Rectory Clo., Stan. 29 E5
Rectory Clo., Surb. 98 F1
Rectory Cres. E11 42 J6
Rectory Fld. Cres. 69 J7
SE7
Rectory Gdns. N8 40 E4
Rectory Gdns. SW4 76 C3
Rectory Gdns., 54 F1
Nthlt.
Rectory Grn., Beck. 95 J1
Rectory Gro. SW4 76 C3
Rectory Gro., Croy. 101 H2
Rectory Gro., 81 F4
Hmptn.
Rectory La. SW17 85 A6
Rectory La., Edg. 30 A6
Rectory La., Loug. 27 D2
Rectory La., Sid. 89 B4
Rectory La., Stan. 29 E5
Rectory La., Surb. 98 E1
Rectory La., Wall. 101 C3
Rectory Orchard 84 B4
SW19
Rectory Pk. Ave., 54 E3
Nthlt.
Rectory Pl. SE18 70 D4
Rectory Rd. E12 52 C5
Rectory Rd. E17 42 B3
Rectory Rd. N16 50 C2
Rectory Rd. SW13 74 G2
Rectory Rd. W3 65 B1
Rectory Rd., Beck. 96 A1
Rectory Rd., Dag. 53 G6
Rectory Rd., Hayes 54 A6
Rectory Rd., Houns. 72 B1
Rectory Rd., Kes. 104 A7
Rectory Rd., Sthl. 63 F3
Rectory Sq. E1 59 G5
Reculver Ms. N18 33 D4
Lyndhurst Rd.
Reculver Rd. SE16 68 G5

Red Anchor Clo. SW3 18 G6
Red Barracks Rd. 70 C4
SE18
Red Cedars Rd., 97 H7
Orp.
Red Hill, Chis. 88 E5
Red Ho. La., Bexh. 80 D4
Red Ho. Rd., Croy. 94 D6
Red La., Esher 98 D6
Red Lion Ct. EC4 21 B5
Red Lion Ct. EC4 12 F4
Red Lion Ct. EC4 58 G6
Red Lion Hill N2 39 G2
Red Lion La. SE18 79 D1
Red Lion Pl. SE18 79 D1
Shooter's Hill Rd.
Red Lion Rd., Surb. 98 J2
Red Lion Row SE17 21 A5
Red Lion Row SE17 67 A5
Red Lion Sq. WC1 12 C2
Red Lion Sq. WC1 58 F5
Red Lion St. WC1 12 C1
Red Lion St. WC1 58 F5
Red Lion St., Rich. 73 G5
Red Lion Yd. W1 15 C3
Red Lo. Rd., 103 C1
W.Wick.
Red Oak Clo., Orp. 104 E3
Red Path E9 50 J6
Eastway
Red Pl. W1 11 B5
Red Post Hill SE21 104 E3
Red Post Hill SE24 77 A4
Redan Pl. W2 10 A4
Redan Pl. W2 58 E6
Redan St. W14 66 A3
Redan Ter. SE5 76 J2
Flaxman Rd.
Redberry Bro. SE26 86 F3
Redbourne Ave. N3 39 D1
Redbridge Gdns. SE5 68 B7
Redbridge La. E., 43 A6
Ilf.
Redbridge La. W. 42 H6
E11
Redburn St. SW3 18 J5
Redburn St. SW3 66 J6
Redcar Clo., Nthlt. 45 H6
Redcar St. SE5 67 J7
Redcastle Clo. E1 59 F7
Redchurch St. E2 9 F5
Redchurch St. E2 59 C4
Redcliffe Gdns. 18 B4
SW10
Redcliffe Gdns. 66 E5
SW10
Redcliffe Gdns., 52 D1
Ilf.
Redcliffe Ms. SW10 18 B4
Redcliffe Ms. SW10 66 E5
Redcliffe Pl. SW10 18 C6
Redcliffe Pl. SW10 66 F6
Redcliffe Rd. SW10 18 C4
Redcliffe Rd. SW10 66 F5
Redcliffe Sq. SW10 18 B4
Redcliffe Sq. SW10 66 E5
Redcliffe St. SW10 18 B5
Redcliffe St. SW10 66 E6
Redclose Ave., 93 D5
Mord.
Chalgrove Ave.
Redclyffe Rd. E6 60 J1
Redcroft Rd., Sthl. 54 J7
Redcross Way SE1 17 A3
Redcross Way SE1 67 J2
Reddings, The NW7 30 F3
Reddings Clo. NW7 30 G1
Reddins Rd. SE15 21 G7
Reddins Rd. SE15 68 D6
Reddons Rd., Beck. 86 H7
Rede Pl. W2 57 D6
Chepstow Pl.
Redesdale Gdns., 64 D7
Islw.
Redesdale St. SW3 18 H5
Redesdale St. SW3 66 H6
Redfern Ave., 72 G7
Houns.
Redfern Rd. NW10 47 E7
Redfern Rd. SE6 78 C7
Redfield La. SW5 66 D4
Redford Ave., 94 F4
Th.Hth.
Redford Ave., Wall. 101 E6
Redford Wk. N1 58 H1
Britannia Row
Redgate Dr., Brom. 103 H2
Redgate Ter. SW15 75 A6
Lytton Gro.
Redgrave Clo., 95 C6
Croy.
Redgrave Rd. SW15 75 A3
Redhill Dr., Edg. 38 C2

Redhill St. NW1 7 E3
Redhill St. NW1 58 B2
Redington Gdns. NW3
Redington Rd. NW3 48 E4
Redlands Ct., Brom. 87 F7
Redlands Gdns., 90 F4
W.Mol.
Dunstable Rd.
Redlands Rd., Enf. 25 H1
Redlands Way SW2 76 F7
Redlaw Way SE16 21 J4
Redleaf Clo., Belv. 71 G6
Redlees Clo., Islw. 73 D4
Redman Clo., Nthlt. 54 C2
Redman's Rd. E1 113 J5
Redmead La. E1 17 H2
Redmore Rd. W6 65 H4
Redpoll Way, Erith 71 D2
Redriff Est. SE16 68 H3
Redriff Rd. SE16 68 G3
Redriff Rd., Rom. 44 H2
Redriffe Rd. E13 60 F1
Redroofs Clo., 96 B1
Beck.
Redruth Clo. N22 32 F7
Palmerston Rd.
Redruth Rd. E9 59 F1
Redstart Clo. E6 61 B5
Columbine Ave.
Redstart Clo. SE14 68 H7
Southergnate Way
Redston Rd. N8 40 C4
Redvers Rd. N22 40 G2
Redvers St. N1 9 E3
Redwald Rd. E5 50 G4
Redway Dr., Twick. 72 J7
Redwing Path SE28 70 G2
Whinchat Rd.
Redwood Clo. N14 24 D7
The Vale
Redwood Clo. SE16 68 H1
Redwood Clo., Wat. 28 C4
Redwood Est. 63 B6
Houns.
Redwood Twr. E11 51 D3
Redwood Wk., Surb. 98 G1
Redwood Way, Barn. 23 A5
Redwoods SW15 83 G1
Redwoods Clo., 34 H2
Buck.H.
Beech La.
Reece Ms. SW7 18 E1
Reece Ms. SW7 66 G4
Reed Ave., Orp. 104 H3
Reed Clo. E16 60 G5
Reed Clo. SE12 78 G5
Reed Rd. N17 41 C2
Reede Rd., Dag. 53 G6
Reede Way, Dag. 53 H6
Reedham Clo. N17 41 E4
Reedham St. SE15 77 D2
Reedholm Vill. N16 50 A4
Winston Rd.
Reeds Pl. NW1 49 C7
Royal College St.
Reedworth St. SE11 20 F2
Reedworth St. SE11 67 G4
Reenglass Rd., 29 G4
Stan.
Rees Gdns., Croy. 95 C6
Rees St. N1 58 J1
Reesland Clo. E12 52 D6
Reets Fm. Clo. NW9 38 E6
Reeves Ave. NW9 38 D7
Reeves Cor., Croy. 101 H2
Roman Way
Reeves Ms. W1 11 B6
Reeves Ms. W1 58 A4
Reeves Rd. E3 60 B4
Reeves Rd. SE18 70 E6
Reform Row N17 41 C2
Reform St. SW11 75 J2
Regal Clo. E1 13 J1
Regal Clo. W5 55 G5
Regal Ct. N18 33 C5
College Rd.
Regal Cres., Wall. 101 B3
Regal La. NW1 58 A1
Regents Pk. Rd.
Regal Way, Har. 37 H6
Regan Way N1 9 D2
Regan Way N1 59 B2
Regency Clo. W5 55 H6
Regency Clo., Chig. 35 F5
Regency Lo., 81 F5
Hmptn.
Regency Ms. NW10 47 G6
High Rd.

Regency Ms., Beck. 96 C1
Regency Ms., Islw. 73 B5
Queensbridge Rd.
Regency Pl. SW1 19 J1
Regency St. SW1 19 J1
Regency St. SW1 67 D4
Regency Wk., Croy. 95 H6
Regency Way, Bexh. 80 D3
Regent Clo. N12 31 F5
Nether St.
Regent Clo., Har. 37 H6
Regent Clo., Houns. 72 B1
Regent Gdns., Ilf. 44 A6
Regent Pl. W1 11 G5
Regent Pl., Croy. 102 C1
Grant Rd.
Regent Rd. SE24 76 H6
Regent Rd., Surb. 91 J5
Regent Sq. E3 60 B3
Regent Sq. WC1 8 B4
Regent Sq. WC1 58 E3
Regent Sq., Belv. 71 H4
Regent St. NW10 57 H3
Kilburn La.
Regent St. SW1 11 H6
Regent St. SW1 58 D7
Regent St. W1 11 E3
Regent St. W1 58 B6
Regent St. W4 65 A5
Regents Ave. N13 32 G5
Regents Bri. Gdns. 20 B7
SW8
Regents Bri. Gdns. 67 E7
SW8
Regents Clo., 102 B6
S.Croy.
Regents Dr., Kes. 104 A5
Regents Ms. NW8 6 D1
Regents Pk. NW1 6 J2
Regents Pk. NW1 57 J2
Regents Pk. Est. 7 F4
NW1
Regents Pk. Rd. N3 39 C4
Regents Pk. Rd. NW1 48 J7
Regents Pk. Ter. 58 B1
NW1
Oval Rd.
Regent's Pl. SE3 78 G2
Regents Row E8 59 D1
Regina Clo., Barn. 23 A3
Regina Rd. N4 49 F1
Regina Rd. SE25 95 D3
Regina Rd. W13 64 D1
Regina Rd., Sthl. 63 E4
Regina Ter. W13 64 E1
Reginald Rd. E7 51 G6
Reginald Rd. SE8 69 A7
Reginald Sq. SE8 69 A7
Regis Rd. NW5 49 B5
Regnart Bldgs. NW1 7 G5
Reid Clo., Pnr. 36 A4
Reidhaven Rd. SE18 70 H4
Reigate Ave., Sutt. 100 D2
Reigate Rd., Brom. 87 F3
Reigate Rd., Ilf. 52 J2
Reigate Way, Wall. 101 E5
Reighton Rd. E5 50 D3
Relay Rd. W12 65 J1
Relf Rd. SE15 77 D3
Relko Gdns., Sutt. 100 G5
Relton Ms. SW7 14 H5
Rembrandt Clo. E14 69 D3
Rembrandt Clo. SW1 19 B2
Rembrandt Rd. SE13 78 E4
Rembrandt Rd., Edg. 38 A2
Remington Rd. E6 61 B6
Remington Rd. N15 41 A6
Remington St. N1 8 H2
Remington St. N1 58 H2
Remnant St. WC2 12 C3
Rempstone Ms. N1 9 C1
Remus Rd. E3 51 A7
Monier Rd.
Rendlesham Clo., 96 J1
Brom.
Rendlesham Rd. E5 50 D4
Rendlesham Rd., 24 H1
Enf.
Renforth St. SE16 68 F2
Renfrew Clo. E6 61 D7
Renfrew Rd. SE11 20 G1
Renfrew Rd. SE11 67 H4
Renfrew Rd., Houns. 72 D2
Renfrew Rd., 83 B7
Kings.T.
Renmuir St. SW17 84 J6
Rennell St. SE13 78 C3
Renness Rd. E17 41 H3
Rennets Clo. SE9 79 H5
Rennets Wd. Rd. SE9 79 G5
Rennie Est. SE16 68 E4
Rennie St. SE1 16 G1
Rennie St. SE1 67 H1

Renown Clo., Croy. 101 H1
Renown Clo., Rom. 44 G1
Rensburg Rd. E17 41 G5
Renshaw Clo., Belv. 71 F6
Grove Rd.
Renters Ave. NW4 38 J6
Renwick Rd., Bark. 62 B4
Repens Way, Hayes 54 D4
Stipularis Dr.
Rephidim St. SE1 17 C6
Replingham Rd. 84 C1
SW18
Reporton Rd. SW6 75 B1
Repository Rd. SE18 70 C6
Repton Ave., Wem. 46 F4
Repton Clo., Cars. 100 H5
Repton Ct. E5 50 H3
Repton Ct., Beck. 96 B1
Repton Gro., Ilf. 43 C1
Repton Rd., Har. 37 J4
Repton St. E14 59 H6
Repulse Clo., Rom. 44 H1
Reservoir Rd. N14 24 C5
Reservoir Rd. SE4 77 H2
Resolution Wk. SE18 70 C3
Venus Rd.
Restell Clo. SE3 69 E6
Reston Pl. SW7 14 C4
Restons Cres. SE9 79 G6
Restormel Clo., 72 G5
Houns.
Retcar Clo. N19 49 B2
Retcar Pl. N19 49 B2
Darmouth Pk. Hill
Retford St. N1 9 E2
Retingham Way E4 34 B2
Retreat, The NW9 38 A5
Retreat, The SW14 74 E3
South Worple Way
Retreat, The, Har. 36 G7
Retreat, The, Surb. 91 J6
Retreat, The, 95 A4
Th.Hth.
Retreat, The, 99 H2
Wor.Pk.
Retreat Clo., Har. 37 F5
Retreat Pl. E9 50 F6
Retreat Rd., Rich. 73 G5
Retreat Way, Chig. 54 E7
Reunion Row E1 59 E7
Pennington St.
Reveley Sq. SE16 68 H2
Howland Way
Revell Ri. SE18 70 J6
Revell Rd., 92 B2
Kings.T.
Revell Rd., Sutt. 100 C6
Revelon Rd. SE4 77 H3
Revelstoke Rd. SW18 84 C2
Reventlow Rd. SE9 88 F1
Reverdy Rd. SE1 21 H2
Reverdy Rd. SE1 68 D4
Reverend Clo., Har. 45 H3
Revesby Rd., Cars. 93 G6
Review Rd. NW2 47 F2
Review Rd., Dag. 62 H1
Rewell St. SW6 66 F7
Rewley Rd., Cars. 93 G6
Rex Pl. W1 11 C6
Reydon Ave. E11 42 J6
Reynard Clo., Brom. 97 C3
Reynard Dr. SE19 86 C7
Reynardson Rd. N17 32 J7
Reynolds Ave. E12 52 D5
Reynolds Ave., 98 H7
Chess.
Reynolds Ave., Rom. 44 C7
Reynolds Clo. NW11 39 E7
Reynolds Clo. SW19 93 G1
Reynolds Clo., 100 J1
Cars.
Reynolds Ct. E11 51 F3
Cobbold Rd.
Reynolds Dr., Edg. 37 J3
Reynolds Pl. SE3 69 H7
Reynolds Pl., Rich. 73 J6
Cambrian Rd.
Reynolds Rd. SE15 77 F5
Reynolds Rd. W4 65 C3
Reynolds Rd., Hayes 54 C4
Reynolds Rd., 92 D7
N.Mal.
Reynolds Way, 102 B4
Croy.
Rheidol Ms. N1 8 J1
Rheidol Ter. N1 8 H1
Rheidol Ter. N1 58 J1
Rheola Clo. N17 41 C1
Rhoda St. E2 9 G5
Rhodes Ave. N22 40 C1
Rhodes Moorhouse 93 D6
Ct., Mord.
Rhodes St. N7 49 F5
Mackenzie Rd.
Rhodesia Rd. E11 51 D2

Rhodesia Rd. SW9 76 E2
Rhodeswell Rd. E14 59 H5
Rhodrons Ave., 98 H5
Chess.
Rhondda Gro. E3 59 H3
Rhyl Rd., Grnf. 55 C2
Rhyl St. NW5 49 A6
Rhys Ave. N11 32 D7
Rialto Rd., Mitch. 94 A2
Ribble Clo., 34 J6
Wdf.Grn.
Prospect Rd.
Ribblesdale Ave., 45 H6
Nthlt.
Ribblesdale Rd. N8 40 F4
Ribblesdale Rd. 85 B6
SW16
Ribchester Ave., 55 C3
Grnf.
Ribston Clo., Brom. 104 A1
Ricardo St. E14 60 B6
Ricards Rd. SW19 84 C5
Rich La. SW5 18 A4
Rich St. E14 59 J7
Richard Clo. SE18 70 B4
Richard Foster Clo. 41 J7
E17
Richard St. E1 59 E6
Commercial Rd.
Richards Ave., Rom. 44 J5
Richards Clo., Har. 37 D5
Richards Pl. E17 42 A3
Richards Pl. SW3 10 H1
Richardson Clo. E8 59 C1
Clarissa St.
Richardson Rd. E15 60 E2
Richardson's Ms. W1 7 F6
Richbell Pl. WC1 12 C1
Richborne Ter. SW8 20 D7
Richborne Ter. SW8 67 F7
Richborough Rd. 48 B4
NW2
Riches Rd., Ilf. 52 F2
Richford Rd. E15 60 F1
Richford St. W6 65 J2
Richlands Ave., 99 G4
Epsom
Richmond Ave. E4 34 D5
Richmond Ave. N1 58 F1
Richmond Ave. 47 J6
NW10
Richmond Ave. 93 B1
SW20
Richmond Bri., 73 G5
Rich.
Richmond Bri., 73 G6
Twick.
Richmond Bldgs. W1 11 H4
Richmond Clo. E17 41 J6
Richmond Cres. E4 34 D5
Richmond Cres. N1 58 F1
Richmond Cres. N9 33 D1
Richmond Gdns. 38 G5
NW4
Richmond Gdns., 29 C7
Har.
Richmond Grn., 101 E3
Croy.
Richmond Gro. N1 49 H7
Richmond Gro., 91 J6
Surb.
Alpha Rd.
Richmond Hill, Rich. 73 H6
Richmond Hill Ct., 73 H6
Rich.
Richmond Ms. W1 11 H4
Richmond Pk. 83 C4
Heights, Kings.T.
Richmond Pk. Rd. 74 C5
SW14
Richmond Pk. Rd., 91 H1
Kings.T.
Richmond Pl. SE18 70 F4
Richmond Rd. E4 34 D1
Richmond Rd. E7 51 H5
Richmond Rd. E8 50 C7
Richmond Rd. E11 51 D2
Richmond Rd. N2 39 F2
Richmond Rd. N11 32 E6
Richmond Rd. N15 41 B6
Richmond Rd. SW20 92 H1
Richmond Rd. W5 64 H2
Richmond Rd., Barn. 23 E5
Richmond Rd., Croy. 101 E3
Richmond Rd., Ilf. 52 F3
Richmond Rd., Islw. 73 D3
Richmond Rd., 82 G5
Kings.T.
Richmond Rd., 94 H3
Th.Hth.
Richmond Rd., 82 D1
Twick.
Richmond St. E13 60 G2

Richmond Ter. SW1	16	A3
Richmond Ter. SW1	67	E2
Richmond Way E11	51	G2
Richmond Way W12	66	A2
Richmond Way W14	66	A2
Richmount Gdns. SE3	78	G3
Rickard Clo. NW4	38	G4
Rickard Clo. SW2	85	G1
Rickards Clo.,	98	H1
Surb.		
Rickett St. SW6	66	D6
Rickman St. E1	59	F3
Mantus Rd.		
Rickmansworth Rd.,	36	B2
Pnr.		
Rickthorne Rd. N19	49	E2
Landseer Rd.		
Rickyard Path SE9	79	B4
Ridding La., Grnf.	46	C5
Riddons Rd. SE12	87	J3
Ride, The, Brent.	64	E5
Ride, The, Enf.	25	F3
Rideout St. SE18	70	C4
Rider Clo., Sid.	79	H6
Ridgdale St. E3	60	A2
Ridge, The, Bex.	80	F7
Ridge, The, Orp.	104	G2
Ridge, The, Surb.	92	A5
Ridge, The, Twick.	73	A7
Ridge Ave. N21	24	J7
Ridge Clo. NW4	39	A2
Ridge Clo. NW9	38	D4
Ridge Crest, Enf.	24	F1
Ridge Hill NW11	48	B1
Ridge Rd. N8	40	F6
Ridge Rd. N21	32	J1
Ridge Rd. NW2	48	C3
Ridge Rd., Mitch.	85	B7
Ridge Rd., Sutt.	100	B1
Ridge Way SE19	86	B6
Central Hill		
Ridge Way, Felt.	81	E3
Ridgebrook Rd. SE3	78	J3
Ridgecroft Clo.,	89	J1
Bex.		
Ridgemont Gdns.,	30	C4
Edg.		
Ridgemount Ave.	102	G2
Croy.		
Ridgemount Clo.	86	E7
SE20		
Anerley Pk.		
Ridgemount Gdns.,	24	H3
Enf.		
Ridgeview Clo.,	23	A6
Barn.		
Ridgeview Rd. N20	31	E3
Ridgeway, Brom.	103	G2
Ridgeway, Wdf.Grn.	34	J4
Ridgeway, The E4	34	B2
Ridgeway, The N3	31	E7
Ridgeway, The N11	31	J4
Ridgeway, The N14	32	E2
Ridgeway, The NW7	30	G3
Ridgeway, The NW9	38	E4
Ridgeway, The NW11	48	C1
Ridgeway, The W3	65	A3
Ridgeway, The,	101	F3
Croy.		
Ridgeway, The, Enf.	24	G1
Ridgeway, The, Har.	36	F5
Ridgeway, The	37	F6
(Kenton), Har.		
Ridgeway, The,	36	A7
Ruis.		
Ridgeway, The,	29	F6
Stan.		
Ridgeway, The,	100	G6
Sutt.		
Ridgeway Ave.,	23	J6
Barn.		
Ridgeway Cres.,	104	H3
Orp.		
Ridgeway Cres.	104	H2
Gdns., Orp.		
Ridgeway Dr., Brom.	87	H5
Ridgeway E., Sid.	79	J5
Ridgeway Gdns. N6	40	C7
Ridgeway Gdns.,	43	B5
Ilf.		
Ridgeway Rd. SW9	76	H3
Ridgeway Rd., Islw.	64	B7
Ridgeway Rd. N.,	64	B6
Islw.		
Ridgeway W., Sid.	79	H5
Ridgewell Clo. N1	58	J1
Basire St.		
Ridgewell Clo.,	62	H1
Dag.		
Ridgewell Rd. E16	60	J5
Ridgmount Gdns.	11	H1
WC1		
Ridgmount Pl. WC1	11	H1

Ridgmount Rd.	75	E5
SW18		
Ridgmount St. WC1	11	H1
Ridgway SW19	83	J7
Ridgway Gdns.	84	A7
SW19		
Ridgway Pl. SW19	84	B6
Riding, The NW11	39	C7
Golders Grn. Rd.		
Riding Ho. St. W1	11	E2
Riding Ho. St. W1	58	C5
Ridings, The W5	55	J4
Ridings, The, Sun.	90	A1
Ridings, The, Surb.	92	A5
Ridings Ave. N21	24	H4
Ridings Clo. N6	40	C7
Hornsey La. Gdns.		
Ridley Ave. W13	64	E3
Ridley Rd. E7	51	J4
Ridley Rd. E8	50	C5
Ridley Rd. NW10	56	G2
Ridley Rd. SW19	84	E7
Ridley Rd., Brom.	96	F3
Ridley Rd., Well.	80	B1
Ridley Several SE3	78	H2
Blackheath Pk.		
Ridsdale Rd. SE20	95	E1
Riefield Rd. SE9	79	F4
Riesco Dr., Croy.	102	F6
Riffel Rd. NW2	47	J5
Rifle Pl. SE11	20	F5
Rifle Pl. W11	66	A1
Rifle St. E14	60	B5
Rigault Rd. SW6	75	B2
Rigby Clo., Croy.	101	G3
Rigby Ms., Ilf.	52	E2
Cranbrook Rd.		
Rigden St. E14	60	B6
Rigeley Rd. NW10	56	G3
Rigg App. E10	50	G1
Rigge Pl. SW4	76	D4
Riggindale Rd. SW16	85	D4
Riley Rd. SE1	17	F5
Riley Rd. SE1	68	C3
Riley St. SW10	18	E7
Riley St. SW10	66	G7
Rinaldo Rd. SW12	76	B7
Ring, The W2	10	A5
Ring, The W2	57	G7
Ring Clo., Brom.	87	H7
Garden Rd.		
Ringcroft St. N7	49	G5
Ringers Rd., Brom.	96	G3
Ringford Rd. SW18	75	C5
Ringlewell Clo.,	25	E2
Enf.		
Central Ave.		
Ringmer Ave. SW6	75	B1
Ringmer Gdns. N19	49	E2
Sussex Way		
Ringmer Pl. N21	25	A5
Ringmer Way, Brom.	97	C5
Ringmore Ri. SE23	77	F7
Ringslade Rd. N22	40	F2
Ringstead Rd. SE6	78	B7
Ringstead Rd.,	100	G4
Sutt.		
Ringway N11	32	C6
Ringway, Sthl.	63	D5
Ringwold Clo.,	86	H7
Beck.		
Ringwood Ave. N2	39	J2
Ringwood Ave.,	94	E7
Croy.		
Ringwood Clo., Pnr.	36	C3
Ringwood Gdns.	83	G2
SW15		
Ringwood Rd. E17	41	J6
Ringwood Way N21	32	H1
Ringwood Way,	81	G4
Hmptn.		
Ripley Clo., Brom.	97	C5
Ringmer Way		
Ripley Clo., Croy.	103	C6
Ripley Gdns. SW14	74	D3
Ripley Gdns., Sutt.	100	F4
Ripley Ms. E11	42	E7
Wadley Rd.		
Ripley Rd. E16	60	J6
Ripley Rd., Belv.	71	G4
Ripley Rd., Enf.	24	J1
Ripley Rd., Hmptn.	81	G7
Ripley Rd., Ilf.	52	J2
Ripley Vill. W5	55	F6
Castlebar Rd.		
Riplington Ct. SW15	74	G7
Longwood Dr.		
Ripon Clo., Nthlt.	45	G5
Ripon Gdns., Chess.	98	G5
Ripon Gdns., Ilf.	43	B7
Ripon Rd. N9	25	E7
Ripon Rd. N17	41	A3
Ripon Rd. SE18	70	E6

Ripon Way, Borwd.	22	C5
Rippersley Rd.,	80	A1
Well.		
Ripple Rd., Bark.	61	G1
Ripple Rd., Dag.	62	D1
Rippleside Rd.	62	B2
Est., Bark.		
Ripplevale Gro. N1	49	F7
Rippolson Rd. SE18	70	J5
Risborough Dr.,	92	G7
Wor.Pk.		
Risborough St. SE1	16	H3
Risdon St. SE16	68	F2
Renforth St.		
Rise, The E11	42	G5
Rise, The N13	32	G4
Rise, The NW7	30	F6
Rise, The NW10	47	D4
Rise, The, Bex.	80	C7
Rise, The, Buck.H.	27	A7
Rise, The, Edg.	30	B5
Rise, The, Grnf.	46	D6
Rise, The, Sid.	80	C7
Risedale Rd., Bexh.	80	H3
Riseldine Rd. SE23	77	H6
Rising Sun Ct. EC1	12	H2
Risinghill St. N1	8	E1
Risinghill St. N1	58	F2
Risingholme Clo.,	37	B1
Har.		
Risingholme Rd.,	37	B2
Har.		
Risings, The E17	42	D4
Risley Ave. N17	40	J1
Rita Rd. SW8	20	B6
Rita Rd. SW8	67	E6
Ritches Rd. N15	40	J5
Ritchie Rd., Croy.	95	E6
Ritchie St. N1	8	F1
Ritchie St. N1	58	G2
Ritchings Ave. E17	41	H4
Ritherdon Rd. SW17	85	A2
Ritson Rd. E8	50	D6
Ritter St. SE18	70	D6
Rivaz Pl. E9	50	H6
Rivenhall Gdns. E18	42	F4
River Ave. N13	32	H3
River Ave., T.Ditt.	91	D7
River Bank N21	24	J7
River Bank, E.Mol.	91	B3
River Bank, T.Ditt.	91	C5
River Bank, W.Mol.	90	F3
River Barge Clo. E14	69	C2
Stewart St.		
River Clo. E11	42	J6
River Clo., Surb.	91	G5
Catherine Rd.		
River Front, Enf.	25	A3
River Gdns., Cars.	101	A3
River Gdns., Felt.	72	B4
River Gro. Pk.,	95	J1
Beck.		
River La., Rich.	82	G1
River Meads Ave.,	81	G3
Twick.		
River Pk. Gdns.,	87	D7
Brom.		
River Pk. Rd. N22	40	F2
River Pl. N1	49	J7
River Reach, Tedd.	82	F5
River Rd., Bark.	61	H2
River Rd., Buck.H.	35	B1
River Rd. Business	61	J3
Pk., Bark.		
River St. EC1	8	E3
River St. EC1	58	G3
River Ter. W6	65	J5
Crisp Rd.		
River Vw., Enf.	24	J3
Chase Side		
River Vw. Gdns.,	82	C2
Twick.		
River Wk., Walt.	90	A6
River Way SE10	69	F3
River Way, Epsom	99	D6
River Way, Loug.	27	C6
River Way, Twick.	81	H2
Riverbank Way,	64	F6
Brent.		
Rivercourt Rd. W6	65	H4
Riverdale SE13	78	C3
Lewisham High St.		
Riverdale Gdns.,	73	F6
Twick.		
Riverdale Rd. SE18	70	J5
Riverdale Rd., Bex.	80	E7
Riverdale Rd.,	71	H5
Erith		
Riverdale Rd.,	81	F4
Felt.		
Riverdale Rd.,	73	F6
Twick.		
Riverdene, Edg.	30	C3

Riverdene Rd., Ilf.	52	D3
Riverhead Clo. E17	41	G2
Rivermead Clo.,	82	E5
Tedd.		
Rivermead Ct. SW6	75	C3
Rivernook Clo.,	90	C5
Walt.		
Riversdale Rd. N5	49	H3
Riversdale Rd.,	91	D6
T.Ditt.		
Riversfield Rd.,	25	B3
Enf.		
Riverside NW4	38	H7
Riverside SE7	69	H3
Anchor & Hope La.		
Riverside, Twick.	82	E1
Riverside Ave.,	91	A5
E.Mol.		
Riverside Clo. E5	50	F1
Riverside Clo. W7	55	B4
Riverside Clo.,	91	G4
Kings.T.		
Riverside Clo.,	101	B3
Wall.		
Riverside Ct. E4	26	B6
Chelwood Clo.		
Riverside Ct. SW8	19	J5
Riverside Ct. SW8	67	D6
Riverside Dr. NW11	39	B6
Riverside Dr. W4	65	D7
Riverside Dr.,	93	H5
Mitch.		
Riverside Dr.,	82	E2
Rich.		
Riverside Gdns. W6	65	H5
Riverside Gdns.,	24	J2
Enf.		
Riverside Gdns.,	55	H2
Wem.		
Riverside Ind.	62	A3
Est., Bark.		
Riverside Rd. E15	60	C2
Riverside Rd. N15	41	D6
Riverside Rd. SW17	84	E4
Riverside Rd., Sid.	89	E3
Riverside Wk. SE1	16	D1
Riverside Wk., Bex.	80	D7
Riverside Wk.,	73	B3
Islw.		
Riverside Wk.,	91	G2
Kings.T.		
High St.		
Riverton Clo. W9	57	C3
Riverview Gdns.	65	H6
SW13		
Riverview Gro. W4	65	B6
Riverview Pk. SE6	87	A6
Riverview Rd. W4	65	B6
Riverview Rd.,	99	D5
Epsom		
Riverway N13	32	G4
Riverwood La.,	97	G1
Chis.		
Rivington Ave.,	43	A2
Wdf.Grn.		
Rivington Ct. NW10	56	G1
Rivington Cres. NW7	30	F7
Rivington Pl. EC2	9	E4
Rivington St. EC2	9	D4
Rivington St. EC2	59	B3
Rivington Wk. E8	59	D1
Wilde Clo.		
Rivulet Rd. N17	32	J7
Rixon Ho. SE18	70	E6
Barnfield Rd.		
Rixsen Rd. E12	52	B5
Roach Rd. E3	51	A7
Roads Pl. N19	49	E2
Hornsey Rd.		
Roan St. SE10	69	B7
Robb Rd., Stan.	29	D6
Robert Adam St. W1	11	B3
Robert Adam St. W1	58	A6
Robert Clo. W9	6	D6
Robert Clo., Chig.	35	J5
Robert Dashwood	20	J2
Way SE17		
Robert Dashwood	67	J4
Way SE17		
Robert Gentry Ho.	66	B5
W14		
Comeragh Rd.		
Robert Keen Clo.	77	D1
SE15		
Cicely Rd.		
Robert Lowe Clo.	68	G7
SE14		
Robert Owen Ho.	75	A1
SW6		
Robert St. E16	70	E1
Robert St. NW1	7	E4
Robert St. NW1	58	B3
Robert St. SE18	70	G5

Robert St. WC2	12	B6
Roberta St. E2	9	J4
Roberta St. E2	59	D3
Roberton Dr., Brom.	96	J1
Roberts Clo. SE9	88	G1
Roberts Clo., Pnr.	36	B5
Field End Rd.		
Roberts Clo., Sutt.	100	A7
Roberts Ms. SW1	**15**	**B6**
Robert's Pl. EC1	**8**	**F5**
Roberts Rd. E17	42	B1
Roberts Rd. NW7	31	B6
Roberts Rd., Belv.	71	G5
Roberts St., Croy.	101	J3
High St.		
Robertsbridge Rd.,	100	F1
Cars.		
Robertson Rd. E15	60	C1
Robertson St. SW8	76	B3
Robeson St. E3	59	J5
Ackroyd Dr.		
Robin Clo. NW7	30	E3
Robin Clo., Hmptn.	81	E5
Robin Ct. SE16	**21**	**H1**
Robin Ct. SE16	68	D4
Robin Cres. E6	61	B5
Robin Gro. N6	49	A2
Robin Gro., Brent.	64	F6
Robin Gro., Har.	37	J6
Robin Hill Dr.,	88	B6
Chis.		
Robin Hood Dr.,	29	C7
Har.		
Robin Hood La. E14	60	C6
Robin Hood La. SW15	83	E4
Robin Hood La.,	80	E5
Bexh.		
Robin Hood La.,	100	D5
Sutt.		
Robin Hood Rd. SW19	83	H5
SW19		
Robin Hood Way	83	E4
SW15		
Robin Hood Way	83	E4
SW20		
Robin Hood Way,	46	C6
Grnf.		
Robina Clo., Bexh.	80	D4
Robinhood Clo.,	94	C4
Mitch.		
Robinhood La.,	94	C3
Mitch.		
Robinia Clo., Chig.	35	H5
Robins Ct. SE12	87	J3
Robins Gro.,	103	G3
W.Wick.		
Robinscroft Ms. SE10	78	B1
Sparta St.		
Robinson Cres.	28	J1
(Bushey), Wat.		
Robinson Rd. E2	59	F2
Robinson Rd. SW17	84	H6
Robinson Rd., Dag.	53	G4
Robinson St. SW3	**18**	**J5**
Robinson's Clo. W13	55	D5
Robinwood Pl. SW15	83	D4
Robsart St. SW9	76	F2
Robson Ave. NW10	56	G1
Robson Clo. E6	61	B6
Linton Gdns.		
Robson Clo., Enf.	24	H2
Robson Rd. SE27	85	H3
Roch Ave., Edg.	37	J2
Rochdale Rd. E17	42	A7
Rochdale Rd. SE2	71	B5
Rochdale Way SE8	69	A7
Idonia St.		
Roche Rd. SW16	94	E1
Roche Wk., Cars.	93	G6
Rochelle Clo. SW11	75	G4
Rochelle St. E2	**9**	**F4**
Pownall Rd.		
Rochemont Wk. E8	59	C1
Rochester Ave. E13	60	J1
Rochester Ave.,	96	H2
Brom.		
Rochester Clo. SW16	85	E7
Rochester Clo.,	25	B1
Enf.		
Rochester Clo.,	80	B6
Sid.		
Rochester Dr., Bex.	80	F6
Rochester Dr., Pnr.	36	D5
Rochester Gdns.,	102	B3
Croy.		
Rochester Gdns.,	43	C7
Ilf.		
Rochester Ms. NW1	49	C7
Rochester Pl. NW1	49	C6
Rochester Rd. NW1	49	C6
Rochester Rd.,	100	J4
Cars.		
Rochester Row SW1	**19**	**G1**

Rochester Row SW1	67	C4
Rochester Sq. NW1	49	C7
Rochester St. SW1	**15**	**H6**
Rochester St. SW1	67	D3
Rochester Ter. NW1	49	C6
Rochester Wk. SE1	**17**	**B1**
Rochester Way SE3	78	J2
Rochester Way SE9	79	C3
Rochester Way	78	H1
Relief Rd. SE3		
Rochester Way	78	J4
Relief Rd. SE9		
Rochford Ave.,	27	F3
Loug.		
Rochford Ave., Rom.	44	C5
Rochford Clo. E6	61	A2
Boleyn Rd.		
Rochford Grn.,	27	F3
Loug.		
Rochford St. NW5	48	J5
Rochford Wk. E8	50	D7
Wilman Gro.		
Rochford Way, Croy.	94	E6
Rock Ave. SW14	74	D3
South Worple Way		
Rock Gdns., Dag.	53	H5
Rockwell Rd.		
Rock Gro. Way SE16	**21**	**J1**
Rock Gro. Way SE16	68	E4
Blue Anchor La.		
Rock Hill SE26	86	C4
Rock St. N4	49	G2
Rockbourne Rd. SE23	86	G1
Rockells Pl. SE22	77	E6
Rockford Ave.,	55	D2
Grnf.		
Rockhall Rd. NW2	48	A4
Rockhampton Clo.	85	G4
SE27		
Rockhampton Rd.		
Rockhampton Rd.	85	G4
SE27		
Rockhampton Rd.,	102	B6
S.Croy.		
Rockingham Clo.	74	F4
SW15		
Rockingham Est. SE1	**16**	**J6**
Rockingham Est. SE1	67	J3
Rockingham St. SE1	**16**	**J6**
Rockingham St. SE1	67	J3
Rockland Rd. SW15	75	B4
Rocklands Dr.,	37	E2
Stan.		
Rockley Rd. W14	66	A2
Rockmount Rd. SE18	70	J5
Rockmount Rd. SE19	86	A6
Rocks La. SW13	74	G3
Rockware Ave.,	55	B1
Grnf.		
Rockways, Barn.	22	F6
Rockwell Rd., Dag.	53	H5
Rockwells Gdns.	86	B4
SE19		
Rockwood Pl. W12	65	J2
Shepherds Bush Grn.		
Rocliffe St. N1	**8**	**H2**
Rocmoale Way SE8	69	A7
Octavius St.		
Rocombe Cres. SE23	77	F7
Rocque La. SE3	78	F3
Rodborough Rd.	48	D1
NW11		
Roden Ct. N6	40	D7
Hornsey La.		
Roden Gdns., Croy.	95	B6
Roden St. N7	49	F3
Roden St., Ilf.	52	D3
Rodenhurst Rd. SW4	76	C6
Roderick Rd. NW3	48	J4
Roding Ave.,	35	B6
Wdf.Grn.		
Roding La., Buck.H.	35	A1
Roding La., Chig.	35	E2
Roding La. N.,	35	B6
Wdf.Grn.		
Roding La. S., Ilf.	43	A4
Roding La. S.,	43	A3
Wdf.Grn.		
Roding Ms. E1	**17**	**J1**
Roding Rd. E5	50	H4
Roding Rd. E6	61	E5
Roding Rd., Loug.	27	B5
Roding Trd. Est.,	52	E7
Bark.		
Roding Vw., Buck.H.	35	A1
Rodings, The,	34	J6
Wdf.Grn.		
Rodmarton St. W1	**11**	**A2**
Rodmarton St. W1	57	J5
Rodmell Clo., Hayes	54	E4
Rodmell Slope N12	31	C5
Rodmere St. SE10	69	E5
Trafalgar Rd.		
Rolls Pk. Ave. E4	34	A6

Rodmill La. SW2	76	E7
Rodney Clo., Croy.	101	H1
Rodney Clo., N.Mal.	92	E5
Rodney Clo., Pnr.	36	E7
Rodney Ct. W9	**6**	**D5**
Rodney Gdns., Pnr.	36	B5
Rodney Gdns.,	103	G4
W.Wick.		
Rodney Pl. E17	41	H2
Rodney Pl. SE17	**21**	**A1**
Rodney Pl. SE17	67	J4
Rodney Pl. SW19	93	F1
Rodney Rd. E11	42	H4
Rodney Rd. SE17	**21**	**A1**
Rodney Rd. SE17	67	J4
Rodney Rd., Mitch.	93	H2
Rodney Rd., N.Mal.	92	E5
Rodney Rd., Twick.	72	D6
Rodney St. N1	**8**	**D1**
Rodney St. N1	58	F2
Rodney Way, Rom.	44	G1
Rodway Rd. SW15	74	G2
Rodway Rd., Brom.	96	H1
Rodwell Clo., Ruis.	45	C1
Rodwell Pl., Edg.	30	A6
Whitchurch La.		
Rodwell Rd. SE22	77	C6
Roe End NW9	38	C4
Roe Grn. NW9	38	C5
Roe La. NW9	38	B4
Roe Way, Wall.	101	E7
Roebourne Way E16	70	D2
Roebuck Clo., Felt.	81	B4
Roebuck La. N17	33	C6
High Rd.		
Roebuck La.,	26	J7
Buck.H.		
Roebuck Rd., Chess.	99	A5
Roedean Ave., Enf.	25	F1
Roedean Clo., Enf.	25	F1
Roedean Cres. SW15	74	G6
Roehampton Clo.	74	G4
SW15		
Roehampton Dr.,	88	F6
Chis.		
Roehampton Gate	74	E6
SW15		
Roehampton High St.	74	G7
SW15		
Roehampton La.	74	G4
SW15		
Roehampton Vale	83	F3
SW15		
Roffey St. E14	69	C2
Rogate Ho. E5	50	D3
Muir Rd.		
Roger St. WC1	**8**	**D6**
Roger St. WC1	58	F4
Rogers Gdns., Dag.	53	G5
Rogers Rd. E16	60	F6
Rogers Rd. SW17	84	G4
Rogers Rd., Dag.	53	G5
Rogers Wk. N12	31	E3
Brook Meadow		
Rojack Rd. SE23	86	G1
Rokeby Gdns.,	42	G1
Wdf.Grn.		
Rokeby Pl. SW20	83	H7
Rokeby Rd. SE4	77	J2
Rokeby St. E15	60	D1
Rokesby Clo., Well.	79	G2
Rokesby Pl., Wem.	46	G5
Rokesly Ave. N8	40	E5
Roland Gdns. SW7	**18**	**D3**
Roland Gdns. SW7	66	F5
Roland Gdns., Felt.	81	F3
Roland Ms. E1	59	G5
Stepney Grn.		
Roland Rd. E17	42	D4
Roland Way SE17	**21**	**C4**
Roland Way SE17	68	A5
Roland Way SW7	**18**	**D3**
Roland Way, Wor.Pk.	96	F2
Roles Gro., Rom.	44	D4
Rolfe Clo., Barn.	23	H4
Rolinsden Way, Kes.	104	A4
Roll Gdns., Ilf.	43	D5
Rollesby Rd.,	99	A6
Chess.		
Rollesby Way SE28	62	C7
Rolleston Ave.,	97	E6
Orp.		
Rolleston Clo.,	97	E7
Orp.		
Rolleston Rd.,	102	A7
S.Croy.		
Rollins St. SE15	68	F6
Rollit Cres.,	72	G5
Houns.		
Rollit St. N7	49	F5
Hornsey Rd.		
Rolls Bldgs. EC4	**12**	**E3**
Rolls Pk. Rd. E4	34	B5

Rolls Pk. Rd. E4	34	B5
Rolls Pas. EC4	**12**	**E3**
Rolls Rd. SE1	**21**	**G3**
Rolls Rd. SE1	68	C5
Rollscourt Ave.	76	J5
SE24		
Rolt St. SE8	68	H6
Rolvenden Gdns.,	88	A7
Brom.		
Rolvenden Pl. N17	41	D1
Manor Rd.		
Roma Read Clo.	74	H7
SW15		
Bessborough Rd.		
Roma Rd. E17	41	H3
Roman Clo., Felt.	72	C5
Roman Ri. SE19	86	A6
Roman Rd. E2	59	F3
Roman Rd. E3	59	H2
Roman Rd. E6	61	A4
Roman Rd. N10	32	B7
Roman Rd. W4	65	F4
Roman Rd., Ilf.	52	E6
Roman Sq. SE28	71	A1
Roman Way N7	49	F6
Roman Way SE15	68	F7
Clifton Way		
Roman Way, Croy.	101	H2
Roman Way, Enf.	25	C5
Roman Way Ind. Est.	49	F7
N1		
Offord St.		
Romanhurst Ave.	96	E4
Brom.		
Romanhurst Gdns.,	96	E4
Brom.		
Romany Gdns. E17	41	H1
McEntee Ave.		
Romany Gdns., Sutt.	93	D7
Romberg Rd. SW17	85	A3
Romborough Gdns.	78	C5
SE13		
Romborough Way	78	C5
SE13		
Romero Clo. SW9	76	F3
Stockwell Rd.		
Romero Sq. SE3	78	J4
Romeyn Rd. SW16	85	F3
Romford Rd. E7	51	F5
Romford Rd. E12	52	B4
Romford Rd. E15	51	E6
Romford St. E1	**13**	**J2**
Romford St. E1	59	D5
Romilly Dr., Wat.	28	C4
Romilly Rd. N4	49	H2
Romilly St. W1	**11**	**H5**
Romilly St. W1	58	D7
Rommany Rd. SE27	86	A4
Romney Clo. N17	41	E1
Romney Clo. NW11	48	F1
Romney Clo. SE14	68	F7
Kender St.		
Romney Clo., Chess.	98	H4
Romney Clo., Har.	36	G7
Romney Dr., Brom.	88	A7
Romney Dr., Har.	36	G7
Romney Gdns., Bexh.	80	F1
Romney Ms. W1	8	B6
Romney St. SW1	67	E3
Romola Rd. SE24	85	H1
Romsey Clo., Orp.	104	E4
Romsey Gdns., Dag.	62	D1
Romsey Rd. W13	55	D7
Romsey Rd., Dag.	62	D1
Rona Rd. NW3	49	A4
Rona Wk. N1	50	A6
Marquess Est.		
Ronald Ave. E15	60	E3
Ronald Clo., Beck.	95	J4
Ronald St. E1	59	F6
Devonport St.		
Ronalds Rd. N5	49	G5
Ronalds Rd., Brom.	96	G1
Ronaldstone Rd.,	79	H6
Sid.		
Ronart St., Har.	37	C3
Stuart Rd.		
Rondu Rd. NW2	48	B5
Ronelean Rd., Surb.	98	J3
Ronver Rd. SE12	87	G1
Baring Rd.		
Rood La. EC3	**13**	**D5**
Rood La. EC3	59	B7
Rook Wk. E6	61	B6
Allhallows Rd.		
Rooke Way SE10	69	F5
Rookeries Clo.,	81	B3
Felt.		
Rookery Clo. NW9	38	F5
Rookery Cres., Dag.	53	H7

Rookery Dr., Chis. 97 D1
Rookery La., Brom. 97 A6
Rookery Rd. SW4 76 C4
Rookery Way NW9 38 F5
Rookfield Ave. N10 40 C4
Rookfield Clo. N10 40 C4
  Cranmore Way
Rookstone Rd. SW17 84 J5
Rookwood Ave., 27 F3
  Loug.
Rookwood Ave., 92 G4
  N.Mal.
Rookwood Ave., 101 D4
  Wall.
Rookwood Gdns. E4 34 F1
  Whitehall Rd.
Rookwood Gdns., 27 F3
  Loug.
  St. Marys
Rookwood Rd. N16 41 C7
Rope St. SE16 68 H3
Rope Wk., Sun. 90 C3
Rope Wk. Gdns. E1 13 J3
Rope Yd. Rails SE18 70 E3
Ropemaker Rd. SE16 68 H2
Ropemaker St. EC2 13 B1
Ropemaker St. EC2 59 A5
Ropemakers Flds. 59 J7
  E14
  Narrow St.
Roper La. SE1 17 E4
Roper St. SE9 79 C6
Roper Way, Mitch. 94 A2
Ropers Ave. E4 34 B5
Ropers Wk. SW2 76 G7
  Brockwell Pk. Gdns.
Ropery St. E3 59 J4
Ropley St. E2 9 H2
Ropley St. E2 59 D2
Rosa Alba Ms. N5 49 J4
  Kelross Rd.
Rosaline Rd. SW6 66 B7
Rosamond St. SE26 86 E3
Rosary Clo., Houns. 30 B2
Rosary Gdns. SW7 18 C2
Rosary Gdns. SW7 66 F4
Rosaville Rd. SW6 66 C7
Roscoe St. EC1 9 A6
Roscoff Clo., Edg. 38 C1
Rose All. SE1 17 A1
Rose All. SE1 67 J1
Rose & Crown Ct. 12 J3
  EC2
Rose & Crown Yd. 15 G1
  SW1
Rose Ave. E18 42 H2
Rose Ave., Mitch. 93 J1
Rose Ave., Mord. 93 F5
Rose Bates Dr. NW9 38 A4
Rose Ct. E1 59 B5
  Sandys Row
Rose Ct. SE26 86 E2
Rose Ct., Pnr. 36 C3
  Nursery Rd.
Rose Dale, Ash. 104 E2
Rose Dale, Orp. 104 E2
Rose End, Wor.Pk. 100 A1
Rose Gdn. Clo., 29 H6
  Edg.
Rose Gdns. W5 64 G3
Rose Gdns., Felt. 81 A2
Rose Gdns., Sthl. 54 G4
Rose Glen NW9 38 D4
Rose Hill, Sutt. 100 E3
Rose La., Rom. 44 D3
Rose Lawn (Bushey), 28 J1
  Wat.
Rose St. WC2 12 A5
Rose Wk., Surb. 92 B5
Rose Wk., W.Wick. 103 C2
Rose Way SE12 78 G5
Roseacre Clo. W13 55 E5
  Middlefielde
Roseacre Rd., Well. 80 B3
Rosebank SE20 86 E7
Rosebank Ave., 46 C4
  Wem.
Rosebank Clo. N12 31 H5
Rosebank Gdns. E3 59 J2
Rosebank Gro. E17 41 J3
Rosebank Rd. E17 42 B6
Rosebank Rd. W7 64 B2
Rosebank Vill. E17 42 A4
Rosebank Wk. NW1 49 D7
  Maiden La.
Rosebank Way W3 56 D6
Roseberry Gdns. N4 40 H6
Roseberry Gdns., 104 H3
  Orp.
Roseberry Pl. E8 50 C6
Roseberry St. SE16 68 E4
Rosebery Ave. E12 52 B6

Rosebery Ave. EC1 8 E5
Rosebery Ave. EC1 58 G4
Rosebery Ave. N17 41 D2
Rosebery Ave., Har. 45 E4
Rosebery Ave., 92 F2
  N.Mal.
Rosebery Ave., Sid. 79 H7
Rosebery Ave., 94 J2
  Th.Hth.
Rosebery Clo., Mord. 93 A6
Rosebery Gdns. N8 40 E5
Rosebery Gdns. W13 55 D6
Rosebery Gdns., 100 E4
  Sutt.
Rosebery Ms. N10 40 C2
Rosebery Ms. SW2 76 E6
  Rosebery Rd.
Rosebery Rd. N9 33 D3
Rosebery Rd. N10 40 C2
Rosebery Rd. SW2 76 E6
Rosebery Rd., 72 J5
  Houns.
Rosebery Rd., 92 B2
  Kings.T.
Rosebery Rd., Sutt. 100 C6
Rosebery Sq. EC1 8 E6
Rosebery Sq., 92 B2
  Kings.T.
Rosebine Ave. 73 A7
  Twick.
Rosebury Rd. SW6 75 E2
Rosebury Vale, 45 A2
  Ruis.
Rosecourt Rd., 94 F6
  Croy.
Rosecroft Ave. NW3 48 D3
Rosecroft Gdns. NW2 47 G3
Rosecroft Gdns., 82 A1
  Twick.
Rosecroft Rd., 54 G4
  Sthl.
Rosecroft Wk., Pnr. 36 D5
Rosecroft Wk., Wem. 46 G5
Rosedale Clo. W7 64 C2
  Boston Rd.
Rosedale Clo., 29 E6
  Stan.
Rosedale Ct. N5 49 H4
  Panmure Clo.
Rosedale Gdns., 53 B7
  Dag.
Rosedale Rd. E7 51 J5
Rosedale Rd., Dag. 53 B7
Rosedale Rd., Epsom 99 G5
Rosedale Rd., Rich. 73 H4
Rosedale Rd., Rom. 44 J2
Rosedene NW6 57 A1
Rosedene Ave. SW16 85 F3
Rosedene Ave., 94 E7
  Croy.
Rosedene Ave., 54 G3
  Grnf.
Rosedene Ave., 93 D5
  Mord.
Rosedene Gdns., 43 D4
  Ilf.
Rosedene Ter. E10 51 B2
Rosedew Rd. W6 66 A6
Rosefield Clo., 100 H5
  Cars.
  Alma Rd.
Rosefield Gdns. E14 60 A7
Roseford Ct. W12 66 A2
  Shepherds Bush Grn.
Rosehart Ms. W11 57 D6
  Westbourne Gro.
Rosehatch Ave., 44 D3
  Rom.
Roseheath Rd., 72 F5
  Houns.
Rosehill, Esher 98 D6
Rosehill, Hmptn. 90 G1
Rosehill Ave., 100 F1
  Sutt.
Rosehill Gdns., 46 C5
  Grnf.
Rosehill Gdns., 100 E2
  Sutt.
Rosehill Pk. W., 100 E1
  Sutt.
Rosehill Rd. SW18 75 F6
Roseland Clo. N17 33 A7
  Cavell Rd.
Roseleigh Ave. N5 49 H4
Roseleigh Clo., 73 G6
  Twick.
Rosemary Ave. N3 39 E2
Rosemary Ave. N9 33 E1
Rosemary Ave., Enf. 25 A1
Rosemary Ave., 72 D2
  Houns.
Rosemary Ave., 90 G3
  W.Mol.

Rosemary Dr. E14 60 D6
Rosemary Dr., Ilf. 43 A5
Rosemary Gdns., 98 H4
  Chess.
Rosemary Gdns., 53 F1
  Dag.
Rosemary La. SW14 74 C3
Rosemary Pl. N1 59 A1
  Shepperton Rd.
Rosemary Rd. SE15 21 G7
Rosemary Rd. SE15 68 C7
Rosemary Rd. SW17 84 F3
Rosemary Rd., Well. 79 J1
Rosemary St. N1 59 A1
  Shepperton Rd.
Rosemead NW9 38 F7
Rosemead Ave., 94 C2
  Mitch.
Rosemead Ave., 46 H5
  Wem.
Rosemont Ave. N12 31 F6
Rosemont Rd. NW3 48 F6
Rosemont Rd. W3 56 B7
Rosemont Rd., 73 J2
  N.Mal.
Rosemont Rd., Rich. 73 H6
Rosemont Rd., Wem. 55 H1
Rosemoor St. SW3 18 J2
Rosemoor St. SW3 66 J4
Rosemount Clo., 35 C6
  Wdf.Grn.
  Chapelmount Rd.
Rosemount Dr., 97 C4
  Brom.
Rosemount Rd. W13 55 D6
Rosemount Rd., 92 C3
  Kings.T.
Rosenau Cres. SW11 75 H1
Rosenau Rd. SW11 75 H1
Rosendale Rd. SE21 76 J7
Rosendale Rd. SE24 76 J7
Roseneath Ave. N21 32 H1
Roseneath Rd. SW11 76 A6
Roseneath Wk., Enf. 25 A4
Rosens Wk., Edg. 30 B3
Rosenthal Rd. SE6 78 B6
Rosenthorpe Rd. 77 G2
  SE15
Roserton St. E14 69 C2
Rosery, The, Croy. 95 G6
Roses, The, 34 F7
  Wdf.Grn.
Rosethorn Clo. SW12 76 D7
Rosetta Clo. SW8 67 E7
  Kenchester Clo.
Roseveare Rd. SE12 87 J4
Roseville Ave., 72 G5
  Houns.
Roseville Rd., 63 A5
  Hayes
Rosevine Rd. SW20 92 J1
Roseway SE21 77 A6
Rosewood Ave., 46 D5
  Grnf.
Rosewood Clo., Sid. 89 C3
Rosewood Ct., Brom. 96 J1
Rosewood Gdns. 78 C2
  SE13
  Lewisham Rd.
Rosewood Gro., 100 F2
  Sutt.
Rosewood Sq. W12 56 G6
  Primula St.
Rosher Clo. E15 51 D7
Rosina St. E9 50 G5
Roskell Rd. SW15 75 A3
Roslin Rd. W3 65 B3
Roslin Way, Brom. 87 G5
Roslyn Clo., Mitch. 93 G2
Roslyn Rd. N15 41 A5
Rosmead Rd. W11 57 B7
Rosoman Pl. EC1 8 F5
Rosoman St. EC1 8 F4
Rosoman St. EC1 58 G3
Ross Ave. NW7 31 B5
Ross Ave., Dag. 53 F2
Ross Clo., Har. 28 J7
Ross Ct. SW15 75 A7
Ross Par., Wall. 101 B6
Ross Rd. SE25 95 A3
Ross Rd., Twick. 81 H1
Ross Rd., Wall. 101 C5
Ross Way SE9 79 B3
Rossall Cres. NW10 55 J3
Rossdale, Sutt. 100 H5
Rossdale Dr. N9 25 F6
Rossdale Dr. NW9 47 C1
Rossdale Rd. SW15 74 J4
Rosse Ms. SE3 78 E1
Rossendale St. E5 50 E2
Rossendale Way 58 C1
  NW1
Rossetti Rd. SE16 68 E5

Rossignol Gdns., 101 A2
  Cars.
Rossindel Rd., 72 G5
  Houns.
Rossington St. E5 50 D2
  Barn.
Rossiter Flds., 23 B6
  Barn.
Rossiter Rd. SW12 85 B1
Rossland Clo., Bexh. 80 H5
Rosslyn Ave. E4 34 F2
Rosslyn Ave. SW13 74 E3
Rosslyn Ave., Barn. 23 H6
Rosslyn Ave., Dag. 44 F7
Rosslyn Ave., Felt. 72 A6
Rosslyn Clo., 103 F3
  W.Wick.
Rosslyn Cres., Har. 37 C4
Rosslyn Cres., Wem. 46 H4
Rosslyn Hill NW3 48 G4
Rosslyn Ms. NW3 48 G4
  Rosslyn Hill
Rosslyn Pk. Ms. NW3 48 G5
  Lyndhurst Rd.
Rosslyn Rd. E17 42 C4
Rosslyn Rd., Bark. 52 G7
Rosslyn Rd., Twick. 73 F6
Rossmore Rd. NW1 6 H6
Rossmore Rd. NW1 57 H4
Rosswood Gdns., 101 B6
  Wall.
Rostella Rd. SW17 84 F3
Rostrevor Ave. N15 41 C6
Rostrevor Gdns., 63 E5
  Sthl.
Rostrevor Ms. SW6 75 C1
  Rostrevor Rd.
Rostrevor Rd. SW6 75 C1
Rostrevor Rd. SW19 84 D5
Rotary St. SE1 16 G5
Roth Wk. N7 49 F3
  Durham Rd.
Rothbury Gdns., 64 D7
  Islw.
Rothbury Rd. E9 50 J7
Rothbury Wk. N17 33 D7
  Northumberland Gro.
Rotherfield Rd., 101 A4
  Cars.
Rotherfield St. N1 49 J7
Rotherham Wk. SE1 16 G2
Rotherhill Ave. 85 D6
  SW16
Rotherhithe New Rd. 21 J4
  SE16
Rotherhithe New Rd. 68 E5
  SE16
Rotherhithe Old Rd. 68 G4
  SE16
Rotherhithe St. 68 F2
  SE16
Rotherhithe Tunnel 68 G1
  E1
Rotherhithe Tunnel 59 H7
  App. E14
Rotherhithe Tunnel 68 F2
  App. SE16
Rothermere Rd., 101 F5
  Croy.
Rotherwick Hill W5 55 J4
Rotherwick Rd. NW11 39 D7
Rotherwood Clo. 93 B1
  SW20
Rotherwood Rd. 75 A3
  SW15
Rothery St. N1 58 H1
  Gaskin St.
Rothery Ter. SW9 67 H7
  Foxley Rd.
Rothesay Ave. SW20 93 B2
Rothesay Ave., 46 A6
  Grnf.
Rothesay Ave., 74 B4
  Rich.
Rothesay Rd. SE25 95 A4
Rothsay Rd. E7 51 J7
Rothsay St. SE1 17 D5
Rothsay St. SE1 68 B3
Rothsay Wk. E14 69 A4
  Charnwood Gdns.
Rothschild Rd. W4 65 C3
Rothschild St. SE27 85 H4
Rothwell Gdns., 53 C7
  Dag.
Rothwell Rd., Dag. 62 C1
Rothwell St. NW1 57 J1
Rotten Row SW1 14 J3
Rotten Row SW1 14 H3
Rotten Row SW7 66 H2
Rotterdam Dr. E14 69 C3
Rouel Rd. SE16 17 H6
Rouel Rd. SE16 68 D3
Rougemont Ave., 93 D6
  Mord.

Name	Page	Grid
Round Gro., Croy.	95	G7
Round Hill SE26	86	F3
Roundaway Rd., Ilf.	43	C1
Roundhay Clo. SE23	86	G2
Roundhill Dr., Enf.	24	F4
Roundmead Ave., Loug.	27	D2
Roundmead Clo., Loug.	27	D3
Roundtable Rd., Brom.	87	F3
Roundtree Rd., Wem.	46	E6
Roundway, The N17	40	J1
Roundway, The, Esher	98	C6
Roundwood, Chis.	97	E2
Roundwood Rd. NW10	47	F6
Rounton Rd. E3	60	A4
Roupell Rd. SW2	85	F1
Roupell St. SE1	**16**	**F2**
Roupell St. SE1	67	G1
Rous Rd., Buck.H.	35	B1
Rousden St. NW1	49	C7
Rouse Gdns. SE21	86	B4
Routh Rd. SW18	75	H7
Routh St. E6	61	C5
Routledge Clo. N19	49	D1
Rover Ave., Ilf.	35	J6
Rowallan Rd. SW6	66	B7
Rowan Ave. E4	33	J6
Rowan Clo. SW16	94	C1
Rowan Clo. W5	64	H2
Rowan Clo., N.Mal.	92	E2
Rowan Clo., Stan.	29	C6
Woodlands Dr.		
Rowan Clo., Wem.	46	D3
Rowan Ct. E8	50	C7
Rowan Cres. SW16	94	C1
Rowan Dr. NW9	38	G3
Rowan Gdns., Croy.	102	C3
Radcliffe Rd.		
Rowan Ind. Est., Croy.	95	B7
Rowan Rd. SW16	94	C2
Rowan Rd. W6	66	A4
Rowan Rd., Bexh.	80	E3
Rowan Rd., Brent.	64	E7
Rowan Ter. W6	66	A4
Bute Gdns.		
Rowan Wk. N2	39	F5
Rowan Wk. N19	49	C2
Bredgar Rd.		
Rowan Wk. W10	57	B4
Droop St.		
Rowan Wk., Brom.	104	C3
Rowan Way, Rom.	44	C3
Rowans, The N13	32	H3
Rowans Way, Loug.	27	C4
Rowantree Clo. N21	33	A1
Rowantree Rd. N21	33	A1
Rowantree Rd., Enf.	24	H2
Rowanwood Ave., Sid.	89	A3
Rowben Clo. N20	31	E1
Rowberry Clo. SW6	65	J7
Rowcross St. SE1	**21**	**G3**
Rowcross St. SE1	68	C5
Rowdell Rd., Nthlt.	54	G1
Rowden Rd. E4	34	A6
Rowden Rd., Beck.	95	H1
Rowden Rd., Epsom	99	B4
Rowditch La. SW11	76	A2
Rowdon Ave. NW10	47	H7
Rowdowns Rd., Dag.	62	F1
Rowe Gdns., Bark.	61	J2
Rowe La. E9	50	F5
Rowe Wk., Har.	45	G3
Rowena Cres. SW11	75	H2
Rowfant Rd. SW17	85	A1
Rowhill Rd. E5	50	E4
Rowington Clo. W2	**10**	**A1**
Rowington Clo. W2	57	E5
Rowland Ave., Har.	37	F3
Rowland Ct. E16	60	F4
Rowland Cres. Chig.	35	H4
Rowland Hill Ave. N17	32	J7
Rowland Hill St. NW3	48	H5
Rowland Way SW19	93	E1
Hayward Clo.		
Rowlands Ave., Pnr.	28	G5
Rowlands Clo. N6	40	A6
North Hill		
Rowlands Clo. NW7	30	G7
Rowlands Rd., Dag.	53	F2
Rowley Ave., Sid.	80	B7
Rowley Clo., Wem.	46	J7
Rowley Gdns. N4	49	J7
Rowley Grn. Rd., Barn.	22	F5
Rowley Ind. Est. W3	65	B3
Rowley La., Barn.	22	E4
Rowley La., Borwd.	22	D1
Rowley Rd. N15	40	J5
Rowley Way NW8	57	E1
Rowlls Rd., Kings.T.	91	J3
Rowney Gdns., Dag.	53	C6
Rowney Rd., Dag.	53	B6
Rowntree Path SE28	62	B7
Booth Clo.		
Rowntree Rd., Twick.	82	B1
Rowse Clo. E15	60	C1
Rowsley Ave. NW4	38	J3
Rowstock Gdns. N7	49	D5
Rowton Rd. SE18	70	F7
Roxborough Ave., Har.	37	B7
Roxborough Ave., Islw.	64	C7
Roxborough Pk., Har.	37	B7
Roxborough Rd., Har.	37	A5
Roxbourne Clo., Nthlt.	45	D6
Roxburgh Rd. SE27	85	H5
Roxby Pl. SW6	66	D6
Roxeth Grn. Ave., Har.	45	H3
Roxeth Gro., Har.	45	H4
Roxeth Hill, Har.	46	A3
Roxley Rd. SE13	78	B6
Roxton Gdns., Croy.	103	A5
Roxwell Rd. W12	65	G2
Roxwell Rd., Bark.	62	A2
Roxwell Trd. Pk. E10	41	H7
Roxwell Way, Wdf.Grn.	34	J7
Roxy Ave., Rom.	44	C7
Roy Gdns., Ilf.	43	H4
Roy Gro., Hmptn.	81	H6
Roy Sq. E14	59	H7
Narrow St.		
Royal Albert Dock E16	61	B7
Royal Albert Dock Spine Rd. E16	61	A7
Royal Arc. W1	**11**	**F6**
Royal Ave. SW3	**18**	**J3**
Royal Ave. SW3	66	J5
Royal Ave., Wor.Pk.	99	E2
Royal Circ. SE27	85	G3
Royal Clo., Ilf.	44	A7
Royal Clo., Wor.Pk.	99	E2
Royal College St. NW1	49	C7
Royal Ct. SE16	68	J3
Finland St.		
Royal Cres. W11	66	A1
Royal Cres., Ruis.	45	E4
Royal Cres. Ms. W11	66	A1
Queensdale Rd.		
Royal Ex. EC3	**13**	**C4**
Royal Ex. EC3	59	A6
Royal Ex. Ave. EC3	**13**	**C4**
Royal Ex. Bldgs. EC3	**13**	**C4**
Royal Hill SE10	69	C7
Royal Hospital Rd. SW3	**18**	**J5**
Royal Hospital Rd. SW3	66	J6
Royal London Est., The N17	33	D6
Royal London Ind. Est. NW10	56	D2
North Acton Rd.		
Royal Mint Ct. EC3	**13**	**G6**
Royal Mint Ct. EC3	59	C7
Royal Mint Pl. E1	**13**	**G5**
Royal Mint St. E1	**13**	**G5**
Royal Mint St. E1	59	C7
Royal Mt., Ct., Twick.	82	B3
Royal Naval Pl. SE14	68	J7
Royal Oak Pl. SE22	77	E6
Royal Oak Rd. E8	50	E6
Royal Oak Rd., Bexh.	80	F5
Royal Opera Arc. SW1	**15**	**H1**
Royal Orchard Clo. SW18	75	B7
Royal Par. SE3	78	F2
Royal Par. W5	55	H3
Western Ave.		
Royal Par., Chis.	88	F7
Royal Par. Ms. SE3	78	F2
Royal Par.		
Royal Par. Ms., Chis.	88	F7
Royal Pl. SE10	69	C7
Royal Rd. E16	60	J6
Royal Rd. SE17	**20**	**G5**
Royal Rd. SE17	67	H6
Royal Rd., Sid.	89	D3
Royal Rd., Tedd.	91	E5
Royal Route, Wem.	47	A4
Royal St. SE1	**16**	**D5**
Royal St. SE1	67	F3
Royal Victor Pl. E3	59	G2
Royal Victoria Dock E16	60	G7
Royal Wk., Wall.	101	B3
Prince Charles Way		
Royalty Ms. W1	**11**	**H4**
Roycraft Ave., Bark.	61	J2
Roycraft Clo., Bark.	61	J2
Roycroft Clo. E18	42	H1
Roydene Rd. SE18	70	H6
Roydon Clo. SW11	76	B1
Reform St.		
Roydon Clo., Loug.	27	B7
Roydon St. SW11	76	B1
Southolm St.		
Royle Cres. W13	55	D4
Royston Ave. E4	34	A5
Royston Ave., Sutt.	100	G3
Royston Ave., Wall.	101	D4
Royston Clo., Houns.	72	B1
Royston Ct. SE24	76	J6
Burbage Rd.		
Royston Ct., Rich.	73	J1
Lichfield Rd.		
Royston Ct., Surb.	99	A3
Hook Ri. N.		
Royston Gdns., Ilf.	43	A6
Royston Gro., Pnr.	28	G6
Royston Par., Ilf.	43	A6
Royston Pk. Rd., Pnr.	28	F6
Royston Rd. SE20	95	G1
Royston Rd., Rich.	73	H5
Royston St. E2	59	F2
Roystons, The, Surb.	92	B5
Rozel Ct. N1	59	B1
Rozel Rd. SW4	76	C3
Rubastic Rd., Sthl.	63	C3
Rubens Rd., Nthlt.	54	C2
Rubens St. SE6	86	J2
Ruberoid Rd., Enf.	25	J3
Ruby Ms. E17	42	A3
Ruby Rd.		
Ruby Rd. E17	42	A3
Ruby St. SE15	68	E6
Ruby Triangle SE15	68	E6
Sandgate St.		
Ruckholt Clo. E10	51	B3
Ruckholt Rd. E10	51	B4
Rucklidge Ave. NW10	56	F2
Rudall Cres. NW3	48	G4
Willoughby Rd.		
Ruddstreet Clo. SE18	70	E4
Rudland Rd., Bexh.	80	H3
Rudloe Rd. SW12	76	C7
Rudolph Rd. E13	60	F2
Rudolph Rd. NW6	57	D2
Rudyard Gro. NW7	30	C6
Ruffetts, The, S.Croy.	102	E7
Ruffetts Clo., S.Croy.	102	E7
Rufford Clo., Har.	37	D6
Rufford St. N1	58	E1
Rufford Twr. W3	65	B1
Rufus Clo., Ruis.	45	E3
Rufus St. N1	**9**	**D4**
Rugby Ave. N9	33	C1
Rugby Ave., Grnf.	46	A6
Rugby Ave., Wem.	46	E5
Rugby Clo., Har.	37	B4
Rugby Gdns., Dag.	53	C6
Rugby Rd. NW9	38	A4
Rugby Rd. W4	65	E2
Rugby Rd., Dag.	53	B6
Rugby Rd., Islw.	73	B5
Rugby Rd., Twick.	73	B5
Rugby St. WC1	**8**	**C6**
Rugby St. WC1	58	F4
Rugg St. E14	60	A7
Ruislip Clo., Grnf.	54	H4
Ruislip Rd., Grnf.	54	G3
Ruislip Rd., Nthlt.	54	C1
Ruislip Rd. E. W7	55	A4
Ruislip Rd. E. W13	55	A4
Ruislip Rd. E., Grnf.	55	A4
Ruislip St. SW17	84	J4
Rum Clo. E1	59	F7
Rumbold Rd. SW6	66	E7
Rumsey Clo., Hmptn.	81	F6
Rumsey Rd. SW9	76	F3
Runbury Circ. NW9	47	D2
Runcorn Clo. N17	41	E4
Runcorn Pl. W11	57	B7
Rundell Cres. NW4	38	H5
Runnel Fld., Har.	46	B3
Runnymede SW19	93	F1
Runnymede Clo., Twick.	72	H7
Runnymede Ct., Croy.	102	C2
Runnymede Cres. SW16	94	D1
Runnymede Gdns., Grnf.	55	A2
Runnymede Gdns., Twick.	72	H7
Runnymede Rd., Twick.	72	H6
Runway, The, Ruis.	45	B5
Rupack St. SE16	68	F2
St. Marychurch St.		
Rupert Ave., Wem.	46	H5
Rupert Ct. W1	**11**	**H5**
Rupert Gdns. SW9	76	H2
Rupert Rd. N19	49	D3
Holloway Rd.		
Rupert Rd. NW6	57	C2
Rupert Rd. W4	65	E7
Rupert St. W1	**11**	**H5**
Rupert St. W1	58	D7
Rural Way SW16	85	B7
Ruscoe Rd. E16	60	F6
Rush Grn. Gdns., Rom.	53	J1
Rush Grn. Rd., Rom.	53	J1
Rush Gro. St. SE18	70	C4
Rush Hill Ms. SW11	76	A3
Rush Hill Rd.		
Rush Hill Rd. SW11	76	A3
Rusham Rd. SW12	75	J6
Rushbrook Cres. E17	41	J1
Rushbrook Rd. SE9	88	F2
Rushcroft Rd. E4	34	A7
Rushcroft Rd. SW2	76	G4
Rushden Clo. SE19	86	A7
Rushden Gdns. NW7	30	J6
Rushden Gdns., Ilf.	43	D2
Rushdene SE2	71	C3
Rushdene Ave., Barn.	23	H7
Rushdene Clo., Nthlt.	54	C2
Rushdene Cres., Nthlt.	54	C2
Rushdene Rd., Pnr.	36	D6
Rushen Wk., Cars.	100	G1
Paisley Rd.		
Rushett Clo., T.Ditt.	98	E1
Rushett Rd., T.Ditt.	91	E7
Rushey Clo., N.Mal.	92	D4
Rushey Grn. SE6	78	B7
Rushey Hill, Enf.	24	F4
Rushey Mead SE4	78	A5
Rushford Rd. SE4	77	J6
Rushgrove Ave. NW9	38	E5
Rushley Clo., Kes.	104	A4
Rushmead E2	59	E3
Florida St.		
Rushmead, Rich.	82	E3
Croftway		
Rushmead Clo., Croy.	102	C4
Rushmere Ct., Wor.Pk.	99	G2
Rushmoor Clo., Pnr.	36	B4
Rushmore Clo., Brom.	97	B3
Rushmore Rd. E5	50	F4
Rusholme Ave., Dag.	53	G3
Rusholme Gro. SE19	86	B5
Rusholme Rd. SW15	75	A6
Rushout Ave., Har.	37	E6
Rushton St. N1	**9**	**C1**
Rushton St. N1	59	A2
Rushworth Ave. NW4	38	G3
Rushworth Gdns.		
Rushworth Gdns. NW4	38	G3
Rushworth St. SE1	**16**	**H3**
Rushworth St. SE1	67	H2
Ruskin Ave. E12	52	B6
Ruskin Ave., Rich.	65	H7
Ruskin Ave., Well.	80	A2
Ruskin Clo. NW11	39	E6
Ruskin Dr., Orp.	104	H3
Ruskin Dr., Well.	80	A3

Ruskin Dr., Wor.Pk.   99 H2
Ruskin Gdns. W5   55 G4
Ruskin Gdns., Har.   37 J4
Ruskin Gro., Well.   80 A2
Ruskin Pk. Ho. SE5   77 A3
Ruskin Rd. N17   41 C1
Ruskin Rd., Belv.   71 G4
Ruskin Rd., Cars.   100 J5
Ruskin Rd., Croy.   101 H2
Ruskin Rd., Islw.   73 C3
Ruskin Rd., Sthl.   54 E7
Ruskin Wk. N9   33 D2
  Durham Rd.
Ruskin Wk. SE24   76 J5
Ruskin Way SW19   93 G1
Rusland Ave., Orp.   104 G3
Rusland Pk. Rd.,   37 H4
  Har.
Rusper Clo. NW2   47 J3
Rusper Clo., Stan.   29 F4
Rusper Rd. N22   40 H2
Rusper Rd., Dag.   53 C6
Russell Ave. N22   40 G2
Russell Clo. NW10   47 C7
Russell Clo. SE7   69 J7
Russell Clo., Beck.   96 B3
Russell Clo., Bexh.   80 G4
Russell Clo., Ruis.   45 C2
Russell Ct. SW1   **15 G2**
Russell Gdns. N20   31 H2
Russell Gdns. NW11   39 B6
Russell Gdns. W14   66 B3
Russell Gdns.,   82 F2
  Rich.
Russell Gdns. Ms.   66 B2
  W14
Russell Gro. NW7   30 E5
Russell Gro. SW9   76 G1
Russell Kerr Clo. W4   65 C7
  Burlington La.
Russell La. N20   31 H2
Russell Mead, Har.   29 C7
Russell Pl. NW3   48 H5
  Aspern Rd.
Russell Pl. SE16   68 H3
  Onega Gate
Russell Rd. E4   33 J4
Russell Rd. E10   42 B6
Russell Rd. E16   60 G6
Russell Rd. E17   41 J3
Russell Rd. N8   40 D6
Russell Rd. N13   32 F6
Russell Rd. N15   41 B5
Russell Rd. N20   31 H2
Russell Rd. NW9   38 F6
Russell Rd. SW19   84 D7
Russell Rd. W14   66 B3
Russell Rd., Buck.H.   34 H1
Russell Rd., Mitch.   93 H3
Russell Rd., Nthlt.   45 J5
Russell Rd., Twick.   73 C6
Russell Rd., Walt.   90 A6
Russell Sq. WC1   **8 A4**
Russell Sq. WC1   58 E4
Russell St. WC2   **12 B5**
Russell St. WC2   58 E7
Russell Wk., Rich.   73 J4
  Park Hill
Russell Way, Sutt.   100 D5
Russell's Footpath   85 E5
  SW16
Russet Dr., Croy.   102 H1
Russett Way SE13   78 B2
  Conington Rd.
Russetts Clo. E4   34 D4
  Larkshall Rd.
Russia Ct. EC2   **13 A4**
Russia Dock Rd.   68 H1
  SE16
Russia La. E2   59 F2
Russia Row EC2   **13 A4**
Russia Wk. SE16   68 G2
  Archangel St.
Rust Sq. SE5   **21 B7**
Rust Sq. SE5   68 A7
Rusthall Ave. W4   65 D4
Rusthall Clo.,   95 F6
  Croy.
Rustic Ave. SW16   85 B7
Rustic Pl., Wem.   46 G4
Rustington Wk.,   93 C7
  Mord.
Ruston Ave., Surb.   92 B7
Ruston Gdns. N14   30 A4
  Farm La.
Ruston Ms. W11   57 B6
  St. Marks Rd.
Ruston St. E3   59 J1
Rutford Rd. SW16   85 E5
Ruth Clo., Stan.   37 F2
Rutherford Clo.,   100 G6
  Sutt.

Rutherford St. SW1   **19 H1**
Rutherford St. SW1   67 D4
Rutherford Twr.,   54 H6
  Sthl.
Rutherford Way   29 A1
  (Bushey), Wat.
Rutherford Way,   47 A3
  Wem.
Rutherglen Rd. SE2   71 A6
Rutherwyke Clo.,   99 G6
  Epsom
Ruthin Rd. SE3   69 G6
Ruthven St. E9   59 G1
  Lauriston Rd.
Rutin Clo. NW9   38 E6
Rutland Ave., Sid.   80 A7
Rutland Clo. SW14   74 B3
Rutland Clo. SW19   84 H7
  Rutland Rd.
Rutland Clo., Bex.   89 D1
Rutland Clo.,   98 J6
  Chess.
Rutland Ct., Enf.   25 E5
Rutland Dr., Mord.   93 C6
Rutland Dr., Rich.   82 G1
Rutland Gdns. N4   40 H6
Rutland Gdns. SW7   **14 H4**
Rutland Gdns. SW7   66 H2
Rutland Gdns. W13   55 D5
Rutland Gdns.,   102 B4
  Croy.
Rutland Gdns., Dag.   53 C5
Rutland Gdns. Ms.   **14 H4**
  SW7
Rutland Gate SW7   **14 H4**
Rutland Gate SW7   66 H2
Rutland Gate, Belv.   71 H5
Rutland Gate, Brom.   96 F4
Rutland Gate Ms.   **14 G4**
  SW7
Rutland Gro. W6   65 H5
Rutland Ms. NW8   57 E1
  Boundary Rd.
Rutland Ms. E. SW7   **14 G5**
Rutland Ms. S. SW7   **14 G5**
Rutland Pk. NW2   47 J6
Rutland Pk. SE6   86 J2
Rutland Pl. EC1   **12 H1**
Rutland Pl.   29 A1
  (Bushey), Wat.
  The Rutts
Rutland Rd. E7   52 A7
Rutland Rd. E9   59 F1
Rutland Rd. E11   42 H5
Rutland Rd. E17   42 A6
Rutland Rd. SW19   84 H7
Rutland Rd., Har.   36 J6
Rutland Rd., Ilf.   52 E4
Rutland Rd., Sthl.   54 G4
Rutland Rd., Twick.   82 A2
Rutland St. SW7   **14 H5**
Rutland St. SW7   66 H3
Rutland Wk. SE6   86 J2
Rutley Clo. SE17   **20 G5**
Rutlish Rd. SW19   93 D1
Rutter Gdns.,   93 G4
  Mitch.
Rutts, The   29 A1
  (Bushey), Wat.
Rutts Ter. SE14   77 G1
Ruvigny Gdns. SW15   75 A3
Ruxley Clo., Epsom   99 B5
Ruxley Clo., Sid.   89 E6
Ruxley Cor. Ind.   89 D6
  Est., Sid.
Ruxley Cres., Esher   98 E6
Ruxley La., Epsom   99 B6
Ruxley Ms., Epsom   99 B5
Ruxley Ridge, Esher   98 D7
Ryalls Ct. N20   31 J3
Ryan Clo. SE3   78 J4
Ryan Clo., Ruis.   45 B1
Ryan Dr., Brent.   64 D6
Ryarsh Cres., Orp.   104 H4
Rycott Path SE22   77 D7
  Lordship La.
Rycroft Way N17   41 C3
Ryculff Sq. SE3   78 F2
Rydal Clo. NW4   39 A1
Rydal Cres., Grnf.   55 E3
Rydal Dr., Bexh.   80 F2
Rydal Dr., W.Wick.   103 E2
Rydal Gdns. NW9   38 E5
Rydal Gdns. SW15   83 E5
Rydal Gdns., Houns.   72 H6
Rydal Gdns., Wem.   46 F1
Rydal Rd. SW16   85 D4
Rydal Way, Enf.   25 F6
Rydal Way, Ruis.   45 C4
Rydal Pl., Twick.   73 F6
Ryde Vale Rd. SW12   85 B2
Ryder Clo., Brom.   87 H5
Ryder Ct. SW1   **15 G1**

Ryder St. SW1   **15 G1**
Ryder St. SW1   67 C1
Ryder Yd. SW1   **15 G1**
Rydon St. N1   59 H1
  St. Paul St.
Rydons Clo. SE9   79 B3
Rydston Clo. N7   49 F7
  Sutterton St.
Rye, The N14   24 C7
Rye Clo., Bex.   80 H6
Rye Hill Est. SE15   77 F4
Rye Hill Pk. SE15   77 F4
Rye La. SE15   77 D2
Rye Pas. SE15   77 D3
Rye Rd. SE15   77 G4
Rye Wk. SW15   75 A5
  Chartfield Ave.
Rye Way, Edg.   29 J6
Ryecotes Mead SE21   86 B1
Ryecroft Ave., Ilf.   43 E2
Ryecroft Ave.,   72 H7
  Twick.
Ryecroft Cres., Barn.   22 H5
Ryecroft Rd. SE13   78 B5
Ryecroft Rd. SW16   85 G6
Ryecroft Rd., Orp.   97 G6
Ryecroft St. SW6   75 E1
Ryedale SE22   77 E6
Ryefield Path SW15   83 G1
Ryefield Rd. SE19   85 J6
Ryelands Cres. SE12   78 J6
Ryfold Rd. SW19   84 D3
Ryhope Rd. N11   32 B4
Ryland Ho., Croy.   101 J3
Ryland Rd. NW5   49 B6
Rylandes Rd. NW2   47 G3
Rylett Cres. W12   65 F2
Rylett Rd. W12   65 F3
Rylston Rd. N13   33 A3
Rylston Rd. SW6   66 C6
Rymer Rd., Croy.   95 B7
Rymer St. SE24   76 H6
Rymill St. E16   70 D1
Rysbrack St. SW3   **14 J5**
Rysbrack St. SW3   66 J3
Rythe Ct., T.Ditt.   91 D7
Rythe Rd., Esher   98 A5

S

Sabbarton St. E16   60 F6
  Victoria Dock Rd.
Sabella Ct. E3   59 J2
  Mostyn Gro.
Sabine Rd. SW11   75 J3
Sable Clo., Houns.   72 C3
Sable St. N1   49 H7
  Canonbury Rd.
Sach Rd. E5   50 E2
Sackville Ave.,   103 G1
  Brom.
Sackville Clo.,   46 A3
  Har.
Sackville Est. SW16   85 E3
Sackville Gdns.,   52 C1
  Ilf.
Sackville Rd.,   100 D7
  Sutt.
Sackville St. W1   **11 G6**
Sackville St. W1   58 C7
Sackville Way SE22   86 D1
  Dulwich Common
Saddlers Clo.,   22 D6
  Borwd.
  Farriers Way
Saddlers Clo., Pnr.   28 G6
Saddlers Ms., Wem.   46 C4
  The Boltons
Saddlescombe Way   31 D5
  N12
Sadler Clo., Mitch.   93 J2
Sadlers Ride,   90 H3
  W.Mol.
Saffron Ave. E14   60 D7
Saffron Clo. NW11   39 C5
Saffron Hill EC1   **12 F1**
Saffron Hill EC1   58 G5
Saffron Rd., Rom.   44 J2
Saffron St. EC1   **12 F1**
Saffron Way, Surb.   98 G1
Sage St. E1   69 H1
  Cable St.
Sage Way WC1   **8 C4**
Saigasso Clo. E16   61 A6
  Royal Rd.
Sail St. SE11   **20 D1**
Sail St. SE11   67 F4
Sainfoin Rd. SW17   85 A2
Sainsbury Rd. SE19   86 B5
St. Agathas Dr.,   82 J6
  Kings.T.

St. Agathas Gro.,   100 J1
  Cars.
St. Agnes Clo. E9   59 F1
  Gore Rd.
St. Agnes Pl. SE11   **20 F6**
St. Agnes Pl. SE11   67 H6
St. Aidans Rd. SE22   77 E6
St. Aidans Rd. W13   64 E2
St. Albans Ave. E6   61 C3
St. Alban's Ave. W4   65 D3
St. Albans Ave.,   81 D5
  Felt.
St. Albans Clo.   48 D1
  NW11
St. Albans Cres. N22   40 G1
St. Albans Cres.,   34 G1
  Wdf.Grn.
St. Alban's Gdns.,   82 D5
  Tedd.
St. Albans Gro. W8   **14 B5**
St. Albans Gro. W8   66 E3
St. Albans Gro.,   93 H7
  Cars.
St. Albans La. NW11   48 D1
  West Heath Dr.
St. Albans Ms. W2   **10 F1**
St. Alban's Pl. N1   58 H1
St. Albans Rd. NW5   49 A3
St. Albans Rd. NW10   56 E1
St. Albans Rd.,   23 A1
  Barn.
St. Albans Rd.,   52 J1
  Ilf.
St. Albans Rd.,   82 H6
  Kings.T.
St. Alban's Rd.,   100 C4
  Sutt.
St. Albans Rd.,   34 G7
  Wdf.Grn.
St. Albans St. SW1   **11 H6**
St. Albans Ter. W6   66 B6
  Margravine Rd.
St. Albans Twr. E4   33 J6
St. Albans Twr. E4   33 J6
St. Alfege Pas.   69 C6
  SE10
St. Alfege Rd. SE7   70 A6
St. Alphage Gdns.   **13 A2**
  EC2
St. Alphage Wk.,   38 C2
  Edg.
St. Alphege Rd. N9   25 F7
St. Alphonsus Rd.   76 D4
  SW4
St. Amunds Clo. SE6   87 A4
St. Andrew St. EC4   **12 F2**
St. Andrew St. EC4   58 G5
St. Andrews Ave.,   46 D4
  Wem.
St. Andrew's Clo.   31 F4
  N12
  Woodside Ave.
St. Andrews Clo.   47 H3
  NW2
St. Andrew's Clo.,   73 A1
  Islw.
St. Andrews Clo.,   45 D2
  Ruis.
St. Andrews Clo.,   37 F2
  Stan.
St. Andrew's Ct.   84 F2
  SW18
  Waynflete St.
St. Andrews Dr.,   37 F1
  Stan.
St. Andrews Gro.   50 A1
  N16
St. Andrew's Hill   **12 H5**
  EC4
St. Andrew's Hill   58 H7
  EC4
St. Andrews Ms. N16   50 B1
St. Andrews Ms. SE3   69 G7
  Mycenae Rd.
St. Andrews Pl. NW1   **7 E5**
St. Andrews Rd. E11   42 E6
St. Andrews Rd. E13   60 H3
St. Andrews Rd. E17   41 G2
St. Andrews Rd. N9   25 F7
St. Andrews Rd. NW9   47 D1
St. Andrews Rd.   47 H6
  NW10
St. Andrews Rd.   39 C6
  NW11
St. Andrews Rd. W3   56 E6
St. Andrews Rd. W7   64 B2
  Church Rd.
St. Andrews Rd. W14   66 B6
St. Andrews Rd.,   100 H3
  Cars.
St. Andrews Rd.,   101 J4
  Croy.
  Lwr. Coombe St.

St. Andrews Rd., 25 A3
Enf.
St. Andrews Rd., 43 C7
Ilf.
St. Andrews Rd., 89 D3
Sid.
St. Andrews Rd., 91 G6
Surb.
St. Andrews Rd., 28 D3
Wat.
  Bird Rd.
St. Andrews Sq. W11 57 B6
  St. Marks Rd.
St. Andrews Sq., 91 G6
Surb.
St. Andrews Twr., 54 J7
Sthl.
St. Andrews Way E3 60 B4
St. Annes Clo. N6 49 A3
  Highgate W. Hill
St. Anne's Clo., 28 C4
Wat.
St. Anne's Ct. W1 11 H4
St. Annes Gdns. 55 J3
NW10
St. Anne's Ho. N16 50 B1
St. Annes Pas. E14 59 J6
  Newell St.
St. Annes Rd. E11 51 D2
St. Anne's Rd., 46 G5
Wem.
St. Anne's Row E14 59 J6
St. Anne's St. E14 59 J6
  Commercial Rd.
St. Ann's, Bark. 61 F1
St. Ann's Cres. 75 E6
SW18
St. Ann's Gdns. NW5 49 A6
  Queens Cres.
St. Ann's Hill SW18 75 E5
St. Ann's La. SW1 15 J5
St. Ann's Pk. Rd. 75 F6
SW18
St. Ann's Pas. SW13 74 E3
  Cross St.
St. Anns Rd. N9 33 C2
St. Anns Rd. N15 40 H5
St. Ann's Rd. SW13 74 F2
St. Anns Rd. W11 57 A7
St. Ann's Rd., Bark. 61 F1
  Axe St.
St. Ann's Rd., Har. 37 B6
St. Ann's St. SW1 15 J5
St. Ann's Ter. NW8 6 F1
St. Ann's Ter. NW8 57 G2
St. Ann's Vill. W11 66 A1
St. Anns Way, 101 H6
S.Croy.
St. Anselm's Pl. W1 11 D4
St. Anthonys Ave., 34 J6
Wdf.Grn.
St. Anthonys Clo. E1 17 H1
St. Anthonys Clo. 84 H2
SW17
  College Gdns.
St. Antony's Rd. E7 51 H7
St. Arvans Clo., 102 B3
Croy.
St. Asaph Rd. SE4 77 G3
St. Aubyn's Ave. 84 C5
SW19
St. Aubyns Ave. 72 G5
Houns.
St. Aubyns Clo., 104 J3
Orp.
St. Aubyns Gdns. 104 J2
Orp.
St. Aubyn's Rd. 86 C6
SE19
St. Audrey Ave., 80 G2
Bexh.
St. Augustine's 55 H2
Ave. W5
St. Augustines 97 B5
Ave., Brom.
St. Augustines 101 J6
Ave., S.Croy.
St. Augustines 46 H3
Ave., Wem.
St. Augustines Rd. 49 D7
NW1
St. Augustine's 71 F4
Rd., Belv.
St. Austell Clo., 37 J2
Edg.
St. Austell Rd. 78 C2
SE13
St. Awdry's Rd., 52 G7
Bark.
St. Barnabas Clo. 96 C2
Beck.
St. Barnabas Ct., Har. 36 J1

St. Barnabas Rd. 42 A6
E17
St. Barnabas Rd., 85 A7
Mitch.
St. Barnabas Rd., 100 G5
Sutt.
St. Barnabas Rd., 42 H1
Wdf.Grn.
St. Barnabas St. 19 C3
SW1
St. Barnabas St. 67 A5
SW1
St. Barnabas Ter. 50 G5
E9
St. Barnabas Vill. 76 E1
SW8
St. Bartholomews 86 E4
Clo. SE26
St. Bartholomew's 61 C2
Rd. E6
St. Benedict's Clo. 85 A5
SW17
  Church La.
St. Benet Gro., 93 F7
Cars.
St. Benet's Clo. 84 H2
SW17
  College Gdns.
St. Benet's Pl. EC3 13 C5
St. Bernards, Croy. 102 B3
St. Bernard's Clo. 86 A4
SE27
St. Bernard's Rd. 61 A1
E6
St. Blaise Ave., 96 H2
Brom.
St. Botolph Row EC3 13 F4
St. Botolph St. EC3 13 F3
St. Botolph St. EC3 59 C6
St. Bride St. EC4 12 G3
St. Bride St. EC4 58 H6
St. Brides Ave., 37 J1
Edg.
St. Brides Clo., Erith 71 D2
  St. Katherines Rd.
St. Bride's Pas. EC4 12 G4
St. Catherines 84 H2
SW17
  College Gdns.
St. Catherines Dr. 77 G2
SE14
  Kitto Rd.
St. Catherine's Ms. 18 J1
SW3
St. Catherines Rd. 34 A2
E4
St. Chads Gdns., 44 E7
Rom.
St. Chad's Pl. WC1 8 B3
St. Chad's Pl. WC1 58 E3
St. Chads Rd., Rom. 44 E6
St. Chad's St. WC1 8 B3
St. Chad's St. WC1 58 E3
St. Charles Pl. W10 57 B5
  Chesterton Rd.
St. Charles Sq. W10 57 B5
St. Christopher's 73 B1
Clo., Islw.
St. Christophers 94 G3
Gdns., Th.Hth.
St. Christophers 101 C5
Ms., Wall.
St. Christopher's 11 C3
Pl. W1
St. Clair Dr., 99 H3
Wor.Pk.
St. Clair Rd. E13 60 H2
St. Claire Clo., 43 C2
Ilf.
St. Clair's Rd., 102 C2
Croy.
St. Clare St. EC3 13 F4
St. Clements Ct. N7 49 G6
  Arundel Sq.
St. Clements 86 D3
Heights SE26
St. Clement's La. 12 D4
WC2
St. Clements St. N1 49 G6
St. Clements St. N7 49 G6
St. Cloud Rd. SE27 85 J4
St. Crispins Clo. 48 H4
NW3
St. Crispin's Clo., 54 F6
Sthl.
St. Cross St. EC1 12 F1
St. Cross St. EC1 58 G5
St. Cuthberts Gdns., 28 F7
Pnr.
  Westfield Pk.
St. Cuthberts Rd. 48 C6
NW2

St. Cyprian's St. 84 J4
SW17
St. Davids Clo., 47 C3
Wem.
St. Davids Clo., 96 B7
W.Wick.
St. David's Ct. E17 42 C3
St. Davids Dr., 37 J1
Edg.
St. Davids Pl. NW4 38 H7
St. Denis Rd. SE27 86 A4
St. Dionis Rd. SW6 75 C2
St. Donatts Rd. 77 J1
SE14
St. Dunstan's All. 13 D6
EC3
St. Dunstans Ave. 56 D7
W3
St. Dunstan's Ct. 58 G6
EC4
  Fleet St.
St. Dunstans Gdns. 56 D7
W3
  St. Dunstans Ave.
St. Dunstan's Hill 13 D6
EC3
St. Dunstan's Hill 59 B7
EC3
St. Dunstan's Hill, 100 B5
Sutt.
St. Dunstan's La. 13 D6
EC3
St. Dunstans La., 96 C6
Beck.
St. Dunstan's Rd. 51 J6
E7
St. Dunstans Rd. 95 C4
SE25
St. Dunstans Rd. W6 66 A5
St. Dunstans Rd. W7 64 B2
St. Dunstans Rd., 72 B2
Houns.
St. Edmunds Clo. 57 J1
NW8
  St. Edmunds Ter.
St. Edmunds Clo. 84 H2
SW17
  College Gdns.
St. Edmunds Clo., 71 D2
Erith
  St. Katherines Rd.
St. Edmunds Dr., 37 D1
Stan.
St. Edmund's La., 72 H7
Twick.
St. Edmunds Rd. N9 25 D7
St. Edmunds Rd., 43 C6
Ilf.
St. Edmunds Ter. 6 H1
NW8
St. Edmunds Ter. 57 H1
NW8
St. Edwards Clo. 39 D6
NW11
St. Egberts Way E4 34 C1
St. Elmo Rd. W12 65 F1
St. Elmos Rd. SE16 68 G2
St. Erkenwald Rd., 61 G1
Bark.
St. Ermin's Hill 15 H5
SW1
St. Ervans Rd. W10 57 C5
St. Fabian Twr. E4 33 J6
St. Faiths Clo., 24 J1
Enf.
St. Faith's Rd. 85 H1
SE21
St. Fillans Rd. SE6 87 C1
St. Francis Clo., 97 H6
Orp.
St. Francis Clo., 28 B1
Wat.
St. Francis Rd. 77 B4
SE22
St. Francis Twr. E4 33 J6
St. Gabriel's Clo. 51 H1
E11
St. Gabriels Rd. 48 A5
NW2
St. George St. W1 11 E5
St. George St. W1 58 B7
St. Georges Ave. E7 51 H7
St. Georges Ave. N7 49 D4
St. Georges Ave. 38 C4
NW9
St. George's Ave. 64 G2
W5
St. Georges Ave., 54 F7
Sthl.
St. Georges Circ. 16 G5
SE1
St. Georges Circ. 67 H3
SE1

St. Georges Clo. 39 C6
NW11
St. Georges Clo., 46 D3
Wem.
St. Georges Ct. E6 61 C4
St. Georges Ct. SW7 14 C5
St. Georges Dr. 19 E2
SW1
St. George's Dr. 67 B4
SW1
St. Georges Dr., 28 E3
Wat.
St. Georges Flds. 10 H4
W2
St. Georges Flds. 57 H6
W2
St. George's Gdns., 99 B2
Surb.
  Hamilton Ave.
St. Georges Gro. 84 G3
SW17
St. Georges Gro. 84 G3
Est. SW17
St. Georges Ind. 32 H7
Est. N17
St. Georges La. EC3 13 C5
St. Georges Ms. NW1 48 J7
  Regents Pk. Rd.
St. Georges Pl., 82 D1
Twick.
  Church La.
St. Georges Rd. E7 51 H6
St. Georges Rd. E10 51 C3
St. Georges Rd. N9 33 D3
St. Georges Rd. N13 33 C3
St. Georges Rd. 39 C6
NW11
St. Georges Rd. SE1 16 F5
St. Georges Rd. SE1 67 G3
St. George's Rd. 84 C7
SW19
St. Georges Rd. W4 65 D2
St. Georges Rd. W7 64 C1
St. George's Rd., 96 B1
Beck.
St. Georges Rd., 97 C2
Brom.
St. Georges Rd., 53 E5
Dag.
St. George's Rd., 81 D4
Felt.
St. Georges Rd., 43 C7
Ilf.
St. George's Rd., 83 A7
Kings.T.
St. George's Rd., 94 B3
Mitch.
St. Georges Rd., 97 G6
Orp.
St. Georges Rd., 73 J3
Rich.
St. Georges Rd., 89 D6
Sid.
St. Georges Rd., 73 E5
Twick.
St. Georges Rd., 101 B5
Wall.
St. Georges Rd. W., 97 B1
Brom.
St. Georges Sq. E7 51 H7
St. Georges Sq. E14 59 H7
St. Georges Sq. SE8 68 J4
St. George's Sq. 19 H4
SW1
St. George's Sq. 67 D5
SW1
St. George's Sq., 92 E3
N.Mal.
  High St.
St. George's Sq. 19 H4
Ms. SW1
St. George's Sq. 67 D5
Ms. SW1
St. Georges Ter. 48 J7
NW1
  Regents Pk. Rd.
St. Georges Wk., 101 J3
Croy.
St. Georges Way 21 D6
SE15
St. Georges Way 68 B6
SE15
St. Gerards Clo. 76 C5
SW4
St. Germans Pl. SE3 78 G1
St. Germans Rd. 86 H1
SE23
St. Giles Ave., Dag. 53 H7
St. Giles Clo., Dag. 53 H7
  St. Giles Ave.
St. Giles Clo., Orp. 104 G5
St. Giles High St. 11 J3
WC2

St. Giles High St. 58 D6
WC2
St. Giles Pas. WC2 11 J4
St. Giles Rd. SE5 68 B7
St. Gilles Ho. E2 59 G2
Mace St.
St. Gothard Rd. SE27 86 A4
St. Gregory Clo., 45 C4
Ruis.
St. Helena Rd. SE16 68 G4
St. Helena St. WC1 8 E4
St. Helen's Cres. 94 F1
SW16
St. Helens Gdns. 57 A5
W10
St. Helens Pl. EC3 13 D3
St. Helens Rd. SW16 94 F1
St. Helen's Rd. W13 64 E1
Dane Rd.
St. Helens Rd., Erith 71 D2
St. Helens Rd., Ilf. 43 C6
St. Helier Ave., 93 F7
Mord.
St. Heliers Ave., 72 G5
Houns.
St. Heliers Rd. E10 42 C6
St. Hildas Clo. NW6 57 A1
St. Hildas Clo. SW17 84 H2
St. Hilda's Rd. SW13 65 H6
St. Hughe's Clo. 84 H2
SW17
College Gdns.
St. Hughs Rd. SE20 95 E1
Ridsdale Rd.
St. James Ave. E2 59 F2
St. James Ave. N20 31 H3
St. James Ave. W13 64 D1
St. James Ave., 95 H3
Beck.
St. James Ave., 100 D5
Sutt.
St. James Clo. N20 31 H3
St. James Clo. SE18 70 F5
Congleton Gro.
St. James Clo., 92 F5
N.Mal.
St. James Clo., 45 C2
Ruis.
St. James Gdns. W11 66 B1
St. James Gdns., 46 G7
Wem.
St. James Gate NW1 49 D7
St. Pauls Cres.
St. James Ms. E14 59 C3
St. James Rd. E15 51 F5
St. James Rd. N9 33 E2
Queens Rd.
St. James Rd., 100 H3
Cars.
St. James Rd., 85 A7
Mitch.
St. James Rd., 91 G6
Surb.
St. James Rd., 100 D5
Sutt.
St. James St. W6 65 J5
St. James Wk. SE15 68 C7
Sumner Est.
St. James Way, Sid. 89 E5
St. James's SE14 77 H1
St. James's Ave., 95 H3
Beck.
St. James's Ave., 81 J5
Hmptn.
St. James's Clo. 84 J2
SW17
St. James's Dr.
St. James's Cotts., 73 G5
Rich.
Paradise Rd.
St. James's Ct. SW1 15 G5
St. James's Ct. SW1 67 C3
St. James's Cres. 76 G3
SW9
St. James's Dr. 84 J1
SW17
St. James's Gro. 75 J2
SW11
Reform St.
St. James's La. N10 40 B4
St. James's Mkt. 11 H6
SW1
St. James's Pk. SW1 15 H5
St. James's Pk. SW1 67 C2
St. James's Pk., 94 J7
Croy.
St. James's Pas. EC3 13 E4
St. James's Pl. SW1 15 F2
St. James's Pl. SW1 67 C1
St. James's Rd. SE1 21 J5
St. James's Rd. SE1 68 D5
St. James's Rd. 17 J5
SE16

St. James's Rd. 68 D3
SE16
St. James's Rd., 94 H7
Croy.
St. James's Rd., 81 H5
Hmptn.
St. James's Rd., 91 G2
Kings.T.
St. James's Row EC1 8 G5
St. James's Sq. SW1 15 G1
St. James's Sq. SW1 67 D1
St. James's St. E17 41 H5
St. James's St. SW1 15 F1
St. James's St. SW1 67 C1
St. James's Ter. 6 J1
NW8
St. James's Ter. 57 J1
Ms. NW8
St. James's Wk. EC1 8 G5
St. James's Wk. EC1 58 H4
St. Joans Rd. N9 33 C1
St. John Fisher 71 D3
Rd., Erith
St. John St. EC1 8 G3
St. John St. EC1 58 G2
St. Johns Ave. N11 31 J5
St. John's Ave. 56 F1
NW10
St. John's Ave. 75 A5
SW15
St. John's Ch. Rd. 50 F5
E9
St. John's Clo. SW6 66 D7
Dawes Rd.
St. John's Clo., 46 H5
Wem.
St. John's Cotts. 86 F7
SE20
Maple Rd.
St. Johns Cotts., 73 H4
Rich.
Kew Foot Rd.
St. Johns Ct., 34 H1
Buck.H.
St. John's Ct., 73 C2
Islw.
St. John's Cres. SW9 76 G3
St. Johns Dr. SW18 84 E1
St. Johns Est. N1 9 C2
St. Johns Est. N1 59 A2
St. John's Est. SE1 17 F4
St. Johns Gdns. W11 57 B7
St. Johns Gro. N19 49 C2
St. Johns Gro. SW13 74 F2
Terrace Gdns.
St. Johns Gro., 73 H4
Rich.
Kew Foot Rd.
St. John's Hill 75 G4
SW11
St. John's Hill 75 G4
Gro. SW11
St. John's La. EC1 8 G6
St. John's La. EC1 58 H4
St. John's Ms. W11 57 D6
Ledbury Rd.
St. Johns Par., Sid. 89 A4
Church Rd.
St. John's Pk. SE3 69 F7
St. Johns Pas. SE23 86 F1
Davids Rd.
St. John's Pas. SW19 84 B6
Ridgway Pl.
St. John's Path EC1 8 G6
St. Johns Pathway 86 F1
SE23
Devonshire Rd.
St. John's Pl. EC1 8 G6
St. John's Rd. E4 38 B3
St. Johns Rd. E6 61 B1
St. Johns Rd. E16 60 G6
St. John's Rd. E17 42 B2
St. John's Rd. N15 41 B6
St. John's Rd. NW11 39 C6
St. John's Rd. SE20 86 F7
St. John's Rd. SW11 75 H4
St. John's Rd. SW19 84 B6
St. John's Rd., 61 H1
Bark.
St. Johns Rd., 100 H3
Cars.
St. Johns Rd., 101 H3
Croy.
Sylverdale Rd.
St. Johns Rd., 91 A4
E.Mol.
St. John's Rd., 81 E4
Felt.
St. Johns Rd., Har. 37 C6
St. Johns Rd., Ilf. 43 G7
St. John's Rd., Islw. 73 B2
St. Johns Rd., 91 F2
Kings.T.

St. Johns Rd., Loug. 27 C2
St. John's Rd., 92 C3
N.Mal.
St. Johns Rd., Orp. 97 G6
St. Johns Rd., 73 H4
Rich.
St. Johns Rd., Sid. 89 B4
St. Johns Rd., 63 E3
Sthl.
St. Johns Rd., 100 D2
Sutt.
St. John's Rd., 80 B3
Well.
St. John's Rd., 46 H5
Wem.
St. John's Sq. EC1 8 G6
St. John's Ter. E7 51 H6
St. Johns Ter. SE18 70 F6
St. John's Ter. W10 57 A4
Harrow Rd.
St. Johns Vale SE8 78 A2
St. Johns Vill. N19 49 D2
St. Johns Way N19 49 C2
St. John's Wd. Ct. 6 F4
NW8
St. John's Wd. High 6 F2
St. NW8
St. John's Wd. High 57 G2
St. NW8
St. John's Wd. Pk. 57 G1
NW8
St. John's Wd. Rd. 6 E5
NW8
St. John's Wd. Rd. 57 G4
NW8
St. John's Wd. Ter. 6 F1
NW8
St. John's Wd. Ter. 57 G2
NW8
St. Josephs Clo. 57 B5
W10
Bevington Rd.
St. Josephs Clo., 104 J4
Orp.
St. Joseph's Ct. 69 H6
SE7
St. Josephs Dr., 63 E1
Sthl.
St. Joseph's Gro. 38 H4
NW4
St. Josephs Rd. N9 25 E7
St. Joseph's Vale 78 D3
SE3
St. Jude St. N16 50 B5
St. Jude's Rd. E2 59 E2
St. Julian's Clo. 85 G4
SW16
St. Julian's Fm. 85 G4
Rd. SE27
St. Julian's Rd. 57 D1
NW6
St. Katharines Prec. 7 D1
NW1
St. Katharine's Way 17 G1
E1
St. Katharine's Way 68 D1
E1
St. Katherines Rd., 71 D2
Erith
St. Katherine's Row 13 E5
EC3
St. Keverne Rd. SE9 88 B4
St. Kilda Rd. W13 64 D1
St. Kilda Rd., Orp. 104 J1
St. Kilda's Rd. N16 50 A1
St. Kildas Rd., 37 B6
Har.
St. Kitts Ter. SE19 86 B5
St. Laurence Clo. 57 A1
NW6
St. Lawrence Clo., 29 J7
Edg.
St. Lawrence Dr., 36 B5
Pnr.
St. Lawrence St. 69 C1
E14
St. Lawrence Ter. 57 B5
W10
St. Lawrence Way 76 G2
SW9
St. Leonards Ave. E4 34 D6
St. Leonards Ave., 37 F5
Har.
St. Leonard's Clo., 80 A3
Well.
Hook La.
St. Leonards Ct. N1 9 C3
St. Leonard's Gdns. 72 E1
Houns.
St. Leonards Gdns., 52 F5
Ilf.
St. Leonards Ri., 104 H4
Orp.

St. Leonards Rd. 60 B5
E14
St. Leonards Rd. 56 D4
NW10
St. Leonard's Rd. 74 B3
SW14
St. Leonards Rd. 55 F6
W13
St. Leonards Rd., 101 H3
Croy.
St. Leonards Rd., 98 C6
Esher
St. Leonards Rd., 91 G5
Surb.
St. Leonards Rd., 91 D6
T.Ditt.
St. Leonards Sq. 49 A6
NW5
St. Leonards Sq., 91 G5
Surb.
St. Leonards Rd.
St. Leonards St. E3 60 B3
St. Leonard's Ter. 18 J4
SW3
St. Leonard's Ter. 66 J5
SW3
St. Leonards Wk. 85 F7
SW16
St. Loo Ave. SW3 18 H5
St. Loo Ave. SW3 66 H6
St. Louis Rd. SE27 85 J4
St. Loys Rd. N17 41 B2
St. Luke's Ave. SW4 76 D4
St. Lukes Ave., Ilf. 52 E5
St. Lukes Clo. SE25 95 E6
St. Luke's Est. EC1 9 B4
St. Luke's Est. EC1 59 A3
St. Lukes Ms. W11 57 C6
Basing St.
St. Lukes Pas., 91 J1
Kings.T.
St. Lukes Rd. W11 57 C5
St. Lukes Sq. E16 60 F6
St. Luke's SW3 18 H3
St. Luke's St. SW3 66 H5
St. Luke's Yd. W9 57 C3
St. Malo Ave. N9 33 F3
St. Margarets, 61 F1
Bark.
St. Margarets Ave. 40 H4
N15
St. Margarets Ave. 31 F1
N20
St. Margarets Ave., 45 J3
Har.
St. Margarets Ave., 88 G3
Sid.
St. Margaret's Ave., 100 B3
Sutt.
St. Margaret's Ct. 17 B2
SE1
St. Margarets Cres. 74 H5
SW15
St. Margarets Dr., 73 E5
Twick.
St. Margaret's Gro. 51 F3
E11
St. Margaret's Gro. 70 F6
SE18
St. Margarets Gro., 73 D6
Twick.
St. Margarets Pas. 78 E3
SE13
Church Ter.
St. Margaret's Rd. 51 J2
E12
St. Margarets Rd. 41 B3
N17
St. Margaret's Rd. 56 J3
NW10
St. Margarets Rd. 77 J4
SE4
St. Margarets Rd., 64 B2
W7
St. Margarets Rd., 95 G4
Beck.
St. Margarets Rd., 30 B5
Edg.
St. Margarets Rd., 73 E6
Twick.
St. Margarets Rd. 77 J4
SE4
Adelaide Ave.
St. Margaret's St. 16 A4
SW1
St. Margaret's St. 67 E2
SW1
St. Margaret's Ter. 70 F5
SE18
St. Mark St. E1 13 G4
St. Mark St. E1 59 C6
St. Marks Clo. SE10 69 C7
Ashburnham Pl.

St. Marks Clo. W11	57	B6
Lancaster Rd.		
St. Marks Clo.,	23	E3
Barn.		
St. Marks Cres. NW1	58	A1
St. Marks Gate E9	50	J7
Cadogan Ter.		
St. Mark's Gro.	**18**	**B7**
SW10		
St. Mark's Gro.	66	E6
SW10		
St. Marks Hill,	91	H6
Surb.		
St. Marks Pl. SW19	84	C6
Wimbledon Hill Rd.		
St. Marks Pl. W11	57	B6
St. Marks Ri. E8	50	C5
St. Marks Rd. SE25	95	G4
Coventry Rd.		
St. Mark's Rd. W5	64	H1
The Common		
St. Marks Rd. W7	64	B2
St. Marks Rd. W10	57	A5
St. Marks Rd. W11	57	B6
St. Marks Rd.,	96	H3
Brom.		
St. Marks Rd., Enf.	25	C5
St. Marks Rd.,	93	J2
Mitch.		
St. Marks Rd.,	82	E7
Tedd.		
St. Marks Sq. NW1	58	A1
Regents Pk. Rd.		
St. Martins Ave. E6	61	A2
St. Martin's Clo.	58	C1
NW1		
St. Martins Clo.,	25	E1
Enf.		
St. Martins Clo.,	71	D2
Erith		
St. Helens Rd.		
St. Martin's Clo.,	28	C4
Wat.		
Muirfield Rd.		
St. Martin's Ct. WC2	**12**	**A5**
St. Martins Est. SW2	85	G1
St. Martin's La. WC2	**12**	**A5**
St. Martin's La. WC2	58	E7
St. Martin's Pl. WC2	**12**	**A6**
St. Martin's Pl. WC2	58	E7
St. Martins Rd. N9	33	E2
St. Martin's Rd. SW9	76	F2
St. Martin's St. WC2	**11**	**J6**
St. Martins Way	84	F3
SW17		
St. Martin's-le-Grand	**12**	**J3**
EC1		
St. Martin's-le-Grand	58	J6
EC1		
St. Mary Abbots Pl.	66	C3
W8		
St. Mary Abbots	66	C3
Ter. W14		
St. Mary at Hill EC3	**13**	**D6**
St. Mary at Hill EC3	59	B7
St. Mary Ave.,	101	A3
Wall.		
St. Mary Axe EC3	**13**	**D4**
St. Mary Axe EC3	59	B6
St. Mary Rd. E17	42	A4
St. Mary St. SE18	70	D4
St. Marychurch St.	68	F2
SE16		
St. Marys, Bark.	61	G1
St. Marys App. E12	52	C5
St. Mary's Ave. E11	42	H6
St. Mary's Ave. N3	39	B2
St. Mary's Ave.,	96	E3
Brom.		
St. Mary's Ave.,	63	G4
Sthl.		
St. Marys Ave.,	82	C6
Tedd.		
St. Marys Clo.,	98	J7
Chess.		
St. Marys Clo.,	99	G7
Epsom		
St. Mary's Clo., Sun.	90	A4
Green Way		
St. Marys Ct. E6	61	C4
St. Mary's Ct. SE7	70	A7
St. Mary's Ct. W5	64	G2
St. Mary's Rd.		
St. Marys Cres. NW4	38	H3
St. Marys Cres.,	64	A7
Islw.		
St. Mary's Gdns.	**20**	**F1**
SE11		
St. Mary's Gdns.	67	G4
SE11		
St. Mary's Gro. N1	49	H6
St. Mary's Gro.	74	H3
SW13		

St. Mary's Gro. W4	65	B6
St. Mary's Gro.,	73	J4
Rich.		
St. Marys Mans. W2	**10**	**E1**
St. Marys Mans. W2	57	G5
St. Mary's Ms. NW6	48	E7
Priory Rd.		
St. Marys Path N1	58	H1
St. Mary's Pl. SE9	79	D6
Eltham High St.		
St. Mary's Pl. W5	64	G2
St. Mary's Rd.		
St. Marys Rd. E10	51	C3
St. Marys Rd. E13	60	H2
St. Marys Rd. N8	40	E4
High St.		
St. Marys Rd. N9	33	E1
St. Marys Rd. NW10	56	E1
St. Marys Rd. NW11	39	B7
St. Mary's Rd. SE15	77	F1
St. Mary's Rd. SE25	95	B3
St. Mary's Rd.	84	B5
(Wimbledon) SW19		
St. Mary's Rd. W5	64	G2
St. Mary's Rd.,	23	J7
Barn.		
St. Marys Rd., Bex.	89	J1
St. Marys Rd.,	91	A5
E.Mol.		
St. Marys Rd., Ilf.	52	F2
St. Marys Rd.,	91	G6
Surb.		
St. Marys Rd. (Long	91	F7
Ditton), Surb.		
St. Mary's Rd.,	99	E2
Wor.Pk.		
St. Marys Sq. W2	**10**	**E1**
St. Marys Sq. W2	57	G5
St. Mary's Sq. W5	64	G2
St. Mary's Rd.		
St. Marys Ter. W2	**10**	**E1**
St. Marys Ter. W2	57	G5
St. Marys Vw., Har.	37	F5
St. Mary's Wk. SE11	**20**	**F1**
St. Mary's Wk. SE11	67	G4
St. Mary's Way,	35	D5
Chig.		
St. Matthew St. SW1	**15**	**H6**
St. Matthews Ave.,	98	H1
Surb.		
St. Matthew's Dr.,	97	C3
Brom.		
St. Matthew's Rd.	76	F4
SW2		
St. Matthews Rd. W5	64	H1
The Common		
St. Matthew's Row	**9**	**H5**
E2		
St. Matthew's Row	59	D3
E2		
St. Matthias Clo.	38	F5
NW9		
St. Maur Rd. SW6	75	C1
St. Merryn Clo.	79	G7
SE18		
St. Michael's All. EC3	**13**	**C4**
St. Michaels Ave.	25	F7
N9		
St. Michael's Ave.,	47	A6
Wem.		
St. Michaels Clo.	61	A5
E16		
Long Mark Rd.		
St. Michael's Clo.	39	C2
N3		
St. Michael's Clo.	31	H5
N12		
St. Michaels Clo.	97	B3
Brom.		
St. Michaels Clo.	71	D2
Erith		
St. Helens Rd.		
St. Michaels Clo.,	99	F2
Wor.Pk.		
St. Michaels Cres.	36	E6
Pnr.		
St. Michaels Gdns.	57	B5
W10		
St. Lawrence Ter.		
St. Michaels Rd.	47	J4
NW2		
St. Michael's Rd.	76	F2
SW9		
St. Michaels Rd.,	101	J1
Croy.		
St. Michaels Rd.,	101	C6
Wall.		
St. Michaels Rd.,	80	B3
Well.		
St. Michaels St. W2	**10**	**F3**
St. Michaels St. W2	57	G6
St. Michaels Ter.	40	E2
N22		

St. Mildred's Ct.	**13**	**B4**
EC2		
St. Mildreds Rd.	78	F7
SE12		
St. Nicholas Glebe	85	A5
SW17		
St. Nicholas La.,	97	B1
Chis.		
St. Nicholas Rd.	70	J5
SE18		
St. Nicholas Rd.,	100	E5
Sutt.		
St. Nicholas Rd.,	91	C6
T.Ditt.		
St. Nicholas St.	77	J1
SE8		
Lucas St.		
St. Nicholas Way,	100	E4
Sutt.		
St. Ninian's Ct.	31	J3
N20		
St. Norbert Grn.	77	H4
SE4		
St. Norbert Rd. SE4	77	G5
St. Olaf's Rd. SW6	66	B7
St. Olaves Ct. EC2	**13**	**B4**
St. Olave's Est. SE1	**17**	**E3**
St. Olaves Gdns.	**20**	**E1**
SE11		
St. Olaves Rd. E6	61	D1
St. Olave's Wk.	94	C2
SW16		
St. Olav's Sq. SE16	68	F2
Albion St.		
St. Oswald's Pl.	**20**	**C4**
SE11		
St. Oswald's Pl.	67	F5
SE11		
St. Oswald's Rd.	94	H1
SW16		
St. Oswulf St. SW1	**19**	**J2**
St. Pancras Way	49	C7
NW1		
St. Patrick's Ct.,	34	E7
Wdf.Grn.		
St. Paul St. N1	58	J1
St. Paul's All. EC4	58	H6
St. Paul's Chyd.		
St. Paul's Ave. NW2	47	J6
St. Paul's Ave.	68	G1
SE16		
St. Pauls Ave.,	37	J5
Har.		
St. Paul's Chyd. EC4	**12**	**H4**
St. Paul's Chyd. EC4	58	H6
St. Paul's Clo. SE7	70	A5
St. Paul's Clo. W5	64	J2
St. Pauls Clo.	100	H1
Cars.		
St. Pauls Clo.,	98	G4
Chess.		
St. Pauls Clo.,	72	E2
Houns.		
St. Paul's Ct. W14	66	A4
Colet Gdns.		
St. Pauls Ctyd. SE8	69	A7
Deptford High St.		
St. Pauls Cray Rd.,	97	G1
Chis.		
St. Pauls Cres. NW1	49	D7
St. Pauls Dr. E15	51	D5
St. Paul's Ms. NW1	49	D7
St. Pauls Cres.		
St. Paul's Pl. N1	50	A6
St. Pauls Ri. N13	32	H6
St. Pauls Rd. N1	49	H6
St. Paul's Rd. N17	33	D7
St. Paul's Rd.,	61	F1
Bark.		
St. Paul's Rd.,	64	G6
Brent.		
St. Paul's Rd.,	71	J7
Erith		
St. Paul's Rd.,	73	J3
Rich.		
St. Paul's Rd.,	94	J3
Th.Hth.		
St. Paul's	50	A6
Shrubbery N1		
St. Pauls Sq.,	96	G2
Brom.		
St. Pauls St. E3	59	J5
St. Paul's Ter. SE17	**20**	**H5**
St. Pauls Twr. E10	42	C7
St. Pauls Wk.,	83	A7
Kings.T.		
Alexandra Rd.		
St. Pauls Way E3	59	H5
St. Pauls Way N3	31	E7
St. Pauls Wd. Hill,	97	H2
Orp.		
St. Peter's All. EC3	**13**	**C4**
St. Peter's Ave. E2	**9**	**J2**

St. Peter's Ave.	42	E4
E17		
St. Peters Ave. N18	33	D4
St. Peter's Clo. E2	**9**	**J2**
St. Peter's Clo. E2	59	D2
St. Peters Clo.	84	H2
SW17		
College Gdns.		
St. Peters Clo.,	22	H5
Barn.		
St. Peters Clo.,	88	G7
Chis.		
St. Peters Clo.,	43	H4
Ilf.		
St. Peters Clo.,	45	D2
Ruis.		
St. Peters Clo.	29	A1
(Bushey), Wat.		
St. Peter's Ct. NW4	38	J5
St. Peters Ct. SE3	78	F4
Eltham Rd.		
St. Peters Ct. SE4	77	J2
Wickham Rd.		
St. Peter's Gdns.	85	G3
SE27		
St. Peters Gro. W6	65	G4
St. Peters Rd. N9	33	E1
St. Peters Rd. N9	33	F1
St. Peters Rd. W6	65	G5
St. Peters Rd.,	102	A4
Croy.		
St. Peters Rd.,	92	A2
Kings.T.		
St. Peters Rd.,	61	C6
Sthl.		
St. Peters Rd.,	73	E5
Twick.		
St. Peters Rd.,	90	G4
W.Mol.		
St. Peter's Sq. E2	**9**	**J2**
St. Peters Sq. W6	65	G5
St. Peters St. N1	58	H1
St. Peter's St.,	102	A5
S.Croy.		
St. Peters Ter. SW6	66	C7
St. Peters Vill. W6	65	G4
St. Peter's Way N1	50	B7
St. Peters Way W5	55	G5
St. Petersburgh Pl.	**10**	**A5**
W2		
St. Petersburgh Ms.	57	E7
W2		
St. Petersburgh Pl.	**10**	**A5**
W2		
St. Petersburgh Pl.	57	E7
W2		
St. Philip Sq. SW8	76	B2
St. Philip St. SW8	76	B2
St. Philip's Ave.,	99	H2
Wor.Pk.		
St. Philip's Rd. E8	50	D6
St. Philips Rd.,	91	G6
Surb.		
St. Philip's Way N1	58	J1
Linton St.		
St. Quentin Rd.,	79	J3
Well.		
St. Quintin Ave.,	56	J5
W10		
St. Quintin Gdns.	56	J5
W10		
St. Quintin Rd. E13	60	H2
St. Raphael's Way	47	C5
NW10		
St. Regis Clo. N10	40	B2
St. Ronans Cres.,	34	G7
Wdf.Grn.		
St. Rule St. SW8	76	C2
St. Saviour's Est.	**17**	**F5**
SE1		
St. Saviour's Est.	68	C3
SE1		
St. Saviour's Rd.	76	F5
SW2		
St. Saviours Rd.,	94	H6
Croy.		
St. Silas Pl. NW5	49	A6
St. Silas St. Est.	49	A6
NW5		
St. Simons Ave.	74	J5
SW15		
St. Stephens Ave.	42	C5
E17		
St. Stephens Ave.	65	H2
W12		
St. Stephens Ave.	55	E6
W13		
St. Stephens Clo.	42	B5
E17		
St. Stephens Clo.	57	H1
NW8		
St. Stephens Clo.,	54	G5
Sthl.		

St. Stephens Cres. 57 D6
W2
  Talbot Rd.
St. Stephens Cres., 94 G3
Th.Hth.
St. Stephens Gdn. 57 D6
Est. W2
  Shrewsbury Rd.
St. Stephens Gdns. 75 C5
SW15
  Manfred Rd.
St. Stephens Gdns. 57 D6
W2
St. Stephen's 73 F6
Gdns., Twick.
St. Stephens Gro. 78 C3
SE13
St. Stephens Ms. W2 57 D5
  Chepstow Rd.
St. Stephen's Pas., 73 F6
Twick.
  Richmond Rd.
St. Stephens Rd. E3 59 H1
St. Stephens Rd. E6 51 J7
St. Stephen's Rd. 42 B5
E17
  Grove Rd.
St. Stephens Rd. 55 E6
W13
St. Stephen's Rd., 23 A5
Barn.
St. Stephens Rd., 72 G6
Houns.
St. Stephens Row 13 B5
EC4
St. Stephens Ter. 67 F7
SW8
St. Stephen's Wk. 18 C1
SW7
St. Swithin's La. EC4 13 B5
St. Swithin's La. 59 A7
EC4
St. Swithun's Rd. 78 D5
SE13
St. Thomas Ct., 80 G7
Bex.
St. Thomas Dr., 104 F1
Orp.
St. Thomas Dr., 36 E1
Pnr.
St. Thomas Gdns., 52 F6
Ilf.
St. Thomas Pl. NW1 49 D7
  Maiden La.
St. Thomas Rd. E16 60 G6
St. Thomas Rd. N14 24 D7
St. Thomas Rd., 71 J2
Belv.
St. Thomas Rd. SE1 17 C2
St. Thomas St. SE1 68 A1
St. Thomas's Gdns. 49 A6
NW5
  Queens Cres.
St. Thomas's Pl. E9 50 F7
St. Thomas's Rd. N4 49 G2
St. Thomas's Rd. 56 E1
NW10
St. Thomas's Rd. W4 65 C6
St. Thomas's Sq. E9 50 F7
St. Thomas's Way 66 C7
SW6
St. Ursula Gro., 36 D5
Pnr.
St. Ursula Rd., 54 G6
Sthl.
St. Vincent Clo. 85 H5
SE27
St. Vincent Rd., 72 J6
Twick.
St. Vincent St. W1 11 C2
St. Wilfrids Clo., 23 G5
Barn.
  East Barnet Rd.
St. Wilfrid's Rd., 23 G5
Barn.
  East Barnet Rd.
St. Winifreds Clo., 35 F5
Chig.
St. Winifreds Rd., 82 E6
Tedd.
St. Winifride's 37 J4
Ave. E12
Saints Dr. E7 52 A5
Salamanca Pl. SE11 20 C2
Salamanca St. SE11 20 C2
Salamanca St. SE11 67 F4
Salcombe Dr., Mord. 100 A1
Salcombe Dr., Rom. 44 F6
Salcombe Gdns. 30 J6
NW7
Salcombe Rd. E17 41 J7
Salcombe Rd. N16 50 B5
Salcombe Way, Ruis. 45 A2

Salcott Rd. SW11 75 H5
Salcott Rd., Croy. 101 E3
Sale Pl. W2 10 G2
Sale Pl. W2 57 H6
Sale St. E2 9 J5
Sale St. E2 59 D4
Salehurst Clo., 37 H5
Har.
Salehurst Rd. SE4 77 J6
Salem Pl., Croy. 101 J3
Salem Rd. W2 10 B5
Salem Rd. W2 57 E7
Salford Rd. SW2 85 D1
Salhouse Clo. SE28 62 C6
  Rollesby Way
Salisbury Ave. N3 39 C3
Salisbury Ave., 52 G7
Bark.
Salisbury Ave., 100 C6
Sutt.
Salisbury Clo. SE17 21 B1
Salisbury Clo., 99 F3
Wor.Pk.
Salisbury Ct. EC4 12 F4
Salisbury Ct. EC4 58 H6
Salisbury Gdns. 84 B7
SW19
Salisbury Gdns., 35 A2
Buck.H.
Salisbury Hall 34 A6
Gdns. E4
Salisbury Ho. E14 60 B6
  Hobday St.
Salisbury Ms. SW6 66 C7
  Dawes Rd.
Salisbury Pl. SW9 67 H7
Salisbury Pl. W1 10 J1
Salisbury Pl. W1 57 J5
Salisbury Rd. E4 34 A3
Salisbury Rd. E7 51 G6
Salisbury Rd. E10 51 C2
Salisbury Rd. E12 52 A5
Salisbury Rd. E17 42 C5
Salisbury Rd. N4 40 H5
Salisbury Rd. N9 33 D3
Salisbury Rd. N22 40 H1
Salisbury Rd. SE25 95 D6
Salisbury Rd. SW19 84 B7
Salisbury Rd. W13 64 D2
Salisbury Rd., 23 B3
Barn.
Salisbury Rd., Bex. 89 G1
Salisbury Rd., 97 B5
Brom.
Salisbury Rd., 100 J6
Cars.
Salisbury Rd., Dag. 53 H6
Salisbury Rd., 81 C1
Felt.
Salisbury Rd., Har. 37 A5
Salisbury Rd., 72 C3
Houns.
Salisbury Rd., Ilf. 52 H2
Salisbury Rd., 92 D3
N.Mal.
Salisbury Rd., Pnr. 36 A4
Salisbury Rd., 73 H4
Rich.
Salisbury Rd., 63 E4
Sthl.
Salisbury Rd., 99 D4
Wor.Pk.
Salisbury Sq. EC4 12 F4
Salisbury St. NW8 6 G6
Salisbury St. W3 65 C2
Salisbury Ter. SE15 77 F3
Salisbury Wk. N19 49 C2
Salix Clo., Sun. 81 B7
  Oak Gro.
Salliesfield, 73 A6
Twick.
Salmen Rd. E13 60 F2
Salmon La. E14 59 H6
Salmon Rd., Belv. 71 G5
Salmon St. E14 59 J6
  Salmon La.
Salmon St. NW9 47 B1
Salmond Clo., Stan. 29 D6
  Robb St.
Salmons Rd. N9 33 J1
Salmons Rd., Chess. 98 G6
Salomons Rd. E13 60 J5
  Chalk Rd.
Salop Rd. E17 41 G6
Saltash Clo., Sutt. 100 C4
Saltash Rd., Ilf. 35 G7
Saltash Rd., Well. 80 C1
Saltash Rd. W4 65 E2
Saltcroft Clo., 47 B1
Wem.
Salter Rd. SE16 68 G1
Salter St. E14 60 A7

Salter St. NW10 56 G3
Salterford Rd. SW17 85 A6
Salters Hall Ct. EC4 13 B5
Salters Hill SE19 86 A5
Salters Rd. E17 42 D4
Salters Rd. W10 57 A4
Salterton Rd. N7 49 E3
Saltoun Rd. SW2 76 E1
Saltram Clo. N15 41 C4
Saltram Cres. W9 57 C3
Saltwell St. E14 60 A7
Saltwood Gro. SE17 21 B4
Salusbury Rd. NW6 57 B1
Salvia Gdns., Grnf. 55 D2
  Selborne Gdns.
Salvin Rd. SW15 75 A3
Salway Clo., 34 F7
Wdf.Grn.
Salway Pl. E15 51 E6
  Broadway
Salway Rd. E15 51 D6
Sam Bartram Clo. 69 J5
SE7
Samantha Clo. E17 41 J7
Sambruck Ms. SE6 87 B2
  Inchmery Rd.
Samels Ct. W6 65 G5
  South Black Lion La.
Samford St. NW8 6 G6
Samford St. NW8 57 H4
Samos Rd. SE20 95 E2
Sampson Ave., Barn. 23 A5
Sampson Clo., Belv. 71 D3
  Carrill Way
Sampson St. E1 17 J2
Sampson St. E1 68 D1
Samson St. E13 60 J2
Samuel Clo. E8 59 C1
  Pownall Rd.
Samuel Clo. SE14 68 G6
Samuel Clo. SE18 70 B4
Samuel Johnson Clo. 85 G4
SW16
  Curtis Fld. Rd.
Samuel Lewis Trust 50 D4
Dws. E8
  Amhurst Rd.
Samuel Lewis Trust 49 G7
Dws. N1
  Liverpool Rd.
Samuel Lewis Trust 18 G2
Dws. SW3
Samuel Lewis Trust 66 D7
Dws. SW6
Samuel St. SE18 70 C4
Sancroft Clo. NW2 47 H3
Sancroft Rd., Har. 37 C2
Sancroft St., Stan. 37 C2
Sancroft St. SE11 20 D3
Sancroft St. SE11 67 F5
Sanctuary, The SW1 15 J5
Sanctuary, The, 80 D6
Bex.
Sanctuary, The, 93 E6
Mord.
  Green La.
Sanctuary, The, 93 E6
Mord.
Sanctuary St. SE1 17 A4
Sandal Rd. N18 33 D5
Sandal Rd., N.Mal. 92 D5
Sandal St. E15 60 E1
Sandale Clo. N16 50 A3
  Stoke Newington Ch. St.
Sandall Clo. W5 55 H4
Sandall Rd. NW5 49 C6
Sandall Rd. W5 55 H4
Sandalwood Clo. E1 59 H4
  Solebay St.
Sandalwood Rd., 81 B3
Felt.
Sandbach Pl. SE18 70 F5
Sandbourne Ave. 93 E2
SW19
Sandbourne Rd. SE4 77 H2
Sandbrook Clo. NW7 30 D6
Sandbrook Rd. N16 50 B3
Sandby Grn. SE9 79 B3
Sandell St. SE1 16 E3
Sanders Clo., 81 J5
Hmptn.
Sanders La. NW7 30 J7
Sanders Way N19 49 D1
  Sussex Way
Sanderson Clo. NW5 49 B4
Sanderstead Ave. 48 B2
NW2
Sanderstead Clo. 76 C7
SW12
  Atkins Rd.
Sanderstead Rd. E10 50 H1
Sanderstead Rd., 102 A7
S.Croy.

Sandfield Gdns., 94 H3
Th.Hth.
Sandfield Ind. Est., 90 F1
Hmptn.
Sandfield Pas., 94 J3
Th.Hth.
Sandfield Rd., 94 H3
Th.Hth.
Sandford Ave. N22 40 J1
Sandford Ave., 27 E3
Loug.
Sandford Clo. E6 61 C4
Sandford Ct. N16 50 B1
  Bethune Rd.
Sandford Rd. E6 61 B3
Sandford Rd. N22 40 J1
Sandford Rd., Bexh. 80 E4
Sandford Rd., Brom. 96 G3
Sandford St. SW6 66 E7
  Kings Rd.
Sandgate La. SW18 84 H1
Sandgate Rd., Well. 71 C7
Sandgate St. SE15 68 E6
Sandham Pt. SE18 70 E4
  Troy Ct.
Sandhills, Wall. 101 D4
Sandhurst Ave., 36 H6
Har.
Sandhurst Ave., 92 B7
Surb.
Sandhurst Clo. NW9 38 A3
Sandhurst Dr., Ilf. 52 J4
Sandhurst Rd. N9 25 F6
Sandhurst Rd. NW9 38 A3
Sandhurst Rd. SE6 87 D1
Sandhurst Rd., Bex. 80 D5
Sandhurst Rd., Sid. 88 J3
Sandhurst Way, 102 B7
S.Croy.
Sandiford Rd., Sutt. 100 C2
Sandiland Cres., 103 F2
Brom.
Sandilands, Croy. 102 D2
Sandilands Rd. SW6 75 E1
Sandison St. SE15 77 C3
Sandland St. WC1 12 D2
Sandland St. WC1 58 F5
Sandling Ri. SE9 88 C3
Sandlings, The N22 40 G2
Sandmere Rd. SW4 76 E5
Sandon Clo., Esher 91 A7
Sandown Ave., Dag. 55 C7
Sandown Clo., 72 A1
Houns.
Sandown Rd. SE25 95 E5
Sandown Way, Nthlt. 45 E6
Sandpit Pl. SE7 70 B5
Sandpit Rd., Brom. 87 E5
Sandpits Rd., Croy. 102 G4
Sandpits Rd., Rich. 82 G2
Sandra Clo. N22 40 J1
  New Rd.
Sandra Clo., Houns. 72 H5
Sandridge Clo., 37 B4
Har.
  Queens Dr.
Sandridge St. N19 49 C2
Sandringham Ave. 93 B1
SW20
Sandringham Clo., 25 B2
Enf.
Sandringham Clo., 43 F3
Ilf.
Sandringham Ct. W9 6 D4
Sandringham Cres., 45 G2
Har.
Sandringham Dr., 79 H2
Well.
Sandringham Gdns. 40 E6
N8
Sandringham Gdns. 31 F6
N12
Sandringham Gdns., 72 A1
Houns.
Sandringham Gdns., 43 F3
Ilf.
Sandringham Rd. E7 51 J5
Sandringham Rd. E8 50 C5
Sandringham Rd. 42 D6
E10
Sandringham Rd. 40 J3
N22
Sandringham Rd. 47 H6
NW2
Sandringham Rd. 39 B7
NW11
Sandringham Rd., 52 J6
Bark.
Sandringham Rd., 87 G5
Brom.
Sandringham Rd., 45 G7
Nthlt.

Sandringham Rd., 94 J5
  Th.Hth.
Sandringham Rd., 99 G3
  Wor.Pk.
Sandrock Pl., Croy. 102 G4
Sandrock Rd. SE13 78 A3
Sand's End La. SW6 75 E1
Sands Way, Wdf.Grn. 35 C6
Sandstone Pl. N19 49 B2
  Dartmouth Pk. Hill
Sandstone Rd. SE12 87 H2
Sandtoft Rd. SE7 69 H6
Sandwell Cres. NW6 48 D6
Sandwich St. WC1 8 A4
Sandwich St. WC1 58 E3
Sandy Bury, Orp. 104 G3
Sandy Hill Ave. SE18 70 E5
Sandy Hill Rd. SE18 70 E5
Sandy La., Har. 37 J6
Sandy La., Kings.T. 91 E1
Sandy La., Mitch. 94 A1
Sandy La., Rich. 82 F2
Sandy La., Sid. 89 D7
Sandy La., Sutt. 100 B7
Sandy La., Tedd. 82 D7
Sandy La., Walt. 90 B6
Sandy La. Est., 82 G2
  Rich.
Sandy La. N., Wall. 101 D6
Sandy Ridge, Chis. 88 D6
Sandy Rd. NW3 48 E2
Sandy Way, Croy. 102 J3
Sandycombe Rd., 81 A1
  Felt.
Sandycombe Rd., 74 A3
  Rich.
Sandycombe Rd., 73 F6
  Twick.
Sandycroft SE2 71 A6
Sandyhill Rd., Ilf. 52 E4
Sandymount Ave., 29 F5
  Stan.
Sandys Row E1 13 E2
Sandys Row E1 59 B5
Sanford La. N16 50 C3
  Stoke Newington
  High St.
Sanford St. SE14 68 H6
Sanford Ter. N16 50 C2
Sanford Wk. N16 50 C2
Sanford Wk. SE14 68 H6
  Cold Blow La.
Sanger Ave., Chess. 98 H5
Sangley Rd. SE6 78 B7
Sangley Rd. SE25 95 B4
Sangora Rd. SW11 75 G4
Sans Wk. EC1 8 F5
Sans Wk. EC1 58 G4
Sansom Rd. E11 51 F2
Sansom St. SE5 68 A7
Santley St. SW4 76 E4
Santos Rd. SW18 75 D5
Santway, The, Stan. 29 B5
Sapphire Clo. E6 61 D6
Sapphire Clo., Dag. 53 C1
Sapphire Rd. SE8 68 H5
Sara Ct., Beck. 96 B1
  Albemarle Rd.
Saracen Clo., Croy. 95 A6
Saracen St. E14 60 A6
Saracen's Head Yd. 13 F4
  EC3
Sarah Ho. SW15 74 F4
  Arabella Dr.
Sarah St. N1 9 E3
Saratoga Rd. E5 50 F4
Sardinia St. WC2 12 C4
Sarita Clo., Har. 37 A2
Sarjant Path SW19 84 A2
  Queensmere Rd.
Sark Clo., Houns. 63 G7
Sark Wk. E16 60 H6
Sarnesfield Ho. SE15 68 E6
  Pencraig Way
Sarnesfield Rd., 25 A3
  Enf.
  Church St.
Sarre Rd. NW2 48 C5
Sarsen Ave., Houns. 72 F2
Sarsfield Rd. SW12 84 J2
Sarsfield Rd., 55 E2
  Grnf.
Sartor Rd. SE15 77 G4
Satanita Clo. E16 61 A6
  Aleston Beck Rd.
Satchwell Mead NW9 38 F1
Satchwell Rd. E2 9 G4
Satchwell St. E2 9 G4
Sauls Grn. E11 51 E3
  Napier Rd.
Saunders Ness Rd. 69 C5
  E14

Saunders Rd. SE18 70 J5
Saunders Way SE28 62 B7
  Oriole Way
Saunderton Rd., 46 E5
  Wem.
Savage Gdns. E6 61 C6
Savage Gdns. EC3 13 E6
Savernake Rd. N9 25 D6
Savernake Rd. NW3 48 J4
Savile Clo., N.Mal. 92 E5
Savile Gdns., Croy. 102 C2
Savile Row W1 11 F5
Savile Row W1 57 C7
Savill Gdns. SW20 92 G3
  Bodnant Gdns.
Savill Row, 34 F6
  Wdf.Grn.
Saville Rd. E16 70 B1
Saville Rd. W4 65 D3
Saville Rd., Rom. 44 F6
Saville Rd., Twick. 82 C1
Saville Row, Brom. 103 F1
Saville Row, Enf. 25 G2
  Green St.
Savona Clo. SW19 84 B7
Savona Est. SW8 67 C7
Savona St. SW8 67 C7
Savoy Bldgs. WC2 12 C6
Savoy Clo. E15 60 E1
  Arthingworth St.
Savoy Clo., Edg. 30 A5
Savoy Ct. WC2 12 B6
Savoy Hill WC2 12 C6
Savoy Pl. WC2 12 B6
Savoy Pl. WC2 58 E7
Savoy Row WC2 12 C6
Savoy Steps WC2 12 C6
Savoy St. WC2 12 C6
Savoy St. WC2 58 E7
Savoy Way WC2 12 C6
Sawkins Clo. SW19 84 B2
Sawley Rd. W12 65 F1
Sawtry Clo., Cars. 93 G7
Sawyer Clo. N9 33 D2
  Lion Rd.
Sawyer St. SE1 16 J3
Sawyer St. SE1 67 J2
Sawyers Clo., Dag. 53 J6
Sawyer's Hill, 73 J7
  Rich.
Sawyers Lawn W13 55 C6
Saxby Rd. SW2 76 E7
Saxham Rd., Bark. 61 J2
Saxlingham Rd. E4 34 D3
Saxon Ave., Felt. 81 E2
Saxon Clo., Surb. 91 G6
Saxon Dr. W3 56 B6
Saxon Rd. E3 59 J2
Saxon Rd. E6 61 C4
Saxon Rd. N22 40 H1
Saxon Rd. SE25 95 A5
Saxon Rd., Brom. 87 F1
Saxon Rd., Ilf. 52 E6
Saxon Rd., Sthl. 63 E1
Saxon Rd., Wem. 47 C3
Saxon Wk., Sid. 89 C6
  Cray Rd.
Saxon Way N14 24 D6
Saxonbury Ave., 90 B3
  Sun.
Saxonbury Clo., 93 G3
  Mitch.
Saxonbury Gdns., 98 F1
  Surb.
Saxton Clo. SE13 78 D3
Sayers Wk., Rich. 73 J7
  Stafford Pl.
Sayes Ct. SE8 68 J5
  Sayes Ct. St.
Sayes Ct. St. SE8 68 J6
Scads Hill Clo., 97 J6
  Orp.
Scala St. W1 11 G1
Scala St. W1 58 C5
Scales Rd. N17 41 C3
Scampston Ms. W10 57 A6
Scandrett St. E1 68 E1
  Marquess Rd.
Scarborough Rd. E11 51 D1
Scarborough Rd. N4 40 G7
Scarborough Rd. N9 25 F7
Scarborough St. E1 13 G4
Scarbrook Rd., 101 J3
  Croy.
Scarle Rd., Wem. 46 G6
Scarlet Rd. SE6 78 G4
Scarlette Manor Way 76 G7
  SW2
  Papworth Way
Scarsbrook Rd. SE3 79 A3
Scarsdale Pl. W8 14 A5
Scarsdale Rd., Har. 45 J3

Scarsdale Vill. W8 66 D3
Scarth Rd. SW13 74 F3
Scawen Rd. SE8 68 H5
Scawfell St. E2 9 G2
Scawfell St. E2 59 C2
Scaynes Link N12 31 D5
Sceaux Est. SE5 77 B1
Sceaux Gdns. SE5 77 C1
Sceptre Rd. E2 59 F3
Schofield Wk. SE3 69 H7
  Dornberg Clo.
Scholars Rd. E4 34 C1
Scholars Rd. SW12 85 C1
Scholefield Rd. N19 49 D2
Scholes Cres. SW2 85 G1
School Ho. La., 82 E7
  Tedd.
School La. SE23 86 E2
School La., 91 F1
  Kings.T.
School La., Pnr. 36 E4
School La., Surb. 98 J1
School La., Well. 80 B3
School Pas., 91 J2
  Kings.T.
School Pas., Sthl. 63 F1
School Rd. E12 52 C4
School Rd. NW10 56 D4
School Rd., Chis. 97 F1
School Rd., Dag. 62 C1
School Rd., E.Mol. 91 A4
School Rd., Hmptn. 81 J6
School Rd., 77 J3
  Kings.T.
School Rd. Ave., 81 J6
  Hmptn.
School Way N12 31 F4
  High Rd.
Schoolbell Ms. E3 59 H2
  Arbery Rd.
Schoolhouse La. E1 59 G7
Schoolway N12 31 G6
Schoolway, Dag. 53 C3
Schooner Clo. SE16 68 G2
  Kinburn St.
Schubert Rd. SW15 75 C5
Sclater St. E1 9 F5
Sclater St. E1 59 C4
Scoble Pl. N16 50 C4
  Amhurst Rd.
Scoresby St. SE1 16 G2
Scoresby St. SE1 67 H1
Scorton Ave., Grnf. 55 D2
Scot Gro., Pnr. 28 D7
Scotch Common 55 D5
  W13
Scoter Clo., Wdf.Grn. 34 H7
  Mallards Rd.
Scotland Grn. N17 41 C2
Scotland Grn. Rd., 25 G5
  Enf.
Scotland Grn. Rd. N. 25 G4
  Enf.
Scotland Pl. SW1 16 A2
Scotland Rd., 34 J1
  Buck.H.
Scotsdale Clo., 97 H4
  Orp.
Scotsdale Clo., 100 B7
  Sutt.
Scotsdale Rd. SE12 78 H5
Scotswood St. EC1 8 F5
Scotswood Wk. N17 33 D7
Scott Clo. SW16 94 F1
Scott Clo., Epsom 99 C5
Scott Cres., Har. 45 H1
Scott Ellis Gdns. 6 E4
  NW8
Scott Ellis Gdns. 57 G3
  NW8
Scott Fm. Clo., 98 E1
  T.Ditt.
Scott Gdns., Houns. 63 D7
Scott Ho. N18 33 D5
Scott Lidgett Cres. 17 H4
  SE16
Scott Lidgett Cres. 68 D2
  SE16
Scott Russell Pl. E14 69 B5
  Westferry Rd.
Scott St. E1 59 E4
Scottes La., Dag. 53 D1
  Valence Ave.
Scotts Ave., Brom. 96 D2
Scotts Dr., Hmptn. 81 H7
Scotts Fm. Rd., 99 C6
  Epsom
Scotts La., Brom. 96 D3
Scotts Rd. E10 51 C1
Scotts Rd. W12 65 H2
Scotts Rd., Brom. 87 G7
Scotts Rd., Sthl. 63 C3

Scott's Yd. EC4 13 B5
Scoulding Rd. E16 60 G6
Scout App. NW10 47 K4
Scout La. SW4 76 C3
  Old Town
Scout Way NW7 30 D4
Scovell Cres. SE1 16 J4
Scovell Rd. SE1 16 J4
Scrattons Ter., Bark. 62 D1
Scriven St. E8 59 C1
Scrooby St. SE6 78 B6
Scrubs La. NW10 56 G3
Scrubs La. W10 56 H5
Scrutton Clo. SW12 76 D7
Scrutton St. EC2 9 D6
Scrutton St. EC2 59 B4
Scudamore La. NW9 38 C4
Scutari Rd. SE22 77 F5
Scylla Rd. SE15 77 E3
Seabright St. E2 59 E3
  Bethnal Grn. Rd.
Seabrook Dr., 103 E2
  W.Wick.
Seabrook Gdns., 44 G7
  Rom.
Seabrook Rd., Dag. 53 D3
Seacoal La. EC4 12 G4
Seacoal La. EC4 58 H6
Seacole Clo. W3 56 D5
Seacourt Rd. SE2 71 D2
Seacroft Gdns., 28 D3
  Wat.
Seafield Rd. N11 32 C2
Seaford Rd. E17 42 B3
Seaford Rd. N15 41 A4
Seaford Rd. W13 64 E1
Seaford Rd., Enf. 25 B4
Seaford St. WC1 8 B4
Seaford St. WC1 58 F3
Seaforth Ave., 92 H5
  N.Mal.
Seaforth Cres. N5 49 J5
Seaforth Gdns. N21 24 F7
Seaforth Gdns., 99 F4
  Epsom
Seaforth Gdns., 34 J5
  Wdf.Grn.
Seaforth Pl. SW1 15 G5
Seager Pl. E3 59 J5
  Burdett Rd.
Seagrave Rd. SW6 66 D6
Seagry Rd. E11 42 G6
Seal St. E8 50 C4
Searle Pl. N4 49 F1
  Evershot Rd.
Searles Clo. SW11 66 H7
Searles Rd. SE1 21 C1
Searles Rd. SE1 68 A4
Sears St. SE5 21 B7
Sears St. SE5 68 A7
Seasprite Clo., Nthlt. 54 D3
  Ruislip Rd.
Seaton Ave., Ilf. 52 H5
Seaton Clo. E13 60 H4
  New Barn St.
Seaton Clo. SE11 20 G3
Seaton Clo. SW15 83 H1
Seaton Clo., Twick. 73 A6
Seaton Gdns., Ruis. 45 A3
Seaton Pl. NW1 7 F5
Seaton Pl. E5 50 D4
  Nolan Way
Seaton Rd., Mitch. 93 H2
Seaton Rd., Twick. 72 J6
Seaton Rd., Well. 71 C7
Seaton Rd., Wem. 55 H2
Seaton St. N18 33 D5
Sebastian St. EC1 8 H3
Sebastian St. EC1 58 H3
Sebastopol Rd. N9 33 D4
Sebbon St. N1 49 H7
Sebert Rd. E7 51 H5
Sebright Pas. E2 9 J2
Sebright Rd., Barn. 23 A2
Secker Cres., Har. 36 J1
Secker St. SE1 16 E2
Second Ave. E12 52 B4
Second Ave. E13 60 G3
  First Ave.
Second Ave. E17 42 A5
Second Ave. N18 33 F4
Second Ave. NW4 39 A4
Second Ave. SW14 74 E3
Second Ave. W3 65 F1
Second Ave. W10 57 B4
Second Ave., Dag. 62 H1
Second Ave., Enf. 25 A5
Second Ave., Rom. 44 C5
Second Ave., Walt. 90 B6
Second Ave., Wem. 46 G2
Second Clo., W.Mol. 90 J4
Second Cross Rd., 82 A2
  Twick.

Second Way, Wem. 47 B4
Sedan Way SE17 21 D3
Sedcombe Clo., Sid. 89 B4
  Knoll Dr.
Sedcote Rd., Enf. 25 F5
Sedding St. SW1 19 B1
Sedding St. SW1 67 A1
Seddon Rd., Mord. 93 G5
Seddon St. WC1 8 D4
Sedge Rd. N17 33 F7
Sedgebrook Rd. SE3 79 A2
Sedgecombe Ave., 37 F5
  Har.
Sedgeford Rd. W12 65 F1
Sedgehill Rd. SE6 87 A4
Sedgemere Ave. N2 39 F3
Sedgemere Rd. SE2 71 C3
Sedgemoor Dr., Dag. 53 G4
Sedgeway SE6 87 F1
Sedgewood Clo., 96 F7
  Brom.
Sedgmoor Pl. SE5 68 B7
Sedgwick Rd. E10 51 C2
Sedgwick St. E9 50 G5
Sedleigh Rd. SW18 75 C6
Sedlescombe Rd. 66 C6
  SW6
Sedley Pl. W1 11 D4
Sedley Ri., Loug. 27 C2
Seeley Dr. SE21 86 B4
Seelig Ave. NW9 37 G7
Seely Rd. SW17 85 A6
Seething La. EC3 13 E5
Seething La. EC3 59 B7
Seething Wells La., 91 F6
  Surb.
Sefton Ave. NW7 30 D6
Sefton Ave., Har. 37 A1
Sefton Clo., Orp. 97 J4
Sefton Clo., Croy. 102 D1
Sefton Rd., Orp. 97 J4
Sefton Rd. SW15 74 J3
Segal Clo. SE23 77 F7
Sekforde St. EC1 8 G6
Sekforde St. EC1 58 H4
Selan Gdns., Hayes 54 B5
Selbie Ave. NW10 47 F5
Selborne Ave. E12 52 D4
  Walton Rd.
Selborne Ave. E17 41 J4
Selborne Ave., Bex. 89 E1
Selborne Gdns. NW4 53 G4
Selborne Gdns., 55 D2
  Grnf.
Selborne Rd. E17 41 J5
Selborne Rd. N14 32 E3
Selborne Rd. N22 40 F1
Selborne Rd. SE5 77 A2
  Denmark Hill
Selborne Rd., Croy. 102 B3
Selborne Rd., Ilf. 52 D2
Selborne Rd., N.Mal. 92 E2
Selborne Rd., Sid. 89 B4
Selbourne Ave., 91 J2
  Surb.
Selby Chase, Ruis. 45 B2
Selby Clo. E6 61 B5
  Linton Gdns.
Selby Clo., Chess. 98 H7
Selby Clo., Chis. 88 D6
Selby Gdns., Sthl. 54 G4
Selby Grn., Cars. 93 H7
Selby Rd. E11 51 E3
Selby Rd. E13 60 H5
Selby Rd. N17 33 B6
Selby Rd. SE20 95 D2
Selby Rd. W5 55 C4
Selby Rd., Cars. 93 H7
Selby St. E1 9 J6
Selby St. E1 59 D4
Selden Rd. SE15 77 F2
Selden Wk. N7 49 F2
  Durham Rd.
Selhurst New Rd. 95 B6
  SE25
Selhurst Pl. SE25 95 B6
Selhurst Rd. N9 33 A3
Selhurst Rd. SE25 95 B5
Selinas La., Dag. 44 E7
Selkirk Rd. SW17 84 H4
Selkirk Rd., Twick. 81 J2
Sellers Clo., 22 C1
  Borwd.
Sellers Hall Clo. N3 31 D7
Sellincourt Rd. 84 H5
  SW17
Sellindge Clo., Beck. 86 J7
Sellon Ms. SE11 20 D2
Sellons Ave. NW10 56 F1
Sellwood Dr., Barn. 23 A5
Selsdon Ave., 102 A6
  S.Croy.
  Selsdon Rd.

Selsdon Clo., Rom. 44 J1
Selsdon Clo., Surb. 91 H5
Selsdon Rd. E11 42 G7
Selsdon Rd. E13 60 J1
Selsdon Rd. NW2 47 F2
Selsdon Rd. SE27 85 H3
Selsdon Rd., 102 A5
  S.Croy.
Selsdon Rd. Ind. 102 A6
  Est., Croy.
  Selsdon Rd.
Selsdon Way E14 69 B3
Selsea Pl. N16 50 B5
  Crossway
Selsey Cres., Well. 80 D1
Selsey St. E14 60 A5
Selvage La. NW7 30 D5
Selway Clo., Pnr. 36 B3
Selwood Pl. SW7 18 E3
Selwood Rd., Chess. 98 G4
Selwood Rd., Croy. 102 E2
Selwood Rd., Sutt. 100 C1
Selwood Ter. SW7 18 E3
Selworthy Clo. E11 42 G5
Selworthy Rd. SE6 86 J3
Selwyn Ave. E4 34 C6
Selwyn Ave., Ilf. 43 J6
Selwyn Ave., Rich. 73 H3
Selwyn Clo., Houns. 72 E4
Selwyn Ct. SE3 78 F3
Selwyn Cres., Well. 80 B3
Selwyn Rd. E3 59 J2
Selwyn Rd. E13 60 H1
Selwyn Rd. NW10 47 D7
Selwyn Rd., N.Mal. 92 D5
Semley Gate E9 50 J6
  Eastway
Semley Pl. SW1 19 C2
Semley Pl. SW1 67 A4
Semley Rd. SW16 94 E2
Senate St. SE15 77 F2
Senator Wk. SE28 70 G3
  Broadwater Rd.
Seneca Rd., Th.Hth. 94 J4
Senga Rd., Wall. 101 A1
Senhouse Rd., Sutt. 100 A3
Senior St. W2 10 A1
Senior St. W2 57 E5
Senlac Rd. SE12 87 H1
Sennen Rd., Enf. 25 C7
Sennen Wk. SE9 88 B3
  Nunnington Clo.
Senrab St. E1 59 G6
Sentinel Clo., Nthlt. 54 E4
Sentinel Sq. NW4 38 J4
  Brent St.
September Way, 29 E6
  Stan.
Sequoia Clo. 29 A1
  (Bushey), Wat.
  Giant Tree Hill
Sequoia Gdns., Orp. 97 J7
Sequoia Pk., Pnr. 28 H6
Serbin Clo. E10 42 C7
Serjeants Inn EC4 12 F4
Serle St. WC2 12 D3
Serle St. WC2 58 F6
Sermon La. EC4 58 J6
  Carter La.
Serpentine Rd. W2 14 J2
Serpentine Rd. W2 66 J1
Serviden Dr., Brom. 97 A1
Setchell Rd. SE1 21 F1
Setchell Way SE1 21 F1
Seth St. SE16 68 F2
  Swan Rd.
Seton Gdns., Dag. 53 C7
Settle Pt. E13 60 G2
  London Rd.
Settle St. E1 13 J2
Settle St. E1 59 D5
  London Rd.
Settles St. E1 13 J2
Settrington Rd. SW6 75 E2
Seven Acres, Cars. 100 H2
Seven Acres, Nthwd. 28 A6
Seven Acres, Cars. 100 H2
Seven Kings Rd., 52 J1
  Ilf.
Seven Sisters Rd. 40 J7
  N4
Seven Sisters Rd. 49 F3
  N7
Seven Sisters Rd. 41 A6
  N15
Sevenoaks Clo., 80 H4
  Bexh.
Sevenoaks Ho. SE25 95 D3
Sevenoaks Rd. SE4 77 H3
Sevenoaks Rd., Orp. 104 J4
Sevenoaks Rd. 104 J7
  (Green St. Grn.), Orp.

Sevenoaks Way, Sid. 89 C7
Seventh Ave. E12 52 C4
Severn Dr., Esher 98 D2
Severn Way NW10 47 F5
Severnake Clo. E14 69 A4
Severus Rd. SW11 75 H4
Seville St. SW1 15 A4
Seville St. SW1 66 J2
Sevington Rd. NW4 38 H6
Sevington St. W9 6 A6
Sevington St. W9 57 E4
Seward Rd. W7 64 D2
Seward Rd., Beck. 95 G2
Seward St. EC1 8 H4
Seward St. EC1 58 H4
Sewardstone Gdns. 26 B5
  E4
Sewardstone Rd. E2 59 F2
Sewardstone Rd. E4 26 B7
Sewdley St. E5 50 G4
Sewell Rd. SE2 71 A4
Sewell St. E13 60 G3
Sextant Ave. E14 69 D4
Seymour Ave. N17 41 D2
Seymour Ave., Mord. 93 A7
Seymour Clo., 90 J5
  E.Mol.
Seymour Clo., Pnr. 36 F1
Seymour Ct. E4 34 F2
Seymour Dr., Brom. 104 C1
Seymour Gdns. SE4 77 H3
Seymour Gdns., 81 C4
  Felt.
Seymour Gdns., Ilf. 52 C1
Seymour Gdns., 45 D1
  Ruis.
Seymour Gdns., 91 J5
  Surb.
Seymour Gdns., 73 E7
  Twick.
Seymour Ms. W1 11 B3
Seymour Ms. W1 58 A6
Seymour Pl. SE25 95 E4
Seymour Pl. W1 10 H1
Seymour Pl. W1 57 H5
Seymour Rd. E4 34 B1
Seymour Rd. E6 61 A2
Seymour Rd. E10 50 J1
Seymour Rd. N3 31 E7
Seymour Rd. N8 40 H5
Seymour Rd. N9 33 E2
Seymour Rd. SW18 75 C7
Seymour Rd. SW19 84 A3
Seymour Rd. W4 65 C4
Seymour Rd., Cars. 101 A5
Seymour Rd., E.Mol. 90 J5
Seymour Rd., Hmptn. 81 J5
Seymour Rd., 91 J1
  Kings.T.
Seymour Rd., Mitch. 94 A7
Seymour Rd., W.Mol. 90 J5
Seymour St. W1 10 J4
Seymour St. W1 57 J6
Seymour St. W2 10 J4
Seymour St. W2 57 J6
Seymour Ter. SE20 95 E1
Seymour Vill. SE20 95 E1
Seymour Wk. SW10 18 C5
Seymour Wk. SW10 66 F6
Seymours, The, 27 D1
  Loug.
Seyssel St. E14 69 C4
Shaa Rd. W3 56 D7
Shacklegate La., 82 B4
  Tedd.
Shackleton Clo. 86 E2
  SE23
Shackleton Rd., Sthl. 54 F7
Shacklewell Grn. E8 50 C4
  Shacklewell La.
Shacklewell La. E8 50 C5
Shacklewell La. N16 50 C4
Shacklewell Row E8 50 C4
Shacklewell St. E2 9 G5
Shacklewell St. E2 59 C3
Shad Thames SE1 17 F2
Shad Thames SE1 68 C2
Shadbolt Clo., 99 F2
  Wor.Pk.
Shadwell Dr., 54 F3
  Nthlt.
Shadwell Pierhead 59 F7
  E1
  Glamis Rd.
Shadwell Pl. E1 59 F6
  Martha St.
Shaef Way, Tedd. 82 D7
Shafter Rd., Dag. 53 J6
Shaftesbury, Loug. 27 A3
Shaftesbury Ave. W1 11 H5
Shaftesbury Ave. W1 58 H7
Shaftesbury Ave. 11 H6
  WC2

Shaftesbury Ave. 58 D7
  WC2
Shaftesbury Ave., 23 F3
  Barn.
Shaftesbury Ave., 25 G2
  Enf.
Shaftesbury Ave., 72 A6
  Felt.
Shaftesbury Ave., 37 G5
  Har.
Shaftesbury Ave. 45 H1
  (Kenton), Har.
Shaftesbury Ave., 63 G4
  Sthl.
Shaftesbury Circle, 45 J1
  Har.
  Shaftesbury Ave.
Shaftesbury Ms. W8 66 D3
  Stratford Rd.
Shaftesbury Pt. E13 60 H2
  High St.
Shaftesbury Rd. E4 34 D1
Shaftesbury Rd. E7 51 J7
Shaftesbury Rd. E10 51 A1
Shaftesbury Rd. E17 42 B6
Shaftesbury Rd. N18 33 B6
Shaftesbury Rd. N19 49 E1
Shaftesbury Rd., 95 J2
  Beck.
Shaftesbury Rd., 93 G7
  Cars.
Shaftesbury Rd., 73 H3
  Rich.
Shaftesbury St. N1 9 A2
Shaftesbury St. N1 58 J2
Shaftesbury Way, 82 A3
  Twick.
Shaftesbury Waye, 54 C5
  Hayes
Shaftesburys, The, 61 F2
  Bark.
Shafto Ms. SW1 14 J6
Shafton Rd. E9 59 G1
Shaftsbury Rd., 95 J2
  Beck.
Shakespeare Ave. 32 C5
  N11
Shakespeare Ave. 56 D1
  NW10
Shakespeare Ave., 72 A6
  Felt.
Shakespeare Ave., 54 A4
  Hayes
Shakespeare Cres. 52 C6
  E12
Shakespeare Cres. 56 D1
  NW10
Shakespeare Dr., 37 J6
  Har.
Shakespeare Gdns. 39 J4
  N2
Shakespeare Ho. N14 32 D2
  High St.
Shakespeare Rd. E17 41 G2
Shakespeare Rd. N3 39 D1
  Popes Dr.
Shakespeare Rd. 30 F4
  NW7
Shakespeare Rd. 76 H5
  SE24
Shakespeare Rd. W3 65 C1
Shakespeare Rd. W7 55 C7
Shakespeare Rd., 80 E1
  Bexh.
Shakespeare Sq. 35 F6
  Ilf.
Shakespeare Wk. 50 B4
  N16
Shakespeare Way, 81 C4
  Felt.
Shalcomb St. SW10 18 D6
Shalcomb St. SW10 66 F6
Shaldon Dr., Mord. 93 B5
Shaldon Dr., Ruis. 45 C3
Shaldon Rd., Edg. 37 J2
Shalfleet Dr. W10 57 A7
Shalford Clo., Orp. 104 F4
  Isabella Dr.
Shalimar Gdns. W3 56 C7
Shalimar Rd. W3 56 C7
  Hereford Rd.
Shallons Rd. SE9 88 E4
Shalston Rd. SW14 74 B3
Shalston Vill., 91 J1
  Surb.
Shamrock Rd., Croy. 94 B6
Shamrock St. SW4 76 D3
Shamrock Way N14 32 B1
Shand St. SE1 17 E2
Shand St. SE1 68 B2
Shandon Rd. SW4 76 C6
Shandy St. E1 59 G5
Shanklin Gdns., Wat. 28 C4

Shanklin Rd. N8	40	D5
Shanklin Rd. N15	41	D4
Shanklin Way SE15	68	C7
Pentride St.		
Shannon Clo. NW2	48	A3
Shannon Clo., Sthl.	63	D5
Shannon Gro. SW9	76	F4
Shannon Pl. NW8	**6**	**H1**
Shannon Way, Beck.	87	B6
Shap Cres., Cars.	100	J3
Shap St. E2	59	C1
Laburnum St.		
Shapland Way N13	32	F5
Shardcroft Ave.	76	H5
SE24		
Shardeloes Rd. SE14	77	J2
Sharman Ct., Sid.	89	A4
Sharnbrooke Clo.,	80	C3
Well.		
Sharon Clo., Surb.	98	F1
Sharon Gdns. E9	59	F1
Sharon Rd. W4	65	D5
Sharon Rd., Enf.	25	H2
Sharpe Clo. W7	55	C5
Templeman St.		
Sharpleshall St.	48	J7
NW1		
Sharpness Clo.,	54	E5
Hayes		
Sharratt St. SE15	68	F6
Sharsted St. SE17	**20**	**G4**
Sharsted St. SE17	67	H5
Shavers Pl. SW1	**11**	**H6**
Shaw Ave., Bark.	62	E2
Shaw Clo. SE28	71	B1
Shaw Clo. (Bushey),	29	B2
Wat.		
Shaw Dr., Walt.	90	C7
Shaw Gdns., Bark.	62	E2
Shaw Rd., Brom.	87	F3
Shaw Rd., Enf.	25	G1
Shaw Sq. E17	41	H1
Shaw Way, Wall.	101	E7
Shawbrooke Rd. SE9	78	J5
Shawbury Rd. SE22	77	F3
Shawfield Pk.,	97	A2
Brom.		
Shawfield St. SW3	**18**	**H4**
Shawfield St. SW3	66	H5
Shawford Ct. SW15	74	G7
Shawford Rd., Epsom	99	D6
Shaws Cotts. SE23	86	H3
Shearing Dr., Cars.	93	F7
Stavordale Rd.		
Shearling Way N7	49	E6
Shearman Rd. SE3	78	F4
Shearsmith Ho. E1	**13**	**J5**
Sheaveshill Ave.	38	E4
NW9		
Sheen Common Dr.,	74	A4
Rich.		
Sheen Ct., Rich.	74	A4
Sheen Rd.		
Sheen Ct. Rd.,	74	A4
Rich.		
Sheen Gate Gdns.	74	C3
SW14		
Sheen Gro. N1	58	G1
Richmond Ave.		
Sheen La. SW14	74	C5
Sheen Pk., Rich.	73	H4
Sheen Rd., Orp.	97	J4
Sheen Rd., Rich.	73	H5
Sheen Way, Wall.	101	F5
Sheen Wd. SW14	74	C5
Sheendale Rd.,	73	H4
Rich.		
Sheenewood SE26	86	E5
Sheep La. E8	59	E1
Sheep Wk. Ms. SW19	84	B6
Sheepcote Clo.,	63	A7
Houns.		
Sheepcote La. SW11	75	J2
Sheepcote Rd., Har.	37	C6
Sheepcotes Rd.,	44	D4
Rom.		
Sheephouse Way,	99	D1
N.Mal.		
Sheerwater Rd. E16	61	A5
Sheffield Sq. E3	59	J3
Malmesbury Rd.		
Sheffield St. WC2	**12**	**C4**
Sheffield Ter. W8	66	D1
Shefton Ri., Nthwd.	28	A7
Shelbourne Clo.,	36	F3
Pnr.		
Shelbourne Rd. N17	41	E2
Shelburne Rd. N7	49	F4
Shelbury Clo., Sid.	89	A3
Shelbury Rd. SE22	77	E5
Sheldon Ave. N6	39	H7
Sheldon Ave., Ilf.	43	E2
Sheldon Clo. SE12	78	H5

Sheldon Clo. SE20	95	E1
Sheldon Rd. N18	33	B4
Sheldon Rd. NW2	48	A4
Sheldon Rd., Bexh.	80	F1
Sheldon Rd., Dag.	53	E7
Sheldon St., Croy.	101	J3
Wandle Rd.		
Sheldrake Pl. W8	66	D2
Sheldrick Clo. SW19	93	G2
Shelduck Clo. NW9	38	E2
Swan Dr.		
Sheldwich Ter.,	97	B6
Brom.		
Turpington La.		
Shelford Pl. N16	50	A3
Stoke Newington		
Ch. St.		
Shelford Ri. SE19	86	C7
Shelford Rd., Barn.	22	J5
Shelgate Rd. SW11	75	H5
Shell Clo., Brom.	97	B6
Shell Rd. SE13	78	B3
Shelley Ave. E12	52	B6
Shelley Ave., Grnf.	55	A3
Shelley Clo., Edg.	30	A4
Shelley Clo., Grnf.	55	A3
Shelley Clo., Hayes	54	A5
Shelley Clo., Orp.	104	H3
Shelley Clo.,	72	D1
Houns.		
Shelley Cres.,	54	F6
Sthl.		
Shelley Dr., Well.	79	H1
Shelley Gdns., Wem.	46	F2
Shelley Gro., Loug.	27	C4
Shelley Way SW19	84	G6
Shellgrove Est. N16	50	B5
Shellness Rd. E5	50	E5
Shellwood Rd. SW11	75	J2
Shelmerdine Clo. E3	60	A5
Shelton Rd. SW19	93	D1
Shelton St. WC2	**12**	**A4**
Shelton St. WC2	58	E6
Shenfield Ho. SE18	70	A7
Shooter's Hill Rd.		
Shenfield Rd.,	34	H7
Wdf.Grn.		
Shenfield St. N1	**9**	**E2**
Shenfield St. N1	59	B2
Shenley Rd. SE5	77	B1
Shenley Rd., Borwd.	22	A4
Shenley Rd., Houns.	72	E1
Shepherd Mkt. W1	**15**	**D2**
Shepherd St. W1	**15**	**D2**
Shepherdess Pl. N1	**9**	**A3**
Shepherdess Wk. N1	**9**	**A2**
Shepherds Bush Grn.	58	J2
W12		
Shepherds Bush Grn.	65	J2
W12		
Shepherds Bush Mkt.	65	J2
W12		
Uxbridge Rd.		
Shepherds Bush Pl.	66	A2
W12		
Shepherds Bush Rd.	65	J3
W6		
Shepherds Clo. N6	40	B6
Shepherds Clo.,	44	D5
Rom.		
Shepherds Ct. W12	66	A2
Shepherds Bush Grn.		
Shepherds Grn.,	88	G7
Chis.		
Shepherds Hill N6	40	B6
Shepherds La. E9	50	G6
Shepherds Pl. W1	**11**	**B5**
Shepherds Wk. NW2	47	G2
Shepherds Wk. NW3	48	G4
Shepherds Wk.	29	A2
(Bushey), Wat.		
Shepherds Way,	102	G7
S.Croy.		
Shepley Clo., Cars.	101	A3
Sheppard Clo.,	91	H4
Kings.T.		
Beaufort Rd.		
Sheppard Dr. SE16	68	E5
Sheppard St. E16	60	F4
Shepperton Clo.,	22	D1
Borwd.		
Shepperton Rd. N1	58	J1
Shepperton Rd.,	97	G6
Orp.		
Sheppey Gdns., Dag.	53	C7
Sheppey Rd.		
Sheppey Rd., Dag.	53	B7
Sheppey Wk. N1	49	J7
Marquess Est.		
Sherard Rd. SE9	79	B5
Sheraton Business	55	E2
Cen., Grnf.		
Sheraton St. W1	**11**	**H4**

Sherborne Ave.,	25	F2
Enf.		
Sherborne Ave.,	63	G4
Sthl.		
Sherborne Gdns.	38	A3
NW9		
Sherborne Gdns.	55	E5
W13		
Sherborne La. EC4	**13**	**B5**
Sherborne Rd.,	98	H5
Chess.		
Sherborne Rd., Orp.	97	J4
Sherborne Rd.,	100	D2
Sutt.		
Sherborne St. N1	59	A1
Sherboro Rd. N15	41	C6
Ermine Rd.		
Sherbourne Cres.,	93	H7
Cars.		
Sherbrook Gdns.	24	H7
N21		
Green Las.		
Sherbrooke Clo.,	80	G4
Bexh.		
Sherbrooke Rd. SW6	66	B7
Shere Clo., Chess.	98	G5
Shere Rd., Ilf.	43	D5
Sheredan Rd. E4	34	D5
Sherfield Gdns.	74	F6
SW15		
Sheridan Ct.,	72	F5
Houns.		
Vickers Way		
Sheridan Cres.,	97	E2
Chis.		
Sheridan Gdns.,	37	G6
Har.		
Sheridan Pl. SW13	74	F2
Brookwood Ave.		
Sheridan Pl.,	90	H1
Hmptn.		
Sheridan Rd. E7	51	F3
Sheridan Rd. E12	52	B5
Sheridan Rd. SW19	93	C1
Sheridan Rd., Belv.	71	G4
Sheridan Rd., Bexh.	80	E3
Sheridan Rd., Rich.	82	F3
Sheridan St. E1	59	E6
Watney St.		
Sheridan Ter.,	45	H5
Nthlt.		
Whitton Ave. W.		
Sheridan Wk. NW11	39	D6
Sheridan Wk., Cars.	100	J5
Carshalton Pk. Rd.		
Sheridan Way, Beck.	95	J1
Turners Meadow		
Way		
Sheringham Ave.	52	C4
E12		
Sheringham Ave.	24	D5
N14		
Sheringham Ave.,	81	A3
Felt.		
Sheringham Ave.,	44	J6
Rom.		
Sheringham Ave.,	81	F1
Twick.		
Sheringham Dr.,	52	J5
Bark.		
Sheringham Rd. N7	49	F6
Sheringham Rd.	95	F3
SE20		
Sheringham Twr.	54	H7
Sthl.		
Sherington Ave.	28	G7
Pnr.		
Sherington Rd. SE7	69	H6
Sherland Rd.,	73	C7
Twick.		
Sherlies Ave., Orp.	104	H2
Sherlock Ms. W1	**11**	**B1**
Sherman Rd., Brom.	96	G1
Shernhall St. E17	42	C3
Sherrard Rd. E7	51	J6
Sherrard Rd. E12	52	A6
Sherrards Way,	23	D5
Barn.		
Sherrick Grn. Rd.	47	H5
NW10		
Sherriff Rd. NW6	48	D6
Sherrin Rd. E10	51	A4
Sherringham Ave.	41	D2
N17		
Sherrock Gdns. NW4	38	G4
Sherwin Rd. SE14	77	G1
Sherwood Ave. E18	42	H3
Sherwood Ave.	85	C7
SW16		
Sherwood Ave.,	46	B6
Grnf.		
Sherwood Ave.,	54	B4
Hayes		

Sherwood Clo. SW13	74	H3
Lwr. Common S.		
Sherwood Clo. W13	64	E1
Sherwood Clo., Bex.	80	C6
Sherwood Gdns. E14	69	A4
Sherwood Gdns.,	52	G7
Bark.		
Sherwood Pk. Ave.,	80	A7
Sid.		
Sherwood Pk. Rd.,	94	C4
Mitch.		
Sherwood Pk. Rd.,	100	D5
Sutt.		
Sherwood Rd. NW4	38	J3
Sherwood Rd. SW19	84	C7
Sherwood Rd., Croy.	95	E7
Sherwood Rd.,	81	J5
Hmptn.		
Sherwood Rd., Har.	45	J2
Sherwood Rd., Ilf.	43	G4
Sherwood Rd., Well.	79	H3
Sherwood St. N20	31	G3
Sherwood St. W1	**11**	**G5**
Sherwood Ter. N20	31	G3
Green Rd.		
Sherwood Way,	103	B2
W.Wick.		
Shetland Clo.,	22	D6
Borwd.		
Percheron Rd.		
Shetland Rd. E3	59	J2
Shield Dr., Brent.	64	D6
Shield Hill St. SE7	71	C4
Shifford Path SE23	86	G3
Shillibeer Pl. W1	**10**	**H2**
Shillibeer Wk.,	35	J3
Chig.		
Shillingford St. N1	49	H7
Cross St.		
Shillitoe Rd. N13	32	H5
Shinfield St. W12	56	J6
Shinglewell Rd.,	71	G6
Erith		
Shinners Clo. SE25	95	D5
Stanger Rd.		
Ship and Mermaid	**17**	**C3**
Row SE1		
Ship La. SW14	74	C3
Ship St. SE8	78	A1
Ship Tavern Pas. EC3	**13**	**D5**
Shipka Rd. SW12	85	B1
Shipman Rd. E16	60	H6
Shipman Rd. SE23	86	G2
Shipton Clo., Dag.	53	D3
Shipton St. E2	**9**	**G3**
Shipton St. E2	59	C2
Shipwright Rd. SE16	68	H2
Shirburn St. SE23	77	F7
Tyson Rd.		
Shirbutt St. E14	60	B7
Shire Ct., Erith	71	D3
St. John Fisher Rd.		
Shirebrook Rd. SE3	79	A3
Shirehall Clo. NW4	39	A6
Shirehall Gdns. NW4	39	A6
Shirehall La. NW4	39	A6
Shirehall Pk. NW4	39	A6
Shires, The, Rich.	82	H4
Shirland Ms. W9	57	C3
Shirland Rd. W9	57	C3
Shirley Ave., Bex.	80	D7
Shirley Ave., Croy.	102	F1
Shirley Ave., Sutt.	100	G4
Shirley Ch. Rd.,	102	F3
Croy.		
Shirley Clo. E17	42	B5
Addison Rd.		
Shirley Clo.,	72	J5
Houns.		
Shirley Ct., Croy.	102	G3
Shirley Cres.,	95	H4
Beck.		
Shirley Dr., Houns.	72	J5
Shirley Gdns. W7	64	C1
Shirley Gdns.,	52	H6
Bark.		
Shirley Gro. N9	25	F7
Shirley Gro. SW11	76	A3
Shirley Hills Rd.,	102	G5
Croy.		
Shirley Ho. Dr. SE7	69	J7
Shirley Oaks Rd.,	102	G1
Croy.		
Shirley Pk. Rd.,	102	E1
Croy.		
Shirley Rd. E15	51	E7
Shirley Rd. W4	65	D2
Shirley Rd., Croy.	95	E7
Shirley Rd., Enf.	24	J3
Shirley Rd., Sid.	88	H3
Shirley St. E16	60	F6
Shirley Way, Croy.	102	H3
Shirlock Rd. NW3	48	J4

Shobden Rd. N17 41 A1
Shoe La. EC4 **12** **F3**
Shoe La. EC4 58 G6
Shoebury Rd. E6 52 C7
Shoot Up Hill NW2 48 B5
Shooters Ave., Har. 37 F4
Shooter's Hill SE18 79 D1
Shooter's Hill, Well. 79 F2
Shooter's Hill Rd. SE3 78 F1
Shooter's Hill Rd. SE18 79 A1
Shooters Rd., Felt. 24 H1
Shore Clo., Felt. 72 A7
Shore Clo., Hmptn. 81 E5
  Stewart Clo.
Shore Gro., Felt. 81 G2
Shore Pl. E9 50 F7
Shore Rd. E9 50 F7
Shoreditch High St. E1 **9** **E6**
Shoreditch High St. E1 59 B4
Shoreham Clo. SW18 75 E5
  Ram St.
Shoreham Clo., Bex. 89 D1
  Stansted Cres.
Shoreham Clo., Croy. 95 F5
Shoreham Way, Brom. 96 G6
Shorncliffe Rd. SE1 **21** **F3**
Shorncliffe Rd. SE1 68 C5
Shorndean St. SE6 87 C1
Shorne Clo., Sid. 80 B6
Shornefield Clo., Brom. 97 D3
Shornells Way SE2 71 C5
  Willrose Cres.
Shorrolds Rd. SW6 66 C7
Short Gate N12 31 C4
Short Hedges, Houns. 72 G1
  Lampton Ave.
Short Path SE18 70 E6
  Westdale Rd.
Short Rd. E11 51 E2
Short Rd. E15 60 D1
Short Rd. W4 65 E6
Short St. NW4 38 J4
  New Brent St.
Short St. SE1 **16** **F3**
Short Wall E15 60 D3
  Bisson Rd.
Short Way N12 31 H6
Short Way SE9 79 B3
Short Way, Twick. 72 J7
Shortcroft Rd., Epsom 99 F7
Shortcrofts Rd., Dag. 53 F6
Shorter St. E1 **13** **G5**
Shorter St. E1 59 C7
Shortland Rd. E10 42 B7
Shortlands W6 66 A4
Shortlands Clo. N18 33 A3
Shortlands Gdns., Brom. 96 E2
Shortlands Gro., Brom. 96 D3
Shortlands Rd., Brom. 96 D3
Shortlands Rd., Kings.T. 82 J7
Shorts Cft. NW9 38 B4
Shorts Gdns. WC2 **12** **A4**
Shorts Gdns. WC2 58 E6
Shorts Rd., Cars. 100 H4
Shotfield, Wall. 101 B6
Shott Clo., Sutt. 100 F5
  Turnpike La.
Shottendane Rd. SW6 75 D1
Shottery Clo. SE9 88 B3
Shottfield Ave. SW14 74 E4
Shoulder of Mutton All. E14 59 H7
  Narrow St.
Shouldham St. W1 **10** **H2**
Shouldham St. W1 57 H5
Showers Way, Hayes 63 A1
Shrapnel Clo. SE18 70 B7
Shrapnel Rd. SE9 79 C3
Shrewsbury Ave. SW14 74 C4
Shrewsbury Ave., Har. 37 H4
Shrewsbury Clo., Surb. 98 H2
Shrewsbury Cres. NW10 56 D1

Shrewsbury La. SE18 79 E1
Shrewsbury Ms. W2 57 D5
  Chepstow Rd.
Shrewsbury Rd. E7 52 A5
Shrewsbury Rd. N11 32 C6
Shrewsbury Rd. W2 57 D6
Shrewsbury Rd., Beck. 95 H3
Shrewsbury Rd., Cars. 93 H6
Shrewsbury Wk., Islw. 73 D3
  South St.
Shrewton Rd. SW17 84 J7
Shroffold Rd., Brom. 87 E4
Shropshire Clo., Mitch. 94 E4
Shropshire Pl. WC1 **7** **G6**
Shropshire Rd. N22 32 F7
Shroton St. NW1 **10** **G1**
Shroton St. NW1 57 H5
Shrubberies, The E18 42 G2
Shrubberies, The, Chig. 35 F5
Shrubbery Clo. N1 58 J1
  St. Paul St.
Shrubbery Gdns. N21 24 H7
Shrubbery Rd. N9 33 D3
Shrubbery Rd. SW16 85 E4
Shrubbery Rd., Sthl. 63 F1
Shrubland Gro., Wor.Pk. 99 J3
Shrubland Rd. E8 59 C1
Shrubland Rd. E10 42 A7
Shrubland Rd. E17 42 A5
Shrublands Ave., Croy. 103 A4
Shrublands Clo. N20 31 G1
Shrublands Clo. SE26 86 F3
Shrublands Clo., Chig. 35 F6
Shuna Wk. N1 50 A6
  St. Pauls Rd.
Shurland Ave., Barn. 23 G6
Shurland Gdns. SE15 **21** **G7**
Shurlock Dr., Orp. 104 F4
Shuters Sq. W14 66 C5
  Sun Rd.
Shuttle Clo., Sid. 79 J7
Shuttle St. E1 **9** **H6**
Shuttlemead, Bex. 89 F4
Shuttleworth Rd. SW11 75 G2
Sibella Rd. SW4 76 D2
Sibley Clo., Bexh. 80 E5
Sibley Gro. E12 52 B7
Sibthorp Rd., Mitch. 93 J2
Sibthorpe Rd. SE12 78 H6
Sibton Rd., Cars. 93 H7
Sicilian Ave. WC1 **12** **B2**
Sidbury St. SW6 75 B1
Sidcup Bypass, Orp. 89 B6
Sidcup Bypass, Sid. 88 H4
Sidcup High St., Sid. 89 A4
Sidcup Hill, Sid. 89 B4
Sidcup Hill Gdns., Sid. 89 C5
  Sidcup Hill
Sidcup Pl., Sid. 89 A5
Sidcup Rd. SE9 88 J7
Sidcup Rd. SE12 78 H5
Sidcup Technology Cen., Sid. 89 D5
Siddons La. NW1 **7** **A6**
Siddons Rd. N17 41 D1
Siddons Rd. SE23 86 H2
Siddons Rd., Croy. 101 G3
Side Rd. E17 41 J5
Sidewood Rd. SE9 88 G1
Sidford Pl. SE1 **16** **D6**
Sidings, The E11 51 C1
Sidmouth Ave., Islw. 73 B2
Sidmouth Clo., Wat. 28 B2
Sidmouth Dr., Ruis. 45 A3
Sidmouth Rd. E10 51 C3
Sidmouth Rd. NW2 47 H7
Sidmouth Rd. SE15 77 C1
Sidmouth Rd., Well. 71 C7
Sidmouth St. WC1 **8** **B4**
Sidmouth St. WC1 58 F3
Sidney Ave. N13 32 F5
Sidney Elson Way E6 61 D2
  Edwin Ave.
Sidney Est. E1 59 F6

Sidney Gdns., Brent. 64 F6
Sidney Gro. EC1 **8** **G2**
Sidney Rd. E7 51 G3
Sidney Rd. N22 32 F7
Sidney Rd. SE25 95 D5
Sidney Rd. SW9 76 F2
Sidney Rd., Beck. 95 H2
Sidney Rd., Har. 36 J3
Sidney Rd., Twick. 73 D6
Sidney Rd., Walt. 90 A7
Sidney Sq. E1 59 F5
Sidney St. E1 59 F5
Sidworth St. E8 50 E7
Siebert Rd. SE3 69 G6
Siemens Rd. SE18 70 A3
Sigdon Rd. E8 50 D5
Sigers, The, Pnr. 36 B6
Signmakers Yd. NW1 58 B1
  Delancey St.
Silbury Ave., Mitch. 93 H1
Silbury St. N1 **9** **B3**
Silchester Rd. W10 57 A6
Silecroft Rd., Bexh. 80 G1
Silesia Bldgs. E8 50 E7
  London La.
Silex St. SE1 **16** **H4**
Silex St. SE1 67 H2
Silk Clo. SE12 78 C2
Silk Mills Path SE13 78 C2
Silk St. EC2 **13** **A1**
Silk St. EC2 58 J5
Silkfield Rd. NW9 38 E5
Silkin Ho., Wat. 28 C3
Silkstream Rd., Edg. 38 C1
Silsoe Rd. N22 40 F2
Silver Birch Ave. E4 33 J6
Silver Birch Clo. N11 32 A6
Silver Clo. SE14 68 H7
  Southerngate Way
Silver Clo., Har. 29 A7
Silver Cres. W4 65 B4
Silver Jubilee Way, Houns. 72 B2
Silver La., W.Wick. 103 D2
Silver Pl. W1 **11** **G5**
Silver Rd. W12 57 A7
Silver Spring Clo., Erith 71 H6
Silver St. N18 33 A4
Silver St., Enf. 25 A3
Silver Wk. SE16 68 J1
Silver Way, Rom. 44 H3
Silverbirch Wk. NW3 49 A6
  Queens Cres.
Silvercliffe Gdns., Barn. 23 H4
Silverdale SE26 86 F4
Silverdale, Enf. 24 E4
Silverdale Ave., Ilf. 43 H5
Silverdale Clo. W7 64 B1
  Cherington Rd.
Silverdale Clo., Nthlt. 45 F5
Silverdale Clo., Sutt. 100 C4
Silverdale Dr. SE9 88 B2
Silverdale Dr., Sun. 90 B2
Silverdale Gdns., Hayes 63 A2
Silverdale Rd. E4 34 D6
Silverdale Rd., Bexh. 80 H2
Silverdale Rd. (Petts Wd.), Orp. 97 F4
Silverhall St., Islw. 73 D3
Silverholme Clo., Har. 37 H7
Silverland St. E16 70 C1
Silverleigh Rd., Th.Hth. 94 F4
Silvermere Rd. SE6 78 B6
Silverst Clo., Nthlt. 45 H6
Silverston Way, Stan. 29 F6
Silverthorn Gdns. E4 34 A2
Silverthorne Rd. SW8 76 B2
Silverton Rd. W6 66 A6
Silvertown Way E16 60 E6
Silvertree La., Grnf. 55 A3
  Cowgate Rd.
Silverwood Clo., Beck. 87 A7

Silvester Rd. SE22 77 C5
Silvester St. SE1 **17** **B4**
Silwood Est. SE16 68 F4
  Millender Wk.
Silwood St. SE16 68 F4
Simla Clo. SE14 68 H6
  Chubworthy St.
Simla Ho. SE1 **17** **C4**
Simmil Rd., Esher 98 B5
Simmons Clo. N20 31 H1
Simmons La. E4 34 D1
Simmons Rd. SE18 70 E5
Simmons Way N20 31 H2
Simms Clo., Cars. 100 H2
Simms Rd. SE1 **21** **J2**
Simms Rd. SE1 68 D4
Simnel Rd. SE12 78 H7
Simon Clo. W11 57 C7
  Portobello Rd.
Simonds Rd. E10 51 A2
Simone Clo., Brom. 97 A1
Simons Wk. E15 51 D5
  Alma St.
Simpson Dr. W3 56 D6
Simpson Rd., Houns. 72 F6
Simpson Rd., Rich. 82 F4
Simpson St. SW11 75 H2
Simpsons Rd. E14 60 B7
Simpsons Rd., Brom. 96 G3
Sims Wk. SE3 78 F4
  Lee Rd.
Sinclair Ct., Beck. 87 A7
Sinclair Gdns. W14 66 A2
Sinclair Gro. NW11 39 A6
Sinclair Rd. E4 33 H5
Sinclair Rd. W14 66 A2
Sinclare Clo., Enf. 25 C1
Singapore Rd. W13 64 D1
Singer St. EC2 **9** **C4**
Singleton Clo. SW17 84 J7
Singleton Clo., Croy. 94 J7
  St. Saviours Rd.
Singleton Rd., Dag. 53 F5
Singleton Scarp N12 31 D5
Sinnott Rd. E17 41 G1
Sion Rd., Twick. 73 E7
Sir Alexander Clo. W3 65 F1
Sir Alexander Rd. W3 65 F1
Sir Thomas More Est. SW3 **18** **F6**
Sirdar Rd. N22 40 H3
Sirdar Rd. W11 57 A7
Sirdar Rd., Mitch. 85 A6
  Grenfell Rd.
Sirinham Pt. SW8 **20** **C6**
Sirinham Pt. SW8 67 F6
Sirus Rd., Nthwd. 28 A5
Sise La. EC4 **13** **B4**
Siskin Clo., Borwd. 22 A4
Sisley Rd., Bark. 61 H1
Sispara Gdns. SW18 75 C6
Sissinghurst Rd., Croy. 95 D7
Sister Mabel's Way SE15 **21** **H7**
Sisters Ave. SW11 75 J3
Sistova Rd. SW12 85 B1
Sisulu Pl. SW9 76 G3
Sittingbourne Ave., Enf. 25 A6
Sitwell Gro., Stan. 29 C5
Sivill Ho. E2 **9** **G3**
Sivill Ho. E2 59 C3
Siviter Rd., Dag. 53 H7
Siviter Way, Dag. 53 H7
Siward Rd. N17 41 A1
Siward Rd. SW17 84 F3
Siward Rd., Brom. 96 H3
Six Acres Est. N4 49 G2
Sixth Ave. E12 52 C4
Sixth Ave. W10 57 B3
Sixth Cross Rd., Twick. 81 J3
Skardu Rd. NW2 48 B5
Skeena Hill SW18 75 B7
Skeffington Rd. E6 61 C1
Skelbrook St. SW18 84 E2
Skelgill Rd. SW15 75 C4
Skelley Rd. E15 51 F7
Skelton Clo. E8 50 C6
  Buttermere Wk.
Skelton Rd. E7 51 G6
Skeltons La. E10 42 B7
Skalwith Rd. W6 65 J6
Skenfrith Ho. SE15 68 E6
  Commercial Way
Skerne Rd., Kings.T. 82 G7
Sketchley Gdns. SE16 68 G5

Name	Page	Grid
Sketty Rd., Enf.	25	B3
Skiers St. E15	60	E1
Skiffington Clo. SW2	85.	G1
Skinner Ct. E2	59	E2
Parmiter St.		
Skinner Pl. SW1	**19**	**B2**
Skinner St. EC1	**8**	**F4**
Skinner St. EC1	58	G3
Skinners La. EC4	**13**	**A5**
Skinners La.	72	H1
Houns.		
Skinner's Row SE10	78	B1
Blackheath Rd.		
Skipsey Ave. E6	61	C3
Skipton St. SE1	**16**	**H6**
Skipworth Rd. E9	59	F1
Skomer Wk. N1	49	J6
Clephane Rd.		
Sky Peals Rd.,	34	D7
Wdf.Grn.		
Slade, The SE18	70	H6
Slade Ho., Houns.	72	F6
Slade Twr. E10	51	A2
Slade Wk. SE17	**20**	**J5**
Sladebrook Rd. SE3	79	A3
Sladedale Rd. SE18	70	H5
Sladen Pl. E5	50	E4
Clarence Rd.		
Slades Clo., Enf.	24	G3
Slades Dr., Chis.	88	F3
Slades Gdns., Enf.	24	G2
Slades Hill, Enf.	24	G3
Slades Ri., Enf.	24	G3
Slagrove Pl. SE13	78	B5
Ladywell Rd.		
Slaidburn St. SW10	**18**	**D6**
Slaidburn St. SW10	66	F6
Slaithwaite Rd.	78	C4
SE13		
Slaney Pl. N7	49	Gb
Hornsey Rd.		
Sleaford Grn., Wat.	28	D3
Sleaford St. SW8	**19**	**F7**
Sleaford St. SW8	67	C7
Slievemore Clo. SW4	76	D3
Slingsby Pl. WC2	**12**	**A5**
Slippers Pl. SE16	68	E3
Sloane Ave. SW3	**18**	**H2**
Sloane Ave. SW3	66	H4
Sloane Ct. E. SW3	**19**	**B3**
Sloane Ct. E. SW3	67	A5
Sloane Ct. W. SW3	**19**	**B3**
Sloane Ct. W. SW3	67	A5
Sloane Gdns. SW1	**19**	**B2**
Sloane Gdns. SW1	67	A4
Sloane Gdns., Orp.	104	F3
Partridge Dr.		
Sloane Sq. SW1	**19**	**A2**
Sloane Sq. SW1	66	J4
Sloane St. SW1	**15**	**A5**
Sloane St. SW1	66	J2
Sloane Ter. SW1	**19**	**A1**
Sloane Ter. SW1	66	J4
Sloane Wk., Croy.	95	J6
Slocum Clo. SE28	62	C7
Woodpecker Rd.		
Slough La. NW9	38	C5
Sly St. E1	59	E6
Cannon St. Rd.		
Smallberry Ave.,	73	C2
Islw.		
Smallbrook Ms. W2	**10**	**E4**
Smalley Clo. N16	50	C3
Smalley Rd. Est.	50	C3
N16		
Smalley Clo.		
Smallwood Rd. SW17	84	G4
Smardale Rd. SW18	75	F5
Alma Rd.		
Smarden Clo., Belv.	71	G5
Essenden Rd.		
Smarden Gro. SE9	88	C4
Smart St. E2	59	G3
Smarts La., Loug.	27	A4
Smarts Pl. N18	33	D5
Fore St.		
Smart's Pl. WC2	**12**	**B3**
Smeaton Rd. SW18	75	D7
Smeaton Rd.,	35	C5
Wdf.Grn.		
Smeaton St. E1	68	E1
Smedley St. SW4	76	D2
Smedley St. SW8	76	D2
Smeed Rd. E3	51	A7
Smiles Pl. SE13	78	C2
Smith Clo. SE16	68	G1
Smith Sq. SW1	**16**	**A6**
Smith Sq. SW1	67	E3
Smith St. SW3	**18**	**J3**
Smith St. SW3	66	J5
Smith St., Surb.	91	J6
Smith Ter. SW3	**18**	**J4**
Smith Ter. SW3	66	J5
Smithfield St. EC1	**12**	**G2**
Smithies Ct. E15	51	C5
Clays La.		
Smithies Rd. SE2	71	B4
Smith's Ct. W1	**11**	**G5**
Smiths Fm. Est.,	54	G2
Nthlt.		
Smiths Way NW2	47	G2
Smiths Yd. SW18	84	F2
Summerley St.		
Smith's Yd., Croy.	101	J3
St. Georges Wk.		
Smithson Rd. N17	41	A1
Smithwood Clo.	84	B1
SW19		
Smithy St. E1	59	F5
Smock Wk., Croy.	94	J6
Smugglers Way	75	E4
SW18		
Smyrks Rd. SE17	**21**	**E4**
Smyrks Rd. SE17	68	B5
Smyrna Rd. NW6	48	D7
Smythe St. E14	60	B7
Snag La., Sev.	104	G1
Snakes La., Barn.	24	C3
Snakes La. E.,	34	J6
Wdf.Grn.		
Snakes La. W.,	34	G6
Wdf.Grn.		
Snaresbrook Dr.,	29	G4
Stan.		
Snaresbrook Rd. E11	42	E4
Snarsgate St. W10	56	J5
Sneath Ave. NW11	39	C7
Snells Pk. N18	33	C6
Sneyd Rd. NW2	47	J4
Snow Hill EC1	**12**	**G2**
Snow Hill EC1	58	H5
Snow Hill Ct. EC1	**12**	**H3**
Snowbury Rd. SW6	75	E2
Snowden St. EC2	**9**	**D6**
Snowden St. EC2	59	B4
Snowdon Dr. NW9	38	E6
Snowdown Clo.	95	G1
SE20		
Snowdrop Clo.,	81	G6
Hmptn.		
Gresham Rd.		
Snowman Ho. NW6	48	F7
Snowsfields SE1	**17**	**C3**
Snowsfields SE1	68	A2
Snowshill Rd. E12	52	B5
Snowy Fielder Waye,	73	E2
Islw.		
Soames St. SE15	77	C3
Soames Wk., N.Mal.	92	E1
Socket La., Brom.	96	H6
Soho Sq. W1	**11**	**H3**
Soho Sq. W1	58	D6
Soho St. W1	**11**	**H3**
Solebay St. E1	59	H4
Solent Rd. NW6	48	D5
Soley Ms. WC1	**8**	**E3**
Solna Ave. SW15	74	J5
Solna Rd. N21	33	A1
Solomon's Pas. SE15	77	E4
Solon New Rd. SW4	76	E4
Solon New Rd. Est.	76	E4
SW4		
Solon New Rd.		
Solon Rd. SW2	76	E4
Solway Clo. E8	50	C6
Buttermere Wk.		
Solway Clo., Houns.	72	E3
Solway Rd. N22	40	H1
Solway Rd. SE22	77	D4
Somaford Gro.,	23	G6
Barn.		
Somali Rd. NW2	48	C5
Somerby Rd., Bark.	52	G7
Somercoates Clo.,	23	H3
Barn.		
Somerfield Rd. N4	49	H2
Somerford Clo.,	36	A4
Pnr.		
Somerford Gro. N16	50	C4
Somerford Gro. N17	33	D7
Somerford Gro. Est.	50	C4
N16		
Somerford Gro.		
Somerford St. E1	59	E4
Somerford Way	68	H2
SE16		
Somerhill Ave.,	80	B7
Sid.		
Somerhill Rd.,	80	B2
Well.		
Somerleyton Pas.	76	H4
SW9		
Somerleyton Rd.	76	G4
SW9		
Somers Clo. NW1	**7**	**H1**
Somers Cres. W2	10	G4
Somers Cres. W2	57	H6
Somers Ms. W2	**10**	**G4**
Somers Pl. SW2	76	F7
Somers Rd. E17	41	J4
Somers Rd. SW2	76	F6
Somersby Gdns.,	43	C5
Ilf.		
Somerset Ave.	92	H2
SW20		
Somerset Ave.,	98	G4
Chess.		
Somerset Ave.,	79	J5
Well.		
Somerset Clo.,	92	E6
N.Mal.		
Somerset Clo.,	42	G1
Wdf.Grn.		
Somerset Est. SW11	75	G1
Somerset Gdns. N6	40	A7
Somerset Gdns.	78	B2
SE13		
Somerset Gdns.	94	F3
SW16		
Somerset Gdns.,	82	B5
Tedd.		
Somerset Rd. E17	42	A5
Somerset Rd. N17	41	C3
Somerset Rd. N18	33	C5
Somerset Rd. NW4	38	J4
Somerset Rd. SW19	84	A3
Somerset Rd. W4	65	D3
Somerset Rd. W13	64	E1
Somerset Rd., Barn.	23	E5
Somerset Rd.,	64	G6
Brent.		
Somerset Rd., Har.	36	J6
Somerset Rd.,	91	J2
Kings.T.		
Somerset Rd., Sthl.	54	F6
Somerset Rd., Tedd.	82	B5
Somerset Sq. W14	66	B2
Somerset Waye,	63	E7
Houns.		
Somersham Rd.,	80	E2
Bexh.		
Somerton Ave.,	74	B3
Rich.		
Somerton Rd. NW2	47	A3
Somerton Rd. SE15	77	E4
Somertrees Ave.	87	H2
SE12		
Somervell Rd., Har.	45	F5
Somerville Rd. SE20	86	G7
Somerville Rd.,	44	C6
Rom.		
Sondes St. SE17	**21**	**B5**
Sondes St. SE17	68	A6
Sonia Ct., Har.	37	C6
Sonia Gdns. N12	31	F4
Woodside Ave.		
Sonia Gdns. NW10	47	F4
Sonia Gdns., Houns.	63	G7
Sonning Gdns.,	81	E6
Hmptn.		
Sonning Rd. SE25	95	D6
Soper Clo. E4	33	J5
Sophia Clo. N7	49	F6
Mackenzie Rd.		
Sophia Rd. E10	51	B1
Sophia Rd. E16	60	H6
Sopwith Ave.	98	H5
Chess.		
Sopwith Rd., Houns.	63	C7
Sopwith Way,	91	H1
Kings.T.		
Sorrel Clo. SE28	71	A1
Sorrell Clo. SE14	68	H7
Southerngate Way		
Sorrell Gdns. E6	61	B5
Sorrento Rd., Sutt.	100	D3
Sotheby Rd. N5	49	J3
Sotheran Clo. E8	59	D1
Sotheron Rd. SW6	66	E7
Soudan Rd. SW11	75	J1
Souldern Rd. W14	66	A3
South Access Rd.	41	H7
E17		
South Acre NW9	38	F2
South Africa Rd.	65	H1
W12		
South Audley St. W1	**11**	**C6**
South Audley St. W1	58	A7
South Ave. E4	26	B7
South Ave., Cars.	101	A7
South Ave., Rich.	73	G1
Sandycombe Rd.		
South Ave., Sthl.	54	F7
South Ave. Gdns.,	54	F7
Sthl.		
South Bank, Chis.	88	F3
South Bank, Surb.	91	H6
South Bank Ter.,	91	H6
Surb.		
South Birkbeck Rd.	51	D3
E11		
South Black Lion	65	G5
La. W6		
South Bolton Gdns.	**18**	**B3**
SW5		
South Bolton Gdns.	66	E5
SW5		
South Carriage Dr.	66	H2
SW1		
South Carriage Dr.	**14**	**G3**
SW7		
South Carriage Dr.	66	H2
SW7		
South Clo. N6	40	B6
South Clo., Barn.	23	C3
South Clo., Bexh.	80	D4
South Clo., Dag.	62	G1
South Clo., Mord.	93	D6
Green La.		
South Clo., Pnr.	36	F7
South Clo., Twick.	81	G3
South Colonnade	69	A1
E14		
South Countess Rd.	41	J3
E17		
South Cres. WC1	**11**	**H2**
South Cres. WC1	58	D5
South Cross Rd.,	43	F5
Ilf.		
South Croxted Rd.	86	A3
SE21		
South Dagenham Rd.,	53	J7
Dag.		
South Dene NW7	30	D3
South Dr., Orp.	104	H5
South Ealing Rd. W5	64	G2
South Eastern Ave.	33	C3
N9		
South Eaton Pl. SW1	**19**	**C1**
South Eaton Pl. SW1	67	A4
South Eden Pk. Rd.,	96	D0
Beck.		
South Edwardes Sq.	66	C3
W8		
South End W8	**14**	**B5**
South End, Croy.	101	J4
South End Clo. NW3	48	H4
South End Rd. NW3	48	H4
South End Row W8	**14**	**B5**
South End Row W8	66	E3
South Esk Rd. E7	51	J6
South Gdns. SW19	84	G7
South Gipsy Rd.	80	D3
Well.		
South Glade, The,	89	F1
Bex.		
Camden Rd.		
South Grn. NW9	38	E1
Clayton Fld.		
South Gro. E17	41	J5
South Gro. N6	49	A1
South Gro. N15	41	A5
South Gro. Ho. N6	49	A1
Highgate W. Hill		
South Hill, Chis.	88	C6
South Hill Ave.,	45	J3
Har.		
South Hill Gro.,	46	B4
Har.		
South Hill Pk. NW3	48	H4
South Hill Pk.	48	H4
Gdns. NW3		
South Hill Rd.,	96	E3
Brom.		
South Huxley N18	33	A5
South Island Pl.	67	F7
SW9		
South Lambeth Pl.	**20**	**B5**
SW8		
South Lambeth Pl.	67	E6
SW8		
South Lambeth Rd.	**20**	**B7**
SW8		
South Lambeth Rd.	67	E6
SW8		
South La., Kings.T.	91	G3
South La., N.Mal.	92	D4
South La. W.,	92	D4
N.Mal.		
South Lo. Ave.,	94	E4
Mitch.		
South Lo. Cres.,	24	D4
Enf.		
South Lo. Dr. N14	24	D4
South Mall N9	33	D3
Plevna Rd.		
South Mead NW9	38	F1
South Mead, Epsom	99	E7
South Meadows,	46	H5
Wem.		

Name	Page	Ref
South Molton La. W1	11	D4
South Molton La. W1	58	B6
South Molton Rd. E16	60	G6
South Molton St. W1	11	D4
South Molton St. W1	58	B6
South Norwood Hill SE25	95	B1
South Oak Rd. SW16	85	F4
South Par. SW3	18	F3
South Par. SW3	66	G5
South Par. W4	65	D4
South Pk. Cres. SE6	87	F1
South Pk. Cres., Ilf.	52	G3
South Pk. Dr., Ilf.	52	H3
South Pk. Gro., N.Mal.	92	C4
South Pk. Hill Rd., S.Croy.	102	A5
South Pk. Ms. SW6	75	E3
South Pk. Rd. SW19	84	D6
South Pk. Rd., Ilf.	52	G3
South Pk. Ter., Ilf.	52	H3
South Pk. Way, Ruis.	45	C6
South Penge Pk. Est. SE20	95	E2
South Pl. EC2	13	C2
South Pl. EC2	59	A5
South Pl., Enf.	25	F5
South Pl., Surb.	91	J7
South Pl. Ms. EC2	13	C2
South Rd. N9	33	D1
South Rd. SE23	86	G2
South Rd. SW19	84	F6
South Rd. W5	64	G4
South Rd., Edg.	38	B1
South Rd., Felt.	81	D5
South Rd., Hmptn.	81	E6
South Rd., Rom. (Chadwell Heath)	44	E6
South Rd., Rom. (Little Heath)	44	B5
South Rd., Sthl.	63	F2
South Rd., Twick.	82	A3
South Row SE3	78	F2
South Sea St. SE16	68	J3
South Side W6	65	F3
South Side Common SW19	83	J6
South Sq. NW11	39	E6
South Sq. WC1	12	E2
South St. W1	15	C1
South St., W1	67	A1
South St., Brom.	96	G2
South St., Enf.	25	F5
South St., Islw.	73	D3
South St., Rain.	62	J2
South Tenter St. E1	13	G4
South Tenter St. E1	59	C7
South Ter. SW7	18	G1
South Ter. SW7	66	H4
South Ter., Surb.	91	H6
South Vale SE19	86	B6
South Vale, Har.	46	B4
South Vw., Brom.	96	H2
South Vw. Dr. E18	42	H3
South Vw. Rd. N8	40	D3
South Vw., Loug.	27	C6
South Vw. Rd., Pnr.	28	B6
South Vill. NW1	49	D6
South Wk., W.Wick.	103	E3
South Way N9	33	F2
South Way N11 *Ringway*	32	C6
South Way, Brom.	96	G7
South Way, Croy.	102	H3
South Way, Har.	36	G4
South Way, Wem.	47	A5
South W. India Dock Entrance E14	69	C2
South Western Rd., Twick.	73	D6
South Wf. Rd. W2	10	E3
South Wf. Rd. W2	57	G6
South Woodford to Barking Relief Rd., Bark.	52	D4
South Worple Ave. SW14 *South Worple Way*	74	E3
South Worple Ave. SW14	74	D3
Southacre Way, Pnr.	36	C1
Southall La., Houns.	63	B6
Southall Pl. SE1	17	B4
Southall Pl. SE1	68	A2
Southam St. W10	57	B3
Southampton Bldgs. WC2	12	E2
Southampton Gdns., Mitch.	94	E5
Southampton Pl. WC1	12	B2
Southampton Pl. WC1	58	E5
Southampton Rd. NW5	48	J5
Southampton Row WC1	12	B1
Southampton Row WC1	58	E5
Southampton St. WC2	12	B5
Southampton St. WC2	58	E7
Southampton Way SE5	21	C7
Southampton Way SE5	68	A7
Southbank, T.Ditt.	91	E7
Southborough Clo., Surb.	98	G1
Southborough La., Brom.	97	B5
Southborough Rd. E9	50	G7
Southborough Rd., Brom.	97	B3
Southborough Rd., Surb.	98	H1
Southbourne, Brom.	96	G7
Southbourne Ave. NW9	38	C2
Southbourne Clo., Pnr.	36	E7
Southbourne Cres. NW4	39	B4
Southbourne Gdns. SE12	78	H5
Southbourne Gdns., Ilf.	52	F5
Southbourne Gdns., Ruis.	45	B1
Southbridge Pl., Croy.	101	J4
Southbridge Rd., Croy.	101	J4
Southbridge Way, Sthl.	63	E2
Southbrook Ms. SE12	78	F6
Southbrook Rd. SE12	78	F6
Southbrook Rd. SW16	94	E1
Southbury Ave., Enf.	25	D5
Southbury Rd., Enf.	25	A3
Southchurch Rd. E6	61	C2
Southcombe St. W14	66	B4
Southcote Ave. Surb.	92	B7
Southcote Rd. E17	41	G5
Southcote Rd. N19	49	C4
Southcote Rd. SE25	95	E5
Southcroft Ave. Well.	79	H3
Southcroft Ave. W.Wick.	103	C2
Southcroft Rd. SW16	85	B6
Southcroft Rd. SW17	85	A6
Southcroft Rd., Orp.	104	H3
Southdale, Chig.	35	G6
Southdean Gdns. SW19	84	C2
Southdown Ave. W7	64	D3
Southdown Cres., Har.	45	J1
Southdown Cres., Ilf.	43	H5
Southdown Dr. SW20 *Crescent Rd.*	84	A7
Southdown Rd. SW20	93	A1
Southend Clo. SE9	79	E6
Southend Cres. SE9	79	E6
Southend La. SE6	87	A4
Southend La. SE26	86	J4
Southend Rd. E6	52	C7
Southend Rd. E17	42	D1
Southend Rd. E18	42	F2
Southend Rd., Beck.	87	A7
Southend Rd., Wdf.Grn.	42	J2
Southern Ave. SE25	95	C3
Southern Ave., Felt.	81	A1
Southern Dr., Loug.	27	C6
Southern Gro. E3	59	J3
Southern Rd. E13	60	H2
Southern Rd. N2	39	J4
Southern Row W10	57	B4
Southern St. N1	8	C1
Southern St. N1	58	F2
Southern Way, Rom.	44	G6
Southgate Way SE14	68	H7
Southernhay, Loug.	27	A4
Southerton Rd. W6	65	J3
Southey Rd. N15	41	B5
Southey Rd. SW9	76	G1
Southey Rd. SW19	84	D7
Southey St. SE20	86	G7
Southfield, Barn.	23	A6
Southfield Cotts. W7 *Oaklands Rd.*	64	C2
Southfield Gdns., Twick.	82	C4
Southfield Pk., Har.	36	H4
Southfield Rd. N17	41	B2
Southfield Rd. W4	65	D2
Southfield Rd., Chis.	97	J3
Southfield Rd., Enf.	25	E6
Southfields NW4	38	H3
Southfields, E.Mol.	91	B6
Southfields Ct. SW19	84	B1
Southfields Pas. SW18 *Southfields Rd.*	75	D6
Southfields Rd. SW18	75	D6
Southfleet Rd., Orp.	104	H3
Southgate Circ. N14 *The Bourne*	32	D1
Southgate Gro. N1	50	A7
Southgate Rd. N1	59	A1
Southholme Clo. SE19	95	C1
Southill La., Pnr.	36	B4
Southill Rd., Chis.	88	B6
Southill St. E14 *Chrisp St.*	60	B6
Southland Rd. SE18	70	J7
Southland Way, Houns.	73	A5
Southlands Ave. Orp.	104	G4
Southlands Gro., Brom.	97	B3
Southlands Rd., Brom.	96	J5
Southly Clo., Sutt.	100	D3
Southmead Rd. SW19	84	B1
Southmont Rd., Esher	98	B2
Southmoor Way E9	50	J6
Southold Ri. SE9	88	C3
Southolm St. SW11	76	B1
Southover N12	31	D3
Southover, Brom.	87	G5
Southport Rd. SE18	70	G4
Southridge Pl. SW20	84	A7
Southsea Rd., Kings.T.	91	H4
Southspring, Sid.	79	G7
Southvale Rd. SE3	78	E2
Southview Ave. NW10	47	F5
Southview Clo. Bex.	80	F6
Southview Cres. Ilf.	43	E6
Southview Gdns., Wall.	101	C7
Southview Rd., Brom.	87	D4
Southville SW8	76	D1
Southville Rd., T.Ditt.	91	D7
Southwark Bri. EC4	13	A6
Southwark Bri. EC4	67	J1
Southwark Bri. SE1	13	A6
Southwark Bri. SE1	67	H3
Southwark Bri. Rd. SE1	16	J4
Southwark Bri. Rd. SE1	67	H3
Southwark Gro. SE1	16	J2
Southwark Pk. Est. SE16	68	E4
Southwark Pk. Rd. SE16	21	G1
Southwark Pk. Rd. SE16	68	C4
Southwark Pl., Brom. *St. Georges Rd.*	97	C3
Southwark St. SE1	16	H1
Southwark St. SE1	67	H1
Southwater Clo. E14	59	J6
Southwater Clo., Beck.	87	B7
Southway N20	31	D2
Southway NW7	30	G7
Southway NW11	39	E5
Southway SW20	92	J4
Southway, Wall.	101	C4
Southwell Ave., Nthlt.	45	G6
Southwell Gdns. SW7	14	C6
Southwell Gdns. SW7	66	F4
Southwell Gro. Rd. E11	51	E2
Southwell Rd. SE5	76	J3
Southwell Rd., Croy.	94	G6
Southwell Rd., Har.	37	G6
Southwest Rd. E11	51	D1
Southwick Ms. W2	10	F3
Southwick Pl. W2	10	G4
Southwick Pl. W2	57	H6
Southwick St. W2	10	G3
Southwick St. W2	57	H6
Southwold Dr. Bark.	53	A5
Southwold Rd. E5	50	E2
Southwold Rd., Bex.	80	H6
Southwood Ave. N6	40	B7
Southwood Ave., Kings.T.	92	C1
Southwood Clo. Brom.	97	C4
Southwood Clo., Wor.Pk. *Carters Clo.*	100	A1
Southwood Dr., Surb.	92	C7
Southwood Gdns., Esher	98	D3
Southwood Gdns., Ilf.	43	E4
Southwood La. N6	40	A7
Southwood Lawn Rd. N6	40	A7
Southwood Rd. SE9	88	E2
Southwood Rd. SE28	71	B1
Sovereign Clo. E1	59	E7
Sovereign Clo. W5	55	F5
Sovereign Ms. E2	9	F1
Sovereign Pk. NW10	56	B4
Sowerby Clo. SE9	79	B5
Spa Clo. SE25	95	B1
Spa Hill SE19	95	A1
Spa Rd. SE16	17	F6
Spa Rd. SE16	68	C3
Space Waye, Felt.	72	A5
Spafield St. EC1	8	E5
Spalding Rd. NW4	38	J6
Spalding Rd. SW17	85	B5
Spanby Rd. E3	60	A4
Spaniards Clo. NW11	48	G1
Spaniards End NW3	48	F1
Spaniards Rd. NW3	48	F3
Spanish Pl. W1	11	C3
Spanish Pl. W1	58	A6
Spanish Rd. SW18	75	F5
Spareleaze Hill, Loug.	27	B5
Sparkbridge Rd., Har.	37	B4
Sparks Clo. W3 *Joseph Ave.*	56	D6
Sparks Clo., Hmptn. *Victors Dr.*	81	E6
Sparrow Clo., Hmptn.	81	E6
Sparrow Dr., Orp.	104	F1
Sparrow Fm. Dr., Felt.	72	C6
Sparrow Fm. Rd., Epsom	99	G4
Sparrow Grn., Dag.	53	H3
Sparrows La. SE9	79	F7
Sparrows Way (Bushey), Wat. *Sparrows Herne*	28	J1
Sparsholt Rd. N19	49	F1
Sparsholt Rd., Bark.	61	H1
Sparta St. SE10	78	C1
Spear Ms. SW5	66	D4
Spearman St. SE18	70	D6
Spearpoint Gdns., Ilf.	43	J4
Spears Rd. N19	49	E1
Speart La., Houns.	63	E7
Spedan Clo. NW3	48	E3

Speedwell St. SE8 69 A7
Comet St.
Speedy Pl. WC1 8 A4
Speer Rd., T.Ditt. 91 C7
Speke Ho. SE5 67 J7
Speke Rd., Th.Hth. 95 A2
Spekehill SE9 88 C3
Speldhurst Clo., Brom. 96 G5
Speldhurst Rd. E9 50 G7
Speldhurst Rd. W4 65 D3
Spellbrook Wk. N1 58 J1
Basire St.
Spelman St. E1 13 H1
Spelman St. E1 59 D5
Spencer Ave. N13 32 F6
Spencer Ave., Hayes 54 A5
Spencer Clo. N3 39 D2
Spencer Clo. NW10 55 J3
Spencer Clo., Orp. 104 H2
Spencer Clo., Wdf.Grn. 34 J5
Spencer Ct. NW8 6 C1
Spencer Dr. N2 39 F6
Spencer Gdns. SE9 79 C5
Spencer Gdns. SW14 74 C5
Spencer Hill SW19 84 B6
Spencer Hill Rd. SW19 84 B7
Spencer Ms. W6 66 B6
Greyhound Rd.
Spencer Pk. SW18 75 G5
Spencer Pas. E2 59 E2
Pritchard's Rd.
Spencer Pl., Croy. 95 A7
Gloucester Rd.
Spencer Ri. NW5 49 B4
Spencer Rd. E6 61 A1
Spencer Rd. E17 42 C2
Spencer Rd. N8 40 F5
Spencer Rd. N11 32 B4
Spencer Rd. N17 41 D1
Spencer Rd. SW18 75 G4
Spencer Rd. SW20 92 H1
Spencer Rd. W3 65 C1
Spencer Rd. W4 65 C7
Spencer Rd., Brom. 87 F7
Spencer Rd., E.Mol. 91 A4
Spencer Rd., Har. 37 B2
Spencer Rd., Ilf. 52 J1
Spencer Rd., Islw. 72 J1
Spencer Rd., Mitch. 94 A3
Spencer Rd. Mitch. (Beddington), 94 A7
Spencer Rd., S.Croy. 102 B5
Spencer Rd., Twick. 82 B3
Spencer Rd., Wem. 46 F2
Spencer St. EC1 8 G4
Spencer St. EC1 58 H3
Spencer St., Sthl. 63 D2
Spencer Wk. SW15 75 A4
Spenser Gro. N16 50 B4
Spenser Rd. SE24 76 G5
Spenser St. SW1 15 G5
Spenser St. SW1 67 C3
Spensley Wk. N16 50 A3
Clissold Rd.
Speranza St. SE18 70 J5
Sperling Rd. N17 41 B2
Spert St. E14 59 H7
Spey St. E14 60 C5
Speyside N14 24 C6
Spezia Rd. NW10 56 G2
Spicer Clo. SW9 76 H2
Spicer Clo., Walt. 90 C6
Spices Yd., Croy. 101 J4
Spiers Clo., N.Mal. 92 F6
Spigurnell Rd. N17 41 A1
Spikes Bri. Rd., Sthl. 54 E6
Spilsby Clo. NW9 38 E2
Kenley Ave.
Spindlewood Gdns., Croy. 102 B4
Spindrift Ave. E14 69 A4
Spinel Clo. SE18 70 J5
Spinnells Rd., Har. 45 F1
Spinney, The N21 24 G7
Spinney, The SW16 85 C3
Spinney, The, Barn. 23 E2
Spinney, The, Sid. 89 E4
Spinney, The, Stan. 29 H4
Spinney, The, Sun. 90 A1
Spinney, The, Sutt. 99 J4
Spinney, The, Wem. 46 D3
Spinney Clo., N.Mal. 92 E5
Spinney Gdns. SE19 86 C5
Spinney Gdns., Dag. 53 E5
Spinney Oak, Brom. 97 B2
Spinneys, The, Brom. 97 C2
Spirit Quay E1 17 J1
Spital Sq. E1 13 E1
Spital Sq. E1 59 B5
Spital St. E1 9 H6
Spital St. E1 59 D5
Spital Yd. E1 13 E1
Spitalfields Mkt. E1 13 F1
Spitalfields Mkt. E1 59 C5
Spitfire Est., Houns. 63 C5
Spitfire Way, Houns. 63 C5
Spode Wk. NW6 48 E6
Lymington Rd.
Spondon Rd. N15 41 D4
Spooner Wk., Wall. 101 D5
Sportsbank St. SE6 78 C7
Spottons Gro. N17 40 J1
Gospatrick Rd.
Spout Hill, Croy. 103 A5
Spratt Hall Rd. E11 42 G6
Spray La., Twick. 73 B6
Kneller Rd.
Spray St. SE18 70 E4
Spreighton Rd., W.Mol. 90 H4
Sprimont Pl. SW3 18 J3
Sprimont Pl. SW3 66 J4
Spring Bri. Rd. W5 55 G7
Spring Clo., Barn. 23 A5
Spring Clo., Borwd. 22 A1
Spring Clo., Dag. 53 D1
Spring Clo. La., Sutt. 100 B6
Spring Cotts., Surb. 91 G5
St. Leonards Rd.
Spring Ct., Sid. 89 A3
Station Rd.
Spring Dr., Pnr. 36 A6
Eastcote Rd.
Spring Gdns. SW1 15 J1
Spring Gdns., Rom. 44 J5
Spring Gdns., Wall. 101 C5
Spring Gdns., W.Mol. 90 J5
Spring Gdns., Wdf.Grn. 34 J7
Spring Gdns. Ind. Est., Rom. 44 J5
Spring Gro. W4 65 A5
Spring Gro., Hmptn. 90 H1
Plevna Rd.
Spring Gro., Loug. 27 A6
Spring Gro., Mitch. 94 A1
Spring Gro. Cres., Houns. 72 J1
Spring Gro. Rd., Houns. 72 H1
Spring Gro. Rd., Islw. 73 A1
Spring Gro. Rd., Rich. 73 J5
Spring Hill E5 41 D7
Spring Hill SE26 86 F4
Spring Lake, Stan. 29 E4
Spring La. E5 41 E7
Spring La. SE25 95 E6
Spring Ms. W1 11 A1
Spring Pk. Ave., Croy. 102 G2
Spring Pk. Dr. N4 49 J1
Spring Pk. Rd., Croy. 102 G2
Spring Pas. SW15 75 A3
The Embk.
Spring Path NW3 48 G5
Spring Pl. NW5 49 B5
Spring St. W2 10 E4
Spring St. W2 57 G6
Spring Ter., Rich. 73 H5
Spring Vale, Bexh. 80 H4
Spring Vill. Rd., Edg. 30 A7
Spring Wk. E1 13 J1
Springall St. SE15 68 E7
Springbank N21 24 F6
Springbank Rd. SE13 78 D6
Springbank Wk. NW1 49 D7
Agar Gro.
Springbourne Ct., Beck. 96 C1
Springclose La., Sutt. 100 B6
Springcroft Ave. N2 39 J4
Springdale Rd. N16 50 A4
Springfield E5 50 E1
Springfield (Bushey), Wat. 29 A1
Springfield Ave. N10 40 C3
Springfield Ave. SW20 93 C3
Springfield Ave., Hmptn. 81 H6
Springfield Clo. N12 31 E5
Springfield Clo., Stan. 29 D3
Springfield Dr., Ilf. 43 F6
Springfield Gdns. E5 50 E1
Springfield Gdns. NW9 38 D5
Springfield Gdns., Brom. 97 C4
Springfield Gdns., Ruis. 45 B1
Springfield Gdns., W.Wick. 103 B2
Springfield Gdns., Wdf.Grn. 34 J7
Springfield Gro. SE7 69 J6
Springfield La. NW6 57 E1
Springfield Mt. NW9 38 D5
Springfield Ri. SE26 86 E3
Springfield Rd. E4 34 E1
Springfield Rd. E6 52 C7
Springfield Rd. E15 60 E3
Springfield Rd. E17 41 J6
Springfield Rd. N11 32 B5
Springfield Rd. N15 41 D4
Springfield Rd. NW8 57 F1
Springfield Rd. SE26 86 E5
Springfield Rd. SW19 84 C5
Springfield Rd. W7 64 B1
Springfield Rd., Bexh. 80 H3
Springfield Rd., Brom. 97 C4
Springfield Rd., Har. 37 B6
Springfield Rd., Hayes 63 C1
Springfield Rd., Kings.T. 91 H3
Springfield Rd., Tedd. 82 D5
Springfield Rd., Th.Hth. 94 J1
Springfield Rd., Twick. 81 G1
Springfield Rd., Wall. 101 A5
Springfield Rd., Well. 80 B3
Springfield Wk. NW6 57 E1
Springhill Clo. SE5 77 A3
Springhurst Clo., Croy. 102 J4
Springpark Dr., Beck. 96 C3
Springpond Rd., Dag. 53 E5
Springrice Rd. SE13 78 D6
Springvale Ave., Brent. 64 H5
Springvale Est. W14 66 B3
Blythe Rd.
Springvale Ter. W14 66 A3
Springwater Clo. SE18 79 D1
Springwell Ave. NW10 56 F1
Springwell Clo. SW16 85 G4
Etherstone Rd.
Springwell Ct., Houns. 72 D2
Springwell Rd. SW16 85 G4
Springwell Rd., Houns. 72 D2
Springwood Cres., Edg. 30 B2
Sprowston Ms. E7 51 G6
Sprowston Rd. E7 51 G5
Spruce Ct. W4 65 D2
Spruce Ct. W5 64 H3
Elderberry Rd.
Spruce Hills Rd. E17 42 C2
Spruce Pk., Brom. 96 F4
Cumberland Rd.
Sprucedale Gdns., Croy. 102 G4
Sprules Rd. SE4 77 H2
Spur Rd. N15 41 A4
Philip La.
Spur Rd. SW1 15 F4
Spur Rd. SW1 67 C2
Spur Rd., Bark. 61 F3
Spur Rd., Edg. 29 H4
Spur Rd., Felt. 72 B5
Spur Rd., Islw. 64 E7
Spur Rd. Est., Edg. 29 J4
Spurfield, W.Mol. 90 H3
Spurgeon Ave. SE19 95 A1
Spurgeon Rd. SE19 95 A1
Spurgeon St. SE1 17 B6
Spurgeon St. SE1 68 A3
Spurling Rd. SE22 77 C4
Spurling Rd., Dag. 53 F6
Spurstowe Rd. E8 50 E6
Marcon Pl.
Spurstowe Ter. E8 50 E5
Square, The W6 65 J5
Square, The, Cars. 101 A5
Square, The, Ilf. 43 D7
Square, The, Rich. 73 G5
Square, The, Wdf.Grn. 34 G5
Square Rigger Row SW11 75 F3
York Pl.
Squarey St. SW17 84 F3
Squires Ct. SW19 84 D4
Squires La. N3 39 E2
Squires Mt. NW3 48 G3
East Heath Rd.
Squires Wd. Dr., Chis. 88 C7
Bullers Wd. Dr.
Squirrel Clo., Houns. 72 C3
Squirrels, The SE13 78 D3
Belmont Hill
Squirrels, The, Pnr. 36 F3
Squirrels Clo. N12 31 F4
Woodside Ave.
Squirrels Grn., Wor.Pk. 99 G2
The Ave.
Squirrels La., Buck.H. 35 A3
Squirrels Ms. W13 55 D7
Squirries St. E2 9 J3
Squirries St. E2 59 D3
Stable Clo., Nthlt. 54 G2
Hotspur Rd.
Stable Wk. N2 39 G1
Old Fm. Rd.
Stable Way W10 56 J6
Latimer Rd.
Stable Yd. SW1 15 F3
Stable Yd. SW9 76 F2
Broomgrove Rd.
Stable Yd. Rd. SW1 15 G3
Stable Yd. Rd. SW1 67 C2
Stables, The, Buck.H. 26 J7
Stables End, Orp. 104 F3
Stables Ms. SE27 85 J5
Stables Way SE11 20 E3
Stables Way SE11 67 G5
Stacey Ave. N18 33 F4
Stacey Clo. E10 42 D5
Halford Rd.
Stacey St. WC2 11 J4
Stacey St. WC2 58 D6
Stackhouse St. SW3 14 J5
Stacy Path SE5 68 B7
Harris St.
Stadium Rd. NW2 38 J7
Stadium Rd. SE18 70 C7
Stadium St. SW10 66 F7
Stadium Way, Wem. 46 J4
Staff St. EC1 9 C4
Staffa Rd. E10 50 G1
Stafford Clo. N14 24 C5
Stafford Clo. NW6 57 D3
Stafford Clo., Sutt. 100 B6
Stafford Ct. W8 66 D3
Kensington High St.
Stafford Cross Ind. Est., Croy. 101 F5
Stafford Gdns., Croy. 101 F5
Stafford Pl. SW1 15 F5
Stafford Pl. SW1 67 C3
Stafford Pl., Rich. 73 J7
Stafford Rd. E3 59 J2
Stafford Rd. E7 51 J7
Stafford Rd. NW6 57 D3
Stafford Rd., Croy. 101 G4
Stafford Rd., Har. 28 J7
Stafford Rd., N.Mal. 92 C3
Stafford Rd., Sid. 88 H4
Stafford Rd., Wall. 101 B6
Stafford St. W1 15 F1
Stafford St. W1 67 C1
Stafford Ter. W8 66 D2

Staffordshire St. SE15	77	D1
Stag Clo., Edg.	38	B2
Stag La. NW9	38	C3
Stag La. SW15	83	F2
Stag La., Buck.H.	34	H2
Stag La., Edg.	38	B2
Stag Pl. SW1	**15**	**F5**
Stag Pl. SW1	67	C3
Stag Ride SW19	83	F3
Stags Way, Islw.	64	C6
Stainbank Rd., Mitch.	94	B3
Stainby Rd. N15	41	C4
Stainer St. SE1	**17**	**C2**
Stainer St. SE1	68	A1
Staines Ave., Sutt.	100	A2
Staines Rd., Felt.	72	C5
Staines Rd. (TW3), Houns.	72	G3
Staines Rd. (TW4), Houns.	72	C5
Staines Rd., Ilf.	52	G4
Staines Rd., Twick.	81	G3
Staines Rd. E., Sun.	81	A7
Staines Wk., Sid. *Evry Rd.*	89	C6
Stainforth Rd. E17	42	A4
Stainforth Rd., Ilf.	43	G7
Staining La. EC2	**13**	**A3**
Staining La. EC2	58	J6
Stainmore Clo., Chis.	97	G1
Stainsbury St. E2 *Royston St.*	59	F2
Stainsby Pl. E14	60	A6
Stainsby Rd. E14	60	A6
Stainton Rd. SE6	78	D6
Stainton Rd., Enf.	25	F1
Stalbridge St. NW1	**10**	**H1**
Stalham St. SE16	68	E3
Stambourne Way SE19	86	B7
Stambourne Way, W.Wick.	103	C3
Stamford Brook Ave. W6	65	F3
Stamford Brook Rd. W6	65	F3
Stamford Clo. N15	41	D4
Stamford Clo., Har.	29	B7
Stamford Clo., Sthl.	54	G7
Stamford Ct. W6 *Goldhawk Rd.*	65	F4
Stamford Dr., Brom.	96	F4
Stamford Gdns., Dag.	53	C7
Stamford Gro. E. N16 *Oldhill St.*	50	D1
Stamford Gro. W. N16 *Oldhill St.*	50	D1
Stamford Hill N16	50	C2
Stamford Hill Est. N16	50	C1
Stamford Rd. E6	61	B1
Stamford Rd. N1	50	B7
Stamford Rd. N15	41	D4
Stamford Rd., Dag.	62	B1
Stamford St. SE1	**16**	**E2**
Stamford St. SE1	67	G1
Stamp Pl. E2	**9**	**F3**
Stamp Pl. E2	59	C3
Stanard Clo. N16	41	B7
Stanborough Clo., Hmptn.	81	F6
Stanborough Pas. E8 *Abbot St.*	50	C6
Stanborough Rd., Houns.	73	A3
Stanbridge Pl. N21	32	H2
Stanbridge Rd. SW15	74	J3
Stanbrook Rd. SE2	71	B2
Stanbury Rd. SE15	77	E1
Stancroft NW9	38	E5
Standard Ind. Est. E16	70	C2
Standard Pl. EC2	**9**	**E4**
Standard Rd. NW10	56	C4
Standard Rd., Belv.	71	G5
Standard Rd., Bexh.	80	E4
Standard Rd., Houns.	72	E3
Standen Rd. SW18	75	C7
Standfield Gdns., Dag. *Standfield Rd.*	53	G6
Standfield Rd., Dag.	53	G5

Standish Rd. W6	65	G4
Standlake Pt. SE23	86	G3
Stane Clo. SW19	93	E1
Hayward Clo.		
Stane Way SE18	70	B7
Stanfield Rd. E3	59	H2
Stanford Clo., Hmptn.	81	F6
Stanford Clo., Rom.	44	H6
Stanford Clo., Wdf.Grn.	35	B5
Stanford Ho., Bark.	62	B2
Stanford Pl. SE17	**21**	**D2**
Stanford Rd. N11	31	J5
Stanford Rd. SW16	94	D2
Stanford Rd. W8	**14**	**B5**
Stanford Rd. W8	66	E3
Stanford St. SW1	**19**	**H2**
Stanford Way SW16	94	D2
Stangate Cres., Borwd.	22	D5
Stangate Gdns., Stan.	29	E4
Stanger Rd. SE25	95	D4
Stanhope Ave. N3	39	C3
Stanhope Ave., Brom.	103	F1
Stanhope Ave., Har.	37	A1
Stanhope Clo. SE16	68	G2
Middleton Dr.		
Stanhope Gdns. N4	40	H6
Stanhope Gdns. N6	40	B6
Stanhope Gdns. NW7	30	F5
Stanhope Gdns. SW7	**18**	**D1**
Stanhope Gdns. SW7	66	F4
Stanhope Gdns., Dag. *Stanhope Rd.*	53	F3
Stanhope Gdns., Ilf.	52	C1
Stanhope Gate W1	**15**	**C1**
Stanhope Gate W1	67	A1
Stanhope Gro., Beck.	95	J5
Stanhope Ms. E. SW7	**18**	**D1**
Stanhope Ms. E. SW7	66	F4
Stanhope Ms. S. SW7	**18**	**D2**
Stanhope Ms. W. SW7	**18**	**D1**
Stanhope Ms. W. SW7	66	F4
Stanhope Par. NW1	**7**	**F3**
Stanhope Pk. Rd., Grnf.	54	J4
Stanhope Pl. W2	**10**	**J4**
Stanhope Pl. W2	57	J7
Stanhope Rd. E17	42	B5
Stanhope Rd. N6	40	C6
Stanhope Rd. N12	31	F5
Stanhope Rd., Barn.	22	J5
Stanhope Rd., Bexh.	80	E2
Stanhope Rd., Cars.	101	A7
Stanhope Rd., Croy.	102	B3
Stanhope Rd., Dag.	53	F2
Stanhope Rd., Grnf.	54	J5
Stanhope Rd., Sid.	89	A4
Stanhope Row W1	**15**	**D2**
Stanhope St. NW1	**7**	**F3**
Stanhope St. NW1	58	C3
Stanhope Ter. W2	**10**	**F5**
Stanhope Ter. W2	57	G7
Stanier Clo. W14 *Aisgill Ave.*	66	C5
Stanlake Ms. W12	65	J1
Stanlake Rd. W12	65	J1
Stanlake Vill. W12	65	J1
Stanley Ave., Bark.	61	J2
Stanley Ave., Beck.	96	C2
Stanley Ave., Dag.	53	F1
Stanley Ave., Grnf.	54	J1
Stanley Ave., N.Mal.	92	G5
Stanley Ave., Wem.	46	H7
Stanley Clo. SW8	**20**	**C6**
Stanley Clo. SW8	80	F6
Stanley Clo., Wem.	46	H7
Stanley Cres. W11	57	C7
Stanley Gdns. NW2	47	J5
Stanley Gdns. SW17	85	A6
Ashbourne Rd.		
Stanley Gdns. W3	65	E2
Stanley Gdns. W11	57	C7
Stanley Gdns., Wall.	101	C6
Stanley Gdns. Ms. W11 *Stanley Cres.*	57	C7

Stanley Gdns. Rd., Tedd.	82	B5
Stanley Gro. SW8	76	A2
Stanley Gro., Croy.	94	G6
Stanley Pk. Dr., Wem.	55	J1
Stanley Pk. Rd., Cars.	100	H7
Stanley Pk. Rd., Wall.	101	B6
Stanley Pas. NW1	**8**	**A2**
Stanley Rd. E4	34	D1
Stanley Rd. E10	42	B6
Stanley Rd. E12	52	B5
Stanley Rd. E15	60	D1
Stanley Rd. E18	42	F1
Stanley Rd. N2	39	G3
Stanley Rd. N9	33	C1
Stanley Rd. N10	32	B7
Stanley Rd. N11	32	D6
Stanley Rd. N15	40	H4
Stanley Rd. NW9 *West Hendon Bdy.*	38	G7
Stanley Rd. SW14	74	B4
Stanley Rd. SW19	84	D7
Stanley Rd. W3	65	C3
Stanley Rd., Brom.	96	H4
Stanley Rd., Cars.	101	A7
Stanley Rd., Croy.	94	G2
Stanley Rd., Enf.	25	B3
Stanley Rd., Har.	45	J2
Stanley Rd., Houns.	72	J4
Stanley Rd., Ilf.	52	G2
Stanley Rd., Mitch.	85	A7
Stanley Rd., Mord.	93	D4
Stanley Rd., Nthwd.	36	A1
Stanley Rd., Sid.	89	A3
Stanley Rd., Sthl.	54	E7
Stanley Rd., Sutt.	100	E6
Stanley Rd., Tedd.	82	B4
Stanley Rd., Twick.	82	A3
Stanley Rd., Wem.	46	J6
Stanley St. SE8	68	J7
Stanley Ter. N19	49	E2
Stanleycroft Clo., Islw.	73	A1
Stanmer St. SW11	75	H1
Stanmore Gdns., Rich.	73	J3
Stanmore Gdns., Sutt.	100	F3
Stanmore Hill, Stan.	29	D3
Stanmore Pl. NW1 *Arlington Rd.*	58	B1
Stanmore Rd. E11	51	H1
Stanmore Rd. N15	40	H4
Stanmore Rd., Belv.	71	J4
Stanmore Rd., Rich.	73	J3
Stanmore St. N1 *Caledonian Rd.*	58	F1
Stanmore Ter., Beck.	96	A2
Stanmore Way, Loug.	27	D1
Stannard Rd. E8	50	D6
Stannary Pl. SE11	**20**	**F4**
Stannary St. SE11	**20**	**F5**
Stannary St. SE11	67	G6
Stannington Path, Borwd. *Warenford Way*	22	A1
Stansfeld Rd. E6	61	A5
Stansfield Rd. SW9	76	F3
Stansfield Rd., Houns.	72	B2
Stansgate Rd., Dag.	53	G2
Stanstead Clo., Brom.	96	F5
Stanstead Gro. SE6	86	J1
Catford Hill		
Stanstead Manor, Sutt.	100	D6
Stanstead Rd. E11	42	H5
Stanstead Rd. SE6 *Catford Hill*	86	J1
Stanstead Rd. SE23	86	G1
Stansted Cres., Bex.	89	D1
Stanswood Gdns. SE5 *Sedgmoor Pl.*	68	B7
Stanthorpe Clo. SW16	85	E5
Stanthorpe Rd. SW16	85	E5
Stanton Ave., Tedd.	82	B5
Stanton Clo., Epsom	99	B5
Stanton Clo., Wor.Pk.	100	A1
Stanton Rd. SE26 *Stanton Way*	86	J4
Stanton Rd. SW13	74	F2

Stanton Rd. SW20	93	A1
Stanton Rd., Croy.	94	J7
Stanton Sq. SE26 *Stanton Way*	86	J4
Stanton St. SE15	77	D1
Stanton Way SE26	86	J4
Stanway Clo., Chig.	35	H5
Stanway Gdns. W3	65	A1
Stanway Gdns., Edg.	30	C6
Stanway St. N1	**9**	**E1**
Stanway St. N1	59	B2
Stanwick Rd. W14	66	C4
Stanworth St. SE1	**17**	**F4**
Stanworth St. SE1	68	C2
Stanwyck Dr., Chig.	35	F5
Stapenhill Rd., Wem.	46	E3
Staple Inn Bldgs. WC1	**12**	**E2**
Staple St. SE1	**17**	**C4**
Staple St. SE1	68	A2
Staplefield Clo. SW2	85	E1
Staplefield Clo., Pnr.	28	E7
Stapleford Ave., Ilf.	43	H5
Stapleford Clo. E4	34	C3
Stapleford Clo. SW19 *Beaumont Rd.*	75	B7
Stapleford Clo., Kings.T.	92	A3
Stapleford Rd., Wem.	46	G7
Stapleford Way, Bark.	62	B3
Staplehurst Rd. SE13	78	E5
Staplehurst Rd., Cars.	100	H7
Staples Clo. SE16	68	H1
Staples Cor. NW2	47	H1
Staples Cor. Business Pk. NW2	47	G1
Staples Rd., Loug.	27	A3
Stapleton Gdns., Croy.	101	G5
Stapleton Hall Rd. N4	49	F1
Stapleton Rd. SW17	85	A3
Stapleton Rd., Bexh.	71	F7
Stapleton Rd., Orp.	104	J3
Stapley Rd., Belv.	71	G5
Stapylton Rd., Barn.	23	B3
Star & Garter Hill, Rich.	82	H1
Star La. E16	60	E4
Star Rd. W14	66	C6
Star Rd., Islw.	73	A2
Star St. E16	60	F5
Star St. W2	**10**	**F3**
Star St. W2	57	H6
Star Yd. WC2	**12**	**E3**
Starboard Way E14	69	A3
Starch Ho. La., Ilf.	43	G2
Starcross St. NW1	**7**	**G4**
Starcross St. NW1	58	C3
Starfield Rd. W12	65	G2
Starkleigh Way SE16 *Egan Way*	68	E5
Starling Clo., Buck.H.	34	G1
Starling Clo., Pnr.	36	C3
Starling Ms. SE28 *Whinchat Rd.*	70	C2
Starling Wk., Hmptn. *Oak Ave.*	81	E6
Starts Clo., Orp.	104	D3
Starts Hill Ave., Orp.	104	E4
Starts Hill Rd., Orp.	104	D3
State Fm. Ave., Orp.	104	E4
Staten Gdns., Twick.	82	C1
Statham Gro. N16 *Green Las.*	49	J4
Statham Gro. N18 *Tanners End La.*	33	B5
Station App. E7	51	H4
Station App. *Woodford Rd.*		
Station App. (Snaresbrook) E11 *High St.*	42	G5
Station App. N11	32	B5
Station App. (Woodside Pk.) N12 *Holden Rd.*	31	E4
Station App. N16 (Stoke Newington) *Stamford Hill*	50	C2

Station App. NW10	56	F3
Station Rd.		
Station Rd. SE3	78	H3
Kidbrooke Pk. Rd.		
Station App.	88	C1
(Mottingham) SE9		
Station App. SE26	86	F4
Sydenham Rd.		
Station App. SW6	75	B3
Station App. SW16	85	D5
Station App. W7	64	B1
Station App., Bex.	80	G7
Bexley High St.		
Station App., Bexh.	80	E2
Avenue Rd.		
Station App., Bexh.	80	J2
(Barnehurst)		
Station App., Brom.	103	G1
Station App.,	35	A4
Buck.H.		
Cherry Tree Ri.		
Station App., Chis.	97	D1
Station App., Chis.	88	B6
(Elmstead Wds.)		
Station App., Epsom	99	F5
(Stoneleigh)		
Station App., Esher	98	C3
(Hinchley Wd.)		
Station App., Grnf.	46	A7
Station App.,	90	G1
Hmptn.		
Milton Rd.		
Station App., Har.	27	B7
Station App., Ilf.	43	G3
Station App.,	92	A2
Kings.T.		
Station App., Loug.	27	B5
Station App., Loug.	27	F4
(Debden)		
Station App., Orp.	104	J2
Station App., Pnr.	36	E4
Station App., Pnr.	28	G7
(Hatch End)		
Uxbridge Rd.		
Station App., Rich.	74	A1
Station App., Ruis.	45	B5
Station App., Sid.	89	A2
Station App., Sun.	90	A1
Station App., Sutt.	100	B7
(Cheam)		
Station App., Wat.	28	D3
Prestwick Rd.		
Station App., Well.	80	A2
Station App., Wem.	46	E6
Station App. Rd. W4	65	C7
Station Ave. SW9	76	H3
Coldharbour La.		
Station Ave.,	92	E3
N.Mal.		
Station Ave., Rich.	74	A1
Station Clo. N3	39	D1
Station Rd.		
Station Clo.,	90	H1
Hmptn.		
Station Cres. N15	41	A4
Station Cres. SE3	69	G5
Station Cres., Wem.	46	E6
Station Est., Beck.	95	G4
Elmers End Rd.		
Station Est. Rd.,	81	B1
Felt.		
Station Gdns. W4	65	C7
Station Gro., Wem.	46	H6
Station Hill, Brom.	103	G2
Station Ho., Wem.	47	B7
Station Par. E11	42	G5
Station Par. N14	32	D1
High St.		
Station Par. NW2	47	J6
Station Par. W3	56	A6
Station Par., Bark.	52	F7
Station Pas. E18	42	H2
Maybank Rd.		
Station Path E8	50	E6
Amhurst Rd.		
Station Pl. N4	49	G2
Seven Sisters Rd.		
Station Ri. SE27	85	H2
Norwood Rd.		
Station Rd.	34	C1
(Chingford) E4		
Station Rd. E7	51	G4
Station Rd. E10	51	C3
Station Rd. E12	52	A4
Station Rd. E17	41	H6
Station Rd. N3	39	D1
Station Rd. N11	32	B5
Station Rd. N17	41	D3
Hale Rd.		
Station Rd. N19	49	C3
Station Rd. N21	32	H1
Station Rd. N21	32	H1
(Winchmore Hill)		
Station Rd. N22	40	E2
Station Rd. NW4	38	G6
Station Rd. NW7	30	E5
Station Rd. NW10	56	F2
Station Rd. SE20	86	F6
Station Rd. SE25	95	C4
(Norwood Junct.)		
Station Rd. SW13	74	F2
Station Rd. SW19	93	F1
Station Rd. W5	55	J6
Station Rd.	64	B1
(Hanwell) W7		
Station Rd., Barn.	23	E5
Station Rd., Belv.	71	G3
Station Rd., Bexh.	80	E3
Station Rd., Borwd.	22	A4
Station Rd., Brom.	96	G1
Station Rd., Brom.	96	E2
(Shortlands)		
Station Rd., Cars.	100	J4
Station Rd., Chess.	98	H5
Station Rd., Chig.	35	E3
Station Rd., Croy.	102	A2
(East Croydon)		
Station Rd., Croy.	101	J1
(West Croydon)		
Station Rd., Edg.	30	A6
Station Rd., Enf.	24	J3
Station Rd., Esher	98	A2
Station Rd.	98	A5
(Claygate), Esher		
Station Rd., Hmptn.	90	G1
Station Rd., Har.	37	C4
Station Rd. (North	36	H5
Harrow), Har.		
Station Rd., Houns.	72	H4
Station Rd., Ilf.	52	E3
Station Rd.	43	G3
(Barkingside), Ilf.		
Station Rd.,	92	A1
Kings.T.		
Station Rd., Kings.T.	91	G1
(Hampton Wick)		
Station Rd., Loug.	27	B4
Station Rd., N.Mal.	92	H5
(Motspur Pk.)		
Station Rd., Orp.	104	J2
Station Rd., Rom.	53	D1
(Chadwell Heath)		
Station Rd., Sid.	89	A4
Station Rd., Sun.	81	A7
Station Rd., Tedd.	82	C5
Station Rd.,	91	C7
T.Ditt.		
Station Rd., Twick.	82	C1
Station Rd.,	103	C2
W.Wick.		
Station Rd. N.,	71	H3
Belv.		
Station Sq.	97	F5
(Petts Wd.), Orp.		
Station St. E15	51	D7
Station St. E16	70	E1
Station Ter. NW10	57	A2
Station Ter. SE5	76	J1
Station Vw., Grnf.	55	A1
Station Way, Buck.H.	34	J4
(Roding Valley)		
Station Way	98	B6
(Claygate), Esher		
Station Way	100	B6
(Cheam), Sutt.		
Station Yd., Twick.	73	D7
Staunton Rd.,	82	H6
Kings.T.		
Staunton St. SE8	68	B1
Stave Yd. Rd. SE16	68	H1
Staveley Clo. E9	50	F5
Churchill Wk.		
Staveley Clo. N7	49	E4
Penn Rd.		
Staveley Clo. SE15	77	E1
Asylum Rd.		
Staveley Gdns. W4	74	D1
Staveley Rd. W4	65	C6
Staverton Rd. NW2	47	J7
Stavordale Rd. N5	49	H4
Stavordale Rd.	100	F1
Cars.		
Stayners Rd. E1	59	G4
Stayton Rd., Sutt.	100	D3
Stead St. SE17	**21**	**B2**
Stead St. SE17	68	A4
Steadfast Rd.,	91	G1
Kings.T.		
Stean St. E8	59	C1
Stebbing Way, Bark.	62	A2
Stebondale St. E14	69	C5
Stedham Pl. WC1	**12**	**A3**
Steedman St. SE17	**20**	**J2**
Steeds Rd. N10	39	J1
Steeds Way, Loug.	27	B3
Steele Rd. E11	51	E4
Steele Rd. N17	41	B3
Steele Rd. NW10	56	C2
Steele Rd. W4	65	C3
Steele Rd., Islw.	73	D4
Steeles Ms. N. NW3	48	J6
Steeles Rd.		
Steeles Ms. S. NW3	48	J6
Steeles Rd.		
Steeles Rd. NW3	48	J6
Steen Way SE22	77	B5
East Dulwich Gro.		
Steep Clo., Orp.	104	J6
Steep Hill SW16	85	D3
Steep Hill, Croy.	102	B4
Steeple Clo. SW6	75	B2
Steeple Clo. SW19	84	B5
Steeple Ct. E1	59	E4
Coventry Rd.		
Steeple Wk. N1	58	J1
Basire St.		
Steeplestone Clo.	32	J5
N18		
Steerforth St. SW18	84	F2
Steers Way SE16	68	H2
Stella Rd. SW17	84	J6
Stellar Ho. N17	33	D6
Stellman Clo. E5	50	D3
Stembridge Rd. SE20	95	E2
Stephan Clo. E8	59	D1
Stephen Clo., Orp.	104	H2
Stephen Ms. W1	**11**	**H2**
Stephen Rd., Bexh.	80	J3
Stephen St. W1	**11**	**H2**
Stephen's Rd. E15	60	D5
Stephendale Rd.	75	E3
SW6		
Stephen's Rd. E15	60	E1
Stephenson Rd. W7	55	C6
Stephenson Rd.,	72	G7
Twick.		
Stephenson St. E16	60	E4
Stephenson St.	56	E3
NW10		
Stephenson Way	**7**	**G5**
NW1		
Stephenson Way	58	C4
NW1		
Stepney Causeway	59	G6
E1		
Stepney Grn. E1	59	F5
Stepney High St. E1	59	G5
Stepney Way E1	59	F5
Sterling Ave., Edg.	29	J4
Sterling Ind. Est.,	53	H4
Dag.		
Sterling Pl. W5	64	H4
Sterling Rd., Enf.	25	A1
Sterling St. SW7	**14**	**H4**
Sterling Way N18	33	A4
Sterndale Rd. W14	66	A3
Sterne St. W12	66	A2
Sternhall La. SE15	77	D3
Sternhold Ave. SW2	85	D2
Sterry Cres., Dag.	53	G6
Alibon Rd.		
Sterry Dr., Epsom	99	E4
Sterry Dr., T.Ditt.	91	B6
Sterry Gdns., Dag.	53	G6
Sterry Rd., Bark.	61	J1
Sterry Rd., Dag.	53	G4
Sterry St. SE1	**17**	**B4**
Sterry St. SE1	68	A2
Steucers La. SE23	86	H1
Steve Biko La. SE6	87	A4
Steve Biko Way,	72	G3
Houns.		
Stevedale Rd.,	80	C2
Well.		
Stevenage Rd. E6	52	D6
Stevenage Rd. SW6	66	F6
Stevens Ave. E9	50	F6
Stevens Clo., Beck.	86	A5
Stevens Clo.,	81	E6
Hmptn.		
Stevens Clo., Pnr.	36	C5
Bridle Rd.		
Stevens Grn.	28	J1
(Bushey), Wat.		
Stevens La., Esher	98	D7
Stevens Rd., Dag.	53	B3
Stevens St. SE1	**17**	**E5**
Stevens Way, Chig.	35	H4
Stevenson Cres.	**21**	**J3**
SE16		
Stevenson Cres.	68	D5
SE16		
Steventon Rd. W12	56	F7
Steward St. E1	**13**	**E1**
Steward St. E1	59	B5
Stewart Clo. NW9	38	C6
Stewart Clo., Chis.	88	E5
Stewart Clo.,	81	E6
Hmptn.		
Stewart Rainbird	52	D5
Ho. E12		
Stewart Rd. E15	51	C4
Stewart St. E14	69	C2
Stewart's Gro. SW3	**18**	**G3**
Stewart's Gro. SW3	66	H5
Stewart's Rd. SW8	67	C7
Stewartsby Clo. N18	32	J5
Steyne Rd. W3	65	B1
Steyning Gro. SE9	88	C4
Steyning Way,	72	C4
Houns.		
Steynings Way N12	31	D5
Steynton Ave., Bex.	89	D2
Stickland Rd.,	71	G4
Belv.		
Picardy Rd.		
Stickleton Clo.,	54	H3
Grnf.		
Stile Hall Gdns. W4	65	A5
Stile Path, Sun.	90	A3
Stilecroft Gdns.,	46	E3
Wem.		
Stiles Clo., Brom.	97	C6
Stillingfleet Rd.	65	G6
SW13		
Stillington St. SW1	**19**	**G1**
Stillington St. SW1	67	C4
Stillness Rd. SE23	77	H6
Stilton Cres. NW10	17	Q7
Celtic St., NW10	17	Q?
Stipularis Dr.,	54	D4
Hayes		
Stirling Clo. SW16	94	C1
Stirling Rd. E13	60	H2
Stirling Rd. E17	41	H3
Stirling Rd. N17	41	D1
Stirling Rd. N22	40	H1
Stirling Rd. SW9	76	E2
Stirling Rd. W3	65	B3
Stirling Rd., Har.	37	C3
Stirling Rd., Hayes	54	B7
Stirling Rd.,	72	G7
Twick.		
Stirling Rd. Path	41	H3
E17		
Stirling Wk.,	92	C5
N.Mal.		
Green La.		
Stirling Wk., Surb.	92	B6
Stirling Way,	22	D6
Borwd.		
Stirling Way, Croy.	94	E7
Stiven Cres., Har.	45	F3
Stock Orchard Cres.	49	F5
N7		
Stock Orchard St.	49	F5
N7		
Stock St. E13	60	G2
Stockbury Rd.,	95	F6
Croy.		
Stockdale Rd., Dag.	53	F2
Stockdove Way,	55	C3
Grnf.		
Stockfield Rd. SW16	85	F3
Stockfield Rd.,	98	B5
Esher		
Stockholm Rd. SE16	68	F5
Stockhurst Clo.	74	J2
SW15		
Stockingswater La.,	25	H3
Enf.		
Stockport Rd. SW16	94	D1
Stocks Pl. E14	59	J7
Grenade St.		
Stocksfield Rd. E17	42	C3
Stockton Gdns. N17	32	J7
Stockton Rd.		
Stockton Gdns. NW7	30	G8
Stockton Rd. N17	32	J7
Stockton Rd. N18	33	D6
Stockwell Ave. SW9	76	F3
Stockwell Clo.,	96	H2
Brom.		
Stockwell Gdns. SW9	76	F1
Stockwell Gdns.	76	E2
Est. SW9		
Stockwell Grn. SW9	76	F2
Stockwell La. SW9	76	F2
Stockwell Ms. SW9	76	F2
Stockwell Rd.		
Stockwell Pk. Cres.	76	F2
SW9		
Stockwell Pk. Est.	76	F2
SW9		
Stockwell Pk. Rd.	76	F1
SW9		
Stockwell Pk. Wk.	76	F3
SW9		
Stockwell Rd. SW9	76	F2
Stockwell St. SE10	69	C6

Stockwell Ter. SW9	76	F1
Stodart Rd. SE20	95	F1
Stofield Gdns. SE9	88	A3
Aldersgrove Ave.		
Stoford Clo. SW19	75	B7
Stoke Newington Ch.	50	A3
St. N16		
Stoke Newington	50	C3
Common N16		
Stoke Newington	50	C3
High St. N16		
Stoke Newington Rd.	50	C5
N16		
Stoke Pl. NW10	56	F3
Stoke Rd., Kings.T.	83	C7
Stokenchurch St.	75	E1
SW6		
Stokes Rd. E6	61	B4
Stokes Rd., Croy.	95	G6
Stokesby Rd.,	98	J6
Chess.		
Stokesley St. W12	56	F6
Stoll Clo. NW2	47	J3
Stoms Path SE6	87	A5
Sedgehill Rd.		
Stonard Rd. N13	32	G3
Stonard Rd., Dag.	53	B5
Stonards Hill,	27	C6
Loug.		
Stondon Pk. SE23	77	H6
Stondon Wk. E6	61	A2
Abbots Rd.		
Stone Bldgs. WC2	**12**	**D2**
Stone Bldgs. WC2	58	F6
Stone Clo. SW4	76	C2
Larkhall Ri.		
Stone Clo., Dag.	53	F2
Stone Hall Rd. N21	24	F7
Stone Ho. Ct. EC3	**13**	**E3**
Stone Pk. Ave.,	96	A4
Beck.		
Stone Pl., Wor.Pk.	99	G2
Stone Rd., Brom.	96	F5
Stone St., Croy.	101	G5
Stone Yd. La. E14	60	B7
Poplar High St.		
Stonebanks, Walt.	90	A7
Stonebridge	50	C7
Common E8		
Mayfield Rd.		
Stonebridge Pk.	47	D7
NW10		
Stonebridge Rd. N15	41	C5
Stonebridge Way,	47	B6
Wem.		
Stonechat Sq. E6	61	B5
Peridot St.		
Stonecot Clo.,	100	B1
Sutt.		
Stonecot Hill,	100	B1
Sutt.		
Stonecroft Rd.,	71	J7
Erith		
Stonecroft Way,	94	E7
Croy.		
Stonecutter St. EC4	**12**	**G3**
Stonecutter St. EC4	58	H6
Stonefield Clo.,	80	G3
Bexh.		
Stonefield Clo.,	45	E5
Ruis.		
Stonefield St. N1	58	G1
Stonefield Way SE7	70	A7
Greenbay Rd.		
Stonefield Way,	45	E4
Ruis.		
Stonegrove, Edg.	29	H4
Stonegrove Est.,	29	H4
Edg.		
Stonegrove Gdns.,	29	H5
Edg.		
Stonehall Ave.,	43	B6
Ilf.		
Stoneham Rd. N11	32	C5
Stonehill Clo. SW14	74	D5
Stonehill Grn. Rd.,	89	J7
Dart.		
Birchwood Rd.		
Stonehill Rd. SW14	74	C5
Stonehill Rd. W4	65	A5
Wellesley Rd.		
Stonehill Wds.	89	H6
Caravan Pk., Sid.		
Stonehills Ct. SE21	86	B3
Stonehorse Rd. E17	25	F5
Enf.		
Stonehouse St. SW4	76	D4
Stoneleigh Ave.	99	G3
Wor.Pk.		
Stoneleigh Cres.,	99	F5
Epsom		
Stoneleigh Pk. Ave.,	95	G6
Croy.		

Stoneleigh Pk. Rd.,	99	F6
Epsom		
Stoneleigh Pl. W11	57	A7
Stoneleigh Rd. N17	41	C3
Stoneleigh Rd.,	93	H7
Cars.		
Stoneleigh Rd., Ilf.	43	B3
Stoneleigh St. W11	57	A7
Stoneleigh Ter. N19	49	B2
Dartmouth Pk. Hill		
Stonells Rd. SW11	75	J5
Chatham Rd.		
Stonenest St. N4	49	F1
Stones End St. SE1	**16**	**J4**
Stones End St. SE1	67	J2
Stoney All. SE18	79	D2
Stoney La. E1	**13**	**F3**
Stoney La. SE19	86	C6
Church Rd.		
Stoney St. SE1	**17**	**B1**
Stoney St. SE1	68	A1
Stoneyard La. E14	60	B7
Poplar High St.		
Stoneycroft Clo.	78	F7
SE12		
Stoneycroft Rd.,	35	B6
Wdf.Grn.		
Stoneydeep, Tedd.	82	D4
Twickenham Rd.		
Stoneydown E17	41	H4
Stoneydown Ave.	41	H4
E17		
Stoneyfields Gdns.,	30	C4
Edg.		
Stoneyfields La.,	30	C5
Edg.		
Stonhouse St. SW4	76	D3
Stonor Rd. W14	66	C4
Stony Path, Loug.	27	C1
Stopford Rd. E13	60	G1
Stopford Rd. SE17	**20**	**H4**
Stopford Rd. SE17	67	H5
Store Rd. E16	70	D2
Store St. E15	51	D5
Store St. WC1	**11**	**H2**
Store St. WC1	58	D5
Storers Quay E14	69	D4
Storey Rd. E17	41	J4
Storey Rd. N6	39	J6
Storey St. E16	70	D1
Storey's Gate SW1	**15**	**J4**
Storey's Gate SW1	67	D2
Stories Ms. SE5	77	B2
Stories Rd. SE5	77	B3
Stork Rd. E7	51	F6
Storks Rd. SE16	**17**	**J6**
Storks Rd. SE16	68	D3
Storksmead Rd.,	30	E7
Edg.		
Stormont Rd. N6	39	J7
Stormont Rd. SW11	76	A3
Stormont Way,	98	F5
Chess.		
Storrington Rd.,	102	C1
Croy.		
Story St. N1	49	F7
Carnoustie Dr.		
Stothard Pl. EC2	**13**	**E1**
Stothard St. E1	59	F4
Colebert Ave.		
Stoughton Ave.,	100	A5
Sutt.		
Stoughton Clo. SE11	**20**	**D2**
Stoughton Clo.	83	G1
SW15		
Bessborough Rd.		
Stour Ave., Sthl.	63	G3
Stour Clo., Kes.	103	J4
Stour Rd. E3	51	A7
Stour Rd., Dag.	53	G2
Stourcliffe St. W1	**10**	**J4**
Stourcliffe St. W1	57	J6
Stourhead Clo.	75	A7
SW19		
Castlecombe Dr.		
Stourhead Gdns.	92	G3
SW20		
Stourton Ave.,	81	F4
Felt.		
Stow Cres. E17	33	H7
Stowage SE8	69	A6
Stowe Gdns. N9	33	C1
Latymer Rd.		
Stowe Pl. N15	41	B3
Stowe Rd. W12	65	H2
Stowting Rd., Orp.	104	H4
Stox Mead, Har.	34	A1
Stracey Rd. E7	51	G4
Stracey Rd. NW10	56	D1
Strachan Pl. SW19	83	J6
Woodhayes Rd.		
Stradbroke Dr.,	35	D6
Chig.		

Stradbroke Gro.,	35	A1
Buck.H.		
Stradbroke Gro.,	43	B3
Ilf.		
Stradbroke Pk.,	35	E6
Chig.		
Stradbroke Rd. N5	49	J4
Stradella Rd. SE24	76	J6
Strafford Ave.,	43	D2
Ilf.		
Strafford Rd. W3	65	C2
Strafford Rd.,	23	B3
Barn.		
Strafford Rd.,	72	F3
Houns.		
Strafford Rd.,	73	D7
Twick.		
Strafford St. E14	69	A2
Strahan Rd. E3	59	H3
Straight, The,	63	D2
Sthl.		
Straightsmouth SE10	69	C7
Strait Rd. E6	61	B7
Straker's Rd. SE15	77	E4
Strand WC2	**12**	**A6**
Strand WC2	58	E7
Strand La. WC2	**12**	**D5**
Strand on the Grn.	65	A6
W4		
Strand Pl. N18	33	B4
Strand Sch. App. W4	65	A6
Strandfield Clo.	70	H5
SE18		
Strangways Ter. W14	66	C3
Melbury Rd.		
Stranraer Way N1	49	E7
Strasburg Rd. SW11	76	B1
Stratfield Pk. Clo.	24	H7
N21		
Stratford Ave. W8	66	D3
Stratford Rd.		
Stratford Cen., The	51	D7
E15		
Broadway		
Stratford Clo.,	53	A7
Bark.		
Stratford Clo.,	53	J7
Dag.		
Stratford Ct., N.Mal.	92	D4
Kingston Rd.		
Stratford Gro. SW15	75	A4
Stratford Pl. W1	**11**	**D4**
Stratford Pl. W1	58	B6
Stratford Rd. E13	60	F1
Stratford Rd. W3	65	C2
Bollo Bri. Rd.		
Stratford Rd. W8	66	D3
Stratford Rd.,	54	B4
Hayes		
Stratford Rd.,	63	E4
Sthl.		
Stratford Rd.,	94	G4
Th.Hth.		
Stratford Vill. NW1	49	C7
Strath Ter. SW11	75	H4
Stratham Clo. SW18	75	B6
Strathaven Rd. SE12	78	H6
Strathblaine Rd.	75	G5
SW11		
Strathbrook Rd.	85	F7
SW16		
Strathcona Rd.,	46	G2
Wem.		
Strathdale SW16	85	F5
Strathdon Dr. SW17	84	G3
Strathearn Ave.,	81	H1
Twick.		
Strathearn Pl. W2	**10**	**G5**
Strathearn Pl. W2	57	H7
Strathearn Rd. SW19	84	D5
Strathearn Rd.,	100	D5
Sutt.		
Stratheden Rd. SE3	78	G1
Strathfield Gdns.,	52	D6
Bark.		
Strathleven Rd. SW2	76	E4
Strathmore Gdns. N3	39	E1
Strathmore Gdns.	66	D1
W8		
Palace Gdns. Ter.		
Strathmore Gdns.,	38	B2
Edg.		
Strathmore Rd.	84	D3
SW19		
Strathmore Rd.,	94	J7
Croy.		
Strathmore Rd.,	82	B4
Tedd.		
Strathnairn St. SE1	**21**	**J2**
Strathnairn St. SE1	68	D4
Strathray Gdns. NW3	48	H6
Strathville Rd.	84	D2
SW18		

Strathyre Ave. SW16	94	G3
Stratton Clo. SW19	93	D2
Stratton Clo.,	80	E3
Bexh.		
Stratton Clo., Edg.	29	J6
Stratton Clo.,	72	F1
Houns.		
Stratton Dr., Bark.	52	J5
Stratton Gdns.,	54	F6
Sthl.		
Stratton Rd. SW19	93	D2
Stratton Rd., Bexh.	80	E3
Stratton St. W1	**15**	**E1**
Stratton St. W1	67	B1
Strattondale St.	69	C3
E14		
Strauss Rd. W4	65	D2
Strawberry Hill,	82	C3
Twick.		
Strawberry Hill	82	C4
Clo., Twick.		
Strawberry Hill	82	C3
Rd., Twick.		
Strawberry La.,	100	J3
Cars.		
Strawberry Vale N2	39	G1
Strawberry Vale,	82	C3
Twick.		
Streakes Fld. Rd.	47	G2
NW2		
Stream La., Edg.	30	B5
Streamway, Belv.	71	F6
Streamdale SE2	71	A6
Streamside Clo. N9	33	C1
Streamside Clo.,	96	G4
Brom.		
Streatfield Ave. E6	61	C1
Streatfield Rd.,	37	F3
Har.		
Streatham Clo. SW16	85	E2
Streatham Common	85	E5
N. SW16		
Streatham Common	85	E6
S. SW16		
Streatham Ct. SW16	85	E3
Streatham High Rd.	85	E5
SW16		
Streatham Hill SW2	85	E2
Streatham Pl. SW2	76	E7
Streatham Rd.,	94	A1
Mitch.		
Streatham St. WC1	**12**	**A3**
Streatham Vale	94	C1
SW16		
Streathbourne Rd.	85	A2
SW17		
Streatley Pl. NW3	48	F4
New End Sq.		
Streatley Rd. NW6	48	C7
Streeters La.,	101	D3
Wall.		
Streetfield Ms. SE3	78	G3
Streimer Rd. E15	60	C2
Strelley Way W3	56	E7
Stretton Rd., Croy.	95	B7
Stretton Rd., Rich.	82	F2
Strickland Rd.,	71	G4
Belv.		
Strickland Row SW18	75	D4
Strickland St. SE8	78	A1
Strickland Way,	104	J4
Orp.		
Stride Rd. E13	60	F2
Strode Clo. N10	32	A7
Pembroke Rd.		
Strode Rd. E7	51	G4
Strode Rd. N17	41	B2
Strode Rd. NW10	47	G6
Strode Rd. SW6	66	B7
Strone Rd. E7	52	H6
Strone Rd. E12	52	A6
Strone Way, Hayes	54	E4
Strongbow Cres. SE9	79	C5
Strongbow Rd. SE9	79	C5
Strongbridge Clo.,	45	G1
Har.		
Stronsa Rd. W12	65	F2
Stroud Cres. SW15	83	G3
Stroud Fld., Nthlt.	45	E6
Stroud Gate, Har.	45	H4
Stroud Grn. Gdns.,	95	F7
Croy.		
Stroud Grn. Rd. N4	49	F1
Stroud Grn. Way,	95	E7
Croy.		
Stroud Rd. SE25	95	D6
Stroud Rd. SW19	84	D3
Stroudes Clo.,	92	E7
Wor.Pk.		
Stroudley Wk. E3	60	B3
Strouts Pl. E2	**9**	**F3**
Strutton Grd. SW1	**15**	**H5**
Strutton Grd. SW1	67	D3

Name	Page	Grid
Strype St. E1	13	F2
Stuart Ave. NW9	38	G7
Stuart Ave. W5	64	J1
Stuart Ave., Brom.	103	G1
Stuart Ave., Har.	45	F3
Stuart Cres., Croy.	102	J4
Stuart Evans Clo., Well.	80	C3
Stuart Gro., Tedd.	82	B5
Stuart Pl., Mitch.	93	J1
Stuart Rd. NW6	57	D3
Stuart Rd. SE15	77	F4
Stuart Rd. SW19	84	D3
Stuart Rd. W3	65	C1
Stuart Rd., Bark.	52	J7
Stuart Rd., Barn.	23	H7
Stuart Rd., Har.	37	C3
Stuart Rd., Rich.	82	E2
Stuart Rd., Th.Hth.	94	J4
Stuart Rd., Well.	80	B1
Stuart Twr. W9	6	C4
Stuart Twr. W9	57	F3
Stubbs Dr. SE16	68	E5
Stubbs Pt. E13	60	G4
Stubbs Way SW19	93	G1
Brangwyn Cres.		
Stucley Pl. NW1	49	B7
Hawley Cres.		
Stucley Rd., Houns.	63	J7
Studd St. N1	58	H1
Studdridge St. SW6	75	D2
Studholme St. NW3	48	D4
Studholme St. SE15	68	E7
Studio Pl. SW1	15	A4
Studio Way, Borwd.	22	C2
Studland SE17	21	B3
Studland Clo., Sid.	88	J3
Studland Rd. SE26	86	G5
Studland Rd. W7	55	A6
Studland Rd., Kings.T.	82	H6
Studland St. W6	65	H4
Studley Ave. E4	34	D7
Studley Clo. E5	50	H5
Studley Ct., Sid.	89	B5
Studley Dr., Ilf.	43	A6
Studley Est. SW4	76	E1
Studley Gra. Rd. W7	64	B2
Studley Rd. E7	51	H6
Studley Rd. SW4	76	E1
Studley Rd., Dag.	53	D7
Stukeley Rd. E7	51	H7
Stukeley St. WC2	12	B3
Stukeley St. WC2	58	E6
Stumps Hill La., Beck.	87	A6
Sturdy Rd. SE15	77	E2
Sturge Ave. E17	42	B1
Sturge St. SE1	16	J3
Sturgeon Rd. SE17	20	J4
Sturgeon Rd. SE17	67	H5
Sturges Fld., Chis.	88	G6
Sturgess Ave. NW4	38	G7
Sturmer Way N7	49	F5
Stock Orchard Cres.		
Sturrock Clo. N15	41	A4
Sturry St. E14	60	B6
Sturt St. N1	9	A2
Sturt St. N1	58	J2
Stutfield St. E1	13	J4
Stutfield St. E1	59	D6
Styles Gdns. SW9	76	H3
Styles Way, Beck.	96	C4
Sudbourne Rd. SW2	76	E5
Sudbrook Gdns., Rich.	82	H3
Sudbrook La., Rich.	82	H1
Sudbrooke Rd. SW12	75	J6
Sudbury Ave., Wem.	46	F5
Sudbury Ct. S5	50	H4
Sudbury Ct. Dr., Har.	46	C3
Sudbury Ct. Rd., Har.	46	C3
Sudbury Cres., Brom.	87	G6
Sudbury Cres., Wem.	46	E5
Sudbury Cft., Wem.	46	C4
Sudbury Gdns., Croy.	102	B4
Langton Way		
Sudbury Heights Ave., Grnf.	46	C5
Sudbury Hill, Har.	46	B2
Sudbury Hill Clo., Wem.	46	C4
Sudbury Meadows, Wem.	46	F3
Sudbury Rd., Bark.	52	J5
Sudeley St. N1	8	H2
Sudeley St. N1	58	H2
Sudlow Rd. SW18	75	D5
Sudrey St. SE1	16	J4
Suez Ave., Grnf.	55	C2
Suez Rd., Enf.	25	H4
Suffield Rd. E4	34	B3
Suffield Rd. N15	41	C5
Suffield Rd. SE20	95	F2
Suffolk Clo., Borwd.	22	D5
Clydesdale Clo.		
Suffolk Ct. E10	42	A7
Suffolk Ct., Ilf.	43	H6
Suffolk La. EC4	13	B5
Suffolk Pk. Rd. E17	41	H4
Suffolk Pl. SW1	15	J1
Suffolk Rd. E13	60	G3
Suffolk Rd. N15	41	A6
Suffolk Rd. NW10	47	E7
Suffolk Rd. SE25	95	C4
Suffolk Rd. SW13	65	F7
Suffolk Rd., Bark.	52	G7
Suffolk Rd., Dag.	53	J5
Suffolk Rd., Enf.	25	E5
Suffolk Rd., Har.	36	F6
Suffolk Rd., Ilf.	43	H6
Suffolk Rd., Sid.	89	C6
Suffolk Rd., Wor.Pk.	99	F2
Suffolk St. E7	51	G5
Suffolk St. SW1	11	J6
Sugar Bakers Ct. EC3	13	E4
Sugar Ho. La. E15	60	C2
Sugar Loaf Wk. E2	59	F3
Victoria Pk. Sq.		
Sugden Rd. SW11	76	A3
Sugden Rd., T.Ditt.	95	E1
Sugden Way, Bark.	51	J2
Sulgrave Gdns. W6	65	J2
Sulgrave Rd.		
Sulgrave Rd. W6	65	J3
Sulina Rd. SW2	76	E7
Sulivan Ct. SW6	75	D2
Sulivan Rd. SW6	75	D3
Sullivan Ave. E16	61	A5
Sullivan Clo. SW11	75	H3
Sullivan Clo., W.Mol.	90	G3
Victoria Ave.		
Sullivan Rd. SE11	20	F1
Sullivan Rd. SE11	67	G4
Sultan Rd. E11	42	H4
Sultan St. SE5	20	J7
Sultan St. SE5	67	J7
Sultan St., Beck.	95	G2
Sumatra Rd. NW6	48	D5
Sumburgh Rd. SW12	76	A6
Summer Ave., E.Mol.	91	B5
Summer Gdns., E.Mol.	91	B5
Summer Hill, Borwd.	22	A5
Summer Hill, Chis.	97	D2
Summer Hill Vill., Chis.	97	D1
Summer Ho. Rd. N16	50	B2
Stoke Newington Ch. St.		
Summer Rd., E.Mol.	91	B5
Summer Rd., T.Ditt.	91	C5
Summer Trees, Sun.	90	B1
The Ave.		
Summercourt Rd. E1	59	F6
Summerdene Clo. SW16	85	C7
Bates Cres.		
Summerfield Ave. NW6	57	B2
Summerfield La., Surb.		
Summerfield Rd. W5	55	E4
Summerfield Rd., Loug.	27	A6
Summerfield St. SE12	78	F7
Summerhill Clo., Orp.	104	H3
Summerhill Gro., Enf.	25	B6
Summerhill Rd. N15	41	A4
Summerhill Way, Mitch.	94	A1
Summerhouse Ave., Houns.	72	E1
Summerland Gdns. N10	40	B3
Summerlands Ave. W3	56	C7
Summerlee Ave. N2	39	J4
Summerlee Gdns. N2	39	J4
Summerley St. SW18	84	E2
Summers Clo., Sutt.	100	D7
Overton Rd.		
Summers Clo., Wem.	47	B1
Summers La. N12	31	G7
Summers Row N12	31	H6
Summers St. EC1	8	E6
Summersby Rd. N6	40	B6
Summerstown SW17	84	F3
Summerton Way SE28	62	D7
Summerville Gdns., Sutt.	100	C6
Summerwood Rd., Islw.	73	C5
Summit, The, Loug.	27	C1
Summit Ave. NW9	38	D5
Summit Clo. N14	32	C2
Summit Clo. NW9	38	D4
Summit Clo., Edg.	30	A7
Summit Ct. NW2	48	B5
Summit Dr., Wdf.Grn.	43	A2
Summit Est. N16	41	D7
Summit Rd. E17	42	B4
Summit Rd., Nthlt.	45	G7
Summit Way N14	32	B2
Summit Way SE19	86	B7
Sumner Ave. SE15	77	C1
Sumner Rd.		
Sumner Clo., Orp.	104	F4
Sumner Est. SE15	68	C7
Sumner Gdns., Croy.	101	G1
Sumner Pl. SW7	18	F2
Sumner Pl. Ms. SW7	18	F2
Sumner Rd. SE15	21	G6
Sumner Rd., Croy.	101	G1
Sumner Rd., Har.	36	J7
Sumner Rd. S., Croy.	101	G1
Sumner St. SE1	16	H1
Sumner St. SE1	67	H1
Sumpter Clo. NW3	48	H6
Sun Ct. EC3	13	C4
Sun La. SE3	69	H7
Sun Pas. SE16	17	H5
Sun Rd. W14	66	C5
Sun St. EC2	13	C1
Sun St. EC2	59	A5
Sun St. Pas. EC2	13	D1
Sunbeam Rd. NW10	56	D4
Sunbury Ave. NW7	30	D5
Sunbury Ave. SW14	74	D4
Sunbury Ct., Sun.	90	D2
Sunbury Ct. Rd., Sun.	90	C2
Sunbury Gdns. NW7	30	D5
Sunbury La. SW11	75	G1
Sunbury La., Walt.	90	A6
Sunbury Rd., Sutt.	100	A3
Sunbury St. SE18	70	C3
Sunbury Way, Felt.	81	C5
Suncroft Pl. SE26	86	F3
Sunderland Ct. SE22	77	D7
Sunderland Rd. SE23	86	G1
Sunderland Rd. W5	64	G3
Sunderland Rd. W2	10	A3
Sunderland Ter. W2	57	E6
Sunderland Way E12	52	A2
Sundew Ave. W12	56	G7
Sundial Ave. SE25	95	C3
Sundorne Rd. SE7	69	H5
Sundra Wk. E1	59	G4
Beaumont Gro.		
Sundridge Ave., Brom.	97	A2
Sundridge Ave., Chis.	88	B7
Sundridge Ave., Well.	79	G2
Sundridge Ho., Brom.	87	H5
Burnt Ash La.		
Sundridge Rd., Croy.	95	C7
Sunfields Pl. SE3	69	H7
Sunland Ave., Bexh.	80	E4
Sunleigh Rd., Wem.	55	H1
Sunley Gdns., Grnf.	55	D1
Sunmead Rd., Sun.	90	A3
Sunna Gdns., Sun.	90	B2
Sunningdale N14	32	D5
Wilmer Way		
Sunningdale Ave. W3	56	E7
Sunningdale Ave., Bark.	61	G1
Sunningdale Ave., Felt.	81	E2
Sunningdale Ave., Ruis.	45	C1
Sunningdale Clo. E6	61	C3
Ascot Rd.		
Sunningdale Clo., Stan.	29	D7
Sunningdale Gdns. NW9	38	C5
Sunningdale Gdns. W8	66	D3
Lexham Ms.		
Sunningdale Rd., Brom.	97	B4
Sunningdale Rd., Sutt.	100	C4
Sunningfields Cres. NW4	38	H2
Sunningfields Rd. NW4	38	H3
Sunninghill Rd. SE13	78	B2
Sunny Bank SE25	95	D3
Sunny Cres. NW10	47	C7
Sunny Gdns. Rd. NW4	38	H2
Sunny Hill NW4	38	H3
Sunny Nook Gdns., S.Croy.	102	A6
Selsdon Rd.		
Sunny Rd., The, Enf.	25	G1
Sunny Side, Walt.	90	C5
Sunny Vw. NW9	38	D5
Sunny Way N12	31	H7
Sunnycroft Rd. SE25	95	D3
Sunnycroft Rd., Houns.	72	H2
Sunnycroft Rd., Sthl.	54	G5
Sunnydale, Orp.	104	D2
Sunnydale Gdns. NW7	30	D6
Sunnydale Rd. SE12	78	H5
Sunnydene Ave. E4	34	D5
Sunnydene Ave., Ruis.	45	A1
Sunnydene Gdns., Wem.	46	F6
Sunnydene St. SE26	86	H4
Sunnyfield NW7	30	F4
Sunnyhill Rd. SW16	85	E4
Sunnyhurst Clo., Sutt.	100	D3
Sunnymead Ave., Mitch.	94	C3
Sunnymead Rd. NW9	38	D7
Sunnymead Rd. SW15	74	H5
Sunnymede Dr., Ilf.	43	E5
Sunnyside NW2	48	C3
Sunnyside SW19	84	B6
Sunnyside Dr. E4	26	C7
Sunnyside Pas. SW19	84	B6
Sunnyside Rd. E10	51	A1
Sunnyside Rd. N19	40	D7
Sunnyside Rd. W5	64	G1
Sunnyside Rd., Ilf.	52	F3
Sunnyside Rd., Tedd.	81	J4
Sunnyside Rd. E. N9	33	D3
Sunnyside Rd. N. N9	33	C3
Sunnyside Rd. S. N9	33	C3
Sunray Ave. SE24	77	A4
Sunray Ave., Brom.	97	B6
Sunray Ave., Surb.	99	B2
Sunrise Clo., Felt.	81	F3
Exeter Rd.		
Sunset Ave. E4	34	B1
Sunset Ave., Wdf.Grn.	34	F4
Sunset Gdns. SE25	95	C2
Sunset Rd. SE5	76	J4
Sunset Vw., Barn.	23	B2
Sunshine Way, Mitch.	93	J2
Sunwell Clo. SE15	77	E2
Gordon Rd.		
Surbiton Ct., Surb.	91	F6
Surbiton Cres., Kings.T.	91	H5
Surbiton Hall Clo., Kings.T.	91	H4
Surbiton Hill Pk., Surb.	91	J5
Surbiton Hill Rd., Surb.	91	H4
Surbiton Rd., Kings.T.	91	G4
Surlingham Clo. SE28	62	D7
Surr St. N7	49	E5
Surrendale Pl. W9	57	D4
Surrey Canal Rd. SE14	68	G6
Surrey Canal Rd. SE15	68	F6
Surrey Cres. W4	65	A5
Surrey Gro. SE17	21	D4
Surrey Gro., Sutt.	100	G3

Surrey La. SW11 75 H1
Surrey La. Est. 75 H1
SW11
Surrey Lo. SE1 16 E6
Surrey Ms. SE27 86 B4
Hamilton Rd.
Surrey Mt. SE23 86 E1
Surrey Quays Rd. 68 F3
SE16
Surrey Rd. SE15 77 G5
Surrey Rd., Bark. 52 H7
Surrey Rd., Dag. 53 H5
Surrey Rd., Har. 36 J5
Surrey Rd., W.Wick. 103 B1
Surrey Row SE1 16 G3
Surrey Row SE1 67 H2
Surrey Sq. SE17 21 D3
Surrey Sq. SE17 68 B5
Surrey St. E13 60 H3
Surrey St. WC2 12 D5
Surrey St. WC2 58 F7
Surrey St., Croy. 101 J2
Surrey Ter. SE17 21 E3
Surrey Ter. SE17 68 B4
Surrey Water Rd. 68 G1
SE16
Surridge Gdns. SE19 86 A6
Hancock Rd.
Susan Clo., Rom. 44 J3
Susan Rd. SE3 78 H2
Susan Wd., Chis. 97 D1
Susannah St. E14 60 B6
Sussex Ave., Islw. 73 B3
Sussex Clo. N19 49 E2
Cornwallis Rd.
Sussex Clo., Ilf. 43 C6
Sussex Clo., N.Mal. 92 E4
Sussex Clo., Twick. 73 E6
Westmorland Clo.
Sussex Cres., 45 G6
Nthlt.
Sussex Gdns. N4 40 J5
Sussex Gdns. N6 39 J5
Great N. Rd.
Sussex Gdns. W2 10 E5
Sussex Gdns. W2 57 G6
Sussex Gdns., 98 G6
Chess.
Sussex Ms. E. W2 10 F4
Sussex Ms. W. W2 10 F5
Sussex Pl. NW1 6 J4
Sussex Pl. NW1 57 J4
Sussex Pl. W2 10 F4
Sussex Pl. W2 57 G6
Sussex Pl., W6 65 J5
Sussex Pl., Erith 71 H7
Sussex Pl., N.Mal. 92 E4
Sussex Ring N12 31 D5
Sussex Rd. E6 61 D1
Sussex Rd., Cars. 100 J6
Sussex Rd., Erith 71 H7
Sussex Rd., Har. 36 J5
Sussex Rd., Mitch. 94 E5
Lincoln Rd.
Sussex Rd., N.Mal. 92 E4
Sussex Rd., Sid. 89 B5
Sussex Rd., S.Croy. 102 A6
Sussex Rd., Sthl. 63 D3
Sussex Rd., W.Wick. 103 B1
Sussex Sq. W2 10 F5
Sussex Sq. W2 57 G7
Sussex St. E13 60 H3
Sussex St. SW1 19 E4
Sussex St. SW1 67 B5
Sussex Wk. SW9 76 H4
Sussex Way N7 49 E2
Sussex Way N19 49 E1
Sussex Way, Barn. 24 B5
Sutcliffe Clo. NW11 39 E5
Sutcliffe Ho., 54 A6
Hayes
Sutcliffe Rd. SE18 70 H6
Sutcliffe Rd., 80 C2
Well.
Sutherland Ave. W9 57 D4
Sutherland Ave. W13 55 E6
Sutherland Ave., 63 A4
Hayes
Sutherland Ave., 97 J6
Orp.
Sutherland Ave., 79 H4
Well.
Sutherland Clo., 38 B4
Barn.
Sutherland Ct. NW9 38 B4
Sutherland Dr. SW19 93 G1
Brangwyn Cres.
Sutherland Gdns. 74 E3
SW14
Sutherland Gdns., 92 H7
Wor.Pk.
Sutherland Gro. 75 B6
SW18

Sutherland Gro., 82 B5
Tedd.
Sutherland Pl. W2 57 D6
Sutherland Pt. E5 50 E4
Tiger Way
Sutherland Rd. E17 41 G2
Sutherland Rd. N17 33 D7
Sutherland Rd. W4 65 E6
Sutherland Rd. W13 55 D6
Sutherland Rd., 71 G3
Belv.
Sutherland Rd., 94 G7
Croy.
Sutherland Rd., 25 G5
Enf.
Sutherland Rd., 54 F6
Sthl.
Sutherland Rd. Path 41 G3
E17
Sutherland Row 19 E3
SW1
Sutherland Row 67 B5
SW1
Sutherland Sq. SE17 20 J4
Sutherland Sq. SE17 67 J5
Sutherland St. SW1 19 D3
Sutherland St. SW1 67 B5
Sutherland Wk. SE17 21 A4
Sutherland Wk. SE17 67 J5
Sutlej Rd. SE7 69 J7
Sutterton St. N7 49 F6
Sutton Arc., Sutt. 100 E5
Throwley Way
Sutton Clo., Beck. 90 B1
Albemarle Rd.
Sutton Clo., Loug. 27 B7
Sutton Clo., Pnr. 36 A5
Sutton Common Rd., 93 C7
Sutt.
Sutton Clo. W4 65 C6
Sutton Ct. Rd. E13 60 J3
Sutton Ct. Rd. W4 65 C7
Sutton Ct. Rd., 100 F6
Sutt.
Sutton Cres., Barn. 23 A5
Sutton Dene, Houns. 72 H1
Sutton Est. N1 49 H7
Upper St.
Sutton Est. SW3 18 H3
Sutton Est. SW3 66 H5
Sutton Est. W10 56 J5
Sutton Gdns., Bark. 61 H1
Sutton Rd.
Sutton Gdns., Croy. 95 C5
Sutton Gro., Sutt. 100 G4
Sutton Hall Rd., 63 G7
Houns.
Sutton La. W4 65 C5
Sutton La., Houns. 72 F3
Sutton La. S. W4 65 C6
Sutton Pk. Rd., 100 E6
Sutt.
Sutton Path, Borwd. 22 A2
Stratfield Rd.
Sutton Pl. E9 50 F5
Sutton Rd. E13 60 F4
Sutton Rd. E17 41 G1
Sutton Rd. N10 40 A1
Sutton Rd., Bark. 61 H2
Sutton Rd., Houns. 62 F5
Sutton Row W1 11 J3
Sutton Row W1 58 D6
Sutton Sq. E9 50 F5
Urswick Rd.
Sutton Sq., Houns. 72 F1
Sutton St. E1 59 F7
Sutton Way W10 56 J5
Sutton Way, Houns. 72 F1
Sutton's Way EC1 9 A6
White Hart La.
Swaffield Rd. SW18 75 E7
Swain Rd., Th.Hth. 94 J5
Swains La. N6 49 A1
Swains Rd. SW17 84 J7
Swainson Rd. W3 65 F2
Swallands Rd. SE6 87 A3
Swallow Clo. SE14 77 G1
Swallow Clo. 28 J1
(Bushey), Wat.
Swallow Dr. NW10 47 D6
Kingfisher Way
Swallow Dr., Nthlt. 54 G2
Swallow Pas. W1 11 E4
Swallow Pl. W1 11 E4
Swallow St. E6 61 B5
Swallow St. W1 11 G6
Swallowfield Rd. 69 H5
SE7
Swan App. E6 61 B5
Swan Clo. E17 41 H1
Banbury Rd.

Swan Clo., Croy. 95 B7
Swan Clo., Felt. 81 E4
Swan Ct. SW3 18 H4
Swan Dr. NW9 38 E2
Swan La. EC4 13 B6
Swan La. N20 31 F3
Swan Mead SE1 17 D6
Swan Mead SE1 68 B3
Swan Ms. SW9 76 F1
Swan Pl. SW13 74 F2
Swan Rd. SE16 68 F2
Swan Rd. SE18 70 A3
Swan Rd., Felt. 81 E5
Swan Rd., Sthl. 54 H6
Swan St. SE1 17 A5
Swan St. SE1 67 J3
Swan St., Islw. 73 E3
Swan Wk. SW3 18 J5
Swan Wk. SW3 66 J6
Swan Way, Enf. 25 G2
Swan Yd. N1 49 H6
Highbury Sta. Rd.
Swanage Rd. E4 34 C7
Swanage Rd. SW18 75 F6
Swanage Waye, 54 C6
Hayes
Swanbridge Rd., 80 G1
Bexh.
Swandon Way SW18 75 E4
Swanfield St. E2 9 F4
Swanfield St. E2 59 C3
Swanley Rd., Well. 80 C1
Swanscombe Rd. W4 65 E5
Swanscombe Rd. 66 A1
W11
Swansea Rd., Enf. 25 F4
Swanshope, Loug. 27 E2
Swansland Gdns. E17 41 H1
McEntee Ave.
Swanston Path, Wat. 28 C3
Swanton Gdns. 84 A1
SW19
Swanton Rd., Erith 71 H7
Swanwick Clo. SW15 74 F7
Swaton Rd. E3 60 A4
Swaylands Rd., 71 G6
Belv.
Swaythling Clo. N18 33 E4
Sweden Gate SE16 68 H3
Swedenborg Gdns. 59 D7
E1
Sweeney Cres. SE1 17 G4
Sweeney Cres. SE1 68 C2
Sweet Briar Grn. N9 33 C3
Sweet Briar Gro. N9 33 C3
Sweet Briar Wk. N18 33 C4
Sweetmans Ave., 36 D3
Pnr.
Sweets Way N20 31 G2
Swete St. E13 60 G2
Swetenham Wk. 70 F5
SE18
Sandbach Pl.
Sweyn Pl. SE3 78 G2
Swift Clo. E17 33 H7
Banbury Rd.
Swift Clo., Har. 45 H2
Swift Rd., Felt. 81 D4
Swift Rd., Sthl. 63 F3
Swift St. SW6 75 C1
Swiftsden Way, 87 E6
Brom.
Swinbrook Rd. W10 57 B5
Swinburne Ct. SE5 77 A4
Basingdon Way
Swinburne Cres., 95 F6
Croy.
Swinderby Rd., Wem. 46 H6
Swindon Clo., Ilf. 52 H2
Salisbury Rd.
Swindon St. W12 65 H1
Swinfield Clo., 81 E4
Felt.
Swinford Gdns. SW9 76 H3
Swingate La. SE18 70 H7
Swinnerton St. E9 50 H5
Swinton Clo., Wem. 47 B1
Swinton Pl. WC1 8 C3
Swinton Pl. WC1 58 F3
Swinton St. WC1 8 C3
Swinton St. WC1 58 F3
Swires Shaw, Kes. 104 A4
Swiss Ter. NW6 48 G7
Swithland Gdns. SE9 88 D4
Swyncombe Ave. W5 64 G4
Swynford Gdns. NW4 38 G4
Handowe Clo.
Sybil Ms. N4 40 H6
Lothair Rd. N.
Sybil Thorndike Ho. 49 J6
N1
Clephane Rd.

Sybourn St. E17 41 J7
Sycamore Ave. W5 64 G3
Sycamore Ave., Sid. 79 J6
Sycamore Clo. E16 60 E4
Clarence Rd.
Sycamore Clo. N9 33 D4
Pycroft Way
Sycamore Clo. SE9 88 B2
Sycamore Clo., 23 G6
Barn.
Sycamore Clo., 100 J4
Cars.
Sycamore Clo., 81 A3
Felt.
Sycamore Clo., 54 E1
Nthlt.
Sycamore Gdns. W6 65 H2
Sycamore Gdns., 93 G2
Mitch.
Sycamore Gro. NW9 38 C7
Sycamore Gro. SE6 78 C6
Sycamore Gro. SE20 86 D7
Sycamore Gro., 92 D3
N.Mal.
Sycamore Hill N11 32 A6
Sycamore Rd. SW19 83 J6
Sycamore Rd., Tedd. 82 F6
Sycamore St. EC1 8 J6
Sycamore Wk. W10 57 B4
Fifth Ave.
Sycamore Wk., Ilf. 43 F4
Civic Way
Sycamore Way, 94 G5
Th.Hth.
Grove Rd.
Sydenham Ave. SE26 86 E5
Sydenham Cotts. 87 J2
SE12
Sydenham Hill SE23 86 E1
Sydenham Hill SE26 86 C4
Sydenham Hill Est. 86 D3
SE26
Sydenham Pk. SE26 86 F3
Sydenham Pk. Rd. 86 F3
SE26
Sydenham Ri. SE23 86 E2
Sydenham Rd. SE26 86 G5
Sydenham Rd., 101 J1
Croy.
Sydmons Ct. SE23 77 F7
Sydner Ms. N16 50 C4
Sydner Rd.
Sydner Rd. N16 50 C4
Sydney Clo. SW3 18 F2
Sydney Clo. SW3 66 G4
Sydney Gro. NW4 38 J5
Sydney Ms. SW3 18 F2
Sydney Pl. SW7 18 F2
Sydney Pl. SW7 66 G4
Sydney Rd. E11 42 H6
Mansfield Rd.
Sydney Rd. N8 40 G4
Sydney Rd. N10 40 A1
Sydney Rd. SE2 71 C3
Sydney Rd. SW20 93 A2
Sydney Rd. W13 64 D1
Sydney Rd., Bexh. 80 D4
Sydney Rd., Enf. 25 A3
Sydney Rd., Felt. 81 A1
Sydney Rd., Ilf. 43 F2
Sydney Rd., Rich. 73 H4
Sydney Rd., Sid. 88 H4
Sydney Rd., Sutt. 100 D4
Sydney Rd., Tedd. 82 C5
Sydney Rd., 34 G4
Wdf.Grn.
Sydney St. SW3 18 G3
Sydney St. SW3 66 H5
Sylvan Ave. N3 39 D2
Sylvan Ave. N22 32 F7
Sylvan Ave. NW7 30 F6
Sylvan Ave., Rom. 44 H6
Sylvan Est. SE19 95 C1
Sylvan Gdns., Surb. 91 G7
Sylvan Gro. SE15 68 E6
Sylvan Hill SE19 95 B1
Sylvan Rd. E7 51 G6
Sylvan Rd. E11 42 G5
Sylvan Rd. E17 42 A5
Sylvan Rd. SE19 95 C1
Sylvan Wk., Brom. 97 C3
Sylvan Way, Dag. 53 B3
Sylvan Way, 103 E4
W.Wick.
Sylverdale Rd., 101 H3
Croy.
Sylvester Ave., 88 C6
Chis.
Sylvester Path E8 50 E6
Sylvester Rd.
Sylvester Rd. E8 50 E6
Sylvester Rd. E17 41 J7
Sylvester Rd. N2 39 F2

Sylvester Rd., Wem. 46 F5
Sylvestrus Clo., 92 A1
  Kings.T.
Sylvia Ave., Pnr. 28 E6
Sylvia Gdns., Wem. 47 B7
Symes Ms. NW1 7 F1
Symons St. SW3 19 A2
Symons St. SW3 66 J4
Syon Gate Way, 64 D7
  Brent.
Syon La., Islw. 64 C6
Syon Pk. Gdns., 64 C7
  Islw.
Syon Vista, Rich. 73 G1
  Kew Rd.

T

Tabard Gdn. Est. SE1 17 C4
Tabard Gdns. Est. SE1 68 A2
Tabard St. SE1 17 B4
Tabard St. SE1 68 A2
Tabernacle Ave. E13 60 G4
  Barking Rd.
Tabernacle St. EC2 9 C6
Tabernacle St. EC2 59 A4
Tableer Ave. SW4 76 C5
Tabley Rd. N7 49 E4
Tabor Gdns., Sutt. 100 C6
Tabor Gro. SW19 84 B7
Tabor Rd. W6 65 H3
Tachbrook Est. SW1 19 J4
Tachbrook Est. SW1 67 D5
Tachbrook Ms. SW1 19 F1
Tachbrook Rd., 63 D4
  Sthl.
Tachbrook St. SW1 19 G2
Tachbrook St. SW1 67 C4
Tack Ms. SE4 68 A3
Tadema Rd. SW10 66 F7
Tadmor St. W12 66 A1
Tadworth Ave., 92 F5
  N.Mal.
Tadworth Rd. NW2 47 G2
Taeping St. E14 69 B4
Taffy's How, Mitch. 93 H3
Taft Way E3 60 B2
  St. Leonards St.
Tait Rd., Croy. 95 B7
Talacre Rd. NW5 49 A6
Talbot Ave. N2 39 G3
Talbot Clo. N15 41 C4
Talbot Ct. EC3 13 C5
Talbot Cres. NW4 38 G5
Talbot Gdns., Ilf. 53 A2
Talbot Ho. E14 60 B6
  Giraud St.
Talbot Pl. SE3 78 E2
Talbot Rd. E6 61 D2
Talbot Rd. E7 51 G4
Talbot Rd. N6 40 A6
Talbot Rd. N15 41 C4
Talbot Rd. N22 40 C4
Talbot Rd. W2 57 D6
Talbot Rd. W11 57 C6
Talbot Rd. W13 55 D7
Talbot Rd., Brom. 96 H4
  Masons Hill
Talbot Rd., Cars. 101 A5
Talbot Rd., Dag. 53 F6
Talbot Rd., Har. 37 C2
Talbot Rd., Islw. 73 D4
Talbot Rd., Sthl. 63 E4
Talbot Rd., Th.Hth. 95 A4
Talbot Rd., Twick. 82 B1
Talbot Rd., Wem. 46 G5
Talbot Sq. W2 10 F4
Talbot Sq. W2 57 G6
Talbot Wk. NW10 47 E6
  Garnet Rd.
Talbot Wk. W11 57 B6
Talbot Yd. SE1 17 B2
Talfourd Pl. SE15 77 C1
Talfourd Rd. SE15 77 C1
Talgarth Rd. W6 66 A5
Talgarth Rd. W14 66 A5
Talgarth Wk. NW9 38 E5
Talisman Clo., Ilf. 53 B1
Talisman Sq. SE26 86 D4
Talisman Way, Wem. 46 J3
Tall Elms Clo., 96 F5
  Brom.
Tall Trees SW16 94 F3
Tallack Rd. E10 50 J1
Tallis Gro. SE7 69 H6
Tallis St. EC4 12 F5
Tallis St. EC4 58 G7
Tallis Vw. NW10 47 D6
  Mitchellbrook Way
Tally Ho Cor. N12 31 F5

Talma Gdns., Twick. 73 B6
Talma Rd. SW2 76 G4
Talmage Clo. SE23 77 F7
  Tyson Rd.
Talman Gro., Stan. 29 G6
Talwin St. E3 60 B3
Tamar Sq., Wdf.Grn. 34 H6
Tamar St. SE7 70 B3
Tamar Way N17 41 C3
Tamarind Yd. E1 17 J1
Tamarisk Sq. W12 56 F7
Tamesis Gdns., 99 E2
  Wor.Pk.
Tamian Est., Houns. 72 C4
Tamian Way, Houns. 72 C4
Tamworth Ave., 34 E6
  Wdf.Grn.
Tamworth Gdns., 36 B2
  Pnr.
Tamworth La., 94 A2
  Mitch.
Tamworth Pk., 94 B4
  Mitch.
Tamworth Pl., Croy. 101 J2
Tamworth Rd., 101 H2
  Croy.
Tamworth St. SW6 66 D6
Tancred Rd. N4 40 H6
Tandridge Dr., Orp. 104 G1
Tanfield Ave. NW2 47 F4
Tanfield Rd., Croy. 101 J2
Tangier Rd., Rich. 74 B4
Tanglebury Clo. 97 R4
  Brom.
Tanglewood Clo., 102 F3
  Croy.
Tanglewood Clo., 29 B2
  Stan.
Tanglewood Way, 81 B3
  Felt.
Tangley Gro. SW15 74 F7
Tangley Pk. Rd., 81 F5
  Hmptn.
Tangmere Gdns., 54 C2
  Nthlt.
Tangmere Way NW9 38 E2
Tanhurst Wk. SE2 71 D3
  Alsike Rd.
Tankerton Rd., 98 J2
  Surb.
Tankerton St. WC1 8 B4
Tankerville Rd. 85 D7
  SW16
Tankridge Rd. NW2 47 H2
Tanner St. SE1 17 E4
Tanner St. SE1 68 B2
Tanner St., Bark. 52 F6
Tanners Clo., Walt. 90 B6
Tanners End La. N18 33 B4
Tanners Hill SE8 77 J1
Tanners La., Ilf. 43 F3
Tannery Clo., Beck. 95 G5
Tannery Clo., Dag. 53 H3
Tannsfeld Rd. SE26 86 G5
Tansley Clo. N7 49 D5
  Hilldrop Rd.
Tanswell Est. SE1 16 F4
Tanswell St. SE1 16 E4
Tansy Clo. E6 61 D6
Tant Ave. E16 60 F6
Tantallon Rd. SW12 85 A1
Tantony Gro., Rom. 44 D3
Tanyard La., Bex. 80 G7
  Bexley High St.
Tapestry Clo., 100 E7
  Sutt.
Taplow NW3 48 G7
Taplow SE17 21 C3
Taplow SE17 68 A5
Taplow Rd. N13 32 J4
  North Circular Rd.
Taplow St. N1 9 A2
Taplow St. N1 58 J2
Tapp St. E1 59 E4
Tappesfield Rd. 77 F3
  SE15
Tapster St., Barn. 23 C3
Tarbert Rd. SE22 77 B5
Tarbert Wk. E1 59 F7
  Juniper St.
Tariff Rd. N17 33 D6
Tarleton Gdns. SE23 86 E1
Tarling Clo., Sid. 89 B3
Tarling Rd. E16 60 F6
Tarling Rd. N2 39 F2
Tarling St. E1 59 E6
Tarling St. Est. E1 59 F6
Tarn St. SE1 16 J6
Tarnbank, Enf. 24 E5
Tarnwood Pk. SE9 79 C7
Tarquin Ho. SE26 86 D4
Tarragon Gro. SE26 86 G6

Tarrant Pl. W1 10 J2
Tarrington Clo. 85 D3
  SW16
Tarry La. SE8 68 H5
Tarver Rd. SE17 20 H4
Tarver Rd. SE17 67 H5
Tarves Way SE10 69 B7
Tash Pl. N11 32 B5
  Woodland Rd.
Tasker Ho., Bark. 61 G2
  Dovehouse Mead
Tasker Rd. NW3 48 J5
Tasman Rd. SW9 76 E3
Tasman Wk. E16 61 A6
  Royal Rd.
Tasmania Ter. N18 32 J4
Tasso Rd. W6 66 B6
Tatam Rd. NW10 47 D7
Tate Rd. E16 70 C1
  Newland St.
Tate Rd., Sutt. 100 D5
Tatnell Rd. SE23 77 H6
Tattersall Clo. SE9 79 B5
Tatton Cres. N16 41 C7
  Clapton Common
Tatum St. SE17 21 C2
Tatum St. SE17 68 A4
Taunton Ave. SW20 92 H2
Taunton Ave., 72 J2
  Houns.
Taunton Clo., Ilf. 35 J6
Taunton Clo., Sutt. 100 D1
Taunton Ct. N17 33 B7
Taunton Dr. N2 39 F3
Taunton Dr., Enf. 24 G3
Taunton Ms. NW1 6 J6
Taunton Pl. NW1 6 J5
Taunton Pl. NW1 57 J4
Taunton Rd. SE12 78 E5
Taunton Rd., Grnf. 54 H1
Taunton Way, Stan. 37 H2
Tavern La. SW9 76 G2
Taverner Sq. N5 49 J4
  Highbury Gra.
Taverners Clo. W11 66 B1
  Addison Ave.
Taverners Way E4 34 E1
  Douglas Rd.
Tavistock Ave. E17 41 G3
Tavistock Ave., 55 D2
  Grnf.
Tavistock Clu. N16 50 B5
  Crossway
Tavistock Cres. W11 57 C5
Tavistock Cres., 94 E4
  Mitch.
Tavistock Gdns., 52 H4
  Ilf.
Tavistock Gate, 102 A1
  Croy.
Tavistock Gro., 95 A7
  Croy.
Tavistock Ms. E18 42 G4
  Avon Way
Tavistock Ms. W11 57 C6
  Lancaster Rd.
Tavistock Pl. E18 42 G3
  Avon Way
Tavistock Pl. N14 24 B7
  Chase Side
Tavistock Pl. WC1 8 A5
Tavistock Pl. WC1 58 E4
Tavistock Rd. E7 51 F4
Tavistock Rd. E15 51 F6
Tavistock Rd. E18 42 G3
Tavistock Rd. N4 41 A6
Tavistock Rd. NW10 56 F2
Tavistock Rd. W11 57 C6
Tavistock Rd., 96 F4
  Brom.
Tavistock Rd., 100 G1
  Cars.
Tavistock Rd., 102 A1
  Croy.
Tavistock Rd., Edg. 38 A1
Tavistock Rd., 80 C1
  Well.
Tavistock Sq. WC1 7 J5
Tavistock Sq. WC1 58 D4
Tavistock St. WC2 12 B5
Tavistock St. WC2 58 E7
Tavistock Ter. N19 49 D3
Tavistock Wk., 100 G1
  Cars.
  Tavistock Rd.
Taviton St. WC1 7 H5
Taviton St. WC1 58 D4
Tavy Bri. SE2 71 C3
Tavy Clo. SE11 20 F3
Tawney Rd. SE28 62 B7
Tawny Clo., Felt. 81 A3
  Chervil Clo.
Tawny Way SE16 68 G4
Tayben Ave., Twick. 73 B6

Taybridge Rd. SW11 76 A3
Tayburn Clo. E14 60 C6
Taylor Ave., Rich. 74 B2
Taylor Clo. N17 33 D7
Taylor Clo., Hmptn. 81 J5
Taylor Clo., Orp. 104 J4
Taylor Ct. E15 51 C5
Taylor Rd., Mitch. 84 H7
Taylor Rd., Wall. 101 B5
Taylors Bldgs. SE18 70 E4
  Spray St.
Taylors Clo., Sid. 88 J4
Taylors Grn. W3 56 E6
  Long Dr.
Taylors La. NW10 47 E7
Taylors La. SE26 86 E4
Taylors La., Barn. 23 C1
Taymount Ri. SE23 86 F2
Tayport Clo. N1 49 E7
Tayside Dr., Edg. 30 B3
Taywood Rd., Nthlt. 54 F3
  Invicta Gro.
Teak Clo. SE16 68 H1
Teal Clo. E16 61 A5
  Fulmer Rd.
Teale St. E2 9 J1
Teale St. E2 59 D2
Tealing Dr., Epsom 99 D4
Teasel Clo., Croy. 102 G1
Teasel Way E15 60 E3
Tebworth Rd. N17 33 C7
Tedder Clo., Chess. 98 F6
Tedder Rd., S.Croy. 102 F7
Teddington Pk., 82 C5
  Tedd.
Teddington Pk. Rd., 82 C4
  Tedd.
Tedworth Gdns. SW3 18 J4
Tedworth Sq. SW3 18 J4
Tedworth Sq. SW3 66 J5
Tee, The W3 56 E6
Tees Ave., Grnf. 55 B2
Teesdale Ave., 73 D1
  Islw.
Teesdale Clo. E2 9 J2
Teesdale Clo. E2 59 D2
Teesdale Gdns. SE25 95 B2
  Grange Hill
Teesdale Gdns., 73 D1
  Islw.
Teesdale Rd. E11 42 F6
Teesdale St. E2 59 E2
Teeswater Ct., 71 D3
  Erith
  Middle Way
Teevan Clo., Croy. 95 D7
Teevan Rd., Croy. 102 D5
Teignmouth Clo. 76 D4
  SW4
Teignmouth Clo., 37 J2
  Edg.
Teignmouth Gdns., 55 C2
  Grnf.
Teignmouth Rd. NW2 48 A5
Teignmouth Rd., 80 C2
  Well.
Telegraph Hill NW3 48 E3
Telegraph La., 98 C6
  Esher
Telegraph Ms., Ilf. 53 A1
Telegraph Rd. SW15 74 H7
Telegraph St. EC2 13 B3
Telemann Sq. SE3 78 H3
Telephone Pl. SW6 66 C6
  Lillie Rd.
Telfer Clo. W3 65 C2
  Church Rd.
Telferscot Rd. SW12 85 D1
Telford Ave. SW2 85 D1
Telford Clo. SE19 86 C6
  St. Aubyn's Rd.
Telford Clo. W3 65 C2
  Church Rd.
Telford Dr., Walt. 90 C7
Telford Rd. N11 32 C6
Telford Rd. NW9 38 G6
  West Hendon Bdy.
Telford Rd. SE9 88 G2
Telford Rd. W10 57 B5
Telford Rd., Sthl. 54 H7
Telford Rd., Twick. 72 G7
Telford Ter. SW1 19 F5
Telford Ter. SW1 67 C5
Telford Way W3 56 E5
Telford Way, Hayes 54 E5
Telfords Yd. E1 13 J6
Telham Rd. E6 61 D2
Tell Gro. SE22 77 C4
Tellson Ave. SE18 79 A1
Telscombe Clo., 104 H2
  Orp.
Temeraire St. SE16 68 F2
  Swan Rd.

Temperley Rd. SW12	76	A7
Templar Dr. SE28	62	D6
Templar Ho. NW2	48	C6
Shoot Up Hill		
Templar Pl., Hmptn.	81	G7
Templar St. SE5	76	D4
Templars Ave. NW11	39	C6
Templars Cres. N3	39	D2
Templars Dr., Har.	29	A6
Temple EC4	**12**	**E5**
Temple Ave. EC4	**58**	**F5**
Temple Ave. EC4	58	C7
Temple Ave. N20	23	G7
Temple Ave., Croy.	102	J2
Temple Ave., Dag.	53	G1
Temple Clo. E11	42	E7
Wadley Rd.		
Temple Clo. N3	39	C2
Cyprus Rd.		
Temple Clo. SE28	70	F3
Temple Fortune Hill	39	D5
NW11		
Temple Fortune La.	39	C5
NW11		
Temple Gdns. NW11	39	C6
Temple Gdns., Dag.	53	D3
Temple Gro. NW11	39	D6
Temple Gro., Enf.	24	H3
Temple La. EC4	**12**	**F4**
Temple Mead Clo.,	29	E6
Stan.		
Temple Mill La. E15	51	A4
Temple Pl. WC2	**12**	**D5**
Temple Pl. WC2	58	F7
Temple Rd. E6	61	B1
Temple Rd. N8	40	F4
Temple Rd. NW2	47	J4
Temple Rd. W4	65	C3
Temple Rd. W5	64	G3
Temple Rd., Croy.	102	A4
Temple Rd., Houns.	72	H4
Temple Rd., Rich.	73	J2
Temple Sheen SW14	74	B4
Temple Sheen Rd.	74	B4
SW14		
Temple St. E2	59	E2
Temple Way, Sutt.	100	G3
Temple W. Ms. SE11	**16**	**G6**
Temple W. Ms. SE11	67	H3
Templecombe Rd. E9	59	F1
Templecombe Way,	93	B5
Mord.		
Templehof Ave. NW2	38	J7
Templeman Rd. W7	55	C5
Templemead Clo. W3	56	E6
Templeton Ave. E4	34	A4
Templeton Clo. SE19	95	A1
Templeton Pl. SW5	66	D4
Templeton Rd. N15	41	A6
Templewood W13	55	E5
Templewood Ave.	48	E3
NW3		
Templewood Gdns.	48	E3
NW3		
Tempsford Ave.,	22	D4
Borwd.		
Tempsford Clo.,	24	J3
Enf.		
Gladbeck Way		
Temsford Clo., Har.	36	J2
Tenbury Clo. E7	52	A5
Romford Rd.		
Tenbury Ct. SW2	85	D1
Tenby Ave., Har.	37	E2
Tenby Clo. N15	41	C4
Hanover Rd.		
Tenby Clo., Rom.	44	E6
Tenby Clo., Nthlt.	46	E6
Tenby Rd. E17	41	H5
Tenby Rd., Edg.	37	J1
Tenby Rd., Enf.	25	F3
Tenby Rd., Rom.	44	E6
Tenby Rd., Well.	80	D1
Tench St. E1	68	E1
Tenda Rd. SE16	68	E4
Roseberry St.		
Tendring Way, Rom.	44	C5
Tenham Ave. SW2	85	D2
Tenison Ct. W1	**11**	**F5**
Tenison Way SE1	**16**	**D2**
Tenison Way SE1	67	F1
Tenniel Clo. W2	**10**	**C5**
Tennis Ct. La.,	91	C3
E.Mol.		
Hampton Ct. Way		
Tennis St. SE1	**17**	**B3**
Tennis St. SE1	68	A2
Tennison Ave.,	22	B5
Borwd.		
Tennison Rd. SE25	95	C4
Tenniswood Rd.,	25	B1
Enf.		
Tennyson Ave. E11	42	G7
Tennyson Ave. E12	52	B7
Tennyson Ave. NW9	38	C3
Tennyson Ave.,	92	H5
N.Mal.		
Tennyson Ave.,	82	C1
Twick.		
Tennyson Clo.,	79	J1
Well.		
Tennyson Rd. E10	51	B1
Tennyson Rd. E15	51	E7
Tennyson Rd. E17	41	J6
Tennyson Rd. NW6	57	C1
Tennyson Rd. NW7	30	G5
Tennyson Rd. SE20	86	G7
Tennyson Rd. SW19	84	F6
Tennyson Rd. W7	55	C7
Tennyson Rd.,	72	J2
Houns.		
Tennyson Rd., Well.	79	J1
Tennyson Rd. SW8	76	B2
Tent St. E1	59	E4
Tenter Grd. E1	**13**	**F2**
Tenterden Clo. NW4	39	A3
Tenterden Clo. SE9	88	C4
Tenterden Dr. NW4	39	A3
Tenterden Gdns.	39	A3
NW4		
Tenterden Gdns.,	95	D7
Croy.		
Tenterden Gro. NW4	39	A3
Tenterden Rd. N17	33	C7
Tenterden Rd.,	95	D7
Croy.		
Tenterden Rd., Dag.	53	F2
Tenterden St. W1	**11**	**E4**
Tenterden St. W1	58	B6
Terborch Way SE22	77	B5
East Dulwich Gro.		
Teresa Ms. E17	42	A4
Teresa Wk. N10	40	B5
Connaught Gdns.		
Terling Clo. E11	51	F3
Terling Rd., Dag.	53	G2
Terling Wk. N1	58	J1
Britannia Row		
Terminus Pl. SW1	**15**	**E6**
Terminus Pl. SW1	67	B3
Terrace, The E4	34	E3
Chingdale Rd.		
Terrace, The N3	39	C2
Hendon La.		
Terrace, The NW6	57	D1
Terrace, The SW13	74	E2
Terrace, The,	34	G6
Wdf.Grn.		
Terrace Gdns. SW13	74	F2
Terrace La., Rich.	73	H6
Terrace Rd. E9	50	F7
Terrace Rd. E13	60	G1
Terrace Rd., Walt.	90	A7
Terrace Wk., Dag.	53	E5
Terrapin Rd. SW17	85	B3
Terretts Pl. N1	49	H7
Upper St.		
Terrick Rd. N22	40	E1
Terrick St. W12	56	H6
Terrilands, Pnr.	36	F3
Terront Rd. N15	40	J5
Tessa Sanderson Pl.	76	B3
SW8		
Heath Rd.		
Tessa Sanderson	46	A5
Way, Grnf.		
Lilian Board Way		
Testerton Wk. W11	57	A7
Whitchurch Rd.		
Tetbury Pl. N1	58	H1
Upper St.		
Tetcott Rd. SW10	**18**	**C7**
Tetcott Rd. SW10	66	F7
Tetherdown N10	40	A3
Tetterby Way SE16	**22**	**J4**
Tetty Way, Brom.	96	G2
Teversham La. SW8	76	E1
Teviot Clo., Well.	80	B1
Teviot St. E14	60	C5
Tewkesbury Ave.	77	E7
SE23		
Tewkesbury Ave.,	36	E5
Pnr.		
Tewkesbury Clo. N15	41	A6
Tewkesbury Rd.		
Tewkesbury Gdns.	38	B3
NW9		
Tewkesbury Rd. N15	41	A6
Tewkesbury Rd.	55	D7
W13		
Tewkesbury Rd.,	100	G1
Cars.		
Tewkesbury Ter. N11	32	C6
Tewson Rd. SE18	70	H4
Teynham Ave., Enf.	25	A6
Teynham Grn.,	96	G5
Brom.		
Teynton Ter. N17	40	J1
Thackeray Ave. N17	41	D2
Thackeray Clo. SW19	84	A7
Thackeray Dr., Ilf.	44	A7
Thackeray Dr., Rom.	44	A7
Thackeray Rd. E6	61	A2
Thackeray Rd. SW8	76	B2
Thackeray St. W8	**14**	**B4**
Thackeray St. W8	66	E2
Thackery Clo., Har.	45	G1
Thakeham Clo. SE26	86	E5
Thakrah Clo. N2	39	F2
Thalia Clo. SE10	69	D6
Feathers Pl.		
Thame Rd. SE16	68	G2
Thames Ave. SW10	75	F1
Thames Ave., Dag.	62	G4
Thames Ave., Grnf.	55	C2
Thames Bank SW14	74	C2
Thames Clo., Hmptn.	90	H2
Thames Clo., W.Mol.	90	H2
Thames Mead, Walt.	90	A7
Thames Meadow,	90	G2
W.Mol.		
Thames Rd. E16	70	A1
Thames Rd. W4	65	A6
Thames Rd., Bark.	60	A3
Thames Rd. Ind.	70	A1
Est. E16		
Thames Side,	91	G1
Kings.T.		
Thames Side, Tedd.	82	G7
Thames St. SE10	69	B6
Thames St., Hmptn.	90	H1
Thames St.,	91	G2
Kings.T.		
Thames St., Sun.	90	A4
Thames Vill. W4	74	C1
Thamesbank Pl.	62	C6
SE28		
Thamesgate Clo.,	82	E4
Rich.		
Locksmeade Rd.		
Thameshill Ave.,	44	J2
Rom.		
Thameside, Tedd.	82	F7
Thameside Ind. Est.	70	B2
E16		
Thameside Wk. SE28	62	B6
Thamesmead, Walt.	90	A7
Thamesmere Dr.	62	A7
SE29		
Thamesvale Clo.,	72	G2
Houns.		
Thane Vill. N7	49	F3
Thanescroft Gdns.,	102	B3
Croy.		
Thanet Dr., Kes.	104	A3
Phoenix Dr.		
Thanet Pl., Croy.	101	J4
Thanet Rd., Bex.	80	G7
Thanet St. WC1	**8**	**A4**
Thanet St. WC1	58	E3
Thanington Ct. SE9	79	H6
Thant Clo. E10	51	B3
Tharp Rd., Wall.	101	D5
Thatcham Gdns.	23	F7
N20		
Thatchers Clo.,	27	F2
Loug.		
Thatchers Way,	73	A5
Islw.		
Thatches Gro., Rom.	44	E4
Thavies Inn EC1	**12**	**F3**
Thaxted Pl. SW20	84	A7
Thaxted Rd. SE9	88	F2
Thaxted Rd.,	27	A7
Buck.H.		
Thaxton Rd. W14	66	C6
Thayer St. W1	**11**	**C2**
Thayer St. W1	58	A5
Thayers Fm. Rd.,	95	H1
Beck.		
Theatre St. SW11	75	J3
Theberton St. N1	58	G1
Theed St. SE1	**16**	**F2**
Theed St. SE1	67	G1
Thelma Gdns. SE3	79	A1
Thelma Gdns., Felt.	81	E3
Theobald Clo., Tedd.	82	D6
Theobald Cres.,	36	H1
Har.		
Theobald Rd. E17	41	J7
Theobald Rd., Croy.	101	H2
Theobald St. SE1	**17**	**B6**
Theobalds Ave. N12	31	F4
Theobalds Ct. N4	49	J2
Queens Dr.		
Theobald's Rd. WC1	**12**	**B2**
Theobald's Rd. WC1	58	F5
Theodore Rd. SE13	78	D6
Therapia La., Croy.	94	D7
Therapia Rd. SE22	77	F6
Theresa Rd. W6	65	G4
Therfield Ct. N4	49	J2
Brownswood Rd.		
Thermopylae Gate	69	B4
E14		
Theseus Wk. N1	**8**	**H2**
Thesiger Rd. SE20	86	G7
Thessaly Rd. SW8	67	C7
Thetford Clo. N13	32	H6
Thetford Gdns.,	53	D7
Dag.		
Thetford Rd., Dag.	53	D7
Thetford Rd.,	92	D6
N.Mal.		
Thetis Ter., Rich.	65	A6
Theydon Gro.,	34	J6
Wdf.Grn.		
Theydon Pk. Rd.,	27	H1
Epp.		
Theydon Rd. E5	50	F2
Theydon St. E17	41	J7
Thicket Cres.,	100	F4
Sutt.		
Thicket Gro., Dag.	53	C6
Thicket Rd. SE20	86	D7
Thicket Rd., Sutt.	100	F4
Third Ave. E12	52	B4
Third Ave. E13	60	G3
Third Ave. E17	42	A5
Third Ave. W3	65	F1
Third Ave. W10	57	B3
Third Ave., Dag.	62	H1
Third Ave., Enf.	25	C5
Third Ave., Rom.	44	C6
Third Ave., Wem.	46	G2
Third Clo., W.Mol.	90	H4
Third Cross Rd.,	82	A2
Twick.		
Third Way, Wem.	47	B4
Thirleby Rd. SW1	**15**	**G6**
Thirleby Rd. SW1	67	C3
Thirleby Rd., Edg.	38	D1
Thirlmere Ave.,	55	F3
Grnf.		
Thirlmere Gdns.,	46	F1
Wem.		
Thirlmere Ho.,	73	C5
Islw.		
Thirlmere Ri.,	87	F6
Brom.		
Thirlmere Rd. N10	40	B1
Thirlmere Rd. SW16	85	D4
Thirlmere Rd.,	80	J2
Bexh.		
Thirsk Clo., Nthlt.	45	G6
Thirsk Rd. SE25	95	A4
Thirsk Rd. SW11	76	A3
Thirsk Rd., Mitch.	85	A7
Thistle Gro. SW10	**18**	**D3**
Thistle Gro. SW10	66	F5
Thistle Mead, Loug.	27	D3
Thistlebrook SE2	71	C3
Thistlecroft Gdns.,	37	G1
Stan.		
Thistledene, T.Ditt.	91	B6
Thistledene Ave.,	45	E3
Har.		
Thistlemead, Chis.	97	E2
Thistlewaite Rd. E5	50	E3
Thistlewood Clo. N7	49	F2
Thistleworth Clo.,	64	A7
Islw.		
Thomas à Beckett	46	C4
Clo., Wem.		
Thomas Baines Rd.	75	G3
SW11		
Thomas Darby Ct.	57	B6
W11		
Thomas Doyle St.	**16**	**H5**
SE1		
Thomas Doyle St.	67	H3
SE1		
Thomas Hardy Ho.	32	F7
N22		
Thomas La. SE6	78	A7
Thomas More St. E1	**13**	**H6**
Thomas More St. E1	59	D7
Thomas More Way	39	F3
N2		
Thomas Rd. E14	59	J6
Thomas St. SE18	70	E4
Thompson Ave.,	74	A3
Rich.		
Thompson Clo., Ilf.	52	F2
High Rd.		
Thompson Rd. SE22	77	C6
Thompson Rd., Dag.	53	F3
Thompson's Ave.	**20**	**J7**
SE5		

Thompson's Ave. SE5 67 J7
Thomson Cres., Croy. 101 G1
Thomson Rd., Har. 37 B3
Thorburn Sq. SE1 21 H2
Thorburn St. SE1 68 D4
Thorburn Way SW19 93 G1
Phipps Bri. Rd.
Thoresby St. N1 9 A3
Thoresby St. N1 58 J3
Thorkhill Gdns., T.Ditt. 98 D1
Thorkhill Rd., T.Ditt. 98 D1
Thorn Ave. (Bushey), Wat. 28 J1
Thorn Clo., Brom. 97 D6
Thorn Clo., Nthlt. 54 F3
Thorn Ho., Beck. 95 H1
Thornaby Gdns. N18 33 D6
Thornbury Ave., Islw. 64 A7
Thornbury Gdns., Borwd. 22 C3
Thornbury Rd. SW2 76 E6
Thornbury Rd., Islw. 64 A7
Thornby Rd. E5 50 F3
Thorncliffe Rd. SW2 76 E6
Thorncliffe Rd., Sthl. 63 F5
Thorncombe Rd. SE22 77 B5
Thorncroft Rd., Sutt. 100 E4
Thorncroft St. SW8 67 E7
Thorndean St. SW18 84 F2
Thorndene Ave. N11 32 A1
Thorndike Ave., Nthlt. 54 D1
Thorndike Clo. SW10 18 C7
Thorndike Clo. SW10 66 F7
Thorndike St. SW1 19 H2
Thorndike St. SW1 67 D4
Thorndon Clo., Orp. 97 J2
Thorndon Gdns., Epsom 99 E5
Thorndon Rd., Orp. 97 J2
Thorndyke Ct., Pnr. 28 F7
Westfield Pk.
Thorne Clo. E11 51 E4
Thorne Clo. E16 60 F6
Thorne Clo., Erith 71 J6
Thorne Pas. SW13 74 E2
Thorne Rd. SW8 67 E7
Thorne St. SW13 74 E3
Thorneloe Gdns., Croy. 101 G5
Thornes Clo., Beck. 96 C3
Thornet Wd. Rd., Brom. 97 D3
Thorney Cres. SW11 66 G7
Thorney Hedge Rd. W4 65 B4
Thorney St. SW1 20 A1
Thorney St. SW1 67 E4
Thorneycroft Clo., Walt. 90 C5
Thornfield Ave. NW7 39 B1
Thornfield Rd. W12 65 H2
Thornford Rd. SE13 78 C5
Thorngate Rd. W9 57 D4
Thorngrove Rd. E13 60 H1
Thornham Gro. E15 51 D5
Thornham St. SE10 69 B6
Thornhaugh Ms. WC1 7 A6
Thornhaugh St. WC1 11 J1
Thornhaugh St. WC1 58 D5
Thornhill Ave. SE18 70 H7
Thornhill Bri. Wf. N1 58 F1
Caledonian Rd.
Thornhill Cres. N1 49 F7
Thornhill Gdns. E10 51 J2
Thornhill Gdns., Bark. 52 H7
Thornhill Gro. N1 49 F7
Lofting Rd.
Thornhill Ho. N1 49 G7
Thornhill Rd.
Thornhill Rd. E10 51 B2
Thornhill Rd. N1 49 G7
Thornhill Rd., Croy. 94 J7
Thornhill Rd., Surb. 98 H2
Thornhill Sq. N1 49 F7
Thornlaw Rd. SE27 85 G4
Thornley Clo. N17 33 D7
Thornley Dr., Har. 45 H2

Thornley Pl. SE10 69 E5
Caradoc St.
Thornsbeach Rd. SE6 87 C1
Thornsett Pl. SE20 95 E2
Thornsett Rd. SE20 95 E2
Thornsett Rd. SW18 84 E1
Thornside, Edg. 30 A6
High St.
Thornton Ave. SW2 85 D1
Thornton Ave. W4 65 E4
Thornton Ave., Croy. 94 F6
Thornton Ct. SW20 93 A5
Thornton Dene, Beck. 96 A2
Thornton Gdns. SW12 85 D1
Thornton Gro., Pnr. 28 G6
Thornton Hill SW19 84 B7
Thornton Pl. W1 10 J1
Thornton Pl. W1 57 J5
Thornton Rd. E11 51 D2
Thornton Rd. N18 33 F3
Thornton Rd. SW12 76 D7
Thornton Rd. SW14 74 D3
Thornton Rd. SW19 84 A6
Thornton Rd., Barn. 23 B3
Thornton Rd., Belv. 71 H4
Thornton Rd., Brom. 87 G5
Thornton Rd., Cars. 100 G1
Thornton Rd., Croy. 94 F7
Thornton Rd., Ilf. 52 E4
Thornton Rd. 94 G5
Th.Hth.
Thornton Rd. E. SW19 84 A6
Thornton Rd.
Thornton Row, Th.Hth. 94 G5
London Rd.
Thornton St. SW9 76 G2
Thornton Way NW11 39 E5
Thorntons Fm. Ave., Rom. 53 J1
Thorntree Rd. SE7 70 A5
Thornville St. SE8 78 A1
Thornwood Clo. E18 42 H2
Thornwood Rd. SE13 78 E5
Thorogood Gdns. E15 51 E5
Thorold Rd. N22 32 E7
Thorold Rd., Ilf. 52 E2
Thorparch Rd. SW8 76 D1
Thorpe Clo. W10 57 B6
Cambridge Gdns.
Thorpe Clo., Orp. 104 H2
Thorpe Cres. E17 41 J2
Thorpe Hall Rd. E17 42 C1
Thorpe Rd. E6 61 C1
Thorpe Rd. E7 51 F4
Thorpe Rd. E17 42 C2
Thorpe Rd. N15 41 B6
Thorpe Rd., Bark. 52 G7
Thorpe Rd., Kings.T. 82 H7
Thorpebank Rd. W12 65 G1
Thorpedale Gdns., Ilf. 43 D4
Thorpedale Rd. N4 49 E2
Thorpewood Ave. SE26 86 E2
Thorsden Way SE19 86 B4
Oaks Ave.
Thorverton Rd. NW2 48 B3
Thoydon Rd. E3 59 H2
Thrale Rd. SW16 85 C4
Thrale St. SE1 17 A2
Thrale St. SE1 67 J1
Thrasher Clo. E8 59 C1
Stean St.
Thrawl St. E1 13 G2
Thrawl St. E1 59 C5
Threadneedle St. EC2 13 C4
Threadneedle St. EC2 59 A6
Three Colt St. E14 59 J6
Three Colts La. E2 59 E4
Three Cors., Bexh. 80 H2
Three Cups Yd. WC1 12 D2
Three Kings Rd., Mitch. 94 A3
Three Kings Yd. W1 11 D5
Three Kings Yd. W1 58 B7
Three Mill La. E3 61 A3
Three Oak La. SE1 17 F3
Threshers Pl. W11 57 B7
Thriftwood SE26 86 F3
Thrift Fm. La., Borwd. 22 C2
Thrigby Rd., Chess. 98 H3
Throckmorten Rd. E16 60 H6

Throgmorton Ave. EC2 13 C3
Throgmorton Ave. EC2 59 A6
Throgmorton St. EC2 13 C3
Throgmorton St. EC2 59 A6
Throwley Clo. SE2 71 C3
Throwley Rd., Sutt. 100 E5
Throwley Way, Sutt. 100 E4
Thrupp Clo., Mitch. 94 B2
Thrush Grn., Har. 36 G4
Thrush St. SE17 20 J3
Thurbarn Rd. SE6 87 A5
Thurland Rd. SE16 17 H5
Thurland Rd. SE16 68 D3
Thurlby Clo., Har. 37 D6
Gayton Rd.
Thurlby Clo., Wdf.Grn. 35 C5
Thurlby Rd. SE27 85 G4
Thurlby Rd., Wem. 46 G6
Thurleigh Ave. SW12 76 A6
Thurleigh Rd. SW12 75 J7
Thurleston Ave., Mord. 93 B5
Thurlestone Ave. N12 31 J6
Thurlestone Ave., Ilf. 52 J4
Thurlestone Rd. SE27 85 G3
Thurloe Clo. SW7 18 G1
Thurloe Clo. SW7 66 H4
Thurloe Pl. SW7 18 F1
Thurloe Pl. SW7 66 G4
Thurloe Pl. Ms. SW7 18 F1
Thurloe Sq. SW7 18 G1
Thurloe Sq. SW7 66 H4
Thurloe St. SW7 18 F1
Thurloe St. SW7 66 G4
Thurlow Clo. E4 34 B6
Higham Sta. Ave.
Thurlow Gdns., Ilf. 35 G6
Thurlow Gdns., Wem. 46 G5
Thurlow Hill SE21 85 J1
Thurlow Pk. Rd. SE21 85 H1
Thurlow Rd. NW3 48 G5
Thurlow Rd. W7 64 D2
Thurlow St. SE17 20 J3
Thurlow St. SE17 68 A5
Thurlow Ter. NW5 49 A5
Thurlston Rd., Ruis. 45 A3
Thurnby Ct., Twick. 82 B3
Thursland Rd., Sid. 89 E5
Thursley Cres., Croy. 103 C7
Thursley Gdns. SW19 84 A2
Thursley Rd. SE9 88 C3
Thurso St. SW17 84 E4
Thurstan Rd. SW20 83 H7
Thurston Rd. SE13 78 B2
Thurston Rd., Sthl. 54 F6
Thwaite Clo., Erith 71 J6
Thyra Gro. N12 31 E6
Tibbatts Rd. E3 60 B4
Tibbenham Wk. E13 60 F2
Stride Rd.
Tibberton Sq. N1 49 J7
Popham Rd.
Tibbets Clo. SW19 84 A1
Tibbet's Cor. SW19 75 A7
Tibbet's Ride SW19 75 A7
Tiber Gdns. N1 58 F1
Treaty St.
Ticehurst Clo., Orp. 89 A7
Grovelands Rd.
Ticehurst Rd. SE23 86 H2
Tickford Clo. SE2 71 C2
Ampleforth Rd.
Tidal Basin Rd. E16 60 F7
Tidenham Gdns., Croy. 102 B3
Tideswell Rd. SW15 74 J4
Tideswell Rd., Croy. 103 A3
Tideway Clo., Rich. 82 E4
Locksmeade Rd.
Tidey St. E3 60 A5
Tidford Rd., Well. 79 J2
Tidworth Rd. E3 60 A4
Tiepigs La., Brom. 103 F1
Tiepigs La., W.Wick. 103 E2
Tierney Rd. SW2 76 E7
Tiger La., Brom. 96 H4
Tiger Way E5 50 E4

Tilbrook Rd. SE3 78 J3
Tilbury Clo. SE15 21 E7
Tilbury Rd. E6 61 C2
Tilbury Rd. E10 42 C7
Tildesley Rd. SW15 74 J6
Tile Fm. Rd., Orp. 104 G3
Tile Kiln La. N6 49 C1
Winchester Rd.
Tile Kiln La. N13 32 J5
Tile Kiln La., Bex. 89 J2
Tile Yd. E14 59 J6
St. Anne's St.
Tile Yd. E14 59 J6
Commercial Rd.
Tilehurst Rd. SW18 84 G1
Tilehurst Rd., Sutt. 100 B5
Tileyard Rd. N7 49 E7
Tilford Ave., Croy. 103 C7
Tilford Gdns. SW19 84 A1
Tilia Rd. E5 50 E4
Clarence Rd.
Tiller Rd. E14 69 A3
Tillett Clo. NW10 47 C6
Tillett Way E2 9 H3
Tilling Rd. NW2 47 J1
Tillingbourne Gdns. N3 39 C3
Tillingbourne Grn., Orp. 97 J4
Tillingbourne Way N3 39 C3
Tillingham Way N12 31 D4
Tillman St. E1 59 E6
Bigland St.
Tilloch St. N1 49 F7
Carnoustie Dr.
Tillotson Rd. N9 33 C2
Tillotson Rd., Har. 28 H7
Tillotson Rd., Ilf. 43 D7
Tilney Ct. EC1 9 A5
Tilney Dr., Buck.H. 34 G2
Tilney Gdns. N1 50 A6
Baxter Rd.
Tilney Rd., Dag. 53 F6
Tilney Rd., Sthl. 63 C4
Tilney St. W1 15 C1
Tilney St. W1 67 A1
Tilson Gdns. SW2 76 E7
Tiloon Ho. SW2 76 E7
Tilson Gdns.
Tilson Rd. N17 41 D1
Tilt Yd. App. SE9 79 C6
Tilton St. SW6 66 B6
Tiltwood, The W3 56 C7
Acacia Rd.
Timber Clo., Chis. 97 D2
Timber Mill Way SW4 76 D3
Timber Pond Rd. SE16 68 G1
Timber St. EC1 8 J5
Timbercroft, Epsom 99 E4
Timbercroft La. SE18 70 H6
Timberdene NW4 39 A2
Timberdene Ave., Ilf. 43 F1
Timberland Rd. E1 59 E6
Timberwharf Rd. N16 41 D6
Times Sq., Sutt. 100 E5
High St.
Timothy Rd. E3 59 J5
Timsbury Wk. SW15 83 G1
Tindal St. SW9 76 H1
Tinderbox All. SW14 74 D3
Tine Rd., Chig. 35 H5
Tinsley Rd. E1 59 F5
Tintagel Cres. SE22 77 C4
Tintagel Dr., Stan. 29 G4
Tintern Ave. NW9 38 B3
Tintern Clo. SW15 75 B5
Tintern Clo. SW19 84 F7
Tintern Gdns. N14 24 E7
Tintern Path NW9 38 E6
Ruthin Clo.
Tintern Rd. N22 40 J1
Tintern Rd., Cars. 100 G1
Tintern St. SW4 76 E4
Tintern Way, Har. 45 H1
Tinto Rd. E16 60 G4
Tinwell St., Borwd. 22 C5
Cranes Way
Tinworth St. SE11 20 B3
Tinworth St. SE11 67 E5
Tippetts Clo., Enf. 24 J1
Tipthorpe Rd. SW11 76 A3
Tipton Dr., Croy. 102 B4
Tiptree Clo. E4 34 C3
Tiptree Cres., Ilf. 43 D3
Tiptree Dr., Enf. 25 A4
Tiptree Est., Ilf. 43 D3

Tiptree Rd., Ruis. 45 B4
Tirlemont Rd., 101 J7
S.Croy.
Tirrell Rd., Croy. 94 B3
Tisbury Ct. W1 11 H5
Tisbury Rd. SW16 94 E2
Tisdall Pl. SE17 21 C2
Tisdall Pl. SE17 68 A4
Titchborne Row W2 10 H4
Titchfield Rd. NW8 57 J1
Titchfield Rd., 100 G1
Cars.
Titchfield Wk., Cars. 93 G7
Titchfield Rd.
Titchwell Rd. SW18 75 G7
Tite St. SW3 18 J4
Tite St. SW3 66 J6
Tithe Barn Clo., 91 J1
Kings.T.
Tithe Barn Way, 54 B2
Nthlt.
Tithe Clo. NW7 38 G1
Tithe Fm. Ave., 45 G3
Har.
Tithe Fm. Clo., 45 G3
Har.
Tithe Wk. NW7 38 G1
Titley Clo. E4 34 A5
Titmuss Ave. SE28 62 B7
Titmuss St. W12 65 H2
Tiverton Ave., Ilf. 43 D3
Tiverton Rd. SE9 88 F1
Tiverton Rd. N15 41 A6
Tiverton Rd. N18 33 B5
Tiverton Rd. NW10 57 A1
Tiverton Rd., Edg. 37 J2
Tiverton Rd., 72 J2
Houns.
Tiverton Rd., Ruis. 45 A3
Tiverton Rd., 94 G5
Th.Hth.
Willett Rd.
Tiverton Rd., Wem. 55 H2
Tiverton St. SE1 16 J6
Tiverton St. SE1 67 J3
Tiverton Way, 98 F5
Chess.
Tivoli Ct. SE16 68 J2
Tivoli Gdns. SE18 70 B4
Tivoli Rd. N8 40 D5
Tivoli Rd. SE27 85 J5
Tivoli Rd., Houns. 72 E4
Tobacco Quay E1 59 E7
Wapping La.
Tobago St. E14 69 A2
Manilla St.
Tobin Clo. NW3 48 H7
Toby La. E1 59 H4
Todds Wk. N7 49 F2
Tokenhouse Yd. EC2 13 B3
Tokyngton Ave., 47 A6
Wem.
Toland Sq. SW15 74 G5
Tolcarne Dr., Pnr. 36 A2
Toley Ave., Wem. 37 H7
Tollbridge Clo. W10 57 B4
Kensal Rd.
Tollesbury Gdns., 43 G3
Ilf.
Tollet St. E1 59 G4
Tollgate Dr. SE21 86 B2
Tollgate Gdns. NW6 6 A1
Tollgate Gdns. NW6 57 E2
Tollgate Rd. E6 61 A5
Tollgate Rd. E16 60 J5
Tollhouse Way N19 49 C2
Tollington Pk. N4 49 F2
Tollington Pl. N4 49 F2
Tollington Rd. N7 49 F4
Tollington Way N7 49 E3
Tolmers Ms. N7 9 G5
Tolpuddle St. N1 8 E1
Tolpuddle St. N1 58 G2
Tolsford Rd. E5 50 E5
Tolson Rd., Islw. 73 D3
Tolverne Rd. SW20 92 J1
Tolworth Clo., 99 B1
Surb.
Tolworth Gdns., 44 D5
Rom.
Tolworth Pk. Rd., 98 J2
Surb.
Tolworth Ri. N., 92 D6
Surb.
South La.
Tolworth Ri. S., 92 D6
Surb.
South La.
Tolworth Rd., Surb. 98 H2
Tom Coombs Clo. 79 B4
SE9
Well Hall Rd.
Tom Cribb Rd. SE28 70 F3

Tom Hood Clo. E15 51 D5
Maryland St.
Tom Mann Clo., 61 H1
Bark.
Tom Smith Clo. SE10 69 E6
Maze Hill
Tomahawk Gdns., 54 D3
Nthlt.
Javelin Way
Tomlins Gro. E3 60 A3
Tomlins Orchard, 61 F1
Bark.
Tomlins Ter. E14 59 J5
Rhodeswell Rd.
Tomlins Wk. N7 49 F2
Briset Way
Tomlinson Clo. E2 9 G4
Tomlinson Clo. E2 59 C3
Tomlinson Clo. W4 65 B5
Oxford Rd. N.
Tompion St. EC1 8 G4
Tomswood Hill, Ilf. 35 E7
Tomswood Rd., Chig. 35 D6
Tonbridge Cres., 37 H4
Har.
Tonbridge Ho. SE25 95 D3
Tonbridge Rd., 90 E4
W.Mol.
Tonbridge St. WC1 8 A3
Tonbridge St. WC1 58 E3
Tonbridge Wk. WC1 8 A3
Tonfield Rd., Sutt. 100 C1
Tonge Clo., Beck. 96 A5
Tonsley Hill SW18 75 E5
Tonsley Pl. SW18 75 E5
Tonsley Rd. SW18 75 E5
Tonsley St. SW18 75 E5
Tonstall Rd., 94 A2
Mitch.
Tooke Clo., Pnr. 36 E1
Took's Ct. EC4 12 E3
Tooley St. SE1 17 C1
Tooley St. SE1 58 B1
Toorack Rd., Har. 37 A2
Tooting Bec Gdns. 85 D4
SW16
Tooting Bec Rd. 85 B4
SW16
Tooting Bec Rd. 85 A5
SW17
Tooting Gro. SW17 84 H5
Tooting High St. 84 H6
SW17
Tootswood Rd., 96 E5
Brom.
Top Ho. Ri. E4 26 C7
Parkhill Rd.
Top Pk., Beck. 96 G5
Topcliffe Dr., Orp. 104 G5
Topham Sq. N17 40 J1
Topham St. EC1 8 E5
Topiary Sq., Rich. 73 J3
Topley St. SE9 79 A4
Topp Wk. NW2 47 J2
Topsfield Rd. N8 40 E5
Topsham Rd. SW17 84 J3
Tor Gdns. W8 66 D2
Tor Rd., Well. 80 C1
Torbay Rd. NW6 48 C7
Torbay Rd., Har. 45 E2
Torbay St. NW1 49 B7
Hawley Rd.
Torbridge Clo., 29 H7
Edg.
Torbrook Clo., Bex. 80 E6
Torcross Dr. SE23 86 F2
Torcross Rd., Ruis. 45 B3
Tormead Clo., Sutt. 100 D6
Tormount Rd. SE18 70 H6
Toronto Ave. E12 52 C4
Toronto Rd. E11 51 D4
Toronto Rd., Ilf. 52 E1
Torquay Gdns., Ilf. 43 A4
Torquay St. W2 10 A2
Torr Rd. SE20 86 G7
Torre Wk., Cars. 100 H1
Torrens Rd. E15 51 F6
Torrens Rd. SW2 76 F5
Torrens Sq. E15 51 F6
Torrens St. EC1 8 F2
Torrens St. EC1 58 C2
Torriano Ave. NW5 49 D5
Torriano Cotts. NW5 49 C5
Torriano Ave.
Torridge Gdns. SE15 77 F4
Torridge Rd., 94 H5
Th.Hth.
Torridon Rd. SE6 78 D7
Torridon Rd. SE13 78 E7
Torrington Ave. N12 31 G5
Torrington Clo. N12 31 G4
Torrington Clo., 98 B6
Esher

Torrington Dr., 45 H4
Har.
Torrington Dr., 27 F4
Loug.
Torrington Gdns. 32 C6
N11
Torrington Gdns., 55 F1
Grnf.
Torrington Gdns., 27 F4
Loug.
Torrington Gro. N12 31 H5
Torrington Rd. N15 31 F5
Torrington Pl. E1 17 J2
Torrington Pl. E1 50 B6
Torrington Pl. WC1 11 G1
Torrington Pl. WC1 58 D5
Torrington Rd. E18 42 G3
Torrington Rd., 53 F1
Dag.
Torrington Rd., 98 B6
Esher
Torrington Rd., 55 F1
Grnf.
Torrington Sq. WC1 7 J6
Torrington Sq. WC1 58 D4
Torrington Sq., 95 A7
Croy.
Tavistock Gro.
Torrington Way, 93 D7
Mord.
Torver Rd., Har. 37 B4
Torver Way, Orp. 104 G2
Torwood Rd. SW15 74 G5
Tothill St. SW1 15 H4
Tothill St. SW1 67 D2
Totnes Rd., Well. 71 B7
Totnes Wk. N2 39 G4
Tottenhall Rd. N13 32 G6
Tottenham Ct. Rd. 7 G6
W1
Tottenham Ct. Rd. 58 C4
W1
Tottenham Grn. E. 41 C4
N15
Tottenham La. N8 40 E5
Tottenham Rd. N1 50 B6
Tottenham St. W1 11 G1
Tottenham St. W1 58 C5
Totterdown St. SW17 84 J4
Totteridge Common 30 G2
N20
Totteridge Grn. N20 31 D2
Totteridge La. N20 31 D2
Totteridge Village 31 B1
N20
Totternhoe Clo., 37 F5
Har.
Totton Rd., Th.Hth. 94 G3
Toulmin St. SE1 16 J4
Toulmin St. SE1 67 J4
Toulon St. SE5 20 J7
Toulon St. SE5 67 J7
Tournay Rd. SW6 66 C7
Toussaint Wk. SE16 17 J5
Tovil Clo. SE20 95 E2
Towcester Rd. E3 60 B4
Tower Bri. E1 17 F2
Tower Bri. E1 68 C1
Tower Bri. SE1 17 F2
Tower Bri. SE1 68 C1
Tower Bri. App. E1 17 F2
Tower Bri. App. E1 68 C1
Tower Bri. Rd. SE1 17 D6
Tower Bri. Rd. SE1 68 B3
Tower Clo. NW3 48 G5
Lyndhurst Rd.
Tower Clo. SE20 86 E7
Tower Clo., Ilf. 35 E6
Tower Clo., Orp. 104 J2
Tower Ct. WC2 12 A4
Tower Gdns. Rd. N17 40 J1
Tower Hamlets Rd. 51 F4
E7
Tower Hamlets Rd. 42 A3
E17
Tower Hill EC3 13 F6
Tower Hill EC3 59 B7
Tower Ms. E17 42 A4
Tower Pl. EC3 13 E6
Tower Pt., Enf. 25 A4
Tower Ri., Rich. 73 H3
Jocelyn Rd.
Tower Rd. NW10 47 G7
Tower Rd., Belv. 71 J4
Tower Rd., Bexh. 80 G4
Tower Rd., Orp. 104 J2
Tower Rd., Twick. 82 C3
Tower Royal EC4 13 A5
Tower St. WC2 11 J4
Tower St. WC2 58 D6
Tower Ter. N22 40 F2
Mayes Rd.

Tower Vw., Croy. 95 G7
Towers Pl., Rich. 73 H5
Eton St.
Towers Rd., Pnr. 28 E7
Towers Rd., Sthl. 54 G4
Towfield Rd., Felt. 81 F2
Towing Path Wk. N1 58 D1
York Way
Town, The, Enf. 25 A3
Town Ct. Path N4 49 J1
Town Hall App. Rd. 41 C4
N15
Town Hall Ave. W4 65 D5
Town Hall Rd. SW11 75 J3
Town Meadow, 64 G7
Brent.
Town Quay, Bark. 61 E1
Town Rd. N9 33 E2
Towncourt La., Orp. 97 G6
Towney Mead, Nthlt. 54 F2
Townholm Cres. W7 64 C3
Townley Ct. E15 51 F6
Townley Rd. SE22 77 B5
Townley Rd., Bexh. 80 F6
Townley St. SE17 21 B3
Townmead Rd. SW6 75 E3
Townmead Rd., Rich. 74 B2
Townsend Ave. N14 32 D4
Townsend Ind. Est. 56 C2
NW10
Townsend La. NW9 38 D7
Townsend Rd. N15 41 C5
Townsend Rd., Sthl. 63 E1
Townsend St. SE17 21 D1
Townsend St. SE17 68 A4
Townsends Yd. N6 49 A1
Townshend Clo., 89 B6
Sid.
Townshend Est. NW8 6 G1
Townshend Est. NW8 57 H2
Townshend Rd. NW8 57 H1
Townshend Rd., 88 E5
Chis.
Townshend Rd., 73 J4
Rich.
Townshend Ter., 73 J4
Rich.
Townson Ave., 54 A3
Nthlt.
Townson Way, Nthlt. 54 A2
Townson Ave.
Towton Rd. SE27 85 J2
Toynbec Clo., Chis. 88 E4
Beechwood Ri.
Toynbee Rd. SW20 93 B1
Toynbee St. E1 13 F2
Toynbee St. E1 59 C5
Toyne Way N6 39 J6
Gaskell Rd.
Tracey Ave. NW2 47 J5
Tracy Ct., Stan. 29 F7
Tradescant Rd. SW8 67 E7
Trading Est. Rd. 56 C4
NW10
Trafalgar Ave. N17 33 B6
Trafalgar Ave. SE15 21 G4
Trafalgar Ave. SE15 68 C5
Trafalgar Ave., 100 A1
Wor.Pk.
Trafalgar Business 61 J4
Cen., Bark.
Trafalgar Clo. SE16 68 H4
Greenland Quay
Trafalgar Gdns. E1 59 G5
Trafalgar Gro. SE10 69 D6
Trafalgar Pl. E11 42 G4
Trafalgar Pl. N18 33 D5
Trafalgar Rd. SE10 69 D6
Trafalgar Rd. SW19 84 E7
Trafalgar Rd., 82 A2
Twick.
Trafalgar Sq. WC2 15 J1
Trafalgar Sq. WC2 67 D1
Trafalgar St. SE17 21 B3
Trafalgar St. SE17 68 A5
Trafalgar Ter., 46 B1
Har.
Nelson Rd.
Trafalgar Way E14 69 C1
Trafalgar Way, 101 F2
Croy.
Trafford Clo. E15 51 B5
Trafford Clo., Ilf. 35 J6
Trafford Rd., 94 F5
Th.Hth.
Tramway Ave. E15 51 E7
Tramway Ave. N9 25 E7
Tramway Path, 93 H4
Mitch.
Tranby Pl. E9 50 G5
Homerton High St.
Tranley Ms. NW3 48 H5
Fleet Rd.

Tranmere Rd. N9 25 C7
Tranmere Rd. SW18 84 F1
Tranmere Rd., 72 H7
Twick.
Tranquil Pas. SE3 78 F2
Tranquil Vale
Tranquil Vale SE3 78 E2
Transay Wk. N1 50 A6
Marquess Rd.
Transept St. NW1 10 H2
Transept St. NW1 57 H5
Transmere Clo., 97 F6
Orp.
Transom Sq. E14 69 B4
Transport Ave., 64 D5
Brent.
Tranton Rd. SE16 17 J5
Tranton Rd. SE16 68 D3
Traps Hill, Loug. 27 C3
Traps La., N.Mal. 92 E1
Travellers Way, 72 C2
Houns.
Travers Clo. E17 41 G1
Travers Rd. N7 49 G3
Treacy Clo. 28 J2
(Bushey), Wat.
Treadgold St. W11 57 A7
Treadway St. E2 59 E2
Treaty St. N1 58 F1
Trebeck St. W1 15 D1
Trebovir Rd. SW5 66 D5
Treby St. E3 59 J4
Trecastle Way N7 49 D4
Carleton Rd.
Tredegar Ms. E3 59 J3
Tredegar Rd. E3 59 J2
Tredegar Rd. N11 32 D7
Tredegar Sq. E3 59 J3
Tredegar Ter. E3 59 J3
Trederwen Rd. E8 59 V1
Tredown Rd. SE26 86 F5
Tredwell Clo., 97 B4
Brom.
Tredwell Rd. SE27 85 H4
Tree Clo., Rich. 82 G1
Tree Rd. E16 60 J6
Treen Ave. SW13 74 E3
Treetops Clo. SE2 71 E5
Treeview Clo. SE19 95 B1
Treewall Gdns., 87 H4
Brom.
Trefgarne Rd., Dag. 53 G2
Trefil Wk. N7 49 E4
Trefoil Rd. SW18 75 F5
Tregaron Ave. N8 40 E6
Tregaron Gdns., 92 E4
N.Mal.
Avenue Rd.
Tregarvon Rd. SW11 76 A4
Tregenna Ave., Har. 45 F4
Tregenna Clo. N14 24 C5
Tregenna Ct., Har. 45 G4
Trego Rd. E9 51 A7
Tregothnan Rd. SW9 76 E3
Tregunter Rd. SW10 18 B5
Tregunter Rd. SW10 66 F6
Trehearn Rd., Ilf. 35 G7
Trehern Rd. SW14 74 D3
Treherne Ct. SW9 76 G1
Eythorne Rd.
Treherne Ct. SW17 85 A4
Trehurst St. E5 50 H5
Trelawn Rd. E10 51 C3
Trelawn Rd. SW2 76 G5
Trelawney Est. E9 50 F6
Trelawney Rd., Ilf. 35 G7
Trellick Twr. W10 57 C4
Trellis Sq. E3 59 J3
Malmesbury Rd.
Treloar Gdns. SE19 86 A6
Hancock Rd.
Tremadoc Rd. SW4 76 D4
Tremaine Clo. SE4 78 A2
Tremaine Rd. SE20 95 E2
Trematon Pl., Tedd. 82 F7
Tremlett Gro. N19 49 C3
Tremlett Ms. N19 49 C3
Junction Rd.
Trenance Gdns., 53 A3
Ilf.
Trench Yd. Ct., 93 E6
Mord.
Green La.
Trenchard Ave., 45 B4
Ruis.
Trenchard Clo., 29 D6
Stan.
Trenchard Ct., 93 E6
Mord.
Trenchard St. SE10 69 D5
Trenchold St. SW8 20 A6
Trenchold St. SW8 67 E6

Trenholme Clo. SE20 86 E7
Trenholme Rd. SE20 86 E7
Trenholme Ter. SE20 86 E7
Trenmar Gdns. 56 H3
NW10
Trent Ave. W5 64 F3
Trent Gdns. N14 24 B6
Trent Rd. SW2 76 F5
Trent Rd., Buck.H. 34 H1
Trent Way, Wor.Pk. 99 J3
Trentbridge Clo., 35 J6
Ilf.
Trentham St. SW18 84 D1
Trentwood Side, 24 F3
Enf.
Treport St. SW18 75 E7
Tresco Clo., Brom. 87 E6
Tresco Gdns., Ilf. 53 A2
Tresco Rd. SE15 77 E4
Trescoe Gdns., Har. 36 E7
Tresham Cres. NW8 6 G5
Tresham Cres. NW8 57 H4
Tresham Rd., Bark. 52 J7
Tresham Wk. E9 50 F5
Churchill Wk.
Tressell Clo. N1 49 H7
Sebbon St.
Tressillian Cres. SE4 78 A3
Tressillian Rd. SE4 77 J4
Trestis Clo., Hayes 54 E5
Jollys La.
Treswell Rd., Dag. 62 E1
Tretawn Gdns. NW7 30 F4
Tretawn Pk. NW7 30 E4
Trevanion Rd. W14 66 B4
Treve Ave., Har. 36 J7
Trevelyan Ave. E12 52 C4
Trevelyan Cres., 37 G7
Har.
Trevelyan Gdns. 56 J1
NW10
Trevelyan Rd. E15 51 F4
Trevelyan Rd. SW17 84 A5
Treveris St. SE1 16 H2
Treverton St. W10 57 B4
Treville St. SW15 74 H7
Treviso Rd. SE23 86 G2
Farren Rd.
Trevithick St. SE8 69 A6
Trevone Gdns., Pnr. 36 E6
Trevor Clo., Barn. 23 G6
Trevor Clo., Brom. 96 F7
Trevor Clo., Har. 29 C7
Kenton La.
Trevor Clo., Islw. 73 C5
Trevor Clo., Nthlt. 54 C2
Trevor Gdns., Edg. 38 D1
Trevor Gdns., 54 C2
Nthlt.
Trevor Pl. SW7 7 H4
Trevor Pl. SW7 66 H2
Trevor Rd. SW19 84 B7
Trevor Rd., Edg. 38 D1
Trevor Rd., 34 G7
Wdf.Grn.
Trevor Sq. SW7 10 J4
Trevor Sq. SW7 66 H3
Trevor St. SW7 7 H4
Trevor St. SW7 66 H2
Trevose Rd. E17 42 D7
Trevose Way, Wat. 28 C3
Trewenna Dr., 98 G5
Chess.
Trewince Rd. SW20 92 A1
Trewint St. SW18 84 F2
Trewsbury Rd. SE26 86 G5
Triandra Way, Hayes 54 D5
Triangle, The N13 32 G4
Triangle, The, 90 J1
Hmptn.
High St.
Triangle, The, 92 C2
Kings.T.
Kenley Rd.
Triangle Ct. E16 61 A5
Tollgate Rd.
Triangle Pas. 23 F4
Barn.
Station Rd.
Triangle Pl. SW4 76 D4
Triangle Rd. E8 59 E1
Trident Gdns., 54 D3
Nthlt.
Jetstar Way
Trident St. SE16 68 G4
Trident Way, Sthl. 63 B3
Trigon Rd. SW8 20 D7
Trigon Rd. SW8 67 F7
Trilby Rd. SE23 86 G2
Trimmer Wk., Brent. 64 H6
Netley Rd.
Trinder Gdns. N19 49 E1
Trinder Rd.

Trinder Rd. N19 49 E1
Trinder Rd., Barn. 22 J5
Tring Ave. W5 64 J1
Tring Ave., Sthl. 54 F6
Tring Ave., Wem. 47 A6
Tring Clo., Ilf. 43 G5
Trinidad St. E14 59 J7
Trinity Ave. N2 39 G3
Trinity Ave., Enf. 25 C6
Trinity Ch. Pas. 65 H6
SW13
Trinity Ch. Rd. 65 H6
SW13
Trinity Ch. Sq. SE1 17 A5
Trinity Ch. Sq. SE1 67 J3
Trinity Clo. E11 51 E2
Trinity Clo. NW3 48 G4
Hampstead High St.
Trinity Clo. SE13 78 D4
Wisteria Rd.
Trinity Clo., Brom. 104 B1
Trinity Clo., 72 E4
Houns.
Trinity Cotts., 73 J3
Rich.
Trinity Rd.
Trinity Ct. N1 50 B7
Downham Rd.
Trinity Ct. SE7 70 A4
Charlton La.
Trinity Cres. SW17 84 J2
Trinity Gdns. E16 60 F5
Trinity Gdns. SW9 76 F4
Trinity Gro. SE10 78 C1
Trinity Ms. W10 57 A6
Cambridge Gdns.
Trinity Pl., Bexh. 80 F4
Trinity Ri. SW2 85 G1
Trinity Rd. N2 39 G3
Trinity Rd. N22 32 E7
Whittington Rd.
Trinity Rd. SW17 84 J2
Trinity Rd. SW18 75 G5
Trinity Rd. SW19 84 D6
Trinity Rd., Ilf. 43 F3
Trinity Rd., Rich. 73 J3
Trinity Rd., Sthl. 63 E1
Trinity Sq. EC3 13 E6
Trinity Sq. EC3 59 B7
Trinity Sq. E16 60 G5
Vincent St.
Trinity St. SE1 17 A4
Trinity St. SE1 67 J2
Trinity St., Enf. 24 J2
Trinity Wk. NW3 48 F6
Trinity Way E4 33 J6
Trinity Way W3 56 E7
Trio Pl. SE1 17 A4
Tristan Ct. SE8 78 E3
Tristram Clo. E17 42 D3
Tristram Rd., Brom. 87 F4
Triton Sq. NW1 7 F5
Triton Sq. NW1 58 C4
Tritton Ave., Croy. 101 E4
Tritton Rd. SE21 86 A3
Triumph Ho., Bark. 62 A3
Triumph Rd. E6 61 C6
Trojan Way, Croy. 101 F3
White Horse Rd.
Trosley Rd., Belv. 71 G6
Trossachs Rd. SE22 77 B5
Trothy Rd. SE1 21 J2
Trott Rd. N10 31 J7
Trott St. SW11 75 G1
Trotwood, Chig. 35 G6
Troughton Rd. SE7 69 H5
Troutbeck Rd. SE14 77 H1
Trouville Rd. SW4 76 C6
Trowbridge Est. E9 50 J6
Trowbridge Rd. E9 50 J6
Trowlock Ave., 82 F6
Tedd.
Trowlock Way, 82 G6
Tedd.
Troy Ct. SE18 70 E4
Troy Rd. SE19 86 A6
Troy Town SE15 77 D3
Truesdale Rd. E6 61 C6
Trulock Rd. N17 33 D7
Trulock Rd. N17 33 D7
Truman Clo., Edg. 30 B7
Pavilion Way
Truman's Rd. N16 50 B5
Trump St. EC2 13 A4
Trumpers Way W7 64 B2
Trumpington Rd. E7 51 F4
Trundle St. SE1 16 J3
Trundlers Way 29 B1
(Bushey), Wat.
Trundleys Rd. SE8 68 G5
Trundleys Ter. SE8 68 G4
Truro Gdns., Ilf. 43 B7

Truro Rd. E17 41 J4
Truro Rd. N22 32 E7
Truro St. NW5 49 A6
Truslove Rd. SE27 85 G5
Trussley Rd. W6 65 J3
Trust Wk. SE21 85 H1
Peabody Hill
Tryfan Clo., Ilf. 43 A5
Tryon St. SW3 18 J3
Tryon St. SW3 66 J5
Trystings Clo., 98 D6
Esher
Tuam Rd. SE18 70 G6
Tubbenden Clo., 104 H2
Orp.
Tubbenden Dr., Orp. 104 G4
Tubbenden La., Orp. 104 G4
Tubbenden La. S., 104 G5
Orp.
Tubbs Rd. NW10 56 F2
Tudor Ave., Hmptn. 81 G6
Tudor Ave., Wor.Pk. 99 H3
Tudor Clo. N6 40 C7
Tudor Clo. NW3 48 H5
Tudor Clo. NW7 30 G6
Tudor Clo. NW9 47 C2
Tudor Clo. SW2 76 F6
Elm Pk.
Tudor Clo., Chess. 98 H5
Tudor Clo., Chig. 35 D4
Tudor Clo., Chis. 97 C1
Tudor Clo., Pnr. 36 A5
Tudor Clo., Sutt. 100 B6
Tudor Clo., Wall. 101 C7
Tudor Clo., 34 H5
Wdf.Grn.
Tudor Ct. E17 41 J7
Tudor Ct., Felt. 81 C4
Tudor Ct. N., Wem. 47 A5
Tudor Ct. S., Wem. 47 A5
Tudor Cres., Enf. 24 J1
Tudor Cres., Ilf. 35 E6
Tudor Dr., Kings.T. 82 G5
Tudor Dr., Mord. 93 A6
Tudor Est. NW10 56 B3
Tudor Gdns. NW9 47 C2
Tudor Gdns. SW13 74 E3
Treen Ave.
Tudor Gdns. W3 56 A5
Tudor Gdns., Twick. 82 C1
Tudor Gdns., 103 C3
W.Wick.
Tudor Gro. E9 50 F7
Tudor Pl. W1 11 H3
Tudor Pl., Mitch. 84 H7
Tudor Rd. E4 34 B6
Tudor Rd. E6 60 J1
Tudor Rd. E9 59 E1
Tudor Rd. N9 25 E7
Tudor Rd. SE19 86 C7
Tudor Rd. SE25 95 E5
Tudor Rd., Bark. 61 J1
Tudor Rd., Barn. 23 D3
Tudor Rd., Beck. 96 B3
Tudor Rd., Hmptn. 81 G7
Tudor Rd., Har. 37 A2
Tudor Rd., Houns. 73 A4
Tudor Rd., Kings.T. 83 A7
Tudor Rd., Pnr. 36 C2
Tudor Rd., Sthl. 54 E7
Tudor St. EC4 12 F5
Tudor St. EC4 58 G7
Tudor Wk., Bex. 80 E6
Tudor Way N14 32 D1
Tudor Way W3 65 A2
Tudor Way, Orp. 97 G6
Tudor Well Clo., 29 E5
Stan.
Tudway Rd. SE3 78 H3
Tufnell Pk. Rd. N7 49 D4
Tufnell Pk. Rd. N19 49 C4
Tufter Rd., Chig. 35 J5
Tufton Gdns., 90 H2
W.Mol.
Tufton Rd. E4 34 A4
Tufton St. SW1 16 B6
Tufton St. SW1 67 D3
Tugela Rd., Croy. 95 A6
Tugela St. SE6 86 J2
Tuilerie St. E2 9 H1
Tulip Clo., Croy. 102 G1
Tulip Clo., Hmptn. 81 F6
Partridge Rd.
Tulip Ct., Pnr. 36 C3
Tulse Clo., Beck. 96 C3
Tulse Hill SW2 76 G6
Tulse Hill Est. SW2 76 G6
Tulsemere Rd. SE27 85 J2
Tumbling Bay, Walt. 90 A6
Tummons Gdns. 95 B2
SE25
Tuncombe Rd. N18 33 B4
Tunis Rd. W12 65 H1

Tunley Rd. NW10 56 E1
Tunley Rd. SW17 85 A1
Tunmarsh La. E13 60 H3
Tunnanleys E6 61 D6
　Horse Leaze
Tunnel Ave. SE10 69 D2
Tunnel Gdns. N11 32 C7
Tunnel Rd. SE16 68 F2
　Church St.
Tunstall Clo., Orp. 104 H4
Tunstall Rd. SW9 76 F4
Tunstall Rd., Croy. 102 B1
Tunstall Wk. 64 H6
　Brent.
　Ealing Rd.
Tunstock Way, Belv. 71 E3
Tunworth Clo. NW9 38 C6
Tunworth Cres. 74 F6
　SW15
Turenne Clo. SW18 75 F4
Turin Rd. N9 25 F7
Turin St. E2 9 H4
Turin St. E2 59 D3
Turkey Oak Clo. 95 B1
　SE19
Turk's Head Yd. EC1 12 G1
Turks Row SW3 19 A3
Turks Row SW3 66 J5
Turle Rd. N4 49 F1
Turle Rd. SW16 94 E2
Turlewray Clo. N4 49 F1
Turley Clo. E15 60 E1
Turnagain La. EC4 12 G3
Turnage Rd., Dag. 53 E1
Turnberry Ct., Wat. 28 C3
Turnberry Quay E14 69 B3
　Pepper St.
Turnberry Way, 104 G1
　Orp.
Turnchapel Ms. SW4 76 B3
　Cedars Rd.
Turner Ave. N15 41 B4
Turner Ave., Mitch. 93 J1
Turner Ave., Twick. 81 J3
Turner Clo. NW11 39 E6
Turner Dr. NW11 39 E6
Turner Rd. E17 42 C3
Turner Rd., Edg. 37 H2
Turner Rd., N.Mal. 92 D7
Turner St. E1 59 E5
Turner St. E16 60 F6
Turners Meadow 95 J1
　Way, Beck.
Turners Rd. E3 59 J5
Turners Way, Croy. 101 G2
Turners Wd. NW11 48 F1
Turneville Rd. W14 66 C6
Turney Rd. SE21 76 J7
Turnham Grn. Ter. 65 E4
　W4
Turnham Grn. Ter. 65 E4
　Ms. W4
　Turnham Grn. Ter.
Turnham Rd. SE4 77 H5
Turnmill St. EC1 8 F6
Turnmill St. EC1 58 G4
Turnpike Clo. SE8 68 J7
　Amersham Vale
Turnpike Ho. EC1 8 H4
Turnpike La. N8 40 F4
Turnpike La., Sutt. 100 F5
Turnpike Link, 102 B2
　Croy.
Turnpin La. SE10 69 C6
Turnston Clo. NW9 38 E2
　Kestrel Clo.
Turnstone Clo. E13 60 G3
Turpentine La. SW1 19 E4
Turpin Way, Wall. 101 B7
Turpington Clo., 97 B6
　Brom.
Turpington La., 97 B7
　Brom.
Turpins La., 35 C5
　Wdf.Grn.
Turquand St. SE17 21 A2
Turret Gro. SW4 76 C3
Turton Rd., Wem. 46 H5
Turville St. E2 9 G5
Tuscan Rd. SE18 70 G5
Tuskar St. SE10 69 E5
Tustin Est. SE15 68 F6
Tuttlebee La., 34 G2
　Buck.H.
Tweedale St. E15 51 C5
Tweedale Rd., Cars. 100 G1
Tweedmouth Rd. E13 60 H2
Tweedy Rd., Brom. 96 G1
Tweezer's All. WC2 12 E5
Twelvetrees Cres. 60 C4
　E3
Twentyman Clo., 34 G5
　Wdf.Grn.

Twickenham Bri., 73 F5
　Rich.
Twickenham Bri., 73 F5
　Twick.
Twickenham Clo., 101 F3
　Croy.
Twickenham Gdns., 46 D5
　Grnf.
Twickenham Gdns., 29 B7
　Har.
Twickenham Rd. E11 51 D2
Twickenham Rd., 81 F3
　Felt.
Twickenham Rd., 73 D5
　Islw.
Twickenham Rd., 73 F5
　Rich.
Twickenham Rd., 82 D4
　Tedd.
Twickenham Trd. 73 C6
　Est., Twick.
Twilley St. SW18 75 E7
Twine Ct. E1 59 F7
Twineham Grn. N12 31 D4
　Tillingham Way
Twining Ave., 81 J3
　Twick.
Twinn Rd. NW7 31 B6
Twisden Rd. NW5 49 B4
Twybridge Way 47 C7
　NW10
Twyford Abbey Rd. 55 J3
　NW10
Twyford Ave. N2 39 J3
Twyford Ave. W3 56 A7
Twyford Cres. W3 65 A1
Twyford Pl. WC2 12 C3
Twyford Rd., Cars. 100 G1
Twyford Rd., Har. 45 H1
Twyford Rd., Ilf. 52 F5
Twyford St. N1 58 F1
Tyas Rd. E16 60 F4
Tybenham Rd. SW19 93 C3
Tyberry Rd., Enf. 25 E3
Tyburn La., Har. 37 B7
Tyburn Way W1 11 H4
Tycehurst Hill, 27 C4
　Loug.
Tye La., Orp. 104 F5
Tyers Est. SE1 17 D3
Tyers Est. SE1 68 B2
Tyers Gate SE1 17 D4
Tyers St. SE11 20 C4
Tyers St. SE11 67 F5
Tyers Ter. SE11 20 C4
Tyers Ter. SE11 67 F5
Tyeshurst Clo. SE2 71 E5
Tylecroft Rd. SW16 94 E2
Tylehurst Gdns., 52 F5
　Ilf.
Tyler Clo. E2 9 F1
Tyler Clo. E2 59 C2
Tyler St. SE10 69 E5
Tylers Clo., Loug. 27 B7
Tyler's Ct. W1 11 H4
Tylers Gate, Har. 37 H6
Tylers Path, Cars. 100 J4
Tynan Clo., Felt. 81 A1
　Sandycombe Rd.
Tyndale Ct. E14 69 B5
Tyndale La. N1 49 H7
　Upper St.
Tyndale Ter. N1 49 H7
　Tyndale La.
Tyndall Rd. E10 51 C2
Tyndall Rd., Well. 79 J3
Tyne St. E1 13 G3
Tyneham Rd. SW11 76 A2
Tynemouth Rd. N15 41 C4
Tynemouth Rd., 85 A7
　Mitch.
Tynemouth St. SW6 75 F2
Type St. E2 59 G2
Tyrawley Rd. SW6 75 E1
Tyrell Clo., Har. 46 B4
Tyrell Ct., Cars. 100 J4
Tyrell Sq., Mitch. 93 H1
Tyron Way, Sid. 88 H4
Tyrone Rd. E6 61 C2
Tyrrel Way NW9 38 F7
Tyrrell Ave., Well. 80 A5
Tyrrell Rd. SE22 77 D4
Tyrwhitt Rd. SE4 78 A3
Tysoe St. EC1 8 E4
Tyson Rd. SE23 77 F7
Tyssen Pas. E8 50 C6
　Tyssen Rd.
Tyssen Rd. N16 50 C3
Tyssen St. E8 50 C6

Tyssen St. N1 9 E2
Tytherton Rd. N19 49 D3

U

Uamvar St. E14 60 B5
Uckfield Gro., Mitch. 94 A1
Udall St. SW1 19 G2
Udney Pk. Rd., 82 D5
　Tedd.
Uffington Rd. NW10 56 G1
Uffington Rd. SE27 85 G4
Ufford Clo., Har. 28 H7
　Ufford Rd.
Ufford Rd., Har. 28 H7
Ufford St. SE1 16 F3
Ufford St. SE1 67 G2
Ufton Gro. N1 50 A7
Ufton Rd. N1 50 A7
Ujima Ct. SW16 85 E1
　Sunnyhill Rd.
Ullathorne Rd. SW16 85 C4
Ulleswater Rd. N14 32 E4
Ullin St. E14 60 C5
　St. Leonards Rd.
Ullswater Clo. SW15 83 D4
Ullswater Clo., 87 E7
　Brom.
Ullswater Cres. 83 D4
　SW15
Ullswater Rd. SE27 85 H2
Ullswater Rd. SW13 65 G7
Ulster Gdns. N13 32 J4
Ulster Pl. NW1 7 D6
Ulster Ter. NW1 7 D5
Ulundi Rd. SE3 69 E6
Ulva Rd. SW15 75 A5
　Ravenna Rd.
Ulverscroft Rd. 77 C5
　SE22
Ulverston Rd. E17 42 D2
Ulverstone Rd. SE27 85 H2
Ulysses Rd. NW6 48 C5
Umbria St. SW15 74 G6
Umfreville Rd. N4 40 H6
Undercliff Rd. SE13 78 A3
Underhill, Barn. 23 D5
Underhill Pas. NW1 58 B1
　Camden High St.
Underhill Rd. SE22 77 D5
Underhill St. NW1 58 B1
　Camden High St.
Underne Ave. N14 32 B2
Undershaft EC3 13 D4
Undershaft EC3 59 B6
Undershaw Rd., 87 F3
　Brom.
Underwood, Croy. 103 C5
Underwood, The 88 C2
　SE9
Underwood Rd. E1 9 H6
Underwood Rd. E1 59 D4
Underwood Rd. E4 34 B5
Underwood Rd., 34 J7
　Wdf.Grn.
Underwood Row N1 9 A3
Underwood Row N1 58 J3
Underwood St. N1 9 A3
Underwood St. N1 58 J3
Undine Rd. E14 69 B4
Undine St. SW17 84 J5
Uneeda Dr., Grnf. 55 A1
Union Cotts. E15 51 E7
　Hay Clo.
Union Ct. EC2 13 D3
Union Ct., Rich. 73 H5
　Eton St.
Union Dr. E1 59 H4
　Solebay St.
Union Gro. SW8 76 D2
Union Rd. N11 32 D6
Union Rd. SW4 76 D2
Union Rd. SW8 76 D2
Union Rd., Brom. 97 A5
Union Rd., Croy. 94 J7
Union Rd., Nthlt. 54 G2
Union Rd., Wem. 46 H6
Union Sq. N1 58 J1
Union St. E15 60 C1
Union St. SE1 16 H2
Union St. SE1 67 H1
Union St., Barn. 23 B4
Union St., Kings.T. 91 G2
Union Wk. E2 9 E3
Unity Clo. NW10 47 G6
Unity Way SE18 70 B3
University Clo. NW7 30 F7
University Pl., 71 H7
　Erith
　Belmont Rd.
University Rd. SW19 84 G6
University St. WC1 7 G6
University St. WC1 58 C4

Unwin Clo. SE15 21 H6
Unwin Clo. SE15 68 D6
Unwin Rd. SW7 14 E5
Unwin Rd., Islw. 73 B3
Upbrook Ms. W2 10 D4
Upcerne Rd. SW10 66 F7
Upchurch Clo. SE20 86 E7
Upcroft Ave., Edg. 30 C5
Updale Rd., Sid. 88 J4
Upfield, Croy. 102 E2
Upfield Rd. W7 55 C4
Upgrove Manor Way 76 G7
　SW2
　Trinity Rd.
Uphall Rd., Ilf. 52 E5
Upham Pk. Rd. W4 65 E4
Uphill Dr. NW7 30 E5
Uphill Dr. NW9 38 C5
Uphill Gro. NW7 30 E4
Uphill Rd. NW7 30 E4
Upland Rd. E13 60 F4
　Sutton Rd.
Upland Rd. SE22 77 D7
Upland Rd., Bexh. 80 F3
Upland Rd., S.Croy. 102 A5
Upland Rd., Sutt. 100 G6
Uplands, Beck. 96 A2
Uplands, The, 27 C3
　Loug.
Uplands, The, Ruis. 45 A1
Uplands Clo. SW14 74 B5
　Monroe Dr.
Uplands End, 35 B7
　Wdf.Grn.
Uplands Pk. Rd., 24 G3
　Enf.
Uplands Rd. E17 41 G2
　Blackhorse La.
Uplands Rd. N8 40 F5
Uplands Rd., Barn. 24 A7
Uplands Rd., Rom. 44 D3
Uplands Rd., 35 B7
　Wdf.Grn.
Uplands Trd. Est. 41 G3
　E17
Uplands Way N21 24 G5
Upney La., Bark. 52 H6
Upnor Way SE17 21 E3
Uppark Dr., Ilf. 43 F6
Upper Abbey Rd., 71 F4
　Belv.
Upper Addison Gdns. 66 B2
　W14
Upper Bardsey Wk. 49 J6
　N1
　Marquess Est.
Upper Belgrave St. 15 C5
　SW1
Upper Belgrave St. 67 A3
　SW1
Upper Berkeley St. 10 J4
　W1
Upper Berkeley St. 57 J6
　W1
Upper Beulah Hill 95 B1
　SE19
Upper Brighton Rd. 91 G6
　Surb.
Upper Brockley Rd. 77 J2
　SE4
Upper Brook St. W1 11 B6
Upper Brook St. W1 58 A7
Upper Butts, Brent. 64 F6
Upper Caldy Wk. N1 49 J6
　Marquess Est.
Upper Camelford Wk. 57 B6
　W11
　Lancaster Rd.
Upper Cavendish 39 D3
　Ave. N3
Upper Cheyne Row 18 G6
　SW3
Upper Cheyne Row 66 H6
　SW3
Upper Clapton Rd. 50 E1
　E5
Upper Clarendon Wk. 57 B6
　W11
　Lancaster Rd.
Upper Dengie Wk. N1 58 J1
　Popham Rd.
Upper Elmers End 95 H4
　Rd., Beck.
Upper Fern. Rd. 90 F4
　W.Mol.
Upper Fosters NW4 38 J5
　New Brent St.
Upper Grn. E., 93 J2
　Mitch.
Upper Grn. W., 93 J2
　Mitch.
Upper Grosvenor St. 11 B6
　W1

Upper Grosvenor St. W1	58	A7
Upper Grotto Rd., Twick.	82	C2
Upper Grd. SE1	**16**	**E1**
Upper Grd. SE1	67	G1
Upper Gro. SE25	95	B4
Upper Gro. Rd., Belv.	71	F6
Upper Gulland Wk. N1	49	J6
Marquess Est.		
Upper Ham Rd., Rich.	82	G4
Upper Handa Wk. N1	50	A6
Marquess Est.		
Upper Harley St. NW1	**7**	**C6**
Upper Harley St. NW1	58	A4
Upper Hawkwell Wk. N1	58	J1
Popham Rd.		
Upper Hitch, Wat.	28	E1
Upper Holly Hill Rd., Belv.	71	H5
Upper James St. W1	**11**	**G5**
Upper John St. W1	**11**	**G5**
Upper Lismore Wk. N1	49	J6
Marquess Est.		
Upper Mall W6	65	G5
Upper Marsh SE1	**16**	**D5**
Upper Marsh SE1	67	F2
Upper Montagu St. W1	**10**	**J1**
Upper Montagu St. W1	57	J5
Upper Mulgrave Rd., Sutt.	100	B7
Upper N. St. E14	60	A5
Upper Palace Rd., E.Mol.	90	J3
Upper Pk., Loug.	27	A4
Upper Pk. Rd. N11	32	B5
Upper Pk. Rd. NW3	48	J6
Upper Pk. Rd., Belv.	71	H4
Upper Pk. Rd., Brom.	96	H1
Upper Pk. Rd., Kings.T.	83	A6
Upper Phillimore Gdns. W8	66	D2
Upper Ramsey Wk. N1	50	A6
Marquess Est.		
Upper Rawreth Wk. N1	58	J1
Popham Rd.		
Upper Richmond Rd. SW15	74	F4
Upper Richmond Rd. W. SW14	74	D4
Upper Richmond Rd. W., Rich.	74	A4
Upper Rd. E13	60	G3
Upper Rd., Wall.	101	D5
Upper St. Martin's La. WC2	**12**	**A5**
Upper St. Martin's La. WC2	58	E7
Upper Selsdon Rd., S.Croy.	102	B7
Upper Sheppey Wk. N1	49	J7
Marquess Est.		
Upper Sheridan Rd., Belv.	71	G4
Coleman Rd.		
Upper Shirley Rd., Croy.	102	F2
Upper St. N1	49	H6
Upper Sunbury Rd., Hmptn.	90	E1
Upper Sutton La., Houns.	63	G7
Upper Tachbrook St. SW1	**19**	**G7**
Upper Tachbrook St. SW1	67	C4
Upper Tail, Wat.	28	E3
Upper Talbot Wk. W11	57	B6
Lancaster Rd.		
Upper Teddington Rd., Kings.T.	82	F7
Upper Ter. NW3	48	F3
Upper Thames St. EC4	**12**	**H5**
Upper Thames St. EC4	58	J7
Upper Tollington Pk. N4	40	G2

Upper Tooting Pk. SW17	84	J2
Upper Tooting Rd. SW17	84	J4
Upper Town Rd., Grnf.	54	H4
Upper Tulse Hill SW2	76	F7
Upper Vernon Rd., Sutt.	100	G5
Upper Walthamstow Rd. E17	42	D4
Upper Wickham La., Well.	80	B3
Upper Wimpole St. W1	**11**	**C1**
Upper Wimpole St. W1	58	A5
Upper Woburn Pl. WC1	**7**	**J4**
Upper Woburn Pl. WC1	58	D3
Upperton Rd., Sid.	88	J5
Upperton Rd. E. E13	60	J3
Inniskilling Rd.		
Upperton Rd. W. E13	60	J3
Uppingham Ave., Stan.	37	E1
Upsdell Ave. N13	32	G6
Upstall St. SE5	76	H1
Upton Ave. E7	51	G7
Upton Clo., Bex.	80	F6
Upton Dene, Sutt.	100	E7
Upton Gdns., Har.	37	E5
Upton La. E7	51	H6
Upton Pk. Rd. E7	51	H7
Upton Rd. N18	33	D5
Upton Rd. SE18	70	F6
Upton Rd., Bex.	80	F6
Upton Rd., Bexh.	80	E4
Upton Rd., Houns.	72	G3
Upton Rd., Th.Hth.	95	A2
Upton Rd. S., Bex.	80	F6
Upway N12	31	H7
Upwood Rd. SE12	78	G6
Upwood Rd. SW16	94	E1
Urlwin St. SE5	**35**	**J6**
Urlwin St. SE5	67	J6
Urlwin Wk. SW9	76	G1
Urmston Dr. SW19	84	B1
Ursula St. SW11	75	H1
Urswick Gdns., Dag.	53	E7
Urswick Rd.		
Urswick Rd. E9	50	F5
Urswick Rd., Dag.	53	D7
Usborne Ms. SW8	**20**	**D7**
Usborne Ms. SW8	67	F7
Usher Rd. E3	59	J2
Usk Rd. SW11	75	F4
Usk St. E2	59	G3
Utopia Village NW1	58	A1
Chalcot Rd.		
Uvedale Rd., Dag.	53	G3
Uvedale Rd., Enf.	25	A5
Uverdale Rd. SW10	66	F7
Uxbridge Gdns., Felt.	81	D2
Marlborough Rd.		
Uxbridge Rd. W3	65	A1
Uxbridge Rd. W5	55	J7
Uxbridge Rd. W7	64	C1
Uxbridge Rd. W12	65	G1
Uxbridge Rd., Felt.	61	C1
Uxbridge Rd., Hmptn.	81	G4
Uxbridge Rd., Har.	29	A7
Uxbridge Rd., Hayes	54	A6
Uxbridge Rd., Kings.T.	91	G4
Uxbridge Rd., Pnr.	36	C2
Uxbridge Rd., Sthl.	63	G1
Uxbridge Rd., Stan.	29	C6
Uxbridge St. W8	66	D7
Uxendon Cres., Wem.	41	H1
Uxendon Hill, Wem.	46	J1

V

Valan Leas, Brom.	96	E3
Valance Ave. E4	34	E1
Vale, The N10	40	A1
Vale, The N14	24	D7
Vale, The NW11	48	A3
Vale, The SW3	**18**	**E6**
Vale, The SW3	66	C6
Vale, The W3	65	D1
Vale, The, Croy.	102	G2
Vale, The, Felt.	72	B6
Vale, The, Houns.	63	E6
Vale, The, Ruis.	45	C4

Vale, The, Sun.	81	A6
Ashridge Way		
Vale, The, Wdf.Grn.	34	G7
Vale, Ave., Borwd.	22	B5
Vale Clo. W9	**6**	**C4**
Vale Clo., Orp.	104	D4
Vale Ct. W9	**6**	**C4**
Vale Cres. SW15	83	E3
Vale Cft., Pnr.	36	E5
Vale Dr., Barn.	23	C4
Vale End SE22	77	B4
Grove Vale		
Vale Gro. N4	40	J7
Vale Gro. W3	65	D1
The Vale		
Vale of Health NW3	48	G3
East Heath Rd.		
Vale Ri. NW11	48	C1
Vale Rd. E7	51	H6
Vale Rd. N4	40	J7
Vale Rd., Brom.	97	D2
Vale Rd., Epsom	99	F4
Vale Rd., Mitch.	94	D3
Vale Rd., Sutt.	100	E4
Vale Rd., Wor.Pk.	99	F3
Vale Rd. N., Surb.	98	H2
Vale Rd. S., Surb.	98	H2
Vale Row N5	49	H3
Gillespie Rd.		
Vale Royal N7	49	E7
Vale St. SE27	86	A3
Vale Ter. N4	40	H6
Valence Ave., Dag.	53	D1
Valence Circ., Dag.	53	D3
Valence Wd. Rd., Dag.	53	D3
Valencia Rd., Stan.	29	F4
Valentia Pl. SW9	76	G4
Brixton Sta. Rd.		
Valentine Ave., Bex.	89	E2
Valentine Ct. SE23	86	G2
Valentine Pl. SE1	**16**	**G3**
Valentine Pl. SE1	67	H2
Valentine Rd. E9	50	G6
Valentine Rd., Har.	45	J3
Valentine Row SE1	**16**	**G4**
Valentines Rd., Ilf.	52	E1
Valerian Way E15	60	E3
Valeswood Rd., Brom.	87	F5
Valetta Gro. E13	60	G2
Valetta Rd. W3	65	E2
Valette St. E9	50	E6
Valiant Clo., Nthlt.	54	D3
Ruislip Rd.		
Valiant Clo., Rom.	44	G2
Valiant Ho. SE7	69	J5
Valiant Way E6	61	C5
Vallance Rd. E1	**13**	**J1**
Vallance Rd. E1	59	D4
Vallance Rd. E2	**9**	**J5**
Vallance Rd. E2	59	D3
Vallance Rd. N22	40	C2
Vallentin Rd. E17	42	C4
Valley Ave. N12	31	G4
Valley Clo., Loug.	27	C6
Valley Clo., Pnr.	36	B2
Alandale Dr.		
Valley Dr. NW9	38	A6
Valley Flds. Cres., Enf.	24	G3
Valley Gdns. SW19	84	G7
Valley Gdns., Wem.	46	J7
Valley Gro. SE7	69	J5
Valley Hill, Loug.	27	B7
Valley Link Est., Enf.	25	H6
Valley Ms., Twick.	82	D2
Cross Deep		
Valley Rd. SW16	85	F5
Valley Rd., Belv.	71	H4
Valley Rd., Brom.	96	E2
Valley Side E4	34	A2
Valley Vw., Barn.	23	B6
Valley Wk., Croy.	102	F2
Valleyfield Rd. SW16	85	F5
Valliere Rd. NW10	56	G3
Valliers Wd. Rd., Sid.	88	G1
Vallis Way W13	55	D5
Vallis Way, Chess.	95	G4
Valmar Rd. SE5	76	J1
Valnay St. SW17	84	J5
Valognes Ave. E17	41	H1
Valonia Gdns. SW18	75	C6
Vambery Rd. SE18	70	F6
Van Dyck Ave., N.Mal.	92	D7

Vanbrough Cres., Nthlt.	54	C1
Vanbrugh Clo. E16	61	A5
Fulmer Rd.		
Vanbrugh Dr., Walt.	90	C7
Vanbrugh Flds. SE3	69	F6
Vanbrugh Hill SE3	69	F6
Vanbrugh Hill SE10	69	F6
Vanbrugh Pk. SE3	69	F7
Vanbrugh Pk. Rd. SE3	69	F7
Vanbrugh Pk. Rd. W. SE3	69	F7
Vanbrugh Rd. W4	65	D3
Vanbrugh Ter. SE3	78	F1
Vanburgh Clo., Orp.	104	H1
Vancouver Rd. SE23	86	H2
Vancouver Rd., Edg.	38	B3
Vancouver Rd., Hayes	54	B4
Vancouver Rd., Rich.	82	F4
Vanderbilt Rd. SW18	84	E1
Vandome Clo. E16	60	H6
Vandon Pas. SW1	**15**	**G5**
Vandon St. SW1	**15**	**G5**
Vandon St. SW1	67	C3
Vandy St. EC2	**9**	**D6**
Vandyke Clo. SW15	75	A6
Vandyke Cross SE9	79	B5
Vane Clo. NW3	48	G4
Vane Clo., Har.	37	J6
Vane St. SW1	**19**	**G1**
Vanessa Clo., Belv.	71	G5
Vanguard Clo., Croy.	101	H1
Vanguard Clo., Rom.	44	H2
Vanguard St. SE8	78	A1
Vanguard Way, Wall.	101	E7
Vanoc Gdns., Brom.	87	G4
Vansittart Rd. E7	51	F4
Vansittart St. SE14	68	H7
Vanston Pl. SW6	66	D7
Vant Rd. SW17	84	J5
Varcoe Rd. SE16	68	E5
Varden Clo. W3	56	D6
Varden St. E1	59	E6
Vardens Rd. SW11	75	G4
Vardon Clo. N3	39	B1
Claremont Pk.		
Varley Par. NW9	38	E4
Varley Rd. E16	60	H6
Varley Way, Mitch.	93	G2
Varna Rd. SW6	66	D7
Varna Rd., Hmptn.	90	H1
Varndell St. NW1	**7**	**F3**
Varndell St. NW1	58	C3
Vartry Rd. N15	41	A6
Vassall Rd. SW9	67	G7
Vauban Est. SE16	**17**	**G6**
Vauban Est. SE16	68	C3
Vauban St. SE16	**17**	**G6**
Vauban St. SE16	68	C3
Vaughan Ave. NW4	38	G5
Vaughan Ave. W6	65	F4
Vaughan Gdns., Ilf.	43	C7
Vaughan Rd. E15	51	F6
Vaughan Rd. SE5	76	J3
Vaughan Rd., Har.	36	J7
Vaughan Rd., T.Ditt.	91	E7
Vaughan Rd., Well.	79	J2
Vaughan Way E1	**13**	**H6**
Vaughan Way E1	59	D7
Vaughan Williams Clo. SE8	69	A7
Watson's St.		
Vauxhall Bri. SE1	**20**	**A4**
Vauxhall Bri. SE1	67	E5
Vauxhall Bri. SW1	**20**	**A4**
Vauxhall Bri. SW1	67	E5
Vauxhall Bri. Rd. SW1	**19**	**G1**
Vauxhall Bri. Rd. SW1	67	C3
Vauxhall Gdns., S.Croy.	101	J6
Vauxhall Gdns. Est. SE11	**20**	**D4**
Vauxhall Gdns. Est. SE11	67	F5
Vauxhall Gro. SW8	**20**	**B5**
Vauxhall Gro. SW8	67	F6
Vauxhall St. SE11	**20**	**D4**
Vauxhall St. SE11	67	F5
Vauxhall Wk. SE11	**20**	**C3**
Vauxhall Wk. SE11	67	F5
Vawdrey Clo. E1	59	F4
Veals Mead, Mitch.	93	H1
Vectis Gdns. SW17	85	B6
Vectis Rd.		
Vectis Rd. SW17	85	B6

Veda Rd. SE13 78 A4
Velde Way SE22 77 B5
East Dulwich Gro.
Velletri Ho. E2 59 G2
Mace St.
Vellicoe Rd. E13 60 G4
Jutland Rd.
Vellum Dr., Cars. 101 A3
Venables Clo., Dag. 53 H4
Venables St. NW8 **6 F6**
Venables St. NW8 57 G4
Vencourt Pl. W6 65 G4
Venetia Rd. N4 40 H4
Venetia Rd. W5 64 G2
Venetian Rd. SE5 76 J2
Venn St. SW4 76 C4
Venner Rd. SE26 86 F6
Ventnor Ave., Stan. 37 E1
Ventnor Dr. N20 31 E3
Ventnor Gdns., 52 H6
Bark.
Ventnor Rd. SE14 68 G7
Ventnor Rd., Sutt. 100 E7
Venture Clo., Har. 80 E7
Venue St. E14 60 C5
Venus Rd. SE18 70 C3
Vera Ave. N21 24 G5
Vera Lynn Clo. E7 51 G4
Dames Rd.
Vera Rd. SW6 75 B1
Verbena Gdns. W6 65 G5
Verdant La. SE6 87 E1
Verdayne Ave., 102 G1
Croy.
Verdun Rd. SE18 71 A6
Verdun Rd. SW13 65 G6
Vere Rd., Loug. 27 F4
Vere St. W1 **11 D4**
Vere St. W1 58 B6
Vereker Dr., Sun. 90 A3
Vereker Rd. W14 66 B5
Verity Clo. W11 57 B6
Vermont Rd. SE19 86 A6
Vermont Rd. SW18 75 E6
Vermont Rd., Sutt. 100 E3
Verney Gdns., Dag. 53 E4
Verney Rd. SE16 **21 J5**
Verney Rd. SE16 68 D6
Verney Rd., Dag. 53 E4
Verney St. NW10 47 D3
Verney Way SE16 68 E5
Vernham Rd. SE18 70 F6
Vernon Ave. E12 52 G4
Vernon Ave. SW20 93 A2
Vernon Ave., 34 H7
Wdf.Grn.
Vernon Clo., Epsom 99 C6
Vernon Ct., Stan. 37 E1
Vernon Dr.
Vernon Cres., Barn. 24 A6
Vernon Dr., Stan. 37 D1
Vernon Ms. E17 41 J4
Vernon Rd.
Vernon Ms. W14 66 B4
Vernon St.
Vernon Pl. WC1 **12 B2**
Vernon Pl. WC1 58 E5
Vernon Ri. WC1 **8 D3**
Vernon Ri. WC1 58 F3
Vernon Ri., Grnf. 46 A5
Vernon Rd. E3 59 J2
Vernon Rd. E11 51 E1
Vernon Rd. E15 51 E7
Vernon Rd. E17 41 J4
Vernon Rd. N8 40 G3
Vernon Rd. SW14 74 D3
Vernon Rd., Ilf. 52 J1
Vernon Rd., Sutt. 100 F5
Vernon Sq. WC1 **8 D3**
Vernon St. W14 66 B4
Vernon Yd. W11 57 C7
Portobello Rd.
Veroan Rd., Bexh. 80 E2
Verona Dr., Surb. 98 H2
Verona Rd. E7 51 G7
Upton La.
Veronica Gdns. SW16 94 C1
Veronica Rd. SW17 85 B3
Veronique Gdns., 43 F5
Ilf.
Verran Rd. SW12 76 B7
Balham Gro.
Versailles Rd. SE20 86 D7
Verulam Bldgs. WC1 **12 D1**
Verulam Ave. E17 41 J6
Verulam Rd., Grnf. 54 G4
Verulam St. WC1 **12 E1**
Verwood Rd., Har. 36 J2
Vesey Path E14 60 B6
East India Dock Rd.
Vespan Rd. W12 65 G2
Vesta Rd. SE4 77 H2
Vestris Rd. SE23 86 G2

Vestry Ms. SE5 77 B1
Vestry Rd. E17 42 B4
Vestry Rd. SE5 77 B1
Vestry St. N1 **9 B3**
Vestry St. N1 59 A3
Vevey St. SE6 86 J2
Veysey Gdns., Dag. 53 G3
Oglethorpe Rd.
Viaduct, The E18 42 G2
Viaduct Pl. E2 59 E3
Viaduct St.
Viaduct St. E2 59 E3
Vian St. SE13 78 B3
Vibart Gdns. SW2 76 F7
Vibart Wk. N1 58 E1
Outram Pl.
Vicarage Ave. SE3 69 G7
Vicarage Clo., 71 J6
Erith
Vicarage Clo., 54 F1
Nthlt.
Vicarage Ct. W8 **14 A3**
Vicarage Cres. SW11 75 G1
Vicarage Dr. SW14 74 D5
Vicarage Dr., Bark. 52 F7
Vicarage Fm. Rd., 72 E2
Houns.
Vicarage Flds., 90 C6
Walt.
Vicarage Gdns. W8 66 D1
Vicarage Gate
Vicarage Gdns., 93 H3
Mitch.
Vicarage Gate W8 **14 A3**
Vicarage Gate W8 66 E1
Vicarage Gro. SE5 77 A1
Vicarage La. E6 61 C3
Vicarage La. E15 51 E7
Vicarage La., Chig. 35 F2
Vicarage La., Ilf. 52 G1
Vicarage Pk. SE18 70 F5
Vicarage Path N8 40 D7
Vicarage Rd. E10 42 A7
Vicarage Rd. E15 51 F7
Vicarage Rd. N17 33 D7
Vicarage Rd. NW4 38 G6
Vicarage Rd. SE18 70 F5
Vicarage Rd. SW14 74 D5
Vicarage Rd., Bex. 89 H1
Vicarage Rd., Croy. 101 G3
Vicarage Rd., Dag. 53 H7
Vicarage Rd., 91 G2
Kings.T.
Vicarage Rd. 91 F1
(Hampton Wick),
Kings.T.
Vicarage Rd., Sutt. 100 E4
Vicarage Rd., Tedd. 82 D5
Vicarage Rd., 82 B2
Twick.
Vicarage Rd. 72 J6
(Whitton), Twick.
Vicarage Rd., 35 B7
Wdf.Grn.
Vicarage Way NW10 47 D3
Vicarage Way, Har. 36 G7
Vicars Bri. Clo., 55 H2
Wem.
Vicars Clo. E9 59 F1
Victoria Pk. Rd.
Vicars Clo. E15 60 G1
Vicars Clo., Enf. 25 B2
Vicars Hill SE13 78 B4
Vicars Moor La. N21 24 G7
Vicars Oak Rd. SE19 86 B6
Vicars Rd. NW5 49 A5
Vicars Wk., Dag. 53 B3
Viceroy Clo. N2 39 H4
Market Pl.
Viceroy Ct. NW8 **6 H1**
Viceroy Rd. SW8 76 E1
Vickers Way, Houns. 72 E5
Victor Gro., Wem. 46 H7
Victor Rd. NW10 56 H2
Victor Rd. SE20 86 G7
Victor Rd., Har. 36 J3
Victor Rd., Tedd. 82 B4
Victor Vill. N9 33 A3
Victoria Ave. E6 61 A1
Victoria Ave. EC2 **13 E2**
Victoria Ave. N3 39 C1
Victoria Ave., 23 G4
Barn.
Victoria Rd.
Victoria Ave., 72 F5
Houns.
Victoria Ave., 91 G6
Surb.
Victoria Ave., 101 A3
Wall.
Victoria Ave., Wem. 47 B6
Victoria Ave., 90 G3
W.Mol.

Victoria Clo., 23 G4
Barn.
Victoria Clo., 90 G3
W.Mol.
Victoria Ave.
Victoria Cotts., 73 J1
Rich.
Victoria Ct., Wem. 47 A6
Victoria Cres. N15 41 B5
Victoria Cres. SE19 86 B6
Victoria Cres. SW19 84 C7
Victoria Dock Rd. 60 G7
E16
Victoria Dr. SW19 75 D7
Victoria Embk. EC4 **12 E5**
Victoria Embk. EC4 58 G7
Victoria Embk. SW1 **16 B3**
Victoria Embk. SW1 67 E2
Victoria Embk. WC2 **12 D6**
Victoria Embk. WC2 58 F7
Victoria Gdns. W11 66 D1
Victoria Gdns., 72 E1
Houns.
Victoria Gro. N12 31 G5
Victoria Gro. W8 **14 C5**
Victoria Gro. W8 66 F3
Victoria Ind. Est. 56 E3
NW10
Victoria La., Barn. 23 C4
Victoria Ms. NW6 57 D1
Victoria Ms. SW4 76 B4
Victoria Ri.
Victoria Pk. E9 59 H1
Victoria Pk. Rd. E9 59 F1
Victoria Pk. Sq. E2 59 F3
Victoria Pas. NW8 **6 E5**
Victoria Pl., Rich. 73 G5
Victoria Pt. E13 60 G2
Victoria Rd.
Victoria Ri. SW4 76 B3
Victoria Rd. E4 34 E1
Victoria Rd. E11 51 E4
High Rd. Leytonstone
Victoria Rd. E13 60 G2
Victoria Rd. E17 42 C2
Victoria Rd. E18 42 H2
Victoria Rd. N4 40 F7
Victoria Rd. N9 33 C3
Victoria Rd. N15 41 D4
Victoria Rd. N18 33 C4
Victoria Rd. N22 40 C1
Victoria Rd. NW4 38 J4
Victoria Rd. NW6 57 C2
Victoria Rd. NW7 30 F5
Victoria Rd. NW10 56 E4
Victoria Rd. SW14 74 D3
Victoria Rd. W3 56 D5
Victoria Rd. W5 55 E5
Victoria Rd. W8 **14 C4**
Victoria Rd. W8 66 F2
Victoria Rd., Bark. 52 E6
Victoria Rd., Barn. 23 G4
Victoria Rd., Bexh. 80 G4
Victoria Rd., Brom. 97 A5
Victoria Rd., 35 A2
Buck.H.
Victoria Rd., Chis. 88 D5
Victoria Rd., Dag. 53 H5
Victoria Rd., Felt. 81 B1
Victoria Rd., 91 J2
Kings.T.
Victoria Rd., 84 H7
Mitch.
Victoria Rd., Ruis. 45 A1
Victoria Rd., Sid. 88 J3
Victoria Rd., Sthl. 63 F3
Victoria Rd., Surb. 91 G6
Victoria Rd., Sutt. 100 G5
Victoria Rd., Tedd. 82 D6
Victoria Rd., 73 E7
Twick.
Victoria Rd. 28 H1
(Bushey), Wat.
Victoria Sq. SW1 **15 E5**
Victoria Sta. SW1 **19 E1**
Victoria Sta. SW1 67 B4
Victoria Steps, 64 J6
Brent.
Kew Bri. Rd.
Victoria St. E15 51 E7
Victoria St. SW1 **15 F6**
Victoria St. SW1 67 C3
Victoria St., Belv. 71 F5
Victoria Ter. N4 49 G1
Victoria Ter., Har. 46 B1
Victoria Vill., 73 J3
Rich.
Victoria Way SE7 69 H5
Victorian Gro. N16 50 B4
Victorian Rd. N16 50 B3
Victors Dr., Hmptn. 81 E6
Victors Way, Barn. 23 C3
Victory Ave., Mord. 93 F5

Victory Business 73 C4
Cen., Islw.
Victory Pl. SE17 **21 A1**
Victory Pl. SE17 67 J4
Victory Pl. SE19 86 B6
Westow St.
Victory Rd. SW19 84 F7
Victory Rd., Rain. 63 C5
Victory Way, Houns. 63 C5
Victory Way, Rom. 44 H2
Vienna Clo., Ilf. 43 B2
Coburg Gdns.
View, The SE2 71 E5
View Clo. N6 39 J7
View Clo., Chig. 35 G5
View Clo., Har. 37 A4
View Rd. N6 39 J7
Viewfield Clo., 37 H7
Har.
Viewfield Rd. SW18 75 C6
Viewfield Rd., Bex. 89 C1
Viewland Rd. SE18 70 J5
Viga Rd. N21 24 G6
Vigilant Clo. SE26 86 D4
Vignoles Rd., Rom. 44 G7
Vigo Rd. W1 **11 F6**
Vigo St. W1 58 C7
Viking Clo. E3 59 H2
Selwyn Rd.
Viking Ct. SW6 66 D6
Viking Rd., Sthl. 54 E7
Viking Way, Belv. 71 J3
Villa Rd. SW9 76 G3
Villa St. SE17 **21 C4**
Villa St. SE17 68 A5
Villacourt Rd. SE18 71 A7
Village, The SE7 69 J6
Village Arc. E4 34 D1
Station Rd.
Village Clo. E4 34 C5
Village Heights, 34 F5
Wdf.Grn.
Village Ms. NW9 47 D2
Village Rd. N3 39 B2
Village Rd., Enf. 25 A7
Village Row, Sutt. 100 D7
Village Way NW10 47 D4
Village Way SE21 77 A6
Village Way, Beck. 96 A3
Village Way, Pnr. 36 E7
Village Way E., 36 G7
Har.
Villas Rd. SE18 70 F4
Villiers Ave., 91 J5
Surb.
Villiers Ave., 81 F1
Twick.
Villiers Clo. E10 51 A2
Villiers Clo., 91 J4
Surb.
Villiers Ct. N20 23 F7
Buckingham Ave.
Villiers Path, 91 H5
Surb.
Villiers Rd. NW2 47 G6
Villiers Rd., Beck. 95 G2
Villiers Rd., Islw. 73 B2
Villiers Rd., 91 J4
Kings.T.
Villiers Rd., Sthl. 63 F1
Villiers St. WC2 **16 B1**
Villiers St. WC2 67 E1
Vincam Clo., Twick. 72 G7
Vince St. EC1 **9 C4**
Vince St. EC1 59 A3
Vincent Ave., Surb. 99 B1
Vincent Clo. SE16 68 H2
Vincent Clo., Barn. 23 E3
Vincent Clo., Brom. 96 H4
Vincent Clo., Ilf. 38 H1
Vincent Gdns. NW2 47 F3
Vincent Rd. E4 34 D6
Vincent Rd. N15 40 J4
Vincent Rd. N22 40 G2
Vincent Rd. SE18 70 E4
Vincent Rd. W3 65 C3
Vincent Rd., Croy. 95 B7
Vincent Rd., Dag. 53 E7
Vincent Rd., Houns. 72 D2
Vincent Rd., Islw. 73 A1
Vincent Rd., 92 A3
Kings.T.
Vincent Rd., Wem. 46 J7
Vincent Row, Hmptn. 81 J6
Vincent Sq. SW1 **19 H1**
Vincent Sq. SW1 67 C4
Vincent St. E16 60 F5
Vincent St. SW1 **19 H1**
Vincent St. SW1 67 D4
Vincent Ter. N1 **8 G1**

Vincent Ter. N1 58 H2
Vine Clo., Surb. 91 J6
Vine Clo., Sutt. 100 F3
Vine Ct. E1 13 J2
Vine Pl., Har. 37 H6
Vine Gdns., Ilf. 52 F5
Vine Hill EC1 8 E6
Vine La. SE1 17 E2
Vine Pl. W5 64 H1
The Common
Vine Pl., Houns. 72 H4
Vine Rd. E15 51 F7
Vine Rd. SW13 74 F3
Vine Rd., E.Mol. 90 J4
Vine Rd., Orp. 104 J6
Vine Sq. W14 66 C5
Vine St. EC3 13 F4
Vine St. W1 11 G6
Vine St., Rom. 44 J4
Vine St. Bri. EC1 8 F6
Vine St. Bri. EC1 58 G4
Vine Yd. SE1 17 A4
Vinegar All. E17 42 B4
Vinegar St. E1 68 E1
Reardon Path
Vinegar Yd. SE1 17 D3
Viner Clo., Walt. 90 C6
Vineries, The N14 24 C5
Vineries, The, Enf. 25 B3
Vineries Bank NW7 30 H5
Vineries Clo., Dag. 53 G6
Heathway
Vinson Ave. N9 20 E1
Viney Rd. SE13 78 B3
Vineyard, The, 73 H5
Rich.
Vineyard Ave. NW7 31 B7
Vineyard Clo. SE6 87 A1
Vineyard Hill Rd. 84 C4
SW19
Vineyard Pas., Rich. 73 H5
Paradise Rd.
Vineyard Path SW14 74 D3
Vineyard Rd., Felt. 81 A3
Vineyard Row, 91 F1
Kings.T.
Vineyard Wk. EC1 8 E5
Vining St. SW9 76 G4
Vintners Pl. EC4 13 A5
Viola Ave. SE2 71 B4
Viola Ave., Felt. 72 C6
Viola Sq. W12 56 F7
Violet Clo., Wall. 101 A1
Violet Gdns., Croy. 101 H5
Violet Hill NW8 6 C2
Violet Hill NW8 57 F2
Violet La., Croy. 101 H6
Violet Rd. E3 60 B4
Violet Rd. E17 42 A6
Violet Rd. E18 42 H2
Violet St. E2 59 E4
Three Colts La.
Virgil Pl. W1 10 J2
Virgil St. SE1 16 D5
Virgil St. SE1 67 F3
Virginia Clo., 92 C4
N.Mal.
Willow Rd.
Virginia Rd. E2 9 F4
Virginia Rd. E2 59 C3
Virginia Rd., 94 H1
Th.Hth.
Virginia St. E1 13 J6
Virginia St. E1 59 D7
Virginia Wk. SW2 76 F6
Beechdale Rd.
Viscount Dr. E6 61 C5
Viscount Gro., 54 D3
Nthlt.
Wayfarer Rd.
Viscount St. EC1 12 J1
Vista, The SE9 79 A6
Vista, The, Sid. 88 J5
Langdon Shaw
Vista Ave., Enf. 25 G2
Vista Dr., Ilf. 43 A5
Vista Way, Har. 37 H6
Vivian Ave. NW4 38 G5
Vivian Ave., Wem. 47 A5
Vivian Clo., Wat. 28 A1
Vivian Gdns., Wat. 28 A1
Vivian Gdns., Wem. 47 A5
Vivian Rd. E3 59 H2
Vivian Sq. SE15 77 E3
Scylla Rd.
Vivian Way N2 39 G5
Vivien Clo., Chess. 98 H7
Vivienne Clo., 73 G6
Twick.
Voce Rd. SE18 70 G7
Voewood Clo., 92 F6
N.Mal.

Volta Way, Croy. 101 F1
Voltaire Rd. SW4 76 D3
Voluntary Pl. E11 42 G6
Vorley Rd. N19 49 C2
Voss Ct. SW16 85 E6
Voss St. E2 9 J4
Voss St. E2 59 D3
Vulcan Clo., Wall. 101 F7
De Havilland Rd.
Vulcan Gate, Enf. 24 G3
Vulcan Rd. SE4 77 J2
Vulcan Ter. SE4 77 J2
Vulcan Way N7 49 F6
Vyne, The, Bexh. 80 H3
Vyner Rd. W3 56 D7
Vyner St. E2 59 E1
Vyse Rd., Barn. 22 J4

W

Wadding St. SE17 21 B2
Wadding St. SE17 68 A4
Waddington Rd. E15 51 D5
Waddington St. E15 51 D6
Waddington Way 85 J7
SE19
Waddon Clo., Croy. 101 G3
Waddon Ct. Rd., 101 G4
Croy.
Waddon Marsh Way,101 F1
Croy.
Waddon New Rd., 101 H3
Croy.
Waddon Pk. Ave., 101 G3
Croy.
Waddon Rd., Croy. 101 G3
Waddon Way, Croy. 101 G6
Wade Rd. E16 60 J6
Leyes Rd.
Wades Gro. N21 24 G7
Wades Hill N21 24 G6
Wades La., Tedd. 82 D5
High St.
Wades Ms. N21 24 G7
Wades Hill
Wades Pl. E14 60 B7
Wadeson St. E2 59 E2
Wadeville Ave., 44 F6
Rom.
Wadeville Clo., 71 G5
Belv.
Wadham Ave. E17 34 B7
Wadham Gdns. NW3 48 H7
Wadham Gdns., Grnf. 46 A6
Wadham Rd. E17 42 B1
Wadham Rd. SW15 75 B4
Wadhurst Clo. SE20 95 E2
Wadhurst Rd. W4 65 D3
Wadhurst Rd. SW8 76 C1
Wadley Rd. E11 42 E7
Wadsworth Clo., 25 G5
Enf.
Falcon Rd.
Wadsworth Clo., 55 F2
Grnf.
Wadsworth Rd., 55 E2
Grnf.
Wager St. E3 59 J4
Waghorn Rd. E13 60 J1
Waghorn Rd., Har. 37 G3
Waghorn St. SE15 77 D3
Wagner St. SE15 68 F7
Wagtail Clo. NW9 38 E2
Swan Dr.
Waights Ct., 91 H1
Kings.T.
Wainfleet Ave., 44 J2
Rom.
Wainford Clo. SW19 84 A1
Windlesham Gro.
Wainwright Gro., 73 A4
Islw.
Waite Davies Rd. 78 F7
SE12
Waite St. SE15 21 F5
Waite St. SE15 68 C6
Waithman St. EC4 12 G4
Wakefield Gdns. 86 B7
SE19
Wakefield Gdns., 43 B6
Ilf.
Wakefield Ms. WC1 8 B4
Wakefield Rd. N11 32 D5
Wakefield Rd. N15 41 C5
Wakefield Rd., 73 G5
Rich.
Wakefield St. E6 61 A1
Wakefield St. N18 33 D5
Wakefield St. WC1 8 B4
Wakefield St. WC1 58 E3
Wakeham St. N1 50 A6
Wakehams Hill, Pnr. 36 F3
Wakehurst Rd. SW11 75 H5

Wakelin Rd. E15 60 E2
Wakeling Rd. W7 55 C5
Templeman Rd.
Wakeling St. E14 59 H6
Wakeman Rd. NW10 56 J3
Wakemans Hill Ave. 38 D5
NW9
Wakering Rd., Bark. 52 F6
Wakerley Clo. E6 61 C6
Truesdale Rd.
Wakley St. EC1 8 G3
Wakley St. EC1 58 H3
Walberswick St. SW8 67 E7
Walbrook EC4 13 B5
Walbrook EC4 59 A7
Walbrook Ho. N9 33 F2
Walburgh St. E1 59 E6
Bigland St.
Walcorde Ave. SE17 21 A2
Walcot Rd., Enf. 25 J2
Walcot Sq. SE11 20 F1
Walcot Sq. SE11 67 G4
Walcott St. SW1 19 G1
Waldeck Gro. SE27 85 H3
Waldeck Rd. N15 40 H4
Waldeck Rd. SW14 74 C3
Lwr. Richmond Rd.
Waldeck Rd. W4 65 A6
Waldeck Rd. W13 55 E6
Waldegrave Ave., 82 C5
Tedd.
Waldegrave Rd.
Waldegrave Gdns., 82 C2
Twick.
Waldegrave Pk., 82 C4
Twick.
Waldegrave Rd. N8 40 G3
Waldegrave Rd. SE19 86 C7
Waldegrave Rd. W5 55 J7
Waldegrave Rd., 97 B4
Brom.
Waldegrave Rd., 53 C2
Dag.
Waldegrave Rd., 82 C4
Tedd.
Waldegrave Rd., 82 C2
Twick.
Waldegrove, Croy. 102 C3
Waldemar Ave. SW6 75 B1
Waldemar Ave. W13 64 F1
Waldemar Rd. SW19 84 D5
Walden Ave. N13 32 J4
Walden Ave., Chis. 88 C4
Walden Clo., Belv. 71 F5
Walden Gdns., 94 F4
Th.Hth.
Walden Rd. N17 41 A1
Walden Rd., Chis. 88 C6
Walden St. E1 59 E6
Walden Way NW7 31 A6
Walden Way, Ilf. 35 H7
Waldenshaw Rd. 86 F1
SE23
Waldo Clo. SW4 76 C5
Waldo Pl., Mitch. 84 H1
Waldo Rd. NW10 56 G3
Waldo Rd., Brom. 97 A3
Waldram Cres. SE23 86 F1
Waldram Pk. Rd. 86 G1
SE23
Waldram Pl. SE23 86 F1
Waldrist Way, Erith 71 F2
Waldron Gdns., 96 D3
Brom.
Waldron Ms. SW3 18 F5
Waldron Rd. SW18 84 F3
Waldron Rd., Har. 46 B1
Waldronhyrst, 101 H4
S.Croy.
Waldrons, The, 101 H4
Croy.
Waleran Clo., Stan. 29 C6
Chenduit Way
Waleran Rd SE13 78 C2
Wales Ave., Cars. 100 H5
Wales Fm. Rd. W3 56 D5
Waley St. E1 59 H5
Walfield Ave. N20 23 E7
Walford Rd. N16 50 B4
Walfrey Gdns., Dag. 53 E7
Walham Gro. SW6 66 C5
Walham Ri. SW19 84 B6
Walham Yd. SW6 66 D7
Walham Gro.
Walkden Rd., Chis. 88 D5
Walker Clo. N11 32 C4
Walker Clo. SE18 70 F4
Walker Clo. W7 64 B1
Walker Clo., Hmptn. 81 F6
Fearnley Cres.
Walkers Ct. E8 50 D6
Wilton Way

Walkers Ct. W1 11 H5
Walkers Pl. SW15 75 B3
Felsham Rd.
Walkerscroft Mead 85 J1
SE21
Walkford Way SE15 68 C7
Daniel Gdns.
Walks, The N2 39 G3
Wall End Rd. E6 52 D7
Wall St. N1 50 A6
Wallace Clo. SE28 62 D7
Haldane Rd.
Wallace Cres., 100 J5
Cars.
Wallace Rd. N1 49 J6
Wallbutton Rd. SE4 77 H2
Wallcote Ave. NW2 48 A1
Waller Dr., Nthwd. 36 A2
Waller Rd. SE14 77 G1
Wallers Clo., Dag. 62 E1
Wallers Clo., 35 C5
Wdf.Grn.
Waller's Hoppit, 27 B2
Loug.
Wallflower St. W12 56 F7
Wallgrave Rd. SW5 18 A1
Wallgrave Rd. SW5 66 E4
Wallingford Ave. 57 A5
W10
Wallington Rd., 43 J7
Ilf.
Wallis All. SE1 17 A4
Wallis Clo. SW11 75 G2
Wallis Rd. E9 50 J6
Wallis Rd., Sthl. 54 H6
Walliss Cotts. SW2 76 E7
Wallorton Gdns. 74 D4
SW14
Wallwood Rd. E11 51 D1
Wallwood St. E14 59 J5
Walm La. NW2 47 J6
Walmar Clo., Barn. 23 G1
Walmer Clo. E4 34 B2
Walmer Clo., Rom. 44 H2
Walmer Gdns. W13 64 D2
Walmer Ho. N9 33 C1
Walmer Pl. W1 10 J1
Walmer Rd. W10 57 B7
Walmer Rd. W11 57 B7
Walmer St. W1 10 J1
Walmer Ter. SE18 70 F4
Walmgate Rd., Grnf. 55 E1
Walmington Fold 31 D6
N12
Walney Wk. N1 49 J6
Clephane Rd.
Walnut Clo. SE8 68 J6
Clyde St.
Walnut Clo., Cars. 100 J5
Walnut Clo., Ilf. 43 F4
Civic Way
Walnut Ct. W5 64 H2
Walnut Gro., E15 51 E4
Burgess Rd.
Walnut Gro., Enf. 25 A5
Walnut Ms., Sutt. 100 F7
Walnut Tree Ave. 93 H3
Mitch.
Dearn Gdns.
Walnut Tree Clo. 74 F1
SW13
Walnut Tree Clo., 97 F1
Chis.
Walnut Tree Rd. 69 E5
SE10
Walnut Tree Rd., 64 H6
Brent.
Walnut Tree Rd., 53 D2
Dag.
Walnut Tree Rd., 63 F6
Houns.
**Walnut Tree Wk. 20 E1
SE11**
Walnut Tree Wk. 67 G4
SE11
Walnut Way, Buck.H. 35 A3
Walnut Way, Ruis. 45 C6
Walpole Ave., Rich. 73 J2
Walpole Clo. W13 64 F2
Walpole Clo., Pnr. 28 G6
Walpole Cres., 82 C5
Tedd.
Walpole Gdns. W4 65 C5
Walpole Gdns., 82 B2
Twick.
Walpole Pk. W5 64 F1
Walpole Pl., Tedd. 82 C5
Walpole Rd. E6 51 J7
Walpole Rd. E17 41 H4
Walpole Rd. E18 42 F1
Walpole Rd. N17 40 J3
Walpole Rd. N17 40 J2
Walpole Rd. SW19 84 G6

Walpole Rd., Brom. 97 A5
Walpole Rd., Croy. 102 A2
Walpole Rd., Surb. 91 H7
Walpole Rd., Tedd. 82 C5
Walpole Rd., Twick. 82 B2
Walpole St. SW3 18 J3
Walpole St., Wem. 66 J5
Walrond Ave., Wem. 46 H5
Walsham Clo. N16 41 D7
Braydon Rd.
Walsham Clo. SE28 62 D7
Walsham Rd. SE14 77 G2
Walsham Rd., Felt. 72 B7
Walsingham Gdns., 99 E4
Epsom
Walsingham Pk., 97 G2
Chis.
Walsingham Rd. E5 50 D3
Walsingham Rd. 64 D1
W13
Walsingham Rd., 25 A4
Enf.
Walsingham Rd., 93 J5
Mitch.
Walsingham Wk., 71 G6
Belv.
Walter St. E2 59 G3
Walter St., Kings.T. 91 H1
Sopwith Way
Walter Ter. E1 59 G6
Walter Wk., Edg. 30 C6
Walters Ho. SE17 20 G6
Walters Rd. SE25 95 B4
Walters Rd., Enf. 25 F5
Walters Way SE23 77 G6
Walters Yd., Brom. 96 G2
Walterton Rd. W9 57 C4
Waltham Ave. NW9 38 A6
Waltham Dr., Edg. 38 A2
Waltham Pk. Way 42 A1
E17
Waltham Rd., Cars. 93 G7
Waltham Rd., Sthl. 63 E3
Waltham Rd., 35 B6
Wdf.Grn.
Waltham Way E4 33 J4
Walthamstow Ave. 33 H5
E4
Walthamstow 42 C2
Business Cen. E17
Waltheof Ave. N17 41 A1
Waltheof Gdns. N17 41 A1
Walton Ave., Har. 45 F5
Walton Ave., N.Mal. 92 F4
Walton Ave., Sutt. 100 B3
Walton Clo. E5 50 G3
Orient Way
Walton Clo. NW2 47 H2
Walton Clo. SW8 20 B7
Walton Clo. SW8 67 E7
Walton Clo., Har. 37 A4
Walton Cres., Har. 45 F4
Walton Dr. NW10 47 D6
Mitchellbrook Way
Walton Dr., Har. 37 A4
Walton Gdns. W3 56 B5
Walton Gdns., Wem. 46 H2
Walton Pl. SW3 14 J5
Walton Rd. E12 52 D4
Walton Rd. E13 60 J2
Walton Rd. N15 41 C4
Walton Rd., E.Mol. 90 E4
Walton Rd., Har. 37 A4
Walton Rd., Sid. 89 C2
Walton Rd., Walt. 90 C5
Walton Rd., W.Mol. 90 E4
Walton St. SW3 18 H1
Walton St. SW3 66 H4
Walton St., Enf. 25 A1
Walton Way W3 56 B5
Walton Way, Mitch. 94 C4
Walworth Pl. SE17 21 A4
Walworth Pl. SE17 67 J5
Walworth Rd. SE1 20 J2
Walworth Rd. SE1 67 J4
Walworth Rd. SE17 20 J2
Walworth Rd. SE17 67 J4
Walwyn Ave., Brom. 97 A3
Wanborough Dr. 83 H1
SW15
Wandle Bank SW19 84 G7
Wandle Bank, Croy. 101 E3
Wandle Ct., Epsom 99 C4
Wandle Ct. Gdns., 101 E3
Croy.
Wandle Rd. SW17 84 H2
Wandle Rd., Croy. 101 J3
Wandle Rd. 101 E3
(Waddon), Croy.
Wandle Rd., Mord. 93 F4
Wandle Rd., Wall. 101 B2
Wandle Side, Croy. 101 F3

Wandle Side, Wall. 101 B3
Wandle Way SW18 84 E1
Wandle Way, Mitch. 93 J5
Wandon Rd. SW6 66 E7
Wandsworth Bri. 75 E3
SW6
Wandsworth Bri. 75 E3
SW18
Wandsworth Bri. Rd. 75 E1
SW6
Wandsworth 55 F2
Business Cen., Grnf.
Wandsworth 75 J7
Common SW12
Wandsworth 75 F5
Common (North Side)
SW18
Wandsworth 75 F5
Common (West Side)
SW18
Wandsworth High St. 75 D5
SW18
Wandsworth Plain 75 D5
SW18
Wandsworth Rd. 20 A5
SW8
Wandsworth Rd. 76 B3
SW8
Wangey Rd., Rom. 44 D7
Wanless Rd. SE24 76 J3
Wanley Rd. SE5 77 A4
Wanlip Rd. E13 60 H4
Wannock Gdns., Ilf. 35 E7
Wansbeck Rd. E9 50 J7
Wansdown Pl. SW6 18 A7
Wansey St. SE17 21 A2
Wansey St. SE17 67 J4
Wansford Pk., 22 D4
Borwd.
Wansford Rd., 42 J1
Wdf.Grn.
Wanstead Clo., 96 J2
Brom.
Wanstead La., Ilf. 43 B6
Wanstead Pk. Ave. 52 A2
E12
Wanstead Pk. Rd., 43 B6
Ilf.
Wanstead Pl. E11 42 G6
Wanstead Rd., Brom. 96 J2
Wansunt Rd., Bex. 89 J1
Wantage Rd. SE12 78 F5
Wantz Rd., Dag. 53 H4
Wapping Dock St. E1 68 E1
Cinnamon St.
Wapping High St. E1 17 J2
Wapping High St. E1 68 D1
Wapping La. E1 59 E7
Wapping Wall E1 68 E1
Warbank La., 83 F7
Kings.T.
Warbeck Rd. W12 65 H2
Warberry Rd. N22 40 F2
Warboys App., 83 B6
Kings.T.
Warboys Cres. E4 34 C5
Warboys Rd., 83 B6
Kings.T.
Warburton Clo., 29 A6
Har.
Warburton Rd. E8 59 E1
Warburton Rd., 81 H1
Twick.
Warburton Ter. E17 42 B2
Ward Rd. E15 60 D1
Ward Rd. N19 49 C3
Wardalls Gro. SE14 68 F7
Wardell Clo. NW7 32 E3
Wardell Fld. NW9 38 E1
Warden Ave., Har. 45 F1
Warden Rd. NW5 49 A6
Wardens Gro. SE1 16 J2
Wardle St. E9 50 G5
Wardley St. SW18 75 E7
Garratt La.
Wardo Ave. SW6 75 B1
Wardour Ms. W1 11 G4
Wardour St. W1 11 G3
Wardour St. W1 58 C6
Wardrobe Pl. EC4 12 H4
Wardrobe Ter. EC4 12 H5
Wards Rd., Ilf. 43 G7
Wareham Clo., 72 H4
Houns.
Waremead Rd., Ilf. 43 E5
Warenford Way, 22 A1
Borwd.
Warepoint Dr. SE28 70 G2
Warfield Rd. NW10 57 A3
Warfield Rd., 90 H1
Hmptn.
Warfield Yd. NW10 57 A3
Warfield Rd.

Wargrave Ave. N15 41 C6
Wargrave Rd., Har. 45 J3
Warham Rd. N4 40 G5
Warham Rd., Har. 37 C2
Warham Rd., 101 H5
S.Croy.
Warham St. SE5 20 H7
Warham St. SE5 67 H7
Waring Clo., Orp. 104 J6
Waring Dr., Orp. 104 J6
Waring Rd., Sid. 89 C6
Waring St. SE27 85 J4
Warkworth Gdns., 64 D7
Islw.
Warkworth Rd. N17 33 A7
Warland Rd. SE18 70 G7
Warley Ave., Dag. 44 F7
Warley Ave., Hayes 54 A6
Warley Rd. N9 33 F2
Warley Rd., Hayes 54 A6
Warley Rd., Ilf. 43 D1
Warley Rd., 34 H7
Wdf.Grn.
Warley St. E2 59 G3
Warlingham Rd., 94 H4
Th.Hth.
Warlock Rd. W9 57 C4
Warlters Clo. N7 49 E4
Warlters Rd.
Warlters Rd., The 49 E4
N7
Warltersville Rd. 40 E7
N19
Warmington Clo. E5 50 G3
Orient Way
Warmington Rd. 76 J6
SE24
Warmington St. E13 60 G4
Barking Rd.
Warminster Gdns. 95 D2
SE25
Warminster Rd. 95 D3
SE25
Warminster Way, 94 B1
Mitch.
Warndon St. SE16 68 F4
Warneford Rd., Har. 37 G3
Warneford St. E9 59 E1
Warner Ave., Sutt. 100 B2
Warner Clo. E15 51 E5
Warner Clo. NW9 38 F7
Warner Pl. E2 9 J2
Warner Pl. E2 59 D2
Warner Rd. E17 41 H4
Warner Rd. N8 40 D4
Warner Rd. SE5 76 J1
Warner Rd., Brom. 87 F7
Warner St. EC1 8 E6
Warner St. EC1 58 G4
Warner Yd. EC1 8 E6
Warners Clo., 34 G5
Wdf.Grn.
Warners La., 82 G5
Kings.T.
Warners Path, 34 G5
Wdf.Grn.
Warnford Rd., Orp. 104 J5
Warnham Ct. Rd., 100 J7
Cars.
Warnham Rd. N12 31 G5
Warple Ms. W3 65 E2
Warple Way
Warple Way W3 65 E2
Warren, The E12 52 B4
Warren, The, Hayes 54 A6
Warren, The, Houns. 63 F7
Warren, The, 99 D4
Wor.Pk.
Warren Ave. E10 51 C3
Warren Ave., Brom. 87 E7
Warren Ave., Orp. 104 J5
Warren Ave., Rich. 74 B4
Warren Ave., 102 G7
S.Croy.
Warren Clo. N9 25 G7
Warren Clo. SE21 76 J7
Lairdale Clo.
Warren Clo., Wem. 46 G2
Warren Ct., Chig. 35 G4
Warren Cres. N9 25 C7
Warren Cutting, 83 D7
Kings.T.
Warren Dr., Grnf. 54 H4
Warren Dr., Ruis. 36 D7
Warren Dr., The E11 42 J7
Warren Dr. N., 99 B1
Surb.
Warren Dr. S., 99 C1
Surb.
Warren Flds., Stan. 29 F4
Valencia Rd.
Warren Footpath, 82 F1
Twick.

Warren Gdns. E15 51 D5
Ashton Rd.
Warren Gro., Borwd. 22 D4
Warren Hill, Loug. 26 J5
Warren Ho. E3 60 B3
Bromley High St.
Warren La. SE18 70 E3
Warren La., Stan. 29 C3
Warren Ms. W1 7 F6
Warren Pk., 83 C6
Kings.T.
Warren Pk. Rd., 100 G6
Sutt.
Warren Pl. E1 59 G6
Pitsea St.
Warren Pond Rd. E4 34 F1
Warren Ri., N.Mal. 92 D1
Warren Rd. E4 34 C2
Warren Rd. E10 51 C3
Warren Rd. E11 42 J6
Warren Rd. NW2 47 F2
Warren Rd. SW19 84 H6
Warren Rd., Bexh. 80 G5
Warren Rd., Brom. 103 G2
Warren Rd., Croy. 102 B1
Warren Rd., Ilf. 43 G5
Warren Rd., 83 C6
Kings.T.
Warren Rd., Orp. 104 J5
Warren Rd., Sid. 89 C3
Warren Rd., Twick. 72 J6
Warren Rd. 28 J1
(Bushey), Wat.
Warren St. W1 7 E6
Warren St. W1 58 C4
Warren Ter., Rom. 44 D4
Warren Wk. SE7 69 J6
Warren Way NW7 31 B6
Warrender Rd. N19 49 C3
Warrender Way, 36 A7
Ruis.
Warrens Shawe La., 30 B2
Edg.
Warriner Gdns. 75 J1
SW11
Warrington Cres. W9 6 C6
Warrington Cres. W9 57 F4
Warrington Gdns. W9 6 C6
Warrington Pl. E14 69 C1
Yabsley St.
Warrington Rd., 101 H3
Croy.
Warrington Rd., 53 D2
Dag.
Warrington Rd., 37 B5
Har.
Warrington Rd., 73 G5
Rich.
Warrington Sq., 53 D2
Dag.
Warrington St. E13 60 G4
Doherty Rd.
Warrior Sq. E12 52 D4
Warsaw Clo., Ruis. 45 B6
Glebe Ave.
Warsdale Dr. NW9 38 D5
Mardale Dr.
Warspite Rd. SE18 70 A3
Warton Rd. E15 51 C7
Warwall E6 61 E6
Warwick Ave. W2 10 D1
Warwick Ave. W2 57 F5
Warwick Ave. W9 6 B6
Warwick Ave. W9 57 E4
Warwick Ave., Edg. 30 B3
Warwick Ave., Har. 45 F4
Warwick Clo., Barn. 23 G5
Warwick Clo., Bex. 80 F7
Warwick Clo., 81 J7
Hmptn.
Warwick Ct. SE15 77 D2
Warwick Ct. WC1 12 D2
Warwick Cres. W2 10 C1
Warwick Cres. W2 57 F5
Warwick Dene W5 64 H1
Warwick Dr. SW15 74 H3
Warwick Est. W2 10 B2
Warwick Est. W2 57 E5
Warwick Gdns. N4 40 J5
Warwick Gdns. W14 66 C3
Warwick Gdns., Ilf. 52 E1
Warwick Gdns., 91 C5
T.Ditt.
Warwick Gro. E5 50 E1
Warwick Gro., Surb. 91 J7
Warwick Ho. St. SW1 15 J1
Warwick Ho. St. SW1 67 D1
Warwick La. EC4 12 H4
Warwick La. EC4 58 H6
Warwick La. W5 66 G2
Warwick Rd.
Warwick Pl. W9 10 C1
Warwick Pl. W9 57 F5

Warwick Pl. N. SW1	19	F2	Watergate EC4	12	G5	Watford Clo. SW11	75	H1
Warwick Pl. N. SW1	67	C4	Watergate, Wat.	28	D2	*Petworth St.*		
Warwick Rd. E4	34	A5	Watergate St. SE8	69	A6	Watford Rd. E16	60	G5
Warwick Rd. E11	42	H5	**Watergate Wk. WC2**	12	B6	Watford Rd., Har.	37	D7
Warwick Rd. E12	52	B5	Waterhall Ave. E4	34	E4	Watford Rd., Wem.	46	D2
Warwick Rd. E15	51	F6	Waterhall Clo. E17	41	G1	Watford Rd. NW4	38	G4
Warwick Rd. E17	41	J1	Waterhouse Clo. E16	61	A5	Watford Way NW7	30	E4
Warwick Rd. N11	32	D6	Waterhouse Clo.	48	G5	Watkin Rd., Wem.	47	B3
Warwick Rd. N18	33	B4	NW3			Watkinson Rd. N7	49	F6
Warwick Rd. SE20	95	E3	*Lyndhurst Rd.*			**Watling Ave., Edg.**	38	C1
Warwick Rd. SW5	66	D5	Waterhouse Clo. W6	66	A4	**Watling Ct. EC4**	13	A4
Warwick Rd. W5	64	G2	*Great Ch. La.*			Watling Gdns. NW2	48	B6
Warwick Rd. W14	66	C4	**Waterloo Bri. SE1**	12	C6	**Watling St. EC4**	12	C4
Warwick Rd., Barn.	23	E4	Waterloo Bri. SE1	67	F1	Watling St. EC4	58	J6
Warwick Rd., Borwd.	22	D3	**Waterloo Bri. WC2**	12	C6	Watling St., Bexh.	80	H4
Warwick Rd., Houns.	91	F1	Waterloo Bri. WC2	58	F7	Watlings, The,	95	H6
Warwick Rd.,	91	F1	Waterloo Clo. E9	50	F5	Croy.		
Kings.T.			*Churchill Wk.*			Watlington Gro.	86	H5
Warwick Rd., N.Mal.	92	C3	Waterloo Est. E2	59	F2	SE26		
Warwick Rd., Sid.	89	B5	Waterloo Gdns. E2	59	F2	Watney Mkt. E1	59	E6
Warwick Rd., Sthl.	63	F3	Waterloo Pas. NW6	48	C7	*Commercial Rd.*		
Warwick Rd., Sutt.	100	F4	**Waterloo Pl. SW1**	15	H1	Watney Rd. SW14	74	C3
Warwick Rd.,	91	C5	Waterloo Pl. SW1	67	D1	Watney St. E1	59	E6
T.Ditt.			Waterloo Rd. E6	51	J7	Watneys Rd., Mitch.	94	D5
Warwick Rd.,	94	G3	Waterloo Rd. E10	42	A7	Watson Ave. E6	52	D7
Th.Hth.			Waterloo Rd. NW2	47	G1	Watson Ave., Sutt.	100	B3
Warwick Rd., Twick.	82	B1	**Waterloo Rd. SE1**	16	E3	Watson Clo. N16	50	A5
Warwick Rd., Well.	80	C3	Waterloo Rd. SE1	67	G1	*Matthias Rd.*		
Warwick Row SW1	15	E5	Waterloo Rd., Ilf.	43	F2	Watson Clo. SW19	84	H6
Warwick Row SW1	67	B3	Waterloo Rd., Sutt.	100	G5	Watson St. E13	60	H1
Warwick Sq. EC4	12	H3	Waterloo Ter. N1	49	H7	Watsons Ms. W1	10	H2
Warwick Sq. SW1	19	F3	Waterlow Ct. NW11	39	E7	Watsons Rd. N22	40	G1
Warwick Sq. SW1	67	C5	*Heath Clo.*			*North Circular Rd.*		
Warwick Sq. Ms.	19	H2	Waterlow Rd. N19	49	C1	Watsons Yd. NW2	47	F2
SW1			Waterman St. SW15	75	A3	*North Circular Rd.*		
Warwick St. W1	11	G5	Waterman Way E1	68	E1	Wattisfield Rd. E5	50	F3
Warwick St. W1	58	C7	Waterman's Clo.,	82	H7	Watts Gro. E3	60	B5
Warwick Ter. SE18	70	G6	Kings.T.			Watts La., Chis.	97	E1
Warwick Way SW1	19	E3	*Woodside Rd.*			Watts La., Tedd.	82	D5
Warwick Way SW1	67	B5	Watermans Wk.	68	H1	Watts Rd., T.Ditt.	91	D7
Warwick Yd. EC1	9	A6	SE16			Watts St. E1	68	G1
Warwickshire Path	68	J7	*Redriff Rd.*			**Watts Way SW7**	14	F5
SE8			Watermead Rd. SE6	87	B4	Wauthier Clo. N13	32	H5
Washington Ave. E12	52	B4	Watermead Way N17	41	D3	Wavel Ms. N8	40	D4
Washington Rd. E6	51	J7	Watermen's Sq.	86	F7	Wavel Ms. NW6	48	E7
St. Stephens Rd.			SE20			*Acol Rd.*		
Washington Rd. E18	42	F2	Watermill Clo.,	82	F3	Wavel Pl. SE26	86	C4
Washington Rd.	65	G7	Rich.			*Sydenham Hill*		
SW13			Watermill La. N18	33	B5	Wavell Dr., Sid.	79	H6
Washington Rd.,	92	A2	Watermill Way SW19	93	F1	Wavendon Ave. W4	65	D5
Kings.T.			Watermill Way,	81	F2	Waveney Ave. SE15	77	E4
Washington Rd.,	99	H2	Felt.			**Waveney Clo. E1**	17	J1
Wor.Pk.			Watermint Quay N16	41	D6	Waverley Ave. E4	33	J4
Wastail Clo. NW9	38	E2	Waters Gdns., Dag.	53	G5	Waverley Ave. E17	42	D3
Swan Dr.			*Sterry Rd.*			Waverley Ave.,	92	B6
Wastdale Rd. SE23	86	G1	Waters Rd. SE6	87	E3	Surb.		
Wat Tyler Rd. SE3	78	D2	Waters Rd.,	92	B2	Waverley Ave.,	100	E2
Wat Tyler Rd. SE10	78	C2	Kings.T.			Sutt.		
Watchfield Ct. W4	65	C5	Waters Sq.,	92	B3	Waverley Ave.,	81	F1
Watcombe Cotts.,	65	A6	Kings.T.			Twick.		
Rich.			Watersedge, Epsom	99	C4	Waverley Ave.,	46	J5
Watcombe Pl. SE25	95	E5	Watersfield Way,	29	G7	Wem.		
Albert Rd.			Edg.			Waverley Clo. E18	42	J1
Watcombe Rd. SE25	95	E5	**Waterside Clo. SE16**	17	J4	Waverley Clo.,	97	A5
Water Gdns., Stan.	29	E6	Waterside Clo.,	53	A4	Brom.		
Water La. E15	51	E6	Bark.			Waverley Cres. SE18	70	G6
Water La. NW1	49	B7	Waterside Clo.,	54	F3	Waverley Gdns. E6	61	B5
Kentish Town Rd.			Nthlt.			*Oliver Gdns.*		
Water La. SE14	68	F7	Waterside Clo.,	98	H2	Waverley Gdns.	55	J2
Water La., Ilf.	52	H3	Surb.			NW10		
Water La., Kings.T.	91	G1	*Culsac Rd.*			Waverley Gdns.,	61	H2
Water La., Rich.	73	G5	Waterside Dr.,	90	A5	Bark.		
Water La., Sid.	89	F3	Walt.			Waverley Gdns., Ilf.	43	F2
Water La., Twick.	82	D1	Waterside Pl. NW1	58	A1	Waverley Gdns.,	36	A1
Water Rd., Wem.	55	J1	*Princess Rd.*			Nthwd.		
Water St. WC2	12	D5	Waterside Pt. SW11	66	H7	Waverley Gro. N3	39	A3
Water Twr. Hill,	102	A4	Waterside Rd.,	63	G3	Waverley Ind. Pk.,	37	A3
Croy.			Sthl.			Har.		
Waterbank Rd. SE6	87	B3	Waterside Way	84	F4	Waverley Pl. N4	49	H2
Waterbeach Rd.,	53	C6	SW17			*Adolphus Rd.*		
Dag.			Watersmeet Way	62	C6	**Waverley Pl. NW8**	6	E1
Waterbrook La. NW4	38	J5	SE28			Waverley Pl. NW8	50	G2
Watercress Pl. N1	50	B7	**Waterson St. E2**	9	E3	Waverley Rd. E17	42	C3
Hertford Rd.			Waterson St. E2	59	B3	Waverley Rd. E18	42	J1
Waterdale Rd. SE2	71	A6	Watersplash Clo.,	91	H3	Waverley Rd. N8	40	E6
Waterden Rd. E15	51	A5	Kings.T.			Waverley Rd. N17	33	E7
Waterer Ri., Wall.	101	D6	Watersplash La.,	63	A4	Waverley Rd. SE18	70	F5
Waterfall Clo. N14	32	C3	Hayes			Waverley Rd. SE25	95	E4
Waterfall Cotts.	84	G6	*North Hyde Rd.*			Waverley Rd., Enf.	24	H4
SW19			Watersplash La.,	63	B5	Waverley Rd.,	99	G6
Waterfall Rd. N11	32	B4	Houns.			Epsom		
Waterfall Rd. N14	32	C3	Waterview Ho. E14	59	H5	Waverley Rd., Har.	45	E1
Waterfall Rd. SW19	84	G6	*Carr St.*			Waverley Rd., Sthl.	64	B3
Waterfall Ter. SW17	84	H6	Waterworks La. E5	50	G2	Waverley Vill. N17	41	C2
Waterfield Clo.	71	B1	Waterworks Rd. SW2	76	E6	Waverley Wk. W2	57	D5
SE28			Waterworks Yd.,	101	J3	Waverley Way,	100	H6
Waterfield Clo.,	71	G3	Croy.			Cars.		
Belv.			*Surrey St.*			Waverton Ho. E3	59	J1
Waterfield Gdns.	95	A4	Watery La. SW20	93	C2	Waverton Rd. SW18	75	F1
SE25			Watery La., Nthlt.	54	C2	**Waverton St. W1**	15	D1
Waterford Rd. SW6	66	E7	Watery La., Sid.	89	B6	Waverton St. W1	54	A5
Watergardens, The,	83	C6	Wates Way, Mitch.	93	J6	Wavertree Ct. SW2	85	F1
Kings.T.			Wateville Rd. N17	40	J1	*Streatham Hill*		

Wavertree Rd. E18	42	G7
Wavertree Rd. SW2	85	E1
Waxlow Cres., Sthl.	54	G6
Waxlow Rd. NW10	56	C2
Waxwell Clo., Pnr.	36	D2
Waxwell La., Pnr.	36	D2
Waye Ave., Houns.	72	A1
Wayfarer Rd.,	54	D3
Nthlt.		
Wayfield Link SE9	79	G6
Wayford St. SW11	75	H2
Wayland Ave. E8	50	D5
Waylands Mead,	96	B1
Beck.		
Wayleave, The SE28	62	B7
Oriole Way		
Waylett Pl. SE27	85	H3
Waylett Pl., Wem.	46	G3
Wayman Ct. E8	50	E6
Wayne Clo., Orp.	104	J3
Waynflete Ave.,	101	H3
Croy.		
Waynflete Sq. W10	57	A6
Waynflete St. SW18	84	F2
Wayside NW11	48	B1
Wayside SW14	74	C5
Wayside Clo. N14	24	C6
Wayside Commercial	62	A2
Est., Bark.		
Wayside Ct., Twick.	73	F6
Wayside Ct., Wem.	47	A3
Oakington Ave.		
Wayside Gdns. SE9	99	C1
Wayside Gro.		
Wayside Gdns., Dag.	53	G5
Wayside Gro. SE9	88	C4
Wayside Ms., Ilf.	43	D5
Gaysham Ave.		
Weald, The, Chis.	88	C6
Weald Clo. SE16	68	E5
Stevenson Cres.		
Weald Clo., Brom.	104	B2
Weald La., Har.	37	A2
Weald Ri., Har.	29	C7
Weald Sq. E5	50	E2
Rossington St.		
Weald Way, Rom.	44	H6
Wealdstone Rd.,	100	C2
Sutt.		
Wealdwood Gdns.,	28	H6
Pnr.		
Highbanks Rd.		
Weale Rd. E4	34	D3
Wear Pl. E2	59	E3
Weardale Gdns.,	25	A1
Enf.		
Weardale Rd. SE13	78	D4
Wearside Rd. SE13	78	B5
Weatherley Clo. E3	59	J5
Weaver St. E1	9	H6
Weaver St. E1	59	D4
Weaver Wk. SE27	85	J4
Weavers Clo., Islw.	73	B4
Weavers Ter. SW6	66	D6
Micklethwaite Rd.		
Weavers Way NW1	49	D7
Webb Est. E5	41	D7
Webb Gdns. E13	60	G4
Kelland Rd.		
Webb Pl. NW10	56	F3
Old Oak La.		
Webb Rd. SE3	69	F6
Webb St. SE1	17	D6
Webb St. SE1	68	B3
Webber Row SE1	16	F4
Webber Row SE1	67	G2
Webber St. SE1	16	G4
Webber St. SE1	67	G2
Webbs Rd. SW11	75	J4
Webbs Rd., Hayes	54	B3
Webbscroft Rd.,	53	H4
Dag.		
Webster Gdns. W5	64	G1
Webster Rd. E11	51	C3
Webster Rd. SE16	17	J6
Webster Rd. SE16	68	D3
Wedderburn Rd.	48	G5
NW3		
Wedderburn Rd.,	61	G1
Bark.		
Wedgewood Wk.	48	E5
NW6		
Lymington Rd.		
Wedgewood Way	85	J7
SE19		
Wedgwood Ms. W1	11	J4
Wedlake St. W10	57	B4
Kensal Rd.		
Wedmore Ave., Ilf.	43	D2
Wedmore Gdns. N19	49	D2
Wedmore Ms. N19	49	D3
Wedmore St.		
Wedmore Rd., Grnf.	55	A3

Wedmore St. N19	49	D3
Weech Rd. NW6	48	D4
Weedington Rd. NW5	49	A5
Weekley Sq. SW11	75	G3
Thomas Baines Rd.		
Weigall Rd. SE12	78	G4
Weighouse St. W1	**11**	**C4**
Weighouse St. W1	58	A6
Weighton Rd. SE20	95	E2
Weighton Rd., Har.	37	A1
Weihurst Gdns., Sutt.	100	D3
Weimar St. SW15	75	B3
Weir Est. SW12	76	C7
Weir Hall Ave. N18	33	A6
Weir Hall Gdns. N18	33	A5
Weir Hall Rd. N17	33	A6
Weir Hall Rd. N18	33	A5
Weir Rd. SW12	76	C7
Weir Rd. SW19	84	E3
Weir Rd., Bex.	80	H7
Weir Rd., Walt.	90	A6
Weirdale Ave. N20	31	J2
Weir's Pas. NW1	**7**	**J3**
Weir's Pas. NW1	58	A3
Weiss Rd. SW15	75	A3
Welbeck Ave., Brom.	87	G4
Welbeck Ave., Hayes	54	B4
Welbeck Ave., Sid.	89	A1
Welbeck Clo. N12	31	G5
Torrington Pk.		
Welbeck Clo., Borwd.	22	A3
Welbeck Clo., Epsom	99	G7
Welbeck Clo., N.Mal.	92	F5
Welbeck Rd. E6	61	A3
Welbeck Rd., Barn.	23	G6
Welbeck Rd., Cars.	100	H1
Welbeck Rd., Har.	45	H1
Welbeck Rd., Sutt.	100	G2
Welbeck St. W1	**11**	**C2**
Welbeck St. W1	58	A5
Welbeck Way W1	**11**	**D3**
Welbeck Way W1	58	B6
Welby St. SE5	76	H1
Weld Pl. N11	32	B5
Weldon Clo., Ruis.	45	B6
Weldon Dr., W.Mol.	90	F4
Welfare Rd. E15	51	E7
Welford Clo. E5	50	G3
Denton Way		
Welford Pl. SW19	84	B4
Welham Rd. SW16	85	B6
Welham Rd. SW17	85	A5
Welhouse Rd., Cars.	100	H1
Well App., Barn.	22	J5
Well Clo. SW16	85	F4
Well Clo., Ruis.	45	E3
Parkfield Cres.		
Well Cottage Clo. E11	42	J7
Well Ct. EC4	**13**	**A4**
Well Ct. SW16	85	F4
Well Gro. N20	23	F7
Well Hall Rd. SE9	79	B3
Well La. SW14	74	C5
Well Pas. NW3	48	G3
Well Rd. NW3	48	G3
Well Rd., Barn.	22	J5
Well St. E9	50	F7
Well St. E15	51	E6
Well Wk. NW3	48	G4
Wellacre Rd., Har.	37	E6
Wellan Clo., Well.	80	B5
Welland Gdns., Grnf.	55	C2
Welland Ms. E1	**17**	**J1**
Welland St. SE10	69	C6
Wellands Clo., Brom.	97	C2
Wellbrook Rd., Orp.	104	D4
Wellclose Sq. E1	**13**	**J5**
Wellclose Sq. E1	59	D7
Wellclose St. E1	**13**	**J6**
Welldon Cres., Har.	37	B6
Weller St. SE1	**16**	**J3**
Wellers Ct. NW1	**8**	**A2**
Wellesley Ct. W9	**6**	**C3**
Wellesley Ct. Rd., Croy.	102	A2
Wellesley Cres., Twick.	82	B2
Wellesley Gro., Croy.	102	A2
Wellesley Pl. NW1	**7**	**H4**
Wellesley Rd. E11	42	G5
Wellesley Rd. E17	42	A6
Wellesley Rd. N22	40	G2
Wellesley Rd. NW5	49	A5
Wellesley Rd. W4	65	A5
Wellesley Rd., Croy.	101	J1
Wellesley Rd., Har.	37	B5
Wellesley Rd., Ilf.	52	E2
Wellesley Rd., Sutt.	100	F6
Wellesley Rd., Twick.	82	A3
Wellesley St. E1	59	G5
Wellesley Ter. N1	**9**	**A3**
Wellesley Ter. N1	58	J3
Wellfield Ave. N10	40	B3
Wellfield Rd. SW16	85	E4
Wellfield Wk. SW16	85	F5
Wellfields Rd., Loug.	27	D3
Wellfit St. SE24	76	H3
Milkwood Rd.		
Wellgarth, Grnf.	46	E6
Wellgarth Rd. NW11	48	E1
Wellhouse La., Barn.	22	J4
Wellhouse Rd., Beck.	95	J4
Welling High St., Well.	80	A3
Welling Way SE9	79	G3
Welling Way, Well.	79	H3
Wellings Ho., Hayes	63	B1
Wellington Ave. E4	34	A2
Wellington Ave. N9	33	E3
Wellington Ave. N15	41	C6
Wellington Ave., Houns.	72	G5
Wellington Ave., Pnr.	36	F1
Wellington Ave., Sid.	80	A6
Wellington Ave., Wor.Pk.	99	J3
Wellington Bldgs. SW1	**19**	**C4**
Wellington Clo. SE14	77	G1
Wild Goose Dr.		
Wellington Clo. W11	57	D6
Ledbury Rd.		
Wellington Clo., Dag.	53	J7
Wellington Ct. NW8	**6**	**E2**
Wellington Cres., N.Mal.	92	C3
Wellington Dr., Dag.	53	J7
Wellington Gdns. SE7	69	J5
Wellington Gdns., Twick.	82	A4
Wellington Ms. SE22	77	D4
Peckham Rye		
Wellington Pk. Ind. Est. NW2	47	G1
Wellington Pas. E11	42	G5
Wellington Rd.		
Wellington Pl. N2	39	H5
Great N. Rd.		
Wellington Pl. NW8	**6**	**F3**
Wellington Pl. NW8	57	G3
Wellington Rd. E6	61	C1
Wellington Rd. E7	51	F4
Wellington Rd. E10	50	H1
Wellington Rd. E11	42	G5
Wellington Rd. E17	41	H3
Wellington Rd. NW8	**6**	**E1**
Wellington Rd. NW8	57	G2
Wellington Rd. NW10	57	A3
Wellington Rd. SW19	84	D2
Wellington Rd. W5	64	F3
Wellington Rd., Belv.	71	F5
Wellington Rd., Bex.	80	D5
Wellington Rd., Brom.	96	J4
Wellington Rd., Croy.	94	H7
Wellington Rd., Enf.	25	B4
Wellington Rd., Hmptn.	82	A5
Wellington Rd., Har.	37	B3
Wellington Rd., Pnr.	28	F7
Wellington Rd., Twick.	82	A4
Wellington Rd. N., Houns.	72	F3
Wellington Rd. S., Houns.	72	F4
Wellington Row E2	**9**	**G3**
Wellington Row E2	59	C3
Wellington Sq. SW3	66	A5
Wellington St. SE18	70	D4
Wellington St. WC2	**12**	**B5**
Wellington St. WC2	58	E7
Wellington St., Bark.	61	F1
Axe St.		
Wellington Ter. E1	68	E1
Waterman Way		
Wellington Ter., Har.	46	A1
Wellington Way E3	60	A3
Wellmeadow Rd. SE6	78	E7
Wellmeadow Rd. SE13	78	E6
Wellmeadow Rd. W7	64	D4
Wellow Wk., Cars.	100	G1
Whitland Rd.		
Wells, The N14	24	D7
Wells Clo., Nthlt.	54	C3
Yeading La.		
Wells Dr. NW9	47	D1
Wells Gdns., Dag.	53	H5
Pondfield Rd.		
Wells Gdns., Ilf.	53	B6
Wells Ho. Rd. NW10	56	E5
Wells Ms. W1	**11**	**G2**
Wells Pk. Rd. SE26	86	D3
Wells Ri. NW8	57	J1
Wells Rd. W12	65	J2
Wells Rd., Brom.	97	C2
Wells Sq. WC1	**8**	**C4**
Wells St. W1	**11**	**F2**
Wells St. W1	58	C5
Wells Ter. N4	49	G2
Wells Way SE5	**21**	**C5**
Wells Way SE5	68	B6
Wells Way SW7	**14**	**E5**
Wells Way SW7	66	G3
Wells Yd. N7	49	G5
Holloway Rd.		
Wellside Clo., Barn.	22	J4
Wellsmoor Gdns., Brom.	97	D3
Wellsprings Cres., Wem.	47	B3
Wellstead Ave. N9	25	F7
Wellstead Rd. E6	61	D2
Wellwood Rd., Ilf.	53	A1
Welsford St. SE1	**21**	**H3**
Welsford St. SE1	68	D5
Welsh Clo. E13	60	G1
Welsh Side Wk. NW9	38	E6
Fryent Gro.		
Welshpool Ho. E8	59	D1
Benjamin Clo.		
Welshpool St. E8	59	E1
Broadway Mkt.		
Weltje Rd. W6	65	G4
Welton Rd. SE18	70	H7
Welwyn St. E2	59	F3
Globe Rd.		
Wembley Commercial Cen., Wem.	46	G2
Wembley Hill Rd., Wem.	46	J5
Wembley Pk. Business Cen., Wem.	47	B3
Wembley Pk. Dr., Wem.	46	J4
Wembley Rd., Hmptn.	81	G7
Wembley Way, Wem.	47	B6
Wemborough Rd., Stan.	37	E1
Wembury Rd. N6	40	B7
Wemyss Rd. SE3	78	F2
Wendela Ct., Har.	46	B3
Wendell Rd. W12	65	F3
Wendling Rd., Sutt.	100	G1
Wendon St. E3	59	J1
Wendover SE17	**21**	**D3**
Wendover Clo., Hayes	54	E4
Kingsash Dr.		
Wendover Dr., N.Mal.	92	F6
Wendover Rd. NW10	56	F2
Wendover Rd. SE9	79	A3
Wendover Rd., Brom.	96	H3
Wendover Way, Well.	80	A5
Wendy Clo., Enf.	25	C6
Wendy Way, Wem.	55	H1
Wenlock Ct. N1	**9**	**C2**
Wenlock Gdns. NW4	38	G4
Rickard Clo.		
Wenlock Rd. N1	**8**	**J2**
Wenlock Rd. N1	58	J2
Wenlock Rd., Edg.	30	B7
Wenlock St. N1	**9**	**A2**
Wenlock St. N1	58	J2
Wennington Rd. E3	59	G2
Wensley Ave., Wdf.Grn.	34	F7
Wensley Clo. SE9	79	C6
Wensley Rd. N18	33	E6
Wensleydale Ave., Ilf.	43	B2
Wensleydale Gdns., Hmptn.	81	H7
Wensleydale Pas., Hmptn.	90	G1
Wensleydale Rd., Hmptn.	81	G6
Wentland Clo. SE6	87	D2
Wentland Rd.		
Wentland Rd. SE6	87	D2
Wentworth Ave. N3	31	D7
Wentworth Clo. N3	31	E7
Wentworth Clo., Mord.	93	D7
Wentworth Clo., Orp.	104	H5
Wentworth Clo., Surb.	98	G2
Wentworth Cres. SE15	68	D7
Wentworth Dr., Pnr.	36	A5
Wentworth Gdns. N13	32	H4
Wentworth Hill, Wem.	46	J1
Wentworth Ms. E3	59	J3
Eric St.		
Wentworth Pk. N3	31	D7
Wentworth Pl., Stan.	29	E6
Greenacres Dr.		
Wentworth Rd. E12	52	A4
Wentworth Rd. NW11	39	C6
Wentworth Rd., Barn.	23	A3
Wentworth Rd., Croy.	94	G7
Wentworth Rd., Sthl.	63	C4
Wentworth St. E1	**13**	**F3**
Wentworth St. E1	59	C6
Wentworth Way, Pnr.	36	D4
Wenvoe Ave., Bexh.	80	H2
Wernbrook St. SE18	70	F6
Werndee Rd. SE25	95	D4
Werneth Hall Rd., Ilf.	43	C3
Werrington St. NW1	**7**	**G2**
Werrington St. NW1	58	C2
Werter Rd. SW15	75	B4
Wesley Ave. NW10	56	D3
Wesley Ave., Houns.	72	E2
Wesley Clo. N7	49	F2
Wesley Clo. SE17	**20**	**H2**
Wesley Clo., Har.	45	J2
Wesley Rd. E10	42	C7
Wesley Rd. NW10	56	C1
Hillside		
Wesley Rd. SE17	**20**	**H2**
Wesley Rd., Hayes	54	A7
Wesley Sq. W11	57	B6
Bartle Rd.		
Wesley St. W1	**11**	**C2**
Wesleyan Pl. NW5	49	B4
Gordon Ho. Rd.		
Wessex Ave. SW19	93	D2
Wessex Clo., Ilf.	43	H6
Wessex Clo., Kings.T.	92	B1
Gloucester Rd.		
Wessex Dr., Pnr.	28	E7
Wessex Gdns. NW11	48	B1
Wessex La., Grnf.	55	A2
Wessex St. E2	59	F3
Wessex Way NW11	48	B1
West App., Orp.	97	F5
West Arbour St. E1	59	F6
West Ave. E17	42	B4
West Ave. N3	31	D6
West Ave. NW4	39	A5
West Ave., Pnr.	36	F6
West Ave., Sthl.	54	F7
West Ave., Wall.	101	G5
West Ave. Rd. E17	42	A4
West Bank N16	41	B7
West Bank, Bark.	61	L1
Highbridge Rd.		
West Bank, Enf.	24	J2
West Barnes La. SW20	92	G5
West Barnes La., N.Mal.	92	H3
West Carriage Dr. W2	**10**	**G6**

Name	Pg	Ref
West Carriage Dr. W2	57	G7
West Cen. St. WC1	**12**	**A3**
West Chantry, Har.	36	H1
Chantry Rd.		
West Clo. N9	33	C3
West Clo., Barn.	22	H5
West Clo. (Cockfosters), Barn.	24	A4
West Clo., Grnf.	54	J2
West Clo., Wem.	46	J1
West Common Rd., Brom.	103	G2
West Cotts. NW6	48	D5
West Ct. SE18	79	C1
Prince Imperial Rd.		
West Ct., Wem.	46	F2
West Cromwell Rd. SW5	66	C4
West Cromwell Rd. W14	66	C5
West Cross Route W10	57	A7
West Cross Route W11	66	A1
West Cross Way, Brent.	64	E6
West Dene, Sutt.	100	B6
Park La.		
West Dr. SW16	85	C4
West Dr., Har.	29	A6
West Dr. Gdns., Har.	29	A6
West Eaton Pl. SW1	**19**	**B1**
West Eaton Pl. SW1	67	A4
West Eaton Pl. Ms. SW1	**15**	**B6**
West Ella Rd. NW10	47	E7
West End Ave. E10	42	D5
West End Ave., Pnr.	36	D4
West End Ct., Pnr.	36	D4
West End Gdns., Nthlt.	54	C2
Edward Clo.		
West End La. NW6	48	D5
West End La., Barn.	23	A4
West End La., Pnr.	36	D3
West End Rd., Nthlt.	45	C7
West End Rd., Ruis.	45	A4
West End Rd., Sthl.	63	E1
West Gdns. E1	59	E7
West Gdns. SW17	84	H6
West Gate W5	55	H3
West Grn. Rd. N15	40	H4
West Gro. SE10	78	C1
West Gro., Wdf.Grn.	34	J6
West Halkin St. SW1	**15**	**B5**
West Halkin St. SW1	67	A3
West Hall Rd., Rich.	74	B1
West Hallowes SE9	88	B1
West Ham La. E15	51	D7
West Ham Pk. E7	51	F7
West Hampstead Ms. NW6	48	E6
West Harding St. EC4	**12**	**F3**
West Heath Ave. NW11	48	D1
West Heath Clo. NW3	48	D3
West Heath Dr. NW11	48	D1
West Heath Gdns. NW3	48	D2
West Heath Rd. NW3	48	D1
West Heath Rd. SE2	71	C6
West Hendon Bdy. NW9	38	F6
West Hill SW15	75	A7
West Hill SW18	75	A7
West Hill, Har.	46	B2
West Hill, Wem.	46	J1
West Hill Ct. N6	49	A3
West Hill Pk. N6	48	J2
Merton La.		
West Hill Rd. SW18	75	C6
West Hill Way N20	31	E1
West Holme, Erith	80	J1
West Ho. Clo. SW19	84	B1
West India Ave. E14	69	A1
West India Dock Rd. E14	59	J6
West Kentish Town Est. NW5	49	A6
Warden Rd.		
West La. SE16	68	A2
West Lo. Ave. W3	65	A1
West Mall W8	66	D1
Palace Gdns. Ter.		
West Mead, Epsom	95	E4
West Mead, Ruis.	45	C4
West Ms. N17	33	E6
West Ms. SW1	**19**	**F2**
West Oak, Beck.	96	D1
West Pk. SE9	88	B2
West Pk. Ave., Rich.	74	A1
West Pk. Clo., Rom.	44	D5
West Pk. Rd., Rich.	74	A1
West Pier E1	68	E1
Wapping High St.		
West Pl. SW19	83	J5
West Poultry Ave. EC1	**12**	**G2**
West Quarters W12	56	G6
Du Cane Rd.		
West Quay Dr., Hayes	54	E5
West Ridge Gdns., Grnf.	54	J2
West Rd. E15	60	F1
West Rd. N17	33	E6
West Rd. SW3	**19**	**A4**
West Rd. SW3	66	J5
West Rd. SW4	76	D5
West Rd. W5	55	H5
West Rd., Barn.	24	A7
West Rd., Kings.T.	92	C1
West Rd., Rom. (Chadwell Heath)	44	D6
West Row W10	57	B4
West Sheen Vale, Rich.	73	J4
West Side Common SW19	83	J6
West Smithfield EC1	**12**	**G2**
West Smithfield EC1	58	H5
West Sq. SE11	**16**	**G6**
West Sq. SE11	67	H3
West St. E2	59	E2
Clare St.		
West St. E11	51	E3
West St. E17	42	B5
Grove Rd.		
West St. WC2	**11**	**J5**
West St., Bexh.	80	F4
West St., Brent.	64	F6
West St., Brom.	96	G1
West St., Cars.	100	J3
West St., Croy.	101	J4
West St., Har.	46	A1
West St., Sutt.	100	E5
West St. La., Cars.	100	J4
West Temple Sheen SW14	74	B4
West Tenter St. E1	**13**	**G4**
West Tenter St. E1	59	C6
West Twrs., Pnr.	36	D6
West Vw. NW4	38	J4
West Vw., Loug.	27	C4
West Wk. W5	55	H5
West Wk., Barn.	24	A7
West Wk., Hayes	63	A1
West Warwick Pl. SW1	**19**	**F2**
West Warwick Pl. SW1	67	C4
West Way N18	33	A4
West Way NW10	47	D4
West Way, Croy.	102	H2
West Way, Edg.	30	B6
West Way, Houns.	63	F7
West Way, Pnr.	36	D4
West Way, W.Wick.	96	D6
West Way Gdns., Croy.	102	G2
West Woodside, Bex.	80	E7
West World W5	55	H3
Westacott Clo. N19	49	D1
Westall Rd., Loug.	27	E3
Westbank Rd., Hmptn.	81	J6
Westbeech Rd. N22	40	G3
Westbere Dr., Stan.	29	G4
Westbere Rd. NW2	48	B4
Westbourne Ave. W3	56	D6
Westbourne Ave., Sutt.	100	B2
Westbourne Bri. W2	**10**	**C2**
Westbourne Bri. W2	57	F5
Westbourne Clo., Hayes	54	B4
Westbourne Cres. W2	**10**	**E5**
Westbourne Cres. W2	57	G7
Westbourne Cres. Ms. W2	**10**	**E5**
Westbourne Dr. SE23	86	G2
Westbourne Gdns. W2	**10**	**A3**
Westbourne Gdns. W2	57	E6
Westbourne Gro. W2	57	D6
Westbourne Gro. W11	57	C7
Westbourne Gro. Ms. W11	57	D6
Westbourne Gro.		
Westbourne Gro. Ter. W2	**10**	**A4**
Westbourne Gro. Ter. W2	57	E6
Westbourne Pk. Ms. W2	**10**	**A3**
Westbourne Pk. Pas. W2	57	D5
Westbourne Pk. Rd. W2	57	D5
Westbourne Pk. Rd. W11	57	B6
Westbourne Pk. Vill. W2	57	D5
Westbourne Rd. N7	49	F6
Westbourne Rd. SE26	86	G6
Westbourne Rd., Bexh.	71	D7
Westbourne Rd., Croy.	95	C6
Westbourne St. W2	**10**	**E5**
Westbourne St. W2	57	G7
Westbourne Ter. W2	**10**	**C3**
Westbourne Ter. W2	57	F6
Westbourne Ter. Ms. W2	**10**	**C3**
Westbourne Ter. Ms. W2	57	F6
Westbourne Ter. Rd. W2	**10**	**C2**
Westbourne Ter. Rd. W2	57	F5
Westbridge Rd. SW11	75	G1
Westbrook Ave., Hmptn.	81	F7
Westbrook Clo., Barn.	23	G3
Westbrook Cres., Barn.	23	G3
Westbrook Rd. SE3	78	H1
Westbrook Rd., Houns.	63	F7
Westbrook Rd., Th.Hth.	95	A1
Westbrook Sq., Barn.	23	G3
Westbrooke Cres.		
Westbrooke Cres., Well.	80	C3
Westbrooke Rd., Sid.	88	G2
Westbrooke Rd., Well.	80	B3
Westbury Ave. N22	40	H3
Westbury Ave., Esher	98	C6
Westbury Ave., Sthl.	54	G4
Westbury Ave., Wem.	46	H7
Westbury Clo., Ruis.	36	A7
Westbury Gro. N12	31	D6
Westbury La., Buck.H.	26	J2
Westbury Lo. Clo., Pnr.	36	D3
Westbury Ms. E17	42	A4
Westbury Rd.		
Westbury Rd. E7	51	H5
Westbury Rd. E17	41	J4
Westbury Rd. N11	32	E6
Westbury Rd. N12	31	D6
Westbury Rd. SE20	95	H6
Westbury Rd. W5	55	H6
Westbury Rd., Bark.	61	G1
Westbury Rd., Beck.	95	H3
Westbury Rd., Brom.	97	A1
Westbury Rd., Buck.H.	34	J2
Westbury Rd., Croy.	95	A6
Westbury Rd., Felt.	81	H7
Westbury Rd., Ilf.	52	D2
Westbury Rd., N.Mal.		
Westbury Rd., Wem.	46	H7
Westbury St. SW8	76	C2
Westbury Ter. E7	51	H6
Westchester Dr. NW4	39	A3
Westcombe Ave., Croy.	94	E6
Westcombe Ct. SE3	69	F7
Westcombe Pk. Rd.		
Westcombe Dr., Barn.	23	D5
Westcombe Hill SE3	69	G6
Westcombe Hill SE10	69	G5
Westcombe Pk. Rd. SE3	69	E6
Westcoombe Ave. SW20	92	F1
Westcote Rd. SW16	85	C5
Westcott Clo. N15	41	C6
Ermine Rd.		
Westcott Clo., Brom.	97	B5
Ringmer Way		
Westcott Cres. W7	55	B6
Westcott Rd. SE17	**20**	**H5**
Westcott Rd. SE17	67	H6
Westcourt, Sun.	90	B2
Westcroft Clo. NW2	48	B4
Westcroft Gdns., Mord.	93	C3
Westcroft Rd., Cars.	101	A4
Westcroft Rd., Wall.	101	A4
Westcroft Sq. W6	65	G4
Westcroft Way NW2	48	B4
Westdale Pas. SE18	70	E6
Westdale Rd.		
Westdale Rd. SE18	70	E6
Westdean Ave. SE12	87	H1
Westdean Clo. SW18	75	E5
Westdown Rd. E15	51	C4
Westdown Rd. SE6	78	A7
Westel Ho. W5	55	F7
Westerdale Rd. SE10	69	G5
Westerfield Rd. N15	41	C5
Westergate Rd. SE2	71	E4
Westerham Ave. N9	33	A3
Westerham Dr., Sid.	80	B6
Westerham Rd. E10	42	B6
Westerham Rd., Kes.	104	A7
Westerley Cres. SE26	86	J5
Western Ave. NW11	39	A6
Western Ave. W3	56	A4
Western Ave. W5	55	J4
Western Ave., Dag.	53	J6
Western Ave., Grnf.	55	B2
Western Ave., Nthlt.	54	F1
Western Ave., Ruis.	54	F3
Western Ct. N3	31	D4
Huntley Dr.		
Western Gdns. W5	56	A7
Western Gateway E16	60	G7
Western Ho. W5	55	H3
Western La. SW12	76	A7
Western Ms. W9	57	C4
Great Western Rd.		
Western Pl. SE16	68	F2
Canon Beck Rd.		
Western Rd. E13	60	J1
Western Rd. E17	42	C5
Western Rd. N2	39	J4
Western Rd. N22	40	F2
Western Rd. NW10	56	C4
Western Rd. SW9	76	G3
Western Rd. SW19	93	G1
Western Rd. W5	55	G7
Western Rd., Mitch.	93	H1
Western Rd., Sthl.	63	C4
Western Rd., Sutt.	100	D5
Western Ter. W6	65	G5
Chiswick Mall		
Western Trd. Est. NW10	56	B4
Western Way SE28	70	G3
Western Way, Barn.	23	D6
Westernville Gdns., Ilf.	43	F7
Westferry Circ. E14	69	A1
Westferry Rd. E14	69	A2
Westfield, Loug.	26	J5
Westfield Clo. NW9	25	H3
Westfield Clo., Enf.		
Westfield Clo., Sutt.	100	C4
Westfield Dr., Har.	37	G4
Westfield Gdns., Har.	37	G4
Westfield La., Har.	37	G4
Westfield Pk., Pnr.	28	F7
Westfield Rd. NW7	30	D3
Westfield Rd. W13	64	D1
Westfield Rd., Beck.	95	J2
Westfield Rd., Bexh.	80	J2
Westfield Rd., Croy.	101	H2
Westfield Rd., Dag.	53	E4
Westfield Rd., Mitch.	93	J2

Westfield Rd., Surb. 91 G5
Westfield Rd., Sutt. 100 C4
Westfield Rd., Walt. 90 E7
Westfield St. SE18 70 A3
Westfields SW13 74 F3
Westfields Ave. SW13
Westfields Rd. W3 56 B5
Westgate Rd. SE25 95 E4
Westgate Rd., Beck. 96 C1
Westgate St. E8 59 E1
Westgate Ter. SW10 18 B4
Westgate Ter. SW10 66 E5
Westglade Ct., Har. 37 G5
Westgrove La. SE10 78 C1
Westhay Gdns. SW14 74 B5
Westholm NW11 39 E4
Westholme, Orp. 97 H7
Westholme Gdns., Ruis. 45 A1
Westhorpe Gdns. NW4 38 J3
Westhorpe Rd. SW15 74 J3
Westhurst Dr., Chis. 88 E5
Westlake Clo. N13 32 G3
Westlake Clo., Hayes 54 E4
Lochan Clo.
Westland Dr., Brom. 103 F2
Westland Pl. N1 9 B3
Westland Clo. 59 A3
Westlands Clo., 63 A4
Hayes
Granville Rd.
Westlands Ter. SW12 76 C6
Gaskarth Rd.
Westlea Rd. W7 64 D3
Westleigh Ave. SW15 74 H5
Westleigh Dr., 97 B1
Brom.
Westleigh Gdns., 38 A1
Edg.
Westmead SW15 74 H7
Westmead Rd., Sutt. 100 G4
Westmede, Chig. 35 F6
Westmere Dr. NW7 30 D3
Westmill Ct. N4 49 J2
Brownswood Rd.
Westminster Ave. 94 H2
Th.Hth.
Westminster Bri. 16 B4
SE1
Westminster Bri. 67 F2
SE1
Westminster Bri. 16 B4
SW1
Westminster Bri. 67 E2
SW1
Westminster Bri. 16 D4
Rd. SE1
Westminster Bri. 67 F2
Rd. SE1
Westminster 15 F6
Cathedral Piazza
SW1
Westminster Clo. 43 G2
Ilf.
Westminster Clo., 82 D5
Tedd.
Westminster Dr. N13 32 E5
Westminster Gdns. 34 E1
E4
Westminster Gdns., 61 H2
Bark.
Westminster Gdns., 43 F2
Ilf.
Westminster Rd. N9 33 E1
Westminster Rd. W7 64 B1
Westminster Rd., 100 G2
Sutt.
Westmoat Clo., 87 C7
Beck.
Westmont Rd., Esher 98 B2
Westmoor Gdns. 25 G2
Enf.
Westmoor Rd., Enf. 25 G2
Westmoor Rd. SE7 70 A3
Westmoreland Ave. 79 H3
Well.
Westmoreland Pl. 19 E4
SW1
Westmoreland Pl. 67 B5
SW1
Westmoreland Pl. 55 G5
W5
Mount Ave.

Westmoreland Rd. 37 J3
NW9
Westmoreland Rd. 21 B5
SE17
Westmoreland Rd. 68 A6
SE17
Westmoreland Rd. 74 F1
SW13
Westmoreland Rd., 96 E5
Brom.
Westmoreland St. 11 C2
W1
Westmoreland St. 58 A5
W1
Westmoreland Ter. 19 E4
SW1
Westmoreland Ter. 67 B5
SW1
Westmoreland Wk. 21 B5
SE17
Westmorland Clo. 52 A2
E12
Westmorland Clo., 73 E6
Twick.
Westmorland Rd. E17 42 A6
Westmorland Rd., 36 H5
Har.
Westmorland Way, 94 D4
Mitch.
Westmount Rd. SE9 79 C2
Westoe Rd. N9 33 E2
Weston Ave., 91 B7
T.Ditt.
Weston Ave., W.Mol. 90 E3
Weston Ct. N4 49 J3
Queens Dr.
Weston Dr., Stan. 37 E1
Weston Gdns., Islw. 73 A1
Weston Grn., Dag. 53 F4
Weston Grn., T.Ditt. 98 B1
Weston Grn. Rd., 98 A1
Esher
Weston Grn. Rd., 98 B1
T.Ditt.
Weston Gro., Brom. 87 F7
Weston Pk. N8 40 E6
Weston Pk., 91 H2
Kings.T.
Fairfield W.
Weston Pk., T.Ditt. 98 B1
Weston Pk. Clo., 98 B1
T.Ditt.
Weston Pk.
Weston Ri. WC1 8 D2
Weston Ri. WC1 58 F3
Weston Rd. W4 65 C3
Weston Rd., Brom. 87 F7
Weston Rd., Enf. 25 A1
Weston Rd., T.Ditt. 98 B1
Weston St. SE1 17 C3
Weston St. SE1 68 A2
Mare St.
Weston Wk. E8 50 E7
Westover Hill NW3 48 D2
Westover Rd. SW18 75 F7
Westow Hill SE19 86 B6
Westow St. SE19 86 B6
Westpoint Trd. Est. 56 A4
W3
Westpole Ave., 24 A4
Barn.
Westport Rd. E13 60 H4
Westport St. E1 59 G6
Westrow SW15 74 J6
Westrow Dr., Bark. 53 A5
Westrow Gdns., Ilf. 52 J2
Westside NW4 38 H2
Westview Clo. NW10 47 F5
Westview Clo. W7 55 B6
Westview Cres. N9 25 B7
Westview Dr., 43 G2
Wdf.Grn.
Westville Rd. W12 65 G2
Westville Rd., 98 D1
T.Ditt.
Westward Rd. E4 33 H5
Westward Way, Har. 37 H6
Westway NW7 30 G7
Westway SW20 92 H3
Westway W2 57 D5
Westway W9 57 D5
Westway W10 57 B6
Westway W12 56 F7
Westway, Orp. 97 J3
Westway Clo. SW20 92 H3
Westways, Epsom 99 F4
Westwell Rd. SW16 85 E6
Westwick Gdns. W14 66 A2
Westwick Gdns. 72 B2
Houns.
Westwood Ave. SE19 94 J1
Westwood Ave., Har. 45 H4

Westwood Clo., 97 A3
Brom.
Westwood Gdns. 74 F3
SW13
Westwood Hill SE26 86 D5
Westwood La., Sid. 80 A5
Westwood La., Well. 79 J3
Westwood Pk. SE23 77 E7
Westwood Rd. E16 69 H1
Westwood Rd. SW13 74 F3
Westwood Rd., Ilf. 52 J1
Wetheral Dr., Stan. 37 F1
Wetherby Clo., 45 H6
Nthlt.
Wetherby Gdns. 18 C2
SW5
Wetherby Gdns. 66 F4
SW5
Wetherby Ms. SW5 18 B3
Wetherby Pl. SW7 18 C2
Wetherby Pl. SW7 66 F4
Wetherby Rd., Enf. 24 J1
Wetherby Way, 98 H7
Chess.
Wetherden St. E17 41 J7
Wetherell Rd. E9 59 G1
Wetherill Rd. N10 40 A1
Wexford Rd. SW12 75 J7
Wey Ct., Epsom 99 C4
Weybourne St. 84 F2
SW18
Weybridge Pt. SW11 75 J2
Weybridge Rd., 94 G4
Th.Hth.
Weydown Clo. SW19 84 B1
Weyhill Rd. E1 13 J3
Weylond Rd., Dag. 53 E3
Weyman Rd. SE3 78 J1
Weymouth Ave. NW7 30 E5
Weymouth Ave. W5 64 F3
Weymouth Ct., Sutt. 100 D7
Weymouth Ms. W1 11 D1
Weymouth Ms. W1 58 B5
Weymouth St. W1 11 C2
Weymouth St. W1 58 A5
Weymouth Ter. E2 9 G1
Weymouth Ter. E2 59 C2
Weymouth Wk. 29 D6
Stan.
Whadcote St. N4 49 G2
Seven Sisters Rd.
Whalebone Ave., 44 F6
Rom.
Whalebone Ct. EC2 13 C3
Whalebone Gro., 44 F6
Rom.
Whalebone La. E15 51 E7
West Ham La.
Whalebone La. N., 44 E2
Rom.
Whalebone La. N., 44 F7
Dag.
Whalebone La. S., 44 F6
Rom.
Wharf La., Twick. 82 D1
Wharf Pl. E2 59 D1
Wharf Rd. E15 60 D1
Wharf Rd. N1 8 J2
Wharf Rd. N1 58 J2
Wharf Rd., Enf. 25 H6
Wharf Rd. Ind. 25 H6
Est., Enf.
Wharf St. E16 60 E5
Wharfdale Ct. E5 50 G4
Rushmore Rd.
Wharfdale Rd. N1 8 B1
Wharfdale Rd. N1 58 E2
Wharfedale Gdns., 94 F4
Th.Hth.
Wharfedale St. SW10 18 A4
Wharfside Rd. E16 60 E5
Wharncliffe Dr., 64 A1
Sthl.
Wharncliffe Gdns. 95 B2
SE25
Wharncliffe Rd. SE25 95 B2
Wharton Clo. NW10 47 E6
Wharton Rd., Brom. 96 H1
Wharton St. WC1 8 D4
Wharton St. WC1 58 F3
Whateley Rd. SE20 86 D7
Whateley Rd. SE22 77 C5
Whatley Ave. SW20 93 A3
Whatman Rd. SE23 77 G7
Wheatfield Way, 91 H2
Kings.T.
Wheatfields, Enf. 25 H2
Wheathill Rd. SE20 95 E2
Wheatlands, Houns. 63 G6
Wheatlands Rd. 85 A3
SW17
Stapleton Rd.
Wheatley Clo. NW4 38 G2

Wheatley Cres. 54 A7
Hayes
Wheatley Gdns. N9 33 B2
Wheatley Rd., Islw. 73 C3
Wheatley St. W1 11 C2
Wheatsheaf Clo., 45 E5
Nthlt.
Wheatsheaf La. SW6 65 J7
Wheatsheaf La. SW8 20 A7
Wheatsheaf La. SW8 67 E7
Wheatsheaf Ter. 66 C7
SW6
Bishops Rd.
Wheatstone Clo., 93 H1
Mitch.
Wheatstone Rd. W10 57 B6
Portobello Rd.
Wheel Fm. Dr., Dag. 53 J3
Wheeler Gdns. N1 58 E1
Outram Pl.
Wheelers Cross, 61 G2
Bark.
Wheelwright St. N7 49 F7
Whelan Way, Wall. 101 D3
Wheler St. E1 9 F6
Wheler St. E1 59 C4
Whellock Rd. W4 65 E3
Whenman Ave., Bex. 89 J2
Whernside Clo. SE28 62 C7
Whetstone Clo. N20 31 G2
Oakleigh Rd.
Whetstone Pk. WC2 12 C3
Whetstone Rd. SE3 78 J2
Whewell Rd. N19 49 E2
Whichcote St. SE1 16 C2
Whidborne Clo. SE8 78 A2
Cliff Ter.
Whidborne St. WC1 8 B4
Whidborne St. WC1 58 E3
Whimbrel Clo. SE28 62 C7
Whinchat Rd. SE28 70 G3
Whinfell Clo. SW16 85 D5
Whinyates Rd. SE9 79 B3
Whipps Cross Rd. 42 D5
E11
Whiskin St. EC1 8 G4
Whiskin St. EC1 58 H3
Whisperwood Clo., 29 B7
Har.
Whistler Gdns., Edg. 37 J2
Whistler St. N5 49 H4
Whistler Wk. SW10 18 D7
Whistlers Ave. SW11 56 G2
Whiston Rd. E2 59 C2
Whitakers Way, 27 C1
Loug.
Whitbread Clo. N17 41 D1
Whitbread Rd. SE4 77 H4
Whitburn Rd. SE13 78 B4
Whitby Ave. NW10 56 B3
Whitby Gdns. NW9 38 A3
Whitby Gdns., Sutt. 100 G2
Whitby Rd. SE18 70 C4
Whitby Rd., Har. 45 J3
Whitby Rd., Ruis. 45 B3
Whitby Rd., Sutt. 100 G2
Whitby St. E1 9 F5
Whitcher Clo. SE14 68 H6
Chubworthy St.
Whitcher Pl. NW1 49 C7
Rochester Rd.
Whitchurch Ave. 29 J7
Edg.
Whitchurch Clo. 29 J6
Edg.
Whitchurch Gdns. 29 J6
Edg.
Whitchurch La., Edg. 29 G7
Whitchurch Rd. W11 57 A7
Whitcomb Ct. WC2 58 D7
Whitcomb St.
Whitcomb St. WC2 11 J6
Whitcomb St. WC2 58 D7
White Acre NW9 38 E2
White Adder Way 69 B4
Spindrift Ave.
White Bear Pl. NW3 48 G4
New End Sq.
White Ch. La. E1 13 H3
White Ch. La. E1 59 D6
White Ch. Pas. E1 13 H3
White City Clo. W12 56 J7
White City Rd. W12 56 H7
White City Rd. W12 56 H7
White Conduit St. 8 F1
N1
White Craig Clo., 28 G5
Pnr.
White Gdns., Dag. 53 G6
Sterry Rd.
White Gate Gdns., 29 C7
Har.

White Hart La. N17 32 J7
White Hart La. N22 40 G1
White Hart La. NW10 47 F6
  Church Rd.
White Hart La. SW13 74 E2
White Hart La., 44 G1
  Rom.
White Hart Rd. SE18 70 H4
White Hart Slip, 96 G2
  Brom.
White Hart St. SE11 20 F3
White Hart St. SE11 67 G5
White Hart Yd. SE1 17 B2
White Horse Hill, 88 C4
  Chis.
White Horse La. E1 59 G4
White Horse Rd. E1 59 H6
White Horse Rd. E6 61 C3
White Horse St. W1 15 E2
White Horse St. W1 67 B1
White Ho. Dr., 29 F4
  Stan.
White Kennet St. E1 13 E3
White Lion Ct. EC3 13 D4
White Lion Hill EC4 58 H7
White Lion Hill EC4 12 H5
White Lion St. N1 8 E2
White Lion St. N1 58 G2
White Lion Yd. W1 11 D5
White Lo. SE19 85 H7
White Lo. Clo. N2 39 G6
White Lo. Clo., 100 F7
  Sutt.
White Oak Dr., 96 C2
  Beck.
White Orchards N20 23 C7
White Orchards, 29 D5
  Stan.
White Post La. E9 50 J7
White Post La. SE13 70 A3
White Post St. SE15 68 F7
White Rd. E15 51 E7
White St., Sthl. 63 D2
White Swan Ms. W4 65 E6
  Bennett St.
Whiteadder Way E14 69 B4
  Spindrift Ave.
Whitear Wk. E15 51 D6
Whitebarn La., Dag. 62 E7
Whitebeam Ave., 97 D7
  Brom.
Whitebeam Clo. SW9 67 F7
  Clapham Rd.
Whitebeam Twr. E17 41 H3
Whitebutts Rd., 45 D3
  Ruis.
**Whitechapel High 13 G3
  St. E1**
Whitechapel High 59 C6
  St. E1
Whitechapel Rd. E1 13 H2
Whitechapel Rd. E1 59 D5
Whitecote Rd., 54 J6
  Sthl.
Whitecroft Clo., 96 D4
  Beck.
Whitecroft Way, 96 C5
  Beck.
Whitecross Pl. EC2 13 C1
Whitecross St. EC1 9 A5
Whitecross St. EC1 58 J4
Whitecross St. EC2 13 A1
Whitecross St. EC2 58 J5
Whitefield Ave. NW2 38 J7
Whitefield Clo. 75 B6
  SW15
Whitefoot La., 87 C4
  Brom.
Whitefoot Ter., 87 E3
  Brom.
Whitefriars Ave., 37 B2
  Har.
Whitefriars Dr., Har. 37 A2
  Whitefriars Ave.
Whitefriars St. EC4 12 F4
Whitefriars St. EC4 58 G6
Whitehall SW1 16 A1
Whitehall SW1 67 E1
Whitehall Ct. SW1 16 B2
Whitehall Ct. SW1 67 E1
Whitehall Cres., 98 G5
  Chess.
Whitehall Gdns. E4 34 D1
Whitehall Gdns. SW1 16 A2
Whitehall Gdns. W3 65 A1
Whitehall Gdns. W4 65 B6
Whitehall La., 32 C2
  Buck.H.
Whitehall Pk. N19 49 C1
Whitehall Pk. Rd. 65 B6
  W4
Whitehall Pl. SW1 16 A2
Whitehall Pl. SW1 67 E1

Whitehall Pl., Wall. 101 B4
  Bernard Rd.
Whitehall Rd. E4 34 E2
Whitehall Rd. W7 64 D2
Whitehall Rd., 97 A5
  Brom.
Whitehall Rd., Har. 37 B7
Whitehall Rd., 94 G6
  Th.Hth.
Whitehall Rd., 34 F2
  Wdf.Grn.
Whitehall St. N17 33 C7
Whitehaven Clo. 96 G4
  Brom.
Whitehaven St. NW8 6 G6
Whitehead Clo. N18 33 A5
Whitehead Clo. 75 F7
  SW18
**Whitehead's Gro. 18 H3
  SW3**
Whitehead's Gro. 66 H5
  SW3
Whitehills Rd., 27 D3
  Loug.
Whitehorn Gdns., 102 E2
  Croy.
Whitehorse Rd. SE1 16 F5
Whitehorse Rd., 94 J7
  Croy.
Whitehorse Rd., 95 A4
  Th.Hth.
Whitehouse Ave 22 B3
  Borwd.
Whitehouse La., 24 J1
  Enf.
  Brigadier Hill
Whitehouse Way 32 B2
  N14
Whiteledgcs W13 55 F6
Whitelegg Rd. E13 60 F2
Whiteley Rd. SE19 86 A5
Whiteleys Cotts. 66 C4
  W14
Whiteleys Way, 81 G3
  Felt.
Whiteoak Gdns., 79 J7
  Sid.
Whiteoaks La., 55 A2
  Grnf.
Whites Ave., Ilf. 43 H6
Whites Dr., Brom. 96 F7
Whites Grds. SE1 17 E4
Whites Grds. SE1 68 B2
**Whites Grds. SE1 17 E3
  SE1**
White's Row E1 13 F2
White's Row E1 59 C5
White's Sq. SW4 76 D4
  Nelson's Row
Whitestile Rd., 64 F5
  Brent.
Whitestone La. NW3 48 F3
  Heath St.
Whitestone Wk. NW3 48 F3
  North End Way
Whitethorn Gdns., 25 A5
  Enf.
Whitethorn St. E3 60 A4
Whitewebbs Way, 97 J1
  Orp.
Whitfield Pl. W1 7 F6
Whitfield Rd. E6 51 J7
Whitfield Rd. SE3 78 D1
Whitfield Rd., 71 F7
  Bexh.
Whitfield St. W1 7 F6
Whitfield St. W1 58 C4
Whitford Gdns., 93 J3
  Mitch.
Whitgift Ave., 101 H5
  S.Croy.
Whitgift St. SE11 20 C1
Whitgift St. SE11 67 F4
Whitgift St., Croy. 101 J3
  High St.
Whiting Ave., Bark. 52 E7
Whitings, Ilf. 43 G5
Whitings Rd., Barn. 22 J5
Whitings Way E6 61 D5
Whitland Rd., Cars. 100 G1
Whitley Rd. N17 41 B2
Whitlock Dr. SW19 75 B7
Whitman Rd. E3 59 H4
Whitmead Clo., 102 B6
  S.Croy.
Whitmore Clo. N11 32 B5
Whitmore Gdns. 56 J2
  NW10
Whitmore Rd. N1 59 E1
Whitmore Rd., Beck. 95 J3
Whitmore Rd., Har. 36 J7
Whitnell Way SW15 74 J5

Whitney Ave., Ilf. 43 A4
Whitney Rd. E10 42 A7
Whitney Wk., Sid. 89 E6
Whitstable Clo., 95 J1
  Beck.
Whitta Rd. E12 52 A4
Whittaker Ave., 73 G5
  Rich.
  Hill St.
Whittaker Rd. E6 52 A7
Whittaker Rd., 100 C3
  Sutt.
Whittaker St. SW1 19 B2
Whittaker St. SW1 67 A4
Whittaker Way SE1 21 J2
Whittell Gdns. SE26 86 F3
Whittingstall Rd. 75 C1
  SW6
**Whittington Ave. 13 D4
  EC3**
Whittington Ct. N2 39 J5
Whittington Rd. N22 32 E7
Whittington Way, 36 E5
  Pnr.
Whittle Clo., Sthl. 54 H6
Whittle Rd., Houns. 63 C7
Whittlebury Clo., 100 J7
  Cars.
Whittlesea Clo., 28 J7
  Har.
  Whittlesea Rd.
Whittlesea Path, 36 J1
  Har
Whittlesea Rd., 36 J1
  Har.
Whittlesey St. SE1 16 F2
Whitton Ave. E., 46 B5
  Grnf.
Whitton Ave. W., 46 A5
  Grnf.
Whitton Ave. W., 45 H5
  Nthlt.
Whitton Clo., Grnf. 46 D6
Whitton Dene, 72 H5
  Houns.
Whitton Dene, Islw. 73 A5
Whitton Dr., Grnf. 46 D6
Whitton Manor Rd., 72 D5
  Islw.
Whitton Rd., Houns. 72 H4
Whitton Rd., Twick. 73 C6
Whitton Wk. E3 60 A3
Whitton Waye, 72 G6
  Houns.
Whitwell Rd. E13 60 G3
Whitworth Pl. SE18 70 E4
Whitworth Rd. SE18 70 D6
Whitworth Rd. SE25 95 B3
Whitworth St. SE10 55 H7
Whorlton Rd. SE15 77 E3
Whymark Ave. N22 40 G3
Whytecroft, Houns. 63 D7
Whyteville Rd. E7 51 H6
Wick La. E3 50 D5
Wick Rd. E9 50 G6
Wick Rd., Tedd. 82 E7
Wick Sq. E9 50 J6
  Eastway
Wicker St. E1 59 E6
  Burslem St.
Wickers Oake SE19 86 C4
Wickersley Rd. SW11 76 A2
Wicket, The, Croy. 103 A5
Wicket Rd., Grnf. 55 D3
Wickets Way, Ilf. 35 J6
Wickford St. E1 59 F5
Wickford Way E17 41 G4
Wickham Ave., Croy. 102 H2
Wickham Ave., Sutt. 99 J5
Wickham Chase, 103 D1
  W.Wick.
Wickham Clo., Enf. 25 E3
Wickham Clo., 92 F5
  N.Mal.
Wickham Ct. Rd., 103 C2
  W.Wick.
Wickham Cres., 103 C2
  W.Wick.
Wickham Gdns. SE4 77 J3
Wickham Ho. E1 59 F5
  Jamaica St.
Wickham La. SE2 71 A5
Wickham Ms. SE4 77 J2
Wickham Rd. E4 34 C7
Wickham Rd. SE4 77 J3
Wickham Rd., Beck. 96 B2
Wickham Rd., Croy. 102 F2
Wickham Rd., Har. 37 A2
Wickham St. SE11 20 C3
Wickham St. SE11 67 F5
Wickham St., Well. 79 H2
Wickham Way, Beck. 96 C4
Wickliffe Ave. N3 39 B2

Wickliffe Gdns., 47 B2
  Wem.
Wicklow St. WC1 8 C3
Wicklow St. WC1 58 F3
Wicks Clo. SE9 88 A4
Wicksteed Ho., 64 J5
  Brent.
Wickwood St. SE5 76 H2
Widdecombe Ave., 45 E2
  Har.
Widdenham Rd. N7 49 F4
Widdin St. E15 51 D7
Wide Way, Mitch. 94 D3
Widecombe Gdns., 43 B4
  Ilf.
Widecombe Rd. SE9 88 B3
Widecombe Way N2 39 G5
Widegate St. E1 13 E2
Widenham Clo., Pnr. 36 C5
  Bridle Rd.
Widgeon Clo. E16 60 H6
  Maplin Rd.
Widley Rd. W9 57 D3
Widmore Lo. Rd., 97 A2
  Brom.
Widmore Rd., Brom. 96 G2
Wieland Rd., Nthwd. 28 A7
Wigan Ho. E5 50 F7
  Warwick Gro.
Wigeon Path SE28 70 G3
Wiggington Ave., 47 B6
  Wem.
Wiggins Mead NW9 30 F7
Wigham Ho., Bark. 52 F7
Wightman Rd. N4 40 G4
Wightman Rd. N8 40 G4
Wigley Rd., Felt. 81 D2
Wigmore Pl. W1 11 D3
Wigmore Pl. W1 58 B6
Wigmore Rd., Cars. 100 G2
Wigmore St. W1 11 B4
Wigmore St. W1 58 A6
Wigram Rd. E11 42 J6
Wigram Sq. E17 42 D2
Wigston Rd. E13 60 H4
Wigston Gdns., Stan. 37 H1
Wigton Pl. SE11 20 F4
Wigton Rd. E17 41 J1
Wilberforce Rd. N4 49 H2
Wilberforce Rd. NW9 38 G6
Wilberforce Way 84 A6
  SW19
Wilbraham Pl. SW1 19 A1
Wilbraham Pl. SW1 66 J4
Wilbury Way N18 33 A6
Wilby Ms. W11 66 C1
Wilcox Clo. SW8 20 B7
Wilcox Clo. SW8 67 E7
Wilcox Clo., Borwd. 22 C1
Wilcox Pl. SW1 15 G6
Wilcox Rd. SW8 20 A7
Wilcox Rd. SW8 67 E7
Wilcox Rd., Sutt. 100 E4
Wilcox Rd., Tedd. 82 A4
Wild Ct. WC2 12 C3
Wild Ct. WC2 58 E5
Wild Goose Dr. SE14 77 F1
Wild Hatch NW11 39 D6
Wild St. WC2 12 B4
Wild St. WC2 58 E6
Wildcroft Gdns., 29 G6
  Edg.
Wildcroft Rd. SW15 74 J7
Wilde Clo. E8 59 D1
Wilde Pl. N13 32 H6
  Medesenge Way
Wilde Pl. SW18 75 G7
  Heathfield Rd.
Wilder Clo., Ruis. 45 B1
Wilderness, The, 81 H4
  Hmptn.
  Park Rd.
Wilderness Rd., 88 E7
  Chis.
Wilderton Rd. N16 41 B7
Wildfell Rd. SE6 78 B7
Wild's Rents SE1 17 D5
Wild's Rents SE1 68 B3
Wildwood Clo. SE12 78 F7
Wildwood Gro. NW3 48 F1
  North End Rd.
Wildwood Ri. NW11 48 F1
Wildwood Rd. NW11 39 E6
Wildwood Ter. NW3 48 F1
Wilford Clo., Enf. 25 A3
Wilfred Owen Clo. 84 F6
  SW19
  Tennyson Rd.
Wilfred St. SW1 15 F5
Wilfred St. SW1 67 C3
Wilfred Turney Est. 65 H3
  W6
  Sycamore Gdns.

Wilfrid Gdns. W3 56 C5
Wilkes St. E1 13 G1
Wilkes St. E1 59 C5
Wilkie Way SE22 86 D1
  Lordship La.
Wilkin St. NW5 49 B6
Wilkin St. Ms. NW5 49 B6
  Wilkin St.
Wilkins Clo., 93 H1
  Mitch.
Wilkinson Rd. E16 60 J6
Wilkinson St. SW8 67 F7
Wilkinson Way W4 65 D2
  Southfield Rd.
Wilks Pl. N1 9 E2
Will Crooks Gdns. 78 J4
  SE9
Willan Rd. N17 41 A2
Willan Wall E16 60 F7
  Victoria Dock Rd.
Willard St. SW8 76 B3
Willcocks Clo., 98 H3
  Chess.
Willcott Rd. W3 65 B1
Willenhall Ave., 23 F6
  Barn.
Willenhall Rd. SE18 70 E5
Willersley Ave., 104 G3
  Orp.
Willersley Ave., 88 J1
  Sid.
Willersley Clo., 88 J1
  Sid.
Willes Rd. NW5 49 B6
Willesden La. NW2 47 J6
Willesden La. NW6 57 C1
Willet Way SE16 68 E5
  Egan Way
Willett Clo., 54 C3
  Nthlt.
  Broomcroft Ave.
Willett Clo., Orp. 97 H6
Willett Pl., 94 G5
  Th.Hth.
  Willett Rd.
Willett Rd., 94 G5
  Th.Hth.
Willett Way, Orp. 97 G5
William Barefoot Dr. 88 C4
  SE9
William Bonney Est. 76 D4
  SW4
William Booth Rd. 95 D1
  SE20
William Carey Way, 37 B6
  Har.
William Clo., Rom. 44 J1
William Dunbar Ho. 57 C2
  NW6
William Ellis Way 17 J4
  SE16
William IV St. WC2 12 A6
William IV St. WC2 58 E7
William Gdns. SW15 74 H5
William Guy Gdns. 60 B3
  E3
  Talwin St.
William Margrie Clo. 77 D2
  SE15
  Moncrieff St.
William Morris Clo. 61 A1
  E17
William Pl. E3 59 J2
  Roman Rd.
William Rd. NW1 7 F4
William Rd. NW1 58 C3
William Rd. SW19 84 B7
William Rd., Sutt. 100 F5
William Saville Ho. 57 C2
  NW6
William St. E10 42 B6
William St. N17 33 C7
William St. SW1 15 A4
William St. SW1 66 J2
William St., Bark. 52 F7
William St., Cars. 100 H3
Williams Ave. E17 41 J1
Williams Bldgs. E2 59 F4
Williams Clo. N8 40 D6
  Coolhurst Rd.
Williams Gro. N22 40 G1
William's La. SW14 74 C3
Williams La., Mord. 93 F5
Williams Rd. W13 55 D7
Williams Rd., Sthl. 63 E4
Williams Ter., 101 G6
  Croy.
Williamson Clo. 69 F4
  SE10
  Lenthorp Rd.

Williamson Rd. N4 40 H6
Williamson St. N7 49 E4
Williamson Way 31 B6
  NW7
Willifield Way NW11 39 C4
Willingale Clo., 27 F2
  Loug.
  Willingale Rd.
Willingale Clo., 34 J6
  Wdf.Grn.
Willingale Rd., Loug. 27 F1
Willingdon Rd. N22 40 H2
Willingham Ter. NW5 49 C5
  Leighton Rd.
Willingham Way, 92 A3
  Kings.T.
Willington Ct. E5 50 H3
  Mandeville St.
Willington Rd. SW9 76 E3
Willis Ave., Sutt. 100 H7
Willis Rd. E15 60 F2
Willis Rd., Croy. 94 J7
Willis Rd., Erith 71 J4
Willis St. E14 60 H6
Willmore End SW19 93 E1
Willoughby Ave., 101 F4
  Croy.
Willoughby Gro. N17 33 E7
Willoughby La. N17 33 E6
Willoughby Pk. Rd. 33 E7
  N17
Willoughby Rd. N8 40 G3
Willoughby Rd. NW3 48 G4
Willoughby Rd., 91 J1
  Kings.T.
Willoughby Rd., 73 G6
  Twick.
Willoughby St. WC1 12 A2
Willoughby Way SE7 69 H4
Willow Ave. SW13 74 F2
Willow Ave., Sid. 80 A6
Willow Bank SW6 75 B3
Willow Bank, Rich. 82 E3
Willow Bri. Rd. N1 49 J6
Willow Clo. W5 55 G5
Willow Clo., Bex. 80 F6
Willow Clo., Brent. 64 F6
Willow Clo., Brom. 97 C5
Willow Clo., 35 A3
  Buck.H.
Willow Clo., 94 G6
  Th.Hth.
Willow Cotts., 94 C3
  Mitch.
Willow Ct., Edg. 29 H4
Willow Dene, Pnr. 36 D2
Willow Dr., Barn. 23 B4
Willow End N20 31 D2
Willow End, Nthwd. 28 A6
Willow End, Surb. 98 H1
Willow Gdns., 72 G1
  Houns.
Willow Grn. NW9 38 E1
  Clayton Fld.
Willow Gro. E13 60 G2
  Lettsom Wk.
Willow Gro., Chis. 88 D6
Willow La., Mitch. 93 J6
Willow Mt., Croy. 102 B3
  Langton Way
Willow Pl. SW1 19 G1
Willow Pl. SW1 67 C4
Willow Rd. NW3 48 G4
Willow Rd. W5 64 H2
Willow Rd., Enf. 25 B3
Willow Rd., N.Mal. 92 C4
Willow Rd., Rom. 44 E6
Willow Rd., Wall. 101 B7
Willow St. E4 26 D7
Willow St. EC2 9 D5
Willow St. EC2 59 B4
Willow St., Rom. 44 J4
Willow Tree Clo. 84 E1
  SW18
  Cargill Rd.
Willow Tree Clo., 54 C4
  Hayes
Willow Tree La., 54 C4
  Hayes
Willow Tree Wk., 96 H1
  Brom.
Willow Vale W12 65 G1
Willow Vale, Chis. 88 E6
Willow Vw. SW19 93 G1
Willow Wk. E17 41 J5
Willow Wk. N2 39 G2
  Central Ave.
Willow Wk. N15 40 H5
Willow Wk. N21 24 F6
Willow Wk. SE1 21 E1
Willow Wk. SE1 68 B4
Willow Wk., Orp. 104 E3
Willow Wk., Sutt. 100 C3

Willow Way N3 31 E7
Willow Way SE26 86 E3
Willow Way W11 57 A7
  St. Anns Rd.
Willow Way, Epsom 99 D6
Willow Way, Sun. 90 A4
Willow Way, Twick. 81 H2
Willow Way, Wem. 46 D3
Willow Wd. Cres. 95 B6
  SE25
Willowbrook Rd. 21 G6
  SE15
Willowbrook Rd. 68 C6
  SE15
Willowbrook Rd., 63 G3
  Sthl.
Willowcourt Ave., 37 E5
  Har.
Willowdene N6 39 J7
  Denewood Rd.
Willowdene Clo., 72 J7
  Twick.
Willowhayne Dr., 90 B7
  Walt.
Willowhayne Gdns., 99 J3
  Wor.Pk.
Willowmead Clo. W5 55 G5
Willows, The, 35 A3
  Buck.H.
Willows, The, Esher 98 B6
  Albany Cres.
Willows Ave., Mord. 93 E5
Willows Clo., Pnr. 36 C2
Willrose Cres. SE2 71 B5
Wills Cres., Houns. 72 H6
Wills Gro. NW7 30 G5
Wilman Gro. E8 50 D7
Wilmar Gdns., 103 B1
  W.Wick.
Wilmcote Ho. W2 57 D5
Wilmer Clo., 82 J5
  Kings.T.
Wilmer Cres., 82 J5
  Kings.T.
Wilmer Gdns. N1 59 B1
Wilmer Lea Clo. E15 51 C7
Wilmer Way N14 32 D5
Wilmington Ave. W4 65 D7
Wilmington Gdns., 59 B1
  Bark.
Wilmington Sq. WC1 8 E4
Wilmington Sq. WC1 58 G3
Wilmington St. WC1 8 E4
Wilmot Clo. N2 39 F2
Wilmot Clo. SE15 68 D7
Wilmot Pl. NW1 49 C7
Wilmot Pl. W7 64 B1
  Boston Rd.
Wilmot Rd. E10 51 B2
Wilmot Rd. N17 41 A3
Wilmot Rd., Cars. 100 J5
Wilmot St. E2 59 E4
Wilmount St. SE18 70 E4
Wilna Rd. SW18 75 F7
Wilsham St. W11 66 A1
Wilshaw St. SE14 78 A1
Wilsmere Dr., Har. 29 B7
Wilsmere Dr., 45 E6
  Nthlt.
Wilson Ave., Mitch. 84 H7
Wilson Clo., Wem. 37 J7
Wilson Dr., Wem. 37 J7
Wilson Gdns., Har. 36 J7
Wilson Gro. SE16 68 E2
Wilson Rd. E6 61 A3
Wilson Rd. SE5 77 B1
Wilson Rd., Chess. 98 J6
Wilson Rd., Ilf. 43 C7
Wilson St. E17 42 C5
Wilson St. EC2 13 C1
Wilson St. EC2 59 A5
Wilson St. N21 24 G7
Wilsons Pl. E14 59 J6
  Salmon La.
Wilsons Rd. W6 66 A5
Wilstone Clo., 54 E4
  Hayes
  Kingsash Dr.
Wilthorne Gdns., 53 H7
  Dag.
  Acre Rd.
Wilton Ave. W4 65 E5
Wilton Cres. SW1 15 B4
Wilton Cres. SW1 67 A2
Wilton Cres. SW19 93 C1
Wilton Gdns., 90 G3
  W.Mol.
Wilton Gro. SW19 93 C1
Wilton Gro., N.Mal. 92 F6
Wilton Ms. SW1 15 C5
Wilton Ms. SW1 67 A3
Wilton Par., Felt. 81 A2
  Highfield Rd.

Wilton Pk. Ct. SE18 79 D1
  Prince Imperial Rd.
Wilton Pl. SW1 15 B4
Wilton Pl. SW1 67 A2
Wilton Rd. N10 40 A2
Wilton Rd. SE2 71 C4
Wilton Rd. SW1 15 E6
Wilton Rd. SW1 67 C4
Wilton Rd. SW19 84 H7
Wilton Rd., Barn. 23 J4
Wilton Rd., Houns. 72 D3
Wilton Rd., Ilf. 52 E3
Wilton Row SW1 15 B4
Wilton Row SW1 67 A2
Wilton Sq. N1 59 A1
Wilton St. SW1 15 D5
Wilton St. SW1 67 B3
Wilton Ter. SW1 15 B5
Wilton Ter. SW1 67 A3
Wilton Vill. N1 59 A1
Wilton Way E8 50 D6
Wiltshire Clo. SW3 18 J2
Wiltshire Gdns. N4 40 J6
Wiltshire Gdns., 81 J1
  Twick.
Wiltshire Rd. SW9 76 G3
Wiltshire Rd., Th.Hth. 94 G3
Wiltshire Row N1 59 A1
Wilverley Cres., 92 E6
  N.Mal.
Wimbart Rd. SW2 76 F7
Wimbledon Bri. 84 C6
  SW19
Wimbledon Hill Rd. 84 B6
  SW19
Wimbledon Pk. Est. 84 C1
  SW19
Wimbledon Pk. Rd. 84 C1
  SW18
Wimbledon Pk. Rd. 84 B2
  SW19
Wimbledon Pk. Side 84 A2
  SW19
Wimbledon Rd. 84 F4
  SW17
Wimbledon Sta. 84 C6
  SW19
  The Bdy.
Wimbolt St. E2 9 H3
Wimbolt St. E2 59 D3
Wimborne Ave. 54 B6
  Hayes
Wimborne Ave., Orp. 97 J3
Wimborne Ave., 63 G4
  Sthl.
Wimborne Clo. SE12 78 F5
Wimborne Clo., 34 J2
  Buck.H.
Wimborne Clo., 99 J1
  Wor.Pk.
Wimborne Dr. NW9 38 A3
Wimborne Dr., Pnr. 36 D7
Wimborne Gdns. 55 E5
  W13
Wimborne Rd. N9 33 D2
Wimborne Rd. N17 41 B2
Wimborne Way, 95 G4
  Beck.
Wimbourne St. N1 9 B1
Wimbourne St. N1 59 A2
Wimpole Clo., Brom. 96 J4
Wimpole Clo., 91 J2
  Kings.T.
Wimpole Ms. W1 11 D1
Wimpole Ms. W1 58 B5
Wimpole St. W1 11 D2
Wimpole St. W1 58 B6
Winans Wk. SW9 76 G2
Wincanton Cres., 45 G5
  Nthlt.
Wincanton Gdns., 43 E3
  Ilf.
Wincanton Rd. SW18 75 C7
Winchcomb Gdns. 79 A3
  SE9
Winchcombe Rd. 100 G2
  Cars.
Winchelsea Ave., 71 F7
  Bexh.
Winchelsea Clo. 75 A5
  SW15
Winchelsea Rd. E7 51 G4
Winchelsea Rd. N17 41 B3
Winchelsea Rd. 56 D1
  NW10
Winchelsey Ri., 102 C6
  S.Croy.
Winchendon Rd. 66 C7
  SW6
Winchendon Rd., 82 A4
  Tedd.

Name	Page	Grid
Winchester Ave. NW6	57	B1
Winchester Ave. NW9	37	J3
Winchester Ave., Houns.	63	F6
Winchester Clo. E6	61	B6
Boultwood Rd.		
Winchester Clo. SE17	**20**	**H2**
Winchester Clo. SE17	67	H4
Winchester Clo., Brom.	96	F3
Winchester Clo., Enf.	25	B5
Winchester Clo., Kings.T.	83	B7
Winchester Dr., Pnr.	36	D5
Winchester Ho. SE18	70	A7
Shooter's Hill Rd.		
Winchester Ms. NW3	48	G7
Winchester Rd.		
Winchester Pk., Brom.	96	F3
Winchester Pl. N6	49	B1
Cromwell Ave.		
Winchester Pl. W3	65	C2
Avenue Rd.		
Winchester Rd. E4	34	C7
Winchester Rd. N6	40	B7
Winchester Rd. N9	33	D2
Winchester Rd. NW3	48	G7
Winchester Rd., Bexh.	80	D2
Winchester Rd., Brom.	96	F3
Winchester Rd., Felt.	81	F3
Winchester Rd., Har.	37	H4
Winchester Rd., Ilf.	52	G3
Winchester Rd., Twick.	73	E7
Winchester Sq. SE1	**17**	**B1**
Winchester St. SW1	**19**	**E3**
Winchester St. SW1	67	B5
Winchester St. W3	65	C2
Winchester Wk. SE1	**17**	**B1**
Winchester Wk. SE1	68	A1
Winchfield Clo., Har.	37	F6
Winchfield Rd. SE26	86	H5
Winchilsea Cres., W.Mol.	90	J2
Winchmore Hill Rd. N14	32	D1
Winchmore Hill Rd. N21	24	F7
Winckley Clo., Har.	37	J5
Wincott St. SE11	**20**	**F2**
Wincott St. SE11	67	G4
Wincrofts Dr. SE9	79	G4
Windborough Rd., Cars.	101	A7
Windermere Ave. N3	39	D3
Windermere Ave. NW6	57	B1
Windermere Ave. SW19	93	E3
Windermere Ave., Har.	37	F7
Windermere Ave., Ruis.	36	C7
Windermere Ave., Wem.	37	F7
Windermere Clo., Orp.	104	E3
Windermere Ct. SW13	65	F6
Windermere Gdns., Ilf.	43	B5
Windermere Gro., Wem.	46	F1
Windermere Ave.		
Windermere Ho., Islw.	73	C5
Windermere Rd. N10	40	A1
Windermere Rd. N19	49	C2
Holloway Rd.		
Windermere Rd. SW15	83	E4
Windermere Rd. SW16	94	C1
Windermere Rd. W5	64	F3
Windermere Rd., Bexh.	80	J2
Windermere Rd., Croy.	102	C1
Windermere Rd., Sthl.	54	F5
Windermere Rd., W.Wick.	103	E2
Winders Rd. SW11	75	H2
Windfield Clo. SE26	86	G4
Windham Rd., Rich.	73	J3
Winding Way, Dag.	53	C3
Winding Way, Har.	46	B4
Windlass Pl. SE8	68	H4
Windlesham Gro. SW19	84	A1
Windley Clo. SE23	86	F2
Windmill Clo. SE13	78	C2
Windmill Clo., Surb.	98	F1
Windmill Ct. NW2	48	B6
Windmill Dr. SW4	76	B5
Windmill Dr., Kes.	103	J4
Windmill Gdns., Enf.	24	G3
Windmill Gro., Croy.	94	J6
Windmill Hill NW3	48	F3
Windmill Hill, Enf.	24	H3
Windmill La. E15	51	D6
Windmill La., Barn.	22	F6
Windmill La., Grnf.	54	J5
Windmill La., Islw.	64	B4
Windmill La., Sthl.	63	J2
Windmill La., Surb.	91	E6
Windmill La. (Bushey), Wat.	29	A1
Windmill Ms. W4	65	E4
Chiswick Common Rd.		
Windmill Pas. W4	65	E4
Chiswick Common Rd.		
Windmill Ri, Kings.T.	83	B7
Windmill Rd. N18	33	A4
Windmill Rd. SW18	75	G6
Windmill Rd. SW19	83	J3
Windmill Rd. W4	65	E4
Windmill Rd. W5	64	F4
Windmill Rd., Brent.	64	G5
Windmill Rd., Croy.	94	J7
Windmill Rd., Hmptn.	81	H5
Windmill Rd., Mitch.	94	C5
Windmill Row SE11	**20**	**E4**
Windmill St. W1	67	G5
Windmill St. W1	**11**	**H2**
Windmill St. W1	58	D5
Windmill St. (Bushey), Wat.	29	B1
Windmill Wk. SE1	**16**	**F2**
Windmill Wk. SE1	67	G2
Windover Ave. NW9	38	D4
Windrose Clo. SE16	68	G2
Windrush Clo. SW11	75	G4
Maysoule Rd.		
Windrush Clo. W4	74	C1
Windrush La. SE23	86	G3
Windsor Ave. E17	41	H2
Windsor Ave. SW19	93	F1
Windsor Ave., Edg.	30	B4
Windsor Ave., N.Mal.	92	C5
Windsor Ave., Sutt.	100	B3
Windsor Ave., W.Mol.	90	G3
Windsor Clo. N3	39	B2
Windsor Clo. SE27	85	J4
Windsor Clo., Borwd.	38	A1
Warrenford Way		
Windsor Clo., Brent.	64	E6
Amalgamated Dr.		
Windsor Clo., Chis.	88	E5
Windsor Clo., Har.	45	G3
Windsor Cres.		
Windsor Clo., Nthwd.	36	A2
Windsor Ct. N14	24	C7
Windsor Ct., Sun.	81	A6
Windsor Rd.		
Windsor Cres., Har.	45	G3
Windsor Cres., Wem.	47	B3
Windsor Dr., Barn.	23	J6
Windsor Gdns. W9	57	D5
Windsor Gdns., Croy.	101	E3
Richmond Rd.		
Windsor Gro. SE27	85	J4
Windsor Pl. SW1	**15**	**G6**
Windsor Rd. E4	34	B4
Chivers Rd.		
Windsor Rd. E7	51	H5
Windsor Rd. E10	51	B2
Windsor Rd. E11	51	G1
Windsor Rd. N3	39	B2
Windsor Rd. N7	49	E3
Windsor Rd. N13	32	G3
Windsor Rd. N17	41	D2
Windsor Rd. NW2	47	H6
Windsor Rd. W5	55	H7
Windsor Rd., Barn.	23	A6
Windsor Rd., Bexh.	80	E4
Windsor Rd., Dag.	53	E3
Windsor Rd., Har.	37	A1
Windsor Rd., Houns.	72	B2
Windsor Rd., Ilf.	52	E4
Windsor Rd., Kings.T.	82	H7
Windsor Rd., Rich.	73	J2
Windsor Rd., Sthl.	63	F3
Windsor Rd., Sun.	81	A6
Windsor Rd., Tedd.	82	A5
Windsor Rd., Th.Hth.	94	H2
Windsor Rd., Wor.Pk.	99	G2
Windsor St. N1	58	H1
Windsor Ter. N1	**9**	**A3**
Windsor Ter. N1	58	J3
Windsor Wk. SE5	77	A2
Windsor Way W14	66	A4
Windsors, The, Buck.H.	35	B2
Windspoint Dr. SE15	68	E6
Ethnard Rd.		
Windus Rd. N16	50	C1
Windus Wk. N16	50	C1
Alkham Rd.		
Windy Ridge, Brom.	97	B1
Windyridge Clo. SW19	84	A5
Wine Clo. E1	59	F7
Wine Office Ct. EC4	**12**	**F4**
Winefride's Rd. E12	52	C5
Winford Ho. E3	50	J7
Jodrell Rd.		
Winforton St. SE10	78	C1
Winfrith Rd. SW18	75	F7
Wingate Cres., Croy.	94	D6
Wingate Rd. W6	65	H3
Wingate Rd., Ilf.	52	E5
Wingate Rd., Sid.	89	C6
Wingate Trd. Est. N17	33	C7
Wingfield Ms. SE15	77	D3
Wingfield St.		
Wingfield Rd. E15	51	E4
Wingfield Rd. E17	42	B5
Wingfield Rd., Kings.T.	83	A6
Wingfield St. SE15	77	D3
Wingfield Way, Ruis.	66	A6
Wingford Rd. SW2	76	E6
Wingmore Rd. SE24	76	J3
Wingrave Rd. W6	65	J6
Wingrove Rd. SE6	87	E2
Winifred Gro. SW11	75	J4
Winifred Rd. SW19	93	D1
Winifred Rd., Dag.	53	E2
Winifred Rd., Hmptn.	81	G4
Winifred St. E16	70	C1
Winifred Ter., Enf.	25	C7
Edward Clo.		
Winkfield Rd. E13	60	H2
Winkfield Rd. N22	40	G1
Winkley St. E2	59	E2
Winlaton Rd., Brom.	87	D4
Winmill Rd., Dag.	53	F3
Winn Common Rd. SE18	70	H6
Winn Rd. SE12	87	H1
Winnett St. W1	**11**	**H5**
Winnington Clo. N2	39	G6
Winnington Rd. N2	48	G1
Winns Ave. E17	41	H3
Winns Ter. E17	42	A2
Winsbeach E17	42	D2
Winscombe Cres. W5	55	G4
Winscombe St. N19	49	B2
Winscombe Way, Stan.	29	D5
Winsford Rd. SE6	86	J3
Winsford Ter. N18	33	A5
Winsham Gro. SW11	76	A5
Winslade Rd. SW2	76	E5
Winslade Way SE26	78	B7
Rushey Grn.		
Winsland Ms. W2	**10**	**E3**
Winsland St. W2	**10**	**E3**
Winsland St. W2	57	G6
Winsley St. W1	**11**	**F3**
Winsley St. W1	58	C6
Winslow SE17	**21**	**D4**
Winslow Clo. NW10	47	E3
Neasden La. N.		
Winslow Clo., Pnr.	36	B6
Winslow Gro. E4	34	E2
Winslow Rd. W6	65	J6
Winslow Way, Felt.	81	D3
Winsor Ter. E6	61	D5
Winstanley Est. SW11	75	G3
Winstanley Rd. SW11	75	G3
Winstead Gdns., Dag.	53	J5
Winston Ave. NW9	38	E7
Winston Clo., Har.	29	C6
Winston Clo., Rom.	44	H4
Winston Ct., Har.	28	H7
Winston Rd. N16	50	A4
Winston Wk. W4	65	D4
Clement Clo.		
Winston Way, Ilf.	52	E3
Winstre Rd., Borwd.	22	C1
Winter Ave. E6	61	B1
Winter Box Wk., Rich.	73	J4
Winterborne Ave., Orp.	104	G3
Winterbourne Rd. SE6	86	J1
Winterbourne Rd., Dag.	53	C2
Winterbourne Rd., Th.Hth.	94	G4
Winterbrook Rd. SE24	76	J6
Winterfold Clo. SW19	84	B2
Wintergreen Clo. E6	61	B5
Yarrow Cres.		
Winters Rd., T.Ditt.	91	E7
Winterstoke Gdns. NW7	30	G5
Winterstoke Rd. SE6	86	J1
Winterton Ho. E1	59	E6
Winterton Pl. SW10	**18**	**D5**
Winterwell Rd. SW2	76	E5
Winthorpe Rd. SW15	75	B4
Winthrop St. E1	59	E5
Winton Ave. N11	32	C7
Winton Clo. N9	25	G7
Winton Gdns., Edg.	29	J7
Winton Rd., Orp.	104	E4
Winton Way SW16	85	G5
Wisbeach Rd., Croy.	95	A5
Wisdons Clo., Dag.	53	H1
Wise La. NW7	30	G5
Wise Rd. E15	60	D1
Wiseman Ct. SE19	86	C5
Wiseman Rd. E10	51	A2
Wiseton Rd. SW17	84	H1
Wishart Rd. SE3	79	A2
Wisley Rd. SW11	76	A5
Wisley Rd., Orp.	89	A7
Wisteria Clo., Orp.	104	E2
Wisteria Rd. SE13	78	D4
Witan St. E2	59	E3
Witham Clo., Loug.	27	B6
Witham Rd. SE20	95	F3
Witham Rd. W13	64	D1
Witham Rd., Dag.	53	G5
Witham Rd., Islw.	73	A1
Witherby Clo., Croy.	102	B5
Witherfield Way SE16	77	E3
Egan Way		
Witheridge Rd. N5	49	G5
Withers Mead NW9	38	F1
Witherston Way SE9	88	D2
Withy Mead E4	34	D3
Withycombe Rd. SW19	75	A7
Witley Cres., Croy.	103	C6
Witley Gdns., Sthl.	63	F4
Witley Rd. N19	49	C2
Holloway Rd.		
Witney Clo., Pnr.	28	F6
Witney Path SE23	86	G3
Inglemere Rd.		
Wittenham Way E4	34	D3
Wittersham Rd., Brom.	87	F5
Wivenhoe Clo. SE15	77	E3
Wivenhoe Ct., Houns.	72	F4
Wivenhoe Rd., Bark.	62	A2
Wiverton Rd. SE26	86	F6
Wix Rd., Dag.	62	D1
Wixs La. SW4	76	B3
Woburn Clo. SW19	84	F6
Tintern Clo.		
Woburn Pl. WC1	**7**	**J5**
Woburn Pl. WC1	58	D4
Woburn Rd., Cars.	100	H1
Woburn Rd., Croy.	101	J1
Woburn Sq. WC1	**7**	**J6**
Woburn Sq. WC1	58	D4
Woburn Wk. WC1	**7**	**J4**
Woffington Clo., Kings.T.	91	F1
Woking Clo. SW15	74	F4
Woldham Rd., Brom.	96	E4
Wolds Dr., Orp.	104	D4
Wolfe Clo., Brom.	96	G6
Wolfe Clo., Hayes	54	B3
Ayles Rd.		

Wolfe Cres. SE7 70 A5
Wolfe Cres. SE16 68 G2
Wolferton Rd. E12 52 C4
Wolffe Gdns. E15 51 F6
Wolffram Clo. SE13 78 E5
Wolfington Rd. SE27 85 H4
Wolftencroft Clo. 75 G3
  SW11
Wollaston Clo. SE1 20 J1
Wolmer Clo., Edg. 30 B4
Wolmer Gdns., Edg. 30 A3
Wolseley Ave. SW19 84 D2
Wolseley Gdns. W4 65 B6
Wolseley Rd. E7 51 H7
Wolseley Rd. N8 40 D6
Wolseley Rd. N22 40 F1
Wolseley Rd. W4 65 C4
Wolseley Rd., Har. 37 B3
Wolseley Rd., Mitch. 94 A7
Wolseley St. SE1 17 G4
Wolseley St. SE1 68 D2
Wolsey Ave. E6 61 D3
Wolsey Ave. E17 41 J3
Wolsey Ave., T.Ditt. 91 C5
  Aragon Ave.
Wolsey Clo. SW20 83 H7
Wolsey Clo., Houns. 72 J4
Wolsey Clo., Kings.T. 92 B1
Wolsey Clo., Sthl. 63 J3
Wolsey Clo., Wor.Pk. 99 G4
Wolsey Cres., Mord. 93 B7
Wolsey Dr., Kings.T. 82 H5
Wolsey Gdns., Ilf. 35 E6
Wolsey Gro., Edg. 30 D7
Wolsey Ms. NW5 49 C6
Wolsey Ms., Orp. 104 J5
  Osgood Ave.
Wolsey Rd. N1 50 A5
Wolsey Rd., E.Mol. 91 A4
Wolsey Rd., Enf. 25 E2
Wolsey Rd., Hmptn. 81 H6
Wolsey St. E1 59 F5
  Sidney St.
Wolsey Way, Chess. 99 A5
Wolstonbury N12 31 D5
Wolvercote Rd. SE2 71 D2
Wolverley St. E2 59 E3
  Bethnal Grn. Rd.
Wolverton SE17 21 D3
Wolverton Ave., 92 A1
  Kings.T.
Wolverton Gdns. W5 55 J7
Wolverton Gdns. W6 66 A4
Wolverton Rd., Stan. 29 E6
Wolverton Way N14 24 C5
Wolves La. N13 32 G6
Wolves La. N22 32 G7
Womersley Rd. N8 40 F6
Wonford Clo., 92 E1
  Kings.T.
  Greenman St.
Wontner Rd. SW17 84 J2
Wood Clo. E2 9 H5
Wood Clo. E2 59 D4
Wood Clo. NW9 38 D7
Wood Clo., Har. 37 A7
Wood Dr., Chis. 88 B6
Wood End Ave., Har. 45 H4
Wood End Clo., Nthlt. 46 A5
Wood End Gdns., 45 J5
  Nthlt.
Wood End La., Nthlt. 45 H6
Wood End Rd., Har. 46 A4
Wood End Way 45 J5
  Nthlt.
Wood La. N6 40 B6
Wood La. NW9 38 D7
Wood La. W12 56 J6
Wood La., Dag. 53 C4
Wood La., Islw. 64 B6
Wood La., Stan. 29 D3
Wood La., Wdf.Grn. 34 F4
Wood Lo. Gdns., 88 B7
  Brom.
Wood Lo. La., 103 C3
  W.Wick.
Wood Pt. E16 60 G5
  Fife Rd.
Wood Ride, Barn. 23 G1
Wood Ride, Orp. 97 G4
Wood St. E16 60 H7
  Ethel Rd.
Wood St. E17 42 C3
Wood St. EC2 13 A4
Wood St. EC2 58 J6
Wood St. W4 65 E5
Wood St., Barn. 22 J4
Wood St., Kings.T. 91 H1
Wood St., Mitch. 94 A7
Wood Vale N10 40 C5
Wood Vale SE23 86 E1
Wood Vale Est. SE23 77 F6

Wood Way, Orp. 104 D2
Woodall Rd., Enf. 25 G6
Woodbank Rd., 87 F3
  Brom.
Woodbastwick Rd. 86 G5
  SE26
Woodberry Ave. N21 32 G2
Woodberry Ave., 36 H4
  Har.
Woodberry Clo., Sun. 81 A6
  Ashridge Way
Woodberry Cres. N10 40 B3
Woodberry Down N4 40 J7
Woodberry Down 40 J7
  Est. N4
Woodberry Gdns. 31 F6
  N12
Woodberry Gro. N4 40 J7
Woodberry Gro. N12 31 F6
Woodberry Way E4 34 C1
Woodberry Way N12 31 F6
Woodbine Clo., 82 A2
  Twick.
Woodbine Gro. SE20 86 E7
Woodbine La., 99 H3
  Wor.Pk.
Woodbine Pl. E11 42 G6
Woodbine Rd., Sid. 88 H1
Woodbine Ter. E9 50 F6
  Morning La.
Woodbines Ave., 91 G3
  Kings.T.
Woodborough Rd. 74 H4
  SW15
Woodbourne Ave. 85 D3
  SW16
Woodbourne Clo. 85 E3
  SW16
  Woodbourne Ave.
Woodbourne Dr., 98 C6
  Esher
Woodbourne Gdns., 101 B7
  Wall.
Woodbridge Clo. N7 49 F2
Woodbridge Clo. 47 G3
  NW2
Woodbridge Ct., 35 B7
  Wdf.Grn.
Woodbridge Rd., 52 J5
  Bark.
Woodbridge St. EC1 8 G5
Woodbridge St. EC1 58 H4
Woodbrook Rd. SE2 71 A6
Woodburn Clo. NW4 39 A5
Woodbury Clo. E11 42 H4
Woodbury Clo., 102 C2
  Croy.
Woodbury Hill, 27 B3
  Loug.
Woodbury Hollow, 27 B2
  Loug.
Woodbury Pk. Rd. 55 E4
  W13
Woodbury Rd. E17 42 B4
Woodbury St. SW17 84 H5
Woodchester Sq. W2 10 A1
Woodchester Sq. W2 57 E5
Woodchurch Clo., 88 G3
  Sid.
Woodchurch Dr., 88 A7
  Brom.
Woodchurch Rd. 48 D7
  NW6
Woodclyffe Dr., Chis. 97 D2
Woodcock Ct., Har. 37 H7
Woodcock Dell Ave., 37 G7
  Har.
Woodcock Hill, Har. 37 F5
Woodcombe Cres. 86 F1
  SE23
Woodcote Ave. NW7 30 J6
Woodcote Ave., 94 H4
  Th.Hth.
Woodcote Clo., Enf. 25 F6
Woodcote Clo., 82 J5
  Kings.T.
Woodcote Dr., Orp. 104 G1
Woodcote Ms., Wall. 101 B6
Woodcote Pl. SE27 85 H5
Woodcote Rd. E11 42 G7
Woodcote Rd., Wall. 101 B6
Woodcroft N21 32 F1
Woodcroft SE9 88 C3
Woodcroft, Grnf. 46 D6
Woodcroft Ave. NW7 30 D7
Woodcroft Ave., 37 C1
  Stan.
Woodcroft Rd., 94 H5
  Th.Hth.
Woodedge Clo. E4 34 F1
Woodend SE19 85 J6
Woodend, Sutt. 100 F2
Woodend Gdns., Enf. 24 E4

Woodend Rd. E17 42 C2
Wooder Gdns. E7 51 G4
Wooderson Clo. 95 B4
  SE25
Woodfall Ave., Barn. 23 C5
Woodfall Rd. N4 49 G1
Woodfall St. SW3 18 J4
Woodfall St. SW3 66 J5
Woodfarrs SE5 77 A4
Woodfield Ave. NW9 38 E4
Woodfield Ave. 85 D3
  SW16
Woodfield Ave. W5 55 F4
Woodfield Ave., 101 A6
  Cars.
Woodfield Ave., 46 F3
  Wem.
Woodfield Clo. SE19 85 J7
Woodfield Clo., Enf. 25 B4
Woodfield Cres. W5 55 G4
Woodfield Dr., Barn. 24 A7
Woodfield Gdns. W9 57 C5
  Woodfield Rd.
Woodfield Gdns., 92 F5
  N.Mal.
Woodfield Gro. 85 D3
  SW16
Woodfield La. SW16 85 D3
Woodfield Pl. W9 57 C4
Woodfield Rd. W5 55 F4
Woodfield Rd. W9 57 C5
Woodfield Rd., 72 B2
  Houns.
Woodfield Rd., T.Ditt. 98 C2
Woodfield Way N11 32 D7
Woodford Ave., Ilf. 43 B3
Woodford Bri. Rd., 43 A3
  Ilf.
Woodford Ct. W12 66 A2
  Shepherds Bush Grn.
Woodford Cres., 36 B2
  Pnr.
Woodford New Rd. 42 E4
  E17
Woodford New Rd. 42 E2
  E18
Woodford New Rd. 34 F7
  Wdf.Grn.
Woodford Pl., Wem. 46 H1
Woodford Rd. E7 51 H4
Woodford Rd. E18 42 G4
Woodford Trd. Est., 43 A2
  Wdf.Grn.
Woodgate Ave., 98 G5
  Chess.
Woodgate Cres., 28 A6
  Nthwd.
Woodger Rd. W12 65 J2
  Goldhawk Rd.
Woodget Clo. E6 61 B6
  Remington Rd.
Woodgrange Ave. 31 G6
  N12
Woodgrange Ave. 65 A1
  W5
Woodgrange Ave., 25 D6
  Enf.
Woodgrange Ave., 37 F5
  Har.
Woodgrange Clo., 37 G5
  Har.
Woodgrange Gdns., 25 D6
  Enf.
Woodgrange Rd. E7 51 H5
Woodgrange Ter., 25 D6
  Enf.
  Great Cambridge Rd.
Woodhall Ave. SE21 86 C3
Woodhall Ave., Pnr. 36 E2
Woodhall Dr. SE21 86 C3
Woodhall Dr., Pnr. 36 D1
Woodhall Gate, Pnr. 28 D7
Woodhall La., Wat. 28 D3
Woodhall Rd., Pnr. 28 D7
Woodham Ct. E18 42 F4
Woodham Rd. SE6 87 C3
Woodhatch Clo. E6 61 B5
  Leamouth Rd.
Woodhaven Gdns., 43 F3
  Ilf.
  Brandville Gdns.
Woodhayes Rd. 83 J7
  SW19
Woodhead Dr., Orp. 104 H2
  Sherlies Ave.
Woodheyes Rd. 47 D5
  NW10
Woodhill SE18 70 B4
Woodhill Cres., Har. 37 G6
Woodhouse Ave., 55 C2
  Grnf.
Woodhouse Clo., 55 C2
  Grnf.

Woodhouse Eaves, 28 A5
  Nthwd.
Woodhouse Gro. E12 52 B6
Woodhouse Rd. E11 51 F3
Woodhouse Rd. N12 31 F4
Woodhurst Ave., 97 F6
  Orp.
Woodhurst Rd. SE2 71 A5
Woodhurst Rd. W3 56 C7
Woodington Clo. SE9 79 D6
Woodison St. E3 59 H4
Woodknoll Dr., 97 C1
  Chis.
Woodland Clo. NW9 38 C6
Woodland Clo. SE19 86 B6
  Woodland Hill
Woodland Clo., 99 E6
  Epsom
Woodland Clo., 34 H3
  Wdf.Grn.
Woodland Cres. 69 E6
  SE10
Woodland Gdns. N10 40 B5
Woodland Gdns., 73 B3
  Islw.
Woodland Gro. SE10 69 E5
Woodland Hill SE19 86 B6
Woodland Ri. N10 40 B4
Woodland Ri., Grnf. 46 D6
Woodland Rd. E4 34 C1
Woodland Rd. N11 32 B5
Woodland Rd. SE19 86 C5
Woodland Rd., Loug. 27 B3
Woodland Rd., 94 G4
  Th.Hth.
Woodland St. E8 50 C6
  Dalston La.
Woodland Ter. SE7 70 B4
Woodland Ter. SE18 70 B4
Woodland Wk. NW3 48 H5
  Aspern Rd.
Woodland Wk., 87 E4
  Brom.
Woodland Way N21 32 G2
Woodland Way NW7 30 E6
Woodland Way SE2 71 D4
Woodland Way, 102 H1
  Croy.
Woodland Way, 85 A7
  Mitch.
Woodland Way, 93 C4
  Mord.
Woodland Way, 97 F4
  Orp.
Woodland Way, 99 B2
  Surb.
Woodland Way, 103 B4
  W.Wick.
Woodland Way, 34 H3
  Wdf.Grn.
Woodlands NW11 39 B6
Woodlands SW20 92 J4
Woodlands, Har. 36 G4
Woodlands, The N14 32 B1
Woodlands, The 78 D7
  SE13
Woodlands, The 85 J7
  SE19
Woodlands, The, 73 C2
  Islw.
Woodlands Ave. E11 51 G1
Woodlands Ave. N3 31 F7
Woodlands Ave. W3 65 B1
Woodlands Ave., 92 C1
  N.Mal.
Woodlands Ave., 44 E6
  Rom.
Woodlands Ave., 36 C7
  Ruis.
Woodlands Ave., 88 H1
  Sid.
Woodlands Ave., 99 F2
  Wor.Pk.
Woodlands Clo. 39 B5
  NW11
Woodlands Clo., 22 B4
  Borwd.
Woodlands Clo., 97 C2
  Brom.
Woodlands Clo., 98 C7
  Esher
Woodlands Dr., Stan. 29 C6
Woodlands Dr., Sun. 90 C2
Woodlands Gro., 73 B2
  Islw.
Woodlands Pk. Bex. 89 J4
Woodlands Pk. Rd. 40 H5
  N15
Woodlands Pk. Rd. 69 E6
  SE10
Woodlands Rd. E11 51 E2
Woodlands Rd. E17 42 C3
Woodlands Rd. N9 33 F1

Woodlands Rd. SW13 — 74 F3
Woodlands Rd., Bexh. — 80 E3
Woodlands Rd., Brom. — 97 B2
Woodlands Rd., Har. — 37 C5
Woodlands Rd., Ilf. — 52 F3
Woodlands Rd., Islw. — 73 A3
Woodlands Rd., Sthl. — 63 D1
Woodlands Rd., Surb. — 91 G7
Woodlands St. SE13 — 78 D7
Woodlands Way SW15 — 75 C5
  Oakhill Rd.
Woodlawn Clo. SW15 — 75 C5
Woodlawn Cres., Twick. — 81 H2
Woodlawn Dr., Felt. — 81 D2
Woodlawn Rd. SW6 — 66 A7
Woodlea Dr., Brom. — 96 E5
Woodlea Rd. N16 — 50 B3
Woodleigh Ave. N12 — 31 H6
Woodleigh Gdns. SW16 — 85 E3
Woodley Clo. SW17 — 84 J7
  Arnold Rd.
Woodman La. E4 — 26 E5
Woodman Path, Chig. — 35 H6
Woodman St. E16 — 70 D1
Woodmans Gro. NW10 — 47 F5
Woodmans Ms. W12 — 56 J5
  Wood La.
Woodmansterne Rd. SW16 — 85 C7
Woodmere SE9 — 79 C7
Woodmere Ave., Croy. — 95 F7
Woodmere Clo. SW11 — 76 A3
  Lavender Hill
Woodmere Clo., Croy. — 95 G7
Woodmere Gdns., Croy. — 95 F7
Woodmere Way, Beck. — 96 D5
Woodnook Rd. SW16 — 85 B5
Woodpecker Clo. N9 — 25 E6
Woodpecker Clo. (Bushey), Wat. — 28 J1
Woodpecker Rd. SE14 — 68 H6
Woodpecker Rd. SE28 — 62 C7
Woodquest Ave. SE24 — 76 J5
Woodridge Clo., Enf. — 24 G1
Woodridings Ave., Pnr. — 36 F1
Woodridings Clo., Pnr. — 28 F7
Woodriffe Rd. E11 — 42 D7
Woodrise, Pnr. — 36 A5
Woodrow SE18 — 70 C4
Woodrow Clo., Grnf. — 46 E7
Woodrow Ct. N17 — 33 E7
  Heybourne Rd.
Woodrush Clo. SE14 — 68 H7
  Southerngate Way
Woodrush Way, Rom. — 44 D4
Woods, The, Nthwd. — 28 A5
Woods Clo. SE19 — 86 B6
  Woodland Hill
Woods Ms. W1 — 11 B5
Woods Ms. W1 — 58 A7
Woods Pl. SE1 — 17 E6
Woods Rd. SE15 — 77 E1
Woodseer St. E1 — 13 G1
Woodseer St. E1 — 59 C5
Woodsford SE17 — 21 B4
Woodsford Sq. W14 — 66 B2
Woodshire Rd., Dag. — 53 H3
Woodside NW11 — 39 D5
Woodside SW19 — 84 C6
Woodside, Buck.H. — 34 J2
Woodside Ave. N6 — 39 J5
Woodside Ave. N10 — 40 A4
Woodside Ave. N12 — 31 F4
Woodside Ave. SE25 — 95 E6
Woodside Ave., Chis. — 88 F5
Woodside Ave., Esher — 91 B7
Woodside Ave., Wem. — 55 H1

Woodside Clo., Stan. — 29 E5
Woodside Clo., Surb. — 99 C1
Woodside Clo., Wem. — 55 H1
Woodside Ct. N12 — 31 F4
  Woodside Ave.
Woodside Ct. Rd., Croy. — 95 D7
Woodside Cres., Sid. — 88 H3
Woodside End, Wem. — 55 H1
Woodside Gdns. E4 — 34 B5
Woodside Gdns. N17 — 41 B2
Woodside Gra. Rd. N12 — 31 E4
Woodside Grn. SE25 — 95 D6
Woodside Gro. N12 — 31 F3
Woodside La. N12 — 31 E3
Woodside La., Bex. — 80 D6
Woodside Pk. SE25 — 95 D5
Woodside Pk. Ave. E17 — 42 D4
Woodside Pk. Rd. N12 — 31 E4
Woodside Pl., Wem. — 55 H1
Woodside Rd. E13 — 60 J4
Woodside Rd. N22 — 32 F7
Woodside Rd. SE25 — 95 E6
Woodside Rd., Brom. — 97 B5
Woodside Rd., Kings.T. — 34 G4
  Kings.T.
Woodside Rd., N.Mal. — 92 D2
Woodside Rd., Sid. — 88 H3
Woodside Rd., Sutt. — 100 F3
Woodside Rd., — 34 G4
  Wdf.Grn.
Woodside Way, Croy. — 95 E6
Woodside Way, Mitch. — 94 B1
Woodsome Rd. NW5 — 49 A3
Woodspring Rd. SW19 — 84 B2
Woodstead Gro., Edg. — 29 H4
Woodstock Ave. NW11 — 48 B1
Woodstock Ave. W13 — 64 D3
Woodstock Ave., Islw. — 73 D5
Woodstock Ave., Sthl. — 54 F3
Woodstock Ave., Sutt. — 93 C7
Woodstock Clo., Bex. — 80 F7
Woodstock Clo., Stan. — 37 H2
Woodstock Ct. SE12 — 78 G6
Woodstock Cres. N9 — 25 E6
Woodstock Gdns., Beck. — 96 B1
Woodstock Gdns., Ilf. — 53 A2
Woodstock Gro. W12 — 66 A2
Woodstock La. S., Surb. — 98 F2
Woodstock La. S., Chess. — 98 F4
Woodstock La. S., Esher — 98 E5
Woodstock Ms. W1 — 11 C2
Woodstock Ri., Sutt. — 93 C7
Woodstock Rd. E7 — 51 J7
Woodstock Rd. E17 — 42 D2
Woodstock Rd. N4 — 49 G1
Woodstock Rd. NW11 — 39 C7
Woodstock Rd. W4 — 65 E3
Woodstock Rd., Cars. — 101 A5
Woodstock Rd., Croy. — 102 A3
Woodstock Rd., Wem. — 46 J7
Woodstock St. E16 — 60 E6
  Victoria Dock Rd.
Woodstock St. W1 — 11 D4
Woodstock Ter. E14 — 60 B7
Woodstock Way, Mitch. — 94 B2
Woodstone Ave., Epsom — 99 G5
Woodsyre SE26 — 86 C4
Woodthorpe Rd. SW15 — 74 H4
Woodtree Clo. NW4 — 38 J2
  Ashley La.
Woodvale Ave. SE25 — 95 C3
Woodvale Wk. SE27 — 85 J5
Woodvale Way NW2 — 48 A3
  The Vale
Woodview Ave. E4 — 34 C4
Woodview Clo. N4 — 40 H7

Woodview Clo. SW15 — 83 D4
Woodview Clo., Kings.T. — 83 D4
Woodville SE3 — 78 H1
Woodville Clo. SE12 — 78 G5
Woodville Clo., Tedd. — 82 D4
Woodville Gdns. NW11 — 39 A7
  Hendon Way
Woodville Gdns. W5 — 55 H6
Woodville Gdns., Ilf. — 43 E3
Woodville Gro., Well. — 80 A3
Woodville Rd. E11 — 51 F1
Woodville Rd. E17 — 41 H4
Woodville Rd. E18 — 42 H2
Woodville Rd. N16 — 50 B5
Woodville Rd. NW6 — 57 C2
Woodville Rd. NW11 — 39 A7
Woodville Rd. W5 — 55 G6
Woodville Rd., Barn. — 23 E3
Woodville Rd., Mord. — 93 D4
Woodville Rd., Rich. — 82 E3
Woodville Rd., Th.Hth. — 94 J4
Woodville St. SE18 — 70 B4
  Woodhill
Woodward Ave. NW4 — 38 G5
Woodward Gdns., Dag. — 53 C7
  Woodward Rd.
Woodward Gdns., Stan. — 29 C7
Woodward Rd., Dag. — 53 B7
Woodwarde Rd. SE22 — 77 B6
Wooday Cres., Har. — 37 D6
Woodwell St. SW18 — 75 F5
  Huguenot Pl.
Woodyard Clo. NW5 — 49 A5
  Gillies St.
Woodyard La. SE21 — 77 B7
Woodyates Rd. SE12 — 78 G6
Wool Rd. SW20 — 83 H7
Woolacombe Rd. SE3 — 78 J1
Wooler St. SE17 — 21 B4
Wooler St. SE17 — 68 A5
Woolf Clo. SE28 — 71 B1
Woollaston Rd. N4 — 40 H6
Woolmead Ave. NW9 — 57 H1
Woolmer Gdns. N18 — 33 D6
Woolmer Rd. N18 — 33 D5
Woolmore St. E14 — 60 C7
Woolneigh St. SW6 — 75 E3
Woolstaplers Way SE16 — 21 H1
  Riverhead Clo.
Woolston Clo. E17 — 41 G2
Woolstone Rd. SE23 — 86 H2
Woolwich Ch. St. SE18 — 70 B3
Woolwich Common SE18 — 70 D6
Woolwich Garrison SE18 — 70 D5
  Repository Rd.
Woolwich High St. SE18 — 70 D3
Woolwich Ind. Est. SE28 — 70 H3
  Hadden Rd.
Woolwich Manor Way E16 — 61 E7
Woolwich New Rd. SE18 — 70 E4
Woolwich Rd. SE2 — 71 D6
Woolwich Rd. SE7 — 69 F5
Woolwich Rd. SE10 — 69 H5
Woolwich Rd., Belv. — 71 F4
Woolwich Rd., Bexh. — 80 G4
Wooster Gdns. E14 — 60 D6
Woosters Ms., Har. — 36 J3
  Fairfield Dr.
Wootton Gro. N3 — 39 D1
Wootton St. SE1 — 16 F2
Wootton St. SE1 — 67 G1
Worbeck Rd. SE20 — 95 F2
Worcester Ave. N17 — 33 D7
Worcester Clo., Croy. — 102 J2
Worcester Clo., Mitch. — 94 A2
Worcester Cres. NW7 — 30 E3
Worcester Cres., Wdf.Grn. — 34 J4
Worcester Gdns., Grnf. — 45 J6
Worcester Gdns., Ilf. — 43 B7

Worcester Gdns., Wor.Pk. — 99 E2
Worcester Ms. NW6 — 48 E6
  Lymington Rd.
Worcester Pk. Rd., Wor.Pk. — 99 C3
Worcester Pl. EC4 — 13 A5
Worcester Rd. E12 — 52 C4
Worcester Rd. E17 — 41 G2
Worcester Rd. SW19 — 84 C5
Worcester Rd., Sutt. — 100 D7
Wordsworth Ave. E12 — 52 B7
Wordsworth Ave. E18 — 42 F3
Wordsworth Ave., Grnf. — 55 A3
Wordsworth Dr., Sutt. — 99 J4
Wordsworth Rd. N16 — 50 B5
Wordsworth Rd. SE1 — 21 F2
Wordsworth Rd. SE20 — 86 G7
Wordsworth Rd., Hmptn. — 81 F4
Wordsworth Rd., Wall. — 101 C6
Wordsworth Rd., Well. — 79 H1
Wordsworth Wk. NW11 — 39 C4
Worfield St. SW11 — 16 H7
Worgan St. SE11 — 20 C3
Worgan St. SE11 — 67 F5
Worland Rd. E15 — 51 E7
World Trade Cen. E1 — 13 G6
World Trade Cen. E1 — 59 C7
World's End Est. SW10 — 18 E7
World's End La. N21 — 24 F5
Worlds End La., Enf. — 24 F4
Worlds End La., Orp. — 104 J6
World's End Pas. SW10 — 18 E7
World's End Pl. SW10 — 18 D7
Worlidge St. W6 — 65 J5
Worlingham Rd. SE22 — 77 C4
Wormholt Rd. W12 — 65 G1
Wormwood St. EC2 — 13 D3
Wormwood St. EC2 — 59 B6
Wornington Rd. W10 — 57 B4
Woronzow Rd. NW8 — 57 G1
Worple Ave. SW19 — 84 A7
Worple Ave., Islw. — 73 D5
Worple Clo., Har. — 45 F1
Worple Rd. SW19 — 84 B7
Worple Rd. SW20 — 92 J2
Worple Rd., Islw. — 73 D4
Worple Rd. Ms. SW19 — 84 C6
Worple St. SW14 — 74 D3
Worple Way, Har. — 45 F1
Worple Way, Rich. — 73 H5
Worship St. EC2 — 9 C6
Worship St. EC2 — 59 A4
Worslade Rd. SW17 — 84 G4
Worsley Bri. Rd. SE26 — 86 J4
Worsley Bri. Rd., Beck. — 87 A5
Worsley Rd. E11 — 51 E4
Worsopp Dr. SW4 — 76 C5
Worth, Clo., Orp. — 104 H4
Worth Gro. SE17 — 21 B4
Worthfield Clo., Epsom — 99 D7
Worthing Clo. E15 — 60 E2
  Mitre Rd.
Worthing Rd., Houns. — 63 F6
Worthington Rd., Surb. — 98 J1
Worthy Down Ct. SE18 — 79 D1
  Prince Imperial Rd.
Wortley Rd. E6 — 52 A7
Wortley Rd., Croy. — 94 G7
Worton Gdns., Islw. — 73 A2
Worton Hall Est., Islw. — 73 B4
Worton Pk. Ind. Est., Islw. — 74 H3
Worton Rd., Islw. — 73 A4
Worton Way, Islw. — 73 A2
Wotton Rd. NW2 — 47 J3
Wotton Rd. SE8 — 68 J6
Wouldham Rd. E16 — 60 F6

Wragby Rd. E11 | 51 | E3
Wrampling Pl. N9 | 33 | D2
  Croyland Rd.
Wrangthorn Wk., | 101 | G4
  Croy.
  Epsom Rd.
Wray Ave., Ilf. | 43 | D3
Wray Cres. N4 | 49 | E2
Wrayfield Rd., Sutt. | 100 | A3
Wraysbury Clo., | 72 | E5
  Houns.
  Dorney Way
Wrekin Rd. SE18 | 70 | F7
Wren Ave. NW2 | 47 | J5
Wren Ave., Sthl. | 63 | F4
Wren Clo. E16 | 60 | F6
  Ibbotson Ave.
Wren Cres. | 28 | J1
  (Bushey), Wat.
Wren Gdns., Dag. | 53 | D5
Wren Landing E14 | 69 | A1
  Cabot Sq.
Wren Path SE28 | 70 | G3
Wren Rd. SE5 | 77 | A1
Wren Rd., Dag. | 53 | D5
Wren Rd., Sid. | 89 | C4
Wren St. WC1 | **8** | **D5**
Wren St. WC1 | 58 | F4
Wrentham Ave. | 57 | A2
  NW10
Wrenthorpe Rd., | 87 | E4
  Brom.
Wrenwood Way, Pnr. | 36 | B4
Wrexham Rd. E3 | 60 | A2
Wricklemarsh Rd. | 78 | J1
  SE3
Wrigglesworth St. | 68 | G7
  SE14
Wright Rd., Houns. | 63 | C7
Wrights All. SW19 | 83 | J6
Wrights Clo. SE13 | 69 | F4
  Wisteria Rd.
Wrights Clo., Dag. | 53 | H4
Wrights Grn. SW4 | 76 | D4
  Nelson's Row
Wrights La. W8 | **14** | **A5**
Wrights La. W8 | 66 | E3
Wrights Pl. NW10 | 47 | C6
  Mitchell Way
Wrights Rd. E3 | 59 | J2
Wrights Rd. SE25 | 95 | B3
Wrights Row, Wall. | 101 | B4
Wrights Wk. SW14 | 74 | D3
  North Worple Way
Wrigley Clo. E4 | 34 | D5
Wrotham Rd. NW1 | 49 | C7
  Agar Pl.
Wrotham Rd. W13 | 64 | E1
  Mattock La.
Wrotham Rd., Barn. | 23 | B2
Wrotham Rd., Well. | 80 | C1
Wroths Path, Loug. | 27 | C1
Wrottesley Rd. | 56 | G2
  NW10
Wrottesley Rd. SE18 | 70 | F6
Wroughton Rd. | 75 | J5
  SW11
Wroughton Ter. NW4 | 38 | H4
Wroxall Rd., Dag. | 53 | C6
Wroxham Gdns. N11 | 32 | C7
Wroxham Rd. SE28 | 62 | D7
Wroxton Rd. SE15 | 77 | E2
Wrythe Grn., Cars. | 100 | J3
Wrythe Grn. Rd., | 100 | J3
  Cars.
Wrythe La., Cars. | 93 | F7
Wulfstan St. W12 | 56 | F5
Wyatt Clo., Hayes | 54 | A5
Wyatt Pk. Rd. SW2 | 85 | E2
Wyatt Rd. E7 | 51 | G6
Wyatt Rd. N5 | 49 | J3
Wyatts La. E17 | 42 | C3
Wybert St. NW1 | **8** | **A4**
Wyborne Way NW10 | 47 | C7
Wyburn Ave., Barn. | 23 | C2
Wych Elm Pas., | 91 | J1
  Kings.T.
Wyche Gro., S.Croy. | 102 | A7
Wycherley Clo. SE3 | 69 | F7
Wycherley Cres., | 23 | E6
  Barn.
Wychwood Ave., | 29 | G6
  Edg.
Wychwood Ave., | 94 | J3
  Th.Hth.
Wychwood Clo., Edg. | 29 | G6
Wychwood End N6 | 40 | C7
Wychwood Gdns., | 43 | C4
  Ilf.
Wychwood Way | 86 | A6
  SE19
  Central Hill
Wyclif St. EC1 | **8** | **G4**

Wycliffe Clo., Well. | 79 | J1
Wycliffe Rd. SW11 | 76 | A2
Wycliffe Rd. SW19 | 84 | E6
Wycombe Gdns. | 38 | D2
  NW11
Wycombe Pl. SW18 | 75 | F6
Wycombe Rd. N17 | 41 | D1
Wycombe Rd., Ilf. | 43 | C5
Wycombe Rd., Wem. | 56 | A1
Wydehurst Rd., | 95 | D7
  Croy.
Wydell Clo., Mord. | 93 | A6
Wydeville Manor Rd. | 87 | H4
  SE12
Wye Clo., Orp. | 97 | J7
Wye St. SW11 | 75 | G2
Wyemead Cres. E4 | 34 | E3
Wyevale Clo., Pnr. | 36 | A3
Wyfields, Ilf. | 43 | E1
  Ravensbourne Gdns.
Wyfold Rd. SW6 | 75 | B1
Wyhill Wk., Dag. | 53 | J6
Wyke Clo., Islw. | 64 | C6
Wyke Gdns. W7 | 64 | C3
Wyke Rd. E3 | 51 | A7
Wyke Rd. SW20 | 92 | J2
Wykeham Ave., Dag. | 53 | C6
Wykeham Grn., Dag. | 53 | C6
Wykeham Hill, Wem. | 46 | J1
Wykeham Ri. N20 | 31 | B1
Wykeham Rd. NW4 | 38 | J5
Wykeham Rd., Har. | 37 | E4
Wyld Way, Wem. | 47 | B6
Wyldes Clo. NW11 | 48 | F1
  Wildwood Rd.
Wyldfield Gdns. N9 | 33 | C2
  Latymer Rd.
Wyleu St. SE23 | 77 | H7
Wylie Rd., Sthl. | 63 | G3
Wyllen Clo. E1 | 59 | F4
Wymering Rd. W9 | 57 | D3
Wymond St. SW15 | 74 | J3
Wynan Rd. E14 | 69 | B5
Wynaud Ct. N22 | 32 | F6
  Palmerston Rd.
Wyncham Ave., Sid. | 88 | H1
Wynchgate N14 | 32 | D1
Wynchgate N21 | 24 | E7
Wynchgate, Har. | 29 | B7
Wyncroft Clo., Brom. | 97 | C3
Wyndale Ave. NW9 | 38 | A6
Wyndcliff Rd. SE7 | 69 | H6
Wyndcroft Clo., Enf. | 24 | H3
Wyndham Clo., Orp. | 104 | F1
Wyndham Clo., Sutt. | 100 | D7
Wyndham Cres. N19 | 49 | C3
Wyndham Cres., | 72 | G6
  Houns.
Wyndham Est. SE5 | **20** | **J7**
Wyndham Est. SE5 | 67 | J7
Wyndham Ms. W1 | **10** | **J2**
Wyndham Pl. W1 | **10** | **J2**
Wyndham Pl. W1 | 57 | J5
Wyndham Rd. E6 | 52 | A7
Wyndham Rd. SE5 | 67 | J7
Wyndham Rd. W13 | 64 | E3
Wyndham Rd., Barn. | 31 | J1
Wyndham Rd., | 82 | J7
  Kings.T.
Wyndham St. W1 | **10** | **J1**
Wyndham St. W1 | 57 | J5
Wyndham Yd. W1 | **10** | **J2**
Wyneham Rd. SE24 | 77 | A5
Wynell Rd. SE23 | 86 | G3
Wynford Pl., Belv. | 71 | G6
Wynford Rd. N1 | **8** | **C1**
Wynford Rd. N1 | 58 | F2
Wynford Way SE9 | 88 | C3
Wynlie Gdns., Pnr. | 36 | B2
Wynndale Rd. E18 | 42 | H1
Wynne Rd. SW9 | 76 | G2
Wynns Ave., Sid. | 80 | A5
Wynnstay Gdns. W8 | 66 | D3
Wynter St. SW11 | 75 | F4
Wynton Gdns. SE25 | 95 | B5
Wynton Pl. W3 | 56 | B6
Wynyard Ter. SE11 | **20** | **D3**
Wynyard Ter. SE11 | 67 | F5
Wynyatt St. EC1 | **8** | **G4**
Wyre Gro., Edg. | 30 | B3
Wyre Gro., Hayes | 63 | A4
Wyresdale Cres., | 55 | C3
  Grnf.
Wythburn Pl. W1 | **10** | **J4**
Wythens Wk. SE9 | 79 | E6
Wythenshawe Rd., | 53 | G3
  Dag.
Wythes Clo., Brom. | 97 | C2
Wythes Rd. E16 | 70 | B1
Wythfield Rd. SE9 | 78 | C6
Wyvenhoe Rd., Har. | 45 | J3
Wyvil Est. SW8 | **20** | **A7**
Wyvil Rd. SW8 | **20** | **A6**

Wyvil Rd. SW8 | 67 | E6
Wyvis St. E14 | 60 | B5

Y

Yabsley St. E14 | 69 | C1
Yalding Rd. SE16 | **17** | **H6**
Yalding Rd. SE16 | 68 | D3
Yale Clo., Houns. | 72 | F5
  Bramley Way
Yarborough Rd. | 93 | G1
  SW19
  Runnymede
Yardley Clo. E4 | 26 | B5
Yardley La. E4 | 26 | B5
Yardley St. WC1 | **8** | **E4**
Yardley St. WC1 | 58 | G3
Yarmouth Cres. N17 | 41 | E5
Yarmouth Pl. W1 | **15** | **D2**
Yarnfield Sq. SE15 | 77 | D1
  Clayton Rd.
Yarnton Way SE2 | 71 | D2
Yarnton Way, Erith | 71 | D2
Yarrow Cres. E6 | 61 | B5
Yateley St. SE18 | 70 | A3
Yates Ct. NW2 | 48 | A6
Yeading Ave., Har. | 45 | E2
Yeading Fork, Hayes | 54 | B5
Yeading Gdns., | 54 | B5
  Hayes
Yeading La., Hayes | 54 | B6
Yeading La., Nthlt. | 54 | C3
Yeames Clo. W13 | 55 | D6
Yeate St. N1 | 50 | A7
Yeatman Rd. N6 | 39 | J6
Yeats Clo. SE13 | 78 | D2
  Eliot Pk.
Yeldham Rd. W6 | 66 | A5
Yellow Hammer Ct. | 38 | E2
  NW9
  Eagle Dr.
Yelverton Rd. SW11 | 75 | G2
Yenston Clo., Mord. | 93 | D6
Yeo St. E3 | 60 | B5
Yeoman Clo. SE27 | 85 | H3
Yeoman Clo. E6 | 61 | D5
Yeoman St. SE8 | 68 | H4
Yeomans Acre, Ruis. | 36 | A6
Yeomans Row SW3 | 14 | H6
Yeoman's Row SW3 | 66 | H3
Yeomans Way, Enf. | 25 | F2
Yeomans Yd. E1 | **13** | **G5**
Yeomen Way, Ilf. | 35 | F6
Yeovil Clo., Orp. | 104 | H2
Yerbury Rd. N19 | 49 | D3
Yester Dr., Chis. | 88 | B7
Yester Pk., Chis. | 88 | C7
Yester Rd., Chis. | 88 | B7
Yew Clo., Buck.H. | 35 | A2
Yew Gro. NW2 | 48 | A4
Yew Tree Clo. N21 | 24 | G7
Yew Tree Clo., Well. | 80 | A1
Yew Tree Clo., | 99 | E1
  Wor.Pk.
Yew Tree Gdns. | 44 | E5
  (Chadwell Heath),
  Rom.
Yew Tree Rd. W12 | 56 | F7
Yew Tree Wk., | 72 | F5
  Houns.
Yew Wk., Har. | 46 | B1
Yewdale Clo., Brom. | 87 | E6
Yewfield Rd. NW10 | 47 | F6
Yewtree Clo. N22 | 40 | C1
Yewtree Rd., Beck. | 95 | J3
Yoakley Rd. N16 | 50 | B2
Yoke Clo. N7 | 49 | E6
  Ewe Clo.
Yolande Gdns. SE9 | 79 | B5
Yonge Pk. N4 | 49 | G3
York Ave. SW14 | 74 | C5
York Ave. W7 | 64 | B1
York Ave., Sid. | 88 | H2
York Ave., Stan. | 37 | E1
York Bri. NW1 | **7** | **B5**
York Bri. NW1 | 58 | A4
York Bldgs. WC2 | **12** | **B6**
York Clo. E6 | 61 | C6
  Boultwood Rd.
York Clo., Mord. | 93 | E4
York Cres., Borwd. | 22 | D2
York Cres., Loug. | 24 | E7
York Gate NW1 | **7** | **B6**
York Gate NW1 | 58 | A4
York Gate N14 | 24 | E7
York Gro. SE15 | 77 | F1
York Hill SE27 | 85 | H3
York Hill, Loug. | 27 | B3
York Hill Est. SE27 | 85 | H3
York Ho., Wem. | 46 | J4
York Ho. Pl. W8 | **14** | **A3**

York Ho. Pl. W8 | 66 | E2
York Ms. NW5 | 49 | B5
  Kentish Town Rd.
York Ms., Ilf. | 52 | D3
York Par., Brent. | 64 | G5
York Pl. SW11 | 75 | F3
York Pl. WC2 | **12** | **B6**
York Pl., Dag. | 53 | J6
York Pl., Ilf. | 52 | D2
  York Rd.
York Ri. NW5 | 49 | B3
York Ri., Orp. | 104 | H1
York Rd. E4 | 34 | A5
York Rd. E7 | 51 | G6
York Rd. E10 | 51 | C3
York Rd. E17 | 41 | G5
York Rd. N11 | 32 | D6
York Rd. N18 | 33 | E6
York Rd. N21 | 25 | A7
York Rd. SE1 | **16** | **D2**
York Rd. SE1 | 67 | F2
York Rd. SW11 | 75 | F4
York Rd. SW18 | 75 | F4
York Rd. SW19 | 84 | F6
York Rd. W3 | 56 | C6
York Rd. W5 | 64 | F3
York Rd., Barn. | 23 | F5
York Rd., Brent. | 64 | G5
York Rd., Croy. | 94 | G7
York Rd., Houns. | 72 | H3
York Rd., Ilf. | 52 | D3
York Rd., Kings.T. | 82 | J7
York Rd., Nthwd. | 36 | A2
York Rd., Rich. | 73 | J5
  Albert Rd.
York Rd., Sutt. | 100 | D6
York Rd., Tedd. | 82 | B4
York Sq. E14 | 59 | H6
York St. W1 | **10** | **J2**
York St. W1 | 57 | J5
York St., Bark. | 61 | F1
  Abbey Rd.
York St., Mitch. | 94 | A7
York St., Twick. | 82 | D1
York Ter. E. NW1 | **7** | **C6**
York Ter. E. NW1 | 58 | A4
York Ter. W. NW1 | **7** | **B6**
York Ter. W. NW1 | 58 | A4
York Way N1 | 58 | E1
York Way N7 | 49 | D6
York Way N20 | 31 | J3
York Way, Borwd. | 22 | D2
York Way, Chess. | 98 | H7
York Way, Felt. | 81 | F3
York Way Ct. N1 | 58 | E1
Yorkland Ave., Well. | 79 | J3
Yorkshire Clo. N16 | 50 | B3
Yorkshire Gdns. N18 | 33 | E5
Yorkshire Grey Pl. | 48 | F4
  NW3
  Heath St.
Yorkshire Grey Yd. | **12** | **C2**
  WC1
Yorkshire Rd. E14 | 59 | H6
Yorkshire Rd., | 94 | E5
  Mitch.
Yorkton St. E2 | **9** | **H2**
Yorkton St. E2 | 59 | D2
Young Rd. E16 | 60 | J6
Young St. W8 | **14** | **A4**
Young St. W8 | 66 | E2
Youngmans Clo., | 24 | J1
  Enf.
Young's Bldgs. EC1 | **9** | **A5**
Youngs Rd., Ilf. | 43 | G5
Yoxley App., Ilf. | 43 | F6
Yoxley Dr., Ilf. | 43 | F6
Yukon Rd. SW12 | 76 | B7
Yuletide Clo. NW10 | 47 | E7
Yunus Khan Clo. E17 | 42 | A5

Z

Zampa Rd. SE16 | 68 | F5
Zander Ct. E2 | **9** | **J3**
Zangwill Rd. SE3 | 79 | A1
Zealand Rd. E3 | 59 | H2
Zennor Rd. SW12 | 85 | C1
Zenoria St. SE22 | 77 | C4
Zermatt Rd., Th.Hth. | 94 | J4
Zetland St. E14 | 60 | B5
Zion Pl., Th.Hth. | 95 | A4
Zion Rd., Th.Hth. | 95 | A5
Zoar St. SE1 | **16** | **J1**
Zoffany St. N19 | 49 | D2